2003 SONG WRITER'S MARKET®

1,200 PLACES TO MARKET YOUR SONGS

EDITED BY IAN BESSLER

WRITER'S DIGEST BOOKS
CINCINNATI, OH

If you would like to be considered for a listing in the next edition of *Songwriter's Market*, send a SASE (or SAE and IRC) with your request for a questionnaire to *Songwriter's Market*—QR, 4700 East Galbraith Road, Cincinnati OH 45236. Please indicate in which section you would like to be included.

Supervisory Editor, Annuals Department: Alice Pope
Editorial Director, Annuals Department: Barbara Kuroff

Writer's Market website: www.WritersMarket.com
Writer's Digest website: www.writersdigest.com

International Standard Serial Number 0161-5971
International Standard Book Number 1-58297-123-4

Cover image © Miguel S. Salmeron/Getty Images/FPG

Attention Booksellers: This is an annual directory of F&W Publications. Return deadline for this edition is December 31, 2003.

contents at a glance

Contents

RESOURCES

From the Editor

Every year when I put this book together, I'm startled by the realization not only of how much there is to learn about the music industry, but also by how much it's possible to gain from a fresh look at topics you thought you had thoroughly grasped long ago. There is always some new perspective or detail to examine, and experienced artists of all types—songwriters, painters, sculptors, etc.—recognize the constant re-examination and application of the basics of their particular crafts as the road to mastery.

In that spirit, this year's new offerings among the upfront articles include two new pieces exploring basic aspects of the music industry: **Understanding Performing & Mechanical Rights Organizations 101**, on page 29, and **Song Sharks, Single-Song Marketing & Collaboration 101**, on page 40. Both of these articles are by music publisher, manager, consultant and educator Rusty Gordon of Rustron Music Productions & Publishing. Rusty has been active in the music industry for over 40 years and has an encyclopedic knowledge of the inner workings of the music industry.

For the more experienced among you, we have **Collaborative Chemistry: The Art of Co-Writing**, by Dan Kimpel (page 25). More and more of the songs that make it onto radio (not written by the recording artist) are written by teams of collaborating songwriters (up to five different songwriters are sometimes credited). Read this article and get inside information from professional songwriters on how their experiences collaborating with writing partners over the years.

For those of you who mainly write and perform your own material, we have another article from producer Scott Mathews, entitled **Keeping Your Bearings in the Studio** (page 36). A lot of performing songwriters (and bands) are producing and recording their own albums, either to promote themselves or to license. Producing your own recording can still be a relatively expensive proposition, even if you restrict yourself to mid-level studios, and you can easily get lost during the process. Read this handy guide for advice on preparing yourself to enter a studio, and get more bang for your buck.

So, I hope you get a lot out of this year's edition. But, amid all the talk of networking, royalties and radio play, and all the strategies for marketing and for making yourself more knowledgeable and competitive, never forget that, in the end, it comes down to you, the blank page and whatever vision and skill you have at your disposal. In short, it all comes down to the song. You (along with, maybe, your collaborator) will eventually be left alone to bring that song into the world or have it slip from your grasp. But, if you succeed in that task, and your song has what it takes to be that one hit song that carries an album or launches a career, then it will find its place and so will you.

Ian C. Bessler
songmarket@fwpubs.com
www.writersdigest.com

Songwriter's Market
Feedback

If you have a suggestion for improving *Songwriter's Market*, or would like to take part in a reader survey we conduct from time to time, please make a photocopy of this form (or cut it out of the book), fill it out, and return it to:

    Songwriter's Market Feedback
    4700 East Galbraith Road
    Cincinnati OH 45236
    Fax: (513)531-2686

☐ Yes! I'm willing to fill out a short survey by mail or online to provide feedback on *Songwriter's Market* or other books on songwriting.

☐ Yes! I would like to subscribe to the *Songwriter's Market* newsletter (be sure to include your e-mail address if you wish to receive it online).

☐ Yes! I have a suggestion to improve *Songwriter's Market* (attach a second sheet if more room is necessary):

_____

_____

_____

_____

_____

_____

_____

_____

_____

Name:_____

Address:_____

City:_____ State:_____ Zip:_____

Phone:_____ Fax:_____

E-mail:_____ Website:_____

I am a
☐ songwriter
☐ performing songwriter
☐ musician
☐ other_____

Quick-Start

If the business of marketing your songs is a new experience, this book may seem overwhelming. This "Quick-Start" will take you step by step through the process of preparing you and your songs to be heard by music industry professionals. It points you to the different places in *Songwriter's Market* that contain information on specific marketing and business subjects.

Use this as a guide to launch your songwriting career. When you are finished looking it over, read through the referred articles in their entirety. They will reinforce what you already know and introduce you to facets of the industry you have yet to encounter. Good luck!

1. Join a songwriting organization. This is the most important first step for a songwriter. Organizations provide opportunities to learn about the music business, polish your craft, and make indispensable contacts who can take you to the next level.
  - Organizations, page 411

2. Educate yourself about the music business. Before you leap, read up on what you are getting yourself into. Attend songwriting workshops and music conferences. Don't learn the ins and outs the hard way.
  - The Structure of the Music Business, page 11
  - Royalties, page 12
  - If You Write Lyrics, But Not Music sidebar, page 10
  - Frequently Asked Questions About This Book sidebar, page 5
  - The Business of Songwriting, page 20
  - Understanding Performing & Mechanical Rights Organizations 101, page 29
  - Song Sharks, Single-Song Marketing & Collaboration 101, page 40
  - Workshops & Conferences, page 438
  - Publications of Interest, page 457

3. Prepare yourself and your songs for marketing. Get letterhead, get criticism, make contacts and subscribe to songwriting/music magazines; then start building a following and a strong catalog.
  - Improving Your Craft, page 10
  - Organizations, page 411
  - Workshops & Conferences, page 438
  - Publications of Interest, page 457
  - Collaborative Chemistry: The Elusive Art of Co-Writing, page 25
  - Using the Internet to Get Your Songs Heard, page 44
  - Taking Stock & Making Plans: Advice for Long-Distance Nashville Songwriters, page 48

4. Choose three songs you feel are ready to be marketed and make a demo.
  - Submitting Your Songs, page 13
  - What Music Professionals Look for In a Demo sidebar, page 15
  - Keeping Your Bearings in the Studio, page 36

5. Decide which arm(s) of the music business you will submit your songs to.
  - Where Should I Send My Songs?, page 6
  - Music Publishers Section Introduction, page 57
  - Record Companies Section Introduction, page 139
  - Record Producers Section Introduction, page 223

- Managers & Booking Agents Section Introduction, page 265
- Advertising, Audiovisual & Commercial Music Firms Section Introduction, page 331
- Contests & Awards Section Introduction, page 396

6. Find the companies open to your style of music and level of experience or use your contacts to get a referral and permission to submit. Be picky about where you send your material. It's a waste of your effort and money to send to every company listed in this book without regard to whether or not they want to hear your songs.

- Narrowing Your Search, page 8
- Openness to Submissions sidebar, page 8

7. Locate the companies closest to where you live. It's easier to have a relationship when the company is within driving distance.

- Geographic Index, page 484

8. Decide which companies you to want to submit your song to and whether they are appropriate markets for you (pay special attention to the information under the **Music** subhead and also the royalty percentage they pay). Do additional research through trade publications, Internet, other songwriters.

- The Markets, pages 55
- Publications of Interest, page 457
- Websites of Interest, page 462

9. Find out how to submit. Read the information under the **How to Contact** subhead.

- Sample Reply Postcard, page 14
- How to Send Your Demos, page 9
- Quiz: Are You Professional?, page 18

10. Call the companies and verify that their submission policy has not changed; also check to make sure the contact person is still there.

11. Send out your submission package according to each company's directions.

- Quiz: Are You Professional?, page 18
- Submitting Your Songs, page 13

12. Decide whether you want to sign with a company (if they reply and are interested in working with you). Just because they want to sign you doesn't mean you should.

- The Rip-Offs, page 23
- Song Sharks, Single-Song Marketing & Collaboration 101, page 40

13. Have an entertainment attorney look over any contract before you sign.

- Contracts, page 21
- Publishing Contracts, page 59
- Record Company Contracts, page 142

14. After signing, how do you get paid?

- Royalties, page 12
- Understanding Performing & Mechanical Rights Organizations 101, page 29

How to Use *Songwriter's Market* to Get Your Songs Heard

Songwriter's Market is designed to help you make good decisions about submitting your songs—whether you're approaching music publishers, record companies, producers, managers, chamber music groups, or theater companies.

If you're new to the business of marketing your music, a good place to start—after this article, but before you dive into the market listings—is with Quick-Start on page 3 and Getting Started, on page 10. If you're an old hand at this, you might wish to begin with a quick brush-up in The Business of Songwriting, on page 20. In either case, the other articles, Insider Report interviews, and section introductions throughout the book should prove informative and inspiring.

Getting to know this book. *Songwriter's Market* is divided into Markets and Resources. The Markets section contains all the companies (music publishers, record companies, etc.) seeking new material and is the part of the book you will concentrate on when submitting songs. If you're uncertain about which markets might have the most interest in your material, review the introductory explanations at the beginning of each section. They will clarify the various functions of each segment of the music industry and help you narrow your list of possible submissions. The Resources section contains listings and information on organizations, workshops, retreats/colonies, publications and websites to help you learn more about the music industry and the craft of songwriting.

Frequently Asked Questions About This Book

1. What's the deal with listing companies that don't take unsolicited submissions?

We want to provide you with the most complete songwriting resource. To do this, you should be aware of the companies that are not open to unsolicited submissions so you can take one of two actions: either 1) don't submit to them; or 2) work to establish a relationship with them to earn a solicited submission. If the major companies that are closed to submissions weren't in here, wouldn't you wonder what their policy was? Also, it's important to read these listings every year to keep informed about the industry.

2. How do these companies get listed in the book anyway?

No company pays to be included—all listings are free. Every company has to fill out a detailed questionnaire about their services. All questionnaires are screened to make sure the companies meet our requirements (see The Rip-Offs on page 23). Each year we contact every company in the book and have them update their information.

3. Why aren't other companies I know about listed in this book?

We may have sent these companies a questionnaire, but they never returned it. Or if they did return a questionnaire, we may have decided not to include them based on our requirements (see The Rip-Offs on page 23).

4. I sent a company a demo tape, and they said in their listing they take unsolicited submissions. My demo was returned unopened. What happened?

At the time we contacted the company they were open to submissions, but things change fast in this business and their policy may have changed by the time you sent your demo. It's always a good idea to call a company to check on their policy before sending them anything.

WHERE SHOULD I SEND MY SONGS?

It depends. Who are you writing your music for? Are you writing songs for an act you now belong to? Are you hoping to have your music accepted and recorded by an artist? Take a look at the How Songs Are Recorded and Released flow chart on page 7. It shows the different paths a songwriter can take to get her music recorded (the Key to this chart is below).

The performing songwriter. If you are writing songs for an existing group or for yourself as a solo artist, you're probably trying to advance the career of your act. If that's the case, and you're seeking a recording contract, the Record Companies section will be the place to start. Look also at the Record Producers section. Independent record producers are constantly on the lookout for up-and-coming artists. They may also have strong connections with record companies looking for acts, and will pass your demo on or recommend the act to a record company. And if your act doesn't yet have representation, your demo submission may be included as part of a promotional kit sent to a prospective manager listed in the Managers & Booking Agents section.

The nonperforming songwriter. If you are a songwriter seeking to have your songs recorded by other artists, you may submit to some of the same markets as the performing songwriter, but for different reasons. The Record Producers section contains mostly independent producers who work regularly with particular artists, rather than working fulltime for one record company. Because they work closely with a limited number of clients, they may be willing to consider songs written with a specific act in mind. The independent producer is often responsible for picking cuts for a recording project. The Managers & Booking Agents section may be useful for the same reason. Many personal managers are constantly seeking new material for the acts they represent, and a good song sent at the right time can mean a valuable cut for the songwriter. The primary market for songwriters not writing with particular artists in mind will be found in the Music Publishers section. Music publishers are the jacks-of-all-trades in the industry, having knowledge about and keeping abreast of developments in all other segments of the music business. They act as the first line of contact between the songwriter and the music industry.

Key to How Songs Are Recorded and Released (page 7)

A and B—options for non-performing songwriters
C—avenue for both performing and non-performing songwriters
D and E—processes for performing songwriters

Artist—band or singer who performs the music
Artist's Manager—works with the artist to manage her career; locates songs to record if the artist does not write her own material
Independent Producer—not affiliated with a record company; works in the studio and records songs; may have an affiliation with an artist
Producer—affiliated with a record company or music publisher; works in the studio and records songs
Publisher—evaluates songs for commercial potential, finds artists to record them, finds other uses (such as TV or film) for the songs, collects income generated by the songs and protects copyrights from infringement
Record Company—signs artists to its label, finances recording, promotion and touring, and releases songs/albums to radio and TV

How Songs Are Recorded and Released

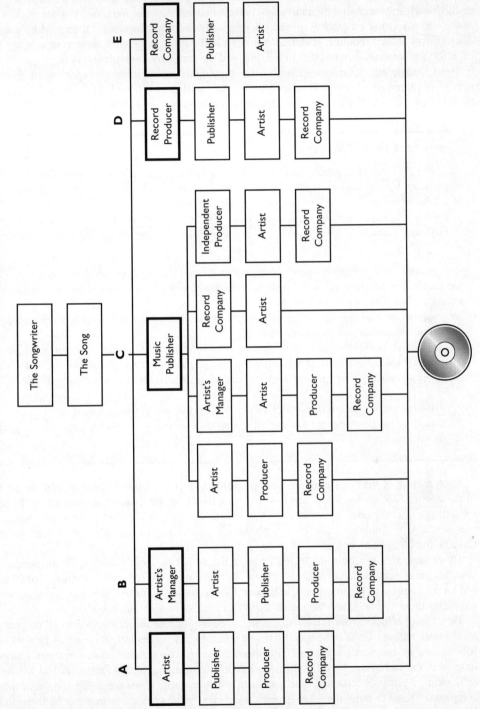

NARROWING YOUR SEARCH

After you've identified the type of companies you're going to send demos to, the next step is to research each section to find the individual markets that will be most interested in your work. Refer to the sample listing on page 9 to see where specific information can be found. Most users of *Songwriter's Market* should first check three items in the listings: location of the company, the type of music the company is interested in hearing, and the company's submission policy.

Next, decide which best describes you as a songwriter: beginner or experienced. Companies have indicated which type of songwriter they wish to work with by a symbol in front of their listing (⬜ ◨ ◪ ◫). See the Openness to Submissions sidebar below.

Openness to Submissions

Improve the chances of getting your music heard by locating companies open to your level of experience. Listings in the Music Publishers, Record Companies, Record Producers, and Managers & Booking Agents sections were asked how open they are to submissions. You can quickly find listings open to your level of experience by checking one of two sources: 1. Openness to Submissions Index on page 475; or 2. the openness icon (⬜ ◨ ◪ or ◫) at the beginning of the listing.

⬜ indicates the company is open to beginners' submissions, regardless of past success.

◨ means the company is mostly interested in previously published songwriters/well-established acts*, but will consider beginners.

◪ these companies are not interested in submissions from beginners, only from previously published songwriters/well-established acts*.

◫ companies with this icon only accept material referred to them by a reputable industry source**. [Note: We still include these listings so you know *not* to send them material. You must get an industry referral in order for these companies to listen to your songs.]

* Well-established acts are those with a following, permanent gigs or previous record deal.
** Reputable industry sources include managers, entertainment attorneys, performing rights organizations, etc.

Each section of the book contains listings from all over the United States as well as the rest of the world. If location is important to you, check the Geographic Index at the back of the book for listings of companies by state and other countries. To quickly find those markets located outside the U.S., look for these two symbols: ⯐ appears before the titles of all listings from Canada and ⊞ appears before all overseas listings.

Other important symbols are ᴺ indicating a listing is new to this edition; ✔ meaning there is a change in contact name, address, phone, fax or e-mail; ☆ for award-winning companies; and ⯐ for companies placing songs in film or TV (excluding commercials). For quick reference regarding these symbols, see the inside front and back covers of this book.

Don't mail blindly. Your music isn't going to be appropriate for submission to all companies. Most music industry firms have specific music interests and needs, and you want to be sure your submissions are being seen and heard by companies who have a genuine interest in them. Category Indexes at the end of the Music Publishers, Record Companies, Record Producers and Managers & Booking Agents sections will clue you in to which musical styles are being sought by which companies. (Keep in mind these are general categories. Some companies may not be listed in the Category Index because they either accept all types of music or the music they are looking for doesn't fit into any of the general categories.) Within each listing, under the **Music** subhead, you will find, in **bold** type, a more detailed list of the styles of music a company is seeking.

Pay close attention to the types of music described. For instance, if the music you write fits the category of "rock," there can be many variations on that style. Our sample above is interested in **hard rock**, another listing may be looking for **country rock**, and another, **soft rock**. These are three very different styles of music, but they all fall under the same general category. The Category Index is there to help you narrow down the listings within a certain music genre; it is up to you to narrow them down even further to fit the type of music you write. The music styles in each listing are *in descending order of importance*; if your particular specialty is country music, you may want to seek out those companies that list country as their first priority as your primary targets for submissions.

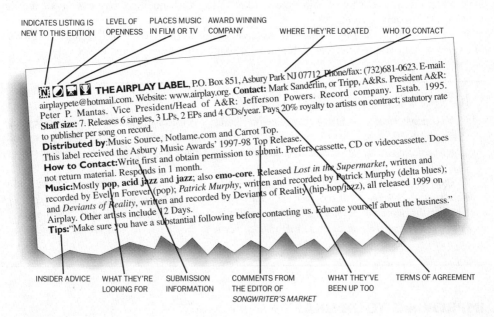

You will note that some market listings contain editorial comments and are marked by a bullet (●). Editorial comments give you additional information such as special submission requirements, any awards a company may have won, and other details that will be helpful in narrowing down your list of companies to submit to.

HOW TO SEND YOUR DEMOS

Finally, when you've placed the most likely listings geographically and identified their music preferences and openness to submissions, read the **How to Contact** subhead. As shown in the sample listing above, it will give you pertinent information about what to send as part of a demo submission, how to go about sending it and when you can expect to hear back from them.

Read carefully! Not all of the markets listed in *Songwriter's Market* accept unsolicited submissions (indicated by ⊘ in front of the listing), so it's important to read this information closely. Most companies have carefully considered their submission policies, and packages that do not follow their directions are returned or discarded without evaluation. Follow the instructions: it will impress upon the market your seriousness about getting your work heard.

You've now identified markets you feel will have the most interest in your work. Read the complete listing carefully before proceeding. Many of the listings include individualized information important for the submitting songwriter. Then, it's time for you to begin preparing your demo submission package to get your work before the people in the industry. For further information on that process, turn to Getting Started on page 10.

Getting Started

Breaking in and thriving in the competitive music industry without being overwhelmed is perhaps the biggest challenge facing songwriters. Those who not only survive but also succeed have taken the time before entering the market to learn as much as they can about the inner workings of the music industry.

Reading, studying and using the information contained in sourcebooks such as *Songwriter's Market* will help you market yourself and your work professionally and effectively.

If You Write Lyrics, But Not Music

You must find a collaborator. The music business is looking for the complete package: music plus lyrics. If you don't write music, find a collaborator who does. The best way to find a collaborator is through songwriting organizations. Check the Organizations section (pages 411) for songwriting groups near you.

Don't get ripped-off. "Music mills" advertise in the back of magazines or solicit you through the mail. For a fee they will set your lyrics or poems to music. The rip-off is that they may use the same melody for hundreds of lyrics and poems, whether it sounds good or not. Publishers recognize one of these melodies as soon as they hear it. (Also see the Rip-Offs on page 23).

IMPROVING YOUR CRAFT

There is no magic formula for success in the music business. If you want to make it, you must begin by believing in yourself and your talent. Develop your own personal vision and stick with it. Why do you write songs? Is it because you want to be rich or because you love the process? Is every song you write an attempt to become famous or a labor of love? Every effort you make to discern your motives and clarify your goals will be a step in the right direction. Successful songwriters usually believe they have a talent that deserves to be heard, whether by 2 or 2,000 people. Songwriting is a craft, like woodworking or painting. Talent is involved, of course, but with time and practice the craft can be improved and eventually mastered.

Organizations. While working on songs, look for support and feedback wherever you can. A great place to start is a local songwriting organization, which can offer friendly advice, support from other writers, and a place to meet collaborators. (For more information on songwriting organizations, see the Organizations section on page 411.) Many organizations offer song critique sessions to help you identify strengths and weaknesses in your material and give you guidance to improve your craft. Use the criticism you receive in such sessions to fine-tune your writing style. Your songwriting will improve, and you will be creating connections within the industry and continuing your education not only in the craft of songwriting but in the business as well.

Books. Books can also be helpful in matters of craft and business. Books are available to help you write better melodies, stronger lyrics and songs that sell. Many books cover the business side of music, explaining the intricacies of how the business works and giving valuable tips on how to network with people in the business. Music catalogs such as Music Books Plus (call (800)265-8481 for a catalog or visit www.musicbooksplus.com) or online booksellers like Amaz on.com and barnesandnoble.com carry hundreds of books about songwriting and the music industry.

Magazines. Magazines can keep you up-to-date on the latest trends and happenings in today's ever-changing music business. From industry trade magazines like *Billboard* and *Variety* to more specific magazines such as *Performing Songwriter* and *JazzTimes*, there is a magazine catering to just about every segment of the industry and type of music you can imagine. Since this is a trend-oriented business, weekly and monthly magazines can help you stay abreast of what's hot and what's not. For some suggestions, see Publications of Interest on page 457.

The Internet. The Internet can be another valuable source of information. Not only are many record companies, publishers and magazines online, but a growing number of music sites exist where artists can showcase their songs for an unlimited audience, chat with other songwriters and musicians from all over the world, and even sell their product online. See Websites of Interest on page 462 for a list of some current music-oriented websites as well as Using the Internet to Get Your Songs Heard on page 44. New ones are popping up every day, so surfing the Web frequently will help you learn what's available.

THE STRUCTURE OF THE MUSIC BUSINESS

The music business in the U.S. revolves around three major hubs: New York, Nashville and Los Angeles. Power is concentrated in those areas because that's where most record companies, publishers, songwriters and performers are. Many people trying to break into the music business move to one of those three cities to be close to the people and companies they want to contact. From time to time a regional music scene will heat up in a non-hub city such as Austin, Chicago or Seattle. When this happens, songwriters and performers in that city experience a kind of musical Renaissance complete with better-paying gigs, a creatively charged atmosphere and intensified interest from major labels.

All this is not to say that a successful career cannot be nurtured from any city in the country, however. It can be, especially if you are a songwriter. By moving to a major music hub, you may be closer physically to major companies, but you'll also encounter more competition than you would back home. Stay where you're comfortable; it's probably easier (and more cost-effective) to conquer the music scene where you are than it is in Los Angeles or Nashville. There are many smaller, independent companies located in cities across the country. Most international careers are started on a local level, and some may find a local career more satisfying, in its own way, than the constant striving to gain the attention of major companies.

For more advice on whether you are ready to move to a major music center, specifically Nashville, see Taking Stock & Making Plans: Advice for Long-Distance Nashville Songwriters on page 48.

Making contact. If you are interested in obtaining a recording contract, you will need to make contact with A&R reps, producers, publishers and managers. Getting your material to these professionals and establishing relationships with as many people in the industry as you can should be your main goal as a songwriter. The more people who hear your songs, the better your chances of getting them recorded.

A&R reps, producers and managers. Consumer support, in the form of money spent on records, concert tickets and other kinds of musical entertainment, keeps the music industry in business. Because of that, record companies, publishers and producers are eager to give the public what they want. To stay one step ahead of public tastes, record companies hire people who have a knack for spotting musical talent and anticipating trends, and put them in charge of finding and developing new talent. These talent scouts are called A&R representatives. "A&R" stands for "artist and repertoire," which simply means they are responsible for discovering new talent and matching songs to particular artists. The person responsible for the recording artist's product—the record—is called the producer. The producer's job is to develop the artist's work and come out of the studio with a good-sounding, saleable product that represents the artist in the best way possible. His duties sometimes include choosing songs for a particular project, so record producers are also great contacts for songwriters. Managers are interested in developing an artist's career as a whole, and are typically on the prowl for material suitable for the performers they represent.

Music publishers. Producers, A&R reps, and managers are aided in their search for talent by the music publisher. A publisher works as a songwriter's advocate who, for a percentage of the profits (typically 50% of all earnings from a particular song), attempts to find commercially profitable uses for the songs he represents. A successful publisher stays in contact with several A&R reps, finding out what upcoming projects are in need of new material, and whether any songs he represents will be appropriate.

ROYALTIES

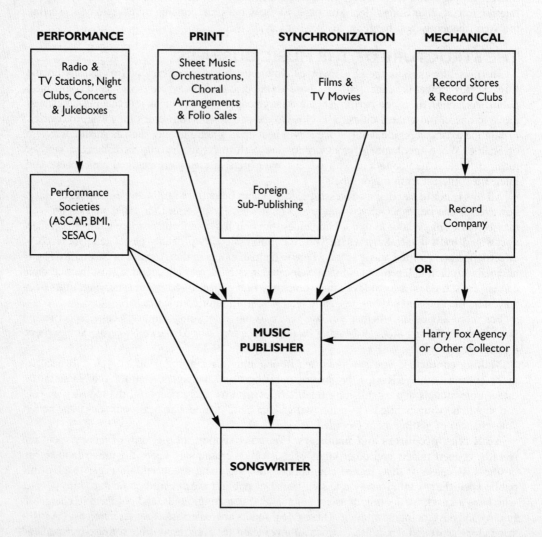

ROYALTIES

When a song is recorded and released to the public, the recording artist, songwriter, record company, producer and publisher all stand to profit. Recording artists earn a negotiated royalty from a record company based on the number of records sold. Producers are usually paid either a negotiated royalty based on sales or a flat fee at the time of recording. Publishers and songwriters earn mechanical royalties (money a record company pays a publisher based on record sales) and performance royalties, which are based on radio airplay and live performances. Look at the royalties flow chart above. It shows where royalties come from and where they go before landing in the songwriter's pocket. As the chart shows, a music publisher is an invaluable resource for songwriters to earn royalties (see the Music Publishers section on page 57).

For More Information

Songwriter's Market lists music publishers, record companies, producers and managers (as well as advertising firms, play producers and classical performing arts organizations) along with specifications on how to submit your material to each. If you can't find a certain person or company you're interested in, there are other sources of information you can try. *The Recording Industry Sourcebook*, an annual directory published by Norris-Whitney Communications, lists record companies, music publishers, producers and managers, as well as attorneys, publicity firms, media, manufacturers, distributors and recording studios around the U.S. Trade publications such as *Billboard* or *Variety*, available at most local libraries and bookstores, are great sources for up-to-date information. These periodicals list new companies as well as the artists, labels, producers and publishers for each song on the charts. CD booklets and cassette j-cards can be valuable sources of information, providing the name of the record company, publisher, producer and usually the manager of an artist or group. Use your imagination in your research and be creative—any contacts you make in the industry can only help your career as a songwriter. See Publications of Interest on page 457.

SUBMITTING YOUR SONGS

When it comes to presenting your material, the tool of the music industry is a demonstration recording—a demo. Cassette tapes have been the standard in the music industry for decades because they're so convenient. Songwriters use demos to present their songs, and musicians use them to showcase their performance skills. Demos are submitted to various professionals in the industry, either by mail or in person. Be sure to read the sidebar What Music Professionals Look for in a Demo on page 15 for specifics. Also read Quiz: Are You Professional? on page 18.

Demo quality

The production quality of demos can vary widely, but even simple guitar/vocal or piano/vocal demos must sound clean, with the instrument in tune and lyrics sung clearly. Many songwriters invest in home recording equipment, such as multitrack recorders, and record demos themselves. Other writers prefer to book studio time, hire musicians, and get professional input from an engineer or producer. Demo services are also available to record your demo for a fee. It's up to you to decide what you can afford and feel most comfortable with, and what you think best represents your song. Once a master recording is made of your song, you're ready to make cassette copies and start pitching your song to the contacts you've researched.

Some companies indicate that you may send a videocassette of your act in performance or a group performing your songs, instead of the standard cassette demo. Most of the companies listed in *Songwriter's Market* have indicated that a videocassette is not required, but have indicated their preferred format should you decide to send one. Television systems vary widely from country to country, so if you're sending a video to a foreign listing check with them for the system they're using. For example, a VHS format tape recorded using the U.S. system (called NTSC) will not play back on a standard British VCR (using the PAL system), even if the recording formats are the same. It is possible to transfer a video from one system to another, but the expense in both time and money may outweigh its usefulness. Systems for some countries include: NTSC—U.S., Canada and Japan; PAL—United Kingdom, Australia and Germany; and SECAM—France.

SAMPLE REPLY POSTCARD

I would like to hear:
☐ "Name of Song"   ☐ "Name of Song"   ☐ "Name of Song"

I prefer:
☐ cassette   ☐ DAT   ☐ CD   ☐ videocassette

With:
☐ lyric sheet   ☐ lead sheet   ☐ either   ☐ both

☐ I am not looking for material at this time, try me in _____ weeks/months.
☐ I am not interested.

_____   _____
Name   Title

Submitting by mail

When submitting material to companies listed in this book:

☑ Read the listing carefully and submit *exactly* what a company asks for in the exact way it asks that it be submitted. It's always a good idea to call first, just in case a company has changed its submission policy.

☑ Listen to each demo before sending to make sure the quality is satisfactory.

☑ Enclose a brief, typed cover letter to introduce yourself. Indicate what songs you are sending and why you are sending them. If you're a songwriter pitching songs to a particular artist, state that in the letter. If you're an artist/songwriter looking for a recording deal, you should say so. Be specific.

☑ Include typed lyric sheets or lead sheets if requested. Make sure your name, address and phone number appear on each sheet.

☑ Neatly label each tape with your name, address and phone number along with the names of the songs in the sequence in which they appear on the tape.

What Music Professionals Look for in a Demo

- **Format**. The cassette is still the preferable format for demos, although CDs are becoming more popular. Music executives are busy people and whenever they have a chance, they will listen to demos. Cassette players are what they have the easiest access to, whether in their office, car or home. Cassettes are also cheaper to duplicate than CDs or DATs, and are cheaper and easier to mail. If they like what they hear on the cassette they can always ask you for a DAT or CD later.
- **Number, order and length of songs**. The consensus throughout the industry is that three songs is sufficient. Most music professionals don't have time to listen to more than three, and they figure if you can't catch their attention in three songs, your songs probably don't have hit potential.

  Put three complete songs on the tape, not just snippets of your favorites, and remember to put your best, most commercial song first on the tape. If it's an up-tempo number, that makes it even easier to catch someone's attention. All songs should be on the same side of the tape, and none of them should be longer than four minutes. Cue the tape to the beginning of the first song so no time will be wasted fast-forwarding or rewinding.
- **Production**. How elaborate a demo has to be lies in the type of music you write, and what an individual at a company is looking for. Usually, up-tempo pop, rock and dance demos need to be more fully produced than pop ballads and country demos. Many of the companies listed in *Songwriter's Market* tell you what type of demo they prefer to receive, and if you're not sure you can always call and ask what their preference is. Either way, make sure your demo is clean and clear, and the vocals are up front.

  If you are an artist looking for a record deal, obviously your demo needs to be as fully produced as possible to convey your talent as an artist. Many singer/songwriters record their demos as if they were going to be released as an album. That way, if they have already recorded three or four CD-quality demo tapes but haven't heard anything from the labels they've been submitting to, they can put those demos together and release a CD or cassette on their own. They end up with a professional-looking product, complete with album cover graphics and liner notes, to sell at shows and through mail order without spending a lot of money to re-record the songs.
- **Performance**. If you can't sing well, you may want to find someone who can. It pays to find a good vocalist and good musicians to record your demos, and there are many places to find musicians and singers willing to work with you. Check out local songwriting organizations, music stores and newspapers to find musicians in your area you can hire to play on your demo. Many singers who don't write their own songs will sing on demos in exchange for a copy of the tape they can use as their own demo to help further their performing careers.

  If you can't find local musicians, or don't want to go through the trouble of putting together a band just for the purposes of recording your demo, you may want to try a demo service. For a fee, a demo service will produce your songs in their studio using their own singers and musicians. Many of these services advertise in music magazines, songwriting newsletters and bulletin boards at local music stores. If you decide to deal with a demo service, make sure you can hear samples of work they've done in the past. Many demo services are mail-order businesses—you send them either a rough tape of your song or the sheet music and they'll produce and record a demo within a month or two. Be sure you find a service that will let you have creative control over how your demo is to be produced, and make sure you tell them exactly how you want your song to sound. As with studios, shop around and find the demo service that best suits your needs and budget.

☑ If the company returns material (many do not; be sure to read each listing carefully), include a SASE for the return. Your return envelope to countries other than your own should contain a self-addressed envelope (SAE) and International Reply Coupon (IRC), available at your local post office. Be sure the return envelope is large enough to accommodate your material, and include sufficient postage for the weight of the package.

☑ Wrap the package neatly and write (or type on a shipping label) the company's address and your return address so they are clearly visible. Your package is the first impression a company has of you and your songs, so neatness is important.

☑ Mail first class. Stamp or write "First Class Mail" on the package and on the SASE you enclose. Don't send by registered or certified mail unless it is specifically requested by the company.

☑ Keep records of the dates, songs and companies you submit to.

If you are writing to inquire about a company's needs or to request permission to submit (many companies ask you to do this first), your query letter should be typed, brief and pleasant. Explain the kind of material you have and ask for their needs and submission policy.

To expedite a reply, enclose a self-addressed, stamped postcard requesting the information you are seeking. Your typed questions (see the Sample Reply Postcard on the previous page) should be direct and easy to answer. Place the company's name and address in the upper left hand space on the front of the postcard so you'll know which company you queried. Keep a record of the queries you send for future reference.

Simultaneous submissions and holds. It's acceptable to submit your songs to more than one person at a time (this is called simultaneous submission). The exception to this is when a publisher, artist or other industry professional asks if he may put a song of yours "on hold." This means he intends to record it and doesn't want you to give the song to anyone else. Your song may be returned to you without ever having been recorded, even if it's been on hold for months. Or, it may be recorded but not used on an album. If either of these things happens, you're free to pitch your song to other people again. (You can, and should, protect yourself from having a song on hold indefinitely. Establish a deadline for the person who asks for the hold, e.g., "You can put my song on hold for [number of] months." Or modify the hold to specify that you will pitch the song to other people, but you will not sign a deal without allowing the person who has the song on hold to make you an offer.) When someone publishes your song and you sign a contract, you grant that publisher exclusive rights to your song and you may not pitch it to other publishers. You can, however, pitch it to any artists or producers interested in recording the song without publishing it themselves.

Following up. If a company doesn't respond within several weeks after you've sent your demo, don't despair. As long as your demo is in their hands, there is a chance someone is reviewing it. If after a reasonable amount of time you still haven't received word on your submission (check the reporting time each company states in its listing), follow up with a friendly letter or phone call. Many companies do not return submissions, so don't expect a company that states "Does not return material" to send your materials back to you.

Submitting in person

Planning a trip to one of the major music hubs will give you insight into how the music industry works. Whether you decide to visit New York, Nashville or Los Angeles, have specific goals in mind and set up appointments to make the most of your time there. It will be difficult to get in to see some industry professionals as many of them are extremely busy and may not feel meeting out-of-town writers is a high priority. Other people are more open to, and even encourage, face-to-face meetings. They may feel that if you take the time to travel to where they are and you're organized enough to schedule meetings beforehand, you're more professional than many aspiring songwriters who blindly submit inappropriate songs through the mail. (For listings of companies by state, see the Geographic Index at the back of the book.)

What to take. Take several cassette copies and lyric sheets of each of your songs. More than one of the companies you visit may ask that you leave a copy to review. There's also a good chance that the person you have an appointment with will have to cancel (expect that occasionally) but wants you to leave a copy of the songs so he can listen and contact you later. Never give someone the last or only copy of your material—if it is not returned to you, all the hard work and money that went into making that demo will be lost.

Where to network. Another good place to meet industry professionals face-to-face is at seminars such as the yearly South by Southwest Music and Media Conference in Austin, the National Academy of Songwriters' annual Songwriters Expo in Los Angeles, or the Nashville Songwriters Association's Spring Symposium, to name a few (see the Workshops & Conferences section on page 438 for further ideas). Many of these conferences feature demo listening sessions, where industry professionals listen to demos submitted by songwriters attending the seminars.

Dealing with rejection. Many good songs have been rejected simply because they weren't what the particular publisher or record company was looking for at the time, so don't take rejection personally. Realize that if a few people don't like your songs, it doesn't mean they're not good. However, if there seems to be a consensus about your work—for instance, the feel of a song isn't right or the lyrics need work—give the advice serious thought. Listen attentively to what the reviewers say and use their criticism constructively to improve your songs.

Quiz: Are You Professional?

OK, everybody! Take out your submission package and let's take a look. Hmm . . . very interesting. I think you're well on your way, but you should probably change a few things.

We asked record companies, music publishers and record producers, "What do songwriters do in correspondence with your company (by phone, mail or demo) that screams 'amateur'?" Take this quiz and find out how professional you appear to those on the receiving end of your submission. The following are common mistakes songwriters make all the time. They may seem petty, but, really, do you want to give someone an excuse not to listen to your demo? Check off the transgressions you have committed.

BY MAIL YOU SENT:

☐ anything handwritten (lyrics, cover letters, labels for cassettes). Today there is no excuse for handwritten materials. Take advantage of your local library's typewriters or businesses that charge by the hour to use a computer. And don't even think about using notebook paper.

☐ materials without a contact name *and* phone number. Put this information on *everything*.

☐ lyrics only. Music companies want music and words. See the If You Write Lyrics, But Not Music sidebar on page 10.

☐ insufficient return postage, an envelope too small to return materials, no SASE at all, or a "certified mail" package. If you want materials returned, don't expect the company to send it back on their dime with their envelope—give them what they need. Certified mail is unnecessary and annoying; first class will suffice.

☐ long-winded, over-hyped cover letters, or no cover letter at all. Companies don't need (or want) to hear your life story, how many instruments you play, how many songs you've written, how talented you are or how all your songs are sure-fire hits. Briefly explain why you are sending the songs (e.g., your desire to have them published) and let the songs speak for themselves. Double check your spelling too.

☐ over-packaged materials. Do not use paper towels, napkins, foil or a mountain of tape to package your submission. Make the investment in bubble wrap or padded envelopes.

☐ photos of your parents or children. As much as you love them, your family's pictures or letters of recommendation won't increase your chances of success (unless your family is employed by a major music company).

☐ songs in the style the company doesn't want. Do not "shotgun" your submissions. Read the listings carefully to see if they want your style of music.

YOU CALLED THE CONTACT PERSON:

☐ to check on the submission only a couple days after it was received. Read the listings to see how soon (or if) they report back on submissions. Call them only after that time has elapsed. If they are interested, they will find a way to contact you.

☐ excessively. It's important to be proactive, but check yourself. Make sure you have given them enough time to respond before you call again. Calling every week is inappropriate.

☐ armed with an angry or aggressive tone of voice. A bad attitude will get you nowhere.

WITH THE DEMO YOU PROVIDED:

☐ no lyric sheet. A typed sheet of lyrics for each song is required.

☐ poor vocals and instrumentation. Spending a little extra for professionals can make all the difference.

☐ a poor-quality cassette. The tape should be new and have a brand name.

☐ long intros. Don't waste time—get to the heart of the song.

☐ buried vocals. Those vocals should be out front and clear as a bell.

☐ recordings of sneezes or coughs. Yuck.

SCORING

If you checked 1-3: Congratulations! You're well within the professional parameters. Remedy the unprofessional deeds you're guilty of and send out more packages.

If you checked 4 or more: Whoa! Overhaul your package, let someone check it over, and then fire away with those impeccably professional submissions!

The Business of Songwriting

Familiarizing yourself with standard music industry practices will help you toward your goal of achieving and maintaining a successful songwriting career. The more you know, the less likely you'll be to make a mistake when dealing with contracts, agreements and the other legal and business elements that make up the *business* side of your songwriting career.

COPYRIGHT

Copyright protection is extended to your songs the instant they are put down in fixed form. This protection lasts for your lifetime (or the lifetime of the last surviving author, if you co-wrote the song) plus 70 years. When you prepare demos, place notification of copyright on all copies of your song—the lyric sheets, lead sheets and cassette labels. The notice is simply the word "copyright" or the symbol © followed by the year the song was created (or published) and your name: © 2001 by John L. Public.

Registering your copyright

For the best protection, you may want to consider registering your copyright with the Library of Congress. Although a song is copyrighted whether or not it is registered, registration establishes a public record of your copyright and could prove useful in any future litigation involving the song. Registration also entitles you to a potentially greater settlement in a copyright infringement suit.

To register your song, request government form PA from the Copyright Office. Call the 24-hour hotline at (202)707-9100 and leave your name and address on the recorder. Once you receive the PA form, you will be required to return it, along with a registration fee and a tape or lead sheet of your song, to the Register of Copyrights, Copyright Office, Library of Congress, Washington DC 20559. It may take as long as four months to receive your certificate of registration from the Copyright Office, but your songs are protected from the date of creation, and the date of registration will reflect the date you applied for registration. For additional information about registering your songs, call the Copyright Office's Public Information Office at (202)707-3000 or visit their website at http://lcweb.loc.gov/copyright.

> **ℹ️ For More Information**
>
> The Library of Congress's copyright website is your best source for current, complete information on the subject of copyright. Not only can you learn all you could possibly wish to know about intellectual property rights and U.S. copyright law (the section of the U.S. Code dealing with copyright is reprinted there in its entirety), but you can also download copyright forms directly from the site. The site also includes links to other copyright-related web pages, many of which will be of interest to songwriters, including ASCAP, BMI, SESAC, and the Harry Fox Agency. Check it out at **http://lcweb.loc.gov/copyright**.

Copyright infringement is rarer than most people think, but if you ever feel that one of your songs has been stolen—that someone has unlawfully infringed on your copyright—you must prove that you created the work. Copyright registration is the best proof of a date of creation. You *must* have your copyright registered in order to file a copyright infringement lawsuit. One way writers prove a work is original is to keep their rough drafts and revisions of songs, either on paper or on tape.

Be forewarned there is one potential unintended consequence of registering your song with the Library of Congress. Because copyright registration establishes a public record of your songwriting, unethical music companies, or "song sharks" (see the Rip-Offs on page 23, and Song Sharks, Single-Song Marketing & Collaboration 101 on page 40), often search the copyright indexes and mail solicitations to songwriters with registered songs who live out away from the major music centers such as Nashville, and who may not know any better and therefore be easy prey for these unethical companies. *Do not allow this possibility to dissuade you from registering your songs with the copyright office!* Simply be aware and educate yourself about what you should expect from a legitimate ethical music company.

CONTRACTS

You will encounter several types of contracts as you deal with the business end of songwriting. You may sign a legal agreement between you and a co-writer establishing percentages of the writer's royalties each of you will receive, what you will do if a third party (e.g., a recording artist) wishes to change your song and receive credit as a co-writer, and other things. As long as the issues at stake are simple and co-writers respect each other and discuss their business philosophy in advance of writing a song, they can write up an agreement without the aid of a lawyer. In other situations— when a publisher, producer or record company wants to do business with you—you should always have the contract reviewed by a knowledgeable entertainment attorney.

Single song contracts

This is a common contract and is likely to be the first you will encounter in your songwriting career. A music publisher offers a single song contract when he wants to sign one or more of your songs but doesn't want to hire you as a staff writer. You assign your rights to a particular song to the publisher for an agreed-upon number of years (usually the life of the copyright).

Typical components. Every single song contract should contain this basic information: the publisher's name, the writer's name, the song's title, the date and the purpose of the agreement. The songwriter also declares that the song is an original work and he is the creator of the work. The contract must specify the royalties the songwriter will earn from various uses of the song, including performance, mechanical, print and synchronization royalties.

Splits and royalties. The songwriter should receive no less than 50% of the income his song generates. That means that whatever the song earns in royalties, the publisher and songwriter should split 50/50. The songwriter's half is called the "writer's share" and the publisher's half is called the "publisher's share." If there is more than one songwriter, the songwriters split the writer's share. Sometimes successful songwriters will bargain for a percentage of the publisher's share, negotiating what is in fact a co-publishing agreement. For a visual explanation of royalties, see the flow chart on page 12.

"Holds" and reversion clauses. Songwriters should also negotiate for a reversion clause. This calls for the rights to the song to revert to the songwriter if some provision of the contract is not met. The typical reversion clause covers the failure to secure a commercial release of a song within a specified period of time (usually one or two years). If nothing happens with the song, the rights will revert back to the songwriter, who can then give the song to a more active publisher if he so chooses. Some publishers will agree to this, figuring that if they don't get some action on the song in the first year, they're not likely to ever have much luck with it. Other publishers are reluctant to agree to this clause. They may invest a lot of time and money in a song, re-demoing it and pitching it to a number of artists; they may be actively looking for ways to exploit the song. If a producer puts a song on hold for a while and goes into a lengthy recording project, by the time the record company (or artist or producer) decides which songs to release as singles, a year can easily go by. That's why it's so important to have a good working relationship with your publisher. You need to trust that he has your best interests in mind and be flexible if the situation calls for it.

Ten Basic Points Your Contract Should Include

The following list, taken from a Songwriters Guild of America publication, enumerates the basic features of an acceptable songwriting contract:

1. **Work for Hire.** When you receive a contract covering just one composition, you should make sure the phrases "employment for hire" and "exclusive writer agreement" are *not* included. Also, there should be no options for future songs.

2. **Performing Rights Affiliation.** If you previously signed publishing contracts, you should be affiliated with either ASCAP, BMI or SESAC. All performance royalties must be received directly by you from your performing rights organization and this should be written into your contract.

3. **Reversion Clause.** The contract should include a provision that if the publisher does not secure a release of a commercial sound recording within a specified time (one year, two years, etc.), the contract can be terminated by you.

4. **Changes in the Composition.** If the contract includes a provision that the publisher can change the title, lyrics or music, this should be amended so that only with your consent can such changes be made.

5. **Royalty Provisions.** You should receive fifty percent (50%) of all publisher's income on all licenses issued. If the publisher prints and sells his own sheet music, your royalty should be ten percent (10%) of the wholesale selling price. The royalty should not be stated in the contract as a flat rate ($.05, $.07, etc.).

6. **Negotiable Deductions.** Ideally, demos and all other expenses of publication should be paid 100% by the publisher. The only allowable fee is for the Harry Fox Agency collection fee, whereby the writer pays one half of the amount charged to the publisher for mechanical rights. The current rate charged by the Harry Fox Agency is 7.55 cents per cut for songs under 5 minutes; and 1.45 cents per minute for songs over 5 minutes.

7. **Royalty Statements and Audit Provision.** Once the song is recorded, you are entitled to receive royalty statements at least once every six months. In addition, an audit provision with no time restriction should be included in every contract.

8. **Writer's Credit.** The publisher should make sure that you receive proper credit on all uses of the composition.

9. **Arbitration.** In order to avoid large legal fees in case of a dispute with your publisher, the contract should include an arbitration clause.

10. **Future Uses.** Any use not specifically covered by the contract should be retained by the writer to be negotiated as it comes up.

Additional clauses. Other issues a contract should address include whether or not an advance will be paid to the songwriter and how much it will be; when royalties will be paid (quarterly or semiannually); who will pay for demos—the publisher, songwriter or both; how lawsuits against copyright infringement will be handled, including the cost of such lawsuits; whether the publisher has the right to sell the song to another publisher without the songwriter's consent; and whether the publisher has the right to make changes in a song, or approve of changes written by someone else, without the songwriter's consent. In addition, the songwriter should have the right to audit the publisher's books if the songwriter deems it necessary and gives the publisher reasonable notice. (For more information on music publishers, see the Music Publishers section introduction on page 57.)

SGA's Popular Songwriter's Contract. While there is no such thing as a "standard" contract, The Songwriters Guild of America (SGA) has drawn up a Popular Songwriter's Contract which it believes to be the best minimum songwriter contract available. The Guild will send a copy of the contract at no charge to any interested songwriter upon request. (See the Songwriters Guild of America listing in the Organizations section on page 433.) SGA will also review free of charge any contract offered to its members, checking it for fairness and completeness. For a thorough discussion of the somewhat complicated subject of contracts, see these two books published by Writer's Digest Books: *The Craft and Business of Songwriting*, by John Braheny and *Music Publishing: A Songwriter's Guide*, by Randy Poe.

THE RIP-OFFS

As in any business, the music industry has its share of dishonest, greedy people who try to unfairly exploit the talents and aspirations of others. Most of them use similar methods of attack that you can learn to identify and avoid. "Song sharks," as they're called, prey on beginners—those writers who are unfamiliar with ethical industry standards. Song sharks will take any songs—quality doesn't count. They're not concerned with future royalties, since they get their money upfront from songwriters who think they're getting a great deal (for additional information see Song Sharks, Single-Song Marketing & Collaboration 101 on page 40.)

Here are some guidelines to help you recognize these "song sharks":

- **Never pay to have your music "reviewed"** by a company that may be interested in publishing, producing or recording it. Reputable companies review material free of charge.
- **Never pay to have your songs published**. A reputable company interested in your songs assumes the responsibility and cost of promoting them, in hopes of realizing a profit once the songs are recorded and released.
- **Avoid paying a fee to have a publisher make a demo of your songs**. Some publishers may take demo expenses out of your future royalties, but you should reconsider paying upfront for demo costs for a song that is signed to a publisher. See the sidebar Publishers That Charge on the next page for more information.
- **No record company should ask you to make or pay for a demo**. Their job is to make records and decide which artists to sign *after* listening to demo submissions.
- **Never pay to have your lyrics or poems set to music**. "Music mills"—for a price— may use the same melody for hundreds of lyrics and poems, whether it sounds good or not. Publishers recognize one of these melodies as soon as they hear it (see the sidebar If You Write Lyrics, But Not Music on page 10.)
- **Avoid CD compilation deals where a record company asks you to pay a fee** to be included on a CD to be sent to radio stations, producers, etc. It's primarily a money-maker for the company involved, and radio station programmers and other industry professionals just don't listen to these things to find new artists.
- **Read all contracts carefully before signing** and don't sign any contract you're unsure about or that you don't fully understand. It is well worth paying an attorney for the time it takes him to review a contract if you can avoid a bad situation that may cost you thousands of dollars in potential income.
- **Don't pay a company to pair you with a collaborator**. A better way is to contact songwriting organizations that offer collaboration services to their members.
- **Don't sell your songs outright**. It's unethical for anyone to offer such a proposition.
- **If you are asked by a record company or other music-industry company to pay expenses upfront, be careful**. A record producer may charge upfront to produce your record, or a small indie label may ask you to pay recording costs. Each situation is different, and it's up to you to decide whether or not it will be beneficial. Talk to other artists who have signed similar contracts before signing one yourself. Research the company and its track record by finding out what types of product they have released, and what kind of

distribution they have. Visit their website on the Internet, if they have one. Beware of any company that won't let you know what it has done in the past. If it has had successes and good working relationships with other writers and artists, it should be happy to brag about them.

- **Before participating in a songwriting contest, read the rules carefully**. Be sure that what you're giving up in the way of entry fees, etc., is not greater than what you stand to gain by winning the contest. See the Contests & Awards section introduction on page 396 for more advice on this.
- **Verify any situation about an individual or company if you have any doubts at all**. Contact the performing rights society with which it is affiliated. Check with the Better Business Bureau in the town where it is located or the state's attorney general's office. Contact professional organizations you're a member of and inquire about the reputation of the company.

Publishers That Charge

Songwriter's Market feels if a publisher truly believes in you and your music, they will invest in a professional demo. This book only lists publishers that do not charge for this service. If you have found a publisher through this book that charges for demo services, write to the editor at: *Songwriter's Market*, 4700 E. Galbraith Road, Cincinnati OH 45236.

There are smaller publishing companies with demo services as part of their organization. They may request a professional demo and give you the option of using their services or those of an outside company. This doesn't necessarily mean the publishing company is ripping you off. Use your best judgement and know there are many other publishing companies that will not charge for this service.

RECORD KEEPING

As your songwriting career continues to grow, you should keep a ledger or notebook containing all financial transactions relating to your songwriting. It should include a list of income from royalty checks as well as expenses incurred as a result of your songwriting business: cost of tapes, demo sessions, office supplies, postage, traveling expenses, dues to organizations, class and workshop fees and any publications you purchase pertaining to songwriting. It's also advisable to open a checking account exclusively for your songwriting activities, not only to make record keeping easier, but to establish your identity as a business for tax purposes.

Any royalties you receive will not reflect taxes or any other mandatory deductions. It is your responsibility to keep track of income and file the appropriate tax forms. Contact the IRS or an accountant who serves music industry clients for specific information.

INTERNATIONAL MARKETS

Everyone talks about the world getting smaller, and it's true. Modern communication technology has brought us to the point at which information can be transmitted around the globe instantly. No business has enjoyed the fruits of this progress more than the music industry. American music is heard in virtually every country in the world, and having a hit song in other countries as well as in the United States can greatly increase a songwriter's royalty earnings.

While these listings may be a bit more challenging to deal with than domestic companies, they offer additional avenues for songwriters looking for places to place their songs. To find international listings, see the Geographical Index at the back of the book. You might also flip through the pages and look for listings preceded by 🌐 which indicates an international market.

Collaborative Chemistry: The Elusive Art of Co-Writing

BY DAN KIMPEL

It is an enduring cliché: two songwriters huddled in a tiny cubicle, pouring their emotions into one song. Today, in this era of instant computer communication and transferable sound files, it is no longer necessary for songwriters to be on the same continent— let alone in the same room—to collaborate. Still, what has not changed is the elusive chemistry that creates hit songs.

As in every historical decade of modern popular music, today's charts reveal the dominance of co-writes in all popular formats. Tunesmiths in the songwriting capitol of Nashville plan their creative lives around painstakingly scheduled co-writing appointments. In pop and dance music, writer-producers and self-proclaimed "song doctors" are often brought in to collaborate with artists. Hip-hip and rap songs often utilize samples—snippets of pre-existent songs—as well as writer-producers. Consequently, these lengthy credits frequently resemble the rosters of Manhattan law firms.

Dan Kimpel

Cultivating collaborations is an undeniable key to future successes for emerging artists and new songwriters. Choosing the right partner or partners is probably the most crucial decision a songwriter can make. "Competition demands that each element of the song—melody, lyric and groove—be the best they can be, says John Braheny, author of the best-selling book *The Craft & Business of Songwriting* (Writer's Digest.) And, he adds, "Few writers can do it all." Clearly, co-writing is not only about the art but also the politics. Writing a song with an established songwriter, an up and coming act or the next chart-topping producer may be the best possible way to open doors. But most successful songwriting collaborations still retain a trace of the mystical about them: two songwriters, bonded in their respective processes, distilling their souls into the absolute essence of a song.

PARTNERS IN RHYME

Stephanie Bentley and Holly Lamar grew up in adjacent small Southern towns. When they reconnected years later in Nashville, their first co-writing effort blossomed into a chart-topping song, "Breathe," recorded by Faith Hill. Bentley is still relatively new to the songwriting world; she was first a performer, vocalist and recording artist. Today, as a Grammy and ACM-nominated songwriter, she is in much demand as a collaborator.

"Because of 'Breathe' I've been able to be put with some great writers," she says, "but I'm

DAN KIMPEL *is the author of the best-selling book* Networking in the Music Business *(Writer's Digest Books). Since 1998, he has taught a course based on his book at Sir Paul McCartney's Liverpool Institute for Performing Arts (LIPA) in the U.K. He contributes to a variety of print mediums, and passengers on United Airlines hear Kimpel's interviews with songwriters and recording artists on the United Entertainment Network. He lives in Los Angeles, California.*

always going through this process, 'Am I going to be on today?' There are days when it just doesn't come as easily. If I have a day like that with Holly, or someone I normally write with, it's OK; we'll go shopping or have lunch. With a new person, there's more pressure. It's a tightrope—but it's exciting."

Songwriter Allan Rich agrees that he too experiences his most uncomfortable moments when meeting a potential collaborator. "It's like taking your clothes off before you know the person, it's that vulnerable," he explains. Rich is a Hollywood-based gold/platinum writer responsible for co-writing the *NSYNC smash, "I Drive Myself Crazy," Barbra Streisand's "Lessons to be Learned," and two Academy Award-nominated songs, "Run to You" recorded by Whitney Houston on the 23-million selling *Bodyguard* soundtrack, and "For the First Time" from *One Fine Day*, a song covered by both Kenny Loggins and Rod Stewart.

When working with a new co-writer Rich takes a personal path. "I talk and get to know the person a bit first. Then, when I feel comfortable I always say, 'Let's agree that we will throw out every idea even if it's stupid,' because you have to throw out the stupid stuff to get to the good stuff. But it's like a date; you want to make a good impression, make them like you, especially if you're recommended."

Both of Rich's Oscar-nominated songs were penned with his longtime collaborator, Jud Friedman. "Jud and I have been working together for 11 or 12 years and will continue to work together," says Rich. "But Jud and I also both write with other people as well, out of necessity and for our own personal growth. We have to allow each other the freedom to express different sides of ourselves. Other people bring things to the party with Jud that I can't and vice versa. Why should we be limited in expressing ourselves?" It was Rich's notable collaboration with Rick Nowels and Ellen Shipley that resulted in *NSYNC's "I Drive Myself Crazy."

Steve Seskin, a songwriter based in Northern California, has mined country gold by co-writing such emotionally-charged smashes as "Don't Laugh at Me" for Mark Wills and "Grown Men Don't Cry" for country superstar Tim McGraw. He too uses the dating metaphor. "Why would you go out on a date with someone? You think they're interesting to talk to, you like the way they look. And then you go out on a date and it's not what you thought it would be. Sometimes it's true love and other times you're going, 'Can I get out of here? What time is it?' With co-writing it's the same thing."

Rich adds, "If you meet with someone to write and there's fireworks and chemistry you can have a hot passionate writing affair, then wake up in the morning and never see them again. Writing can be a series of magic one night stands."

Seskin cautions, "But if you get in the room with someone and all those factors are there, that doesn't mean two people can write well together. It's such a personal experience and we all have different processes. Sometimes two people who respect each other get together in a room and they each do it so differently they can't do it together."

AFTER THE HONEYMOON

And just as in real life, there are those rare occasions when dating leads to something more long term. Rich reveals, "I think you have to have trust, because it's literally a marriage. The same things that come up in relationships between two people in a personal relationship also come up between collaborators, especially if you have a long time writing relationship. Jealousy, for instance. If you start working with another collaborator it can get touchy, if there is a possessiveness."

Speaking of his long association with Jud Friedman, Rich continues, "Jud and I have different processes and we don't always agree, but I always respect and admire the person he is. We both have to remember that we're different people and our needs are different. He's very work oriented, and my work ethic is more like a butterfly. Jud's married and I'm single; he has a family and I have more freedom. All of that comes to play when we sit down to work because we are two very distinctive personalities. As long as we come to the table with the same goals we do well. And I couldn't sustain a writing relationship with a person if I didn't trust him, or have faith in him, and know he's an honest, fair person. From that point you can open yourself up in a relationship and take chances."

Stephanie Bentley also seeks this emotional resonance, since songwriting is contingent upon revealing a depth of honesty. She says, "If you're writing songs, it's better that you know somebody well because you can be totally honest and let down all the barriers. You have to be comfortable enough with someone to bare your soul, lay it on the line, and get laughed at occasionally. The most important thing is that your personalities click. It's great to hook up with new writers, but every friend of mine who's a writer says the same thing: the people you always come back to are the people you've been writing with the longest, because these are the people you feel the most comfortable with. The chemistry is the most important thing."

Allan Rich notes that in writing partnerships there are inevitable ebbs and flows. "You constantly have to work on writing partnerships to propel them forward," he says. "At the same time, you have to let them flow and let go. I think there have been those moments for both Jud and me. He's my friend; I love his family. But I don't think you necessarily have to be a good friend in order to write a great song with somebody."

Extending Allan Rich's songwriting partnership as marriage concept one step further, there was a notable occasion when his presence formed a creative triumvirate that lit a fire between two long-time hit collaborators, Rick Nowels and Ellen Shipley. The song was "I Drive Myself Crazy."

Rich explains: "With Ellen and Rick, they had done such incredible work but were looking for a little bridge between the two of them; maybe a little outside energy to re-ignite their relationship at that moment. I wanted to work with both of them so we got together. They played me some tracks of things they had started and they were stuck on. They played me the chorus, 'I lie awake and I drive myself crazy/ I drive myself crazy thinking of you.' And I interjected 'Made a mistake when I let you go baby' and that was the spark that was needed to ignite the collaboration. That was just sitting in a room. We've never written another song. I've written with both Ellen and Rick separately, but not together. That's an example of a magic moment."

CHANGING PARTNERS

There is specialization within songwriting; some writers are more adept at lyrics, others more comfortable in composing music. Hip-hop and rap are often configured with the track recorded first, then the lyrics constructed later. As John Braheny notes, "You see a lot of collaborations with artists and writers or writer-producers that are specifically tailored for the style of the artist. We see a lot of songs in the R&B/hip-hop and dance music genres that are collaborations with producers who may not be great lyricists or melody writers, but who are experts at creating great tracks as a foundation for the song. In that case, they find writer/singers who create melodies and or lyrics on top of the tracks."

Surprisingly, given her formidable presence in Nashville, Stephanie Bentley doesn't consider herself married to the genre of country music. She notes "Breathe" was selected as BMI's Pop Song of the Year and explains, "I grew up on all kinds of music—jazz, country, pop. I like not doing only one thing. It's fun to be freer with lyrics and music than Nashville can allow you to. I love writing music for Nashville, but it's more conservative, more restrained. It's fun to get out of that box a little bit sometimes." Many of her recent collaborators have been European writers, based in London, and the new pop mecca, Stockholm, Sweden. "Some people only work one way," Bentley confides. "I try to be a chameleon and go with the flow. Some people like to start with the melody and go from there; some have to have an idea before they think of a melody or lyric. Everyone works a different way. It's interesting for me because it lets me work with other writers. There's never one particular scenario that's going to make a great song."

Seskin also changes his approach, depending on the situation. "I write with some people who couldn't be in the same room together, but they both work with me separately. There's something in my personality that allows for that. I enjoy getting to know people who are different than me." One of Seskin's collaborators is hit writer Bob DiPiero, one of Music City's most enduring writers, with cuts including "American Made" (Oak Ridge Boys); "Wink (Neal McCoy); "Cleopatra, Queen of Denial" (Pam Tillis); and "Daddy's Money" (Ricochet), which he penned with Seskin. "Have you seen the Woody Allen movie *Zelig*?" queries DiPiero. "If Woody Allen was standing with black jazz musicians, he'd become one; if he was standing around priests, he'd become a holy man. Well I'm like a musical Zelig. Whatever my co-writers are into, I gravitate to that."

PLEASE PLACE YOUR TRAY TABLES IN THEIR UPRIGHT POSITIONS

In the past 15 years, having made 125 separate songwriting trips from his home in Northern California to Nashville to write, Steve Seskin could be a poster boy for both frequent flyer miles and songwriting collaborations. "I write an average of 50 songs a year," he notes, " and I write 40 of them in 60 days. I don't like to write all the time; I have other things to do." Does he come into a collaboration with ideas and concepts? "It's always different," he says. "It depends on who I write with. Alan Shamblin (co-writer of "Don't Laugh at Me") is a keeper of ideas. He always has a notebook of 50 titles and a couple of starts on those titles. I know he'll have an idea. Lisa Drew, a lyricist, will always have three or four ideas. I might not like any of them, but then we'll go to ground zero and just talk. Annie Roboff (co-writer of "This Kiss" for Faith Hill) is way more of a music person than a lyricist, but she doesn't keep a lot of ideas around. If I'm going to write with her I'll make sure I have an idea that at least I'm excited about. I've come up with songs out of nothing, just sitting there talking. Other times I have an idea that's burning a hole in me."

Seskin, a recording artist and performer himself, rarely writes solo. "Not entire songs," he qualifies. "I'll come up with something while I'm home and then go to Nashville or L.A. and write with someone and bring out that tidbit to get it rolling. I've only written three songs by myself in the past ten years. I've become somewhat addicted to co-writing—it comes under the heading of 'If it ain't broke don't fix it.' "

And for Seskin, co-writing all comes back to the personal bond. "You're attracted to their material and the part of the human being you're going to spend six hours in a room with. I'm not sure we're going to be prolific every day, so I like writing with someone I can hang with. I think that's a key first thing."

MAKING CONTACT

Where can you meet potential collaborators? Clubs, classes and songwriting organizations will offer the most immediate results. On-line, websites such as www.tonos.com and performing rights organizations ASCAP, BMI and SESAC often hook up writers as well. Lyricist Pamela Phillips-Oland who authored *The Art of Writing Great Lyrics* (Allworth Press) advises, "Collaborators may be advertised for in magazines such as *Music Connection* and *American Songwriter*," but she notes that meeting potential collaborators is a contact sport. "Speak to everyone you know. You'd be surprised who has a friend who is a songwriter, and people are only too happy to introduce friends to friends. Attend seminars, join local songwriting organizations, take songwriting classes offered through community college extension courses and elsewhere. Don't be afraid to approach a stranger whose work you admire. Someone has to make the first move!"

Understanding Performing & Mechanical Rights Organizations 101

BY RUSTY GORDON

PERFORMING RIGHTS ORGANIZATIONS
What do PROs do?

The work of these PROs is the backbone of the music industry. Without them songwriters would have no method for keeping track of the "use" of their songs and absolutely no dependable method or process for the collection of royalties earned as a result of that "use" nationally or internationally. The long road out from under the tons of paperwork resulting from the "pen to paper" method of accounting has given way to computer databases. This has led to extremely efficient data entry and tabulations and has shortened the waiting time for royalty checks to reach the songwriters and the publishers. Today's PROs are at the peak of technical efficiency and accountability. All three PROs offer the same services, adhere to the same fixed statutory rates for royalty collections and pay the royalties due the publishers and the songwriters: 50 percent to publishers and 50 percent to the songwriters.

Rusty Gordon

Who are the major PROs?

In the USA there are only three Performance Rights Organizations. They are: **Broadcast Music Incorporated (BMI)**, **The American Society of Composers, Authors and Publishers (ASCAP)** and the **Society of European Stage Authors and Composers (SESAC)**. They use

---

Contact Information for Performance Rights Organizations

BMI: New York City: (212)586-2000, West Hollywood: (310)659-9109, Nashville: (800)925-8451, Miami: (305)266-3636, London: 44-171-486-2036, e-mail: www.bmi.com

ASCAP: New York City: (212)621-6000, Nashville: (615)742-5000, Miami Beach: (305)673-3446, Los Angeles: (323)883-1000, Hato Rey, Puerto Rico: (787)281-0782, e-mail: www.ascap.com

SESAC: New York City: (212)489-5699, Nashville: (615)320-0055, Santa Monica: (310)393-9671, e-mail: www.sesac.com

---

RUSTY GORDON *has been an artist's consultant and manager, record producer, song publisher, lyricist, event producer/promoter and the creator of a college course entitled "The Business of Music." She has been presenting music business seminars and songwriter's workshops since 1970. Her company, Rustron-Whimsong Music Productions specializes in the production of benefits, music festivals and special events.*

all available technology to keep their services cutting edge. The documentation, databases and the dedicated staff of BMI, ASCAP and SESAC keep the royalty wheels turning while they provide the muscle and backbone to the business of music.

How do PROs collect the money?

There are more than 100,000 radio and television stations, nightclubs, hotels, amusement parks, concert halls, theaters, cruise ships and establishments that present music to the public for profit. PROs acquire the rights from publishers and songwriters and then grant users of music licenses to use their entire song database. PROs collect fees from each user of music they license and then pay the earned royalties to the writers and publishers, minus a small service fee.

What specific areas do PROs watch over?

Performance Rights: This is the right granted under the U.S. Copyright Act to owners of musical works (songwriters and publishers) to license these works to be publicly performed for profit.

Broadcast Performances: Every time a popular song is played on commercial radio, it generates 12¢. If that song reaches the Top Ten on the *Billboard* magazine charts, the number of plays multiplied by 12¢ will generate an enormous amount of money. The 12¢ is split between the publisher's 50 percent and the songwriter's 50 percent minus the PRO service fee. Any song that is identified on the *Billboard* charts is making significant royalties. Even songs that don't make it to the *Billboard* charts can generate thousands of dollars. Broadcast performance royalties are paid in the following four categories: commercial radio, classical radio, college radio and national public radio. The rates vary in the different categories. Performances of classical music generate royalties based on the length of airplay time for the performance. The minimum rate starts at 32¢ per minute. College stations generate a minimum of 6¢ for each song played. National public radio rates are variable based on the amount of the license fees received by the PROs in the given year from NPR stations.

U.S. Radio Theme Music: A work of music (with/without words) that is used at the opening and closing of a regularly scheduled radio program, that runs not less than 25 minutes, earns 6¢ each time the program is aired.

U.S. Television Royalties: The PROs monitor all network and local television stations, public television and cable stations. These royalties are broken down in many creative ways: feature performances (visual with vocal, instrumental only or background vocal), background performances, theme performances, logo performances, infomercial performances, promotional announcements and commercial jingle performances.

Foreign Radio and Television Royalties: All three U.S. PROs have agreements with all the international foreign PROs for collecting royalties for U.S. PRO publishers and songwriters. Royalties earned in foreign countries will be collected and then transmitted to the U.S. PROs for payment to the U.S. publishers and songwriters. International PROs collect a small service fee for this service. U.S. PROs will convert the foreign exchange to U.S. currency.

Compulsory License Fees:
- **Distant Signal Broadcast Television (broadcast signals transmitted by satellite carriers):** Once a year the U.S. Copyright Office pays royalties to PROs for music performed on DSBT Stations that are carried by cable television systems. Royalties are also collected from manufacturers and distributors of audio home recording devices and media.
- **Pay-Per-View Services:** This is an extension of the payment formula used for cable television. Information regarding what has been played is provided by the pay-per-view licensee to the PROs.
- **Internet Uses:** This is a new and very exciting area for collecting royalties. Websites using music become licensed with agreements as to how performances will be tabulated and royalties distributed. This growing medium is viewed as a major source of new income.
- **Commercial Music Services:** The digital/cable music suppliers (AEI, Muzak and 3M, among

others) use all types of music and pay license fees to the PROs for the rights to use the music.

- **Live Concert Royalties:** Pop concerts are monitored by independent sources who create databases which are used to solicit concert set lists. These set lists enable the PROs to identify the songs they will be paying royalties for. License fees are collected from concert promoters and venue administrators.

SONGWRITERS AND PROs

What does "affiliation" mean?

PRO Publisher Affiliation: PROs license publishers to be in the business of publishing songs. All song publishers in the U.S. are required under federal law to become an affiliate publisher with one of the three PROs. No song publisher is in the legitimate business of song publishing if they are not affiliated. There would be no way they could collect royalties or be aware of the track record of their songs without the PROs.

PRO Songwriter Affiliation: If a songwriter has written a song with words and music or an instrumental alone or in collaboration with other writers and the song is commercially published or recorded or otherwise likely to be performed for profit, the songwriter(s) are eligible to join the PRO of their choice. Once the choice of a PRO is made, contact the songwriter administration of that PRO and request a songwriter's application for membership. An unpublished songwriter can join as an associate member and a published songwriter as a professional member writer. When an associate member has a song published, they become a professional member. PRO affiliation contracts are renewed automatically and can be cancelled by the songwriter by written notification of the decision to end the PRO affiliation. Sometimes songwriter's decide to switch from one PRO to another. When this happens the songwriter's catalog of songs is switched to the new PRO for administration.

Songwriters Affiliated as Both Writer & Publisher: Once a songwriter becomes affiliated with a PRO, that affiliation will last indefinitely. The songwriter will be able to work with any publisher who is also affiliated with the PRO they belong to. As the songwriter's career evolves, there is always the possibility that they may want to become a publisher themselves. If the criteria for publishing ownership is met, the songwriter can start their own publishing company.

Can songwriters affiliate as publishers?

There are many songwriter self-owned publishing companies in business in the U.S. and some of them are doing very well. To apply to become the owner of a publishing company, contact your PRO and request the publisher affiliation packet. Publishing companies are also owned by music business professionals who are not songwriters.

It is important to understand that a publishing company is the administrative backbone of the songwriting industry and all the forms and contracts related to songwriting would be needed to do the business of a song publisher—song marketing and promotion. An in-depth knowledge of the Library of Congress copyright registration forms is also necessary.

New song publishers should try to build relationships with established marketing publishers who can help with administrative responsibilities and offer co-publishing or split-publishing opportunities as a result of their established contact base in the music industry. A new publisher can also become a subsidiary of a marketing publisher and that brings financial support.

What information do I receive when I affiliate?

When you receive your songwriter or publishing company PRO application packet, you will receive information booklets that answer all your questions about PROs. You will then have the ability to educate and pass on the information to other non-affiliated songwriters you know. You will become a resource having all the information at your fingertips.

Other points of interest

Song Clearance Forms: Songwriters and publishers fill out PRO clearance forms for each song they want to add to the PRO database. The registration of songs is extremely important if the song is being performed live before the public or is included in a sound recording (CD or cassette) that is being distributed and/or sold to the public. Clearance information can be filed on the PRO's paper form or electronically.

Register Independent Releases

Warning: Sound recordings that are independently produced by songwriters and sold to the public are capable of showing up anywhere in the world that people take them. If a song is picked up by a producer in the U.S. or in another country and is recorded there and manages to generate radio air play, royalties will be earned. If the song title and songwriter identification are not listed in the database of any of the U.S. PROs, no royalty payments will be received by the songwriter.

Collaborating Songwriters & PROs: A PRO-affiliated songwriter can collaborate on a song with other songwriters who are affiliated with one of the other two PROs. Each collaborator's information will be on the clearance form for each of the PROs involved. The songwriters will be paid the percentage of royalties each earned through their own PRO. If a songwriter collaborates with another writer who is not affiliated with a PRO, that writer will have no way to collect royalties in the absence of any PRO representation.

Songwriter Contact Information: Every time a PRO-affiliated songwriter changes residence, it is essential that the change of address be reported to their PRO immediately. A current address must always be in the database. A songwriter can reside outside of the U.S., as long as they are a U.S. citizen.

Songwriters Without A Publisher: As an unpublished songwriter, any royalties earned from the "use" of an unpublished song will be paid to the songwriter(s). All songs cleared with the PROs must be copyrighted with the U.S. Library of Congress, either as a single song or in a copyrighted collection of songs. PROs divide royalty payments equally between the publisher and the songwriter(s). In the absence of a publisher the songwriter(s) get the total amount collected.

MECHANICAL RIGHTS ORGANIZATIONS
What do MROs do?

The true backbone of the American and the international record and song publishing industry is the work and services of the mechanical rights organizations. MROs are empowered with the most awesome task of accounting imaginable. They must keep track of every song assigned to them by American publishing companies. They keep an extensive database of songs and the record labels that have recorded them. They monitor record sales in the U.S. and collect royalty payments for their affiliated publishers. The publishers are paid the statutory rate of 8¢ for each song that has generated record sales. Royalty payments are received quarterly. MROs also collaborate with foreign MROs and transmit those royalties to affiliated publishers, after conversion to U.S. currency and the collection of their service fees.

MROs issue licenses to record companies, giving them the right to record and release compositions to the public for sale. MROs collect mechanical license fees from record companies. MROs may also conduct periodic audits of record company sales, usually as a result of the record companies not paying the mechanical fees timely or in some cases not paying at all. When a record company continues to ignore its responsibility to pay mechanicals, they can be cited legally and they can be stopped from distributing any more record products until they straighten out their financial obligations and make compliance with mechanical rights.

Who are the major MROs?

The *International Buyer's Guide*, published by *Billboard* Magazine/Books, identifies only three mechanical rights organizations: The Harry Fox Agency, Inc. (HFA), the American Mechanical Rights Agency (AMRA) and the Songwriter's Guild of America (SGA). The Harry Fox Agency is the largest mechanical rights organization in the world.

The Harry Fox Agency (HFA) only pays royalties to publishers. It is the publisher's responsibility to send half of what they receive to the songwriter within 30 days of receipt from HFA. The Harry Fox Agency is the most aggressive in the area of audits.

The American Mechanical Rights Agency (AMRA) remits equal royalty payments to the publishers and the songwriters. AMRA will accept the affiliation of publishers who are publishing songs that are distributed on independent releases. They will also collect the royalties for songwriters who own the exclusive rights to their songs, but have not signed with a publisher. AMRA is progressive and has an interest in the American independent record and publishing market.

The Songwriters Guild of America (SGA) can offer a limited catalog administration plan for the worldwide administration of the publishing rights of its songwriter members who are also publishers. SGA has made it possible for songwriters who publish their own songs to receive mechanical royalty administration. A Guild member who is a writer/publisher is not required to pay a service fee for publishing administration. The Guild only collects their service fee from the royalties earned by songwriters.

Contact Information for the Mechanical Rights Organizations

The Harry Fox Agency, Inc. (HFA): New York City (212)370-5330, e-mail: pr@nmpa.org

American Mechanical Rights Agency (AMRA): Los Angeles (310)440-8778, e-mail: amra calif@aol.com

Songwriters Guild of America (SGA): New York City: (212)768-7902, Hollywood: (323)462-1108, Nashville: (615)329-1782, Weehawken, NJ: (201)867-7603, e-mail: song news@aol.com, website: www.Songwriters.org

---

How do mechanical rights, royalties and compulsory licensing work?

When a published song is recorded, manufactured and distributed by a record (independent, mid-size or major) the songs on that record product each earn 8¢ for every record produced for sale to the public. The 8¢ is divided equally between the songwriter and the song's publisher.

Mechanical royalties are federally established as a statutory rate. This rate will change slightly periodically every few years. The new rate established in 2002 is 8¢, up ½¢ from the previous 7½¢ rate. The independent record labels that record songs owned by publishers must report the use of that song to the publisher and must be able to pay the statutory royalty rate to that publisher based on the number of CD and/or cassette products they produce for sale.

Only the sound recordings produced to sell are accountable for the 8¢ royalty from limited distribution products. It is important to keep 10-20 percent of short runs for "demo-not-for-sale" use. This is a rule of thumb for first-run products in limited distribution that do not exceed 1000 units. The "demo-not-for-sale" status is to be given away and never sold. They are used only for promotion, marketing and in demo packs sent to industry contacts to secure paid gigs or to get publishers or administrative record labels interested. If a songwriter wants to record a popular song as a "cover" on their own CD or cassette, they must file a "Notice of Use" with the owner of exclusive rights to the song. The owner of exclusive rights is the publisher. Failure to notify the publisher that their song is in "use" would be an infringement and constitute a violation of the law of "Compulsory Licensing" which is clearly established in the International Copyright Convention and the Berne Copyright Convention.

The Law of Compulsory Licensing

"A 'Compulsory License' grants the privilege of making and recording a musical arrangement of a song to the extent necessary to conform it to the style or manner of the creative interpretation of the performance involved, but the arrangement shall not change the basic melody or lyric or fundamental character of the song and shall not be subject to protection as a derivative work under this title, except with the express consent of the copyright owner in writing."

For "Compulsory Licensing" to be applied effectively, the owner of the exclusive rights to a song—the publisher, or if there is no publisher, the songwriter—must copyright the song with the Library of Congress to start the exclusive rights ownership for the author's life plus 70 years. This is the only way to assure that any user of music who decides to arrange and record a song can locate the owner of exclusive rights to that song by searching the Library of Congress' database. If a song does not exist as an officially copyrighted song, it will be invisible to the international music industry.

THE SONGWRITER AND MECHANICAL RIGHTS

Singer-songwriters and freelance songwriters are all trying very hard to get their songs selected for recording and released for public sale. Today's busy record market is the combination of large corporate record labels, corporate mid-size record labels and independent labels that are usually owned by the songwriters who create the songs for the records. The independent record label business is also home to music business record producers, business entrepreneurs and the owners of song publishing companies. The Small Business Administration and the IRS have been observing a steady increase, over the past 15 years, in the forming of small business music production companies, independent record labels and small publishing companies.

How much money can mechanical royalties add up to?

For songwriters and publishers with commercially successful songs or songs that have become standards and have been covered and arranged for many different artists on many record labels over time, including conversion to foreign languages, the collection of mechanical royalties can be mind-boggling. Between the mechanical and performing rights royalties earned by a very successful song, the writers and the publishers will reach far beyond the "American dream."

What if a songwriter is independently releasing CDs or cassettes?

Independent singer/songwriters who create their own cassettes or CDs to sell at their own performances are usually involved with limited distribution of their sound recordings. Mechanical royalties are only earned when the songs are recorded by a record label not owned by the songwriter.

COPYRIGHT AND PERFORMING/MECHANICAL RIGHTS

It is extremely important that songwriters who are distributing or selling their songs on CD's or cassettes to the public secure the exclusive rights to their songs by registering them for copyright with the Library of Congress. The songs on a sound recording, if all songs are written by the same songwriter, can be registered together in a collection on the PA form for $30. The CDs or cassettes songwriters independently produce should be registered for copyright on the SR form. That way they establish exclusive rights ownership of the product they have created. The SR form secures the rights to the arrangements of the songs on the sound recording. This is the form that record labels use. The PA form is for songwriters and publishers. It secures the rights to the basic melody of a song and the lyrics if there are any. It is just good common sense to protect the rights of the creators of music.

Keeping Your Bearings in the Studio

BY SCOTT MATHEWS

Scott Mathews

Today's recording studio is much more versatile than one of even a year ago. But, if you are producing yourself or entering a studio for the first time, and you are not prepared with a vision and a plan to fulfill that vision, you risk what I call option overload—that feeling of "I am faced with more choices and possibilities than I have time to hear! I don't know what direction to go in!"

Any technological device that can help get ideas out of our heads and to the listener is our friend. However, let's not lose sight that first and foremost these pieces of technology are there to *support* our creativity, not *be* our creativity. With all of this equipment, the temptation is to go off track from your goal and get lost in endless tweaking or perpetual auditioning of instrument sounds, technical tricks and special effects.

Now that relatively affordable systems with infinite tracks and options are available, even in many home studios, the playing field is finally leveled between professional and project studios. It is now possible for a wide range of songwriters and artists to gain access to a black box that can:

a) take in ghastly out of tune vocals and spit them out in perfect tune;

b) take a drummer who's idea of successful time keeping is not falling off his stool and make his meter as smooth as a Swiss watch; and

c) take a mix with no direction and make it a mix going in 1001 different directions at once.

In fact, the rapid development of technology has been so staggering it can be argued that music itself is having a hard time keeping up. As songwriters and record makers, it's our job to accentuate what makes us individual and showcases our vision as artists, rather than showing how good we are at programming a piece of equipment.

To illustrate, I get demos for production consideration that have been made on amazingly powerful computer based recorders/editors/mixers and I often have trouble finding any emotion in them. I don't want to downplay the possibilities of this equipment—any medium is fine as long as there is a vision to get across, and I DO want a strong, professional-sounding recording when I complete a project and walk out of the studio. But, in the beginning I just want to hear the nuts and bolts of the song and know there is an individual voice attached. If there is any distinct personality there, I'll pick up on it. Content is king.

At the same time, if I'm at all successful as a producer, it's from having done it for a while. I know the phase of experimenting is a natural part of getting comfortable with a modern studio and the things it can do. I do not want to discourage that, but you must also be aware of the dangers and not get lost when the clock is ticking. For those of you starting out and a little

Multi-platinum contributor **SCOTT MATHEWS** *of Hit or Myth Productions has produced, recorded or performed with a range of artists including John Hiatt, Van Morrison, Keith Richards and John Lee Hooker. His songs have been cut by a diverse range of artists including Barbra Streisand and Dave Edmunds. See his listing in the Record Producers section. "Not affiliated with any other impostors using 'Scott Mathews.'" He can be e-mailed at hitormyth@aol.com.*

unclear about the whole process, I want you to be able to bang out a song that sounds great because it's coming from you and not a machine.

THE DANGERS OF OPTION OVERLOAD
The Devil's in the details

Obsessing on details that don't factor prominently into the big picture is a common mistake to people who are new to the studio. For example, anyone who has seen drum sample sound libraries knows there are often literally hundreds (or more!) of kick drum sounds one can choose from. Does that mean you want to spend studio time starting at sound #1 and scrolling to #999? Life is much too short, so I want to know how to find the sound I am aiming for. If my final mix is heard by a program director at an influential radio station and it provokes them to comment, "Great kick sound," I know I have failed. I'm not selling kick drums! I'm selling amazing performances by artists who have something to say with real songs that move people.

Compromised live performance

Competition is fierce. Careers are built on more than just what we pull out of the studio and record execs often want to know an act can deliver onstage before they'll open their wallets. It is equally true that what happens on stage, in front of the camera, in interviews and other areas of our career weigh heavily when it comes to our ability to make fans or not.

Smart artists make sure their material, approach and strengths are developed before offering it to the masses. Why not stay home and work out the kinks, then test it out on real people in a live setting—before going into the studio? Unfortunately, you may find the ease of operation in the studio with all its "help" does quite the opposite for your stage performance. It's called learning the hard way how much you have relied on bells and whistles to sound acceptable. It is unreasonable for an artist to believe hot rod studio devices are going to do much good in these respects.

Production Tip #1—Cut to a Click

Anyone at all, professional ears or layperson, can tell if a tempo is not steady. And when you don't nail down a solid foundation of drums in the studio, there is nothing to build on top of with all the other instruments. It's useless to try. If timekeeping is indeed found to be a problem spot, and the drummer addresses it head on and practices hard on keeping rhythm with a click track, it will become second nature in the studio. The band will have a great start to their recordings, as well as a much tighter stage performance. It can even hone the drummer's sense of time to where he doesn't require a click. But don't forget, you've got to start with tracks keeping perfect time if you wish to take advantage of the fantastic digital editing possibilities in the studio.

If you think it compromises "feel" to perform with perfect time, you probably haven't worked with the right drummer. Great drummers can play side by side to a click and be as expressive and solid as the groove could ever want. Most professional drummers actually prefer recording to click tracks. It frees them up to not worry about time and just get the feel, while the click does all the work staying steady.

Lost in the money pit

As a producer, I keep a very watchful eye out for how the budget is spent. If I ever spend $1,500 a day in the studio scrolling for a bloody sound, consider it a cry for help and please—someone—carry me away. I don't want my artists to have to recoup one more dollar than they have to before they see royalties. This not only gives hope to the idea they will make money; it increases the odds they will be offered better deals because labels then don't have to risk ridiculous sums to get incredible masters. Let this also serve as a warning to those of you producing your own sessions (and spending your own money, either directly or through the backdoor of the accounting department).

When it comes to the price tag it is my job to ensure that what is spent in the studio does not put the artist in any unwanted position financially. I want all my artists to have not just a couple big selling records that recoup and see royalties, but careers sustained due (in no small part) to the ability to deliver world-class masters to their labels in a cost-effective way.

SOLUTIONS—PLAN AHEAD BEFORE YOU PRESS THE "RED"
Establish your vision—look inside so you can pull it out

Wasted hours/days/weeks/years can be spared if you arm yourself with direction (a recording session roadmap) and you know where you are going. Once you have discovered your true vision as an artist, you are well on your way to fulfilling that vision efficiently in the studio. (It IS important to experiment and grow every time you begin a new song and/or recording. Otherwise, you've already done it and it's high time to hang it up!) When you allow yourself a roadmap, you may then employ the endless options and tools in the studio to your benefit without becoming bogged down.

If you are efficient in recording, able to take charge of the studio and get the sound you want—without breaking the bank and growing old trying—you will be that much more attractive to those you want financing future projects. (If that is your desire. But, since any money advanced to you in the first place is recoupable, it's always *your* money.)

Hone on your own—before you hurt the studio's microphone

The studio is a very telling place. When you hear your voice played back and it's consistently out of tune, I would suggest some singing lessons (or at least more practice) to see how much you can improve before you market yourself as a recording artist. First, you have got your voice—and your general skill as a musician—in shape to perform without total embarrassment. Then you can use that hot rod gear to push it even further over the top where it retains all your nuance and feeling, but it's fine-tuned to fit perfectly in place in the overall blend of the final mix.

Truth is, everyone you hear on any new release is using some sort of performance enhancement. But much like good plastic surgeons, we producers are supposed to correct it without being detected. If a singer sings a slightly off-key note, it is reasonable to assume it can be fixed with a tuner in the studio. But if that note has to be shifted too far, there are distracting artifacts accompanying the voice that make it sound more like a keyboard than a human voice.

Production Tip #2—Break Down Your Sound

Before entering the studio take the group and have "sectional" rehearsals. That is to say, have the bass and drums play the tunes without any other players, just the voice. See how that supports the phrasing of the vocal. Then take the vocalist out (I know you've always wanted to do that anyway) and see how it flies. You will be surprised.

The same goes for all the other players on the session. Rehearse in sections and make sure all the voicing of the chords compliment each other from instrument to instrument and that the lead and hook lines work to full effect.

Build that dream team

If you look around, you'll notice many artists rely on the same team when they record—The Beatles, for instance, teamed with George Martin in the studio throughout their career as a group. Working with an effective creative team provides a familiarity and comfort to the proceedings that is reflected in the work. If the team works, stay with it. Like minded people can be hard to find, as you know if you are in a band!

Also, when I bring new projects to record companies, it is common for them to ask how long it took to get the results they are hearing. They want to know what kind of investment they are looking at if they want to pursue signing the act. In my case, I am adamant about keeping costs as low as possible while never compromising the making of world-class masters. I've got to be able to keep budgets low and studio time down to a relatively short amount.

One way I accomplish this is by having my own studio and a team of assistants I can work with on almost every project. The ease of operation is built in because of our long-standing relationship. Styles and approaches change radically from one project to the next, but there is always a clear understanding that keeps things moving at a fun, creative pace. We have plenty of time for trying practically any idea we can think of because we know how to get to that idea in specific terms and the ability to articulate it both musically and sonically.

As an example of teamwork in action, take real string arrangements. This is a place where budgets commonly go straight through the roof. If you want to fill a studio with quality string players, have an arranged score written, pay copyists, etc., you have added a tremendous gouge to your budget. As an alternative, I have an engineer on my team who is one of the most musical people I've worked with, and it happens he knows his way around a violin, viola and cello. I will come up with an idea for strings, lay down a track on a mellotron or another string sample, and part by part we redo the guide with real strings. An hour after getting the original idea, we are sitting back hearing the glorious sounds of several tracks of strings mixed and placed into the mix.

So, how do you build this dream team? I look for the quality of people at least as much as talent. A group of people who work well together is more often about chemistry than it is a roomful of geniuses. You will have a much better chance of getting things to work if the people all respect one another and have the right frame of mind and appreciation for the common goal. And don't forget, when you are on the road, there are maybe two hours where you'll be on stage each day. That makes twenty-two hours you've got to be around these people off stage. Being friends and being able to be open and just hang out with ease makes for a tighter knit group.

As a producer, I have my antenna up sky high in respect to direction when auditioning bands. If it's not obvious to me that they are all for one, they are off my list. Steering the ship is not going to happen if I am constantly pulled in six different directions by six different band members.

IT'S NOT THE GEAR, IT'S THE HEART AND THE EAR!

If we were to find one word to define what we as artists are here to do, I believe that word is communicate. Within that all-encompassing word are all the subtexts (such as entertain, move, enlighten, and of course just plain rock!). But it all stems from our ability to communicate. Getting a strong hold on what we feel inside and therefore need to communicate in our work sets us on our way to "how." We have to know both what we want and (just as importantly) what we *don't* want, so as to not loose focus and go off track. The many pitfalls we encounter along the way are inevitable, but are more easily sidestepped when we are headed where we know we need to go.

So, listen to your heart, believe in your ear and your music will soar no matter what gear you use to record it with.

See ya on the charts . . .

Song Sharks, Single-Song Marketing & Collaboration 101

BY RUSTY GORDON

SONG SHARKS, CON ARTISTS AND SCAMS

The music industry marketplace has always been bedeviled by people who try to take advantage of others and use deceptions, manipulations and schemes to accomplish their goals. These people often exist on the fringes of the legitimate music industry, but some of them work their way into jobs and positions in the music business that give them valuable cover for their disreputable activities.

It is very important for people trying to break into the music industry creatively to be able to identify a scam or a scammer. Here are some things to be aware of.

Rusty Gordon

Are they a real business?

When a person provides a service to the music industry, they should be involved with a legitimate business. Anyone who is working "out of pocket" will in many cases be leaving little or no paper trail of their transactions. Some will tell you they are just starting out and haven't gotten around to getting their company registered with the IRS. Others will fabricate a business they work for, claiming they are a field representative looking for new talent.

If they do have an office they work out of and you go to their office, look on the walls of the office or on the desks for a Business Certificate. If you can find it, check to see if the name of the business this person is with is on it. Also note the employer ID number on the certificate.

People who do not work for or own a company registered with the IRS as a small business (sole proprietorship, partnership or limited partnership) or as a corporation, should throw up a yellow caution light. The government requires every properly registered business in the U.S. to display their business registration certificate with employer ID number in plain sight, at their place of business, so customers or clients can easily see it.

If you don't see the certificate, ask the person if the company or business they are with is registered with the IRS. If they say "yes," call the IRS and ask for verification from them that this business is actually registered to do business in the U.S. If the business is not registered, it's time to walk away. If the person tells you the business is not registered with the IRS, ask why not. Pay careful attention to what they tell you and remember it is your obligation to yourself to question people and get answers that you can live with if you plan to enter into a business arrangement with them.

RUSTY GORDON *has been an artist's consultant and manager, record producer, song publisher, lyricist, event producer/promoter and the creator of a college course entitled "The Business of Music." She has been presenting music business seminars and songwriter's workshops since 1970. Her company, Rustron-Whimsong Music Productions, specializes in the production of benefits, music festivals and special events.*

Verify claims of music industry involvement

You must establish proof of existing track record and definite relationship with nationally known artists or professional music business people. If you meet someone who tells you they are an artist's manager, a booking agent, a producer, a record label owner or a song publisher, get ready to verify what they tell you. Some people will tell you they have been active and successful in the music business and they will throw out the names of artists or industry professionals that you recognize to impress you.

Once this happens, you have a way to determine if they were telling you the truth. Try to find out exactly what kind of relationship they had with the people they mention. With that information you can go directly to the source and verify the validity of the relationship. You can also use either of the directory sources listed below to contact the people themselves and find out if the information you were given is fact or fiction.

Other sources to check

There are music industry guides and directories that can help you establish the truth or uncover lies and deceit. The *Talent & Touring Directory* provided by *Billboard* magazine, has contact information for all the musical artists who perform in the U.S. The listings include their managers, booking agents and record labels with addresses, phone and fax numbers and usually e-mail addresses.

The *International Buyer's Guide*, also from *Billboard*, is the worldwide resource for music industry businesses. All legitimate song publishers and major or independent record companies are listed, along with all the contact information and the names of the primary executives and staff. Both guides are published and updated annually. Use these guides to verify the existence of a company and remember, the purpose of a music industry business is to make money. Any company that chooses invisibility has a reason for doing that; it may indicate there is something to hide. It pays to be cautious.

The "classic" song shark

"Song sharks" can be found lurking in the ad section of *Popular Mechanics* magazine or any other magazine unrelated to the music business. They often throw their bait to people who write what they refer to as "song poems." They offer to create melodies for the song poems. Then, when people respond by sending their song poems, they are hooked into the "success by illusion" scheme the song sharks thrive on. The song shark sends back to the writer a brief, but positive reaction to the quality and creativity of the song poems that were submitted. This is a form letter meant to stroke the ego and set up the writer for services the song shark wants to be paid for. They offer to create melodies for the song poems and the charade begins.

There is a price for every service the song shark offers. Sharks allude to, but never actually say they can help the writer get a hit song. They simply want the fees they charge for melodies, demo sound recordings and arrangers' fees. The melodies they come up with are used again and again on different song poems. They try to shape them into lyrics and the composer of the melody functions as a "work-for-hire." The song shark composers refuse to claim co-collaboration with the writers and most of them refuse to have their name listed as "author" on the copyright form. Sometimes the song shark will give the writer a fictitious name for the composer, just to satisfy their curiosity. (Song sharks also have people on staff who create lyrics for submitted melodies. But, there are no prize-winning professional lyric writers or composers working for song sharks.)

The type of persons easily scammed by a song shark are senior citizens, songwriters who have copyrighted for the first time, and people whose lifestyle and life experience have no common ground with the music industry, making them vulnerable to the manipulations of song sharks.

Song sharks in the U.S. continually vary their scams and rip-offs. It is not uncommon to find them pretending to have a connection to a publishing company. This is another ploy to get people to spend more money. **No legitimate BMI, ASCAP or SESAC publisher would get involved with a song shark.** If they did, and this came to the attention of the performing rights organizations, that publisher would lose its performing rights licensing and be out of business. **Publishing companies cannot charge songwriters for any of the services they provide. If they do they can lose their performing rights affiliation.**

Song sharks will probably always be alive and well and taking advantage of uninformed aspiring songwriters and lyricists. Please share what you have learned in this article. *Songwriter's Market* is the only resource for the U.S. music industry that provides a wide range of music business listings, including all contact information and submission guidelines—use it!

SINGLE-SONG MARKETING

All songwriters dream of someday writing that one song that somehow develops into a blockbuster, a "standard" that will earn enormous amounts of royalties. Can this really happen to a song written by a songwriter who is new to the music industry and has no special nepotistic contacts to help the process along? It is possible to create a song that is just perfect for a specific recording artist or a song that is so special and universal that it could be arranged in many ways and performed by many different artists. Certain crafting techniques come together more by accident than by design for some writers, and other writers who create top-grossing songs have an understanding of the crafting skills of songwriting and very carefully shape their songs for the commercial market.

Learn to write that "one song"

Album cuts are the meat and potatoes of the recording industry. A ten-song record needs nine album cuts and one hit single to be a successful product. For singer-songwriters who write all their own songs and produce their own sound recordings, the pressure on them is to make sure they have one song that will stand out from all the others. One song that:
- has a melody that works well as an instrumental without words.
- has a carefully crafted concept and well-expressed phrasing.
- tells a simple story beautifully and with emotion.
- has a concept that is very unique and unpredictable.
- holds the attention of an audience because it embraces them and they immediately want to hear it again.

Publishers who are seasoned and instinctive in their ability to seek out these songs—songs that are much more than just album cuts—are the songwriter's salvation. Producers and arrangers, who can single out that "one song" from the new record and give that song the arrangement it demands, are worth their weight in gold.

Knowing this, your goal as a serious and dedicated songwriter should be:
- to choose carefully the songs you submit to publishers and record producers/labels.
- to learn to craft carefully when you identify a certain song as more special than most.
- to avoid burying your song in an arrangement that does not let the words and music breathe together.
- to craft your lyrics carefully to the notes of the melody you create for the song.

Lyric dominant songs are very common. The words drag the melody along with them. **Words and music should not compete, but unite and come together like a good marriage.** A very good marriage! Special songs and special relationships take a lot of effort. Take your time and take your talent and write that "one song."

THE CASE FOR COLLABORATION

For songwriters who come to discover they are lyric dominant writers and for songwriters who are melody dominant writers, the "green light" of collaboration may be flashing. Collaboration of lyricists and composers and the collaborators who add both words and melody to their songs are among the most successful songwriters in the music industry. It is very important to get the very best out of yourself creatively as you shape and mold your songs.

Commercially successful bands often have band members co-writing songs. Performing artists who are not songwriters must seek original songs from many different songwriters and collaborators in the hopes of finding one that will carry them to the charts and success. It should surprise no one that many of the highest grossing songs in all styles of music were written by collaborators. There is magic in the merging of the collaborators' skills, imagination and creative chemistry. They give birth to a song together. Collaboration may work better with some writers than with others. The search for the right person will be more than worth it.

You can also create songs with several different collaborators. Create a contract for each song you assign to a collaborator and allow a fixed time frame for this collaboration. Several collaborators can work on the same song at the same time until one version of the song is selected for copyrighting.

THOUGHTS OF ENCOURAGEMENT

Remember to always take yourself seriously as a songwriter. Every positive contact you make in the pursuit of your career will lead you on to others. Don't wear your heart on your sleeve. One person's rejection of your work can lead to someone who loves what you do. Always concentrate on expanding your songwriting abilities and creative insight.

Don't give up, there's a break out there somewhere and it's waiting for you.

Using the Internet to Get Your Songs Heard

BY CYNTHIA LAUFENBERG

If you're a performing songwriter, the Internet provides infinite possibilities to get your songs heard. You can sell your own CDs on Amazon.com, offer free downloads of your music at MP3 .com, and strut your stuff for industry bigwigs at sites like Farmcl ub.com or LoudEnergy.com. But what if you're not a performer? What if you don't have a CD to sell? What if you're just looking for a publishing deal and want to get your songs cut? Are there resources on the Internet for the non-performing songwriter? Sure there are—you just have to know where to look.

Cynthia Laufenberg

Using the Internet for research and networking

First and foremost, you should look at the Internet as a valuable research tool. It's a great place to research the music industry and network with other songwriters and industry professionals. Brian Austin Whitney, founder of Just Plain Folks (www.jpfolks.com), an organization for songwriters, musicians, and industry professionals, says, "Songwriters should view the Net as a tool in their war chest as opposed to an end-all solution for success. It's a great way to make contacts, research opportunities for appropriate submissions, and learn more about the craft and business of songwriting."

Just about any kind of information for songwriters can be found on the Internet, from free music organizations that you can join to informational sites that provide industry news, updates on trends in the industry, and tips on writing a hit song, finding a collaborator, or recording a demo. There are chat rooms and bulletin boards where songwriters can meet other writers from different parts of the country and the world. David Hooper, President of Kathode Ray Music in Nashville, likens logging onto the Internet to visiting a vast library. "The best thing about the Internet is the trading of information," he says. "You can't learn everything you need to know about the music business from the Net, but it is a good primer."

The amount of information about the music industry and the songwriting community available on the Internet grows every day, and it pays to take advantage of all of the free information provided, no matter what type of music you write. According to Whitney, "You can visit great online resource sites like the Muse's Muse (www.musesmuse.com), read information sites like the Mi2N network (www.Mi2N.com), use the vast services of TAXI, one of the earliest music entities on the Internet (www.taxi.com), set up an info page on MP3.com, and learn all you can directly from the sites of music industry educators like Jason Blume (www.jasonblume.com), among many others."

CYNTHIA LAUFENBERG *was editor of* Songwriter's Market *from 1991-1996. She currently lives in Princeton, New Jersey.*

While the Internet can provide songwriters with an introduction to a world that's beyond their front door, it's important to remember that it can never be as effective as actual face-to-face interaction with people in the industry. "The most successful writers use the tools the Internet offers to supplement their in-person visits and phone calls with publishers, labels, artists and other writers. But, these new tools cannot replace that human contact," Whitney says. "Even the best tool in a mechanic's toolbox can't repair an engine alone. The same principle applies to songwriting success. Songwriters need to learn to use all their tools in concert, adding new technology to their existing arsenal for the greatest possible success."

Jodi Krangle, owner of The Muse's Muse, agrees. "Internet services are great, but they shouldn't take the place of networking in person," she says. "This isn't to say that you should move to Nashville, L.A. or New York. It's only to say that if you have a local songwriting association, get involved with it. Audience feedback is essential to writing good songs. Sharing your songs with others and getting them to tell you what works and what doesn't is also a great way to get to know people with the potential to help you get your music heard. As I always say, it's all about relationships. Go after them— nurture them—and you will ultimately be successful, whether you perform your own songs or not."

Sending e-mails and conducting business from the privacy of your own home can be effective and quick, but don't get complacent with the convenience of electronic communication and forget about the human factor that's so important when networking in the music business. "While you're making contacts and promoting your work, never forget to do all the traditional things that many using the Net have stopped doing," Whitney says. "Send an actual letter, typed and signed by hand, in a real envelope sent to a specific real person as a follow-up. Just as e-mail was a novelty three years ago, sending a real letter—not a form letter—to someone is now a novelty itself. Use that to your advantage. A writer on the Net is at her most powerful when she uses the vast array of Internet and technological tools available but never forgets that human interaction—especially face-to-face—can never be replaced and can never be improved on. Never put all your eggs in one basket—and that goes for the Internet. Be sure to balance e-mails with phone calls and in-person meetings. Balance digital files with actual hardcopy CDs. Balance a general mailing list announcement with a simple personal letter to a specific person. Just as a balanced diet positively affects your health, balanced online and off-line efforts will positively affect the health of your career."

Do you need your own website?

Definitely. A website is like a press kit for the new millennium. Design your own website so interested writers, artists, publishers, and industry professionals can learn about your music and hear your songs. "Purchase your name as a domain name and set up a simple and classy info/bio page. Include a nice photograph," Whitney says, "because pictures humanize the face-lessness of the Internet. Also, learning the very simple basics of making your own website is a must," Whitney says. "And don't be intimidated, because it's much easier than anyone initially thinks, in most cases being as simple as using a word processor. Consider this your online business card/press kit." There are literally hundreds of books available now that can help you set up your own website, no matter what your skill level is (see the sidebar at the end of this article for some book suggestions).

Once you've created a killer website with cool graphics, photos, and biographical information about yourself, you can't just post the lyrics to your songs and expect anyone to pay attention. "A non-performing artist still needs a demo," Krangle says. "Just because they don't perform their own material doesn't mean non-performing artists don't have to set their words and music down in some sort of format others can listen to. It's virtually impossible these days to sell a song based on lyrics alone." And if you can't sing, by all means, don't! Find someone who can and record a professional-sounding demo. "The lead vocal on a demo is hugely important," says Krangle. "Let's face it—if you're wincing through a recording, it'll be a great deal more difficult to hear the song's potential. This doesn't have to cost a lot of money. A tape recorder in someone's living room with a guitar and a friend who has a good voice will do it, or consider having a professionally recorded demo of your best songs done." And be sure to copyright your songs before putting them on the Internet. "It's good to know you have some protection when you're putting your songs on the Internet for a lot of anonymous people to hear," Krangle says.

Learn how to add your own digital files to your website so people can hear that fabulous demo you spent your last two months' salary creating. Hooper finds having a website to go to after he's met with a songwriter can be a valuable way to stay on top of what a writer is doing. "Personally, I don't like to take demos over the Net," he says. "It's great if I was talking to you and you had a website that I could go to and listen to your music."

Using the Internet as a song plugger

You've done your research and know which publishers are interested in the music you write. You've made a fabulous, professional demo of your songs. Your website is up and running, featuring info about you and clips of your songs. Now it's time to start sending out those tapes and making visits to publishers' offices, right? Sure it is. But the Web can also help you pitch your songs to interested parties. Brett Perkins, owner of Brett Perkins Presents and former CEO of the National Academy of Songwriters, sees the Internet as yet another way to pitch songs. "I find one of the greatest tools—which I teach in my workshops—is the sending of song submissions by e-mail sound file to companies seeking songs who list in reputable publications," he says. "It saves time and postage, and often generates a faster response in my experience, evidenced recently by a publisher in the Philippines who liked my e-mailed song, and now we're negotiating for usage by one of their groups." Learn how to download your demos onto the Web for easy access. "One tip for this usage," says Perkins, "is to offer up two forms of download—a standard MP3 and also a faster/lower streaming sample—so the receiver isn't kept waiting." Whitney concurs. "Nothing is faster, cheaper or as easy to duplicate to many recipients as e-mail and digital song files," he says.

Using the Internet, you can discover valuable information about companies who use the type of music you write and what kind of writers they work with. Listen to songs from those artists to get an idea of the quality and style of music they are using. This will also give you an idea of the production value each company may expect from you when you send them a demo of your songs.

Research the companies you want to submit to and contact them via email to introduce yourself, along with a link to your website that features your songs. "Explain that you are sending them a CD or cassette copy of your demo, but wanted them to have access to the songs immediately if it was convenient for them to listen via the Internet," Whitney suggests. "Never assume how your listener wants to receive their music. Instead, send them the link and a real-life copy." Continue to use e-mail to follow up, but don't send spam mail or form letters. "Write short personal notes directly to the person you are building your relationship with," Whitney says. "Only send information to your contacts that is specifically applicable for them, and is compelling for them as well. This means they will benefit by having read this information. If only you benefit, it is a waste of their time."

Not only can you post your songs to your own website for anyone to hear, but you can also post your songs on other sites industry professionals visit to search for new songs. These sites multiply daily, so you need to constantly check the Web to see what's out there and to find the right places for you and your songs. There are many services available on the Internet that will list your songs in a database for industry professionals to search through. Start with the established sites and link from there. Some well-known sites include TAXI (www.taxi.com), which has been around since 1992. It offers a yearly subscription to writers and artists along with personal feedback from top industry professionals. Every two weeks, TAXI members receive an updated list of what people in the industry are looking, giving you the opportunity to pitch your songs to those interested parties. SongScope (www.songscope.com), which bills itself as the "World's First On-Line Independent Songwriter's Song Shopping Catalog," and SongCatalog (www.SongCatalog.com) let you list your catalog of songs on their sites for industry professionals to access. These are just a few of the sites out there that can help you pitch your songs to industry professionals. However, pay close attention to the fees these sites charge; some charge monthly fees, and others charge per song downloaded. It's up to you to decide what will work best for you.

The Internet offers a variety of ways for non-performing songwriters to get their music heard and into the hands of industry professionals who can get their songs recorded. Research your options wisely to find the best sites and contacts that will help you find the songwriting success you've been searching for!

For More Information
Print Resources
Here is a list of books to help you learn more about promoting your songs on the Internet and setting up your own website: Building a Web Site for Dummies, by David and Rhonda Crowder (Hungry Minds, Inc., 2000); Creating Web Pages for Dummies, by Bud E. Smith, Arthur Bebak, and Kevin Werbach (Hungry Minds, Inc., 1999); How to Promote Your Music Successfully on the Internet: The Musicians Guide to Effective Music Promotion on the Internet, by David Nevue (Midnight Rain Productions, 2001); MP3 for Musicians: Promote Your Music Career Online, by John V. Hedtke and Sandy Bradley (Top Floor Publishing, 2000); MP3 for Dummies, by Andy Rathbone (Hungry Minds, Inc., 1999)

Web Resources
This select list of websites for songwriters is only the tip of the iceberg when it comes to promoting your songs online. The Internet is constantly growing and changing, so you need to keep up-to-date on the latest sites.
www.getsigned.com
www.indiebiz.com
www.jpfolks.com
www.mp3.com
www.musesmuse.com
www.songcatalog.com
www.songlink.com
www.songscope.com
www.taxi.com
www.unisong.com

Taking Stock & Making Plans: Advice for Long-Distance Nashville Songwriters

BY JIM MELKO

"If you want to become a successful songwriter in Nashville, you gotta move here!" If you're an aspiring songwriter who has ever visited or even called Nashville, you have undoubtedly heard that statement many times. But if you're never going to make that move, must you give up the dream of success at songwriting?

Jim Melko

No, but recognize that no one gives any special breaks to the out-of-towner, that you have to compete with the very best professional songwriters in Nashville, and you have much less access to the people you need to see. To make it in "Music City" without actually living there, you must:

- make a careful assessment of where you stand,
- figure out what you need to achieve,
- and plan carefully for achieving it.

Success in Nashville is rarely just around the corner. It lies at the top of a long flight of stairs. This article is intended to help you figure out where you are on that staircase and what steps you need to take to move closer to the top. In the following sections, *choose the level for each category that best describes you, and develop realistic goals and deadlines based upon the recommendations for that level.*

CRAFT & QUALITY
Level one

You enjoy your own songs, but you have never played them for anyone other than family and friends. You do not belong to any songwriters' groups, and your songs have never been critiqued by someone truly knowledgeable in the craft.

What to Do

 If you haven't already joined NSAI, that should be your first step. The Nashville Songwriters Association International (NSAI) is dedicated to educating songwriters around the world in the craft and business of songwriting, and it provides a wealth of resources and information. I believe becoming a member of NSAI is critical to the long-distance writer's chances of success.

JIM MELKO *has been a staff writer for a Nashville publisher and has also been a co-ordinator since 1993 for the Songwriters Workshop at SouthBrook, the Dayton/Cincinnati chapter for NSAI (Nashville Songwriters Association International). See the NSAI listing in the Organizations section of this book.*

☑ If you are an NSAI member, you need to make regular use of the NSAI critiquing service. NSAI members may send in a song on cassette along with a lyric sheet, and a professional songwriter will record his or her critique on the tape itself.

☑ Set the goal of having a song submitted for critiquing at all times; as soon as one is returned, send the next one in. If necessary, submit even old songs of dubious quality; you may find that the critiquer finds something worth salvaging from them.

☑ Consult with NSAI and find out if there is a local area workshop in proximity to you. If not, then consider forming your own (contact NSAI for more information). There may also be non-NSAI local groups in your area (check with your local colleges, newspapers, music stores, and radio stations); the important thing is to find one that maintains high standards for song critiques.

☑ If there is a workshop nearby, attend regularly. If you truly want to become successful in songwriting, don't confuse inconvenient with impossible! Make your personal schedule bend around your workshop schedule, and do not allow your non-songwriting obligations to limit your ability to attend on a regular basis.

Level two

You have been submitting songs fairly often to NSAI, and you present songs regularly at a local workshop. The feedback almost always includes suggestions for improvement, often requiring major structural changes.

What to Do

☑ Rewrite! Rewrite! Rewrite! Then, resubmit! Far too many writers go on to write new songs without seriously attempting to rewrite songs that were critiqued. Until you learn to improve your songs, you will not learn how to write them properly from the start.

☑ Collaborate with other writers at your level or slightly above your level of writing.

☑ Visit Nashville and get feedback from publishers and the performing rights organizations (ASCAP, BMI, and SESAC).

Level three

You have been submitting songs fairly often to NSAI and to your local group, and the feedback is positive. The criticisms you receive don't tend to require major rewrites, and the NSAI critiques keep saying things like, "This one is almost there."

What to Do

☑ Attend one of the NSAI Song Camps.

☑ Start working with collaborators who are better in some ways than you. (Skip down to the sections below concerning discipline and Nashville networking.)

☑ Remember: *You may be "almost there" but there are probably many new levels of development ahead of you.*

PRODUCTIVITY

Level one

You love to write a song but can't find the time to do it often. You must feel inspired to write. You are amazed to hear of professionals who write a song or more a day. Your biggest problem seems to be your inability to finish a song, which you manage to do only every two or three months. You believe you have creative cycles that at their peaks allow you to be highly productive, and at their lows render you incapable of writing anything.

What to Do

☑ Set aside one night a week—or more—that is absolutely your time to work on music.

☑ Ask your family or friends to challenge you to make effective use of that time, to help you avoid procrastinating or being lazy.

☑ If you can collaborate with someone, meet regularly and agree upon the mutual goal of finishing what you start.

☑ Work on revisions as soon as possible after receiving critiques.

☑ Attend local workshops on a regular basis.

☑ Remember: *If you can write songs, you can become a disciplined writer. It's simply a behavior, a habit, not an innate talent or disposition.*

Level two

You have several unfinished songs at any time, but you also finish at least a song or two a month. You maintain a regular time for writing and squeeze more writing in at other times. You have a few collaborators at your level of quality, and hopefully at least one who is much better. You still cope with "creative cycles," but they are shorter in duration and you can "turn on" your creativity when you collaborate. You have at least one or two songs that received positive critiques suggesting only minor revisions, but you have not made professional demos of your songs.

What to Do

☑ Set up a regular routine just for finishing projects—late at night after everyone is in bed, or extra early in the morning, maybe an hour before you go to work.

☑ Discipline yourself either to finish a song or to make significant progress every time.

☑ Get your finished songs professionally demoed. Demos provide a sense of completion, allowing you to look ahead to the new songs you will write.

Level three

You either have a regular work schedule for songwriting, or you spend a significant amount of writing throughout the week. Several projects are underway at any time, but you are also adept at finishing them. Most writers you know are willing to collaborate with you because they respect your craft and ability. You have several professionally produced demos.

What to Do

☑ If most of your best songs are already published through single-song contracts, concentrate on writing new and better songs to build your available catalog.

☑ Use your contacts to find Nashville collaborators.

☑ When your catalog is better developed, meet with the writer relations professional at your performing rights organization and ask for referrals and advice.

☑ Develop friendships within the music business, at least one professional contact willing to meet with you over a meal or after business hours.

BUSINESS KNOWLEDGE
Level one

You know little about the music business. You're not sure how much money a hit song makes, but you suspect that one could set you up for life. You don't really know how a staff writing position works. If you were to make a trip to Nashville, you wouldn't know what to do. You are unable to name many hit songwriters or publishers.

What to Do

☑ Browse through the music business sections in your local bookstore, buy books and read them. NSAI offers several books to its members through its bookstore.

☑ Look through *Songwriter's Market* for publishers with cuts by recognizable artists, and read the articles.

☑ Attend an NSAI Symposium this year. The Symposium is rich in information about the music business, and you'll be surrounded by long-distance songwriters like yourself. NSAI also sponsors Tin Pan South, a week in which the very best songwriters perform every night in several clubs throughout Nashville, allowing you to become familiar with the most respected songwriters in the industry.

Level two

You've read a few books and understand how the business works. You've attended at least one NSAI symposium and met with one or two publishers, or with someone at the performing rights organizations.

What to Do

☑ Attend more Symposiums in Nashville.

☑ Read the trade journals such as *Billboard* and track writers and publishers whose songs appear on the charts. Try to see those publishers.

☑ Set up appointments to get feedback and talk about your aspirations with writers relations staff at ASCAP, BMI, and SESAC.

☑ Get a "feel" for the competition. Visit Nashville as frequently as possible and go to see acts at the Bluebird Café and other establishments that feature songwriters.

Level three

You know the business directly through your relationships with publishers and the performing rights organizations. You've attended several NSAI symposiums, and much of what's presented is "old hat" to you.

What to Do

☑ Start using your connections. Determine the kind of publisher you want to have, and begin cultivating the relationships which interest you most. Remember that *Nashville is built on friendships*. It's not enough to be a name or face the publisher will recognize; you need to become friends with the publisher.

☑ Have an entertainment attorney lined up now to consult with quickly if you are offered a contract.

EXPOSURE
All levels

You should be able to play an instrument and perform your songs if at all possible. There are professional writers who are unable to play an instrument or perform, but none of them would regard their lack of skill as an advantage.

☑ Perform locally and learn to entertain and read how your audiences react to your songs. Once you're comfortable on stage, participate in open mic nights in Nashville and audition for establishments like the Bluebird Café where writers can showcase their material.

☑ Consider entering songwriting contests. While such contests are not likely to make you an overnight success, they can improve your confidence, win you the attention of other writers and any involved reputable publishers, and of course earn you money or prizes. However, Songwriting contests can create problems with your copyright ownership if they are not reputable, so be very cautious about entering them.

☑ It is likewise unlikely you will earn a hit record through "cassette roulette" — sending song submissions to publishers through the mail with their permission. Nevertheless, it is possible that you might capture the interest of a publisher and begin a relationship that could prove beneficial later on. If you aren't visiting Nashville regularly and you have no special contacts, cassette roulette is certainly better than nothing. However, *never submit through the mail without first obtaining permission.* Your call to obtain that permission can be the start of a relationship.

NETWORKING
Level one

You've never visited publishers or the performing rights organizations in Nashville.

What to Do

☑ If the quality of your work is at Level One as described earlier, this is probably not the time for you to visit publishers or the performing rights organizations. You need to be writing songs of sufficient quality to show a publisher that you are serious and have some promise. Instead, use the NSAI critiquing process and your local workshop critiques to improve your quality to Level Two. If you have good contacts, save them; *don't blow them by presenting inferior material!*

☑ If you are at higher levels of quality, start making the trip. Make an appointment with writer's relations staff at BMI, ASCAP, and SESAC. If one believes you're ready, he or she will refer you to publishers. At the least you'll get some good advice.

☑ Use *Songwriter's Market* to find publishers who will meet with you and listen to your songs. Even if you are not offered a contract, you should consider your visit a success if you are at least invited to come back when you have new material.

☑ If you can get in to see the publisher at companies with major hits, be careful to present yourself well. Cultivate those relationships as well as the ones you establish with the still struggling publishers. You never know which relationships could pay off later.

☑ If you've been procrastinating about visiting Nashville, ask yourself why. Is it because you are afraid to face rejection? If so, then you are indeed facing a major crisis because you will not find success without making the visits, and you will suffer a lot of rejection. *Rejection is the only constant in the business of songwriting!*

Level two

You've made some visits to Nashville and you've been invited to revisit some publishers when you have new material. You have contacts in the performing rights organizations who will meet with you when you're in town. You've not yet earned a publishing contract.

What to Do

☑ Work hard on developing the quality of your songs, and maintain regular contact with your publishing contacts both by phone and in person. Your publishing contacts want to know if you are serious, so don't disappoint them or procrastinate.

☑ If you are eventually offered a single-song contract, enjoy the experience and the excitement of knowing that success could happen at any time. But keep in mind, too, that publishers sometimes offer such contracts more for the sake of encouraging you to come back and to see what you will be able to do next.

Level three

You've earned a few single-song contracts either with a single publisher or with several, but no staff contract seems to be on the horizon. You may be frustrated that no one has heard your entire catalog because the best songs have been awarded contracts and scattered among various publishers.

What to Do

☑ Your contacts at your performing rights organization would probably be willing at this stage to sit down and review a more comprehensive presentation of your work, including already published songs. Nevertheless, you need to have a catalog of both strong and available songs if you are going to earn a staff contract.

☑ Stop signing individual contracts and work hard on developing your catalog.

☑ When your catalog is ready, use your résumé of publishing contracts to open new doors to other publishers.

Conclusion

There is a saying in Nashville that "a good song will find its way." In that philosophy is hope for the long-distance songwriter who believes that merit can prevail over geographical location. But a good song isn't really "good" unless it's heard—and it will only find its way among the people who hear it. For the Nashville resident, it's much easier to believe in that saying because the song is already in the right place to be heard. But if you don't live there, you need to make your own way before your song will ever have the chance it needs to break through the long-distance barrier.

The Markets

Important Information on Market Listings

- Although every listing in *Songwriter's Market* is updated, verified or researched prior to publication, some changes are bound to occur between publication and the time you contact any listing. You may want to call a company before sending them material to make sure their submission policy has not changed.
- Listings are based on interviews and questionnaires. They are not advertisements, nor are markets reported here necessarily endorsed by the editor.
- Every listing in *Songwriter's Market* is screened for unethical practices. If a listing does not meet our ethical requirements, they will be excluded from the book.
- Companies that appeared in the 2002 edition of *Songwriter's Market*, but do not appear this year, are listed in the General Index at the back of the book along with a code explaining why they do not appear in this edition.
- A word of warning. Don't pay to have your song published and/or recorded or to have your lyrics—or a poem—set to music. Read "Rip-Offs" in The Business of Songwriting section to learn how to recognize and protect yourself from the "song shark."
- If you have found a song shark through this book, write to us at 4700 East Galbraith Road, Cincinnati OH 45236, with an explanation and copies of documentation of the company's unethical practices.
- Songwriter's Market *reserves the right to exclude any listing which does not meet its requirements.*

Key to Abbreviations

SASE—self-addressed, stamped envelope
SAE—self-addressed envelope
IRC—International Reply Coupon, for use in countries other than your own.

- For definitions of terms and abbreviations relating specifically to the music industry, see the Glossary in the back of the book.
- For explanations of symbols, see the inside front and back covers of the book. Also see pages 8.

Complaint Procedure

If you feel you have not been treated fairly by a listing in *Songwriter's Market*, we advise you to take the following steps:

- First try to contact the listing. Sometimes one phone call or a letter can quickly clear up the matter.
- Document all your correspondence with the listing. When you write to us with a complaint, provide the details of your submission, including the date of your first contact with the listing, the nature of your subsequent correspondence, and copies of any documentation.
- We will enter your letter into our files and attempt to contact the listing.
- The number and severity of complaints will be considered in our decision whether or not to delete the listing from the next edition.

Music Publishers

Finding songs and getting them recorded—that's the main function of a music publisher. Working as an advocate for you and your songs, a music publisher serves as a song plugger, administrator, networking resource and more. The knowledge and personal contacts a music publisher can provide may be the most valuable resources available for a songwriter just starting in the music business.

HOW MUSIC PUBLISHERS WORK

Music publishers attempt to derive income from a song through recordings, use in TV and film soundtracks and other areas. While this is their primary function, music publishers also handle administrative tasks such as copyrighting songs, collecting royalties for the songwriter, negotiating and issuing synchronization licenses for use of music in films, television programs and commercials, arranging and administering foreign rights, auditing record companies and other music users, suing infringers, and producing new demos of the music submitted to them. In a small, independent publishing company, one or two people may handle all these jobs. Larger publishing companies are more likely to be divided into the following departments: creative (or professional), copyright, licensing, legal affairs, business affairs, royalty, accounting and foreign.

The *creative department* is responsible for finding talented writers and signing them to the company. Once a writer is signed, it is up to the creative department to develop and nurture the writer so he will write songs that create income for the company. Staff members often put writers together to form collaborative teams. And, perhaps most important, the creative department is responsible for securing commercial recordings of songs and pitching them for use in film and other media. The head of the creative department, usually called the professional manager, is charged with locating talented writers for the company. Once a writer is signed, the professional manager arranges for a demo to be made of the writer's songs. Even though a writer may already have recorded his own demo, the publisher will often re-demo the songs using established studio musicians in an effort to produce the highest-quality demo possible.

Once a demo is produced, the professional manager begins shopping the song to various outlets. He may try to get the song recorded by a top artist on his or her next album or get the song used in an upcoming film. The professional manager uses all the contacts and leads he has to get the writer's songs recorded by as many artists as possible. Therefore, he must be able to deal efficiently and effectively with people in other segments of the music industry, including A&R personnel, recording artists, producers, distributors, managers and lawyers. Through these contacts, he can find out what artists are looking for new material, and who may be interested in recording one of the writer's songs.

WHERE THE MONEY COMES FROM

After a writer's songs are recorded, the other departments at the publishing company come into play.

- The *licensing and copyright departments* are responsible for issuing any licenses for use of the writer's songs in film or TV and for filing various forms with the copyright office.
- The *legal affairs department and business affairs department* works with the professional department in negotiating contracts with its writers.
- The *royalty and accounting departments* are responsible for making sure that users of music are paying correct royalties to the publisher and ensuring the writer is receiving the

proper royalty rate as specified in the contract and that statements are mailed to the writer promptly.

- Finally, the *foreign department*'s role is to oversee any publishing activities outside of the United States, to notify subpublishers of the proper writer and ownership information of songs in the catalogue and update all activity and new releases, and to make sure a writer is being paid for any uses of his material in foreign countries.

LOCATING A MUSIC PUBLISHER

How do you go about finding a music publisher that will work well for you? First, you must find a publisher suited to the type of music you write. If a particular publisher works mostly with alternative music and you're a country songwriter, the contacts he has within the industry will hardly be beneficial to you. Each listing in this section details, in order of importance, the type of music that publisher is most interested in; the music types appear in **boldface** to make them easier to locate. It's also very important to submit only to companies interested in your level of experience (see the Openness to Submissions sidebar on page 8). You will also want to refer to the Category Index at the end of this section, which lists companies by the type of music they work with. Publishers placing music in film or TV will be proceded by a 🎬 (see the Film & TV Index for a complete list of these companies).

Additional Publishers

There are **MORE PUBLISHERS** located in other sections of the book! On page 129 use the list of Additional Publishers to find listings within other sections who are also music publishers.

Do your research!

It's important to study the market and do research to identify which companies to submit to.

- Many record producers have publishing companies or have joint ventures with major publishers who fund the signing of songwriters and who provide administration services. Since producers many times have an influence over what is recorded, targeting the producer/publisher can be a useful avenue.
- Since most publishers don't open unsolicited material, try to meet the publishing representative in person (at conferences, speaking engagements, etc.) or try to have an intermediary intercede on your behalf (for example, an entertainment attorney; a manager, an agent, etc.).
- As to demos, submit no more than 3 songs.
- As to publishing deals, co-publishing deals (where a writer owns part of the publishing share through his or her own company) are relatively common if there is interest in a writer.
- Are you targeting a specific artist to sing your songs? If so, find out if that artist even considers outside material. Get a copy of the artist's latest album, and see who wrote most of the songs. If they were all written by the artist, he's probably not interested in hearing material from outside writers. If the songs were written by a variety of different writers, however, he may be open to hearing new songs.
- Check the album liner notes, which will list the names of the publishers of each writer. These publishers obviously have had luck pitching songs to the artist, and they may be able to get your songs to that artist as well.
- If the artist you're interested in has a recent hit on the *Billboard* charts, the publisher of that song will be listed in the "Hot 100 A-Z" index. Carefully choosing which publishers will work best for the material you write may take time, but it will only increase your chances of getting your songs heard. "Shotgunning" your demo packages (sending out

many packages without regard for music preference or submission policy) is a waste of time and money and will hurt, rather than help, your songwriting career.

Once you've found some companies that may be interested in your work, learn what songs have been successfully handled by those publishers. Most publishers are happy to provide you with this information in order to attract high-quality material. Ask the publisher for the names of some of their staff writers, and give them a call. Ask their opinion of how the publisher works. Keep in mind as you're researching music publishers how you get along with them personally. If you can't work with a publisher on a personal level, chances are your material won't be represented as you would like it to be. A publisher can become your most valuable connection to all other segments of the music industry, so it's important to find someone you can trust and feel comfortable with.

Independent or major company?

Also consider the size of the publishing company. The publishing affiliates of the major music conglomerates are huge, handling catalogs of thousands of songs by hundreds of songwriters. Unless you are an established songwriter, your songs probably won't receive enough attention from such large companies. Smaller, independent publishers offer several advantages. First, independent music publishers are located all over the country, making it easier for you to work face-to-face rather than by mail or phone. Smaller companies usually aren't affiliated with a particular record company and are therefore able to pitch your songs to many different labels and acts. Independent music publishers are usually interested in a smaller range of music, allowing you to target your submissions more accurately. The most obvious advantage to working with a smaller publisher is the personal attention they can bring to you and your songs. With a smaller roster of artists to work with, the independent music publisher is able to concentrate more time and effort on each particular project.

For More Information

For more instructional information on the listings in this book, including explanations of symbols (ⓝ ☑ ⬇ ⬆ ☑ ⊞ ◯ ⬗ ☑ ⊘), read the article How to Use *Songwriter's Market* to Get Your Songs Heard on page 5.

SUBMITTING MATERIAL TO PUBLISHERS

When submitting material to a publisher, always keep in mind that a professional, courteous manner goes a long way in making a good impression. When you submit a demo through the mail, make sure your package is neat and meets the particular needs of the publisher. Review each publisher's submission policy carefully, and follow it to the letter. Disregarding this information will only make you look like an amateur in the eyes of the company you're submitting to.

Listings of companies in Canada are preceded by a ☑ , and international markets are designated with a ⊞ . You will find an alphabetical list of these companies at the back of the book, along with an index of publishers by state.

PUBLISHING CONTRACTS

Once you've located a publisher you like and he's interested in shopping your work, it's time to consider the publishing contract—an agreement in which a songwriter grants certain rights to a publisher for one or more songs. The contract specifies any advances offered to the writer, the rights that will be transferred to the publisher, the royalties a songwriter is to receive and the length of time the contract is valid.

- When a contract is signed, a publisher will ask for a 50-50 split with the writer. This is standard industry practice; the publisher is taking that 50% to cover the overhead costs of running his business and for the work he's doing to get your songs recorded.
- It is always a good idea to have a publishing contract (or any music business contract) reviewed by a competent entertainment lawyer.
- There is no "standard" publishing contract, and each company offers different provisions for their writers.

Make sure you ask questions about anything you don't understand, especially if you're new in the business. Songwriter organizations such as the Songwriters Guild of America (SGA) provide contract review services, and can help you learn about music business language and what constitutes a fair music publishing contract. Be sure to read The Business of Songwriting on page 20 for more information on contracts. See the Organizations section of this book for more information on the SGA and other songwriting groups.

When signing a contract, it's important to be aware of the music industry's unethical practitioners. The "song shark," as he's called, makes his living by asking a songwriter to pay to have a song published. The shark will ask for money to demo a song and promote it to radio stations; he may also ask for more than the standard 50% publisher's share or ask you to give up all rights to a song in order to have it published. Although none of these practices is illegal, it's certainly not ethical, and no successful publisher uses these methods. *Songwriter's Market* works to list only honest companies interested in hearing new material. (For more on "song sharks," see The Rip-Offs on page 23.)

☑ ⊘ ○ **A TA Z MUSIC**, P.O. Box 1014, St. George VT 84771-1014. Phone/fax: (435)688-1818. E-mail: info@acecrazy.com. Website: www.acecrazy.com. **Contact:** Kyle Garrett, professional manager (pop/r&b/hip-hop). Music publisher. Estab. 1999. Publishes 8 songs/year; publishes 2 new songwriters/year. Staff size: 4. Pays standard royalty.
How to Contact: *We only accept material referred to us by a reputable industry source (manager, entertainment attorney, etc.)* Prefers CD/CDR or VHS videocassette with lyric sheet. "Be sure to include lyric sheets!" Include SASE.
Music: Mostly **pop**, **r&b** and **hip-hop**; also **rock**, **dance** and **alternative**. Does not want country. Published "Five Thousand New Angels" (single by Ace); and "Power of USA" (single by Ace) from *9-11* (album), recorded by Ace (pop), released 2001 on Diferent.
Tips: "Put a lot of effort into your submission . . . it'll show. Never take a submission lightly . . . it'll show! Go to as many songwriter workshops as possible and refine your craft. Send only great songs . . . *not* good songs."

☑ ○ **ABALONE PUBLISHING**, 29355 Little Mack, Roseville MI 48066. (586)775-6533. E-mail: jtrupi4539@aol.com. Website: members.aol.com/jtrupi4539/index.html. **Contact:** Jack Timmons, director. Music publisher and record company (L.A. Records). Estab. 1984. Publishes 20-30 songs/year; publishes 20-30 new songwriters/year. Staff size: 12. Hires staff songwriters. Pays standard royalty.
Affiliate(s): BGM Publishing, AL-KY Music and Bubba Music (BMI).
How to Contact: Submit demo tape by mail. Unsolicited submissions are OK. Prefers cassette with 1-5 songs and lyric sheet. "Include cover letter describing your goals." Include SASE with first class postage. All others, please include $1 to cover fluctuating postal rates. Responds in 3 months.
Music: Mostly **rock**, **pop** and **alternative**; also **dance**, **pop/rock** and **country**. Does not want rap, alternative or rave. Published *Mad About You*, written and recorded by Joey Harlow (techno), released 2000; *The Torch* (album by Robbi Taylor/The Sattellites), recorded by The Sattellites (rock); "The Web" (single by Jay Collins), recorded by The Net (rock); and "Passion" (single by R. Gibb), recorded by Notta (blues), all on L.A. Records.

Tips: "Follow stipulations for submission 'to a tee.' Not conforming to our listing exactly constitutes return of your submission. Write what you feel; however, don't stray too far from the trends that are currently popular. Lyrical content should depict a definite story line and paint an accurate picture in the listener's mind."

ALCO MUSIC (BMI), P.O. Box 18197, Panama City Beach FL 32417. Professional Manager: Ann McEver (country, alternative, rock). **Contact:** A&R Dept. Music publisher. Estab. 2000. Staff size: 2. Pays standard royalty.

How to Contact: Submit demo tape by mail. Unsolicited submissions are OK. Prefers cassette or CD with 3 songs, lyric sheet and cover letter. Include SASE. Responds in 3 weeks.

Music: Mostly **pop/rock**, **country** and **alternative**; also **gospel**. Does not want instrumentals. Published "Hungry Now" (single by Jack Bennion) from *Hungry and How* (album), recorded by Snack Bar (alternative), released 2001 on Alco; "Treat Mama Good" (single by Willie Burk) from *Willie Burk* (album), recorded by Willie Burk (country), released 2001 on Alco.

Tips: "Make sure your submission meets our submission requirements. We are looking for songs that can compete at a Nashville or Los Angeles level and strong enough for major artists."

ALEXANDER SR. MUSIC (BMI), PMB 364, 7100 Lockwood Blvd., Boardman OH 44512. (330)782-5031. Fax: (330)782-6954. E-mail: dap@netdotcom.com. Website: www.dapenterta inment.com. **Contact:** LaVerne Chambers, promotions. Owner: Darryl Alexander. Music publisher, record company (DAP Entertainment), music consulting, distribution and promotional services and record producer. Estab. 1992. Publishes 12-22 songs/year; publishes 2-4 new songwriters/year. Staff size: 3. Pays standard royalty.

How to Contact: *Write first and obtain permission to submit.* Prefers cassette with 4 songs and lyric sheet. "We will accept finished masters (cassette or CD) for review." Include SASE. Responds in 2 months. "No phone calls or faxes please."

Film & TV: Places 2 songs in TV/year. Music Supervisor: Darryl Alexander. Recently published "Feel Your Love" and "You Are So Beautiful" for the film *The Doctor Is Upstairs*, both written and recorded by Darryl Alexander.

Music: Mostly **contemporary jazz** and **urban gospel**; also **R&B**. Does not want rock, gangsta rap, heavy metal or country. Published "Take A Chance" (single by Darryl Alexander/Shiela Hayes), recorded by Shiela Hayes (urban jazz), released 2001; "Nothing But the 405" (single by Herb McMullen), recorded by Darryl Alexander (urban jazz), released 2002 on DAP Entertainment; and "Feel Your Love" (single by Darryl Alexander), recorded by Darryl Alexander (urban jazz), released 2001 on DAP Entertainment.

Tips: "Send only music in styles that we review. Submit your best songs and follow submission guidelines. Finished masters open up additional possibilities. Lead sheets may be requested for material we are interested in. Must have SASE if you wish to have cassette returned. No phone calls, please."

ALEXIS (ASCAP), P.O. Box 532, Malibu CA 90265. (323)463-5998. **Contact:** Lee Magid, president. Music publisher, record company, personal management firm, and record and video producer. Member AIMP. Estab. 1950. Publishes 50 songs/year; publishes 20-50 new songwriters/year. Pays standard royalty.

Affiliate(s): Marvelle (BMI), Lou-Lee (BMI), D.R. Music (ASCAP) and Gabal (SESAC).

**FOR EXPLANATIONS OF THESE SYMBOLS,
SEE THE INSIDE FRONT AND BACK COVERS OF THIS BOOK.**

How to Contact: Submit a demo tape by mail. Unsolicited submissions are OK. Prefers cassette or VHS videocassette with 1-3 songs and lyric sheet. "Try to make demo as clear as possible—guitar or piano should be sufficient. A full rhythm and vocal demo is always better." Does not return material. Responds in 2 months only if interested.

Music: Mostly **R&B**, **jazz**, **MOR**, **pop** and **gospel**; also **blues**, **church/religious**, **country**, **dance-oriented**, **folk** and **Latin**. Published "Jesus Is Just Alright" (single by Reynolds), recorded by D.C. Talk on Forefront Records (pop); "Blues For the Weepers" (single by Rich/Magid), recorded by Lou Rawls on Capitol Records (pop/blues); and "What Shall I Do" (single by Q. Fielding), recorded by Tramaine Hawkins on EMI/Sparrow Records (ballad).

Tips: "Try to create a good demo, vocally and musically. A good home-recorded tape will do."

☑ ○ **ALIAS JOHN HENRY TUNES (BMI)**, 11 Music Square E., Suite 607, Nashville TN 37203. (615)582-1782. E-mail: bobbyjohn@spencemanor.com/BJH. Website: spencemanor.com. **Contact:** Bobby John Henry, owner. Music publisher, record producer and music hotel (The Spence Manor Suites). Estab. 1996. Publishes 3 songs/year; publishes 1 new songwriter/year. Staff size: 3. Pays standard royalty.

How to Contact: *Call first and obtain permission to submit.* Prefers cassette with 3 songs and lyric sheet. Does not return material. Responds in 6 months only if interested.

Music: Mostly **country**, **rock** and **alternative**. Does not want rap. Published *Mr. Right Now* (album by Kari Jorgensen), recorded by "Hieke" on Warner Bros. (rock); and *Nothing to Me* (album by B.J. Henry), recorded by Millie Jackson on Spring.

Tips: "Focus and rewrite, rewrite, rewrite."

⊕ ○ **ALL ROCK MUSIC**. Phone: (31) 186-604266. Fax: (32) 0186-604366. E-mail: sales@colle ctorrec.com. Website: www.collectorrec.com. **Contact:** Cees Klop, president. Music publisher, record company (Collector Records) and record producer. Estab. 1967. Publishes 40 songs/year; publishes several new songwriters/year. Staff size: 3. Pays standard royalty.

Affiliate(s): All Rock Music (England).

How to Contact: Submit demo tape by mail. Unsolicited submissions are OK. Prefers cassette. SAE and IRC. Responds in 2 months.

Music: Mostly **'50s rock**, **rockabilly** and **country rock**; also **piano boogie woogie**. Published "Hey Now Baby" (single), from *Second Time Rockin'* (album), written and recorded by Billy Lee (rocka-billy), released 2001 on Collector Records; "Good Better Best" (single), from *R & R with Piano* (album), written and recorded by Wallace Waters ('50s rock), released 2001 on Collector Records; and "Bingo Boogie" (single by R. Turner) from *High Steppin' Daddy* (album), recorded by Tommy Mooney ('50s hillbilly), released 2000 on Collector Records.

Tips: "Send only the kind of material we issue/produce as listed."

☑ ○ **ALLEGHENY MUSIC WORKS**, 1611 Menoher Blvd., Johnstown PA 15905. (814)255-4007. E-mail: TunedOnMusic@aol.com. Website: www.alleghenymusicworks.com. **Contact:** Al Rita, managing director. Music publisher and record company (Allegheny Records). Estab. 1991. Staff size: 2. Pays standard royalty.

Affiliate(s): Allegheny Music Works Publishing (ASCAP) and Tuned on Music (BMI).

How to Contact: *Write first and obtain permission to submit.* "Include SASE for reply. E-mail queries are acceptable. Responds in 1 week to regular mail requests and usually within 48 hours to e-mail queries."

Music: Mostly **country**; also **pop**, **A/C**, **R&B**, **novelty**, **Halloween** and **inspirational**. Does not want rap, metal or x-rated lyrics. Published "Flying In the Sky" (single by Penny Towers Wilber) from *Halloween Bash* (album), recorded by Victor R. Vampire (pop/novelty/Halloween), released 2000 on Allegheny.

Tips: "Bookmark our website and check it regularly, clicking on *Songwriter Opportunities*. Each month, as a free service to songwriters, we list a new artist or company looking for songs. Complete contact information is included. For a deeper insight into the type of material our company publishes, we invite you to read the customer reviews on amazon.com to our 2000 best seller Halloween album release, *Halloween Bash*."

◑**ALLISONGS INC. (ASCAP, BMI)**, 1603 Horton Ave., Nashville TN 37212. (615)292-9899. Website: www.allisongs.com. President: Jim Allison. Professional Manager: Bill Renfrew. Music publisher, record company (ARIA Records) and record producer (Jim Allison). Estab. 1985. Publishes 50 songs/year. Staff size: 4. Pays standard royalty.
Affiliate(s): Jim's Allisongs (BMI), Songs of Jim Allison (BMI) and Annie Green Eyes Music (BMI).
  • Reba McEntire's "What Am I Gonna Do About You," published by AlliSongs, Inc., was included on her triple-platinum album, *Greatest Hits*.
How to Contact: Submit demo tape by mail. Unsolicited submissions are OK. Send CD and lyric sheet. Does not return material. Responds in 6 weeks only if interested.
Music: Mostly **country** and **pop**. Published "Beautiful World" (single by Anne Delana Reeves/Billy Montana/Jim Allison) from *Beautiful World* (album), recorded by Sheri Porter (alternative country), released 2001 on ARIA Records; and "Montgomery to Memphis" (single by Anne Delana Reeves/ Billy Montana) from *Lee Ann Womack* (album), recorded by Lee Ann Womack (country), released 1997 on Decca Records.
Tips: "Send your best—we will contact you if interested. No need to call us. It will be listened to."

☑ ⬚ ◑**ALPHA MUSIC INC. (BMI)**, 747 Chestnut Ridge Rd., Chestnut Ridge NY 10977. (845)356-0800. Fax: (845)356-0895. E-mail: alpha@trfmusic.com. **Contact:** Michael Nurko. Music publisher. Estab. 1931. Pays standard royalty.
Affiliate(s): Dorian Music Corp. (ASCAP) and TRF Music Inc.
How to Contact: "We accept submissions of new compositions. Submissions are not returnable."
Music: All categories, mainly **instrumental** and **acoustic**; also **theme music** for television and film. "Have published over 50,000 titles since 1931."

☑ ◑**AMEN, INC.**, 2035 Pleasanton Rd., San Antonio TX 78221-1306. (210)932-AMEN. E-mail: manny@amenmusic.com. Music publisher and record company (AMC Records). Estab. 1963. Pays standard royalty.
Affiliate(s): CITA Music (BMI).
How to Contact: Submit demo tape by mail. Unsolicited submissions are OK. Accepts Spanish music only. Prefers cassette and lyric sheet. "Allow three to four weeks before calling to inquire about submission." Include SASE. Responds in 4 months.
Music: Evangelical Christian gospel in Spanish. Published "Imponme Tus Manos" (by Jesus Yorba Garcia), recorded by Rudy Guerra; "Jesucristo" (by Enrique Alvarez), recorded by Kiko Alvarez; and "Hey, Hey, Hey" (by Manny R. Guerra), all on AMC Records. Administers Voz En Zion.

◑**AMERICATONE INTERNATIONAL**, 1817 Loch Lomond Way, Las Vegas NV 89102-4437. (702)384-0030. Fax: (702) 382-1926. President: Joe Jan Jaros. Estab. 1975. Publishes 25 songs/year. Pays variable royalty.
Affiliate(s): Americatone Records International, Christy Records International USA, Rambolt Music International (ASCAP).
How to Contact: Submit demo tape by mail. Unsolicited submissions OK. Prefers cassettes, "studio production with top sound recordings." Include SASE. Responds in 1 month.
Music: Mostly **country**, **R&B**, **Spanish** and **classic ballads**. Published "Romantic Music," written and recorded by Chuck Mymit; "Explosion" (by Ray Sykora), recorded by Sam Trippe; and "From Las Vegas" (by Ladd Staide), recorded by Robert Martin, all on Americatone International Records.

◐**ARAS MUSIC (ASCAP)**, P.O. Box 100215, Palm Bay FL 32910-0215. Phone/fax: (208)441-6559. E-mail: savmusic@juno.com. President: Bill Young. **Contact:** Amy Young (country, contemporary Christian, pop, alternative, jazz and latin) or Bruce Marion (piano and instrumental). Music publisher and record company (Outback Records). Member Academy of Country Music, Country Music Association. Estab. 1996. Pays standard royalty.
Affiliate(s): SAV Music (BMI), Outback Records and PARDO Music (SESAC).

How to Contact: Submit demo tape by mail. Unsolicited submissions are OK. Prefers cassette or CD with 3 songs and typed lyric sheet. Include SASE. "Make sure enough postage is included to return demo." Responds in 3 months.

Music: Mostly **country**, **contemporary Christian** and **jazz**; also music suitable for motion pictures. Does not want rap or classical. Published "Once Upon A Time" (single by R. Cook), recorded by Curtis Grant (country), released 2002 on AMI Records; "Under the Influence" (single by R. Calhoun/ S. Collins) from *The Deal Is Done* (album), recorded by John Coibert (country), released 2001 on Outback Records; and "To Find Saving Grace" (single by B. Fuller/S. Blackmon) from *Bare My Soul* (album), recorded by Brian Fuller (Christian), released 2001 on Outback Records/Universal UK.

Tips: "When recording a demo, have an artist in mind. We pitch to major labels and major artists, so please submit studio-quality demos with typed lyric sheets. If you submit a marketable product, we will put forth 100% effort for you."

☑ ◻ **AUDIO MUSIC PUBLISHERS (ASCAP)**, 449 N. Vista St., Los Angeles CA 90036. (818)362-9853. Fax: (323)653-7670. E-mail: parlirec@aol.com. Website: www.parlirec.com. **Contact:** Len Weisman, professional manager. Owner: Ben Weisman. Music publisher, record company and record producer (The Weisman Production Group). Estab. 1962. Publishes 25 songs/year; publishes 10-15 new songwriters/year. Staff size: 10. Pays standard royalty.

How to Contact: Submit demo tape by mail. Unsolicited submissions are OK. "No permission needed." Prefers cassette with 3-10 songs and lyric sheet. "We do not return unsolicited material without SASE. Don't query first; just send tape." Responds in 6 weeks. "We listen; we don't write back. If we like your material we will telephone you."

Music: Mostly **pop**, **R&B** and **rap**; also **dance**, **funk**, **soul** and **gospel**. Does not want heavy metal. "Crazy About You" (single) and *Where Is Love* (album), both written by Curtis Womack; and *Don't Make Me Walk Away* (album by Debe Gunn), all recorded by Valerie (R&B) on Kon Kord.

◻ **AVALON MUSIC (ASCAP, BMI)**, P.O. Box 121626, Nashville TN 37212. **Contact:** A&R Review Department. Professional Manager: Avalon Hughes. Music publisher, record company (Avalon Recording Group) and record producer (Avalon Productions). Estab. 2001. Staff size: 3. Pays standard royalty.

How to Contact: Submit demo tape by mail. Unsolicited submissions are OK. Prefers cassette or CD with 3 songs and lyric sheet. Include SASE. Responds in 3 weeks.

Music: Mostly **rock**, **country**, and **alternative**; also **R&B** and **hip hop**. Published "Paradise" (single by Allude) from *Allude To This* (album), recorded by Allude (alternative), released 2001 on Avalon; "Who Knows" (single by Jim Hughes) from *Madrid*, recorded by Madrid (rock), released 2001 on Avalon.

Tips: "Send songs suitable for today's market."

◖ **BAGATELLE MUSIC PUBLISHING CO. (BMI)**, P.O. Box 925929, Houston TX 77292. (713)680-2160 or (800)845-6865. **Contact:** Byron Benton, President. Music publisher, record company and record producer. Publishes 40 songs/year; publishes 2 new songwriters/year. Pays standard royalty.

Affiliate(s): Floyd Tillman Publishing Co.

How to Contact: Submit demo tape by mail. Unsolicited submissions are OK. Prefers cassette (or videocassette) with any number of songs and lyric sheet. Include SASE.

Music: Mostly **country**; also **gospel** and **blues**. Published "Everything You Touch" (single), written and recorded by Johnny Nelms; "This Is Real" and "Mona from Daytona" (singles), written and recorded by Floyd Tillman, all on Bagatelle Records.

◖ **BAITSTRING MUSIC (ASCAP)**, 2622 Kirtland Rd., Brewton AL 36426. (334)867-2228. **Contact:** Roy Edwards, president. Music publisher and record company (Bolivia Records). Estab. 1972. Publishes 20 songs/year; publishes 10 new songwriters/year. Hires staff songwriters. Pays standard royalty.

Affiliate(s): Cheavoria Music Co. (BMI)

How to Contact: Submit demo tape by mail. Unsolicited submissions are OK. Prefers cassette with 3 songs and lyric sheet. Does not return material. Responds in 1 month.
Music: Mostly **R&B**, **pop** and **easy listening**; also **country**. Published "Forever and Always," written and recorded by Jim Portwood (pop); and "Make Me Forget" (by Horace Linsley) and "Never Let Me Go" (by Cheavoria Edwards), both recorded by Bobbie Roberson (country), all on Bolivia Records.

◐ **BAL & BAL MUSIC PUBLISHING CO. (ASCAP)**, P.O. Box 369, LaCanada CA 91012-0369. (818)548-1116. E-mail: balmusic@pacbell.net. **Contact:** Adrian P. Bal, President or Berdella M. Bal, Vice President/Secretary-Treasurer. Music publisher, record company (Bal Records) and record producer. Member AGAC and AIMP. Estab. 1965. Publishes 2-6 songs/year; publishes 2-4 new songwriters/year. Staff size: 2. Pays standard royalty.
Affiliate(s): Bal West Music Publishing Co. (BMI).
How to Contact: *Write or call first and obtain permission to submit.* Prefers cassette with 3 songs and lyric sheet. Include SASE. Responds in 3 months.
Music: Mostly **MOR**, **country**, **rock** and **gospel**; also **blues**, **church/religious**, **easy listening**, **jazz**, **R&B**, **soul** and **top 40/pop**. Does not want heavy metal or rap. Published *Special Day* (album), written and recorded by Rhonda Johnson on Bal Records (gospel).
Tips: "Send what you believe to be commercial—who will buy the product?"

N ◐ **BALMUR ENTERTAINMENT**, 1105 17th Ave. S., Nashville TN 37212-2203. (615)329-1431. Fax: (615)321-0240. **Contact:** Cyndi Forman, creative director. Music publisher. Publishes 100 songs/year; publishes 2-3 new songwriters/year. Hires staff songwriters. Pays standard royalty.
Affiliate(s): Willdawn Music, A Little Good News Music (ASCAP), Pugwash Music (BMI) and Paddy's Head Music (SOCAN).
How to Contact: Does not accept any unsolicited submissions.
Music: Mostly **country**, **pop** and **rock**. Published "Chain of Love" (single), recorded by Clay Walker (country); and "People Like Us" (single), recorded by Aaron Tippin (country).

◖ **BARKIN' FOE THE MASTER'S BONE**, 1111 Elm St. #520, Cincinnati OH 45210-2271. (513)721-4965. Website: www.1stbook.com. Company Owner (rock, R&B): Kevin Curtis. Professional Managers: Shonda Barr (country, jazz, pop, rap); Betty Barr (gospel, soul, soft rock). Music publisher. Estab. 1989. Publishes 4 songs/year; publishes 1 new songwriter/year. Staff size: 4. Pays standard royalty.
Affiliate(s): Beat Box Music (ASCAP) and Feltstar (BMI).
How to Contact: Submit demo tape by mail. Unsolicited submissions are OK. Prefers cassette (or VHS videocassette) with 3 songs. Include SASE. Responds in 2 weeks.
Music: Mostly **country**, **soft rock** and **pop**; also **soul**, **gospel**, **rap** and **jazz**. Does not want classical. Published "Bird's Eye View" (single by Chris Payne), "Can I Go Again" (single by Chris Payne) and "Tony" (single by Chris Payne), all from *Bird's Eye View* (album), recorded by Chris Payne, released 2001 on Valley Media.

◖ **BARREN WOOD PUBLISHING (BMI)**, 2426 Auburn Ave., Dayton OH 45406-1928. Phone/fax: (937)275-4221. President: Jack Froschauer. Music publisher and record company (Emerald City Records). Estab. 1992. Publishes 5-6 songs/year; publishes 3-4 new songwriters/year. Staff size: 1. Pays standard royalty.
Affiliate(s): MerryGold Music Publishing (ASCAP).
How to Contact: Submit demo by mail. Unsolicited submissions are OK. Prefers CD with 1 song and lyric or lead sheet. "Studio quality demo please." Include SASE. Responds in 3 months.

TO HELP YOU UNDERSTAND and use the information in these listings, see "How to Use *Songwriter's Market* to Get Your Songs Heard," on page 5.

Music: Mostly **country**, **A/C** and **Christian**. Does not want alternative. Published "We Can't Go Home" and "She's Married" (singles by D. Walton) from *Relish* (album), recorded by My 3 Sons (rock), released 2000 on Emerald City.

Tips: "Recognize that songwriting is a business. Present yourself and your material in a professional, businesslike mannner."

○ **BAY RIDGE PUBLISHING CO. (BMI)**, P.O. Box 5537, Kreole Station, Moss Point MS 39563-1537. (228)475-0059. Estab. 1974. **Contact:** Doris M. Mitchell, president. Vice President: Justin F. Mitchell. Vice President/Manager: Joe F. Mitchell. Music publisher and record company (Missile Records).

How to Contact: *Write or call first to obtain permission before you submit.* Include #10 business-size SASE to respond to your request to submit material. **After you receive permission to submit, include with submission SASE with sufficient postage to return all materials.** No reply without SASE or return of material without sufficient return postage. "No collect calls; not reviewing unsolicited material. All songs sent for review MUST include sufficient return postage. **Absolutely *no* reply postcards, only SASE.** If you only write lyrics, do not submit. We only accept completed songs, so you must find a musical collaborator. We are not interested in reviewing homemade recordings." Prefers CD (first choice) or cassette with 3-8 songs and lyrics to songs submitted. Responds in 2 months.

Music: **Country**, **hardcore**, **folk**, **contemporary**, **alternative**, **gospel**, **rap**, **heavy metal**, **jazz**, **bluegrass**, **R&B**; also **ballads**, **reggae**, **world**, **soul**, **MOR**, **blues**, **rock** and **pop**. Published "Excuse Me, Lady," "When She Left Me" (singles by Rich Wilson), "Everyone Gets A Chance (To Lose in Romance)" and "I'm So Glad We Found Each Other" (singles by Joe F. Mitchell), recorded by Rich Wilson (country), released on Missile Records.

Tips: "Outstanding singers with outstanding songs, well-produced, well-written and ready for the market will be shopped to major labels or given consideration for release on Missile Records. Give us a call. We have the connections to get you to the next level where you need to be. We will give consideration to new exceptionally talented artists with a fan base and some backing."

⊞ **BEAVERWOOD AUDIO-VIDEO (BMI)**, 133 Walton Ferry, Hendersonville TN 37075. (615)824-2820. Fax: (615)824-2833. E-mail: beaverwd@bellsouth.net. Owner: Clyde Beavers. Music publisher, record company (Kash Records, JCL Records), record producer, audio-video duplication. Estab. 1976. Pays standard royalty.

Affiliate(s): Jackpot Music (BMI).

How to Contact: Submit demo tape by mail. Unsolicited submissions are OK. Prefers cassette, DAT or videocassette with 1-5 songs. Does not return material.

Music: Mostly **gospel** and **country**. Published "Mary Had a Little Lamb," *Listen to My Story* and *I Heard His Call*, all written and recorded by Lawrence Davis on JCL Records (gospel).

✓ ◐ **HAL BERNARD ENTERPRISES, INC.**, 2612 Erie Ave., P.O. Box 8385, Cincinnati OH 45208. (513)871-1500. Fax: (513)871-1510. E-mail: halbernard@cinci.rr.com. **Contact:** Sammy, assistant. President: Stan Hertzman. Professional Manager: S. Monian. Music publisher, record company (Strugglebaby), record producer and management firm (Umbrella Artists Management). Publishes 12-24 songs/year; 1-2 new songwriters/year. Pays standard royalty.

Affiliate(s): Sunnyslope Music (ASCAP), Bumpershoot Music (BMI), Apple Butter Music (ASCAP), Carb Music (ASCAP), Saiko Music (ASCAP), Smorgaschord Music (ASCAP), Clifton Rayburn Music (ASCAP) and Robert Stevens Music (ASCAP).

How to Contact: *Write or call first and obtain permission to submit.* Prefers cassette with 3 songs and lyric sheet. Include SASE. Responds in 6 weeks only if interested.

Music: Mostly **rock**, **R&B** and **top 40/pop**. Published *Through My Eyes* (album by Paul Bromwell), recorded by Bromwell-Diehl Band, released 2001 on Bash; *Car Caught Fire* (album), written and recorded by The Bears, released 2001 on ABP; and *The Greenhornes* (album), written and recorded by The Greenhornes, released 2000 on Telstar.

Tips: "Best material should appear first on demo. Cast your demos. If you, as the songwriter, can't sing it—don't. Get someone who can present your song properly, use a straight rhythm track and keep it as naked as possible. If you think it still needs something else, have a string arranger, etc. help you but still keep the *voice up* and the *lyrics clear.*"

☑ ▣ ◑ **BIG FISH MUSIC PUBLISHING GROUP**, 11927 Magnolia Blvd., Suite 3, N. Hollywood CA 91607. (818)984-0377. CEO: Chuck Tennin. Producer: Gary Black (country, pop, adult contemporary, rock, crossover songs, other styles). Professional Music Manager: Lora Sprague (jazz, New Age, instrumental, pop rock, R&B). Music publisher, record company (California Sun Records) and production company. Estab. 1971. Publishes 10-20 songs/year; publishes 5-10 new songwriters/year. Staff size: 6. Pays standard royalty. "We also license songs and music to users."
Affiliate(s): Big Fish Music (BMI) and California Sun Music (ASCAP).
How to Contact: *Write first and obtain permission to submit.* Include SASE for reply. "*Please do not call.* After permission to submit is confirmed, we will assign and forward to you a submission code number allowing you to submit up to 4 songs maximum, preferably on CD or cassette. Include a properly addressed cover letter, signed and dated, with your source of referral (*Songwriter's Market*) with your assigned submission code number and SASE for reply and/or return of material. Include lyrics. *Unsolicited material will not be accepted.* That is our Submission Policy to review outside and new material." Responds in 2 weeks.
Film & TV: Places 6 songs in TV/year. Recently published "Even the Angels Knew" (by Cathy Carlson/Craig Lackey/Marty Axelrod); "Stop Before We Start" (by J.D. Grieco); "Oh Santa" (by Christine Bridges/John Deaver), all recorded by The Black River Girls in *Passions* (NBC); licensed "A Christmas Wish" (by Ed Fry/Eddie Max), used in *Passions* (NBC); and "Girls Will Be Girls" (single by Cathy Carlson/John LeGrande), recorded by The Black River Girls, used in *All My Children* (ABC).
Music: **Country**, including **country pop**, **country A/C** and **country crossover** with a cutting edge; also **pop**, **pop ballads**, **adult contemporary**, **uplifting**, **inspirational adult contemporary gospel** with a powerful message, **instrumental background and theme music** for TV & films, New Age/instrumental jazz and **novelty type songs** for all kinds of commercial use. Published "If Wishes Were Horses" (single by Billy O'Hara); "Purple Bunny Honey" (single by Robert Lloyd/Jim Love); "Leavin' You For Me" (single by J.D. Griew); "Move That Train" (single by Robert Porter); "Happy Landing" (by T. Brawley/B. Woodrich); "Girls Will Be Girls" (single by Cathy Carlson/John LeGrande); "You Should Be Here With Me" (single by Ken McMeans); and "Stop Before We Start" (single by J.D. Grieco), all recorded by Black River Girls on California Sun Records.
Tips: "Demo should be professional, high quality, clean, simple, dynamic, and must get the song across on the first listen. Good clear vocals, a nice melody, a good musical feel, good musical arrangement, strong lyrics and chorus—a unique, catchy, clever song that sticks with you. Looking for unique country and pop songs with a different edge that can crossover to the mainstream market for ongoing Nashville music projects and songs for a hot female country trio that crosses over to adult contemporary and pop with great lush, warm harmonies that reach out to middle America and baby boomers and their grown up children (25 to 65). Also, catchy uptempo songs with an attitude, meaningful lyrics (Shania Twain style) for upcoming album projects. Also, soundtrack music of all types for new Film Production Company and upcoming film projects."

☑ ▣ ◑ **BIXIO MUSIC GROUP & ASSOCIATES/IDM MUSIC (ASCAP)**, 111 E. 14th St., Suite 140, New York NY 10003. (212)695-3911. Fax: (212)967-6284. E-mail: sales@bixio.com and mail@idmmusic.com. Website: www.bixio.com and www.idmmusic.com. General Manager: Johannes in der Muhlen. Administrator: Miriam Westercappel (all styles). A&R Director: Tomo (all styles). Office Manager: Courtney Stack-Slutsky. Administrative Assistant: Karlene Evans (soundtracks). Creative Director: Robert Draghi (all styles). Senior Creative Director/Producer: Tomo. A&R: Claudene Neysmith (world/New Age). Music publisher, record company and rights clearances. Estab. 1985. Publishes a few hundred songs/year; publishes 2 new songwriters/year. Staff size: 6. Pays standard royalty.
How to Contact: *Does not accept unsolicited material.*

Music: Mostly **soundtracks**. Published "La Strada Nel Bosco," included in the TV show *Ed* (NBC); "La Beguine Du Mac," included in the TV show *The Chris Isaac Show* (Showtime); and "Alfonsina Delle Camelie," included in the TV show *UC: Undercover* (NBC).

N **⊠** **○** **BLACK MARKET ENTERTAINMENT RECORDINGS (ASCAP, BMI)**, 936 Harwell St. NW, Atlanta GA 30314. (404)522-8000. Fax: (404)522-7643. E-mail: sloanem@mindspring.com. **Contact:** Sloane L. Molot, A&R assistant. Music publisher and record company (B.M.E. Records). Estab. 1992. Publishes 20 new songs/year; publishes 20 new songwriters/year. Staff size: 7. **Affiliate(s):** SWOLE Music (ASCAP).

How to Contact: Submit demo tape by mail. Unsolicited submissions are OK. Prefers CD/CDR with cover letter. "Please do not call; enclose mailing and e-mail address." Does not return material. Responds in 1 month.

Film & TV: Places 3 songs in film and 1 song in TV/year. Music Supervisor: Vincent Phillips. Recently published "I Like Dem" (by J. Smith/S. Norris), recorded by Li'l Jon and the Eastside Boyz; "Kissable Spot" (by Jonathan Smith), recorded by Devon, both placed in *Big Momma's House*; and "Trick Busta" (by Hardnett/Anderson/Bryon), recorded by Lyrical Giants, placed in *Sex and the City*.

Music: Mostly **rap** and **r&b**; also **rock** and **alternative**. Published "Bia' Bia' (single by J. Smith/S. Norris/T. Shaw/S. Martin) from *Put Yo Hood Up* (album), recorded by Lil Jon and the Eastside Boyz (rap), released 2001 on BME/TVT; "Shut Up" (single by R. McDowell/J. Jones/D. Green/R. Lewis) from *Right Quick* (album), recorded by Jim Crow (rap), released 2001 on Noontime/Interscope; and "I Like Dem" (single by J. Smith/S. Norris) from *We Still Crunk* (album), recorded by Lil Jon and the Eastside Boyz (rap), released 2000 on BME Recordings.

Tips: "Put your best foot forward. Submit only the best stuff you have. First impressions are important."

○ **BLUE DOG PUBLISHING AND RECORDS**, P.O. Box 3438, St. Louis MO 63143. (314)646-0191. Fax: (314)646-8005. E-mail: chillawack@worldnet.att.net. Website: www.bluedogpublishing.com. **Contact:** James Pedigo, president (rock/pop/commercial/alternative). Music publisher and record company. Estab. 1999. Publishes 3 songs/year; publishes 3 new songwriters/year. Staff size: 5. Pays standard royalty or payment negotiable.

How to Contact: Submit demo tape by mail. Unsolicited submissions are OK. Prefers cassette or CD with 3 songs, lyric sheet and cover letter. "Call to make sure we received material. We do call back." Does not return material. Responds in 1 month.

Music: Mostly **rock**, **pop/commercial** and **alternative**. Published "All Fall Down" (single by Bob Bender/Matt Davis/Steve Gendron) from *Phone Home* (album), recorded by 5th Degree (heavy/hard); "Still in Love With You" (single by Tiffany Kappler) from *Ariel* (album), recorded by Ariel (pop); and *All That and More* (album), written and recorded by Jeff Reulback (country/ballad), all released 2000 on Blue Dog Publishing and Records.

Tips: "Send a quality demo. Even a two-track demo is fine. Vocals should be clear and upfront. Be professional and stay motivated."

⊕ **○** **BME PUBLISHING**, P.O. Box 450224, Cologne Germany 50877. Phone: (049)221-9472000. Fax: (049)221-9502278. E-mail: info@BME-Records.de. Website: www.BME-Records.de. **Contact:** Dr. Dietmar Barzen. Music publisher, record company and record producer. Estab. 1993. Pays standard royalty to artists on contract.

How to Contact: Submit demo tape by mail. Unsolicited submissions are OK. Prefers cassette, DAT or CDR with 3-5 songs and lyric sheet. SAE and IRC. Responds in 1 month.

Music: Mostly **pop/AC**, **rock** and **commercial dance/hip-hop**; also **MOR**.

✓ **∅** **BMG MUSIC PUBLISHING**, 1540 Broadway, 28th Floor, New York NY 10036-4098. (212)930-4000. Fax: (212)930-4263. Website: www.bmgentertainment.com. Beverly Hills office: 8750 Wilshire Blvd., Beverly Hills CA 90211. (310)358-4700. Fax: (310)358-4727. **Contact:** Scott Francis, president BMG songs. Vice President of Film & Music: Ron Broitman. Nashville office: 1400 18th Ave. S., Nashville TN 37212. (615)858-1300. Fax: (615)858-1330. Music publisher.

How to Contact: BMG Music Publishing does not accept unsolicited submissions.
Music: Published "All Night Long" (single by F. Evans/R. Lawrence/S. Combs/S. Crawford), recorded by Faith Evans featuring Puff Daddy on Bad Boy; and "Ain't Enough Roses" (single by L. Brokop/S. Hogin/B. Reagan), recorded by Lisa Brokop on Columbia (country).

☑ ⊘ **BOURNE CO. MUSIC PUBLISHERS (ASCAP)**, 5 W. 37th St., New York NY 10018. (212)391-4300. Fax: (212)391-4306. E-mail: bourne@bournemusic.com. Website: www.bournemusi c.com. **Contact:** Professional Manager. Music publisher. Estab. 1917. Publishes educational material and popular music.
Affiliate(s): ABC Music, Ben Bloom, Better Half, Bogat, Burke & Van Heusen, Goldmine, Harborn, Lady Mac and Murbo Music.
How to Contact: *Does not accept unsolicited submissions.*
Music: **Piano/vocal**, **band pieces** and **choral pieces**. Published "Amen" and "Mary's Little Boy Child" (singles by Hairston); "When You Wish Upon a Star" (single by Washington/Harline); and "Unforgettable" (single by Irving Gordon).

◖ **ALLAN BRADLEY MUSIC (BMI)**, 1325 Marengo Ave., South Pasadena CA 91030. (626)441-4453. E-mail: melodi4ever@aol.com. Website: http://allanlicht.ontheweb.com. **Contact:** Allan Licht, Owner. Music publisher, record company (ABL Records) and record producer. Estab. 1993. Publishes 10 songs/year; publishes 5 new songwriters/year. Staff size: 2. Pays standard royalty.
Affiliate(s): Holly Ellen Music (ASCAP).
How to Contact: Submit demo tape by mail. Unsolicited submissions are OK. Prefers cassette with 3 songs and lyric sheet. "Send only unpublished works." Does not return material. Responds in 2 weeks only if interested.
Music: Mostly **A/C**, **pop** and **R&B**; also **country** and **Christian contemporary**. Does not want hard rock. Published *Time to Go* (album), written and recorded by Alan Douglass; *The Sun that Follows the Rain* (album by R.K. Holler/Rob Driggers), recorded by Michael Cavanaugh (pop), released 1999; and *Only In My Mind* (album by Jonathon Hansen), recorded by Allan Licht, all on ABL Records.
Tips: "Be open to suggestions from well-established publishers. Please send only songs that have Top 10 potential. Only serious writers are encouraged to submit."

◖ **BRANSON COUNTRY MUSIC PUBLISHING (BMI)**, P.O. Box 2527, Broken Arrow OK 74013. (918)455-9442. Fax: (918)451-1965. E-mail: bransoncm@aol.com. **Contact:** Betty Branson, A&R. Music publisher. Estab. 1997. Publishes 20 songs/year; publishes 4-5 new songwriters/year. Pays standard royalty.
How to Contact: Submit demo tape by mail with lyric sheet. Send photo and bio if looking for artist promotion. Unsolicited submissions are OK. Prefers CD or cassette with 3-5 songs and lyric sheet. Does not return material. Responds in 3 weeks only if interested.
Music: Mostly **traditional country** and **upbeat country**. Published "Sharin' Sharon" (CD single), written and recorded by Roger Wayne Manard (country), released 2001; "Focus" (single), written and recorded by B.J. Rimbon, released 2001; and "Houston, We've Got a Problem" and "Synchronized Rednecks" (CD singles), written and recorded by Travis Ogle, released 2002.
Tips: "Send good quality demo capable of competing with airplay top 40. Put your 'attention getter' up front and build from that point as the listener will give you about 10-15 seconds to continue listening or turn you off. Use a good hook and keep comming back to it."

☑ 🖼 ⊘ **BRENTWOOD-BENSON MUSIC PUBLISHING (ASCAP,BMI,SESAC)**, 741 Cool Springs Blvd., Franklin TN 37067. (615)261-3300. Fax: (615)261-3384. Professional Managers:

MARKET CONDITIONS are constantly changing! If you're still using this book and it is 2004 or later, buy the newest edition of *Songwriter's Market* at your favorite bookstore or order directly from Writer's Digest Books at (800)289-0963.

Holly Zabka, creative director; James Rueger, creative director; Marty Wheeler, vice president of creative affairs. **Contact:** Leslie Linebaugh, assistant to vice president. Music publisher. Estab. 1901. Publishes 600 songs/year. Staff size: 6; 15 staff writers; 50 artist writers. Pays standard royalty.
Affiliate(s): New Spring Publishing, Inc. (ASCAP), Bridge Building Music, Inc. (BMI) and Designer Music, Inc. (SESAC).
How to Contact: Does not accept unsolicited material.
Film & TV: Places 5-10 songs in film and 3 songs in TV/year. Music Supervisor: Marty Wheeler, vice president of creative affairs.
Music: Contemporary Christian, southern gospel, inspirational, praise and **worship.**

☑ ♥ **BRIAN SONG MUSIC CORP. (BMI)**, P.O. Box 1376, Pickens SC 29671. (864)878-7217. Fax: (864)878-6274. E-mail: braines105@aol.com. **Contact:** Brian E. Raines, president. Music publisher, record company (Palmetto Records), record producer and artist management. Estab. 1985. Publishes 5 songs/year; publishes 2-3 new songwriters/year. Staff size: 3. Pays standard royalty.
How to Contact: *Write first and obtain permission to submit.* Prefers CD or VHS videocassette with 3 songs and lyric sheet. "Unsolicited material not accepted, and will be returned. Demo must be good quality, lyrics typed. Send photo if an artist; send bio on writer or artist." Does not return material. Responds in 1 month.
Music: Mostly **country, gospel** and **country/gospel**; also **country/blues.** Published *I Wasn't There* (album), written and recorded by Dale Cassell on Mark V (gospel); and *From the Heart* (album), written and recorded by Jim Hubbard on Hubbitt (gospel).

⚑ ☒ ○ **BSW RECORDS (BMI)**, P.O. Box 2297, Universal City TX 78148. (210)599-0022. Fax: (210)653-3989. E-mail: bswr18@txdirect.net. Website: www.bswrecords.com. **Contact:** Frank Willson, President. Music publisher, record company and record producer (Frank Willson). Estab. 1987. Publishes 26 songs/year; publishes 14 new songwriters/year. Staff size: 5. Pays standard royalty.
Affiliate(s): WillTex Music and Universal Music Marketing (BMI).
• This company has been named Record Label of the Year ('94-'01) by the Country Music Association of America.
How to Contact: Submit demo tape or CD by mail. Unsolicited submissions are OK. Prefers cassette or CD with 3 songs, lyric sheet and cover letter. Include SASE. Responds in 2 months.
Film & TV: Places 2 songs in film/year.
Music: Mostly **country, blues** and **soft rock.** Does not want rap. Published *These Four Walls* (album), written and recorded by Dan Kimmel (country); and *I Cried My Last Tear* (album by T. Toliver), recorded by Candeeland (country), both released 1999 on BSW Records.

Ⓝ ○ **BUCKEYE MUSIC GROUP (ASCAP)**, 5695 Cherokee Rd., Cleveland OH 44124-3047. (440)442-7777. Fax:(440)442-1904. **Contact:** John J. Selvaggio (country) or Joseph R. Silver (rock and roll). Music publisher. Estab. 1998. Publishes 1 song/year. Staff size: 4. Pays standard royalty.
How to Contact: Submit demo tape by mail. Unsolicited submissions are OK. Prefers cassette or CD/CDR along with VHS videocassette. "Send your best three songs with a lead sheet." Include SASE. Responds in 3 weeks.
Music: Mostly **country, rock** and **r&b**; also **jingles** and **ballads.**
Tips: "Write from the heart, not from the head. Strive to be different."

Ⓝ ⊘ **BUG MUSIC, INC. (ASCAP, BMI)**, 6777 Hollywood, Los Angeles CA 90028-4676. (323)466-4352. Fax: (323)466-2366. E-mail: buginfo@bugmusic.com. Website: www.bugmusic.com. Vice President of Creative: Eddie Gomez. Creative Director: Jonathan Palmer; Creative Assistant: Sasha Ross. Nashville office: 1026 16th Ave. S., Nashville TN 37212. (615)726-0782. Fax: (615)726-0784. Creative Director: John Allen; Creative Manager: Drew Hale. London office: 31 Milson Rd., West Kensington, London W14 0LJ. Phone: 0207-602-0727. Fax: 0207-603-7483. Creative Manager: Paul Jordan. New York office: 1776 Broadway, Suite 1708, New York NY 10019. (212)765-2172. Fax: (212)765-2691. Senior Vice President: Garry Valletri. Music publisher. Estab. 1975. Other offices: Nashville contact John Allen and London contact Paul Jordan. "We handle administration."
Affiliate(s): Bughouse (ASCAP).

How to Contact: *Does not accept unsolicited submissions.*
Music: All genres. Published "You Were Mine" (by E. Erwin/M. Seidel), recorded by Dixie Chicks on Monument.

○ **BURIED TREASURE MUSIC (ASCAP)**, 524 Doral Country Dr., Nashville TN 37221. **Contact:** Scott Turner, owner/manager. Music publisher and record producer (Aberdeen Productions). Estab. 1972. Publishes 30-50 songs/year; publishes 3-10 new songwriters/year. Pays standard royalty.
Affiliate(s): Captain Kidd Music (BMI).
How to Contact: Submit demo tape by mail. Unsolicited submissions are OK. Prefers cassette or VHS videocassette with 1-4 songs and lyric sheet. Responds in 2 weeks. "Always enclose SASE if answer is expected."
Music: Mostly **country**, **country/pop** and **MOR**. Does not want rap, hard rock, metal, hip-hop or alternative. "One Heart" (single by Scott Turner/Doc Pomus) and "September Hearts" (single by Buddy Holly/Scott Turner) both from *September Hearts* (album), recorded by Colin Cook (pop/MOR), released 2001; and "Please Mr. Music Man" (single by Audie Murphy/Scott Turner) from *The Entrance* (album), recorded by Lea Brennan (country), released 2000.
Tips: *"Don't* send songs in envelopes that are 15"x 20", or by registered mail. The post office will not accept tapes in regular business-size envelopes."

N ○ **BURNSONGS (ASCAP)**, 1110 17th Ave. S. #3, Nashville TN 37212-2221. (615)239-8053. E-mail: songs@burnsongs.com. Website: www.burnsongs.com. **Contact:** Ernie Petrangelo. Music publisher, record company (Da'ville Records, and record producer (Ernie Petrangelo). Estab. 1986. Publishes 13 songs/year; publishes 3 new songwriters/year. Staff size: 1. Pays standard royalty.
Affiliate(s): Raproductions.com (BMI).
How to Contact: Submit demo tape by mail. Unsolicited submissions are OK. Prefers cassette or CD/CDR with 3 songs, lyric sheet and cover letter. Include SASE. Responds in 2-3 weeks only if interested.
Film and TV: Places 2 songs in film/year. Music supervisor: Ernie Petrangelo. Recently published "Instruments Of Destruction" and "Aw S#!t What Are We Gonna Do Now!" (by Burns/Serpa/Ward), recorded by NRG2 in *Transformers—The Movie* (released to DVD.)
Music: Mostly **hip-hop**, **rap** and **r&b**; also **urban pop**, **rock/rap** and **pop/rock/alternative**. Does not want country, "unless it's very different, edgy and hip." Recently published "Instruments Of Destruction," "Aw S#!t What Are We Gonna Do Now!" (singles by Burns/Serpa/Ward) and "Come And Get It" (single by Burns/Ward) from *Transformed* (album), recorded by NRG2 (heavy metal), released 2001 on Da'Ville Records.
Tips: "Please submit the best quality demo you can afford. We are interested in hit quality material with great hooks. Raps must be interesting & have meaning. No thugged-out material please. No excessive profanity. If you are an artist, please send a photo and bio with your package."

○ **CALIFORNIA COUNTRY MUSIC (BMI)**, 112 Widmar Pl., Clayton CA 94517. (925)833-4680. **Contact:** Edgar J. Brincat, owner. Music publisher and record company (Roll On Records). Estab. 1985. Publishes 30 songs/year; publishes 2-4 new songwriters/year. Staff size: 1. Pays standard royalty.
Affiliate(s): Sweet Inspirations Music (ASCAP).
How to Contact: Submit demo tape by mail. Unsolicited submissions are OK. Do not call or write. Prefers cassette with 3 songs and lyric sheet. Any calls will be returned collect to caller. Include SASE. Responds in 6 weeks.
Music: Mostly **MOR**, **contemporary country** and **pop**; also **R&B**, **gospel** and **light rock**. Does not want rap, metal or rock. Published *For Realities Sake* (album by F.L. Pittman/R. Barretta) and *Maddy* (album by F.L. Pittman/M. Weeks), both recorded by Ron Banks & L.J. Reynolds on Life & Bellmark Records; and *Quarter Past Love* (album by Irwin Rubinsky/Janet Fisher), recorded by Darcy Dawson on NNP Records.

N ◑ **CAMEX MUSIC**, 535 Fifth Ave., New York NY 10017. (212)682-8400. **Contact:** Alex Benedetto, A&R director. Music publisher, record company and record producer. Estab. 1970. Publishes 100 songs/year; publishes 10 new songwriters/year. Query for royalty terms.

How to Contact: Submit demo CD by mail. Unsolicited submissions are OK. Prefers CD/CDR with 5-10 songs and lyric sheet or lead sheet. Include SASE. Responds in 6 months.
Music: Mostly **alternative rock**, **pop** and **hard rock**; also **R&B**, **MOR** and **movie themes**.

⊘ CHEAVORIA MUSIC CO. (BMI), 2622 Kirtland Rd., Brewton AL 36426. (334)867-2228. **Contact:** Roy Edwards, president. Music publisher, record company (Bolivia Records) and record producer (Known Artist Production). Estab. 1972. Publishes 20 new songwriters/year. Pays standard royalty.
Affiliate(s): Baitstring Music (ASCAP).
How to Contact: *Write first and obtain permission to submit.* Prefers cassette with 3 songs and lyric sheet. Does not return material. Responds in 1 month.
Music: Mostly **R&B**, **pop** and **country**; also **ballads**. Published "Forever and Always" (single), written and recorded by Jim Portwood on Bolivia Records (country).

⊠ ⊘ CHERRI/HOLLY MUSIC (BMI), 1859 Acton Court, Simi Valley CA 93065-2205. (805)527-4082. Professional Managers: John G. Goske (MOR, top 40, jazz); Holly Rose Lawrence (R&B, new and traditional country, dance/pop); Pat (Big Red) Silzer (Southern gospel, Christian contemporary). Vice President: Helen Goske; Engineer: Cherri (Pete Segar type rock). Music publisher, record company (Whirlwind Label) and record producer (Helen and John G. Goske). Estab. 1961. Publishes 200-300 songs/year; publishes 75-100 new songwriters/year. Staff size: 3-4. Pays standard royalty.
Affiliate(s): Blue Sapphire Music (ASCAP).
How to Contact: Submit professional studio demo by mail with SASE. Unsolicited submissions are OK. Prefers cassette or CD with 3 songs and typed lyric sheet and cover letter. Must be copyrighted. "Absolutely no phone calls. Put name, address and phone number on everything. Important to hear lyrics above music. Please submit cover letter overview with cassette. Lyrics should be typed. Photo would be good. Please include SASE." Does not return material. Responds in 2 months only if interested.
Music: Mostly **traditional country**, **contemporary country with crossover edge**, **honky-tonk country**, **pop ballads** ala Diane Warren; also **Southern Christian and contemporary Christian gospel** and **film and TV music**. No grunge or gangster rap. Published "Non Stop Flight" and "Big Money Blues" (singles by Randall Rutledge) from *Non Stop Flight* (album), recorded by Randall Rutledge (country), released 2001 by Whirlwind; "Regina" (single by Ron McManaman), recorded by Ronnie Kimbal, released on WIR Records; "Dance Like You Love Her" (single by Ron McManaman), recorded by Ronnie Kimbal, released on Woodrich Records; "Morocco" (single), written and recorded by Joe Striffolino on Retrieve Records; and "I Want Everyone to Know" (single by John G. Goske/John Wm. LaRocca), recorded by various artists in Germany, Netherlands, Switzerland and Austria.
Tips: "Submit well-crafted songs with killer hooks ala hits on radio. Must be copyrighted with symbol and year. Also looking for radio-ready masters."

☑ ⊠ ⊘ CHRISTMAS & HOLIDAY MUSIC (BMI), 7461 El Dorado Dr., Buena Park CA 90620. (714)523-1583. E-mail: justinwilde@christmassongs.com. Website: www.christmassongs.c om. **Contact:** Justin Wilde, president. Music publisher. Estab. 1980. Publishes 8-12 songs/year; publishes 8-12 new songwriters/year. Staff size: 1. "All submissions must be complete songs (i.e., music and lyrics)." Pays standard royalty.
   ● Christmas & Holiday Music is relocating their office this year. See their website for most
   current address before mailing.
Affiliate(s): Songcastle Music (ASCAP).
How to Contact: Submit demo tape by mail. Unsolicited submissions are OK. Do *not* call. "First class mail only. Registered or certified mail not accepted." Prefers cassette with no more than 3 songs and lyric sheet. Do not send lead sheets or promotional material, bios, etc." Include SASE but does not return material out of the US. Responds only if interested.
Film & TV: Places 4-5 songs in TV/year. Published "Mr. Santa Claus" in *Casper's Haunted Christmas*.

Music: Strictly **Christmas music** (and a little Hanukkah and Halloween) in every style imaginable: easy listening, rock, R&B, pop, blues, jazz, country, reggae, rap, children's secular or religious. *Please do not send anything that isn't a holiday song.* Published "It Must Have Been the Mistletoe" (single by Justin Wilde/Doug Konecky) from *Christmas Memories* (album), recorded by Barbra Streisand (pop Christmas), released 2001 by Columbia; "What Made the Baby Cry?" (single by Toby Keith) and "You've Just Missed Christmas" (single by Penny Lea/Buzz Smith/Bonnie Miller) from *The Vikki Carr Christmas Album* (album), recorded by Vikki Carr (holiday/Christmas), released 2000 on Delta; and "Mr. Santa Claus" (single by James Golseth) from *Casper's Haunted Christmas* soundtrack (album), recorded by Scotty Blevins (Christmas), released 2000 on Koch International.
Tips: "We only sign one out of every 100 submissions. Please be selective. If a stranger can hum your melody back to you after hearing it twice, it has 'standard' potential. Couple that with a lyric filled with unique, inventive imagery, that stands on its own, even without music. Combine the two elements, and workshop the finished result thoroughly to identify weak points. Only when the song is polished to perfection, then cut a master quality demo that sounds like a record or pretty close to it. Submit positive lyrics only. Avoid negative themes like 'Blue Christmas.' "

☑ ☑ SONNY CHRISTOPHER PUBLISHING (BMI), P.O. Box 9144, Ft. Worth TX 76147-2144. (817)367-0860. Website: www.silverbucklepublishing.com. **Contact:** Sonny Christopher, CEO. Music publisher, record company and record producer. Estab. 1974. Publishes 20-25 new songs/year; publishes 3-5 new songwriters/year. Staff size: 1. Pays standard royalty.
How to Contact: *Write first, then call and obtain permission to submit.* Prefers cassette with lyric sheet. Include SASE (#10 or larger). Responds in 3 months.
Music: Mostly **country**, **rock** and **blues**. Published *Did They Judge Too Hard* (album by Sonny Christopher), recorded by Ronny Collins (collins@abilene.com.) on Sonshine Records.
Tips: "Be patient. I will respond as soon as I can. A songwriter should have a studio-cut demo with a super vocal. I am one who can hear a song with just acoustic guitar. Don't be hesitant to do a rewrite. To the young songwriter: *never, never* quit."

☒ ☑ CHRYSALIS MUSIC, 8500 Melrose Ave., Suite 207, Los Angeles CA 90069. (310)652-0066. Fax: (310)652-2024. Website: www.chrysalismusic.com. **Contact:** Mark Friedman, vice president of creative services. Music publisher. Estab. 1968.
How to Contact: *Chrysalis Music does not accept any submissions.*
Music: Published "Sum 41" (single by Outcast); "Light Ladder" (single by David Gray). Administer David Lee Roth; Andrea Boccelli.

☒ ☑ CIMIRRON MUSIC (BMI), 607 Piney Point Rd., Yorktown VA 23692. (757)898-8155. E-mail: lpuckett@lx.netcom.com. President: Lana Puckett. Music publisher, record company (Cimirron/Rainbird Records) and record producer. Estab. 1986. Publishes 10-20 songs/year. "Royalty depends on song and writer."
How to Contact: *Write or call first and obtain permission to submit.* Prefers cassette with 1-3 songs and lyric sheet. Does not return material. Responds in 3 months.
Music: Mostly **country**, **acoustic**, **folk** and **bluegrass**. Published *Cornstalk Pony* (by Lana Puckett/K. Person), recorded by Lana Puckett; "Turning for Home," written and recorded by Ron Fetner; "Memories of Home," written and recorded by Code Bluegrass Band; and "Pictures," written and recorded by Stephen Bennett, all on Cimirron Records.

☒ ☑ COFFEE AND CREAM PUBLISHING COMPANY (ASCAP), 1138 E. Price St., Philadelphia PA 19138. (215)842-3450. **Contact:** Bolden Abrams, Jr., president. Music publisher and record producer (Coffee and Cream Productions). Publishes 20 songs/year; publishes 4 new songwriters/year. Pays standard royalty.

REMEMBER: Don't "shotgun" your demo tapes. Submit only to companies interested in the type of music you write. For more submission hints, refer to Getting Started on page 10.

How to Contact: Submit demo tape by mail. Unsolicited submissions are OK. Prefers cassette or VHS videocassette with 1-4 songs and lyric or lead sheets. Include SASE. Responds in 2 weeks only if interested.

Music: Mostly **dance**, **pop** and **R&B**; also **gospel** and **country**. Published "If I Let Myself Go" (by Jose Gomez/Sheree Sano), recorded by Chuck Jackson and Dionne Warwick; "You Are My Life" (by Sean Chhangur), recorded by Chuck Jackson, both on RCA-BMG Records; and "Sweet Lover" (by Maxine Bachnia), recorded by Ron Hevener on RMB Records.

☑ ◑ **CORELLI'S MUSIC BOX (BMI)**, P.O. Box 2314, Tacoma WA 98401-2314. (253)798-5281. **Contact:** Jerry Corelli, Owner. Music publisher. Estab. 1996. Publishes 10 songs/year; publishes 3 new songwriters/year. Staff size: 2. Pays standard royalty.

How to Contact: Submit demo tape by mail. Unsolicited submissions are OK. Prefers cassette or CD with 1-3 songs and lyric sheet. "We want songs with a message and overtly Christian. Make sure all material is copyrighted." Include SASE. Responds in 2 months.

Music: Mostly **contemporary Christian** and **Christmas**. Does not want rap. Published *This Child* (album by Bert Boone), recorded by Jerry Corelli (Christmas); *Easter Sunday* (album), written and recorded by Earl Richards and Dave Gonzalez (contemporary Christian); and *Too Good for This World* (album by Stuart Logan), recorded by Jerry Corelli (Christian), all released 2000 on Omega III Records.

☑ ◑ **THE CORNELIUS COMPANIES (BMI, ASCAP, SESAC)**, Dept. SM, 1719 West End Ave., Suite 805-E, Nashville TN 37203. (615)321-5333. E-mail: corneliuscomps@aol.com. Website: www.corneliuscompanies.com. **Contact:** Ron Cornelius, owner/manager. Music publisher and record producer (Ron Cornelius). Estab. 1986. Publishes 60-80 songs/year; publishes 2-3 new songwriters/year. Occasionally hires staff writers. Pays standard royalty.

Affiliate(s): RobinSparrow Music (BMI), Strummin' Bird Music (ASCAP) and Bridgeway Music (SESAC).

How to Contact: *Write or call first and obtain permission to submit.* Submit demo tape by mail. Unsolicited submissions are OK. Prefers CD, DAT or cassette with 2-3 songs. Include SASE. Responds in 2 months.

Music: Mostly **country** and **pop**; also **positive country**, **gospel** and **alternative**. Published songs by Confederate Railroad, Faith Hill, David Allen Coe, Alabama and over 50 radio singles in the positive Christian/country format.

Tips: "Looking for material suitable for film."

[N] ◑ **COTTON TOWN MUSIC COMPANY (BMI)**, P.O. Box 804, Commerce GA 30529. **Contact:** A&R Review Department. Professional Manager: James Viola. Music Publisher. Estab. 2002. Staff size: 2. Pays standard royalty.

How to Contact: Submit demo tape by mail. Unsolicited submissions are OK. Prefers cassette or CD/CDR with 2-3 songs and lyric sheet and cover letter. "Please put name and address clearly on outside of package." Include SASE. Responds in 5 weeks.

Music: Mostly **alternative**, **country** and **rock**; also **blues**, **gospel** and **pop**.

Tips: "We are looking for song material in many formats. Songs must be unique, but they must still fit with markets such as Atlanta, Nashville, Los Angeles, and New York."

[N] ◑ **COUNTRY SHOWCASE AMERICA (BMI)**, 14134 Brighton Dam Rd., Clarksville MD 21029. (301)854-2917. **Contact:** Francis Gosman. Music publisher, record company and record producer. Estab. 1971. Publishes 9 songs/year; publishes 1 new songwriter/year. Pays standard royalty.

How to Contact: Submit demo tape by mail. Unsolicited submissions are OK. Prefers cassette with 2 songs and lyric sheet. Does not return material. Responds only if interested.

Music: Mostly **country**. Published "If You Think" (by J. Owens), recorded by Harry Wade on CSA Records (country).

N ◨ **COUNTRY STAR MUSIC (ASCAP)**, 439 Wiley Ave., Franklin PA 16323. (814)432-4633. **Contact:** Norman Kelly, president. Music publisher, record company (Country Star, Process, Mersey and CSI) and record producer (Country Star Productions). Estab. 1970. Publishes 15-20 songs/year; publishes 4-6 new songwriters/year. Pays standard royalty.
Affiliate(s): Kelly Music Publications (BMI) and Process Music Publications (BMI).
● See the listing for Country Star International in the Record Companies section, Country Star Productions in the Record Producers section and Country Star Attractions in the Managers & Booking Agents section.
How to Contact: Submit demo tape by mail. Unsolicited submissions are OK. Prefers cassette with 1-4 songs and typed lyric or lead sheet. SASE. Reports in 2 weeks. "No SASE no return."
Music: Mostly **country**; also **rock**, **gospel**, **MOR** and **r&b**. Published "Holiday Waltz" (single by F. Stelzer), recorded by Debbie Sue (country), released on Star Records; "Climbing Mountains" (single by Delamer-Gihara), recorded by Sugar Belle, released on Mersey Records; and "Teardrops Still Fall" (single by Kelly/Barbaria), recorded by Larry Pieper (country), released on Star Records.
Tips: "Send only your best songs-ones you feel are equal to or better than current hits. Typed or printed lyrics, please. For return of demo, send mailing label and return postage."

N ▧ ○ **CROWE ENTERTAINMENT (ASCAP, BMI, SESAC)**, 1010 16th Ave. S., Nashville TN 37212. (615)255-7900. E-mail: jcrowe7349@aol.com. Website: www.croweentertainment.com. **Contact:** Jo Crowe. Music publisher. Estab. 1988. Publishes 75 songs/year; publishes 75 new songwriters/year. Staff size: 4. Pays "writer's share" royalty.
Affiliate(s): Midnight Crow (ASCAP), Cro Jo (BMI), and JacAce21 (SESAC).
● Crowe Entertainment received the 2000 Hallman Award from TSAI.
How to Contact: Submit demo tape by mail. Unsolicited submissions are OK. Prefers CD/CDR with 4 songs, lyric sheet, and cover letter. Include SASE. Responds in 6 weeks.
Film & TV: Places 1 song in TV/year. Recently published "I've Been There" (by Rick Tiger), recorded by Shay for commercial use.
Music: All types. Published "What Will You Do With Me" (single by Rick Tiger and Craig Martin) from *Back to America* (album), recorded by Western Flyer (country), released 1996 on Step One; "No Sir" (single by Ellis/Montana/Dean) from *No Sir* (album), recorded by Darryl & Don Ellis (adult contemporary), released 1994 on Sony; and "Who Are They" (single by Seay), recorded by Leann Rimes on Curb Records.
Tips: "Send only hit songs. Submit only if you are serious about your songwriting."

⊕ ☑ ▧ ◨ **CTV MUSIC (GREAT BRITAIN)**, Television Centre, St. Helier, Jersey JE1 3ZD Channel Islands Great Britain. Phone: (1534)816816. Fax: (1534)816817. E-mail: soles@channeltv. co.uk. Website: www.channeltv.co.uk. **Contact:** Gordon De Ste. Croix, managing director. Music publisher of music for TV commercials, TV programs and corporate video productions. Estab. 1986. Staff size: 1. Pays standard royalty.
How to Contact: *Does not accept unsolicited submissions.*
Music: Mostly **instrumental**, for TV commercials and programs.

▼ ○ **CUPIT MUSIC (ASCAP, BMI)**, P.O. Box 121904, Nashville TN 37212. (615)731-0100. Fax: (615)731-3005. E-mail: cupit@cupitmusic.com. Website: www.cupitmusic.com. **Contact:** Denise Roberts, creative assistant. Music publisher, record producer and recording studio. Estab. 1986. Staff size: 8. Pays standard royalty.
Affiliate(s): Cupit Memaries (ASCAP) and Cupit Music (BMI).
● Cupit Music's "What If He's Right" was number 1 on CCRB Christian Country Chart for ten consecutive weeks, and was named Song of the Year."
How to Contact: *Please visit www.cupitmusic.com for our submission policy.* Prefers CD with lyric sheet. "We will return a response card." Include SASE. Responds in 2 months.
Music: Mostly **country**. Does not want rap, hard rock or metal. Published "What If He's Right" (single by Jerry Cupit) from *Memarie* (album), recorded by Memarie (Christian country), released

2000 on HotSong.com Records; and "I'm Not Homeless" (single by Jerry Cupit/Ken Mellons/Randy Roberts) from *Wings of a Dove* (album), recorded by Ken Mellons (Christian country), released 2000 on Curb Records.

◯ DAGENE MUSIC (ASCAP), P.O. Box 410851, San Francisco CA 94141. (415)822-1530. President: David Alston. Music publisher, record company (Cabletown Corp.), management firm (Golden City Int.) and record producer (Classic Disc Production). Estab. 1988. Hires staff songwriters. Pays standard royalty.
Affiliate(s): 1956 Music.
How to Contact: *Write first and obtain permission to submit.* Prefers cassette or CD with 2-3 songs and lyric sheet. "Be sure to obtain permission before sending any material." Include SASE. Responds in 1 month.
Music: Mostly **R&B/rap**, **dance** and **pop**. Published "To Know You Better" (single by David Alston), recorded by Rare Essence on Cabletown Records; "Let's Get It On" (single), written and recorded by Chapter One on Dagene Records; and "Why Can't I Be Myself" (single), written and recorded by David Alston on E-lect-ric Recordings.

◯ DAPMOR PUBLISHING (ASCAP, BMI, SESAC), Box 121, Kenner LA 70065. (504)468-9820. **Contact:** Kelly Jones, President. Music publisher, record company and record producer. Estab. 1977. Publishes 10 songs/year. Publishes 3 new songwriters/year. Hires staff songwriters. Pays standard royalty.
How to Contact: *Write first and obtain permission to submit.* Prefers 10-song professionally-recorded CD. Does not return material. Responds in 6 weeks.
Music: Mostly **R&B**, **soul**, and **pop**; also **top 40**, **country** and **rap**. Published "Tell Me, Tell Me" (single) (R&B); and "Sisco" (single) (R&B), both written and recorded by Kelly Jones on Justice Recordings.
Tips: "If accepted you must sign a contract. Learn to accept rejection and keep trying."

☑ ◷ JOF DAVE MUSIC (ASCAP), 1055 Kimball Ave., Kansas City KS 66104. (913)593-3180. Fax: (816)584-9916. **Contact:** David Johnson, president. Music publisher, record company (Cymbal Records). Estab. 1984. Publishes 10 songs/year; publishes 2 new songwriters/year. Pays standard royalty.
How to Contact: *Contact first and obtain permission to submit.* Prefers cassette or CD. Include SASE. Responds in 1 month.
Music: Mostly **gospel**, **blues** and **R&B**. Published "The Woman I Love" (single) from *Sugar Bowl* (album), written and recorded by King Alex, released 2001 on Cymbal Records.

☑ ⌂ ◷ THE EDWARD DE MILES MUSIC COMPANY (BMI), 28 E. Jackson Bldg., 10th Floor, #S627, Chicago IL 60604-2263. (773)509-6381. Fax: (312)922-6964. **Contact:** Professional Manager. Music publisher, record company (Sahara Records), record producer, management, bookings and promotions. Estab. 1984. Publishes 50-75 songs/year; publishes 5 new songwriters/year. Hires staff songwriters. Pays standard royalty.
How to Contact: *Write first and obtain permission to submit.* Prefers cassette with 1-3 songs and lyric sheet. Does not return material. Reponds in 1 month.
Music: Mostly **top 40 pop/rock**, **R&B/dance** and **country**; also **musical scores for TV, radio, films and jingles**. Published "Dance Wit Me" and "Moments" (singles), written and recorded by Steve Lynn on Sahara Records (R&B).
Tips: "Copyright all songs before submitting to us."

Ⓝ ◷ DEL CAMINO MUSIC PUBLISHING (BMI), 5010 S. Twelfth Ave., Tucson AZ 85706. (520)573-7274. Fax: (520)573-3325. **Contact:** Luis Lopez, president. Music publisher and record producer. Estab. 1985. Pays standard royalty.
How to Contact: Submit demo tape by mail. Unsolicited submissions are OK. Prefers cassette with 3 songs and lyric and lead sheet. "Include copy of properly copyrighted form." Does not return material. Responds in 1 month.

Music: Mostly **Latin/Spanish**, **Tex-Mex/pop** and **country rock**. Published "Te Quiero Tanto, Tanto" (single by Epifanio Gonzalez) from *La Leyenda Viva* (album), recorded by Lorenzo De Monteclaro, released 2001 on Fonovisa Records; "Mi Mejor Regalo" (single by Armando Antonio Negrete) from *De Chichuahua Para Ti* (album), recorded by Polo Urias Y Su Maquina Norteña, released 2001 on Fonovisa Records; and "Tu Llegada" (single by Martin Miranda) from *Juego Peligroso* (album), recorded by Amenaza Norteña, released 2001 on Sony Records.

Tips: "Make sure your songs have good commercial potential. Have a clean sounding demo and clearly typed lyric sheet."

○ **DELEV MUSIC COMPANY**, 7231 Mansfield Ave., Philadelphia PA 19138-1620. (215)276-8861. Fax: (215)276-4509. E-mail: delevmusic@cs.com. President/CEO: W. Lloyd Lucas. A&R: Darryl Lucas. Music publisher. Publishes 6-10 songs/year; publishes 6-10 new songwriters/year. Pays standard royalty.

Affiliate(s): Sign of the Ram Music (ASCAP), Gemini Lady Music (SESAC) and Delev Music (BMI).

How to Contact: *Does not accept unsolicited material.* Prefers cassette or VHS videocassette with 1-3 songs and lyric sheet. "We will not accept certified mail." Does not return material. Responds in 3 months.

Music: Mostly **R&B ballads** and **dance-oriented**; also **pop ballads**, **crossover** and **country/western**. Published "Angel Love" (single by Barbara Heston/Geraldine Fernandez) from *The Silky Sounds of Debbie G* (album), recorded by Debbie G (light R&B/easy listening), released 2000 on Blizzard Records.

Tips: "Persevere regardless if it is sent to our company or any other company. Believe in yourself."

◐ **FRANK DELL MUSIC**, P.O. Box 7171, Duluth MN 55807. (218)626-9044. E-mail: f_dell@hotmail.com. **Contact:** Frank Dell, president. Music publisher, record company (Music Services and Marketing), record producer and management. Estab. 1980. Publishes 2 songs/year. Pays standard royalty.

Affiliate(s): Albindell Music (BMI).
● Frank Dell's record label, Music Services and Marketing, can be found in the Record Companies section.

How to Contact: Submit demo tape by mail. Unsolicited submissions are OK. Prefers cassette. Include SASE. Responds in 3 months.

Music: Mostly **country**, **gospel** and **pop**. Published *I Can Tell* (album by F. Dell/Linda Kay), recorded by Frank Dell on Country Legends Records (country).

Ⓝ ⊕ ◐ **DEMI MONDE RECORDS & PUBLISHING LTD.**, Foel Studio, Llanfair Caereinion, POWYS, Wales. Phone/fax: (01938)810758. E-mail: demi-monde@dial.pipex.com. Website: www.demi.monde.co.uk/demimonde. **Contact:** Dave Anderson, managing director. Music publisher, record company (Demi Monde Records & Publishing Ltd.), record producer (Dave Anderson). Member MCPS. Estab. 1983. Publishes 50-70 songs/year; publishes 10-15 new songwriters/year. Pays standard royalty.

How to Contact: Submit demo tape by mail. Unsolicited submissions are OK. Prefers cassette or VHS videocassette with 3-4 songs. Does not return material. Responds in 6 weeks.

Music: Mostly **rock**, **R&B** and **pop**. Published "I Feel So Lazy" (by D. Allen), recorded by Gong (rock); "Phalarn Dawn" (by E. Wynne), recorded by Ozric Tentacles (rock); and "Pioneer" (by D. Anderson), recorded by Amon Dual (rock), all on Demi Monde Records.

REFER TO THE CATEGORY INDEX (at the end of this section) to find exactly which companies are interested in the type of music you write.

N ♥ DISNEY MUSIC PUBLISHING (ASCAP, BMI), 500 S. Buena Vista St., Burbank CA 91521-6182. (818)569-3228. Fax: (818)845-9705. **Contact:** Brian Rawlings, vice president of music publishing; Edwin Oliver, director of music publishing; Noah Dewey, A&R, music publishing. Music publisher.
Affiliate(s): Seven Peaks Music and Seven Summits Music.
How to Contact: *Call first and obtain permission to submit.* Does not return material.

O BUSTER DOSS MUSIC (BMI), 341 Billy Goat Hill Rd., Winchester TN 37398. (931)649-2577. Fax: (615)649-2732. E-mail: cbb@vallnet.com. Website: http://stardustcountrymusic.com. **Contact:** Buster Doss, president. Music publisher, record producer, management firm and record company (Stardust). Estab. 1959. Publishes 500 songs/year; publishes 50 new songwriters/year. Staff size: 62. Pays standard royalty.
How to Contact: *Write or call first and obtain permission to submit.* Prefers cassette with 2 songs and lyric sheet. Include SASE. Responds in 1 week.
Music: Mostly **country**; also **rock**. Does not want rap or hard rock. Published *The Heart* (album), written and recorded by Bryant Miller (country); *Do I Ever Cross Your Mind* (album), written and recorded by Michael Apidgian; and *Down South* (album), written and recorded by Rooster Quantrell, all on Stardust Records.

☑ O DREAM SEEKERS PUBLISHING (BMI), 21 Coachlight Dr., Danville IL 61832-8240. (615)822-1160. **Contact:** Jerry Webb, professional manager. President: Sally Sidman. Music publisher. Estab. 1993. Publishes 25-50 songs/year; publishes 15-20 new songwriters/year. Pays standard royalty.
Affiliate(s): Dream Builders Publishing (ASCAP).
How to Contact: Submit demo tape by mail. Unsolicited submissions are OK. "Please do not call to request permission—just submit your material. There are no code words. We listen to everything." Prefers cassette or CD with 2 songs and lyric sheet. "If one of your songs is selected for publishing, we prefer to have it available on CD for dubbing off copies to pitch to artist." Include SASE. Responds in 6 weeks.
Music: Mostly **country**. "All types of **country** material, but mostly in need of uptempo songs, preferably with positive lyrics." Does not want rap, jazz, classical, children's, hard rock, instrumental or blues. Published "Starting Tonight" (single by Sam Storey), recorded by Wayne Horsburgh on Rotation Records (country); "I Can Still See it From Here" (single by John Pearson), recorded by Matt Caldwell on RMC Records; and "An Elvis Night Before Christmas" (single by Keith Collins), recorded by C.C. McCartney on Rotation Records (country).
Tips: "Be willing to work hard to learn the craft of songwriting. Be persistent. Nobody is born a hit songwriter. It often takes years to achieve that status."

Ø DREAMWORKS SKG MUSIC PUBLISHING, 9268 W. 3rd St., Beverly Hills CA 90210. (310)234-7700. Music publisher and record company (DreamWorks Records).
How to Contact: *DreamWorks SKG Music Publishing does not accept unsolicited submissions.*

N O DRIVE MUSIC, INC. (BMI), 10451 Jefferson Blvd., Culver City CA 90232. (310)815-4900. Fax: (310)815-4908. E-mail: driveentertainment@earthlink.net. Website: www.driveentertainm ent.com. **Contact:** Stephen Powers, president and CEO. Music publisher and record company (Drive Entertainment). Estab. 1993. Publishes 25 songs/year. Pays negotiated royalty. "Seeks single songs for representation. Acquires catalogs, large and small."
Affiliate(s): Donunda Music (ASCAP), Fairyland Music (ASCAP) and Licette Music (ASCAP).
How to Contact: *Does not accept unsolicited submissions.*
Music: Mostly **dance**, **pop** and **rock**; also **R&B**. Published all Sharon, Lois and Bram products (children's).

O DUANE MUSIC, INC. (BMI), 382 Clarence Ave., Sunnyvale CA 94086. (408)739-6133. **Contact:** Garrie Thompson, President. Music publisher and record producer. Publishes 10-20 songs/ year; publishes 1 new songwriter/year. Pays standard royalty.

Affiliate(s): Morhits Publishing (BMI).
How to Contact: Submit demo tape by mail. Unsolicited submissions are OK. Prefers cassette with 1-2 songs. Include SASE. Responds in 2 months.
Music: Mostly **blues**, **country**, **disco** and **easy listening**; also **rock**, **soul** and **top 40/pop**. Published "Little Girl" (single), recorded by The Syndicate of Sound & Ban (rock); "Warm Tender Love" (single), recorded by Percy Sledge (soul); and "My Adorable One" (single), recorded by Joe Simon (blues).

☑ ◯ **EARITATING MUSIC PUBLISHING (BMI)**, P.O. Box 1101, Gresham OR 97030. Website: www.earitating.com. Music publisher. Estab. 1979. Pays individual per song contract, usually greater than 50% to writer.
How to Contact: Submit demo tape by mail. Unsolicited submissions are OK. Prefers CD or CD-R with lyric sheet. "Submissions should be copyrighted by the author. We will deal for rights if interested." Does not return material. Responds only if interested.
Music: Mostly **rock**, **country** and **folk**. Does not want rap.
Tips: "Melody is most important, lyrics second. Style and performance take a back seat to these. A good song will stand with just one voice and one instrument. Also, don't use staples on your mailers."

☑ ◯ **EAST COAST MUSIC PUBLISHING (BMI)**, P.O. Box 12, Westport MA 02790-0012. (508)679-4272. Fax: (508)673-1235. E-mail: eastcoastmusic@hotmail.com. Website: www.keytomusicsuccess.com. **Contact:** Mary-Ann Thomas, president. Professional Managers: Michael Thomas (hip-hop, rock, jazz); Lisa Medeiros (pop, electronic, dance, country); Noel James (R&B, rap, alternative). Music publisher. Estab. 1996. Publishes 20 songs/year; publishes 10 new songwriters/year. Staff size: 9. Pays standard royalty.
Affiliate(s): New England Sound (BMI).
How to Contact: Submit demo tape by mail. Unsolicited submissions are OK. Prefers cassette with 3-5 songs and lyric or lead sheet. "If you send a SASE I will get back to you within one month. If no SASE I will only respond if interested. We keep submissions in case we decide to publish the song at a future date." Does not return material. Responds only if interested.
Music: Mostly **pop**, **country** and **rock**; also **R&B**, **alternative**, **dance**, **hip-hop** and **rap**. Published "Hard to Believe" (single by Ronnie Neilan/Paul Rogers) from *Play Hard* (album), recorded by Black Knights (hip-hop), released 2001 on Prolific Records; "I'll Fight for You" (single by Patricia Santos) from *Living for the Moment* (album), recorded by Drama Queen (rock), released 2001 on East Coast Records; and "I've Never Felt This" (single by Ashly Williams/Jake Jones/Maureen Jones) from *Passion* (album), recorded by Dreamers (pop), released 2001 on Prolific Records.
Tips: "We are seeking very radio friendly songs like Britney Spears, Destiny's Child or N*Sync. Something real now. We are not seeking non-commercial material. We also have a free monthly newsletter with over 1,000 members. It tells people what's going on at East Coast Music Publishing, gives helpful music business advice and allows members to announce things. The way to subscribe is online and it's absolutely free. Just send e-mail to: eastcoastmusic-subscribe@yahoogroups.com."

⊕ ◯ **EDITION ROSSORI**, Hietzinger Hptstr 94, Vienna A-1130 Austria. Phone: (01)8762400. Fax: (01)8795464. E-mail: mario_rossori@compuserve.com. Website: www.poppate.com. **Contact:** Mario Rossori, manager. Music publisher and management agency. Estab. 1990. Publishes 150 songs/year; publishes 10 new songwriters/year. Staff size: 2. Pays negotiable royalty.
How to Contact: Submit demo tape by mail. Unsolicited submissions are OK. Does not return material. Responds in 2 months.
Music: Mostly **pop, dance** and **rock**. Does not want jazz. Published *Welsfischer au Wolpedelta* (album), written and recorded by Heinz on Universal (rock).

[N] ◯ **EGYPTIANMAN PRODUCTIONS (ASCAP)**, (formerly May Peace Be Upon You Music), 4740 E. Warner Rd., Suite 2-157, Phoenix AZ 85044. (602)212-6735. Fax: (775)942-0589. E-mail: carlosmuhammad@egyptianmanproductions.com. Website: www.egyptianmanproductions.com. CEO/Writer/Publisher/President: Carlos C. Muhammad. Music publisher. Estab. 1996.
Affiliate(s): May Peace Be Upon You Music (ASCAP).

How to Contact: Submit demo CD by mail. Unsolicited submissions are OK. Prefers CD with 3-4 songs, lyric sheet, 8×10 b&w glossy and bio on a floppy disk. "Do not call. In cover letter say whether you are seeking a publishing or record deal." Include SASE. Responds in 3 weeks.
Music: Mostly **r&b**, **pop/r&b**, **hip-hop**, **rap**, **heavy metal**, **rock**, **punk rock**, **pop**, **alternative**; also **soft rock**, **Latin**, **contemporary country**, **inspirational** and **jazz**.

○ **EMANDELL TUNES**, 10220 Glade Ave., Chatsworth CA 91311. (818)341-2264. Fax: (818)341-1008. **Contact:** Leroy C. Lovett, Jr., president/administrator. Music Publisher. Estab. 1979. Publishes 6-12 songs/year; publishes 3-4 new songwriters/year. Pays standard royalty.
Affiliate(s): Ben-Lee Music (BMI), Birthright Music (ASCAP), Em-Jay Music (ASCAP), Northworth Songs, Chinwah Songs, Gertrude Music (all SESAC), Alvert Music (BMI), Andrask Music, Australia (BMI), Nadine Music, Switzerland.
How to Contact: *Write first and obtain permission to submit.* Prefers cassette, videocassette or CD with 4-5 songs and lead or lyric sheet. Include bio of writer, singer or group. Include SASE. Responds in 6 weeks.
Music: Mostly **inspirational**, **contemporary gospel** and **choral**; also **strong country** and **light top 40**. Published "Under My Skin" and "Colorada River" (singles by Diana/Kim Fowley), recorded by Diana, released 2001 on WFL Records; and "Runaway Love" (single by Gil Askey), recorded by Linda Clifford (new gospel), released 2001 on Sony Records.
Tips: "We suggest you listen to current songs. Imagine how that song would sound if done by some other artist. Keep your ear tuned to new groups, bands, singers. Try to analyze what made them different, was it the sound? Was it the song? Was it the production? Ask yourself these questions: Do they have that 'hit' feeling? Do you like what they are doing?"

N ○ **EMF PRODUCTIONS**, 1000 E. Prien Lake Rd., Suite D, Lake Charles LA 70601. Phone/fax: (337)474-0435. E-mail: emfprod@aol.com. Website: www.emfproductions.com. President: Ed Fruge. Music publisher and record producer. Estab. 1984. Pays standard royalty.
How to Contact: Submit demo tape by mail. Unsolicited submissions are OK. Prefers cassette or VHS videocassette with 4 songs and lyric sheet. Does not return material. Responds in 6 weeks.
Music: Mostly **R&B**, **pop** and **rock**; also **country** and **gospel**.

○ **EMI CHRISTIAN MUSIC PUBLISHING**, P.O. Box 5085, Brentwood TN 37024. (615)371-4400. Fax: (615)371-6897. Website: www.emicmg.com. Music publisher. Publishes 100 songs/year; publishes 2 new songwriters/year. Hires staff songwriters. Pays standard royalty.
Affiliate(s): Birdwing Music (ASCAP), Sparrow Song (BMI), His Eye Music (SESAC), Ariose Music (ASCAP), Straightway Music (ASCAP), Shepherd's Fold Music (BMI), Songs of Promise (SESAC), Dawn Treader Music (SESAC), Meadowgreen Music Company (ASCAP), River Oaks Music Company (BMI), Stonebrook Music Company (SESAC), Bud John Songs, Inc. (ASCAP), Bud John Music, Inc. (BMI), Bud John Tunes, Inc. (SESAC).
How to Contact: *"We do not accept unsolicited submissions."*
Music: Published "Concert of the Age" (by Jeffrey Benward), recorded by Phillips, Craig & Dean; "God Is In Control," written and recorded by Twila Paris, both on StarSong Records; and "Faith, Hope and Love" (by Ty Lacy), recorded by Point of Grace on Word Records.
Tips: "Come to Nashville and be a part of the fastest growing industry. It's nearly impossible to get a publisher's attention unless you know someone in the industry that is willing to help you."

N ○ **EMI MUSIC PUBLISHING**, 1290 Avenue of the Americas, 42nd Floor, New York NY 10104. (212)830-2000. Fax: (212)586-2794. Santa Monica office: 2700 Colorado Ave., Suite 100, Santa Monica CA 90404. (310)586-2700. Fax: (310)586-2758. Website: www.emimusic.com. Contact: Jodi Gerson; Sharona Sabbag; Big Jon; Carla Ondrasik. Music publisher.
How to Contact: *EMI does not accept unsolicited material.*

THE TYPES OF MUSIC each listing is interested in are printed in **boldface**.

Music: Published "All Night Long" (by F. Evans/R. Lawrence/S. Combs), recorded by Faith Evans featuring Puff Daddy on Bad Boy; "You" (by C. Roland/J. Powell), recorded by Jesse Powell on Silas; and "I Was" (by C. Black/P. Vassar), recorded by Neal McCoy on Atlantic.
Tips: "Don't bury your songs. Less is more—we will ask for more if we need it. Put your strongest song first."

◖ EMSTONE, INC. MUSIC PUBLISHING (BMI), Box 1287, Hallandale FL 33008. (305)936-0412. E-mail: emstoneinc@yahoo.com. **Contact:** Michael Gary, Creative Director. President: Mitchell Stone. Vice President: Madeline Stone. Music publisher. Estab. 1997. Pays standard royalty.
How to Contact: Submit demo CD by mail. Unsolicited submissions are OK. Prefers CD with any number of songs and lyric sheet. Does not return material. Responds within 1 week if interested.
Music: Everything except classical, jazz and opera. Published "Say Goodbye To Yesterday" (single by Diane Corrado, Faith Rice and Paul Cecere); "Is It Now?" (single by Milinda Allen); and "My Heart Is A Pretender" (single by Allen A. Forella and John H. Smith), all pop/rock recorded by Jaden Michaels on the album *XOXO* on Backstage Records.
Tips: "Avoid writing an explanation of the songs on your demo; if the music is great, it'll speak for itself. We sign only songs that display a spark of genius—anything less can not compete in the music industry. We do not return any materials and will contact you when we want you to sign our publishing contract."

⊕ ◖ EVER-OPEN-EYE MUSIC (PRS), Wern Fawr Farm, Pencoed, MID, Glam CF356NB United Kingdom. Phone: (01656)860041. **Contact:** M.R. Blanche, managing director. Music publisher and record company (Red-Eye Records). Member PPL and MCPS. Estab. 1980. Publishes 6 songs/year. Staff size: 3. Pays negotiable royalty.
How to Contact: Submit demo tape by mail. Unsolicited submissions are OK. Prefers CD. Does not return material. Responds in 2 months.
Music: Mostly **R&B**, **gospel** and **pop**; also **swing**. Published "Snake Hips" and "Eclection" (singles by Burton/Jones); and "Life Insurance" (single by Steve Finn), all recorded by Tiger Bay on Red-Eye Records.

▨ ◖ FAMOUS MUSIC PUBLISHING COMPANIES, 10635 Santa Monica Blvd., Suite 300, Los Angeles CA 90025. (310)441-1300. Fax: (310)441-4722. Website: www.syncsite.com. President: Ira Jaffe. Vice President, Film and TV: Stacey Palm. Vice President/Urban: Brian Postelle. Senior Creative Director: Carol Spencer (rock/pop/alternative). Senior Creative Director/Latin: Claribell Cuevas. New York office: 1633 Broadway, 11th Floor, New York NY 10019. (212)654-7433. Fax: (212)654-4748. Chairman and CEO: Irwin Z. Robinson. Executive Vice President, Finance and Administration: Margaret Johnson. Vice President Catalogue Development: Mary Beth Roberts. Creative Director: Tanya Brown. Nashville office: 65 Music Square East, Nashville TN 37212. (615)329-0500. Fax: (615)321-4121. Vice President: Pat Finch (country). Senior Creative Director: Curtis Green. Music Publisher. Estab. 1929. Publishes 500 songs/year. Hires staff songwriters. Staff size: 100. Pays standard royalty.
Affiliate(s): Famous Music (ASCAP) and Ensign Music (BMI).
How to Contact: *Famous Music does not accept unsolicited submissions.*
Film & TV: Famous Music is a Paramount Pictures' company. Music Supervisors: Stacey Palm and Delly Ramin. Published "My Heart Will Go On" (by James Homer/Wil Jennings), recorded by Celine Dion in *Titanic*.
Music: Mostly **rock**, **urban**, **R&B**, **country** and **Latin**. Published "I Hope You Dance" (single by Tia Sellers/Michael Dulaney), recorded by Lee Ann Womack; and "He Wasn't Man Enough" (single by Fred Jerkins III), recorded by Toni Braxton.

▨ ◖ FAVERETT GROUP, 1502 18th Ave. S., Nashville TN 37212. (615)292-4602. Fax: (615)292-5339. E-mail: FaverettGroup@aol.com. Website: www.DanSchafer.com. **Contact:** Dan Schafer, creative director. Music publisher and record company (Bridge Records, Inc.). Estab. 1994. Pays standard royalty.
Affiliate(s): Faverett Tracks (BMI), Virginia Borden Rhythms (ASCAP).

insider report

Songwriter finds success in 'Wide Open Spaces'

When she signed her song "Wide Open Spaces" with the Dixie Chicks as the title track for their first album, Susan Gibson put the Dixie Chicks and herself on the musical map. The CD boasts some of the most coveted music statistics: It sold 11 million copies, was the biggest selling album in history by a country music group, one of the top-100 selling albums of all time and the biggest selling country debut album ever. "Wide Open Spaces" also led the Dixie Chicks to Grammys, *Billboard*, ACM and CMA awards, among many others.

Susan Gibson

Amazingly, Gibson was fairly new to songwriting. "Wide Open Spaces" was one of the first twenty songs she had written, and the story of the song's birth sounds like a songwriter's fairy-tale. She had just come home from her first semester of school at the University of Montana in Missoula and was experiencing the particular claustrophobia common to children of even the most well-meaning parents. Her mother had asked her a simple, motherly question, "What did you do last night?" and, boom, the song was born. "I'd been away three months and thought I could do it all," she said. "I sat down at my mom's kitchen table and wrote it in 15-20 minutes. It wasn't crafted," she said "It was just a blurted out diary entry."

In fact, she forgot about the song as quickly as she'd written it. Back at school, her mother sent her a care package "full of t-shirts, probably a poster of Scott Baio in lip gloss and the notebook," as Gibson remembers it, laughing. That night, while hanging out with friends, she played a riff she had been working on and one of her friends said it reminded her of her grandfather's ranch there in Montana. Her comment reminded Gibson of the lyrics in her notebook and she was able to fit the two together. "It was a perfect fit," she said. "I had to fiddle with some of the music but it just fit together."

That Christmas, she went home and began singing backup with the Groobies, a band out of Amarillo, Texas. In the summer, they recorded a demo tape of "Wide Open Spaces" and sent it to Lloyd Maines, a popular Lubbock musician and producer. Maines enjoyed the song and gave a copy to his wife and to his daughters. One of his daughters, Natalie, was also a young musician who had just joined the Dixie Chicks, a budding band at the time. Soon the Dixie Chicks were regularly covering the song in their shows. But it wasn't until Natalie's bachelorette party that all of the pieces came together. Emily, Martie, Natalie and Natalie's sister, Kim, were celebrating in Lubbock, Texas, and came into a bar where the Groobies were playing. During the show they sent a napkin up, requesting they play "Wide Open Spaces." The Groobies honored the request and after the show the Dixie Chicks came up to talk with them—and asked if they could put the song on their album.

"I was so flattered, of course," Gibson said about her response at the time, "but I couldn't say yes right then. I was so protective of that song. I thought, 'If I turn it loose, it's loose.' I wish someone would have shaken my shoulders and said, 'Susan, you don't need to think that hard.' But I didn't know that's how people make careers."

Gibson said the permissions process was "all really simple." She accepted the common industry royalties rate so there really wasn't very much negotiation involved. With the permissions completed and agreed upon, things were ready to go, but the Dixie Chicks' producer in Nashville initially didn't want the song on the album. It wasn't country enough. Gibson said she doesn't remember who exactly to attribute the quote to, but thinks the response went something like "Well, if you're so good at your job, can't you make it country enough?"

From there the song skyrocketed. Soon Gibson was hearing it in the grocery store and as muzak in the elevator with an oboe playing the melody. "The funny thing was," Gibson said, "here I'd wanted to be so big and my mom had to send the notebook to me to begin with!"

How did Gibson feel about the new production of the song? "I loved it. They made some changes; they took out a verse and changed the last line. At first it hurt my feelings but I realized that if I wanted control over it I shouldn't have turned it loose." People told her it sounded "more produced" than her version. "Of course it sounded more produced," she answered, laughing. "They have beautiful voices—they don't smoke two packs of cigarettes a day. Their voices make the chorus huge. It's the difference between having your arms at your sides, and having them spread out up in the air."

Gibson thinks of her experience with "Wide Open Spaces" as a gift. If it wouldn't have been for Lloyd Maines, the only person they knew in the music industry, the song might not have made it out of Amarillo. "I didn't intend to write an anthem about moving away from home," she said. "If I would have stepped aside to be aware of it, it wouldn't have happened." After the success of "Wide Open Spaces," the Groobies tried to send more music in the Nashville direction, but didn't receive the response they had hoped for. "After being exposed to Nashville and having it work, I realize how lucky I am," Gibson said. "I can't recreate that situation; it was a perfect marriage. It just makes me realize how lucky all of it was."

Regarding the process of songwriting, Gibson says, "Songwriting has taught me you gotta realize nobody else can do it like you can. There may be better or worse [songwriters], but they aren't like you." She remembers a friend once checked a book about songwriting out of the library and let her borrow it. "It absolutely said everything I would never say," she said. "Teaching people [to write songs] is like teaching them to paint—there's painting by number in a book, and there's oil painting with gravel and dog hair for added texture. There's no way to study it; you have to practice telling the truth in a way." The lyrics may change for various reasons, she says, "but the heart of a song has to be true. You've gotta mean it and if you mean it, you've gotta say it."

What's Gibson's advice for beginning songwriters? When it comes to the music industry, she says, "No one's going to do things for you. If you want it done you have to do it." But when it comes to hanging in there in the long dry spells, she says, "You have to do it for the joy of playing. That's your paycheck. I am an instant gratification girl. I don't know what I'd do if I had a job where people didn't clap every four or five minutes." Gibson feels lucky to have someone like Maines in her corner. "He gave lots of good advice by not giving much," she said. When asked if she'd ever heard any really bad advice, Gibson said, "I don't really think so. If anyone has turned me in a wrong direction, I should thank them. I'm happy where I am."

—*Amy Ratto*

How to Contact: *Write or call first and obtain permission to submit.* Prefers cassette or CDR with up to 5 songs and lyric sheet. Include SASE. Responds ASAP.

Music: Accepts **all styles**; lyrics only.

◖ **FIFTH AVENUE MEDIA, LTD.**, 19 W. 21st St., #603A, New York NY 10010. (516)295-3922. Fax: (516)295-6872. E-mail: fifthavmed@aol.com. Website: www.thefirm.com/fifthavenue. Professional Managers: Bruce E. Colfin (rootsy bluesy rock/reggae); Jeffrey E. Jacobson (hip-hop/R&B/dance); Daniel Weiss (alternative rock/heavy metal). Music publisher and record company (Fifth Avenue Media, Ltd.). Estab. 1995. Publishes 2 songs/year. Staff size: 4. Pays standard royalty.

Music: Published "Analog" (single by Paul Byrne) from *Paul Byrne & the Bleeders* (album), recorded by Paul Byrne (pop rock), released 2001 on Independent.

▦ ⌧ ◖ **FIRST TIME MUSIC (PUBLISHING) U.K. (PRS)**, Sovereign House, 12 Trewartha Road, Praa Sands, Penzance, Cornwall TR20 9ST United Kingdom. Phone: (01736)762826. Fax: (01736)763328. E-mail: panamus@aol.com. Website: www.songwriters-guild.com. **Contact:** Roderick G. Jones, managing director. Music publisher, record company (First Time Records), record producer (Panama Music Library) and management firm (First Time Management and Production Co.). Member MCPS. Estab. 1986. Publishes 500-750 songs/year; 20-50 new songwriters/year. Staff size: 6. Hires staff writers. Pays standard royalty; "50-60% to established and up-and-coming writers with the right attitude."

Affiliate(s): Scamp Music Publishing, Panama Music Library, Musik Image Library, Caribbean Music Library, Psi Music Library, ADN Creative Music Library, Heraldic Production Music Library, Promo Sonor International, Eventide Music, Melody First Music Library, Panama Music Ltd.

How to Contact: Submit demo tape by mail. Unsolicited submissions are OK. Prefers cassette, CD/CDR or VHS videocassette "of professional quality" with unlimited number of songs and lyric or lead sheets. Responds in 1 month. SAE and IRC required for reply.

Film & TV: Places 58 songs in film and TV/year. Published "Atmos," written and recorded by Bob Brimley for the BBC; "Maciek," written and recorded by Henryk Wozniacki for World Wide Pictures; and "Haunted House" (by Frank Millum), recorded by Colin Eade for Carlton Television.

Music: All styles. Published "The Place For Me" (single by Peter Arnold) from *Birmingham, The Place For Me* (album), recorded by Keith Slater (spiritual/inspirational), released 2001 on Rooftop Records; "Oh No It's Christmas" (single by Peter Arnold) from *Santa's Top 20*, recorded by Mike Berry (pop), released 2001 on Delta Music PLC); and "Vayri Dzarig" (Wild Flower) (single by Melikian/Mancuclian) from *World Music*, recorded by Rosey Armen (world music), released by Kbox Records 2001.

Tips: "Have a professional approach—present well produced demos. First impressions are important and may be the only chance you get. Writers are advised to join the Guild of International Songwriters and Composers in the United Kingdom."

◐ **FLYING RED HORSE PUBLISHING (BMI)**, 2932 Dyer St., Dallas TX 75205. (214)691-5318. Fax: (214)692-1392. E-mail: barbe@texasmusicgroup.com. Website: texasmusicgroup.com. **Contact:** Barbara McMillen, creative director. Music publisher, record company (Remarkable Records) and record producer (Texas Fantasy Music). Estab. 1993. Publishes 15-30 songs/year; publishes 6-10 new songwriters/year. Pays standard royalty.

Affiliate(s): Livin' the Life Music (ASCAP).

How to Contact: Submit demo tape by mail between March and July only. Unsolicited submissions are OK. Prefers cassette with 3 songs and lyric sheet. Include SASE. Responds in 6 months.

Music: Mostly **children's and special occasion songs and stories**. Published *Teardrops to Rainbows* (album by Rollie Anderson/Richard Theisen); *Little Lost Note* (album by Lauren Shapiro/Richard Theisen); and "The Dinosaur Rag" (single by Beverly Houston), recorded by the Dixie Chicks (country), all on Remarkable Records.

Tips: "Even when a song is written for children, it should still meet the criteria for a well-written song—and be pleasing to adults as well."

□ ○ FRESH ENTERTAINMENT (ASCAP), 1315 Simpson Rd., Atlanta GA 30314. Phone/fax: (770)642-2645. E-mail: whunter1122@yahoo.com. **Contact:** Willie W. Hunter, managing director. Music publisher and record company. Publishes 5 songs/year. Staff size: 4. Hires staff songwriters. Pays standard royalty.
Affiliate(s): !Hserf Music (ASCAP), Blair Vizzion Music (BMI) and Santron Music (BMI).
How to Contact: Submit demo tape by mail. Unsolicited submissions are OK. Prefers cassette or videocassette with 3 songs and lyric sheet. "Send photo if available." Include SASE. Responds in 6 weeks.
Film & TV: Places 1 song in TV/year. Published the theme song for BET's *Comic Vue* (by Charles E. Jones), recorded by Cirocco.
Music: Mostly **rap**, **R&B** and **pop/dance**. Published "You Betta Duck" (single by Big James/Noble/Nations) from *Bankhead Boyz* (album), recorded by Bankhead Boyz (hip-hop/rap), released 2001 on The Big Boy Records; "We Hate Pastor Troy" (single by W. Jackson/Javou/Chosen One) from *Ready For War* (album), recorded by Swat Team (rap/hip-hop), released 2000 on Armageddon/Milltyme; "Erase the Color Line" (single by M. Warner/J. Smith/J. Lewis) from *EMQ-Non Pilation* (album), recorded by Michael Warner/JS-1/Noray (R&B/hip-hop), released 2000 on EMQ Entertainment; and "Live Your Fantasy" (single by B. Miles/E. Davis) from *Nubian Woman* (album), recorded by Bob Miles (jazz), released 2000 on Sheets of Sounds.

○ BOB SCOTT FRICK ENTERPRISES, 404 Bluegrass Ave., Madison TN 37115-5307. (615)865-6380. Fax: (615)865-6380. **Contact:** Bob Frick, owner. Music publisher, record company (R.E.F.) and record producer. Estab. 1961. Publishes 25 songs/year; publishes 2 new songwriters/year. Staff size: 2. Pays standard royalty.
Affiliate(s): Sugarbakers Music (ASCAP) and Frick Music Publishing Co. (BMI).
How to Contact: Submit demo tape by mail. Unsolicited submissions are OK. Prefers cassette with 2 songs and lyric sheet. Include SASE. Responds in 3 weeks.
Music: Mostly **Christian** and **country**. Does not want rock. Published *Come Home Daddy* (album by Bill Herold) (country); *It's All Right* (album by Gerald Cunningham) (country); and *If You Need A Miracle* (album by Don Blunkall) (gospel), all recorded by Bob Scott Frick on R.E.F.

◘ FRICON MUSIC COMPANY (BMI), 11 Music Square E, Suite 301, Nashville TN 37203. (615)726-0090. Fax: (615)826-0500. E-mail: fricon@home.com. President: Terri Fricon. **Contact:** Madge Benson, professional manager. Music publisher. Estab. 1981. Publishes 25 songs/year; publishes 1-2 new songwriters/year. Staff size: 6. Pays standard royalty.
Affiliate(s): Fricout Music Company (ASCAP) and Now and Forever Songs (SESAC).
How to Contact: *Contact first and obtain permission to submit.* Prefers cassette with 1-2 songs and lyric or lead sheet. "Prior permission must be obtained or packages will be returned." Include SASE. Responds in 2 months.
Music: Mostly **country**.

☑ ◘ FROZEN INCA MUSIC, P.O. Box 20387, Atlanta GA 30325. (404)931-9049. Fax: (404)351-8714. E-mail: mrland@mindspring.com. Website: www.landsliderecords.com. **Contact:** Eddie Cleveland, vice president. President: Michael Rothschild. Music publisher, record company (Landslide Records) and record producer. Estab. 1981. Publishes 12 songs/year; publishes 3 new songwriters/year. Pays standard royalty.
Affiliate(s): Landslide Records.
How to Contact: Submit demo tape by mail. Unsolicited submissions are OK. Prefers cassette with 3-12 songs. Responds only if interested. Demos not returned.
Music: Mostly **blues**, **swing**, **rock** and **roots music**. Published "A Quitter Never Wins" (single by Ellis/Sampson); "Cold Cold Ground" (single by Sean Costello); and "Who's Been Cheating Who" (single by Costello/Cleveland), all recorded by Sean Costello (blues/rock); and "Alright" (single by Rob Roper) from *Out of the Madness* (album), recorded by Derek Trucks Band, released 2000 on House of Blues.

◻ **FURROW MUSIC (BMI)**, P.O. Box 4121, Edmond OK 73083-4121. **Contact:** G.H. Derrick, owner/publisher. Music publisher, record company (Gusher Records) and record producer. Estab. 1984. Publishes 10-15 songs/year. Staff size: 1. Pays standard royalty.

How to Contact: Submit demo tape by mail. Unsolicited submissions are OK. Prefers cassette, VHS videocassette or CD with 1 song and lyric sheet. "One instrument and vocal is OK for demo." Include SASE. Responds in 2 weeks.

Music: Mostly **country** and **cowboy**. Released 5 original songs on Devin Derrick's CD in 2000. Looking for original songs for his second CD for 2002.

Tips: "Have your song critiqued by other writers (or songwriter organizations) prior to making the demo. Only make and send demos of songs that have a universal appeal. Make sure the vocal is out front of the music. Never be so attached to a lyric or tune that you can't rewrite it. Don't forget to include your SASE with all submissions."

◙ **G MAJOR MUSIC (BMI)**, P.O. Box 3331, Fort Smith AR 72913-3331. Fax: (501)782-0842. E-mail: JerryGlidewell@juno.com. Professional Managers: Alex Hoover (country/southern rock/gospel); Jerry Glidewell (contemporary country/pop). Music publisher. Estab. 1992. Publishes 10 songs/year; publishes 3 new songwriters/year. Staff size: 2. Pays standard royalty.

How to Contact: Submit demo tape by mail. Unsolicited submissions are OK. Prefers cassette or CD. Submit up to 3 songs. Include SASE. Responds in 3 weeks.

Music: Mostly **country**, **traditional country** and **pop**; also **contemporary Christian**. Published *In Competition With a Truck* (album by Elaine Woolsey), recorded by Libby Benson (country); "Question of Heart" (single by Jerry Glidewell), recorded by Brian Bateman (country); and "Step Out Into the Sun" (single by Chad Little/Jerry Glidewell), recorded by Libby Benson (Christian contemporary), all on MBS.

Tips: "We are looking for radio-friendly hits for the country market. We use a top songplugger in Nashville. Remember, your song has to be so good that people will spend their hard earned money to hear it over and over again."

◻ **ALAN GARY MUSIC (ASCAP, BMI)**, P.O. Box 179, Palisades Park NJ 07650. President: Alan Gary. Creative Director: Fran Levine. Creative Assistant: Harold Green. Music publisher. Estab. 1987. Publishes a varying number of songs/year. Staff size: 3. Pays standard royalty.

How to Contact: Submit demo tape by mail. Unsolicited submissions are OK. Prefers cassette or VHS videocassette with lyric sheet. Include SASE.

Music: Mostly **pop**, **R&B** and **dance**; also **rock**, **A/C** and **country**. Published "Liberation" (single by Gary/Julian), recorded by Les Julian on Music Tree Records (A/C); "Love Your Way Out of This One" (single by Gary/Rosen), recorded by Deborah Steel on Bad Cat Records (contemporary country); and "Dueling Rappers" (single by Gary/Free), recorded by Prophets of Boom on You Dirty Rap! Records (rap/R&B).

◻ **GLAD MUSIC CO. (ASCAP, BMI, SESAC)**, 14340 Torrey Chase, Suite 380, Houston TX 77014. (281)397-7300. Fax: (281)397-6206. E-mail: wesdaily@gladmusicco.com. Website: www.gladmusicco.com. **Contact:** Wes Daily, A&R Director (country). Music publisher, record company and record producer. Estab. 1958. Publishes 10 songs/year; publishes 10 new songwriters/year. Staff size: 4. Pays standard royalty.

Affiliate(s): Bud-Don (ASCAP) and Rayde (SESAC).

How to Contact: *Write first and obtain permission to submit or to arrange personal interview.* Prefers cassette or CD with 3 songs, lyric sheet and cover letter. Does not return material. Responds in 2 weeks.

Music: Mostly **country**. Does not want weak songs. Published *Love Bug* (album by C. Wayne/W. Kemp), recorded by George Strait, released 1995 on MCA; *Walk Through This World With Me* (album), written and recorded by George Jones and *Race Is On* (album by D. Rollins), recorded by George Jones, both released 1999 on Asylum.

▨◻ **AUGUST GOLDEN MUSIC (BMI)**, 6666 Brookmont Terrace #705, Nashville TN 37205. Phone/fax: (615)353-8134. **Contact:** Marie Golden (pop/film/country). Music publisher. Estab. 1998. Staff size: 3.

How to Contact: *Write, call or fax first and obtain permission to submit.* Prefers cassette or CD with 3 songs and lyric sheet. Does not return material. Responds in 3 weeks.
Music: Mostly **country**, **pop** and **rock**; also **film music** and **Latin music**. Does not want rap.
Tips: "Have a professional studio demo and the guts to be different."

☑ ◯ **THE GOODLAND MUSIC GROUP INC.**, P.O. Box 24454, Nashville TN 37202. (615)269-7071. Fax: (615)269-0131. E-mail: jonwalk@aristomedia.com. Website: www.aristomedia. com. **Contact:** John Walker, Publishing Coordinator. Music publisher. Estab. 1988. Publishes 50 songs/year; 5-10 new songwriters/year. Pays standard royalty.
Affiliate(s): Goodland Publishing Company (ASCAP), Marc Isle Music (BMI) and Gulf Bay Publishing (SESAC).
How to Contact: Submit demo tape by mail. Unsolicited submissions are OK. Include SASE with first class postage "for reply only."
Music: Mostly **country/Christian**, but open to **all styles**. "We are now listening to **pop, hip-hop, rock, dance** for publishing consideration." Published "Where Does Love Go When It's Gone?" (single by Barton/Byram), recorded by Warren Johnson on MDL Records; "Swingin' for the Fences" (single by Myers/Meier) and "The Best Mistake" (single by Primamore), both recorded by Daniel Glidwell on Starborn Records.

◪ ◖ **GOODNIGHT KISS MUSIC (BMI)**, 10153½ Riverside Dr. #239, Toluca Lake CA 91601. (323)969-9993. E-mail: staff@goodnightkiss.com. Website: www.goodnightkiss.com. **Contact:** Janet Fisher, managing director. Music publisher, record company and record producer. Estab. 1986. Publishes 6-8 songs/year; publishes 4-5 new songwriters/year. Pays standard royalty.
 • Goodnight Kiss Music specializes in placing music in movies and TV, but also pitches major label acts.
Affiliate(s): Scene Stealer Music (ASCAP).
How to Contact: "Check our website or subscribe to free newsletter (www.goodnightkiss.com) to see what we are looking for and to obtain codes. Packages must have proper submission codes, or they are discarded." Prefers CD or cassette with 1-3 songs and lyric sheet. Send SASE for reply. Does not return material. Responds in 6 months.
Film & TV: Places 3-5 songs in film/year. Published "I Do, I Do, Love You" (by Joe David Curtis), recorded by Ricky Kershaw in *Road Ends*; "Bee Charmer's Charmer" (by Marc Tilson) for the MTV movie *Love Song*; "Right When I Left" (by B. Turner/J. Fisher) in the movie *Knight Club*.
Music: **All modern styles**. Published and produced *And to All a Goodnight* (Christmas comp. CD); produced *I'm Gonna Lasso Santa* (album) and *When Sunny Gets Blues, Scarlet Ribbons, and Other Songs I Wrote* (album by Jack Segal), both released 2001 on Goodnight Kiss Records.
Tips: "The absolute best way to keep apprised of the company's needs is to subscribe to the online newsletter. Only specifically requested material is accepted, as listed in the newsletter (what the industry calls us for is what we request from writers). We basically use an SGA contract, and there are never fees to be considered for specific projects or albums. However, we are a real music company, and the competition is just as fierce as with the majors."

◙ **GREEN ONE MUSIC (BMI)**, Rockin' Chair Center Suite 102, 1033 W. State Highway 76, Branson MO 65616. (417)334-2336. Fax: (417)334-2306. **Contact:** George J. Skupien, president. Music publisher, record label and recording studio. Estab. 1992. Publishes 6-12 songs/year. Pays standard royalty.
How to Contact: *Write or fax first and obtain permission to submit.* Prefers CD, cassette or DAT with 2-4 songs. "We *only* accept professional studio demo tapes. This means that your tape has been performed, recorded and produced by someone with music industry experience, who will represent

---

REFER TO THE CATEGORY INDEX (at the end of this section) to find exactly which companies are interested in the type of music you write.

your songs with the quality of a master recording." Does not return material. "For your protection, all tapes, lyrics or other material that is received, that are not accepted, are immediately destroyed to protect the songwriters." Responds in 3 months.

Music: Mostly **country**, **MOR** and **light rock**; also **American polka music**, **waltzes** and **comedy— fun songs**. Published "Today May Be Too Late" (single by Billy Rice/Matt Row'd), recorded by Billy Rice, released 2000 on Green Bear Records; and "Love Is Why I Feel This Way" (single by G. Skupien/Sara Wright), from *Country Compilation 102* (album), recorded by Buddy Thomas, released 2000 on Green Bear Records.

Tips: "Always put your best song first on your tapes submitted. Be sure your vocal is clear!"

G-STRING PUBLISHING (BMI, SOCAN), P.O. Box 1096, Hudson, Quebec J0P 1H0 Canada. (514)869-3236. Fax: (450)458-2819. E-mail: LA_Record@excite.com. Website: www.r adiofreedom.com. Music Coordinator: Ms. T. Hart. Music publisher, record company (L.A. Records), record producer. Estab. 1991. Publishes 20 songs; publishes 5-10 new songwriters/year. Pays standard royalty.

How to Contact: Submit demo tape by mail. Unsolicited submissions are OK. Does not return material. Prefers cassette or DAT with 3 songs and lyric sheet.

Music: Mostly **commercial rock**, **A/C** and **dance**; also **country**. Published "No White in the Blues" and "Big Daddy" (singles by M. Lengies), recorded by Joe King.

Tips: "Know your craft; songs must have great lyrics and good melody, and create a strong emotional reaction. They must be under four minutes and must be radio friendly."

R.L. HAMMEL ASSOCIATES, INC., P.O. Box 531, Alexandria IN 46001-0531. E-mail: rlh@rlhammel.com. Website: www.rlhammel.com. **Contact:** A&R Department. President: Randal Hammel. Music publisher, record producer and consultant. Estab. 1974. Staff size: 3-5. Pays standard royalty.

Affiliate(s): Ladnar Music (ASCAP) and Lemmah Music (BMI).

How to Contact: Submit demo tape by mail. Unsolicited submissions are OK. Prefers cassette, DAT or VHS/8mm videocassette with 3 songs and typed lyric sheet. Does not return material. Responds ASAP.

Music: Mostly **pop**, **Christian** and **R&B**; also **MOR**, **rock** and **country**. Published *Lessons For Life* (album by Kelly Hubbell/Jim Boedicker) and *I Just Want Jesus* (album by Mark Condon), both recorded by Kelly Connor on Impact Records.

HAPPY MELODY, VZW, Paul Gilsonstraat 31, 8200 St-Andries, Belgium. Phone: (050)31- 63-80. **Contact:** Eddy Van Mouffaert, general manager. Music publisher, record company (Jump Records) and record producer (Jump Productions). Member SABAM S.V., Brussels. Publishes 100 songs/year; publishes 8 new songwriters/year. Staff size: 2. Pays standard royalty via SABAM S.V.

How to Contact: Submit demo tape by mail. Unsolicited submissions are OK. Prefers cassette. Does not return material. Responds in 2 weeks.

Music: Mostly **easy listening**, **disco** and **light pop**; also **instrumentals**. Published *Dikke Berta* and *Da Da Da* (albums by Ricky Mondes), both recorded by Guy Dumon on BM Studio (Flemish); and *Onze Vader* (album by David Linton), recorded by De Korenaar on Korenaar (profane).

Tips: "Music wanted with easy, catchy melodies (very commercial songs)."

HES FREE PRODUCTIONS & PUBLISHING COMPANY, 3709 E. 29th, P.O. Box 1214, Bryan TX 77806-1214. (979)268-3263. Fax: (979)589-2575. E-mail: hesfreeprodandpubco@ yahoo.com. Website: http://home1.gte.net/jbhes/. Executive Producer/CEO/Owner: Brenda M. Freeman-Heslip (gospel); Producer of songwriting: Jamie Heslip. Assistant Producer: Rochelle Heslip (r&b). Director of A&R: Damion Turner (rap). Music publisher and record producer. Estab. 2001. Staff size: 30. Pays 25% "due to our company supplying everything."

How to Submit: *We only accept material referred to us by a reputable industry source (manager, entertainment attorney, etc.).* Include CD/CDR. Does not return submissions. Responds in 4-6 weeks only if interested. "Make sure you copyright all of your material through the Library of Congress in Washington, D.C."

Music: Mostly **r&b**, **gospel** and **rap**; also **rock**. Does not want country. Published "Texas Boys" (single by Chris Idlebird) from *Texas Boys* (album), recorded by Chris Idlebird and Vicki Diggs (rap), released 2002; "Controversial Crossover" (single by Ray Brooks) from *Controversial Crossover* (album), recorded by "Mike-Ray" Ray Brooks (r&b), released 2002; "Walk through the Rays" (single by Donell Travis), from *Dontray the Ghetto Prophet* (album), recorded by Donell Travis and Ralatraneka Mercer (rap), released 2002.

Tips: "We will ensure that each project is complete with professionalism, with the highest technology methods possible. Additionally, our goal is to publish and record over 200 songs annually."

HEUPFERD MUSIKVERLAG GmbH, Ringwaldstr. 18, Dreieich 63303 Germany. Phone/fax: (06103)86970. E-mail: heupferd@t-online.de. **Contact:** Christian Winkelmann, general manager. Music publisher and record company (Viva La Difference). GEMA. Publishes 60 songs/year. Staff size: 3. Pays "royalties after GEMA distribution plan."
Affiliate(s): Song Bücherei (book series). "Vive La Difference!" (label).
How to Contact: *Does not accept unsolicited submissions.*
Film & TV: Places 1 song in film/year. Published "El Grito Y El Silencio" (by Thomas Hickstein), recorded by Tierra in *Frauen sind was Wunderbares*.
Music: Mostly **folk**, **jazz** and **fusion**; also **New Age**, **rock** and **ethnic music**. Published "West Coast of Clare" (single by Andy Irvine) from *Celtic Dreams* (album), recorded by The Wacking Shillelaghs (folk), released 2001 on BMG; and *Havana-Colores Del Amor* (album), written by Kurt Klose, recorded by Havana (Latin), released 2001 on Vive La Difference.

HICKORY LANE PUBLISHING AND RECORDING (ASCAP, SOCAN), 19854 Butternut Lane, Pitt Meadows, British Columbia V3Y 2S7 Canada. (604)465-1258. **Contact:** Chris Urbanski, president. Music publisher, record company and record producer. Estab. 1988. Hires staff writers. Publishes 30 songs/year; publishes 5 new songwriters/year. Pays standard royalty.
How to Contact: *Does not accept unsolicited submissions.*
Music: Mostly **country** and **country rock**. Published *Mama Liked the Roses* (album), "She Misses Me" (single) and "Love Letters" (single), all recorded by Chris Michaels (country), released 2002 on Hickory Lane Records.
Tips: "Send us a professional quality demo with the vocals upfront. We are looking for hits, and so are the major record labels we deal with. Be original in your approach, don't send us a cover tune."

HIGH-MINDED MOMA PUBLISHING & PRODUCTIONS (BMI), P.O. Box 959, Coos Bay OR 97420. **Contact:** Kai Moore Snyder, president. Music publisher and production company. Pays standard royalty.
How to Contact: Prefers 7½ ips reel-to-reel, CD or cassette with 4-8 songs and lyric sheet. Include SASE. Responds in 1 month.
Music: Mostly **country**, **MOR**, **rock (country)**, **New Age** and **top 40/pop**.

HIS POWER PRODUCTIONS AND PUBLISHING (ASCAP, BMI), 1304 Canyon, Plainview TX 79072-4740. (806)296-7073. Fax: (806)296-7111. E-mail: dcarter@o-c-s.com. Website: www.hppp.com. Professional Managers: Darryl Carter (R&B, gospel, country rock); T. Lee Carter (pop, new rock, classic rock). Music publisher, record company (Lion and Lamb), record producer and management and booking agency (End-Time Management & Booking Agency). Estab. 1995. Publishes 4-10 songs/year; publishes 3 new songwriters/year. Staff size: 4. Hires staff songwriters. Pays negotiable royalty.
Affiliate(s): Love Story Publishing (BMI).
• The song "Heal Me," published by His Power, was awarded a 1998, 1999, 2000, 2001 and 2002 ASCAP Popular Award.
How to Contact: *Write or call first and obtain permission to submit.* Prefers cassette, CD or DAT with 1-5 songs and lyric sheet. Include SASE. Responds in 4 months.
Music: Mostly **power gospel**, **pop**, **new rock**, **classic rock**, **country rock gospel** and **adult contemporary gospel**; also **R&B**, **jazz**, **Christ-oriented Christmas music**, **pro-life and family** and **southern gospel**. Does not want negative-based lyrics of any kind. Published "She Used to Be Me"

(single), written and recorded by Crystal Cartier on Love Story (blues); "It's His Life" (single), written and recorded by Mike Burchfield (country gospel), released on Lion and Lamb Records; and "I Didn't Say The I Love Yous" (single), written and recorded by Joe Copeland (country), released on Tex Sound Records.

Tips: "Be serious. We are only interested in those who have meaning and substance behind what is created. Music is an avenue to change the world. Submit what comes from the heart. Don't be in a hurry. Good music has no time limits. And yet, time will reward the desire you put into it. Be willing to embark on newly designed challenges that will meet a new century of opportunity and needs never before obtainable through conventional music companies."

◯ HITSBURGH MUSIC CO. (BMI), P.O. Box 1431, 233 N. Electra, Gallatin TN 37066. (615)452-0324. Promotional Director: Kimolin Crutcher. A&R Director: K'leetha Gilbert. Executive Vice President: Kenneth Gilbert. **Contact:** Harold Gilbert, President/General Manager. Music publisher. Estab. 1964. Publishes 12 songs/year. Staff size: 4. Pays standard royalty.
Affiliate(s): 7th Day Music (BMI).
How to Contact: Submit demo tape by mail. Unsolicited submissions are OK. Prefers cassette or quality videocassette with 2-4 songs and lead sheet. Prefers studio produced demos. Include SASE. Responds in 6 weeks.
Music: Mostly **country gospel** and **MOR**. Published "Georgia Boy" (single by Donald Layne), recorded by The Swingsters (MOR), released 2000 on Southern City; and "Disorder at the Border" (single), written and recorded by Donald Layne, released 2001 on Southern City.

☑ ◯ HITSOURCE PUBLISHING (BMI), 1324 Oakton, Evanston IL 60202. (847)328-4203. Fax: (847)328-4236. E-mail: hitsource@earthlink.net. **Contact:** Al Goldberg, president. Music publisher. Estab. 1986. Publishes 3-12 songs/year; publishes 1-2 new songwriters/year. Pays standard royalty.
Affiliate(s): Grooveland Music (ASCAP) and KidSource Publishing (BMI).
How to Contact: *Write or e-mail first and obtain permission to submit.* "Sometimes we are not actively plugging songs." Prefers CD or cassette with 3 songs and lyric sheet. Does not return material. Responds in 2 months.
Music: Mostly **pop**, **country** and **rock**.
Tips: "Ask yourself the following questions: Does this song come from the heart? Will an artist be willing to risk his career by recording this song? Have you critiqued the song yourself and rewritten it yet?"

▨ ◯ HOLY SPIRIT MUSIC (BMI), P.O. Box 31, Edmonton KY 42129. (270)432-3183. **Contact:** W. Junior Lawson, president. Music publisher. Member GMA, International Association of Gospel Music Publishers and Southern Gospel Music Association. Estab. 1973. Publishes 4 songs/year; publishes 2 new songwriters/year. Staff size: 1. Pays standard royalty.
How to Contact: Submit demo tape by mail. Unsolicited submissions are OK. Prefers cassette with 2 songs and lyric sheet. Include SASE. Responds in 3 weeks.
Film & TV: Places 1 song in film and 1 song in TV/year. Published "I'm Making Plans To See Jesus" (by Gregory A. Pollard), recorded by The Florida Boys in *Saved By Grace*.
Music: Mostly **Southern gospel** and **country gospel**. Does not want rock gospel or contemporary gospel. Published "God Gave Us Teardrops" (single by Barbara Jean Smith) and "He's My Rock for the Ages" (single by Charles E. Cox) from *Circle of Love* (album), recorded by Isabelle Marie (gospel), released 2001 on Independent; "He Can Say Peace" (single by Malcolm G. Burton) from *He's the Rock* (album), recorded by One Voice (mixed quartet), released 2001 on Independent.
Tips: Send "good clear cut tape with typed copy of lyrics."

▦ ◑ INSIDE RECORDS/OK SONGS, St.-Jacobsmarkt 76, 2000 Antwerp 6 Belgium. Phone: (32)+3+226-77-19. Fax: (32)+3+226-78-05. **Contact:** Jean Ney, MD. Music publisher and record company. Estab. 1989. Publishes 50 songs/year; publishes 30-40 new songwriters/year. Hires staff writers. Royalty varies "depending on teamwork."

How to Contact: Submit demo tape by mail. Unsolicited submissions are OK. Prefers cassette with complete name, address, telephone and fax number. SAE and IRC. Responds in 2 months.
Music: Mostly **dance, pop** and **MOR contemporary**; also **country, reggae** and **Latin**. Published *Fiesta De Bautiza* (album by Andres Manzana); *I'm Freaky* (album by Maes-Predu'homme-Robinson); and *Heaven* (album by KC One-King Naomi), all on Inside Records.

◯ INTERPLANETARY MUSIC (BMI), 584 Roosevelt, Gary IN 46404. (219)886-2003. Fax: (219)886-1000. CEO: James R. Hall III. A&R Director (hip-hop, R&B, jazz): Martin Booker. A&R (R&B, gospel): Bryant Henderson. Music publisher, record company (Interplanetary Records) and record producer. Estab. 1972. Staff size: 5. Publishes 10 songs/year; publishes 4 new songwriters/year. Pays standard royalty.
How to Contact: *Call first and obtain permission to submit.* Prefers cassette. Include SASE. Responds in 1 month.
Music: Mostly **R&B**, **rap** and **Top 40/urban contemporary**. Does not want country. Published "Beneath the Sheets" (single by James Hall) and "Good Times" (single by Bernard Tucker), both recorded by Subliminal on Interplanetary Records.
Tips: "Please submit a good quality cassette recording of your best work."

☑ ◯ IRON SKILLET MUSIC, 6337 Murray Lane, Brentwood TN 37027. (615)371-0646. Fax: (615)370-0353. E-mail: jschneiderassoc@aol.com. **Contact:** Jack Schneider, president. Vice President: Claude Southall. Office Manager: Nell Tolson. Music publisher, record company (Rustic Records Inc.) and record producer. Estab. 1984. Publishes 20 songs/year. Pays standard royalty.
Affiliate(s): Covered Bridge Music (BMI), Town Square Music (SESAC).
How to Contact: Submit demo tape by mail. Unsolicited submissions are OK. Prefers cassette with 3 songs and lyric sheet. Include SASE. Responds in 3 months.
Music: Mostly **country**. Published "Bear Huggin" (single by Colte Bradley/Judi Davis); "Ain't It Amazing" (single by C. Southall/J. Schneider); and "To Love Another Woman" (single by Bobby Reed), recorded by Colte Bradley (country), released 2001 on Rustic Records.
Tips: "Send three or four traditional country songs, story songs or novelty songs with strong hook. Enclose SASE (manilla envelope)."

�'ⁿ JANA JAE MUSIC (BMI), P.O. Box 35726, Tulsa OK 74153. (918)786-8896. Fax: (918)786-8897. E-mail: janajae@janajae.com. Website: www.janajae.com. **Contact:** Kathleen Pixley, secretary. Music publisher, record company (Lark Record Productions, Inc.) and record producer (Lark Talent and Advertising). Estab. 1980. Publishes 5-10 songs/year; publishes 1-2 new songwriters/year. Staff size: 8. Pays standard royalty.
How to Contact: Submit demo tape by mail. Unsolicited submissions are OK. Prefers cassette or VHS videocassette with 3-4 songs and typed lyric and lead sheet if possible. Does not return material. Responds only if accepted for use.
Music: Mostly **country**, **bluegrass**, **jazz** and **instrumentals** (**classical** or **country**). Published *Mayonnaise* (album by Steve Upfold), recorded by Jana Jae; and *Let the Bible Be Your Roadmap* (album by Irene Elliot) recorded by Jana Jae, both on Lark Records.

[N] [▣] ◯ JAELIUS ENTERPRISES (ASCAP, BMI), P.O. Box 459, Royse City TX 75189. (972)636-9230. Fax: (972)636-0036. E-mail: jaelius@flash.net. Website: www.jaelius.com. **Contact:** James Cornelius, managing director. Music publisher. Publishes 3-5 songs/year; publishes 3 new songwriters/year. Staff size: 2. Pays standard royalty.
Affiliate(s): Jaelius Music (ASCAP), Hitzgalore Music (BMI), Air Rifle Music (ASCAP) and Bee Bee Gun Music (BMI).

● **A BULLET** introduces comments by the editor of *Songwriter's Market* indicating special information about the listing.

How to Contact: *Write or call first and obtain permission to submit*. Prefers cassette. Include SASE. Responds in 6 weeks.

Film & TV: Places 2 songs in film/year. Recently published "Night Has a Thousand Eyes" (by Wayne/Weisman/Garrett), recorded by Anita Kelsey in *Dark City*; and "Feeling in Love," written and recorded by J.J. Cale in *Lawn Dogs*.

Music: Mostly **pop**, **country** and **gospel**; also **R&B**. Does not want rap. Published "Make a Joyful Noise" and "I Know" (singles), recorded by Olivia Mojica (gospel); "Where Would I Be Without Your Love" (single), recorded by Lee Mays (gospel); "God Gives His Love International" (single), recorded by Michelle Deck (gospel).

Tips: "Today's market requires good demos. Strong lyrics are a must."

⊕ ☑ ◯ **JA/NEIN MUSIKVERLAG GMBH**, Oberstr. 14 A, D-20144, Hamburg Germany. Fax: (+49)40 448850. E-mail: janeinmv@aol.com. General Manager: Mary Dostal. Music publisher, record company and record producer. GEMA. Publishes 100 songs/year; publishes 20 new songwriters/year. Staff size: 3. Pays 60% royalty.

Affiliate(s): Pinorrekk Mv., Star-Club Mv., Wunderbar Mv. and Sempex Mv. (GEMA).

How to Contact: Submit audio (visual) carrier by mail. Unsolicited submissions are OK. Prefers cassette, CDR or VHS videocassette. Enclose SAE and IRC or e-mail address. Responds in 2 months.

Music: Mostly **jazz**, **klezmer**, **pop**, **rap** and **rock**. Published "Dem Melekh's Nigh" (single by Alan Bern), recorded by Brave New World (klezmer), released on ÿ Pinorrekk Records; "Wenn Ich Robert DeNiro Waer" (single), written and recorded by Bernd Huber (pop), released on Lux Records; and "Just Before the Break of Day" (single), written and recorded by Axel Zwingenberger and Big Joe Duskin (boogie woogie), released on Vagabond Records.

Tips: "If no SAE and IRC or e-mail address are enclosed, we only reply if we have fallen in love. We do not return submitted material. Send A-Side songs or extraordinary works only, please. Write what you expect from collaboration. If artist, include photo. If CS, leave three seconds between tracks. Enclose lyrics. Be fantastic!"

☑ ◖ **JASPER STONE MUSIC (ASCAP)/JSM SONGS (BMI)**, 10 Deepwell Farms Rd., South Salem NY 10590. E-mail: gcrecords@aol.com. Website: www.goldcitymusic.com. President: Chris Jasper. Vice President/General Counsel: Margie Jasper. Music publisher. Estab. 1986. Publishes 20-25 songs/year. "Each contract is worked out individually and negotiated depending on terms." Staff size: 5. Pays standard royalty.

How to Contact: Submit demo tape by mail. Unsolicited submissions are OK. Prefers cassette, CD or DAT with maximum of 3 songs and lyric sheets. Include SASE. Responds in 6 weeks.

Music: Mostly **R&B/pop**, **rap** and **rock**. Does not want country, classical or children's. Published "And I Love Her" (single by J. Lennon/P. McCartney), recorded by Brothaz By Choice on Gold City Records (R&B).

Tips: "Keep writing. Keep submitting tapes. Be persistent. Don't give up. Send your best songs in the best form (best production possible)."

◖ **JERJOY MUSIC (BMI)**, P.O. Box 1264, 6020 W. Pottstown Rd., Peoria IL 61654-1264. (309)673-5755. Fax: (309)673-7636. E-mail: uarltd@unitedcyber.com. Website: www.unitedcyber.com/uarltd. **Contact:** Jerry Hanlon, professional manager. Music publisher and record company (Universal-Athena Records). Estab. 1978. Publishes 6 songs/year; publishes 6 new songwriters/year. Staff size: 3. Pays standard royalty.

Affiliate(s): Kaysarah Music (BMI).

How to Contact: "We accept unsolicited submissions. We do not return phone calls." Prefers cassette or CD with 4-8 songs and lyric sheet. Include SASE. "We do not critique work unless asked." Responds in 2 weeks.

Music: Mostly **country**. Published "The Girl From Central High" (single by Ron Czikall) from *Right Here In Tennessee* (album), recorded by Tracy Wells (country); "Too Late to Put the Bottle Down" (single by Cliff Thigpen) from *Hello Mr. Heartache* (album), recorded by Jerry Hanlon (country); and "New Jerusalem" (single by Diane Kemp Pantel) from *Country Nights* (album), recorded by Garry Johnson (country), all released 2000 on UAR.

Tips: "Don't submit any song that you don't honestly feel is well constructed and strong in commercial value. Be honest and sincere."

N JODA MUSIC (BMI), P.O. Box 100, Spirit Lake IA 51360. (712)336-2859. President: John Senn. A&R Director: Wes Weller. Music publisher and record company. Estab. 1970. Publishes 10 songs/year. Pays standard royalty.
Affiliate(s): Okoboji Music (BMI).
How to Contact: Prefers cassette with no more than 4 songs and lyric sheet. "Keep demos short." Include SASE. Responds in 3 weeks.
Music: Mostly **light rock**, **country** and **gospel**. Published "Beer & Popcorn" (by Dave Peterson), recorded by Ralph Lundquist (country); "Change is Going to Come" (by Roger Hughes), recorded by Silver $ Band (pop); and *Time Keeps Taking You*, written and recorded by Wes Weller (country), all on IGL Records.

N ⬤ AL JOLSON BLACK & WHITE MUSIC (BMI), 116 17th Ave. S., Nashville TN 37203. (615)244-5656. **Contact:** Johnny Drake, general manager. Music publisher. Estab. 1981. Publishes 600 songs/year; publishes 50 new songwriters/year. Pays standard royalty.
Affiliate(s): Jolie House Music (ASCAP).
How to Contact: Submit a demo tape by mail. Unsolicited submissions are OK. Prefers cassette with 3 songs and lyric sheet. Send: Attn. Johnny Drake. Include SASE. Responds in 6 weeks.
Music: Mostly **country crossover**, **light rock** and **pop**. Published "Come Home to West Virginia" (single by Scott Phelps), recorded by Kathy Mattea; "Ten Tiny Fingers, Ten Tiny Toes" (single by David John Hanley), recorded by Kelly Dawn; and "Indiana Highway" (single), recorded by Staggerlee, both on ASA Jolson Records (country).
Tips: "Make sure it has a strong hook. Ask yourself if it is something you would hear on the radio five times a day. Have good audible vocals on demo tape."

N ⬤ QUINCY JONES MUSIC, 3800 Barham Blvd., Suite 503, Los Angeles CA 90068. (818)972-9494. E-mail: info@quincyjonesmusic.com. Music publisher.
How to Contact: *Quincy Jones Music does not accept unsolicited submissions.*

☑ ◯ JPMC MUSIC INC. (BMI), P.O. Box 526, Burlington VT 05402. (802)860-7110. Fax: (802)860-7112. E-mail: music@jpmc.com. Website: www.jpmc.com. **Contact:** Jane Peterer, president. Music publisher, record company (JPMC Records) and book publisher. Estab. 1989. Publishes 20 songs/year; publishes 10 new songwriters/year. Pays standard royalty.
Affiliate(s): GlobeSound Publishing (ASCAP) and GlobeArt Publishing Inc. (BMI).
How to Contact: Submit a demo tape by mail. Unsolicited submissions are OK. Prefers "professional" DAT, CD or cassette with 3 songs and lyric sheet. "If submitting a CD, indicate which three tracks to consider, otherwise only the first three will be considered." Include SASE. Responds in 2 months. See website for complete guidelines.
Music: Mostly **pop/R&B**, **jazz** and **gospel**; also **country** and **instrumental**. Published "Ode to Ireland" (single by Breschi), recorded by Breschi/Cassidy on Pick Records (instrumental); and "Ici Paris" (single), written and recorded by Michael Ganian.
Tips: "We are in constant communication with record and film producers and will administer your work on a worldwide basis. We also publish songbooks for musicians and fans, as well as educational and method books for students and teachers."

⬤ JUKE MUSIC (BMI), P.O. Box 120277, Nashville TN 37212. **Contact:** Becky Gibson, songwriter coordinator. Professional Manager: Jack Cook. Music publisher. Estab. 1987. Publishes 60-150 songs/year; publishes 3-25 new songwriters/year. Pays standard royalty.
How to Contact: Submit demo tape by mail. Unsolicited submissions are OK. Prefers CD or cassette with 3 songs and lyric sheet. "Send only radio-friendly material." Does not return material. Responds in 8 months.
Music: Mostly **country/pop** and **rock**; also **alternative adult** and **Christian**. Does *not* want theatrical, improperly structured, change tempo and feel, poor or no hook. Published "Cross on the High-

way" (single) from *Sumner Country Drive Inn* (album), written and recorded by Ronnie McDowell, released 2001 on Portland; "April Fool" (single by Phil Delberg) from *Georgia Rockitt* (album), recorded by Tuscaloosa (southern rock/country), released 2000 on Blackstone; and "King & Queen of Love" (single by Ralph Lake) from *Running Scared 2001*, recorded by Michael Sheahan (pop/rock), released 2001 on Daydreamer.

Tips: "Do your homework, craft the song, be sure you're willing to gamble your songwriting integrity on this song or songs you're sending. We recommend songwriters attend workshops or conferences before submitting material. Help us cut through the junk. Send *positive, uptempo, new country* for best results. It seems most of our submitters read what we *do not* want and send that! *Please* listen to country radio."

N JUST A NOTE (ASCAP, BMI), P.O. Box 39261, Louisville KY 40233. (502)777-4539. E-mail: TalkToHeath@home.com. Website: www.heath&assoc.com. **Contact:** John V. Heath, general partner. Music publisher, record companies (Hillview, Estate) and record producer (MVT Productions). Estab. 1979. Publishes 35 songs/year; publishes 10-15 new songwriters/year. Pays standard royalty.
Affiliate(s): Two John's Music (ASCAP).
How to Contact: Submit demo tape by mail. Unsolicited submissions are OK. "Or e-mail me." Prefers cassette, 7½ ips reel-to-reel or VHS videocassette with 3 songs and lead sheet. Include SASE. Responds in 1 month.
Music: Mostly **pop**, **country**, **R&B** and **MOR**; also **gospel**. Published *Old Age* and *Rose*, written and recorded by Mark Gibbs on Hillview Records; and *Area Code 502*, written and recorded by Adonis on Estate Records.
Tips: "As we are an international company, please have access to lead sheet. Since this takes time to do, we do charge for this service. Our sub-publishers require lead sheets."

☑ ○ KANSA RECORDS CORPORATION, 11716 Manor Rd., Leawood KS 66211. (913)661-0233. E-mail: kansarec@aol.com. **Contact:** Kit Johnson, secretary and treasurer/general manager. Music publisher, record company and record producer. Estab. 1972. Publishes 50-60 songs/year; publishes 8-10 new songwriters/year. Pays standard royalty.
Affiliate(s): Great Leawood Music, Inc. (ASCAP) and Twinsong Music (BMI).
How to Contact: Submit demo tape by mail. Unsolicited submissions are OK. Prefers cassette with 4 songs and lyric sheet. Does not return material. Responds in 2 months.
Music: Mostly **country**, **MOR** and **country rock**; also **R&B** (leaning to country) and **Christian**. Does not want hard rock. Published *Louisiana Hop*; *Big Hurt*; *Seasons of Our Love* (albums by Walter Leise), all recorded by Jerry Piper on Kansas Records.

○ KAUPPS & ROBERT PUBLISHING CO. (BMI), P.O. Box 5474, Stockton CA 95205. (209)948-8186. Fax: (209)942-2163. Website: www.makingmusic4u.com. **Contact:** Kristy Ledford, A&R coordinator (all styles). Production Manager (country, pop, rock): Rick Webb. Professional Manager (country, pop, rock): Bruce Boun. President: Nancy L. Merrihew. Music publisher, record company (Kaupp Records), manager and booking agent (Merri-Webb Productions and Most Wanted Bookings). Estab. 1990. Publishes 15-20 songs/year; publishes 5 new songwriters/year. Pays standard royalty.
How to Contact: *Write first and obtain permission to submit.* Prefers cassette or VHS videocassette (if available) with 3 songs maximum and lyric sheet. "If artist, send PR package." Include SASE. Responds in 6 months.
Music: Mostly **country**, **R&B** and **A/C rock**; also **pop**, **rock** and **gospel**. Published "Prisoner of Love" (single by N. Merrihew/Rick Webb), recorded by Nanci Lynn (country/rock/pop); "Excuse Me, But That Ain't Country"; "I Thank You Father" and "On the Other Side" (singles by N. Merrihew/B. Bolin), recorded by Bruce Bolin (country/rock/pop); and "Did You Think That I Thought That You Liked Me" (single by N. Merrihew/B. Bolin), recorded by Nanci Lynn (country/rock/pop) and Cheryl (country/rock/pop), all released on Kaupp Records.
Tips: "Know what you want, set a goal, focus in on your goals, be open to constructive criticism, polish tunes and keep polishing."

KAYSARAH MUSIC (ASCAP), (formerly Jerjoy Music), P.O. Box 1264, 6020 W. Potts-town Rd., Peoria IL 61654-1264. (309)673-5755. Fax: (309) 673-7636. E-mail: uarltd@unitedcyber.c om. Website: www.unitedcyber.com. **Contact:** Jerry Hanlon, owner/producer. Music Publisher, record company, and record producer. Estab. 2000. Publishes 2 new songwriters/year. Staff size: 3. Pays standard royalty.
Affiliate(s): Jerjoy Music (BMI).
How to Contact: Submit demo tape by mail. Unsolicited submissions are OK. Prefers cassette or CD with 4 songs and lyric sheet and cover letter. Include SASE. Responds in 2 weeks.
Music: Mostly **traditional country**, **modern country** and **country gospel**; also **Irish country**, **Irish ballads** and **Irish folk/traditional**. Recently published "It's Too Late For Goodbye" (single by Dorothy Wallace) and "A World Without You" (single by Sue Rapp) from *Candlelight and Wine* (album), recorded by Jackie Nelson (modern country), released 2001 on Irish Records.
Tips: "Be honest in comparing your material to commercially recorded works."

 KEYSHAVON MUSIC PUBLISHING (BMI), 530 Broadway St., Platteville WI 53818. (608)348-7419. E-mail: Topcat@mhct.net. **Contact:** Christopher Isabell, owner. Music Publisher. Estab. 2001. Pays standard royalty.
How to Contact: Submit demo tape by mail. Unsolicited submissions are OK. Prefers cassette or CD with 5 songs and lyric and lead sheet. "Please copyright your songs." Include SASE. Responds in 1 month.
Music: All types.
Tips: "Make sure your song is well written with a professional demo. We need hits. Also, please read all you can about the music industry."

 LAKE TRANSFER PRODUCTIONS & MUSIC (ASCAP, BMI), 11300 Hartland St., North Hollywood CA 91605. (818)508-7158. **Contact:** Jim Holvay, professional manager (pop, R&B, soul); Tina Antoine (hip-hop, rap); Steve Barri Cohen (alternative rock, R&B). Music publisher and record producer (Steve Barri Cohen). Estab. 1989. Publishes 11 songs/year; publishes 3 new songwriters/ year. Staff size: 6. Pay "depends on agreement, usually 50% split."
Affiliate(s): Lake Transfer Music (ASCAP) and Transfer Lake Music (BMI).
How to Contact: *Does not accept unsolicited submissions.*
Music: Mostly **alternative pop**, **R&B/hip-hop** and **dance**. Does not want country & western, classical, New Age, jazz or swing. Published "Here On Out" (single by Rico/The "SBC") from *The Movement* (album), recorded by Rico (rap/hip-hop), released 2002 on Lost Empire/Interscope; "Beautiful Woman" (single by Patrice Rushen/Sheree Brown/The "SBC") from *Beautiful Women the Album* (album), recorded by SBPR, Sisters Being Positively Real (hip-hop/soul), released 2001 by Brown Baby/Hidden Beach; "It's Not Fair" (single by M. Weitzel/The "SBC"/Rico) from *TBA* (album), recorded by TBA (Latina/hip-hop), released 2002 by Lost Empire/Interscope.
Tips: "All our staff are songwriters/producers. Jim Holvay has written hits like 'Kind of a Drag' and 'Hey Baby They're Playin our Song' for the Buckinghams. Steve Barri Cohen has worked with every one from Evelyn 'Champaigne' King, Patrice Rushen to Phantom Planets (Geffen)." "Good songs are not enough—you must be a complete artist and writer."

 LARI-JON PUBLISHING (BMI), 325 W. Walnut, Rising City NE 68658. (402)542-2336. **Contact:** Larry Good, owner. Music publisher, record company (Lari-Jon Records), management

FOR EXPLANATIONS OF THESE SYMBOLS,
SEE THE INSIDE FRONT AND BACK COVERS OF THIS BOOK.

firm (Lari-Jon Promotions) and record producer (Lari-Jon Productions). Estab. 1967. Publishes 20 songs/year; publishes 2-3 new songwriters/year. Staff size: 1. Pays standard royalty.

How to Contact: Submit demo tape by mail. Unsolicited submissions are OK. Prefers cassette with 5 songs and lyric sheet. "Be professional." Include SASE. Responds in 2 months.

Music: Mostly **country**, **Southern gospel** and **'50s rock**. Does not want rock, hip-hop, pop or heavy metal. Published "Bluegrass Blues" and "Carolina Morning" (singles by Larry Good) from *Carolina Morning* (album), recorded by Blue Persuasion (country), released 2002 by Bullseye; "Those Rolling Hills of Glenwood" (single by Tom Campbell) from *Single* (album), recorded by Tom Campbell (country), released 2001 by Jeffs-Room-Productions.

☑ ◯ **TRIXIE LEIGH MUSIC**, 1728 Crimson Tree Way #D, Edgewood MD 21040. (410)538-8262. **Contact:** Rick Solimini, Music Publisher. E-mail: cherasnyelijah@webtv.net. Music publisher and record company (Cherasny Records). Estab. 1997. Publishes 4 songs/year; publishes 4 new songwriters/year. Hires staff writers. Staff size: 4. Pays standard royalty.

How to Contact: *Write first and obtain permission to submit.* Prefers cassette with 3 songs and lyric and lead sheets. Include SASE. Responds in 1 month.

Music: **Contemporary Christian**. Does not want secular, rap, opera or hard rock. Published *Paid In Full* (album), recorded by Redemption (contemporary Christian), released 2001 on Cherasny Records.

Tips: "Be consistent in learning the craft of songwriting."

☑ ◯ **LES MUSIC GROUP**, 6301 N. O'Connor, Irving TX 75039. E-mail: chris@dallastexas.cc. Website: www.studiosatlascolinas.com. Professional Managers: Chris Christian (pop/Christian); Sharon Clark. Music publisher, record company and record producer. Estab. 1981. Publishes 2,000 songs/year. Staff size: 35. Hires staff songwriters. Pays standard royalty.

Affiliate(s): Home Sweet Home Music/Bug and Bear Music (ASCAP), Chris Christian Music (BMI) and Monk and Tid (SESAC).

How to Contact: Submit demo tape by mail. Unsolicited submissions are OK. Prefers CD, DAT or videocassette. Include name, phone number and e-mail on CD or tape. Does not return material. Responds if interested.

Music: Does not want quartet music.

Tips: "Keep writing until you get good at your craft. Co-write with the best you can—always put phone number on tape or CD's."

◢ **LEXINGTON ALABAMA MUSIC PUBLISHING (BMI)**, 3596 County Rd. 136, Lexington AL 35648. Phone/fax: (256)229-8814. Email: LampMusic@cs.com. **Contact:** Darrell Glover, owner. Professional Managers: Roy Crabb (R&B); Ann Glover (country); Grady Glover (rock). Music publisher and record company (Lamp Records). Estab. 1981. Publishes 35 songs/year; publishes 5 new songwriters/year. Staff size: 4. Pays standard royalty.

Affiliate(s): Northwest Alabama Music Publishing (BMI).

How to Contact: Submit demo tape by mail. Unsolicited submissions are OK. Prefers CD or CD-R with 3 songs, lyric sheet and cover letter. "Find a new way of expressing old ideas." Does not return material. Responds only if interested.

Music: Mostly **country**, **southern rock** and **R&B**; also **comedy**, **gospel** and **Christmas**. Does not want rap, hard rock and classical. Published "Candlelight Opera" (single), written and recorded by Mark Narmore (country); *Let's Make the World Noisy* (album by Curtis Hall), recorded by Apul (rock), both released 2000 on Lamp Records; and "He Pours Out His Spirit" (single), written and recorded by Gary Springer (gospel), released 2001 on Lamp Records.

◪ ▨ ◢ **LILLY MUSIC PUBLISHING (SOCAN)**, 61 Euphrasia Dr., Toronto, Ontario M6B 3V8 Canada. (416)782-5768. Fax: (416)782-7170. **Contact:** Panfilo DiMatteo, president. Music publisher and record company (P. & N. Records). Estab. 1992. Publishes 20 songs/year; publishes 8 new songwriters/year. Staff size: 3. Pays standard royalty.

Affiliate(s): San Martino Music Publishing and Paglieta Music Publishing (CMRRA).
How to Contact: Submit demo tape by mail. Unsolicited submissions are OK. Prefers cassette (or videocassette if available) with 3 songs and lyric and lead sheets. "We will contact you only if we are interested in the material." Responds in 1 month.
Film & TV: Places 12 songs in film/year.
Music: Mostly **dance**, **ballads** and **rock**; also **country**. Published *Only This Way* (album), recorded by Zoe Skylar (dance), released on P&N Records.

☑ ◑ **LINEAGE PUBLISHING CO. (BMI)**, P.O. Box 211, East Prairie MO 63845. (573)649-2211. **Contact:** Tommy Loomas, professional manager. Staff: Alan Carter and Joe Silver. Music publisher, record producer, management firm (Staircase Promotions) and record company (Capstan Record Production). Pays standard royalty.
How to Contact: Submit demo tape by mail. Unsolicited submissions are OK. Prefers cassette with 2-4 songs and lyric sheet; include bio and photo if possible. Include SASE. Responds in 2 months.
Music: Mostly **country**, **easy listening**, **MOR**, **country rock** and **top 40/pop**. Published "Let It Rain" (single by Roberta Boyle), recorded by Vicarie Arcoleo on Treasure Coast Records; "Country Boy" (single), written and recorded by Roger Lambert; and "Boot Jack Shuffle" (single by Zachary Taylor), recorded by Skid Row Joe, both on Capstan Records.

N LITA MUSIC (ASCAP), 2831 Dogwood Place, Nashville TN 37204. (615)269-8682. Fax: (615)269-8929. Website: http://songsfortheplanet.com. **Contact:** Justin Peters, president. Music publisher. Estab. 1980.
Affiliate(s): Justin Peters Music, Platinum Planet Music and Tourmaline (BMI).
How to Contact: Submit demo by mail. Unsolicited submissions are OK. Prefers CD with 5 songs and lyric sheet. Does not return material. "Place code '2003' on each envelope submission."
Music: Mostly **Southern gospel/Christian** and **country**; also **classic rock**. Published "No Less Than Faithful" (single by Don Pardoe/Joel Lyndsey), recorded by Ann Downing on Daywind Records, Jim Bullard on Genesis Records and Melody Beizer (#1 song) on Covenant Records; "No Other Like You" (single by Mark Comden/Paula Carpenter), recorded by Twila Paris and Tony Melendez (#5 song) on Starsong Records; "Making A New Start" and "Invincible Faith" (singles by Gayle Cox), recorded by Kingdom Heirs on Sonlite Records; and "I Don't Want To Go Back" (single by Gail Cox), recorded by Greater Vision on Benson Records.

◑ **HAROLD LUICK & ASSOCIATES MUSIC PUBLISHER (BMI)**, P.O. Box 368, Carlisle IA 50047. (515)989-3748. Fax: (515)989-0235. E-mail: haroldl@cmshowcase.org. Website: www.cm showcase.org. President (country, bluegrass, blues, contemporary Christian): Harold L. Luick. Vice President (cajun, gospel, country, blues): Barbara A. Luick. Professional Manager: Frank Gallagher (MOR, contemporary country). Music publisher, record company, record producer and music industry consultant. Publishes 25-30 songs/year; publishes 5-10 new songwriters/year. Pays standard royalty.
How to Contact: *Write or call first about your interest, or for more information on CMSI.* Prefers cassette with 3-5 songs and lyric sheet. Include SASE. Responds in 3 weeks.
  ● Harold Luick & Associates is now owned and operated by Country Music Showcase International Inc.
Music: Mostly **traditional country** and **hard core country**. Does not want hip-hop or rap. Published "Ballad of Deadwood L.P." (single), written and recorded by Don Laughlin on Kajac Records (historical country); "He Thought She Always Knew" (single by Frank Gallagher/Scott Hoff), recorded by Scott Hoff (country), released 2000 on Door Knob Records; and "Adios, Sayonara, Goodbye" (single by Hank Sasaki/Frank Gallagher), recorded by Hank Sasaki (Japanese EMI country artist), released 2000 on EMI Japan. (Note: mp3 samples available at www.cmsh owcase.org/setarecord.htm.)

Tips: "It takes just as much of your time and money to pitch a good song as a bad one, so concentrate on the potential of the good ones. Join nonprofit educational songwriters associations (like CMSI) that can help you write better songs through critiques, evaluations, seminars and workshops."

N ⚪ M & T WALDOCH PUBLISHING, INC. (BMI), 4803 S. Seventh St., Milwaukee WI 53221. (414)482-2194. VP, Creative Management (rockabilly, pop, country): Timothy J. Waldoch. Professional Manager (country, top 40): Mark T. Waldoch. Music publisher. Estab. 1990. Publishes 2-3 songs/year; publishes 2-3 new songwriters/year. Staff size: 2. Pays standard royalty.
How to Contact: Submit demo tape by mail. Unsolicited submissions are OK. Prefers cassette with 3-6 songs and lyric or lead sheet. "We prefer a studio produced demo tape." Include SASE. Responds in 3 months.
Music: Mostly **country/pop**, **rock**, **top 40 pop**; also **melodic metal**, **dance**, **R&B**. Does not want rap. Published "It's Only Me" and "Let Peace Rule the World" (by Kenny LePrix), recorded by Brigade on SBD Records (rock).
Tips: "Study the classic pop songs from the 1950s through the present time. There is a reason why good songs stand the test of time. Today's hits will be tomorrow's classics. Send your *best* well-crafted, polished song material."

N ⚪ MAJOR ENTERTAINMENT (BMI), (formerly Majestic Control), 331 W. 57th St. #173, New York NY 10019. (212)489-1500. Fax: (212)489-5660. E-mail: info@majorentertainment.com. CEO: Matt "Half Pint" Davis. President: Tatiana Sampson. Music publisher, promotions and public relations. Estab. 1983.
How to Contact: Submit demo tape by mail. Unsolicited submissions are OK. Prefers CD with 3 songs. Include SASE. Responds in 2 months.
Music: Mostly **rap** and **R&B**. Artists include Soul IV Real, Father MC and Tre-8.

✔ ⚪ MAKERS MARK GOLD (ASCAP), 534 W. Queen Lane, Philadelphia PA 19144. (215)849-7633. E-mail: MakersMark@verizon.net. Website: www.prolificrecords.com. Producer: Paul Hopkins. Music publisher and record producer. Estab. 1991. Pays standard royalty.
How to Contact: Submit demo CD or tape by mail. Unsolicited submissions are OK. Prefers 2-4 songs. Does not return material. Responds in 6 weeks if interested.
Music: Mostly **R&B**, **hip-hop**, **gospel**, **pop** and **house**. Published "Silent Love," "Why You Want My Love" and "Something for Nothing," (singles), written and recorded by Elaine Monk, released on Black Sands Records/Metropolitan Records; "Get Funky" (single), written and recorded by Larry Larr, released on Columbia Records; "He Made A Way" (single by Kenyatta Arrington); "We Give All Praises Unto God" (single by Jacqueline D. Pate); "I Believe He Will" (single by Pastor Alyn E. Waller); and "Psalms 146" (single by Rodney Roberson), all songs recorded by The Enon Tabernacle Mass Choir from *Pastor Alyn E. Waller Presents: The Enon Tabernacle Mass Choir*, released on ECDC Records (www.enontab.org).
Tips: "I prefer to work with those with representation."

⚐ ⚪ MANUITI L.A. (ASCAP), 4007 W. Magnolia Blvd., Burbank CA 91505. (818)843-2628. Fax: (818)843-4480. E-mail: manuitila@aol.com. **Contact:** Steven Rosen, president. Music publisher and record producer. "The exclusive music publishing company for writer/producer Guy Roche."
How to Contact: *Does not accept unsolicited material.*
Film & TV: Recently published "As If," recorded by Blaque in *Bring It On*; "Turn the Page," recorded by Aaliyah in *Music of the Heart*; and "While You Were Gone," recorded by Kelly Price in *Blue Streak*.
Music: Mostly **pop** and **R&B**. Published "What A Girl Wants," single recorded by Christina Aguilera (pop); "Almost Doesn't Count," single recorded by Brandy (R&B) on Atlantic; "Beauty," single recorded by Dru Hill (R&B) on Island; and "Under My Tree," single recorded by *NSync on RCA.

Tips: "Do your homework on who you are contacting and what they do. Don't waste yours or their time by not having that information."

MARKEA MUSIC/GINA PIE MUSIC (BMI, SESAC), P.O. Box 121396, Nashville TN 37212. (615)329-1111. Fax: (615)329-4121. E-mail: keatonmusic@mindspring.com. Professional Managers: Chris Keaton (country/folk/R&B); Kent Martin (folk/pop). Music publisher. Estab. 1995. Publishes 19 songs/year; publishes 1 new songwriter/year. Staff size: 2. Hires staff songwriters. Pays standard royalty.
Affiliate(s): Markea Music (BMI) and Gina Pie Music (SESAC).
How to Contact: *Call first and obtain permission to submit.* Prefers cassette or CD with 3 songs and lyric sheet. Does not return material. Responds in 6 weeks.
Film & TV: Places 1 song in film and 1 song in TV/year. Published "Keep Coming Back," written and recorded by Mike Younger in *Time of Your Life*; and "If By Chance . . .," written and recorded by Mike Younger in *A Galaxy, Far, Far Away.*
Music: Mostly **country**, **folk** and **pop**; also **R&B**. Published "I'm Happy" (single by Ronna Reeves/Tom McHugh) from *Ronna Reeves* (album), recorded by Ronna Reeves (pop/country), released 2000 on Hello.
Tips: "Send your best."

JOHN WELLER MARVIN PUBLISHING (ASCAP), 863 Sarcee Ave., Suite 1, Akron OH 44305. (330)733-8585. Fax: (330)733-8595. E-mail: stephanie_jwm@yahoo.com. **Contact:** Stephanie Arble, President. Music Publisher. Estab. 1996. Pays standard royalty.
How to Contact: Submit demo tape by mail. Unsolicited submissions are OK. Prefers cassette, CD or VHS and lyric or lead sheet. Responds in 6 weeks.
Music: All genres, mostly **pop**, **R&B**, **rap**; also **rock**, and **country**. Published "Downloading Files" (single by S. Arble/R. Scott), recorded by Ameritech Celebration Choir (corporate promotional). "We work with a promoter booking major label artists and with some television and corporate promotional recordings."

MASTER SOURCE (ASCAP, BMI), 13903 Sherman Way, Suite 14, Van Nuys CA 91405. (818)994-3400. Fax: (818)994-3443. E-mail: mastersource@mastersource.net. Website: www.mastersource.net. Owner: Marc Ferrari. Creative Director: Josh Kessler. Music publisher. Estab. 1993. Publishes 100 songs/year; publishes 20 new songwriters/year. Pays standard royalty.
Affiliate(s): Red Engine Music (ASCAP) and Revision West (BMI).
How to Contact: *Call first and obtain permission to submit.* Prefers CD with up to 5 songs and lyric sheet. No guaranteed response.
Film & TV: Published music for *As Good As It Gets* (film); *Wag The Dog* (film); and *Touched By An Angel* (TV).
Music: All contemporary styles. Mostly **reggae/salsa**, **rap/urban** and **ethnic**; also **country**, **jazz** and **world beat**.
Tips: "We specialize in film and TV placements. Master quality recordings a must!"

MAVERICK MUSIC, 8730 Sunset Blvd., Suite 420, Los Angeles CA 90069. (310)652-6300. Music publisher and record company (Maverick).
How to Contact: *Maverick Music does not accept unsolicited submissions.*

MAYFAIR MUSIC (BMI), 2600 John St., Unit 219, Markham, Ontario L3R 3W3 Canada. (905)475-1848. **Contact:** John Loweth, A&R director. Music publisher, record company (MBD

REFER TO THE GEOGRAPHIC INDEX (at the back of this book) to find listings of companies by state, as well as foreign listings.

insider report

Songwriter lands publishers through diligence and research

Charles Hurowitz had been writing songs for over twenty years when he recently decided to pursue publishing opportunities. "The rest," as his website says, "is history!" Seven of his songs have since been signed on with leading publishing companies, including Emstone Inc. Music Publishing and Transition Music Corporation.

Such success was a long time coming. Hurowitz started playing guitar at the age of twelve and began writing his own songs when he was sixteen. "Some of those early songs were, of course, not very good, but a few of them I actually rewrote into decent songs." Hurowitz kept writing, eventually amassing a catalog of almost thirty songs. "Over the years I always wanted to do something with them, but I never knew what to do. I

Charles Hurowitz

wanted to find a band or someone who could put these things down, make them sound good, just so I could hear what they sounded like on a professional recording." Realizing his strength lies in writing rather than performing, Hurowitz hired a live band to record a demo. "The owner of the studio also helped produce and arrange the tunes, made some suggestions, moved things around and changed things. We ended up doing twelve songs."

After recording the songs, Hurowitz began researching publishers by using, among other things, *Songwriter's Market*. "I thought what I really wanted to do was learn how to market my music, so I started going through *Songwriter's Market*, building spreadsheets to keep track of different publishers, the music they liked, names, and addresses," Hurowitz says. He then compiled a list of 150 publishers and sent demos to each, but didn't receive many responses at first. "I got smarter. In the beginning, I submitted to just anybody that would take a demo. Then I started always sending out cards or e-mails to ask if it was okay, even if they said unsolicited was okay. I found it was a lot more efficient; if they didn't answer, it wasn't worth it. And over the course of this, I started weeding out publishers that seemed small-time. I also began building lists and sending out demos based on publications by *Billboard* magazine, as well as various directories of film music supervisors. These resources opened up a whole new set of contacts, and initial feedback on demos has been real positive. Also, the Bandit Newsletter at www.banditnewsletter.com has been a great source of leads."

In addition to systematically researching *Songwriter's Market* and other directories, Hurowitz joined Nashville Songwriters Association (NSAI). Although their critiques are often harsh, he says, they are also beneficial. "It's still good to hear what they have to say; if they pick up on something, somebody else—a publisher for example—might have the same problem with the song." But he also takes those critiques with a grain of salt. "I have a song called 'The Agreement,' and NSAI trashed its story line. They said 'This is ridiculous!' Then a publisher sent me back a letter on the song, and although they didn't accept it, they said 'By the way, that's a great story line.' "

Hurowitz also uses the Internet as a promotional platform, maintaining a website, caseysong s.com, which features a bio and samples of his music. "But one of the problems I've found is that there aren't very many people in the industry who will go to your website," he says. "They want a submission on CD first. It would save a lot of problems and time and effort if I could get publishers or record producers to sample the tunes on the website, but it doesn't seem to attract publishers."

After signing a publishing deal, Hurowitz says one of the difficulties he has faced is the lack of information about the ongoing process of selling the song. "Once you sign a publishing deal, you don't get a lot of information. The publisher will tell me they're pushing the song, they're working on it, and they'll let me know. What I don't get is any more detail than that." His deal with Transition Music is one in which the publisher is specifically looking to place his songs in film or television, and Hurowitz has a piece of advice for beginning songwriters interested in a similar deal: make sure to obtain performance rights to the recordings on the demo. "When I first had my demos done, it didn't even occur to me to think about the performance rights to those actual recordings. But for film and television, usually they're interested in the finished product and they won't re-record the songs. I found out that I was nowhere if I didn't have full performance rights. Since it turned out the guys who did my demo had legitimate reasons they couldn't grant me full performance rights, I ended up having to go back to have songs redone to get performance rights."

He also advises beginners to keep track of their submissions. "Let's say I have twenty songs; you can usually send about three or four at a time. I wanted to make sure I knew exactly who I sent demos to and when. This also allows me to follow up. Many times publishers won't respond even if you include an SASE. If a month or two after you submit you give them a call, it sometimes pushes them to at least tell you where you stand."

Hurowitz admits that it can sometimes be difficult to find the right niche for your music, especially if you're writing in a genre with a smaller market. "It's frustrating that unless you're writing country or hip-hop, there's not as much market for you. I get a lot of positive response from people in the 40- to 50-year-old group who say, 'Hey, it's Beatles-like!' But that's both a plus and minus for me. Some people will say my music is too '60s and Beatles-ish." Even with the disappointment of rejection, he notes, beginning songwriters can still learn valuable lessons; it's a matter of finding the right kind of publisher. "There are a couple of publishers I enjoy working with, who, even when they reject my submissions, at least give me a feeling as to what's going on. I learn a lot from them.

But, in conjunction with his long-standing musical leanings, he has also come to recognize the value of collaboration. "I've been doing a lot more co-writing lately," he says. "It expands opportunities, opens up new ideas and even allows me to work in other genres. Right now, I'm doing lyrics for an R&B song and an AAA/MOR tune, and this is helping me expand beyond the rock genre."

Hurowitz has also pursued collaboration opportunities on the Internet, including member-ship in TAXI (www.taxi.com), Tonos (www.tonos.com) and Broadjam.com (www.broadjam. com). "Tonos has helped me make valuable connections with other songwriters all over the world," he says. "After joining Tonos, I was contacted by an Australian lyricist who had lyrics for a song called 'Adrenaline.' We collaborated on the song, posted on Tonos for a demo studio. We ended up with a great demo and what everyone says is my best song to date. We already have interest from publishers and a New York City entertainment law firm. I am also working with a Greek songwriter who needed English lyrics to his song. I wrote English lyrics to his melody, and we are getting ready to have the song recorded for a demo. We are very excited about marketing this one in the U.S. for film or TV."

"If you're really a beginner," Hurowitz says, "definitely get some feedback, whether it's by NSAI or another service. If you have a good song, get a really good demo made by a live band. You have to be committed!" And once you're ready to start submitting, know your market's needs; it can make the difference between a sale and a rejection. "At the time I submitted to Transition Music, they felt like they needed some '60s-style songs in their catalog. I hit them at the right time." With perseverance and intelligent marketing strategies, you can find the right place.

—Travis Adkins

Records), music print publisher (Music Box Dancer Publications), record producer and distributor. Member CMPA, CIRPA, CRIA. Estab. 1979. Publishes 20-30 songs/year; publishes 3-5 new songwriters/year. Pays standard royalty.

How to Contact: Submit demo CD/CDR by mail. Unsolicited submissions are OK. Prefers CD/CDR with 2-5 songs. Does not return material. Responds in 3 weeks.

Music: Mostly **instrumental**.

Tips: "Strong melodic choruses and original-sounding music receive top consideration."

⊘ MCA MUSIC PUBLISHING. 2440 Sepulveda Blvd., Suite 100, Los Angeles CA 90064. (310)235-4700. Fax: (310)235-4900.

● In 1999, MCA Music Publishing and PolyGram Music Publishing merged into Universal Music Publishing.

How to Contact: *MCA Music Publishing does not accept unsolicited submissions.*

☑ ☒ ☐ McCONKEY ARTISTS AGENCY MUSIC PUBLISHING (BMI), Hollywood Media Center Blgd., 1604 N. Cahuenga, Suite 108, Hollywood CA 90028-6267. (323)463-7141. Fax: (323)463-2558. E-mail: info@vinegowerrecords.com or mcconkeyagency@msn.com. Website: www .vinegowerrecords.com. **Contact:** Mack K. McConkey, managing director. Music publisher. Estab. 1998. Publishes 12 songs/year; publishes 5 new songwriters/year. Staff size: 5. Pays standard royalty.

Affiliate(s): Vinegower Music (ASCAP).

How to Contact: Submit CD by mail. Unsolicited submissions are OK. Prefers CD with 1-5 songs and lyric sheet and cover letter. "Please send us a professional CD, as well as a typed or computer-printed lyric sheet and cover letter." Does not return material. Responds in 6 months.

Film & TV: Places 2 songs in TV/year. Published "Freaky World" (single by Sosa/Keesee/McConkey), recorded by The Mess (alternative rock) in an indie film production *Employee of the Month* to be released 2002 and in a MTV series *The Osbournes* to be released 2002. Also published "Chinese Cowboy" (singles by Sosa/Keesee/McConkey), recorded by The Mass (alternative rock) in a MTV series *The Osbournes* to be released 2002.

Music: **All types**. Published "Oh Sweet Time" (single by Kevin Los) from *Strychnine: The First Hit*, recorded by Strychnine (modern rock), released 2001 on Vinegower Records; "All That You Are" (single by Kevin Kos) from *Strychnine II* (album), recorded by Strychnine (modern rock), released 2002 on Vinegower Records; and "Freaky World" (single by Nestor Sosa/John Keesee/Mack McConkey) from *The Mess*, recorded by The Mess (alternative), released 2002 on Vinegower Records.

Tips: "Provide the best quality package on your songs. Also send the songs you feel are hits. Do not bother sending album filler material."

☐ JIM McCOY MUSIC (BMI), Rt. 2, Box 2910, Berkeley Springs WV 25411. (304)258-9381. **Contact:** Bertha and Jim McCoy, Owners. Music publisher, record company (Winchester Records) and record producer (Jim McCoy Productions). Estab. 1973. Publishes 20 songs/year; publishes 3-5 new songwriters/year. Pays standard royalty.

Affiliate(s): New Edition Music (BMI).

How to Contact: Submit demo tape by mail. Unsolicited submissions are OK. Prefers cassette, 7½ or 15 ips reel-to-reel (or VHS or Beta videocassette) with 6 songs. Include SASE. Responds in 1 month.

Music: Mostly **country**, **country/rock** and **rock**; also **bluegrass** and **gospel**. Published "One Time" (single by T. Miller), recorded by J.B. Miller on Hilton Records (country); and "Like Always" (single by J. Alford), recorded by Al Hogan on Winchester Records (country).

N **⬛** **◎** **McJAMES MUSIC INC. (BMI)**, 1724 Stanford St., Suite B, Santa Monica CA 90404. Also: 701 Hollow Rd., Nashville TN 37205. (615)356-0094. E-mail: info@mcjamesmusic.com. Website: www.mcjamesmusic.com. Professional Managers: Tim James (country/pop); Steven McClintock (pop/country). Music publisher, record company (37 Records) and record producer (Steven McClintock). Estab. 1977. Publishes 10 songs/year. Staff size: 3. Pays standard royalty. Does administration and collection for all foreign markets for smaller publishers and writers.

Affiliate(s): 37 Records (ASCAP) and McJames Music, Inc. (BMI).

How to Contact: *Only accepts material referred by a reputable industry source.* Prefers cassette with 2 songs and cover letter. Does not return material. Responds in 6 months.

Film & TV: Places 2 songs in film and 3 songs in TV/year. Music Supervisor: Tim James. Recently published "Christmas Needs Love" (by S. McClintock), recorded by Andy Williams in Special; "Woman On the Run," written and recorded by Fran Lucci in Special; and "Blinded By Love," written and recorded by Paul Jefferson in CBS Movie of the Week. New feature release "A Little Inside" with three cuts by writers, "I Wanna Live Like That" by Cathy Anne Whitworth, "She's Way Too Cute for Him," by Matt and Gunner Nelson and "Look at Me Now" by Steve Mandile and Steve Mcclintock.

Music: Mostly **country**, **pop** and **dance**; also **bluegrass** and **alternative**. Does not want rap or classical. Published *That's What Love Is* (by S. McClintock/T. Douglas), recorded by Mark Vance (country) on Sony; *Keeps Bringing Me Back* (by S. McClintock/V. Shaw), recorded by Victoria Shaw (easy listening) on Taffita; and *Don't Let This Plan* (by S. McClintock/R. Irving), recorded by Steven McClintock (country) on 37 Records. Recent cover by ATC on BMG/Universal with "If Love is Blind," selling over 300,000 CDs in less than 6 months; single by new Warner Bros. act Six Wire called "Look At Me Now," recent duet by Victoria Shaw and Richard Schneider on Universal Holland with the song "Loved By You." Place three songs in the new Sony Play Station with the writer/artist Chad Petry.

Tips: "Write a song we don't have in our catalog or write an undeniable hit. We will know it when we hear it."

◻ **MELLOW HOUSE MUSIC (BMI)**, P.O. Box 423618, San Francisco CA 94142. (415)776-8430. **Contact:** Darren Brown, president. Music publisher, record company (Mellow House Recordings) and record producer. Estab. 1992. Publishes 10 songs/year; publishes 10 new songwriters/year. Hires staff writers. Staff size: 7. Pays standard royalty.

How to Contact: Submit demo tape by mail. Unsolicited submissions are OK. Prefers cassette, DAT or CD with 3 songs and lyric sheet. Include SASE. Responds in 2 months.

Music: Mostly **funk**, **R&B** and **hip-hop**; also **pop/rock**, **alternative jazz** and **gospel**. Published "Soul Reflection" and "Love Parade" (singles), both written and recorded by Bobby Beale on Mellow House Recordings (jazz).

◎ **MELODY HILLS RANCH PUBLISHING CO. (BMI)**, 804 N. Trenton, Ruston LA 71270. (318)255-7127. Fax: (318)255-3050. E-mail: melodyhills@altavista.com. Owners: Jim Ball and Jane Ball. Music publisher. Estab. 1996. Publishes 2-3 songs/year; publishes 1-2 new songwriters/year. Staff size: 5. Pays standard royalty.

OPENNESS TO SUBMISSIONS: ◻ beginners; ◖ beginners and experienced; ◖ experienced only; ◎ no unsolicited submissions/industry referrals only.

How to Contact: *Write first and obtain permission to submit.* Prefers cassette with 3-4 songs and lyric sheet. Does not return material. Responds in 6 weeks.
Music: Mostly **traditional country**, **southern rock** and **pop**. Does not want rap or rock. Published *Hungover Heart* and *Last Call for Alcohol* (albums), both written and recorded by Jim Ball; and *Peter Filed Chapter 13* and *Lovin' On* (albums), both written and recorded by Monty Russell on Melody Hills (traditional country).

⊕ ✓ ⬚ MENTO MUSIC GROUP, Symphony House, Winterhuder Weg 142, D-22085, Hamburg Germany. Phone: (040)22716552 + -53. Fax: (040)22716554. E-mail: mento_music@t-online. de. **Contact:** Arno H. Van Vught, general manager. Professional Manager: Michael Frommhold. Music publisher and record company (Playbones Records). Estab. 1970. Pays standard royalty.
Affiliate(s): Auteursunie, Edition Lamplight, Edition Melodisc, Massimo Jauch Music Productions and Marathon Music.
How to Contact: Submit demo tape by mail. Unsolicited submissions are OK. Prefers cassette with 3-4 songs. "Put your strongest/best song first. Put your name and address on the inside sleeve of the tape. If you have a fax number, inform us. Tell us in a typed cover letter what you want/what you are looking for." Does not return material. Responds in 3 weeks.
Music: Mostly **instrumental**, **pop**, **MOR**, **country**, **background music** and **film music**. Does not want classical. Published "Vergessen wir die Mark" (single by DP/Volker Frank), recorded by Volker Frank (pop), released 2001; *Paradise* (album), written and recorded by Anna C. Nova (pop), released 2001 on Playbones Records; *Lord of the Dance* (album), written and recorded by Wolfgang Bauer (world music), released 2001 on Playbones Records.

Ⓝ ⬚ ⬚ MIDI TRACK PUBLISHING (BMI)/ALLRS MUSIC PUBLISHING CO. (ASCAP), P.O. Box 1545, Smithtown NY 11787. (718)767-8995. E-mail: allrsmusic@aol.com. Website: www.geocities.com/allrsmusic. **Contact:** Renee Silvestri, president. Music publisher, record company (MIDI Track Records), music consultant, artist management. Voting member of NARAS (The Grammy Awards), CMA, SGMA, SGA. Estab. 1994. Staff size: 5. Publishes 3 songs/year; publishes 2 new songwriters/year. Pays standard royalty.
Affiliate(s): Midi-Track Publishing Co. (BMI).
How to Contact: *Call or e-mail first to obtain permission to submit.* Prefers CD or cassette with 3 songs, lyric sheet and cover letter. "Make sure your CD or cassette tape is labeled with your name, mailing address, telephone number, and e-mail address. We do not return material." Responds via e-mail in 3 months.
Film & TV: Places 1 song in film/year. Published "Why Can't You Hear My Prayer" (single by F. John Silvestri/Leslie Silvestri), recorded by Iliana Medina in a documentary by Silvermine Films.
Music: Mostly **country**, **gospel**, **top 40**, **r&b**, **MOR** and **pop**. Does not want showtunes, jazz, classical or rap. Published "Why Can't You Hear My Prayer" (single by F. John Silvestri/Leslie Silvestri), recorded by four-time Grammy nominee Huey Dunbar of the group DLG (Dark Latin Groove), released on Trend Records (other multiple releases, also recorded by Iliana Medina and released 2002 on MIDI Track Records); "Chasing Rainbows" (single by F. John Silvestri/Leslie Silvestri), recorded by Tommy Cash (country), released on MMT Records (including other multiple releases); "Because of You" (single by F. John Silvestri/Leslie Silvestri), recorded by Iliana Medina, released 2002 on MIDI Track Records, also recorded by three-time Grammy nominee Terri Williams, released on KMA Records; also recorded by Vicki Leigh (country) from Grand Ole Opry member Ernie Ashworth's *Ernie Ashworth and Friends* (album), released 2001 on KMA Records; and "Why Do You Lie Next to Me" (single by F. John Silvestri/Leslie Silvestri), recorded by Terri Williams, released 2002 on International Productions.
Tips: "Attend workshops, seminars, join songwriters organizations and keep writing, you will achieve your goal."

⬚ THE MIGHTY BLUE MUSIC MACHINE, 2016 Douglas Ave., Clearwater FL 33755. Fax: (727)449-8814. E-mail: mightyblue@earthlink.net. **Contact:** Tony Blue, GM. Music publisher. Estab. 1995. Staff size: 3-5. Pays standard royalty.
Affiliate(s): Earth Groovz (ASCAP) and Songs From Out of the Blue (BMI).

How to Contact: *Write first and obtain permission to submit.* Include SASE. "No phone calls, please." Prefers cassette or CD with 1-3 songs and lyric sheets. "Send 'studio' quality demo with typed lyric sheets." Include SASE. Responds in 3 months. "We do not return tapes or CDs."
Music: Mostly **rock (acoustic)**, **country** and **pop**; also **blues**, **Christian/gospel**, **R&B**, **jazz** and **dance**. Does not want violent lyrics. "Be positive—be original."
Tips: "Submit only professional 'studio' quality demos (invest in your craft) and be very patient."

N ⊘ **MONK FAMILY MUSIC GROUP (ASCAP, BMI, SESAC)**, P.O. Box 150768, Nashville TN 37215-0768. (615)292-6811. Fax: (615)292-7266. **Contact:** Irving Telder or McKenna Monk, professional managers. Music publisher. Estab. 1983. Hires staff songwriters. Pays standard royalty.
Affiliate(s): Charlie Monk Music (ASCAP), Monk Family Music (BMI), and Monkids Music (SESAC).
• Received the 1998 "Publisher of the Year" Award from SESAC and the 2001 Performance Award from ASCAP.
How to Contact: *Contact first and obtain permission to submit.* "We only accept material referred to us by a reputable industry source (manager, entertainment attorney, etc.)" Does not return submissions.
Music: Mostly **country**. Published "Kiss This" (single by Philip Douglas/Thea Tippin/Aaron Tippin) from *People Like Us* (album), recorded by Aaron Tippin (country), released 2000 on Lyric Street; "Commitment" (single by Tony Martin/Bubby Wood/Tony Colton) from *Sittin' On Top of the World* (album), recorded by Leann Rimes (country), released 1998 on Curb Records; and "Until We Fall Back In Love Again" (single by Philip Douglas/Jim Weatherly/Jeff Carson) from *Real Life* (album), recorded by Jeff Carson (country), released 2001 on Curb Records.

⋮⋮ ◐ **MONTINA MUSIC (SOCAN)**, Box 702, Snowdon Station, Montreal, Quebec H3X 3X8 Canada. **Contact:** David P. Leonard, professional manager. Music publisher and record company (Monticana Records). Estab. 1963. Pays negotiable royalty.
Affiliate(s): Saber-T Music (SOCAN).
How to Contact: *Write first and obtain permission to submit or submit demo tape by mail.* Unsolicited submissions are OK. Prefers CD, cassette, phonograph record or VHS videocassette. SAE and IRC. Responds in 3 months.
Music: Mostly **top 40**; also **bluegrass**, **blues**, **country**, **dance-oriented**, **easy listening**, **folk**, **gospel**, **jazz**, **MOR**, **progressive**, **R&B**, **rock** and **soul**. Does not want heavy metal, hard rock, jazz, classical or New Age.
Tips: "Maintain awareness of styles and trends of your peers who have succeeded professionally. Understand the markets to which you are pitching your material. Persevere at marketing your talents. Develop a network of industry contacts, first locally, then regionally, nationally and internationally."

◻ **MOON JUNE MUSIC (BMI)**, 4233 SW Marigold, Portland OR 97219. (507)777-4621. Fax: (503)277-4622. **Contact:** Bob Stoutenburg, President. Music publisher. Estab. 1971. Staff size: 1. Pays standard royalty.
How to Contact: Submit demo tape by mail. Unsolicited submissions are OK. Prefers cassette or CD with 2-10 songs. Include SASE. Responds in 6 weeks.
Music: Mostly **country**, **top 40**, **blues**, **Christmas** and **novelty**. Does not want rap, Christian, world, folk or New Age.

⊘ **THE MUSIC BRIDGE (ASCAP, BMI)**, P.O. Box 661918, Los Angeles CA 90066-1918. (310)398-9650. Fax: (310)398-4850. E-mail: thebridge@aol.com. Website: http://themusicbridge.com. **Contact:** David G. Powell, president. Music publisher and music supervision. Estab. 1992.

THE OPENNESS TO SUBMISSIONS INDEX at the back of this book lists all companies in this section by how open they are to submissions.

How to Contact: *Only accepts material referred by a reputable industry source.* Does not return material. Responds in 2 months.

◉ THE MUSIC ROOM PUBLISHING GROUP, P.O. Box 219, Redondo Beach CA 90277. (310)316-4551. **Contact:** John Reed, president/owner. Music publisher and record producer. Estab. 1982. Pays standard royalty.
Affiliate(s): MRP (BMI).
How to Contact: *Not accepting unsolicited material.*
Music: Mostly **pop/rock/R&B** and **crossover**.

◖ MUSIKUSER PUBLISHING (ASCAP), 15030 Ventura Blvd., Suite 425, Sherman Oaks CA 91403. (818)783-2182. Fax: (818)783-3204. E-mail: musikuser@aol.com. **Contact:** John Sloate, president. Music publisher. Estab. 1974. Publishes 20 songs/year; publishes 3 new songwriters/year. Pays standard royalty.
How to Contact: *Write first and obtain permission to submit.* "No phone calls." Prefers DAT with lyric and lead sheet. Does not return material.
Music: All styles. Published *Thief of Hearts* (album by Hattler/Kraus), recorded by Tina Turner on Virgin Records.

▣ ◉ NAKED JAIN RECORDS (ASCAP), P.O. Box 4132, Palm Springs CA 92263-4132. (760)325-8663. Fax: (760)320-4305. E-mail: info@nakedjainrecords.com. Website: www.nakedjainr ecords.com. **Contact:** Dena Banes, vice president/A&R. Music publisher, record company and record producer (Dey Martin). Estab. 1991. Publishes 40 songs/year; publishes 2 new songwriters/year. Staff size: 5. Pays standard royalty.
Affiliate(s): Aven Deja Music (ASCAP).
How to Contact: *Write or call first and obtain permission to submit or to arrange personal interview.* Prefers cassette or CD with 3 songs, lyric sheet and cover letter. Does not return material. Responds in 2 weeks.
Film & TV: Places 10 songs in TV/year. Music Supervisors: Dey Martin (alternative). Recently published "Yea Right" (single), written and recorded by Lung Cookie in Fox Sports TV; "Just Ain't Me" (single), written and recorded by Lung Cookie in ESPN-TV; and "Speak Easy" (single), written and recorded by Lung Cookie in ESPN-TV.
Music: Mostly **alternative rock**. Does not want country.
Tips: "Write a good song."

▣ ⊕ ◻ NERVOUS PUBLISHING, 5 Sussex Crescent, Northolt, Middx. UB5 4DL England. Phone: +44(0208)423 7373. Fax: +44(0208)423 7773. E-mail: nervous@compuserve.com. Website: www.nervous.co.uk. **Contact:** Roy Williams, owner. Music publisher, record company (Nervous Records) and record producer. MCPS, PRS and Phonographic Performance Ltd. Estab. 1979. Publishes 100 songs/year; publishes 25 new songwriters/year. Pays standard royalty; royalties paid directly to US songwriters.
 ● Nervous Publishing's record label, Nervous Records, is listed in the Record Companies
   section.
How to Contact: Submit demo tape by mail. Unsolicited submissions are OK. Prefers cassette with 3-10 songs and lyric sheet. "Include letter giving your age and mentioning any previously published material." SAE and IRC. Responds in 3 weeks.
Music: Mostly **psychobilly**, **rockabilly** and **rock** (impossibly fast music—e.g.: Stray Cats but twice as fast); also **blues**, **country**, **R&B** and **rock** ('50s style). Published *Trouble*, recorded by Dido Bonneville (rockabilly); *Rockabilly Comp*, recorded by various artists; and *Nervous Singles Collection*, recorded by various artists, all on Nervous Records.
Tips: "Submit *no* rap, soul, funk—we want *rockabilly.*"

▣ ◻ NEW CLARION MUSIC GROUP (ASCAP, BMI, SESAC), P.O. Box 158518, Nashville TN 37215. Phone/fax: (615)269-8669. **Contact:** Sue K. Patton, CEO/president. Music Publisher, record producer. Estab. 1984.

Affiliate(s): Lac Grand Musique, Inc., Golden Reed Music, Inc., Little Admiral Music (ASCAP); Lac de Charles Musique, Inc., Triumvirate Music, Inc., Little General Music (BMI); Grand Staff Music, Inc. (SESAC).

- New Clarion Music Group has received a number of ASCAP and BMI song awards, in addition to Grammy nominations.

How to Contact: *Write first to obtain permission to submit a demo.* Prefers cassette, CD, or DAT with 3 songs and lyric sheet. Include SASE. Responds in 6 weeks.

Music: Mostly **country**, **adult contemporary** and **pop/rock**. "We are also interested in anything superior. Send what you consider your best material, regardless of genre. A work tape with guitar or piano and vocal is fine; a demo is not necessary. If it's a hit, we'll hear it."

Tips: "Write from the heart, but write smartly. Work diligently on your craft. Keep in touch. Perseverance and progress are everything. Be open to an outside opinion of your work and consider suggestions for improvement."

☑ ⊘ **A NEW RAP JAM PUBLISHING**, P.O. Box 683, Lima OH 45802. E-mail: just_chilling_2 002@yahoo.com. Professional Managers: William Roach (rap, clean); James Milligan (country, 70s music, pop). **Contact:** A&R Dept. Music publisher and record company (New Experience/Grand Slam Records and Pump It Up Records). Estab. 1989. Publishes 30 songs/year; publishes 2-3 new songwriters/year. Hires staff songwriters. Staff size: 6. Pays standard royalty.

Affiliate(s): Party House Publishing (BMI) and Creative Star Management.

How to Contact: *Write first to arrange personal interview or submit demo tape by mail.* Unsolicited submissions are OK. Prefers cassette with 3-5 songs and lyric or lead sheet. Include SASE. Responds in 5 weeks.

Music: Mostly **R&B**, **pop** and **rock/rap**; also **contemporary**, **gospel**, **country** and **soul**. Published "Can't Play a Playa" and "Get Your Own" (singles by David Fawcett) from *Enter the Mind* (album), recorded by Devious 01 (rap), released 2002 on Pump It Up Records; "The Broken Hearted" (single by Carl Milligan/James Milligan) from *The Final Chapter* (album), recorded by T.M.C. the milligan conection (r&b gospel), released 2001/2002 on New Experience/Pump It Up Records.

Tips: "We are seeking hit artists of the 1970s and 1980s who would like to be re-signed, as well as new talent and female solo artists. Send any available information supporting the group or act. We are a label that does not promote violence, drugs or anything that we feel is a bad example for our youth. Establish music industry contacts, write and keep writing and most of all believe in yourself. Use a good recording studio but be very professional. Just take your time and produce the best music possible. Sometimes you only get one listen. Make sure you place your best song on your demo first. This will increase your chances greatly. If you're the owner of your own small label and have a finished product, please send it. And if there is interest we will contact you."

⊘ **NORTHWEST ALABAMA MUSIC PUBLISHING CO. (BMI)**, 3596 County Rd. 136, Lexington AL 35648. Phone/fax: (256)229-8814. E-mail: LampMusic@cs.com. Professional Managers: Erica Hand (country, soft rock); Kimberley Glover (gospel, R&B); D. Glover (rock, pop). Music Publisher and record company (Harmony House Records). Estab. 2000. Publishes 10 songs/year; publishes 2 new songwriters/year. Staff size: 3. Hires staff writers. Pays standard royalty.

Affiliate(s): Lexington Alabama Music Publishing (BMI).

How to Contact: Submit demo tape by mail. Unsolicited submissions are OK. Prefers cassette or CD with 3 songs, a lyric sheet and cover letter. "If you send unsolicited materials please label it as such in correspondence. List the name of your manager or contact person and the phone number as well as address with SASE for response." Does not return material. Responds only if interested.

Music: Mostly **country**, **pop** and **rock**; also **R&B**, **gospel** and **southern rock**. Does not want classical. Published "Let It Go" (single by Mark Terry), recorded by Mark Anthony (country); "Heirlooms" (single), written and recorded by Kellie Flippo (pop); and "Southern Girls" (single by Teena Hartsfield), recorded by Rex & the Rockets (R&B), all released 2000 on Harmony House Records.

Tips: "Don't try to critique your own songs."

⊠ ⊘ **OLD SLOWPOKE MUSIC (BMI)**, P.O. Box 52681, Tulsa OK 74152. (918)742-8087. E-mail: ryoung@cherrystreetrecords.com. Website: www.cherrystreetrecords.com. **Contact:** Steve

Hickerson, Professional Manager. President: Rodney Young. Music publisher and record producer. Estab. 1977. Publishes 24-36 songs/year; publishes 2-3 new songwriters/year. Staff size: 2. Pays standard royalty.

How to Contact: *Does not accept unsolicited submissions.*

Film & TV: Places 1 song in film/year. Recently published "Samantha," written and recorded by George W. Carroll in *Samantha*.

Music: Mostly **rock**, **country** and **R&B**; also **jazz**. Published *Promise Land* (album), written and recorded by Richard Neville on Cherry Street Records (rock).

Tips: "Write great songs. We sign only artists who play an instrument, sing and write songs."

◯ **ONTRAX COMPANIES (ASCAP)**, P.O. Box 769, Crown Point IN 46308. (219)736-5815. **Contact:** Professional Manager. Music publisher and record producer. Estab. 1991. Publishes 30 songs/year; 7 new songwriters/year. Staff size: 7. Pays standard royalty.

How to Contact: Submit demo tape by mail. Unsolicited submissions are OK. Prefers CD (but will accept cassette) with 1-6 songs. "Tapes should be mailed in as small a package as possible, preferrably in a small bubble mailer. All items must be labeled and bear the proper copyright notice. We listen to all submissions in the order they arrive. No phone calls please." Does not return submissions. Responds only if interested.

Music: Mostly **pop/rock**, **country** and **crossover country**. Does not want heavy metal or rap. Published "Worlds Will Collide" (single by E. Casper/J. Porte) from *Win-Win* (album), recorded by Maowna (pop/rock), released 2001 on Simpletoon; "Heart Don't Fail Me Now" (single by D. Archer/S.B. Mesich/B. Auburn) from *Tolling Belle* (album), recorded by Southern Fried (country), released 2001 on Songmill; and "The Morning After Noon" (single by M. Carlson/M.T. Kitsler) from *Cold November Rain* (album), recorded by All Picked Out (crossover country), released 2001 on Staff.

Tips: "Please do not include SASEs or response cards. We will not respond unless interested in publishing the song. You need not request permission to submit. Again, small packages please, 6×9 maximum."

◢ **ORCHID PUBLISHING (BMI)**, Bouquet-Orchid Enterprises, P.O. Box 1335, Norcross GA 30091. (770)814-2420. **Contact:** Bill Bohannon, president. Music publisher, record company, record producer (Bouquet-Orchid Enterprises) and artist management. Member: CMA, AFM. Publishes 10-12 songs/year; publishes 3 new songwriters/year. Pays standard royalty.

How to Contact: Submit demo tape by mail. Unsolicited submissions are OK. Prefers cassette or CD with 3-5 songs and lyric sheet. "Send biographical information if possible—even a photo helps." Include SASE. Responds in 1 month.

Music: Mostly **religious** ("Amy Grant, etc., contemporary gospel"); **country** ("Garth Brooks, Trisha Yearwood-type material"); and **top 100/pop** ("Bryan Adams, Whitney Houston-type material"). Published "Blue As Your Eyes" (single), written and recorded by Adam Day; "Spare My Feelings" (single by Clayton Russ), recorded by Terri Palmer; and "Trying to Get By" (single by Tom Sparks), recorded by Bandoleers, all on Bouquet Records.

🅽◯ **OYSTER BAY MUSIC PUBLISHING (BMI)**, 504 Northridge Oval, Cleveland OH 44144-3256. **Contact:** Daniel Bischoff, professional manager. Music Publisher. Estab. 1990. Publishes 6 new songwriters/year. Staff size: 2. Pays standard royalty.

Affiliate(s): East Meadow Music Publishing Company (ASCAP).

How to Contact: Submit demo tape by mail. Unsolicited submissions are OK. Prefers cassette, CD/CDR, or videotape with 2 songs on tape or 6 songs on CD and lyric sheet and cover letter. Include SASE. Responds in one month.

Music: Mostly **country**, **rap** and **pop/rock**; also **blues** and **r&b**. Recently published "Just A Simple Bouquet" (single by Daniel Workman and Jim Ward) and "The King Went On A Journey" (single by Marjorie Lambert) from *Johnny Wright* (album), recorded by Johnny Wright (country), released 2002 on DTM Records.

Tips: "Please send your best songs."

⊕ ▣ ⊘ **PAS MAL PUBLISHING SARL**, 283 Fbg St. Antoine, Paris 75020 France. Phone: 011(33)1 43485151. Fax: 011(33)1 43485753. E-mail: patrickjammes@compuserve.com. Website: www.intoxygene.com or www.theyounggods.com. **Contact:** Jammes Patrick, managing director. Music publisher. Estab. 1990. Staff size: 2. Publishes 5-10 songs/year. Pays 60% royalty.
How to Contact: *Does not accept unsolicited submissions.*
Film & TV: Places 3 songs in film and 2 songs in TV/year.
Music: Mostly **new industrial** and **metal**. Does not want country, pop or jazz. Published *Second Nature Lucidogen Astromic* (album), written and recorded by The Young Gods (alternative), released October 2000 on Intoxygene.

◯ **PECOS VALLEY MUSIC (BMI)**, 2709 W. Pine Lodge, Roswell NM 88201. (505)622-2008. E-mail: willmon5@bigfoot.com. **Contact:** Ray Willmon, president. Professional Manager: Jack Bush. Music publisher. Estab. 1989. Publishes 10-15 songs/year; publishes 2-3 new songwriters/year. Staff size: 3. Pays standard royalty.
How to Contact: Submit demo tape with lyrics by mail. Unsolicited demos are OK. "No phone calls please. No demo tapes will be returned unless we offer you a contract."
Music: Country music only please. Does not want rock & roll. Published "Wait on Me" (single), written and recorded by Mel Farmer (country); and "So It's Over" (single), written and recorded by Joe Farmer (country), both on SunCountry Records.
Tips: "Listen to what's being recorded today and write with these in mind. Learn proper song structure (AAAA, ABAB, AABA, etc.) Make the best demo you can."

⊕ ☑ ◉ **PEGASUS MUSIC**, P.O. Box 127, Otorohanga 2564, New Zealand. E-mail: peg.music @xtra.co.nz. Professional Managers: Errol Peters (country, rock); Ginny Peters (gospel, pop). Music publisher and record company. Estab. 1981. Publishes 20-30 songs/year; publishes 5 new songwriters/year. Pays standard royalty.
How to Contact: Submit demo tape by mail. Unsolicited submissions are OK. Prefers cassette with 3-5 songs and lyric sheet. SAE and IRC. Responds in 1 month.
Music: Mostly **country**; also **bluegrass**, **easy listening** and **top 40/pop**. Published "Rocking Horse" (single by Ginny Peters) from *The Land of Waltzing Matilda* (album), recorded by Brian Letton (country), released 2001 on LBS; "Before I Say Goodbye" (single by Yvonne Marsh) from *Faded Love* (album), recorded by Dennis Marsh (MOR), released 2001 on Manuka; and "We Almost Touched" (single by Russ Rouselle/Ginny Peters) from *The Northern United Steel Company* (album), recorded by Russ Rouselle (country), released 2001 on Rooster Records.
Tips: "Get to the meat of the subject without too many words. Less is better."

▣ ◯ **PEN MUSIC GROUP, INC. (ASCAP, BMI, SESAC, CCLI)**, 1608 N. Las Palmas Ave., Los Angeles CA 90028-6112. (323)993-6542. Fax: (323)468-0519. E-mail: submission@penmusic.com. Website: www.penmusic.com. Professional Managers: Jennifer Herbig, manager film & TV (film & TV); Michael Eames, president (all styles). **Contact:** Karri Bowman, office manager. Music publisher and publishing administrator. Estab. 1994. Publishes 100 songs/year; publishes 15 new songwriters/year. Staff size: 5. Pay varies depending on situation.
Affiliate(s): Pensive Music (ASCAP) and Penname Music (BMI).
How to Contact: *E-mail or write first and obtain permission to submit.*
Film & TV: Places over 200 songs in various projects per year.
Music: Publishes **all styles** of music with songs on both major label and independent releases worldwide.
Tips: "Present yourself professionally and then let the music speak for itself."

☑ ⊘ **PERLA MUSIC (ASCAP)**, 122 Oldwick Rd., Whitehouse Station NJ 08889-5014. (908)439-2336. Fax: (908)439-9119. E-mail: perlamusic@pmrecords.org. Website: www.pmrecords.org. **Contact:** Gene Perla (jazz). Music publisher, record company (P.M. Records, Inc.), record producer (BPProductions.org) and Internet Design and Hosting. Estab. 1971. Publishes 5 songs/year. Staff size: 1. Pays 75%/25% royalty.
Music: Mostly **jazz**.

◑JUSTIN PETERS MUSIC (BMI), P.O. Box 271056, Nashville TN 37227. (615)269-8682. Fax: (615)269-8929. Website: http://songsfortheplanet.com. **Contact:** Justin Peters, president. Music publisher. Estab. 1981.

Affiliate(s): Platinum Planet Music, Tourmaline (BMI) and LITA Music (ASCAP).

How to Contact: Submit demo by mail. Unsolicited submissions are OK. Prefers CD with 5 songs and lyric sheet. Does not return material. "Place code '2003' on each envelope submission."

Music: Mostly **pop**, **reggae**, **country** and **comedy**. Published "Saved By Love" (single), recorded by Amy Grant on A&M Records; "Love's Not a Game" (single), recorded by Kashief Lindo on VP Records; "A Gift That She Don't Want," (single), recorded by Bill Engvall on Warner Brother Records; and "I Wanna Be That Man" (single), recorded by McKameys on Pamplin Records, all written by Justin Peters.

◗ PIANO PRESS (ASCAP), P.O. Box 85, Del Mar CA 92014-0085. (858)481-5650. Fax: (858)755-1104. E-mail: pianopress@aol.com. Website: www.pianopress.com. **Contact:** Elizabeth C. Axford, M.A., owner. Music publisher. Publishes songbooks & CD's for music students and teachers. Estab. 1999. Publishes 32-100 songs/year; publishes 1-24 new songwriters/year. Staff size: 5. Pays standard print music and/or mechanical royalty; composer retains rights to songs.

How to Contact: *Write or call first and obtain permission to submit.* Prefers cassette or CD with 1-3 songs, lyric and lead sheet, cover letter and sheet music/piano arrangements. "Looking for children's songs for young piano students and arrangements of public domain folk songs of any nationality." Currently accepting submissions for *Kidtunes*. Include SASE. Responds in 2 months.

Music: Mostly **children's**, **folk songs** and **funny songs**; also **piano arrangements**, **lead sheets with melody, chords and lyrics** and **songbooks**. Does not want commercial pop, R&B, etc. Published "I Can" (single by Tom Gardner) from *Kidtunes* (album), recorded by The Uncle Brothers (children's), released 2002 by Piano Press; "Rock & Roll Teachers" (single by Bob King) from *Kidtunes* (album), recorded by Bob King & Friends (children's), released 2002 by Piano Press; and "It Really Isn't Garbage" (single by Danny Einbender) from *Kidtunes* (album), recorded by Danny Eibender/Pete Seeger/et al. (children's), released 2002 by Piano Press.

Tips: "Songs should be simple, melodic and memorable. Lyrics should be for a juvenile audience and well-crafted."

Ⓝ PLATINUM GOLD MUSIC (ASCAP), 18653 Ventura Blvd., Suite 292, Tarzana CA 91356. (661)268-0404. E-mail: platinumgold@aol.com. Managers: Steve Cohen and David Cook. Music publisher. Estab. 1981.

How to Contact: "Platinum Gold discourages unsolicited submissions. You may write or call first to obtain permission to submit a demo." Prefers cassette with no more than 4 songs. Does not return material. Responds in 3 weeks.

Music: Mostly **R&B**, **pop** and **hip hop**; also **country** and **rock**. Published *Misunderstanding* (by Steven Russell), recorded by The Whispers on Capitol Records (R&B); *My Music* (by R. Warren/R. Benford/J. Harreld), recorded by Troop on Atlantic Records (R&B); and *Come To Me* (by L.A. McNeil), recorded by Michael Cooper on Warner Bros. Records (R&B).

Ⓝ PLATINUM PLANET MUSIC, INC. (BMI), 2831 Dogwood Place, Nashville TN 37204. (615)269-8682. Fax: (615)269-8929. Website: http://songsfortheplanet.com. **Contact:** Justin Peters, president. Music publisher. Estab. 1997.

Affiliate(s): Justin Peters Music, Tourmaline (BMI) and LITA Music (ASCAP).

How to Contact: Submit demo by mail. Unsolicited submissions are OK. Prefers CD with 5 songs and lyric sheet. Does not return material. "Place code '2003' on each envelope submission."

Music: Mostly **r&b**, **dance** and **country**; also represents many Christian artists/writers. Published "Happy Face" (single by Dez Dickerson/Jordan Dickerson), recorded by Squirt on Absolute Records;

THE FILM & TV INDEX found at the back of this book lists companies placing music in film and TV (excluding TV commercials).

"Welcome To My Love" (single by Mike Hunter), recorded by Kyndl on PPMI; "Dog The Nine" and "White House" (singles), written and recorded by Bride for Absolute Records; and "Loud" (single), written and recorded by These Five Down on Absolute Records.

POLLYBYRD PUBLICATIONS LIMITED (ASCAP, BMI, SESAC), P.O. Box 8442, Universal CA 91608. (818)506-8533. Fax: (818)506-8534. E-mail: pplzmi@aol.com. Branch office: 333 Proctor St., Carson City NV 89703. (818)884-1946. Fax: (818)882-6755. **Contact:** Dakota Hawk, vice president. Professional Managers: Cisco Blue (country, pop, rock); Tedford Steele (hip-hop, R&B). Music publisher, record company (PPL Entertainment) and Management firm (Sa'mall Management). Estab. 1979. Publishes 100 songs/year; publishes 25-40 new songwriters/year. Hires staff writers. Pays standard royalty.
Affiliate(s): Kellijai Music (ASCAP), Pollyann Music (ASCAP), Ja'Nikki Songs (BMI), Velma Songs International (BMI), Lonnvanness Songs (SESAC), PPL Music (ASCAP), Zettitalia Music, Butternut Music (BMI), Zett Two Music (ASCAP), Plus Publishing and Zett One Songs (BMI).
How to Contact: *Write first and obtain permission to submit.* Prefers cassette or VHS videocassette with 4 songs and lyric and lead sheet. Include SASE. Responds in 2 months.
Music: Published "Believe" (single by J. Jarrett/S. Cuseo) from *Time* (album), recorded by Lejenz (pop), released 2001 on PRL/Credence; *Rainbow Gypsy Child* (album), written and recorded by Riki Hendrix (rock), released 2001 on PRL/Sony; and "What's Up With That" (single by Brandon James/Patrick Bouvier) from *Outcast* (album), recorded by Condottieré (hip-hop), released 2001 on Bouvier.
Tips: "Make those decisions—are you really a songwriter? Are you prepared to starve for your craft? Do you believe in delayed gratification? Are you commercial or do you write only for yourself? Can you take rejection? Do you want to be the best? If so, contact us—if not, keep your day job."

POLYGRAM MUSIC PUBLISHING. 1416 N. La Brea Ave., Los Angeles CA 90028. In 1999, PolyGram Music Publishing and MCA Music Publishing merged into Universal Music Publishing.
How to Contact: *Polygram Music Publishing does not accept unsolicited submissions.*

PORTAGE MUSIC (BMI), 16634 Gannon W., Rosemount MN 55068. (952)432-5737. President: Larry LaPole. Music publisher. Publishes 5-20 songs/year. Pays standard royalty.
How to Contact: *Does not accept unsolicited submissions.*
Music: Mostly **country** and **country rock**. Published "Lost Angel," "Think It Over" and "Congratulations to Me" (by L. Lapole), all recorded by Trashmen on Sundazed.
Tips: "Keep songs short, simple and upbeat with positive theme."

THEODORE PRESSER CO. (ASCAP, BMI, SESAC), 588 N. Gulph Rd., King of Prussia PA 19406. (610)525-3636. Fax: (610)527-7841. E-mail: presser@presser.com. Website: www.presser.com. **Contact:** Debbie Oranzi, Editorial Assistant. Music publisher. Estab. 1783. Publishes 200 songs/year; publishes 3 new songwriters/year. Staff size: 51. Pays standard royalty; 10% on print.
Affiliate(s): Theodore Presser, Beekman, Oliver Ditson, John Church, Elkan-Vogel (ASCAP), Merion Music (BMI) and Mercury Music (SESAC).
How to Contact: Submit demo tape by mail. Unsolicited submissions are OK. Prefers cassette and score. Include SASE. Responds in 2 months.
Film & TV: Places 12 songs in film and 14 songs in TV/year.
Music: Mostly **serious concert music**, **sacred and secular choral** and **educational music**. Does not want popular music.
Tips: "Write honest, high quality music and send it to us, following our submission guidelines which you can receive via e-mail."

PRITCHETT PUBLICATIONS (BMI), P.O. Box 725, Daytona Beach FL 32114-0725. (904)252-4848. Fax: (904)252-7402. E-mail: CharlesVickers@USALink.com. Website: www.ZYWorld.com/CharlesVickers. **Contact:** Charles Vickers, Vice President. Music publisher and record company (King of Kings Record Co., Pickwick/Mecca/International Records). Estab. 1975. Publishes 21 songs/year; publishes 12 new songwriters/year.

Affiliate(s): Alison Music (ASCAP), Charles H. Vickers Music Associates (BMI) and QuickSilver Encrease Records Inc.

How to Contact: *Write first and obtain permission to submit.* Prefers cassette with 6 songs and lyric or lead sheet. Does not return material.

Music: Mostly **gospel**, **rock-disco** and **country**.

☑ ☒ ◯ **QUARK, INC.**, P.O. Box 7320, New York NY 10150-7320. Fax: (845)708-0113. E-mail: quarkent@aol.com. **Contact:** Curtis Urbina, manager. Professional Manager: Michelle Harris (alternative/pop). Music publisher, record company (Quark Records) and record producer (Curtis Urbina). Estab. 1984. Publishes 12 songs/year; 2 new songwriters/year. Staff size: 4. Pays standard royalty.

Affiliate(s): Quarkette Music (BMI), Freedurb Music (ASCAP), Pacific Time Entertainment and Quark Records.

How to Contact: *Call first and obtain permission to submit.* Prefers CD only with 2 songs. No cassettes. Include SASE. Responds in 2 months.

Film & TV: Places 10 songs in film/year. Music Supervisor: Curtis Urbina (pop/dance).

Music: Mostly **pop**. Does not want anything short of a hit. Published "Keep on Keeping On" (single by M. Serio) from *Entertainers* (album), recorded by Bel Mondo (pop), released 2002 on Pacific Time Entertainment; "Your Lucky Day" (single by K. Katahgiotis) from *Your Lucky Day* (album), recorded by Kimon (pop/rock), released 2002 on Ultrascene Entertainment; and "Throwback" (single by E. Cohen) from *Party Time* (album), recorded by DJ Strobe (dance), released 2002 on Quark Records.

Tips: "Write strong songs with commercial appeal. Trust your instincts."

🌐 ◐ **R.J. MUSIC**, 'The Return', 10A Margaret Rd., Barnet, Herts. EN4 9NP United Kingdom. Phone: (020)440-9788. **Contact:** Roger James and Susana Boyle, Managing Directors. Music publisher and management firm (Roger James Management). PRS. Pays negotiable royalty (up to 50%).

How to Contact: Submit demo tape by mail. Unsolicited submissions are OK. Prefers cassette with 1 song and lyric or lead sheet. "Will return cassettes, but only with correct *full* postage!"

Music: Mostly **MOR**, **blues**, **country** and **rock**; also **chart material**. Does not want disco or rap.

🌐 ☑ ◯ **R.T.L. MUSIC**, White House Farm, Shropshire TF9 4HA England. Phone: (01630)647374. Fax: (01630)647612. **Contact:** Tanya Woof, A&R manager. Professional Managers: Ron Lee (rock/rock 'n roll); Katrine LeMatt (MOR/dance); Xavier Lee (heavy metal); Tanya Lee (classical/other types). Music publisher, record company (Le Matt Music) and record producer. Estab. 1971. Publishes approximately 30 songs/year. Pays standard royalty.

Affiliate(s): Lee Music (publishing), Swoop Records, Grenouille Records, Check Records, Zarg Records, Pogo Records, R.T.F.M. (all independent companies).

How to Contact: Submit demo tape or CD by mail. Unsolicited submissions are OK. Prefers CD, cassette or MDisc (also VHS 625/PAL system videocassette) with 1-3 songs and lyric and lead sheets; include still photos and bios. "Make sure name and address are on CD or cassette." Send IRC. Responds in 6 weeks.

Music: **All types**. Published "Time Bombs" (single by Phill Dunn), recorded by Orphan (rock), released 2000 on Pogo; *Phobias* (album), recorded by Orphan (rock), released 2000 on Pogo; and *The Best Of* (album), recorded by Emmitt Till (rock/blues), released 2000 on Swoop.

☒ ◐ **RAINBOW MUSIC CORP. (ASCAP)**, 45 E. 66 St., New York NY 10021. (212)988-4619. **Contact:** Fred Stuart, vice president. Music publisher. Estab. 1990. Publishes 25 songs/year. Staff size: 2. Pays standard royalty.

Affiliate(s): Tri-Circle (ASCAP).

How to Contact: *Only accepts material referred by a reputable industry source.* Prefers cassette with 2 songs and lyric sheet. Include SASE. Responds in 1 week.

Film & TV: Published "Break It To Me Gently" (by Diane Lampert/Joe Seneca), recorded by Brenda Lee in *Trees Lounge*; and "Nothin' Shakin' (But Leaves on the Tree)" (by Diane Lampert/Eddie Fontaine), recorded by The Beatles in *Beatles TV Special*.

Music: Mostly **pop**, **R&B** and **country**; also **jazz**.

☑ ⚲ ⊘ **REN ZONE MUSIC (ASCAP)**, P.O. Box 3153, Huntington Beach CA 92605. (714)596-6582. Fax: (714)596-6577. E-mail: renzone@socal.rr.com. **Contact:** Keith Wolzinger, president. Music publisher. Estab. 1998. Publishes 14 songs/year; publishes 2 new songwriters/year. Staff size: 2. Pays standard royalty.
   ● This company won a Parents Choice 1998 Silver Honor Shield.
How to Contact: *Does not accept unsolicited submissions.*
Music: Mostly **children's**. Does not want rap or punk. Published "Walk Like the Animals" (single by Dayle Lusk) from *Tumble 'n' Tunes* (album), recorded by Dayle Lusk/Danielle Ganya (children's); "Surf Town" (single by Dayle Lusk) from *City Song at Huntington Beach* (album), recorded by Lisa Worshaw (pop); and "Snowboardin' (single by Stephanie Donatoni) from *Sea Cliff Tunes*, recorded by Lisa Worshaw (children's), all released 2000 on Ren Zone.
Tips: "Submit well-written lyrics that convey important concepts to kids on good quality demos with easy to understand vocals."

Ⓝ ⊘ **RHYTHMS PRODUCTIONS (ASCAP)**, P.O. Box 34485, Los Angeles CA 90034. **Contact:** Ruth White, president. Music and multimedia publisher. Member NARAS. Publishes 4 titles/year. Pays negotiable royalty.
Affiliate(s): Tom Thumb Music.
How to Contact: Submit tape with letter outlining background in educational children's music. Include SASE. Responds in 2 months.
Music: "We're only interested in **children's songs** and interactive programs that have educational value. Our materials are sold in schools and homes, so artists/writers with an 'edutainment' background would be most likely to understand our requirements." Published "Professor Whatzit®" series including "Adventures of Professor Whatzit & Carmine Cat" (cassette series for children); "Musical Math," "Musical Reading" and "Theme Songs."

Ⓝ ○ **RIDGE MUSIC CORP. (ASCAP, BMI)**, 38 Laurel Ledge Court, Stamford CT 06903. E-mail: pmtannen@optonline.net. President/General Manager: Paul Tannen. Music publisher. Estab. 1961. Member CMA. Publishes 6 songs/year. Pays standard royalty.
Affiliate(s): Tannen Music Inc. and Deshufflin, Inc.
How to Contact: Submit demo tape by mail. Unsolicited submissions OK. Prefers cassette with 3 songs and lyric sheet. Include SASE. Responds in 2 months.
Music: Mostly **country**, **rock**, **top 40/pop** and **jazz**. Published "Forever," written and recorded by Mark Whitfield on Verve Records (jazz).

⊘ **ROCK N METAL MUSIC PUBLISHING CO.**, P.O. Box 325, Fort Dodge IA 50501-0325. **Contact:** James E. Hartsell Jr., Owner. Music publisher. Estab. 1996. Publishes 1-4 songs/year. Pays standard royalty.
How to Contact: *Write first and obtain permission to submit.* Prefers cassette and bio with 3 songs and lead sheet. Include SASE. Responds in 3 weeks.
Music: **Heavy metal**, **hard rock** and **hard alternative** only.
Tips: "We are looking for new and established songwriters and artists. We will help musicians who need to collaborate with a lyricist. Please follow the guidelines and be patient. Remember the louder, the faster, the better."

☑ ⊘ **ROCKER MUSIC/HAPPY MAN MUSIC (BMI, ASCAP)**, 4696 Kahlua Lane, Bonita Springs, FL 34134. (941)947-6978. E-mail: obitts@bellsouth.net. **Contact:** Dick O'Bitts, executive producer. Estab. 1960. Music publisher, record company (Happy Man Records, Condor Records and Air Corp Records), record producer (Rainbow Collections Ltd.) and management firm (Gemini Complex). Publishes 25-30 songs/year; publishes 8-10 new songwriters/year. Staff size: 2. Pays standard royalty.

How to Contact: Submit demo tape by mail. Unsolicited submissions are OK. Prefers cassette, VHS videocassette or CD with 4 songs and lyric or lead sheet. Include SASE. Do not call. Responds in 1 month.

Music: Mostly **country**, **rock**, **pop**, **gospel**, **Christian** and **off-the-wall**. Does not want hip-hop. Published *Got the T Shirt* (album), recorded by The Thorps, released 2001 on Happy Man; and *In The Distance* (album), recorded by 4 Harmonee, released 2001 on Happy Man.

⊘ ROCKFORD MUSIC CO. (ASCAP, BMI), 150 West End Ave., Suite 6-D, New York NY 10023. **Contact:** Danny Darrow, manager. Music publisher, record company (Mighty Records), record and video tape producer (Danny Darrow). Publishes 1-3 songs/year; publishes 1-3 new songwriters/year. Staff size: 3. Pays standard royalty.

Affiliate(s): Corporate Music Publishing Company (ASCAP) and Stateside Music Company (BMI).

How to Contact: Submit demo tape by mail. Unsolicited submissions are OK. "No phone calls and do not write for permission to submit." Prefers cassette with 3 songs and lyric sheet. Does not return material. Responds in 2 weeks.

Music: Mostly **MOR** and **top 40/pop**; also **adult pop**, **country**, **adult rock**, **dance-oriented**, **easy listening**, **folk** and **jazz**. Does not want rap. Published "Let There Be Peace" (single by Danny Darrow) from *Let There Be Peace* (album), recorded by Danny Darrow (spiritual); "Doomsday" (single by Danny Darrow/Robert Lee Lowery) from *Doomsday* (album), recorded by Danny Darrow (Euro jazz); and "Impulse" (single by Danny Darrow) from *Impulse* (album), recorded by Danny Darrow (Euro jazz), all released 2001 on Mighty Records.

Tips: "Listen to Top 40 and write current lyrics and music."

⟦N⟧ ⊘ RONDOR MUSIC INTERNATIONAL/ALMO/IRVING MUSIC, A UNIVERSAL MUSIC GROUP COMPANY, 2440 Sepulveda Blvd., Suite 119, Los Angeles CA 90064. (310)235-4800. Fax: (310)235-4801. New York office: 111 W. 57th St., 9th Floor, New York NY 10019. (212)265-8866. Fax: (212)265-3096. Nashville office: 1904 Adelicia Ave., Nashville TN 37212. (615)321-0820. Fax: (615)327-1018. Creative Staff Assistant: Alana Downey. Music publisher. Estab. 1965. Hires staff writers. Royalty amount depends on deal.

Affiliates: Almo Music Corp. (ASCAP) and Irving Music, Inc. (BMI).

How to Contact: *Does not accept unsolicited submissions.*

⟦N⟧ ⊘ ROSEBOWL MUSIC, Rembrandtstrasse 14, 81245 Munich, Germany. Phone: +49-172-7344661. E-mail: musicfarm@hotmail.com. **Contact:** Robert Klug, managing director. A&R: Ken Rose. "Pop/Rock/Alternative song-oriented music only." Music publisher and production company. Estab. 1995. Publishing advances paid on top-line material.

How to Contact: Submit demo CD by mail. Prefers CD with 2 songs only. "No MP3 files. Songs are judged wholly on songwriting and the writer's/band's ability to mix artistic ideas, well-crafted lyrics and songs with commercial potential. Submissions are not returned and senders are contacted if we are interested in the submitted material."

Music: Song-oriented music of **all genres**. "We currently have Top 10 songs in 3 major markets."

Tips: "Rosebowl Music is run by established songwriters and producers who are listening for originality, vibe, and that 'special something.' We do listen to everything that comes in, but please submit your best 2 songs only!"

⟦C⟧ RUSTRON MUSIC PUBLISHERS (BMI), 1156 Park Lane, West Palm Beach FL 33417-5957. (561)686-1354. E-mail: gordon-whims@juno.com. **Contact:** any professional manager. Professional Managers: Rusty Gordon (adult contemporary, acoustic, New Age fusions, children's, cabaret);

MARKETS THAT WERE listed in the 2002 edition of *Songwriters Market* but do not appear this year are listed in the General Index with a notation explaining why they were omitted.

Ron Caruso (all styles); Davilyn Whims (folk fusions, country, blues). Music publisher, record company, management firm and record producer (Rustron Music Productions). Estab. 1972. Publishes 100-150 songs/year; publishes 10-20 new songwriters/year. Staff size: 9. Pays standard royalty.
Affiliate(s): Whimsong Publishing (ASCAP).
How to Contact: Submit demo tape or CD by mail. Unsolicited submissions are OK. For freelance songwriters we prefer cassette with 1-3 songs and typed lyric or lead sheet. For performing songwriters we prefer CD with up to 15 songs. "Clearly label your tape container or jewel box. Include cover letter. We don't review songs on websites." SASE required for all correspondence. Responds in 4 months.
Music: Mostly **pop** (ballads, blues, theatrical, cabaret), **progressive country** and **folk/rock**; also **R&B** and **New Age** instrumental fusions with classical, jazz or pop themes and women's music. Does not publish rap, hip-hop, new wave, youth music, hard rock, heavy metal or punk. Published "Rainbow" (single by Eric Shaffer/Rusty Gordon) from *The Triangle and The Rainbow* (album), recorded by Song n a Whim (folk/rock), released 2001 on Rustron Records; "America and Her Enemies" (single by Stacie Jubal) from *Time for Topical Again* (album), recorded by Stacie Jubal (folk-rock), released 2001 on Whimsong Records; and "Take a Closer Look" (single by Jeremy White) from *Back On the Island* (album), recorded by Jeremy White (yankee reggae), released 2001 on Whimsong Records.
Tips: "Accepting songwriter's CD for full product review of all songs on CD. Write strong hooks. Keep song length 3½ minutes or less. Avoid predictability—create original lyric themes. Tell a story. Compose definitive melody. Tune in to the trends and fusions indicative of commercially viable new music for the new millennium. Songs reviewed for single-song marketing must be very carefully crafted."

◻ **SABTECA MUSIC CO. (ASCAP)**, P.O. Box 10286, Oakland CA 94610. (510)465-2805. Fax: (510)832-0464. Professional Managers: Sean Herring (pop, R&B, jazz); Lois Shayne (pop, R&B, soul, country). **Contact:** Duane Herring, president. Music publisher and record company (Sabteca Record Co., Andre Romare). Estab. 1980. Publishes 8-10 songs/year; 1-2 new songwriters/year. Pays standard royalty.
Affiliate(s): Toyiabe Publishing (BMI).
How to Contact: *Write first and obtain permission to submit.* Prefers cassette with 2 songs and lyric sheet. Include SASE. Responds in 1 month.
Music: Mostly **R&B**, **pop** and **country**. Published "I Miss You Baby" (single by Walt Coleman), recorded by Lois Shayne (r&b), released 2001 on Sabteca; "Lost Somewhere In Time" (single), written and recorded by Reggie Walker (r&b), released 2000 on Sabteca; and "Rappin' Mama" (single), written and recorded by Lois Shayne (rap), released 2001 on Sabteca.
Tips: "Listen to music daily, if possible. Keep improving writing skills."

▣ ☑ ▣ ◻ **SADDLESTONE PUBLISHING (BMI, SOCAN)**, 6260-130 St., Surrey British Columbia V3X 1R6 Canada. (604)572-4232. Fax: (604)572-4252. E-mail: saddles@telus.net. Website: http://saddlestone.ontheweb.nu. **Contact:** Candice James (country), CEO. President: Grant Lucas (rock). Professional Manager: Sharla Cuthbertson (pop, R&B). Music publisher, record company (Saddlestone) and record producer (Silver Bow Productions). Estab. 1988. Publishes 100 songs/year; publishes 12-30 new songwriters/year. Pays standard royalty.
Affiliate(s): Silver Bow Publishing (SOCAN, ASCAP).
How to Contact: Submit demo tape by mail. Unsolicited submissions are OK. Prefers cassette with 3 songs and lyric sheet. "Make sure vocal is clear." Does not return material. Responds in 3 months.
Film & TV: Places 1 song in film and 2 songs in TV/year. Music Supervisors: Janet York; John McCullough. Recently published "Midnite Ride" (by Cam Wagner), recorded by 5 Star Hillbillies in *North of Pittsburgh*.
Music: Mostly **country**, **rock** and **pop**; also **gospel** and **R&B**. Published *That's Real Love*, written and recorded by Darrell Meyers (country), released 2000; *Hopeless Believer* (by Diane Baumgartner), recorded by Echo 200 (pop); and "Silent River" (single by John Reilly), recorded by Wolfe Milestone, released 2001, all on Independent Records.

Tips: "Submit clear demos, good hooks and avoid long intros or instrumentals. Have a good singer do vocals."

N ○ SCHAFER MUSIC (ASCAP), 3236 Cloverwood Dr., Nashville TN 37214. (615)883-7086. (615)292-9117. E-mail: schafermusic1@aol.com. Website: www.danschafer.com. **Contact:** Dan Schafer, creative director. Music publisher, record producer (Schafer Music) and record company (Oh Dee Records). Estab. 1974. Publishes 200 songs/year; publishes 2 new songwriters/year. Staff size: 1. Pays standard royalty.
● Also see listing for Schafer Music in the Record Producers section. Schafer Music received the #1 Song Award in 1998 from Word/Idea Publishing.
Affiliate(s): Schafer Music (ASCAP), Virginia Borden Rhythms (ASCAP), and Faverett Tracks (BMI).
How to Contact: Submit demo tape by mail. Unsolicited submissions are OK. Prefers cassette or CD/CDR with lyric sheet. "Just lyrics accepted." Does not return material. Responds only if interested.
Music: Mostly **pop**, **country** and **smooth jazz**; also **gospel** and **folk**. Does not want hip-hop or rap.
Tips: "Never Give up."

○ TIM SCOTT MUSIC GROUP (BMI), The Associate Group, L.L.C., P.O. Box 91079, Springfield MA 01139. Phone/fax: (509)351-4379. E-mail: simpleandsafe@aol.com. **Contact:** Timothy Scott, president. Music publisher and record company (Keeping It Simple and Safe). Estab. 1993. Publishes 20-50 songs/year. Staff size: 20. Hires staff writers. Pays standard royalty.
Affiliates: Tim Scott Music (ASCAP).
How to Contact: Submit demo tape by mail. Unsolicited submissions are OK. Prefers cassette with 3-5 songs and lyric sheet. Include SASE. Responds in 3 months.
Music: Mostly **R&B** and **pop**; also **country**, **rock** and **gospel**. Published "Crime of Love" (single by Dante Johnson/David Smooth) from *Crime of Love* (album), recorded by The Lawyers and the Judges (top 40), released 2001 on Night Owl Records; "Not in My House" (single by Don "Poorman" Williams) from *Empty Pockets* (album), recorded by The Poor Folks (r&b), released 2001 on Night Owl Records; and "Sweet Candy Love" (single by Mary McNeil/Sandy McNeil/Hazel Jackson) from *Sweet Love Forever* (album), recorded by Sweet Honey (r&b), released 2001 on Night Owl Records.

N ▼ ○ SDM (ASCAP, BMI), 740 N. La Brea, Los Angeles CA 90038. (323)933-9977. Fax: (323)933-0633. E-mail: sbe740@earthlink.net. **Contact:** Laurent Besencon, A&R. Music publisher, record company (Sunset Boulevard) and manager. Publishes 1,000 songs/year; publishes 5 new songwriters/year. Hires staff songwriters. Pays standard royalty.
Affiliate(s): Playhard Music and Plaything Music (ASCAP), Playful Music and Music Pieces (BMI).
● SDM has received BMI and ASCAP awards as well as several Gold and Platinum certifications.
How to Contact: *Call first and obtain permission to submit.* Prefers CD with 3 songs and lyric sheet. Include SASE. Responds in 1 month.
Music: Mostly **pop**, **R&B** and **rock**. Published "Love Train" (by Felton Pilate), recorded by Dru Hill; and "A Little Bit of Love" (by Claude Glaubette), recorded by Celine Dion.

◑ SEGAL'S PUBLICATIONS (BMI), P.O. Box 507, Newton MA 02159. (617)969-6196. **Contact:** Charles Segal. Music publisher and record producer (Segal's Productions). Estab. 1963. Publishes 80 songs/year; publishes 6 new songwriters/year. Pays standard royalty.
Affilate(s): Charles Segal's Publications (BMI) and Charles Segal's Music (SESAC).
How to Contact: Submit demo tape by mail. Unsolicited submissions are OK. Prefers CD or VHS videocassette with 3 songs and lyric or lead sheet. Does not return material. Responds only if interested.
Music: Mostly **rock**, **pop** and **country**; also **R&B**, **MOR** and **children's songs**. Published "A Time to Care" (by Brilliant/Segal), recorded by Rosemary Wills (MOR); "Go to Bed" (by Colleen Segal), recorded Susan Stark (MOR); and "Only In Dreams" (by Chas. Segal), recorded by Rosemary Wills (MOR), all on Spin Records.

Tips: "Besides making a good demo cassette, include a lead sheet of music—words, melody line and chords. Put your name and phone number on CD."

◓ **SELLWOOD PUBLISHING (BMI)**, 170 N. Maple, Fresno CA 93702. Phone/fax: (559)255-1717. E-mail: tracsell@aol.com. **Contact:** Stan Anderson, owner. Music publisher, record company (TRAC Record Co.) and record producer. Estab. 1972. Publishes 10 songs/year; publishes 3 new songwriters/year. Pays standard royalty.
How to Contact: Submit demo tape—unsolicited submissions are OK. Prefers cassette or VHS videocassette with 2 songs and lyric sheet. Include SASE. Responds in 3 weeks. "Submit professional studio demos only."
Music: Mostly **traditional country**, **southern gospel** and **country**. Does not want rock 'n' roll, rap or heavy metal. Published *Reno* (album); *Let the Music Play* (album); and *Remember the Love* (album), all written and recorded by Kevin B. Willard (country), all released 2000 on TRAC Records.
Tips: "We're looking for all styles of country, especially uptempo dance types."

☑ ◓ **SHAWNEE PRESS, INC.**, 49 Waring Dr., P.O. Box 690, Delaware Water Gap PA 18327. (570)476-0550. Fax: (570)476-1250. E-mail: shawnee-info@shawneepress.com. Website: www.ShawneePress.com. **Contact:** Cherie Troester, Editorial Assistant. Editor (church choral music): Joseph M. Martin. Professional Managers: Greg Gilpin (educational choral); Ed Esposito (instrumental, no strings); David Angerman (handbell music); Joseph Martin (piano-sacred only). Music publisher. Estab. 1917. Publishes 150 songs/year. Staff size: 35. Pays negotiable royalty.
Affiliate(s): Glory Sound, Harold Flammer Music, Mark Foster Music, Wide World Music, Concert Works.
How to Contact: Submit manuscript. Unsolicited submissions are OK. See website for guidelines. Prefers manuscript; recording required for instrumental submissions; recordings optional for choral submissions. Include SASE. Responds in 4 months.
Music: Mostly **church/liturgical**, **educational choral** and **instrumental. No musicals or contatas.**
Tips: "Submission guidelines appear on our website."

☑ ▦ ◓ **SHU'BABY MONTEZ MUSIC**, P.O. Box 28816, Philadelphia PA 19151. (215)473-5527. Fax: (215)473-8895. E-mail: schubaby@att.net. Website: www.geocities.com/SunsetStrip/Cabaret/2810. President: Leroy Schuler. Music publisher. Estab. 1986. Publishes 25 songs/year; publishes 10 new songwriters/year. Pays standard royalty.
How to Contact: *Contact first and obtain permission to submit.* Prefers cassette with 3 songs and lyric sheet. Include SASE. Responds in 5 weeks.
Film & TV: Places 9 songs in film/year. Music Supervisor: Paul Roberts. Recently published "Sweaty and Nakey" (single by Martin "Martygraw" Schuler), recorded by Color Blind; "Baby With Blues" and "A Chance to Love Again" (singles by Lou Leggerie), recorded by Marie Davenport.
Music: Mostly **R&B**, **dance**, **hip-hop** and **pop**. Does not want country. Published "Situation" (single by Shaun/Trigger/Hollywood/Jamaine) from *MVP for Life*, recorded by MVP (rap); and "Be My Valentine" (single by Lou Leggerie), recorded by Cubby St. Charles (r&b/pop), both released 2002 on Urban Logic Records.
Tips: "Keep the music simple, but with nice changes. Don't be afraid to use altered chords."

Ⓝ 🌐 **SIEGEL MUSIC COMPANIES**, Marstallst. 8, 80539, Munich Germany. Phone: +49-89-29069-0. Fax: +49-89-29060-277. E-mail: jupiter-records@writeme.com. Website: www.jupiter-records.de. President (pop/MOR): Ralph Siegel. Managing Director (pop/MOR): Joachim Neubauer. Professional Manager (rock/heavy metal): Walter Wicha. Professional Manager (pop/dance): Maria Glauben. Professional Manager (pop/MOR): Helfard V. Schenckendorff. Professional Manager (pop/dance): Sonja Jeschke. Music publisher, record company, (Jupiter Records and 69-Records) and record producer. Estab. 1948. GEMA. Publishes 1,500 songs/year; publishes 50 new songwriters/year. Hires staff songwriters. Pays 60% according to the rules of GEMA.
Affiliate(s): Sounds of Jupiter, Inc. (USA), Gobian Music (ASCAP) and Symphonie House Music (ASCAP).

How to Contact: Submit demo tape or CD by mail. Unsolicited submissions are OK. SAE and IRC. Responds in 2 months.

Music: Mostly **pop**, **rock** and **dance**; also **soul** and **black music**. Published "Privacy" (by Ralph Siegel/John O'Flynn), recorded by Bianca Shomburg (pop); and "Abrakadabra" (by Ralph Siegel/Nicole Seibert), recorded by Nicole, both on Jupiter; and "Dormi" (by Giacomo Puccini), recorded by Albano Carrisi on WEA Records (classical).

Tips: "If you believe that your song could be a #1 in the charts, please submit it!"

◯ SILICON MUSIC PUBLISHING CO. (BMI), 222 Tulane St., Garland TX 75043-2239. President: Gene Summers. Vice President: Deanna L. Summers. Public Relations: Steve Summers. Music publisher and record company (Front Row Records). Estab. 1965. Publishes 10-20 songs/year; publishes 2-3 new songwriters/year. Pays standard royalty.

How to Contact: Submit demo tape by mail. Unsolicited submissions are OK. Prefers cassette with 1-2 songs. Does not return material. Responds ASAP.

Music: Mostly **rockabilly** and **'50s material**; also **old-time blues/country** and **MOR**. Published "Almost Persuaded," "Someone Somewhere," and "Who Stole The Marker," all recorded by Gene Summers on Crystal Clear Records (rockabilly). Also published "I'm Gonna Find Me Some Neon"; and "Mr. Radio Race" (singles), written and recorded by Joe Hardin Brown, released 2002 on Mister Rock Records. New CD to be released in 2002 with 10 newly published Silicon songs.

Tips: "We are very interested in '50s rock and rockabilly *original masters* for release through overseas affiliates. If you are the owner of any '50s masters, contact us first! We have releases in Holland, Switzerland, England, Belgium, France, Sweden, Norway and Australia. We have the market if you have the tapes! Our staff writers include James McClung, Gary Mears (original Casuals), Robert Clark, Dea Summers, Shawn Summers, Joe Hardin Brown, Bill Becker and Dan Edwards."

▨ ◎ SILVER BLUE MUSIC/OCEANS BLUE MUSIC, 3940 Laurel Canyon Blvd., Suite 441, Studio City CA 91604. (818)980-9588. E-mail: jdiamond20@aol.com. **Contact:** Joel Diamond, president. Music publisher and record producer (Joel Diamond Entertainment). Estab. 1971. Publishes 50 songs/year. Pays standard royalty.

How to Contact: *Does not accept unsolicited material.* "No tapes returned."

Film & TV: Places 4 songs in film and 6 songs in TV/year.

Music: Mostly **pop** and **R&B**; also **rap**. Does not want country, jazz or classical. Published "After the Lovin" (by Bernstein/Adams), recorded by Engelbert Humperdinck. Other artists include David Hasselhof, Kari (Curb Records), Ike Turner, Andrew Dice Clay, Gloria Gaynor, Kaci, Tony Orlando, Ike Turner, Katie Cassidy and Vaneza.

◎ SILVER THUNDER MUSIC GROUP, P.O. Box 41335, Nashville TN 37204. (615)391-5035. **Contact:** Rusty Budde, president. Music publisher and record producer (Rusty Budde Productions). Estab. 1985. Publishes 200 songs/year. Publishes 5-10 new songwriters/year. Hires staff songwriters. Pays standard royalty.

How to Contact: *Write first and obtain permission to submit.* Prefers cassette or VHS videocassette. Does not return material.

Music: Mostly **country**, **pop** and **R&B**. Published *Rock N Cowboys* (album), written and recorded by Jeff Samules on STR Records; *This Ain't the Real Thing* (album by Rusty Budde), recorded by Les Taylor on CBS Records; and "Feel Again" (single by Rusty Budde/Shara Johnson), recorded by Shara Johnson on Warner Bros. Records.

Tips: "Send clear, clean recording on cassette with lyric sheets."

FOR BOOKS ON THE CRAFT AND BUSINESS of songwriting, check out the website for Writer's Digest Books at www.writersdigest.com.

◘ SIMPLY GRAND MUSIC, INC. (ASCAP, BMI), P.O. Box 41981, Memphis TN 38174-1981. (901)763-4787. Fax: (901)763-4883. E-mail: wahani@aol.com. President: Linda Lucchesi. Music publisher. Estab. 1965. Pays standard royalty.
Affiliate(s): Memphis Town Music, Inc. (ASCAP) and Beckie Publishing Co. (BMI).
How to Contact: Submit demo tape by mail. Unsolicited submissions are OK. Prefers cassette with 1-3 songs and lyric sheet. Include SASE. Responds in 1 month. "Please do not send demos by certified or registered mail. Include enough postage for return of materials."
Music: Mostly **pop**, **soul**, **country**, **soft rock**, **children's songs**, **jazz** and **R&B**.

⊕ ✓ ◘ SINUS MUSIK PRODUKTION, ULLI WEIGEL, Geitnerweg 30a, D-12209, Berlin Germany. +49-30-7159050. Fax: +49-30-71590522. E-mail: ulli.weigel@arcor.de. Website: www.ulli-weigel.de. **Contact:** Ulli Weigel, owner. Music publisher, record producer and screenwriter. Member: GEMA, GVL. Estab. 1976. Publishes 20 songs/year; publishes 6 new songwriters/year. Staff size: 3. Pays standard royalty.
Affiliate(s): Sinus Musikverlag H.U. Weigel GmbH.
How to Contact: Submit demo tape or CD by mail. Unsolicited submissions are OK. Prefers cassette or CD-R with up to 10 songs and lyric sheets. Responds in 2 months. "If material should be returned, please send an International Reply Coupon (IRC). No stamps."
Music: Mostly **rock**, **pop** and **New Age**; also **background music for movies**. Published "Simple Story" (single), recorded by MAANAM on RCA (Polish rock); *Die Musik Maschine* (album by Klaus Lage), recorded by CWN Productions on Hansa Records (pop/German); and "Maanam" (single by Jakowskyl/Jakowska), recorded by CWN Productions on RCA Records (pop/English).
Tips: "Take more time working on the melody than on the instrumentation. Since December of 1999, I am a provider of 'Music-On-Demand.' This is an online record service of the Deutsche Telekom in Germany, Austria and Switzerland. I am also looking for master-quality recordings for non-exclusive release on my label."

ℕ SIZEMORE MUSIC (BMI), P.O. Box 23275, Nashville TN 37202. (256)845-5003. Fax: (256)845-0054. E-mail: gary@sizemoremusic.com. Website: www.sizemoremusic.com. Contact: Gary Sizemore. Music publisher, record company (The Gas Co.) and record producer (Gary Sizemore). Estab. 1960. Publishes 5 songs/year; 1 new songwriter/year. Pays standard royalty.
How to Contact: Submit demo tape by mail. Unsolicited submissions are OK. Prefers cassette or VHS videocassette with lyric sheets. Does not return material. Responds in 2 weeks.
Music: Mostly **soul** and **R&B**; also **blues**, **pop** and **country**. Published "Liquor and Wine" and "The Wind," written and recorded by K. Shackleford on Heart Records (country); and "She's Tuff" (by Jerry McCain), recorded by The Fabulous Thunderbirds on Chrysalis Records (blues).

◉ SONY MUSIC PUBLISHING, 550 Madison Ave., 18th Floor, New York NY 10022. (212)833-4729. Fax: (212)833-5552. Santa Monica office: 2100 Colorado Ave., Santa Monica CA 90404. (310)449-2545. Nashville office: 8 Music Square W. (615)726-8300. Fax: (615)244-6387. Music publisher.
How to Contact: *Sony Music does not accept unsolicited submissions.*
Music: Published "Angel" (by S. McLachlan/P. Marchand), recorded by Sarah McLachlan on Arista; "Doo Wop (That Thing)," written and recorded by Lauryn Hill on Ruffhouse; and "I Can't Get Over You" (by R. Dunn/T. McBride), recorded by Brooks & Dunn on Arista Nashville.

✓ ◘ SOUND CELLAR MUSIC, 703 N. Brinton Ave., Dixon IL 61021. (815)288-2900. Fax: (815)288-2867. E-mail: tjoos@essexl.com. Website: www.cellarrecords.com. **Contact:** Todd Joos (country, pop, Christian), president. Professional Managers: James Miller (folk, adult contemporary); Mike Thompson (metal, hard rock, alternative). Music publisher, record company (Sound Cellar Records), record producer and recording studio. Estab. 1987. Publishes 15-25 songs/year. Publishes 5 or 6 new songwriters/year. Staff size: 7. Pays standard royalty.
How to Contact: Submit demo tape by mail. Unsolicited submissions are OK. Prefers cassette with 3 or 4 songs and lyric sheet. Does not return material. "We contact by phone in 3-4 weeks only if we want to work with the artist."

Music: Mostly **metal**, **country** and **rock**; also **pop** and **blues**. Published "Problem of Pain" (single by Shane Sowers) from *Before the Machine* (album), recorded by Junker Jorg (alternative metal/rock), released 2000; "Vaya Baby" (single by Joel Ramirez) from *It's About Time* (album), recorded by Joel Ramirez and the All-Stars (latin/R&B), released 2000; and "X" (single by Jon Pomplin) from *Project 814* (album), recorded by Project 814 (progressive rock), released 2001, all on Cellar Records.

◻ SOUTHERN MOST PUBLISHING COMPANY (BMI), P.O. Box 1461446, Laurie MO 65038. (573)374-1111. Fax: (275)522-1533. E-mail: mashred@yahoo.com. **Contact:** Dann E. Haworth, president/owner. Music publisher and record producer (Haworth Productions). Estab. 1985. Publishes 10 songs/year; 3 new songwriters/year. Hires staff songwriters. Pays standard royalty.
Affiliate(s): Boca Chi Key Publishing (ASCAP).
How to Contact: Submit demo CD or tape by mail. Unsolicited submissions are OK. Prefers CD or cassette with 3 songs and lyric sheet. Include SASE. Responds in 2 weeks.
Music: Mostly **rock**, **R&B** and **country**; also **gospel** and **New Age**.
Tips: "Keep it simple and from the heart."

◪ SPRADLIN/GLEICH PUBLISHING (BMI), 4234 N. 45th St., Phoenix AZ 85018-4307. **Contact:** Lee Gleich (rock, pop, movie, country); Paul Spradlin (country), managers. Music publisher. Estab. 1988. Publishes 4-10 songs/year; 2-4 new songwriters. Staff size: 2. Pays standard royalty.
Affiliate(s): Paul Lee Publishing (ASCAP).
How to Contact: *Write first and obtain permission to submit.* Prefers cassette with 3 songs and lyric or lead sheet. "It must be very good material, as I only have time for promoting songwriters who really care." Include SASE. Responds in 6 weeks.
Music: Mostly **country** geared to the US and European country markets; also **pop**, **rock** and **movie**. Published "Going Slow" (single by Paul Spradlin) from *Goosecreek* (album), recorded by Goosecreek Symphony, released 2000 on Capital; and "Blue Ain't As Blue" and "Frosty Morning" (singles by Kurt McFarland) from *Big Sky* (album), recorded by Kurt McFarland, released 2000 on Big Sky Records.
Tips: "I need radio type songs. Please send me only your best. I have pitches to major stars but need great songs. I cannot train writers!"

◪ STARBOUND PUBLISHING CO. (BMI), Dept. SM, 207 Winding Rd., Friendswood TX 77546. Phone/fax: (281)482-2346. E-mail: bh207@msn.com. **Contact:** Buz Hart, president. Music publisher, record company (Juke Box Records, Quasar Records and Eden Records) and record producer (Lonnie Wright and Buz Hart). Estab. 1970. Publishes 35-100 songs/year; publishes 5-10 new songwriters/year. Pays standard royalty.
How to Contact: *Write or call first and obtain permission to submit.* Prefers cassette with 3 songs and lyric sheet. Include SASE. Responds in 2 months.
Music: Mostly **country**, **R&B** and **gospel**. Does not want rap. Published "If I Had Another Heart" (single by Larry Wheeler/Buz Hart) from *Day One* (album), recorded by Waylon Adams (country), released 1999 on Jukebox Records; "My Biggest Thrill" and "Old Fashioned Girl" (singles by Phil Hamm/Buz Hart) from *This and That* (album), recorded by Raiders of the Lost Heart (country), released 2000 on MP3.com.

✓ ◪ STELLAR MUSIC INDUSTRIES (ASCAP, BMI), P.O. Box 54700, Atlanta GA 30308-0700. (770)454-1011. Fax: (770)454-8088. E-mail: stellarmusicind@aol.com. Website: www.goldwax.com. **Contact:** Jimmie McClendon, A&R. President: E.W. Clark. Vice President: Elliot Clark. Music publisher and record company (Goldwax Record Corporation). Estab. 1963. Staff size: 4. Publishes 100 songs/year; publishes 60 new songwriters/year. Hires staff songwriters. Pays standard royalty.
Affiliate(s): Rodanca Music (ASCAP), Bianca Music (BMI) and Urban Assault Records.
How to Contact: *Write or call first and obtain permission to submit.* Prefers cassette, CD/CDR, DAT or videocassette with 4 songs and lyric sheet. Include SASE. Responds in 6 weeks.

Music: Mostly **R&B/hip hop**, **pop/rock** and **jazz**; also **blues**, **contemporary country** and **contemporary gospel**. Published "Rude" (by A. Clark), recorded by 3-4-U, released 2000 on Urban Assault Records; *Long Journey* (by G. Harris), released 2000 on Gold Wax Records; and *We're Rollin* (by J.&C. Harris), released 1999 on Rap/N/Wax Records.

RAY STEVENS MUSIC (BMI), 1707 Grand Ave., Nashville TN 37212. (615)327-4629. Fax: (615)321-5455. E-mail: raystevens@raystevens.com. Website: www.raystevens.com. **Contact:** Ramona Smith, Assistant Manager. Professional Manager: Randy Cullers (country/pop/R&B). Music publisher. Publishes 40 songs/year; publishes 3 new songwriters/year. Staff size: 5. Hires staff songwriters. Pays standard royalty.
Affiliate(s): Ahab Music Co., Inc. (ASCAP) and Grand Ave. Music (BMI).
How to Contact: *Does not accept unsolicited submissions.*
Film & TV: Places 3 songs in film/year. Recently published "Injurin Joe" and "From The Very First Moment" (by Ray Stevens/C.W. Kalb, Jr.), recorded by Ray Stevens in *Tom Sawyer*.
Music: Mostly **country**, **pop** and **R&B**. Published *After Hours* (by Suzi Ragsdale), recorded by Pam Tillis on Arista (country); *Troublemaker* (by Suzi Ragsdale), recorded by Mila Mason on Atlantic (country); and *Bad Little Boy* (by C.W. Kalb Jr.), recorded by Ray Stevens on MCA (country).

STILL WORKING MUSIC GROUP (ASCAP, BMI, SESAC), 1625 Broadway, Nashville TN 37203. (615)242-4201. Fax: (615)242-4202. Music publisher and record company (Orby Records, Inc.). Estab. 1994.
Affiliate(s): Still Working for the Woman Music (ASCAP), Still Working for the Man Music (BMI) and Still Working for All Music (SESAC).
How to Contact: *Does not accept unsolicited submissions.*
Film & TV: Published "First Noel," recorded by The Kelions in *Felicity*.
Music: Mostly **rock**, **country** and **pop**; also **dance** and **R&B**. Published "If You See Him/If You See Her" (by Tommy Lee James), recorded by Reba McIntire/Brooks & Dunn; "Round About Way" (by Wil Nance), recorded by George Strait on MCA; and "Wrong Again" (by Tommy Lee James), recorded by Martina McBride on RCA (country).
Tips: "If you want to be a country songwriter you need to be in Nashville where the business is. Write what is in your heart."

JEB STUART MUSIC CO. (BMI), P.O. Box 6032, Station B, Miami FL 33101-6032. (305)547-1424. **Contact:** Jeb Stuart, president. Music publisher, record producer (Esquire International) and management firm. Estab. 1975. Publishes 4-6 songs/year. Pays standard royalty.
How to Contact: Submit demo tape by mail. Unsolicited submissions are OK. Prefers cassette or CD with 2-4 songs and lead sheet. Include SASE. Responds in 1 month.
Music: Mostly **gospel**, **jazz/rock**, **pop**, **R&B** and **rap**; also **blues**, **church/religious**, **country**, **disco** and **soul**. Published "Love in the Rough," "Guns, Guns (No More Guns)" and "Come On Cafidia" (singles), all written and recorded by Jeb Stuart on Esquire Int'l Records.

SUCCES, Pijnderslaan 84, 9200 Dendermonde Belgium. (052)21 89 87. Fax: (052)21 89 87. **Contact:** Deschuyteneer Hendrik, director. Music publisher, record company and record producer. Estab. 1978. Publishes 400 songs/year. Hires staff songwriters. Staff size: 4. Pays standard royalty.
How to Contact: Submit demo tape by mail. Unsolicited submissions are OK. Prefers cassette or VHS videocassette with 3 songs. SAE and IRC. Responds in 2 months.
Film & TV: Places songs in TV. Recently released "Werkloos" (by Deschuyteneer), recorded by Jacques Vermeire in *Jacques Vermeire Show*.
Music: Mostly **pop**, **dance** and **variety**; also **instrumental** and **rock**. Published "Hoe Moet Dat Nou" (single by Henry Spider), recorded by Monja (ballad), released 2001 on MN; "Liefde" (single by H. Spider), recorded by Rudy Silvester (rock), released 2001 on Scorpion; and "Bel Me Gauw" (single by H. Spider), recorded by Guy Dumon (ballad), released 2001 on BM Records.

SUN STAR SONGS, P.O. Box 1387, Pigeon Forge TN 37868. (865)428-4121. Fax: (865)908-4121. E-mail: sunstarsng@aol.com. **Contact:** Tony Glenn Rast, president. Music publisher. Estab. 1965. Pays standard royalty.

How to Contact: Submit demo tape by mail. Unsolicited submissions are OK. Prefers cassette with 3 songs and lyric sheets. Include SASE. Responds in 3 weeks.

Music: Mostly **country**, **Christian country-gospel** and **bluegrass**; also **comedy**. Published "Tonight Is Mine" (single by Stampley/Shirley/Alderman), from *Rockin' Country Party* (album), recorded by Confederate Railroad (country), released 2000 on Atlantic; and "Red White and Blue" (single by Tony Glenn Rast), recorded by Fox Brothers, released 2001 on Mercy Street.

Tips: "Submit quality demos. Also interested in good lyrics for co-writing."

☑ ◑ **SUNSONGS MUSIC (BMI)/DARK SUN MUSIC (SESAC)**, Administrator for WDA Music (ASCAP), 52 N. Evarts Ave., Elmsford NY 10523. (914)592-2563. Fax: (914)592-6905. E-mail: mberman438@aol.com. **Contact:** Michael Berman (pop, country, rock); John Henderson (R&B, hip-hop), professional managers. Music publisher, record producer and talent agency (Hollywood East Entertainment). Estab. 1981. Publishes 20 songs/year; publishes 10 new songwriters/year. Staff size: 6. Pays standard royalty; co-publishing deals available for established writers.

How to Contact: Submit demo tape by mail. Unsolicited submissions are OK. Prefers CD, cassette with 3-4 songs and lyric sheet. Include SASE. Responds in 1 month.

Music: Mostly **dance-oriented** and **R&B**; also **rock (all styles)** and **top 40/pop**. Does not want hard core rap or heavy metal. Published "My First Love" (single by William Duvall/Kevin Ceballo/John Henderson), recorded by Kevin Ceballo (pop), released 2001 on Universal; and "Como Fuecapaz" (single by William Duvall) from *Mi Primer Amor* (album), recorded by Kevin Ceballo (latin), released 2001 on RMM.

Tips: "Submit material with strong hook and know the market being targeted by your song."

◑ **T.C. PRODUCTIONS/ETUDE PUBLISHING CO. (BMI)**, 121 Meadowbrook Dr., Somerville NJ 08876. (908)359-5110. Fax: (908)359-1962. E-mail: tcproductions@ren.com. Website: www.vmgmusic.com. President: Tony Camillo. Professional Manager (R&B): Jacqui Collins. Professional Manager (dance): Gene Serina. Music publisher and record producer. Estab. 1992. Publishes 25-50 songs/year; publishes 3-6 new songwriters/year. Pays negotiable royalty.

Affiliate(s): We Iz It Music Publishing (ASCAP) and Etude/Barcam (BMI).

How to Contact: *Write or call first and obtain permission to submit.* Prefers cassette with 3-4 songs and lyric sheet. Include SASE. Responds in 1 month.

Music: Mostly **R&B** and **dance**; also **country** and **outstanding pop ballads**. Published "Living in the Light" (single by Michelle Parto), recorded by Michelle Parto (pop), released 2001 on Wee Be Records; *God Loves You* (album), recorded by Faith (spiritual), released 2001 on Faith Records.

Ⓝ ◑ **TALBOT MUSIC GROUP (ASCAP, BMI)**, 2 Music Circle S., Nashville TN 37203. (615)244-6200. Fax: (615)254-8860. E-mail: talbotmusi@aol.com. Music publisher. Estab. 1984. Publishes 40 songs/year. Hires staff songwriters. Pays standard royalty.

Affiliate(s): Plainspoken Music Publishing, Inc. (ASCAP) and Harbot (SESAC).

How to Contact: *Talbot Music Group does not accept unsolicited submissions.*

Music: Published "Austin" (single by David Kent/Kirsti Manna) from *Blake Shelton* (album), recorded by Blake Shelton (country), released 2001 on Giant/Warner Bros.

✦ ◯ **THIRD WAVE PRODUCTIONS LIMITED**, P.O. Box 563, Gander, Newfoundland A1V 2E1 Canada. (709)256-8009. Fax: (709)256-7411. Website: www.buddywasisname.com. **Contact:** Arch. Bonnell, president. Music publisher, record company (Third Wave/Street Legal), distribution and marketing company. Estab. 1986. Publishes 20 songs/year; publishes 2 new songwriters/year.

How to Contact: Submit demo tape by mail. Unsolicited submissions are OK. Prefers cassette or DAT with lyric sheet. Include SASE. Responds in 2 months.

✦ ⊕ **SENDING TO A COUNTRY** other than your own? Be sure to send International Reply Coupons (IRCs) instead of stamps for replies or return of your materials.

Music: Mostly **traditional Newfoundland**, **Celtic/Irish**, **folk**; also **bluegrass**, **country** and **pop/rock**. Published *Salt Beef Junkie* and *He's a Part of Me* (albums by Buddy Wosisname), recorded by The Other Fellers (traditional); and *Nobody Never Told Me* (album), written and recorded by The Psychobilly Cadillacs (country), all on Third Wave Productions.

N TOURMALINE MUSIC, INC. (BMI), 2831 Dogwood Place, Nashville TN 37204. (615)269-8682. Fax: (615)269-8929. Website: http://songsfortheplanet.com. **Contact:** Justin Peters, president. Music publisher. Estab. 1980.
Affiliate(s): Justin Peters Music (BMI), LITA Music (ASCAP) and Platinum Planet Music.
How to Contact: Submit demo by mail. Unsolicited submissions are OK. Prefers CD with 5 songs and lyric sheet. Does not return material. "Place code '2003' on each envelope submission."
Music: Mostly **worship**, **country** and some **classic rock**. Published "Making War In The Heavenlies" (single by George Searcy), recorded by Ron Kenoly on Integrity Records; "The Hurt Is Worth The Chance" (single by Justin Peters/Billy Simon), recorded by Gary Chapman on RCA/BMG Records; and "For So Long" (single by Monroe Jones/Chris McCollum), recorded by GLAD on Benson Records (also recorded by DMB Band, Connie Scot).

☑ ☒ ◑ TOWER MUSIC GROUP 50 Music Square W., Suite 201, Nashville TN 37203. (615)320-7003. Fax: (615)320-7006. E-mail: castleua@bellsouth.net. Website: www.castlerecords.com. **Contact:** Dave Sullivan, A&R Director. Professional Managers: Ed Russell; Eddie Bishop. Music publisher, record company (Castle Records) and record producer. Estab. 1969. Publishes 50 songs/year; publishes 10 new songwriters/year. Staff size: 15. Pays standard royalty.
Affiliate(s): Cat's Alley Music (ASCAP) and Alley Roads Music (BMI).
How to Contact: *See submission policy on website.* Prefers cassette with 3 songs and lyric sheet. Does not return material. "You may follow up via e-mail." Responds in 3 months only if interested.
Film & TV: Places 2 songs in film and 26 songs in TV/year. Published "Run Little Girl" (by J.R. Jones/Eddie Ray), recorded by J.R. Jones in *Roadside Prey*.
Music: Mostly **country** and **R&B**; also **blues**, **pop** and **gospel**. Published "If You Broke My Heart" (single by Condrone) from *If You Broke My Heart* (album), recorded by Kimberly Simon (country); "I Wonder Who's Holding My Angel Tonight" (single) from *Up Above* (album), recorded by Carl Butler (country); and "Psychedelic Fantasy" (single by Paul Sullivan/Priege) from *The Hip Hoods* (album), recorded by The Hip Hoods (power/metal/y2k), all released 2001 on Castle Records.
Tips: "Please contact us via e-mail with any other demo submissions questions."

⊕ ☒ ◑ TRANSAMERIKA MUSIKVERLAG KG, Wilhelmstrasse 10, 23611 Bad Schwartau, Germany. Phone: 0049-451-21530. E-mail: transamerika@online.de. Website: www.TRANSAMERIKAmusik.de. General Manager: Pia Kaminsky. **Hamburg:** Isestrasse 77, 20149 Hamburg, Germany. Phone: 0049-40-46961527. E-mail: transamerika@t-online.de. Professional Manager: Kirsten Jung. Member: GEMA, PRS, KODA, NCB, APRA. Music publisher and administrator. Estab. 1978. Staff size: 3. Pays 50% royalty if releasing a record; 85% if only administrating.
Affiliate(s): German Fried Music, Screen Music Services Ltd. (London), Cors Ltd. (London), MCI Ltd. (London), Leosong Music Australia Rty. Ltd. (Sydney) and MCS Music Ltd. (USA, London).
How to Contact: "We accept only released materials—no demos!" Submit CD or VHS videocassette. Does not return material. Responds only if interested.
Film & TV: Places several songs in film and 2 songs in TV/year.
Music: Mostly **pop**; also **rock**, **country**, **film music** and **reggae**. Published "T'estimo (I Love you")" (single), written and recorded by José Carreras.
Tips: "We are specializing in administering (filing, registering, licensing and finding unclaimed royalties, and dealing with counter-claims) publishers worldwide."

☑ ☒ ◑ TRANSITION MUSIC CORPORATION (ASCAP, BMI, SESAC), 2690 N. Beachwood Ave., Los Angeles CA 90068. (323)860-7074. Fax: (323)860-7986. E-mail: onestopmus@aol.com. Director of Film and Television Music: Jennifer Brown. President: Donna Ross-Jones. Vice President: David Jones. Administration: Mike Dobson. Music publisher. Estab. 1988. Publishes 250 songs/year; publishes 20 new songwriters/year. Variable royalty based on song placement and writer.

Affiliate(s): Pushy Publishing (ASCAP), Creative Entertainment Music (BMI) and One Stop Shop Music (SESAC).
How to Contact: Address submissions to: New Submissions Dept. Submit demo tape by mail. Unsolicited submissions are OK. Prefers cassette, DAT or CD with 3 songs. Include SASE. Responds in 3 weeks.
Film & TV: "TMC provides music for film, TV and commercials."
Music: All styles.
Tips: "Supply master quality material with great songs."

⬤ **ULTIMATE PEAK MUSIC (BMI)**, P.O. Box 707, Nashville TN 37076. E-mail: greenzebra@h ome.com. Website: http://members.home.net/greenzebra/. **Contact:** Danny Crader, creative manager. Music publisher. Estab. 1992. Publishes 35 songs/year; publishes 4 new songwriters/year. Hires staff writers. Staff size: 4. Pays standard royalty.
How to Contact: Submit demo tape by mail. Unsolicited submissions are OK. Prefers cassette with 1-6 songs and lyric sheet. Include SASE. Responds in 6 weeks.
Music: Mostly **country** and **MTV pop/rock**. Published "Right In The Heart" (single by Rob Sparks) from *That's It* (album), recorded by King Cone (country), released 2001 on Ah! Records; "I Wanna Be Free" (single by Jordan Mycoskie) from *Jordan Mycoskie* (album), recorded by Jordan Mycoskie (Americana), released 2002 on Ah! Records; "I Love Animals" (single by Carla Rhodes) from *Carla's Golden Hits Volume 6* (album), recorded by Carla Rhodes, released 2002 on Green Zebra.
Tips: "Listen to the radio and compare your songs to the hits—not for recording quality, but for substance and content and structure—and be objective and realistic and honest with yourself."

⬤ **UNIVERSAL MUSIC PUBLISHING**, 12 Music Circle S., Nashville TN 37203.
 • In 1999, MCA Music Publishing and PolyGram Music Publishing merged into Universal Music Publishing.
How to Contact: *Does not accept unsolicited submissions.*

[N] ⬤ **UNKNOWN SOURCE MUSIC (ASCAP)**, 907 Baltimore St., Mobile AL 36605. (251)716-6995. E-mail: platinumforce@hotmail.com. **Contact:** Domonic La Force, A&R. Music publisher, record company (Smokin Ya Productions) and record producer. Estab. 1993. Publishes 5-10 songs/year; publishes 1-2 new songwriters/year. Hires staff songwriters. Staff size: 5. Pays standard royalty.
Affiliate(s): Sundance Records (ASCAP), Critique Records.
How to Contact: Submit demo tape by mail. Unsolicited submissions are OK. Prefers cassette with 3 songs. Does not return material. Responds in 6 weeks.
Music: Mostly **rap/hip-hop**, **R&B** and **alternative**. Published "Luv 4 Money," written and recorded by DaForce; "I Don't Know," written and recorded by Cluster; and *Smokeout Queen* (single by T. Harris), all released 1999 on Unknown Source Records.
Tips: "Keep working with us, be patient, be willing to work hard. Send your very best work."

⬤ **VAAM MUSIC GROUP (BMI)**, P.O. Box 29550, Hollywood CA 90029-0550. Phone/fax: (323)664-7765. E-mail: pmarti3636@aol.com. **Contact:** Pete Martin, president. Music publisher and record producer (Pete Martin/Vaam Productions). Estab. 1967. Publishes 9-24 new songs/year. Pays standard royalty.
Affiliate(s): Pete Martin Music (ASCAP).
How to Contact: Prefers cassette with 2 songs and lyric sheet. Include SASE. Responds in 1 month. "Small packages only."
Music: Mostly **top 40/pop**, **country** and **R&B**. "Submitted material must have potential of reaching top 5 on charts."
Tips: "Study the top 10 charts in the style you write. Stay current and up-to-date with today's market."

N ◯ VALIANT RECORDS & MANAGEMENT, P.O. Box 180099, Dallas TX 75218-0099. (214)327-0808. Fax: (214)324-5567. E-mail: Vvance@flash.net. Website: www.vincevance.com and www.vincevance.net. **Contact:** Andy Stone, president. Music Publisher. Estab. 1971. Publishes 20 songs/year; publishes 1 new songwriter/year. Staff size: 5. Pays standard royalty of 50%.
Affiliate(s): Brightstone Publishing (ASCAP) and Brightstone Music Publishing (SESAC).
How to Contact: Submit demo tape by mail. Unsolicited submissions are OK. Prefers cassette, CD, videocassette with a maximum of 4 songs and lyric sheet, lead sheet, and cover letter. SASE. "No guarantees!" Does not return submissions. Responds only if interested.
Music: Mostly **parodies** and **top 40 country**; also **adult contemporary**, **top 40**, **children's** and **novelty**. No rap or X-rated material. Published "Cruising the Coast" (single by Terry Houle/Troy Powers/Andy Stone) and "Contents Under Pressure" (single by Troy Powers) from *Cruising the Coast* (album), recorded by Vince Vance (rock), released 2001 on Valiant Records; and "My Valentine" (single by Troy Powers/Ed Loftus/Andy Stone), recorded by Vince Vance (AC), released 2002 on Valiant Records.
Tips: "Submit clear recordings where we can hear the lyrics, melody, chord structure. Your expertise as an arranger is appreciated, but we find that producers have their own ideas. We have had the best luck with novelty, parodies, holiday songs and mainstream country, but we are looking for hits!"

◯ VOKES MUSIC PUBLISHING (BMI), Box 12, New Kensington PA 15068-0012. (724)335-2775. President: Howard Vokes. Music publisher, record company, booking agency and promotion company.
How to Contact: Submit cassette with 3 songs and lyric or lead sheet. Include SASE. Responds in 1 week.
Music: Mostly **traditional country/bluegrass** and **gospel**. Published "A Million Tears" (single by Duke & Null), recorded by Johnny Eagle Feather on Vokes Records; "I Won't Be Your Honky Tonk Queen" (single by Vokes/Wallace), recorded by Bunnie Mills on Pot-Of-Gold Records; and "Break The News" (single by Vokes/Webb), recorded by Bill Beere on Oakhill Records.
Tips: "We're always looking for country songs that tell a story, and only interested in hard-traditional-bluegrass, country and country gospel songs. Please no 'copy-cat songwriters.' "

N ▼ ◯ WARNER/CHAPPELL MUSIC, INC., 10585 Santa Monica Blvd., Third Floor, Los Angeles CA 90025-4950. (310)441-8600. Fax: (310)470-3232. New York office: 1775 Broadway, 23rd Floor, New York NY 10019. (212)419-2600. Fax: (212)419-2633. Music publisher.
How to Contact: *Warner/Chappell does not accept unsolicited material.*

✓ ◯ WEAVER OF WORDS MUSIC (BMI), P.O. Box 803, Tazewell VA 24651. (276)988-6267. **Contact:** H.R. Cook, president. Music publisher and record company (Fireball Records). Estab. 1978. Publishes 12 songs/year. Pays standard royalty.
Affiliate(s): Weaver of Melodies Music (ASCAP).
How to Contact: Submit demo tape by mail. Unsolicited submissions are OK. Prefers cassette with 3 songs and lyric or lead sheets. Include SASE. Responds in 3 weeks.
Music: Mostly **country**. Published "Winds of Change" (single), written and recorded by Cecil Surrett; "Texas Saturday Night" and "Old Flame Burning" (singles), written and recorded by H.R. Cook, all on Fireball Records (country).

◯ WEMAR MUSIC CORP. (BMI), 836 N. La Cienega Blvd., #276, W. Hollywood CA 90069. Phone/fax: (323)692-1037. **Contact:** Stuart Wiener, President. Music publisher. Estab. 1940. Publishes 30 songs/year; publishes 30 new songwriters/year. Pays standard royalty.
Affiliate(s): Grand Music Corp. (ASCAP).
How to Contact: Submit demo tape by mail. Unsolicited submissions are OK. "No phone calls." Include SASE. Responds in 2 months.
Music: Mostly **pop**, **country**, **R&B** and **dance**. Published "Pearl" and "Heavy Hitter" (singles), written and recorded by Geri Verdi on Mills Records (blues); and "Meat Street" (single), written and recorded by Neal Fox on Gravity Records (Broadway Show).

⊕ ✓ ◐ BERTHOLD WENGERT (MUSIKVERLAG), Hauptstrasse 36, D-76327, Pfinztal-Sollingen, Germany. **Contact:** Berthold Wengert. Music publisher. Pays standard GEMA royalty.
How to Contact: Prefers cassette and complete score for piano. SAE and IRC. Responds in 1 month. "No cassette returns!"
Music: Mostly **light music** and **pop**.

▣ ◐ WESTWOOD MUSIC GROUP (ASCAP, BMI), 1031 Amboy Ave., Suite 202, Edison NJ 08837. (732)225-8600. Fax: (732)225-8644. E-mail: music@westwoodmusicgroup.com. Website: www.westwoodmusicgroup.com. President: Victor Kaply. Vice President/Creative Services: Steve Willoughby. **Film & TV Dept.:** 521 Fifth Ave., Suite 1700, New York NY 10175. (212)619-3500. Fax: (212)619-3588. E-mail: filmmusic@westwoodmusicgroup.com. **Contact:** Steve Willoughby, director of film/TV music. Music publisher. Publishes 30 songs/year; publishes 2 new songwriters/year. Staff size: 4. Pays standard royalty.
How to Contact: *Write first and obtain permission to submit.* Prefers CD with 3 songs and lyric sheet. Include SASE. Responds in 6 weeks.
Music: Mostly **rock**; also **pop**. Published "History" (single), written and recorded by Geoff Byrd (pop), released 2001 on Chrome Records; "She Let Me Go" (single), written and recorded by Brian Clayton (country), released 2001 on Westwood Records; and "Starlight Dancing" (single), written and recorded by Stephen Kaminski and featured in the ABC original movie "When Billie Beat Bobby," released 2001 on ACB-TV.
Tips: Submit a "neat promotional package with bio and lyrics."

◐ WHITE CAT MUSIC, P.O. Box 19720, Fountain Hills AZ 85269. (480)951-3115. Fax: (480)951-3074. Professional Manager: Frank Fara. Producer: Patty Parker. Music publisher, record company and record producer. Member CMA, CCMA, BCCMA and BBB. Estab. 1978. Publishes 12 songs/year; publishes 5 new songwriters/year. Staff size: 2. "50% of our published songs are from non-charted and developing writers." Pays standard royalty.
Affiliate(s): Rocky Bell Music (BMI), How The West Was Sung Music (BMI) and Crystal Canyon Music (ASCAP).
● Fara and Parker are authors of the book *How to Open Doors in the Music Industry—the Independent Way.*
How to Contact: Submit demo tape by mail. Unsolicited submissions are OK. Prefers cassettes with 2-4 songs and include lyric sheet. Include SASE. Responds in 2 weeks.
Music: All styles of **country**—traditional to crossover. Published "Great American Country" (single by Paula Mengarelli/Tom Mengarelli/Jaff Hansel), recorded by Paula Mengarelli (country), released 2001 on Comstock; "She's Bad News" (single by Roy G. Ownbey/Alexandria Sheraton), recorded by Jentille (country), released 2001 on Comstock; and "Give Your Love to Me" (single by Michael Ray) from *Reason to Believe* (album), recorded by Derek Carle (country), released 2001 on Comstock.
Tips: "Have an out front vocal presentation so lyric can be heard. Go easy on long instrumental intros and breaks which distract. Send only two to four songs—medium to up tempo are always in demand. This helps stack the odds in your favor for getting heard."

◐ WHITING MUSIC (ASCAP, BMI), P.O. Box 110002, Nashville TN 37211. (615)331-8945. Fax: (615)315-9391. E-mail: musicnash@aol.com. Website: www.whitingmusic.com. Publisher: James Whiting. **Contact:** Lisa Dey, professional manager. Music publisher and record producer (Jamey Whiting). Estab. 1982. Publishes 12 songs/year; publishes 4 new songwriters/year. Staff size: 2. Hires staff songwriters. Pays standard royalty.
Affiliate(s): James Whiting Music (ASCAP) and Moody Judy Music (BMI).
How to Contact: Submit demo tape by mail. Unsolicited submissions are OK. Prefers cassette or CD with 3 songs, lyric sheet and cover letter. Include SASE. Responds in 3 weeks.

▨ ⊕ SENDING TO A COUNTRY other than your own? Be sure to send International Reply Coupons (IRCs) instead of stamps for replies or return of your materials.

Music: Mostly **country**, **pop** and **rock**; also **blues**, **jazz** and **reggae**. Published "Long Haul" (single), written and recorded by Marcus Vickers (country) on Viking; *Guilty* (album by B. Loomis/P. Loomis), recorded by B. Loomis (country); and *Hear Me Now (For All the Things Never Said)* (album by J. Fischer/J. Whiting), recorded by Joice Walton (blues) on Pinnacle.

Tips: "Songs should be less than 3½ minutes long, should have a clear title or hook, and should be presented with a clean vocal with simple demo."

☑ ◑ WILCOM PUBLISHING (ASCAP), Box 4456, West Hills CA 91308. (661)285-8032. Fax: (661)285-8032. E-mail: info@wilcompublishing.com. Website: www.wilcompublishing.com. **Contact:** William Clark, Owner. Music publisher. Estab. 1989. Publishes 10-15 songs/year; publishes 1-2 new songwriters/year. Staff size: 2. Pays standard royalty.

How to Contact: *Write or call first and obtain permission to submit.* Prefers cassette with 1-2 songs and lyric sheet. Include SASE. Responds in 3 weeks.

Music: Mostly **R&B**, **pop** and **rock**; also **country**. Does not want rap. Published "Girl Can't Help It" (single by W. Clark/D. Walsh/P. Oland), recorded by Stage 1 on Rockit Records (top 40).

▧ ♥ WINSTON & HOFFMAN HOUSE MUSIC PUBLISHERS (ASCAP, BMI), P.O. Box 1415, Burbank CA 91507-1415. Fax: (323)462-8342. E-mail: sixties1@aol.com. **Contact:** Lynne Robin Green, president. Music publisher. Estab. 1958. Publishes 25 songs/year. Staff size: 2. Pays standard royalty.

Affiliate(s): Lansdowne Music Publishers (ASCAP), Bloor Music (BMI) and Ben Ross Music (ASCAP), "also administers 26 other firms."

How to Contact: Submit demo tape by mail. Unsolicited submissions are OK. "*Do not query first. Do not call.*" Prefers cassette with 3 songs maximum and lyric sheet. "*Must include SASE, or no reply!*" Responds in 1 month.

Film & TV: Places 45 songs in film and 25 songs in TV/year. Recently published "Hard Work" (by J. Handy) for *The Bernie Mac Show*; theme and cues (by G. Farias) for *The Christian Show* (Universion Network) and for *The Ritmo Latin Music Awards 2001* (Telemundo network); "Dooley" (by Dillard/Jayne) in *Baby Blues*; "Closer Walk With Thee" (by Craver/Henderson) in *Smiling Fish and Goat on Fire*; "Born to Jump" (by Larry Dunn) in *Olympics 2000*.

Music: Mostly **R&B dance**, **ballads**, **hip hop**, **vocal jazz**, **alternative rock** and **R&B**; also **bluegrass**, **Spanish pop** and **pop ballads**. Published "Mom Praying" (single by Scales/Grant/Smith/Jordan) from *The Reason* (album), recorded by Beanie Siegel (hip-hop), released 2001 on Universal-DEF Jam Records; "Penetration" (single by Stephen Leonard), recorded by The Ventures (surf rock), released 2001 on Varese Sarabande; "Old Home Place" (single by Dean Webb/Mitch Jayne) from *Slack Family Bluegrass* (album), recorded by Slack Family Bluegrass Band (bluegrass), released 1999 on Planetary Records; and "Souljacker Part 1" (single by Everette/Norton/Siegel), recorded by Souljacker-The EELS (rock/alternative), released 2001 on Universal/Dreamworks.

Tips: "Be selective in what you send. Be realistic about which artist it suits! Be patient in allowing time to place songs. Be open to writing for films—be interesting lyrically and striking melodically."

◒ WORLD FAMOUS MUSIC CO. (ASCAP), 1364 Sherwood Rd., Highland Park IL 60035. (847)831-3123. E-mail: getchip@interacess.com. **Contact:** Chip Altholz, president. Music publisher and record producer. Estab. 1986. Publishes 25 songs/year; 3-4 new songwriters/year. Pays standard royalty.

How to Contact: *E-mail first to obtain permission to submit.* Submit demo tape by mail. Unsolicited submissions are OK. Prefers cassette with 3 songs and lyric sheet. Include SASE. Responds in 1 month.

Music: Mostly **pop**, **R&B** and **rock**. Published "Harmony" (single by Altholz/Faldner), recorded by Barry Faldner on Amertel Records (ballad); and "Running" and "Serious" (singles), both written and recorded by Nick Bak on Pink Street Records.

Tips: "Have a great melody, a lyric that is visual and tells a story and a commercial arrangement."

▧ ◒ YOUR BEST SONGS PUBLISHING, P.O. Box 488, Auburn WA 98071. E-mail: jcmark @earthlink.net. General Manager: Craig Markovich. Music publisher. Estab. 1988. Publishes 1-5 songs/year; publishes 1-3 new songwriters/year. Query for royalty terms.

How to Contact: *Write first and obtain permission to submit.* Prefers cassette with 1-3 songs and lyric sheet. "Submit your 1-3 best songs per type of music. Use separate cassettes per music type and indicate music type on each cassette." Include SASE. Responds in 3 months.

Music: Mostly **country**, **rock/blues** and **pop/rock**; also **progressive**, **A/C**, some **heavy metal** and **New Age**. Published "Sea of Dreams," written and recorded by J.C. Mark on Cybervoc Productions (New Age).

Tips: "We just require good lyrics, good melodies and good rhythm in a song. We absolutely do not want music without a decent melodic structure. We do not want lyrics with foul language or lyrics that do not inspire some form of imaginative thought."

☑ ☒ ◙ **ZETTITALIA MUSIC INTERNATIONAL (ASCAP, BMI)**, P.O. Box 8442, Universal City CA 91618. (818)506-8533. Fax: (818)506-8534. E-mail: zettworks@aol.com. Website: www.pplzmi.com. **Contact:** Cheyenne Phoenix, A&R. Assistant, A&R: Kaitland Diamond. Music publisher. Estab. 1995. Publishes 40 songs/year; publishes 2 new songwriters/year. Staff size: 2. Hires staff songwriters. Pays standard royalty.

Affiliate(s): Zett One Songs (ASCAP) and Zett Two Music (BMI).

How to Contact: *Write to obtain permission to submit.* "Include SASE or e-mail." Prefers cassette or CD with 3 songs. Include SASE. Responds in 6 weeks.

Film & TV: Places 2 songs in film and 4 songs in TV/year.

Music: Mostly **pop**, **film music**, **country**, **instrumental** and **R&B**. Does not want gangster rap or heavy metal. Published *Wings of Faith* (album), written and recorded by Karen Heart (Christian), released 2000 on KGM Records.

Tips: "In art, be a good student and stay true to your instincts. In business, be thorough, realistic, flexible and straightforward. Finally, The Golden Rule rules."

Ⓝ ◙ **ZITEL PUBLISHING CO. (BMI)**, 4102 Buffalo Gap Rd. Suite 5, Abilene TX 79605. (915)692-9197. E-mail: zitel@juno.com. **Contact:** Karen McKelvain, CEO (christian/children's); Tony Lowe, President (R&B, pop, rock); Larry Donnelly, Vice President (country). Music publisher. Estab. 2002. Staff size: 3.

How to Contact: Submit demo tape by mail. Unsolicited submissions are OK. Prefers cassette or CD with 2-4 songs and lyric sheet. Does not return material. Responds in two months to submissions only if interested.

Music: Mostly **Christian**, **country** and **rock**; also **pop**, **children's** and **r&b**. Recently published *The Other Side of Jordan* (album by Henry Burleson), recorded by Heaven's Jubilee (country/gospel); *Carnival of Faith* (album), written and recorded by Kaitlyn Martin (Christian/children's); and *Heart & Soul* (album by Glover/Babb/Swafford), recorded by Heart and Soul Group (Christian R&B).

◙ **ZOMBA MUSIC PUBLISHING (ASCAP, BMI)**, 137-139 W. 25th St., New York NY 10001. (212)727-0016. West Hollywood office: 9000 Sunset Blvd., Suite 300, West Hollywood CA 90069. Music publisher. Publishes 5,000 songs/year.

Affiliate(s): Zomba Enterprises, Inc. (ASCAP); Zomba Songs, Inc. (BMI).

How to Contact: *Zomba Music Publishing does not accept unsolicited material.* "Contact us through management or an attorney."

Music: Mostly **R&B**, **pop** and **rap**; also **rock** and **alternative**. Published ". . . Baby One More Time" (single by M. Martin), recorded by Britney Spears on Jive; "Home Alone" (single by R. Kelly/K. Price/K. Murray), recorded by R. Kelly featuring Keith Murray on Jive; and "Taking Everything" (single by G. Levert/D. Allamby/L. Browder/A. Roberson), recorded by Gerald Levert on EastWest.

Additional Music Publishers

The following companies are also music publishers, but their listings are found in other sections of the book. See the General Index for page numbers, then read the listings for submission information.

"A" Major Sound Corporation
A.P.I. Records
Aberdeen Productions
ABL Records
ACR Productions
Afterschool Publishing Company/Records, Inc.
Allegheny Music Works
American Artists Entertainment
Ariana Records
Arkadia Entertainment Corp.
Atlan-Dec/Grooveline Records
Avita Records
Bagatelle Record Company
Baird Enterprises, Ron
Bal Records
Banana Records
Barrett Rock 'n' Roll Enterprises, Paul
Blue Gem Records
Blue Wave Productions
Blues Alley Records
Boulevard Music & Publishing
Brentwood Records/Diadem Records
BSW Records
Butler Music, Bill
Cacophony Productions
Cambria Records & Publishing
Capstan Record Production
Cellar Records
Celt Musical Services, Jan
Chattahoochee Records
Cherry Street Records
Chucker Music Inc.
Cimirron/Rainbird Records
Circuit Rider Talent & Management Co.
Class Act Productions/Management
Coffee and Cream Productions
Coppin, Johnny/Red Sky Records
Cosmotone Records
CPA Records
Criss-Cross Industries
Cupit Productions, Jerry
DAP Entertainment
Dagene/Cabletown Company
De Miles, Edward
Diamond Entertainment, Joel
Discmedia
Disc-tinct Music, Inc.
Drive Entertainment
Ellis International Talent Agency, The
Emerald City Records
Enterprize Records-Tapes
Esquire International
Eternal Song Agency, The
Factory Beat Records, Inc.

Fireant
Fish of Death Records and Management
Flat Records
Fresh Entertainment
Front Row Records
Gallery II Records/Jumpin' Jack Records
Generic Records, Inc.
Gig Records
Glocc Cocced Records
Golden Guru Entertainment
Golden Triangle Records
Goldwax Record Corporation
Green Bear Records
Groove Makers' Recordings
Gueststar Entertainment Agency/Records, Inc.
Hailing Frequency Music Productions
Happy Man Records
Hardison International Entertainment Corporation
Haworth Productions
Heads Up Int., Ltd.
Heart Consort Music
Heart Music, Inc.
Hi-Bias Records Inc.
Horizon Records, Inc.
Hot Wings Entertainment
Hottrax Records
Huge Production, Inc., A
Hupp Enterprises, Joe
J & V Management
James Management, Roger
Jay Jay Publishing & Record Co.
Joey Records
Jump Productions
Kaupp Records
Kingston Records and Talent
Knight Agency, Bob
Known Artist Productions
Kuper Personal Management
L.A. Entertainment, Inc.
L.A. Records (Canada)
L.A. Records (Michigan)
Lawrence, Ltd., Ray
Levy Management, Rick
Lock
Lucifer Records, Inc.
M.B.H. Music Management
Mac-Attack Productions
Magid Productions, Lee
Major Entertainment, Inc.
Marvel Records, Andy
Mathews, d/b/a Hit or Myth Productions, Scott
Mighty Records
Montgomery Management, Gary F.
Muse Artists Inc.

New Experience Records
Noteworthy Enterprises
NPO Records, Inc.
On the Level Music!
Only New Age Music, Inc.
P. & N. Records
PGE Platinum Groove Entertainment
Philly Breakdown Recording Co.
Pickwick/Mecca/International Records
Pierce, Jim
Playbones Records
PPL Entertainment Group
Precision Management
Presence Records
Rainbow Collection Ltd.
Rampant Records
RAVE Records, Inc.
Red-Eye Records
Riohcat Music
RN'D Productions
Roll On Records®
Ruffnation Records
Sahara Records and Filmworks Entertainment
Sa'Mall Management
Satellite Music
Sea Cruise Productions, Inc.
Serge Entertainment Group
Silver Bow Management
Silver Thunder Music Group
Sound Management Direction
Sound Works Entertainment Productions Inc.
SRS Productions/Hit Records Network

Staircase Promotion
Stardust
Stormin' Norman Productions
Street Records
Stuart Audio Services
Studio Seven
SunCountry Records
Sureshot Records
Swift River Productions
T.J. Booker Ltd.
Tangent® Records
Tari, Roger Vincent
Tas Music Co./Dave Tasse Entertainment
Texas Fantasy Music Group
3rd Stone Records
Third Wave Productions Ltd.
TMC Productions
TVT Records
Umpire Entertainment Enterprizes
Universal Music Marketing
Van Pol Management, Hans
Vickers Music Association, Charles
Wall Street Music
Warehouse Creek Recording Corp.
Warner Productions, Cheryl K.
Weisman Production Group, The
Wemus Entertainment
Westpark Music - Records, Production & Publishing
Wilder Artists' Management, Shane
Williams Management, Yvonne
World Wide Management
X.R.L. Records/Music

Category Index

The Category Index is a good place to begin searching for a market for your songs. Below is an alphabetical list of 20 general music categories. If you write country songs and are looking for a publisher to pitch them, check the Country section in this index. There you will find a list of music publishers interested in hearing country songs. Once you locate the entries for those publishers, read the music subheading *carefully* to determine which companies are most interested in the type of country music you write. Some of the markets in this section do not appear in the Category Index because they have not indicated a specific preference. Most of these said they are interested in "all types" of music. Listings that were very specific, or whose description of the music they're interested in doesn't quite fit into these categories, also do not appear here.

Adult Contemporary (also easy listening, middle of the road, AAA, ballads, etc.)

Alexis
Allegheny Music Works
Baitstring Music
Bal & Bal Music Publishing Co.
Barkin' Foe the Master's Bone
Barren Wood Publishing
Bay Ridge Publishing Co.
Big Fish Music Publishing Group
BME Publishing
Bradley Music, Allan
Buried Treasure Music
California Country Music
Camex Music
Duane Music, Inc.
Emstone, Inc. Music Publishing
Gary Music, Alan
Green One Music
G-String Publishing
Hammel Associates, Inc., R.L.
Happy Melody
High-Minded Moma Publishing & Productions
Hitsburgh Music Co.
Inside Records/OK Songs
Ja/Nein Musikverlag GmbH
Just a Note
Kansa Records Corporation
Kaupps & Robert Publishing Co.
Lineage Publishing Co.
Mento Music Group
MIDI Track Publishing/ALLRS Music Publishing Co.
Montina Music
New Clarion Music Group
New Rap Jam Publishing, A
Pegasus Music
R.J. Music
Rockford Music Co.
Rondor Music International/Almo/Irving Music, A Universal Music Group Company
Rosebowl Music
Segal's Publications
Silicon Music Publishing Co.
Your Best Songs Publishing

Alternative (also modern rock, punk, college rock, new wave, hardcore, new music, industrial, ska, indie rock, garage, etc.)

A Ta Z Music
Abalone Publishing
Alco Music
Alias John Henry Tunes
Avalon Music
Bay Ridge Publishing Co.
Black Market Entertainment Recordings
Blue Dog Publishing and Records
Burnsongs
Camex Music
Cornelius Companies, The
Cotton Town Music Company
East Coast Music Publishing
Egyptianman Productions
Faverett Group
Juke Music
Lake Transfer Productions & Music
McJames Music Inc.
Mellow House Music
Montina Music
Pas Mal Publishing Sarl
Rock N Metal Music Publishing Co.
Rondor Music International/Almo/Irving Music, A Universal Music Group Company
Rosebowl Music
Unknown Source Music
Winston & Hoffman House Music Publishers
Zomba Music Publishing

Blues
Alexis
Bagatelle Music Publishing Co.
Bal & Bal Music Publishing Co.
Bay Ridge Publishing Co.
Brian Song Music Corp.
BSW Records
Christopher Publishing, Sonny
Cotton Town Music Company
Dave Music, Jof
Duane Music, Inc.
Frozen Inca Music
Ja/Nein Musikverlag GmbH
Mighty Blue Music Machine, The
Montina Music
Moon June Music
Nervous Publishing
Oyster Bay Music Publishing
R.J. Music
Rosebowl Music
Silicon Music Publishing Co.
Sizemore Music
Sound Cellar Music
Stellar Music Industries
Stuart Music Co., Jeb
Tower Music Group
Whiting Music

Children's
Flying Red Horse Publishing
Mayfair Music
Piano Press
Ren Zone Music
Rhythms Productions
Rosebowl Music
Segal's Publications
Simply Grand Music, Inc.
Zitel Publishing Co.

Classical (also opera, chamber music, serious music, choral, etc.)
Jae Music, Jana
Presser Co., Theodore

Country (also western, C&W, bluegrass, cowboy songs, western swing, honky-tonk, etc.)
Abalone Publishing
Alco Music
Alexis
Alias John Henry Tunes
All Rock Music
Allegheny Music Works
AlliSongs Inc.
Americatone International
ARAS Music
Avalon Music
Bagatelle Music Publishing Co.
Baitstring Music
Bal & Bal Music Publishing Co.
Balmur Entertainment

Barkin' Foe the Master's Bone
Barren Wood Publishing
Bay Ridge Publishing Co.
Beaverwood Audio-Video
Big Fish Music Publishing Group
Bradley Music, Allan
Branson Country Music Publishing
Brian Song Music Corp.
BSW Records
Buckeye Music Group
Buried Treasure Music
California Country Music
Cheavoria Music Co. (BMI)
Cherri/Holly Music
Christopher Publishing, Sonny
Cimirron Music
Coffee and Cream Publishing Company
Cornelius Companies, The
Cotton Town Music Company
Country Showcase America
Country Star Music
Cupit Music
Dapmor Publishing
De Miles Music Company, The Edward
Del Camino Music Publishing
Delev Music Company
Dell Music, Frank
Doss Music, Buster
Dream Seekers Publishing
Duane Music, Inc.
Earitating Music Publishing
East Coast Music Publishing
Egyptianman Productions
Emandell Tunes
EMF Productions
Emstone, Inc. Music Publishing
Famous Music Publishing Companies
Faverett Group
Frick Enterprises, Bob Scott
Fricon Music Company
Furrow Music
G Major Music
Gary Music, Alan
Glad Music Co.
Golden Music, August
Goodland Music Group Inc., The
Green One Music
G-String Publishing
Hammel Associates, Inc., R.L.
Hickory Lane Publishing and Recording
High-Minded Moma Publishing & Productions
Hitsburgh Music Co.
Hitsource Publishing
Inside Records/OK Songs
Iron Skillet Music
Jae Music, Jana
Jaelius Enterprises
Jerjoy Music
JoDa Music
Jolson Black & White Music, Al
JPMC Music Inc.

Juke Music
Just a Note
Kansa Records Corporation
Kaupps & Robert Publishing Co.
Kaysarah Music
Lari-Jon Publishing
Lexington Alabama Music Publishing
Lilly Music Publishing
Lineage Publishing Co.
Luick & Associates Music Publisher, Harold
M & T Waldoch Publishing, Inc.
Markea Music/Gina Pie Music
Marvin Publishing, John Weller
Master Source
McConkey Artists Agency Music Publishing
McCoy Music, Jim
McJames Music Inc.
Melody Hills Ranch Publishing Co.
Mento Music Group
MIDI Track Publishing/ALLRS Music Publishing
    Co.
Mighty Blue Music Machine, The
Monk Family Music Group
Montina Music
Moon June Music
Nervous Publishing
New Clarion Music Group
New Rap Jam Publishing, A
Northwest Alabama Music Publishing
Old Slowpoke Music
Ontrax Companies
Orchid Publishing
Oyster Bay Music Publishing
Pecos Valley Music
Pegasus Music
PEN Music Group, Inc.
Peters Music, Justin
Platinum Gold Music
Platinum Planet Music, Inc.
Portage Music
Pritchett Publications
R.J. Music
Rainbow Music Corp.
Ridge Music Corp.
Rocker Music/Happy Man Music
Rockford Music Co.
Rosebowl Music
Rustron Music Publishers
Sabteca Music Co.
Saddlestone Publishing
Schafer Music Group
Scott Music Group, Tim
Segal's Publications
Sellwood Publishing
Silicon Music Publishing Co.
Silver Thunder Music Group
Simply Grand Music, Inc.
Sizemore Music
Sound Cellar Music
Southern Most Publishing Company
Spradlin/Gleich Publishing

Starbound Publishing Co.
Stellar Music Industries
Stevens Music, Ray
Still Working Music Group
Stuart Music Co., Jeb
Sun Star Songs
T.C. Productions/Etude Publishing Co.
Third Wave Productions Limited
Tourmaline Music, Inc.
Tower Music Group
Transamerika Musikverlag KG
Ultimate Peak Music
Vaam Music Group
Vokes Music Publishing
Weaver of Words Music
Wemar Music Corp.
White Cat Music
Whiting Music
Wilcom Publishing
Winston & Hoffman House Music Publishers
Your Best Songs Publishing
Zettitalia Music International
Zitel Publishing Co.

Dance (also house, hi-NRG, disco, club, rave, techno, trip-hop, trance, etc.)
A Ta Z Music
Abalone Publishing
Alexis
Audio Music Publishers
Better Than Sex Music
BME Publishing
Cherri/Holly Music
Coffee and Cream Publishing Company
Dagene Music
De Miles Music Company, The Edward
Delev Music Company
Drive Music, Inc.
Duane Music, Inc.
East Coast Music Publishing
Edition Rossori
Fresh Entertainment
Gary Music, Alan
Goodland Music Group Inc., The
G-String Publishing
Happy Melody
Inside Records/OK Songs
Lake Transfer Productions & Music
Lilly Music Publishing
M & T Waldoch Publishing, Inc.
Makers Mark Gold
McJames Music Inc.
Mighty Blue Music Machine, The
Montina Music
Platinum Planet Music, Inc.
Pritchett Publications
Rockford Music Co.
Rosebowl Music
Shu'Baby Montez Music
Siegel Music Companies
Still Working Music Group

Stuart Music Co., Jeb
Succes
Sunsongs Music/Dark Son Music
T.C. Productions/Etude Publishing Co.
Valiant Records & Management
Wemar Music Corp.
Winston & Hoffman House Music Publishers

Folk (also acoustic, Celtic, etc.)
Alexis
Bay Ridge Publishing Co.
Cimirron Music
Earitating Music Publishing
Heupferd Musikverlag GmbH
Markea Music/Gina Pie Music
Montina Music
Piano Press
Rockford Music Co.
Rosebowl Music
Rustron Music Publishers
Schafer Music Group
Third Wave Productions Limited

Instrumental (also background music, musical scores, etc.)
Alpha Music Inc.
Big Fish Music Publishing Group
CTV Music (Great Britain)
Happy Melody
Jae Music, Jana
JPMC Music Inc.
Mayfair Music
Mento Music Group
PEN Music Group, Inc.
Rosebowl Music
Rustron Music Publishers
Shawnee Press, Inc.
Succes
Zettitalia Music International

Jazz (also fusion, bebop, swing, etc.)
Alexander Sr. Music
Alexis
ARAS Music
Bal & Bal Music Publishing Co.
Barkin' Foe the Master's Bone
Bay Ridge Publishing Co.
Egyptianman Productions
Heupferd Musikverlag GmbH
His Power Productions and Publishing
Jae Music, Jana
JPMC Music Inc.
Master Source
McConkey Artists Agency Music Publishing
Mellow House Music
Mighty Blue Music Machine, The
Montina Music
Old Slowpoke Music
Perla Music
Rainbow Music Corp.
Ridge Music Corp.

Rockford Music Co.
Rosebowl Music
Schafer Music Group
Simply Grand Music, Inc.
Stellar Music Industries
Stuart Music Co., Jeb
Whiting Music
Winston & Hoffman House Music Publishers

Latin (also Spanish, salsa, Cuban, conga, Brazilian, cumbja, rancheras, Mexican, merengue, Tejano, Tex Mex, etc.)
Alexis
Amen, Inc.
Americatone International
Del Camino Music Publishing
Egyptianman Productions
Famous Music Publishing Companies
Golden Music, August
Inside Records/OK Songs
Rosebowl Music

Metal (also thrash, grindcore, heavy metal, etc.)
Bay Ridge Publishing Co.
Egyptianman Productions
M & T Waldoch Publishing, Inc.
Pas Mal Publishing Sarl
Rock N Metal Music Publishing Co.
Rosebowl Music
Sound Cellar Music
Your Best Songs Publishing

New Age (also ambient)
Heupferd Musikverlag GmbH
High-Minded Moma Publishing & Productions
Rosebowl Music
Rustron Music Publishers
Sinus Musik Produktion, Ulli Weigel
Southern Most Publishing Company
Your Best Songs Publishing

Novelty (also comedy, humor, etc.)
Allegheny Music Works
Big Fish Music Publishing Group
Green One Music
Lexington Alabama Music Publishing
Moon June Music
Peters Music, Justin
Piano Press
Rosebowl Music
Sun Star Songs

Pop (also top 40, top 100, popular, chart hits, etc.)
A Ta Z Music
Abalone Publishing
Alco Music
Alexis
Allegheny Music Works
AlliSongs Inc.

Westwood Music Group
Whiting Music
Wilcom Publishing
Winston & Hoffman House Music Publishers
World Famous Music Co.
Your Best Songs Publishing
Zettitalia Music International
Zitel Publishing Co.
Zomba Music Publishing

R&B (also soul, black, urban, etc.)

A Ta Z Music
Alexander Sr. Music
Alexis
Allegheny Music Works
Americatone International
Audio Music Publishers
Avalon Music
Baitstring Music
Bal & Bal Music Publishing Co.
Barkin' Foe the Master's Bone
Bay Ridge Publishing Co.
Bernard Enterprises, Inc., Hal
Better Than Sex Music
Black Market Entertainment Recordings
Bradley Music, Allan
Buckeye Music Group
Burnsongs
California Country Music
Camex Music
Cheavoria Music Co. (BMI)
Coffee and Cream Publishing Company
Country Star Music
Dagene Music
Dapmor Publishing
Dave Music, Jof
De Miles Music Company, The Edward
Delev Music Company
Demi Monde Records & Publishing Ltd.
Drive Music, Inc.
Duane Music, Inc.
East Coast Music Publishing
Egyptianman Productions
EMF Productions
Emstone, Inc. Music Publishing
Ever-Open-Eye Music
Famous Music Publishing Companies
Fresh Entertainment
Frozen Inca Music
Gary Music, Alan
Hammel Associates, Inc., R.L.
Hes Free Productions & Publishing Company
His Power Productions and Publishing
Interplanetary Music
Jaelius Enterprises
Jasper Stone Music (ASCAP)/JSM Songs (BMI)
JPMC Music Inc.
Just a Note
Kansa Records Corporation
Kaupps & Robert Publishing Co.
Lake Transfer Productions & Music

Lexington Alabama Music Publishing
M & T Waldoch Publishing, Inc.
Major Entertainment
Makers Mark Gold
Manuiti L.A.
Markea Music/Gina Pie Music
Marvin Publishing, John Weller
McConkey Artists Agency Music Publishing
Mellow House Music
MIDI Track Publishing/ALLRS Music Publishing Co.
Mighty Blue Music Machine, The
Montina Music
Music Room Publishing Group, The
Nervous Publishing
New Rap Jam Publishing, A
Northwest Alabama Music Publishing
Old Slowpoke Music
Oyster Bay Music Publishing
PEN Music Group, Inc.
Platinum Gold Music
Platinum Planet Music, Inc.
Rainbow Music Corp.
Rondor Music International/Almo/Irving Music, A Universal Music Group Company
Rosebowl Music
Rustron Music Publishers
Sabteca Music Co.
Saddlestone Publishing
Scott Music Group, Tim
SDM
Segal's Publications
Shu'Baby Montez Music
Siegel Music Companies
Silver Blue Music/Oceans Blue Music
Silver Thunder Music Group
Simply Grand Music, Inc.
Sizemore Music
Southern Most Publishing Company
Starbound Publishing Co.
Stellar Music Industries
Stevens Music, Ray
Still Working Music Group
Stuart Music Co., Jeb
Sunsongs Music/Dark Son Music
T.C. Productions/Etude Publishing Co.
Tower Music Group
Unknown Source Music
Vaam Music Group
Valiant Records & Management
Wemar Music Corp.
Wilcom Publishing
Winston & Hoffman House Music Publishers
World Famous Music Co.
Your Best Songs Publishing
Zettitalia Music International
Zitel Publishing Co.
Zomba Music Publishing

Rap (also hip-hop, bass, etc.)

A Ta Z Music
Audio Music Publishers
Avalon Music
Barkin' Foe the Master's Bone
Bay Ridge Publishing Co.
Better Than Sex Music
Black Market Entertainment Recordings
BME Publishing
Burnsongs
Dagene Music
Dapmor Publishing
East Coast Music Publishing
Egyptianman Productions
Fresh Entertainment
Goodland Music Group Inc., The
Hes Free Productions & Publishing Company
Interplanetary Music
Jasper Stone Music (ASCAP)/JSM Songs (BMI)
Lake Transfer Productions & Music
Major Entertainment
Makers Mark Gold
Marvin Publishing, John Weller
Master Source
Mellow House Music
New Rap Jam Publishing, A
Oyster Bay Music Publishing
PEN Music Group, Inc.
Platinum Gold Music
Rosebowl Music
Shu'Baby Montez Music
Silver Blue Music/Oceans Blue Music
Stellar Music Industries
Stuart Music Co., Jeb
Unknown Source Music
Valiant Records & Management
Winston & Hoffman House Music Publishers
Zomba Music Publishing

Religious (also gospel, sacred, Christian, church, hymns, praise, inspirational, worship, etc.)

Alco Music
Alexander Sr. Music
Alexis
Allegheny Music Works
Amen, Inc.
ARAS Music
Audio Music Publishers
Bagatelle Music Publishing Co.
Bal & Bal Music Publishing Co.
Barkin' Foe the Master's Bone
Barren Wood Publishing
Bay Ridge Publishing Co.
Beaverwood Audio-Video
Big Fish Music Publishing Group
Bradley Music, Allan
Brentwood-Benson Music Publishing
Brian Song Music Corp.
California Country Music
Cherri/Holly Music

Coffee and Cream Publishing Company
Corelli's Music Box
Cornelius Companies, The
Cotton Town Music Company
Country Star Music
Dave Music, Jof
Dell Music, Frank
Egyptianman Productions
Emandell Tunes
EMF Productions
Ever-Open-Eye Music
Frick Enterprises, Bob Scott
G Major Music
Goodland Music Group Inc., The
Hammel Associates, Inc., R.L.
Hes Free Productions & Publishing Company
His Power Productions and Publishing
Hitsburgh Music Co.
Holy Spirit Music
Jaelius Enterprises
JoDa Music
JPMC Music Inc.
Juke Music
Just a Note
Kansa Records Corporation
Kaupps & Robert Publishing Co.
Lari-Jon Publishing
Leigh Music, Trixie
Lexington Alabama Music Publishing
Makers Mark Gold
McCoy Music, Jim
Mellow House Music
MIDI Track Publishing/ALLRS Music Publishing Co.
Mighty Blue Music Machine, The
Montina Music
New Rap Jam Publishing, A
Northwest Alabama Music Publishing
Orchid Publishing
Pritchett Publications
Rocker Music/Happy Man Music
Rosebowl Music
Saddlestone Publishing
Schafer Music Group
Scott Music Group, Tim
Sellwood Publishing
Shawnee Press, Inc.
Southern Most Publishing Company
Starbound Publishing Co.
Stellar Music Industries
Stuart Music Co., Jeb
Sun Star Songs
Tourmaline Music, Inc.
Tower Music Group
Vokes Music Publishing
Zitel Publishing Co.

Rock (also rockabilly, AOR, rock 'n' roll, etc.)

Burnsongs
A Ta Z Music
Abalone Publishing

Alco Music
Alias John Henry Tunes
All Rock Music
Americatone International
Avalon Music
Bal & Bal Music Publishing Co.
Balmur Entertainment
Bay Ridge Publishing Co.
Bernard Enterprises, Inc., Hal
Better Than Sex Music
Black Market Entertainment Recordings
Blue Dog Publishing and Records
BME Publishing
BSW Records
Buckeye Music Group
California Country Music
Camex Music
Christopher Publishing, Sonny
Cotton Town Music Company
Country Star Music
De Miles Music Company, The Edward
Del Camino Music Publishing
Demi Monde Records & Publishing Ltd.
Doss Music, Buster
Drive Music, Inc.
Duane Music, Inc.
Earitating Music Publishing
East Coast Music Publishing
Edition Rossori
Egyptianman Productions
EMF Productions
Famous Music Publishing Companies
Frozen Inca Music
Gary Music, Alan
Golden Music, August
Goodland Music Group Inc., The
Green One Music
G-String Publishing
Hammel Associates, Inc., R.L.
Hes Free Productions & Publishing Company
Heupferd Musikverlag GmbH
Hickory Lane Publishing and Recording
High-Minded Moma Publishing & Productions
Hitsource Publishing
Ja/Nein Musikverlag GmbH
Jasper Stone Music (ASCAP)/JSM Songs (BMI)
JoDa Music
Jolson Black & White Music, Al
Juke Music
Kaupps & Robert Publishing Co.
Lari-Jon Publishing
Lexington Alabama Music Publishing
Lilly Music Publishing
M & T Waldoch Publishing, Inc.
Marvin Publishing, John Weller
McConkey Artists Agency Music Publishing
McCoy Music, Jim
Mellow House Music
Melody Hills Ranch Publishing Co.

Mighty Blue Music Machine, The
Montina Music
Music Room Publishing Group, The
Nervous Publishing
New Clarion Music Group
New Rap Jam Publishing, A
Northwest Alabama Music Publishing
Old Slowpoke Music
Ontrax Companies
Oyster Bay Music Publishing
PEN Music Group, Inc.
Platinum Gold Music
Portage Music
Pritchett Publications
R.J. Music
Ridge Music Corp.
Rocker Music/Happy Man Music
Rockford Music Co.
Rondor Music International/Almo/Irving Music, A
  Universal Music Group Company
Rosebowl Music
Saddlestone Publishing
Scott Music Group, Tim
SDM
Segal's Publications
Siegel Music Companies
Silicon Music Publishing Co.
Simply Grand Music, Inc.
Sinus Musik Produktion, Ulli Weigel
Sound Cellar Music
Southern Most Publishing Company
Stellar Music Industries
Still Working Music Group
Stuart Music Co., Jeb
Succes
Sunsongs Music/Dark Son Music
Third Wave Productions Limited
Tourmaline Music, Inc.
Transamerika Musikverlag KG
Ultimate Peak Music
Valiant Records & Management
Westwood Music Group
Whiting Music
Wilcom Publishing
World Famous Music Co.
Your Best Songs Publishing
Zitel Publishing Co.
Zomba Music Publishing

World Music (also reggae, ethnic, calypso, international, world beat, etc.)
Bay Ridge Publishing Co.
Heupferd Musikverlag GmbH
Inside Records/OK Songs
Kaysarah Music
Master Source
Peters Music, Justin
Rosebowl Music
Transamerika Musikverlag KG
Whiting Music

Record Companies

Record companies release and distribute records, cassettes and CDs—the tangible products of the music industry. They sign artists to recording contracts, decide what songs those artists will record, and determine which songs to release. They are also responsible for providing recording facilities, securing producers and musicians, and overseeing the manufacture, distribution and promotion of new releases.

MAJOR LABELS & INDEPENDENT LABELS

Major labels and independent labels—what's the difference between the two? Major labels are defined as those record companies distributed by one of the "Big 5" distribution companies: BMG Distribution, EMI Music Distribution (EMD), Sony Music Distribution, Warner/Elektra/Atlantic Distribution (WEA) and Universal Music and Video Distribution (UMVD). Distribution companies are wholesalers that sell records to retail outlets. If a label is distributed by one of these major companies, you can be assured any release coming out on that label has a large distribution network behind it. It will most likely be sent to most major retail stores in the United States. Independent labels go through smaller distribution companies to distribute their product. They usually don't have the ability to deliver records in massive quantities as the major distributors do. However, that doesn't mean independent labels aren't able to have hit records just like their major counterparts. A record label's distributors are found in the listings after the **Distributed by** heading.

Many of the companies listed in this section are independent labels. They are usually the most receptive to receiving material from new artists. Major labels spend more money than most other segments of the music industry; the music publisher, for instance, pays only for items such as salaries and the costs of making demos. Record companies, at great financial risk, pay for many more services, including production, manufacturing and promotion. Therefore, they must be very selective when signing new talent. Also, the continuing fear of copyright infringement suits has closed avenues to getting new material heard by the majors. Most don't listen to unsolicited submissions, period. Only songs recommended by attorneys, managers and producers who record company employees trust and respect are being heard by A&R people at major labels (companies with a referral policy have a ⊘ preceding their listing). But that doesn't mean all major labels are closed to new artists. With a combination of a strong local following, success on an independent label (or strong sales of an independently produced and released album) and the right connections, you could conceivably get an attentive audience at a major label.

But the competition is fierce at the majors, so you shouldn't overlook independent labels. Since they're located all over the country, indie labels are easier to contact and can be important in building a local base of support for your music (consult the Geographic Index at the back of the book to find out which companies are located near you). Independent labels usually concentrate on a specific type of music, which will help you target those companies your submissions should be sent to. And since the staff at an indie label is smaller, there are fewer channels to go through to get your music heard by the decision makers in the company.

The Case for Independents

If you're interested in getting a major label deal, it makes sense to look to independent record labels to get your start. Independent labels are seen by many as a stepping stone to a major recording contract. Very few artists are signed to a major label at the start of their careers; usually, they've had a few independent releases that helped build their reputation in the industry. Major labels watch independent labels closely to locate up-and-coming bands and new trends. In the current economic atmosphere at major labels—with extremely high overhead costs for developing new bands and the fact that only 10% of acts on major labels actually make any profit—they're not willing to risk everything on an unknown act. Most major labels won't even consider signing a new act that hasn't had some indie success.

But independents aren't just farming grounds for future major label acts; many bands have long term relationships with indies, and prefer it that way. While they may not be able to provide the extensive distribution and promotion that a major label can (though there are exceptions), indie labels can help an artist become a regional success, and may even help the performer to see a profit as well. With the lower overhead and smaller production costs an independent label operates on, it's much easier to "succeed" on an indie label than on a major.

HOW RECORD COMPANIES WORK

Independent record labels can run on a small staff, with only a handful of people running the day-to-day business. Major record labels are more likely to be divided into the following departments: A&R, sales, marketing, promotion, product management, artist development, production, finance, business/legal and international.

- The *A&R department* is staffed with A&R representatives (reps) who search out new talent. They go out and see new bands, listen to demo tapes, and decide which artists to sign. They also look for new material for already signed acts, match producers with artists and oversee recording projects. Once an artist is signed by an A&R rep and a record is recorded, the rest of the departments at the company come into play.
- The *sales department* is responsible for getting a record into stores. They make sure record stores and other outlets receive enough copies of a record to meet consumer demand.
- The *marketing department* is in charge of publicity, advertising in magazines and other media, promotional videos, album cover artwork, in-store displays, and any other means of getting the name and image of an artist to the public.
- The *promotion department*'s main objective is to get songs from a new album played on the radio. They work with radio programmers to make sure a product gets airplay.
- The *product management department* is the ringmaster of the sales, marketing and promotion departments, assuring that they're all going in the same direction when promoting a new release.
- The *artist development department* is responsible for taking care of things while an artist is on tour, such as setting up promotional opportunities in cities where an act is performing.
- The *production department* handles the actual manufacturing and pressing of the record and makes sure it gets shipped to distributors in a timely manner.
- People in the *finance department* compute and distribute royalties, as well as keep track of expenses and income at the company.
- The *business/legal department* takes care of contracts, not only between the record company and artists but with foreign distributors, record clubs, etc.
- And finally, the *international department* is responsible for working with international companies for the release of records in other countries.

LOCATING A RECORD LABEL

With the abundance of record labels out there, how do you go about finding one that's right for the music you create? First, it helps to know exactly what kind of music a record label releases. Become familiar with the records a company has released, and see if they fit in with what you're doing. Each listing in this section details the type of music a particular record company is interested in releasing. You will want to refer to the Category Index, located at the end of this section, to help you find those companies most receptive to the type of music you write. You should only approach companies open to your level of experience (see the Openness to Submissions sidebar on page 8). Visiting a company's website can also provide valuable information about a company's philosophy, the artists on the label and the music they work with.

Networking

Recommendations by key music industry people are an important part of making contacts with record companies. Songwriters must remember that talent alone does not guarantee success in the music business. You must be recognized through contacts, and the only way to make contacts is through networking. Networking is the process of building an interconnecting web of acquaintances within the music business. The more industry people you meet, the larger your contact base becomes, and the better are your chances of meeting someone with the clout to get your demo into the hands of the right people. If you want to get your music heard by key A&R representatives, networking is imperative.

Networking opportunities can be found anywhere industry people gather. A good place to meet key industry people is at regional and national music conferences and workshops. There are many held all over the country for all types of music (see the Workshops and Conferences section for more information). You should try to attend at least one or two of these events each year; it's a great way to increase the number and quality of your music industry contacts.

Creating a buzz

Another good way to attract A&R people is to make a name for yourself as an artist. By starting your career on a local level and building it from there, you can start to cultivate a following and prove to labels that you can be a success. A&R people figure if an act can be successful locally, there's a good chance they could be successful nationally. Start getting booked at local clubs, and start a mailing list of fans and local media. Once you gain some success on a local level, branch out. All this attention you're slowly gathering, this "buzz" you're generating, will not only get to your fans but to influential people in the music industry as well.

For More Information

For more instructional information on the listings in this book, including explanations of symbols ( ), read the article How to Use *Songwriter's Market* to Get Your Songs Heard on page 5.

SUBMITTING TO RECORD COMPANIES

When submitting to a record company, major or independent, a professional attitude is imperative. Be specific about what you are submitting and what your goals are. If you are strictly a songwriter and the label carries a band you believe would properly present your song, state that in your cover letter. If you are an artist looking for a contract, showcase your strong points as a performer. Whatever your goals are, follow submission guidelines closely, be as neat as possible and include a top-notch demo. If you need more information concerning a company's requirements, write or call for more details. (For more information on submitting your material, see the article Getting Started on page 10, What Music Professionals Look for in a Demo sidebar on page 15 and Quiz: Are You Professional? on page 18.)

Additional Record Companies

There are **MORE RECORD COMPANIES** located in other sections of the book! On page 214 use the list of Additional Record Companies to find listings within other sections who are also record companies.

RECORD COMPANY CONTRACTS

Once you've found a record company that is interested in your work, the next step is signing a contract. Independent label contracts are usually not as long and complicated as major label ones, but they are still binding, legal contracts. Make sure the terms are in the best interest of both you and the label. Avoid anything in your contract that you feel is too restrictive. It's important to have your contract reviewed by a competent entertainment lawyer. A basic recording contract can run from 40-100 pages, and you need a lawyer to help you understand it. A lawyer will also be essential in helping you negotiate a deal that is in your best interest.

Recording contracts cover many areas, and just a few of the things you will be asked to consider will be: What royalty rate is the record label willing to pay you? What kind of advance are they offering? How many records will the company commit to? Will they offer tour support? Will they provide a budget for video? What sort of a recording budget are they offering? Are they asking you to give up any publishing rights? Are they offering you a publishing advance? These are only a few of the complex issues raised by a recording contract, so it's vital to have an entertainment lawyer at your side as you negotiate.

○ **A.P.I. RECORDS**, P.O. Box 7041, Watchung NJ 07061-0741. (908)753-1601. Fax: (908)753-3724. E-mail: apirecord@aol.com. Website: www.apirecords.com. **Executive Vice President:** Meg Poltorak. Vice President: Kevin Ferd. Record company, music publisher (Humbletunes, Inc.) and record producer (August Productions, Inc.). Estab. 1989. Staff size: 5. Releases 5 singles, 6 LPs and 6 CDs/year. Pays negotiable royalty to artists on contract; statutory rate to publisher per song on record.
How to Contact: Submit demo tape by mail. Unsolicited submissions are OK. Prefers cassette, CD, DAT or VHS videocassette with 3 songs and lyric sheet. Does not return material. Responds in 6 months if interested.
Music: Mostly **pop/rock**, **jazz** and **classical**. Released "When Will I See You" (single by Micheals/Keyes) from *Kassy Micheals* (album), recorded by Kassy Micheals (pop), released 2001; "Under the Big Top" (single by Patrick Bamburak) from *Coming Attractions* (album), recorded by Bait-Oven (pop); "It Is Written" (single by Bamburek/Aversano/Keyes) from *Fun Haus* (album), recorded by Fun Haus (pop-rock), all released 2001 on API.
Tips: "Looking for well-crafted material. Packaging and production are not important."

⊘ **A&M RECORDS**, 825 Eighth Ave., 29th Floor, New York NY 10019.
● As a result of the PolyGram and Universal merger, A&M Records has been folded into Interscope Records. See the Interscope/Geffen/A&M Records listing is this section for further information.

Ⓝ ○ **ABL RECORDS**, 1325 Marengo Ave., South Pasadena CA 91030. (626)441-4453. E-mail: melodi4ever@earthlink.net. Website: allanlicht.ontheweb.com. **Contact:** Allan Licht, owner. Record company and music publisher (Allan Bradley Music/BMI and Holly Ellen Music/ASCAP). Estab. 1993. Staff size: 2. Releases 10 singles/year. Pays 50% royalty to artists on contract; statutory rate to publisher per song on record.

How to Contact: Submit demo tape by mail. Unsolicited submissions are OK. Prefers cassette with 3 songs and lyric sheet. Does not return material. Responds in 1 month.

Music: Mostly **A/C**, **pop** and **R&B**; also **country** and **Christian contemporary**. Released *I'll Keep the Change* (by Betty Kay Miller/Marcia McCaslin), recorded by Dakota Brad (country), released 1999 on ABL Records. Other artists include Tracy Todd, Sam Morrison, Donna West, Jill J. Switzer and Michael Cavanaugh.

Tips: "Submit top-notch material with great demos."

AFTERSCHOOL RECORDS, INC., P.O. Box 14157, Detroit MI 48214. (313)894-8855. **Contact:** Genesis Act, MCP, director/producer. Record company, music publisher (Afterschool Publishing Co., Inc.) and record producer (Feel Production, MCP). Estab. 1969. Releases 6 singles, 1 LP and a variable number of CDs/year. Pays negotiable royalty to artists on contract; statutory rate to publisher per song on record.

Distributed by: Afterschool, Fermata, Cancopy, CMRAA, NCB, AMRA, MCPS and BMG.

How to Contact: Submit demo tape by mail. Unsolicited submissions are OK. Prefers cassette, CD, DAT or videocassette with 1 song and lyric and lead sheets. Include SASE. Responds in 1 month.

Music: **All types.** Mostly **pop**, **dance** and **rap**; also **jazz**. Artists include P.M. Dawn, 2 Hyped Brothers and a Dog, 2 Live Crew, Beats International, Miss Jones, Luke, Cut-N-Move, Rockman, Kinsui, Jazzy Jeff & Fresh Prince, Whodini, M.C. Hammer, Betty Wright, Body & Soul, Gloria Estefan & Miami Sound Machine.

Tips: "Contracts are non-exclusive. Artists must have legal representation when submitting. Afterschool Records does not have pre-drafted documents."

THE AIRPLAY LABEL, P.O. Box 851, Asbury Park NJ 07712. Phone/fax: (732)681-0623. E-mail: airplaypete@hotmail.com. Website: www.airplay.org. **Contact:** Tracy Spencer, A&R. President A&R: Peter P. Mantas. Vice President/Head of A&R: Jefferson Powers. Record company. Estab. 1995. Staff size: 7. Releases 6 singles, 3 LPs, 2 EPs and 4 CDs/year. Pays 20% royalty to artists on contract; statutory rate to publisher per song on record.

Distributed by: Music Source, Notlame.com, Valley and Redeye.

• This label received the Asbury Music Awards' 1997-98 Top Release.

How to Contact: *Write first and obtain permission to submit.* Prefers cassette, CD or videocassette. Does not return material. Responds in 1 month.

Music: Mostly **pop**, **acid jazz** and **jazz**; also **emo-core**. Released *Good to Be Alive* (album), written and recorded by Evelyn Forever (pop), released 2001 on Airplay; "Eve to Noam" (single by Sassaris) from *Eve to Noam* (album), recorded by Eve to Noam (rock), released 2001 on Airplay; and "Free" (single by Simprini) from *Pop 2K* (album), recorded by Kitty in the Tree (pop), released 2001 on Airplay.

Tips: "Hard work pays off."

ALBATROSS RECORDS, P.O. Box 540102, Houston TX 77254-0102. (713)521-2616. Fax: (713)529-4914. E-mail: rpds2405@aol.com. Website: www.rndproductions.com. A&R: Byron Gates. Record company. Estab. 1990. Staff size: 4. Releases 20 singles, 10 LPs and 10 CDs/year. Pays negotiable royalty to artists on contract; statutory rate to publisher per song on record.

FOR EXPLANATIONS OF THESE SYMBOLS, SEE THE INSIDE FRONT AND BACK COVERS OF THIS BOOK.

Distributed by: Select-O-Hits and Bayside.

How to Contact: Submit demo tape by mail. Unsolicited submissions are OK. Prefers CD and pictures. Does not return material. Responds in 3 weeks.

Music: Mostly **R&B**, **rap** and **Latino/TexMex pop**; also **jazz**, **country**, **rock** and **blues**. Released *Lines & Spaces* (album), recorded by Shades of Brown (jazz); *Remi n Alize* (album), recorded by Mr. International (rap); and *Screw Theory Vol. 2* (album), recorded by various (rap), all on Albatross Records. Other artists include Nu Ground, D.G.I. Posse, Hollister Fraucus, 4-Deep and McBreed.

○ **ALCO RECORDINGS**, P.O. Box 18197, Panama City Beach FL 32417. **Contact:** Ann McEver, president. Record company. Estab. 2000. Staff size: 2. Pays standard royalty to artists on contract; statutory rate to publisher per song on record.

How to Contact: Submit demo tape by mail. Unsolicited submissions are OK. Prefers cassette or CD with 2-3 songs, lyric sheet and cover letter. Include SASE. Responds in 3 weeks.

Music: Mostly **pop/rock**, **country** and **alternative**. Also **gospel**. Does not want instrumentals. Released "Hungry Now" (single by Jack Benning) from *Hungry and How* (album), recorded by Snack Bar (alternative), released 2001 on Alco; "Treat Mama Good" (single), written and recorded by Willie Burk (country) on his self-titled album, released 2001 on Alco.

Tips: "Think about your submission. Make sure it meets our submission requirements. We are looking for artists or groups who could compete at a national level."

☑ **ALL STAR RECORD PROMOTIONS**, 1229 S. Prospect St., Marion OH 43302-7267. (740)382-5939. E-mail: allstarmanage@msn.com. **Contact:** John Simpson, president. Record promoter. Estab. 1980.

How to Contact: *Contact and obtain permission to submit.*

Music: Mostly **country** and **Christian country**; also **gospel**.

☑ ○ **ALLEGHENY MUSIC WORKS**, 1611 Menoher Blvd., Johnstown PA 15905. (814)255-4007. E-mail: TunedOnMusic@aol.com. Website: www.alleghenymusicworks.com. **Contact:** Al Rita, managing director. Labels include Allegheny Records. Record company and music publisher (Allegheny Music Works Publishing/ASCAP and Tuned on Music/BMI). Estab. 1991. Pays 10-12% royalty to artists on contract; statutory rate to publisher per song on record.

How to Contact: *Write first and obtain permission to submit.* "Include SASE for reply. E-mail queries are acceptable. Responds in 1 week to regular mail requests and usually within 48 hours to e-mail queries."

Music: Mostly **country (all styles)**; also **pop**, **A/C**, **R&B**, **inspirational**, **novelty** and **Halloween**. Released "That's My Jack O'Lantern" (single), written and recorded by Neil Hartenburg) from *Halloween Bash* (album) (country), released 2000 on Allegheny.

Tips: "Bookmark our website and check it regularly, clicking on *Songwriter Opportunities*. Each month, as a free service to songwriters, we list a new artist or company looking for songs. Complete contact information is included. For a deeper insight into the type of material our company publishes, we invite you to read the customer reviews on amazon.com to our 2000 best seller Halloween album release *Halloween Bash*."

☑ ◙ **AMERICAN RECORDINGS**, 8900 Sunset Blvd., 2nd Floor, West Hollywood CA 90069. (310)288-5300. Website: www.american.recordings.com. A&R: Dino Paredes, George Drakoulias, Antony Bland, Brendon Mendoza. Labels include Too Pure, Infinite Zero, UBL, Venture and Onion. Record company.

Distributed by: Sony.

How to Contact: Submit demo tape by mail. Unsolicited submissions are OK. Prefers CD, cassette or videocassette with lyric and lead sheet.

Music: Released *Unchained*, recorded by Johnny Cash on American Recordings. Other artists include Slayer, System of a Down, The Black Crowes, Jayhawks, Loudermilk, Unida, American Head Charge, Man Made God, Saul Williams, Nusvat Fatch Ali Khan, Rohat Fetch Ali Khan.

●**AMERICATONE RECORDS INTERNATIONAL USA**, 1817 Loch Lomond Way, Las Vegas NV 89102-4437. (702)384-0030. Fax: (702)382-1926. E-mail: jjj@americatone.com. Website: www.americatone.com. Estab. 1985. **Contact:** A&R Director. Labels include The Rambolt Music International (ASCAP), Americatone (BMI) and Christy Records International. Record company, producer and music publisher. Releases 8 CDs and cassettes/year. Pays 10% royalty.
Distributed by: Big Band, Otter, Dist., North County, General, Harbor Export, International Dist., Twinbrook Dist., Gibson Dist.
How to Contact: Submit demo tape by mail. Unsolicited submissions are OK. Prefers cassette or CD. Include SASE. Responds in 1 month.
Music: Mostly **jazz**, **rock**, **Spanish** and **classic ballads**. Released *After All These Years*, written and recorded by Brent Blount; and *The Ramblers*, written and recorded by Brad Sauders, both on Americatone International Records. Other artists include Mark Masters Jazz Orchestra, Raoul Romero and His Jazz Stars Orchestra, Ladd McIntosh Big Band, Dick Shearer and His Stan Kenton Spirits, Gabriel Rosati from Roma Italy, Lee Gibson with John Reddick and his Jazz Orchestra from BBC London, Explosion Sam Trippe, Bill Perkins Jazz Quintet, Caribbean Jazz, Jazz in the Rain, Americatone is also music published of Top Sheet Music Orchestrations and Piano Publishers.

○**AMIGOS MUSIC & MARKETING**, 81 Pondfield Rd., Suite 266, Bronxville NY 10708. Phone/fax: (718)548-7366. E-mail: amigosrcd@aol.com or andygrullon@yolandaduke.com. Website: www.yolandaduke.com. **Contact:** Andy Grullon, director. Labels include Amigos, Tataiba, 3×2 Son, and Flamenco. Record company. Estab. 1990. Staff size: 10. Releases 5 singles, 3 LPs and 3 CDs/year. Pays 6¼% royalty to artists on contract or negotiable; statutory rate to publisher per song on record.
Distributed by: UMVD.
How to Contact: Submit demo tape by mail. Unsolicited submissions are OK. Prefers cassette, CD or VHS videocassette with 3 songs and lyric sheet. Does not return materials. Responds in 6 weeks if interested.
Music: Mostly **Latin**. Released "Marinero De Luces Live!" (single by Jose L. Perales) from *Yolanda Duke Live!* (album), recorded by Yolanda Duke (salsa); "El Heurfano" (single) from *El Huerfano* (album), recorded by Manny Valenz (merengue); and "Tu Perro Guardian" (single by Juan Lanfranco) from *Perias de Amor*, recorded by Juan Lanfranco (bachata), all released 2001 on Amigos Music.
Tips: "Put together lyrics that make sense with a good melody. We are noted for releasing Latin music."

⊕ ●**AMP RECORDS & MUSIC**, Box BM Fame, London WC1N 3XX United Kingdom. Phone/fax: (0044)(0)208 889 0616. E-mail: info@ampmusic.demon.co.uk. Website: www.ampmusic.demon.co.uk. **Contact:** Mark Jenkins, A&R (New Age, instrumental, ambient, progressive rock). Record company. Estab. 1985. Staff size: 10. Releases 12 CDs/year. Pays negotiable royalty to artists on contract; negotiable rate to publisher per song on record.
Distributed by: Shellshock (UK), Eurock/ZNR/NSA (USA), MP (Italy) and Crystal Lake (France).
How to Contact: Submit demo tape by mail. Unsolicited submissions are OK. Prefers cassette, CD or DAT with cover letter and press clippings. Does not return material. Responds in 2 months.
Music: Mostly **New Age**, **instrumental** and **ambient**; also **progressive rock**, **synthesizer** and **ambient dance**. Does not want ballads, country or AOR. Released *Changing States*, recorded by Keith Emerson (progressive rock); *Tyranny of Beauty*, written and recorded by Tangerine Dream (synthesizer); and *Spirit of Christmas*, written and recorded by various artists (instrumental compilation), all on AMP Records.
Tips: "Send a relevant style of music."

TO HELP YOU UNDERSTAND and use the information in these listings, see "How to Use *Songwriter's Market* to Get Your Songs Heard," on page 5.

N ◎ ANGEL/EMI RECORDS, 304 Park Ave. S, New York NY 10010. (212)253-3200. Fax: (212)253-3011. Website: www.angelrecords.com. Record company. Labels include EMI Classics and Virgin Classics.

Distributed by: EMI.

How to Contact: *Angel/EMI Records does not accept unsolicited submissions.*

Music: Artists include Sarah Brightman, Paul McCartney and Bernadette Peters.

☑ ○ ANISETTE RECORDS, 34 Rutland Sq., Apt. 3, Boston MA 02118-3174. Phone/fax: (213)365-9495. E-mail: anisette@earthlink.net. Website: www.anisetterecords.com. A&R Chief: M-K O'Connell. Record company. Estab. 1998. Staff size: 2. Releases 2 CDs/year. Pays negotiable royalty to artists on contract; statutory rate to publisher per song on record.

Distributed by: NAIL, Darla, Carrot Top, Surefire, Scratch and Parasol.

How to Contact: *E-mail before submitting. No unsolicited submissions.* Prefers cassette or CD. Does not return material. Responds in 2 weeks.

Music: Mostly **rock**, **pop** and **rap**. Released *Greatest Moments of Doubt* (album by Kevin Castillo), recorded by Retriever; *The Miracle of Flight* (album), written and recorded by Stratotanker; and *El Rey* (album), recorded by The Lassie Foundation (rock), all on Anisette.

Tips: "Send the material and follow up with an e-mail."

☑ ○ ARIANA RECORDS, 1336 S. Avenida Polar #C-208, Tucson AZ 85710. (520)790-7324. E-mail: jgasper1596@earthlink.net. Website: www.arianarecords.com. **Contact:** James M. Gasper, president. Vice President (pop, rock): Tom Dukes. Partners: Tom Privett (funk, experimental, rock); Scott Smith (pop, rock, AOR). Labels include Egg White Records. Record company, music publisher (Myko Music/BMI) and record producer. Estab. 1980. Staff size: 4. Releases 2 singles, 4 LPs and 1 compilation/year. Pays negotiable royalty to artists on contract; negotiable rate to publisher per song on record.

Distributed by: Impact Music Distributors and Care Free Music.

How to Contact: "We are only interested in finished CD projects. No tapes. No demos." Unsolicited submissions are OK. Include SASE. Responds in 6 months.

Music: Mostly **rock**, **funk**, **jazz**, **anything weird**, **strange** or **lo-fi** (must be mastered to CD). Released "Be Yourself" (single by J. Gasper/T. Broline/M. Smart) from *Be Yourself* (album), recorded by Thank God F4 Fingers (pop strange), released 2002 on Ariana Records; "22nd Street Funk" (single by T. Dukes/T. Privett/J. Gasper) from *Z Trax* (album), recorded by Z Trax (instrumental funk/jazz), released 2002 on Egg White Records; and "Lazy Girlfriend" (single by A. Musika/Mr. Jimi/Alex Stone) from *This Is* (album), recorded by The Whereabouts (pop rock), released 2003 on Ariana Records. Other artists include The Krossing Guards, Radiant Grub, The Rakeheads, Mary's Purse and New World Slavery.

Tips: "We're a small company, but working your material is our job. If we like it, we'll sell it! It's a tough business. Keep trying."

◎ ARISTA RECORDS, 6 W. 57th St., New York NY 10019. (212)489-7400. Fax: (212)977-9843. Website: www.aristarec.com. Beverly Hills office: 8750 Wilshire Blvd., 3rd Floor, Beverly Hills CA 90211. (310)358-4600. Nashville office: 7 Music Circle North, Nashville TN 37203. (615)846-9100. Fax: (615)846-9192. Labels include Bad Boy Records, Arista Nashville and Time Bomb Recordings. Record company.

Distributed by: BMG.

How to Contact: *Does not accept unsolicited material.*

◖ ARKADIA ENTERTAINMENT CORP., 34 E. 23rd St., New York NY 10010. (212)533-0007. Fax: (212)979-0266. E-mail: info@arkadiarecords.com. Website: www.arkadiarecords.com. **Contact:** A&R Song Submissions. Labels include Arkadia Jazz, Arkadia Classical, Arkadia Now and Arkadia Allworld. Record company, music publisher (Arkadia Music), record producer (Arkadia Productions) and Arkadia Video. Estab. 1995.

How to Contact: *Write or call first and obtain permission to submit.*

Music: Mostly **jazz**, **classical** and **pop/R&B**; also **world**.

☑ ◐ **ASTRALWERKS**, 104 W. 29th St., 4th Floor, New York NY 10001. (212)886-7500. Fax: (212)643-5573. Website: www.astralwerks.com. **Contact:** Errol Kolosine, GM. Record company. Estab. 1979. Releases 10-12 12″ singles and 100 CDs/year. Pays varying royalty to artists on contract; statutory rate to publisher per song.
How to Contact: Send submissions to: "Attn: A&R" to address above. No unsolicited phone calls please.
Music: Mostly **alternative/indie/electronic**. Released *You've Come A Long Way* (album), recorded by Fatboy Slim; *Surrender* (album), recorded by Chemical Brothers; and *3 eps* (album), recorded by Beta Band, all on Astralworks.
Tips: "We are open to artists of unique quality and enjoy developing artists from the ground up. We listen to all types of 'alternative' music regardless of genre. It's about the aesthetic and artistic quality first. We send out rejection letters so do not call to find out what's happening with your demo."

◔ **ASYLUM RECORDS NASHVILLE**, 1906 Acklen Ave., Nashville TN 37212. Labels include 143 Records. Record company.
Distributed by: WEA.
How to Contact: *Does not accept unsolicited submissions.*

◯ **ATLAN-DEC/GROOVELINE RECORDS**, 2529 Green Forest Court, Snellville GA 30078-4183. (770)985-1686. Fax: (877)751-5169. E-mail: atlandec@prodigy.net. Website: www.ATLAN-DEC.com. President/Senior A&R Rep: James Hatcher. A&R Rep: Wiletta J. Hatcher. Record company, music publisher and record producer. Estab. 1994. Staff size: 2. Releases 3-4 singles, 3-4 LPs and 3-4 CDs/year. Pays 10-25% royalty to artists on contract; statutory rate to publisher per song on record.
Distributed by: ATLAN-DEC Records.
How to Contact: Submit demo tape by mail. Unsolicited submissions are OK. Prefers cassette and lyric sheet. Does not return material. Responds in 3 months.
Music: Mostly **R&B/urban**, **hip-hop/rap** and **contemporary jazz**; also **soft rock**, **gospel**, **dance** and **new country**. Released *Temptation* (album), recorded by Shawnee (rap/hip-hop); *Skilz to Make Milz* (album), recorded by B-Double-O; and *Enemy of the State* (album), recorded by LowLife, all released 2002 on Atlan-Dec/Grooveline Records. Other artists include Furious D (rap/hip-hop) and Mark Cocker (new country).

◨ ◐ **ATLANTIC RECORDS**, 1290 Avenue of the Americas, New York NY 10104. (212)707-2000. Fax: (212)581-6414. Los Angeles office: 9229 Sunset Blvd., 9th Floor, Los Angeles CA 90069. (310)205-7450. Fax: (310)205-7411. Nashville office: 20 Music Square East, Nashville TN 37203. (615)272-7990. Website: www.atlantic-records.com. Labels include Big Beat Records, LAVA, Nonesuch Records, Atlantic Classics and Rhino Records. Record company. Pays negotiable royalty to artists on contract; negotiable rate to publisher per song on record.
Distributed by: WEA.
How to Contact: *Does not accept unsolicited material.* "No phone calls please."
Music: Released *Yourself or Someone Like You* (album), recorded by Matchbox 20 on LAVA; *Pieces of You* (album), recorded by Jewel on Atlantic; and *Greatest Hits* (album), recorded by John Michael Montgomery on Atlantic (Nashville). Other artists include Sugar Ray, Kid Rock and Brandy.

◯ **AVALON RECORDING GROUP**, P.O. Box 121626, Nashville TN 37212. **Contact:** A&R Review Department. Director: Avalon Hughs. Record company, music publisher (Avalon Music) and record producer (Avalon Productions). Estab. 2001. Staff size: 3. Pays standard royalty to artists on contract.
How to Contact: Submit demo tape by mail. Unsolicited submissions OK. "No phone calls, please." Prefers cassette or CD with 3 songs and lyric sheet. Include SASE. Responds in 3 weeks.
Music: Mostly **rock**, **country**, and **alternative**; also **R&B**, **hip hop** and **gospel**. Released "Paradise" (single by Allude) from *Allude to This* (album), recorded by Allude (alternative), released 2001 on Avalon; "Who Knows" (single by Jim Hughes) from *Madrid* (album), recorded by Madrid (rock), released 2001 on Avalon.

Tips: "Send songs suitable for today's market. We are looking for singers, singer/songwriters and bands that have the potential to go large."

⊘**AVITA RECORDS**, P.O. Box 764, Hendersonville TN 37077-0764. (615) 824-9313. Fax: (615)824-0797. E-mail: Tachoir@bellsouth.net. Website: www.tachoir.com. **Contact:** Robert Kayre, manager. Record company, music publisher (Riohcat Music, BMI) and record producer (Jerry Tachoir). Estab. 1976. Staff size: 8. Releases 2 LPs and 2 CDs/year. Pays negotiable royalty to artists on contract; statutory rate to publisher per song on record.

How to Contact: *Contact first and obtain permission to submit.* We only accept material referred to us by a reputable industry source. Prefers cassette, CD or DAT. Does not return materials. Responds only if interested.

Music: Mostly **jazz**. Released *Improvised Thoughts* (album by Marlene Tachoir/Jerry Tachoir/Van Manakas), recorded by Jerry Tachoir and Van Manakas (jazz), released 2001 on Avita Records. Other artists include Van Manakas.

⊘**AWAL.COM**, P.O. Box 879, Ojai CA 93024. (805)640-7399. Fax: (805)646-6077. E-mail: info @awal.com. Website: www.awal.com. **Contact:** A&R Department. President: Denzyl Feigelson. Record company. Estab. 1996. Staff size: 7. Releases 6 singles, 12 LPs and 12 CDs/year. Pays 50% or negotiable royalty to artists on contract.

Distributed by: Valley and on the Internet.

How to Contact: Submit demo tape by mail. Unsolicited submissions are OK. Prefers CD with 5 songs, lyric sheet, cover letter and press clippings. Does not return materials. Responds in 1 month if interested.

Music: Mostly **pop**, **world** and **jazz**; also **techno**, **teen** and **children's**. Released *Go Cat Go* (album by various), recorded by Carl Perkins on ArtistOne.com; *Bliss* (album), written and recorded by Donna Delory (pop); and *Shake A Little* (album), written and recorded by Michael Ruff, both on Awal Records.

☑◻**AWARE RECORDS**, 2336 W. Belmost Ave., Chicago IL 60618. (773)248-4210. Fax: (773)248-4211. E-mail: aware@awarerecords.com. Website: www.awarerecords.com. A&R: Steve Smith. President: Gregg Latterman. Record company. Distributed by Sony and Redeye. Estab. 1993. Staff size: 8. Releases 5 LPs, 1 EP and 3 CD/year. Pays negotiable royalty to artists on contract; statutory rate to publisher per song on record.

Distributed by: Sony and RED.

How to Contact: Submit demo tape by mail. Unsolicited submissions are OK. Prefers CD with lead sheet, cover letter and press clippings. Does not return material. Responds back only if interested.

Music: Mostly **rock/pop**. Released *Aware 9* (album), written and recorded by various artists (pop/rock); and *More Sounds from Spaghetti Westerns* (album), recorded by Red Elephant, both on Aware Records. Other artists include John Mayer, Five for Fighting, Riddlin Kid, Alice Peacock and Bleu.

☑◻**babysue**, P.O. Box 33369, Decatur GA 30033. (404)320-1178. Website: www.babysue.com. **Contact:** Don W. Seven, president/owner. Record company and management firm. Estab. 1983. Staff size: 1. Releases 2 singles, 5 LPs, 2 EPs and 7 CDs/year. Pays 5-20% royalty to artists on contract; varying royalty to publisher per song on record.

Distributed by: Distributed at website www.babysue.com.

How to Contact: Submit demo tape, CD or CDRW by mail. Unsolicited submissions are OK. Prefers submisison with any number of songs. Does not return material. Responds in 3 months. "We only report back if we are interested in the artist or act."

Music: Mostly **rock**, **pop** and **gospel**; also **heavy metal**, **punk** and **classical**. Released *Mnemonic* (album), recorded by LMNOP on babysue records (rock/pop). Other artists include the Mushcakes, The Shoestrings and The Mommy.

Tips: "We're just into sincere, good stuff."

◉ **BAGATELLE RECORD COMPANY**, P.O. Box 925929, Houston TX 77292. **Contact:** Byron Benton, president. Record company, record producer and music publisher (Bagatelle Music, Floyd Tillman Music Co.). Releases 20 singles and 10 LPs/year. Pays negotiable royalty to artists on contract.
How to Contact: Submit demo tape by mail. Prefers cassette and lyric sheet. Include SASE. Responds in 2 weeks.
Music: Mostly **country**; also **gospel**. Released "This is Real" (single by Floyd Tillman) (country); "Lucille" (single by Sherri Jerrico) (country); and "Everything You Touch" (single by Johnny Nelms) (country). Other artists include Jerry Irby, Bobby Beason, Bobby Burton, Donna Hazard, Danny Brown, Sonny Hall, Ben Gabus, Jimmy Copeland and Johnny B. Goode.

[N] ◯ BANANA RECORDS, 3115 Hiss Ave., Baltimore MD 21234. Phone/fax: (410)663-5915. E-mail: 78couger@home.com. **Contact:** Ron Brown, President. A&R: Brian Batterdan. Record company, music publisher (Infinite Publishing) and record producer (Ronald Brown). Estab. 1990. Releases 30 singles, 20 LPs and 20 CDs/year. Pays standard royalty to artists on contract; statutory rate to publisher per song on record.
How to Contact: Submit demo tape by mail. Unsolicited submissions are OK. Prefers cassette with 3 songs and lyric sheet. Include SASE. Responds in 3 weeks.
Music: Mostly **top 40/commercial**, **pop/ballads** and **alternative**. Released "Crack of the Universe," written and recorded by Jesse Brown (pop) on Global.
Tips: "A good singer works hard at his craft. A hit song has good punch and a lot of talent."

☑ ◉ BELMONT RECORDS, 484 Lexington St., Waltham MA 02452. (781)893-1776. Fax: (781)893-1771. E-mail: jpennycw@aol.com. **Contact:** John Penny, president. Labels include Waverly Records. Record company and record producer. Pays standard royalty to artists on contract; statutory rate to publisher per song on record.
How to Contact: *Write first and obtain permission to submit.* Prefers cassette with 3 songs and lyric sheet. Include SASE. Responds in 3 weeks.
Music: Mostly **country**. Released *Barbara Lawrence* (album), recorded by Barbara Lawrence (c&w), released 1999; and *Listen To Me* (album), recorded by Barbara Lawrence (c&w), released 2000, both on Belmont Records. Other artists include Stan Jr., Tim Barrett, Jackie Lee Williams, Robin Right, Mike Walker and Dwain Hathaway.

◯ BIG BEAT RECORDS, 9229 Sunset Blvd., Los Angeles CA 90069. (323)205-5717. Fax: (323)205-5721. E-mail: mike.caren@atlantic-recording.com. Website: www.atlantic-recordings.com. **Contact:** Michael Caren, director of A&R/staff producer. Record company. Labels include Undeas Records, CWAL and Slip-N-Slide.
Distributed by: WEA.
How to Contact: Submit demo tape by mail. Unsolicited submissions are OK. Prefers cassette, CD or DAT with bio and photo.
Music: Released *www.thug.com* (album), written and recorded by Trick Daddy (rap) on Slip-n-Slide; *Causin' Drama* (album), written and recorded by Drama (rap) on Tight IV Life; and *Any Given Sunday* (album soundtrack), written and recorded by various artists (rap/rock) on Atlantic.

☒ ◉ BIG HEAVY WORLD, P.O. Box 428, Burlington VT 05402-0428. (802)865-1140 or (800)303-1590. E-mail: groundzero@bigheavyworld.com. Website: www.bigheavyworld.com. **Contact:** James Lockridge, founder/A&R director. Record company. Estab. 1996. Staff size: 12. Releases 3 CDs/year. Pays negotiable royalty to artists on contract; pay varies by project to publisher per song on record.

MARKET CONDITIONS are constantly changing! If you're still using this book and it is 2004 or later, buy the newest edition of *Songwriter's Market* at your favorite bookstore or order directly from Writer's Digest Books at (800)289-0963.

● This company was given the 1998 Visionary Award by the Women's Rape Crisis Center. Big Heavy World promotes the music of Burlington, Vermont, and its region. Their compilation CDs vary in genre and theme and often benefit humanitarian services.

How to Contact: *Big Heavy World does not accept unsolicited submissions.*

Music: Compilation projects vary in genre. Released *Pop Pie* (pop); *Pulsecuts Vol II* (alternative); *No Secrets* and *Tonic Two: Core Breach Burlington* (rock/alternative), *242.01 The Bands of Burlington Vermont* (hardcore/punk/alternative); *Hop 3 An Independent Collection of Rhythms and Melodies from the North Upper Most* (downtempo urban); *Hop 4 A Bumpnthump Electronic Loopngroove Compilation from the Green Mountains* (uptempo hip-hop); *Sullivan Square The Contemporary Folk Collection* (folk); *The 10th Annual Los Angeles Music Awards Sonic Sampler* (eclectic). Other artists include ChinHo! (pop) and chainsaws.and.children (industrial).

Tips: "Vermont-based artists are welcome to contact us, both as a record label and online music retail venue."

○ **BLUE GEM RECORDS**, P.O. Box 29550, Hollywood CA 90029. (323)664-7765. E-mail: pmart i3636@aol.com. **Contact:** Pete Martin. Record company, music publisher (Vaam Music Group) and record producer (Pete Martin/Vaam Productions). Estab. 1981. Pays 6-15% royalty to artists on contract; statutory rate to publisher per song on record.

How to Contact: Submit demo tape by mail. Unsolicited submissions are OK. Prefers cassette with 2 songs. Include SASE. Responds in 3 weeks.

Music: Mostly **country** and **R&B**; also **pop/top 40** and **rock**. Released "The Greener Years" (single), written and recorded by Frank Loren (country); "It's a Matter of Loving You" (single by Brian Smith), recorded by Brian Smith & The Renegades (country); and "Two Different Women" (single by Frank Loren/Greg Connor), recorded by Frank Loren (country), all on Blue Gem Records. Other artists include Sherry Weston (country).

☑ ○ **BLUE WAVE**, 3221 Perryville Rd., Baldwinsville NY 13027. (315)638-4286. Fax: (315)635-4757. E-mail: bluewave@localnet.com. Website: www.bluewaverecords.com. **Contact:** Greg Spencer, president/producer. Labels include Blue Wave/Horizon. Record company, music publisher (G.W. Spencer Music/ASCAP) and record producer (Blue Wave Productions). Estab. 1985. Staff size: 1. Releases 3 LPs and 3 CDs/year. Pays variable royalty to artists on contract; statutory rate to publisher per song on record.

Distributed by: Select-O-Hits, Action Music, Burnside Dist.

How to Contact: Submit demo tape by mail. Unsolicited submissions are OK. Prefers cassette or videocassette (live performance only) and as many songs as you like. Include SASE. Responds in 1 month only if interested. "Do not call."

Music: Mostly **blues/blues rock**, **roots rock** and **roots R&B/soul**; also **roots country/rockabilly** or **anything with "soul."** Released "Leave Married Women Alone" (single by Jimmy Cavallo) from *The House Rocker* (album), recorded by Jimmy Cavallo (jump blues), released 2002 on Blue Wave; "Sometimes You Gamble" (single by Kim Simmonds) from *Blues Like Midnight* (album), recorded by Kim Simmonds (blues), released 2001 on Blue Wave; and "Motherless World" (single by Pete McMahon) from *Trouble on the Run* (album), recorded by The Kingsnakes (blues), released 2001 on Blue Wave.

Tips: "Be able to put the song across vocally."

Ⓝ ○ **BMX ENTERTAINMENT**, P.O. Box 10857, Stamford CT 06904. Fax: (203)325-9555. Website: www.bmxrecordsgroup.com. **Contact:** Mauris Gryphon, president. Labels include Red Tape Records. Record company. Estab. 1984. Releases 7 singles, 7 12″ singles, 7 LPs, 7 EPs and 7 CDs/year. Pays 10-12% royalty to artists on contract.

How to Contact: Submit demo tape by mail. Unsolicited submissions are OK. Prefers cassette, CD or VHS videocassette with 4 songs or more. "Send bio, résumé, 8×10 photo, contact information." Include SASE. Responds in 3 weeks.

Music: Mostly **country**, **R&B** and **rock**; also **rap**, **pop**, **jazz**, **classical**, **children's**, **New Age**, **gospel** and **salsa**. Released "Just My Imagination" (by Jobete Music), recorded by Flipside on BMX Entertainment. Other artists include Jazreel and Hardcore Jollies.

◕ **BOLIVIA RECORDS**, 2622 Kirtland Rd., Brewton AL 36246. (334)867-2228. President: Roy Edwards. Labels include Known Artist Records. Record company, record producer (Known Artist Productions) and music publisher (Cheavoria Music Co.). Estab. 1972. Releases 10 singles and 3 LPs/year. Pays 5% royalty to artists on contract; statutory rate to publishers for each record sold.

• Bolivia Records' publishing company, Cheavoria Music, is listed in the Music Publishers section and Known Artist Productions is listed in the Record Producers section.

How to Contact: Submit demo tape by mail. Unsolicited submissions are OK. Prefers cassette with 3 songs and lyric sheet. Include SASE for reply. All tapes will be kept on file. Responds in 1 month.

Music: Mostly **R&B**, **country** and **pop**; also **easy listening**, **MOR** and **soul**. Released "If You Only Knew" (single by Horace Linsky), recorded by Roy Edwards; "Make Me Forget" (single by Horace Linsky), recorded by Bobbie Roberson, both on Bolivia Records; and "We Make Our Reality" (single), written and recorded by Brad Smiley on Known Artist Records. Other artists include Jim Portwood.

N ⊕ ◖ **BOULEVARD MUSIC & PUBLISHING**, 16 Limetrees, Llangattock, Crickhowell NP8 1IL Wales. Phone: (0044)(0)1873 810142. Fax: (0044)(0)1873 811557. E-mail: boulmusic@aol. com. A&R Director: Kevin Holland-King (MOR/jazz). Labels include Silverword, Associate, Mirabeau. Record company and music publisher (Boulevard Publishing). Estab. 1987. Staff size: 2. Releases 8 singles and 25 CDs/year. Pays negotiable royalty to artists on contract; statutory rate to publisher per song on record.

Distributed by: SMG/T.H.E.

How to Contact: Submit demo tape by mail. Unsolicited submissions are OK. Prefers cassette, CD or VHS videocassette with 3 songs, lead sheet and cover letter. SAE and IRC. Responds in 1 month.

Music: Mostly **MOR**, **rock** and **R&B**; also **country** and **jazz**. Released "We Will Stand" (single by McCrory/Kalzaghe) from *We Will Stand* (album), recorded by Lennox Lewis/Joe Kalzaghe/Tony Mortimer (pop), released 2002 on Silverword; *Moves 2 Fast* (album by A. Kyriacon), recorded by Modern Romance (pop/dance), released 2002 on SMG; and *East* (album by Martin Hunter), recorded by Ashmore (pop/dance), released 2002 on SMG. Other artists include Jeff Hooper, Southlanders, Screemer, Modern Romance, Ashmore, Poe-Alley and Richard Beavis.

Tips: "A well-written song is like any masterpiece: hard to find—easy to recognize."

N ◕ **BOUQUET RECORDS**, Bouquet-Orchid Enterprises, P.O. Box 1335, Norcross GA 30091. (770)814-2420. **Contact:** Bill Bohannon, president. Record company, music publisher (Orchid Publishing/BMI), record producer (Bouquet-Orchid Enterprises) and management firm (Bouquet-Orchid Enterprises). Releases 3-4 singles and 2 LPs/year. Pays 5-8% royalty to artists on contract; pays statutory rate to publishers for each record sold.

How to Contact: Submit demo tape by mail. Unsolicited submissions are OK. Prefers cassette or CD with 3-5 songs and lyric sheet. Include SASE. Responds in 1 month.

Music: Mostly **religious** (contemporary or country-gospel, Amy Grant, etc.), **country** ("the type suitable for Clint Black, George Strait, Patty Loveless, etc.") and **top 100** ("the type suitable for Billy Joel, Whitney Houston, R.E.M., etc."); also **rock** and **MOR**. Released *Blue As Your Eyes* (by Bill Bohannon), recorded by Adam Day (country); *Take Care of My World* (by Bob Freeman), recorded by Bandoleers (top 40); and *Making Plans* (by John Harris), recorded by Susan Spencer (country), all on Bouquet Records.

Tips: "Submit 3-5 songs on a cassette tape with lyric sheets. Include a short biography and perhaps a photo. Enclose SASE."

☑ ☒ ◕ **BRENTWOOD RECORDS/DIADEM RECORDS**, 741 Cool Springs Blvd., Franklin TN 37067. (615)261-6500. Fax: (615)261-5903. Website: www.brentwoodrecords.com. Director of A&R: Ed Kee (Christian concept, instrumental). Co-Vice President/General Manager: Dean Diehl (A/C, Christian). Labels include Brentwood Jazz, Diadem Records and Brentwood Kids Company. Record company and music publisher (Brentwood-Benson Publishing). Estab. 1981. Staff size: 9. Releases 18 CDs/year. Pays statutory rate to publisher per song on record.

Distributed by: Provident Music Distribution and BMG.

• Music released by Brentwood Records has been certified Gold by the RIAA; and won the Gospel Music Association's Dove Award.

How to Contact: *Does not accept unsolicited material. Unsolicited material will be returned unopened. "except when negotiated otherwise*

Music: Mostly **Christian praise and worship**, **A/C** and **inspirational**; also **concept-driven projects**. Does not want country, rap, reggae, dance, hip-hop, etc. Released *Tales From The Ark* (animated children's video); *America's Favorite Patriotic Songs* (album); and *My First Worship/My First Christmas* (album), all released 2001 on Brentwood Records.

☑ ☺ ◉ **BROKEN NOTE RECORDS**, 723 Main, #530, Houston TX 77002. (281)658-6484. **Contact:** Tony Avitia, A&R. Record company. Estab. 1993. Staff size: 3. Releases 4 singles, 6 LPs and 6 CDs/year. Pays negotiable royalty to artists on contract; statutory rate to publisher per song on record.

Distributed by: Southwest and Crystal Clear.

• Awarded 1999 Best Local Label by Houston Press

How to Contact: Submit demo tape by mail. Unsolicited submissions are OK. Prefers cassette, CD or VHS videocassette with lyric sheet, cover letter and press clippings. Does not return materials. Responds in 2 months if interested.

Music: Mostly **heavy rock**, **rap** and **techno-rock**; also **surf-instrumental**, **hip hop** and **folk**. Released *The Sultry Sounds of Collision* (album), written and recorded by Cult Ceavers (jazzcore); *The Regal Beagle* (album), written and recorded by I-45 (rap); and *Pogo Au-go-go* (album), written and recorded by Bickley (punk), all on Broken Note.

Tips: "Be persistent."

◉ **BROKEN RECORDS INTERNATIONAL**, 940 S. Grace St., Lombard IL 60148. Phone/fax: (630)693-0719. E-mail: roy@mcguitar.com. Website: www.mcguitar.com/BrokenRecords.htm. International A&R: Roy Bocchieri. Vice President: Jeff Murphy. Record company. Estab. 1984. Payment negotiable.

How to Contact: *Write first and obtain permission to submit.* Prefers cassette or CD with at least 2 songs and lyric sheet. Does not return material. Responds in 2 months.

Music: Mostly **rock**, **pop** and **dance**; also **acoustic** and **industrial**. Released *Figurehead* (album by LeRoy Bocchieri), recorded by Day One (pop/alternative); and *Eitherway* (album by Jeff Murphy/Herb Eimerman), recorded by The Nerk Twins (pop/alternative), both on Broken Records.

◉ **BSW RECORDS**, P.O. Box 2297, Universal City TX 78148. (210)599-0022. Fax: (210)653-3989. E-mail: bswr18@txdirect.net. Website: www.bswrecords.com. President: Frank Willson. Vice Presidents: Frank Weatherly (country, jazz); Regina Willson (blues). Record company, music publisher (BSW Records/BMI), management firm (Universal Music Marketing) and record producer (Frank Willson). Estab. 1987. Staff size: 5. Releases 18 albums/year. Pays standard royalty to artists on contract; statutory rate to publisher per song on record.

How to Contact: Submit demo CD by mail. Unsolicited submissions are OK. Prefers CD (or ¾″ videocassette) with 3 songs and lyric sheet. Include SASE. Responds in 6 weeks.

Music: Mostly **country**, **rock** and **blues**. Released *Memories of Hank Williams, Sr.* (album), recorded by Larry Butler and Willie Nelson. Other artists include Candee Land, Shawn DeLorme, John Wayne and Sonny Marshall.

☑ ◉ **C.P.R.**, 4 West St., Massapequa Park NY 11762. Phone/fax: (516)797-7752. E-mail: d.yannacone@aol.com. **Contact:** Denise Yannacone, A&R. Record company. Estab. 1997. Pays negotiable royalty to artists on contract; statutory rate to publisher per song on record.

How to Contact: Submit demo tape by mail. Unsolicited submissions are OK. Prefers cassette, CD or DAT with 4 songs and lyric sheet. Does not return material. Responds in 3-4 months.

Music: Mostly **uptempos**, **R&B**, **rap**, **rock**, **pop** and **soundtrack**.

Tips: "Keep in mind the sky's the limit. Remember when you feel like quitting, there are no short cuts to success. So please submit songs that are well produced."

◙ **CAMBRIA RECORDS & PUBLISHING**, P.O. Box 374, Lomita CA 90717. (310)831-1322. Fax: (310)833-7442. E-mail: cambruamus@aol.com. **Contact:** Lance Bowling, director of recording operations. Labels include Charade Records. Record company and music publisher. Estab. 1979. Staff size: 3. Pays 5-8% royalty to artists on contract; statutory rate to publisher for each record sold. **Distributed by:** Albany Distribution.
How to Contact: *Write first and obtain permission to submit.* Prefers cassette. Include SASE. Responds in 1 month.
Music: Mostly **classical**. Released *Songs of Elinor Remick Warren* (album) on Cambria Records. Other artists include Marie Gibson (soprano), Leonard Pennario (piano), Thomas Hampson (voice), Mischa Leftkowitz (violin), Leigh Kaplan (piano), North Wind Quintet and Sierra Wind Quintet.

☑ ◙ **CANDYSPITEFUL PRODUCTIONS**, 4202 Co. Rt. 4, Oswego NY 13126. (480)968-7017. E-mail: mandrakerocks@yahoo.com. Website: www.candyspiteful.com. President: William Ferraro. Professional Managers: Lori Wall (all styles), Maxwell Frye (jazz, rock). Record company, music publisher (Candyspiteful Productions), record producer (Candyspiteful Productions). Estab. 2000. Staff size: 3. Produces 6 singles, 2 albums per year. Pays negotiable royalty to artists; statutory to publisher per song on record.
How to Contact: Submit demo tape by mail. Unsolicited submissions are OK. Prefers CD/CDR with 3 songs, lyric sheet and cover letter. "Please include a fact sheet, bio, current play dates, etc." Does not return material. Responds only if interested.
Music: Mostly **progressive rock**, **rock/pop/R&B**and **smooth jazz/rock**. Released *Cloud Nine* (album by Richard Farnsworth), recorded by Thunderhead (hard rock); and "Seven Opus" (single by Sharon Barlow) from *Seven Opus* (album), recorded by Sharon Barlow (pop), both released 2001 on Candyspiteful Productions.

☑ ◙ **CANTILENA RECORDS**, 6548 Via Sereno, Rancho Murieta CA 95683-9226. (916)354-8651. E-mail: llzz@aol.com. Website: www.cantilenarecords.com. A&R: Laurel Zucker. A&R: Davis Sapper. Record company. Estab. 1993. Releases 5 CDs/year. Pays Harry Fox standard royalty to artists on contract; statutory rate to publishers per song on record.
How to Contact: *Write first and obtain permission to submit or to arrange personal interview.* Prefers cassette, CD or DAT. Does not return material.
Music: Mostly **classical**. Released *Answer to a Poem* (album by Alec Wilder) (classical); *Kokopeli* (album by Katherine Hoover) (classical); and *Senario Musicale II* (album by David Kingman) (classical), all recorded by Laurel Zucker. Other artists include Tim Gorman, Prairie Prince, Dave Margen, Israel Philharmonic, Erkel Chamber Orchestra, Samuel Magill, Renee Siebert, Robin Sutherland and Gerald Ranch.

◙ **CAPITOL RECORDS**, 1750 N. Vine St., Hollywood CA 90028-5274. (323)462-6252. Fax: (323)469-4542. Website: www.hollywoodandvine.com. New York office: 304 Park Ave. S., 3rd Floor, New York NY 10010. (212)253-3000. Website: www.hollywoodandvine.com. Nashville office: 3322 West End Ave., 11th Floor, Nashville TN 37203. (615)269-2000. Labels include Blue Note Records, Grand Royal Records, Pangaea Records, The Right Stuff Records and Capitol Nashville Records. Record company.
Distributed by: EMD.
How to Contact: *Capitol Records does not accept unsolicited submissions.*
Music: Artists include Bonnie Raitt, Radiohead, Coldplay, Kylie Minogue and Starsailor.

◙ **CAPRICORN RECORDS**, 83 Walton St., Atlanta GA 30303. (404)954-6600. Fax: (404)954-6688. Record company.
How to Contact: *Write first and obtain permission to submit.*

REMEMBER: Don't "shotgun" your demo tapes. Submit only to companies interested in the type of music you write. For more submission hints, refer to Getting Started on page 10.

☑ ◎ **CAPSTAN RECORD PRODUCTION**, P.O. Box 211, East Prairie MO 63845. (575)649-2211. **Contact:** Joe Silver or Tommy Loomas. Labels include Octagon and Capstan Records. Record company, music publisher (Lineage Publishing Co.), management firm (Staircase Promotion) and record producer (Silver-Loomas Productions). Pays 3-5% royalty to artists on contract.

How to Contact: Unsolicited submissions are OK. Prefers cassette or VHS videocassette with 2-4 songs and lyric sheet. "Send photo and bio." Include SASE. Responds in 1 month.

Music: Mostly **country**, **easy listening**, **MOR**, **country rock** and **top 40/pop**. Released "Country Boy" (single by Alden Lambert); and "Yesterday's Teardrops" and "Round & Round" (single), written and recorded by The Burchetts. Other artists include Bobby Lee Morgan, Skidrow Joe, Vicarie Arcole, Fleming and Scarlett Britoni.

☒ ◎ **CASE ENTERTAINMENT GROUP/C.E.G. RECORDS, INC.**, (formerly C.E.G. Records, Inc.), 102 E. Pikes Peak Ave., #200, Colorado Springs CO 80903. (719)632-0227. Fax: (719)634-2274. E-mail: rac@hpi.net. Website: www.newpants.com and www.oldpants.com. **Contact:** Robert A. Case, president. Record company and music publisher (New Pants Publishing/ASCAP, Old Pants Publishing/BMI). Estab. 1989. Releases 3-4 LPs and 3-4 CDs/year. Pays negotiable royalty to artists on contract.

How to Contact: Submit demo tape by mail. Unsolicited submissions are OK. Prefers CD with 3-5 songs and lyric sheet. "Include a brief history of songwriter's career. Songs submitted must be copywritten or pending with copyright office." Does not return material. "Our representative will contact you if interested in material."

Music: Mostly **pop**, **rock** and **country**. Released *James Becker* (album), recorded by James Becker (folk), released 2001 on New Pants; *Romancing the Blues* (album), by Kathy Watson (pop), released 2001 on New Pants; and *Stephanie Aramburo* (album), recorded by Stephanie Aramburo (pop), released 2001 on Old Pants.

Tips: "Think of the music business as a job interview. You must be able to sell yourself and the music is your baby. You have to be strong and not deal with rejection as a personal thing. It is not a rejection of you, it's a rejection of the music. Most songwriters don't know how to communicate with labels. The best way is to start a friendship with people at the label."

☑ ◯ **CELLAR RECORDS**, 703 N. Brinton Ave., Dixon IL 61021. (815)288-2900. E-mail: tjoos @essex1.com. Website: www.cellarrecords.com. **Contact:** Todd Joos, president (rock, pop, country). Vice President (rock): Bob Brady. Vice President Sales and Marketing: Albert Hurst. A&R: Mike Thompson (metal); Jim Miller (adult contemporary, pop, country); Mark Summers. Record company, music publisher (Sound Cellar Music/BMI) and record producer (Todd Joos). Estab. 1987. Staff size: 7. Releases 6-8 CDs/year. Pays 15-100% royalty to artists on contract; statutory rate to publisher per song on record. Charges in advance "if you use our studio to record."

Distributed by: V&R Distribution, Valley One Stop, Amazon.com and cdnow.com.

How to Contact: Submit demo tape by mail. Unsolicited submissions are OK. Prefers CD with 3-4 songs and lyric sheet. Does not return material. Responds in 1 month only if interested. "If we like it we will call you."

Music: Mostly **metal**, **country** and **rock**; also **pop** and **blues**. "No rap." Released "With Any Luck at All" (single by Tony Stampley/Randy Boudreaux/Joe Stampley) from *With Any Luck At All* (album), recorded by Cal Stage (pop/country); "Sleeping With a Smile" (single by Tony Stampley/Melissa Lyons/Tommy Barnes) from *With Any Luck At All* (album), recorded by Cal Stage (pop/country); and "Speed of My Life" (single by Jon Pomplin/Todd Joss) from *Declassified* (album), recorded by Project 814 (rock), all released 2001 on Cellar Records. Other artists include Eric Topper, Jim Miller, Snap Judgment, Ballistic, Dago Red, Sea of Monsters, Twist of Fate, Rogue, Fusion, Famous Nobodies, Kings, 11¢ Junk, James Miller, Vehement and Noopy Wilson.

Tips: "Make sure that you understand that your band is business and you must be willing to self invest time, effort and money just like any other new business. We can help you but you must also be willing to help yourself."

☑ ◖ **CHATTAHOOCHEE RECORDS**, 2544 Roscomare Rd., Los Angeles CA 90077. (818)788-6863. Fax: (310)471-2089. E-mail: cyardum@prodigy.net. **Contact:** Robyn Meyers, Music Director/A&R. Music Director: Chris Yardum. Record company and music publisher (Etnoc/Conte). Member NARAS. Releases 4 singles/year. Pays negotiable royalty to artists on contract.
How to Contact: Submit demo tape by mail. Unsolicited submissions are OK. Prefers cassette with 2-6 songs and lyric sheet. Does not return material. Responds in 2 months only if interested.
Music: Mostly **rock**. Released *Don't Touch It Let It Drip* (album), recorded by Cream House (hard rock), released 2000 on Chattahoochee Records. Artists include DNA.

◖ **CHERRY STREET RECORDS**, P.O. Box 52681, Tulsa OK 74152. (918)742-8087. E-mail: ryoung@cherrystreetmusic.com. Website: www.cherrystreetrecords.com. President: Rodney Young. Vice President: Steve Hickerson. Record company and music publisher. Estab. 1990. Staff size: 2. Releases 2 CD/year. Pays 50% royalty to artists on contract; statutory rate to publisher per song on record.
Distributed by: Internet.
How to Contact: *Write first and obtain permission to submit.* Prefers cassette or videocassette with 4 songs and lyric sheet. Include SASE. Responds in 4 months.
Music: **Rock**, **country** and **R&B**; also **jazz**. Released *Promise Land* (album), written and recorded by Richard Neville on Cherry Street (rock). Other artists include George W. Carroll and Chris Blevins.
Tips: "We sign only artists who play an instrument, sing and write songs. Send only your best four songs."

◖ **CHIAROSCURO RECORDS**, 830 Broadway, New York NY 10003. (212)473-0479. Fax: (849)279-5025. E-mail: jon@chiaroscurojazz.com. Website: www.ChiaroscuroJazz.com. **Contact:** Jon Bates, A&R/operations manager. Labels include Downtown Sound. Record company and record producer (Hank O'Neal, Andrew Sordoni, Jon Bates). Estab. 1973. Releases 12 CDs/year. Pays negotiable royalty to artists on contract; statutory rate to publisher per song on record.
Distributed by: Allegro and Bayside.
How to Contact: Submit demo tape by mail. Unsolicited submissions are OK. Prefers cassette, CD, DAT or videocassette with 1-3 songs. Include SASE. Responds in 6 weeks.
Music: Mostly **jazz** and **blues**. "A full catalog listing is available on the web at www.chiaroscurojazz. com or by calling (800)528-2582. "New releases scheduled for 2002 include The National Jazz Ensemble, directed by Chuck Israels featuring Bill Evans, Lee Konitz and Tom Harrell, plus 'Sketches Out' with piano phenomenon Mike Jones, and 'Mood Swings' with the magnificent vocals of Kathy Kosin."
Tips: "We are not a pop label. Our average release sells between 3,000-5,000 copies in the first three years. We do not give cash advances or tour support, and our average budget per release is about $15,000 including all production, printing and manufacturing costs."

Ⓝ ◖ **CIMIRRON/RAINBIRD RECORDS**, 607 Piney Point Rd., Yorktown VA 23692. (757)898-8155. E-mail: lpuckett@ix.netcom.com. President: Lana Puckett (country, pop, gospel). Vice President: Kim Person (folk, bluegrass). Record company and music publisher (Cimirron Music). Releases 3-6 CDs and cassettes/year. Pays variable royalty to artists on contract; negotiable rate to publisher per song on record.
Distributed by: Peaches, Plan 9, Plan A, Internet and mail order.
How to Contact: *Write first and obtain permission to submit.* Prefers cassette or CD and lyric sheet. Include SASE. Responds in 2 months.
Music: Mostly **country/acoustic**, **bluegrass** and **singer/songwriter**. Released *Special Delivery* (album), written and recorded by Bill Parson (acoustic); *At Christmas the Heart Goes Home* (album), recorded by Lana Puckett and Kim Person (acoustic); *Turning For Home* (album) by Ron Fetner

---

THE TYPES OF MUSIC each listing is interested in are printed in **boldface**.

(acoustic); *Memories of Home* (album), recorded by Code Bluegrass Band (bluegrass); *Christmas in My Heart* (album), recorded by Rich Follett (acoustic); and *River* (album), recorded by Stephen Bennett, all on Cimirron/Rainbird Records. Other artists include Ron Fetner and Motely.

Tips: "Have a great song. Be hardworking and have a following."

☑ ◐ **CKB RECORDS/HELAPHAT ENTERTAINMENT**, 1908 Estrada Pkwy., Apt. 231, Irving TX 75061-1105. (214)986-5412. Fax: (972)870-1720. E-mail: spoonfedmusik@juno.com. **Contact:** Tony Briggs, A&R director. Record company and record producer (Tony Briggs). Estab. 1999. Staff size: 6. Pays negotiable royalty to artists on contract.

Distributed by: Southwest Distributing.

How to Contact: Submit demo tape by mail. Unsolicited submissions are OK. Prefers cassette, CD or DAT with 4 songs, cover letter and press clippings. Does not return materials. Responds only if interested.

Music: Mostly **rap**, **hip-hop** and **R&B**. Released "Body, Body" (single), recorded by T-Spoon (hip-hop), released 2002 on CKB Records; and "We Can't Be Stopped" (single) from *Ouncified* (album), written and recorded by Tha 40 Clique (hip-hop), released 2002 on CKB. Other artists include Baby Boo and Laticia Love.

Tips: "Be confident, honest and open to ideas."

◐ **CLEOPATRA RECORDS**, 13428 Maxella Ave., PMB 251, Marina del Rey CA 90292. (310)823-0337. Fax: (310)823-5497. **Contact:** Timothy Dooner or Jason Myers. Labels include Hypnotic, Deadline, X-Ray, Cult, Stardust and Purple Pyramid. Record company. Estab. 1991. Releases 5 singles, 10 LPs, 5 EPs and 100 CDs/year. Pays 10-14% royalty to artists on contract; negotiable rate to publisher per song on record.

How to Contact: Submit demo tape by mail. Unsolicited submissions are OK. Prefers CD with 3 songs. Does not return material. Responds in 1 month.

Music: Mostly **industrial**, **gothic** and **trance**; also **heavy metal**, **space rock** and **electronic**.

🌐 ◯ **COLLECTOR RECORDS**, P.O. Box 1200, 3260 AE oud beyerland Holland. Phone: (31)186 604266. Fax: (31)186 604366. E-mail: cees@collectorrec.com. Website: www.collectorrec.com. **Contact:** Cees Klop, president. Manager: John Moore. Labels include All Rock, Downsouth, Unknown, Pro Forma and White Label Records. Record company, music publisher (All Rock Music Publishing) and record producer (Cees Klop). Estab. 1967. Staff size: 4. Release 25 LPs/year. Pays 10% royalty to artist on contract.

How to Contact: Submit demo tape by mail. Unsolicited submissions are OK. Prefers cassette. SAE and IRC. Responds in 2 months.

Music: Mostly **'50s rock**, **rockabilly**, **hillbilly boogie** and **country/rock**; also **piano boogie woogie**. Released "Knocking on the Backside" (single by T. Riedel) from *The Original* (album), recorded by Teddy Redell ('50s rock), released 2001; "Going to California/Bye Bye Sue" (single by T. Riedell) from *The Early Teddy Redell* (album), recorded by Teddy Redell, released 2002; and "Rock Bottom Boogie" (single by Herbert Woolfolk) from *Hokey Pokey Rock* (album), recorded by Herbert Woolfolk (boogie), released 2001, all on Collector Records. Other artists include Henk Pepping.

◉ **COLUMBIA RECORDS**, 550 Madison Ave., 24th Floor, New York NY 10022-3211. (212)833-4000. Fax: (212)833-4389. Santa Monica office: 2100 Colorado Ave., Santa Monica CA 90404. (310)449-2100. Fax: (310)449-2743. Nashville office: 34 Music Square E., Nashville TN 37203. (615)742-4321. Fax: (615)244-2549. E-mail: sonymusiconline@sonymusic.com. Website: www.sony.com/Music/Columbia. Labels include So So Def Records and Ruffhouse Records. Record company.

Distributed by: Sony.

How to Contact: *Columbia Records does not accept unsolicited submissions.*

Music: Released *The Writing's on the Wall* (album), recorded by Destiny's Child; *Marc Anthony* (album), recorded by Marc Anthony; *Affirmation* (album), recorded by Savage Garden; *Ricky Martin* (album), recorded by Ricky Martin, all on Columbia Records. Other artists include Aerosmith and Bob Dylan.

insider report

Brian Perera's Cleopatra:
For the love of Goth

Brian Perera

Can gothic rock become any more theatrical and melodic than Cleopatra Records' recent releases, *A Taste of Sin*, *War of the Worlds & Dracula*, and *Songs of Terror: A Gothic Tribute to Edgar Allen Poe*? "Yes," says CEO/President Brian Perera, and he's actively seeking musicians who can provide original sounds—as long as they don't send candy or incense with their demos. "It's true," says Perera. "We are an eccentric record label, but we still adhere to basic business standards; one of them is to present yourself and your work professionally."

While gifts and gadgets are strongly discouraged, so are bad photographs, bios written in magic marker, and letters of interest riddled with lyrics, pleas for stardom, and claims about being the next Nine-Inch Nails or Ministry.

"As renowned as Nine-Inch has become, we don't need another," says Perera. "Just be yourself, have a vision, and prove you're a part of the evolution of music. At that time we will decide if your musical aspirations fit ours."

The "evolution of music" Perera is speaking of, according to the 2,000 titles now credited to the label group he founded in 1992, spans from industrial, glam/metal and trance to underground hip-hop, jazz and even classical recordings. Where Motorhead and Billie Holiday meet, Perera's philosophy is simple: from the new recordings to the reissues, Cleopatra delivers what music fans desire—all kinds of music. A self-proclaimed nightclub junkie in Los Angeles through the '80s and '90s, Perera developed his own varied musical tastes by immersing himself in all aspects of the business. Seeing a need to challenge the record industry's protocol of carrying just one brand of music, Perera officially launched Cleopatra Records with releases from three eclectic bands: Pressurhed (a space rock band from San Francisco), Motorhead's *On Parole*, which had long been out of print, and most significantly, a series of reissues by electronic forerunners, Kraftwerk.

In the early stages of Cleopatra, dark, surreal releases by Christian Death, Switchblade Symphony and Razed in Black secured the label's reputation of being the single most influential breeder of gothic rock in the '90s, capturing fans from around the globe. And while the style and image of "Goth" music have not changed over the years, asserts Perera, some elements have recently innovated the genre, including keyboards, turntables and the disappearance of distorted vocals.

"Keyboards do dominate gothic and industrial music, but not all artists exploring this brand of sounds need a keyboard in front of them to produce the good quality we ask for," says Perera. "As we are busy nursing our newer imprints which don't necessarily cater to the Goth following, such as the X-Ray imprint and the Stardust imprint, Cleopatra Records remains true to its roots, and we are always looking for edgy tunes—with or without a keyboard."

Considering the label group has earned star-selling status for the distribution giant Caroline for years, Perera's wide expansion of the company with six imprints recently only broadened its favorable reputation. The Cleopatra family now consists of Hypnotic Records, which gained notoriety in two *Billboard* charts with a continuous mix by world famous DJ Paul Oakenfold. Shortly after, the progressive/classic imprint Purple Pyramid surfaced, along with Deadline Records, aggressively slamming out traditional glam rock. Cleopatra's X-Ray, which released the first solo album from SX-10 paired with Cypress Hill's Sen Dog, caters to the electronic dance movement sprouting up in every corner of the world. And as if this assortment wasn't enough, Perera also created the Stardust and Goldenlane imprints, strictly dedicated to the reissue of recordings from the "Marilyn Monroe era."

"Since it's even cheaper to record music today than it was when I first started out—proudly boasting a $2,000-5,000 budget per band—we're recording all the fine music out we possible can," says Perera. Consequently, he doesn't mind praising his releases of the sultry Ella Fitzgerald in the same breath he applauds the "scary, exceptionally dark" chords of Roz Williams.

How fast is the Cleopatra Label Group recording? "The pace is head-spinning, but I have an extremely talented crew of assistants, and the rewards of this business pounce through my door each day," says Perera, who surveys every band, license and deal each day. Over 150 of them occurred in 2000, and the company currently receives approximately 25 demo CDs a week.

"We are excited to open up each demo as it's delivered to us, but we wish that all aspiring artists knew the proper procedure before sending it on its way," says Perera. "Most importantly, if you can't label your work, we will assume it was created by someone imaginary, and secondly, don't be afraid to send us a CD because you think we will steal your music!" And one last thing, demands Perera: "If you are a rap artist, while we may appreciate your lyrics on a demo, we do not appreciate them on our messaging service."

—Candi Lace

☑ ○ **COM-FOUR DISTRIBUTION**, 7 Dunham Place, Brooklyn NY 11211. (718)599-2205. Website: www.com4.com. Distribution Manager: Albert Garzon. Distribution company. Estab. 1985. Distributes over 100,000 different titles including imports.
How to Contact: "Please visit our website for submission information. We accept retail ready product only!"
Music: All genres.
Tips: "We are a distribution company, not a record label. Must have retail ready product!"

☑ ♕ ○ **COMSTOCK RECORDS LTD.**, P.O. Box 19720, Fountain Hills AZ 85269. (480)951-3115. Fax: (480)951-3074. E-mail: fara@comstockrecords.com. Website: www.comstockrecords.com. Production Manager/Producer: Patty Parker. President: Frank Fara. Record company, music publisher (White Cat Music/ASCAP, Rocky Bell Music/BMI, How the West Was Sung Music/BMI), record producer (Patty Parker) and radio promotion. Member CMA, BBB, CCMA, BCCMA, British CMA and AF of M. "Comstock Records, Ltd. has three primary divisions: Production, Promotion and Publishing. We distribute and promote both our own Nashville productions, as well as already completed country or pop/rock CDs. We also offer CD design and mastering and manufacturing for products we promote. We can master from a copy of your DAT master or CD." Staff size: 2. Releases 10-12 CD singles, 10-12 albums/year and 5-6 international sampler CDs. Pays 10% royalty to artists on contract; statutory rate to publishers for each record sold. "Artists pay distribution and promotion fee to press and release their masters."

● Comstock Records was named indie Label of the Year at ECMA of Europe's Country Music Awards for 1998 and 1999. Fara & Parker are also authors of the book *How To Open Doors in the Music Industry—The Independent Way* (available through amazon.com).

How to Contact: Submit demo tape by mail. Unsolicited submissions are OK. Prefers CD or cassette. Include SASE. "Enclose stamped return envelope if demo is to be returned." Responds in 2 weeks.

Music: Released *Weed and Water* (album by Paul Marshall and various co-writers), recorded by Paul Marshall (country), released 2001 on Comstock/Scostepa Music; *George Arlis Highfill* (album by George Highfill and various co-writers), recorded by George Highfill (country), released 2001 on Comstock/Church Street Records; and *Dreaming the Mystery* (album by Shane Russell and Charles John Quarto), recorded by Shane Russell (country), released 2001 on Comstock/Jalapeño Records. Other artists include Rebel Hearts, Mahoney Brothers, Dwight Whitley, Crissy Cummings.

Tips: "Go global—good songs and good singers are universal. Country acts from North America will find a great response in the overseas radio market. Likewise U.S. Radio is open to the fresh new sounds that foreign artists bring to the airwaves."

Ø COSMOTONE RECORDS, PMB 412, 3350-A Highway 6 S., Sugar Land TX 77478. E-mail: marianland@earthlink.net. Website: www.marianland.com/music.html. Record company, music publisher (Cosmotone Music, ASCAP) and record producer (Rafael Brom). Estab. 1984.

Distributed by: marianland.com.

How to Contact: "We do not accept material at this time." Does not return materials.

Music: All types. Released *Angelophany* (album), by Rafael Brom.

[N] Ø COUNTRY STAR INTERNATIONAL, 439 Wiley Ave., Franklin PA 16323. (814)432-4633. **Contact:** Norman Kelly, president. Labels include CSI, Country Star, Process and Mersey Records. Record company, music publisher (Country Star Music/ASCAP, Process and Kelly/BMI), management firm (Country Star Attractions) and record producer (Country Star Productions). Member AFM and AFTRA. Estab. 1970. Releases 5-10 singles and 5-10 LPs/year. Pays 8% royalty to artists on contract; statutory rate to publisher per song on record.

● See the listing for Country Star Music in the Music Publishers section and Country Star Attractions in the Managers & Booking Agents section.

How to Contact: Submit demo tape by mail. Unsolicited submissions are OK. Prefers cassette with 2 songs and typed lyric or lead sheet. SASE. "No SASE no return." Reports in 9 weeks.

Music: Mostly **c&w** and **bluegrass**. Released "Holiday Waltz" (single by F. Seltzer), recorded by Debbie Sue, released on Country Star Records. Other artists include Junie Lou and Bob Stamper.

[N] Ø CPA RECORDS, 15104 Golden Eagle Way, Tampa FL 33625-1545. (813)920-4605. Fax:(813)926-0846. E-mail: 1albert1@gte.net. Website: www.cparecords.com. **Contact:** Sax Kari, director, A&R Dept. Labels include Coffee's Productions and Associates. Record company and music publisher (CPA Music Publishing). Estab. 1999. Staff size: 5. Releases 3 singles and 2 albums/year. Pays negotiable royalty to artists on contract; negotiable royalty to publisher per song on record.

How to Contact: *Write or call first and obtain permission to submit a demo.* Prefers CD/CDR and VHS videocassette with 3 songs, lyric sheet, lead sheet and cover letter. Include SASE. Responds in 2 weeks.

Music: Mostly **gospel/Christian**, **rhythm**, **blues** and **jazz**; also **pop** and **rap**. Does not want country. Released "Mirror Images" and "Break Me Off A Piece" (singles) from *Mirror Images* (album), written and recorded by Coffee (blues), released 2001; and "Living For The Lord"(single by Sax Kari/Andre Walker) from *A Message To Deliver* (album), recorded by Al McDaniel (gospel), released 2000, both on CPA Records. Other artists include Sax Kari, Anthony "Big Lou" McDaniel, and Mike and Anita.

REFER TO THE CATEGORY INDEX (at the end of this section) to find exactly which companies are interested in the type of music you write.

Tips: "Be marketable, creative, committed to achieving success, and willing to work hard to accomplish your goals."

N **○** **CRANK! A RECORD COMPANY**, 1223 Wilshire Blvd. #823, Santa Monica CA 90403. (310)392-8985. Fax: (310)399-7355. E-mail: fan@crankthis.com. Website: www.crankthis.com. **Contact:** Jeff Matlow. Record company. Estab. 1994. Releases 6 singles, 5 LPs, 2 EPs and 5 CDs/year. Pays negotiable royalty to artists on contract.
Distributed by: Southern, Revolver, Lumberjack and Nail.
How to Contact: Submit demo tape by mail. Unsolicited submissions are OK. Prefers CD. "Send whatever best represents your abilities." Does not return material. Responds in 3 weeks.
Music: Mostly **indie/alternative rock** and **pop**. Released *Mono* (album), written and recorded by The Icarus Line (rock/punk); *Down Marriott Lane!* (album), written and recorded by the Get Set (rock/pop); *The Power of Failing*, written and recorded by Mineral (rock); *Boys Life*, written and recorded by Boys Life (rock); and *Such Blinding Stars for Starving Eyes*, written and recorded by Cursive (rock), all on Crank! Other artists include Fireside, Errortype:11, Onelinedrawing, Regrets, Far Apart, Silver Scooter, Sunday's Best and Gloria Record.

○ **CREATIVE IMPROVISED MUSIC PROJECTS (CIMP) RECORDS**, Cadence Building, Redwood NY 13679. (315)287-2852. Fax: (315)287-2860. Website: www.cadencebuilding.com. **Contact:** Bob Rusch, producer. Labels include Cadence Jazz Records. Record company and record producer (Robert D. Rusch). Estab. 1980. Releases 25-30 CDs/year. Pays negotiable royalty to artists on contract; pays statutory rate to publisher per song on record.
Distributed by: North Country Distributors.
  ● CIMP specializes in jazz and creative improvised music.
How to Contact: Submit demo tape or CD by mail. Unsolicited submissions are OK. Prefers cassette or CD. "We are not looking for songwriters but recording artists." Include SASE. Responds in 1 week.
Music: Mostly **jazz** and **creative improvised music**. Released *Mark 'N' Marshall* (album), recorded by Marshall Allen; and *Tag* (album), recorded by Yuko Fujiyama, both on CIMP (improvised jazz). Other artists include Arthur Blyme, John McPhee & David Prentice, Anthony Braxton and Roswell Rudd.
Tips: "CIMP Records are produced to provide music to reward repeated and in-depth listenings. They are recorded live to two-track which captures the full dynamic range one would experience in a live concert. There is no compression, homogenization, eq-ing, post-recording splicing, mixing, or electronic fiddling with the performance. Digital recording allows for a vanishingly low noise floor and tremendous dynamic range. This compression of the dynamic range is what limits the 'air' and life of many recordings. Our recordings capture the dynamic intended by the musicians. In this regard these recordings are demanding. Treat the recording as your private concert. Give it your undivided attention and it will reward you. CIMP Records are not intended to be background music. This method is demanding not only on the listener but on the performer as well. Musicians must be able to play together in real time. They must understand the dynamics of their instrument and how it relates to the others around them. There is no fix-it-in-the-mix safety; either it works or it doesn't. What you hear is exactly what was played. Our main concern is music not marketing."

⊘ **CURB RECORDS**, 47 Music Square E., Nashville TN 37203. (615)321-5080. Fax: (615)327-1964. Website: www.curb.com. **Contact:** Michelle Metzgar, director A&R. Record company.
How to Contact: Curb Records does not accept unsolicited submissions; accepts previously published material only. *Do not submit without permission.*
Music: Released *Everywhere* (album), recorded by Tim McGraw; *Sittin' On Top of the World* (album), recorded by LeAnn Rimes; and *I'm Alright* (album), recorded by Jo Dee Messina, all on Curb Records. Other artists include Mary Black, Bananarama, Junior Brown, Merle Haggard, Kal Ketchum, David Kersh, Lyle Lovett, Tim McGraw, Wynonna and Sawyer Brown.

○ **DAGENE/CABLETOWN COMPANY**, P.O. Box 410851, San Francisco CA 94141. (415)822-1530. **Contact:** David Alston, president. Record company, music publisher (Dagene Music), management firm (Golden City International) and record producer (David-Classic Disc Productions). Estab. 1993. Pays standard royalty to artists on contract; statutory rate to publisher per song on record.

How to Contact: *Write first and obtain permission to submit.* Prefers cassette, CD or VHS videocassette with 2-3 songs and lyric sheet. Include SASE. Responds in 1 month.

Music: Mostly **r&b/rap**, **dance** and **pop**; also **gospel**. Released "Mind Ya Own" (single), recorded by 2 Dominatorz on Dagene Records; "Let's Get It On" (single), written and recorded by Chapter One, released on Dagene Records; "To Know You Better" (single), recorded by Rare Essence on Cabletown Records; and "Why Can't I Be Myself" (single), written and recorded by David Alston on E-lect-ric Recordings.

☑ ◻ **ALAN DALE PRODUCTIONS**, 1630 Judith Lane, Indianapolis IN 46227. (317)786-1630. E-mail: AlanDale2211@aol.com. **Contact:** Alan D. Heshelman, president. Labels include ALTO Records. Record company. Estab. 1990. Pays 10% royalty to artists on contract.

How to Contact: *Write or call first and obtain permission to submit or to arrange personal interview.* Prefers cassette with 3 songs. Does not return material. Responds in 10 weeks.

Music: Mostly **A/C**, **country**, **jazz**, **gospel** and **New Age**.

Tips: "At the present time, we are only looking for vocalists to promote as we promote the songs we write and produce."

☑ ◻ **DEADEYE RECORDS**, P.O. Box 2198, Fallbrook CA 92088-2198. (714)768-0644. E-mail: deadeye@deadeye.com. Website: www.deadeyerecords.com. **Contact:** James Frank, A&R. Record company, record producer and management firm (Danny Federici's Shark River Music). Estab. 1992. Staff size: 2. Releases 3 CDs/year. Pays varying royalty to artists on contract; statutory rate to publisher per song on record.

How to Contact: *Write or e-mail first and obtain permission to submit.* Prefers cassette or videocassette with 3 songs and lyric sheet. Does not return material. Responds in 3 months.

Music: Mostly **country**, **rock** and **blues**. Released *Ragin' Wind* (album by Frank Jenkins), recorded by Diamondback on Deadeye Records (country); and *Flemington*, (album) recorded by Danny Federici (of the E Street Band).

☑ ◻ **DEARY ME RECORDS**, P.O. Box 19315, Cincinnati OH 45219. (513)557-2930. E-mail: jim@dearymerecords.com. Website: www.dearymerecords.com. **Contact:** Jim Farmer, director of business & A&R. Record company. Estab. 1995. Staff size: 2. Releases 3 CDs/year. Pays 50% royalty "after we break even."

How to Contact: Unsolicited submissions are OK. "Please check our website for submission policy."

Music: Mostly **indie rock** and **off-beat punk**. Released *This Is Our ~ Music* (album by Matt Hart/Darren Callahan), recorded by Travel (off-beat punk), released 2000 on Deary Me Records; *Tender Trap* (album), recorded by Fairmount Girls (indie rock), released 2001 on Deary Me Records; and *Black Box Broken* (album), recorded by Chalk (indie rock), released 2001 on Deary Me Records. Other artists include the Greenhomes and the Wolverton Brothers.

Tips: "We are typically not impressed with gimmicks or trends, and are only interested in bands that play gigs on a regular basis. Bands with previously released stuff is a major plus."

☑ ◻ **DEEP SOUTH ENTERTAINMENT**, P.O. Box 17737, Raleigh NC 27619-7737. (919)844-1515. Fax: (919)847-5922. E-mail: info@deepsouthentertainment.com. Website: www.deepsouthentertainment.com. Director of Artist Relations: Amy Cox, associate manager. Record company and management company. Estab. 1996. Staff size: 10. Pays negotiable royalty to artists on contract; statutory rate to publisher per song on record.

Distributed by: Redeye Distribution, Valley, Select-O-Hits, City Hall, AEC/Bassin, Northeast One Stop, Pollstar and Koch International.

How to Contact: Submit demo tape by mail. Unsolicited submissions are OK. Prefers cassette or CD with 3 songs, cover letter and press clippings. Does not return material. Responds only if interested.

Music: Mostly **pop**, **modern rock** and **alternative**; also **swing**, **rockabilly** and **heavy rock**. Does not want rap or R&B. Artists include Bruce Hornsby, Little Feat, Mike Daly, SR-71, Stretch Princess and many more.

DEL-FI RECORDS, INC., 8271 Melrose Ave., Suite 103, Los Angeles CA 90046. (800)993-3534. Fax: (323)966-4805. E-mail: info@del-fi.com. Website: www.del-fi.com. Director of A&R: Bryan Thomas. **Contact:** Bob Keane, owner and president. Labels include Del-Fi, Del-Fi Nashville, Donna, Mustang, Bronco and others. Record company. Estab. 1957. Releases 5-10 LPs and 40 CDs/year. Pays negotiable royalty to artists on contract; statutory rate to publisher per song on record.
Distributed by: Paulstarr Distribution.
  ● Del-Fi's open door policy is legendary.
How to Contact: Submit demo tape by mail. Unsolicited submissions are OK. Prefers cassette or CD. "Please enclose bio information and photo if possible. Send a résumé via fax." Does not return material "unless specified. Allow several weeks." Responds in 1 month.
Music: Mostly **rock**, **surf/drag** and **exotica**. Recently released *Out There in the Dark* (album), written and recorded by Outrageous Cherry (rock); and *Cloud Eleven* (album), written and recorded by Cloud Eleven (rock/pop), both released 1999 on Del-Fi. Other artists include The El Caminos.
Tips: "Be sure you are making/writing music that specifically meets your own artistic/creative demands, and not someone else's. Write/play music from the heart and soul and you will always succeed on a personal rewarding level first. We are *the* surf label . . . home of the 'Delphonic' sound. We've also released many of the music world's best known artists, including Ritchie Valens and the Bobby Fuller Four."

DEMI MONDE RECORDS AND PUBLISHING, LTD., Foel Studio, Llanfair Caereinion, Powys, Wales, United Kingdom. Phone/fax: (01938)810758. E-mail: demi.monde@dial.p ipex.com. Website: www.demimonde.co.uk/demimonde. Managing Director: Dave Anderson. Record company, music publisher (Demi Monde Records & Publishing, Ltd.) and record producer (Dave Anderson). Estab. 1983. Releases 5 12" singles, 10 LPs and 6 CDs/year. Pays 10% royalty to artists on contract; statutory rate to publisher per song on record.
Distributed by: Pinnacle, Magnum and Shellshock.
How to Contact: Submit demo tape by mail. Unsolicited submissions are OK. Prefers cassette with 3-4 songs. Does not return material. Responds in 6 weeks.
Music: Mostly **rock**, **R&B** and **pop**. Released *Hawkwind*, *Amon Duul II & Gong* and *Groundhogs* (by T.S. McPhee), all on Demi Monde Records.

DENTAL RECORDS, P.O. Box 20058 DHCC, New York NY 10017. (212)486-4513. Fax: (212)832-6370. E-mail: rsanford@dentalrecords.com. Website: www.dentalrecords.com. **Contact:** Rick Sanford, owner. Record company. Estab. 1981. Staff size: 2. Releases 1-2 CDs/year. Pays negotiable royalty to artists on contract; statutory rate to publisher per song on record.
Distributed by: Dutch East India Trading.
How to Contact: Submit demo tape by mail. Unsolicited submissions are OK. Prefers CD with any number of songs, lyric sheet and cover letter. "Check our website to see if your material is appropriate." Include SASE. Responds only if interested.
Music: Mostly **weird pop**, **art pop** and **soda pop**. Does not want urban, heavy metal or hard core. Released *Gladolescents* (album), written and recorded by Les Izmor (pop), released 2002 on Dental Records. Other artists include Rick Sanford.

DISCMEDIA, 2134 Newport Blvd., Costa Mesa CA 92627. (949)631-8597. Fax: (949)515-7499. E-mail: irmavideo@hotmail.com. Website: www.discmedia.com. **Contact:** Irma Moller, manager. Producers: Glenn Moller (rock, dance) and Henry Moller (pop). Record company, music publisher (Discmedia) and record producer (Moller Digital Studios). Estab. 1989.
How to Contact: Submit demo tape by mail. Unsolicited submissions are OK. Prefers cassette, CD or VHS with 3 songs, lyric sheet and cover letter. "Do not call after submitting." Does not return materials. Responds only if interested.

Music: Mostly **rock**, **pop** and **dance**; also **bilingual Spanish material** (dance, pop-merengue, rock ballads).

◖ DISCOS FUENTES/MIAMI RECORDS & EDIMUSICA USA, (formerly Miami Records), % Arc Music Group, 254 W. 54th St., 13th Floor, New York NY 10019. (212)246-3333. E-mail: info@arcmusic.com. Website: www.arcmusic.com. **Contact:** Juan Carlos Barguil. Vice President: Jorge Fuentes. President: Alejandro Fuentes. Labels include Discos Fuentes. Record company, music publisher (Edimusica-USA). Estab. 1936. Staff size: 14. Releases 13 singles and 89 CDs/year. Pays negotiable royalty to artists on contract; statutory rate to publisher per song on record.

- Edimusica-USA, Discos Fuentes/Miami Publishing Division entered into an administration deal effective August 18, 2000 with Arc Music Group.

Distributed by: Miami Records.

How to Contact: Submit demo CD/CDR by mail. Unsolicited submissions are OK. Prefers CD/CDR with lyric sheet. Does not return material. Responds only if interested.

Music: Mostly **salsa**, **cumbia** and **vallenato**; also **grupera**, **merengue** and **tropical**. Released *Que Lindo Cu* (album) by Rafael Benitez), recorded by Sonora Dinamita (cumbia); *Mi Libertad* (album by Saulo Sanchez), recorded by Fruko y Sostesos (salsa); and *El Majedro (El Viagra)* (album by Elkin Garcia), recorded by Embajadores Vallenatos (vallenato). Other artists include Sonora Carruseles, The Latin Brothers, Los Chiches Vallenatos, Latinos En La Casa, Chambacu, Pastor Lopez, Grupo Mayoral, Los Titanes and Frank La P & Anthony.

Tips: "Please keep sending us material. Don't give up if we do not use your first demo."

◖ DISC-TINCT MUSIC, INC., P.O. Box 5837, Englewood NJ 07631. (201)568-7066. President: Jeffrey Collins. Labels include Music Station, Echo USA, Dancefloor, Soul Creation and Soul Vibes. Record company, music publisher (Distinct Music, Inc./BMI, Distinct Echo Music/ASCAP) and record producer (Echo USA Productions). Estab. 1985. Releases 50 12″ singles, 10 LPs, 4 EPs and 15 CDs/year. Pays 5-8% royalty to artists on contract; ⅔ statutory rate to publisher per song on record.

How to Contact: Submit demo tape by mail. Unsolicited submissions are OK. Prefers CD, cassette, DVD or VHS videocassette with up to 5 songs. Include SASE. Responds in 1 month.

Music: Mostly **hip-hop**, **R&B**, **dance** and **house/techno**. Released *Your Attitude* (by Jimmie Fox), recorded by Kim Cummings on Music Station Records; and "As Quiet As It's Kept" (by Elis Pacheco), recorded by Colonel Abrams on Soul Creation Records. Other artists include Debbie Blackwell/Cook, Eleanor Grant, Black Rebels, Ready for the World, Llake, George Kerr and Quincy Patrick.

Tips: "Cue your cassettes, which should be labeled clearly."

◖ DREAMWORKS RECORDS, 9268 W. Third St., Beverly Hills CA 90210. (310)288-7700. Fax: (310)288-7750. Website: www.dreamworksrec.com. Nashville office: 1516 16th Ave. S., Nashville TN 37203. (615)463-4600. Fax: (615)463-4601. New York office: 575 Broadway, 6th Floor, New York NY 10012. (212)588-6600. Fax: (212)588-6611. Record company and music publisher (DreamWorks SKG Music Publishing).

How to Contact: Material must be submitted through an agent or attorney. *Does not accept unsolicited submissions.*

◖ DRIVE ENTERTAINMENT, 10451 Jefferson Blvd., Culver City CA 90232. (310)815-4900. Fax: (310)815-4908. E-mail: driveentertainment@earthlink.net. Website: www.driveentertainment.com. **Contact:** Stephen Powers, president and CEO. Labels include Drive Archive, Pagoda Re-

---

● **A BULLET** introduces comments by the editor of *Songwriter's Market* indicating special information about the listing.

cords, Golden Records. Record company and music publisher (Drive Music, Donunda Music). Estab. 1992. Releases 50 LPs and 50 CDs/year. Pays negotiable royalty to artists on contract; statutory rate to publisher per song on record.

Distributed by: Navarre, Fairyland Music, Licette Music, Dorton Music, Great American Gramophone Music, Blue Coast Music.

How to Contact: *Does not accept unsolicted submissions.*

Music: Mostly **pop**, **rock** and **Triple A**; also **dance**. Released *Swing Alive*, written and recorded by various artists (big band); *Singin' The Blues*, written and recorded by various artists (blues); *Talk Memphis to Me*, recorded by Cybill Sheperd; and *Drop Till You Dance*, written and recorded by various artists, all on Drive Entertainment.

◯ DROOL RECORDS, 8306 Wilshire Blvd., #645, Beverly Hills CA 90211. (310)652-1744. Fax: (310)652-1744. E-mail: droolrecords@earthlink.net. President: Kenny Kerner. CEO: Boi. Record company and record producer (Boi). Estab. 1998. Staff size: 4. Releases 3 LPs and 3 CDs/year. Pays negotiable royalty to artists on contract.

Distributed by: City Hall.

How to Contact: Submit demo tape by mail. Unsolicited submissions are OK. Prefers cassette or CD with cover letter. Does not return materials. Responds only if interested.

Music: Mostly **pop**, **glam**, **alternative** and **hip-hop**; also **electronica**. Does not want jazz, new age or classical. Released *Nipples* (album), recorded by Cartoon Boyfriend (pop), released 2000 on Drool Records; and "The End of the World" (single by Joey Rosa/Boi), recorded by Joey Rosa (alternative), released 2000 on Drool Records.

Tips: "Send in CD with cover letter and be patient."

◙ DRUMBEAT INDIAN ARTS, INC., 4143 N. 16th St., Suite 1, Phoenix AZ 85016. (602)266-4823. **Contact:** Bob Nuss, president. Labels include Indian House and Sweet Grass. Record company and distributor of American Indian recordings. Estab. 1984. Staff size: 8. Releases 50 cassettes and 50 CDs/year. Royalty varies with project.

 • Note that Drumbeat Indian Arts is a very specialized label, and only wants to receive submissions by Native American artists.

How to Contact: *Call first and obtain permission to submit.* Prefers cassette or VHS videocassette. Include SASE. Responds in 2 months.

Music: Music by American Indians—any style (must be enrolled tribal members). Does not want New Age "Indian style" material. Released *Pearl Moon* (album), written and recorded by Xavier (native Amerindian), released 2000 on Sweet Grass. Other artists include Black Lodge Singers, R. Carlos Nakai, Lite Foot, Kashtin and Joanne Shenandoah.

Tips: "We deal only with American Indian performers. We do not accept material from others. Please include tribal affiliation."

◯ EDMONDS RECORD GROUP, (formerly Yab Yum Records), 1635 N. Cahenga Blvd., 6th Floor, Los Angeles CA 90028. (323)860-1520. Fax: (323)860-1537. Record company.

Distributed by: Elektra Entertainment.

How to Contact: Submit demo tape by mail. Unsolicited submissions are OK. Any format accepted.

◙ ELEKTRA RECORDS, 345 N. Maple Dr., Suite 123, Beverly Hills CA 90210. (310)288-3800. Fax: (310)246-0347. Website: www.elektra.com. New York office: 75 Rockefeller Plaza, 17th Floor, New York NY 10019. (212)275-4000. Fax: (212)581-4650. Website: www.elektra.com. Labels include Elektra Records, Eastwest Records and Asylum Records. Record company.

Distributed by: WEA.

How to Contact: *Elektra does not accept unsolicited submissions.*

Music: Mostly **alternative/modern rock**. Released *Reload*, recorded by Metallica; *Ophelia*, recorded by Natalie Merchant; and *When Disaster Strikes*, recorded by Busta Rhymes, all on Elektra Entertainment. Other artists include Tracy Chapman, Bryan White, Phish, Björk, The Cure and Natalie Cole.

○ **EMERALD CITY RECORDS**, 2426 Auburn Ave., Dayton OH 45406-1928. Phone/fax: (937)275-4221. President: Jack Froschauer. Record company and publishing company (Barren Wood Publishing). Estab. 1992. Staff size: 1. Pays negotiable royalty to artists on contract; statutory rate to publisher per song on record.
Distributed by: Rotation Record Distributors, Dream Machine Entertainment and GEM.
How to Contact: Submit demo CD by mail. Unsolicited submissions are OK. Prefers CD with 1 song and lyric or lead sheet. "Studio quality please." Include SASE. Responds in 3 months.
Music: Mostly **A/C**, **country** and **contemporary Christian**. Released *Relish* (album by D. Walton), recorded by My 3 Sons (rock), released 2000 on Emerald City Records. Other artists include Cadillac Jack, Mark Vanluvender and Dale Walton.

☑ ○ **EMF PRODUCTIONS**, 1000 E. Prien Lake Rd., Suite D, Lake Charles LA 70601. Phone/fax: (337)474-0435. E-mail: emfprod@aol.com. Website: www.emfproductions.com. **Contact:** Ed Fruge, owner. Record company, music publisher and record producer. Estab. 1977. Releases 3 singles, 3 LPs and 3 CDs/year. Pays 10-14% royalty to artists on contract; statutory rate to publisher per song on record.
● See their listing in the Music Publishers section.
How to Contact: Submit demo tape by mail. Unsolicited submissions are OK. Prefers cassette and lyric sheet. Does not return material. Responds in 6 weeks.
Music: Mostly **pop**, **R&B** and **country**. Released *Trilogy* (album), recorded by ETA (contemporary jazz/New Age/pop), released 2000 on EMF Productions.

○ **EMF RECORDS & AFFILIATES**, 633 Post, Suite #145, San Francisco CA 94109. (415)273-1421. Fax: (415)752-2442. **Contact:** Steven Lassiter, director of operations. Vice President, A&R (all styles): Michael Miller. A&R Supervisor (commercial): Ed Jones. International Producer (world artists): Kimberly Nakamori. Producer/Writer (all or most styles): Joe Tsongo. Labels include Richland Communications, Sky Bent and Urbana Sounds. Record company. Estab. 1994. Staff size: 11. Releases 5 LPs and 5 CDs/year. Pays negotiable royalty to artists on contract; statutory rate to publisher per song on record.
Distributed by: GTI Marketing and Songo Publishing International.
How to Contact: Submit demo tape by mail. Unsolicited submissions are OK. Prefers cassette, CD or DAT with 3 songs and lyric and lead sheets. Does not return material. Responds in 4 months.
Music: Mostly **urban/pop/rock**, **jazz/Latin** and **New Age/classical (crossover)**; also **country**, **world beat** and **ethnic (world)**. Released *Mutual Impact*, written and recorded by Joe Tsongo on EMF Records (New Age); *If I Had Your Love*, written and recorded by Flamé on Richland Communications (soft jazz); and *From The Source* (by B. Flores/A. Jiminez), recorded by Orchestra de Sabor on Urbana Sounds (salsa/Latin jazz). Other artists include Slam Jam.
Tips: "Build your fan base and present good images or professional packages as much as possible."

○ **ENTERPRIZE RECORDS-TAPES**, 1507 Scenic Dr., Longview TX 75604-2319. (903)759-0300. Fax: (903)234-2944. **Contact:** Johnny Patterson, studio manager/A&R (country, gospel). Owner: Jerry Haymes (all styles). Record company and music publisher (Enterprize Entertainment). Estab. 1960. Staff size: 3. Pays negotiable royalty to artists on contract.
Distributed by: Warner Bros Europe.
How to Contact: *Write or call first and obtain permission to submit.* Prefers cassette, CD or videocassette with lyric and lead sheet, cover letter and press clippings. Does not return material. Responds in 1 month.
Music: Mostly **pop (AC)**, **country** and **gospel**; also **rock**. Does not want rap.

Ⓝ ○ **ENTOURAGE MUSIC GROUP**, 11115 Magnolia Blvd., N. Hollywood CA 91601. (818)505-0001. Fax: (818)761-7956. E-mail: emg@primenet.com. Website: www.entouragerecords.com/label. **Contact:** Guy Paonessa, president. Record company and recording studio. Estab. 1986 (studio); 1995 (label). Releases 4 CDs/year. Pays negotiable royalty to artists on contract; statutory rate to publisher per song on record.
Distributed by: Touchwood Distribution.

How to Contact: Submit demo tape by mail. Unsolicited submissions are OK. Prefers cassette, CD, DAT or ½″ videocassette with 3-10 songs. "No phone calls please." Include SASE. Responds in 3 months.

Music: Mostly **rock**, **alternative** and **contemporary jazz**; also **alternative country**. Released *The Mustard Seeds*, written and recorded by The Mustard Seeds (alternative rock); *MacAnanys*, written and recorded by MacAnanys (alternative country); and *P.O.L. Sprockett*, recorded by P.O.L. (rock), all on Entourage Records.

☑ ◎ **EPIC RECORDS**, 550 Madison Ave., 22nd Floor, New York NY 10022. (212)833-8000. Fax: (212)833-4054. Website: www.epicrecords.com. Senior Vice President A&R: Michael Caplan; Senior Vice President A&R: Ben Goldman; Senior Vice President A&R: Peter Ganbard; Vice President A&R: Rose Noone. Santa Monica office: 2100 Colorado Ave., Santa Monica CA 90404. (310)449-2100. Fax: (310)449-2848. E-mail: sonymusiconline@sonymusic.com. Website: www.epic records.com. Senior Vice President A&R: Kaz Utsunomiya; Vice President of A&R: Matthew Marshall. Nashville office: 34 Music Square E., Nashville TN 37203. (615)742-4321. Fax: (615)244-2549. Labels include Epic Soundtrax, LV Records, Immortal Records and Word Records. Record company.

● Epic's *Iron Man*, released by Sabbath won a 1999 Grammy for Best Metal Performance.

Distributed by: Sony Music Distribution.

How to Contact: *Write or call first and obtain permission to submit* (New York office only). Does not return material. Responds only if interested. *Santa Monica and Nashville offices do not accept unsolicited submissions.*

Music: Released *All the Way . . . A Decade of Song* (album), recorded by Celine Dion on 550 Music; *On How Life Is* (album), recorded by Macy Gray on Epic; and *Issues* (album), recorded by Korn on Epic. Other artists include Ghostface Killah, Cappadonna, 7 Mile, Amel Larrieux, TQ and Cha Cha.

Tips: "Do an internship if you don't have experience or work as someone's assistant. Learn the business and work hard while you figure out what your talents are and where you fit in. Once you figure out which area of the record company you're suited for, focus on that, work hard at it and it shall be yours."

◎ **EVIL TEEN RECORDS**, P.O. Box 651, Village Station, New York NY 10014. (212)337-0760. Fax: (212)337-0708. E-mail: info@evilteen.com. Website: www.evilteen.com. **Contact:** Stefani Scamardo, president. Record company. Estab. 1996. Releases 2 singles, 1 LP and 4-6 CDs/year. Pays negotiable royalty to artists on contract; statutory rate to publisher per song on record.

Distributed by: Select-O-Hits.

How to Contact: Submit demo tape by mail. Unsolicited submissions are OK. Prefers cassette, CD, DAT or VHS videocassette. "Send latest musical product with press kit and tour schedule." Include SASE. Responds in 1 month.

Music: Mostly **rock/alternative**, **drum & bass** and **Americana**. Released *For Nearby Stars* (album), recorded by VPN (rock); *Broken Hearts and Auto Parts* (album), recorded by Kevn Kinney (Americana) featuring members of Drivin' 'n' Cryin'; and *Flower and the Knife* (album), recorded by Kevn Kinney (Americana), all released 2002 on Evil Teen Records. Other artists include VPN, Shaft, Benna, Pen Pal and Random.

◎ **FACTORY BEAT RECORDS, INC.**, 521 Fifth Ave., 17th Floor, New York NY 10175. (212)292-4266. Fax: (201)567-3173. E-mail: renalfeeney@webtv.net. Website: www.luma.com./ luma/bands/lucia.rena. Producers: Rena L. Feeney (world, contemporary) and Billy Nichols (soul, r&b). Labels include R&R Records, Inc., Ren Maur Music and Ren Rom Records, Inc. Record company, music publisher and record producer. Estab. 1979. Staff size: 30. Releases 4 singles, 2 LPs, 4 EPs and 2 CDs/year. Pays negotiable royalty to artists on contract.

Distributed by: R&R Records, Inc. and Ren Maur Music.

How to Contact: Submit demo tape by mail. Unsolicited submissions are OK. Prefers cassette with 4 songs. Returns materials if accompanied by SASE. Responds only if interested.

Music: Mostly **r&b**, **contemporary** and **world**; also **soul** and **rap**. Does not want country, rock, heavy metal or rockabilly. Released "Rise Up" (single by Wm. Lee Nichols/Rena L. Feeney), "Once You Fall in Love," "Be Naughty Girl," and "That's Hot" (singles by Wm. Lee Nichols) all from *Rise Up* (album), recorded by Lucia Rena, released 1998 on Factory Beat Records, Inc.

FIREANT, 2009 Ashland Ave., Charlotte NC 28205. Phone/fax: (704)335-1400. E-mail: lewh@fireantmusic.com. Website: www.fireantmusic.com. **Contact:** Lew Herman, owner. Record company, music publisher (Fireant Music) and record producer (Lew Herman). Estab. 1990. Releases several CDs/year. Pays negotiable royalty to artists on contract; statutory royalty to publisher per song on record.
Distributed by: CityHall, North Country and Redeye.
How to Contact: Submit demo tape by mail. Unsolicited submissions are OK. Prefers cassette, DAT or videocassette. Does not return material.
Music: Mostly **progressive**, **traditional** and **musical hybrids**. "Anything except New Age and MOR." Released *Loving the Alien: Athens Georgia Salutes David Bowie* (album), recorded by various artists (rock/alternative/electronic), released 2000 on Fireant; and *Good Enough* (album), recorded by Zen Frisbee. Other artists include Mr. Peters' Belizean Boom and Chime Band.

FIRST TIME RECORDS, Sovereign House, 12 Trewartha Rd., Praa Sands, Penzance, Cornwall TR20 9ST England. Phone: (01736)762826. Fax: (01736)763328. E-mail: panamus@aol.com. Website: www.songwriters-guild.co.uk. **Contact:** Roderick G. Jones, managing director A&R. Labels include Pure Gold Records, Rainy Day Records and Mohock Records, Heraldic Vintage Records, Heraldic Jester Records, Heraldic Creative Disc. Registered members of Phonographic Performance Ltd. (PPL). Record company, music publisher (First Time Music Publishing U.K./MCPS/PRS), management firm and record producer (First Time Management & Production Co.). Estab. 1986. Staff size: 6. Pays variable royalty to artists on contract; statutory rate to publisher per song on record subject to deal.
Distributed by: Media U.K. Distributors.
How to Contact: Submit demo tape by mail. Unsolicited submissions are OK. Prefers cassette or CD with unlimited number of songs and lyric or lead sheets, but not necessary. SAE and IRC. Responds in 3 months.
Music: Released "Lament of the Winged Warrior" (single by Graham D'Ancey) from *Angel of Ages* (album), recorded by Lorne (pop), released 2001 on Heraldic Creative Disc/First Time; "Resurrection Shuffle" (single by Ashton) from *Hoochi Coocha* (album), recorded by Arthur the Moocher (jazz), released 2001 on Heraldic Jester/First Time; and "When Will I Be Loved" (single by Phil Everly) from *Johnny Remember Me* (album), recorded by The Cadillacs (pop), released 2001 on Heraldic Vintage/First Time.

FISH OF DEATH RECORDS AND MANAGEMENT, P.O. Box 245, Westwood MA 02090. (781)326-0143. E-mail: fod@earthlink.net. Website: www.fishofdeath.com. President: Michael D. Andelman. Record company, music publisher and management firm. Estab. 1994. Releases 2-4 singles, 1-2 EPs and 2-4 CDs/year. Pays 18% royalty to artists on contract; statutory rate to publisher per song on record.
Distributed by: MS Distributing, Carrot Top, Nail, Dutch East India and Surefire.
● This label is noted for releasing fun, happy music.
How to Contact: Submit demo tape by mail. Unsolicited submissions are OK. Prefers cassette or CD with 3 songs. "Absolutely no computer or e-mail audio file submissions will be tolerated." Does not return material. Responds in 3 weeks.
Music: Mostly **alternative**, **rock** and **hip-hop**; also **top 40**, **modern rock** and **AAA**. Released *American Made* (album), written and recorded by Hal Lovejoy Circus (alternative/rock); "Kitty Kat Max"

REFER TO THE GEOGRAPHIC INDEX (at the back of this book) to find listings of companies by state, as well as foreign listings.

(single by Kevin Krakower), recorded by 1000 Clowns (rap/pop); and *430 N. Harper Ave* (album by Jude Cristodal), recorded by Jude (folk), all on Fish of Death Records. Other artists include All Miserable Times, The Ghost of Tony Gold, Tiny Buddy and Brown Betty.

Tips: "Be persistent, professional, focused, and not too annoying."

[N] [globe] [O] FLAT RECORDS, P.O. Box 91, Reigate, RH2 0FG England. Phone/fax: (+44)(0)1737-210848. E-mail: panther@dial.pipex.com. Website: www.netlink.co.uk/users/sonic/flat.htm. Producer: Johnny Elmer (industrial, gothic). A&R Managers: Richard Eddington (industrial, rock) and Richard Coppen. Labels include Flat Records, Varia Records, S.E.M.A and Interactive. Record company, music publisher (Flat Music), record producer (Dr. Crippen) and organization. Estab. 1986. Staff size: 10. Releases 1 single, 2 LPs, 1 EP and 2 CDs/year. Pays negotiable royalty to artists under contract; statutory rate to publisher per song on record.

Distributed by: Else, Pinnacle, Polygram and Self.

How to Contact: *Write first and obtain permission to submit.* Unsolicited submissions are OK. Prefers cassette or CD with 2 songs, cover letter and press clippings. Artists should also include photos. Returns materials if accompanied by SASE. Responds in 6 weeks.

Music: Mostly **rock**, **pop** and **dance**; also **industrial**, **electronic** and **techno**. Does not want middle of the road, mainstream or boring music. Released *Divine Inspiration*, written and recorded by various artists (pop/rock) on SEMA; "Just for Kicks" (by Darren Robinson), recorded by Explain (pop/rock) on Interactive; and *Hypnotiki* (by Steel/Andrews), recorded by S.U.N. (techno) on Varia. Other artists include Surfin' Dead, The Borg, J-Faktor, Splodgenessabounds and The Sisters of Merciful Release.

Tips: "Be original, adventurous, hard working and exceptional. Be the best!"

[O] FLOOD RECORDING CORP., 3210 21st St., San Francisco CA 94110. (415)282-4466. Fax: (415)282-4474. E-mail: info@solomusicgroup.com. **Contact:** Jay Siegan, vice president of A&R. Head of A&R: Jeffrey Wood. Record company. Estab. 1995. Releases 2-5 LPs and 2-5 CDs/year. Pays negotiable royalty to artists on contract; statutory rate to publisher per song on record.

Distributed by: ADA and BMG.

How to Contact: Submit demo tape by mail. Unsolicited submissions are OK. Prefers cassette or CD with 2-3 songs and lyric sheet. Does not return material. Responds only if interested.

Music: Mostly **pop**; also **alternative**. Released *Fly* (album), recorded by Hopscotch (pop), released 2001 on Flood Media.

[✓] [O] FLYING HEART RECORDS, Dept. SM, 4026 NE 12th Ave., Portland OR 97212. (503)287-8045. E-mail: flyheart@teleport.com. Website: www.home.teleport.com/~flyheart. **Contact:** Jan Celt, owner. Record company and record producer (Jan Celt). Estab. 1982. Releases 2 CDs/year. Pays variable royalty to artists on contract; negotiable rate to publisher per song on record.

Distributed by: Burnside Distribution Co.

How to Contact: Submit demo tape by mail. Unsolicited submissions are OK. Prefers cassette with 1-10 songs and lyric sheets. Does not return material. "SASE required for *any* response." Responds in 3 months.

Music: Mostly **R&B**, **blues** and **jazz**; also **rock**. Released *Vexatious Progr.* (album), written and recorded by Eddie Harris (jazz); *Juke Music* (album), written and recorded by Thara Memory (jazz); and *Lookie Tookie* (album), written and recorded by Jan Celt (blues), all on Flying Heart Records. Other artists include Janice Scroggins, Tom McFarland, Obo Addy, Snow Bud and The Flower People.

[✓] [O] FRESH ENTERTAINMENT, 1315 Simpson Rd. NW, Suite 5, Atlanta GA 30314. Phone/fax: (770)642-2645. E-mail: whunter1122@yahoo.com. **Contact:** Willie Hunter, managing director. Record company and music publisher (Hserf Music/ASCAP, Blair Vizzion Music/BMI). Releases 5 singles and 2 LPs/year. Pays 7-10% royalty to artists on contract; statutory rate to publisher per song on record.

Distributed by: Ichiban International and Intersound Records.

How to Contact: Submit demo tape by mail. Unsolicited submissions are OK. Prefers cassette or VHS videocassette with at least 3 songs and lyric sheet. Include SASE. Responds in 2 months.

Music: Mostly **R&B**, **rock** and **pop**; also **jazz**, **gospel** and **rap**. Released "We Hate Pastor Troy" (single by W. Jackson/Javou/Chosen One) from *Ready For War*, recorded by Swat Team (rap/hip-hop), released 2000 on Armageddon/Milltyme; "Erase The Color Line" (single by M. Warner/J. Smith/J. Lewis) from *EMG-Non Pilation*, recorded by Michael Warner/JS-1/Noray (R&B/hip-hop), released 2000 on EMQ Entertainment; "Live Your Fantasy" (single by B. Miles/E. Davis) from *Nubian Woman* (album), recorded by Bob Miles (jazz), released 2000 on Sheets of Sounds; and "You Betta Duck" (single by Big James/Noble/Nations) from *Bankhead Boyz* (album), recorded by Bankhead Boyz (hip-hop/rap), released 2001 on The Big Boy Records. Other artists include Cirocco and Invisible Men.

☐ FRONT ROW RECORDS, Ridgewood Park Estates, 222 Tulane St., Garland TX 75043. Website: www.athenet.net/~genevinc/GeneSummers.html. **Contact:** Gene or Dea Summers. Public Relations/Artist and Fan Club Coordinator: Steve Summers. A&R: Shawn Summers. Labels include Juan Records. Record company and music publisher (Silicon Music/BMI). Estab. 1968. Releases 5-6 singles and 2-3 LPs/year. Pays negotiable royalty to artists on contract; standard royalty to songwriters on contract.
Distributed by: Crystal Clear Records.
How to Contact: Submit demo tape by mail. Unsolicited submissions are OK. Prefers cassette or VHS videocassette with 1-3 songs. *"We request a photo and bio with material submission."* Does not return material. Responds ASAP.
Music: Mostly **'50s rock/rockabilly**; also **country**, **bluegrass**, **old-time blues** and **R&B**. Released "Domino" (single), recorded by Gene Summers on Pollytone Records (rockabilly); "Goodbye Priscilla" and "Cool Baby" (singles), both recorded by Gene Summers on Collectables Records.
Tips: "If you own masters of 1950s rock and rockabilly, contact us first! We will work with you on a percentage basis for overseas release. We have active releases in Holland, Switzerland, Belgium, Australia, England, France, Sweden, Norway and the US at the present. We need original masters. You must be able to prove ownership of tapes before we can accept a deal. We're looking for little-known, obscure recordings. We have the market if you have the tapes! We are also interested in country and rockabilly *artists* who have not recorded for awhile but still have the voice and appeal to sell overseas."

N ☐ GALLERY II RECORDS/JUMPIN' JACK RECORDS, 2301 W. 59th St., Los Angeles CA 90043-3233. (323)294-7286. Fax: (323)291-7709. E-mail: jwaller970@aol.com. Website: www.jumpinjackrecords.com. **Contact:** Johno Othello Waller, CEO. Promotion: Byron Rodgers (r&b, hip-hop, salsa, gas, blues, jazz). A&R: Greg McDonald (gospel). Record company, music publisher and record producer. Estab. 1980. Staff size: 3. Pays negotiable royalty to artists on contract; statutory rate to publisher per song on record.
Distributed by: Jumpin' Jack Entertainment Network.
How to Contact: Submit demo tape by mail. Unsolicited submissions are OK. Prefers cassette, CD, DAT or videocassette with lyric sheet and cover letter. Does not return materials. Responds in 3 months.
Music: Mostly **r&b**, **rap**, **gospel** and **salsa**; also **reggae**, **blues** and **jazz**. Released "Better Day" (r&b) and "Jesus Is My Transportation" (gospel) (by Avis D. Winster), recorded by Cheryl Patterson on Gallery II; "Nobody Ride For Free" (by Avis D. Winster), recorded by Jumpin' Jack Committee of Three (rap) on Jumpin' Jack Records; and "American Red, White & Blue" (single), recorded by Vivian Clairborne.

⊘ GEFFEN/DGC RECORDS.
● As a result of the PolyGram and Universal merger, Geffen has been folded into Interscope Records. See the Interscope/Geffen/A&M Records listing in this section for further information.

N ☐ GENERIC RECORDS, INC., 433 Limestone Rd., Ridgefield CT 06877. (203)438-9811. Fax: (203)431-3204. E-mail: hifiadd@aol.com. President (pop, alternative, rock): Gary Lefkowith. A&R (pop, dance, adult contemporary): Bill Jerome. Labels include Outback, GLYN. Record company, music publisher (Sotto Music/BMI) and record producer. Estab. 1976. Staff size: 2. Releases 6 singles and 2 CDs/year. Pays 15% royalty to artists on contract; statutory rate to publisher per song on record.

Distributed by: Dutch East India.

How to Contact: Submit demo tape by mail. Unsolicited submissions are OK. Prefers cassette with 2-3 songs. Include SASE. Responds in 2 weeks.

Music: Mostly **alternative rock**, **rock** and **pop**; also **country** and **rap**. Released "Young Girls" (by Eric Della Penna/Dean Sharenow), recorded by Henry Sugar (alternative/pop); "Rock It," written and recorded by David Ruskay (rock/pop); and *Tyrus*, written and recorded by Tyris (alternative), all on Generic Records, Inc. Other artists include Hifi, Honest, Loose Change and John Fantasia.

Tips: "Love what you're doing. The music comes first."

GIG RECORDS, 520 Butler Ave., Point Pleasant NJ 08742. (732)701-9044. Fax: (732)701-9777. E-mail: Indian@gigrecords.com. Website: www.gigrecords.com. **Contact:** Indian, president. Labels include AMPED. Record company and music publisher (Gig Music). Estab. 1998. Staff size: 8. Releases 2 singles, 2 EPs and 15 CDs/year. Pays negotiable royalty to artists on contract; statutory rate to publisher per song on record.

Distributed by: Amazon, E-Music, CD Now, Nail and Sumthing.

How to Contact: Submit demo tape by mail. Unsolicited submissions are OK. Prefers cassette, CD or VHS videocassette with lyric sheet and cover letter. Does not return materials. Responds ASAP if interested.

Music: Mostly **rock** and **electronic**; also **drum & bass**, **trip-hop** and **hip-hop**. Does not want country. Released *Sweet Conscience* (album by Virginia Traut), recorded by Virginia (pop); *5 Songs* (album), written and recorded by Miles Hunt (pop rock); and *Grace's Period* (album), written and recorded by Michael Ferentino (pop rock), all released 2000 on Gig Releases. Other artists include Ned's Atomic Dustbin, Virginia, The Vibrators, Groundswell UK, Nebula Nine, The Youth Ahead, Dryer and Red Engine Nine.

Tips: "No egos."

GOLD CITY RECORDS, INC., 10 Deepwell Farms Rd., S. Salem NY 10590. (914)533-5096. Fax: (914)533-5097. E-mail: gcrecords@aol.com. Website: www.goldencitymusic.com. President: Chris Jasper. Vice President/General Counsel: Margie Jasper. Labels include Gold City Label. Record company. Estab. 1987. Staff size: 5. Releases 5-10 singles and 3-5 CDs/year. Pays negotiable royalty to artists on contract; statutory rate to publisher per song on record.

How to Contact: Submit demo tape by mail. Unsolicited submissions are OK. Prefers cassette, DAT or CD with 3 songs and lyric sheets. Include SASE. Responds in 6 weeks.

Music: Mostly **R&B**, **contemporary gospel** and **pop**; also **rap**. Released "And I Love Her" (single by P. McCartney/J. Lennon), recorded by Brothaz By Choice (R&B); *Faithful and True* (album), recorded by Chris Jasper (contemporary gospel), released 2001, both on Gold City Records.

GOLDEN TRIANGLE RECORDS, 5501 Camelia St., Pittsburgh PA 15201. E-mail: marcels @salsgiver.com. Website: www.salsgiver.com/people/marcels/main.html. **Contact:** Sunny James Cvetnic, producer. Labels include Rockin Robin and Shell-B. Record company, music publisher (Golden Triangle/BMI) and record producer (Sunny James Cuetnic). Estab. 1987. Staff size: 2. Releases 1 CD/year. Pays standard royalty to artists on contract; statutory rate to publishers per song on record.

How to Contact: Submit demo tape by mail. Unsolicited submissions are OK. Prefers cassette or ½″ VHS videocassette with 3 songs and lyric or lead sheets. Does not return material. Responds in 1 week.

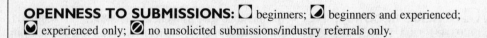

OPENNESS TO SUBMISSIONS: ○ beginners; ◑ beginners and experienced; ● experienced only; ◒ no unsolicited submissions/industry referrals only.

Music: Mostly **progressive R&B**, **rock** and **A/C**; also **jazz** and **country**. Released "My True Story" (single) from *Moon to Millennium* (album), written and recorded by The Marcels on Golden Triangle. Other artists include the T. Jack (blues), Weetman (r&b) and Sunny James (pop/rock).
Tips: "Have patience."

◻ GOLDWAX RECORD CORPORATION, P.O. Box 54700, Atlanta GA 30308-0700. (770)454-1011. Fax: (770)454-8088. E-mail: goldwaxrec@aol.com. Website: www.goldwax.com. **Contact:** Jimmy McClendon, A&R. Labels include Abec, Bandstand USA and Beale Street USA. Record company and music publisher (Stellar Music Industries). Estab. 1963. Staff size: 4. Releases 15 singles, 12 LPs, 4 EPs and 2 CDs/year. Pays negotiable royalty to artists on contract; statutory rate to publisher per song on record.
Distributed by: City Hall Records, Goldwax Distributing.
How to Contact: *Write or call first and obtain permission to submit.* Prefers cassette, CD, DAT or VHS videocassette with 4 songs and lyric sheet. Include SASE. Responds in 6 weeks.
Music: Mostly **R&B/hip-hop**, **pop/rock** and **jazz**; also **blues**, **contemporary country** and **contemporary gospel**. Released *Clifford & Co.* (album) (soul) on Beale Street Records and *Double Deuce* (album) (rap) on Urban Assault Records. Other artists include Double Deuce, Elvin Spenser and Margie Alexander.
Tips: "Songwriters need to provide great melodies; artists need to have commercial appeal."

▣ ◻ GONZO! RECORDS INC., P.O. Box 3688, San Dimas CA 91773. Phone/fax: (909)598-9031. E-mail: gonzorcrds@aol.com. Website: members.aol.com/gonzorcrds. **Contact:** Jeffrey Gonzalez, president. Record company. Estab. 1993. Staff size: 3. Releases 3 singles and 1-6 CDs/year. Pays negotiable royalty to artists on contract; statutory rate to publisher per song on record.
   • Gonzo! Records was awarded Best Indie Label, and Full Frequency was awarded Best Techno/Industrial Band at the 1999 Los Angeles Music Awards.
How to Contact: Submit demo tape by mail. Unsolicited submissions are OK. Prefers cassette or CD. "When submitting, please specify that you got the listing from *Songwriter's Market*." Does not return material. Responds in 6 weeks.
Music: Mostly **commercial industrial**, **dance** and **techno**; also **commercial alternative** and **synth pop**. Released *Hate Breeds Hate* (album), written and recorded by BOL (hard industrial); *Momentum* (album), written and recorded by Full Frequency (commerical industrial); and *Ruth in Alien Corn* (album), written and recorded by Pinch Point (alternative pop), all on Gonzo! Records. Other artists include Turning Keys.
Tips: "If you're going to submit music to me, it must be because you love to write music, not because you want to be a rockstar. That will eventually happen with a lot of hard work."

◻ GRASS ROOTS RECORD & TAPE/LMI RECORDS, P.O. Box 532, Malibu CA 90265. (213)463-5998. **Contact:** Lee Magid, president. Record company, record producer (Lee Magid), music publisher (Alexis/ASCAP, Marvelle/BMI, Lou-Lee/BMI) and management firm (Lee Magid Management Co.). Member AIMP, NARAS. Estab. 1967. Releases 4 LPs and 4 CDs/year. Pays 50% royalty per record sold to artists on contract; statutory rate to publishers per song on record.
   • Grass Roots Record's publishing company, Alexis, is listed in the Music Publishers section, and President Lee Magid is listed in the Record Producers section.
How to Contact: Submit demo tape by mail. Unsolicited submissions are OK. Prefers cassette with 3 songs and lyric sheet. "Please, no 45s." Does not return material. Responds in 2 months.
Music: Mostly **pop/rock**, **R&B**, **country**, **gospel**, **jazz/rock** and **blues**; also **bluegrass**, **children's** and **Latin**. Released "Mighty Hand" (single by C. Rhone), recorded by Cajun Hart on LMI Records (R&B); *Don't You Know* (album by B. Worth), recorded by Della Reese on RCA Records (pop); and *Blues For The Weepers* (album by L. Magid/M. Rich), recorded by Lou Rawls on Capitol Records (R&B). Other artists include John Michael Hides, Julie Miller, Tramaine Hawkins and ZAD.

◎ GREEN BEAR RECORDS, Rockin' Chair Center Suite 103, 1033 W. Main St., Branson MO 65616. Phone/fax: (417)334-2306. **Contact:** George J. Skupien, president. Labels include Green One

Records and Green Bear Records. Record company, music publisher (Green One Music/BMI) and record producer (George Skupien). Estab. 1992. Releases 3-4 singles, 1-10 LPs and 2-6 CDs/year. Pays negotiable royalty to artists on contract; statutory rate to publisher per song on record.

How to Contact: *Write or fax first and obtain permission to submit.* Does not accept unsolicited submissions. "Please send request to submit to address above by mail or fax. If you are approved to send material, songs must be professionally performed and produced. We no longer accept homemade demos. For your protection, all tapes, lyrics and other material that is received and/or rejected will be shredded and destroyed. We do not return material!" Responds on accepted material.

Music: Mostly **country** and **light rock**; also **American polkas**, **southern gospel**, **waltzes**, **comedy** and **fun songs**. Released "Our Last Cowboy Song" (single by Matt Row'd/G. Skupien) from *Memories* (album), recorded by Matt Row'd; and "Love Is Why I Feel This Way" (single by G. Skupien/ Sara Wright) from *Country Compilation 102* (album), recorded by Buddy Thomas, both released 2000 on Green Bear Records. Other artists include D. Mack, B. Jackson, Ted Thomas, Rudy Negron and The Mystics.

☑ ◉ **GRIFFIN MUSIC (a Division of Lakeshore Inc.)**, P.O. Box 1952, Lombard IL 60148. (630)424-0801. Fax: (630)424-0806. E-mail: grifmus@aol.com. Website: griffinmusic.com. **Contact:** Ginger Lord, A&R. Labels include Tango Music, Cyclops and Lakeshore. Record company. Estab. 1992. Staff size: 8. Releases 2 singles, 4 LPs and 24 CDs/year. Pays negotiable royalty to artists on contract; pay to publisher per song on record "depends on artist."

Distributed by: Alliance, Baker & Taylor, Action, Norwalk, H.L. Distribution, MDI, MAD, Digital Waves and Cargo.

How to Contact: Submit demo CD by mail. Unsolicited submissions are OK. Prefers CD with cover letter and press clippings. Does not return material. Responds in 6 weeks.

Music: Mostly **classic rock**, **pop** and **various artists compilations**. Released *In Your Area* (album), recorded by Hawkwind; *All The Hits Plus More* (album), recorded by Herman's Hermits, both released 2001 on Griffin; and *For All We Shared* (album), recorded by Mostly Autumn (pop rock), released 2001 on Cyclops.

Tips: "Have some sort of track history. We are a reissue label and deal mostly with established artists."

☑ ⊘ **GROOVE MAKERS' RECORDINGS**, P.O. Box 271170, Houston TX 77227-1170. Phone/ fax: (281)403-6279. E-mail: imistamadd@aol.com. Website: www.paidnphull.com. **Contact:** Ben Thompson (R&B, rap), CEO. Labels include Paid In Full Entertainment. Record company, music publisher and record producer (Crazy C). Estab. 1994. Staff size: 4. Releases 3 singles, 2 LPs and 2 CDs/year. Pays negotiable royalty to artists on contract; statutory rate to publisher per song on record.

Distributed by: S.O.H. and Southwest Wholesale.

How to Contact: *Write first and obtain permission to submit.* Prefers cassette or CD. Does not return material.

Music: Mostly **rap** and **R&B**. Released "We Thoed" (single by various artists) from *Can I Live* (album), recorded by Mista Madd (rap), released 2000 on Paid In Full Entertainment; and *Soulology: The Genesis* (album), recorded by Sounds of Urban Life (R&B), released 2000 on Soul Muzick Recordings. Other artists include S.O.U.L. and Heather Barrett.

☑ ◯ **GUESTSTAR RECORDS, INC.**, 17321 Ritchie Ave. NE, Sand Lake MI 49343-9475. (616)636-5068. Fax: (775)743-4169. E-mail: gueststarww@wingsisp.com. Website: www.wingsisp. com/mountainmanww/. **Contact:** Marilyn Dietz, office manager. Record company, management firm (Gueststar Entertainment Agency), record producer and music publisher (Sandlake Music/BMI). Estab. 1967. Staff size: 3. Releases 8 singles, 2 LPs and 2 CDs/year. Pays variable royalty to artist on contract, "depending on number of selections on product; 3½¢/per record sold; statutory rate to publisher per song on record."

Distributed by: Guestar Worldwide Music Distributors.

How to Contact: Submit demo tape by mail. Unsolicited submissions are OK. Prefers cassette or VHS videocassette with lyric and lead sheet. "Send a SASE with submissions." Does not return material. Responds in 6 weeks.

Music: Mostly **traditional country**. Released "I'm in Love with a Stranger" (single by Raymond Dietz); and "When Jesus Comes" (single by Raymond Dietz), both from *Best of Mountain Man* (album), recorded by Mountain Man (country), released 2001 on GuestStar. Other artists include Jamie "K" and Sweetgrass Band.

Tips: "Songwriters: send songs like you hear on the radio. Keep updating your music to keep up with the latest trends. Artists: send VHS video and press kit."

○ **HACIENDA RECORDS & RECORDING STUDIO**, 1236 S. Staples St., Corpus Christi TX 78404. (361)882-7066. Fax: (361)882-3943. E-mail: info@haciendarecords.com. Website: www.haciendarecords.com. **Contact:** Rick Garcia, executive vice president. Producers: Carlos Acevedo. Record company, music publisher, record producer. Estab. 1979. Staff size: 10. Releases 12 singles and 15 CDs/year. Pays negotiable royalty to artists on contract; negotiable rate to publisher per song on record.

How to Contact: Submit demo tape by mail. Unsolicited submissions are OK. Prefers cassette with cover letter. Does not return material. Responds in 6 weeks.

Music: Mostly **latin pop/rock**, **tejano** and **salsa**. Released "Chica Bonita" (single), recorded by Albert Zamora and D.J. Cubanito, released 2001 on Hacienda Records; "Si Quieres Verme Llorar" (single) from *Lisa Lopez con Mariachi* (album), recorded by Lisa Lopez (mariachi), released 2002 on Hacienda; "Tartamudo" (single) from *Una Vez Mas* (album), recorded by Peligro (norteno); and "Miento" (single) from *Si Tu Te Vas* (album), recorded by Traizion (tejano), both released 2001 on Hacienda. Other artists include Victoria Y Sus Chikos, Peligro and La Traizion.

Tips: "Submit your best."

☑ ○ **HAPPY MAN RECORDS**, 4696 Kahlua Lane, Bonita Springs FL 34134. (941)947-6978. E-mail: obitts@bellsouth.net. **Contact:** Dick O'Bitts, executive producer. Labels include Condor and Con Air. Record company, music publisher (Rocker Music/BMI, Happy Man Music/ASCAP) and record producer (Rainbow Collection Ltd.). Estab. 1972. Releases 4-6 singles, 4-6 12″ singles, 4-6 LPs and 4 EPs/year. Pays negotiable royalty to artists on contract; statutory rate to publisher per song on record.

Distributed by: V&R.

• Happy Man's publishing company, Rocker Music/Happy Man Music, can be found in the Music Publishers section.

How to Contact: Submit demo tape by mail. Unsolicited submissions are OK. Prefers cassette, CD or VHS videocassette with 3-4 songs and lyric sheet. Include SASE. Responds in 1 month.

Music: **All types**. Released *Got the T-Shirt* (album by Jake Thorp), recorded by The Thorp's; and *In the Distance* (album), written and recorded by 4 Harmonee, both released 2001 on Happy Man Records. Other artists include Ray Pack, Crosswinds, Overdue, The Thorps, Okeefenokee Joe, Colt Gipson, Ron Jeffers and Jim Duff.

● **HEADS UP INT., LTD.**, 23309 Commerce Park Dr., Cleveland OH 44122. (216)765-7381. Fax: (216)464-6037. E-mail: dave@headsup.com. Website: www.headsup.com. **Contact:** Dave Love, president. Record company, music publisher (Heads Up Int., Buntz Music, Musica de Amor) and record producer (Dave Love). Estab. 1980. Staff size: 57. Releases 10 LPs/year. Pays negotiable royalty to artists on contract.

Distributed by: Telarc Int. Corp.

How to Contact: Submit demo tape by mail. Unsolicited submissions are OK. Prefers CD. Does not return material. Responds in one month.

Music: Mostly **jazz**, **R&B** and **pop**. Does not want anything else. Released *Keeping Cool* (album), written and recorded by Joyce Cooling (jazz); *Another Side of Midnight* (album), written and recorded

---

THE OPENNESS TO SUBMISSIONS INDEX at the back of this book lists all companies in this section by how open they are to submissions.

by Marion Meadows (jazz); and *Love Letters* (album), written and recorded by Gerald Veasley (jazz). Other artists include Philip Bailey, Joe McBride, Richard Smith, Robert Perera, Spyro Gyra and Pieces of a Dream.

◙ HEART MUSIC, INC., P.O. Box 160326, Austin TX 78716-0326. (512)795-2375. Fax: (512)795-9573. E-mail: info@heartmusic.com. Website: www.heartmusic.com. **Contact:** Mimi Ali-dor, promotions director. Record company and music publisher (Coolhot Music). Estab. 1989. Staff size: 2. Releases 3 CDs/year. Pays 75% royalty to artists on contract; statutory rate to publisher per song on record.
How to Contact: *Not interested in new material at this time.* Does not return material. Responds only if interested.
Music: Mostly **rock**, **pop** and **jazz**; also **blues**, **urban** and **contemporary folk**. Does not want New Age jazz, smooth jazz or Christian/religious. Released *Mirror* (album), recorded by Monte Montgomery (pop/rock), released June 1999; and *Be Cool Be Kind* (album), recorded by Carla Helm-brecht (jazz), released January 2001, both on Heart Music.

▨ �‌○ HI-BIAS RECORDS INC., 20 Hudson Dr. (side entrance), Maple, Toronto, Ontario L6A 1X3 Canada. Phone/fax: (905)303-9611. E-mail: info@hibias.ca. Website: www.hibias.ca/~hibias. **Contact:** Nick Fiorucci, director. Labels include Tilt, Riff, Toronto Underground, Remedy and Club Culture. Record company, music publisher (Bend 60 Music/SOCAN) and record producer (Nick Fiorucci). Estab. 1990. Staff size: 5. Releases 20-30 singles and 2-5 CDs/year. Pays negotiable royalty to artists on contract; statutory rate to publisher per song on record.
Distributed by: PolyGram/Universal.
How to Contact: Submit demo tape by mail. Unsolicited submissions are OK. Prefers cassette or DAT with 3 songs and lyric sheet. Does not return material. Responds in 6 weeks.
Music: Mostly **dance**, **house**, **club**, **pop** and **R&B**. Released "Hands of Time" (single by N. Fiorucci/B. Cosgrove), recorded by Temperance; "Now That I Found You" (single by B. Farrinco/Cleopatra), recorded by YBZ; and "Lift Me Up" (single), written and recorded by Red 5, all on Hi-Bias (dance/pop). Other artists include DJ's Rule.

✔ ◙ HOLLYWOOD RECORDS, 500 S. Buena Vista St., Old Team Bldg., Burbank CA 91521-1840. (818)560-5670. Fax: (818)845-4313. Website: www.hollywoodrecords.com. Senior Vice President of A&R: Rob Cavallo. Senior Vice President of A&R (soundtracks): Mitchell Leib. Vice Presidents: Jon Lind, Jenny Price, Geoffrey Weiss. New York office: 170 Fifth Ave., 9th Floor, New York NY 10010. (212)645-2722. Fax: (212)741-3016. Website: www.hollywoodrec.com. Executive Director: Jason Jordan. Labels include Acid Jazz Records, Mountain Division Records and Bar/None Records. Record company.
How to Contact: *Hollywood Records does not accept unsolicited submissions.* Queries accepted only from a manager or lawyer.
Music: Released *Sooner or Later* (album), recorded by BB Mak; and *Mission Impossible* soundtrack. Other artists include 3rd Strike, DJ Z-Trip, Rama Duke, Victer Duplaix, Tim James, Lil J, Sheila Nicholls, Calvin Richardson, Scapegoat Wax, Simon & Milo and Alexandria Slate.

◙ HORIZON RECORDS, INC., P.O. Box 610487, San Jose CA 95161-0487. E-mail: info@horizonrecords.com. (408)782-1501. Fax: (408)778-3567. Website: www.horizonrecords.com. **Contact:** Jennifer Linn, vice president. Record company and music publisher (Horizon Music West). Estab. 1996. Staff size: 6. Pays negotiable royalty to artists on contract; statutory rate to publisher per song on record.
Distributed by: Red Eye Distribution.
How to Contact: *Horizon records does not accept unsolicited material.*
Music: Mostly **rock/pop**, **singer/songwriter** and **blues**; also **jazz** and techno. Released *Bohemia* (album), written and recorded by Tommy Elskes on Horizon Records (rock/pop).

◑ **HOT WINGS ENTERTAINMENT**, 429 Richmond Ave., Buffalo NY 14222. (716)884-0248. E-mail: dahotwings@aol.com. **Contact:** Dale Anderson, president. Record company and music publisher (Buffalo Wings Music/BMI). Estab. 1994. Staff size: 1. Releases 2 CDs/year. Pays 10-15% to artists on contract; statutory rate to publisher per song on record.

How to Contact: *Call first and obtain permission to submit.* Prefers cassette or CD with 3 or more songs. Does not return material. Responds in 2 months.

Music: Mostly **folk/acoustic**, **alternative rock** and **jazz**. (Preference to artists from Upstate New York.) Released *Like Being Born* (album), written and recorded by Alison Pipitone (folk/rock); *Flavor* (album by Geoffrey Fitzhugh Perry), recorded by Fitzhugh and the Fanatics (blues/rock); and *Everything Counts* (album), written and recorded by Gretchen Schulz (pop/R&B), all on Hot Wings Records.

◯ **HOTTRAX RECORDS**, 1957 Kilburn Dr., Atlanta GA 30324. (770)662-6661. E-mail: hotwax @hottrax.com. Website: www.hottrax.com. **Contact:** Oliver Cooper, vice president, A&R. Labels include Dance-A-Thon and Hardkor. Record company and music publisher (Starfox Publishing). Staff size: 3. Releases 12 singles and 3-4 CDs/year. Pays 5-15% royalty to artists on contract.

Distributed by: Get Hip Inc.

How to Contact: *Write first and obtain permission to submit.* Prefers cassette with 3 songs and lyric sheet. Does not return material. Responds in 6 months. "When submissions get extremely heavy, we do not have the time to respond/return material we pass on. We do notify those sending the most promising work we review, however."

Music: Mostly **top 40/pop**, **rock** and **country**; also **hardcore punk** and **jazz-fusion**. Released *Starfoxx* (album), written and recorded by Starfoxx (rock); "Cherie, Cherie" (single by A. Janoulis), recorded by Blues Mafia (rock); and *Vol. III, Psychedelic Era* (album by various), recorded by Night Shadows (rock), all released 2000 on Hottrax. Other artists include Big Al Jano.

◑ **IDOL RECORDS**, P.O. Box 720043, Dallas TX 75372. (214)826-4365. Fax: (214)370-5417. E-mail: info@idol-records.com. Website: www.Idol-Records.com. **Contact:** Erv Karwelis, president. Record company. Estab. 1992. Releases 2-3 singles, 30 LPs, 2-3 EPs and 15-20 CDs/year. Pays negotiable royalty to artists on contract; statutory rate to publisher per song on record.

Distributed by: Crystal Clear, Southern, Carrot Top, Disgruntled.

How to Contact: See website at www.idol-records.com for submission policy.

Music: Mostly **rock**, **pop** and **alternative**. Released *Onward Quirky Soldiers* (album), recorded by Chomsky (alternative); *Distance and Clime* (album), recorded by Centro-Matic (alternative); and *Falling Hard in the Key of E* (album), recorded by Macavity (alternative), all released 2001 on Idol Records. Other artists include Pervis, Billyclub, Old 97's, Hoarse, Feisty Cadavers, The American Fuse and Watershed.

☑◯ **IMAGINARY RECORDS**, P.O. Box 66, Whites Creek TN 37189-0066. Phone/fax: (615)299-9237. E-mail: jazz@imaginaryrecords.com. Website: www.imaginaryrecords.com. **Contact:** Lloyd Townsend, proprietor. Labels include Imaginary Records, Imaginary Jazz Records. Record company. Estab. 1981. Staff size: 1. Releases 1-3 CDs/year. Pays negotiable royalty to artists on contract; statutory rate to publisher per song on record.

Distributed by: North Country, Harbor Record Export and Imaginary Distribution.

How to Contact: *Write first to obtain permission to submit.* Prefers cassette or CD with 3-5 songs, cover letter and press clippings. Include SASE. Responds in 4 months if interested.

Music: Mostly **mainstream jazz**, **swing jazz** and **classical**. Does not want country, rap, hip-hop or metal. Released *Fifth House* (album), recorded by New York Trio Project (mainstream jazz), released 2001; *Triologue* (album), recorded by Stevens, Siegel, and Ferguson (mainstream jazz), released 2001; and *Panorama* (album), recorded by Stevens, Siegel, and Ferguson with Valery Poromarev, released 1999, all on Imaginary Jazz.

Tips: "Be patient, I'm slow. I'm primarily considering mainstream jazz or classical—other genre submissions are much less likely to get a response."

⊠ ◐ INNER SOUL RECORDS, INC., P.O. Box 4006, Port Arthur TX 77640. (409)983-5936. Website: www.innersoulrecordsinc.com. **Contact:** Dorie Dorsey, head of A&R dept. Record company. Estab. 1995. Releases 2 singles, 2 LPs/year. Pays negotiable royalty to artists on contract. **How to Contact:** Submit demo tape by mail. Unsolicited submissions are OK. Prefers cassette. Mail submissions to 1240 W. 9th St., Port Arthur TX 77640. Does not return material. Responds in 2 months.
Music: Mostly **rap** and **R&B**. Released "Mr. 25/8" (single by DJ DMD) from *Thirty-Three: Live from Hiroshima* (album), recorded by DJ DMD (hip-hop), released 2001 on Inner Soul Records; "25 Lighters" (single by DJ DMD/Lil Ke Ke/Fat Pat) from *Twenty-Two: P.A. Worldwide* (album), recorded by DJ DMD (hip-hop), released 1998 on Inner Soul/Electra Records; and "So Real" (single by DJ DMD/DJ Screw and Screwed Up Click) from *Eleven* (album), recorded by DJ DMD (hip-hop), released 1996 on Inner Soul.
Tips: "Please be as professional as possible with your submissions. A complete package (bio, cassette, photo) is preferred."

⊠ ◐ INSIDE SOUNDS, 1122 Longreen, Memphis TN 38120, (901)682-2063. Fax: (901)682-2063. E-mail: memphisarc@aol.com. **Contact:** Eddie Dattel, owner. Labels include Inside Memphis, Memphis Archives, Inside Sounds Classic and Psychorock. Record company, music publisher (Inside Sounds Publishing) and record producer (Eddie Dattel). Estab. 1992. Releases 12 CDs/year. Pays negotiable royalty to artists on contract; statutory rate to publisher per song on record.
• Inside Sounds and its affiliated labels are noted for releasing blues recordings from Memphis-area artists.
How to Contact: Submit demo tape by mail. Unsolicited submissions are OK. Prefers cassette or CD. Does not return material. Responds in 3 weeks.
Music: Mostly **blues**, **folk** and **jazz**; also **pop**, **alternative rock** and **comedy**. Released *Diamond In The Bluff* (by Joe Sanders), recorded by Memphis Sheiks (blues); *At The Same Place Twice In Life* (by Klaudia Ploderer), recorded by Klaudia & Rico (alternative); and *Reed Between The Lines*, written and recorded by Carl Wolfe (jazz), all on Inside Memphis. Other artists include Wally Ford and The Lizzard Kings.

⊻ ◎ INTERSCOPE/GEFFEN/A&M RECORDS, 2220 Colorado Ave., Santa Monica CA 90404. (310)855-1000. Fax: (310)855-7908. New York office: 825 Eighth Ave., 29th Floor, New York NY 10019. (212)333-8000. Fax: (212)445-3686. E-mail: interscope@interscoperecords.com. Website: www.interscoperecords.com. Labels include Death Row Records, Nothing Records, Rock Land, Almo Sounds, Aftermath Records and Trauma Records. Record company.
• As a result of the PolyGram and Universal merger, Geffen and A&M Records have been folded into Interscope Records.
How to Contact: *Does not accept unsolicited submissions.*
Music: Released *Fush Yu Mang*, recorded by Smash Mouth; and *The Dirty Boogie*, recorded by The Brian Setzer Orchestra. Other artists include U2 and Marilyn Manson.

◎ ISLAND/DEF JAM MUSIC GROUP, (formerly Mercury Records), 825 Eighth Ave., 19th Floor, New York NY 10019. (212)333-8000. Fax: (212)603-7654. Website: www.defjam.com. Los Angeles office: 8920 Sunset Blvd, 2nd Floor, Los Angeles CA 90069. (310)276-4500. Fax: (310)278-5862. Executive A&R: Paul Pontius; A&R Billy Clark. Nashville office: 66 Music Square W., Nashville TN 37203. (615)320-0110. Fax: (615)327-4856. Labels include Mouth Almighty Records, Worldly/Triloka Records, Blackheart Records, Private Records, Slipdisc Records, Thirsty Ear, Blue Gorilla, Dubbly, Little Dog Records, Rounder and Capricorn Records. Record company.
• In 2001, Island/Def Jam Music Group was bought out by Universal.

THE FILM & TV INDEX found at the back of this book lists companies placing music in film and TV (excluding TV commercials).

How to Contact: *Island/Def Jam Music Group does not accept unsolicited submissions. Do not send material unless requested.*
Music: Artists include Bon Jovi, Ja Rule, Redman and Ludacris.

⊘ JIVE RECORDS, 137-139 W. 25th St., 9th Floor, New York NY 10001. (212)727-0016. Fax: (212)337-0990. Senior Vice President of A&R: Peter Thea. Director of A&R: David Lighty. West Hollywood office: 9000 Sunset Blvd., Suite 300, West Hollywood CA 90069. (310)247-8300. Fax: (310)247-8366. Vice President of A&R: Andy Goldmark. Vice President of Creative Development: Jonathan McHugh. Chicago office: 700 N. Green St., Suite 200, Chicago IL 60622. (312)942-9700. Fax: (312)942-9800. Vice President of A&R: Wayne Williams. Nashville office: 914-916 19th Ave. S., Nashville TN 37212. (615)321-4850. Fax: (615)321-4616. London office: Zomba House, 165-167 High Rd., Willesden, London NW 10 2SG England. Phone: (44) 81-459-8899. Fax: (31) 2153-16785. Record company. Estab. 1982. Releases 23 singles and 23 CDs/year.
Distributed by: BMG.
How to Contact: *Does not accept unsolicited material.* "Contact us through management or an attorney."
Music: Mostly **R&B**, **pop** and **rap**. Artists include Backstreet Boys, Joe, R. Kelly, Britney Spears, Too Short, Petey Pablo and Nivea.
Tips: "Make the best material possible."

[N] [Ⓥ] ⊘ JOEY RECORDS, 6707 W. Commerce, San Antonio TX 78227. (210)432-7893. Fax: (210)436-1511. President: Joes. Lopez. Vice President: Dinah Perez. Labels include Zaz Records. Record company, music publisher (El Zaz Music) and record producer. Estab. 1968. Staff size: 40. Releases 500 LPs and 500 CDs/year. Pays negotiable royalty to artists on contract; statutory rate to publisher per song on record.
Distributed by: Anderson Merchandisers, FRD, Southwest Wholesale and Handleman Co.
  • In 1998, Joey Records won Achievement of Excellence at the Tejano Music Awards.
How to Contact: Submit demo tape by mail. Unsolicited submissions are OK. Prefers CD or VHS videocassette with 10 songs, cover letter and press clippings. Does not return material. Responds in 3 months.
Music: Mostly **regional Mexican**, **Tejano** and **tropical/grupero**. Does not want country. Released *La Rayita* (album writte by Jimmy Garcia/Lena Probadita), recorded by Los Hnos Garcia (Mexican regional); and *Mejores tiempos* (album written by Ramiro Villareal/Ya No Voy Ag), recorded by Michael Salgado (Mexican regional), both released 2000 on Joey Records. Other artists include Amanecer and Los Chacales.
Tips: "Submit information and persist with letters and phone calls and even unexpected visit OK."

[N] ⊘ JUPITER RECORDS, Irmgardstr. 1, 81479 Munchen Germany. E-mail: contact@jupiter-records.de. Website: www.jupiter-records.de. Professional Manager: Helgard von Schenckendorff (pop/MOR). Professional Manager: Peer Schmidt (pop/dance). Record company and record producer.
How to Contact: Submit demo tape or CD by mail. Unsolicited submissions are OK. SAE and IRC. Responds in 2 months.
Music: Mostly **pop**, **rock** and **dance**; also **soul** and **Black music**.
Tips: "If you believe that your song could be No. 1 on the charts, please submit it!"

⊘ KAUPP RECORDS, Box 5474, Stockton CA 95205. (209)948-8186. **Contact:** Nancy L. Merrihew, president. Record company, music publisher (Kaupps and Robert Publishing Co./BMI), management firm (Merri-Webb Productions) and record producer (Merri-Webb Productions). Estab. 1990. Releases 1 single and 4 LPs/year. Pays standard royalty to artists on contract; statutory rate to publisher per song on record.
Distributed by: Merri-Webb Productions and Cal-Centron Distributing Co.
How to Contact: *Write first and obtain permission to submit or to arrange personal interview.* Prefers cassette or VHS videocassette with 3 songs. Include SASE. Responds in 3 months.

Music: Mostly **country**, **R&B** and **A/C rock**; also **pop**, **rock** and **gospel**. Released "I Thank You Father" and "On the Other Side" (singles by N. Merrihew/B. Bolin), recorded by Bruce Bolin; and "Did You Think That I Thought That You Liked Me" (single by N. Merrihew/B. Bolin), recorded by Cheryl, all on Kaupp Records.

♥ KINGSTON RECORDS, 15 Exeter Rd., Kingston NH 03848. (603)642-8493. E-mail: kingston records@ttlc.net. **Contact:** Harry Mann, coordinator. Record company, record producer and music publisher (Strawberry Soda Publishing/ASCAP). Estab. 1988. Releases 3-4 singles, 2-3 12″ singles, 3 LPs and 2 CDs/year. Pays 3-5% royalty to artists on contract; statutory rate to publisher per song.
How to Contact: *Write first and obtain permission to submit.* Prefers cassette, DAT, 15 ips reel-to-reel or videocassette with 3 songs and lyric sheet. Does not return material. Responds in 2 months.
Music: Mostly **rock**, **country** and **pop**; "no heavy metal." Released *Two Lane Highway* and *Armand's Way* (albums), written and recorded by Armand Learay (rock); and *Count the Stars* (album), written and recorded by Doug Mitchell, released 1999, all on Kingston Records.
Tips: "Working only with N.E. and local talent."

◪ ◯ L. A. RECORDS (CANADA), P.O. Box 1096, Hudson, Quebec J0P 1H0 Canada. Phone/fax: (450)458-2819. Pager: (514)869-3236. E-mail: la_records@excite.com. Website: www.radiofree dom.com. Manager (alternative): T. Hart. Producer (rock): M. Lengies. Record company, management firm (M.B.H. Music Management), music publisher (G-String Publishing) and record producer (M. Lengies). Estab. 1991. Releases 20-40 singles and 5-8 CDs/year. Pays negotiable royalty to artists on contract; statutory rate to publishers per song on record.
Distributed by: L.A. Records and Radiofreedom.com.
How to Contact: Submit demo tape by mail. Unsolicited submissions are OK. Prefers cassette or DAT with 3 songs and lyric sheet. Does not return material.
Music: Mostly **commercial rock**, **alternative** and **A/C**; also **country** and **dance**. Released *Zario* (album), written and recorded by Zario on L.A. Records. Other artists include El Vache, General Panic, Brittany and Joe King.

☑ ◯ L.A. RECORDS, 29355 Little Mack, Roseville MI 48066. (810)775-6533. E-mail: jtrupi453 9@aol.com. Website: http://hometown.aol.com/jtrupi4539/larecords.html. President: Jack Timmons. Music Director: John Dudick. Labels include Stark Records, R.C. Records and Fearless. Record company, record producer and music publisher (Abalone Publishing). Estab. 1984. Staff size: 12. Releases 20-30 singles, 1-10 12″ singles, 20-30 LPs, 1-5 EPs and 2-15 CDs/year. Pays 5% royalty to artists on contract; statutory rate to publisher per song on record.
How to Contact: Submit demo tape by mail. Unsolicited submissions are OK. Prefers cassette with 1-10 songs and lyric sheet. "It is very important to include a cover letter describing your objective goals." Responds in 3 months. "Due to fluctuation of postal rates include $1 to cover postage overage above 34¢. All others SASE is acceptable. Packages with 34¢ SASE are not acceptable."
Music: Mostly **rock/hard rock**, **heavy metal** and **pop/rock**; also **country/gospel**, **MOR/ballads**, **R&B**, **jazz**, **New Age**, **dance** and **easy listening**. Released "Mad About You" (single) from *Mad About You* (album), released 2000 on L.A. Records; "Car Crazy" (single) from *Car Crazy* (album), released 1999 on L.A. Records; and "Witemores" (single) from *Nitemoves* (album), released 1999 on L.A. Records, all written and recorded by Joey Harlow. Other artists include The Simmones, Kevin Stark, The Comets and Fearless.

◯ LAMAR MUSIC MARKETING, ℅ 104 Pearsall Dr., Mt. Vernon NY 10552. (914)699-1744. Fax: (914)668-3119. Executive Director: Darlene Barkley. Operations Director: Vernon Wilson. Music Producer: M3. Labels include Lamar, MelVern, Wilson, Pulse Music Publications. Record company, music publisher and workshop organization. Estab. 1984. Staff size: 4. Releases 4 CD singles and 1 LP/year. Pays standard royalty to artists on contract; statutory rate to publisher per song. "We charge only if we are hired to do 'work-for-hire' projects."
How to Contact: "Videotape submissions of performer's actual performance!"
Music: Mostly **R&B**, **rap** and **pop**. Released "I Am So Confused" (single), written and recorded by Eemense; and "Heavenly" (single), recorded by Vern Wilson, both on Lamar Records; and "Feel

Like a Woman" (single by Wilson/Johnson), recorded by Sandra Taylor on MelVern Records (R&B/ballad). Other artists include Barry Manderson and J-Son. Clients include: Hollywood Records, Riviera Film Company and Warner Bros.

Tips: "Unsolicited demo submissions are a waste of time and money. If you choose to spend your money, we suggest that you purchase our video 'From Talent Show to Stardom,' which will tell you everything you need to know about the company and its history. We need to *see* what you can do as well as hear what you can do. We are aware that there are extremely talented producers, but we are looking for extremely talented performers! Those selected will become a part of our music business program. Funding is available for those in the program."

Ⓐ LANDSLIDE RECORDS, P.O. Box 20387, Atlanta GA 30325. (404)931-9049. E-mail: mrland @mindspring.com. Website: http://www.landsliderecords.com. President A&R: Michael Rothschild. Promotions Director/A&R: Eddie Cleveland. Record company, music publisher (Frozen Inca Music/BMI) and record producer. Estab. 1981. Releases 4 LPs and 4 CDs/year. Pays negotiable royalty to artists on contract; negotiable rate to publisher per song on record.
Distributed by: Rock Bottom, Action and Selecto Hits.
How to Contact: Submit demo tape by mail. Unsolicited submissions are OK. Prefers cassette with 6-12 songs and lyric sheet. Demos are not returned.
Music: Mostly **blues** and **roots music**; also **jazz** and **swing**. Released *Moanin' For Molasses* (album), released in 2001 and *Cuttin' In* (album), released in 2000, both written and recorded by Sean Costello (blues); and *Offered Schematics Suggesting Peace* (album), written and recorded by Sound Tribe Sector 9 (jam), released 2001, all on Landslide Records. Other artists include The Steam Donkeys, Colonel Bruce Hampton and Paul McCandless.

Ⓐ LARI-JON RECORDS, 325 W. Walnut, Rising City NE 68658. (402)542-2336. **Contact:** Larry Good, owner. Record company, management firm (Lari-Jon Promotions), music publisher (Lari-Jon Publishing/BMI) and record producer (Lari-Jon Productions). Estab. 1967. Staff size: 1. Releases 15 singles and 5 LPs/year. Pays varying royalty to artists on contract.
How to Contact: Submit demo tape by mail. Unsolicited submissions are OK. Prefers cassette with 5 songs and lyric sheet. Include SASE. Responds in 2 months.
Music: Mostly **country**, **gospel-Southern** and **'50s rock**. Released "Glory Bound Train" (single), written and recorded by Tom Campbell; *The Best of Larry Good* (album), written and recorded by Larry Good (country); and *Her Favorite Songs* (album), written and recorded by Johnny Nace (country), all on Lari-Jon Records. Other artists include Kent Thompson and Brenda Allen.

Ⓐ LARK RECORD PRODUCTIONS, INC., P.O. Box 35726, Tulsa OK 74153. (918)786-8896. Fax: (918)786-8897. E-mail: janajae@janajae.com. Website: www.janajae.com. **Contact:** Kathleen Pixley, vice president. Record company, music publisher (Jana Jae Music/BMI), management firm (Jana Jae Enterprises) and record producer (Lark Talent and Advertising). Estab. 1980. Staff size: 8. Pays negotiable royalty to artists on contract; statutory rate to publisher per song on record.
How to Contact: Submit demo tape by mail. Unsolicited submissions are OK. Prefers cassette or VHS videocassette with 3 songs and lead sheets. Does not return material. Responds only if interested.
Music: Mostly **country**, **bluegrass** and **classical**; also **instrumentals**. Released "Fiddlestix" (single by Jana Jae); "Mayonnaise" (single by Steve Upfold); and "Flyin' South" (single by Cindy Walker), all recorded by Jana Jae on Lark Records (country). Other artists include Syndi, Hotwire and Matt Greif.

Ⓩ LEATHERLAND PRODUCTIONS, 2301 Atlantic St., Hopewell VA 23860. (804)458-1612. E-mail: leatherlandprod@firstsaga.com. Website: www.spudmanfoo.com. **Contact:** Tammy Alexander, owner. Record company, music publisher (Leatherland Productions) and books on tape. Estab. 1997. Pays negotiable royalty to artists on contract; statutory rate to publisher per song on record.
Distributed by: Leatherland Productions.
How to Contact: *No unsolicited submissions accepted.*
Music: **Contemporary Christian**.

◉ ◖ **LOCK**, Coachhouse, Mansion Farm, Liverton Hill, Sandway, Maidstone, Kent ME172NJ England. Phone/fax: (01622)858300. E-mail: info@eddielock.com. **Contact:** Eddie Lock, A&R. Record company, music publisher (Lock 'n' S) and record producer (Carpe Diem). Estab. 1988. Staff size: 2. Releases 10 singles/year. Pays negotiable royalty to artists on contract; statutory rate to publisher per song on record.
Distributed by: Unique, Essential, and Greyhound.
How to Contact: Submit demo tape by mail. Unsolicited submissions are OK. Prefers CD. Does not return material. Responds in 1 week.
Music: Mostly **dance**, **house** and **trance**. Released "Bang to the Beat of the Drum" (single by Eddie Lock/Paul Hutsch/Richard West), recorded by Eddie Lock (tribal/house), released 2001 on Alphabet City/Lock; "Dance to the Music" (single by Eddie Lock and Dylan Burns), recorded by Lock and Burns, released 2001 on Lock/Tempo/Alphabet City; and "Spaced" (single by Eddie Lock/Dylan Burns/Nick Austin), recorded by Lock & Burns (house), released 2001 on Lock.

◉ **LONDON SIRE RECORDS**, 7381 Beverly Blvd., Los Angeles CA 90036. (323)937-4660. Fax: (323)933-7277. Website: www.sirerecords.com. A&R: Jonathon Paley, Andy Paley. New York office: 936 Broadway, New York NY 10010. (212)707-2056. Record company.
Distributed by: WEA.
How to Contact: *Does not accept unsolicited submissions.*
Music: Mostly **rock** and **alternative**.

◉ **LOUD RECORDS**, (formerly Relativity Records), 79 Fifth Ave., 15th Floor, New York NY 10003. (212)337-5300. **Contact:** A&R Dept. Labels include Ruthless Records. Record company.
Distributed by: Sony.
How to Contact: Submit demo tape by mail. Unsolicited submissions are OK. Prefers cassette, CD or DAT. Submit to Attn: A&R Dept.
Music: Released *Heaven'z Movie* (album), recorded by Bizzy Bone on Mo Thugs Records.

◉ **LUCIFER RECORDS, INC.**, P.O. Box 263, Brigantine NJ 08203-0263. (609)266-2623. Fax: (609)266-4870. **Contact:** Ron Luciano, president. Labels include TVA Records. Record company, music publisher (Ciano Publishing and Legz Music), record producer (Pete Fragale and Tony Vallo), management firm and booking agency (Ron Luciano Music Co. and TVA Productions). "Lucifer Records has offices in South Jersey; Palm Beach, Florida; and Las Vegas, Nevada."
How to Contact: *Call or write to arrange personal interview.* Prefers cassette with 4-8 songs. Include SASE. Responds in 3 weeks.
Music: Mostly **dance**, **easy listening**, **MOR**, **rock**, **soul** and **top 40/pop**. Released "I Who Have Nothing," (single), by Spit-N-Image (rock); "Lucky" (single), by Legz (rock); and "Love's a Crazy Game" (single), by Voyage (disco/ballad). Other artists include Bobby Fisher, Jerry Denton, FM, Zeke's Choice, Al Caz, Joe Vee and Dana Nicole.

☑ ◉ **MAJOR ENTERTAINMENT, INC.**, 331 W. 57th St., #173, New York NY 10019. (212)489-1500. Fax: (212)489-5660. E-mail: info@majorentertainment.com. Website: www.majorentertainment.com. **Contact:** Tatiana Sampson, president. A&R Department: Matt "½ Pint" Davis. Record company, music publisher (Major Entertainment/BMI), artist management, distribution and consulting. Estab. 1983.
How to Contact: Submit CD by mail. Unsolicited submissions are OK. Prefers CD with 3 songs. Include SASE. Responds in 2 months.
Music: Mostly **rap** and **R&B**. Released *2 Hot Fa TV* (album by Walter McCullon), recorded by Tre-8 (rap), released 2002 on Major Entertainment; and *No Secrets* (album by Timothy Brown), recorded by Father MC (rap), released 2000 Street Solid.

MARKETS THAT WERE listed in the 2002 edition of *Songwriters Market* but do not appear this year are listed in the General Index with a notation explaining why they were omitted.

☑ ☻ ◉ **MAKOCHÉ RECORDING COMPANY**, 208 N. Fourth St., Bismarck ND 58501. (701)223-7316. Fax: (701)255-8287. E-mail: makoche@aol.com. Website: www.makoche.com. **Contact:** Lisa Dowhaniuk, A&R assistant. Labels include Makoché and Chairmaker's Rush. Record company and recording studio. Estab. 1995. Staff size: 5. Releases 4 CDs/year. Pays negotiable royalty to artists on contract; statutory rate to publisher per song on record.
Distributed by: DNA, Music Design, Four Winds Trading, Zango Music and New Leaf Distribution.
• Makoché is noted for releasing quality music based in the Native American tradition. Recognized by the Grammys, Nammys, New Age Voice Music Awards and C.O.V.R. Music Awards.
How to Contact: *Call first and obtain permission to submit.* "Please submit only fiddle and American Indian-influenced music." Include SASE. Responds in 2 months.
Music: Mostly **Native American**, **flute** and **fiddle**. Released *The Heron Smiled* (album), written and recorded by Annie Humphrey (folk), released 2000 on Makoché; and *Cheyenne Nation* (album), written and recorded by Joseph Fire Crow (Native American flute), released 2000 on Makoché. Other artists include Gary Stroutsos, Bryan Akipa, Keith Bear, Andrew Vasquez, Lakota Thunder, Sissy Goodhouse and Kevin Locke.
Tips: "We are a small label with a dedication to quality."

☑ ☻ **MALACO RECORDS**, 3023 W. Northside Dr., Jackson MS 39213. (601)982-4522. E-mail: jmannery@malaco.com. Website: www.malaco.com. Executive Director: Jerry Mannery. Record company. Estab. 1986. Releases 20 projects/year. Pays variable royalty to artists on contract; statutory rate to publisher per song.
How to Contact: Submit demo tape by mail. Unsolicited submissions are OK. Prefers cassette or CD. Does not return material.
Music: Mostly **traditional** and **contemporary gospel**. Artists include Mississippi Mass Choir, The Bonner Brothers, Lou Rawls, Men of Standard, Mississippi Children's Choir, Bryan Wilson, The Pilgrim Jubilees, Lillian Lilly, Dorothy Norwood, The Sensational Nightengales, The Angelic Gospel Singers, Carolyn Traylor, Christopher Brinson and Rudolph Stanfield & New Revelation.

Ⓝ ☻ **ANDY MARVEL RECORDS**, (formerly Alyssa Records), 302 Bluepoint Rd. W., Holtsville NY 11742. President: Andy Marvel. Labels include Ricochet Records. Record company, music publisher (Andy Marvel Music/ASCAP, Bing Bing Bing Music/ASCAP and Andysongs/BMI) and record producer (Marvel Productions). Estab. 1981. Staff size: 3. Releases 12-15 singles, 1 12" single and 4 LPs/year. Pays standard royalty to artists on contract; statutory rate to publisher per song on record.
How to Contact: Submit demo tape by mail. Unsolicited submissions are OK. Prefers cassette or CD with 3 songs and lyric sheet. Does not return material. "Do not call." Responds in 2 months.
Music: Mostly **pop**, **R&B** and **top 40**; also **country**.

☑ ☻ ◉ **MAVERICK RECORDS**, 9348 Civic Center Dr., Beverly Hills CA 90210. (310)385-7800. Fax: (310)385-7711. Website: www.maverick.com. CEO/Head of A&R: Guy Oseary. A&R: Russ Rieger, Jason Bentley, Danny Strick, Berko Weber, Michael Goldberg. Record company.
Distributed by: WEA.
How to Contact: *Maverick Records does not accept unsolicited submissions.*
Music: Released *Under Rug Swept* (album); *Supposed Former Infatuation Junkie* (album) and *Jagged Little Pill* (album), both recorded by Alanis Morissette; *The Spirit Room* (album), recorded by Michelle Branch; *Tantric* (album), recorded by Tantric; and *Ray of Light* (album), recorded by Madonna. Other artists include Deftones, Home Town Hero, Mest, Michael Lee, Me'shell Ndegeocello, Muse, Onesidezero, Prodigy and Paul Oakenfold.

✦ ☑ ◉ **MAYFAIR MUSIC**, 2600 John St., Unit 219, Markham, Ontario L3R 3W3 Canada. (905)475-1848. **Contact:** John Loweth, A&R. Record company, music publisher (MBD Records). Estab. 1979. Pays 10% royalty to artists on contract; statutory rate to publisher per song on record.
• Mayfair Music is also listed in the Music Publishers section.
How to Contact: Submit demo CD/CDR by mail. Unsolicited submissions are OK. Prefers CD/CDR only with 4 songs. Does not return material. Responds in 3 weeks.
Music: Mostly **instrumental**. Current acts include Frank Mills and Paul Saulnier.

MCA RECORDS, 1755 Broadway, 8th Floor, New York NY 10019. (212)841-8000. Fax: (212)841-8146. Website: www.mca.com/mca_records. Santa Monica office: 2220 Colorado Ave., Santa Monica CA 90404. (310)865-4000. Nashville office: 60 Music Square E., Nashville TN 37203. (615)244-8944. Fax: (615)880-7447. Record company and music publisher (MCA Music).

• In 2000, MCA's The Roots featuring Erykah Badu won a Grammy Award for Best Rap Performance By A Duo or Group ("You Got Me," from *Things Fall Apart*).

How to Contact: MCA Records cannot accept unsolicited submissions. Have your demo recommended to their A&R Department by a well-known manager, agent, producer, radio DJ or other music industry veteran. Create a buzz in your local community at the club label, through local music publications and at your local radio station.

Music: Released *Love Always* (album), recorded by K-Ci & JoJo; *Acquarium* (album), recorded by Aqua; and *Sublime* (album), recorded by Sublime, all on MCA Records. Other artists include Tracy Byrd, George Strait, Vince Gill, The Mavericks and Trisha Yearwood.

METAL BLADE RECORDS, 2828 Cochran St., Suite 302, Simi Valley CA 93065. (805)522-9111. Fax: (805)522-9380. E-mail: metalblade@metalblade.com. Website: www.metalblad e.com. **Contact:** Kim Macleery, vice president creative services. Record company. Estab. 1982. Releases 20 LPs, 2 EPs and 20 CDs/year. Pays negotiable royalty to artists on contract.

How to Contact: Submit demo tape by mail. Unsolicited submissions are OK. Prefers cassette or CD with 3 songs. Does not return material. Responds in 3 months.

Music: Mostly **heavy metal** and **industrial**; also **hardcore**, **gothic** and **noise**. Released "Gallery of Suicide," recorded by Cannibal Corpse; "Voo Doo," recorded by King Diamond; and "A Pleasant Shade of Gray," recorded by Fates Warning, all on Metal Blade Records. Other artists include Grip Inc., Galactic Cowboys, Sacred Reich, Bolt Thrower, Kings X, Mercyful Fate, Flotsam and Jetsam and Six Feet Under.

Tips: "Metal Blade is known throughout the underground for quality metal-oriented acts."

MIGHTY RECORDS, 150 West End, Suite 6-D, New York NY 10023. Manager: Danny Darrow. Labels include Mighty Sounds & Filmworks. Record company, music publisher (Rockford Music Co./BMI, Stateside Music Co./BMI and Corporate Music Publishing Co./ASCAP) and record producer (Danny Darrow). Estab. 1958. Releases 1-2 singles, 1-2 12″ singles and 1-2 LPs/year. Pays standard royalty to artists on contract; statutory rate to publisher per song on record.

How to Contact: Submit demo tape by mail. Unsolicited submissions are OK. "No phone calls." Prefers cassette with 2 songs and lyric sheet. Does not return material. Responds in 1 month only if interested.

Music: Mostly **pop**, **country** and **dance**; also **jazz**. Released "Let There Be Peace" (single by Danny Darrow) from *Let There Be Peace* (album), recorded by Danny Darrow (spiritual); "Doomsday" (single by Robert Lee Lowery and Danny Darrow) from *Doomsday* (album), recorded by Danny Darrow (Euro jazz); and "Impulse" (single by Danny Darrow) from *Impulse* (album), recorded by Danny Darrow (Euro jazz), all released 2001 on Mighty Records.

MISSILE RECORDS, Box 5537, Kreole Station, Moss Point MS 39563-1537. (228)475-0059. "No collect calls." **Contact:** Doris M. Mitchell, president. Vice President: Justin F. Mitchell. Vice President/Manager: Joe F. Mitchell. Record company, music publisher (Bay Ridge Publishing/BMI) and record producer. Estab. 1974. Releases 28 singles and 10 LPs/year. Pays "10-16¢ per song to new artists, higher rate to established artists"; statutory rate to publisher for each record sold.

Distributed by: Big Daddy Music Distribution Co., Hits Unlimited, Action Music Sales, Inc., Allegro Corp., Big Easy Distributing, Select-O-Hits, Total Music Distributors, Music Network, Impact Music, Universal Record Distributing Corporation, Dixie Rak Records & Tapes, Navaree Corporation, Curtis Wood Distributors, Valley Media Distributors, ATM Distributors, HL Distribution, Bayside Distribution, Blue Sky Distribution.

How to Contact: *Write or call first to obtain permission before you submit.* Include #10 business-size SASE to respond to your request to submit material. After you receive permission to submit, include with submission SASE with sufficient postage to return all materials. "All songs sent for review MUST include sufficient return postage; no reply without SASE or return of material without sufficient return postage. No collect calls. **Absolutely no reply post cards, only SASE.** If you only write lyrics, do not submit. We only accept completed songs, so you must find a musical collaborator. We are not interested in reviewing homemade recordings." Prefers CD (first choice) or cassette with 3-8 songs and lyrics to songs submitted. Responds in 2 months.

Music: Country, alternative, gospel, rap, heavy metal, hardcore, folk, contemporary, jazz, bluegrass and R&B; also soul, MOR, blues, ballads, reggae, world, rock and pop. Released "Excuse Me, Lady," "When She Left Me" (singles by Rich Wilson), "Everyone Gets A Chance (To Lose in Romance)" and "I'm So Glad We Found Each Other" (singles by Joe F. Mitchell), recorded by Rich Wilson (country/western); "Rose Up On A Stem" (single by Joe F. Mitchell), recorded by Jerry Piper (country/western), all on Missile Records. Other artists include Moto (reggae), Jackie Lambarella (country pop), Sarah Cooper (pop/R&B), Della Reed (contemporary Christian), Matellica (heavy metal), Coco Hodge (alternative) and Lady Love (rap).

Tips: "Outstanding singers with outstanding songs, well-produced, well-written and ready for the market will be shopped to major labels or given consideration for release on Missile Records. Give us a call. We have the connections to get you to the next level where you need to be. We will give consideration to new exceptionally talented artists with a fan base and some backing."

☑ ◐ **MODAL MUSIC, INC.**™, P.O. Box 6473, Evanston IL 60204-6473. (847)864-1022. E-mail: info@modalmusic.com. Website: www.modalmusic.com. President: Terran Doehrer. Assistant: J. Distler. Record company and agent. Estab. 1988. Staff size: 2. Releases 1-2 LPs/year. Pays negotiable royalty to artists on contract; negotiable rate to publisher per song on record.

How to Contact: Submit demo tape by mail. Unsolicited submissions are OK. Prefers CD or cassette with bio, PR, brochures, any info about artist and music. Does not return material. Responds in 4 months.

Music: Mostly **ethnic** and **world**. Released *Dance The Night Away* (album by T. Doehrer), recorded by Balkan Rhythm Band™; *Sid Beckerman's Rumanian (D. Jacobs)* (album), recorded by Jutta & The Hi-Dukes™; and *Hold Whatcha Got* (album), recorded by Razzmetazz, all on Modal Music Records. Other artists include Ensemble M'chaiya™, Nordland Band™ and Terran's Greek Band™.

Tips: "Please note our focus is ethnic. You waste your time and money by sending us any other type of music. If you are unsure of your music fitting our focus, please call us before sending anything. Put your name and contact info on every item you send!"

▚ ◑ **MONTICANA RECORDS**, P.O. Box 702, Snowdon Station, Montreal, Quebec H3X 3X8 Canada. **Contact:** David P. Leonard, general manager. Labels include Dynacom. Record company, record producer (Monticana Productions) and music publisher (Montina Music/SOCAN). Estab. 1963. Staff size: 1. Pays negotiable royalty to artists on contract.

How to Contact: Submit demo tape by mail. Unsolicited submissions are OK. Prefers CD, phonograph record or VHS videocassette. Include SASE.

Music: Mostly **top 40**, **blues**, **country**, **dance-oriented**, **easy listening**, **folk** and **gospel**; also **jazz**, **MOR**, **progressive**, **R&B**, **rock** and **soul**.

Tips: "Be excited and passionate about what you do. Be professional."

☑ ◎ **DOUG MOODY PRODX**, (formerly Doug Moody Productions), P.O. Box 6271, Oceanside CA 92058-6271. E-mail: dmprodx@aol.com. Website: www.MysticRecordsHQ.com. Labels include Clock. Music publisher (Mystic Records USA & UK, Doug Moody Music USA & UK). Estab. 1968. Releases 8 LPs and 10 CDs/year. Pays 10% royalty to artists on contract.

How to Contact: Only open to groups who perform. Include SASE.

Music: Mystic thrash, **punk** and **blues**, **50s** and **60s** music for Clock Records. Does not want pop, classical, religious. Released *Maximum Rock 'n' Roll* (album), written and recorded by NOFX (mystic); and *Happy Organ* (album), written and recorded by Dave Baby Cortez (clock).

FOR BOOKS ON THE CRAFT AND BUSINESS of songwriting, check out the website for Writer's Digest Books at www.writersdigest.com.

Tips: "Make a master ready for release."

Ⓒ MOTOWN RECORDS, 825 Eighth Ave., New York NY 10019. (212)373-0600. Los Angeles office: 11150 Santa Monica Blvd. #1000, Los Angeles CA 90025. (310)996-7200. Website: www.motown40.com. Labels include BIV Records, Illtown Records and MoJazz Records. Record company.
How to Contact: *Motown Records does not accept unsolicited submissions.*
Music: Artists include Brian McKnight and Erykah Badu.

Ⓝ MUSIC WISE INC., P.O. Box 931, Englewood Cliffs NJ 07632. (914)882-3807. (914)725-0083. E-mail: 18773654718@worldcom.com. CEO (R&B, rap, jazz, pop): John Henry. A&R Director (rap, hip-hop, hardcore): Don Beharry. President of Jazz Division (jazz, fusion): Pedro Berrios. Vice President of A&R: Dirk Miller. Record company, music publisher (Show-Class Music/BMI, Aisha Music/BMI) and artist management. Estab. 1990. Pays negotiable royalty to artists on contract; statutory rate to publisher per song on record.
How to Contact: Submit demo tape by mail. Unsolicited submissions are OK. Prefers CD with 3-4 songs and lyric sheet. "When submitting material please include photos and biography." Include SASE. Responds in 2 weeks.
Music: Mostly **R&B**, **hip hop** and **pop/contemporary**; also **jazz**, **gospel** and **country**.
Tips: "Be very persistent and professional. Have good quality songs, photos and bios and there's a good chance we may do business if the material is hit quality."

☑ Ⓒ NATION RECORDS INC., 6351 W. Montrose 333, Chicago IL 60634. (312)458-9888. Fax: (773)725-5994. E-mail: info@nationrecords.com. Website: www.nationrecords.com. **Contact:** Phil Vaughan, A&R. Record company. Estab. 1996. Releases 5 CDs/year. Pays negotiable royalty to artists on contract; statutory rate to publisher per song on record.
Distributed by: Midwest Artist Distribution.
How to Contact: Submit demo tape by mail. Unsolicited submissions are OK. Prefers cassette or CD with lyric sheet. Does not return material. Responds in 3 months.
Music: All types. Released *American Stories* (album by Bob Young); and *Steve & Johnnie Present* "Life After Dark" (album), both on Nation Records Inc. Other artists include The Buckinghams, Pete Special and World Class Noise.

☑ Ⓒ NEURODISC RECORDS, INC., 3801 N. University Dr., Suite 403, Ft. Lauderdale FL 33351. (954)572-0289. Fax: (954)572-2874. E-mail: info@neurodisc.com. Website: www.neurodisc.com. President: Tom O'Keefe. Label Manager: John Wai. Record company and music publisher. Estab. 1992. Releases 3 singles, 10 LPs and 10 CDs/year. Pays negotiable royalty to artists on contract; 75% "to start" to publisher per song on record.
Distributed by: Capitol Records, Priority/EMI.
How to Contact: Submit demo tape by mail. Unsolicited submissions are OK. Prefers cassette, CD, DAT or VHS videocassette. Include SASE. Responds in 2 months.
Music: Mostly **electronic**, **dance** and **New Age**; also **rap**. Released *Trance Fixed*, 2nd ed. (album), recorded by D.J. Session One; *Trance: the Progressive Experience* (album), recorded by D.J. Vicious Vic; and *Odonata* (album), recorded by Amethystium. Other artists include Eric Hansen, Level X and Get Some Crew.

☑ Ⓒ NIGHT OWL RECORDS., (formerly Keeping It Simple and Safe, Inc.), P.O. Box 91079, Springfield MA 01139-1079. (413)883-2527. E-mail: nightowlrecord@aol.com. **Contact:** New Talent Department. Labels include Grand Jury Records, Second Time Around Records and Southend-Essex Records. Record company. Estab. 1993. Releases 3 singles and 2 CDs/year. Pays 12-25% royalty to artists on contract; statutory rate to publisher per song on record.
Distributed by: Tim Scott Music Group (BMI) music publisher.
How to Contact: Submit demo package by mail. Unsolicited submissions are OK. Prefers cassette or CD with 3-5 songs and lyric sheet. Include SASE. Responds in 1 month.
Music: Mostly **pop**, **R&B**, and **rap**; also **country**, **rock** and **gospel**. Released "Crime of Love" (single by Dante Johnson/David Smooth) from *Crime of Love* (album), recorded by The Lawyers and

Judges (top 40); "Not In My House" (single by Dan "poorman" Williams) from *Empty Pockets* (album), recorded by The Poor Folks (r&b); and "Sweet Candy Love" (single by Mary McNiel/ Sandy McNiel/Hazel Jackson) from *Sweet Love Forever* (album), recorded by Sweet Honey (r&b), all released 2001 on Night Owl Records.

Tips: "Always include in cover letter whether you are asking for a *publishing* or a *recording* deal."

N ⬤ NIGHTMARE RECORDS, 7751 Greenwood Dr., St. Paul MN 55112. Phone/fax: (612)784-9654. E-mail: nightdiscs@aol.com. Website: www.nightmare-records.com. Contact: Lance King. Record company, distributor and management firm (Jupiter Productions). Estab. 1983. Pays 10-15% royalty to artists on contract.

Distributed by: US: Best Buy stores, Sam Goody/Musicland/Media Play/On Cue, Blockbuster Music, Nightmare-Records.com, Dream Disc, Perris Records, Dynasty Music, Two Guys Music, Wildside Imports, Molten Metal, Impulse Music, Alta Mira, Amazon.com, D.S.B. Music, Echo Rider/ Music Works, Generations Underground, Lasers Edge, CD Baby, Outer Limites, Moremetal.com, Sentinel Steel, Restless & Wild, CD's and More, Amazingcds.com, Sounds of Metal, Seven Gates, Must Have Music, Oarfin Records & Distribution, Select-O-Hits, Neh Records, Phoenix Records, Metal Mayhem Music, Century Media, The Sounds of Metal, Rasputin Music, Loud Distribution. Foreign: Bertus Distribution (Netherlands), Bee Bee Records/Distribee (Netherlands), Mega Rock Distribution (Sweden), Nordic Metal (Denmark), Scrape Records (Canada), HMV (Canada), Lament Distribution (Mexico), Steel Gallery (Greece), Sleaszy Rider (Greece), Sun Records, Sounds Machine (Italy), Heavencross (Spain), Leyenda (Spain), The Rock Shop (Spain), JPM Music (Chile), Rising Sun (Germany), Lobel Music (GeK), Concrete (Germany), War of Horns Records (Germany), Discos Sun Records (Spain), Rockhouse Records (Holland), Hellion Records (Germany), DSB (Germany), AOR Basement (UK), Diskheaven (Japan), Sheer Records (Czech Republic), Music Hunter (Finland), Heavy Sound Rock Shop (Sweden), Lament Distributions (Mexico). Christian: Holy Rollers, The Crossing (CDHC), Christian Demo Clearing House, M8, Spring Arbor, C.M.P. (Australia), Rugged Cross, Rad Rockers, Bibles Plus, Ultimatum Music, Blast Beats Music, Nordic Mission, Something More Christian Bookstore, ClassicGod.com.

How to Contact: Submit demo tape by mail. Unsolicited submissions are OK. Prefers cassette or CD with 3 songs. Include brief bio, photo and press clippings (if available). Does not return material. Responds only if interested.

Music: Mostly **hard rock-metal**, with a special interest in **progressive metal**. Released *Untitled* (by King/Barilla), recorded by The Kings Machine (rock); *From Cradle to Grave* (by Petrick/Cassidy), recorded by Malicious (rock); and *Pavlov's Dog's* (by Stevenson/Christensen), recorded by Conditioned Response (rock), all on Nightmare. Current acts include Godhead (Southern fried grunge), Visionary (progressive metal), Balance of Power (progressive metal), Cains Alibi (power metal), Empyria (progressive power metal), Antithesis (progressive thrash metal), USM (Nu-metal) and Sonic Boom (industrial dance).

Tips: "Be patient, persistent and positive! We're busy and we know what were looking for, if we like what we hear, we'll call you ASAP."

✓ ◯ NORTH STAR MUSIC, 22 London St., E. Greenwich RI 02818. (401)886-8888. Fax: (401)886-8880. E-mail: rw@northstarmusic.com. Website: www.northstarmusic.com. **Contact:** Richard Waterman, president. Record company. Estab. 1985. Staff size: 15. Releases 12-16 LPs/year. Pays 9% royalty to artists on contract; ¾ statutory rate to publisher per song on record.

Distributed by: Alliance, Goldenrod and Lady Slipper.

How to Contact: Submit demo CD by mail. Unsolicited submissions are OK. Prefers finished CD. Does not return material. Responds in 2 months.

Music: Mostly **instrumental**, **traditional** and **contemporary jazz**, **New Age**, **traditional world (Cuban, Brasilian, singer/songwriter, Hawaiian and Flamenco)** and **classical**. Released *Mother* (album), written and recorded by Susan McKeown/Cathie Ryan/Robin Spielberg (instrumental); *Mysts of Time* (album), written and recorded by Aine Minogue (Celtic chant); and *Crossing the Waters* (album by Steve Schuch), recorded by Steve Schuch and the Night Heron Consort (contemporary Celtic), all on North Star Music. Other artists include Judith Lynn Stillman, David Osborne, Emilio Kauderer, Gerry Beaudoin, Cheryl Wheeler and Nathaniel Rosen.

◎ **NPO RECORDS, INC.**, P.O. Box 41251, Staten Island NY 10304. Phone/fax: (718)967-6121. E-mail: nporecords@hotmail.com. Website: www.nporecords.com or www.Anomos.com. **Contact:** Erin McCavatelli, vice president. Record company and music publisher (NPO Records and Music Publishing). Estab. 1996. Releases 6 singles, 2 LPs, 2 CDs/year. Pays negotiable royalty to artists on contract; statutory rate to publisher per song on record.

How to Contact: We only accept material referred to us by a reputable industry source (manager, entertainment attorney, etc.).

Music: Mostly **hip-hop** and **dance**. Released "Playing No Games" (single by Anomes/Stealth/Potent Pete) from *From Here On* (album), recorded by Anomos/Stealth (hip-hop); "Show Gee The Money" (single by Gee Money/Potent Pete) from *Show Gee The Money* (album), recorded by Gee Money (hip-hop); and "Something" (single by Allie Gally/Potent Pete) from *The EP* (album), recorded by Allie (R&B), all released 2000 on NPO Records.

Tips: "Be open minded and accepting of constructive criticism. Self-discipline and professionalism are essential."

N ◎ **OGLIO RECORDS**, 507-A Pier Ave., Hermosa Beach CA 90254. (310)791-8600 or (800)266-5237. Fax: (310)791-8670. Contact: Kevin Knight. Record company. Estab. 1992. Releases 20 LPs and 20 CDs/year. Pays negotiable royalty to artist on contract; statutory rate to publisher per song on record.

How to Contact: *Write first and obtain permission to submit.* Accepts demos in all formats. Does not return material. Responds in 6 weeks.

Music: Mostly **alternative rock** and **comedy**.

◎ **OMEGA RECORD GROUP, INC.**, 27 W. 72nd St., New York NY 10023. (212)769-3060. Fax: (212)769-3195. E-mail: info@omegarecords.com. Website: www.omegarecords.com. Sales Manager (pop, jazz, dance): Duane Martuge. Operations Manager (classical, jazz): Frank Burton. Labels include Vanguard Classics and Everest. Record company. Estab. 1989. Releases 5 singles and 60-70 CDs/year. Pays negotiable royalty to artists on contract.

Distributed by: Allegro Corporation.

How to Contact: Submit demo tape by mail. Unsolicited submissions are OK. Prefers cassette, CD or DAT. Include SASE. Responds in 3 weeks.

Music: Mostly **classical** and **jazz**.

◎ **ONLY NEW AGE MUSIC, INC.**, 8033 Sunset Blvd. #472, Hollywood CA 90046. (323)851-3355. Fax: (323)851-7981. E-mail: onam@loop.com. Website: www.newagemusic.com or www.new ageuniverse.com. **Contact:** Suzanne Doucet, president. Record company, music publisher and consulting firm. Estab. 1987.

How to Contact: *Call first and obtain permission to submit.* Does not return material.

Music: Mostly **New Age**; also **world music**.

Tips: "You should have a marketing strategy and at least a small budget for markteing your product."

✔ ◎ **OUTSTANDING RECORDS**, P.O. Box 2111, Huntington Beach CA 92647. (714)377-7447. Fax: (714)377-7468. Website: www.outstandingmusic.com. **Contact:** Earl Beecher, owner. Labels include Morrhythm. Record company, music publisher (Earl Beecher Publishing) and record producer (Earl Beecher). Estab. 1968. Staff size: 1. Releases 20 CDs/year. Pays $2/CD royalty to artists on contract; statutory rate to publisher per song on record.

Distributed by: Sites on the Internet.

How to Contact: Submit demo tape by mail. Unsolicited submissions are OK. Prefers cassette, CD or videocassette (VHS) with 3 songs, lyric sheet, photo and cover letter. Include SASE. Responds in 3 weeks.

Music: Mostly **jazz**, **rock** and **country**; also **everything else especially Latin.** Does not want music with negative, anti-social or immoral messages. Released "Stay With Me" (single by Vic Garcia) from *Sounds of Love* (album), recorded by Ron Brown and Mike Sharp's Balboa Brass (pop), released 2000 on Outstanding; "Hey Mr. Eastwood" (single) from *Gator Brown* (album), written and recorded by Richard Murray (country); and "Timidez" (single) from *Love for the World* (album), written and recorded by Vic Garcia (Latin), both released 2001 on Morrhythm. Other artists include Ron Brown, Paul Smith, Varouge Merdjanian, Greg Doumanian and James Long.

Tips: "Keep selections short (three to three and a half minutes). Short intros and fade outs (if any). No dirty language. Do not encourage listeners to use drugs, alcohol or engage in immoral behavior. I'm especially looking for upbeat, happy, danceable music."

P. & N. RECORDS, 61 Euphrasia Dr., Toronto, Ontario M6B 3V8 Canada. (416)782-5768. Fax: (416)782-7170. **Contact:** Panfilo Di Matteo and Nicola Di Matteo, presidents, A&R. Record company, record producer and music publisher (Lilly Music Publishing). Estab. 1993. Staff size: 2. Releases 10 singles, 20 12″ singles, 15 LPs, 20 EPs and 15 CDs/year. Pays 25-35% royalty to artists on contract; statutory rate to publisher per song on record.

How to Contact: Submit demo tape by mail. Unsolicited submissions are OK. Prefers cassette or videocassette with 3 songs and lyric or lead sheet. Does not return material. Responds in 1 month only if interested.

Music: Mostly **dance**, **ballads** and **rock**. Released *Only This Way* (album), written and recorded by Angelica Castro; *The End of Us* (album), written and recorded by Putz, both on P. & N. Records (dance); and "Lovers" (single by Marc Singer), recorded by Silvana (dance), released 2001 on P. and N. Records.

P.M. RECORDS, P.O. Box 19332, Indianapolis IN 46219-0100. (317)897-2545. E-mail: justtony @indy.net. Website: www.simplytony.com. A&R Directors: John Pelfrey Jr. (country/blues); Tony Mansour (pop, rock). Assistant A&R: Lisa Jack (country); Lori Ellis (rock). Labels include Tomahawk Records. Record company and record producer. Estab. 1998. Staff size: 10. Releases 5 singles, 4 LPs and 4 CDs/year. Pays negotiable royalty to artists on contract; statutory rate to publisher per song on record.

How to Contact: Submit demo tape by mail. Unsolicited submissions are OK. Prefers cassette, CD or videocassette with 3 songs, lyric sheet and lead sheet. "Please specify music style on envelope. Vocals must be clear." Include SASE. Responds in 6 weeks.

Music: Mostly **rock**, **country** and **blues**; also **pop**. Does not want rap. Released "Alibi" (single by Tony Manseur) from *The "Simply Tony" Show* (album), recorded by Simply Tony (pop/rock), released 2000 on P.M. Records; and "All I Wanna Do . . . Is You" (single by John Pelfrey Jr.) from *Cherokee* (album), recorded by J.W. Bach (country rock), released 2000 on Tomahawk.

Tips: "Remember, music is a business. Only serious-minded individuals need apply. Supply as much information as possible."

PACIFIC TIME ENTERTAINMENT, P.O. Box 7320, FDR Station, New York, NY 10150. (212)741-2888. Fax: (845)708-0113. E-mail: pactimeco@aol.com. Website: www.pactimeco. com. **Contact:** Curtis Urbina, president. Record company. Estab. 1998. Staff size: 4. Releases 2 singles and 20 CDs/year. Pays negotiable royalty to artists on contract; ¾ rate to publisher per song on record.

Distributed by: Navarre Corporation.

How to Contact: *Call first and obtain permission to submit.* Prefers CD with 3 songs. Responds in 1 month.

Music: Film scores. Released "The Son's Room" (single by N. Piovani) from *The Son's Room* (album), recorded by Nicola Piovani (soundtrack); and "Keep on Keeping On" (single by M. Serio) from *Entertainers* (album), recorded by Bel Mondo (pop), both released 2001 on Pacific Time Entertainment. Other artists include Nana Simpoulos, Jimmy Earl, Psonica, Mark P. Adler and Scotch Egg.

PAINT CHIP RECORDS, P.O. Box 12401, Albany NY 12212. (518)765-4027. E-mail: paintch ipr@aol.com. **Contact:** Dominick Campana, owner/producer. Record/production company. Estab. 1992. Staff size: 1. Releases 2 CDs/year. Pays negotiable royalty to artists on contract; statutory rate to publisher per song on record.

Distributed by: Paint Chip Records.

How to Contact: Submit demo tape by mail. Unsolicited submissions are OK. Prefers cassette with 4 songs. Does not return material. Responds in several weeks only if interested.

Music: Mostly **"alternative" guitar rock** (bands). Released "Hollywood" (single by Pendergast) from *WEQXclusives* (album), recorded by The Wait (alternative rock), released 2001 on Arms; *Holding on Line One* (album by Pendergast/Barnum), recorded by The Wait, released 2001 on Paint Chip; and *Dear Soul* (album by Pendergast/Barnum), recorded by The Wait, released 2000 on Paint Chip.

Tips: "Do not submit music if you haven't heard of any of the artists on this label. Do not submit music if you are not currently performing. Do not submit music if you don't think your work is absolutely amazing. Do not phone without written permission."

◯ PBM TALENT & PUBLISHING, (formerly Take 2 Records), 107 Music City Cirle, Suite 106, Nashville TN 37214. (615)886-7200. Owner: Michele Mize. A&R (country): Barbara Gauvin. Record company. "PBM also coordinates talent for a country-variety TV show from Nashville and assists in casting for local movies shot in Nashville, TN." Estab. 1990. Releases 1-2 products/year. Pays negotiable royalty to artists on contract; pays statutory rate to publisher per song on record.

Distributed by: PBM Publishing.

How to Contact: *Write or call first and obtain permission to submit.* Prefers CD, cassette or VHS videocassette with lyric sheet, photo and bio. Does not return material. Responds in 8 months. "We do not respond to or return unrequested material."

Music: Mostly **country**. Released "Big Tennessee River" (single), written and recorded by T. Greggs (country), released on Take 2 Records; "Don't Touch Me" (single by Hank Cochran), "Half A Mind" (single by Roger Miller) and "You're Not the Only Heart In Town" (single by Lonnie Wilson), all recorded by Michele Gauvin (country), released on PBM Records. Other artists include Jim Woodrum and Gloria.

Tips: "Please pull shrink wrap from CDs and cassettes submitted."

[N] ◯ PENTACLE RECORDS, P.O. Box 5055, Laguna Beach CA 92652. (949)494-3572. E-mail: pentaclerx@aol.com. Head Honcho: Bara Waters. Production Guru: Robert Cassard. Record company. Estab. 1991. Pays negotiable royalty to artists on contract.

How to Contact: *Write first and obtain permission to submit.* Prefers cassette or CD with lyric sheet. "We like photos and information (bio, etc.) about the artist. Have you performed live? Reviews?" Does not return material. Responds in 6 weeks.

Music: Mostly **AAA**, **modern rock** and **AOR**. Released *Get This* (by Waters/Cassard), recorded by Cassard (rock); *Roux* and "Trying Too Hard" (by Doug Rouhier), both recorded by Roux (rock/AAA), all on Pentacle Records. Other artists include Guillotine, Goose and Love Tribe.

Tips: "We are small and very selective. We look for music that is melodic and interesting with lyrics that reflect a unique point of view. We are looking for artists who can sustain a career of innovative, creative work that changes the way listeners view themselves and their lives. Nothing typical please! If you think, "My stuff sounds as good as the stuff on the radio,' don't bother with us. Move forward until your music is better, different. Push yourself until your music is a contribution to the world, not just more clutter."

◯ PGE PLATINUM GROOVE ENTERTAINMENT, P.O. Box 2877, Palm Beach FL 33480. (561)775-4561. Fax: (561)775-4562. E-mail: Brian@PGEcd.com. Website: www.PGEcd.com or www.561.net. Record company and music publisher (Advantage 1000 Music). Estab. 1993. Staff size: 5. Releases 8 singles, 8 LPs and 7 CDs/year. Pays negotiable royalty to artists on contract; statutory rate to publisher per song on record.

How to Contact: Submit demo tape by mail. Unsolicited submissions are OK. Prefers CD. Does not return material. Responds in 1 month.

◼ ⊕ SENDING TO A COUNTRY other than your own? Be sure to send International Reply Coupons (IRCs) instead of stamps for replies or return of your materials.

Music: Mostly **hip hop, R&B** and **dance**; also **drum n bass** and **alternative**. Does not want rock, country or garbage. Released *Face Off II* (album), written and recorded by various (rap); *Cali Things* (album), written and recorded by various (rap); and *Double Platinum* (album), written and recorded by DJ X. Travagant, all released on Platinum Groove Entertainment (funky breaks/dance).

☑ ◐ **PICKWICK/MECCA/INTERNATIONAL RECORDS**, P.O. Box 725, Daytona Beach FL 32115. (904)252-4849. Fax: (904 or 386)252-7402. E-mail: CharlesVickers@USALink.com. Website: www.ZYWorld.com/CharlesVickers. **Contact:** Clarence Dunklin, president. Record company and music publisher (Pritchett Publications). Estab. 1980. Releases 20 singles, 30 LPs and 30 CDs/year. Pays 5-10% royalty to artists on contract; negotiable rate to publisher per song on record.
How to Contact: Submit demo tape by mail. Unsolicited submissions are OK. Prefers cassette with 12 songs and lyric or lead sheet. Does not return material.
Music: Mostly **gospel, disco** and **rock/pop**; also **country, ballads** and **rap**. Released *Give It To Me Baby* (album by Loris Doby), recorded by Gladys Nighte; *Baby I Love You* (album), written and recorded by Joe Simmon; and *I Love Sweetie* (album by Doris Doby), recorded by Bobby Blane.

☑ ○ **PLATEAU MUSIC**, P.O. Box 947, White House TN 37188. (615)654-8131. Fax: (615)654-8207. E-mail: nville93@aol.com. Website: www.plateaumusicproductions.com. **Contact:** Tony Mantor, owner. Record company and record producer. Estab. 1990. Staff size: 1. Pays negotiable royalty to artists on contract; statutory rate to publisher per song on record.
How to Contact: Submit demo tape by mail. Unsolicited submissions are OK. Prefers cassette with 4 songs and lyric sheet. Does not return material. Responds in 6 weeks.
Music: Mostly **country, R&B** and **rock/pop**. Released *Somewhere in the Neighborhood* (album), recorded by Dobie Toms, released 1999; and *I've Got Love* (album by Sara Majors), recorded by The Weeds, both on PMI Records (country). Other artists include Mark Knight and Carlynne DeVine.
Tips: "We are a music producer that develops talent and shops them to the major labels. We do very few independent releases. Our focus is on getting the artist ready to compete in the major arena. Have dedication and be prepared to work."

⊕ ☑ ◐ **PLAYBONES RECORDS**, Symphony House, Winterhuder Weg 142, D-22085 Hamburg Germany. Phone: (040)22716552 + -53. Fax: (040)22716554. E-mail: mento_music@t-online. de. **Contact:** Michael Frommhold, head of A&R. Producer: Arno van Vught. Labels include Rondo Records. Record company, music publisher (Mento Music Group) and record producer (Arteg Productions). Estab. 1975. Releases 30 CDs/year. Pays 8-16% royalty to artists on contract; statutory rate to publisher per song on record.
How to Contact: Submit demo tape by mail. Unsolicited submissions are OK. Prefers cassette with 3-4 songs. Put your strongest/best song first. "Put your name and address on the inside sleeve of the tape. If you have a fax number, inform us. Tell us in a typed cover letter what you want/what you are looking for." Does not return material. Responds in 3 weeks.
Music: Mostly **instrumentals, country** and **jazz**; also **background music, rock** and **gospel**. Released *Paradise* (album), written and recorded by Anna C. Nova (pop); "Vergessen wir die Mark" (single by DP/Volker Frank), recorded by Volker Frank (pop); and *Lord of the Dance* (album), written and recorded by Wolfgang Bauer (world music), all released 2001 on Playbones Records. Other artists include H.J. Knipphals, Gaby Knies, Jack Hals, H. Hausmann, Crabmeat and M. Frommhold.

◐ **POLYDOR RECORDS**, 1416 N. La Brea Ave., Hollywood CA 90028. New York office: 825 Eighth Ave., 27th Floor, New York NY 10019. Website: www.harmone.com. Labels include Rocket Records. Record company.
How to Contact: Polydor Records does not accept unsolicited submissions.

☑ ○ **POWERBLAST RECORDINGS**, P.O. Box 12911, Cincinnati OH 45212. (513)751-7900. E-mail: ewc@powerblastworldwide.com. Website: www.powerblastworldwide.com. CEO: Ernest W. Coleman. Vice President: M.L. Rogers. Record company. Estab. 1992. Staff size: 6. Releases 4 CDs/year. Pays negotiable royalty to artists on contract; statutory rate to publisher per song on record.
Distributed by: Various one-stop distributors and online e-commerce sites on the Internet.

How to Contact: Submit demo tape by mail. Unsolicited submissions are OK. Prefers CD, cassette or videotape (VHS) with 3 songs and cover letter. Include SASE. Responds in 1 month if interested.

Music: Mostly **hip-hop/rap**, **alternative** and **metal**; also **jazz**, **r&b** and **New Age.** Does not want country. Released *Destructive Communication* (album), written and recorded by Bombthreat (hardcore hip hop); *Death Becomes All of 'Em* (album), written and recorded by Cutty B. Spooky; *Explosive Material* (album), written and recorded by Bombthreat (hardcore hip hop); and *Heat* (album), written, produced and recorded by The G. Other artists include Skin Curtain, Architect Sound Design, DJ Abstrakt, Short Body and Mayhem Stompabitch.

Tips: "Be professional when making contact or approaching our company."

⊙ PPL ENTERTAINMENT GROUP, P.O. Box 8442, Universal City CA 91608. Phone/fax: (818)506-8534. E-mail: pplzmi@aol.com. Website: www.polzmi.com. **Contact:** Cisco Crowe, vice president A&R. Vice President A&R: Jaeson Effantic. Vice President, A&R: Kaitland Diamond. General Manager: Jim Sellavain. President, Creative: Suzette Cuseo. Labels include Bouvier and Credence. Record company, music publisher (Pollybyrd Publications) and management firm (Sa'mall Management). Estab. 1979. Staff size: 3. Releases 10-30 singles, 12 12″ singles, 6 LPs and 6 CDs/year. Pays 10-15% royalty to artists on contract; statutory rate to publisher per song on record.

Distributed by: Sony and The Malibu Trading Company.

How to Contact: *E-mail and obtain permission to submit.* Prefers cassette or videocassette with 2 songs. Include SASE. Responds in 6 weeks.

Music: Released "I Am Sorry" (single) from *JR Perry* (album), written and recorded by JR Perry (gospel), released 2001 on PPL/Sony; "I Don't Want to Be Alone" (single by Jarrett/Cuseo) from *Phyne I Can B.* (album), recorded by Phyne (pop), released 2001 on PPL/Sony; and "Steel Hat, Cold Heart" (single by Ken Allen) from *Destiny* (album), recorded by Buddy Wright (blues), released 2001 on PPL. Other artists include Phuntaine, Condottiere and D.M. Groove.

⊙ PRAVDA RECORDS, 6311 N. Neenah, Chicago IL 60631. (773)563-7509. Fax: (773)763-3252. E-mail: pravdausa@aol.com. Website: pravdamusic.com. **Contact:** Mo Goodman, director of A&R. A&R (pop/rock): Matt Favazza. Labels include Bughouse. Record company. Estab. 1985. Releases 3-6 singles, 1 EP and 5-6 CDs/year. Pays 10-15% royalty to artists on contract; statutory rate to publisher per song on record.

Distributed by: Hep Cat, Columbia House and Carrot Top.

How to Contact: Submit demo tape by mail. Unsolicited submissions are OK. Prefers cassette or CD with 3-4 songs. Does not return material. "Will contact only if interested."

Music: Mostly **rock**. Released "Slipped Away" (single by Dag Juhlin) from *Junior* (album), recorded by The Slugs (pop); "Paralyzed" (single) from *Live In Chicago* (album), written and recorded by Legendary Stardust Cowboy (psychobilly); and "The Freshman 15 (fifteen)" (single) from *Sticky* (album), written and recorded by The New Duncan Imperials (alternative rock), all released 2000 on Pravda. Other artists include Tiny Tim, Frantic Flattops, Gringo, Javelin Boot and cheer-accident.

Tips: "Be nice! Tour behind your release, don't take yourself too seriously."

◯ PRESENCE RECORDS, 67 Candace Lane, Chatham NJ 07928-1115. (201)701-0707. **Contact:** Paul Payton, president. Record company, music publisher (Paytoons/BMI) and record producer (Presence Productions). Estab. 1985. Staff size: 1. Pays 1-2% royalty to artists on contract; statutory rate to publisher per song on record.

Distributed by: Clifton Music.

How to Contact: Submit demo tape by mail. Unsolicited submissions are OK. "No phone calls." Prefers cassette or CD with 2-4 songs and lyric sheet. Include SASE. Responds in 1 month. "Tapes and CDs not returned without prepaid mailer."

Music: Mostly **doo-wop ('50s)**, **rock** and **new wave rock**. "No heavy metal, no 'Christian' or religious rock." Released "Ding Dong Darling," "Bette Blue Moon" and "Davilee/Go On" (singles by Paul Payton/Peter Skolnik), recorded by Fabulous Dudes (doo-wop), all on Presence Records.

Tips: "Would you press and distribute it if it was *your* money? Only send it here if the answer is yes."

⊘ PRIORITY RECORDS, 6430 Sunset Blvd., Suite 900, Hollywood CA 90028. (323)467-0151. Fax: (323)856-8796. Website: www.priorityrec.com. New York office: 32 W. 18th St., 12th Floor, New York NY 10011. (212)627-8000. Fax: (212)627-5555. A&R: Ray/Rae. Labels include No Limit Records, Rawkus Records, Hoo-Bangin' Records and Duck Down Records. Record company.
Distributed by: EMD.
How to Contact: *Does not accept unsolicited submissions.*
Music: Artists include Ice Cube, Snoop Dogg, Big Moe and Dilated Peoples.

[N:] ⊘ Q RECORDS, 1200 Wilson Dr., West Chester PA 19380-4262. (484)701-1580. Fax: (484)701-1988. Senior Director A&R: Dana Kasha-Murray. General Manager: Alan Rubens. A&R: Dana Kasha-Murray. Record company, music publisher. Estab. 1999. Staff size: 8. Releases 16 CDs/ year. Pays negotiable royalty to artists on contract; negotiable rate to publisher per song on record.
Distributed by: Atlantic Records/WEA.
How to Contact: *Write first and obtain permission to submit.* Prefers CD with press clippings. Does not return material. Responds only if interested.
Music: Mostly **rock**, **pop**, **jazz** and **classical**. Released *Footloose: Original Bradway Cast Recording* (album), recorded by the original Broadway cast (soundtrack); and *"American Bandstand" Library of Rock 'n' Roll*, written and recorded by various.

⊘ QUARK RECORDS, P.O. Box 7320, FDR Station, New York NY 10150 or 4 E. 12th St., New York NY 10003. (212)741-2888. E-mail: quarkent@aol.com. **Contact:** Curtis Urbina, president (pop, dance). A&R: Michelle Harris (alternative). Labels include Pacific Time Entertainment. Record company and music publisher (Quarkette Music/BMI and Freedurb Music/ASCAP). Estab. 1984. Releases 6 singles and 3 LPs/year. Pays negotiable royalty to artists on contract; ¾ statutory rate to publisher per song on record.
How to Contact: *Call first and obtain permission to submit.* Prefers CD with 2 songs. Include SASE. Responds in 6 weeks.
Music: Mostly **dance/pop**. Released "Throwback" (single by E. Cohen) from *Party Time* (album), recorded by DJ Strebe (dance); "Being With You" (single by M. Adler) from *Flagstaff, AZ* (album), recorded by Mark P. Adler (pop); and "Ant & The Sky" (single by C. Urbina) from *Highbridge Gardens* (album), recorded by Curtis Urbina (spoken word), all released 2002 on Quark Records.

◯ RADICAL RECORDS, 77 Bleecker St., Suite C2-21, New York NY 10012. (212)475-1111. Fax: (212)475-3676. E-mail: info@radicalrecords.com. Website: www.radicalrecords.com. **Contact:** Johnny Chiba, A&R. Record company. "We also do independent retail distribution for punk, hardcore music." Estab. 1986. Staff size: 7. Releases 1 single and 6 CDs/year. Pays 14% royalty to artists on contract; statutory rate to publisher per song on record.
Distributed by: Caroline, City Hall, Revelation, Select-O-Hits, Revolver, Choke.
How to Contact: *E-mail first for permission to submit demo.* Prefers cassette or CD. Does not return material. Responds in 1 month.
Music: Mostly **punk** and **hardcore**. Released *Too Legit for the Pit—Hardcore Takes the Rap* (album), recorded by various; *Punk's Not Dead—A Tribute to the Exploited* (album), recorded by various; *Fresh Out of Give-a-Fucks* (album), recorded by Submachine; and *East Coast of Oi!* (album), recorded by various. Other artists include The Agents, Social Scare, Blanks 77 and Inspector 7.
Tips: "Create the best possible demos you can and show a past of excellent self-promotion."

◯ RAGS TO RECORDS, INC., P.O. Box 42523, Washington DC 20015. E-mail: info@ragstorec ords.com. Website: www.ragstorecords.com. **Contact:** John Meyer, president, A&R. Record company. Estab. 1997. Releases 1-2 single per CD and 1-4 CDs/year. Pays 10-80% royalties to artists on contract based on sliding scale of total sales and initial company outlay (see website for details); statutory rate to publisher per song on record.
How to Contact: Submit CD or tape by mail. Unsolicited submissions are OK. Prefers CD or tape with 3 or more songs. Does not return material. Responds only if interested.

Music: Mostly **rock**; also **anything loosely classifiable as rock**. Released *Six Pack of Shame* (album), written and recorded by Battery Apple; and *Dakota Floyd* (album), written and recorded by Dakota Floyd, both released 2001, both on Rags To Records.

Tips: "Be confident and be good. RTR is not in the business of holding people's hands while they get their acts together. It is a small company that invests extremely small amounts of money into acts which have already spent considerable time and effort making their music sound good. If you suck, we're not going to call you in the hopes that you get better later on; we're going to ignore you and possibly laugh at you."

RAMPANT RECORDS, 2406 Gates Ave., Redondo Beach CA 90278. (310)546-2896. Fax: (520)396-2515. E-mail: rampant@earthlink.net. Website: www.rampantrecords.com. Vice President of A&R: Paul Grogan. Labels include Slinkey Recordings. Record company, music publisher (Nipple Fish Music Company) and record producer (Paul Grogan). Estab. 1993. Releases 3 LPs, 10 EPs and 2 CDs/year. Pays negotiable royalty to artists on contract; 75% rate to publisher per song on record.

Distributed by: Watts Music, Nemesis Distribution, T.R.C., Syntax, Intergroove and Magestic.

How to Contact: *Check website before submitting.* Submit demo tape by mail. Unsolicited submissions are OK. Prefers cassette with 3 songs. "Supply contact info on cassette and cassette box cover." Does not return material. Responds in 3 weeks.

Music: Mostly **progressive house**, **trance** and **big beat**; also **techno**, **jungle** and **funky breaks**. Does not want pop or electronica. Released *Tempest* (by J. Scotts/J. Blum), recorded by Deepsky (progressive house); and *Hush*, written and recorded by Joshua Ryan and Forefield (trance), both on Slinkey; and *Fly Mutha Beatz* (by Chris Brown), recorded by Brownie on Rampant (big beat/funky breaks). Other artists include Pablo, The Coffee Boys and Ascendance.

Tips: "We are looking for tracks that will rock a dance floor. Solid, well produced, underground tracks only."

RAVE RECORDS, INC., 13400 W. Seven Mile Rd., Detroit MI 48235. E-mail: info@raverecords.com. Website: www.raverecords.com. **Contact:** Carolyn and Derrick, production managers. Record company and music publisher (Magic Brain Music/ASCAP). Estab. 1992. Staff size: 2. Releases 2-4 singles and 2 CDs/year. Pays various royalty to artists on contract; statutory rate to publisher per song on record.

Distributed by: Action Music Sales.

How to Contact: *Does not accept unsolicited submissions.*

Music: Mostly **alternative rock** and **dance**. Artists include Cyber Cryst, Dorothy, Nicole and Bukimi 3.

RAZOR & TIE ENTERTAINMENT, 214 Sullivan St., Suite 4A, New York NY 10012. (212)473-9173. E-mail: info@razorandtie.com. Website: www.razorandtie.com. Record company.

How to Contact: *Does not accept unsolicited material.*

Music: Released *Cry, Cry, Cry* by Dar Williams; *The Sweetheart Collection* by Frankie & The Knockouts; and *Everybody's Normal But Me* by Stuttering John, all on Razor & Tie Entertainment. Other artists include Cledus T. Judd, Graham Parker and Mare Winningham.

RCA RECORDS, 1540 Broadway, 36th Floor, New York NY 10036. (212)930-4000. Fax: (212)930-4447. Website: www.bmg.com/labels/rca.html. A&R: David Bendeth; David Novik; Brian Malouf; Steve Ferrera; Steve Ralbovsky. Beverly Hills office: 8750 Wilshire Blvd., Beverly Hills

**FOR EXPLANATIONS OF THESE SYMBOLS,
SEE THE INSIDE FRONT AND BACK COVERS OF THIS BOOK.**

insider report

Multi-faceted singer-songwriter builds independent career

"Pop is such a fickle word," says Nina Storey, "It's just whatever sells a million records." Indeed, her reviewers have shown the same confusion, using the label "pop" right next to "blues," "gospel," "jazz," "rock," and "soul" in describing her music. Even her venues can't pin her down: Woodstock and Lillith Fair, to the Santa Cruz Blues Festival, to the Montreal International and New Orleans Jazz Festivals. "I enjoy a lot of different sounds," she says and her latest album, *Nina Storey* (Red Lady Records, 2002) serves as new evidence of her eclectic tastes.

Nina Storey

A child in a family of musicians, she grew up surrounded by music. Her father was the sound engineer for Frank Sinatra and Barry Manilow and her mother was a songwriter and producer. But it wasn't until she was 15 years old that she considered the career for herself. Her mother Jan—now also her manager—was working on a production project for MCA that needed a backup singer. Enter Nina. After astounding Leon Ware, award-winning producer, with her voice, the project became her first solo recording, a five-song EP. Since then she has been on many national and international tours, opening for names like Earth, Wind and Fire, The Allman Brothers and Joan Osborne.

All of your work so far had been through your own company. How did you choose to be independent?
Well, being independent was just decided. I mean, all my projects have been on my own, with my own company. I don't know if it was by default or whatever, but it's always been that way. My mom does 99 percent of the work. She does the booking, she runs the office wonderfully, she does everything. I work with her on stuff, but I could never take credit for all the work she does. I also have a film and television music agent in Los Angeles that places music with different projects. But in terms of my role in the company, I kind of go where I'm needed. My dad is the sound engineer and when I tour he's my sound man, so we're a family of multi-taskers.

What kind of international tours have you done?
I did some military tours, played for the troops in Bosnia, Macedonia, and various other safe places. They were unbelievable and pretty intense. You know, being any place so devastated by war is eye opening. We played on an aircraft carrier in the middle of the Mediterranean and that was huge. My sister, my mom and I were the only girls among a thousand men.

You must have needed a lot of connections for these national and international performances. How did these come about, say, for the USO tours?
Well, in that case, someone who was working in the USO contacted us. She said "You should

really try this, this is great," playing overseas for the troops. And it was an opportunity to travel. So we found out who to contact, and it happened.

Do you think taking opportunities such as that help you build a network of connections in the music industry?

Yes. As time goes by you inevitably meet more people and you develop more relationships. So you're constantly trying to expand on that, getting opportunities to work with great musicians. And when you travel you have the opportunity to go and hear other things that expose you to new people. It's definitely a process that takes time. You hear stories all the time where people say "I was just on the subway, then the next day I was on the cover of *Rolling Stone*." That only happens once in a million years. In '99 I played for a ridiculous number of people at Woodstock and the next day I played at a bookstore. It's just a process to go through like anything else.

Would you say that your experiences "with the process" have taught you about the business along the way?

Oh, yeah! You learn more from the wrong choices than the right ones. I've met my share of questionable people and I've met a handful of quality, quality people—the type you try to associate with. Unfortunately, that's the nature of music. But it's like that with anything.

How do you figure out that something is good?

First off, for example, in a situation where someone comes up to you and says, "Hey, I want to manage you," you definitely always have to follow your intuition. I believe in those things. It's easy to quell those feelings and think, "Oh, maybe I'm overreacting." But I also think it's important to research people that you want to work with on a major scale. Meeting musicians that just want to go jam is one thing, but serious business ventures are different. As I tell you these things, I'm telling myself as well—you have to be educated about the decisions. There are a lot of resources now, a lot of industry books about how to protect yourself legally and how to make the right choices. Also, surround yourself with people you trust and people who don't have a vested interest in your career but in you as a person. But even then, sometimes it's a crap-shoot. You just have to say, "Well, let's see what happens!"

You've had quite a bit of commercial success. Has that ever made you feel drawn to write toward the market?

In the span of my writing career I've run the gamut from wacky, experimental to really trying to write a commercial song. Again, what may sound commercial may never sell a million records. If you sell that many records you're inevitably popular. But, because I've written in all these different ways, I try to guide what I'm writing in terms of what I'm trying to get across in that specific song. I try to be true to what feels right in the song, whatever shape it takes. I don't record a lot of 18-minute songs, but in my live show there may a song that explores a lot of different moods, and has an epic feel to it. I'm conscious of the constructs of radio-friendly music, but at the same time I'm always writing what I want to write.

How has your songwriting process changed throughout your career?

I've definitely become more conscious of things. I liken when I first started to painting in the dark. I had some control, but not a lot. But now, the lights are starting to come on. Though the universe is still very, very dark, I'm more conscious of making moves that will give different

> sounds or help the story along. I'm a little more analytical. Sometimes I'll hear a song and think, "Wow. That melody is really cool, why do I like it?" Sometimes, things just come out of your shoe and don't need to be broken apart or anything. I'm in a higher state of consciousness now, which, I guess could be good or bad, but I think it just comes with living. But also, the more you know, the more you realize you don't know.
>
> **What kinds of things are you trying to express in your lyrics?**
> Well, I don't have overall themes with my music or my lyrics. But, there do tend to be things that stand out. Stylistically, there are strong blues influences, there's a strong funky, soulful sound. Lyrically, I've written a lot of music about overcoming personal pain. My new album goes from old school 70's funk to a weird, spacey rock and piano, vocals/theatrical song. I believe that an album always tells a story. The way that the songs are placed even on the record are instrumental in terms of the mood. I always want to be telling a story. I want to be saying something.
> —*Amy Ratto*

CA 90211. (310)358-4000. Fax: (310)358-4040. Senior Vice President of A&R: Bruce Flohr. Nashville office: 1 Music Circle N., Nashville TN 37203. (615)301-4300. Website: www.twangthis.com. A&R Director: Sam Ramage. Director of Artist Development: Debbie Schwartz. Labels include Loud Records, Deconstruction Records and Judgment/RCA Records. Record company.
Distributed by: BMG.

- In 2000, RCA won Grammy Awards for Best Instrumental Arrangement ("Chelsea Bridge," by Don Sebesky); Best Historical Album (*The Duke Ellington Centennial Edition*); and Best Classical Engineered Album (*Stravinsky: Firebird; The Rite of Spring; Persephone*).

How to Contact: *RCA Records does not accept unsolicited submissions.*
Music: Released *'N Sync* (album), recorded by 'N Sync; and *Capitol Punishment* (album), recorded by Big Punisher, both on RCA Records. Other artists include Foo Fighters, Vertical Horizon, Eve 6, Robyn and Dave Matthews Band.

☑ ⊕ ⊘ **RED SKY RECORDS**, P.O. Box 27, Stroud, Glos. GL6 0YQ United Kingdom. Phone: 01453-836877. Fax: 01453-836877. Website: www.redskyrecords.co.uk. **Contact:** Johnny Coppin, producer. Record company and record producer (Johnny Coppin). Estab. 1985. Staff size: 1. Releases 1 album/year. Pays 8-10% to artists on contract; statutory rate to publisher per song on record.
Distributed by: ADA, CM.
How to Contact: *Write first and obtain permission to submit.* Does not return material. Responds in 6 months.
Music: Mostly **rock/singer-songwriters**, **modern folk** and **roots music**. Released *The Dolan Brothers* (album), written and recorded by Dolan Brothers (blues); *A Journey* (album), written and recorded by Johnny Coppin (singer/songwriter); and *Dead Lively!* (album), written and recorded by Paul Burgess (folk) on Red Sky Records. Other artists include David Goodland.

☑ ◯ **REDEMPTION RECORDS**, P.O. Box 10238, Beverly Hills CA 90213. (323)651-0221. Los Angeles: (323)651-0221. E-mail: rkuper@redemption.net. Website: www.redemption.net. A&R Czar: Ryan D. Kuper (hardcore punk, indie rock, power pop). Record company. Estab. 1990. Staff size: varies. Releases 2-3 singles, 2-3 EPs and 2-3 CDs/year. Pays standard royalty to artists on contract; statutory rate to publisher per song on record.
Distributed by: Lumberjack.
How to Contact: Submit demo tape by mail or send mp3 link by e-mail. Prefers e-mail or phone call for permission to submit. "We accept links to websites too. Include band's or artist's goals." Does not return material. Responds only if interested.

Music: Mostly **indie rock** and **power pop**. Artists include Andy Dick & The Bitches of the Century, Not From Space (members of Sunny Day Real Estate, Seaweed, and Verbal Assault), The Eye, Downer, Vendetta Red, Schatzi, Real (members of Supertouch and American Stnadard), With.This.-Life, Citrus and others.

Tips: "Be prepared to tour to support the release. Make sure the current line-up is secure."

RED-EYE RECORDS, Wern Fawr Farm, Pencoed, Mid-Glam CF35 6NB United Kingdom. Phone: (01656)86 00 41. **Contact:** M.R. Blanche, managing director. Record company and music publisher (Ever-Open-Eye Music/PRS). Estab. 1979. Releases 4 singles and 2-3 LPs/year. Pays negotiable royalty to artists on contract; statutory rate to publisher per song on record.

How to Contact: Submit demo tape by mail. Unsolicited submissions are OK. Prefers cassette, VHS videocassette or CD with 4 songs. SAE and IRC. Does not return material.

Music: Mostly **R&B**, **rock** and **gospel**; also **swing**. Released "River River" (single by D. John), recorded by The Boys; and "Billy" (single by G. Williams); and "Cadillac Walk" (single by Moon Martin), both recorded by the Cadillacs, all on Red-Eye Records. Other artists include Cartoon and Tiger Bay.

REPRISE RECORDS, 3300 Warner Blvd., 4th Floor, Burbank CA 91505. (818)846-9090. Fax: (818)840-2389. New York office: 75 Rockefeller Plaza, 21st Floor, New York NY 10019. (212)275-4500. Fax: (212)275-4596. Website: www.repriserec.com. Labels include Duck. Record company.

Distributed by: WEA.

How to Contact: *Reprise Records does not accept unsolicited submissions.*

Music: Released *The Dance* (album), recorded by Fleetwood Mac; *Stunt* (album), recorded by Barenaked Ladies on Reprise; and *Pilgrim* (album), recorded by Eric Clapton on Duck. Other artists include Wilco, Paul Brandt, Chaka Khan, Brady Seals, Arkarna, Dinosaur Jr., Depeche Mode and Green Day.

ROAD RECORDS, P.O. Box 2620, Victorville CA 92393. Website: www.roadrecords.com. **Contact:** Conrad Askland, president. Record company, record producer (Road Records) and music publisher (Askland Publishing). Estab. 1989. Produces 6 singles and 10 albums/year.

How to Contact: *Write or call first and obtain permission to submit.* Prefers at least 3 songs with lyric and lead sheet. Does not return submissions. Responds in 3 weeks.

Music: Mostly **alternative**, **modern country** and **dance**; also **orchestral instrumental**. Does not want jazz. Released "You're the Best Lie" (single by Gailyn Addis and Conrad Askland) from *Gailyn Addis* (album), recorded by Gailyn Addis (pop/AC), released 2001 on Road Records; and *Blues and Me* (album), recorded by Freddy Fender (Tex-Mex), released 2002 on Freddy Records.

Tips: "Do not submit what you think we are looking for. A lot of our projects are 'on the edge.' We are looking for people that have a different, original sound. We supply music to Grand Ole Opry, United Airlines, Knoxbury Farm and G.T.E."

ROBBINS ENTERTAINMENT LLC, 159 W. 25th St., 4th Floor, New York NY 10001. (212)675-4321. Fax: (212)675-4441. E-mail: info@robbinsent.com. **Contact:** John Parker, director of A&R. Record company and music publisher (Rocks, No Salt). Estab. 1996. Staff size: 8. Releases 25 singles and 12-14 CDs/year. Pays negotiable royalty to artists on contract; statutory rate to publisher per song on record.

Distributed by: BMG.

How to Contact: Accepts unsolicited demos as long as it's dance music.

Music: Commercial **dance** only. Released "This Kind of Love" (single by Meg Hentges/Jude O'Nym), and *Brompton's Cocktail* (album by Meg Hentges/Jude O'Nym/Adam Schlesinger), both recorded by Meg Hentges (modern rock); and "When I'm Gone" (single by A. Hammond/H. Payne), recorded by Rockell (dance/pop), all on Robbins Entertainment. Other artists include Ian Van Dahl, Rockell, Dee Dee, Lasgo, Cynthia, Geoprge Lamond, DJ Sammy, Laut Sprecher, Sulk.

Tips: "We are looking for original, but accessible music, with crossover potential."

◘ **ROLL ON RECORDS**®, 112 Widmar Pl., Clayton CA 94517. (925)833-4680. E-mail: rollonrec ords@aol.com. **Contact:** Edgar J. Brincat, owner. Record company and music publisher (California Country Music). Estab. 1985. Releases 2-3 LPs/cassettes/year. Pays 10% royalty to artists on contract; statutory rate to publisher per song on record.
Distributed by: Tower.
How to Contact: Submit demo tape by mail. Unsolicited submissions are OK. Do not call or write. Prefers cassette with 3 songs and lyric sheet. Include SASE. Responds in 6 weeks.
Music: Mostly **contemporary/country**, **MOR** and **R&B**; also **pop**, **light rock** and **modern gospel**. Released "Broken Record" (single by Horace Linsley/Dianne Baumgartner), recorded by Edee Gordon on Roll On Records; *Maddy* and *For Realities Sake* (albums both by F.L. Pittman/Madonna Weeks), recorded by Ron Banks/L.J. Reynolds on Life Records/Bellmark Records.
Tips: "Be patient and prepare to be in it for the long haul. A successful songwriter does not happen overnight. It's rare to write a song today and have a hit tomorrow. If you give us your song and want it back, then don't give it to us to begin with."

✓ ◘ **RUF RECORDS**, 162 N. 8th St., Kenilworth NJ 07033. (908)653-9700. E-mail: rufpublicist @aol.com. **Contact:** Mike DeUrso, marketing manager. General Manager: Ira Leslie. Record company, music publisher and record producer (Thomas Ruf). Estab. 1993. Releases 12 CDs/year. Pays negotiable royalty to artists on contract; statutory rate to publisher per song on record.
Distributed by: IDN.
 • Ruf is known for releasing blues.
How to Contact: Write or call Mike to obtain permission to submit. Does not return material. Responds in 1 week.
Music: Mostly **blues**, **rock** and **R&B**. Released by Nighthawks, Larry Garner and Buddy Miles. Other artists include Walter Trout and Canned Heat.

N ✓ ◘ **RUFFNATION RECORDS**, 101 Charles Dr., 2nd Bldg., Bryn Mawr PA 19010. (610)520-3050. Fax: (610)520-3066. CEO: Chris Schwartz. COO: Kevin Glickman. President: Helen Little. Executive Vice President/General Manager: Robert Dippold. U.K. Office: 3 St. Quintin Ave., London W10 6NX. United Kingdom. 44-208-932-2860. Fax: 44-208-960-0787. E-mail: lucvergier@r uffination.com. Record company, music publisher (Ruffhouse Publishing) and record producer (Joseph "The Butcher" Nicolo). Estab. 1999. Staff size: 20. Releases 20 singles and 6 LPs/year. Pays negotiable royalty to artists on contract.
Distributed by: Warner Bros. Distribution.
How to Contact: Submit demo tape by mail. Unsolicited submissions are OK. Prefers cassette, CD, DAT or videocassette. "Please place phone number on actual listening component." Does not return material. Responds in 3 months.
Music: Mostly **rap**, **R&B** and **rock artists**; also **songwriters of any music style**. Released *Miseducation of Lauryn Hill*, written and recorded by Lauryn Hill on Ruffhouse/Columbia/Sony (rap/R&B). Other artists include Cypress Hill, Kris Kross, The Fugees, Outsidaz, Peacewon, Bobby Ross Avila and Leela James.
Tips: "Be original, spend time on the production of the demo CD not the packaging. Have patience when shopping and let someone else help. If we like the music, we will call you"

◘ **RUSTRON MUSIC PRODUCTIONS**, 1156 Park Lane, West Palm Beach FL 33417-5957. (561)686-1354. E-mail: gordon-whims@juno.com. **Contact:** A&R. Executive Director: Rusty Gordon (folk fusions, blues, women's music, adult contemporary, electric, acoustic, New Age instrumentals, children's, cabaret). Director A&R: Ron Caruso. Associate Director of A&R: Kevin Reeves (pop, country, blues, R&B, jazz). Labels include Rustron Records and Whimsong Records. "Rustron administers 20 independent labels for publishing and marketing." Record company, record producer,

---

TO HELP YOU UNDERSTAND and use the information in these listings, see "How to Use *Songwriter's Market* to Get Your Songs Heard," on page 5.

management firm and music publisher (Whimsong/ASCAP and Rustron Music/BMI). Estab. 1970. Releases 5-10 cassettes and CDs/year. Pays variable royalty to artists on contract. "Artists with history of product sales get higher percent than those with no sales track record." Pays statutory rate to publisher.

How to Contact: *Write or call first to discuss your submission* or submit demo tape or CD by mail. Unsolicited submissions are OK. Prefers CD or cassette with 3 songs and typed lyric sheet. "If singer/ songwriter has independent product (cassette or CD) produced and sold at gigs—send this product." SASE required for all correspondence, no exceptions. Responds in 4 months.

Music: Mostly **mainstream** and **women's music**, **A/C electric acoustic**, **pop (cabaret, blues)** and **blues (R&B, country and folk)**; also **New Age fusions** (instrumentals), **modern folk fusions**, **environmental** and **socio-political**. Released "America and Her Enemies" (single by Stacie Jubal) from *Time For Topical Again* (album), recorded by Stacie Jubal (folk rock), released 2001 on Whimsong Records; "Take a Closer Look" (single by Jeremy White) from *Back on the Island* (album), recorded by Jeremy White (Yankee reggae), released 2001 on Whimsong Records; and "Rainbow" (single by Eric Shaffer and Rusty Gordon) from *The Triangle and the Rainbow* (album), recorded by Song on a Whim (folk rock), released 2001 on Rustron Records.

Tips: "Find your own unique style; write well crafted songs with unpredictable concepts, strong hooks and definitive melody. New Age composers: evolve your themes and add multi-cultural diversity with instruments. Don't be predictable. Don't over-produce your demos and don't drown vocals. Send cover letter clearly explaining your reasons for submitting. Carefully craft songs for single-song marketing."

◻ SABTECA RECORD CO., P.O. Box 10286, Oakland CA 94610. (510)465-2805. Fax: (510)832-0464. E-mail: vitaminsun@aol.com. **Contact:** Duane Herring, president. Production Coordinator (pop, R&B, jazz): Sean Herring. Secretary (pop, R&B, country): Lois Shayne. Labels include André Romare Records. Record company and music publisher (Sabteca Music Co./ASCAP, Toyiabe Music Co./BMI). Estab. 1980. Releases 3 singles and 1 12″ single/year. Pays 10% royalty to artists on contract; statutory rate to publisher per song on record.

Distributed by: Sabteca.

How to Contact: *Write first and obtain permission to submit.* Prefers cassette with lyric sheet. Include SASE. Responds in 1 month.

Music: Mostly **R&B**, **pop** and **country**. Released "On the Good Side" (single by Thomas Roller), recorded by Johnny B (pop), released 2000 on Sabteca. Other artists include Walt Coleman, Lil Brown, Reggie Walker and Lois Shayne.

Tips: "Determination and persistence are vital."

◻ SAFIRE RECORDS, 5617 W. Melvina, Milwaukee WI 53216. Phone/fax: (414)444-3385. **Contact:** Darnell Ellis, president. A&R Representatives: Darrien Kingston (country, pop); Reggie Rodriqez (world, Latin, Irish). Record company, music publisher (Buzz Duzz Duzz), record producer (Darnell Ellis) and management firm (The Ellis International Talent Agency). Estab. 1997. Staff size: 2. Releases 3 singles, 3 LPs, 1 EP and 3 CDs/year. Pays negotiable royalty to artists on contract; statutory rate to publisher per song on record.

How to Contact: Submit demo tape by mail. Unsolicited submissions are OK. Prefers cassette with 3-4 songs. Does not return material. Responds in 2 months. "We will respond only if we are interested."

Music: Mostly **country**, **pop**, **mainstream pop**, all styles of **rock** and anything else except **rap** or **hip-hop**. Artists include Anthony Vincent (country).

Tips: "Songwriters need to get back to the basics of songwriting: great hooklines, strong melodies. We would love to hear from artists and songwriters from all over the world. And remember, just because someone passes on a song it doesn't mean that it's a bad song. Maybe it's a song that the label is not able to market or the timing is just bad."

☑ ▨ ⊘ SAHARA RECORDS AND FILMWORKS ENTERTAINMENT, 28 E. Jackson Bldg., 10th Floor #S627, Chicago IL 60604-2263. (773)509-6381. Fax: (312)922-6964. **Contact:** Edward De Miles, president. Record company, music publisher (EDM Music/BMI, Edward De Miles

Music Company) and record producer (Edward De Miles). Estab. 1981. Releases 15-20 CD singles and 5-10 CDs/year. Pays 9½-11% royalty to artists on contract; statutory rate to publishers per song on record.

How to Contact: *Does not accept unsolicited submissions.*

Music: Mostly **R&B/dance**, **top 40 pop/rock** and **contemporary jazz**; also **TV-film themes**, **musical scores** and **jingles**. Released "Hooked on U," "Dance Wit Me" and "Moments" (singles), written and recorded by Steve Lynn (R&B) on Sahara Records. Other artists include Lost in Wonder, Dvon Edwards and Multiple Choice.

Tips: "We're looking for strong mainstream material. Lyrics and melodies with good hooks that grab people's attention."

SALEXO MUSIC, P.O. Box 18093, Charlotte NC 28218-0093. (704)392-2477. E-mail: salexo @bellsouth.net. **Contact:** Samuel Obie, president. Record company. Estab. 1992. Releases 1 CD/ year.

How to Contact: *Write first and obtain permission to submit.* Prefers cassette with 3 songs and lyric sheet. Include SASE. Responds in 1 month.

Music: Mostly **contemporary gospel** and **jazz**. Released "Make A Joyful Noise" (single by Samuel Obie) from *Edwin Hawkins Music & Arts Seminar/Los Angeles*, recorded by Edwin Hawkins (gospel), released 2001 on World Class Gospel Records.

Tips: "Make initial investment in the best production."

SATELLITE MUSIC, 34 Salisbury St., London NW8 8QE United Kingdom. Phone: (+44)207-402-9111. Fax: (+44)207-723-3064. E-mail: eliot@amimedia.co.uk. Website: www.amime dia.co.uk. **Contact:** Eliot Cohen, CEO. Director: Ray Dorset. Labels include Saraja and Excalibur. Record company and music publisher. Estab. 1976. Staff size: 10. Releases 5 singles, 3 LPs and 3 CDs/year. Pays negotiable royalty to artists on contract; statutory rate to publisher per song on record.

Distributed by: S. Gold & Sons and Total Home Entertainment.

• Satellite Music won two ASCAP awards in 1996 for Top R&B Song of the Year and Top Rap Song of the Year in the U.S.

How to Contact: Submit demo tape by mail. Unsolicited submissions are OK. Prefers cassette, CD, DAT or VHS videocassette with 4 songs, cover letter and press clippings. SAE and IRC. Responds in 6 weeks.

Music: Mostly **dance**, **disco** and **pop**. Does not want blues, jazz or country. Released "In the Snow" (by Ray Dorset), recorded by Mungo Jerry on BME (pop).

SEAFAIR/BOLO RECORDS, (formerly Satin Records), P.O. Box 632, Snohomish WA 98291-0632. (206)546-3038. E-mail: jwiverson@aol.com. **Contact:** John W. Iverson, partner. Labels include Satin Records. Record company and music publisher (Bolmin Publishing/BMI). Estab. 1982. Releases 2 singles, 4 LPs, 1 EP and 4 CDs/year. Pays negotiable royalty to artists on contract; statutory rate to publisher per song on record.

Distributed by: City Hall Records.

How to Contact: *Write first and obtain permission to submit.* Prefers cassette, DAT or CD with lyric sheet. Include SASE. "Will not return materials without SASE." Responds in 2 months.

Music: Mostly **R&B**, **jazz** and **rock**. Released *Private Jungle* (by various), recorded by The Slamhound Hunters (blues/rock); *Sweet Harmony* (by various), recorded by The Main Attraction (R&B), both on Satin Records; *The Transparent Two* (by various), recorded by UNT Two O'Clock Band on Bolo Records (jazz); and *Framed* (album by Lars Emerick/Steve Damm), recorded by Monotone Pictures (modern rock), released 2000 on Seafair-Bolo.

SELECT RECORDS, 19 W. 21st St., Suite 1004, New York NY 10010. (212)691-1200. Fax: (212)691-3375. E-mail: selectrec@aol.com. President, A&R: Fred Munao. Record company and music publisher (ADRA/Hittage). Estab. 1980. Releases 8 singles, 3-4 LPs, 10 singles on CD and 3 albums on CD/year. Pays negotiable royalty to artists on contract; statutory rate to publisher per song on record.

Distributed by: ADA.

How to Contact: *Call first and obtain permission to submit*. Prefers cassette, CD or VHS videocassette with 3-4 songs and lyric sheet. "All bios/information should be typewritten." Does not return material.

Music: Mostly **rap**, **R&B** and **dance**; also **comedy**. Released *Ground Zero* written and recorded by Cash & Computa (rap); *Dirty, Dirty Dawgn*, written and recorded by Mega Thenom (rap); and *The World Ain't Ready*, written and recorded by Ike Dirty (rap).

Tips: "Submit strongest efforts only. Lyrical content is very important, as is the ability to construct strong hooks and being current, music should retain some original flavor."

☑ ◙ **SILTOWN RECORDS**, 1 Park Plaza, Suite 600, Irvine CA 92614. (949)474-5050. Fax: (949)367-1078. E-mail: asp@siltown.com. Website: www.siltown.com. **Contact:** Alban Silva, CEO. Vice President/A&R: Greg Jensen. A&R, Christian/Gospel: Barbara Anderson. A&R, Rap/Hip Hop: Robert Davis. Record company. Estab. 1998. Staff size: 5. Releases 2 singles and 2 CDs/year.
Distributed by: On website.
How to Contact: Submit demo tape by mail. Unsolicited submissions are OK. Prefers CD, DAT with lyric sheet, cover letter and press clipping. Does not return material. Responds in 6 weeks.
Music: Mostly **pop/rock**, **Christian** and **country**; also **rap**, **hip-hop**, **all genres**.
Tips "Submit songs and music that are preferably in digital mode. Submit lyric sheet and send only your best CD. If your are interested in free exposure of your music, submit CD, a recent color photograph of band, and a short biography of thirty words or less. Please visit our website for format."

◙ **SILVER WAVE RECORDS**, P.O. Box 7943, Boulder CO 80306. (303)443-5617. Fax: (303)443-0877. E-mail: info@silverwave.com. Website: www.silverwave.com. **Contact:** James Marienthal. Record company. Estab. 1986. Releases 4-5 CDs/year. Pays varying royalty to artists on contract and to publisher per song on record.
How to Contact: *Write first and obtain permission to submit*. Prefers CD. Include SASE. Responds only if interested.
Music: Mostly **world** and **Native American**.

☑ ◙ **SIN KLUB ENTERTAINMENT, INC.**, P.O. Box 2507, Toledo OH 43606. (419)475-1189. E-mail: es3@worldnet.att.net. Website: www.sinklub.com. (419)475-1189. President/A&R: Edward Shimborske III. Labels include Sin-Ka-Bob Records. Record company, music publisher (Morris St. James Publishing) and record producer (ES3). Estab. 1990. Releases 1 single, 1 LP and 5 CDs/year. Pays negotiable royalty to artists on contract; statutory rate to publisher per song on record.
Distributed by: MAD.
How to Contact: Submit demo tape by mail. Unsolicited submissions are OK. Prefers cassette or CD with 3 songs and lyric sheet. "Send a good press kit (photos, bio, articles, etc.)." Does not return material. Responds in 1 month.
Music: Mostly **harder-edged alternative**, **punk** and **metal/industrial**; also **rap**, **alternative** and **experimental**. Released *Urban Witchcraft* (album), recorded by Thessalonian Dope Gods (industrial), released 1994; *All Balled Up* (album), recorded by Bunjie Jambo (punk), released 1996, both on Sin Klub. Other artists include Kid Rock, Dan Hicks, Lucky Boys Confusion, Crashdog, The Geminus Sect, Evolotto, Kitchen Conspiracy, Valve and Three Below.

🆖 ◙ **SMALL STONE RECORDS**, P.O. Box 02007, Detroit MI 48202. (248)546-1206. Fax: (313)871-4840. E-mail: sstone@smallstone.com. Website: www.smallstone.com. Owner: Scott Hamilton. Record company. Estab. 1995. Staff size: 1. Releases 2 singles, 2 EPs and 10 CDs/year. Pays negotiable royalty to artists on contract; statutory rate to publisher per song on record.
Distributed by: Action, Baker & Taylor.
How to Contact: Submit CD/CD Rom by mail. Unsolicited submissions are OK. Does not return material. Responds in 2 months.
Music: Mostly **alternative**, **rock** and **blues**; also **funk (not R&B)**. Released *Fat Black Pussy Cat*, written and recorded by Five Horse Johnson (rock/blues); *Wrecked & Remixed*, written and recorded by Morsel (indie rock, electronica); and *Only One Division*, written and recorded by Soul Clique (electronica), all on Small Stone Records. Other artists include 36-D, Roundhead, Perplexa.

Tips: "Looking for esoteric music along the lines of Bill Laswell to Touch & Go/Thrill Jockey records material. Only send along material if it makes sense with what we do. Perhaps owning some of our records would help."

SMITHSONIAN FOLKWAYS RECORDINGS, 750 9th St. NW, Suite 4100, Washington DC 20560-0953. (202)275-1144. Fax: (202)275-1164. E-mail: folkways@aol.com. Website: www.fol kways.si.edu. **Contact:** Daniel Sheehy, curator/director. Labels include Smithsonian Folkways, Dyer-Bennet, Cook and Paredon. Record company and music publisher. Estab. 1948. Releases 25 CDs/year. Pays negotiable royalty to artists on contract and to publisher per song on record.
Distributed by: Koch International.
How to Contact: *Write first and obtain permission to submit or to arrange personal interview.* Prefers CD or DAT. Does not return material. Responds in 6 months.
Music: Mostly **traditional US folk music, world music** and **children's music.** Released *Best of Broadside* (album), recorded by various artists (folk); *Vocal Music in Crete* (album), recorded by various artists (world/folk); and *Songs, Rhythms & Chants for the Dance* (album), recorded by Ella Jenkins (children's), all released 2000 on Smithsonian Folkways Recordings. "We only are interested in music publishing associated with recordings we are releasing. Do not send demos of songwriting only."
Tips "If you are a touring artist and singer/songwriter, consider carefully the advantages of a non-museum label for your work. We specialize in ethnographic and field recordings from people around the world."

SOLANA RECORDS, 2440 Great Highway, #5, San Francisco CA 94116. E-mail: solana@ mindspring.com. Website: www.solanarecords.com. **Contact:** Eric Friedmann, president. Record company, music publisher (Neato Bandito Music) and record producer (Eric Friedmann). Estab. 1992. Staff size: 1. Releases 1 single and 2 CDs/year. Pays negotiable royalty to artists on contract; statutory rate to publisher per song on record.
How to Contact: Submit demo tape by mail but *please e-mail for permission first.* Prefers CD with 3-5 songs, photo and cover letter. Include SASE. Responds in 1 month.
Music: Mostly any kind of guitar/vocal-based **rock/pop** and **country.** Does not want rap, hip-hop, metal or canned instrumentation of any sort. Released *Spacious* (by Valerie Moorhead), recorded by Enda (alternative rock); *Livin' the High Life* (by James Cook), recorded by The Wags (hardcore); and *The Grain* (by Rick Ordin), recorded by The Grain (progressive rock). *To Hell with the Road*; and *Live at the Sandbox*, recorded by Delectric (Skiffle).Other artists include The Detonators, Eric Friedman and the Lucky Rubes, The Mudkats and Doormouse.
Tips: "Be honest and genuine. Know how to write a good song, and know how to sing. Don't send my your resumé or life story please. Big bonus points for Telecaster players."

SONAR RECORDS & PRODUCTION, P.O. Box 8095, Fort Worth TX 76112-0001. (817)531-9979. Fax: (817)451-1066. E-mail: sonarrecords@hotmail.com. Website: http://sonarprodu ctions.com. Artist Development: Ken Moody (Moodini). Vice President Urban Music: William Collins. A&R: Geo Clinton and Shana Holyfield. Labels include Sounds of New Artist Recordings. Record producer (Sonar, Moodini). Estab. 1994. Staff size: 4. Releases 3 singles, 1 LP, and 1 CD/year. Pays 12% royalty to artists on contract; statutory rate to publisher per song on record.
Distributed by: WEA.
How to Contact: Submit demo tape by mail. Unsolicited submissions are OK. Prefers CD. Does not return material. Responds in 1 month if interested.
Music: Mostly **positive rap, non-vulgar hip-hop** and **gospel**; also **contemporary gospel.** Artists include Nuwine, Locaine, XL, OX, Peaches and Huzzy, Sons of Abraham and Shank.

MARKET CONDITIONS are constantly changing! If you're still using this book and it is 2004 or later, buy the newest edition of *Songwriter's Market* at your favorite bookstore or order directly from Writer's Digest Books at (800)289-0963.

Tips "Invest in yourself and others will follow."

☑ ◐ **SONIC RECORDS, INC./SRI RECORDS, INC./SRI RECORDS, INC.**, 157 Woodburn Place, Advance NC 27006. (336)940-5736. Fax: (336)940-5736. E-mail: srecords@bellsouth.net. Website: www.sonicrecords.com. **Contact:** George Thompson, Assistant to the President. President: Doug Thurston. Vice President: Bobby Locke. Vice President, Public Relations: Debbie Anderson Locke. Record company and music publisher (Sonrec Music Publisher/BMI). Estab. 1964. Pays negotiable royalty to artists under contract.
Distributed by: Bertus and Self.
How to Contact: Submit demo tape or CD/CDR by mail. Unsolicited submissions are OK. Prefers cassette, CD, DAT or VHS videocassette with up to 3 songs and lyric or lead sheet. Does not return material. Responds ASAP.
Music: Mostly **country**, **gospel alternative** and **rock**. Released "White Wine & Red Roses" (single by Richard Olsen) from *Shooting Star* (album), recorded by Richard Olsen (traditional country), released 2001 on Sonic Records; "I Believe in Miracles" (single by Michael Johnson) from *I Believe in Miracles* (album), recorded by Michael Johnson (gospel), released 2001 on Sonic/SRI; and "Used to Be" (single by Blake Scott) from *Island of Life* (album), recorded by Island of Life (AAA), released 1998 on Sonic.
Tips: "Sonic and SRI are associated with a national television show 'Fast Track To Fame' which is aired weekly via satellite and the AmericaOne television network. Fast Track also has 'Specials' which appear approximately every 4 weekss on 'The National Network' which was formerly the Nashville Network. They also have clips on 'Great American Country' as well as their own network on www.fasttracktofame.tv with live shows Sunday through Wednesday nights at 9:30 eastern/6:30 pacific and continuous music video programming 24 hours a day. Only independent and new artists are broadcast."

✿ ◯ **sonic unyon records canada**, P.O. Box 57347, Jackson Station, Hamilton, Ontario L8P 4X2 Canada. (905)777-1223. Fax: (905)777-1161. E-mail: jerks@sonicunyon.com. Website: www.sonicunyon.com. Co-owners: Tim Potocic; Mark Milne. Record company. Estab. 1992. Releases 2 singles, 2 EPs and 6-10 CDs/year. Pays negotiable royalty to artists on contract; statutory rate to publisher per song on record.
Distributed by: NAIL Distribution.
How to Contact: *Call first and obtain permission to submit.* Prefers cassette or CD. "Research our company before you send your demo. We are small; don't waste my time and your money." Does not return material. Responds in 4 months.
Music: Mostly **rock**, **heavy rock** and **pop rock**. Released *Doberman* (album), written and recorded by Kittens (heavy rock); *What A Life* (album), written and recorded by Smoother; and *New Grand* (album), written and recorded by New Grand on sonic unyon records (pop/rock). Other artists include Tricky Woo, Danko Jones, Crooked Fingers, Frank Black and the Catholics, Jesus Lizard, Chore, Sectorseven, The Dirtmitts, Sianspheric, gorp, Hayden and Poledo.
Tips: "Know what we are about. Research us. Know we are a small company. Know signing to us doesn't mean that everything will fall into your lap. We are only the beginning of an artist's career."

◐ **SOUND GEMS**, P.O. Box 801, South Eastern PA 19339. (215)552-8889. Website: www.soundgems.com. CEO: Frank Fioravanti. A&R Director: Trish Wassel. Record company and music publisher (Melomega Music, Meloman Music). Estab. 1972. Staff size: 3. Pays negotiable royalty to artists on contract; statutory rate to publisher per song on record.
Distributed by: EMI, Sony, Warner.
How to Contact: Submit demo tape by mail. Unsolicited submissions are OK. Prefers cassette, CD with lyric sheet, cover letter and press clipping. "Do not send registered or certified mail." Does not return material. Responds only if interested.
Music: **R&B** only. Released "Be Thankful" (single by William Devaughn) from *Bones* (soundtrack album), recorded by William DeVaughn (r&b), released 2001 on PRI; and "Limo Dream" (single by Hopkins/Rakes/Fioravanti), recorded by Corey (r&b), released 2001 on Sound Gems.
Tips: "Be sure your style fits our catagory. Submit R&B material only."

⬤ **SOUTHLAND RECORDS, INC.**, P.O. Box 1547, Arlington TX 76004-1547. (817)461-3280. E-mail: SteveReed@SouthlandRecords.com. Website: www.SouthlandRecords.com. **Contact:** Steve Reed, president. Record company and record producer (Steve Reed). Estab. 1980. Releases 12 CDs/year. Pays negotiable royalty to artists on contract; statutory rate to publisher per song on record.
How to Contact: Submit demo tape or CD by mail. Unsolicited submissions are OK. Prefers cassette or CD with 4 songs, lyric and lead sheet, cover letter and press clippings. Does not return material. Responds in 3 months.
Music: **Country** only. Artists include Leon Rausch, Rob Dixon, Bob Willis & the Texas Playboys, Ron Gaddis, Tommy Allsup, Jake Hooker, Curtis Potter and Darrell McCall.

✔ ⬤ **SPOTLIGHT RECORDS**, P.O. Box 6055, Hilliard OH 43026-6055. (614)771-5242. Fax: (614)771-5401. E-mail: spotlight3@prodigy.net. Website: ww.spotlightrecords.homestead.com. **Contact:** James Bruce, owner. Record company. Estab. 1994. Staff size: 7. Releases 2 CDs/year. Pays negotiable royalty to artists on contract; statutory rate to publisher per song on record.
How to Contact: Submit demo tape by mail. Unsolicited submissions are OK. Prefers CD or cassette with lyric sheet. Does not return material. Responds only if interested.
Music: Mostly **country**, **pop** and **Christian**. Released *Seasons* (album by Jason Waller), recorded by Mudslut (rock), released 2002 on Spotlight Records; *That's the Way*, recorded by Debbie Collins (country), released 1995 on Spotlight Records; *Only In a Picture* (album by various), recorded by Brandi Lynn Howard (country); and *Sings the Hits* (by various), recorded by Brandi Lynn Howard (country).
Tips: "Submit your best work. Be very professional."

⬤ **STARDUST**, 341 Billy Goat Hill Rd., Winchester TN 37398. (931)649-2577. Fax: (615)649-2732. E-mail: cbd@vallnet.com. Website: www.stardustcountrymusic.com. **Contact:** Barbara Doss, president. Labels include Stardust, Wizard, Doss, Kimbolon, Thunder Hawk, Flaming Star. Record company, music publisher (Buster Doss Music/BMI), management firm (Buster Doss Presents) and record producer (Colonel Buster Doss). Estab. 1959. Releases 50 singles and 25 CDs/year. Pays 8-10% royalty to artists on contract; statutory rate to publisher per song on record.
How to Contact: *Write first and obtain permission to submit.* Prefers cassette with 2 songs and lyric sheet. Include SASE. Responds "on same day received."
Music: Mostly **country**; also **rock**. Released "Come On In" (single), recorded by Duane Hall on Stardust Records and "Rescue Me" (single), recorded by Tommy D on Doss Records. Other artists include Linda Wunder, Rooster Quantrell, Sky, James Bryan, Donna Darlene, Jerri Arnold and "Bronco" Buck Cody.

Ⓝ ⬤ **STARGARD ENTERTAINMENT**, P.O. Box 138, Boston MA 02101. (617)696-7474. E-mail: stargardmusic@cs.com Owner/President: Charles Greenaway. **Contact:** Janice Tritto, artist relations (all types). Labels include Oak Groove Records. Record company, music publisher (Zatco Music/ASCAP and Stargard Publishing/BMI) and record producer. Estab. 1985. Releases 9 singles and 1 LP/year. Pays 5-8% royalty to artists on contract; statutory rate to publisher per song on record.
How to Contact: Submit demo tape by mail. Unsolicited submissions are OK. Prefers cassette and lyric sheet. Include SASE. Responds in 3 months. "Sending bio along with picture or glossies is appreciated but not necessary."
Music: Released "Broken Hearts," written and recorded by Chris Simpson (r&b); and "Darling I" (by Floyd Wilcox), recorded by Lou Bello (r&b), both released 1999 on Stargard Records. Other artists include Tee Rex.

⬤ **STREET RECORDS**, P.O. Box 1356, Folly Beach SC 29439. E-mail: rock@streetrecords.com. Website: www.streetrecords.com. Director of A&R: Tasos. A&R: Conner Lewis; MJ Shutrump; Bettina Torello. Labels include Kretan Sea Records. Record company, music publisher (Kretan Sea Music) and record producer (Tasos). Estab. 1983. Staff size: 5. Releases 4 singles, 2 EPs and 5 CDs/year. Pays negotiable or 13% royalty to artists on contract; statutory rate to publisher per song on record.

Distributed by: Southern Records (USA), Southern Studios (UK and parts of Europe), Sonic Unyon (Canada), Hitch-Hyke (Greece) and WEA (parts of Europe/select releases).
How to Contact: *No unsolicited material. Check website for submission policy.*
Music: Mostly **rock**, **pop** and **punk**; also **folk**, **garage** and **indie**. Does not want rap, metal or country. Released *You Should Enjoy Getting Screamed At!* (album by Thomas Crouch/Bryan Biggart), recorded by F13 (punk); *The Rock Garden* (album by band collective), recorded by Eurogression (rock); and *Hutches of Gunch* (album by Eric Baylies), recorded by Baylies Band (rock), all on Street Records. Other artists include Aberdeen Lizards, Desaru, the Cigs, Onassis and Wax American, Tampered and DeadMeat.
Tips: "Are you ready to tour and give up most luxuries for two years?"

☑ ⊘ **STRUGGLEBABY RECORDING CO.**, 2612 Erie Ave., P.O. Box 8369, Cincinnati OH 45208-8369. (513)871-1500. Fax: (513)871-1510. E-mail: strugglebaby@cinci.rr.com. **Contact:** Sam Richman, A&R/professional manager. Record company, music publisher and record producer (Hal Bernard Enterprises). Estab. 1983. Releases 5-8 CDs/year. Pays negotiable royalty to artists on contract; statutory (per contract) rate to publisher per song on record.
How to Contact: Submit demo tape by mail. Prefers CD with maximum 3 songs. "Positive responses only—no materials returned."
Music: Mostly **modern rock**, **rock** and **R&B**. Released *Through My Eyes* (album), written and recorded by Bromwell-Diehl Band (AAA), released 2001 on Bash; *Live At The Celestial* (album), recorded by Mary Ellen Tanner (jazz), released 2000; and *Stream of Consciousness* (album), recorded by Lee Stolar (jazz), released 2001 by Strugglebaby Recording Co.
Tips: "Keep it simple, honest, with a personal touch. Show some evidence of market interest and attraction value as well as the ability to tour."

☑ ◯ **SUNCOUNTRY RECORDS**, 2709 W. Pine Lodge, Roswell NM 88201. (505)622-2008. E-mail: willmon5@bigfoot.com. **Contact:** Ray Willmon, president, A&R. A&R: Jack Burns. Record company and music publisher (Pecos Valley Music). Estab. 1989. Releases 1-2 singles, 1 CD/year. Pays 2-10% royalty to artists on contract; statutory rate to publisher per song on record.
How to Contact: Submit demo tape by mail. Unsolicited submissions are OK. "No phone calls please—we will accept by mail." Prefers cassette, CD or VHS videocassette with 2 songs maximum and lyric sheet. Include SASE. Responds in 3 months.
Music: County only, some **gospel**. Released "So It's Over" (single by Mel Farmer); "Some Day" (single by Mel Farmer); and "Wait on Me" (single by Mel Farmer), all recorded by Mel Farmer (country), released 2002 on SunCountry Records. Other artists include Joe Farmer and Jack Taylor.

ℕ ◪ **SUNDANCE RECORDS**, 907 Baltimore St., Mobile AL 36605-4653. (251)716-6995. E-mail: arp4ceg@hotmail.com. A&R Director: Mr. Antonio Pritchett. Record company. Estab. 1989. Staff size: 3. Releases 12 singles, 15 LPs, 6 EPs and 15 CDs/year. Pays negotiable royalty to artists on contract; statutory rate to publisher per song on record.
How to Contact: Submit demo tape by mail. Unsolicited submissions are OK. Prefers CD or VHS videocassette with 3-6 songs, lyric sheet, cover letter and press clippings. "Make sure you put your best effort in the product." Include SASE. Responds in 2 months.
Music: Mostly **R&B**, **rap** and **jazz**; also **blues**, **rock** and **gospel**. Released *Poverty to Riches* (by Domonic Laforce), recorded by Da Force (rap); *Alana* (by Antonio R. Pritchett), recorded by Alana (jazz/R&B); and *Messenger*, written and recorded by Messenger (Christian rock), all on SunDance. Other artists include Spice, O.G.K.B., Red T, Mob and Head Rush.

✿ ◪ **SUN-SCAPE ENTERPRISES LIMITED**, P.O. Box 793, Station F, Toronto, Ontario M4Y 2N7 Canada. (905)951-3155. Fax: (905)951-9712. E-mail: info@sun-scape.com. Website: www.sun-scape.com. Estab. 1973. Releases 2 LPs and 2 CDs/year. Pays negotiable royalty to artists on contract.
Distributed by: Christie and Christie, Music Design, Valley Records, New Leaf Distributing and Backroads.
• See the listing for Star-Scape in the Classical & Performing Arts section.

How to Contact: *Call first and obtain permission to submit.* Call for submission requirements. Does not return material. Responds in 1 month.

Music: Mostly **choral**, **new age** and **contemporary classical**. Released *Promethean Fire, Arrival of the Unexpected* and *Let Robots Melt* (albums), all written and recorded by Kenneth G. Mills (New Age); and *Tonal Persuasions, Vol. II* (album), written by Kenneth G. Mills/various, recorded by New Star-Scape Singers (choral), all on Sun-Scape Records.

Ⓩ SURESHOT RECORDS, P.O. Box 9117, Truckee CA 96162. (530)587-0111. E-mail: alanred@ telis.org. Website: www.alanredstone.com. **Contact:** Alan Redstone, owner. Record company, record producer and music publisher. Estab. 1979. Releases 1 LP/year. Pays statutory rate to publisher per song on record.

How to Contact: *Write or call first and obtain permission to submit.* Include SASE. Responds in 1 week.

Music: Mostly **country**, **comedy**, **novelty** and **blues**.

Tips: "Read up and learn to submit properly. Submit like a pro."

◪ ◯ SYNERGY RECORDS, 1609 Harwood St., Suite 7, Vancouver, British Columbia V6G 1Y1, Canada. (604)687-5747. Fax: (604)687-8528. E-mail: darren@synergyrecords.com. Website: www.synergyrecords.com. Project Manager: Darren Staten. Record company, music publisher (Nubian Music) and record producer (Darren Staten). Estab. 1998. Staff size: 3. Releases 2 singles and 2 LPs. Pays negotiable royalty to artists on contract; statutory rate to publisher per song on record.

Distributed by: Fusions Distribution.

How to Contact: Submit demo tape by mail. Unsolicited submissions are OK. Prefers cassette, CD with 3-4 songs, lyric sheet, cover letter and press clipping. Does not return material. Responds in 3 weeks.

Music: Mostly **pop**, **dance**, **rock,** and **R&B**; also **electronica** and **hip-hop**. Does not want punk, hard rock, traditional country.

Tips: "We are looking for great songs with memorable melodies that are perfect for radio and for pop writers/artists. Production is not that important for pop writers/artists. For club-oriented artists, you must be innovative and unique. All potential artists must be *driven, committed, talented* and have an interesting image."

☑ ◯ TANGENT® RECORDS, P.O. Box 383, Reynoldsburg OH 43068-0383. (614)751-1962. Fax: (614)751-6414. E-mail: info@tangentrecords.com. **Contact:** Andrew Batchelor, president. Director of Marketing: Elisa Batchelor. Record company and music publisher (ArcTangent Music/BMI). Estab. 1988. Staff size: 3. Releases 10-12 CDs/year. Pays negotiable royalty to artists on contract; statutory rate to publisher per song on record.

How to Contact: Submit demo tape or CD by mail. Unsolicited submissions are OK. Prefers cassette, CD, DAT or VHS videocassette with minimum of 3 songs and lead sheet if available. "Please include a brief biography/history of artist(s) and/or band, including musical training/education, performance experience, recording studio experience, discography and photos (if available)." Does not return material. Responds in 3 months.

Music: Mostly **artrock** and **contemporary instrumental/rock instrumental**; also **contemporary classical**, **world beat**, **smooth jazz**, **jazz/rock**, **ambient**, **electronic**, and **New Age**.

Tips: "Take the time to pull together a quality cassette or CD demo with package/portfolio, including such relevant information as experience (on stage and in studio, etc.), education/training, biography, career goals, discography, photos, etc. Should be typed. We are *not* interested in generic sounding or 'straight ahead' music. We are seeking music that is innovative, pioneering and eclectic with a fresh, unique sound."

REMEMBER: Don't "shotgun" your demo tapes. Submit only to companies interested in the type of music you write. For more submission hints, refer to Getting Started on page 10.

○ **TEXAS ROSE RECORDS**, P.O. Box 726, Terrell TX 75160-6765. (972)563-3161. Fax: (972)563-2655. E-mail: txrr1@aol.com. Website: www.texasroserecords.com. **Contact:** Nancy Baxendale, president. Record company, music publisher (Yellow Rose of Texas Publishing, Yellow Rose Petal) and record producer (Nancy Baxendale). Estab. 1994. Staff size: 3. Releases 3 CDs/year. Pays negotiable royalty to artists on contract; statutory rate to publisher per song on record.
Distributed by: Honky Tonkin' Music and self distribution.
How to Contact: Submit demo by mail. Unsolicited submissions are OK. Submit maximum of 2 songs on CD and lyrics. Does not return material. Responds in 6 weeks, only if interested.
Music: Mostly **country**, **soft rock** and **blues**; also **pop** and **gospel**. Does not want hip-hop, rap, heavy metal. Released *It Ain't Likely* (album), written and recorded by Jeff Elliot (country); *High on the Hog* (album), written and recorded by Steve Harr (country); and *The Prayer Telephone* (album), written and recorded by Dusty Martin (country/gospel), *Pendulum Dream* (album), written and recorded by Maureen Kelly and "Cowboy Super Hero" (single) written and recorded by Robert Maudlin.
Tips: "We are interested in songs written for today's market with a strong hook. Always use a good vocalist."

▦ ⊕ ○ **3RD STONE RECORDS**, (formerly 3rd Stone Ltd.), Adamson Ltd., P.O. Box 8, Corby, Northants NM7 2XZ United Kingdom. (1536)202295. Fax: (1536)266246. Label Manager: Steve Kalidoski. Labels include Space Age Recordings and Them's Good Records. Record company and music publisher (Heavy Truth Music Publishing). Estab. 1987. Releases 6 singles, 6 LPs, 6 EPs and 20 CDs/year. Pays 50% of net receipts to artists on contract; statutory rate to publisher per song on record.
How to Contact: Submit demo tape by mail. Unsolicited submissions are OK. Prefers cassette or CD with 3-4 songs. "Include contact name and telephone number on CD/tape." SAE and IRC. Responds in 3 weeks.
Music: Mostly **alternative pop/ambient pop**, **space rock/post rock lo-fi** and **punk-melodic**; also **indie/guitar bands**, **experimental electronic** and **psychedelic rock**. Released *Game Over*, written and recorded by Bark Psychosis on 3rd Stone (alternative/rock); *Forever Alien* (by Kember), recorded by Spectrum on Space Age (new electronica); and *Ext. Vacation* (by S.R. Sandall), recorded by Goober Patrol on Them's Good (punk). Other artists include Spacemen 3, Octal, Vanilla Pop, The Popguns, Mali Rain and No-Man.
Tips: "Send material stamped with your own strong identity. 3rd Stone Ltd. is a small, totally independent record label and publisher, signing and developing fledgling acts and looking to conclude world-wide licenses with their releases."

✄ ○ **THIRD WAVE PRODUCTIONS LTD.** P.O. Box 563, Gander Newfoundland A1V 2E1 Canada. (709)256-8009. Fax: (709)256-7411. Website: www.buddywasisname.com. Manager: Wayne Pittman. President: Arch Bonnell. Labels include Street Legal Records. Record company, music publisher, distributor and agent. Estab. 1986. Releases 2 singles, 2 LPs and 2 CDs/year. Pays negotiable royalty to artists on contract; statutory rate to publisher per song on record.
How to Contact: Submit demo tape by mail. Unsolicited submissions are OK. Prefers cassette, DAT and lyric sheet. Include SASE. Responds in 2 months.
Music: Mostly **folk/traditional**, **bluegrass** and **country**; also **pop**, **Irish** and **Christmas**. Released *Salt Beef Junkie* (album), written and recorded by Buddy Wasisname and Other Fellers (folk/traditional); *Newfoundland Bluegrass* (album), written and recorded by Crooked Stovepipe (bluegrass); and *Nobody Never Told Me* (album), written and recorded by The Psychobilly Cadillacs (rockabilly/country), all on Third Wave Productions. Other artists include Lee Vaughn.
Tips: "We are not really looking for songs but are always open to take on new artists who are interested in recording/producing an album. We market and distribute as well as produce albums. Not much need for 'songs' per se, except maybe country and rock/pop."

○ **THUMP RECORDS, INC.**, 3101 Pomona Blvd., Pomona CA 91768. (909)595-2144. Fax: (909)598-7028. E-mail: info@thumprecords.com. Website: www.thumprecords.com. President A&R: Bill Walker. Vice President of A&R and General Manager: Pebo Rodriguez. Labels include Thump

Street and Fama Records. Record company and music publisher (Walk-Lo/ASCAP, On the Note/ BMI). Estab. 1990. Releases 10 singles, 36 LPs, 6 EPs and 36 CDs/year. Pays 10% (negotiable) royalty to artists on contract; ¾ statutory rate to publisher per song on record.
How to Contact: Submit demo tape by mail. Unsolicited submissions are OK. Prefers CD/CDR— do not send mp3s—lyric sheet, biography and 8×10 photo. Include SASE. Responds in 1 month.
Music: Mostly **dance**, **rap** and **ballads**; also **oldies**, **classic rock** and **regional Mexican**. Released "DJ Girl" (single by Katalina). Other artists include Art Banks TDWY, Don Cisco and Jonny Z.
Tips: "Provide Thump with positive upbeat music that has universal appeal."

TOMMY BOY RECORDS, 902 Broadway, 13th Floor, New York NY 10010-6002. (212)388-8300. Fax: (212)388-8465. E-mail: mail@tommyboy.com. Website: www.tommyboy.com. Record company. Labels include Penalty Recordings, Outcaste Records, Timber and Tommy Boy Gospel.
Distributed by: WEA.
How to Contact: Call to obtain current demo submission policy.
Music: Artists include Everlast, Screwball, Amber and Capone-N-Noreaga.

TOPCAT RECORDS, P.O. Box 670234, Dallas TX 75367. (972)484-4141. Fax: (972)620-8333. E-mail: blueman@airmail.net. Website: www.topcatrecords.com. President: Richard Chalk. Record company and record producer. Estab. 1991. Staff size: 1. Releases 3-4 CDs/year. Pays 10-15% royalty to artists on contract; statutory rate to publisher per song on record.
Distributed by: City Hall.
How to Contact: *Call first and obtain permission to submit.* Prefers CD. Does not return material. Responds in 1 month.
Music: Mostly **blues**, **swing** and **R&B**. Released *If You Need Me* (album), written and recorded by Robert Ealey (blues); *Texas Blueswomen* (album by 3 Female Singers), recorded by various (blues/ R&B); and *Jungle Jane* (album), written and recorded by Holland K. Smith (blues/swing), all on Topcat. Released CDs: *Jim Suhler & Alan Haynes—Live*; Bob Kirkpatrick *Drive Across Texas*; *Rock My Blues to Sleep* by Johnny Nicholas; *Walking Heart Attack*, by Holland K. Smith. Other artists include Grant Cook, Muddy Waters, Big Mama Thornton, Big Joe Turner, Geo. "Harmonica" Smith, J.B. Hutto and Bee Houston.
Tips: "Send me blues (fast, slow, happy, sad, etc.) or good blues oriented R&B. No pop."

TRAC RECORD CO., 170 N. Maple, Fresno CA 93702. Phone/fax: (209)255-1717. E-mail: tracsell@aol.com. **Contact:** Stan Anderson, owner. Record company, record producer and music publisher (Sellwood Publishing/BMI). Estab. 1972. Releases 5 singles, 5 LPs and 2 CDs/year.
How to Contact: Submit demo tape by mail. Unsolicited submissions are OK. Prefers cassette or VHS videocassette with 2-3 songs and lyric sheet. "Demo must be clear and professionally recorded." Include SASE. Responds in 3 weeks.
Music: **Country**, **all styles** and **southern gospel**. Released *Sweet Love* (album), written and recorded by Kevin B. Willard, released 2000 on TRAC Records (country). Other artists include Jessica James and Jimmy Walker.

TRIPLE X RECORDS, P.O. Box 862529, Los Angeles CA 90086-2529. (323)221-2204. Fax: (323)221-2778. E-mail: duffxxx@usa.net. Website: www.triple-x.com. Co-owner (punk, skate, ska, reggae): Dean Naleway. Record company. Estab. 1986. Staff size: 5. Releases 25 CDs/year. Royalties not disclosed.
Distributed by: Navarre.
How to Contact: "See our web page for submission policy." Does not return material. Responds in 2 months.
Music: Mostly **rock**, **industrial/goth** and **punk**; also **blues**, **roots** and **noise**.
Tips: "Looking for self-contained units that generate their own material and are willing and able to tour."

TVT RECORDS, 23 E. Fourth St., New York NY 10003. (212)979-6410. Fax: (212)979-6489. Website: www.tvtrecords.com. **Contact:** A&R. Labels include Tee Vee Toons, TVT Soundtrax, 1001

Sundays. Record company and music publisher (TVT Music). Estab. 1986. Releases 25 singles, 20 12″ singles, 40 LPs, 5 EPs and 40 CDs/year. Pays varying royalty to artists on contract; statutory rate to publisher per song on record.

How to Contact: Send e-mail to demo-help@tvtrecords.com to receive information on how to submit your demo.

Music: Mostly **alternative rock**, **rap** and **techno**; also **jazz/R&B**. Released *Home*, recorded by Sevendust; *Hoopla*, recorded by Speeches; and *Retarder*, recorded by The Unband.

Tips: "We look for seminal, ground breaking, genre-defining artists of all types with compelling live presentation. Our quest is not for hit singles but for enduring important artists."

◯ **28 RECORDS**, 19700 NW 86 Court, Miami FL 33015-6917. Phone/fax: (305)829-8142. E-mail: rec28@aol.com. **Contact:** Eric Diaz, president/CEO/A&R. Record company. Estab. 1994. Staff size: 1. Releases 2 LPs and 4 CDs/year. Pays 12% royalty to artists on contract; statutory rate to publisher per song on record.

Distributed by: Rock Bottom-USA.

How to Contact: *Contact first and obtain permission to submit.* Submit demo tape by mail. Unsolicited submissions are OK. Prefers cassette, VHS videocassette or CD (if already released on own label for possible distribution or licensing deals). If possible send promo pack and photo. "Please put Attn: A&R on packages." Does not return material. Responds in 6 weeks.

Music: Mostly **hard rock/modern rock**, **metal** and **alternative**; also **punk** and **death metal**. Released *Julian Day* (album), recorded by Helltown's Infamous Vandal (modern/hard rock); *Fractured Fairy Tales* (album), written and recorded by Eric Knight (modern/hard rock); and *Mantra*, recorded by Derek Cintron (modern rock), all on 28 Records.

Tips: "Be patient and ready for the long haul. We strongly believe in nurturing you, the artist/ songwriter. If you're willing to do what it takes, and have what it takes, we will do whatever it takes to get you to the next level. We are looking for artists to develop. We are a very small label but we are giving the attention that is a must for a new band as well as developed and established acts. Give us a call."

◯ **UAR RECORDS (Universal-Athena Records)**, Box 1264, 6020 W. Pottstown Rd., Peoria IL 61654-1264. (309)673-5755. Fax: (309)673-7636. E-mail: uarltd@unitedcyber.com. Website: www.unitedcyber.com/uarltd. **Contact:** Jerry Hanlon, A&R director. Record company and music publisher (Jerjoy Music/BMI). Estab. 1978. Staff size: 1. Releases 1-2 singles and 1 LP/year. Pays standard royalty to artists on contract; statutory rate to publisher for each record sold.

How to Contact: Unsolicited submissions are OK. Does not return telephone calls. Prefers cassette with 4-8 songs and lyric sheet. Include SASE. "We do not critique work unless asked." Responds in 2 weeks.

Music: Mostly **country**. Released "Hello Mr. Heartache" (single by Harvey Gates) from *Hello Mr. Heartache* (album), recorded by Jerry Hanlon (country); "Country Nights" (single by Matt Dorman) from *Country Nights* (album), recorded by Kent Johnson (country); and "Bang, Bang Goes the Thunder" (single) from *Country Nights* (album), written and recorded by Tim Rehmer (country), all released 2000 and 2001 on UAR. Other artists include Garry Johnson, Jackie Nelson, Willie Morrissey, Tracy Wells and David Clayton Mize.

◉ **UNIVERSAL RECORDS**, 1755 Broadway, 7th Floor, New York NY 10019. (212)373-0600. Fax: (212)373-0688. Website: www.universalrecords.com. Universal City office: 70 Universal City Plaza, 3rd Floor, Universal City CA 91608. (818)777-1000. Contact: A&R Director. Labels include Uptown Records, Mojo Records, Republic Records, Bystorm Records and Gut Reaction Records. Record company.

• As a result of the 1998 PolyGram and Universal merger, Universal is the world's largest record company.

How to Contact: *Universal Records in California does not accept unsolicited submissions.* The New York office *only* allows you to call first and obtain permission to submit.

☑ ⊘ **VALTEC PRODUCTIONS**, P.O. Box 6018, Santa Maria CA 93456. (805)928-8559. **Contact:** J. Anderson and J. Valenta, owner/producers. Record company and record producer (Joe Valenta). Estab. 1986. Releases 20 singles, 15 LPs and 10 CDs/year. Pays negotiable royalty to artists on contract; statutory rate to publisher per song on record.
How to Contact: Submit demo tape by mail. Unsolicited submissions are OK. Prefers DAT with 4 songs and lyric sheet. Does not return material. Responds in 2 months.
Music: Mostly **country**, **top 40** and **A/C**; also **rock**. Released *Just Me* (album by Joe Valenta) and *Hold On* (album by Joe Valenta/J. Anderson), both recorded by Joe Valenta (top 40); and *Time Out (For Love)* (album by Joe Valenta), recorded by Marty K. (country), all on Valtec Records.

🏆 ⊘ **THE VERVE MUSIC GROUP**, 1755 Broadway, 3rd Floor, New York NY 10019. (212)331-2000. Fax: (212)331-2064. Website: www.vervemusicgroup.com. Senior Vice President of A&R: Richard Seidel. A&R Manager: Jason Olaine. A&R Director: Leslie Carr. Los Angeles office (Impulse, Blue Thumb): 100 N. First St., Burbank CA 91502. (818)729-4804. Fax: (818)845-2564. Vice President A&R: Bud Harner. A&R Assistant: George Stamatakis. Record company. Labels include Verve, GRP, Blue Thumb and Impulse! Records.
• Verve's Diana Krall won a 1999 Grammy Award for Best Jazz Vocal Performance; Wayne Shorter won Best Jazz Instrumental Solo; and the Charlie Haden Quartet West won Best Instrumental Arrangement with Vocals.
How to Contact: *The Verve Music Group does not accept unsolicited submissions.*
Music: Artists include Roy Hargrove, Diana Krall, George Benson, Al Jarreau, John Scofield, Natalie Cole, David Sanborn.

🆕 ⊘ **VILLAGE RECORDS**, 35 W. Fourth St., Suite 687, New York NY 10012. (212)998-5398. Fax: (212)995-4560. General Manager (alternative): David Purcell. Director (all styles): Catherine Moore. Record company. Estab. 1988. Staff size: 27. Releases 3 singles, 3 LPs, 1 EP and 3 CDs/year. Pays negotiable royalty to artists on contract; negotiable rate to publisher per song on record.
Distributed by: Big Daddy.
How to Contact: Submit demo tape by mail. Unsolicited submissions are OK. Prefers CD with 2 songs, lyric sheet and cover letter. Include SASE. Responds in 6 months.
Music: Mostly **alternative**, **hip-hop** and **rock**. Does not want classical. New releases by The David Brass Band.

⊘ **VIRGIN RECORDS**, 338 N. Foothill Rd., Beverly Hills CA 90210. (310)278-1181. Fax: (310)278-6231. New York office: 304 Park Ave. S., New York NY 10010. (212)253-3100. Fax: (212)253-3099. Website: www.virginrecords.com. Labels include Rap-A-Lot Records, Pointblank Records, SoulPower Records, AWOL Records, Astralwerks Records, Cheeba Sounds and Noo Trybe Records. Record company.
Distributed by: EMD.
How to Contact: Virgin Records does not accept recorded material or lyrics unless submitted by a reputable industry source. "If your act has received positive press or airplay on prior independent releases, we welcome your written query. Send a letter of introduction accompanied by all pertinent artist information. Do not send a tape until requested. All unsolicited materials will be returned unopened."
Artists include Lenny Kravitz, Janet Jackson, Mick Jagger, Nikka Costa, Ben Harper, Boz Scaggs and Moth.

🏆 ⊘ **VOKES MUSIC RECORD CO.**, P.O. Box 12, New Kensington PA 15068. (724)335-2775. President: Howard Vokes. Labels include Country Boy Records. Record company, booking agency (Vokes Booking Agency) and music publisher (Vokes Music Publishing). Releases 8 singles and 5 LPs/year. Pays 2½-4½% song royalty to artists and songwriters on contract.

THE TYPES OF MUSIC each listing is interested in are printed in **boldface**.

• Mr. Vokes is an inductee of the Country Music Organizations of America's American Eagle Awards' Hall of Fame.

How to Contact: Submit cassette only and lead sheet. Include SASE. Responds in 2 weeks.

Music: Mostly **country**, **bluegrass** and **gospel-old time**. Released *Songs of Tragedy and Disaster* (album), written and recorded by Howard Vokes (country), released on Vokes Records.

☑ ◑ **WALL STREET MUSIC**, 28545 Greenfield, Suite 200, Southfield MI 48075. (248)395-2770. Fax: (248)395-2773. E-mail: a&r@wallstreetmusic.com. Website: www.wallstreetmusic.com. **Contact:** A&R director. Record company, record distributor, record producer and music publisher (Burgundy Bros.). Estab. 1985.

How to Contact: Submit demo package by mail. Include CD, photo, bio, performance history, sales history, reviews and plans to support product. Accepts unsolicited submissions. "Be sure to completely label all items." Does not return material. Responds only if interested.

Music: Mostly **urban**, **rap**, **adult contemporary**, **rock** and **alternative**. Released *Downcity* (album), written and recorded by Mary Ann Rossoni (folk/rock), released 2000 on Wall Street Music *Recognize . . . It's Not A Game . . . ReAL* (album), written and recorded by Money, PMC, Don Juan, Tasherre, and Philpot, released 2002 on Wall Street Music/ReAL Entertainment. Other artists include Tracey Francione, Senator O'Brien, Flux Verde, Todd Harrold Band.

Tips: "The most important attribute we look for is a track record of local performance and any product sales. We are motivated by artists who perform often and have produced and marketed their music locally. You should keep us informed of your success in the industry as a way of helping us keep an eye on you."

◑ **WAREHOUSE CREEK RECORDING CORP.**, P.O. Box 102, Franktown, VA 23354. (757)442-6883. Fax: (757)442-3662. E-mail: warehouse@esva.net. Website: www.warehousecreek.com. President: Billy Sturgis. Record company, music publisher (Bayford Dock Music) and record producer (Billy Sturgis). Estab. 1993. Staff size: 1. Releases 11 singles and 1 CD/year. Pays negotiable royalty to artists on contract; statutory rate to publisher per song on record.

Distributed by: City Hall Records.

How to Contact: Submit demo tape by mail. Unsolicited submissions are OK. Prefers cassette, CD, DAT or VHS videocassette with lyric sheet. Does not return material.

Music: Mostly **R&B**, **blues** and **gospel**. Released *Greyhound Bus* (album by Arthur Crudup); *Going Down in Style* (album by Tim Drummond); and *Something On My Mind* (album by George Crudup), all recorded by Crudup Brothers on Warehouse Creek Records (blues).

☒ ◑ **WARNER BROS. RECORDS**, 3300 Warner Blvd., 4th Floor, N. Bldg., Burbank CA 91505-4694. (818)846-9090. Fax: (818)953-3423. New York office: 75 Rockefeller Plaza, New York NY 10019. (212)275-4500. Fax: (212)275-4595. Vice President of A&R: Che Pope. Senior Vice President A&R: James Dowdall. Director A&R: Brad Kaplan. Nashville office: 20 Music Square E., Nashville TN 37203. (615)748-8000. Fax: (615)214-1523. Website: www.wbr.com. Labels include American Recordings, Eternal Records, Imago Records, Mute Records, Giant Records, Malpaso Records and Maverick Records. Record company.

Distributed by: WEA.

• In 2000, "Scar Tissue," written by Flea, John Frusciante, Anthony Kiedis and Chud Smith, recorded by Red Hot Chili Peppers on Warner Bros. Records received a Grammy Award for Best Rock Song.

How to Contact: *Warner Bros. Records does not accept unsolicited material.* All unsolicited material will be returned unopened. Those interested in having their tapes heard should establish a relationship with a manager, publisher or attorney that has an ongoing relationship with Warner Bros. Records.

Music: Released *Van Halen 3* (album), recorded by Van Halen; *Evita* (soundtrack); and *Dizzy Up the Girl* (album), recorded by Goo Goo Dolls, both on Warner Bros. Records. Other artists include Faith Hill, Tom Petty & the Heartbreakers, Jeff Foxworthy, Porno For Pyros, Travis Tritt, Yellowjackets, Bela Fleck and the Flecktones, Al Jarreau, Joshua Redmond, Little Texas and Curtis Mayfield.

◯ WATERDOG MUSIC, (formerly Waterdog Records), 329 W. 18th St., #313, Chicago IL 60616-1120. (312)421-7499. Fax: (312)421-1848. E-mail: waterdog@waterdogmusic.com. Website: www.waterdogmusic.com. **Contact:** Rob Gillis, label manager. Labels include Whitehouse Records. Record company. Estab. 1994. Staff size: 1. Releases 6 CDs/year. Pays negotiable royalty to artists on contract; statutory rate to publisher per song on record.
Distributed by: Big Daddy Music.
How to Contact: Not accepting unsolicited materials, demos at this time. If submission policy changes, it will be posted at: www.waterdogmusic.com/about.html.
Music: Mostly **rock**, **pop** and **folk**. Released *Pigeon's Throat* (album), written and recorded by Al Rose (rock); *Live Music in the Apartment* (album by Carey OTT), recorded by Torben Floor (rock); and *Framing Caroline* (album), written and recorded by Kat Parsons (rock), all released 1999 on Waterdog Music. Other artists include MysteryDriver, Joel Frankel, Al Rose, Coin, The Good, Spelunkers, The Bad Examples, Ralph Covert, Middle 8, Peter Bernas, Matt Tiegle and Slink Moss and His Flying Aces.
Tips: "We are primarily interested in artists who write their own material and perform live regularly."

N: ⊕ ◯ WESTPARK MUSIC - RECORDS, PRODUCTION & PUBLISHING, P.O. Box 260227, Rathenauplatz 4, 50515 Cologne Germany. Phone: (49)221 247644. Fax: (49)221 231819. E-mail: westparkmusic@aol.com. Website: www.westparkmusic.com. Contact: Ulli Hetscher. Record company and music publisher. Estab. 1986. Staff size: 5. Releases 3-4 singles and 10-12 CDs/year. Pays 9-18% royalty to artists on contract.
Distributed by: BMG Ariola and Indigo.
How to Contact: *Write first and obtain permission to submit* or submit demo tape by mail. Unsolicited submissions are OK. Prefers cassette with 5-6 songs and lyric sheets. Does not return material. Responds in 4 months.
Music: "Check website."
Tips: "Check website first, if possible. Don't send country, mainstream rock/pop or MOR. Mark cassettes clearly. Save yourself money by sending just the CD and booklet (no box and no tray). Don't include stamps (we cannot use them). Send e-mail with brief description first."

◯ WINCHESTER RECORDS, % McCoy, Route 2, Box 114, Berkeley Springs WV 25411. (304)258-9381. Contact: A&R Director. Labels include Master Records and Real McCoy Records. Record company, music publisher (Jim McCoy Music, Clear Music, New Edition Music/BMI), record producer (Jim McCoy Productions) and recording studio. Releases 20 singles and 10 LPs/year. Pays standard royalty to artists; statutory rate to publisher for each record sold.
How to Contact: *Write first and obtain permission to submit.* Prefers 7½ ips reel-to-reel or cassette with 5-10 songs and lead sheet. Include SASE. Responds in 1 month.
Music: Mostly **bluegrass**, **church/religious**, **country**, **folk**, **gospel**, **progressive** and **rock**. Released *Touch Your Heart* (album), written and recorded by Jim McCoy; "Leavin' " (single), written and recorded by Red Steed, both on Winchester Records; and "The Taking Kind" (single by Tommy Hill), recorded by J.B. Miller on Hilton Records. Other artists include Carroll County Ramblers, Bud Arnel, Nitelifers, Jubilee Travelers and Middleburg Harmonizers.

◯ WINDHAM HILL RECORDS, 8750 Wilshire Blvd., 3rd Floor, Beverly Hills CA 90211. (310)358-4800. Fax: (310)358-4127. Website: www.windham.com. Director A&R: Jonathan Miller. Record company.
  • Windham Hill has been folded into RCA Records.

◯ WIND-UP ENTERTAINMENT, 72 Madison Ave., 8th Floor, New York NY 10016. (212)251-9665. Website: www.winduprecords.com. Contact: A&R. Record company. Estab. 1997. Releases 6-7 CDs/year. Pays negotiable royalty to artists on contract; statutory rate to publisher per song on record.
Distributed by: BMG.
How to Contact: *Write first and obtain permission to submit.* Prefers cassette, CD, DAT or video-cassette. Does not return material or respond to submissions.

Music: Mostly **rock**, **folk** and **hard rock**. Released *Weathered* (album) and *Human Clay* (album), written and recorded by Creed (rock); *Sinner* (album) by Drowning Pool; and *Stretch Princess* (album), written and recorded by Stretch Princess (rock), released 1998, all on Wind-Up.
Tips: "We rarely look for songwriters as opposed to bands, so writing a big hit single would be the rule of the day."

Ø **WORD RECORDS & MUSIC**, 25 Music Square W, Nashville TN 37203. (615)457-2000. Website: www.wordrecords.com. Record company.
Distributed by: Epic/Sony.
How to Contact: *Word Records does not accept unsolicited submissions.*
Music: Released *Blaze*, recorded by Code of Ethics; *Steady On*, recorded by Point of Grace; and *Past the Edges*, recorded by Chris Rice, all on Word.

O **WORLD BEATNIK RECORDS**, 20 Amity Lane, Rockwall TX 75087. Fax: (972)771-0853. E-mail: tropikalproductions@juno.com. Website: www.tropikalproductions.com. Producers: J. Towry (world beat, reggae, ethnic, jazz); Jembe (reggae, world beat, ethnic); Arik Towry (ska, pop, ragga, rock). Labels include World Beatnik Records. Record company and record producer (Jimi Towry). Estab. 1983. Staff size: 4. Releases 6 singles, 6 LPs, 6 EPs and 6 CDs/year. Pays negotiable royalty to artists on contract; statutory rate to publisher per song on record.
Distributed by: Midwest Records, Southwest Wholesale, Reggae OneLove, Ejaness Records, Ernie B's, CD Waterhouse and Borders.
How to Contact: Submit demo tape by mail. Unsolicited submissions are OK. Prefers cassette, DAT, mini disk or VHS videocassette with 3 songs and lyric sheet. Include SASE. Responds in 2 weeks.
Music: Mostly **world beat, reggae** and **ethnic**; also **jazz, hip-hop/dance** and **pop**. Released *I and I* (album by Abby I/Jimbe), recorded by Abby I (African pop); *Rastafrika* (album by Jimbe/Richard Ono), recorded by Rastafrika (African roots reggae); and *Vibes* (album by Jimbe/Bongo Cartheni), recorded by Wave (worldbeat/jazz), all released 2001 on World Beatnik. Other artists include Jimi Towry, Wisdom Ogbor (Nigeria), Joe Lateh (Ghana), Dee Dee Cooper, Ras Lyrix (St. Croix), Ras Kumba (St. Kitts), Gary Mon, Darbo (Gambia), Ricki Malik (Jamaica), Arik Miles, Narte's (Hawaii), Gavin Audagnotti (South Africa) and Bongo (Trinidad).

⊕ ☑ O **X.R.L. RECORDS/MUSIC**, White House Farm, Shropshire TF9 4HA England. Phone: (01630)647374. Fax: (01630)647612. **Contact:** Xavier Lee, International A&R Manager. A&R: Tanya Woof. UK A&R Manager: Cathrine Lee. Labels include Swoop, Zarg Records, Genouille, Pogo and Check Records. Record company, record producer and music publisher (Le Matt Music, Lee Music, R.T.F.M. and Pogo Records). Member MPA, PPL, PRS, MCPS, V.P.L. Estab. 1972. Staff size: 11. Releases 30 12″ singles, 20 LPs and 20 CDs/year. Pays negotiable royalty to artists on contract; negotiable rate to publisher for each record sold. Royalties paid to US songwriters and artists through US publishing or recording affiliate.
Distributed by: Lematt Music.
How to Contact: Submit demo tape by mail. Unsolicited submissions are OK. Prefers CD, cassette, MD or VHS 625 PAL standard videocassette with 1-3 songs and lyric sheet. Include bio and still photos. IRC only. Responds in 6 weeks.
Music: Mostly **pop/top 40**; also **bluegrass, blues, country, dance-oriented, easy listening, MOR, progressive, R&B, '50s rock, disco, new wave, rock** and **soul**. Released *Now and Then* (album), written and recorded by Daniel Boone (pop rock), released 2000 on Swoop; *The Creepies* (album), recorded by Nightmare (horror rock), released 2000 on Zarg; and *It's a Very Nice* (album), recorded by Groucho (pop), released 2000 on Swoop. Other artists include Orphan, The Chromatics, Mike Sheriden and the Nightriders, Johnny Moon, Dead Fish, Sight 'N' Sound and Mush.

REFER TO THE CATEGORY INDEX (at the end of this section) to find exactly which companies are interested in the type of music you write.

Tips: "Be original."

☑ ◑ **XEMU RECORDS**, 19 W. 21st St., Suite 503, New York NY 10010. (212)807-0290. Fax: (212)807-0583. E-mail: xemu@xemu.com. Website: www.xemu.com. **Contact:** Dr. Claw, vice president A&R. Record company. Estab. 1992. Staff size: 4. Releases 4 CDs/year. Pays negotiable royalty to artists on contract; statutory rate to publisher per song on record.
Distributed by: Sumthing Distribution.
How to Contact: *Write first and obtain permission to submit.* Prefers cassette with 3 songs. Does not return material. Responds in 2 months.
Music: Mostly **alternative**. Released *A is for Alpha* (album), recorded by Alpha Bitch (alternative rock); *Hold the Mayo* (album), recorded by Death Sandwich (alternative rock); *Madame Apple Sauce* (album), recorded by The Fifth Dementia (alternative rock); and *Happy Suicide Jim* (album), recorded by The Neanderthal Spongecake, all released on Xemu Records. Other artists include Malvert P. Redd.

Additional Record Companies

The following companies are also record companies, but their listings are found in other sections of the book. See the General Index for page numbers, then read the listings for submission information.

Abalone Publishing
ACR Productions
Alert Music, Inc.
Alexander Sr. Music
Alexis
All Rock Music
Allegheny Music Works
AlliSongs Inc.
Amen, Inc.
American Artists Entertainment
Angel Films Company
ARAS Music
Atch Records and Productions
Backstreet Booking
Baird Enterprises, Ron
Baitstring Music
Bal & Bal Music Publishing Co.
Barren Wood Publishing
Barrett Rock 'n' Roll Enterprises, Paul
Bay Ridge Publishing Co.
Big Fish Music Publishing Group
Birthplace Productions
Bixio Music Group & Associates/IDM Music
Black Market Entertainment Recordings
Blue Dog Publishing and Records
Blue Wave Productions
Blues Alley Records
BME Publishing
Bradley Music, Allan
Brian Song Music Corp.
BSW Records
Burnsongs
California Country Music
Camex Music
Celt Musical Services, Jan
Cherri/Holly Music
Christopher Publishing, Sonny
Cimirron Music
Coffee and Cream Productions
Conscience Music
Coppin, Johnny/Red Sky Records
Country Showcase America
Dagene Music
Dapmor Publishing
De Miles, Edward
De Miles Music Company, The Edward
Dell Music, Frank
Drive Music, Inc.
EAO Music Corporation of Canada
Ellis International Talent Agency, The
Eternal Song Agency, The
Ever-Open-Eye Music

Faverett Group
Fifth Avenue Media, Ltd.
First Time Music (Publishing) U.K.
Flying Red Horse Publishing
Fresh Entertainment
Frick Enterprises, Bob Scott
Frozen Inca Music
Furrow Music
Glad Music Co.
Glocc Cocced Records
Golden Guru Entertainment
Green One Music
G-String Publishing
Hailing Frequency Music Productions
Hale Enterprises
Happy Melody
Hardison International Entertainment Corporation
Heart Consort Music
Heupferd Musikverlag GmbH
Hickory Lane Publishing and Recording
His Power Productions and Publishing
Huge Production, Inc., A
Inside Records/OK Songs
Interplanetary Music
Iron Skillet Music
Ja/Nein Musikverlag GmbH
Jay Jay Publishing & Record Co.
JPMC Music Inc.
Kansa Records Corporation
Kaupps & Robert Publishing Co.
Kaysarah Music
Kickstart Music Ltd.
Kingston Records and Talent
Known Artist Productions
L.A. Entertainment, Inc.
Leigh Music, Trixie
Les Music Group
Levy Management, Rick
Lexington Alabama Music Publishing
Lilly Music Publishing
Lineage Publishing Co.
Luick & Associates Music Publisher, Harold
M.B.H. Music Management
Magid Productions, Lee
Makers Mark Music Productions
Mayo & Company, Phil
McCoy Music, Jim
McJames Music Inc.
Mellow House Music
Mento Music Group
Muse Artists Inc.
Naked Jain Records

Neu Electro Productions
New Experience Records
New Rap Jam Publishing, A
Northwest Alabama Music Publishing
Orchid Publishing
OTA Productions
Pacific North Studios Ltd.
Pegasus Music
Philly Breakdown Recording Co.
Pierce, Jim
Pollybyrd Publications Limited
Pritchett Publications
R.T.L. Music
Rainbow Collection Ltd.
Renaissance Entertainment Group
Riohcat Music
RN'D Productions
Road Records
Rocker Music/Happy Man Music
Rockford Music Co.
Saddlestone Publishing
Sa'Mall Management
Satkowski Recordings, Steve
SDM
Sea Cruise Productions, Inc.
Segal's Productions
Sellwood Publishing
Shute Management Pty. Ltd., Phill
Silicon Music Publishing Co.

Silver Bow Management
Silver Thunder Music Group
Sound Cellar Music
Sound Works Entertainment Productions Inc.
SRS Productions/Hit Records Network
Staircase Promotion
Starbound Publishing Co.
Stellar Music Industries
Still Working Music Group
Stormin' Norman Productions
Strictly Forbidden Artists
Studio Seven
Succes
Swift River Productions
Tari, Roger Vincent
Tas Music Co./Dave Tasse Entertainment
Third Wave Productions Limited
TMC Productions
Tower Music Group
Trac Record Co.
Umpire Entertainment Enterprizes
Universal Music Marketing
Unknown Source Music
Van Pol Management, Hans
Vickers Music Association, Charles
Warner Productions, Cheryl K.
WE Records & Management
White Cat Music
Williams Management, Yvonne
World Records

Category Index

The Category Index is a good place to begin searching for a market for your songs. Below is an alphabetical list of 20 general music categories. If you write rock songs and are looking for a record company to submit your songs to, check the Rock section in this index. There you will find a list of record companies interested in hearing rock songs. Once you locate the entries for those record companies, read the music subheading *carefully* to determine which companies are most interested in the type of rock music you write. Some of the markets in this section do not appear in the Category Index because they have not indicated a specific preference. Most of these said they are interested in "all types" of music. Listings that were very specific, or whose description of the music they're interested in doesn't quite fit into these categories, also do not appear here.

Adult Contemporary (also easy listening, middle of the road, AAA, ballads, etc.)
ABL Records
Allegheny Music Works
Banana Records
Bolivia Records
Boulevard Music & Publishing
Bouquet Records
Brentwood Records/Diadem Records
Capstan Record Production
Dale Productions, Alan
Emerald City Records
Enterprize Records-Tapes
Factory Beat Records, Inc.
Fish of Death Records and Management
Golden Triangle Records
Green Bear Records
Kaupp Records
L.A. Records (Canada)
L.A. Records (Michigan)
Leatherland Productions
Lucifer Records, Inc.
Missile Records
Monticana Records
Roll On Records®
Rustron Music Productions
Valtec Productions
Wall Street Music
X.R.L. Records/Music

Alternative (also modern rock, punk, college rock, new wave, hardcore, new music, industrial, ska, indie rock, garage, etc.)
Alco Recordings
AMP Records & Music
Astralwerks
Avalon Recording Group
babysue
Banana Records
Cleopatra Records

Crank! A Record Company
Deary Me Records
Deep South Entertainment
Drool Records
Elektra Records
Entourage Music Group
Evil Teen Records
Fish of Death Records and Management
Flood Recording Corp.
Generic Records, Inc.
Gonzo! Records Inc.
Hot Wings Entertainment
Hottrax Records
Idol Records
Inside Sounds
L.A. Records (Canada)
London Sire Records
Monticana Records
Moody Prodx, Doug
Paint Chip Records
Pentacle Records
PGE Platinum Groove Entertainment
Powerblast Recordings
Radical Records
RAVE Records, Inc.
Redemption Records
Road Records
Sin Klub Entertainment, Inc.
Small Stone Records
Sonic Records, Inc./SRI Records, Inc.
Street Records
Strugglebaby Recording Co.
3rd Stone Records
Triple X Records
TVT Records
28 Records
Village Records
Wall Street Music
X.R.L. Records/Music
Xemu Records

Blues
Albatross Records
Blue Wave
BSW Records
Cellar Records
Chiaroscuro Records
Deadeye Records
Flying Heart Records
Front Row Records
Gallery II Records/Jumpin' Jack Records
Goldwax Record Corporation
Grass Roots Record & Tape/LMI Records
Heart Music, Inc.
Horizon Records, Inc.
Inside Sounds
Landslide Records
Monticana Records
Moody Prodx, Doug
P.M. Records
Rustron Music Productions
Small Stone Records
SunDance Records
Sureshot Records
Texas Rose Records
Topcat Records
Triple X Records
Warehouse Creek Recording Corp.
X.R.L. Records/Music

Children's
Awal.com
BMX Entertainment
Grass Roots Record & Tape/LMI Records
Leatherland Productions
Smithsonian Folkways Recordings

Classical (also opera, chamber music, serious music, choral, etc.)
A.P.I. Records
Arkadia Entertainment Corp.
babysue
BMX Entertainment
Cambria Records & Publishing
Cantilena Records
EMF Records & Affiliates
Imaginary Records
Lark Record Productions, Inc.
North Star Music
Omega Record Group, Inc.
Sun-Scape Enterprises Limited
Tangent® Records

Country (also western, C&W, bluegrass, cowboy songs, western swing, honky-tonk, etc.)
ABL Records
Afterschool Records, Inc.
Albatross Records
Alco Recordings

All Star Record Promotions
Allegheny Music Works
Americatone Records International USA
Atlan-Dec/Grooveline Records
Avalon Recording Group
Bagatelle Record Company
Belmont Records
Blue Gem Records
Blue Wave
BMX Entertainment
Bolivia Records
Boulevard Music & Publishing
Bouquet Records
BSW Records
Capstan Record Production
Case Entertainment Group/C.E.G. Records, Inc.
Cellar Records
Cherry Street Records
Cimirron/Rainbird Records
Collector Records
Country Star International
Dale Productions, Alan
Deadeye Records
Deep South Entertainment
Emerald City Records
EMF Productions
EMF Records & Affiliates
Enterprize Records-Tapes
Entourage Music Group
Front Row Records
Generic Records, Inc.
Golden Triangle Records
Goldwax Record Corporation
Grass Roots Record & Tape/LMI Records
Green Bear Records
Gueststar Records, Inc.
Hottrax Records
Kaupp Records
Kingston Records
L.A. Records (Canada)
L.A. Records (Michigan)
Lari-Jon Records
Lark Record Productions, Inc.
Marvel Records, Andy
Mighty Records
Missile Records
Monticana Records
Music Wise Inc.
Night Owl Records
Outstanding Records
P.M. Records
PBM Talent & Publishing
Pickwick/Mecca/International Records
Plateau Music
Playbones Records
Road Records
Roll On Records®
Rustron Music Productions

Sabteca Record Co.
Safire Records
Siltown Records
Solana Records
Sonic Records, Inc./SRI Records, Inc.
Southland Records, Inc.
Spotlight Records
Stardust
SunCountry Records
Sureshot Records
Texas Rose Records
Third Wave Productions Ltd.
Trac Record Co.
UAR Records
Valtec Productions
Vokes Music Record Co.
Winchester Records
X.R.L. Records/Music

Dance (also house, hi-NRG, disco, club, rave, techno, trip-hop, trance, etc.)
AMP Records & Music
Atlan-Dec/Grooveline Records
Awal.com
Broken Note Records
Broken Records International
Dagene/Cabletown Company
Discmedia
Disc-tinct Music, Inc.
Drive Entertainment
Drool Records
Flat Records
Gig Records
Gonzo! Records Inc.
Hi-Bias Records Inc.
Horizon Records, Inc.
Jupiter Records
L.A. Records (Canada)
L.A. Records (Michigan)
Lock
Lucifer Records, Inc.
Mighty Records
Monticana Records
Neurodisc Records, Inc.
NPO Records, Inc.
P. & N. Records
PGE Platinum Groove Entertainment
Pickwick/Mecca/International Records
Quark Records
Rampant Records
RAVE Records, Inc.
Road Records
Sahara Records and Filmworks Entertainment
Satellite Music
Select Records
Sound Gems
Synergy Records
World Beatnik Records
X.R.L. Records/Music

Folk (also acoustic, Celtic, etc.)
Afterschool Records, Inc.
Broken Note Records
Heart Music, Inc.
Hot Wings Entertainment
Inside Sounds
Missile Records
Monticana Records
Red Sky Records
Rustron Music Productions
Smithsonian Folkways Recordings
Street Records
Third Wave Productions Ltd.
Waterdog Music
Winchester Records
Wind-Up Entertainment

Instrumental (also background music, musical scores, etc.)
AMP Records & Music
Broken Note Records
Lark Record Productions, Inc.
Makoché Recording Company
Mayfair Music
North Star Music
Playbones Records
Road Records
Tangent® Records

Jazz (also fusion, bebop, swing, etc.)
A.P.I. Records
Afterschool Records, Inc.
Airplay Label, The
Albatross Records
Americatone Records International USA
Ariana Records
Arkadia Entertainment Corp.
Atlan-Dec/Grooveline Records
Avita Records
Awal.com
BMX Entertainment
Boulevard Music & Publishing
Candyspiteful Productions
Cherry Street Records
Chiaroscuro Records
CKB Records/Helaphat Entertainment
CPA Records
Creative Improvised Music Projects (CIMP) Records
Dale Productions, Alan
EMF Records & Affiliates
Entourage Music Group
Flying Heart Records
Fresh Entertainment
Gallery II Records/Jumpin' Jack Records
Golden Triangle Records
Goldwax Record Corporation
Grass Roots Record & Tape/LMI Records
Heads Up Int., Ltd.

Heart Music, Inc.
Horizon Records, Inc.
Hot Wings Entertainment
Hottrax Records
Imaginary Records
Inside Sounds
L.A. Records (Michigan)
Landslide Records
Mighty Records
Missile Records
Monticana Records
Music Wise Inc.
North Star Music
Omega Record Group, Inc.
Outstanding Records
Playbones Records
Powerblast Recordings
Q Records
Sahara Records and Filmworks Entertainment
Salexo Music
Seafair/Bolo Records
SunDance Records
Tangent® Records
Topcat Records
TVT Records
World Beatnik Records

Latin (also Spanish, salsa, Cuban, conga, Brazilian, cumbja, rancheras, Mexican, merengue, Tejano, Tex Mex, etc.)
Albatross Records
Americatone Records International USA
Amigos Music & Marketing
BMX Entertainment
Discmedia
Discos Fuentes/Miami Records & Edimusica USA
EMF Records & Affiliates
Grass Roots Record & Tape/LMI Records
Hacienda Records & Recording Studio
Joey Records

Metal (also thrash, grindcore, heavy metal, etc.)
babysue
Cellar Records
Cleopatra Records
Flat Records
L.A. Records (Michigan)
Metal Blade Records
Missile Records
Nightmare Records
Powerblast Recordings
Sin Klub Entertainment, Inc.
28 Records
Wind-Up Entertainment

New Age (also ambient)
AMP Records & Music
BMX Entertainment

Dale Productions, Alan
EMF Records & Affiliates
L.A. Records (Michigan)
Neurodisc Records, Inc.
North Star Music
Only New Age Music, Inc.
Powerblast Recordings
Rustron Music Productions
Sun-Scape Enterprises Limited
Tangent® Records

Novelty (also comedy, humor, etc.)
Inside Sounds
Leatherland Productions
Oglio Records
Select Records
Sureshot Records

Pop (also top 40, top 100, popular, chart hits, etc.)
A.P.I. Records
ABL Records
Afterschool Records, Inc.
Airplay Label, The
Alco Recordings
Allegheny Music Works
Anisette Records
Arkadia Entertainment Corp.
Awal.com
Aware Records
babysue
Banana Records
Blue Gem Records
BMX Entertainment
Bolivia Records
Broken Records International
C.P.R.
Candyspiteful Productions
Capstan Record Production
Case Entertainment Group/C.E.G. Records, Inc.
Cellar Records
CPA Records
Crank! A Record Company
Dagene/Cabletown Company
Deep South Entertainment
Demi Monde Records and Publishing, Ltd.
Dental Records
Discmedia
Drive Entertainment
Drool Records
EMF Productions
EMF Records & Affiliates
Enterprize Records-Tapes
Fish of Death Records and Management
Flat Records
Flood Recording Corp.
Fresh Entertainment
Generic Records, Inc.
Gold City Records, Inc.

Goldwax Record Corporation
Gonzo! Records Inc.
Grass Roots Record & Tape/LMI Records
Griffin Music
Hacienda Records & Recording Studio
Heads Up Int., Ltd.
Heart Music, Inc.
Hi-Bias Records Inc.
Horizon Records, Inc.
Hottrax Records
Idol Records
Inside Sounds
Jive Records
Jupiter Records
Kaupp Records
Kingston Records
L.A. Records (Michigan)
Lucifer Records, Inc.
Marvel Records, Andy
Mayfair Music
Mighty Records
Missile Records
Monticana Records
Music Wise Inc.
Nation Records Inc.
Night Owl Records
P.M. Records
Pickwick/Mecca/International Records
Plateau Music
Q Records
Quark Records
Redemption Records
Roll On Records®
Rustron Music Productions
Sabteca Record Co.
Safire Records
Sahara Records and Filmworks Entertainment
Satellite Music
Siltown Records
Solana Records
sonic unyon records canada
Sound Gems
Spotlight Records
Street Records
SunDance Records
Synergy Records
Texas Rose Records
Third Wave Productions Ltd.
Valtec Productions
Waterdog Music
World Beatnik Records
X.R.L. Records/Music

R&B (also soul, black, urban, etc.)
ABL Records
Albatross Records
Allegheny Music Works
Arkadia Entertainment Corp.
Atlan-Dec/Grooveline Records

Avalon Recording Group
Blue Gem Records
Blue Wave
BMX Entertainment
Bolivia Records
Boulevard Music & Publishing
C.P.R.
Candyspiteful Productions
Cellar Records
Cherry Street Records
CKB Records/Helaphat Entertainment
CPA Records
Dagene/Cabletown Company
Demi Monde Records and Publishing, Ltd.
Disc-tinct Music, Inc.
EMF Productions
EMF Records & Affiliates
Factory Beat Records, Inc.
Flying Heart Records
Fresh Entertainment
Front Row Records
Gallery II Records/Jumpin' Jack Records
Gold City Records, Inc.
Golden Triangle Records
Goldwax Record Corporation
Grass Roots Record & Tape/LMI Records
Groove Makers' Recordings
Heads Up Int., Ltd.
Hi-Bias Records Inc.
Inner Soul Records, Inc.
Jive Records
Jupiter Records
Kaupp Records
L.A. Records (Michigan)
Lucifer Records, Inc.
Major Entertainment, Inc.
Marvel Records, Andy
Missile Records
Monticana Records
Music Wise Inc.
Nation Records Inc.
Night Owl Records
PGE Platinum Groove Entertainment
Plateau Music
Powerblast Recordings
Red-Eye Records
Roll On Records®
Ruffnation Records
Rustron Music Productions
Sabteca Record Co.
Sahara Records and Filmworks Entertainment
Seafair/Bolo Records
Select Records
Sound Gems
Strugglebaby Recording Co.
SunDance Records
Synergy Records
Topcat Records
TVT Records

Warehouse Creek Recording Corp.
X.R.L. Records/Music

Rap (also hip-hop, bass, etc.)
Albatross Records
Anisette Records
Atlan-Dec/Grooveline Records
Avalon Recording Group
BMX Entertainment
Broken Note Records
C.P.R.
CKB Records/Helaphat Entertainment
CPA Records
Dagene/Cabletown Company
Disc-tinct Music, Inc.
Factory Beat Records, Inc.
Fish of Death Records and Management
Fresh Entertainment
Gallery II Records/Jumpin' Jack Records
Generic Records, Inc.
Gig Records
Gold City Records, Inc.
Goldwax Record Corporation
Groove Makers' Recordings
Heart Music, Inc.
Inner Soul Records, Inc.
Jive Records
Jupiter Records
Major Entertainment, Inc.
Missile Records
Neurodisc Records, Inc.
Night Owl Records
NPO Records, Inc.
PGE Platinum Groove Entertainment
Pickwick/Mecca/International Records
Powerblast Recordings
Ruffnation Records
Select Records
Siltown Records
Sin Klub Entertainment, Inc.
Sonar Records & Production
Synergy Records
Triple X Records
TVT Records
Village Records
Wall Street Music
World Beatnik Records

Religious (also gospel, sacred, Christian, church, hymns, praise, inspirational, worship, etc.)
ABL Records
Alco Recordings
All Star Record Promotions
Allegheny Music Works
Atlan-Dec/Grooveline Records
Avalon Recording Group
babysue
Bagatelle Record Company

BMX Entertainment
Bouquet Records
Brentwood Records/Diadem Records
Country Star International
CPA Records
Dagene/Cabletown Company
Dale Productions, Alan
Emerald City Records
Enterprize Records-Tapes
Fresh Entertainment
Gallery II Records/Jumpin' Jack Records
Gold City Records, Inc.
Goldwax Record Corporation
Grass Roots Record & Tape/LMI Records
Green Bear Records
Inner Soul Records, Inc.
Kaupp Records
L.A. Records (Michigan)
Lari-Jon Records
Leatherland Productions
Malaco Records
Missile Records
Monticana Records
Music Wise Inc.
Night Owl Records
Pickwick/Mecca/International Records
Playbones Records
Red-Eye Records
Roll On Records®
Salexo Music
Siltown Records
Sonar Records & Production
Sonic Records, Inc./SRI Records, Inc.
Spotlight Records
SunCountry Records
SunDance Records
Texas Rose Records
Trac Record Co.
Vokes Music Record Co.
Warehouse Creek Recording Corp.
Winchester Records

Rock (also rockabilly, AOR, rock 'n' roll, etc.)
A.P.I. Records
Albatross Records
Alco Recordings
Americatone Records International USA
Anisette Records
Ariana Records
Arkadia Entertainment Corp.
Atlan-Dec/Grooveline Records
Avalon Recording Group
Aware Records
babysue
Blue Gem Records
Blue Wave
BMX Entertainment
Boulevard Music & Publishing
Bouquet Records

Broken Note Records
Broken Records International
BSW Records
C.P.R.
Candyspiteful Productions
Capstan Record Production
Case Entertainment Group/C.E.G. Records, Inc.
Cellar Records
Chattahoochee Records
Cherry Street Records
Collector Records
CPA Records
Deadeye Records
Deary Me Records
Deep South Entertainment
Del-Fi Records, Inc.
Demi Monde Records and Publishing, Ltd.
Discmedia
Drive Entertainment
Drool Records
EMF Records & Affiliates
Enterprize Records-Tapes
Entourage Music Group
Evil Teen Records
Fish of Death Records and Management
Flat Records
Flying Heart Records
Fresh Entertainment
Front Row Records
Generic Records, Inc.
Gig Records
Golden Triangle Records
Goldwax Record Corporation
Grass Roots Record & Tape/LMI Records
Green Bear Records
Griffin Music
Hacienda Records & Recording Studio
Heart Music, Inc.
Horizon Records, Inc.
Hottrax Records
Idol Records
Jupiter Records
Kaupp Records
Kingston Records
L.A. Records (Canada)
L.A. Records (Michigan)
Lari-Jon Records
London Sire Records
Lucifer Records, Inc.
Missile Records
Monticana Records
Night Owl Records
Oglio Records
Outstanding Records

P. & N. Records
P.M. Records
Pentacle Records
Pickwick/Mecca/International Records
Plateau Music
Playbones Records
Pravda Records
Presence Records
Radical Records
Rags to Records, Inc.
Red Sky Records
Red-Eye Records
Roll On Records®
Ruffnation Records
Seafair/Bolo Records
Siltown Records
Small Stone Records
Solana Records
Sonic Records, Inc./SRI Records, Inc.
sonic unyon records canada
Stardust
Street Records
Strugglebaby Recording Co.
SunDance Records
Synergy Records
Tangent® Records
Texas Rose Records
3rd Stone Records
Triple X Records
28 Records
Valtec Productions
Village Records
Wall Street Music
Waterdog Music
Winchester Records
Wind-Up Entertainment
X.R.L. Records/Music

World Music (also reggae, ethnic, calypso, international, world beat, etc.)
Arkadia Entertainment Corp.
Awal.com
EMF Records & Affiliates
Factory Beat Records, Inc.
Gallery II Records/Jumpin' Jack Records
Makoché Recording Company
Missile Records
Modal Music, Inc.™
North Star Music
Only New Age Music, Inc.
Silver Wave Records
Smithsonian Folkways Recordings
Tangent® Records
World Beatnik Records

Record Producers

The independent producer can best be described as a creative coordinator. He's usually the one with the most creative control over a recording project and is ultimately responsible for the finished product. Some record companies have in-house producers who work with the acts on that label (although, in more recent years, such producer-label relationships are often non-exclusive). Today, most record companies contract out-of-house, independent record producers on a project-by-project basis.

WHAT RECORD PRODUCERS DO

Producers play a large role in deciding what songs will be recorded for a particular project and are always on the lookout for new songs for their clients. They can be valuable contacts for songwriters because they work so closely with the artists whose records they produce. They usually have a lot more freedom than others in executive positions and are known for having a good ear for potential hit songs. Many producers are songwriters and musicians themselves. Since they wield a great deal of influence, a good song in the hands of the right producer at the right time stands a good chance of being cut. And even if a producer is not working on a specific project, he is well-acquainted with record company executives and artists and can often get material through doors not open to you.

Additional Record Producers

There are **MORE RECORD PRODUCERS** located in other sections of the book! On page 258 use the list of Additional Record Producers to find listings within other sections who are also record producers.

SUBMITTING MATERIAL TO PRODUCERS

It can be difficult to get your tapes to the right producer at the right time. Many producers write their own songs and even if they don't write, they may be involved in their own publishing companies so they have instant access to all the songs in their catalogs. Also, some genres are more dependent on finding outside songs than others. A producer working with a rock group or a singer-songwriter will rarely take outside songs. It's important to understand the intricacies of the producer/publisher situation. If you pitch your song directly to a producer first, before another publishing company publishes the song, the producer may ask you for the publishing rights (or a percentage thereof) to your song. You must decide whether the producer is really an active publisher who will try to get the song recorded again and again or whether he merely wants the publishing because it means extra income for him from the current recording project. You may be able to work out a co-publishing deal, where you and the producer split the publishing of the song. That means he will still receive his percentage of the publishing income, even if you secure a cover recording of the song by other artists in the future. Even though you would be giving up a little bit initially, you may benefit in the future.

Some producers will offer to sign artists and songwriters to "development deals." These can range from a situation where a Svengali-like producer auditions singers and musicians with the intention of building a group from the ground up, to development deals where a producer signs a band or singer-songwriter to his production company, with the intention of developing an act and producing an album to shop to labels (sometimes referred to as a "baby record deal"). You must carefully consider whether such a deal is right for you. In some cases, such a deal will open doors and propel an act to the next level. In other worst-case scenarios, such a deal can result in loss of artistic and career control, with some acts held in contractual bondage for years at a time. Before you consider any such deal, be clear about your goals, the producer's reputation, and the sort of compromises you are willing to make to reach those goals. If you have any reservations whatsoever, don't do it.

The listings that follow outline which aspects of the music industry each producer is involved in, what type of music he is looking for, and what records and artists he's recently produced. Study the listings carefully, noting the artists each producer works with, and consider if any of your songs might fit a particular artist's or producer's style. Then determine whether they are open to your level of experience (see the Openness to Submissions sidebar on page 8).

Consult the Category Index at the end of this section to find producers who work with the type of music you write, and the Geographic Index at the back of the book to locate producers in your area.

For More Information

For more instructional information on the listings in this book, including explanations of symbols (◼ ✓ ▼ ⬚ ⊕ ◻ ⬭ ⬮ ⬭), read the article How to Use *Songwriter's Market* to Get Your Songs Heard on page 5.

"A" MAJOR SOUND CORPORATION, 80 Corley Ave., Toronto, Ontario M4E 1V2 Canada. (416)690-9552. Fax: (416)690-9482. E-mail: pmilner@sympatico.ca. **Contact:** Paul C. Milner, producer. Record producer and music publisher. Estab. 1989. Produces 2 EPs and 12 CDs/year. Fee derived from sales royalty when song or artist is recorded, or outright fee from recording artist or record company, or investors.
How to Contact: Submit demo tape by mail. Unsolicited submissions are OK. Prefers CD, DAT or VHS videocassette with 5 songs and lyric sheet (lead sheet if available). Does not return material. Responds in 3 months.
Music: Mostly **rock**, **A/C**, **alternative** and **pop**; also **Christian** and **R&B**. Produced *Art of Survival* (album), written and recorded by Nashun (funk/hip-hop), released 2000 on LoFish; *The Sydneys* (album by G. Fayer), recorded by The Sydneys (pop/rock), released 2000 on American Nouveux; and *Innocent Child* (album), written and recorded by Carole Pope (alternative/pop), released 1999 on 077.

ABERDEEN PRODUCTIONS, 524 Doral Country Dr., Nashville TN 37221. (615)646-9750. **Contact:** Scott Turner, executive producer. Record producer and music publisher (Buried Treasure Music/ASCAP, Captain Kidd/BMI). Estab. 1971. Produces 10 singles, 15-20 12″ singles, 8 LPs and 8 CDs/year. Fee derived from outright fee from recording artist.
How to Contact: Submit demo tape by mail. Unsolicited submissions OK. Prefers cassette with maximum 4 songs and lead sheet. Include SASE. "No SASE, no reply." Responds in 2 weeks. No "lyrics only."
Music: Mostly **country**, **MOR** and **rock**; also **top 40/pop**. Produced "All of the Above" (single by Douglas Bush) from *The Entrance* (album), recorded by Lea Brennan (country/MOR), released 2000. Other artists include Jimmy Clanton.
Tips: "Start out on an independent basis because of the heavy waiting period to get on a major label."

☑ ◻ **ACR PRODUCTIONS**, P.O. Box 5636, Midland TX 79704. (615)826-9233 or (915)687-2702. **Contact:** Dwaine Thomas, owner. Record producer, music publisher (Joranda Music/BMI) and record company (ACR Records). Estab. 1986. Produces 120 singles, 8-15 12″ singles, 25 LPs, 25 EPs and 25 CDs/year. Fee derived from sales royalty when song or artist is recorded. "We charge for in-house recording only. Remainder is derived from royalties."
How to Contact: Submit demo tape by mail. Unsolicited submissions are OK. Prefers cassette or VHS videocassette with 5 songs and lyric sheet. Does not return material. Responds in 6 weeks if interested.
Music: Mostly **country swing**, **pop** and **rock**; also **R&B** and **gospel**. Produced *Bottle's Almost Gone* (album) and "Black Gold" (single), written and recorded by Mike Nelson (country), both released 1999 on ACR Records; and *Nashville Series* (album), written and recorded by various (country), released 1998 on ProJam Music.
Tips: "Be professional. No living room tapes!"

◖ **ALCO PRODUCTIONS**, P.O. Box 18197, Panama City Beach FL 32417. **Contact:** Ann McEver, president. Record producer. Estab. 2000. Produces 6 singles and 3 CDs/year. Fee derived from sales royalty when song or artist is recorded.
How to Contact: Submit demo tape by mail. Unsolicited submissions are OK. Prefers cassette or CD with 3 songs and lyric sheet. Include SASE. Responds in 3 weeks.
Music: Mostly **pop/rock**, **country** and **alternative**; also **gospel**. Produced "Hungry Now" (single by Jack Bennion) from *Hungry And How* (album), recorded by Snack Bar (alternative); and "Treat Mama Good" from *Willie Burk* (album), written and recorded by Willie Burke (country), both released 2001 on Alco.
Tips: "Submit your best material. We are looking for artists and groups that are unique and are strong enough to compete at a national level. We are also looking for artists and bands that are different yet ones that would fit into the existing Nashville or Los Angeles music formats."

◖ **STUART J. ALLYN**, 250 Taxter Rd., Irvington NY 10533. (212)486-0856. E-mail: adrstudios@adrinc.org. Associate: Jack Walker. **Contact:** Jack Davis, general manager. President: Stuart J. Allyn. Record producer. Estab. 1972. Produces 6 singles and 3-6 CDs/year. Fee derived from sales royalty and outright fee from recording artist and record company.
How to Contact: *Does not accept unsolicited submissions.*
Music: Mostly **pop**, **rock**, **jazz** and **theatrical**; also **R&B** and **country**. Produced *Thad Jones Legacy* (album), recorded by Vanquard Jazz Orchestra (jazz), released 2000 on New World Records. Other artists include Billy Joel, Aerosmith, Carole Demas, Bob Stewart, The Dixie Peppers, Nora York, Buddy Barnes and various video and film scores.

◻ **ANGEL FILMS COMPANY**, 967 Hwy. 40, New Franklin MO 65274-9778. Phone/fax: (573)698-3900. E-mail: angelfilm@aol.com. Website: www.phoenix.org. **Contact:** Lord Sackville, president. Owner: William H. Hoehne, Jr. Record producer, motion picture company and record company (Angel One). Estab. 1980. Produces 5 LPs, 5 EPs and 5 CDs/year. Fee derived from sales royalty when song or artist is recorded.
How to Contact: Submit demo tape or CD by mail. Unsolicited submissions are OK. Prefers cassette or VHS videocassette with 3 songs. "Send only original material, not previously recorded, and include a bio sheet on artist." Include SASE. Responds in 6 weeks.
Music: Mostly **pop**, **rock** and **rockabilly**; also **jazz** and **R&B**. Produced "March of the Woolley Worms" (single by Bill Otto) from *Empire of the Woolley Worms* (album), recorded by Stephanie Le Gee (childrens), released 2001 on Angel One; "Christmas Is" (single by Stephanie Gee) from *Christ-*

REFER TO THE GEOGRAPHIC INDEX (at the back of this book) to find listings of companies by state, as well as foreign listings.

mas Is (album), recorded by Lee Le (Christmas), released 2002 on Angel One; and *Phoeenix* (album), written and recorded by Phoeenix (MOR), released 2002 on Angel One. Other artists include Julian James, Patrick Donovon,Euttland, B.D.K. and Teddies.

Tips: "Actually listen to what you're doing and ask, 'would I buy that?' "

☑ ⊘ **JONATHAN APPELL PRODUCTIONS, INC.**, 400 Second Ave., #13A, New York NY 10010. (212)725-5613. E-mail: jonathan@appellproductions.com. Website: www.appellproductions. com. **Contact:** Jonathan Appell, producer/engineer. Record producer and audio engineer. Estab. 1989. Produces 2 singles and 5 LPs/year. Fee derived from sales royalty when song or artist is recorded, or outright fee from recording artist or record company.

How to Contact: *Does not accept unsolicited submissions.*

Music: Mostly **rock**, **pop** and **R&B**; also **jazz** and **reggae**. Produced *Mike Fuji* (album); *Piranha Brothers* (album), written and recorded by Piranha Brothers (rock); *Blue Eyed Soul* (album by Chris and Tom O'Connor), recorded by Blue Eyed Soul (pop); and *Roseanne Drucker* (album), recorded by Roseanne Drucker (pop), all on Reload. Other artists include Matt Cohler Band, Lee Drutman Band, YNot and Eric Fleischman.

Tips: "Learn your craft. Ask yourself (honestly), 'Am I good enough to perform alongside whomever the biggest artists are in my genre of music?' If you aren't convinced that you've attained that level of professionalism, you'll never convince a producer or a record company. If you're not ready, get back in there and practice, practice, practice!"

☐ **AVALON PRODUCTIONS**, P.O. Box 121626, Nashville TN 37212. **Contact:** A&R Review Department. Record producer, record company (Avalon Recording Group) and music publisher (Avalon Music). Estab. 2001. Produces 6 singles and 3 albums/year. Fee derived from sales royalty when song or artist is recorded, from outright fee from recording artist, or outright fee from record company.

How to Contact: Submit demo tape by mail. Unsolicited submissions are OK. Prefers cassette or CD with 3 songs and lyric sheet. Include SASE. Responds in 3 weeks.

Music: Mostly **rock**, **country**, and **alternative**; also **R&B**, **rap** and **gospel**. Produced "Paradise" (single by Allude) from *Allude to This* (album), recorded by Allude (alternative), released 2001 on Avalon; "Who Knows" (single by Jim Hughes) from *Madrid* (album), recorded by Madrid (rock), released 2001 on Avalon.

Tips: "Send songs suitable for today's market."

☑ **RON BAIRD ENTERPRISES**, P.O. Box 42, 1 Main St., Ellsworth PA 15331. E-mail: ronssong @charterpa.net. **Contact:** Ron Baird, executive producer. Record producer, record company (La Ron Ltd. Records), music publisher (Baird Music Group). Estab. 1999. Produces 2-5 singles and 1-2 LPs/ year.

How to Contact: Submit demo tape by mail. Unsolicited submissions are OK. "No certified mail." Prefers cassette only with 2-4 songs and lyric sheet. Does not return submissions. Responds only if interested.

Music: Mostly **country** and **country rock**. Does not want hip-hop, gospel/religious or R&B. Produced "Dancin' In Texas" (single by Ronald Lee Baird) from *The Latchem Brothers* (album), recorded by Latchem Brothers (country), released 2001 on LaRow Ltd.; "Trouble Across the River" (single by Ronald Lee Baird), recorded by Corey Christie (country), released 2001 on LaRon Ltd.; and "Jukebox Tears," "Thin Golden Chain," "Security Blanket" and "I'd Better Face It" (singles by Ronald Lee Baird) from *Chapter One* (album), recorded by Justin Temme (country), released 1999 on Door Knob.

Tips: "Our goal is to produce finished masters and shop these for major label deals. We want to produce legitimate hits."

☑ **BAL RECORDS**, P.O. Box 369, LaCanada CA 91012-0369. (818)548-1116. E-mail: balmusic@ pacbell.net. **Contact:** Adrian Bal, president or Berdella M. Bal, vice president. Record producer and music publisher (Bal & Bal Music). Estab. 1965. Produces 1-3 CDs/year. Fee derived from sales royalty when song or artist is recorded.

How to Contact: *Write or call first and obtain permission to submit.* Prefers cassette with 3 songs and lyric sheet. Include SASE. Responds in 3 months.

Music: Mostly **MOR**, **country**, **jazz**, **R&B**, **rock** and **top 40/pop**; also **blues**, **church/religious**, **easy listening** and **soul**. Produced *Special Day* (album), written and recorded by Rhonda Johnson on Bal Records (gospel). Other artists include Kathy Simmons, Paul Richards, Adrian Bal, and Terry Fischer.

☑ ⊘ **HAL BERNARD ENTERPRISES, INC.**, P.O. Box 8369, Cincinnati OH 45208. (513)871-1500. Fax: (513)871-1510. E-mail: halbernard@cinci.rr.com. **Contact:** Stan Hertzman, president. Record producer, record company (Strugglebaby Recording Co.) and music publisher (Sunnyslope Music Inc. and Bumpershoot Music Inc.). Produces 5-8 CDs/year. Fee derived from an advance per project and sales royalty.

How to Contact: Prefers CD with maximum 3 songs. No materials are returned. Responds only if interested.

Music: Produced *Close Enough for Jazz*, recorded by Frank Vincent with Michael Sharfe (jazz); *Get Me Off Or Get Off Me*, written and recorded by Cicada (rock); and *Expresso Bob*, recorded by Bobby Sharp Trio (jazz), released on Strugglebaby Records.

◖ **BIG SKY AUDIO PRODUCTIONS**, 1035 E. Woodland Ave. #2, Springfield PA 19064. (610)328-4709. Fax: (610)328-7728. Website: www.bigskyaudio.com. **Contact:** Drew Raison, producer. Record producer. Estab. 1990. Produces 20-30 CDs/year. Fee derived from sales royalty when song or artist is recorded or outright fee from recording artist or record company.

How to Contact: Submit demo tape by mail. Unsolicited submissions are OK. Prefers CD/CDR with 3 songs and lyric sheet. "Don't send it to us if it isn't copyrighted!" Does not return material. Responds in 6 weeks.

Music: Mostly **rock**, **R&B**, **pop** and **gospel**; also **anything with strong vocals**.

🅽 ◖ **BIRTHPLACE PRODUCTIONS**, P.O. Box 1651, Bristol TN 37621. (423)878-3535. E-mail: stevenp8@prodigy.net. Website: http://pages.prodigy.net/stevenp8. **Contact:** Steve Patrick, president. Record producer and record company (Riverbend Records). Estab. 1994. Produces 12 singles, 10 LPs and 20 CDs/year. Fee derived from outright fee from recording artist or record company.

How to Contact: *Write or call first and obtain permission to submit or to arrange personal interview.* Prefers cassette or videocassette with 10 songs and lyric sheet. Include SASE. Responds in 3 weeks.

Music: Mostly **country**, **gospel** and **folk**. Produced "Jinny Rose" (single), written and recorded by Garry Johnson on Sabteca Records; *Power and Grace* (album), written and recorded by Tommy Bradford on Riverbend Records; and *Light of the World* (album), written and recorded by Steve Warren on S&B Records.

Tips: "Stay focused. Be willing to accept that the commitment you make is determined by your understanding of the business itself."

☑ ◖ **BLUES ALLEY RECORDS**, Rt. 1, Box 288, Clarksburg WV 26301. (304)599-1055. Website: www.bluesalleymusic.com. **Contact:** Joshua Swiger, producer. Record producer, record company and music publisher (Blues Alley Publishing/BMI). New Christian record label (Joshua Tree Records/BMI). Produces 2 singles, 1-2 LPs and 2 EPs/year. Fee derived from sales royalty when song or artist is recorded.

How to Contact: Submit demo tape by mail. Unsolicited submissions are OK. Prefers CD or cassette with 4 songs and lyric and lead sheets. Does not return material. Responds in 6 weeks.

Music: Mostly **Christian**, **alternative** and **pop**. Produced *Casting Stones*, recorded by The New Relics; *Imaginary Friends* (album by Mike Arbogast), recorded by Imaginary Friends (rock) on Blues Alley Records; "I'll Fly Away" (single), written and recorded by J. Nicholson (Christian), released on Blues Alley Records.

🅽 ◖ **CACOPHONY PRODUCTIONS**, 35 Montell St., Oakland CA 94611. (212)777-8763. Producer: Steven Miller. Record producer and music publisher (In Your Face Music). Estab. 1981. Fee derived from sales royalty when song or artist is recorded, or outright fee from recording artist or record company.

How to Contact: *Call first and obtain permission to submit.* Prefers cassette with 3 songs and lyric sheet. "Send a cover letter of no more than three paragraphs giving some background on yourself and the music. Also explain specifically what you are looking for Cacophony Productions to do." Does not return material. Responds only if interested.

Music: Mostly **progressive pop/rock**, **singer/songwriter** and **progressive country**. Produced Dar Williams, Suzanne Vega, John Gorka, Michael Hedges, Juliana Hatfield and Medeski-Martin & Wood.

☑ ⬟ CANDYSPITEFUL PRODUCTIONS, 4202 Co. Rt. 4, Oswego NY 13126. (480)468-7017. E-mail: mandrakerocks@yahoo.com. Website: www.candyspiteful.com. **Contact:** William Ferraro, president. Record producer, record company (Candyspiteful Productions), music publisher (Candyspiteful Productions). Estab. 2000. Produces 12 singles, 2 albums per year. Fee derived from outright fee from recording artist.

How to Contact: Submit demo tape by mail. Unsolicited submissions are OK. Prefers CD/CDR with 3 songs and lyric sheet and cover letter. Does not return material. Responds only if interested.

Music: Mostly **progressive rock**, **rock/pop/R&B** and **smooth jazz/rock**. Produced *Cloud Nine* (album written by David Farnsworth), recorded by Thunderhead (hard rock), released 2001 on Candyspiteful Productions.

⬟ JAN CELT MUSICAL SERVICES, 4026 NE 12th Ave., Portland OR 97212. (503)287-8045. E-mail: flyheart@teleport.com. Website: http://home.teleport.com/~flyheart. **Contact:** Jan Celt, owner. Record producer, music producer and publisher (Wiosna Nasza Music/BMI) and record company (Flying Heart Records). Estab. 1982. Produces 3-5 CDs/year.

How to Contact: Submit demo tape by mail. Unsolicited submissions are OK. Prefers high-quality cassette with 1-10 songs and lyric sheet. "SASE required for any response." Does not return materials. Responds in 4 months.

Music: Mostly **R&B**, **rock** and **blues**; also **jazz**. Produced "Vexatious Progressions" (single), written and recorded by Eddie Harris (jazz); "Bong Hit" (single by Chris Newman), recorded by Snow Bud & the Flower People (rock); and "She Moved Away" (single by Chris Newman), recorded by Napalm Beach, all on Flying Heart Records. Other artists include The Esquires and Janice Scroggins.

⬟ COACHOUSE MUSIC, P.O. Box 1308, Barrington IL 60011. (847)382-7631. Fax: (847)382-7651. E-mail: coachouse1@aol.com. **Contact:** Michael Freeman, president. Record producer. Estab. 1984. Produces 6-8 CDs/year. Fee derived from sales royalty when song or artist is recorded.

How to Contact: *Write first and obtain permission to submit.* Prefers cassette, DAT or CD with 3-5 songs and lyric sheet. Include SASE. Responds in 6 weeks.

Music: Mostly **rock**, **pop** and **blues**; also **alternative rock** and **country/roots**. Produced *Casque Nu* (album), written and recorded by Charlelie Couture on Chrysalis EMI France (contemporary pop); *Time Will Tell*, recorded by Studebaker John on Blind Pig Records (blues); *Where Blue Begins* (album by various/D. Coleman), recorded by Deborah Coleman on Blind Pig Records (contemporary blues) and *Floobie* (album by Dan Ruprecht), recorded by The Pranks on Coachhouse Records (pop). Other artists include Echosend, Eleventh Dream Day, Magic Slim, Amarillo Kings, The Tantrums, The Pranks, Allison Johnson, The Bad Examples, Mississippi Heat and Supermint.

Tips: "Be honest, be committed, strive for excellence."

⬟ COFFEE AND CREAM PRODUCTIONS, 1138 E. Price St., Philadelphia PA 19138. (215)842-3450. **Contact:** Bolden Abrams, Jr., producer. Record producer, music publisher (Coffee and Cream Publishing Company/ASCAP) and record company (Coffee and Cream Records). Produces 12 singles, 12 12" singles and 6 LPs/year. Fee derived from sales royalty or outright fee from recording artist or record company.

How to Contact: Submit demo tape by mail. Unsolicited submissions are OK. Prefers cassette with 1-4 songs and lyric sheet. Include SASE. Responds in 2 weeks.

Music: Mostly **R&B**, **pop** and **country**; also **gospel** and **dance**. Produced "Si Me Dejo Llevar" (by Jose Gomez/Sheree Sano/Julio Hernandez); and "I Can't Wait" (by Abrams/Degrazio/Urbach), both recorded by Melissa Manjom on Misa Records; and "If I Let Myself Go" (by Gomez/Sano), recorded by Ron Hevener on RMB Records. Other artists include Michal Beckham, Robert Benjamin, Darrall Campbell, Elektra, Christopher Shirk, Tony Gilmore, Janine Whetstone, Kissie Darnell and Debra Spice.

☑ ◎ **COLD CREEK RECORDS (CCR)**, (formerly Interstate Records), 2479 Murfreesboro Rd. #327, Nashville TN 37217-3554. (615)361-4438. Fax: (615)361-4438. E-mail: coldcreekent@aol. com. CEO: Jack Batey. President of A&R: Jackson Smith. Record producer and record company. Estab. 2001. Produces 10 singles and 2 CDs/year. Pays negotiable royalty to artist on contract; statutory rate to publisher per song on record.

How to Contact: Submit demo tape or CD by mail. Unsolicited submissions are OK. Prefers CD or cassette with 3-5 songs and lyric sheet. "In screening artists we ask for original material only. Thus we can listen for originality in vocal delivery and judge the strength of writing capabilities. (Please no cover songs or karaoke voice overs)." Does not return material. Responds in 2 months.

Music: Mostly **traditional country**, **bluegrass**, **Texas swing** and **cowboy ballads**. Produced "Bad Love" (single), written and recorded by Barbi Presley; and "Us Cowboys Know How to Take a Fall" (by Larry and Rob Matson), recorded by Bart McEntire, all on Ameri-Star.

Tips: "Be original in your vocals, lyrics and melodies. Submitting full production demos is not necessary. We prefer a vocal with guitar or piano to accompany."

⊕ ◎ **COLLECTOR RECORDS**, P.O. Box 1200, 3260 AE oud beyerland, Holland, The Netherlands. Phone: 186-604266. Fax: 186-604366. E-mail: sales@collectorrec.com. Website: www.collecto rrec.com. **Contact:** Cees Klop, president. Record producer and music publisher (All Rock Music). Produces 25 CDs/year. Fee derived from outright fee from record company.

How to Contact: Submit demo tape by mail. Unsolicited submissions are OK. Prefers cassette. SAE and IRC. Responds in 2 months.

Music: Mostly **'50s rock**, **rockabilly** and **country rock**; also **piano boogie woogie**. Produced "I've Got Nothing" (single by Chester/Ruby) from *Piano Rock and Roll* (album), recorded by Chester and Ruby (rock & roll); "I'm In Love" (single by Berglinsd) from *Hokey Pokey Rock (album), recorded by Frans & the Never Mind Band (50s rock); "Rock Away My Blues" (single by E. Barnett) from Crazy Rockin'* (album), recorded by Sandra Peters (50s rock), all released 2001 on Collector Records.

Tips: "Only send the kind of music we produce."

Ⓝ ⊕ ◎ **JOHNNY COPPIN/RED SKY RECORDS**, P.O. Box 27, Stroud, Glos. GL6 0YQ United Kingdom. Phone/fax: 01453-836877. Record producer, music publisher (PRS) and record company (Red Sky Records). Estab. 1985. Produces 1 album/year. Fee derived from sales royalty when song or artist is recorded.

How to Contact: *Write first and obtain permission to submit.* Does not return material. Responds in 6 months.

Music: Mostly **rock**, **modern folk** and **roots music**. Produced "A Country Christmas" and "Keep the Flame" written and recorded by Johnny Coppin; and "Dead Lively!," written and recorded by Paul Burgess, all on Red Sky Records. Other artists include David Goodland.

Ⓝ ◯ **COTTON TOWN PRODUCTIONS**, P.O. Box 804, Commerce GA 30529. **Contact:** A&R Review Department. Record producer, music publisher (Cotton Town Music Company). Estab 2002. Produces 4 singles and 2 albums/year. Fee derived from sales royalty when song or artist is recorded.

How to Contact: Submit demo tape by mail. Unsolicited submissions are OK. Prefers cassette or CD/CDR with 2-3 songs, lyric sheet and cover letter. "Please put name and address clearly on outside of your package." Include SASE. Responds in 5 weeks.

Music: Mostly **alternative**, **country** and **blues**; also **rock**, **gospel** and **pop**.

OPENNESS TO SUBMISSIONS: ◯ beginners; ◙ beginners and experienced; ◙ experienced only; ◎ no unsolicited submissions/industry referrals only.

Tips: "We are looking for singers, bands, and songs in many formats. We need material and artists who would fit in with markets such as Atlanta, Nashville, Los Angeles, and New York."

N ⊘ COUNTRY STAR PRODUCTIONS, 439 Wiley Ave., Franklin PA 16323. (814)432-4633. **Contact:** Norman Kelly, president. Record company, music publisher (Country Star Music/ASCAP, Kelly Music/BMI and Process Music/BMI) and record company (Country Star, Process, Mersey and CSI Records). Estab. 1970. Releases 5-8 singles and 5-8 LPs/year. Fee derived from sales royalty when song or artist is recorded.
How to Contact: Submit demo tape by mail. Unsolicited submissions are OK. Prefers cassette with 2-4 songs and typed lyric or lead sheet. SASE. Reports in 2 weeks.
Music: Mostly **country**; also **rock**, **gospel**, **MOR** and **r&b**. Produced "Holiday Waltz" (single by Wrightman/Stelzer), recorded by Debbie Sue; "Red Heifer" (single by J. Barbaria), recorded by Bob Stamper, both released on Mersey Records. Other artists include Gary King, Junie Loo, Larry Pieper and Jeffrey Alan Connors.

⊠ ⊘ DOUGLAS CRAIG, (formerly Bewildering Music, Inc.), P.O. Box 302, Locust Valley NY 11560. (516)759-5560. E-mail: bminc@aol.com. Website: http://members.aol.com/bminc/homepage.htm. **Contact:** Douglas W. Craig, producer. Record producer. Estab. 1992. Produces 1 or 2 EPs and 3-5 CDs/year. Fee derived from flat fee or hourly rate.
How to Contact: Prefers cassette, CD or VHS videocassette with photo. All submissions are kept on file.
Music: Mostly **solo artists**, **rock, electronic world beat**; also **remix**, **soundtrack work** (melodic preferred). Artist must live in the New York area and travel to the producer's studio. Other artists include Breakthru and Cuentos Blancos.

✓ ⊘ JERRY CUPIT PRODUCTIONS, Box 121904, Nashville TN 37212. (615)731-0100. Fax: (615)731-3005. E-mail: cupit@cupitmusic.com. Website: www.cupitmusic.com. **Contact:** Denise Roberts, creative assistant. Record producer and music publisher (Cupit Music). Estab. 1984. Fee derived from sales royalty when song or artist is recorded or outright fee from artist.
How to Contact: *Visit website for policy.* Prefers CD with bio and photo. Include SASE. Responds in 2 months.
Music: Mostly **traditional and contemporary uptempo**, **country**, **Southern rock** and **gospel**. Produced "What If He's Right" (single by Jerry Cupit) from *Memarie* (album), recorded by Memarie (Christian country), released 2000 on HotSong.com Records; and "I'm Not Homeless" (single by Jerry Cupit/Ken Mellons/Randy Roberts) from *Wings of a Dove* (album), recorded by Ken Mellons (Christian country), released 2000 on Curb Records. Other artists include Jack Robertson and Jon Nicholson.
Tips: "Be prepared to work hard and be able to take constructive/professional criticism."

○ DAP ENTERTAINMENT, PMB 364, 7100 Lockwood Blvd., Boardman OH 44512. (330)782-5031. Fax: (330)782-6954. Website: www.dapentertainment.com. **Contact:** Darryl Alexander, producer. Record Producer and music publisher (Alexander Sr. Music, BMI). Estab. 1997. Produces 12 singles and 2-4 CDs/year. Fee derived from sales royalty (producer points) when song or artist is recorded or outright fee from recording artist or record company.
How to Contact: *Write first and obtain permission to submit.* Prefers cassette with 2-4 songs and lyric sheet. Include SASE. Responds in 1 month. "No phone calls or faxes will be accepted."
Music: Mostly **contemporary jazz**, **urban contemporary gospel**; also **R&B**. Produced "Take A Chance" (single by Darryl Alexander/Sheila Hayes), recorded by Sheila Hayes (urban jazz), released 2002; and "Feel Your Love" and "You Are So Beautiful" (singles), written recorded by Darryl Alexander Sr. (urban jazz), released 2001 on DAP Entertainment. Other artists include Kathryn Williams.

N ⊡ DAVINCI'S NOTEBOOK RECORDS, 20 Admiral Rd., St. Catharines, Ontario L2P 1G6 Canada. (905)682-5161. E-mail: admin@davincismusic.com. Website: www.davincismusic.com.

insider report

Singer-songwriter builds new groove with producer

Lucky Spaulding grew up in a musical family, including a session musician father who toured with national acts such as Roberta Flack, and played out regularly with his own group, Cincinnati Joe and Mad Lydia. "My whole family played music, " he says. "There were instruments everywhere from the time I was an infant. I quickly caught on." He learned to sing and learned several instruments, including a particular love of bass and drums "I'm a moderate guitar player and keyboard player," he says. "But bass and drums—I'll bite into them!"

Lucky Spaulding

From a young age, he wrote and performed his own personal mix of R&B, rock and reggae with bands in the Cincinnati, Ohio, area. Influenced by bands and artists on the reggae side such as Bob Marley, Steel Pulse, and Black Uhuru, he racked up experience as a live performer and developed a classic smoky reggae vocal tone. At the same time, his parallel interest in classic funk and devotion to studio wizards Steely Dan developed his sense for concise, layered grooves. "Steely Dan were perfectionists," he says. "They have an identity. As soon as you hear the song, you know it's them. In R&B, I also love Earth, Wind & Fire, Parliament, Stevie Wonder—the cream of the '60s and '70s—and even going back to the jazz era, I love Billie Holliday and Ella Fitzgerald."

Spaulding considers this early period to be primarily a learning period, with several false starts and one primary obstacle to moving forward. "Money," he laughs. "Money and not much knowledge of how to do it. I'm sure we could have played three gigs and taken all the money and done it, but I was young. And I'm actually kind of glad that didn't happen, because I want to make an impact with my new stuff where people aren't going to say, 'Oh, it's that reggae guy, what's he doing now?' "

Eventually, Spaulding put together his own band, Lucky and the Zionites, as a focus for his own musical aspirations. With the Zionites backing him up, he released one independent album in 2000, *The Living*. While happy with the album as an artist, he was dissatisfied with the limited profile the album generated as a local, independent release. "It was hardly known. We gave out probably five hundred of them free—we got about a thousand—but the idea wasn't to make money, it was more-or-less to saturate Cincinnati and the surrounding area. We got a great response. The website has done extremely well, and mp3.com asked to use the title track in a world-wide advertisement for their site. There just wasn't really a buzz in the mainstream."

While successful among the band's regional following, the release of the album was also a hard lesson in the difficulties every songwriter and artist experiences at some point in dealing with criticism. He says, "The funny thing about *The Living* album, as far as industry people were concerned, was it got bad responses from critics—too much going on, too much of a blurry sound. Even if you do get mad, you have to look at that and say, 'Cool, I'm going to take this criticism and go back in the studio, spend more time, more money, and do something right. And not take a negative approach to criticism.' "

So, feeling the need for a change, Spaulding put out feelers through his accumulated network of local music industry contacts to see what kind of opportunities might arise. A referral from a former bandmate led to work as a session vocalist in a local studio, singing jingles for clients such as Gold Star Chili, United Bank and Penn Station. During those sessions, he met Cincinnati-based producer Rob Fetters. "Rob hired me to do some jingles. I did the commercials first, and I actually asked Rob, 'Hey are you a producer?' "

As it turned out, Rob Fetters had a considerable track record in the music industry. His résumé includes a longstanding stint in the Bears with renowned guitarist Adrian Belew, a Cincinnati-area native who has toured over the years with artists like King Crimson, Frank Zappa, Talking Heads and David Bowie. "Rob is a funny character," says Spaulding. "He's known internationally. He played with Adrian Belew, the Raisins and the Psychodots. In Cincinnati he's a household name."

Fetters' musical background in more mainstream pop and rock sounds also struck Spaulding as the sort of unlikely match that might offer a new perspective and produce interesting results. "Rob comes from a totally different world," he says. "He comes from a rock, Elvis Costello-type of genre, which is cool. There's a well of good things there. And I said 'OK, I'll take my stuff down and let this guy produce it, and see what he comes up with.' And he's doing this with no strings attached as producer. If it gets signed, and they like him and want to hire him as an independent producer commissioned to produce my stuff, I think that might work out."

The pairing worked, and their sessions together generated *Dinosaur Love*, a six-song EP. The recording gave a new pop gloss and studio sheen to Spaulding's longstanding reggae and R&B stylings, while also stretching into newer, more experimental territory with the title track, "Dinosaur Love." Written by Spaulding's brother and mother—formidable musicians and songwriters in their own right—the song features dinosaur sound effects and signature guitar wizardry courtesy of Belew. "He worked on 'Dinosaur Love,' the one song I feel is going to be the one to get some attention," says Spaulding. "He gave some guitar samples that sound like dinosaur sounds.' "

Spaulding is happy with the results, but is quick to point out the extensive preparation and planning—the hallmark of a productive producer-artist relationship—that went into the sessions. "The aim of this project was to spend the money right to do it right—the right equipment, the right studio. Take more time for each song, and pick the right songs," he says. "And our work started before we even went into the studio. We actually hooked up in a rehearsal spot for a week, and went over the songs, the arrangements, from beginning to end, breakdowns, how we were going to shape the verses, everything. And that way, when we went into the studio, we knew exactly what we were going to do and weren't wasting any time."

However, even with the completion of this step in his music career plan, he recognizes it is only the beginning of a new phase, with new challenges and new opportunities. He also knows part of taking on these new opportunities, especially in the most commercial sectors of the music industry, is the realistic possibility of having to make tradeoffs—and the imminent need for a professional team working on his side. "I think one hell of a business management team and a good lawyer can get you the right deal. My family on my mom's side started radio station WEBN in Cincinnati, and they're all lawyers and radio business people. I think I'll need a bigger manager eventually, and I haven't met anyone yet. And obviously, when you're first starting out, there are going to be things the record company gets and you don't—the list goes on and on—but I think if you can just get a little chunk and get started, then longevity can kick in."

—*Ian Bessler*

Owner: Kevin Richard. Record producer, record company, music publisher, distributor and MIDI recording facility. Estab. 1992. Produces 1 cassette and 1 CD/year. Fee derived from outright fee from artist or commission on sales.

How to Contact: Submit demo CD by mail. Unsolicited submissions are OK. Prefers CD and bio. Does not return material. Responds in 6 weeks.

Music: Mostly **rock**, **instrumental rock**, **New Age** and **progressive-alternative**; also **R&B**, **pop** and **jazz**. Produced *Windows* (by Kevin Hotte/Andy Smith), recorded by Musicom on DaVinci's Notebook Records (power New Age); *Inventing Fire*, written and recorded by Kevin Richard on DNR/Independent (instrumental rock); and *The Cunninghams*, written and recorded by The Cunninghams on Independent (gospel).

Tips: "DNR is an artist-run label. Local bands and performers will receive priority. Be more interested in getting a-foot-in-the-door exposure as opposed to making a fortune. Be satisfied with conquering the world using 'baby steps.' Indie labels don't have large corporate budgets for artist development. We are more about online distribution than artist development. Being a local act means that you can perform live to promote your releases. As an indie artist, selling from the stage is probably going to bring you the biggest volume of sales."

☑ 🖼 ⊘ **EDWARD DE MILES**, 28 E. Jackson Bldg., 10th Floor #S627, Chicago IL 60604-2263. (773)509-6381. Fax: (312)922-6964. **Contact:** Edward De Miles, president. Record producer, music publisher (Edward De Miles Music Co./BMI) and record company (Sahara Records and Filmworks Entertainment). Estab. 1981. Produces 5-10 CDs/year. Fee derived from sales royalty when song or artist is recorded.

How to Contact: *Does not accept unsolicited submissions.*

Music: Mostly **R&B/dance**, **top 40 pop/rock** and **contemporary jazz**; also **country**, **TV and film themes—songs and jingles**. Produced "Moments" and "Dance Wit Me" (singles) (dance), both written and recorded by Steve Lynn; and "Games" (single), written and recorded by D'von Edwards (jazz), all on Sahara Records. Other artists include Multiple Choice.

Tips: "Copyright all material before submitting. Equipment and showmanship a must."

🎵 ⊘ **AL DELORY AND MUSIC MAKERS**, 3000 Hillsboro Rd. #11, Nashville TN 37215. (615)292-2140. Fax: (615)297-6031. **Contact:** Al DeLory, president. Record producer and career consultant (DeLory Music/ASCAP). Estab. 1987. Fee derived from outright fee from recording artist.

• Al DeLory has won two Grammy Awards and has been nominated five times.

How to Contact: *Write or call first and obtain permission to submit or to arrange personal interview.* Prefers CD or VHS videocassette. Include SASE. Responds in 1 month.

Music: Mostly **pop** and **Latin**. Produced "Gentle On My Mind" (single), "By the Time I Get to Phoenix" (single) and "Wichita Lineman" (single), all recorded by Glen Campbell. Other artists include Letter Men and Gary Puckett.

Tips: "Seek advice and council only with professionals with a track record."

🅽 🌐 ⊘ **DEMI MONDE RECORDS & PUBLISHING LTD.**, Foel Studio, Llanfair Caereinion, Powys, SY21 ODS Wales. Phone/fax: 01938-810758. E-mail: demi.monde@dial.pipex.com. Website: www.demi.monde.co.uk/demimonde. **Contact:** Dave Anderson, managing director. Record producer, music publisher (PRS & MCPS) and record company (Demi Monde Records). Estab. 1982. Produces 5 singles, 15 12″ singles, 15 LPs and 10 CDs/year. Fee derived from sales royalty or outright fee from record company.

How to Contact: Submit demo tape by mail. Unsolicited submissions are OK. Prefers cassette with 3 or 4 songs and lyric sheet. Does not return material. Responds in 6 weeks.

THE OPENNESS TO SUBMISSIONS INDEX at the back of this book lists all companies in this section by how open they are to submissions.

Music: Mostly **rock**, **pop** and **blues**. Produced *Average Man*, recorded by Mother Gong (rock); *Frozen Ones*, recorded by Tangle Edge (rock); and *Blue Boar Blues* (by T.S. McPhee), recorded by Groundhogs (rock), all on Demi Monde Records. Other artists include Gong and Hawkwind.

JOEL DIAMOND ENTERTAINMENT, Dept. SM, 3940 Laurel Canyon Blvd., Suite 441, Studio City CA 91604. (818)980-9588. Fax: (818)980-9422. E-mail: jdiamond20@aol.com. **Contact:** Joel Diamond. Record producer, music publisher and manager. Fee derived from sales royalty when song is recorded or outright fee from recording artist or record company.
How to Contact: *Contact first and obtain permission to submit*. Does not return material. Responds only if interested.
Music: Mostly **dance**, **easy listening**, **country**, **R&B**, **rock**, **soul** and **top 40/pop**. Produced "One Night In Bangkok" (single by Robey); "Love is the Reason" (single by Cline/Wilson), recorded by E. Humperdinck and G. Gaynor on Critique Records (A/C); "After the Loving" (single), recorded by E. Humperdinck; I Am What I Am" (single), recorded by Gloria Gaynor; and "Paradise" (single), recorded by Kair.

PHILIP D. DIXON III, ATTORNEY AT LAW, 2501 Parkview Dr. #500, Ft. Worth TX 76102. (817)332-8553. Fax: (817)332-2834. E-mail: pdixon3@yahoo.com. **Contact:** Philip D. Dixon III, attorney. Record producer, artist representative; trademark/copyright protection for artists. Estab. 1995. Fee derived from sales royalty when song or artist is recorded or outright fee from record company. "We do charge for statutory payments made to third parties."
How to Contact: *Write first and obtain permission to submit or write first to arrange personal interview*. Prefers CD with any number of songs and lyric sheet; although cassette and videocassette are OK. SAE ("we pay return postage"). Responds in 1 month.
Music: Mostly **rock**, **country** and **Latino**; also **rap**.
Tips: "Protect your work from a legal standpoint before making any disclosures to anyone. Be vigilant in your creative and business affairs."

COL. BUSTER DOSS PRESENTS, 341 Billy Goat Hill Rd., Winchester TN 37398. **Contact:** Col. Buster Doss, producer. Fax: (931)649-2732. E-mail: cbd@vallnet.com. Website: http://stardustco untrymusic.com. Record producer, record company (Stardust, Wizard), management firm and music publisher (Buster Doss Music/BMI). Estab. 1959. Produces 100 singles, 20 LPs and 20 CDs/year. Fee derived from sales royalty when song or artist is recorded.
How to Contact: *Write first and obtain permission to submit*. Prefers cassette or CD with 2 songs and lyric sheet. Include SASE. Responds in 1 week if interested.
Music: Mostly **country** and **gospel**. Produced *Miss Y2K* (album), written and recorded by Brant Miller; *Ahead of His Time* (album), written and recorded by Rooster Quantrell; and *Lying Again* (album), written and recorded by Bronco Buck Cody, all released 1999 on Stardust Records. Other artists include Troy Cook Jr., Mark Brumfield, Jerri Arnold, Bob Norman, Michael Apidgian, Lolene, Tennessee Bill Foster, Jillian Marie, Mayf Nutter, Billy Swan, Jack Blanchard, Misty Morgan, Billy Grammer, Linda Wunder, Honey James, Rooster Quantrell and Donna Darlene.

ESQUIRE INTERNATIONAL, P.O. Box 6032, Station B, Miami FL 33101-6032. (305)547-1424. **Contact:** Jeb Stuart, president. Record producer, music publisher (Jeb Stuart Music) and management firm. Produces 6 singles and 2 LPs/year. Fee derived from sales royalty or independent leasing of masters and placing songs.
How to Contact: Submit demo tape by mail. Unsolicited submissions are OK. Prefers cassette or CD with 2-4 songs and lead sheet. Include SASE. Responds in 1 month.
Music: Mostly **blues**, **church/religious**, **country**, **dance**, **gospel**, **jazz**, **rock**, **soul** and **top 40/pop**. Produced "Go to Sleep, Little Baby" (single by Jeb Stuart), recorded by Cafidia and Jeb Stuart; "Guns Guns (No More Guns)" (single) and "No One Should Be Alone on Christmas" (single), both written and recorded by Jeb Stuart, all on Esquire Int'l Records. Other artists include Moments Notice and Night Live.

THE ETERNAL SONG AGENCY, P.O. Box 121, Worthington OH 43085. E-mail: submis sions@eternal-song-agency.com. Website: www.eternal-song-agency.com. **Contact:** Attn: A&R. Executive Producer: Leopold Xavier Crawford. Record producer, record company and music publisher (Fragrance Records, Song of Solomon Records, Emerald Records, Lilly Records, Ancient of Days Music and Dynasty Publishing). Estab. 1986. Produces 7-15 singles and 5 CDs/year. Fee derived from sales royalty when song or artist is recorded or outright fee from recording artist or record company.

How to Contact: *Write first and obtain permission to submit.* Prefers cassette or videocassette with 3 songs and lyric or lead sheet. "Type all printed material. Professionalism of presentation will get you an ear with us." Include SASE. Responds in 6 weeks.

Music: Pop, **AOR**, **country**, **contemporary Christian**, **Christian inspirational** and **southern gospel music**. Produced "The Ultimate Answer" (single by Michael Higgins), recorded by Anna Jackson on Fragrance Records. Other artists include Bloodbought, Seventh Dynasty, Streets of Gold and Laura Sanders.

N ☐ **GLOCC COCCED RECORDS**, 117 S. Court St., Irvine KY 40336. (606)723-3078. E-mail: GloccCocced@mail2silver.com. Website: www.GloccCocced.4t.com. **Contact:** Randy A. Moore. Record producer, record company and music publisher. Estab. 2001. Produces 1-4 singles and 2-4 albums/year. Fee derived from outright fee from recording artist.

How to Contact: Submit demo tape by mail. Unsolicited submissions are OK. Prefers CD/CDR with 4 songs and lyric sheet, lead sheet, and cover letter. "Please include a full bio." Does not return material. Responds in 1 month only if interested.

Music: Mostly **gangsta**, **rap** and **hip-hop**; also **r&b**, **dance** and **instrumental**. Does not want rock, jazz, blues, or country. Produced "Gotta Get It" (single by CIX) from *Gotta Get It* (album), recorded by CIX (rap); and "My Life" (single by LoLo/ CIX) from *From Out 99 Pride* (album), recorded by LoLo and CIX, both released on Glocc Cocced Records. Other artists include Lil' C.

Tips: "Be confident. Practice makes perfect, time makes effort."

☑ **HAILING FREQUENCY MUSIC PRODUCTIONS**, 7438 Shoshone Ave., Van Nuys CA 91406. (818)881-9888. Fax: (818)881-0555. E-mail: blowinsmokeband@ktb.net. Website: www.blowinsmokeband.com. President: Lawrence Weisberg. Vice President: Larry Knight. Record producer, record company (Blowin' Smoke Records), management firm (Blowin' Smoke Productions) and music publisher (Hailing Frequency Publishing). Estab. 1992. Produces 3 LPs and 3 CDs/year. Fee derived from sales royalty when song or artist is recorded or outright fee from artist.

How to Contact: *Write or call first and obtain permission to submit.* Prefers cassette or VHS ½″ videocassette. "Write or print legibly with complete contact instructions." Include SASE. Responds in 1 month.

Music: Mostly **contemporary R&B**, **blues** and **blues-rock**; also **songs for film**, **jingles for commercials** and **gospel (contemporary)**. Produced *100% Pure R&B* (album by various), recorded by Blowin' Smoke Rhythm & Blues Band (R&B), released 2000 on Blowin' Smoke Records. Other artists include the Fabulous Smokettes.

☐ **HAWORTH PRODUCTIONS**, Box 1446, Laurie MO 65038. (573)374-1111. Fax: (775)522-1533. E-mail: mashred@yahoo.com. Website: www.geocities.com/mashred. **Contact:** Dann E. Haworth, president/producer. Record producer and music publisher (Southern Most Publishing/BMI). Estab. 1985. Produces 5 singles, 3 12″ singles, 10 LPs, 5 EPs and 10 CDs/year. Fee derived from sales royalty when song or artist is recorded or outright fee from recording artist.

How to Contact: Submit demo tape by mail. Unsolicited submissions are OK. Prefers cassette or 7½ ips or 15 ips reel-to-reel or CD with 3 songs and lyric or lead sheets. Include SASE. Responds in 2 weeks.

Music: Mostly **rock**, **country** and **gospel**; also **jazz**, **R&B** and **New Age**. Produced *Christmas Joy* (album by Esther Kreak) on Serene Sounds Records. Other artists include The Hollowmen, Jordan Border, Jim Wilson, Tracy Creech and Tony Glise.

Tips: "Keep it simple and from the heart."

⚙ **HEART CONSORT MUSIC**, 410 First St. W., Mt. Vernon IA 52314. E-mail: hrtcnsrtms@aol.c om. Website: www.heartconsortmusic.com. **Contact:** Catherine Lawson, manager. Record producer, record company and music publisher. Estab. 1980. Produces 2-3 CDs/year. Fee derived from sales royalty when song or artist is recorded.
How to Contact: Submit demo tape by mail. Unsolicited submissions are OK. Prefers cassette or VHS videocassette with 3 songs and 3 lyric sheets. Include SASE. Responds in 3 months.
Music: Mostly **jazz**, **New Age** and **contemporary**. Produced *New Faces* (album), written and recorded by James Kennedy on Heart Consort Music (world/jazz).
Tips: "We are interested in jazz/New Age artists with quality demos and original ideas. We aim for an international audience."

N ⚙ **HES FREE PRODUCTIONS & PUBLISHING COMPANY**, 3709 E. 29th, P.O. Box 1214, Bryan TX 77806-1214. (979)268-3263. Fax: (979)589-2575. E-mail: hesfreeprodandpubco@y ahoo.com. Website: http://home1.gte.net/jbhes/. Executive Producer/CEO/Owner: Brenda M. Freeman-Heslip. Producer of songwriting: Jamie Heslip. Assistant Producer: Rochelle Heslip. Record producer, music publisher and management agency. Estab. 2001. Fee derived from sales royalty when song or artist is recorded, outright fee from recording artist and outright fee from record company.
How to Submit: *Only accepts material referred by a reputable industry source (manager, entertainment attorney, etc.).* Include CD/CDR. Does not return submissions. Responds in 6 weeks only if interested.
Music: Mostly **r&b**, **gospel** and **rap**; also **rock**. Does not want country. "We will ensure that each project is completed with professionalism, with the highest technology methods possible. Additionally, our goal is to publish and record over 200 songs annually." Produced "Texas Boys" (single by Chris Idlebird) from *Texas Boys* (album), recorded by Chris Idlebird and Vicki Diggs (rap), released 2002; "Controversial Crossover" (single by "Mike-Ray" Ray Brooks) from *Controversial Crossover* (album), recorded by "Mike-Ray" Ray Brooks (r&b), released 2002; "Walk through the Rays" (single by Donell Travis), from *Dontray the Ghetto Prophet* (album), recorded by Donnell Travis and Ralatraneka Mercer (rap), released 2002. Also Donnise Williams; Damion Turner; "Michael-Wayne" Wells.

⚙ **INTEGRATED ENTERTAINMENT**, 3333 Walnut St. #209, Philadelphia PA 19104-3408. (215)417-6921. E-mail: gelboni@aol.com. **Contact:** Lawrence Gelburd, president. Record producer. Estab. 1991. Produces 6 EPs and 6 CDs/year. Fee derived from sales royalty when song or artist is recorded or outright fee from recording artist or record company.
How to Contact: Submit demo tape by mail. Solicited submissions only. Prefers CD with 3 songs. "Draw a guitar on the outside of envelope so we'll know it's from a songwriter." Responds in 2 months.
Music: Mostly **rock** and **pop**. Produced *Gold Record* (album), written and recorded by Dash Rip Rock on Ichiban Records (rock); *Virus* (album), written and recorded by Margin of Error on Treehouse Records (modern rock); and *I Divide* (album), written and recorded by Amy Carr on Evil Twin Records (AAA). Other artists include Land of the Blind, Grimace, Harpoon, Sprawl, Lockdown and Tripe.

⚙ **ALEXANDER JANOULIS PRODUCTIONS/BIG AL JANO PRODUCTIONS**, 1957 Kilburn Dr., Atlanta GA 30324. (770)662-6661. E-mail: ajproductions@hottrax.com. **Contact:** Oliver Cooper, vice president of A&R. CEO: Alex Janoulis. Record producer. Produces 6 singles and 2 CDs/year. Fee derived from sales royalty when song or artist is recorded or outright fee from recording artist or record company.

THE FILM & TV INDEX found at the back of this book lists companies placing music in film and TV (excluding TV commercials).

How to Contact: *Write first and obtain permission to submit.* "Letters should be short, requesting submission permission." Prefers cassette with 1-3 songs. Does not return material. Responds in 6 months.

Music: Mostly **top 40**, **rock** and **pop**; also **black** and **disco**. Produced *Lady That Digs the Blues* (album), recorded by Big Al Jano's Blues Mafia Show; *Everythang & Mo'* (album), written and recorded by Sammy Blue (blues); and *Blues You Can't Refuse* (album), written and recorded by Big Al (blues), both released 2000 on Hottrax Records. Other artists include Bullitthead, Roger Hurricane Wilson, The Bob Page Project, Mike Lorenz and Chesterfield Kings.

JAY BIRD PRODUCTIONS, 5 Highpoint Dr., RR #3, Stouffville, Ontario L4A 7X4 Canada. Phone/fax: (905)640-4104. E-mail: jaybird0@rogers.com. **Contact:** William Wallace, president. Record producer and music publisher (Smokey Bird Publishing). Estab. 1981. Produces 4 singles/year. Fee derived from sales royalty when song or artist is recorded or outright fee from recording artist.

How to Contact: *Write first and obtain permission to submit.* Prefers cassette or VHS videocassette with 3 songs and lyric sheet. Does not return material. Responds in 3 weeks.

Music: Mostly **country**; also **pop/rock**. Produced "Little Lies" (single by W. Wallace), "Dreamin' " (single by Steve Earle) and "Fine Line" (single by W.W.H.G.), all recorded by Lawnie Wallace on MCA Records (country).

JAY JAY PUBLISHING & RECORD CO., P.O. Box 41-4156, Miami FL 33141. Phone/fax: (305)758-0000. Owner: Walter Jagiello. Associate: J. Kozak. Record producer, music publisher (BMI) and record company (Jay Jay Record, Tape and Video Co.). Estab. 1951. Produces 12 singles, 12 LPs and 12 CDs/year. Fee derived from sales royalty when song or artist is recorded.

How to Contact: Submit demo tape by mail. Unsolicited submissions are OK. Prefers cassette or VHS videocassette with 6 songs and lyric and lead sheet. "Quality cassette or reel-to-reel, sheet music and lyrics." Does not return material. Responds in 2 months.

Music: Mostly **ballads**, **love songs**, **country music** and **comedy**; also **polkas**, **hymns**, **gospel** and **waltzes**. Produced "We Love our U.S.A." b/w "Blow Your Whistle"; "United We Stand Polka" (instrumental); "How I Want You Honey" b/w "It's So Exciting" (singles by Walter E. Jagiello) from *Proud to be an American* (album), recorded by Li'l Wally Jagiello, released 2001 on Jay Jay Record, Tape, CD & Video Co. Other artists include Eddie & The Slovenes, Johnny Vandal, Wisconsin Dutchmen and Eddie Zima.

JUMP PRODUCTIONS, 39 Paul Gilsonstraat, 8200 St-Andries Belgium. Phone: (050)137-63-80. **Contact:** Eddy Van Mouffaert, general manager. Record producer and music publisher (Jump Music). Estab. 1976. Produces 25 singles and 2 CDs/year. Fee derived from sales royalty when song or artist is recorded.

• See the listing for Jump Music in the Music Publishers section.

How to Contact: Submit demo tape by mail. Unsolicited submissions are OK. Prefers cassette. Does not return material. Responds in 2 weeks.

Music: Mostly **ballads**, **up-tempo**, **easy listening**, **disco** and **light pop**; also **instrumentals**. Produced *Evelien* (album by Eddy Govert), recorded by Evelien on Quartz Records (Flemish); *Liefde Komt En Liefde Gaat* (album by Les Reed), recorded by Lina on Scorpion Records; and "Father Damiaan" (single by Jan De Vuyst), recorded by Eigentijdse Jeugd on Youth Sound Records.

JUNE PRODUCTIONS LTD., "Toftrees," Church Rd., Woldingham, Surrey CR3 7JH England. Fax: 44(0)1883 652457. E-mail: mackay@dircon.co.uk. **Contact:** David Mackay, producer. Record producer and music producer (Sabre Music). Estab. 1970. Produces 6 singles, 3 LPs and 3 CDs/year. Fee derived from sales royalty.

How to Contact: Submit demo tape by mail. Unsolicited submissions are OK. Prefers CD or cassette with 1-2 songs and lyric sheet. SAE and IRC. Responds in 2 months.

Music: Mostly **MOR**, **rock** and **top 40/pop**. Produced *Web of Love* (by various), recorded by Sarah Jory on Ritz Records (country rock). Other artists include Bonnie Tyler, Cliff Richard, Frankie Miller, Johnny Hallyday, Dusty Springfield, Charlotte Henry and Barry Humphries.

KAREN KANE PRODUCER/ENGINEER. E-mail: mixmama@total.net. Website: www.total .net/~mixmama. **Contact:** Karen Kane, producer/engineer. Record producer and recording engineer. Estab. 1978. Produces 5-10 singles and 5-10 CDs/year. Fee derived from sales royalty when song or artist is recorded or outright fee from recording artist or record company.

How to Contact: *E-mail first and obtain permission to submit.* Unsolicited submissions are *not* OK. "Please note: I am not a song publisher. My expertise is in album production." Does not return material. Responds in 3 weeks.

Music: Mostly **pop**, **alternative**, **R&B/reggae** and **acoustic**. Produced *Permanent Marker*, written and recorded by Ember Swift on Few'll Ignite Sound (alternative/folk/pop); *Topless* (Juno-nominated by various artists), recorded by Big Daddy G on Reggie's Records (blues); and *Dance the Spiral Dance* (album), written and recorded by Ubaka Hill on Ladyslipper Records (African percussion with vocals). Other artists include Tracy Chapman (her first demo), Jack Grunsky, Kyn, Chad Mitchell and Kay Gardner.

Tips: "Get proper funding to be able to make a competitive, marketable product."

KINGSTON RECORDS AND TALENT, 15 Exeter Rd., Kingston NH 03848. (603)642-8493. E-mail: kingstonrecords@ttlc.net. **Contact:** Harry Mann, coordinator. Record producer, music publisher (Strawberry Soda Publishing/ASCAP) and record company (Kingston Records). Estab. 1988. Produces 3-4 singles, 2-3 12″ singles, 2-3 LPs and 1-2 CDs/year. Fee derived from sales royalty when song or artist is recorded. Deals primarily with NE and local artists.

How to Contact: *Write first and obtain permission to submit.* Prefers cassette with 1-2 songs and lyric sheet. Does not return material. Responds in 2 months.

Music: Mostly **rock**, **country** and **pop**; "no heavy metal." Produced *Count the Stars* (album), written and recorded by Doug Mitchell; *Time Machine* (album), written and recorded by Gratefull Ted, both released 1999 on Kingston Records. Other artists include Bob Moore, Candy Striper Death Orgy, Pocket Band, Jeff Walker, J. Evans, NTM, Miss Bliss, Ted Solovicus, Armand LeMay, Four On The Floor and Sumx4.

KNOWN ARTIST PRODUCTIONS, 2622 Kirtland Rd., Brewton AL 36426. (334)867-2228. President: Roy Edwards. Record producer, music publisher (Cheavoria Music Co./BMI, Baitstring Music/ASCAP) and record company (Bolivia Records, Known Artist Records). Estab. 1972. Produces 10 singles and 3 LPs/year. Fee derived from sales royalty when song or artist is recorded.

How to Contact: *Write first and obtain permission to submit.* Prefers cassette with 3 songs and lyric sheet. Responds in 1 month. "All tapes will be kept on file."

Music: Mostly **R&B**, **pop** and **country**; also **easy listening**, **MOR** and **soul**. Produced "Got To Let You Know," "You Are My Sunshine" and "You Make My Life So Wonderful" (singles), all written and recorded by Roy Edwards on Bolivia Records (R&B). Other artists include Jim Portwood, Bobbie Roberson and Brad Smiley.

ROBERT R. KOVACH, P.O. Box 7018, Warner Robins GA 31095-7018. (478)953-2800. **Contact:** Robert R. Kovach, producer. Record producer. Estab. 1976. Produces 6 singles, 2 cassettes and 1 CD/year. Fee derived from sales royalty when song or artist is recorded, or outright fee from record company.

How to Contact: Submit demo tape by mail. Unsolicited submissions are OK. Prefers cassette or CD with 4 songs and lyric sheet. Include SASE. Responds in 4 months.

Music: Mostly **country** and **pop**; also **easy listening**, **R&B**, **rock** and **gospel**. Produced "Pots & Pans" (single), recorded by Theresa Justus (country), and "You Learn A Heart to Break" (single), recorded by Wayne Little (country), both by Roy Robert Dunten; "Lord I've Been Prayin" (single by Robert R. Kovach), recorded by Napolean Starke (gospel), all on Scaramouche; "Sail Out to the Master" (single), written and recorded by Napoleon Starke (gospel), released 2002 on Holy Mackerel. Other artists include Little Rudy.

Tips: "Submit a demo and be patient."

L.A. ENTERTAINMENT, INC., 6367 Selma Ave., Hollywood CA 90028. (323)467-1496. Fax: (323)467-0911. E-mail: info@warriorrecords.com. Website: www.warriorrecords.com. **Contact:**

Jim Ervin, A&R. Record producer, record company (Warrior Records) and music publisher (New Entity Music/ASCAP, New Copyright Music/BMI). Estab. 1988. Fee derived from sales royalty when song or artist is recorded.

How to Contact: Submit demo tape by mail. Unsolicited submissions are OK. Prefers cassette or videocassette with 3 songs, lyric and lead sheet if available. "All written submitted materials (e.g., lyric sheets, letter, etc.) should be typed." Does not return material. Responds in 2 months only via e-mail or SASE.

Music: Mostly **alternative** and **R&B**.

⊘ LARI-JON PRODUCTIONS, 325 W. Walnut, Rising City NE 68658. (402)542-2336. **Contact:** Larry Good, owner. Record producer, music publisher (Lari-Jon Publishing/BMI), management firm (Lari-Jon Promotions) and record company (Lari-Jon Records). Estab. 1967. Produces 10 singles and 5 LPs/year. Fee derived from sales royalty when song or artist is recorded.

How to Contact: Submit demo tape by mail. Unsolicited submissions are OK. "Must be a professional demo." Include SASE. Responds in 2 months.

Music: Mostly **country, gospel-Southern** and **'50s rock**. Produced *Jesus is my Hero* (album), written and recorded by Larry Good on Lari-Jon Records (gospel). Other artists include Brenda Allen, Tom Campbell and Tom Johnson.

◯ LARK TALENT & ADVERTISING, P.O. Box 35726, Tulsa OK 74153. (918)786-8896. Fax: (918)786-8897. E-mail: janajae@janajae.com. Website: www.janajae.com. **Contact:** Kathleen Pixley, vice president. Owner: Jana Jae. Record producer, music publisher (Jana Jae Music/BMI) and record company (Lark Record Productions, Inc.). Estab. 1980. Fee derived from sales royalty when song or artist is recorded.

How to Contact: Submit demo tape by mail. Unsolicited submissions are OK. Prefers cassette or VHS videocassette with 3 songs and lead sheet. Does not return material. Responds in 1 month only if interested.

Music: Mostly **country, bluegrass** and **classical**; also **instrumentals**. Produced "Bussin' Ditty" (single by Steve Upfold); "Mayonnaise" (single by Steve Upfold); and "Flyin' South" (single by Cindy Walker), all recorded by Jana Jae on Lark Records (country). Other artists include Sydni, Hotwire and Matt Greif.

◯ LINEAR CYCLE PRODUCTIONS, P.O. Box 2608, Sepulveda CA 91393-2608. Phone/fax: (818)347-9880. E-mail: LCP@wgn.net. Website: www.westworld.com/lcp/. **Contact:** Manny Pandanceski, producer. Record producer. Estab. 1980. Produces 15-25 singles, 6-10 12″ singles, 15-20 LPs and 10 CDs/year. Fee derived from sales royalty when song or artist is recorded.

How to Contact: Submit demo tape by mail. Unsolicited submissions are OK. Prefers cassette, 7⅛ ips reel-to-reel or ½″ VHS or ¾″ videocassette. Include SASE. Responds in 6 months.

Music: Mostly **rock/pop**, **R&B/blues** and **country**; also **gospel** and **comedy**. Produced "FOP It" (single by Poon), recorded by No Cents (alternative); "My Truck Hasn't Got No Room for You" (single by Hay), recorded by The Tumbleweeds (country), both on Grime Recordings; and "Gim 'M' Shee" (single by Jailboy), recorded by PL238A17 (rap), on Moto Records.

Tips: "We only listen to songs and other material recorded on quality tapes and CDs. We will not accept anything that sounds distorted, muffled and just plain bad! If you cannot afford to record demos on quality stock, or in some high aspects, shop somewhere else!"

⊘ HAROLD LUICK & COUNTRY MUSIC SHOWCASE INTL. ASSOCIATES, Box #368, Carlisle IA 50047. (515)989-3748. Fax: (515)989-0235. E-mail: haroldl@cmshowcase.org. Website: www.cmshowcase.org. Producer: Harold L. Luick. Record producer, music industry consultant, music print publisher and music publisher. Produces 20 singles and 6 LPs/year. Fee derived from sales royalty, outright fee from artist/songwriter or record company, and from consulting fees for information or services.

How to Contact: *Write or call first and obtain permission to submit.* Prefers cassette with 3-5 songs and lyric sheet. Include SASE. Responds in 3 weeks.

Music: Mostly **traditional country**, **gospel**, **contemporary country** and **MOR**. "Over a 12-year period, Harold Luick has produced and recorded 412 singles and 478 albums, 7 of which charted and some of which have enjoyed independent sales in excess of 30,000 units."
Tips: "If you are looking to place a song with us and have it considered for a recording, make sure you have a decent demo, and all legals in order."

☑ ○ **MAC-ATTACK PRODUCTIONS**, 868 NE 81 St., Miami FL 33138. (305)949-1422. E-mail: gomacster@aol.com. **Contact:** Michael McNamee, engineer/producer. Record producer and music publisher (Mac-Attack Publishing/ASCAP). Estab. 1986. Fee derived from outright fee from recording artist or record company.
How to Contact: Submit demo tape by mail. Unsolicited submissions are OK. Prefers CD or cassette or VHS videocassette with 3-5 songs, lyric sheet and bio. Does not return material. Responds in up to 3 months.
Music: Mostly **pop**, **alternative rock** and **dance**. Produced "Hot Potato" (single written and recorded by Tyranny of Shaw) from *Tyranny of Shaw* (punk/metal album), released 2001 on T.O.S. Records; "Minus A Negative" (single written and recorded by Incode) (rock/trans/industrial), released 2002 on Incode Records; and *Kids 'N Salsa* (album), recorded by various (Latin), released 2001 on Co-nect. Other artists include Blowfly, Forget the Name, Nine Llopis, The Lead and Girl Talk.

○ **LEE MAGID PRODUCTIONS**, P.O. Box 532, Malibu CA 90265. (323)463-5998. **Contact:** Lee Magid, president. Record producer, music publisher (Alexis Music, Inc./ASCAP, Marvelle Music Co./BMI and Gabal Music Co./SESAC), record company (Grass Roots Records, LMI Records) and management firm (Lee Magid Management). Estab. 1950. Produces 4 singles, 4 12″ singles, 8 LPs and 8 CDs/year. Fee derived from sales royalty when song or artist is recorded.
How to Contact: Submit demo tape by mail. Unsolicited submissions are OK. "Send cassette giving address and phone number." Prefers cassette or VHS videocassette with 3-6 songs and lyric sheet. "Please only one cassette, and photos if you are an artist/writer." Does not return material. Responds in 6 weeks only if accepted.
Music: Mostly **R&B**, **rock**, **jazz** and **gospel**; also **pop**, **bluegrass**, **church/religious**, **easy listening**, **folk**, **blues**, **MOR**, **progressive**, **soul**, **instrumental** and **top 40**. Produced *I'll Be Seeing You Around* (album by Lorna McGough/John Scott/Mark Newbar), recorded by 2AD on LMI Records (R&B); *It's Only Money* (album by John M. Hides), recorded by J. Michael Hides on Grass Roots Records (pop); and *Blues For the Weepers* (album by Lee Magid/Max Rich), recorded by Bob Stewart on VWC Records (jazz). Other artists include Tramaine Hawkins, Della Reese, Rod Piazza, "Big Joe" Turner, Tom Vaughn and Laura Lee.

☑ ○ **MAKERS MARK MUSIC PRODUCTIONS (ASCAP)**, 534 W. Queen Lane, Philadelphia PA 19144. (215)849-7633. E-mail: Makers.Mark@verizon.net. Website: www.prolificrecords.com or www.mp3.com/paulhopkins. **Contact:** Paul E. Hopkins, producer. Record producer, music publisher and record company (Prolific Records). Estab. 1991. Produces 15 singles, 5 12″ singles and 4 LPs/year. Fee derived from outright fee from recording artist or record company. "We produce professional music videos in VHS and DVD format."
How to Contact: Submit demo tape or CD with bio by mail. Unsolicited submissions are OK. "Explain concept of your music and/or style, and your future direction as an artist or songwriter." Does not return material. Responds in 6 weeks if interested.
Music: Mostly **R&B**, **gospel**, **dance** and **pop**. Produced *All Eyes on the Philosopher* (album by Norman Gilliam/Paul Hopkins), recorded by Norman Gilliam on Prolific Records. Other artists include Larry Larr, Paul Hopkins, Nardo Ranks (international Jamaican artist), Elaine Monk (r&b), New Jerusalem (drama ministry), up-and-coming artists Tatiana (r&b), Sage (r&b artist) and Christin McHenry (pop artist). Also produced *Pastor Alyn E. Waller Presents: The Enon Tabernacle Mass*

MARKETS THAT WERE listed in the 2002 edition of *Songwriters Market* but do not appear this year are listed in the General Index with a notation explaining why they were omitted.

Choir concert album and digital video (*Live from the Tabernacle*), released on ECDC Records/Universal Distributors (www.ebontab.org), Enon Mass Choir (from Philadelphia *Live at the Tabernacle*), New Jerusalem (drama ministry) and Tatiana (R&B).

N: ☻ COOKIE MARENCO, P.O. Box 874, Belmont CA 94002. E-mail: otrstudios@aol.com. (650)595-8475. Fax: (650)598-0915. Studio Manager: Renea Wilfong. Record producer/engineer. Estab. 1981. Produces 10 CDs/year. Fee derived from sales royalty and outright fee from recording artist or record company.
How to Contact: *Write first and obtain permission to submit.* Does not return material. Responds only if interested.
Music: Mostly **alternative modern rock**, **country**, **folk**, **rap**, **ethnic** and **avante-garde**; also **classical**, **pop** and **jazz**. Produced *Off the Beaten Path* (album), written and recorded by Melissa Crabtree (folk), released 2002; *Winter Solstice II* (album), written and recorded by various artists; *Heresay* (album by Paul McCandless); and *Deep At Night* (album by Alex DeGrassi), all on Windham Hill Records (instrumental). Other artists include Tony Furtado Band, Praxis, Oregon, Mary Chapin Carpenter, Max Roach and Charle Haden & Quartet West.

☻ PETE MARTIN/VAAM MUSIC PRODUCTIONS, P.O. Box 29550, Hollywood CA 90029-0550. (323)664-7765. E-mail: vaampubl@aol.com or pmarti3636@aol.com. **Contact:** Pete Martin, president. Record producer, music publisher (Vaam Music/BMI and Pete Martin Music/ASCAP) and record company (Blue Gem Records). Estab. 1982. Produces 12 singles and 5 LPs/year. Fee derived from sales royalty when song or artist is recorded.
How to Contact: Prefers cassette with 2 songs and lyric sheet. Send small packages only. Include SASE. Responds in 1 month.
Music: Mostly **top 40/pop**, **country** and **R&B**. Produced Shay Lynn, Sherry Weston, Vero, Frank Loren, Brian Smith & The Renegades, Victoria Limon, Brandy Rose and Cory Canyon.
Tips: "Study the market in the style that you write. Songs must be capable of reaching top 5 on charts."

☑ ☐ SCOTT MATHEWS, D/B/A HIT OR MYTH PRODUCTIONS, 246 Almonte Blvd., Mill Valley CA 94941. Fax: (415)389-9682. E-mail: hitormyth@aol.com. **Contact:** Mary Ezzell, A&R Director. President: Scott Mathews. Assistant: Mary Ezzell. Record producer, song doctor, studio owner and music publisher (Hang On to Your Publishing/BMI). Estab. 1990. Produces 6-9 CDs/year. Fee derived from sales royalty when artist is recorded, or from recording artist or record company (with royalty points). "*Not affiliated with scottmathews.com or any other imposters using 'Scott Mathews.'* "
   ● Scott Mathews has several gold and platinum awards for sales of over 12 million records.
   He has worked on several Grammy and Oscar winning releases. See his article on page 36.
How to Contact: "*No phone calls or publishing submissions, please.*" Submit demo tape by mail. Unsolicited submissions are OK. Prefers CD (cassette accepted). Include SASE. Responds in 2 months.
Music: Mostly **rock/pop**, **alternative** and **singer/songwriters of all styles**. Produced "The Way We Make a Broken Heart" (single by John Hiatt), recorded by John Hiatt with Rosanne Cash on Capitol (pop); *Slideways* (album), written and recorded by Roy Rogers on E Music (blues); and *How Else Can the Story Go?* (album by Roger Clark), recorded by Lucy Lee on Island (pop). Has produced Roy Orbison, Rosanne Cash, John Hiatt and many more. Has recorded platinum records with everyone from Barbra Streisand to John Lee Hooker, including Keith Richards, George Harrison, Mick Jagger, Van Morrison, Elvis Costello, Bonnie Raitt and Eric Clapton to name but a few, plus several Grammy and Oscar-winning projects.
Tips: "Waiting for a major label to come tap you on the shoulder and say, 'It's your turn,' is the last thing a new artist should even be thinking of. In my humble opinion, today's A&R stands for 'Afraid & Running.' Sorry to all my friends in that department, but the cold truth is, huge corporations are interested only in pleasing the shareholders. Most labels are all about the bottom line, not the music. Recently, I had a president of a major label admit to me that he hates his job because he's not allowed to sign and develop what he wants! So, it's our job to develop our careers by making incredible

masters on our own. Fair deals are born from artists being in control. Set your goal (EP or LP) and budget, find the right producer, and make a stellar CD that can compete with anything on the radio. Early on, you can do more for yourself than a label can. When you prove yourself, they offer the moon. Developing new artists that will sustain long careers is my main focus. Developing new artists who will sustain long careers is my main focus. Let me know if I can help."

A.V. MITTELSTEDT, 9717 Jensen Dr., Houston TX 77093. (713)695-3648. **Contact:** A.V. Mittelstedt, producer. Record producer and music publisher (Sound Masters). Produces 100 singles, 10 LPs and 20 CDs/year. Fee derived from sales royalty and outright fee from recording artist.
How to Contact: Prefers cassette. Include SASE. Responds in 3 weeks.
Music: Mostly **country**, **gospel** and **crossover**; also **MOR** and **rock**. Produced "Too Cold at Home" (single by Bobby Harding), recorded by Mark Chestnutt on Cherry Records (country); "Two Will Be One" (single), written and recorded by Kenny Dale on Axbar Records (country); and "Shake Your Hiney" (single by Gradual Taylor), recorded by Roy Head on Cherry Records (crossover country). Other artists include Randy Cornor, Bill Nash, Ron Shaw, Borderline, George Dearborne and Good, Bad and Ugly.

MONA LISA RECORDS/BRISTOL RECORDING STUDIOS, 169 Massachusetts Ave., Boston MA 02115. (617)247-8689. Fax: (617)421-9977. E-mail: webmaster@bristolstudios.com. Website: www.BristolStudios.com. **Contact:** Ric Poulin, Producer or Craig Burger, Producer. Record producer. Estab. 1987. Produces 50 singles and 10 CDs/year. Fee derived from outright fee from recording company or artist.
How to Contact: Submit through e-mail. Prefers CD and lyric sheet. Responds in 6 weeks.
Music: Mostly **dance**, **R&B** and **pop**; also **jazz** and **rock**. Produced *Future Classics* (album by Ric Poulin/Sean Cooper), recorded by various artists on Mona Lisa Records (dance); "Call the Doctor" (single by Poulin/Yeldham/Poulin), recorded by Bijou on Critique/Atlantic Records (dance); and "Dance to the Rhythm of the Beat" (single by Ric Poulin), recorded by Jennifer Rivers on Associated Artists Int'l (dance). Other artists include Never Never, Sherry Christian, Zina, Damien, Aaron Brown, Amy Silverman and Leah Langfeld.
Tips: "Develop the frame of mind that whatever you do, you are doing it as a professional."

MONTICANA PRODUCTIONS, P.O. Box 702, Snowdon Station, Montreal, Quebec H3X 3X8 Canada. **Contact:** David Leonard, executive producer. Record producer, music publisher (Montina Music) and record company (Monticana Records). Estab. 1963. Fee derived from sales royalty when song or artist is recorded.
How to Contact: Submit demo tape by mail. Unsolicited submissions are OK. Prefers cassette, phonograph record or VHS videocassette with maximum 10 songs and lyric sheet. "Demos should be as tightly produced as a master." Include SASE.
Music: Mostly **top 40**; also **bluegrass**, **blues**, **country**, **dance-oriented**, **easy listening**, **folk**, **gospel**, **jazz**, **MOR**, **progressive**, **R&B**, **rock** and **soul**.
Tips: "Work creatively and believe passionately in what you do and aspire to be. Success comes to those who persevere, have talent, develop their craft and network."

MUSTROCK PRODUCTIONZ WORLDWIDE, 167 W. 81st St., Suite 5C, New York NY 10024-7200. (212)799-9268. E-mail: recordmode@hotmail.com. President: Ivan "DJ/DOC" Rodriguez. Record producer and recording engineer. Estab. 1980. Produces 5 singles, engineers 2 LPs, 3 EPs and 2 CDs/year. Fee derived from sales royalty when song or artist is recorded. "We do not shop deals."
How to Contact: *Call first and obtain permission to submit.* Prefers cassette or VHS videocassette and lyric sheet. Does not return material. Responds in 2 months.
Music: Mostly **hip-hop**, **R&B** and **pop**; also **soul**, **ballads** and **soundtracks**. Produced "Poor Georgie" (by MC Lyte/DJ DOC), recorded by MC Lyte on Atlantic Records (rap). Other artists include Caron Wheeler, The Hit Squad, The Awesome II, Black Steel Music, Underated Productions, EPMD, Redman, Dr. Dre & Ed-Lover, Das-EFX, Biz Markie, BDP, Eric B & Rakim, The Fugees, The Bushwackass, Shai and Pudgee.

Tips: "Services provided include production (pre/post/co), tracking, mixing, remixing, live show tapes, jingles, etc. Additional info available upon request."

◖**NEU ELECTRO PRODUCTIONS**, P.O. Box 1582, Bridgeview IL 60455. (630)257-6289. E-mail: neuelectro@email.com. Website: http://members.nbci.com/neuelectro/index.htm. **Contact:** Bob Neumann, owner. Record producer and record company. Estab. 1984. Produces 16 singles, 16 12″ singles, 20 LPs and 4 CDs/year. Fee derived from outright fee from record company or recording artist.

How to Contact: Submit demo tape by mail. Unsolicited submissions are OK. Prefers cassette or CD with 3 songs and lyric sheet or lead sheet. "Provide accurate contact phone numbers and addresses, promo packages and photos." Include SASE. Responds in 2 weeks. "A production fee estimate will be returned to artist."

Music: Mostly **dance**, **house**, **techno**, **rap** and **rock**; also **experimental**, **New Age** and **top 40**. Produced "Juicy" (single), written and recorded by Juicy Black on Dark Planet International Records (house); "Make Me Smile" (single), written and recorded by Roz Baker (house); *Reactovate-6* (album by Bob Neumann), recorded by Beatbox-D on N.E.P. Records (dance); and *Sands of Time* (album), recorded by Bob Neuman (New Age). Other artists include Skid Marx and The Deviants.

☑◖**NEW EXPERIENCE RECORDS**, P.O. Box 683, Lima OH 45802. E-mail: just_chilling_2 002@yahoo.com. **Contact:** A&R Department. Music Publisher: James L. Milligan Jr. Record producer, music publisher (A New Rap Jam Publishing/ASCAP), management firm (Creative Star Management) and record company (New Experience Records, Grand-Slam Records and Pump It Up Records). Estab. 1989. Produces 15-20 12″ singles, 2 LPs, 3 EPs and 2-5 CDs/year. Fee derived from sales royalty when song or artist is recorded or outright fee from record company, "depending on services required."

How to Contact: *Write first to arrange personal interview.* Address material to A&R Dept. or Talent Coordinator. Prefers cassette with a minimum of 3 songs and lyric or lead sheet (if available). "If tapes are to be returned, proper postage should be enclosed and all tapes and letters should have SASE for faster reply." Responds in 6 weeks.

Music: Mostly **pop**, **R&B** and **rap**; also **gospel**, **contemporary gospel** and **rock**. Produced "Get Your Own" and "Can't Play a Playa" (singles by David Fawcett) from *Enter the Mind* (album), recorded by Devicus 01 (rap), released 2002 on Pump It Up Records; "The Son of God" (single by James Milligan/Anthony Milligan/Melvin Milligan) from *The Final Chapter* (album), recorded by T.M.C. Milligan Conection (r&b gospel), released 2002 on New Experience/Pump It Up Records. Other artists include Qutina Milligan, Melvin Milligan and Venesta Compton.

Tips: "Do your homework on the music business. There are too many sound alikes. Be yourself. I look for what is different, vocal ability, voice range and sound stage presence, etc."

◤☑◖**PACIFIC NORTH STUDIOS LTD.**, Unit 107, 8988 Fraserton Court, Burnaby, British Columbia V5J 1H8 Canada. (604)629-9146. Fax: (604)629-9178. E-mail: patricia@spindigitalmedia. com. Website: www.spindigitalmedia.com. **Contact:** David Jewer, director. Record producer and record company (Lynn Valley Music). Estab. 1993. Produces 4 CDs/year. Fee derived from sales royalty when song or artist is recorded or outright fee from recording artist.

How to Contact: Submit CD by mail. Unsolicited submissions are OK. Accepts CDs only. "Include a bio." Does not return material. Responds in 1 month.

Music: Mostly **world music**, **jazz** and **blues**. Produced *Songs From the Seahorse Hall* (album), written and recorded by David Cory (children's); *Mandala* (album by J. Keating/D. Ritter), recorded by Locos Bravos (world), both on LVM; and *Change In the Weather* (album), written and recorded by Michael Dixon (country).

Tips: "Be a live performer."

FOR BOOKS ON THE CRAFT AND BUSINESS of songwriting, check out the website for Writer's Digest Books at www.writersdigest.com.

☑ ◯ **PANIO BROTHERS LABEL**, P.O. Box 99, Montmartre, Saskatchewan S0G 3M0 Canada. (306)424-2258. Fax: (306)424-2269. **Contact:** John Panio, Jr., executive director. Record producer. Estab. 1977. Produces 1 single and 1 LP/year. Fee derived from sales royalty or outright fee from artist/songwriter or record company.

How to Contact: Submit demo tape by mail. Unsolicited submissions are OK. Prefers cassette with any number of songs and lyric sheet. SAE and IRC. Responds in 1 month.

Music: Mostly **country**, **dance**, **easy listening** and **Ukrainian**. Produced *Ukranian Country* (album), written and recorded by Vlad Panio on PB Records.

☑ **PATTY PARKER**, Comstock Records, Ltd., P.O. Box 19720, Fountain Hills AZ 85269. (480)951-3115. Fax: (480)951-3074. **Contact:** Patty Parker, producer. Record producer, music publisher (White Cat Music) and record company (Comstock Records). Estab. 1978. Produces 6-8 CD singles and 3-4 albums/year. Fee derived from outright fee from recording artist or recording company.

How to Contact: Submit demo tape by mail. Unsolicited submissions are OK. Prefers CD or cassette with 2-4 songs and lyric sheet. Voice up front on demos. Include SASE. Responds in 2 weeks.

Music: Mostly **country—traditional** to **crossover**. Produced "Great American Country" (single by Paula Mengarelli/Tom Mengarelli/Jeff Hansel), recorded by Paula Mengarelli (country); "Down to the Wire" (single by Maria Carmi), recorded by Maria Carmi (country); and "Your Daddy Would be Proud" (single by Paul Gibson) from *Reason to Believe* (album), recorded by Derek Carle (country), all released 2001 on Comstock Records. Other artists include Jentille, R.J. McClintock, Beth Hogan.

Tips: "To catch the ears of radio programmers worldwide, I need good medium to uptempo songs for all the artists coming from Europe, Canada and the U.S. that I produce sessions on in Nashville."

◯ **PHILLY BREAKDOWN RECORDING CO.**, 216 W. Hortter St., Philadelphia PA 19119. (215)848-6725. E-mail: mattcozar@juno.com. **Contact:** Matthew Childs, president. Music Director: Charles Nesbit. Record producer, music publisher (Philly Breakdown/BMI) and record company. Estab. 1974. Produces 3 singles and 2 LPs/year. Fee derived from sales royalty when song or artist is recorded.

How to Contact: *Contact first and obtain permission to submit.* Prefers cassette with 4 songs and lead sheet. Does not return material. Responds in 2 months.

Music: Mostly **R&B**, **hip-hop** and **pop**; also **jazz**, **gospel** and **ballads**. Produced "Lonely River" (single by Clarence Patterson/M. Childs) from *Lonely River* (album), recorded by Gloria Clark; and *Taps* (album), recorded by H Factor, both released 2001 on Philly Breakdown. Other artists include Leroy Christy, Gloria Clark, Jerry Walker, Nina Bundy, Mark Adam, Emmit King, Betty Carol, The H Factor and Four Buddies.

Tips: "If you fail, just learn from your past experience and keep on trying, until you get it done right. Never give up."

☑ **JIM PIERCE**, Dept. SM, 101 Hurt Rd., Hendersonville TN 37075. (615)824-5900. Fax: (615)824-8800. E-mail: jimpierce@bellsouth.net. Website: www.jimpierce.net. **Contact:** Jim Pierce, president. Record producer, music publisher (Strawboss Music/BMI) and record company (Round Robin Records). Estab. 1974. Fee derived from sales royalty or outright fee from recording artist. "Many artists pay me in advance for my services." Has had over 200 chart records to date.

How to Contact: *E-mail first and obtain permission to submit or to arrange personal interview.* Prefers CD with any number of songs and lyric sheet. Will accept cassettes. Does not return material. Responds only if interested. "All submissions should include phone number."

Music: Mostly **country**, **contemporary**, **country/pop**, **gospel** and **traditional country**. Artists include Tommy Cash, George Jones, Jimmy C. Newman, Margo Smith, Bobby Helms, Sammi Smith, Roy Drusky, Charlie Louvin and Melba Montgomery.

Tips: "Industry is seeking good singers who can write songs. Viewing our website is highly suggested."

N QUEEN ESTHER MUSIC PUBLISHERS (ASCAP), 449 N. Vista St., Los Angeles CA 90036. (323)653-0693. E-mail: unclelenny@aol.com. **Contact:** Len Weisman, owner. Record producer, personal manager, music publisher. Estab. 1980. Publishes 30-50 songs/year.
How to Contact: Send demo CD or cassette with 3-10 songs. Include SASE. We only return in prepaid large envelopes.
Music: Mostly **r&b**, **soul**, **rap** and **2nd gospel**. No rock or metal. Now working on "Daniel" CD; "Jusuan" CD; and "Jewel With Love" CD.

✔ ○ REEL ADVENTURES, 9 Peggy Lane, Salem NH 03079. (603)898-7097. Website: www.ree ladventures1.homestead.com. **Contact:** Rick Asmega, chief engineer/producer. Record producer. Estab. 1972. Produces 100 12″ singles, 200 LPs, 5 EPs and 40 CDs/year. Fee derived from sales royalty when song or artist is recorded, or outright fee from recording artist or record company.
How to Contact: Submit demo tape by mail. Unsolicited submissions are OK. Prefers cassette or CD. Include SASE. Responds in 6 weeks.
Music: Mostly **pop**, **funk** and **country**; also **blues**, **Christian**, **reggae** and **rock**. Produced *Funky Broadway* (album), recorded by Chris Hicks; *Testafye* (album), recorded by Jay Williams; and "Acoustical Climate" (single by John G.). Other artists include The Bolz, Second Sinai, Larry Sterling, Broken Men, Melvin Crockett, Fred Vigeant, Monster Mash, Carl Armand, Cool Blue Sky, Ransome, Backtrax, Push, Too Cool for Humans and Burn Alley.

✔ ○ RN'D PRODUCTIONS, (formerly R&D Productions), P.O. Box 540102, Houston TX 77254-0102. (713)521-2616. Fax: (713)529-4914. E-mail: rpds2405@aol.com. Website: www.rndpro ductions.com. **Contact:** Byron Gates, A&R director. National Sales Director: Jeff Troncoso. Record producer, record company (Albatross Records) and distributor, and music publisher (Ryedale Publishing). Estab. 1986. Produces 25 singles, 20 LPs, 4 EPs and 21 CDs/year.
How to Contact: Submit demo CD by mail. Unsolicited submissions are OK. Prefers CD with 4 songs and lyric sheet. Does not return material. Responds in 1 month.
Music: All types. Produced *The Best of Suavehouse* (album), recorded by various (rap), released 2001 on Suavehouse Records; *Doin' It Down South* (album), recorded by 8-Ball & MJG (rap), released 2001 on Suavehouse Records; Untitled album, recorded by NU Ground r&b/pop), released 2000 on Albatross Records. Labels distributed include Suavehouse Records, Albatross Records, Lorelt Records, TDA Music and Ball In' Records.

○ ROAD RECORDS, P.O. Box 2620, Victorville CA 92393. Website: www.roadrecords.com. **Contact:** Conrad Askland, president. Record producer, record company (Road Records) and music publisher (Askland Publishing). Estab. 1989. Produces 6 singles and 10 albums/year. Fee derived from sales royalty when song or artist is recorded.
How to Contact: *Write or call first and obtain permission to submit.* Prefers at least 3 songs with lyric and lead sheet. "We are looking for people that have a different, original sound." Does not return submissions. Responds in 3 weeks.
Music: Mostly **alternative**, **modern country** and **dance**; also **orchestral instrumental**. Does not want jazz. "We supply music to Grand Ole Opry, United Airlines, Knoxbury Farm and G.T.E."
Tips: "Do not submit what you think we are looking for. A lot of our projects are 'on the edge.' "

○ RUSTRON MUSIC PRODUCTIONS, 1156 Park Lane, West Palm Beach FL 33417-5957. (561)686-1354. E-mail: gordon-whims@juno.com. **Contact:** A&R Dept. Executive Director: Rusty Gordon. A&R Director: Ron Caruso. Assistant A&R Director: Kevin Reeves. Record producer, record company, manager and music publisher (Rustron Music Publishers/BMI and Whimsong Publishing/ASCAP). Estab. 1970. Produces 6-10 LP/cassettes and 6 CDs/year. Fee derived from sales royalty when song or artist is recorded or outright fee from record company. "This branch office reviews all material submitted for the home office in Ridgefield, CT."
How to Contact: *Write or call to discuss your submission* or submit demo tape or CD by mail. Prefers CD that was produced to sell at gigs or cassette with 1-3 songs and typed lyric or lead sheet. Also send cover letter clearly explaining your reason for submitting. "Songs should be 3½ minutes

long or less and must be commercially viable for today's market. Exception: New Age fusion compositions 3-10 minutes each, ½ hour maximum. Singer/songwriters and collaborators are preferred." SASE required for all correspondence. Responds in 4 months.

Music: Mostly **progressive country**, **pop** (ballads, blues, theatrical, cabaret), **folk/rock**, and **A/C electric acoustic**; also **r&b**, **New Age fusions**, **folk rock**, **women's music** and **New Age instrumentals**. Produced "Take a Closer Look" (single by Jeremy White) from *Back on the Island* (album), recorded by Jeremy White (yankee reggae), released 2001 on Rustron Records; "Rainbow" (single by Eric Shaffer/Rusty Gordon) from *The Triangle & the Rainbow* (album), recorded by Song on a Whim (folk-rock), released 2001 on Rustron Records; "America and Her Enemies" (single by Stacie Jubal) from *Time for Topical Again* (album), recorded by Stacie Jubal (folk-rock), released 2001 on Whimsong Records. Other artists include Jayne Margo-Reby, Jeremy White, Deb Criss, Robin Plitt, Boomslang Swampsinger.

Tips: "Be open to developing your own unique style. Write well-crafted songs with unpredictable concepts, strong hooks and definitive melodies. New Age composers: evolve your themes and use multiculturally diverse instruments to embellish your compositions/arrangements. Don't be predictable. Experiment with instrumental fusion with jazz and/or classical themes, pop themes and international styles. Send cover letter clearly explaining your reason for submitting."

☑ ◯ **STEVE SATKOWSKI RECORDINGS**, P.O. Box 3403, Stuart FL 34995. (772)225-3128. Engineer/producer: Steven Satkowski. Record producer, recording engineer, management firm and record company. Estab. 1980. Produces 20 CDs/year. Fee derived from outright fee from recording artist or record company.

How to Contact Submit demo tape by mail. Unsolicited submissions are OK. Prefers CD or cassette. Does not return material. Responds in 2 weeks.

Music: Mostly **classical**, **jazz** and **big band**. Produced recordings for National Public Radio and affiliates. Engineered recordings for Steve Howe, Patrick Moraz, Kenny G and Michael Bolton.

N ◯ **SCHAFER MUSIC**, 3236 Cloverwood Dr., Nashville TN 37214. (615)883-7086. (615)292-9117. E-mail: schafermusic1@aol.com. Website: www.danschafer.com. **Contact:** Dan Schafer, creative director. Record producer, record company, and music publisher. Estab. 1974. Produces 2 albums/year. Fee derived from outright fee from recording artist.

• Also see listing for Schafer Music in the Music Publishers section.

How to Contact: Submit demo tape by mail. Unsolicited submissions are OK. Prefers CD/CDR. Does not return material. Responds "ASAP" only if interested.

Music: Mostly **pop**, **country** and **folk**; also **smooth jazz** and **gospel**. Does not want hip-hop or rap. Produced *This Love* (album by various artists), recorded by Linda Scott (country), released 1996 on Oh Dee; *Worth Waiting For*, (album by various artists), recorded by Maryke De Jong (country/pop), released 1997 on Holland; and *Requested Favorites* (album by various artists), recorded by Larry Stevens (adult contemporary), released 1996 on Oh Dee.

Tips: "Never give up."

◉ **SEGAL'S PRODUCTIONS**, 16 Grace Rd., Newton MA 02159. (617)969-6196. Fax: (617)969-6614. **Contact:** Charles Segal. Record producer, music publisher (Segal's Publications/BMI and Samro South Africa) and record company (Spin Records). Produces 6 singles and 6 LPs/year. Fee derived from sales royalty when song or artist is recorded.

How to Contact: *Write first and obtain permission to submit or to arrange personal interview.* Prefers cassette, CD or videocassette with 3 songs and lyric sheet or lead sheet of melody, words, chords. "Please record keyboard/voice or guitar/voice if you can't get a group." Does not return material. Responds in 3 months only if interested.

⚫ ⊕ **SENDING TO A COUNTRY** other than your own? Be sure to send International Reply Coupons (IRCs) instead of stamps for replies or return of your materials.

insider report

Multi-talented international jazz pianist builds music company

Charles Segal

Charles Segal has enjoyed a long and multi-faceted career in the music business in varied roles as pianist, composer, music publisher, producer and teacher. Segal was born in Lithuania and raised in South Africa. He was trained in classical piano performance and composition, and also attained a teacher's Licentiate from the Trinity College of London. American jazz music captured his heart and he developed into an accomplished jazz pianist with a talent for improvisation and composition. Segal's songwriting career started when he won a songwriting competition as a young man. His career later blossomed when he received the South African Grammy equivalent, SARI (South African Record Industry) Award for Song of the Year. His country hit, "My Children, My Wife," reached the Top Ten in South Africa, Germany, Holland, Britain and Israel.

Segal became a household name in South Africa through his many pop hits and his regular appearances on radio and TV. He is the featured artist on over 200 albums, and his work spans a myriad of styles and cultures, including classical, jazz, contemporary, Jewish, African, pop and new age music. He has produced albums with pop groups, traditional African groups and also children's music for his Spin Record label and other international record companies.

He has over 1,000 compositions to his credit, and has written, arranged and produced the music for 11 full-length musicals, several feature films, talk-shows, advertising jingles and soap operas. He wrote the theme music for the "Forsyte Saga" which was broadcast twice a day for three years. Segal's many African compositions, such as "Africa" and "African Fantasy," are considered part of South African traditional music.

Charles Segal Publications was a founding member of SAMRO—the South African Music Rights Organization. Since his move to the USA he has transferred to BMI membership. Charles Segal's Music School was the largest in South Africa and produced the "Instant Series" of music tutor books as well as many easy-to-play sheet music albums. He has also recently published an instructional pamphlet entitled *Easy Tools for Composing*, available through his website (www.charlessegal.com).

When living in South Africa, Segal's record label, Spin Records, associated with various record companies, including EMI, CBS, SABC and RCA. Since moving to the U.S. he has launched the Segal Music label.

Here Charles Segal discusses his music companies and offers advice for aspiring songwriters:

What is your take on the current state of the music industry?
So many of the big record companies are concentrating on rap and heavy rock or commercial

music for teenagers. They are, understandably, not interested in moving away from this money-making machine. So it is up to smaller companies to produce music "for the rest of us."

What kind of new opportunities and markets are you developing through Segal Music?

Segal Music is currently working on a catalogue of 25 easy-listening CD's featuring relaxing music, evergreens, new age, classical, Christmas, Jewish, American patriotic, jazz, children's songs, African themes and others featuring both vocals and instrumental music. These will be released in the U.S. as well as abroad and be available on the Internet at charlessegal.com.

We also are marketing a series of children's musicals ideal for schools and camps. Each show is sold as a package including the script, sheet music, director's notes and a CD of the original sound-track and the backing music for easy rehearsals.

What do you see as the greatest challenge faced by music companies seeking to expand into new markets?

The greatest challenge of breaking into a new market is to find a distributor who is willing to take a chance on new material and artists. The buyers are there, but it is getting the merchandise into their view that is difficult. Record companies and distributors find it easier to work with well-known artists or to link a product with a celebrity, because this cuts down on their promotional costs. So, many newer companies, like our own, have to find alternative means for distribution and advertising. Our company will only take on products that we believe to be marketable in this very tight business.

What sorts of music will be successful in these emerging markets?

Hopefully, after the challenges our country faced on September 11, 2001, the music industry will be moving back to traditional values and music that sends a more positive and tolerant, kinder, gentler message to our young people. This will signal a change and, with change comes openings for new ideas. It is the perfect time for new composers and artists who are persistent and knowledgeable. Segal Music recently released two songs: "Give the World a Chance" and "You're Not Alone" to give encouragement in these difficult times.

What should aspiring songwriters know about successfully submitting to Segal Music?

Because the market changes constantly, there are times when we are only interested in a professionally finished product. At other times we may be willing to work with raw songs and build them into a marketable product.

My best advice is that songwriters should mail a request for permission to submit their material. Describe exactly what form your demo will take. Is it you singing on a cassette or have you made a CD with a group? Give a background of how far you have gone with this material. Include a stamped, self-addressed envelope for the reply. If you do not hear back within 6 weeks, try again. If we cannot take your material this year, try again next year. Persistence is the key.

What sorts of things do you generally see songwriters doing wrong when submitting their work for consideration?

Songwriters waste a lot of time and money because they do not do enough research about the company to which they are submitting material. That is where the request letter is important. Find out specifically what sorts of material that company is accepting at that time.

Most professional companies are not interested in receiving amateurish, shoddy material.- The serious songwriter should do the very best demo possible. A CD is much more impressive than a cassette. Hand-written notes also indicate that you are an amateur. Invest in a letter-head and type a clear, concise letter.

Do NOT ask the company to return your material if they cannot use it. Rather leave it with them. If you are not prepared to lose some money on promoting your material, why should anyone else? The other plus side is that markets are always changing and if they have your material on file, someone may pick it up at a later date.

Some publishers like to have lead sheets of the music. In this case have the music transcribed correctly, with the title at the top of the page, the writers' names in the right hand corner and the copyright date and address at the bottom of the page. A company is impressed if they see that you have gone to the trouble of packaging your product correctly.

What do you think makes a great song?
Of course there are many different opinions about this. In my view, a well-constructed, simple, but memorable melody with the perfect melding of lyrics makes a great song. There should be a "hook" or chorus that repeats several times—this is what the listener waits for.

As a rule, publishers favor evergreens because they can continue earning royalties for many years. Record companies, who make their money from sales, may prefer the gimmicky or currently popular song-types.

In your opinion, what makes a song commercially viable?
The song has to make money or nobody will be in business. To make a song commercially viable, it should fit into a genre or trend that is selling at the moment. For a "hit" song, one should be able to easily imagine a currently popular singer or group performing that song. There are several children's shows that feature music. If a song can fit into one of these shows, it is commercially viable. If there is a trend, a niche your song can fit into, you have a commercial proposition. Of course, there have to be trend-setters and pioneers, but for these to actually make a profit, they have to either have a lot of money or a lot of luck.

What sort of thing makes you reject a song submitted to your company?
I reject a song for the following reasons: If the demonstration package is shoddy and amateurish, or if the arrangement shows a lack of musicality. I'll reject a song if I am not hooked by the melody. If the song is too reminiscent of other songs, then copyright law-suits may follow from the original songwriters. If the song is badly constructed and it is obvious that the writer has no basic musical knowledge. A complicated arrangement in the hands of an amateur comes over as being too messy. A good tip is to keep the arrangements simple and tasteful. Save the harmonies for the chorus.

What should songwriters know about the music business? What are some of the common misconceptions you come across?
There are almost 300 million people living in the U.S.A. and, believe it or not, there are just about 300 million of them who think they have written a hit song and that they will become millionaires overnight.

An overnight success is very rare. In order to be successful, a songwriter will probably have to invest much time and money. The key is that you need to understand the business—how to get your material heard, how you get paid, how royalties work, how much control you have over your material once it is out of your hands. A bonus is if you can get to know people in the music business who can help you succeed.

To truly be successful, budding songwriters have to get the stars out of their eyes and come to grips with the fact that the music business is just that—a business. The people in it want to know: "What's in it for me?" They are interested if they can make money out of your material—that is the simple truth. Like any business, there are contracts to cover the legalities. It is important to spend some money and have a lawyer explain the contract to you before you sign it.

Realize that the money doesn't usually just come rolling in, so don't give up your day job. Even if your song does get recorded, remember that there are many people who will want a piece of the profits from the same song—the writers, the publishers, the performers, the agents, the record companies. The songwriter soon learns that even 1 percent of something is a lot better than 100 percent of nothing!

What kind of advice do you have for beginners to help them get a handle on the music business?
Arm yourself with knowledge, patience and persistence. Start reading everything you can about the music business. Listen to the songs being played on the radio and TV. Go to record stores and observe the merchandise. Take music lessons. Network with other musicians. Once you have perfected your song, copyright it. Register your song with BMI or ASCAP.

If you cannot play an instrument and aren't capable of doing a demo by yourself, make friends with a band who can eventually play your song and get it known locally. Be willing to pay them for extra rehearsals to help you get the song into workable form.

Make an amazing demo CD. Allow experienced musicians to change the song if necessary. Either have them put their names on it, or pay them an outright fee. Respect experienced musicians. They have so much knowledge to offer you.

Think of every angle to get publicity on local TV, radio, or in the newspapers. Every bit of exposure helps to get a resume and a history for the song and you never know who may be listening.

If you are lucky enough to interest an agent, a publisher or record company in handling your song, there will be contracts to sign. Have your lawyer go over this with you. My advice is that you limit the contract to give them the maximum of two years to get the song going. Thereafter, if nothing happens, you will be free to try another agent.

Don't give up. Music is a challenging business, but the rewards of working creatively far outweigh the difficulties. Most people find satisfaction in the business without ever having a hit. There are many avenues in music that are fulfilling and if you are really serious about it, you will find your niche.
—*Ian Bessler*

Music: Mostly **rock**, **pop** and **country**; also **R&B** and **comedy**. Produced "What Is This Love" (single by Paul/Motou), recorded by Julia Manin (rock); "Lovely Is This Memory" (single by Segal/Paul), recorded by Nick Chosn on AU.S. (ballad); and *There'll Come A Time* (album by Charles Segal), recorded by Jill Kirkland on Spin Records (ballad). Other artists include Art Heatley, Dan Hill and Melanie.

Tips: "Make a good and clear production of cassette even if it is only piano rhythm and voice. Also do a lead sheet of music, words and chords."

SHU'BABY MONTEZ MUSIC, 1447 N. 55th St., Philadelphia PA 19131-3901. (215)473-5527. Fax: (215)473-8895. E-mail: schubaby@att.net. Website: www.geocities.com/SunsetStrip/cabaret/2810/. **Contact:** Shubaby, owner. Record producer. Estab. 1986. Produces 6 singles, 6 12″ singles and 3 LPs/year. Fee derived from outright fee from record company.
How to Contact: Submit demo tape by mail. Unsolicited submissions are OK. Prefers cassette with 4 songs and lyric sheet. Include SASE. Responds in 5 weeks.
Music: Mostly **R&B**, **hip-hop** and **funk**. Produced "The Cousins Groove" (single by Ralph Brown/Shubaby Schuler) from *Still on the Run* (album), recorded by Free Style (r&b/jazz), released 2002 on Urban Logic Records; "J-Bon's Jam" (single by J-Bon/Chappy Washington) from *P J-Bon Mason & Phillies Finest* (album), recorded by Hi-Teck Band (jazz), released 2002 on Urban Logic Records; "You Are My Joy" (single by Lou Leggerie) from *Lou Leggerie Greatest Hits* (album), recorded by Cubby St. Charles (pop/r&b), released 2002 on Urban Logic Records. Other artists include Ralph Brown, Wilson Lambert, Martin "Martygraw" Schuler and Waller Wee.
Tips: "Be on time with all projects."

SILVER BOW PRODUCTIONS, 6260 130 St., Surrey, British Columbia V3X 1R6 Canada. (604)572-4232. Fax: (604)572-4252. E-mail: saddles@telus.net. Website: http://silverbow.on theweb.uu. **Contact:** Candice James, A&R. Record producer. Estab. 1986. Produces 16 singles, and 6 CDs/year. Fee derived from outright fee from recording artist.
How to Contact: *Call first and obtain permission to submit.* Prefers cassette with 2 songs and lyric sheet. Does not return material. Responds in 6 weeks.
Music: Mostly **country**, **pop**, and **rock**; also **gospel**, **blues** and **jazz**. Produced *Fragile-Handle With Care*, recorded by Razzy Bailey on SOA Records (country); *High Society*, written and recorded by Darrell Meyers (country); and *Man I Am*, written and recorded by Stang Giles (country crossover), both released 2000 on Saddlestone Records. Other artists include Rex Howard, Gerry King, Joe Lonsdale, Barb Farrell, Dorrie Alexander, Peter James, Matt Audette and Cordel James.

SILVER THUNDER MUSIC GROUP, P.O. Box 41335, Nashville TN 37204. (615)391-5035. President: Rusty Budde. Record producer, record company (Silver Thunder Records), music publisher (Silver Thunder Publishing) and management firm. Estab. 1982. Produces 20 singles, 5-7 LPs and 5-7 CDs/year. Fee derived from sales royalty when song or artist is recorded or outright fee from recording artist or record company.
How to Contact: *Write first and obtain permission to submit or to arrange personal interview.* Prefers cassette. "Artists should submit 8 × 10 photo along with demo tape." Does not return material. Responds in 4 months.
Music: Mostly **country**, **rock** and **R&B**; also **gospel** and **pop**. Produced *What's Not To Love* (album by D.J. Music), recorded by Heather Hartsfield (country); and *Radio Active* (album by G. McCorkel), recorded by J.D. Treece (country), both on STR Records. Other artists include Rod Woodson, Jeff Samules, Jodi Collins and Hank Thompson.

SOUL CANDY PRODUCTIONS, (formerly Poku Productions), 176-B Woodridge Crescent, Ottawa, Ontario K2B 7S9 Canada. (613)820-5715. Fax: (613)820-8736. E-mail: jshakka@h

**FOR EXPLANATIONS OF THESE SYMBOLS,
SEE THE INSIDE FRONT AND BACK COVERS OF THIS BOOK.**

otmail.com. Website: http://stop.at/shakkastop.at/shakka. **Contact:** Jon E. Shakka or Mitchka, co-presidents. Record producer. Estab. 1988. Produces 1 album/year. Fee derived from sales royalty when song or artist is recorded.

How to Contact: *Does not accept unsolicited submissions.*

Music: Mostly **funk**, **rap** and **house music**; also **pop**, **ballads** and **funk-rock**. Produced *I'm My Brother's Keeper* (album), recorded by The Jon E. Shakka Project (funk rap), released 2001 on Poku Records. Other artists include Kim Warnock and James T. Flash.

☑ ◖ **SOUND WORKS ENTERTAINMENT PRODUCTIONS INC.**, 1351 S. Riverview Dr., Gardnerville NV 89410-8923. (775)265-4372. Fax: (775)265-4512. E-mail: music440@charter.net. Website: www.musicjones.com. **Contact:** Michael E. Jones, president. Record producer, record company (Sound Works Records) and music publisher (Sound Works Music). Estab. 1989. Produces 16 singles, 2 LPs and 20 CDs/year. Fee derived from sales royalty when song or artist is recorded or outright fee from recording artist or record company.

How to Contact: Submit demo tape by mail. Unsolicited submissions are OK. Prefers cassette with 3-6 songs and lyric sheet. "Please include short bio and statement of goals and objectives." Does not return material. Responds in 6 weeks.

Music: Mostly **country**, **folk** and **pop**; also **rock**. Produced "Lonelyville," and "Alabama Slammer" (singles), both written and recorded by Wake Eastman; and "Good Looking Loser" (single), written and recorded by Renee Rubach, all on Sound Works Records (country). Other artists include Matt Dorman, Steve Gilmore, The Tackroom Boys, The Los Vegas Philharmonic and J.C. Clark.

Tips: "Put your ego on hold. Don't take criticism personally. Advice is meant to help you grow and improve your skills as an artist/songwriter. Be professional and business-like in all your dealings."

☑ **SPHERE GROUP ONE**, P.O. Box 991, Far Hills NJ 07931-0991. (908)781-1650. Fax: (908)781-1693. E-mail: spheregroupone@att.net. **Contact:** Tony Zarrella, president. Talent Manager: Louisa Pazienza. Record producer, artist development and management firm. Produces 5-6 singles and 3 CDs/year. Estab. 1986.

How to Contact: Submit demo tape by mail. Unsolicited submissions are OK. Prefers cassette, CD or VHS videocassette with 3-5 songs and lyric sheets. "Must include: photos, press, résumé, goals and specifics of project submitted, etc." Does not return material.

Music: Mostly **pop/rock (mainstream)**, **progressive/rock**, **New Age** and **crossover country/pop**; also **film soundtracks**. Produced *Take This Heart*, *It's Our Love* and *You and I* (albums by T. Zarrella), recorded by 4 of Hearts (pop/rock) on Sphere Records. Other artists include Frontier 9 and Bombay Green.

Tips: "Be able to take direction and have trust and faith in yourself, your producer and manager. Currently seeking artists/groups incorporating various styles into a focused mainstream product. Groups with a following are a plus."

☑ ◖ **SRS PRODUCTIONS/HIT RECORDS NETWORK**, (formerly SAS Productions/Hit Records Network), P.O. Box 6235, Santa Barbara CA 93160. (805)964-3035. E-mail: cms@silcom.com. **Contact:** Greg Lewolt, Ernie Orosco and J.C. Martin, producers. Record producer, record company (Night City Records, Warrior Records and Tell International Records), radio and TV promotion and music publisher. Estab. 1984. Produces 4 singles, 2 12″ singles, 4 LPs, 2 EPs and 2-4 CDs/year. Fee derived from outright fee from record company.

How to Contact: Submit demo tape by mail. Unsolicited submissions are OK. Prefers cassette, CD or VHS videocassette with 4-8 songs, photos, bio and lyric sheet. Does not return material. Include SASE. Responds in 2 months.

Music: Mostly **pop-rock**, **country** and **top 40**; also **top 40 funk**, **top 40 rock** and **top 40 country**. Produced "Do You Remember When" (single by Liehengood/B. Faith) from *Legends of Rock* (album), recorded by Bobby Harris (Drifters) and Greg Munford (Strawberry Alarm Clock) (pop), released 2002 on Hit Records Network; "Blond Adventure" (single by JC Martin) from *Blond Adventure* (album), recorded by Black Angel (r&b rock), released 2002 on Outsider-Hit Records Network; "Michael" (single by B. Faith/F. Towles/K. Dyer) from *Anthology* (album), recorded by Brian Faith/

Nic St. Nicholos (Steppenwolf) (pop rock), released 2002 on All American Records. Other artists include New Vision, Jade, Ernie and the Emperors, Hollywood Heros, Tim Bogert (Vanilla Fudge, Jeff Beck), Peter Lewis, Jim Calire (America), Mike Kowalski, Ernie Knapp (Beach Boys) and Jewel.
Tips: "Keep searching for the infectious chorus hook and don't give up."

N ◘ **STUART AUDIO SERVICES**, 134 Mosher Rd., Gorham ME 04038. (207)892-0960. Fax: (207)892-0040. E-mail: jstuart105@aol.com. **Contact:** John A. Stuart, producer/owner. Record producer and music publisher. Estab. 1979. Produces 5-8 CDs/year. Fee derived from sales royalty when song or artist is recorded, outright fee from recording artist or record company, or demo and consulting fees.
How to Contact: *Write or call first and obtain permission to submit or to arrange a personal interview.* Prefers CD with 4 songs and lyric sheet. Include SASE. Responds in 2 months.
Music: Mostly **alternative folk-rock**, **rock** and **country**; also **contemporary Christian**, **children's** and **unusual**. Produced *One of a Kind* (by various artists), recorded by Elizabeth Boss on Bosco Records (folk); *Toad Motel*, written and recorded by Rick Charrette on Fine Point Records (children's); and *Holiday Portrait*, recorded by USM Chamber Singers on U.S.M. (chorale). Other artists include Noel Paul Stookey, Beavis & Butthead (Mike Judge), Don Campbell, Jim Newton and John Angus.

◘ **STUDIO SEVEN**, 417 N. Virginia, Oklahoma City OK 73106. (405)236-0643. Fax: (405)236-0686. E-mail: cope@okla.net. Website: www.lunacyrecords.com. **Contact:** Dave Copenhaver, producer. Record producer, record company (Lunacy Records) and music publisher (VenDome Music). Estab. 1990. Produces 10 LPs and CDs/year. Fee is derived from sales royalty when song or artist is recorded or outright fee from recording artist or record company. "All projects are on a customized basis."
How to Contact: *Contact first and obtain permission to submit.* Prefers cassette with lyric sheet. Include SASE. Responds in 6 weeks.
Music: Mostly **rock**, **jazz-blues** and **world-Native American**; also **country** and **blues**. Produced "Sweet, Long, Cool Drinka' Water (single by Jennifer Lane) from *Sweet, Long, Cool Drinka' Water* (album), recorded by Jennifer Lane (blues/rock), released 2002 on Lunacy Records; "I Ain't Drinkin' Any Less" (single by Rambler) from *Starting Over* (album), recorded by Rambler (country), released 2001 on TDM Entertainment; and "Easier" (single by Sub Roza) from *As the Congregation Grows* (album), recorded by Sub Roza (rock), released 2001 on Lunacy Records. Other artists include Harvey Shelton, Steve Pryor and Ken Taylor.

☑ ◘ **STUDIO VOODOO MUSIC**, (formerly Gary John Mraz), 5703 E. Oakbrook St., Long Beach CA 90815. (562)425-5024. E-mail: studiovoodoo@earthlink.net. Website: www.studiovoodoo music.com. **Contact:** Gary Mraz, owner. Estab. 1984. Record producer. Produces 6-12 12″ singles and 2-6 LPs/year. Fee derived from sales royalty or outright fee from record company.
How to Contact: Submit demo tape by mail. Unsolicited submissions are OK. Prefers cassette or CD/CDR with 3 songs and lyric sheet. Does not return material. Responds in 2 months.
Music: Mostly **dance**, **pop** and **electronica**. Produced "Studio Voodoo," the world's first dts-es surround dvd-audio disc. Other artists include Bush Baby.
Tips: "With today's technology, we are only limited by our own imaginations."

◘ **SWIFT RIVER PRODUCTIONS**, P.O. Box 231, Gladeville TN 37071. (615)316-9479. E-mail: office@andymay.com. Website: www.swiftrivermusic.com. **Contact:** Andy May, producer/owner. Record producer, record company and music publisher. Estab. 1979. Produces 40 singles and 8 CDs/year. Fee derived from outright fee from recording artist or record company.
How to Contact: *Write or call first and obtain permission to submit.* Prefers cassette or CD with 3 songs and lyric sheet. "Demo should be clear and well thought out. Vocal plus guitar or piano is fine. Let us know your present goals and reason for contacting us and include a short bio." Does not return material. Responds in up to 2 months.
Music: Mostly **country**, **singer/songwriters** and **"roots" (folk, acoustic, bluegrass and rock)**; also **instrumental**. Produced "Flyin Fast" (single by May/May/Fast) from *Flyin' Fast* (album), recorded

by Brycen Fast (country), released 2001 on Swift River; "Butterfly" (single by B. Bensing) from *Billy Bensing* (album), recorded by Billy Bensing (progressive rock), released 2001 on Swift River; and "My Apology" (single by Flom/May/May) from *Marinda* (album), recorded by Marinda Flom (country), released 2000 on Swift River. Other artists include Curtis McPeake, Rick Lee and Crossties.

Tips: "I'm interested in artists/writers who are accomplished, self-motivated and able to accept direction. I'm looking for music that is intelligent, creative and in some way contributes something positive."

TAMJAM PRODUCTIONS, 101 N. Citrus Ave., Suite 2, Covina CA 91723-2029. E-mail: tamjam1111@aol.com. **Contact:** John Maellaro, producer. Record producer. Estab. 1985. Produces 10 singles and 5 CDs/year. Fee derived from sales royalty when song or artist is recorded, outright fee from recording artist and record company, depending on project.

How to Contact: Submit demo tape by mail. Unsolicited submissions are OK. Prefers CD with 3 songs and lyric sheet. Clearly label contact name and number on all items submitted. Does not return material. Responds in 3 months.

Music: Mostly **adult contemporary**, **pop** and **R&B**; also **Latin**, **jazz** and **blues**. Produced *If Only I Could Touch You* (album by Arizaga/Maellaro), recorded by Anthony Arizaga (Latin/jazz) on Duende; *Window Seat* (album by Dorsey/Maellaro), recorded by Patty Dorsey (AC/pop) on Saudade; and *Common Ground* (album by Maellaro), recorded by Oddcat (pop/jazz) on Tamjam. Other artists include Magnetic Mary and Kingman.

Tips: "Have a clear idea of your direction and handle things in a business-like manner."

ROGER VINCENT TARI, P.O. Box 576, Piscataway NJ 08855. Phone/fax: (908)222-8978. E-mail: rogervtari@earthlink.net. **Contact:** Roger Vincent Tari, president/producer. Vice President/A&R: Mike Roze. Record producer, record company (VT Records), music publisher (Vintari Music/ASCAP) and magazine publisher. Estab. 1979. Produces 6-8 singles/year. Fee derived from sales royalty when song or artist is recorded or outright fee from recording artist.

How to Contact: Submit demo tape by mail. Unsolicited submissions are OK. Prefers cassette or VHS videocassette with 3 songs and lyric sheet (videocassette is optional). "The artist should send any relevant literature and a simple black and white picture along with the 3-song cassette and lyric sheet." Include SASE. Responds in 1 month.

Music: Mostly **indie-pop**, **new wave**, **synth-pop** and **punk pop**; also **world pop**, **J-pop**, **art rock** and **avant jazz**. Produced "Bad Apple" (single by Reiko Lai/Chung Ho J Lee), recorded by Flush (indie-pop/rock), released 2002 on VT Music/VT Records; "Notice of Death" (single by Scott Cheng), recorded by Scott Cheng (hard rock), released 2002 on VT Music/VT Records; and "No-Way" (single by Roger Vincent Tari), recorded by Scott Cheng/Roger V. Tari (pop/punk), released 2002 on VT Music/VT Records. Other artists include Mind Dope 63, Yaag Yang, Leeji Young, Fractured Glass, N.F. Inc., Ling Ling and East Coast Project (midi inc).

Tips: "We seek artists from around the world. The music should be new and creative regardless of style."

TEXAS FANTASY MUSIC GROUP, 2932 Dyer St., Dallas TX 75205. (214)691-5318. Fax: (214)692-1392. E-mail: barbc@texasmusicgroup.com. Website: www.texasmusicgroup.com. **Contact:** Don Ashley, director of film & TV music. Director of New Age, World and Classical: Richard Theisen. Director of Country, Rock and Classic Rock: Billy Jack Simpson. Creative Director: Barbara McMillen. Record producer and music publisher (Showcat Music and Flying Red Horse Publishing). Estab. 1982. Produces 35 singles/year. Fee derived from sales royalty when song or artist is recorded, or outright fee from record company or recording artist, also sync fees for film/TV.

How to Contact: Submit demo tape by mail. Unsolicited submissions are OK. Prefers CD or cassette with 2 songs and lyric sheet (if applicable). Include SASE. Responds in 6 months. "Submissions accepted between March and July only."

Music: Mostly **instrumental for film** and **all styles**. Produced *When I Was a Dinosaur* (album), recorded by Dixie Chicks and various artists; and *Teardrops To Rainbows & Other New Classic Tales* (album by Richard Theisen/Rollie Anderson), recorded by various artists, both on Remarkable Records (children's).

○ **THEORETICAL REALITY** 52323 Harrisburg, Chesterfield MI 48051. E-mail: erickilgore@m sn.com. **Contact:** Eric Kilgore, chief producer/owner. Record producer. Produces 6 EPs and 2-4 CDs/ year. Fee derived from sales royalty when song or artist is recorded, or individual arrangements with artist.

How to Contact: *Write first and obtain permission to submit.* Prefers cassette with 1-3 songs and legibly printed lyric sheet. Include SASE. Responds in 6 weeks.

Music: Mostly **folk/rock**, **folk** and **acoustic rock**; also **novelty** and **hard to define style combinations**. Produced *Kilgore* (album), written by Kilgore, recorded by Igor Smeghead (spoken word), released 2001 on Theoretical Reality; Untitled album recorded by The Bouncing Perversions (novelty), released 2001 on Theoretical Reality; and *Planet Girth* (album), written by Doom/Mitchell/ Chaz/Krist, recorded by Fatt Haxx (rock), released 2001 on Schizophrenic Recordings. Other artists include Pantheon June, reductive synthesis and O.C. Tolbert.

Tips: "We are a small company that works with a limited amount of acts. We work as hard as we can for our clients, but they must be willing to help themselves also!"

○ **TMC PRODUCTIONS**, P.O. Box 12353, San Antonio TX 78212. (210)829-1909. Website: www.axbarmusic.com. **Contact:** Joe Scates, producer. Record producer, music publisher (Axbar Productions/BMI, Scates & Blanton/BMI and Axe Handle Music/ASCAP), record company (Axbar, Trophy, Jato, Prince and Charro Records) and record distribution and promotion. Produces 3-5 CDs/ year. Fee derived from sales royalty.

How to Contact: *Write or call first and obtain permission to submit.* Prefers cassette with 1-5 songs and lyric sheet. Does not return material. Responds "as soon as possible, but don't rush us."

Music: Mostly **traditional country**; also **blues**, **novelty** and **rock (soft)**. Produced "Chicken Dance" (single) (traditional), recorded by George Chambers and "Hobo Heart" (single), written and recorded by Juni Moon, both on Axbar Records. Other artists include Jim Marshall, Caroll Gilley, Rick Will, Wayne Carter, Kathi Timm, Leon Taylor, Mark Chestnutt and Kenny Dale.

◐ **TRAC RECORD CO.**, 170 N. Maple, Fresno CA 93702. (209)255-1717. E-mail: tracsell@aol.c om. **Contact:** Stan Anderson, Bev Anderson, owners. Record producer, music publisher (Sellwood Publishing/BMI) and record company (TRAC Records). Estab. 1972. Produces 5 12″ singles, 5 LPs and 5 CDs/year. Fee derived from outright fee from recording artist or outside investor.

How to Contact: Submit demo tape by mail. Unsolicited submissions are OK. Prefers cassette with 3 songs and lyric sheet. "Send professional studio demo." Include SASE. Responds in 3 weeks.

Music: Mostly **country, all styles** and **southern gospel**. Produced *All Time Low* (album), written and recorded by Jimmy Walker on TRAC Records (country). Other artists include Jessica James and Kevin Blake Willard.

○ **THE TRINITY STUDIO**, P.O. Box 1417, Corpus Christi TX 78403. (361)854-SING. E-mail: info@trinitystydio.com. Website: www.trinitystudio.com. **Contact:** Jim Wilken, owner. Record producer and recording studio. Estab. 1988. Fee derived from outright fee from recording artist or record company.

How to Contact: Submit demo tape by mail. Unsolicited submissions are OK. Prefers cassette, CD or VHS videocassette. Does not return material. Responds in 1 month.

Music: Mostly **Christian-country**. Produced *Miracle Man* (album), written and recorded by Merrill Lane (country Christian) on TC Records; and *Higher Love* (album by Merrill Lane/Becky Redels), recorded by Becky Redels (country Christian). Other artists include Kerry Patton, Patty Walker, Leah Knight, Lofton Kline, Rockports Gospel Force and Jackie Cole.

TO HELP YOU UNDERSTAND and use the information in these listings, see "How to Use *Songwriter's Market* to Get Your Songs Heard," on page 5.

☑ ◎ **VALTEC PRODUCTIONS**, P.O. Box 6018, Santa Maria CA 93456. (805)928-8559. Website: www.valtec.net. **Contact:** Joe Valenta, producer. Record producer. Estab. 1986. Produces 20 singles and 10 CDs/year. Fee derived from sales royalty when song or artist is recorded.
How to Contact: Submit demo tape by mail. Unsolicited submissions are OK. Prefers cassette, DAT or 8mm videocassette with 3 songs and lyric or lead sheet. Send photo. Does not return material (kept on file for 2 years). Responds in 6 weeks.
Music: Mostly **country**, **pop/AC** and **rock**. Produced *Lisa Sanchez* (album), written and recorded by Lisa Sanchez (country); *John Jacobson* (album), written and recorded by John Jacobson on Valtone Records (pop); and *Taxi* (album), written and recorded by Groupe Taxi on Tesoro Records (Spanish/pop).

◐ **CHARLES VICKERS MUSIC ASSOCIATION**, P.O. Box 725, Daytona Beach FL 32015-0725. (904)252-4849. Fax: (904 or 386)252-7402. E-mail: CharlesVickers@USALink.com. Website: www.ZYWorld.com/CharlesVickers. President: Harold Vickers. Manager: Loris Doby. President/Producer: Dr. Charles H. Vickers D.M. Record producer, music publisher (Pritchett Publication/BMI and Alison Music/ASCAP) and record company (King of Kings Records, L.A. International Records, Quicksilvers/Increase Records Inc. and Bell Records International). Produces 3 singles and 6 LPs/year. Fee derived from sales royalty when song or artist is recorded.
How to Contact: *Call first and obtain permission to submit.* Prefers 7½ ips reel-to-reel or cassette with 1-6 songs. Does not return material. Responds in 6 months.
Music: Mostly **church/religious**, **gospel** and **hymns**; also **bluegrass**, **blues**, **classical**, **country**, **easy listening**, **jazz**, **MOR**, **progressive**, **reggae (pop)**, **R&B**, **rock**, **soul** and **top 40/pop**. Produced *Run to Jesus While You Can* (album), written and recorded by Charles Vickers on Quicksilvers/Increase Records Inc. Other artists include James Franklin, Gladys Nighton and Charles Gardy.

☑ ◯ **THE WEISMAN PRODUCTION GROUP**, 449 N. Vista St., Los Angeles CA 90036. (323)653-0693. E-mail: unclelenny@aol.com. **Contact:** Ben Weisman, owner. Record producer and music publisher (Audio Music Publishers). Estab. 1965. Produces 10 singles/year. Fee derived from sales royalty when song or artist is recorded.
How to Contact: Submit demo CD or tape by mail. Unsolicited submissions are OK. Prefers CD or cassette with 3-10 songs and lyric sheet. Include SASE. "Mention *Songwriter's Market*. Please make return envelope the same size as the envelopes you send material in, otherwise we cannot send everything back. Just send tape." Responds in 6 weeks.
Music: Mostly **R&B**, **soul**, **dance**, **rap** and **top 40/pop**; also **gospel**.

◎ **WESTWIRES DIGITAL USA**, 1042 Club Ave., Allentown PA 18109. (610) 435-1924. E-mail: wayne.becker@westwires.com. Website: www.westwires.com. **Contact:** Wayne Becker, owner/producer. Record producer and production company. Fee derived from outright fee from record company or artist retainer.
How to Contact: Submit demo tape by mail. Unsolicited submissions are OK. Prefers cassette, CD or VHS videocassette with 3 songs and lyric sheet. Does not return material. Responds in 1 month.
Music: Mostly **R&B**, **dance**, **alternative**, **folk** and **eclectic**. Produced *Identity Papers* (album), recorded by Jeff Lee (spoken word) on Drimala Records. Other artists include Weston, Anne Le Baron and Gary Hassay.
Tips: "We are interested in singer/songwriters and alternative artists living in the mid-Atlantic area. Must be able to perform live and take chances."

☑ ◎ **WILBUR PRODUCTIONS**, One University Place 5K, New York NY 10003. (212)255-5544. E-mail: demo@pilotrecording.com. Website: www.pilotrecording.com. **Contact:** Will Schillinger, president. Record producer and recording engineer/studio owner. Estab. 1989. Produces 50 singles, 20 LPs and 20 CDs/year. Fee derived from sales royalty when song or artist is recorded or outright fee from record company or from artist.
How to Contact: Submit demo CD by mail. Prefers CD with 3-5 songs. Does not return material. Responds in 2 weeks.
Music: Mostly **rock**, **jazz** and **alternative**. Worked with Marshall Crenshaw, Vanessa Williams, Sean Lennon, Yoko, Bo Diddley, God's Child, Junior Brown, Warren Zevon, Amy Fairchild, In the Groove, Jack Walrath and many others.

Tips: "Don't worry about your demo quality. Send good songs. Very interested in new bands as well."

✓ ◖ **FRANK WILLSON**, P.O. Box 2297, Universal City TX 78148. (210)599-0022. E-mail: bswr18@txdiret.net. Website: www.BSWRecords.com. **Contact:** Frank Willson, producer. Record producer, management firm (Universal Music Marketing) and record company (BSW Records/Universal Music Records). Estab. 1987. Produces 20-25 albums/year. Fee derived from sales royalty when song or artist is recorded.
   ● Frank Willson's record company, BSW Records, can be found in the Record Companies section and his management firm, Universal Music Marketing, is in the Managers & Booking Agents section.
How to Contact: Submit demo CD by mail. Unsolicited submissions are OK. Prefers cassette with 3-4 songs and lyric sheets. Include SASE. Responds in 1 month.
Music: Mostly **country**, **blues**, **jazz** and **soft rock**. Produced *Follow the Roses* (album), written and recorded by Larry Butler on BSW Records (country). Other artists include Candee Land, Dan Kimmel, Brad Lee, John Wayne and Sonny Marshall.

◖ **WLM MUSIC/RECORDING**, 2808 Cammie St., Durham NC 27705-2020. (919)471-3086. Fax: (919)471-4326. E-mail: wlm.musicrecording@worldnet.att.net. **Contact:** Watts Lee Mangum, owner. Record producer. Estab. 1980. Fee derived from outright fee from recording artist. "In some cases, an advance payment requested for demo production."
How to Contact: Submit demo CD by mail. Unsolicited submissions are OK. Prefers CD with 2-4 songs and lyric or lead sheet (if possible). Include SASE. Responds in 6 months.
Music: Mostly **country**, **country/rock** and **blues/rock**; also **pop**, **rock**, **blues**, **gospel** and **bluegrass**. Produced "911," and "Petals of an Orchid" (singles), both written and recorded by Johnny Scoggins (country); and "Renew the Love" (single by Judy Evans), recorded by Bernie Evans (country), all on Independent. Other artists include Southern Breeze Band and Heart Breakers Band.

◖ **WORLD RECORDS**, 5798 Deer Trail Dr., Traverse City MI 49684. E-mail: jack@worldrec.org. Website: www.worldrec.org. **Contact:** Jack Conners, producer. Record producer, engineer/technician and record company (World Records). Estab. 1984. Produces 1 CD/year. Fee derived from outright fee from recording artist.
How to Contact: *Write first and obtain permission to submit.* Prefers CD with 1 or 2 songs. Include SASE. Responds in 6 weeks.
Music: Mostly **classical**, **folk** and **jazz**. Produced *Perfect World* (album by Jim Davenport/Jack Conners), recorded by JD (pop rock), released 2001 on World Records. Other artists include The Murphy Brothers and The Camerata Singers.

◖ **STEVE WYTAS PRODUCTIONS**, Dept. SM, 11 Custer St., West Hartford CT 06110. (860)953-2834. Contact: Steven J. Wytas. Record producer. Estab. 1984. Produces 4-8 singles, 3 LPs, 3 EPs and 4 CDs/year. Fee derived from outright fee from recording artist or record company.
How to Contact: Submit demo tape by mail. Unsolicited submissions are OK. Prefers CD or VHS videocassette with several songs and lyric or lead sheet. "Include live material if possible." Does not return material. Responds in 3 months.
Music: Mostly **rock**, **pop**, **top 40** and **country/acoustic**. Produced *Already Home* (album), recorded by Hannah Cranna on Big Deal Records (rock); *Under the Rose* (album), recorded by Under the Rose on Utter Records (rock); and *Sickness & Health* (album), recorded by Legs Akimbo on Joyful Noise Records (rock). Other artists include King Hop!, The Shells, The Gravel Pit, G'nu Fuz, Tuesday Welders and Toxic Field Mice.

MARKET CONDITIONS are constantly changing! If you're still using this book and it is 2004 or later, buy the newest edition of *Songwriter's Market* at your favorite bookstore or order directly from Writer's Digest Books at (800)289-0963.

Additional Record Producers

The following companies are also record producers, but their listings are found in other sections of the book. See the General Index for page numbers, then read the listings for submission information.

A.P.I. Records
Afterschool Records, Inc.
Alexander Sr. Music
Alexis
Alias John Henry Tunes
AlliSongs Inc.
Ariana Records
Arkadia Entertainment Corp.
Atlan-Dec/Grooveline Records
Audio Music Publishers
Avita Records
Bacchus Group Productions, Ltd.
Bagatelle Music Publishing Co./Record Company
Bal & Bal Music Publishing Co.
Banana Records
Barrett Rock 'n' Roll Enterprises, Paul
Belmont Records
Big Fish Music Publishing Group
Blowin' Smoke Productions/Records
Blue Wave Productions
BME Publishing
Bouquet Records
Bradley Music, Allan
Brian Song Music Corp.
Buried Treasure Music
Burnsongs
Camex Music
Capstan Record Production
Cellar Records
Cherri/Holly Music
Chiaroscuro Records
Christopher Publishing, Sonny
Chucker Music Inc.
Cimirron Music
CKB Records/Helaphat Entertainment
Cornelius Companies, The
Cosmotone Records
Country Showcase America
Creative Improvised Music Projects (CIMP) Records
Dagene Music
Dapmor Publishing
De Miles Music Company, The Edward
Deadeye Records
Del Camino Music Publishing
Dell Music, Frank
Discmedia
Disc-tinct Music, Inc.
Drool Records
Duane Music, Inc.
Ellis International Talent Agency, The
EMF Productions

Factory Beat Records, Inc.
Fireant
First Time Records/Music (Publishing) U.K.
Flat Records
Flying Heart Records
Flying Red Horse Publishing
Frick Enterprises, Bob Scott
Frozen Inca Music
Furrow Music
Gallery II Records/Jumpin' Jack Records
Generic Records, Inc.
Glad Music Co.
Golden Triangle Records
Green Bear Records
Groove Makers' Recordings
G-String Publishing
Gueststar Entertainment Agency/Records, Inc.
Hammel Associates, Inc., R.L.
Happy Man Records
Happy Melody
Hardison International Entertainment Corporation
Heads Up Int., Ltd.
Hi-Bias Records Inc.
Hickory Lane Publishing and Recording
His Power Productions and Publishing
Interplanetary Music
Iron Skillet Music
Ja/Nein Musikverlag GmbH
Joey Records
Jupiter Records
Kansa Records Corporation
Kaupp Records
Kaysarah Music
Kingston Records
L.A. Records (Canada)
L.A. Records (Michigan)
Lake Transfer Productions & Music
Landslide Records
Les Music Group
Lineage Publishing Co.
Lock
Lucifer Records, Inc.
Luick & Associates Music Publisher, Harold
Makers Mark Gold
Manuiti L.A.
Martin Productions, Rick
Marvel Records, Andy
Mayfair Music
McCoy Music, Jim
McJames Music Inc.
Mega Music Productions
Mellow House Music

Mighty Records
Missile Records
Monticana Records
Music Room Publishing Group, The
Naked Jain Records
New Clarion Music Group
Ontrax Companies
Orchid Publishing
OTA Productions
P. & N. Records
P.M. Records
Perla Music
Plateau Music
Playbones Records
Presence Records
QUARK, Inc.
R.T.L. Music
Rampant Records
Red Sky Records
Renaissance Entertainment Group
Road Records
Rocker Music/Happy Man Music
Rockford Music Co.
Rosebowl Music
Ruffnation Records
Safire Records
Sahara Records and Filmworks Entertainment
Schafer Music Group
Sea Cruise Productions, Inc.
Silver Blue Music/Oceans Blue Music
Silver Thunder Music Group
Sinus Musik Produktion, Ulli Weigel

Sound Cellar Music
Sound Management Direction
Southern Most Publishing Company
Southland Records, Inc.
Sphere Group One
Starbound Publishing Co.
Stardust
Street Records
Stuart Music Co., Jeb
Succes
Sunsongs Music/Dark Son Music
Sureshot Records
T.C. Productions/Etude Publishing Co.
Tiger's Eye Entertainment Management & Consulting
Topcat Records
Tower Music Group
Trac Record Co.
Twentieth Century Promotions
Universal Music Marketing
Unknown Source Music
Valtec Productions
Wagner Agency, William F.
Wall Street Music
Warehouse Creek Recording Corp.
Warner Productions, Cheryl K.
White Cat Music
Whiting Music
Wilder Artists' Management, Shane
Williams Management, Yvonne
World Beatnik Records
World Famous Music Co.
X.R.L. Records/Music

Category Index

The Category Index is a good place to begin searching for a market for your songs. Below is an alphabetical list of 19 general music categories. If you write dance music and are looking for a record producer to pitch them, check the Dance section in this index. There you will find a list of record producers who work with dance music. Once you locate the entries for those producers, read the music subheading *carefully* to determine which companies are most interested in the type of dance music you write. Some of the markets in this section do not appear in the Category Index because they have not indicated a specific preference. Most of these said they are interested in "all types" of music. Listings that were very specific, or whose description of the music they're interested in doesn't quite fit into these categories, also do not appear here.

Adult Contemporary (also easy listening, middle of the road, AAA, ballads, etc.)
"A" Major Sound Corporation
Aberdeen Productions
Bal Records
Diamond Entertainment, Joel
Integrated Entertainment
Jump Productions
June Productions Ltd.
Known Artist Productions
Kovach, Robert R.
Luick & Country Music Showcase Intl. Associates, Harold
Magid Productions, Lee
Mittelstedt, A.V.
Monticana Productions
Panio Brothers Label
Rustron Music Productions
Tamjam Productions
Valtec Productions
Vickers Music Association, Charles

Alternative (also modern rock, punk, college rock, new wave, hardcore, new music, industrial, ska, indie rock, garage, etc.)
"A" Major Sound Corporation
Alco Productions
Avalon Productions
Blues Alley Records
Coachouse Music
Cotton Town Productions
Craig, Douglas
DaVinci's Notebook Records
Kane Producer/Engineer, Karen
L.A. Entertainment, Inc.
Mac-Attack Productions
Marenco, Cookie
Mathews, d/b/a Hit or Myth Productions, Scott
Monticana Productions

Road Records
Stuart Audio Services
Studio Voodoo Music
Tari, Roger Vincent
Vickers Music Association, Charles
Westwires Digital USA
Wilbur Productions

Blues
Bal Records
Celt Musical Services, Jan
Coachouse Music
Cotton Town Productions
Demi Monde Records & Publishing Ltd.
Esquire International
Hailing Frequency Music Productions
Linear Cycle Productions
Magid Productions, Lee
Monticana Productions
Pacific North Studios Ltd.
Reel Adventures
Silver Bow Productions
Studio Seven
Tamjam Productions
TMC Productions
Vickers Music Association, Charles
Willson, Frank
WLM Music/Recording

Children's
Stuart Audio Services

Classical (also opera, chamber music, serious music, choral, etc.)
Lark Talent & Advertising
Marenco, Cookie
Satkowski Recordings, Steve
Vickers Music Association, Charles
World Records

Country (also western, C&W, bluegrass, cowboy songs, western swing, honky-tonk, etc.)

Aberdeen Productions
ACR Productions
Alco Productions
Allyn, Stuart J.
Avalon Productions
Baird Enterprises, Ron
Bal Records
Birthplace Productions
Cacophony Productions
Coachouse Music
Coffee and Cream Productions
Cold Creek Records (CCR)
Cotton Town Productions
Country Star Productions
Cupit Productions, Jerry
De Miles, Edward
Diamond Entertainment, Joel
Dixon III, Philip D., Attorney at Law
Doss Presents, Col. Buster
Esquire International
Eternal Song Agency, The
Haworth Productions
Jay Bird Productions
Jay Jay Publishing & Record Co.
Kingston Records and Talent
Known Artist Productions
Kovach, Robert R.
Lari-Jon Productions
Lark Talent & Advertising
Linear Cycle Productions
Luick & Country Music Showcase Intl. Associates, Harold
Magid Productions, Lee
Marenco, Cookie
Martin, Pete/Vaam Music Productions
Mittelstedt, A.V.
Monticana Productions
Pacific North Studios Ltd.
Panio Brothers Label
Parker, Patty
Pierce, Jim
Reel Adventures
RN'D Productions
Road Records
Rustron Music Productions
Schafer Music
Segal's Productions
Silver Bow Productions
Silver Thunder Music Group
Sound Works Entertainment Productions Inc.
Sphere Group One
SRS Productions/Hit Records Network
Stuart Audio Services
Studio Seven
Swift River Productions

TMC Productions
Trac Record Co.
Trinity Studio, The
Valtec Productions
Vickers Music Association, Charles
Willson, Frank
WLM Music/Recording
Wytas Productions, Steve

Dance (also house, hi-NRG, disco, club, rave, techno, trip-hop, trance, etc.)

Coffee and Cream Productions
De Miles, Edward
Diamond Entertainment, Joel
Esquire International
Glocc Cocced Records
Janoulis Productions, Alexander/Big Al Jano Productions
Jump Productions
Mac-Attack Productions
Makers Mark Music Productions
Mona Lisa Records/Bristol Recording Studios
Monticana Productions
Neu Electro Productions
Panio Brothers Label
Road Records
Soul Candy Productions
Studio Voodoo Music
Weisman Production Group, The
Westwires Digital USA

Folk (also acoustic, Celtic, etc.)

Birthplace Productions
Coppin, Johnny/Red Sky Records
Magid Productions, Lee
Marenco, Cookie
Monticana Productions
Rustron Music Productions
Schafer Music
Sound Works Entertainment Productions Inc.
Swift River Productions
Theoretical Reality
Westwires Digital USA
World Records

Instrumental (also background music, musical scores, etc.)

Eternal Song Agency, The
Glocc Cocced Records
Jump Productions
Lark Talent & Advertising
Magid Productions, Lee
Road Records
Swift River Productions
Texas Fantasy Music Group

WLM Music/Recording
Wytas Productions, Steve

R&B (also soul, black, urban, etc.)
"A" Major Sound Corporation
ACR Productions
Allyn, Stuart J.
Angel Films Company
Appell Productions, Inc., Jonathan
Avalon Productions
Bal Records
Big Sky Audio Productions
Candyspiteful Productions
Celt Musical Services, Jan
Coffee and Cream Productions
Country Star Productions
DAP Entertainment
DaVinci's Notebook Records
De Miles, Edward
Diamond Entertainment, Joel
Esquire International
Glocc Cocced Records
Hailing Frequency Music Productions
Haworth Productions
Hes Free Productions & Publishing
Janoulis Productions, Alexander/Big Al Jano Productions
Kane Producer/Engineer, Karen
Known Artist Productions
Kovach, Robert R.
L.A. Entertainment, Inc.
Linear Cycle Productions
Magid Productions, Lee
Makers Mark Music Productions
Martin, Pete/Vaam Music Productions
Mona Lisa Records/Bristol Recording Studios
Monticana Productions
Mustrock Productionz Worldwide
New Experience Records
Philly Breakdown Recording Co.
Rustron Music Productions
Segal's Productions
Shu'Baby Montez Music
Silver Thunder Music Group
Tamjam Productions
Vickers Music Association, Charles
Weisman Production Group, The
Westwires Digital USA

Rap (also hip-hop, bass, etc.)
Avalon Productions
Dixon III, Philip D., Attorney at Law
Glocc Cocced Records
Hes Free Productions & Publishing
Marenco, Cookie
Mustrock Productionz Worldwide
Neu Electro Productions
New Experience Records

Philly Breakdown Recording Co.
RN'D Productions
Shu'Baby Montez Music
Soul Candy Productions
Weisman Production Group, The

Religious (also gospel, sacred, Christian, church, hymns, praise, inspirational, worship, etc.)
"A" Major Sound Corporation
ACR Productions
Alco Productions
Avalon Productions
Bal Records
Birthplace Productions
Blues Alley Records
Coffee and Cream Productions
Cotton Town Productions
Country Star Productions
Cupit Productions, Jerry
DAP Entertainment
Doss Presents, Col. Buster
Esquire International
Eternal Song Agency, The
Hailing Frequency Music Productions
Haworth Productions
Hes Free Productions & Publishing
Jay Jay Publishing & Record Co.
Kovach, Robert R.
Lari-Jon Productions
Linear Cycle Productions
Luick & Country Music Showcase Intl. Associates, Harold
Magid Productions, Lee
Makers Mark Music Productions
Mittelstedt, A.V.
Monticana Productions
New Experience Records
Philly Breakdown Recording Co.
Schafer Music
Silver Bow Productions
Silver Thunder Music Group
Stuart Audio Services
Trac Record Co.
Trinity Studio, The
Vickers Music Association, Charles
Weisman Production Group, The
WLM Music/Recording

Rock (also rockabilly, AOR, rock 'n' roll, etc.)
"A" Major Sound Corporation
Aberdeen Productions
ACR Productions
Alco Productions
Allyn, Stuart J.
Angel Films Company
Appell Productions, Inc., Jonathan
Avalon Productions

Baird Enterprises, Ron
Bal Records
Big Sky Audio Productions
Cacophony Productions
Candyspiteful Productions
Celt Musical Services, Jan
Coachouse Music
Collector Records
Coppin, Johnny/Red Sky Records
Cotton Town Productions
Country Star Productions
Craig, Douglas
Cupit Productions, Jerry
DaVinci's Notebook Records
Demi Monde Records & Publishing Ltd.
Diamond Entertainment, Joel
Dixon III, Philip D., Attorney at Law
Esquire International
Hailing Frequency Music Productions
Haworth Productions
Hes Free Productions & Publishing
Integrated Entertainment
Janoulis Productions, Alexander/Big Al Jano Productions
Jay Bird Productions
June Productions Ltd.
Kingston Records and Talent
Kovach, Robert R.
Lari-Jon Productions
Linear Cycle Productions
Magid Productions, Lee
Mathews, d/b/a Hit or Myth Productions, Scott
Mittelstedt, A.V.
Mona Lisa Records/Bristol Recording Studios

Monticana Productions
Neu Electro Productions
New Experience Records
Reel Adventures
RN'D Productions
Rustron Music Productions
Segal's Productions
Silver Bow Productions
Silver Thunder Music Group
Soul Candy Productions
Sound Works Entertainment Productions Inc.
Sphere Group One
SRS Productions/Hit Records Network
Stuart Audio Services
Studio Seven
Swift River Productions
Theoretical Reality
TMC Productions
Valtec Productions
Vickers Music Association, Charles
Wilbur Productions
Willson, Frank
WLM Music/Recording
Wytas Productions, Steve

World Music (also reggae, ethnic, calypso, international, world beat, etc.)
Appell Productions, Inc., Jonathan
Craig, Douglas
Kane Producer/Engineer, Karen
Pacific North Studios Ltd.
Reel Adventures
Studio Seven
Tari, Roger Vincent
Vickers Music Association, Charles

Managers & Booking Agents

Before submitting to a manager or booking agent, be sure you know exactly what you need. If you're looking for someone to help you with performance opportunities, the booking agency is the one to contact. They can help you book shows either in your local area or throughout the country. If you're looking for someone to help guide your career, you need to contact a management firm. Some management firms may also handle booking; however, it may be in your best interest to look for a separate booking agency. A manager should be your manager—not your agent, publisher, lawyer or accountant.

MANAGERS

Of all the music industry players surrounding successful artists, managers are usually the people closest to the artists themselves. The artist manager can be a valuable contact, both for the songwriter trying to get songs to a particular artist and for the songwriter/performer. A manager and his connections can be invaluable in securing the right publishing deal or recording contract if the writer is also an artist. Getting songs to an artist's manager is yet another way to get your songs recorded, since the manager may play a large part in deciding what material his client uses. For the performer seeking management, a successful manager should be thought of as the foundation for a successful career.

The relationship between a manager and his client relies on mutual trust. A manager works as the liaison between you and the rest of the music industry, and he must know exactly what you want out of your career in order to help you achieve your goals. His handling of publicity, promotion and finances, as well as the contacts he has within the industry, can make or break your career. You should never be afraid to ask questions about any aspect of the relationship between you and a prospective manager. Always remember that a manager works *for the artist*. A good manager is able to communicate his opinions to you without reservation, and should be willing to explain any confusing terminology or discuss plans with you before taking action. A manager needs to be able to communicate successfully with all segments of the music industry in order to get his client the best deals possible. He needs to be able to work with booking agents, publishers, lawyers and record companies. Keep in mind that you are both working together toward a common goal: success for you and your songs. Talent, originality, professionalism and a drive to succeed are qualities that will attract a manager to an artist—and a songwriter.

BOOKING AGENTS

The function of the booking agent is to find performance venues for their clients. They usually represent many more acts than a manager does, and have less contact with their acts. A booking agent charges a commission for his services, as does a manager. Managers usually ask for a 15-

---

Additional Managers & Booking Agents

There are **MORE MANAGERS & BOOKING AGENTS** located in other sections of the book! On page 323 use the list of Additional Managers & Booking Agents to find listings within other sections who are also managers/booking agents.

20% commission on an act's earnings; booking agents usually charge around 10%. In the area of managers and booking agents, more successful acts can negotiate lower percentage deals than the ones set forth above.

SUBMITTING MATERIAL TO MANAGERS & BOOKING AGENTS

The firms listed in this section have provided information about the types of music they work with and the types of acts they represent. You'll want to refer to the Category Index at the end of this section to find out which companies deal with the type of music you write, and the Geographic Index at the back of the book to help you locate companies near where you live. Then determine whether they are open to your level of experience (see the Openness to Submissions sidebar on page 8). Each listing also contains submission requirements and information about what items to include in a press kit and will also specify whether the company is a management firm or a booking agency. Remember that your submission represents you as an artist, and should be as organized and professional as possible.

> ### ⓘ For More Information
> For more instructional information on the listings in this book, including explanations of symbols (🄽 ☑ 🄵 🄶 🌐 ◖ ◪ ◕ ⊘), read the article How to Use *Songwriter's Market* to Get Your Songs Heard on page 5.

◖**AFTERSCHOOL PUBLISHING COMPANY**, P.O. Box 14157, Detroit MI 48214. (313)894-8855. President: Herman Kelly. Manager: Genesis Act. Management firm, booking agency, record company (Afterschool Co.) and music publisher (Afterschool Pub. Co.). Estab. 1978. Represents individual artists, songwriters, producers, arrangers and musicians from anywhere; currently handles 20 acts. Reviews material for acts.
How to Contact: Submit demo tape by mail. Unsolicited submissions are OK. Prefers cassette with 3 songs and lyric or lead sheet. If seeking management, include cover letter, résumé, proposal, photo, demo tape, lyric sheets, press clippings, video and bio in press kit. Include SASE. Responds in 2 weeks.
Music: Mostly **pop**, **jazz**, **rap**, **country** and **folk**. Works primarily with small bands and solo artists. Current acts include L.L. Cool J, P.M. Dawn, Miss Jones, Whodini, Kinsui, KC and Jimmy B. Horne, T Baby, MC Hammer, Beats International, Cut N Move, Fresh Prince and Jazzy Jeff, 2 Hype, Brothers and a Dog, Brownstone, 2 Live Crew/Luke, Rockman and Gloria Estefan & Miami Sound Machine.

◪**AIR TIGHT MANAGEMENT**, 115 West Rd., P.O. Box 113, Winchester Center CT 06094. (860)738-9139. Fax: (860)738-9135. E-mail: mainoffice@airtightmanagement.com. Website: www.airtightmanagement.com. **Contact:** Jack Forchette, president. A&R: Scott Fairchild. Management firm. Estab. 1969. Represents individual artists, groups or songwriters from anywhere; currently handles 6 acts. Receives 15-20% commission. Reviews material for acts.
How to Contact: *Write first and obtain permission to submit.* Prefers cassette or VHS videocassette. If seeking management, press kit should include photos, bio and recorded material. "Follow up with a fax or e-mail, not a phone call." Does not return material. Responds in 2 weeks.
Music: Mostly **rock**, **country** and **jazz**. Current acts include Johnny Colla (songwriter/producer, and guitarist/songwriter for Huey Lewis and the News), Jason Scheff (lead singer/songwriter for the group "Chicago"), Gary Burr (Nashville songwriter/producer), Nathan East (singer/songwriter/bassist—Eric Clapton, Michael Jackson, Madonna, 4-Play and others), Rocco Prestia (legendary R&B musician, "Tower of Power" bassist), Ilse Delange (singer/songwriter, recording artist) and Marion Meadows (contemporary jazz/urban songwriter/saxophonist, recording artist).

ALERT MUSIC INC., 41 Britain St., Suite 305, Toronto Ontario M5A 1R7 Canada. (416)364-4200. Fax: (416)364-8632. E-mail: contact@alertmusic.com. Website: www.alertmusic.c om. **Contact:** W. Tom Berry, president. Management firm, record company and recording artist. Represents local and regional individual artists and groups; currently handles 5 acts. Reviews material for acts.
How to Contact: *Write first and obtain permission to submit.* Prefers CD. If seeking management, press kit should include finished CD, photo, press clippings and bio. Include SASE.
Music: All types. Works primarily with bands and singer/songwriters. Current acts include Holly Cole (pop vocalist), Kim Mitchell (rock singer/songwriter), Bet E and Stef (bossanova) and Leahy (celtic pop).

ALL STAR MANAGEMENT, 1229 S. Prospect St., Marion OH 43302-7267. (740)382-5939. E-mail: allstarmanage@msn.com. **Contact:** John Simpson, president. Management firm. Estab. 1980. Represents individual artists, groups and songwriters from anywhere; currently handles 9 acts. Receives 20% commission. Reviews material for acts.
How to Contact: Submit demo tape by mail. Unsolicited submissions are OK. Prefers cassette or videocassette with 3 songs and lyric or lead sheet. If seeking management, press kit should include audio cassette with 3 songs, bio, 8×10 photo or any information or articles written about yourself or group, and video if you have one. Does not return material. Responds in 2 months.
Music: Mostly **country**, **Christian**, **adult contemporary** and **smooth jazz**. Works primarily with bands and singers/songwriters. Current acts include Patricia Hoch (singer/songwriter, adult contemporary), Allen Austin (singer/songwriter, country) and Kenney Polson (songwriter/musician, smooth jazz).

ALL STAR TALENT AGENCY, P.O. Box 717, White House TN 37188. (615)643-4208. Fax: (615)643-2228. **Contact:** Joyce Kirby, owner/agent. Booking agency. Estab. 1966. Represents professional individuals, groups and songwriters; currently handles 6 acts. Receives 15% commission. Reviews material for acts.
How to Contact: Submit demo tape by mail. Unsolicited submissions are OK. Prefers cassette or VHS videocassette with 4 songs (can be cover songs) and lead sheet. If seeking management, press kit should include bios, cover letter, press clippings, demo and photos. Does not return material. Does not return long distance phone calls. Responds in 1 month.
Music: Mostly **country**; also **bluegrass**, **gospel**, **MOR**, **rock (country)** and **top 40/pop**. Works primarily with dance, show and bar bands, vocalists, club acts and concerts. Current acts include Alex Houston (MOR), Chris Hartley (country) and Jack Greene (country).

MICHAEL ALLEN ENTERTAINMENT DEVELOPMENT, P.O. Box 111510, Nashville TN 37222. Phone/fax: (615)754-0059. Website: www.michaelallencreates.com. **Contact:** Michael Allen. Management firm and public relations. Represents individual artists, groups and songwriters; currently handles 2 acts. Receives 15-25% commission. Reviews material for acts.
How to Contact: Submit demo tape by mail. Unsolicited submissions are OK. Prefers CD or cassette or VHS videocassette with 3 songs and lyric or lead sheets. If seeking management, press kit should include photo, bio, press clippings, letter and tape. Include SASE. Responds in 3 months.
Music: Mostly **country**, and **pop**; also **rock** and **gospel**. Works primarily with vocalists and bands. Currently doing public relations for Shotgun Red, Ricky Lynn Gregg, Easy Street and Kyle Raines.

AMERICAN ARTISTS ENTERTAINMENT, 21 Chews Landing Rd., Clementon NJ 08021-3843. (856)566-1232. Fax: (856)435-7453. E-mail: ardept@aaeg.com. Website: www.aaeg.c om. **Contact:** A&R Department. Management firm, music publisher (David Music, BMI), record

---

REMEMBER: Don't "shotgun" your demo tapes. Submit only to companies interested in the type of music you write. For more submission hints, refer to Getting Started on page 10.

company (East Coast Records) and record and motion picture distribution. Represents individual artists, groups, actors and models from anywhere; currently handles 3 acts. Receives 20% commission. Reviews material for acts.

How to Contact: Submit demo tape by mail. Unsolicited submissions are OK. Prefers cassette, videocassette or CD with 3 songs. If seeking management, press kit should include bio, press releases, photos, performing, training and background. Include SASE. Responds in 1 month.

Music: Mostly **R&B**, **top 40**, **rap** and **country**; also **modern rock** and motion picture scores. Current acts include The Blue Notes (R&B), The Trammps (disco), Clarice Rose (country) and Bliss (Top 40).

AMERICAN BANDS MANAGEMENT, P.O. Box 840607, Houston TX 77284. (713)785-3700. Fax: (713)785-4641. E-mail: johnblomstrom@aol.com. President: John Blomstrom, Sr. Vice President: Cheryl Byrd. Management firm. Estab. 1973. Represents groups from anywhere; currently handles 3 acts. Receives 15-25% commission. Reviews material for acts.

How to Contact: Submit demo tape by mail prior to making phone contact. Unsolicited submissions are OK. Prefers cassette or CD. If seeking management, press kit should include cover letter, bio, photo, demo tape/CD, press clippings, video, résumé and professional references with names and numbers. Does not return material. Responds in 1 month.

Music: Mostly **rock (all forms)** and **modern country**. Works primarily with bands. Current acts include Captain Pink (Motown), Vince Vance & the Valiants (show band) and Rachel (guitarist/singer/modern folk).

AMOK ARTISTS AGENCY, (formerly Amok Inc.), Box 12, Fergus, Ontario N1M 2W7 Canada. (519)787-1100. Fax: (519)787-0084. E-mail: amok@sentex.net. Website: www.amokmusic.com. **Contact:** Hugo Ranpen, owner. Management firm and booking agency. Estab. 1985. Represents groups from anywhere; currently handles 13 acts. Receives 15-20% commission.

How to Contact: Submit demo tape by mail. Unsolicited submissions are OK. Prefers VHS videocassette or CD with lyric sheet. If seeking management, press kit should include bio, past performances, photo, cassette, CD or video. "Due to the large amount of submissions we receive we can only respond to successful applicants." Does not return material.

Music: Mostly **world beat**, **new roots**, **aboriginal** and **folk**. Works primarily with bands in the world music and new roots field; no mainstream rock/pop. Current acts include Amampondo (world beat, Melt 2000), Lester Quitzau (blues, Festival), Bill Bourne (roots), Madagascar Slim (world), Veda Hille (art rock), Tri-continental (root) and Nash the Slash (art rock).

ANDERSON ASSOCIATES COMMUNICATIONS GROUP, 9291 NW 13th Place, Coral Spring FL 33071. (954)753-5440. Fax: (954)753-9715. E-mail: rjppny@aol.com. Website: http://andersonassociates.com. **Contact:** Richard Papaleo, CEO. Management firm. Estab. 1992. Represents individual artists and groups "only on the East Coast of the US." Currently handles 2 acts. Receives 20% commission. Reviews material for acts.

How to Contact: *Call first and obtain permission to submit.* **"Management Only!"** Submit demo tape by mail. "Call before submitting package." Prefers cassette, bio and/or picture with 3 songs and lead sheet. If seeking management, press kit should include cassette with 3 songs (video OK), bio, cover letter and picture. Does not return material. Responds in 2 months.

Music: Mostly **R&B**, **pop/dance** and **pop/rock**; also **A/C**, **pop/mainstream** and **mainstream rock**. Current acts include Josie D'ambola and Unique (R&B/pop).

Tips: "We are seeking to sign 6-8 acts this year, and we have a management virtual web wall in development."

ARDENNE INT'L INC., 1800 Argyle St., Suite 444, Halifax, Nova Scotia B3J 3N8 Canada. (902)492-8000. Fax: (902)423-2143. E-mail: mardenne@ardenneinternational.com. Website: www.ArdenneInternational.com. **Contact:** Michael Ardenne, president. Management firm. Estab. 1988. Represents local and individual artists; currently handles 2 acts. Receives 20-25% commission. Reviews material for acts.

How to Contact: *Write, call, e-mail or fax first and obtain permission to submit.* Prefers cassette with lyric sheet. "Put name, address, phone number and song list on the tape. Send maximum 3 songs." Send only copywritten material. Does not return materials. Responds as time permits.
Music: Works primarily with vocalists/songwriters. Current acts include Kris Taylor (pop/rock) and The Funken Flames (R&B/soul).

N **ARTIST REPRESENTATION AND MANAGEMENT**, 1257 Arcade St., St. Paul MN 55106. (651)483-8754. Fax: (651)776-6338. E-mail: ra@armentertainment.com. Website: www.arme ntertainment.com. **Contact:** Roger Anderson, agent/manager. Management firm and booking agency. Estab. 1983. Represents artists from anywhere; currently handles 10 acts. Receives 15% commission. Reviews material for acts.
How to Contact: Submit CD and video by mail. Unsolicited submissions are OK. Please include minimum 3 songs. If seeking management, references, current schedule, bio, photo, press clippings should also be included. "Priority is placed on original artists with product who are currently touring." Does not return material. Responds only if interested within 30 days.
Music: Mostly **melodic rock**, **southern rock** and **R&B**. Current acts include Knight Crawler (melodic rock), Crow (R&B, rock), Austin Healy (southern rock) and Pork Chop (blues rock).

N **ATCH RECORDS AND PRODUCTIONS**, 10103 Fondren, Suite 380, Houston TX 77096-4502. (713)981-6540. Fax: (713)981-0083. E-mail: charlesatchison@msn.com. Website: www .atchrecords.com. Chairman/CEO: Charles Atchison. **Contact:** Rodney Gardner, A&R/producer; Christopher "Black" Dilworth, manager/street promotions. Management firm, recording studio and record company. Estab. 1989. Represents local, regional and international individual artists, groups and songwriters; currently handles 5 acts. Receives 20% commission. Reviews material for acts.
How to Contact: Submit demo tape by mail. Unsolicited submissions are OK. Prefers cassette with 2 songs and lyric sheet. If seeking management, include cover letter, bio, photo, demo and lyrics. Does not return material. Responds in 3 weeks.
Music: Mostly **R&B**, **country** and **gospel**; also **pop**, **rap** and **hip-hop**. Works primarily with vocalists and groups. Current acts include Demetris (R&B) and Noble (rap).
Tips: "Send a good detailed demo with good lyrics. Looking for wonderful love stories, dance music, also songs for children."

N **ATLANTIC ENTERTAINMENT GROUP**, 2922 Atlantic Ave., #200, Atlantic City NJ 08401-6396. (609)823-6400. Fax: (609)345-8683. E-mail: aegshows@aol.com. Executive Director of Artist Services: Scott Sherman. A&R: Glenn Guyer. Management, production firm and booking agency. Represents individual artists and groups from anywhere; currently handles over 20 acts. Receives 10-25% commission. Reviews material for acts and management.
How to Contact: Submit demo tape by mail. Unsolicited submissions are OK. Prefers cassette, CD or VHS videocassette with 3 songs. If seeking management, press kit should include bio, cover letter, photo, press clippings, video, résumé, previous listings, demo and reviews. Include SASE. Responds in 2 months only if interested.
Music: Mostly **dance**, **R&B** and **contemporary**; also **specialty**. Current acts include Candace Jourdan (singer/writer), Candy J (singer), C&C Music Factory (dance), Deborah Cooper (R&B vocalist), Candy Girls, Wanda Dee (r&b/dance), the KLF (dance) and Sweet P. Pauline.

N **AUSTEX MUSIC**, 3005 S. Lamar Blvd., D109, Austin TX 78704. (512)480-9790. Fax: (512)480-8789. E-mail: tmcfarl334@aol.com. Owner: T.J. McFarland. Management firm, booking agency, music publisher (True-Tex Music/BMI), record company (Austex Records) and record producer (T.J. McFarland). Estab. 1981. Represents individual artists, groups and songwriters from anywhere; currently handles 3 acts. Reviews material for acts.
How to Contact: Submit demo tape by mail. Unsolicited submissions are OK. Prefers cassette or CD with 3-5 songs and lyric sheet. If seeking management, press kit should include picture and bio. Include SASE. Responds in 2 months.

Music: Mostly **Texas country**, **roots country** and **pop country**; also **swamp rock**. Works primarily with singer/songwriters with bands or small groups. Label support preferred. Current acts include Kimmie Rhodes (pop singer/songwriter with trio), Alvin Crow (fiddler with country roots rock band) and Janet Lynn (singer/songwriter with Texas country band).

Tips: "Learn your craft well. You are competing against aggressive, knowledgeable professionals."

⊘ BACCHUS GROUP PRODUCTIONS, LTD., 5701 N. Sheridan Rd., Suite 8-U, Chicago IL 60660. (773)334-1532. Fax: (773)334-1531. E-mail: bacchusgrp@compuserve.com. Website: www.BacchusGroup.com. **Contact:** D. Maximilian, Managing Director and Executive Producer. Director of Marketing: M. Margarida Rainho. Management firm and record producer (D. Maximilian). Estab. 1990. Represents individual artists or groups from anywhere; currently handles 9 acts. Receives 15-25% commission. Reviews material for acts.

How to Contact: *Does not accept unsolicited submissions.*

Music: Mostly **pop**, **R&B/soul** and **jazz**; also **Latin** and **world beat**. Works primarily with singer/songwriters, composers, arrangers, bands and orchestras. Current acts include Orchestra of the Americas (international dance orchestra), Sorcerers of Swing (big band jazz dance orchestra) and Samba Samba 2000 (Carnival/Mardi Gras worldbeat dance orchestra).

Ⓝ ⊘ BACKSTREET BOOKING, 5658 Kirby Ave., Cincinnati OH 45239. (513)542-9544. Fax: (513)542-9545. E-mail: backstreetbking@aol.com. Website: www.holographicrecords.com/backstreet. **Contact:** James Sfarnas, president. Booking agency. Estab. 1992. Represents individual artists and groups from anywhere; currently handles 8 acts. Receives 10-15% commission. Reviews material for acts.

How to Contact: *Call first and obtain permission to submit.* Accepts only signed acts with product available nationally.

Music: Mostly **niche-oriented music** and **rock**. Current acts include Marky Ramone & The Intruders, Acumen (progressive rock group), Cab (jazz fusion), Spock's Beard (progressive rock) and Basile (comedian).

Tips: "Build a base on your own."

⊘ BARNARD MANAGEMENT SERVICES (BMS), 228 Main St., Suite 3, Venice CA 90291. (310)399-8886. Fax: (310)450-0470. E-mail: bms@barnardus.com. **Contact:** Russell Barnard, president. Management firm. Estab. 1979. Represents artists, groups and songwriters; currently handles 2 acts. Receives 10-20% commission. Reviews material for acts.

How to Contact: *Write first and obtain permission to submit.* Prefers cassette with 3-10 songs and lead sheet. Artists may submit VHS videocassette (15-30 minutes) by permission only. If seeking management, press kit should include cover letter, bio, photo, demo tape/CD, lyric sheets, press clippings, video and résumé. Does not return material. Responds in 2 months.

Music: Mostly **country crossover**, **blues**, **country**, **R&B**, **rock** and **soul**. Current acts include Mark Shipper (songwriter/author) and Sally Rose (R&B band).

Tips: "Semi-produced demos are of little value. Either save the time and money by submitting material 'in the raw,' or do a finished production version."

Ⓝ ⊕ ⊘ PAUL BARRETT ROCK 'N' ROLL ENTERPRISES, 16 Grove Place, Penarth, Vale of Glamorgan CF64 2ND United Kingdom. Phone: 02920-704279. Fax: 01222-709989. **Contact:** Paul Barrett, director. Management firm, booking agency, music publisher (October), record company (Rock 'n' Roll Records) and record producer (Paul Barrett and Ray Thompson). Estab. 1969. Represents individual artists and groups from anywhere; currently handles 30 acts. Receives 10% commission. Reviews material for acts.

● This company only represents acts who perform '50s rock 'n' roll.

How to Contact: Submit demo tape by mail. Unsolicited submissions are OK. Prefers cassette or DAT with picture and bio (for performers). SAE and IRC. Responds in 3 weeks.

THE TYPES OF MUSIC each listing is interested in are printed in **boldface**.

Music: Mostly **50s rock 'n' roll**. Works primarily with "performers plus some writers." Current acts include The Jets (trio), Matchbox (rockabilly) and Ray Campi (American rockabilly hero).
Tips: "We want good original slanted roots music that does not sound British! Performed by cool people with nonmop top, mod squad, silly haircuts or clothes."

○ BASSLINE ENTERTAINMENT, INC., P.O. Box 2394, New York NY 10185. (212)769-6956. E-mail: newbassinc@aol.com. Website: www.basslineinc.com. **Contact:** Clarence Williams, vice president. Senior Consultant for Artist Development: Sharon Williams. Management firm. Estab. 1993. Represents local and regional individual artists, groups and songwriters. Receives 20-25% commission. Reviews material for acts.
How to Contact: Submit demo tape by mail. Unsolicited submissions are OK. Prefers cassette, CD or VHS videocassette. If seeking management, press kit should include cover letter, press clippings, bio, demo (cassette, CD or VHS video), picture and accurate contact telephone number. Include SASE. Responds in 3 weeks.
Music: Mostly **pop**, **R&B**, **club/dance** and **hip-hop/rap**; some **Latin**. Works primarily with singer/ songwriters, producers, rappers and bands. Current acts include Michael Anthony (Latin pop), Dom Pachino (rap) and Jojo p. (r&b).

◑ BIG J PRODUCTIONS, 2516 S. Sugar Ridge, Laplace LA 70068. (504)652-2645. **Contact:** Frankie Jay, agent. Booking agency. Estab. 1968. Represents individual artists, groups and songwriters; currently handles over 50 acts. Receives 15-25% commission. Reviews material for acts.
How to Contact: *Call first and obtain permission to submit* (office hours Monday-Friday: noon-5 pm). Prefers cassette or VHS videocassette with 3-6 songs and lyric or lead sheet. "It would be best for an artist to lip-sync to a prerecorded track. The object is for someone to see how an artist would perform more than simply assessing song content." Artists seeking management should include pictures, biography, tape or CD and video. Does not return material. Responds in 2 weeks.
Music: Mostly **rock**, **pop** and **R&B**. Works primarily with groups with self-contained songwriters. Current acts include Zebra (original rock group), Crowbar (heavy metal) and Kyper (original dance).

◑ BLANK & BLANK, 1 Belmont Ave., Suite 320, Bala Cynwyd PA 19004-1604. (610)664-8200. Fax: (610)664-8201. **Contact:** E. Robert Blank, manager. Management firm. Represents individual artists and groups. Reviews material for acts.
How to Contact: *Contact first and obtain permission to submit.* Prefers videocassette. If seeking management, press kit should include cover letter, demo tape/CD and video. Does not return material.

◑ BLOWIN' SMOKE PRODUCTIONS/RECORDS, 7438 Shoshone Ave., Van Nuys CA 91406-2340. (818)881-9888. Fax: (818)881-0555. E-mail: blowinsmokeband@ktb.net. Website: www.blowinsmokeband.com. **Contact:** Larry Knight, president. Management firm and record producer. Estab. 1990. Represents local and West Coast individual artists and groups; currently handles 7 acts. Receives 15-20% commission. Reviews material for acts.
How to Contact: *Write or call first and obtain permission to submit.* Prefers cassette or CD. If seeking management, press kit should include cover letter, demo tape/CD, lyric sheets, press clippings, video if available, photo, bios, contact telephone numbers and any info on legal commitments already in place. Include SASE. Responds in 1 month.
Music: Mostly **R&B**, **blues** and **blues-rock**. Works primarily with single and group vocalists and a few R&B/blues bands. Current acts include Larry "Fuzzy" Knight (blues singer/songwriter), King Floyd (R&B artist), The Blowin' Smoke Rhythm & Blues Band, The Fabulous Smokettes, and Joyce Lawson.

☑ ○ BLUE WAVE PRODUCTIONS, 3221 Perryville Rd., Baldwinsville NY 13027. (315)638-4286. Fax: (315)635-4757. E-mail: bluewave@localnet.com. Website: www.bluewaverecords.com. **Contact:** Greg Spencer, owner/president. Management firm, music publisher (G.W. Spencer Music/ ASCAP), record company (Blue Wave Records) and record producer (Blue Wave Productions). Estab. 1985. Represents individual artists and/or groups and songwriters from anywhere; currently handles 5 acts. Receives 10% commission. Reviews material for acts.

How to Contact: Submit demo tape by mail. Unsolicited submissions are OK. Prefers CD or VHS videocassette with 3-6 songs. "Just the music first, reviews and articles are OK. No photos or lyrics until later." If seeking management, press kit should include cover letter and demo tape/CD. Include SASE. Responds in 1 month. No phone calls.
Music: Mostly **blues**, **blues/rock** and **roots rock**. Current acts include Kim Lembo (female blues vocalist), Kim Simmonds (blues guitarist and singer/songwriter) and Downchild Bluesband (blues).
Tips: "I'm looking for great singers with soul. Not interested in pop/rock commercial material."

◉ BOUQUET-ORCHID ENTERPRISES, P.O. Box 1335, Norcross GA 30091. (770)814-2420.
Contact: Bill Bohannon, president. Management firm, booking agency, music publisher (Orchid Publishing/BMI) and record company (Bouquet Records). Represents individuals and groups; currently handles 4 acts. Receives 10-15% commission. Reviews material for acts.
How to Contact: Submit demo tape by mail. Unsolicited submissions are OK. Prefers cassette, CD or videocassette with 3-5 songs, song list and lyric sheet. Include brief résumé. If seeking management, press kit should include current photograph, 2-3 media clippings, description of act, and background information on act. Include SASE. Responds in 1 month.
Music: Mostly **country**, **rock** and **top 40/pop**; also **gospel** and **R&B**. Works primarily with vocalists and groups. Current acts include Susan Spencer, Jamey Wells, Adam Day and the Bandoleers.

◉ BROTHERS MANAGEMENT ASSOCIATES, 141 Dunbar Ave., Fords NJ 08863. (732)738-0880. Fax: (732)738-0970. E-mail: bmaent@cs.com. Website: www.bmaent.com. **Contact:** Allen A. Faucera, president. Management firm and booking agency. Estab. 1972. Represents artists, groups and songwriters; currently handles 25 acts. Receives 15-20% commission. Reviews material for acts.
How to Contact: *Write first and obtain permission to submit.* Prefers cassette/CD or VHS videocassette with 3-6 songs and lyric sheets. Include photographs and résumé. If seeking management, include photo, bio, tape and return envelope in press kit. Include SASE. Responds in 2 months.
Music: Mostly **pop**, **rock**, **MOR** and **R&B**. Works primarily with vocalists and established groups. Current acts include Waterfront (R&B), Glen Burtnik (pop rock) and Alisha (pop/dance).
Tips: "Submit very commercial material—make demo of high quality."

☑ ◐ BILL BUTLER MUSIC, P.O. Box 20, Hondo TX 78861-0020. Phone/fax: (830)426-2112.
E-mail: billbutler@aol.com. Owner: Bill Butler. Management firm and music publisher. Estab. 1982. Represents individual artists and songwriters; currently handles 2 acts. Receives 15% commission. Reviews material for acts.
  • They have received a special Citation of Achievement from BMI for One Million Air Plays of "Baby Blue" and Two Million Air Plays of "Love Without End, Amen," by George Strait.
How to Contact: Submit demo by mail. Unsolicited submissions are OK. Prefers cassette or CD with 3 songs and lyric sheet. If seeking management, press kit should include bio, photo, tape or CD with 5 unreleased songs. "No cover tunes please." Does not return material. Responds in 3 months only if interested.
Music: Mostly **country**, **R&B** and **tejano**. Works primarily with singer/songwriters and songwriters. Current acts include Frank Solesbee (country) and Keith Lutz (country).
Tips: "Send quality demos that allow the lyric to be clearly understood. Include lyric sheets. Make sure your name, address and phone number are on both tape or CD and J-card. Don't try to contact us—we will contact you if we're interested."

⊕ ◉ BUXTON WALKER P/L, (formerly Mr. Walker's Company), P.O. Box 2197, St. Kilda West, Vic 3182 Australia. Phone: (+61)3 9537-7155. Fax: (+61)3 9537-7166. E-mail: andrew@buxt onwalker.com. Website: www.buxtonwalker.com. **Contact:** Andrew Walker. Management firm, music publisher (Head Records Publishing) and record company (Head Records). Estab. 1995. Represents individual artists and groups from anywhere; currently handles 5 acts. Management company receives 20% commission.
How to Contact: Submit demo tape by mail. Unsolicited submissions are OK. Cassette or CD only. If seeking management, press kit should include CD, bio and history. "Processing takes time. Contact by fax or e-mail is best as it allows for time differences to be no obstacle." SAE and IRC. Responds in 2 months.

Music: Mostly **rock/pop**, **jazz** and **acoustic**; also **reggae**, **blues** and **world**. Works primarily with singers/songwriters and bands. Current acts include The Jaynes (rock), Black Sorrows (blues and jazz), The Revelators (blues), Tess McKenna (alt rock) and Jen Anderson (scores).

Tips: "We have low need for songs to be supplied to our artists. We are mostly interested in recorded artists/writers looking for distribution/release in Australia/New Zealand."

◯ CHUCKER MUSIC INC., 345 E. 80th St., 15H, New York NY 10021. Fax: (212)879-9621. E-mail: chuckermusic@earthlink.net. Website: www.musiccounselor.com. **Contact:** Chuck Dembrak, president. Management firm, music publisher (Cool 1) and record producer (Chuck Dembrak). Estab. 1984. Represents individual artists, groups and songwriters from anywhere; currently handles 5 acts. Receives 20% commission. Reviews material for acts.

How to Contact: *Write first and obtain permission to submit.* Prefers cassette, VHS videocassette or CD. If seeking management, press kit should include cover letter, bio, demo tape/CD, press clippings, video and photos. Does not return material. Responds in 2 months.

Music: Mostly **R&B**, **top 40** and **dance**; also **jazz**, **rock** and **A/C**. Works primarily with singer/songwriters. Current acts include Kim Waters (jazz), Dr. Zoot (swing), Louis Love (rock) and GAB (rap).

⊕ ✓ ◯ CIRCUIT RIDER TALENT & MANAGEMENT CO., 123 Walton Ferry Rd., Hendersonville TN 37075. (615)824-1947. Fax: (615)264-0462. E-mail: dotwool@bellsouth.net. **Contact:** Linda S. Dotson, president. UK office: 45 Gladstone Road, Melrose Villa House, Watford, Herts WD1 2RA UK. Phone: 011-44-1923-819415. Consultation firm, booking agency and music publisher (Channel Music, Cordial Music). Represents individual artists, songwriters and actors; currently handles 8 acts. Works with a large number of recording artists, songwriters, actors, producers. (Includes multi Grammy-winning producer/writer Skip Scarborough.) Receives 10-15% commission (union rates). Reviews material for acts (free of charge).

How to Contact: *Write or call first and obtain permission to submit.* Prefers cassette or videocassette with 3 songs and lyric sheet. If seeking consultation, press kit should include bio, cover letter, résumé, lyric sheets if original songs, photo and tape with 3 songs. Videocassettes required of artist's submissions. Include SASE. Responds in 2 months.

Music: Mostly **pop**, **country** and **gospel**; also **R&B** and **comedy**. Works primarily with vocalists, special concerts, movies and TV. Current acts include Shauna (R&B dance), Frank White (blues), Alton McClain (gospel), Trina Davis (urban gospel), Sheb Wooley (country) and Todd Taylor (pop/rock instrumentalist).

Tips: "Artists, have your act together. Have a full press kit, videos and be professional. Attitudes are a big factor in my agreeing to work with you (no egotists). This is a business, and we will be building your career."

◯ CLASS ACT PRODUCTIONS/MANAGEMENT, P.O. Box 55252, Sherman Oaks CA 91413. (818)980-1039. Fax: (209)821-4408. E-mail: pkimmel@gr8gizmo.com. **Contact:** Peter Kimmel, president. Management firm, music publisher and production company. Estab. 1985. Currently handles 3 acts. Receives 20% commission. Reviews material for acts.

How to Contact: Submit demo CD by mail. Unsolicited submissions are OK. Include cover letter, pictures, bio, lyric sheets (essential), CD and video in press kit. Include SASE. Responds in 1 month.

Music: All styles. Current acts include Terpsichore (cyber dance/pop), Don Cameron (new country), and Jason Serfling (modern classical).

✓ ◯ CLOCKWORK ENTERTAINMENT MANAGEMENT AGENCY, 227 Concord St., Haverhill MA 01830. (978)373-5677. E-mail: wjm227@hotmail.com. **Contact:** William J. Macek, esq., entertainment attorney, president. Management firm. Represents groups and songwriters throughout New England with mastered product who are looking for label deals and licensing in US and internationally. Fee is negotiated individually; currently handles multiple acts. Commissions vary. Reviews material for acts.

How to Contact: Submit demo tape by mail. Unsolicited submissions are OK. Prefers cassette or CD with 3-12 songs. "Also submit promotion and cover letter with interesting facts about yourself." If seeking management, press kit should include cover letter, tape or CD, photo, bio and press clippings. Include SASE. Responds in 1 month.

Music: Mostly **rock (all types)** and **top 40/pop**. Works primarily with bar bands and original acts. Current acts include Gail Savage (rock singer) and Center Stage (one man show).

CLOUSHER PRODUCTIONS, P.O. Box 1191, Mechanicsburg PA 17055. (717)766-7644. Fax: (717)766-1490. E-mail: clousher@webtv.net. Website: www.clousherentertainment.com. **Contact:** Fred Clousher, owner. Booking agency and production company. Estab. 1972. Represents groups from anywhere; currently handles over 100 acts.

How to Contact: Submit demo tape by mail. Unsolicited submissions are OK. Prefers VHS videocassette. If seeking management, press kit should include press clippings, testimonials, letters, credits, glossies, video demo tape, references, cover letter, résumé and bio. Does not return material. "Performer should check back with us!"

Music: Mostly **country**, **old rock** and **ethnic** (German, Italian, etc.); also **dance bands** (regional) and **classical quartets**. "We work mostly with country, old time R&R, regional variety dance bands, tribute acts, and all types of variety acts." Current acts include Jasmine Morgan (country/pop vocalist), Robin Right (country vocalist) and Island Breeze (ethnic Hawaiian group).

Tips: "The songwriters we work with are entertainers themselves, which is the aspect we deal with. They usually have bands or do some sort of show, either with tracks or live music. We engage them for stage shows, dances, strolling, etc. We do not publish music or submit performers to recording companies for contracts. We strictly set up live performances for them."

CODY ENTERTAINMENT GROUP, P.O. Box 456, Winchester VA 22604. Phone/fax: (540)722-4625. E-mail: codyent@visuallink.com. **Contact:** Phil Smallwood, president. Management firm and booking agency. Estab. 1975. Represents individual artists and groups from anywhere; currently handles 11 acts. Receives 20% commission. Reviews material for acts.

How to Contact: Submit demo tape by mail. Unsolicited submissions are OK. Prefers cassette, DAT or videocassette with 3 songs and lead sheet. If seeking management, press kit should include cover letter, bio, photo, demo tape/CD and video. Does not return material. Responds in 2 months.

Music: Mostly **show acts** and **writers of love songs**. Current acts include The Hutchens (country) and Arlo Haines (writer/performer).

CONCEPT 2000 INC., P.O. Box 2950, Columbus OH 43216-2950. (614)276-2000. Fax: (614)275-0163. Florida office: P.O. Box 2070, Largo FL 33779-2070. (727)585-2922. Fax: (727)585-3835. E-mail: info2k@concept2k.com. Website: www.concept2k.com. **Contact:** Brian Wallace, president. Management firm and booking agency. Estab. 1981. Represents international individual artists, groups and songwriters; currently handles 4 acts. Receives 20% commission. Reviews material for acts.

How to Contact: Submit demo tape by mail. Unsolicited submissions are OK. Prefers cassette with 4 songs. If seeking management, include demo tape, press clips, photo and bio. Does not return material. Responds in 2 weeks.

Music: Mostly **country**, **gospel** and **pop**; also **jazz**, **R&B** and **soul**. Current acts include Bryan Hitch (contemporary gospel), Shades of Grey (R&B/soul), Dwight Lenox (show group) and Gene Walker (jazz).

Tips: "Send quality songs with lyric sheets. Production quality is not necessary."

REFER TO THE CATEGORY INDEX (at the end of this section) to find exactly which companies are interested in the type of music you write.

◐ CONCERTED EFFORTS, INC./FOGGY DAY MUSIC, P.O. Box 600099, Newtonville MA 02460. (617)969-0810. Fax: (617)969-6761. Owner: Paul Kahn. Management firm, booking agency and music publisher (Foggy Day Music). Represents individual artists, groups and songwriters from anywhere; currently handles 5 acts. Commission varies. Reviews material for acts.

How to Contact: Submit demo tape by mail. Unsolicited submissions are OK. Prefers CD, will accept cassette, with lyric sheet. "No management submissions." Does not return material.

Music: Folk, **country** and **rock**; also **world music**, **zydeco** and **blues**. Current acts include Luther Johnson (blues singer), Holmes Brothers and Paul Kahn.

Tips: "Simple recorded demo is OK, with lyrics."

◯ CONSCIENCE MUSIC, P.O. Box 617667, Chicago IL 60661. (312)226-4858. E-mail: towreco rds@aol.com. **Contact:** Karen M. Smith, consultant/personal manager. Management firm and record company (TOW Records). Estab. 1985. Represents individual artists, groups and songwriters from anywhere; currently handles 1 act. Receives 20% commission. Reviews material for acts.

How to Contact: *Write first and obtain permission to submit.* Prefers CD with 2-3 songs and lyric sheet. If seeking management, press kit should include current reviews, demo tape/CD, lyric sheets, list of performance locations, and bio or letter with band or artist objectives. "Cannot overemphasize the importance of having objectives you are ready to discuss with us." Include SASE. Responds in 4 months.

Music: Mostly **rock** and **pop**; also **visual artists**, **writers** and **models**. Works primarily with indie bands in the States and Great Britain. Currently represents Lance Porter (drummer with the Flash Express). "Many clients are on a consulting basis only."

☑ ◐ CORVALAN-CONDLIFFE MANAGEMENT, 1702 Clark Lane, Unit B, Redondo Beach CA 90278. (310)318-2574. Fax: (310)318-6574. E-mail: convcond@earthlink.net. Website: www.pira nharecords.com. **Contact:** Brian Condliffe, manager. Management firm. Estab. 1982. Represents individual artists, groups and songwriters from anywhere; currently handles 2 acts. Receives 15% commission.

How to Contact: *Write or call first and obtain permission to submit.* Prefers cassette with 4-6 songs. If seeking management, press kit should include bio, professional photo, press reviews and demo. Include SASE. Responds in 2 months.

Music: Mostly **pop** and **rock**; also **Latin**. Works primarily with alternative rock and pop/rock/world beat bands. Current acts include Ramiro Medina and Blue Tarantula.

Tips: "Be professional in all aspects of your kit and presentation. Check your grammar and spelling in your correspondence/written material. Know your music and your targeted market (rock, R&B, etc.)."

Ⓝ ◯ COTTON TOWN MANAGEMENT, P.O. Box 804, Commerce GA 30529. **Contact:** James Viola, A&R Department. Management firm. Estab. 2002. Represents individual artists and groups from anywhere. Receives approximately 15% commission. Reviews material for acts.

How to Contact: Submit demo tape by mail. Unsolicited submissions are OK. Prefers cassette or CD/CDR with 2-3 songs and lyric sheet and cover letter along with bio and photos. "Please put name and address clearly on outside of package." Include SASE. Responds in 3-5 weeks.

Music: Mostly **alternative**, **country** and **rock**; also **blues**, **gospel** and **pop**. Works primarily with "bands and singers who are unique."

Tips: "We are looking for unique bands and singers who can compete in the major music markets such as Atlanta, Nashville, Los Angeles, and New York."

Ⓝ COUNTRY STAR ATTRACTIONS, 439 Wiley Ave., Franklin PA 16323. Phone/fax: (814)432-4633. **Contact:** Norman Kelly. Management firm, booking agency, music publisher (Country Star Music/ASCAP), record producer (Country Star Productions) and record company (Country Star, Process, Mersey and CSI Records). Estab. 1970. Represents artists and musical groups; currently handles 6-10 acts. Receives 10-15% commission. Reviews material for acts.

● See the listings for Country Star Music in the Music Publishers section, Country Star International in the Record Companies section and Country Star Productions in the Record Producers section.

How to Contact: Submit demo tape by mail. Unsolicited submissions are OK. Prefers cassette with 2-4 songs and typed lyric or lead sheet; include photo. If seeking management, press kit should include cassette or CD, lyric sheet, brief bio and photo. Include SASE. Responds in 2 weeks.

Music: Mostly **country** (50%); also **gospel** (25%) and **bluegrass** (25%). Works primarily with vocalists. Current acts include Junie Lou, Debbie Sue and Larry Pieper (country singers).

☑ ◐ **COUNTRYWIDE PRODUCERS**, 2466 Wildon Dr., York PA 17403. (717)741-2658. E-mail: denglar@iopener.net. **Contact:** Bob Englar, president. Booking agency. Represents individuals and groups; currently handles 8 acts. Receives 15% commission. Reviews material for acts.

How to Contact: Query or submit demo tape by mail. Unsolicited submissions are OK. If seeking management, press kit should include photo and demo tape. Include SASE. Responds in 1 week.

Music: Bluegrass, **blues**, **classical**, **country** and **disco**; also **folk**, **gospel**, **jazz**, **polka**, **rock (light)**, **soul** and **top 40/pop**. Works primarily with show bands. Current acts include Majestics (50s/60s), Jeff Williams Show (c/w), Osborn Bros (bluegrass) and Star Light Revue Band (c/w).

Ⓝ ⊕ ◐ **CRANIUM MANAGEMENT**, P.O. Box 240, Annandale NSW 2038 Australia. E-mail: cranium@smartchat.net.au. Manager: Peter "Skip" Beaumont-Edmonds. Management firm. Estab. 1992. Represents individual artists, groups and songwriters from anywhere; currently handles 5 acts. Receives 20% commission. Reviews material for acts.

How to Contact: *Write, e-mail or call first and obtain permission to submit.* Send "The minimum number of best songs—don't waste money on being elaborate. Talent will show through. Be sensible—if it doesn't suit us don't send it." If seeking management, press kit should include photo (optional), demo tape, press clippings (minimal), bio and cover letter. Does not return material. Responds in 1 month.

Music: Mostly **alternative** and **pop**; also **country**. Works primarily with pop/rock, alternative bands and singer/songwriters. Current acts include Mental As Anything (pop/rock), Dog Trumpet (alternative roots duo), Adam Harvey (country singer) and David Mason-Cox (singer/songwriter).

☑ ◯ **CREATIVE STAR MANAGEMENT**, 615 E. Second St., Lima OH 45804. E-mail: Just_chilling_2002@yahoo.com. President/Owner: James Milligan. Vice President: Sonya Koger. Management firm, booking agency, music publisher (Party House Publishing/BMI, A New Rap Jam Publishing/ASCAP), record company (New Experience Records/Grand Slam Records). Estab. 1989. Represents individual artists, groups and songwriters from anywhere; currently handles 6 acts. Receives 15-20% commission. Reviews material for acts.

● Creative Star Management's publishing company, A New Rap Jam Publishing (ASCAP), is listed in the Music Publishers section, and their record label, New Experience Records/Grand Slam Records, is listed in the Record Companies section.

How to Contact: *Contact first and obtain permission to submit.* Prefers cassette or VHS videocassette with 3-5 songs and lyric sheet. If seeking management, press kit should include press clippings, bios, résumé, 8×10 glossy photo, any information that will support material and artist. Include SASE. Responds in 6 weeks.

Music: Mostly **R&B**, **pop** and **country**; also **rap**, **contemporary gospel** and **soul/funk**. Current acts include T.M.C. (gospel), David Fawcett (rap) and James Junior (r&b singer).

Tips: "We are seeking '70s and '80s groups looking to re-sign and for management."

◐ **CRISS-CROSS INDUSTRIES**, 24016 Strathern St., West Hills CA 91304. (818)710-6600. Fax: (818)719-0222. **Contact:** Doc Remer, president. Management firm and music publisher (Menachan's Music/ASCAP, Eyenoma Music/BMI). Estab. 1984. Represents individual artists, groups and songwriters from anywhere. Reviews material for acts.

How to Contact: *Write first and obtain permission to submit.* Prefers cassette or VHS videocassette with 3 songs and lyric sheet. If seeking management, press kit should include photo, bio, cover letter, demo tape/CD, video and credits. Include SASE. Responds in 1 month.

Music: Mostly **R&B** and **pop**. Works primarily with vocalists and self contained bands.
Tips: "You must currently be a working act. Make the words to the songs so they can be understood. The music should not be as loud as the vocals."

◢ CROSSFIRE PRODUCTIONS, 304 Braeswood, Austin TX 78704-7200. (512)442-5678. Fax: (512)442-1154. E-mail: vicky@wcclark.com. **Contact:** Vicky Moerbe, president. Management firm. Estab. 1990. Represents local, individual artists and songwriters; currently handles 4 acts. Receives 15% commission. Reviews material for acts.
How to Contact: *Write or call first and obtain permission to submit.* Prefers cassette with any number of songs and lyric sheet. If seeking management, press kit should include biography, press releases/articles/reviews, photograph/discography and copy of current release or demo. Include SASE. Responds in 1 month.
Music: Mostly **blues**, **swing** and **country**; also **soul** and **contemporary rock**. Works primarily with singers and songwriters. Current acts include W.C. Clark (singer/songwriter/touring act; blues/soul), Rusty Weir (songwriter), Steven Fromholz (songwriter) and Haydn Vitera (country/rock singer).
Tips: "Please submit only material to be considered for recordings for blues/soul, swing or country recordings. Our artists are looking for material to be considered for recordings for national releases."

◢ D&M ENTERTAINMENT AGENCY, P.O. Box 19242, Johnston RI 02919. (401)782-0239. **Contact:** Ray DiMillio, president. Management firm and booking agency. Estab. 1968. Represents local groups; currently handles 28 acts. Receives 15% commission. Reviews material for acts.
How to Contact: Submit demo tape by mail. *Write or call to arrange personal interview.* Unsolicited submissions are OK. Prefers cassette or VHS videocassette with 3 songs and lyric or lead sheet. If seeking management, include photo. Does not return material. Responds in 3 weeks.
Music: Mostly **R&B** and **pop**; also **rock**. Current acts include Clique (top 40), Absolute (top 40), xpo (top 40), Sunshine (top 40) and Legit (top 40).

◖ D&R ENTERTAINMENT, 308 N. Park, Broken Bow OK 74728. (580)584-9429. **Contact:** Don Walton, president. Management firm. Estab. 1985. Represents individual artists from anywhere; currently handles 2 acts. Receives 15% commission. Reviews material for acts. Also reviews for other country singers.
How to Contact: Submit demo tape by mail. Unsolicited submissions are OK. Prefers cassette and videocassette with lyric and lead sheet. If seeking management, press kit should include brief background of artist, videotape of performance, cover letter, résumé, photo, press clippings and cassette or CD. "Indicate whether you have any financial or prospective financial backing." Does not return material. Responds in 3 months.
Music: Mostly **country**; also **gospel** and **pop**. Works primarily with young beginning singers. Current acts include Kristi Reed (positive country) and Thomas Wells (contemporary Christian).
Tips: "I need songs (country) that would fit a young singer under 20. In other words no drinking, cheating, marrying songs. A pretty tough choice. Also Christian contemporary songs."

◓ DAS COMMUNICATIONS, LTD., 83 Riverside Dr., New York NY 10024. (212)877-0400. Fax: (212)595-0176. Management firm. Estab. 1975. Represents individual artists, groups and producers from anywhere; currently handles 25 acts. Receives 20% commission.
How to Contact: Responds in 2 months. Prefers demo with 3 songs, lyric sheet and photo. Does not return material.
Music: Mostly **rock**, **pop**, **R&B**, **alternative** and **hip-hop**. Current acts include Joan Osborne (rock), Wyclef Jean (hip-hop), Lady May (hip-hop), Black Eyed Peas (hip-hop), Willa Ford (pop), Diana King (pop) and The Bacon Brothers (rock).

◢ DCA PRODUCTIONS, 330 W. 38th St., Suite 303, New York NY 10018. (212)245-2063. Fax: (212)245-2367. Website: www.dcaproductions.com. **Contact:** Lauren Pellegrino, office manager. President: Daniel Abrahamsen. Vice President: Geraldine Abrahamsen. Management firm. Estab. 1975. Represents individual artists, groups and songwriters from anywhere; currently handles 14 acts.

How to Contact: If seeking management, press kit should include cover letter, bio, photo, demo tape/CD and video. Prefers cassette or VHS videocassette with 2 songs. "All materials are reviewed and kept on file for future consideration. Does not return material. We respond only if interested."
Music: Mostly **acoustic**, **rock** and **mainstream**; also **cabaret** and **theme**. Works primarily with acoustic singer/songwriters, top 40 or rock bands. Current acts include The Word (singers/songwriters), Amelia's Dream (melodic rock) and Gabrielle (singer/songwriter).
Tips: "Please do not call for a review of material."

✓ ◑ **THE EDWARD DE MILES COMPANY**, 28 E. Jackson Bldg., 10th Floor, #S627, Chicago IL 60604-2263. (773)509-6381. Fax: (312)922-6964. **Contact:** Edward de Miles, president. Management firm, booking agency, entertainment/sports promoter and TV/radio broadcast producer. Estab. 1984. Represents film, television, radio and musical artists; currently handles 15 acts. Receives 10-20% commission. Reviews material for acts. Regional operations in Chicago, Dallas, Houston and Nashville through marketing representatives. Licensed A.F. of M. booking agent.
How to Contact: *Write first and obtain permission to submit or to arrange personal interview.* Prefers cassette with 3-5 songs, 8x10 b&w photo, bio and lyric sheet. "Copyright all material before submitting." If seeking management, include cover letter, bio, demo cassette with 3-5 songs, 8×10 b&w photo, lyric sheet, press clippings and video if available in press kit. Include SASE. Does not return material. Responds in 1 month.
Music: Mostly **country**, **dance**, **R&B/soul**, **rock**, **top 40/pop** and **urban contemporary**; also looking for material for television, radio and film productions. Works primarily with dance bands and vocalists. Current acts include Steve Lynn (R&B/dance), Multiple Choice (rap) and D'von Edwards (jazz).
Tips: "Performers need to be well prepared with their presentations (equipment, showmanship a must)."

◑ **BILL DETKO MANAGEMENT**, 378 Palomares Ave., Ventura CA 93003. (805)644-0447. Fax: (805)644-0469. **Contact:** Bill Detko, president. Management firm. Estab. 1984. Represents individual artists, groups and songwriters from anywhere; currently handles 4 acts. Receives 15-20% commission. Reviews material for acts.
How to Contact: *Contact first and obtain permission to submit.* Prefers CD with 3 songs and lyric sheet. If seeking management, press kit should include bio, cover letter, résumé, photo, plus above items and any press or radio action. Does not return material. "Artist must call back."
Music: All styles.

⊕ ✓ ◐ **ANDREW DINWOODIE MANAGEMENT**, P.O. Box 5052, Victoria Point QLD 4165 Australia. Phone: (07)32070502. E-mail: adinwoodie@irrimus.com.au. **Contact:** Andrew Dinwoodie, director. Management firm and booking agency. Estab. 1983. Represents regional (Australian) individual artists, groups and songwriters; currently handles 4 acts. Receives 10-20% commission. Reviews material for acts.
How to Contact: Submit demo tape by mail. Unsolicited submissions are OK. Prefers CD/CDR, cassette or VHS PAL videocassette with lyric sheet. If seeking management, press kit should include cover letter, résumé, bio, photo, goals, audio or videotape and CD if available and anything the artist thinks will help. SAE and IRC. Responds in 1 month.
Music: Mostly **adult contemporary folk**, **country**, **R&B** and **rock/pop**; also **bluegrass**, **swing** and **folk**. Current acts include Spot the Dog (cool and cruisy adult contemporary folk), Bullamakanka (good time Australian music), Donna Heke (blues/soul) and Bluey the Bastard (feral folk).

◐ **DIRECT MANAGEMENT**, 645 Quail Ridge Rd., Aledo TX 76008-2835. Owner: Danny Wilkerson. Management firm and booking agency. Estab. 1986. Represents individual artists and/or groups from anywhere; currently handles 4 acts. Receives 10-20% commission. Reviews material for acts.
How to Contact: Submit demo tape by mail. Unsolicited submissions are OK. Prefers CD or VHS videocassette with 3 songs. If seeking management, press kit should include bio, cassette or CD, photo, lyric sheets, press clippings and video. Does not return material. Responds in 1 month.
Music: Mostly **college rock**, **Christian** and **children's**. Current acts include Waltons (pop/rock), The EPs (rock) and Emily Rogers (country).

N ⬇ ⦿ DIVINE INDUSTRIES, (formerly Gangland Artists), P.O. Box 191, 101-1001 W. Broadway, Vancouver, British Columbia V6H 4E4 Canada. (604)737-0091. Fax: (604)737-3602. E-mail: divine@divineindustries.com. Website: www.divineindustries.com. **Contact:** Allen Moy. Management firm, production house and music publisher. Estab. 1985. Represents artists and songwriters; currently handles 5 acts. Reviews material for acts.
How to Contact: *Write first and obtain permission to submit.* Prefers CD or MP3 with lyric sheet. "Videos are not entirely necessary for our company. It is certainly a nice touch. If you feel your audio cassette is strong—send the video upon later request. Something wildly creative and individual will grab our attention." Does not return material. Responds in 2 months.
Music: Rock, pop and **R&B**. Works primarily with "original rock/left of center" show bands. Current acts include 54-40 (rock/pop), Tom Wilson (folk rock), Chin (r&b) and Pepper Sands (pop).

☑ ⦿ DMR AGENCY, Galleries of Syracuse, Suite 250, Syracuse NY 13202-2416. (315)475-2500. E-mail: dmr@ican.net. Website: www.dmrbooking.com. **Contact:** David M. Rezak. Booking agency. Represents individuals and groups; currently handles 50 acts. Receives 15% commission.
How to Contact: Submit demo tape by mail. Unsolicited submissions are OK. Submit cassette or videocassette with 1-4 songs and press kit. Does not return material.
Music: Mostly **rock (all styles), pop** and **blues**. Works primarily with cover bands. Current acts include Prime Time (R&B), Tom Townsley and the Backsliders (blues) and Los Blancos (blues).
Tips: "You might want to contact us if you have a cover act in our region. Many songwriters in our area have a cover group in order to make money."

⦿ COL. BUSTER DOSS PRESENTS, 341 Billy Goat Hill Rd., Winchester TN 37398. (931)649-2577. Fax: (615)649-2732. **Contact:** Col. Buster Doss, producer. Management firm, booking agency, record company (Stardust Records), record producer and music publisher (Buster Doss Music/BMI). Estab. 1959. Represents individual artists, groups, songwriters and shows; currently handles 14 acts. Receives 15% commission. Reviews material for acts.
How to Contact: *Write first and obtain permission to submit.* Prefers cassette with 2-4 songs and lyric sheet. If seeking management, press kit should include demo, photos, video if available and bio. Include SASE. Responds back on day received.
Music: Mostly **country, gospel** and **progressive**. Works primarily with show and dance bands, single acts and package shows. Current acts include "Rooster" Quantrell, Linda Wunder, The Border Raiders, "Bronco" Buck Cody, Jerri Arnold, Bob Norman, Cindy Lee, John Hamilton, Brant Miller, Troy Cooker, Mark Brumfield and Tennessee Bill Foster.

⬇ ⦿ EAO MUSIC CORPORATION OF CANADA, P.O. Box 1240, Station "M," Calgary, Alberta T2P 2L2 Canada. (403)228-9388. Fax: (403) 229-3598. E-mail: eao@telusphonet.net. **Contact:** Edmund A. Oliverio, president. Management firm and record company. Estab. 1985. Represents individual artists, groups and songwriters from western Canada (aboriginal artists); currently handles 52 acts. Receives 15-20% commission. Reviews material for acts.
How to Contact: Submit demo tape by mail. Unsolicited submissions are OK. Prefers cassette with 3 songs and lyric and lead sheets. If seeking management, press kit should include cover letter, résumé, b&w glossy photo, cassette tape, bio, media clippings and list of venues and festivals performed. SAE and IRC. Responds in 2 weeks.
Music: Mostly **folk** and **native (aboriginal)**; also **rock**. Works primarily with singer/songwriters. Current acts include Activate (funky reggae), Feeding Like Butterflies (folk rock/Celtic), Katrina (country/folk) and Gloria K. MacRae (adult contemporary).
Tips: "Be upfront and honest. Establish your long term goals and short term goals. Have you joined your music associations (i.e., CMA, etc.)? Recent demand for cowboy artists rather than country."

● **A BULLET** introduces comments by the editor of *Songwriter's Market* indicating special information about the listing.

○ **EARTH TRACKS ARTISTS AGENCY**, 4809 Ave. N., Suite 286, Brooklyn NY 11234. E-mail: jewelblues@aol.com. **Contact:** David Krinsky, managing director-artist relations. Management firm. Estab. 1990. Represents individual artists, groups and songwriters from anywhere; currently handles 2 acts. Receives 12-15% commission. Reviews material for acts.
How to Contact: Submit demo CD or tape by mail. Unsolicited submissions are OK. Prefers CD with up to 8 original songs and lyric sheet. If seeking management, press kit should include cover letter, bio, video (if available), 1 group photo, all lyrics with songs, a cassette/CD of original songs and the ages of the artists. "**All submissions must include lyric sheets or material will not be heard.**" Does not return material. Responds in 1 month. "We will contact artist if interested. Include e-mail address for reply. No MP3 files!"
Music: Commercial rock (all kinds), **pop** and **alternative** only. No rap, R&B or metal. Works primarily with commercial, original, solo artists and groups, songwriters in the rock and pop areas. Current acts include Candid (pop/folk-rock) and Spacemonk.
Tips: "I am dedicated to artists I believe in. I act strictly as a personal manager for an artist which means I help them choose songs, submit songs, find a publisher, and/or a record company. Prefer artists who write and perform their own songs but will consider songwriters who can write 'hit' songs for pop/rock markets. I am currently seeking material. CDs, CDRs and CDRWs accepted. I do not handle bookings. Young artists considered for development. Looking for very commercial sounds and looks! Be original!. I charge no upfront fees, but I am very selective about who I represent."

○ **THE ELLIS INTERNATIONAL TALENT AGENCY**, 5617 W. Melvina, Milwaukee WI 53216. Phone/fax: (414)444-3385. **Contact:** Darnell Ellis, A&R rep. Management firm, booking agency, music publisher (Buzz Duzz Duzz Music/ASCAP) record company (Safire Records) and record producer (Darnell Ellis). Estab. 1997. Represents individual artists, groups and songwriters from anywhere; currently handles 2 acts. Receives 15-20% commission. Reviews material for acts.
How to Contact: Submit demo tape by mail. Unsolicited submissions are OK. Prefers cassette or videocassette with 4-6 songs and press kit. If seeking management, press kit should include cassette tape or CD with 4-6 songs (demo), 8×10 photo, video tape and reviews. Does not return material. Responds in 6 weeks. "We will respond only if we are interested."
Music: Mostly **country**, **pop**, **mainstream pop**, **rock** (all styles) and anything else except rap and hip-hop. Works primarily with singers, singer/songwriters, songwriters and bands. Current acts include Anthony Vincent (country), Life As Seen Through (progressive/alternative rock band), Rochelle Major (country/pop), Danny Balkwill (pop/AC) and Tracy Beck (country, folk, blues).

✔ ○ **ENDANGERED SPECIES ARTIST MANAGEMENT**, 4 Berachah Ave., South Nyack NY 10960-4202. (845)353-4001. Fax: (845)353-4332. E-mail: musik@bellatlantic.net. Website: www.endangers.com. President: Fred Porter. Vice President: Suzanne Buckley. Management firm. Estab. 1979. Represents individual artists, groups and songwriters from anywhere; currently handles 3 acts. Receives 20% commission. Reviews material for acts.
How to Contact: *Call first and obtain permission to submit.* Prefers cassette or CD with 10 songs and lyric sheet. "Please include a demo of your music, a clear, recent photograph as well as any current press, if any. A cover letter indicating at what stage in your career you are and expectations for your future. Please label the cassette and/or CD with your name and address as well as the song titles." If seeking management, press kit should include cover letter, bio, photo, demo tape/CD, lyric sheet and press clippings. Include SASE. Responds in 6 weeks.
Music: Mostly **pop**, **rock** and **world**; also **Latin/heavy metal**, **R&B**, **jazz** and **instrumental**. Current acts include Jason Wilson & Tabarruk (pop/reggae, nominated for Juno award 2001), Clear Grey (acoustic rock) and Anna (teen singer).
Tips: "Listen to everything, classical to country, old to contemporary, to develop an understanding of many writing styles. Write with many other partners to keep the creativity fresh. Don't feel your style will be ruined by taking a class or a writing seminar. We all process moods and images differently. This leads to uniqueness in the music."

○ **SCOTT EVANS PRODUCTIONS**, P.O. Box 814028, Hollywood FL 33081-4028. (954)963-4449. E-mail: evansprod@aol.com. Website: www.theentertainmentmall.com. **Contact:** Ted Jones, new artists. Management firm and booking agency. Estab. 1979. Represents local, regional or international individual artists, groups, songwriters, comedians, novelty acts and dancers; currently handles over 150 acts. Receives 10-50% commission. Reviews material for acts.

How to Contact: Submit demo tape by mail. Unsolicited submissions are OK. Prefers cassette and/or ½″ videocassette with 3 songs. If seeking management, include picture, résumé, flyers, cassette or video tape. Does not return material.

Music: Mostly **pop**, **R&B** and **Broadway**. Deals with "all types of entertainers; no limitations." Current acts include Scott Evans and Company (variety song and dance), Dorit Zinger (female vocalist), Jeff Geist, Actors Repertory Theatre, Entertainment Express, Perfect Parties, Joy Deco (dance act), Flashback 2000 Revue (musical song and dance), Everybody Salsa (Latin song and dance) and Around the World (international song and dance).

Tips: "Submit a neat, well put together, organized press kit."

☑ ◎ **EVERGREEN ENTERTAINMENT SERVICES LTD.**, (formerly Professional Artist Management, Ltd.), P.O. Box 755, Shelburne VT 05482. (800)610-7625. Fax: (888)610-7625. E-mail: info@rockandrollaccountant.com. Website: www.rockandrollaccountant.com. **Contact:** Tom Hughes, general manager. President: Brian Keith, CPA. Business management firm. Estab. 1994. Represents Northeast, New York, Tennessee and California individual artists and groups; currently handles 10 acts. Receives 6-10% fee. Reviews material for acts.

How to Contact: Submit demo tape by mail. Unsolicited submissions are OK. Prefers cassette, DAT, mini disc or CD. If seeking management, press kit should include cover letter, bio, demo tape/CD, any commercial releases, reviews and airplay. Does not return material. Responds in 2 months.

Tips: "We are tax advisors and business managers, not a booking agency. We don't shop material to labels."

◎ **EXCLESISA BOOKING AGENCY**, 716 Windward Rd., Jackson MS 39206. (601)366-0220. Fax: (601)987-8777. E-mail: exclesis@bellsouth.net. **Contact:** Roy and Esther Wooten, booking managers/owners. Booking agency. Estab. 1989. Represents groups from anywhere; currently handles 8 acts. Receives 15% commission. Reviews material for acts.

How to Contact: *Call first and obtain permission to submit.* Submit demo tape by mail. Unsolicited submissions are OK. Prefers CD or videocassette. If seeking management, press kit should include CD or cassette, videocassette, pictures, address and telephone contact and bio. Does not return material. Responds in 2 months.

Music: Gospel only. Current acts include Slim & The Supreme Angels, The Mississippi Seminar Choir, The Christianaires, Carolyn Traylor, The Pilgrim Jubilees, Spencer Taylor & the Highway QC's, Evangelist Bertha Jackson, The Annointed Jackson Singers, The Southern Sons and David R. Curry, Jr.

Tips: "Make sure your demo is clear with a good sound so the agent can make a good judgement."

Ⓝ ☑ ◎ **S.L. FELDMAN & ASSOCIATES**, 1505 W. Second Ave. #200, Vancouver, British Columbia V6H 3Y4 Canada. (604)734-5945. Fax: (604)732-0922. E-mail: feldman@slfa.com. Website: www.slfa.com. Management firm and booking agency. Estab. 1970. Represents mostly Canadian artists and groups; currently handles over 200 acts.

How to Contact: *Write or call first to obtain permission to submit a demo.* Prefers CD and lyric sheet. If seeking management, include photo, bio, cassette and video (if available) in press kit. SAE and IRC. Responds in 2 months.

Music: Current acts include Bryan Adams, The Chieftains, Joni Mitchell, Anne Murray, Sarah McLachlan, Diana Krall, Martina McBride, Barenaked Ladies and Nelly Furtado.

☑ ◎ **FRED T. FENCHEL ENTERTAINMENT AGENCY**, 2104 S. Jefferson Avenue, Mason City IA 50401. (641)423-4177. Fax: (641)423-8662. **Contact:** Fred T. Fenchel, president. Booking agency. Estab. 1964. Represents local and international individual artists and groups; currently handles up to 10 acts. Receives 20% commission.

How to Contact: Submit demo tape by mail. Unsolicited submissions are OK. Prefers cassette or videocassette. Does not return material. Responds in 3 weeks.

Music: Mostly **country**, **pop** and some **gospel**. Works primarily with dance bands and show groups; "artists we can use on club dates, fairs, etc." Current acts include The Memories (vocal/musical trio), The Suby's (karaoke) and Black Diamonds (country group). "We deal primarily with established name acts with recording contracts, or those with a label and starting into popularity."

Tips: "Be honest. Don't submit unless your act is exceptional rather than just starting out, amateurish and with lyrics that are written under the pretense of coming from qualified writers."

N ⊠ ⊘ **B.C. FIEDLER MANAGEMENT**, 53 Seton Park Rd., Toronto, Ontario M3C 3Z8 Canada. (416)421-4421. Fax: (416)421-0442. E-mail: bcf@the-wire.com. **Contact:** B.C. Fiedler/Elisa Amsterdam, partners. Management firm, music publisher (B.C. Fiedler Publishing) and record company (Sleeping Giant Music). Estab. 1964. Represents individual artists, groups and songwriters from anywhere; currently handles 4 acts. Receives 20-25% or consultant fees. Reviews material for acts.

How to Contact: *Call first and obtain permission to submit.* Prefers cassette or VHS videocassette with 3 songs and lyric sheet. If seeking management, press kit should include bio, list of concerts performed in past 2 years including name of venue, repertoire, reviews and photos. Does not return material. Responds in 2 months.

Music: Mostly **classical/crossover**, **voice** and **pop**; also **country**. Works primarily with classical/crossover ensembles, instrumental soloists, operatic voice and pop singer/songwriters. Current acts include Gary Guthman (trumpet), The Nylons (a cappella), Johannes Linstada (latin), John Arpin (pianist) and Liona Boyd (classical guitar).

Tips: "Invest in demo production using best quality voice and instrumentalists. If you write songs, hire the vocal talent to best represent your work. Submit tape and lyrics. Artists should follow up 6-8 weeks after submission."

⊕ ⊘ **FIRST TIME MANAGEMENT**, Sovereign House, 12 Trewartha Rd., Praa Sands-Penzance, Cornwall TR20 9ST England. Phone: (01736)762826. Fax: (01736)763328. E-mail: panamus @aol.com. Website: www.songwriters-guild.co.uk. **Contact:** Roderick G. Jones, managing director. Management firm, record company (First Time Records) and music publisher (First Time Music). Estab. 1986. Represents local, regional and international individual aritsts, groups and songwriters; currently handles 114 acts. Receives 15-25% commission. Reviews material for acts.

How to Contact: Submit demo tape by mail. Unsolicited submissions are OK. Prefers cassette, CD or VHS videocassette with 3 songs and lyric sheets. If seeking management, press kit should include cover letter, bio, photo, demo tape/CD, press clippings and anything relevant to make an impression. Does not return material. Responds in 1 month.

Music: Mostly **dance**, **top 40**, **rap**, **country**, **gospel** and **pop**; also **all styles**. Works primarily with songwriters, composers, vocalists, groups and choirs. Current acts include Willow (pop), Animal Cruelty (indie/heavy thrash) and Peter Arnold (folk/roots).

Tips: "Become a member of the Guild of International Songwriters and Composers. Keep everything as professional as possible. Be patient and dedicated to your aims and objectives."

N ⊘ **FIVE STAR ENTERTAINMENT**, 10188 Winter View Dr., Naples FL 34109. (941)566-7701. Fax: (941)566-7702. E-mail: tk5star@aol.com. **Contact:** Sid Kleiner and Trudy Kleiner, co-owners. Booking agency and audiovisual firm (Sid Kleiner Music Enterprises). Estab. 1976. Represents local and regional individual artists and groups; currently handles 400 acts. Receives 15-25% commission. Reviews material for acts.

How to Contact: Submit demo tape by mail. Unsolicited submissions are OK. Accepts CD, cassette, DVD or VHS videocassette. Does not return material.

Music: Mostly **MOR**, **country** and **folk**. Current acts include Dave Kleiner/Liz Pagan (alternative), Sid Kleiner (guitarist) and other acts.

REFER TO THE GEOGRAPHIC INDEX (at the back of this book) to find listings of companies by state, as well as foreign listings.

N 5 STAR MUSIC GROUP/MIKE WADDELL & ASSOCIATES, 4301 S. Carothers Rd., Franklin TN 37064. (615)790-7452. Fax: (615)790-9958. E-mail: mwaddell55@aol.com. President: Mike Waddell. Management firm, music publisher and record producer (James Hudson). Estab. 1977. Represents regional individual artists and songwriters; currently handles 2 acts. Receives variable commission. Reviews material for acts.

How to Contact: Submit demo tape by mail. Unsolicited submissions are OK. Prefers CD with 3 songs and lyric sheet. If seeking management, press kit should include tape, bio, picture and press information. "Should we be interested in any material received, we will contact the writer or artist by telephone or mail. All material should be copyrighted prior to submission." Does not return material. Responds in 3 weeks.

Music: Mostly **country**, **rock** and **Christian**. Current acts include Nathan Whitt (alternative), Gerd Rube (Germany) and Johnathon Bloom (alternative).

Tips: "Research the song market and be confident that your songs will hold up. Do not waste the valuable time of publishers and labels with anything less than professional songs. In past years we have signed songs from submissions via the mail. One of those, Reece Wilson, was named BMI writer of the year in 1995."

N ◑ MITCHELL FOX MANAGEMENT INC., 212 3rd Ave. N., Nashville TN 37201. (615)259-0777. Fax: (615)259-0063. E-mail: mitchell@mitchellfox.com. **Contact:** Mitchell Fox, president. Management firm. Estab. 1980. Represents individual artists, groups and songwriters from anywhere; currently handles 2 acts. Receives 10-15% commission. Reviews material for acts.

How to Contact: *Call or write first for permission to submit a demo.* Prefers cassette with 2 songs and lyric sheet. If seeking management, press kit should include music, pictures and press clippings. Does not return material. Responds in 1 month.

Music: **All styles**.

✔ ◑ ERIC GODTLAND MANAGEMENT, INC., 1040 Mariposa St., Suite 200, San Francisco CA 94107-2520. (415)522-5292. Fax: (415)522-5293. **Contact:** Wayne Ledbetter, manager. Management firm. Estab. 1995. Represents individual artists, groups or songwriters from anywhere; currently handles 8 acts. Receives 20% commission. Reviews material for acts.

How to Contact: Submit demo tape by mail. Unsolicited submissions are OK. Prefers cassette, DAT or CD. If seeking management, press kit should include brief information on how to reach you. Does not return material.

Music: Mostly **pop**, **rock** and **hip-hop**. Works primarily with bands, producers and songwriters. Current acts include Third Eye Blind (pop, rock), The Briefs (punk, rock) and Dakona (pop, rock).

✔ ◯ GOLDEN CITY INTERNATIONAL, Box 410851, San Francisco CA 94141. (415)822-1530. Fax: (415)695-1845. A&R Rep: Adrianna Grays. Management firm, music publisher (Dagene Music/ASCAP) and record company (Dagene/Cabletown Records). Estab. 1993. Represents regional (California area) individual artists and groups; currently handles 3 acts. Receives 15-20% commission. Reviews material for acts.

How to Contact: *Write or call first and obtain permission to submit.* Prefers cassette or VHS videocassette with 2-3 songs. If seeking management, press kit should include a complete bio and current photo along with cassette or CD of recent material. Include SASE. Responds in 1 month.

Music: Mostly **R&B/dance**, **rap** and **pop**; also **gospel** and **dance**. Current clients include Rare Essence (vocal group), Marcus Justice (writer/artist) and David Alston (producer).

N ◑ GOLDEN GURU ENTERTAINMENT, 765 Farnum Rd., Media PA 19063. (610)891-9766. Fax: (610)891-9316. **Contact:** Eric J. Cohen, Esq. and Larry Goldfarb, owners. Management firm and booking agency. Estab. 1988. Represents individual artists, groups and songwriters from anywhere; currently handles 2 acts.

How to Contact: *Call first and obtain permission to submit.* Prefers CD with current work. Responds in 1 month.

Music: Mostly **rock**, **singer/songwriters**, **urban** and **pop**; "anything that is excellent!"

Nina Gordon finds new solo career after Veruca Salt

Nina Gordon spent six years with Veruca Salt, penning their two biggest hits "Seether" from their album *American Thighs* and "Volcano Girls" from *Eight Arms to Hold You*. After six years with Veruca Salt, Gordon struck out on her own with her first solo album, *Tonight and the Rest of My Life*. She's currently touring and recording songs for her next album, due for release around the end of 2002.

Nina Gordon

How did you become involved in writing songs and playing in a band? When did you decide it was something you wanted to pursue as a career? How much musical training did you have?
I started writing songs when I was pretty little. I can remember writing some very silly love songs when I was 11 with a friend of mine. We would just mimic what we heard on the radio—broken hearts and heated passion—things we knew nothing about. We were very dramatic. But I started getting serious about it when I was 17 or 18. I would sit with an acoustic guitar and get pretty deep—and of course "deep" when you are 17 usually means painfully pretentious.

I had no formal music training, but music was a huge part of my family life. My parents had excellent taste and played all the best stuff—Beatles, Stones, The Band, Joni Mitchell, Bob Dylan. They instilled in me the belief that music was as important as anything else—just after family, food, and shelter. I always knew I wanted to sing, but I didn't know if I could write songs. There were certain key people, songwriters, whose songs inspired me to write, and made me believe that I could do it, too. Scott Miller, from a band called Game Theory (and more recently The Loud Family) was one, and Aimee Mann was another. I just connected with their songs and I loved the way they made me feel, so I tried doing it myself.

When I was maybe 23 and living in Chicago, I would sit in my apartment and write songs for myself. I played them for my boyfriend or my brother, but I didn't really think anyone else would ever hear them. At one point, I tried putting an ad in the local music paper, hoping to find some people to play with, but it was fruitless. Then, just by chance, a friend of mine went to a party and met Louise Post, who was writing her own songs and looking for someone to collaborate with. My friend called me immediately and said I must meet this person. So I did, and we really connected, and we formed Veruca Salt, my first (and last) band.

For the first album, Veruca Salt chose to stay with the indie label Minty Fresh Records even after Virgin Records and Geffen Records expressed interest. In what ways did you see that staying with the indie label would be in your best interest?
When we recorded the album for Minty Fresh it was finished before the crazy bidding war

began. We wanted to take things slowly and not have a lot of pressure put on us to have commercial success when we were just getting started. We were such a young band—we had played fewer than 10 shows—and suddenly we were being thrust into the big leagues before we were ready. The idea was to get really good before the whole world heard what we were doing. It didn't really work that way, and we jumped over to Geffen because the record was taking off and we figured we better ride the wave while we had it.

Once Minty Fresh became a part of Geffen Records, what advantages did you have working with a larger label? Any disadvantages?

The advantage of being on a major label is the feeling that you have a lot of power behind you—power to get the songs heard, the videos played, to get the records in the stores, etc. That's all very important. The disadvantage is the pressure to sell more records. And if you don't—and someone else on the label does—you may get lost in the shuffle. It's natural selection, and it's the nature of the business.

As a woman in the music industry, do you feel you faced any particular advantages or disadvantages?

In a way, I lucked out because of my gender. When Veruca Salt first started out we were something of a novelty, because we were two girls writing all the songs, playing guitar, and rocking pretty hard. We got noticed for many reasons, and one big one was because we were girls. There have been times when it was tough getting a song played on the radio because the station already had too many female artists on the playlist—which is totally ridiculous—but other than that I haven't felt that being a woman has held me back at all.

When did the idea of having a solo career first seem appealing? Has it lived up to your expectations? In what ways is it different than working with a band? In what ways do you feel that your audience is different now, if at all?

It can be very difficult being in a band. Especially when there are two songwriters. Things can be totally electrifying at times, but they can be incredibly tense as well. When I left the band to pursue a solo career, it was because I didn't want that drama anymore. I wanted the drama to be in the music, and not in the day to day dealings with the band. I also wanted to see what it felt like to write songs for myself, to stop editing myself and wondering what the rest of the band was going to think. It has been a great experience writing, recording, and performing on my own—no compromises. But it can also be lonely and frustrating. Sometimes you need to bounce ideas off someone, and you miss the inspiration of working with someone else.

Did your first solo album, _Tonight and the Rest of My Life_, turn out the way you hoped it would? What kind of themes emerged? How does that album compare with the album you're currently working on?

Writing and recording _Tonight and the Rest of My Life_ was the greatest experience of my life. I have never felt so grounded and so connected with myself. The theme, if there is one, is my independence, finding my own voice, and looking forward to the rest of my life—life after the band, life after a failed four-year relationship. I am not sure what this next album is going to be about. I am not at the same kind of personal turning point I was last time, and I am finding that my songs are more descriptive of my surroundings and my observations of the world around me. I don't think I am at that turning point yet with this album, though. There is always a cornerstone song that really rocks me, and then I know I have the album.

It's never a single-type song. It's usually more of a sleeper, but it hits me, and then I know I'm ready to record.

What kind of guidance have you had over the years on how to deal with the business side of the music industry?
I was really lucky that I hooked up with some great people at the very beginning: my managers, my lawyer, and my label people. I have gone from Minty Fresh to Geffen to Outpost to Warner Brothers, but I have remained close with a few key people who were there for me along the way, and I know I can trust them. You have to look for the good ones in this industry—they are tough to find, but they do exist.

The music video for "Now I Can Die" was shown on VH1, and your song "Tonight and the Rest of My Life" was featured in the movie *Chocolat* and the movie trailer for *Captain Corelli's Mandolin*. You must have a remarkable management team. Who do you credit for getting your songs out there and publicizing your music?
One of the many benefits of being on a major label is the profile they can generate for you. If you have a powerful company behind you, people are more likely to listen up. Same is true of management. My managers represent artists that are massively successful—Metallica and the Red Hot Chili Peppers—so when they talk about little old me, people pay attention.

How involved have you been in decisions about where to tour? What kind of a plan have you put together with your management team for developing your career as a songwriter, as well as touring and selling records?
Well, at some point I may not want to tour a lot. I may want to chill at home and have a baby or two, in which case it would be nice maybe to write songs for other people. I would love to do that. For the time being I seem to write for myself, but occasionally I will write a song that doesn't really feel like me, and it might be cool to pass it on to another artist.

In what ways do you feel touring is important for you? How would you describe the chemistry or dynamics between you and your audience?
I am actually pretty shy about playing live. I don't get stage fright, but I don't really feel like myself on stage. I am comfortable when I am singing, and I love the feeling you get when you make a real connection with the audience, but the stage banter thing has always been tough for me. The longer a tour goes on, the more comfortable I get, of course.

What was your working relationship with producer Bob Rock like in the studio?
Bob Rock really is a mentor to me. As a producer he pushes me to make my songs stronger—the way a coach would make you do ten more sit-ups! You don't think you have it in you, but he knows you do, and he just gently pushes you in the right direction. He knows so much about music, and the music business, and I trust him completely. He is my greatest champion, and my harshest critic.

What is your songwriting process like? Where have some of your ideas come from?
Generally I just sit down with my guitar and see what happens. I play some chords and if they inspire me to sing a melody, I sing. sometimes the lyrics come out of nowhere just like that. Otherwise I get out one of my millions of notebooks that I fill with words, thoughts, free-associations, and late-night ramblings, and see if that inspires something. Often I will play guitar,

and nothing at all will happen—I get bored, and I walk away. But when I'm lucky, a song happens, and I just sit there and play it over and over, for hours, until it is done. I think the best songs I have written are the ones that come out fully formed, in one sitting. Those songs are the most organic and un-contrived. The ones I tend to labor over for months, tinkering with the chorus, or trying to write the bridge, are never my best work.

Your website said you wrote 30 songs for your next album, and 15 demos were chosen for recording. How did you choose which songs would make the cut?
Well I haven't yet decided which songs I will actually record for the album. I chose thirteen songs to demo, out of the thirty I had written. I chose the ones that were the most meaningful to me. I write lots of songs that I think are pretty good—but I can't really get psyched about them. And if I can't get psyched, then no one else is going to—not my band, not my record label, and definitely not the people buying records. But since making the demos, a few of those thirteen songs have fallen out of my favor, and I have written a few new ones that I am really happy with. Like I said, the best songs are the ones that came easily, and they are also usually the ones that come together easily in the studio.

Do you write songs for other artists? Does the idea of writing on assignment (for a particular artist, for a movie soundtrack, etc.) appeal to you? Have you engaged in any collaborative songwriting?
I never have, but I would love to. A writing assignment is very appealing to me. It would be a challenge to fit the requirements that someone else is imposing, and the pressure would be off to dig deep, and pull something really personal out of myself. I have never had any luck co-writing songs—songwriting is a pretty private process for me, and I have never felt that my best work comes out when I am trying too hard. Being in a room with someone, and trying to write a song together on the spot always feels a little tense to me. That said, it is something I would like to be able to do successfully at some point.

What sort of things do you now know about the music industry that you wish you had known when you started? What was your image of the music industry like at that time vs. how it looks to you now?
It has always looked pretty much the same to me. It would be great if we could all start our own record labels and could be in total control of our careers. Sometimes I wish Louise and I had done that with Veruca Salt. But the truth is, I would rather write and record music I feel passionate about, and let someone else figure out how to sell it. I can't stand worrying about whether I have written "hits" or not, or whether a song is going to do well on radio. That's not how I want to spend my time. It is a nearly impossible business if you aren't writing "hits." And who even knows what a hit is before the fact? No one. It is maddening, but if you love to write songs, you have to play that game to some extent. Unless you are very lucky and enter-prising, and you work around it somehow, the way Ani DiFranco has.

What sort of advice do you have for would-be singer-songwriters on songwriting, putting together a band and working with a producer?
For songwriting, the best thing you can do to write good songs is to write a lot of bad songs! You have to make bad art to make good art. Don't beat yourself up and over-edit yourself. Just keep writing, and exercising those muscles. Try to write something every day. Even if it is just one sentence in a notebook, or a description of a dream you had the night before, write

it down. Once you have some songs that are meaningful to you, I think the best thing you can do is just play out as much as possible. Play your songs for anyone who will listen. Even if they won't listen, keep playing. Make a lot of noise. Move to a city that has a thriving music scene, and just play as much as you can.

—*Rachel Vater*

GREIF-GARRIS MANAGEMENT, 2112 Casitas Way, Palm Springs CA 92264. (760)322-8655. Fax: (760)322-7793. **Contact:** Sid Garris, vice president. Management firm. Estab. 1961. Represents individual artists and/or groups and songwriters from anywhere; currently owns 1 act. Reviews material for acts.
How to Contact: *Write first to obtain permission to submit or to arrange a personal interview.* Submit demo tape by mail. Unsolicited submissions are OK. Prefers cassette. If seeking management, press kit should include demo, cover letter, bio and photo. Include SASE. Responds in 3 weeks.
Music: All types. Current acts include The New Christy Minstrels (folk/pop).

GUESTSTAR ENTERTAINMENT AGENCY, 17321 Ritchie Ave. NE, Sand Lake MI 49343-9475. (616)636-5068. Fax: (775)743-4169. E-mail: gueststarww@wingsisp.com. Website: www.wing sisp.com/mountainmanww/. **Contact:** Raymond G. Dietz, Sr., president. Management firm, booking agency, music publisher (Sandlake Music/BMI), record company (Gueststar Records, Inc.), record producer and record distributor (Gueststar Music Distributors). Represents individual artists, groups, songwriters and bands from anywhere; currently handles 3 acts. Receives 20% commission. Reviews material for acts.
   ● Mr. Dietz is also the editor of several music books, including *Everything You Should Know Before You Get into the Music Business*.
How to Contact: Submit demo tape by mail. Unsolicited submissions are OK. Prefers cassette or VHS videocassette with unlimited songs, but send your best with lyric or lead sheet. If seeking management, press kit should include photo, demo tape, bio, music résumé and VHS videocassette (live on stage) if possible and press clippings. Does not return material. Responds in 6 weeks. SASE required.
Music: Mostly **traditional country.** Current acts include Mountain Man (singer), Jamie "K" (singer) and Sweetgrass (band).

GURLEY & CO., P.O. Box 150657, Nashville TN 37215. (615)269-0474. Fax: (615)385-2052. E-mail: gurleybiz@aol.com. President: Cathy Gurley. Vice President: Meagan Gurley. Management firm and public relations/marketing. Estab. 1985. Represents individual artists, groups and songwriters from anywhere; currently handles 8 acts. Receives 15% commission. Reviews material for acts.
How to Contact: Submit demo tape by mail. Unsolicited submissions are OK. Prefers CD with 3 songs and lyric sheet. Does not return material. Responds in 1 month.
Music: Mostly **country** and **pop.** Current acts include Amy Jayne McCabe (country), Lynn Anderson (country), Andy Tubman (alternative rock), Jay Clementi (country/pop) and Taylor/Martinez (blues/pop).
Tips: "Stay on it. Keep writing."

HALE ENTERPRISES, Rt. 1, Box 49, Worthington IN 47471-9310. (812)875-3664. E-mail: haleenterprises@earthlink.net. **Contact:** Rodger Hale, CEO. Management firm, record company (Projection Unlimited) and recording studio. Estab. 1976. Represents artists, groups, songwriters and studio musicians; currently handles 11 acts. Receives 15% commission for booking, 20% for management. Reviews material for acts.
How to Contact: Submit demo tape by mail. Unsolicited submissions are OK. Prefers cassette or videocassette with 2-10 songs and lyric sheet. If seeking management include cover letter, résumé,

lyric sheets, press clippings, current promo pack *or* photo, video-audio tape, clubs currently performing, short performance history and equipment list (if applicable). Does not return material. Responds in 1 week.

Music: Mostly **country** and **top 40**; also **MOR**, **progressive**, **rock** and **pop**. Works primarily with show bands, dance bands and bar bands. Current acts include Indiana (country show band), Seventh Heaven (top 40 show) and Cotton (show band).

◑ BILL HALL ENTERTAINMENT & EVENTS, 138 Frog Hollow Rd., Churchville PA 18966-1031. (215)357-5189. Fax: (215)357-0320. **Contact:** William B. Hall III, owner/president. Booking agency and production company. Represents individuals and groups; currently handles 20-25 acts. Receives 15% commission. Reviews material for acts.

How to Contact: Submit demo tape by mail. Unsolicited submissions are OK. Prefers cassette or videocassette of performance with 2-3 songs "and photos, promo material and record or tape. We need quality material, preferably before a 'live' audience." Does not return material. Responds only if interested.

Music: Marching band, **circus** and **novelty**. Works primarily with "unusual or novelty attractions in musical line, preferably those that appeal to family groups." Current acts include Fralinger and Polish-American Philadelphia Championship Mummers String Bands (marching and concert group), Erwin Chandler Orchestra (show band), "Mr. Polynesian" Show Band and Hawaiian Revue (ethnic group), the "Phillies Whiz Kids Band" of Philadelphia Phillies Baseball team, Paul Richardson (Phillies' organist/entertainer), Mummermania Musical Quartet, Philadelphia German Brass Band (concert band), Vogelgesang Circus Calliope, Kromer's Carousel Band Organ, Reilly Raiders Drum & Bugle Corps, Hoebel Steam Calliope, Caesar Rodney Brass Band, Rohe Calliope, Philadelphia Police & Fire Pipes Band, Larry Rothbard's Circus Band and Tim Laushey Pep & Dance Band.

Tips: "Please send whatever helps us to most effectively market the attraction and/or artist. Provide something that gives you a clear edge over others in your field!"

⬛ ◑ HANSEN ENTERPRISES, LTD., 855 E. Twain #123411, Las Vegas NV 89109. (702)896-8115. Fax: (702)792-1363. **Contact:** J. Malcom Baird. Management firm. Estab. 1971. Represents individual artists, groups and songwriters from anywhere; currently handles 3 acts. Receives 15-25% commission "or contracted fee arrangement." Reviews material for acts.

How to Contact: Submit demo tape by mail. Unsolicited submissions are OK. Prefers cassette. Include SASE. Responds in 3 weeks. We are looking for potential *hit songs* only: top 40, pop and Spanish. From time to time we need music for TV shows, commercials and films. Send SASE for requirements, which change from time to time depending upon the project(s).

Music: Mostly **'50s & '60s rock** and **Spanish adult contemporary**. Current acts include The Ronettes, Pilita Corrales (top selling female Spanish recording star) and Jackie-Lou Blanco.

☑ ◯ HARDISON INTERNATIONAL ENTERTAINMENT CORPORATION, P.O. Box 1732, Knoxville TN 37901-1732. Phone/fax: (865)688-8680. E-mail: alt1010@aol.com. **Contact:** Dennis K. Hardison, CEO/founder. Management firm, booking agency, music publisher (Denlatrin Music), record company (Denlatrin Records) and record producer. Estab. 1984. Represents individual artists from anywhere; currently handles 3 acts. Receives 20% commission. Reviews material for acts.

• This company has promoted acts including New Edition, Freddie Jackson, M.C. Lyte and Kool Moe Dee.

How to Contact: Submit demo tape by mail. Unsolicited submissions are OK. Prefers cassette or CD with 3 songs. If seeking management, press kit should include bio, promo picture and cassette. Does not return material. Responds in 6 weeks.

OPENNESS TO SUBMISSIONS: ◯ beginners; ◐ beginners and experienced; ◑ experienced only; ◪ no unsolicited submissions/industry referrals only.

Music: Mostly **R&B**, **hip-hop** and **rap**. Current acts include Dynamo (hip-hop), Lil Cola (hip-hop) and Triniti (record producer, Public Enemy).
Tips: "We have an in-house production staff to critique your music."

☑ ⦸ **M. HARRELL & ASSOCIATES**, 5444 Carolina, Merrillville IN 46410. (219)887-8814. Fax: (480)345-2255. E-mail: mhmkbmgs95@hotmail.com. **Contact:** Mary Harrell or Mary Kay Balluch. Management firm and booking agency. Estab. 1984. Represents individual artists, groups, songwriters, all talents—fashion, dancers, etc.; currently handles 40-50 acts. Receives 10-20% commission. Reviews material for acts.
How to Contact: *Call first and obtain permission to submit.* Submit demo tape by mail. Prefers cassette or videocassette with 2-3 songs. If seeking management, press kit should include cover letter, résumé, bio, photo, demo tape/CD and press clippings. "Keep it brief and current." Does not return material. Responds in 1 month.
Music: **All types**, **country**, **R&B**, **jazz**, **gospel**, **Big Band**, **light rock** and **reggae**. Current acts include Bill Shelton & Stormy Weather ('50s music), Bang (r&b and variety) and Johnny Jackson (member of the original Jackson Five, reggae).

⦿ **HAWKEYE ATTRACTIONS**, 102 Geiger St., Huntingburg IN 47542. (812)683-3657. **Contact:** David Mounts, agent. Booking agency. Estab. 1982. Represents individual artists and groups; currently handles 2 acts. Receives 10% commission. Reviews material for acts.
How to Contact: *Call first and obtain permission to submit.* Prefers CD or cassette with 4 songs and lyric sheet. Include SASE. If seeking management, press kit should include bio, press clippings, 8×10 b&w glossy and cassette. Responds in 9 weeks.
Music: Mostly **country** and **western swing**. Works primarily with show bands, Grand Ole Opry style form of artist and music. Current acts include Bill Mounts and His Midwest Cowboys (country/western swing).

Ⓝ ⦸ **HES FREE PRODUCTIONS & PUBLISHING COMPANY**, 3709 E. 29th, P.O. Box 1214, Bryan TX 77806-1214. (979)268-3263. Fax: (979)589-2575. E-mail: hesfreeprodandpubco@yahoo.com. Website: http://home1.gte.net/jbhes/. Executive Producer/CEO/Owner: Brenda M. Freeman-Heslip. Producer of songwriting: Jamie Heslip. Assistant Producer: Rochelle Heslip. Record producer/Director of A&R: Damion Turner. Management agency, record producer and music publisher. Estab. 2001. Represents individual artists, groups, songwriters. Works with individual artists, regional artists in the Bryan, TX and Brazos Valley Area. Currently handles 8 acts. Receives 40% commission.
How to Submit: *We only accept material referred to us by a reputable industry source (manager, entertainment attorney, etc.)* Include CD/CDR with 10 songs and lyric sheet, lead sheet and cover letter. Send resume and updated application for a management firm. Does not return submissions. Responds in 6 weeks only if interested. "Make sure you are serious about your career choice. Only serious clients need to contact us."
Music: Mostly **r&b**, **gospel**, **rap** and **rock**. Does not want country. "We strive to make our professional performing artists the most successful artists possible." Represents "Mike-Ray" Ray Brooks (R&B dancer and singer); Ralatraneka Mercer (R&B and rap singer); Vicki Diggs (R&B and rap singer).
Tips: "Only contact our company if you are seriously considering the entertainment field as a job possibility. Only the seriously inclined clients need apply."

☑ ◯ **HORIZON MANAGEMENT INC.**, P.O. Box 8770, Endwell NY 13762. (607)785-9120. Fax: (607)785-4516. E-mail: hmi67@aol.com. Website: www.musicalonline.com/management/horizon. **Contact:** New Talent Department. Management firm, booking agency and concert promotion. Estab. 1967. Represents regional, national and international artists, groups and songwriters; currently handles over 1,500 acts. Receives 20% commission. Reviews material for acts.
How to Contact: *Call first and obtain permission to submit.* Prefers CD, cassette or VHS videocassette with 1-4 songs and lead sheet. Send cover letter, résumé, lead sheets, photo, bio, lyric sheets, equipment list, demo tape/CD, video, press clippings, reviews, etc. Does not return material. Responds in 1 week.

Music: All styles, originals or covers. Current acts include Pete Best Band (The Beatles original drummer), Sons of Cream and Latin Cadence (6-piece Latin Christian).

N⚑⊘ A HUGE PRODUCTION, INC., 4 Union St., 1C, Salem MA 01970. (978)376-6952. E-mail: rippo@world.std.com. Website: www.rippo.com. **Contact:** Richard M. Gordon, president. Management firm, music publisher (Cat Butt Musik/BMI) and record company (2 Funky International Records). Estab. 1996. Represents regional groups from the northeast; currently handles 2 acts. Receives negotiable commission.

• This company manages Rippopotamus, winner of 1996 Boston Music Award.

How to Contact: *Write first and obtain permission to submit.* Prefers cassette with 3 songs and lyric sheet. If seeking management, press kit should include press, radio tracking, photo and CD. Include SASE. Responds in 1 month.

Music: Mostly **pop/rock** and **funk**. Works with bands exclusively. Current acts include Rippopotamus (8 piece funk band) and There (3-piece power rock).

Tips: "Always call first. Promo packages are expensive, and you should always make sure we're actively seeking material, especially since most modern bands do their own songwriting. Being artists ourselves, we strongly recommend that you be very sure of people you work with and that they have same level of faith and confidence in the project that you do. Never give away the store and always make sure that you are aware of what is transpiring with your career, even if you have someone you trust handling it for you. Ultimately, no one has your interests as much at heart as you do, and thus you should always have your finger on your career's pulse."

N◯ JOE HUPP ENTERPRISES, 4415 S. 449th W. Ave., Jennings OK 74038. (918)865-7026. Fax: (918)865-7403. E-mail: huppent@aol.com (for management) or hippiemus@aol.com (for publishing company). **Contact:** Joe Hupp or Patti Llovet Hupp, presidents. Management firm, booking agency and music publisher (Ol' Hippie Music). Estab. 1984. Represents individual artists, groups and songwriters from anywhere; currently handles 8 acts. Receives 10-20% commission. Reviews material for acts.

How to Contact: For management: huppent@aol.com. Press kit should include photo, bio/fact sheet, cassette or CD and videocassette. For publishing: hippiemus@aol.com. Prefers CD, cassette or VHS videocassette with 1-4 songs and lyric sheets. Does not return material.

Music: Mostly **country**, **rock**, **alternative**; also **folk**, **R&B** and **pop**. Works primarily with bands and singer/songwriters. Current acts include Kelly Spradlin, Patti Hughes, Ron Veytovich and Bryan Tribble.

▣⊘ IMMIGRANT MUSIC INC., 4859 Rue Garnier, Montreal, Quebec H2J 3S8 Canada. Phone/fax: (514)523-5857. E-mail: immigrant@videotron.ca. **Contact:** Dan Behrman, president. Management firm, booking agency and music publisher. Estab. 1979. Represents individual artists, groups and songwriters from anywhere; currently handles 6 acts. Receives 20% commission. Reviews material for acts.

How to Contact: *Call first and obtain permission to submit or to arrange personal interview.* Prefers cassette, VHS videocassette, CD or vinyl with 4 songs. If seeking management, press kit should include bio, press clippings, photo, references, recordings, technical and personal rider and requirements if known. Does not return material. ("I also may use material on my radio program.") Responds in 1 month.

Music: Mostly **world music**, **original ethnic** and **new acoustic music**; also **singer/songwriters**, **folk** and **ethnic/ambient**. Current acts include Simbi (Xenophile Records, vodou-roots band), B'net Houariyat (Gnawa trance music, women ensemble from Morocco), Kristi Stassinopoulou (contemporary Greek world/folk/electronica), La Chango Family (Disques Audiogram, Montreal-based gypsy/reggae/latino/skatro band), Datevik Hovanesian (Armenian world-jazz artist), Atlas-Soul (Gnawafrobeat/latino band from Boston) and Lataye (NYC-based Haitian rodou/roots band).

⊘ INTERNATIONAL ENTERTAINMENT BUREAU, 3612 N. Washington Blvd., Indianapolis IN 46205-3592. (317)926-7566. E-mail: ieb@prodigy.net. Booking agency. Estab. 1972. Represents individual artists and groups from anywhere; currently handles 146 acts. Receives 20% commission.

How to Contact: *No unsolicited submissions.*
Music: Mostly **rock**, **country** and **A/C**; also **jazz**, **nostalgia** and **ethnic**. Works primarily with bands, comedians and speakers. Current acts include Five Easy Pieces (A/C), Doug Lawson (country) and Lordsmen (gospel).

N **INTERNATIONAL PRODUCTION MANAGEMENT**, 12 Dongan Place #201, New York NY 10040. Phone/fax: (212)304-8661. Website: www.lynnmanuell.com. President: Lynn Manuell. Management firm and booking agency. Estab. 1990. Represents individual artists or groups from anywhere; currently handles 10 acts. Receives 15% commission. Reviews material for acts.
How to Contact: Submit demo tape by mail. Unsolicited submissions are OK. Prefers cassette or VHS videocassette with 3 songs and lyric sheet. If seeking management, press kit should include previous reviews and photos. Include SASE. Responds in 3 months.
Music: Mostly **pop**, **classical crossover** and **Broadway**. Works primarily with singers and groups. Current acts include The Cassidys (Irish band).
Tips: "Be thorough in submissions. Clarify your goals."

J & V MANAGEMENT, 143 W. Elmwood, Caro MI 48723. (989)673-2889. Manager/Publisher: John Timko. Management firm, booking agency and music publisher. Represents local, regional or international individual artists, groups and songwriters; currently handles 3 acts. Receives 10% commission. Reviews material for acts.
How to Contact: *Write first and obtain permission to submit.* Prefers CD or cassette with 3 songs maximum and lyric sheet. If seeking management, include short reference bio, cover letter and résumé in press kit. Include SASE. Responds in 2 months.
Music: Mostly **country**. Works primarily with vocalists and dance bands. Current acts include John Patrick (country), Alexander Depue (fiddle) and Most Wanted (country).

JACOBSON TALENT MANAGEMENT (JTM), P.O. Box 0740, Murrieta CA 92564-0740. (909)461-9923. Fax: (909)461-9913. E-mail: jim4097@aol.com. Website: www.jtm-ink.com. **Contact:** Jake Jacobson, owner. Senior Associate: Randi Morgan. Management firm and online consultation service. Estab. 1981. Represents individual artists and groups from anywhere; currently handles 2 acts. Receives 15-20% commission. Reviews material for acts.
How to Contact: *Call first and obtain permission to submit.* Prefers cassette or CD with 5 songs and lyric sheet. If seeking management, press kit should include photo, bio and "anything else you think will help your cause." Include SASE. Responds in 3 weeks.
Music: Mostly **rock**, **R&B/hip-hop** and **country**; also **adult contemporary**. Works primarily with bands and singer/songwriters. Current acts include The Quiet Room (heavy metal) and Glenn Rottmann (guitar instrumental).
Tips: "Work hard. Hold up your end so we can do our jobs. In addition, we find it much easier to work with artists who have a basic working knowledge of the music industry and personal management. Our website provides educational tips for artists and music industry entrepreneurs. Consulting is available for those that do not need full time management, but may be in need of occasional advice and counsel or career direction."

JANA JAE ENTERPRISES, P.O. Box 35726, Tulsa OK 74153. (918)786-8896. Fax: (918)786-8897. E-mail: janajae@janajae.com. Website: www.janajae.com. **Contact:** Kathleen Pixley, agent. Booking agency, music publisher (Jana Jae Publishing/BMI) and record company (Lark Record Productions, Inc.). Estab. 1979. Represents individual artists and songwriters; currently handles 12 acts. Receives 15% commission. Reviews material for acts.
How to Contact: Submit demo tape by mail. Unsolicited submissions are OK. Prefers cassette or videocassette of performance. If seeking management, press kit should include cover letter, bio, photo, demo tape/CD, lyric sheets and press clippings. Does not return material.
Music: Mostly **country**, **classical** and **jazz instrumentals**; also **pop**. Works with vocalists, show and concert bands, solo instrumentalists. Represents Jana Jae (country singer/fiddle player), Matt Greif (classical guitarist), Sydni (solo singer) and Hotwire (country show band).

⊕ ☑ ◐ **ROGER JAMES MANAGEMENT**, The Return, 10A Margaret Rd., Barnet, Herts EN4 9NP England. Phone: 020 844 9788. **Contact:** Susana Boyle, professional manager. Management firm and music publisher (R.J. Music/PRS). Estab. 1977. Represents songwriters. Receives 50% commission (negotiable). Reviews material for acts.
How to Contact: Submit demo tape by mail. Unsolicited submissions are OK. Prefers cassette with 3 songs and lyric sheet. Does not return material.
Music: Mostly **pop**, **country** and "any good song."

❧ ◐ **SHELDON KAGAN INTERNATIONAL**, 35 McConnell, Dorval, Quebec H9S 5L9 Canada. (514)631-2160. Fax: (514)631-4430. E-mail: sheldon@sheldonkagan.com. Website: www.sheldonkagan.com. **Contact:** Sheldon Kagan, president. Booking agency. Estab. 1965. Represents local individual artists and groups; currently handles 17 acts. Receives 10-20% commission. Reviews materials for acts.
How to Contact: Submit demo tape by mail. Unsolicited submissions are OK. Prefers cassette or VHS videocassette with 6 songs. Include SASE. Responds in 5 weeks.
Music: Mostly **top 40**. Works primarily with vocalists and bands. Current acts include Quazz (jazz trio), City Lights (top 40 band), Jeux de Cordes (violin and guitar duo), The Soulmates (top 40) and Boys (top 40).

[N] ◐ **KENDALL WEST AGENCY**, P.O. Box 173776, Arlington TX 76003-3776. (817)468-7800. E-mail: vellucci@flash.net. Contact: Michelle Vellucci. Booking agency and television producer. Estab. 1994. Represents individual artists and groups from anywhere. Receives 10% commission. Reviews material for acts.
How to Contact: *Write first and obtain permission to submit or write to arrange personal interview.* Prefers CD or cassette with 5 songs and lead sheet. If seeking management, press kit should include bio, photo, cover letter, demo tape/CD and résumé. Include SASE. Responds in 1 month.
Music: Mostly **country**, **blues/jazz** and **rock**; also **trios**, dance and **individuals**. Works primarily with bands. Current acts include Way Out West (country band), Breckenridge (variety band) and Jaz-Vil (jazz/blues).

⊕ ☑ ◯ **KICKSTART MUSIC LTD.**, 12 Port House, Square Rigger Row, Plantation Wharf, London SW11 3TY England. Phone: (020)7223 3300. Fax: (020)7223 8777. E-mail: info@kickstart.uk.net. **Contact:** Frank Clark, director. Management/publishing Company. Estab. 1994. Represents individual artists, groups or songwriters from anywhere; currently handles 7 acts. Receives 20-40% commission, "depends on contract." Reviews material for acts.
How to Contact: Submit demo by mail. Unsolicited submissions are OK. Prefers CD, cassette or DAT with 3 songs and lyric and lead sheet. If seeking management, press kit should include photograph and bio. SAE and IRC. Responds in 2 weeks.
Music: All genres including **pop**, **dance**, **rock**, **country** and **blues**. Works primarily with bands who perform a live set of original music and talented singer/songwriters who can cross over to all types of music. Current acts include Pal Joey (rock band), Simon Fox (songwriter) and The Electric Blues Anthology (blues band).
Tips: "We prefer songwriters whose songs can cross over to all types of music, those who do not write in one style only."

[N] ◐ **KITCHEN SYNC**, 8530 Holloway Dr. #208, West Hollywood CA 90069-2475. (310)855-1631. Fax: (310)657-7197. E-mail: ldg@hamptons.com. Contact: Laura Grover. Music production manager. Estab. 1990. Represents individual artists, groups and songwriters from anywhere. Reviews material for acts.
• Kitchen Sync primarily manages the production of music.

THE OPENNESS TO SUBMISSIONS INDEX at the back of this book lists all companies in this section by how open they are to submissions.

How to Contact: *Write first and obtain permission to submit.* Prefers cassette with 3 songs and lyric sheet. If seeking management, press kit should include cover letter, résumé, bio, press clippings, discography and photo. Include SASE. Responds in 1 month.
Music: Mostly **pop/rock**, **country** and **R&B**. Works primarily with producers and singer/songwriters.
Tips: "Have a clear artistic mission statement and career goals. I'm mostly interested in overseeing/ managing production of material, i.e., creating budgets and mapping out recording plan, booking studios, vendors, etc."

🎵 **BOB KNIGHT AGENCY**, 185 Clinton Ave., Staten Island NY 10301. (718)448-8420. **Contact:** Bob Knight, president. Management firm, booking agency, music publisher and royalty collection firm. Estab. 1971. Represents artists, groups and songwriters; currently handles 4 acts. Receives 10-20% commission. Reviews material for acts and for submission to record companies and producers.
How to Contact: Submit demo tape by mail. Unsolicited submissions are OK. Prefers cassette or videocassette (if available) with 5 songs and lead sheet "with bio and references." If seeking management, press kit should include bio, videocassette and audio cassette. Include SASE. Responds in 2 months.
Music: Mostly **top 40/pop**; also **easy listening**, **MOR**, **R&B**, **soul**, **rock (nostalgia '50s and '60s)**, **alternative**, **country**, **country/pop**, **jazz**, **blues** and **folk**. Works primarily with recording and name groups and artists—'50s, '60s and '70s acts, high energy dance and show groups. Current acts include Delfonics (R&B nostalgia), B.T. Express, Brass Construction and Main Ingredient.
Tips: "We're seeking artists and groups with completed albums/demos."

✅⭕ **KUPER PERSONAL MANAGEMENT**, P.O. Box 66274, Houston TX 77266. (713)520-5791. Fax: (713)520-5791. E-mail: kuper@wt.net. Website: www.kupergroup.com. **Contact:** Ivan Kuper, owner. Management firm and music publisher (Kuper-Lam Music/BMI and Uvula Music/ BMI). Estab. 1979. Represents individual artists, groups and songwriters from Texas; currently handles 5 acts. Receives 20% commission. Reviews material for acts.
How to Contact: Submit demo tape by mail. Unsolicited submissions are OK. Prefers cassette. If seeking management, press kit should include cover letter, press clippings, photo, bio (1 page) tearsheets (reviews, etc.) and demo tape/CD. Does not return material. Responds in 2 months.
Music: Mostly **singer/songwriters**, **triple AAA**, **hip-hop** and **Americana**. Works primarily with self-contained and self-produced artists. Current acts include Philip Rodriguez (singer/songwriter), Champ X (rap artist), The Hit Squad (hip-hop), U.S. Representative for The Watchman (Dutch singer/ songwriter) and The Very Girls (Dutch vocal duo).
Tips: "Create a market value for yourself, produce your own master tapes, create a cost-effective situation."

🎵 **LARI-JON PROMOTIONS**, 325 W. Walnut, P.O. Box 216, Rising City NE 68658. (402)542-2336. **Contact:** Larry Good, owner. Management firm, music publisher (Lari-Jon Publishing Co./ BMI) and record company (Lari-Jon Records). Represents individual artists, groups and songwriters; currently handles 3 acts. Receives 15% commission. Reviews material for acts.
How to Contact: Submit demo tape by mail. Unsolicited submissions are OK. Prefers cassette with 5 songs and lyric sheet. If seeking management, press kit should include 8×10 photos, cassette, videocassette and bio sheet. Include SASE. Responds in 2 months.
Music: Mostly **country**, **gospel** and **'50s rock**. Works primarily with dance and show bands. Represents Kent Thompson (singer), Nebraskaland 'Opry (family type country show) and Brenda Allen (singer and comedienne).

🎵 **RAY LAWRENCE, LTD.**, P.O. Box 1987, Studio City CA 91614. (818)508-9022. Fax: (818)508-5672. **Contact:** Ray Lawrence, president. Management firm, booking agency and music publisher (Boha Music/BMI). Estab. 1963. Represents individual artists from anywhere; currently handles 15 acts. Receives 10-15% commission.
How to Contact: Submit demo tape by mail. Unsolicited submissions are OK. Prefers VHS videocassette. If seeking management, press kit should include 8×10 professional photographs and bio. Does not return material. Responds in 2 weeks.

Music: All types. Works primarily with musical and variety acts. Current acts include Trini Lopez (recording artist), Wayland Pickard (recording artist) and Glenn Ash (recording artist).

N ◉ **LEGACY SOUND & ENTERTAINMENT**, 4353 Kostoryz Rd., Corpus Christi TX 78415. (361)852-6412. E-mail: r999a@aol.com. Owner: Robert Alaniz. Booking agency and sound company. Estab. 1993. Represents groups from anywhere. Reviews material for acts.
How to Contact: Submit demo tape by mail. Unsolicited submissions are OK. Prefers cassette or CD with 3-5 songs. Does not return material. Responds in 3 weeks.
Music: Mostly **rock/metal**, **alternative** and **classic rock**. Works primarily with upcoming bands, underground bands and older bands. Current acts include Type O Negative, Fates Warning, Sloppy Seconds, Life of Agony, DRI and Stick.

N ◉ **LENTHALL & ASSOCIATES**, Falcon Ave., Suite 2-2447, Ottawa, Ontario K1V 8C8 Canada. (613)738-2373. Fax: (613)738-0239. **Contact:** Helen Lenthall, CEO. Management firm and record production. Represents individual artists, groups and songwriters from all territories. Reviews material for acts.
How to Contact: *Write first and obtain permission to submit.* Prefers CD or cassette with 3-8 songs maximum and lyric sheet or lead sheet. If seeking management, press kit should include bio, media package, photos, reviews, tracking if available. SAE and IRC. Responds back "only on acts that we consider."
Music: Mostly **soul**, **gospel** and **adult contemporary**. Primarily works with bands and vocalists.

◉ **LEVINSON ENTERTAINMENT VENTURES INTERNATIONAL, INC.**, 1440 Veteran Ave., Suite 650, Los Angeles CA 90024. (323)663-6940. E-mail: leviinc@aol.com. President: Bob Levinson. **Contact:** Jed Leland, Jr. Management firm. Estab. 1978. Represents national individual artists, groups and songwriters; currently handles 4 acts. Receives 15-25% commission. Reviews material for acts.
How to Contact: *Write first and obtain permission to submit.* Prefers cassette or VHS videocassette with 6 songs and lead sheet. If seeking management, press kit should include bio, pictures and press clips. Include SASE. Responds in 1 month.
Music: Mostly **rock**, **MOR**, **R&B** and **country**. Works primarily with rock bands and vocalists.
Tips: "Should be a working band, self-contained and, preferably, performing original material."

☑ ◉ **RICK LEVY MANAGEMENT**, 4250 A1AS, D-11, St. Augustine FL 32080. (904)460-1225. Fax: (904)460-1226. E-mail: ricklevymgmt@att.net. Website: www.ricklevy.com. **Contact:** Rick Levy, president. Management firm, music publisher (Flying Governor Music/BMI) and record company (Luxury Records). Estab. 1985. Represents local, regional or international individual artists and groups; currently handles 7 acts. Receives 15-20% commission. Reviews material for acts.
How to Contact: *Write or call first and obtain permission to submit.* Prefers cassette or VHS videocassette with 3 songs and lyric sheet. If seeking management, press kit should include cover letter, bio, demo tape/CD, VHS video, photo and press clippings. Include SASE. Responds in 2 weeks.
Music: Mostly **R&B** (no rap), **pop**, **country** and **oldies**. Current acts include Jay & the Techniques ('60s hit group), The Original Box Tops ('60s), The Limits (pop), Barbara Lewis ('60s) and Steel Dog Cafe (modern rock). "Rick Levy is currently lead guitarist with Herman's Hermits starring Peter Noone."

◉ **LIVE-WIRE MANAGEMENT**, P.O. Box 653, Morgan Hill, CA 95038. (408)778-3526. Fax: (408)778-3567. E-mail: bruce@L-WM.com. Website: www.L-WM.com. **Contact:** Bruce Hollibaugh, president. Management firm. Estab. 1990. Represents individual artists and groups from anywhere; currently handles 2 acts. Receives 15-25% commission. Reviews material for acts.
How to Contact: Submit demo tape by mail. Unsolicited submissions are OK. Prefers CD or cassette with 3-6 songs and lyric sheet. If seeking management, press kit should include what region you are currently performing in; how often you are doing live shows; any reviews; photos. Does not return material. Responds in 1 month.

Music: Mostly **pop**, **acoustic pop** and **New Age**; also **jazz**, **R&B** and **country**. Works primarily with bands and singer/songwriters. Current acts include Tommy Elskes (singer/songwriter) and Janny Choi (jazz).

[N] [◐] RICHARD LUTZ ENTERTAINMENT AGENCY, 145 N. 46th St., Lincoln NE 68503. (402)475-1900. Fax: (402)475-2299. E-mail: r/94521@navix.net. Website: www.lutzagency.com. **Contact:** Cherie Worley, president. Management firm and booking agency. Estab. 1964. Represents individuals and groups; currently handles 50 acts. Receives 20% commission.
How to Contact: Submit demo tape by mail. Unsolicited submissions are OK. Prefers CD, cassette or videocassette with 5-10 songs "to show style and versatility" and lead sheet. "Send photo, résumé, tape, partial song list and include references. Add comedy, conversation, etc., to your videocassette. Do not play songs in full—short versions preferred." If seeking management, press kit should include audio cassette and photo. Include SASE. Responds in 2 weeks.
Music: Mostly **top 40** and **country**; also **dance-oriented** and **MOR**. "Acts must be uniformed." Current acts include The Calhouns (country), Sweet 'N' Sassy (variety) and Endless Summer (nostalgia).

[N] [▼] [○] M.B.H. MUSIC MANAGEMENT, P.O. Box 1096, Hudson, Quebec J0P 1H0 Canada. (514)869-3236. Fax: (450)458-2819. E-mail: LA_Record@excite.com. Website: www.radiofreedom. com. Manager: T. Hart. Producer: M. Langies. Management firm, publishing company (G-String Publishing) and record company (L.A. Records). Estab. 1982. Works with individual artists and groups from anywhere; currently handles 5 acts. Receives 20-30% commission. Reviews material for acts.
How to Contact: Submit demo tape by mail. Unsolicited submissions are OK. Prefers cassette or DAT with 3 songs and lyric sheet. If seeking management, press kit should include demo, 8×10 glossy, bio/résumé and song list. Does not return material. Responds in 6 months.
Music: Mostly **commercial rock**, **alternative** and **A/C**; also **country** and **dance**. Works primarily with singer/songwriters and solo artists. Current acts include Joe King (Motown), General Panic (alternative/new wave) and Brittany (soda pop).

[◐] MANAGEMENT BY JAFFE, 1560 Broadway, Suite 1103, New York NY 10036-0000. (212)869-6912. Fax: (212)869-7102. E-mail: jerjaf@aol.com. President: Jerry Jaffe. Management firm. Estab. 1987. Represents individual artists and groups from anywhere; currently handles 2 acts. Receives 20% commission. Reviews material for acts "sometimes."
How to Contact: *Write or call first to arrange personal interview.* Prefers CD or cassette and videocassette with 3-4 songs and lyric sheet. Does not return material. Responds in 2 months.
Music: Mostly **rock/alternative**, **pop** and **AAA**. Works primarily with groups and singers/songwriters. Current acts include Joe McIntrye (pop) and Ann Marie Montads (rock).
Tips: "Create some kind of 'buzz' first."

[✓] [◐] MANAGEMENT PLUS, P.O. Box 65089, San Antonio TX 78265. (210)698-8181, ext. 202. Fax: (210)223-3251. E-mail: bill@ynotcall.com or bangelini12@prodigy.net. Website: www.yno tcall.com. **Contact:** Bill Angelini, owner. Management firm and booking agency. Estab. 1980. Represents individual artists and groups from anywhere; currently handles 6 acts. Receives 10-15% commission. Reviews material for acts.
How to Contact: Submit demo tape by mail. Unsolicited submissions are OK. Prefers cassette, VHS videocassette and bio. If seeking management, press kit should include pictures, bio, résumé and discography. Does not return material. Responds in 1 month.
Music: Mostly **Latin American**, **Tejano** and **international**; also **Norteño** and **country**. Current acts include Jay Perez (Tejano), Ram Herrera (Tejano), Rodeo (Tejano) and Grupo Vida (Tejano).

THE FILM & TV INDEX found at the back of this book lists companies placing music in film and TV (excluding TV commercials).

❦ ✓ ◐ **THE MANAGEMENT TRUST LTD.**, 411 Queen St. W, 3rd Floor, Toronto, Ontario M5V 2A5 Canada. (416)979-7070. Fax: (416)979-0505. E-mail: mail@mgmtrust.ca. President: Jake Gold. Assistant to the President: Shelley Stertz. Management firm. Estab. 1986. Represents individual artists and/or groups; currently handles 6 acts.

How to Contact: Submit demo tape by mail. Unsolicited submissions are OK. If seeking management, press kit should include CD or tape, bio, cover letter, photo and press clippings. Does not return material. Responds in 2 months.

Music: All types. Current acts include The Tragically Hip (rock band), The Watchmen (rock band) and Vann (pop/rock/alternative).

✓ ◯ **RICK MARTIN PRODUCTIONS**, 125 Fieldpoint Road, Greenwich CT 06830. Phone/fax: (203)661-1615. E-mail: rick@easywaysystems.com. **Contact:** Rick Martin, president. Personal manager and independent producer. Held the Office of Secretary of the National Conference of Personal Managers from 1975-1997. Represents vocalists and actresses; currently handles 3 acts. Receives 15-25% commission.

How to Contact: Submit 2-3 songs and picture.

Music: Mostly **top 40** and **dance**. Produces vocal groups and female vocalists. Current acts include Jackie Tohn (vocalist/songwriter/actress), Ally Garaio (vocalist) and Anna Rogers (vocalist/songwriter).

Tips: "The songs do not have to be professionally produced—it's really not important what you've done—it's what you can do now that counts."

◐ **PHIL MAYO & COMPANY**, P.O. Box 304, Bomoseen VT 05732. (802)468-2554. Fax: (802)468-8884. E-mail: pmcamgphil@aol.com. **Contact:** Phil Mayo, President. Management firm and record company (AMG Records). Estab. 1981. Represents individual artists, groups and songwriters from anywhere; currently handles 4 acts. Receives 15-20% commission. Reviews material for acts.

How to Contact: *Contact first and obtain permission to submit.* Prefers CD with 3 songs and lyric or lead sheet. If seeking management, include bio, photo and lyric sheet in press kit. Does not return material. Responds in 2 months.

Music: Mostly **rock**, **pop** and **country**; also **blues** and **Christian pop**. Works primarily with dance bands, vocalists and rock acts. Current acts include John Hall, Guy Burlage, Jonell Mosser, Pam Buckland and Orleans.

Ⓝ ◐ **MAZUR ENTERTAINMENT**, (formerly Mazur Public Relations), P.O. Box 2425, Trenton NJ 08607. (609)695-1800. Fax: (609)695-8860. E-mail: michael@mazurpr.com. Website: www.mazurpr.com. **Contact:** Michael Mazur. Management and PR firm. Estab. 1987. Represents groups from anywhere; currently handles 30 acts. Commission varies. Reviews material for acts.

How to Contact: Submit demo tape by mail. Unsolicited submissions are OK. Prefers cassette, CD or VHS videocassette with 2 songs. If seeking management, press kit should include CD/cassette, photo, bio and video. Include SASE. "We try to reply." Responds in 1 month.

Music: Current acts include international and national artists. See website.

✓ ◐ **THE McDONNELL GROUP**, 27 Pickwick Lane, Newtown Square PA 19073. (610)353-8554. E-mail: frankmcdonn@aol.com. **Contact:** Frank McDonnell. Management firm. Estab. 1985. Represents individual artists, groups and songwriters from anywhere; currently handles 6 acts. Receives 20% commission. Reviews material for acts.

How to Contact: *Write first and obtain permission to submit.* Prefers cassette or VHS videocassette with 4 songs and lyric sheet. If seeking management, include cover letter, lyric sheets, press, tape or video, recent photos and bio. Include SASE. Responds in 1 month.

Music: Mostly **rock**, **pop** and **R&B**; also **country** and **jazz**. Current acts include Johnny Bronco (rock group), Mike Forte (producer/songwriter) and Pat Martino (jazz guitarist).

☑ **MEDIA MANAGEMENT**, P.O. Box 3773, San Rafael CA 94912-3773. (415)457-0700. Fax: (415)457-0964. E-mail: mediamanagement9@aol.com. **Contact:** Eugene, proprietor. Management firm. Estab. 1990. Represents local, regional or international individual artists, groups and songwriters; currently handles 4 acts. Receives 15-20% commission. Reviews material for acts.

How to Contact: Submit demo tape by mail. Unsolicited submissions are OK. Prefers cassette or VHS videocassette with lyric sheet. If seeking management, include lyric sheets, demo tape, photo and bio. Does not return material.

Music: Mostly **rock**, **blues** and **pop**; also **jazz** and **R&B**. Works primarily with songwriting performers/bands. Current acts include Zakiya Hooker (r&b/blues/singer/songwriter), Greg Anton/Greggs Eggs (rock songwriter/group), John Lee Hooker Estate (blues) and Natural Four/Ollan Christopher (singer/songwriter/producer and r&b group).

Tips: "Write great *radio-friendly* songs."

☑ ☑ **MEGA MUSIC PRODUCTIONS**, 290 Sunrise Dr., Unit #3-K, Key Biscayne FL 33149. (305)365-8551. Fax: (305)365-8552. E-mail: megamusic1@aol.com. Website: www.megamusicclub. com. **Contact:** Marco Vinicio Carvajal, General Manager. Management firm, booking agency and record producer. Represents individual artists and groups from anywhere; currently handles 7 acts. Receives 25-50% commission. Reviews material for acts.

How to Contact: Submit demo tape by mail. Unsolicited submissions are OK. Prefers cassette, CD or VHS videocassette with 5 songs and lyric sheet. If seeking management, press kit should include cover letter, demo tape/CD, video, photos and bio. Does not return material. Responds in 1 month.

Music: Mostly **rock**, **techno-dance** and **Latin rock**; also **Latin** and **pop**. Works primarily with bands and singers. Current acts include David Summers (Latin pop), Vilma Palma e Vampiros and Filo Paez.

Tips: "Send us compact information and describe your goals."

☑ ◯ **MERRI-WEBB PRODUCTIONS**, P.O. Box 5474, Stockton CA 95205. (209)948-8186. Fax: (209)942-2163. E-mail: kauppmusic@filmmusic.net. Website: www.makingmusic4u.com. **Contact:** Kristy Ledford, A&R coordinator. Management firm, music publisher (Kaupp's & Robert Publishing Co./BMI) and record company (Kaupp Records). Represents regional (California) individual artists, groups and songwriters; currently handles 13 acts. Receives 10-15% commission. Reviews material for acts.

How to Contact: *Write first and obtain permission to submit or to arrange personal interview.* Prefers cassette or VHS videocassette with 3 songs maximum and lyric sheet. Include SASE. Responds in 3 months.

Music: Mostly **country**, **A/C rock** and **R&B**; also **pop**, **rock** and **gospel**. Works primarily with vocalists, bands and songwriters. Current acts include Bruce Bolin (rock/pop singer), Nanci Lynn (country/pop singer) and Rick Webb (country/pop singer).

🅽 ☑ **METRO TALENT GROUP, INC.**, 83 Walton St., Atlanta GA 30303. E-mail: jennifer@me trotalentgroup.com. Website: www.metrotalentgroup.com. **Contact:** Jennifer Hatch. Booking agency. Represents individual artists and groups; currently handles 12-15 acts. Receives 10-15% commission. Reviews material for acts.

How to Contact: *Write or call first and obtain permission to submit.* "We prefer to be contacted via e-mail." Prefers cassette or CD. Include clubs/venues played, guarantees for each show and who you've opened for. Does not return material. Responds in 2 weeks.

Music: Mostly **rock/alternative**, **blues** and **jazz**; also **acoustic**. Visit website for full roster of current acts.

🅽 ◯ **MIDCOAST, INC.**, 1002 Jones Rd., Hendersonville TN 37075. (615)264-3896. E-mail: mid-co@ix.netcom.com. Managing Director: Bruce Andrew Bossert. Management firm and music publisher (MidCoast, Inc./BMI). Estab. 1984. Represents individual artists, groups and songwriters; currently handles 2 acts. Reviews material for acts.

How to Contact: Submit demo tape by mail. Unsolicited submissions are OK. Prefers CD, cassette, VHS videocassette or DAT with 2-4 songs and lyric sheet. If seeking management, press kit should include cover letter, "short" bio, tape, video, photo, press clippings and announcements of any performances in Nashville area. Does not return material. Responds in 6 weeks if interested.

Music: Mostly **rock**, **pop** and **country**. Works primarily with original rock and country bands and artists. Current acts include Room 101 (alternative rock).

N MIDNIGHT MUSIC MANAGEMENT, 816 S. Robertson Blvd., Los Angeles CA 90035. (310)289-3006. Fax: (310)289-3007. Agents: Bob Diamond, Liza Rhima and Stuart Wax. Management firm. Estab. 1989. Represents individual artists, groups, songwriters and indie labels for film and TV; currently handles 10 acts. Receives 15-20% commission. Reviews material for acts.

How to Contact: *Write or call first and obtain permission to submit.* Prefers cassette with 3 songs, lyric sheet and bios and press. If seeking management, press kit should include bio, press, tape and video (if available). Does not return material. Responds in 1 month.

Music: All kinds. Works primarily with R&B/pop songwriters and producers, punk/alternative bands and acoustic rock bands. Current acts include Irene Cara (r&b singer/actress), Nancy Bryan (alternative pop) and Lauran G. (alternative pop). Songwriter: Denise Rich.

☑ ⊘ MIRKIN MANAGEMENT, 906½ Congress Ave., Austin TX 78701. (512)472-1818. Fax: (512)472-6915. E-mail: mirk1@aol.com. Website: www.ianmoore.com. **Contact:** Rebecca Dunlap, administrative assistant. Management firm, ASCAP regional representative. Estab. 1986. Represents individual artists, groups and songwriters from anywhere. Reviews material for acts.

How to Contact: *Write or call first and obtain permission to submit.* Prefers CD with 4 songs. If seeking management, press kit should include photo, press clippings and music. Include SASE.

Music: All types. Current acts include Ian Moore Band (blues/rock) and Kitty Gordon (rock).

N ◯ MONOPOLY MANAGEMENT, 162 N. Milford, Highland MI 48357. **Contact:** Bob Zilli, vice president. Management firm. Estab. 1984. Represents songwriters from anywhere; currently handles 2 acts. Receives 10% commission. Reviews material for acts.

How to Contact: Submit demo tape by mail. Unsolicited submissions are OK. Prefers cassette or VHS videocassette with 4 songs and lyric sheet. If seeking management, press kit should include tape, photo, cover letter and résumé of live performances. Include SASE. Responds in 1 month.

Music: Mostly **country**, **alternative** and **top 40**. Works primarily with singer/songwriters. Current acts include Robert Richmond (songwriter) and The Nashville Sound.

N MONTEREY ARTISTS, INC., 124 12th Ave. S., Nashville TN 37203. (615)321-4444. Fax: (615)321-2446. Booking agency. Represents individual artists, groups from anywhere; currently handles 37 acts. Receives 10% commission. Reviews material for acts.

How to Contact: *Write or call first to arrange personal interview.*

Music: Mostly **country**. Current acts include John Michael Montgomery, Lyle Lovett, The Mavericks, Hal Ketchum, Ricky Skaggs, Sawyer Brown, Junior Brown, Toby Keith and Black Hawk.

⊘ GARY F. MONTGOMERY MANAGEMENT, P.O. Box 5106, Macon GA 31208. (478)749-7259. Fax: (478)757-0002. E-mail: gfmmusic@aol.com. **Contact:** Gary F. Montgomery, president. Management firm, music publisher (g.f.m. Music/ASCAP and 12/31/49 Music/BMI) and production company. Estab. 1981. Represents individual artists, groups, songwriters, record producers and engineers; currently handles 4 acts. Receives 10-20% commission (it varies depending on the act). Reviews material for acts.

How to Contact: *Write or call first and obtain permission to submit.* Prefers CD with 3-5 songs and lyric sheet. If seeking management, press kit should include cover letter, bio, résumé, photo, demo tape/CD, lyric sheets, press clippings and video. "Call first to see if we are accepting new clients." Does not return material. Responds in 2 months only if interested.

Music: All types. Works primarily with singer/songwriters. Current acts include Davis Causey (New Age guitarist), Jan Krist (singer/songwriter), The Night Hawks, Otis Redding III, Jim Dickinson and Bruce Hensal.

N **◑** **MUSE ARTISTS INC.**, (formerly Legend Artists Management), 12 W. 37th St., 5th Floor, New York NY 10018-7404. (212)279-9288. Fax: (212)279-9266. E-mail: sevendigitsbol8@yahoo.c om. **Contact:** Pamela Logan, vice president of A&R, Janice Roeg, president or Kristeen Stelman, production coordinator. Management firm. Estab. 1986. Represents individual artists, groups, songwriters and producers from everywhere; currently handles 6 acts. Receives up to 20% commission. Reviews material for acts.
How to Contact: *Write or call first and obtain permission to submit.* Prefers CD or DAT. If seeking management, press kit should include tape, cover letter and photo. Include SASE. Responds in 6 weeks.
Music: Mostly **pop**, **R&B** and **rock**; also **all styles**. Current acts include Nazarath (rock) and Uranium 235 (rock/electronic/industrial).

⊞ **◯** **MUSIC MARKETING & PROMOTIONS**, (formerly Music Man Promotions), P.O. Box 956, South Perth 6951 Australia. Phone: (618)9450 1199. Fax: (618)9450 8527. E-mail: mmp@global .net.au. Website: www.global.net.au/~mmp/. **Contact:** Eddie Robertson. Booking agency. Estab. 1991. Represents individual artists and/or groups; currently handles 50 acts. Receives 20% commission. Reviews material for acts.
How to Contact: *Write first and obtain permission to submit.* Unsolicited submissions are OK. Prefers cassette or videocassette with photo, information on style and bio. If seeking management, press kit should include photos, bio, cover letter, résumé, press clippings, video, demo, lyric sheets and any other useful information. Does not return material. Responds in 1 month.
Music: Mostly **top 40/pop**, **jazz** and **'60s-'90s**; also **reggae** and **blues**. Works primarily with show bands and solo performers. Current acts include Faces (dance band), N.R.G. (show band) and C.J. & the Thorns (soul).
Tips: "Send as much information as possible. If you do not receive a call after four to five weeks, follow up with letter or phone call."

N **◑** **NIK ENTERTAINMENT CO.**, 274 N. Goodman St., Rochester NY 14607. (585)244-0331. Fax: (585)244-0356. E-mail: nikniceguy@aol.com. Website: www.nikentertainment.com. **Contact:** Dave Lawrence, recording manager. General Manager/President: Gary Webb. Management firm and booking agency. Estab. 1988. Represents groups from anywhere; currently handles 9 acts. Receives 15% commission. Reviews material for acts.
How to Contact: Submit demo tape by mail. Unsolicited submissions are OK. Prefers cassette, VHS videocassette or CD with lyric or lead sheet. If seeking management, press kit should include photo, bio and demo tape. Does not return material. Responds in 3 weeks.
Music: Mostly **mainstream rock** and **pop**. Works primarily with bands. Current acts include Nik and the Nice Guys (pop show band), The Shag-adelics ('60s meets '90s), Fever-The Wrath of Polyester ('70s retro), Alpha Delta Nik (the world's only tribute to *Animal House*), The Blues Family (r&b review), Jazz Nik (basic jazz trio and more), The Bugzappers (swing band), Shamalama (oldies with an edge) and the Rochester Rat Pack (the cocktail culture revival).

◉ **NOTEWORTHY ENTERPRISES**, 3741 Sunny Isles Blvd., N. Miami Beach FL 33160. (305)949-9192. Fax: (305)949-9492. E-mail: ss@noteworthy.net. Website: www.Noteworthy.net. **Contact:** Sheila Siegel, president. Booking agency, music publisher (On the Water Publications/BMI) and talent buyer. Estab. 1987. Represents individual artists, groups and songwriters from anywhere. Receives 20% commission. Reviews material for acts.
How to Contact: *Does not accept unsolicited submissions.* "Request via Internet, please—no faxes or phone calls."

MARKETS THAT WERE listed in the 2002 edition of *Songwriters Market* but do not appear this year are listed in the General Index with a notation explaining why they were omitted.

Music: Mostly **big band**. Works primarily with jazz artists. Current acts include Noteworthy Orchestra (big band), Southlanders Traditional Jazz Band, David Siegel and Jack Siegel. "Complete roster available on website, call for any artists not found."

◖ **NOTEWORTHY PRODUCTIONS**, 124½ Archwood Ave., Annapolis MD 21401. (410)268-8232. Fax: (410)268-2167. E-mail: mcshane@mcnote.com. Website: www.mcnote.com. **Contact:** McShane Glover, president. Management firm and booking agency. Estab. 1985. Represents individual artists, groups and songwriters from everywhere; currently handles 6 acts. Receives 15-20% commission. Reviews material for acts.
How to Contact: *Write first and obtain permission to submit.* Prefers CD/CDR with lyric sheet. If seeking management, press kit should include cassette or CD, photo, bio, venues played and press clippings (preferably reviews). "Follow up with a phone call 3-5 weeks after submission." Does not return material. Responds in 1 month.
Music: Mostly **Americana**, **folk**, and **celtic**. Works primarily with performing singer/songwriters. Current acts include Seamus Kennedy (Celtic/contemporary), Tanglefoot (Canadian) and Clandestine (Texas celtic).

✓ ◖ **ON THE LEVEL MUSIC!**, P.O. Box 508, Owego NY 13827. (607)689-0122. Fax: (607)687-0928. E-mail: fredny2020@yahoo.com. **Contact:** Fred Gage, CEO/president. Management firm, booking agency and music publisher (On The Level Music! Publishing). Estab. 1970. Represents individual artists, groups and songwriters from anywhere; currently handles 30 acts. Receives 15% commission. Reviews material for acts.
How to Contact: Submit demo tape by mail. Unsolicited submissions are OK. Prefers CDs, DAT or VHS videocassette with 4 songs and lyric or lead sheet. If seeking management, press kit should include cover letter, bio, demo tape/CD, lyric sheets, press clippings, 8×10 photo and video. Does not return material. Responds in 1 month.
Music: Mostly **rock**, **alternative** and **jazz**; also **blues**. Current acts include Mule in the Corn, Reynolds and Chase (rock).

N ◖ **OTA PRODUCTIONS**, (formerly PriceClub Productions), 484 Lake Park Ave. #32, Oakland CA 94610. (510)339-3389. Fax: (510)339-0389. E-mail: music@melodia.com. Website: www.melodia.com. **Contact:** Scott Price, director. Management firm, record company and record producer (Scott Price). Estab. 1995. Represents individual artists and groups from anywhere; currently handles 3 acts. Receives 20% commission. Reviews material for acts.
How to Contact: Submit demo tape by mail. Unsolicited submissions are OK. Prefers CD with 5 songs and lyric sheet. If seeking management, press kit should include cover letter, bio, photo, demo/CD, press clippings, video and résumé. Does not return material. Responds in 2 months.
Music: Mostly **jazz**, **Latin** and **pop**. Works primarily with individual artists/groups. Current acts include Omar Sosa (Cuban pianist) and Madhouse (jazz quartet).

♣ ✓ ◖ **OUTLAW ENTERTAINMENT INTERNATIONAL**, #101-1001 W. Broadway, Dept. 400, Vancouver, British Columbia V6H 4E4 Canada. (604)878-1494. Fax: (604)878-1495. E-mail: info@outlawentertainment.com. Website: www.outlawentertainment.com. CEO/President: Tommy Floyd. Assistant President: Suzanne Marie. Management firm. Estab. 1995. Represents individual artists, groups and songwriters from anywhere; currently handles 3 acts. Receives 20% commission. Reviews material for acts.
How to Contact: Submit demo CD by mail. Unsolicited submissions are OK. Prefers CD with 2-3 songs and lyric sheet. If seeking management, press kit should include 8×10 photo, bio and written statement of goals. SAE and IRC. Responds in 1 month.
Music: Mostly **rock**, **metal** and **alt. country**. Works primarily with bands, "but welcomes dynamic singer/songwriters." Current acts include American Dog (hard rock act), Luba Dvorak (alt. country act) and Subsonic (heavy metal act).
Tips: "Clearly define your target market. Write simple, emotional, primal songs."

Ⓝ Ⓜ PERFORMERS OF THE WORLD INC. (P.O.W.), 8901 Melrose Ave., 2nd Floor, Los Angeles CA 90069-5605. (310)205-0366. Fax: (310)205-0365. E-mail: pow-stp@ix.netcom.com. President: Terry Rindal. Agents: Nita Scott, Trip Brown. Booking agency. Estab. 1987. Represents individual artists and groups from anywhere; currently handles 50 acts. Receives 10-15% commission.
How to Contact: *Write or call first and obtain permission to submit.* Prefers cassette or VHS videocassette with several songs and lyric sheet. If seeking management, press kit should include cover letter, photo, bio, press clippings, demo tape/CD and video. Does not return material. Responds in 1 month (depends on quality).
Music: Mostly **rock**, **world music**, **alternative**, **jazz**, **R&B**, **folk** and **pop**. Current acts include Herbie Hancock (jazz legend), Joe Sample (jazz legend), Karla Bonoff (singer/songwriter) and John Cale.
Tips: "Don't harrass us after you submit. We are looking for artistry and quality—if you're not really prepared please don't waste your time (or ours)."

Ⓒ PILLAR RECORDS, P.O. Box 858, Carlisle PA 17013-0858. Phone/fax: (717)249-2536. E-mail: mail@v-domains.com. Website: www.craigkelley.com. **Contact:** A&R Department. Management firm, music publisher and record company. Estab. 1994. Represents individual artists, groups and songwriters from anywhere; currently handles 2 acts. Receives 20% commission. Reviews material for acts.
How to Contact: Submit demo tape by mail. Unsolicited submissions are OK. Prefers CD/CDR with 3 songs and lyric sheet. If seeking management, press kit should include bio, photo, reviews, mailing list, tape or CD. "Please be neat and as professional as possible." Does not return material. Responds in 6 weeks.
Music: Mostly **pop/rock** and **folk/rock**. Works primarily with solo artists and bands. Current acts include the Craig Kelley Band (mainstream rock).
Tips: "Currently looking for a vocals/guitar or vocal/piano act. No band needed."

☑ Ⓞ PRECISION MANAGEMENT, 110 Coliseum Crossing, #158, Hampton VA 23666-5902. Phone/fax: (757)875-0323. E-mail: precisionmanagement@netzero.com. Website: www.angelfire. com/on2/PrecisionManagement. **Contact:** Cappriccieo Scates, operations director. Management firm and music publisher (Mytrell/BMI). Estab. 1990. Represents individual artists and/or groups and songwriters from anywhere; currently handles 3 acts. Receives 20% commission. Reviews material for acts.
How to Contact: Submit demo tape by mail. Unsolicited submissions are OK. Prefers cassette or VHS videocassette with 3-4 songs and lyric sheet. If seeking management, press kit should include photo, bio, demo tape/CD, lyric sheets, press clippings and all relevant press information. Include SASE. Responds in 6 weeks.
Music: Mostly **R&B**, **rap** and **gospel**; also **all types**. Current acts include Surface (R&B act), Joe'I Chancellor (rap artist) amd Desire (R&B).

⊕ Ⓜ PRESTIGE ARTISTES, HighRidge Bath Rd., Farmborough NR Bath BA3 1BR United Kingdom. Phone: 07050 277053. E-mail: drees15066@aol.com. **Contact:** David Rees, proprietor. Management firm and booking agency. Associate company: Lintern Rees Organisation. Estab. 1983. Represents individual artists, groups, songwriters, comedians and specialty acts; currently handles 20 acts. Receives 10-15% commission. Reviews material for acts.
How to Contact: Submit demo tape by mail. Unsolicited submissions are OK. Prefers cassette with 3 songs and lyric sheet. If seeking management, press kit should include good demo tape, cover letter, any references, bio, press clippings, publicity photos and video if available (UK format). Artist should be based in the UK. Does not return material. Responds in 1 month.
Music: Mostly **MOR**, **pop**, **'60s style**, **country** and **rock**. Works primarily with vocal guitarists/keyboards, pop groups, pub/club acts and guitar or keyboard duos. Current acts include Legend (duo), Elvis Presley Junior (vocalist) and Fran DeVere (vocalist).
Tips: "Do not send more than three songs, your best available. Tell us what you want in the UK—be realistic."

N ◑ PRESTIGE MANAGEMENT, 8600 Wilbur Ave., Northridge CA 91324. (818)993-3030. Fax: (818)993-4151. E-mail: prestige@gte.net. **Contact:** Waddell Solomon, vice president. Management firm. Estab. 1987. Represents individual artists, groups and songwriters from anywhere; currently handles 2 acts. Receives 15% commission. Reviews material for acts.

How to Contact: Submit demo tape by mail. Unsolicited submissions are OK. Prefers cassette with 3 songs, photo/bio and lyric sheet. If seeking management, press kit should includ photos, bio, recent show dates and recent show reviews. Does not return material. Responds in 1 month.

Music: Mostly **pop rock**, **hard rock**, **alternative rock**; also **R&B** and **AAA**. Works primarily with pop/rock bands with strong songs and live shows; also songwriters for film/TV projects. Current acts include Neve (modern pop rock), Spinach (ambient rock/pop), Michael Raphael (singer/songwriter) and Skandal.

☑ ◯ PRO TALENT CONSULTANTS, P.O. Box 233, Nice CA 95464. Phone/fax: (707)349-1809. E-mail: pro_talent_artists@yahoo.com. **Contact:** John Eckert, coordinator. Management firm and booking agency. Estab. 1979. Represents individual artists and groups; currently handles 9 acts. Receives 20% commission. Reviews material for acts.

How to Contact: Submit demo tape by mail. Unsolicited submissions are OK. Prefers cassette or VHS videocassette with at least 4 songs and lyric sheet. "We prefer audio cassette (4 songs). Submit videocassette with live performance only." If seeking management, press kit should include an 8×10 photo, a cassette or CD of at least 4-6 songs, a bio on group/artist, references, cover letter, press clippings, video and business card or a phone number with address. Does not return material. Responds in 5 weeks.

Music: Mostly **country**, **country/pop** and **rock**. Works primarily with vocalists, show bands, dance bands and bar bands. Current acts include Jon Richards (country singer), The Golden Leaders of the Rockin' '60s (variety show, various performers) and The Vogues (pop, vocal group).

☑ ◯ RADIOACTIVE TALENT INC., 350 Third Ave., Suite 400, New York NY 10010. (917)733-4700. Website: radiotv.com. **Contact:** Kenjamin Franklin, agent. Booking and talent agency. Estab. 1983. Represents individual artists, groups and broadcasters from anywhere; currently handles 20 acts. Receives 10% commission. Reviews material for acts.

How to Contact: Submit demo tape by mail. Unsolicited submissions are OK. "Please do not phone." Prefers CD, cassette or VHS video with 3 songs and lyric sheet. Press kit should include bio, press clippings, photo, cover letter, résumé, video, e-mail address and 3 radio-friendly original songs on cassettes/CD. "Label all cassettes with phone number and e-mail address." Does not return material. Responds in 3 weeks. "We only call upon further interest."

Music: Mostly **modern rock**, **ballads** and **AAA**; also **A/C** and **CHR/pop**. Current acts include Ambrosia (rock), Les Lokey (alternative) and Kati Mac (AAA).

☑ ◑ RAINBOW COLLECTION LTD., 4696 Kahlua Lane, Bonita Springs FL 34134. (941)947-6978. E-mail: obitts@bellsouth.net. **Contact:** Richard (Dick) O'Bitts, executive producer. Management firm, record company (Happy Man Records) and music publisher (Rocker Music and Happy Man Music). Represents individual artists, groups, songwriters and producers; currently handles 3 acts. Receives 10-20% commission. Reviews material for acts.

How to Contact: Submit demo tape by mail. Unsolicited submissions are OK. Prefers CD or VHS videocassette of live performance with 4 songs and lyric sheet. If seeking management, press kit should include photos, bio and tapes. Include SASE. Responds in 1 month.

Music: Mostly **country**, **pop** and **rock**. Works primarily with writer/artists and groups of all kinds. Current acts include 4 Harmonee (country/pop), The Thorps (country pop), Okefenokee Joe (nature writer and vocalist), Jim Duff (contemporary artist) and Ron Jeffers (country rock).

☑ ◑ RAINBOW TALENT AGENCY, 146 Round Pond Lane, Rochester NY 14662. (585)723-3334. Fax: (585)720-6172. E-mail: rtalent@frontiernet.net. **Contact:** Carl Labate, President. Management firm and booking agency. Represents artists and groups; currently handles 6 acts. Receives 20% commission.

How to Contact: Submit demo tape by mail. Unsolicited submissions are OK. Prefers cassette, CD/CDR with minimum 3 songs and lyric sheet. May send video if available; "a still photo would be good enough to see the type of performance; if you are a performer, it would be advantageous to show yourself or the group performing live. Theme videos are not helpful." If seeking management, include photos, bio, markets established, tape and/or videos. Does not return material. Responds in 1 month.

Music: Blues, **rock** and **R&B**. Works primarily with touring bands and recording artists. Current acts include Nancy Kelley (jazz singer), Uncle Plum (top 40) and Spanky Haschmann Swing Orchestra (high energy swing).

Tips: "My main interest is with groups or performers that are currently touring or ready to do so. And are at least 40% percent original. Strictly songwriters should apply elsewhere."

O RENAISSANCE ENTERTAINMENT GROUP, P.O. Box 1222, Mountainside NJ 07092-1222. E-mail: regroup@hotmail.com. **Contact:** Kevin A. Joy, president/CEO. Management firm, booking agency, record company (Suburan Records) and record producer (Onyx Music and Bo²Legg Productions). Estab. 1992. Represents individual artists, groups and songwriters from anywhere; currently handles 10 acts. Receives 20% commission. Reviews material for acts.

How to Contact: *Write first and obtain permission to submit.* Prefers cassette with 3 songs and lyric or lead sheet. If seeking management, press kit should include cover letter, demo tape/CD, lyric sheets, press clippings, pictures and bio. Does not return material. Responds in 5 weeks.

Music: Mostly **R&B** and **rap**. Works primarily with R&B groups, rap and vocalists. Current acts include Paper Boy (rap), ASU (rap) and A Mother's Child (r&b).

Ø DIANE RICHARDS WORLD MANAGEMENT, INC. E-mail: drworldmgm@aol.com. **Contact:** Diane Richards, president. Management firm. Estab. 1994. Represents individual artists, groups, songwriters and producers from anywhere; currently handles 8 acts. Receives 20% commission. Reviews material for acts.

How to Contact: *Write first (via e-mail) and obtain permission to submit.* If seeking management, press kit should include cover letter, photograph, biography, cassette tape, telephone number and address. Does not return material. Responds in 1 month.

Music: Mostly **dance**, **pop** and **rap**; also **New Age**, **A/C** and **jazz**. Works primarily with pop and dance acts, and songwriters who also are recording artists. Current acts include Sappho (songwriter/artist), Menace (songwriter/producer/artist) and Babygirl (R&B/rap artist).

Ø RIGHT-ON MANAGEMENT, P.O. Box 2627, Dearborn MI 48123. (313)274-7000. Fax: (313)274-9255. E-mail: angel@angelgomez.com. Website: www.angelgomez.com. **Contact:** Angel Gomez, president. Management firm. Estab. 1979. Represents local and international individual artists, groups and songwriters; currently handles 9 acts. Receives 15-20% commission. Reviews material for acts.

How to Contact: *Write first and obtain permission to submit.* Prefers cassette or videocassette of performance with 3-5 songs. If seeking management, include photo, tape/CD, bio, cover letter, press clippings and itinerary of dates. Does not return material. Responds in 2 months.

Music: Mostly **rock**, **pop** and **top 40**; also **funk**. Works primarily with individual artists, groups and songwriters. Current artists include Deena (pop T-40), The Rev. Right Time and the First Cuzins of Funk (new funk) and Bride (rock).

Ø RIOHCAT MUSIC, P.O. Box 764, Hendersonville TN 37077-0764. (615)824-9313. Fax: (615)824-0797. E-mail: tachoir@bellsouth.net. Website: www.tachoir.com. **Contact:** Robert Kayne,

---

FOR BOOKS ON THE CRAFT AND BUSINESS of songwriting, check out the website for Writer's Digest Books at www.writersdigest.com.

manager. Management firm, booking agency, record company (Avita Records) and music publisher. Estab. 1975. Represents individual artists and groups; currently handles 4 acts. Receives 15-20% commission.

How to Contact: *Contact first and obtain permission to submit.* Prefers cassette and lead sheet. If seeking management, press kit should include cover letter, bio, photo, demo tape/CD and press clippings. Does not return material. Responds in 6 weeks.

Music: Mostly **contemporary jazz** and **fusion**. Works primarily with jazz ensembles. Current acts include Group Tachoir (jazz), Tachoir/Manakas Duo (jazz) and Jerry Tachoir (jazz vibraphone artist).

A.F. RISAVY, INC., 1312 Vandalia, Collinsville IL 62234. (618)345-6700. Fax: (618)235-0004. Website: www.swingcitymusic.com. **Contact:** Art Risavy, president. Management firm and booking agency. Divisions include Artco Enterprises, Golden Eagle Records, Swing City Music and Swing City Sound. Estab. 1960. Represents artists, groups and songwriters; currently handles 35 acts. Receives 10% commission. Reviews material for acts.

How to Contact: Submit demo tape by mail. Unsolicited submissions are OK. Prefers CD/CDR, cassette or VHS videocassette with 2-6 songs and lyric sheet. If seeking management, press kit should include pictures, bio and VHS videocassette. Include SASE. Responds in 3 weeks.

Music: Mostly **rock**, **country**, **MOR** and **top 40**.

ROCK OF AGES PRODUCTIONS, 1001 W. Jasmine Dr., Suite K, Lake Park FL 33403-2119. (561)848-1500. Fax: (561)848-2400. President/Agency Director: Joseph E. Larson. Booking agent, literary agency and publisher. Estab. 1980. Represents individual artists and groups from anywhere; currently handles 500 acts. Receives 15-25% commission. Reviews material for acts.

How to Contact: Submit demo tape by mail. Unsolicited submissions are OK. Prefers CD, cassette or VHS videocassette with 3 or more songs and lead sheet. If seeking management, press kit should include videocassette and/or audio cassette, lyric sheets, relevant press, bio, cover letter, résumé and recent photo. Include SASE. Responds in 3 months.

Music: Mostly **top 40**, **country/western** and **rock**; also **gospel** and **opera**. Works primarily with bands, singers, singer/songwriters. Current acts include Andrew Epps (ballad singer/songwriter), John Michael Ferrari (singer/songwriter) and Paola Semprini (opera star).

ROCK WHIRLED MUSIC MANAGEMENT, 1423 N. Front St., Harrisburg PA 17102. (717)236-2386. E-mail: phil.clark@rockwhirled.com. Website: www.rockwhirled.com. **Contact:** Philip Clark, director. Management firm, booking agency and publicists. Estab. 1987. Represents individual artists and/or groups from anywhere; currently handles 12 acts. Receives 10-25% commission. Reviews material for acts.

How to Contact: *Contact first and obtain permission to submit.* Prefers cassette. If seeking management, press kit should include bio, cover letter, demo tape/CD, photo, song list, venue list, description of performance frequency, equipment needed, goals. Include SASE. Responds in 6 weeks.

Music: Mostly **rock**, **alternative** and **folk**. Works primarily with soloist singer/instrumentalists, duo acoustic acts, bands. Current acts include My World (modern rock), Cameron Molloy (country fusion) and Adria (celtic).

Tips: "Be brief, clear, focused in approach. Approach a variety of other agents and managers to get a feel for which companies make the best match. We look for clients who wish to work specifically with us, not just any firm."

ROGUE MANAGEMENT, 2292 S. Railroad Ave., Staten Island NY 10306. Phone/fax: (718)351-8758. E-mail: maurogue@aol.com. **Contact:** Ralph Beauchamp, president. Management firm. Estab. 1992. Represents individual artists, groups and songwriters from anywhere; currently handles 2 acts. Receives 15% commission. Reviews material for acts.

How to Contact: Submit demo tape by mail. Unsolicited submissions are OK. Prefers CD or cassette with 3-5 songs and lyric sheet. If seeking management, press kit should include cover letter, demo tape/CD, lyric sheets, press clippings, photo and bio. Include SASE. Responds in 2 weeks.

Music: Mostly **pop/rock**, **industrial** and **R&B/dance**; also **hard rock**. Works primarily with bands. Current acts include Head (pop/rock), Cheepskates (pop) and Requiem (industrial).

Tips: "Learn that the song comes first, not the image."

◙ **CHARLES R. ROTHSCHILD PRODUCTIONS INC.**, 330 E. 48th St., New York NY 10017. (212)421-0592. **Contact:** Charles R. Rothschild, president. Booking agency. Estab. 1971. Represents individual artists, groups and songwriters from anywhere; currently handles 25 acts. Receives 25% commission. Reviews material for acts.

How to Contact: *Call first and obtain permission to submit.* Prefers cassette, CD or VHS videocassette with 1 song and lyric and lead sheet. If seeking management, include cassette, photo, bio and reviews. Include SASE. Responds in 6 weeks.

Music: Mostly **rock**, **pop**, **family** and **folk**; also **country** and **jazz**. Current acts include Richie Havens (folk singer), Leo Kottke (guitarist/composer), Emmylou Harris (country songwriter), Tom Chapin (kids' performer and folksinger) and John Forster (satirist).

◖ **RUSTRON MUSIC PRODUCTIONS**, Send all artist song submissions to: 1156 Park Lane, West Palm Beach FL 33417-5957. (561)686-1354. E-mail: gordon-whims@juno.com. Main Office: 42 Barrack Hill Rd., Ridgefield CT 06877. ("Main office does not review new material—only South Florida Branch office does.") Executive Director: Rusty Gordon. Artist Consultants: Rusty Gordon and Davilyn Whims. Composition Management: Ron Caruso. Management firm, booking agency, music publisher (Rustron Music Publishers/BMI and Whimsong Publishing/ASCAP), record company and record producer. Estab. 1970. Represents individuals, groups and songwriters; currently handles 20 acts. Receives 10-30% commission. Reviews material for acts.

How to Contact: *Call first to discuss submission.* Send cassette with 3-6 songs (CD/cassette produced for sale preferred). Provide typed lyric or lead sheet for every song in the submission. If seeking management, press kit should include cover letter, bio, demo tape/CD, typed lyric sheets and press clippings. "SASE required for all correspondence." Responds in 4 months.

Music: Mostly **blues** (**country folk/urban**, **Southern**), **country** (**rock**, **blues**, **progressive**), **easy listening**, **Cabaret**, **soft rock** (**ballads**), **women's music**, **R&B**, **folk/rock**; also **New Age instrumentals** and **New Age folk fusion**. Current acts include Jayne Margo-Reby (folk rock), Star Smiley (country), Robin Plitt (historical folk), Lisa Cohen (Cabaret/pop/acapella), Song on A Whim (folk/world music), Jeremy White (yankee reggae) and Boomslang Swampsinger (Florida folk).

Tips: "Send cover letter, typed lyric sheets for all songs. Carefully mix demo, don't drown the vocals, 3-6 songs in a submission. Prefer a for-sale CD made to sell at gigs. Send photo if artist is seeking marketing and/or production assistance. Very strong hooks, definitive melody, evolved concepts, unique and unpredictable themes. Flesh out a performing sound unique to the artist. Stage presence a must!"

✓ ◙ **SAFFYRE MANAGEMENT**, 12801 Lopez Canyon Rd., Kagel Canyon CA 91342. (818)842-4368. E-mail: ebsaffyre@yahoo.com. **Contact:** Esta G. Bernstein, president. Management firm. Estab. 1990. Represents individual artists, groups and songwriters from anywhere; currently handles 3 acts. Receives 15% commission.

How to Contact: *Call first and obtain permission to submit.* If seeking management, press kit should include cover letter, bio, photo, cassette with 3-4 songs and lyric sheets. Does not return material. Responds in 2 weeks only if interested.

Music: Mostly **alternative/modern rock** and **top 40**. "We work only with bands and solo artists who write their own material; our main objective is to obtain recording deals and contracts, while advising our artists on their careers and business relationships." Current artists include Scott Moss (top 40 singer/songwriter), Will Postell (alternative singer/songwriter) and Shoelessjoe (adult alternative group).

Ⓝ ◖ **ST. JOHN ARTISTS**, P.O. Box 619, Neenah WI 54957-0619. (920)722-2222. Fax: (920)725-2405. Website: www.st.john-artists.com/. **Contact:** Jon St. John and Gary Coquoz, agents. Booking agency. Estab. 1977. Represents local and regional individual artists and groups; currently handles 20 acts. Receives 15-20% commission. Reviews material for acts.

How to Contact: *Call first and obtain permission to submit.* Prefers CD or VHS videocassette. If seeking management, press kit should include cover letter, bio, photo, demo tape/CD, video and résumé. Include SASE.

Music: Mostly **rock** and **MOR**. Current acts include Vic Ferrari Band (variety rock), The Groove Hogs (R&B/pop/classic rock), Boom Candle (light rock/classic rock), Competition ('60s-2002), Jegani (r&b/dance) and Shaken Not Stirred (r&b/top 40/dance/'60s-'90s).

◙ SA'MALL MANAGEMENT, P.O. Box 8442, Universal City CA 91608. (310)317-4338. Fax: (818)506-8534. E-mail: samusa@aol.com. Website: www.pplzmi.com. **Contact:** Ted Steele, vice president of talent. Management firm, music publisher (Pollybyrd Publications) and record company (PPL Entertainment Group). Estab. 1990. Represents individual artists, groups and songwriters from anywhere; currently handles 10 acts. Receives 10-25% commission. Reviews material for acts.
How to Contact: *E-mail first and obtain permission to submit.* Prefers cassette with 2 songs and lyric and lead sheet. If seeking management, press kit should include picture, bio and tape. Include SASE. Responds in 2 months.
Music: All types. Current acts include Riki Hendrix (rock), Buddy Wright (blues), Fhyne, Suzette Cuseo, The Band Aka, LeJenz, B.D. Fuoco, Jay Sattiewhite, Paul Allen and J.R. Perry.

N◙ CRAIG SCOTT ENTERTAINMENT, P.O. Box 1722, Paramus NJ 07653-1722. (201)587-1066. Fax: (201)587-0481. E-mail: scott@craigscott.com. Website: www.craigscott.com. Management firm. Estab. 1985. Represents individual artists and/or groups from anywhere. Commission varies. Reviews material for acts.
How to Contact: Submit demo tape by mail. Unsolicited submissions are OK. Prefers cassette or CD. If seeking management, press kit should include tape/CD, bio, picture, relevant press. Does not return material. Responds in 1 month.
Music: All styles.

N◙ SDM, INC., 740 N. La Brea Ave., 1st Floor, Los Angeles CA 90038. (323)933-9977. Fax: (323)933-0633. E-mail: laurent_besencon@sdmmusic.com. **Contact:** Laurent Besencon. Management firm, music publisher and record company. Estab. 1979. Represents individual artists, groups, songwriters from anywhere. Reviews material for acts.
How to Contact: Prefers cassette with lyric sheet. Does not return material. Responds in 3 months.
Music: Current acts include Joe, Alicia Keyes and Luther Vandross.

◙ SEA CRUISE PRODUCTIONS, INC., P.O. Box 1875, Gretna LA 70054-1875. (504)392-4615. Fax: (504)392-4512. E-mail: kenkeene@aol.com. Website: www.frankieford.com. **Contact:** Ken Keene, president/general manager. Management firm, booking agency, music publisher (Sea Cruise Music/BMI), record company (Briarmeade Records) and record producer (Sea Cruise Productions). Estab. 1970. Represents individual artists, groups and songwriters from anywhere; currently handles 12 acts. Receives 15% commission. Reviews material for acts.
How to Contact: Submit demo tape by mail. Unsolicited submissions are OK. Prefers cassette or VHS videocassette with 5-6 songs and lyric or lead sheet. If seeking management, press kit should include cassette, videocassette, CD, publicity photos, bio and press clipping, cover letter, résumé and lyric sheets. Does not return material. "No phone calls." Responds in 2 months "if we are interested in the act."
Music: Mostly **nostalgia '50s/'60s**, **country rock** and **R&B**; also **ballads**, **double entendre** and **novelty songs**. "Most of our acts are '50s, '60s and '70s artists, all of whom have had million selling records, and who are still very active on the concert/night club circuit." Current acts include Frankie Ford (legendary rock 'n' roll singer/pianist), Troy Shondell (singer/songwriter), Jean Knight (Grammy nominated R&B singer), Narvel Felts (country/rockabilly legend) and Dale & Grace (Louisiana's #1 duo).

SENDING TO A COUNTRY other than your own? Be sure to send International Reply Coupons (IRCs) instead of stamps for replies or return of your materials.

SERGE ENTERTAINMENT GROUP, P.O. Box 672216, Marietta GA 30006-0037. (770)850-9560. Fax: (770)850-9646. E-mail: sergeent@aol.com. Website: www.serge.org. **Contact:** Sandy Serge, president. Management and PR firm and song publishers. Estab. 1987. Represents individual artists, groups, songwriters from anywhere; currently handles 15 acts. Receives 15-25% commission. Reviews materials for acts.

How to Contact: *E-mail first for permission to submit.* Submit demo tape or CD by mail. Unsolicited submissions are OK. Prefers cassette or CD with 4 songs and lyric sheet. If seeking management, press kit should include 8×10 photo, bio, cover letter, lyric sheets, max of 4 press clips, VHS videocassette, performance schedule and CD. "All information submitted must include name, address and phone number on each item." Does not return material. Responds in 6 weeks if interested.

Music: Mostly **rock**, **pop** and **country**; also **New Age**. Works primarily with singer/songwriters and bands. Current acts include Dominic Gaudious (New Age), Tom Pau (rock) and Derrik Jordan (A/C).

PHILL SHUTE MANAGEMENT PTY. LTD., Box 273, Dulwich Hill NSW 2203 Australia. Phone: +61 2 95692152. Fax: +61 2 95692152. Website: www.big-rock.com.au. **Contact:** Phill Shute, CEO. Management firm, booking agency and record company (Big Rock Records). Estab. 1979. Represents local individual artists and groups; currently handles 8 acts. Receives 10% commission. Reviews material for acts.

How to Contact: Submit demo tape by mail. Unsolicited submissions are OK. Prefers cassette with 4 songs and lyric sheet. If seeking management, press kit should include cover letter, bio, photo, demo tape/CD, press clippings and résumé. Does not return material. Responds in 1 month.

Music: Mostly **rock**, **pop** and **R&B**; also **country rock**. Works primarily with rock bands, pop vocalists and blues acts (band and vocalists). Current acts include Phill Simmons (country), Two R More (pop/rock) and Now Hear This (rock).

Tips: "Make all submissions well organized (e.g., bio, photo and experience of the act). List areas in which the act would like to work, complete details for contact."

SIDDONS & ASSOCIATES, 584 N. Larchmont Blvd., Hollywood CA 90004. (323)462-6156. Fax: (323)462-2076. E-mail: siddons@earthlink.net. **Contact:** Julia Mays. President: Bill Siddons. Management firm. Estab. 1972. Represents individual artists and groups from anywhere; currently handles 2 acts. Receives 15-20% commission. Reviews material for acts.

How to Contact: *Write first and obtain permission to submit.* Prefers CD or VHS videocassette with 3 songs and lyric sheet. If seeking management, press kit should include cassette of 3 songs, lyric sheet, VHS videocassette if available, biography, past credits and discography. Does not return material. Responds in 3 months.

Music: All styles. Current acts include Elayne Boosler (comedian) and Kurt Bestor (singer/songwriter).

SIEGEL ENTERTAINMENT LTD., 101-1648 W. Seventh Ave., Vancouver British Columbia V6J 1S5 Canada. (604)736-3896. Fax: (604)736-3464. E-mail: siegelent@telus.net. **Contact:** Robert Siegel, president. Management firm and booking agency. Estab. 1975. Represents individual artists, groups and songwriters from anywhere; currently handles more than 100 acts (for bookings). Receives 15-20% commission. Reviews material for acts.

How to Contact: Submit demo CD by mail. Unsolicited submissions are OK. Prefers CD, cassette or VHS videocassette with songlist. If seeking management, press kit should include 8×10 and cassette and/or video. Does not return material. Responds in 1 month.

Music: Mostly **rock**, **pop** and **country**; also **specialty** and **children's**. Current acts include Johnny Ferreira & The Swing Machine, Lee Aaron, Kenny Blues Boss Wayne (boogie) and Tim Brecht (pop/children's).

SILVER BOW MANAGEMENT, 6260 130 St., Surrey, British Columbia V3X 1R6 Canada. (604)572-4232. Fax: (604)572-4252. E-mail: saddles@telus.net. Website: http://silverbow.on theweb.nu. President: Grant Lucas. CEO: Candice James. Management firm, music publisher (Saddlestone Publishing, Silver Bow Publishing), record company (Saddlestone Records) and record producer

(Silver Bow Productions, Krazy Cat Productions). Estab. 1988. Represents individual artists, groups, songwriters from anywhere; currently handles 8 acts. Receives 10% commission. Reviews material for acts.

How to Contact: Submit demo tape by mail. Unsolicited submissions are OK. Prefers cassette with 3 songs and lyric sheet. If seeking management, press kit should include 8 × 10 photo, bio, cover letter, demo tape or CD with lyric sheets, press clippings, video, résumé and current itinerary. "Visuals are everything—submit accordingly." Does not return material. Responds in 2 months.

Music: Mostly **country**, **pop** and **rock**; also **R&B**, **Christian** and **alternative**. Works primarily with bands, vocalists and singer/songwriters. Current acts include Darrell Meyers (country singer/ songwriter), Nite Moves (variety band), Mark Vance (country/pop) and Stan Giles (country).

[N] SIMMONS MANAGEMENT GROUP, P.O. Box 747, Oak Island NC 28465. (919)278-1033. Fax: (919)278-7982. E-mail: HarrySimmons@HarrySimmons.com. President: Harry Simmons. Management firm and music publisher. Represents producers, artists, groups and songwriters; currently handles 4 acts. Receives 15-20% commission. Reviews material for acts.

How to Contact: *Write or call first and obtain permission to submit.* Prefers cassette, CD or VHS videocassette of performance with 3-6 songs and lyric sheet; also submit promotional material, photos and clippings. "Videocassette does not have to be professional. Any information helps." If seeking management, include 3-song demo (tape or CD) and photos in press kit. Does not return material. Responds in 2 months.

Music: Mostly **modern pop**; also **modern rock**, **rock**, **metal**, **R&B**, **industrial**, **country** and **top 40/pop**. Works primarily with "original music recording acts or those that aspire to be." Current acts include Don Dixon (producer, songwriter and recording artist), Marti Jones (recording artist) and Mark Williams (producer).

[O] T. SKORMAN PRODUCTIONS, INC., 3660 Maguire Blvd., Suite 250, Orlando FL 32803. (407)895-3000. Fax: (407)895-1422. E-mail: ted@talentagency.com. Website: www.talentagency.c om. **Contact:** Ted Skorman, president. Management firm and booking agency. Estab. 1983. Represents groups; currently handles 40 acts. Receives 10-25% commission. Reviews material for acts.

How to Contact: *Write or call first for permission to submit.* Prefers cassette with 3 songs, or videocassette of no more than 15 minutes. "Live performance—no trick shots or editing tricks. We want to be able to view act as if we were there for a live show." If seeking management, press kit should include cover letter, bio, photo and demo tape/CD. Does not return material. Responds in 2 months.

Music: Mostly **top 40**, **techno**, **dance**, **MOR** and **pop**. Works primarily with high-energy dance acts, recording acts, and top 40 bands. Current acts include Steph Carse (pop) and Michael Behm (rock).

Tips: "We have many pop recording acts and are looking for commercial material for their next albums."

[N] [O] GARY SMELTZER PRODUCTIONS, 603 W. 13th #2A, Austin TX 78701. (512)478-6020. Fax: (512)478-8979. E-mail: gsptalent@aol.com. **Contact:** Gary Smeltzer, president. Management firm and booking agency. Estab. 1967. Represents individual artists and groups from anywhere. Currently handles 20 acts. "We book about 100 different bands each year—none are exclusive." Receives 20% commission. Reviews material for acts.

How to Contact: Submit demo tape by mail. Unsolicited submissions are OK. Prefers cassette, videocassette or CD. If seeking management, press kit should include cover letter, résumé, cassette or CD, bio, picture, lyric sheets, press clippings and video. Does not return material. Responds in 1 month.

Music: Mostly **alternative**, **R&B** and **country**. Current acts include Ro Tel & the Hot Tomatoes (nostalgic '60s showband).

Tips: "We prefer performing songwriters who can gig their music as a solo or group."

[O] SOUND MANAGEMENT DIRECTION, 152-18 Union Turnpike, Flushing NY 11367. (718)969-0166. Fax: (718)969-8914. E-mail: sounddirection@aol.com. **Contact:** Bob Currie, president. Management firm, consultant, music publisher (Sun Face Music/ASCAP, Shaman Drum/BMI)

insider report

A remarkable songwriter teaches others how it's done

Harriet Schock, a Hollywood, California-based songwriter, performer, teacher and author, theorizes that her multi-disciplinary career was initiated when she skipped fourth grade. "I think I've been trying to catch up ever since," she explains. "Everything I've started took me a while to catch up and actually do. Yes, I had a hit early in my career, but I actually came into my own as a writer much later." The hit Schock refers to is "That Ain't No Way to Treat a Lady," a gold/platinum record and a Grammy-nominated song recorded by Helen Reddy.

Schock, signed to Twentieth Century Fox as a recording artist in the Seventies, continues to record today, delivering such recent releases as *American Romance* and *Rosebud*. "I have people discovering me on the Internet with the new albums and the new

Harriet Schock

fans discovering the old stuff. It's cute how the Internet ties your career up and presents you to be much more important that you really are," she laughs.

Film and television projects are integral pieces of Schock's songwriting successes. Early on she began collaborating with film composers who utilized her skills as a lyricist. Eventually she created songs in their entirety for films. "I love writing for picture," Schock relates. "I like the whole process of using songs to say something that isn't said by the script of the character. When you have the wavelength of music to communicate your message, you can say something that can never be said by the medium of film."

When she was first asked to develop a college course on songwriting at the University of Southern California in Los Angeles, Schock's response was, "Songwriting can't be taught." She recalls, "So they decided not to teach it. Then the next year they asked me again and I said, 'OK.'" She decided the best way to teach was to trick her students into doing what she did naturally. "Two things in a song make an emotional impact. One is telling the truth—not the facts—but the truth. From any situation you're in, you can pull out a universal truth that's worth communicating. But telling the truth is only half the tale; you have to acquire the craft of songwriting. I have a ten-step course that's sort of the Berlitz of songwriting. I teach the craft very quickly. If students just do it according to the steps they'll get it. But if you tell the truth without craft it becomes very self-indulgent and listeners will say 'I don't need to know that much.' With craft, listeners will have their own experience within your personal statement. And so a song will become universal."

Schock now teaches professional—and soon to be professional—songwriters via in-person and correspondence courses. "I teach people who have hit a brick wall," she states. "They want it streamlined; they want the experience of being inspired, but they want it consistently, every time. It's a step-by-step process. One little gradient is easier to confront rather than sitting down and trying to use ten skills at once. People try to get the idea for a song, make it match a melody, have a certain rhythm, have the rhythm of the melody—all these disparate units they're trying to do at one time. They're not fluent enough. I give students one little step they can easily do, then the next steps. Pretty soon they have a song, and their first song is generally better than most people's songs after ten years."

She also believes the process of teaching is a two-way street when it comes to sharpening her own personal grasp of songwriting. "When you teach something you really learn it, so I learn from my students," she professes. "I am so much a better writer now than I used to be, back when everyone discovered me and all was afire." If there are any frustrations for Schock, it's that her other activities often keep her from writing songs herself. "I wish I could make myself write more but I'm so busy," she confides. "In this town it's not just writing, but promoting."

And it's not just Hollywood hype. As a charter member of the Los Angeles music community, Schock has served on innumerable boards and committees for such organizations as the National Academy of Recording Arts & Sciences (NARAS) and Los Angeles Women in Music (LAWIM) for whom she produces a regular show dubbed the "Soiree." She's also arranged events for other non-profit organizations and charities in addition to donating her time as a performer.

Although co-writing is a staple of Schock's creative universe, she says it's not likely she'll sit down in a room and hammer out lyrics. "I'm like a rat with my cheese," she says, "I've got to go off and take whatever my co-writer gave me to get to the place where I need to be. It's very rare that I really write lyrics in the room with somebody. I can work out melodies but I still have to schedule that time for lyrics, too. It's a discipline to do what really needs to be done. What's important is this writing thing, and I have people in my life to remind me. I keep statistics on my production, and I give myself more points for writing than anything else."

What changes has Schock observed in the publishing and songwriting worlds since her emergence? "What I find is that people are bypassing the industry altogether," she says. "I had a fan who put up an MP3 and I thought, 'This is a game I definitely want to play.' But if you're going to bypass the industry and go directly to the public then you really have to be good. A lot of people might think 'The record companies don't want me so I'm going to bypass them.' You have to be good enough—without paying everyone $4 in promotion money to buy a record—to get to the consumer without the hype. So you better have something to say that people want to hear."

What about the trend of writer/producers and artists who have a hand in every song they record? "Songwriting has always been market driven," attests Schock. "What's happening is that everyone wants a piece of the pie. So often there will be one song on an album that's great, written by a real writer. Then the artist, the producer, or a combination thereof will write either with other people or themselves. (Hit songwriters) Barry Mann and Cynthia Weil have said that a song is only as good as the weakest of the writers. When you write with an artist and you don't have control—and they can't write—you don't always get the best product. Sometimes it would be better if the artist just got the song and sang it. Some artists are really wonderful, and I don't mean to offend those who are excellent writers. But producers don't necessarily think like songwriters, and a lot of artists want that songwriting money."

Schock believes melodies are vastly underrated in modern music. "When I hear people talk about Nashville as a town where lyrics dominate, what they don't realize is how melody is still the first thing people hear. Yes, lyrics matter, but it is still melody. I have a segment in my book that says, 'A melody is like a pretty girl at a party who will attract attention.' If she's self-centered or stupid, that's the lyrics. A guy won't talk to her for very long if she is self-centered or stupid, but he wouldn't have talked to her at all if she hadn't been cute. Melodies are the wavelength that communication travels on. If it isn't a pleasant one you're not going to let it in."

Her teaching practice has also taught her a lot about the relationship between melodies and lyrics. "I'll ask people to bring me a lyric and tell me why it's great, and it turns out they're really involved with the melody. They'll bring a lyric that says nothing. On the other hand, some writers consider melody anathema—if they have a good melody then people will think they're trying to be commercial. Some rock bands don't want to do melodies with leaps, just small steps."

Distilling her theories into a book, *Becoming Remarkable, For Songwriters and Those Who Love Songs* (Blue Dolphin), Schock has drawn on her duality as both a successful songwriter and a songwriting teacher with advice on everything from finding the space to write to divining ready sources of inspiration. From her text it is evident she has experienced, first-hand, all of the joy and frustrations inherent to songwriters.

As Schock continues to evolve as a teacher and an author, she realizes it's increasingly essential she maintain a connection with her own performing and songwriting career. "It sounds so self-centered, but there are people who are unhappy that I'm not writing," she confesses. "I went through a long period of thinking 'What do I need to write for? I need to teach.' But my fans came out of the woodwork and said, 'We care that you're not writing.' So now I have a new album coming out."

For more information check out www.harrietschock.com

—*Dan Kimpel*

and record producer. Estab. 1986. Represents individual artists and/or groups, songwriters, producers and engineers from anywhere; currently handles 6 acts. Receives 20% commission. Reviews material for acts.
How to Contact: Submit CD by mail. Unsolicited submissions are OK. Prefers CD or VHS video-cassette with 2 songs and lyric sheet. If seeking management, press kit should include 3 song demo, photo and contact information including phone numbers. "If you want material returned, include SASE." Responds in 3 weeks.
Music: Seeking commercial, contemporary and radio-oriented **rock**, **dance**, **jazz** and **urban**. Works primarily with singer/songwriters and self-contained bands.
Tips: "We only want your best, and be specific with style. Quality, not quantity."

☑ ◪ **SOUTHEASTERN ATTRACTIONS**, 181 W. Valley Ave., Suite 105, Birmingham AL 35209. (205)942-6600. Fax: (205)942-7700. E-mail: staff@seattractions.com. Website: www.seattract ions.com. **Contact:** Agent. Booking agency. Estab. 1967. Represents groups from anywhere; currently handles 200 acts. Receives 20% commission.
How to Contact: Submit demo tape by mail. Unsolicited submissions are OK. Prefers CD or VHS videocassette. Does not return material. Responds in 1 month.
Music: **Rock**, **alternative**, **oldies**, **country** and **dance**. Works primarily with bands. Current acts include Second Hand Jive (contemporary rock), Telluride (Southern rock), Undergrounders (variety to contemporary), Style Band (Motown/dance), The Connection (Motown/dance), Space Wrangler (Widespread Panic cover band), The Spoons (groove band), Skydog Gypsy (groove band) and Horse (rock).

◪ **SP TALENT ASSOCIATES**, P.O. Box 475184, Garland TX 75047. **Contact:** Richard Park, talent coordinator. Management firm and booking agency. Represents individual artists and groups; currently handles 7 acts. Receives 15% commission. Reviews material for acts.

How to Contact: Submit demo tape by mail. Unsolicited submissions are OK. Prefers VHS video-cassette with several songs. Send photo and bio. Does not return material. Responds as soon as possible.

Music: Mostly **rock**, **nostalgia rock** and **country**; also **specialty acts** and **folk/blues**. Works primarily with vocalists and self-contained groups. Current acts include Joe Hardin Brown (country), Rock It! (nostalgia), Renewal (rock group) and Juan Madera & the Supple Grain Seeds.

SPHERE GROUP ONE, P.O. Box 991, Far Hills NJ 07931-0991. (908)781-1650. Fax: (908)781-1693. E-mail: spheregroupone@att.net. President: Tony Zarrella. Talent Manager: Louisa Pazienza. Management firm and record producer. Estab. 1987. Represents individual artists and groups from anywhere; currently handles 5 acts. Receives 20-25% commission.

How to Contact: Send all new submissions to Vision 2000. Submit demo tape by mail. Unsolicited submissions are OK. Prefers CD, cassette or VHS videocassette with 3-5 songs. All submissions must include cover letter, lyric sheets, tape/CD, photo, bio and all press. "Due to large number of submissions we can only respond to those artists which we may consider working with." Does not return material

Music: Mostly **pop/rock**, **pop/country** and **New Age**; also **R&B**. Works primarily with bands and solo singer/songwriters. Current acts include 4 of Hearts (pop/rock), Frontier 9 (pop/rock), Viewpoint (experimental) and Bombay Green (hybrid pop).

Tips: "Develop and create your own style, focus on goals and work as a team and maintain good chemistry with all artists and business relationships."

THE SPOON AGENCY L.L.C., P.O. Box 1539, Wimberley TX 78676. (512)301-7117. Fax: (888)647-4010. E-mail: steve@spoonagency.com. **Contact:** Steve Gladson, managing partner. Management firm and booking agency. Estab. 1969. Represents individual artists, songwriters and groups from anywhere; currently handles 6 acts. Receives 10-20% commission. Reviews material for acts.

How to Contact: Submit demo tape by mail. Unsolicited submissions OK. Prefers cassette, video-cassette or CD and lyric sheet. If seeking management, press kit should include cover letter, demo tape/CD, lyric sheets, press clippings, video, résumé, picture and bio. Does not return material. Responds in 1 month.

Music: Mostly **alternative rock**, **country** and **R&B**; also **classic rock**, **folk** and **Americana**. Works primarily with singer/songwriters and original bands. Current acts include Lou Cabaza (songwriter/producer/manager), Duck Soup (band) and Gaylan Ladd (songwriter/singer).

Tips: "Remember why you are in this biz. The art comes first."

STAIRCASE PROMOTION, P.O. Box 211, East Prairie MO 63845. (573)649-2211. **Contact:** Tommy Loomas, president. Vice President: Joe Silver. Management firm, music publisher (Lineage Publishing) and record company (Capstan Record Production). Estab. 1975. Represents individual artists and groups from anywhere; currently handles 6 acts. Receives 25% commission. Reviews material for acts.

How to Contact: Submit demo tape by mail. Unsolicited submissions are OK. Prefers cassette with 3 songs and lyric sheet. If seeking management, press kit should include bio, photo, audio cassette and/or video and press reviews, if any. "Be as professional as you can." Include SASE. Responds in 2 months.

**FOR EXPLANATIONS OF THESE SYMBOLS,
SEE THE INSIDE FRONT AND BACK COVERS OF THIS BOOK.**

Music: Mostly **country**, **pop** and **easy listening**; also **rock**, **gospel** and **alternative**. Current acts include Skidrow Joe (country comedian, on Capstan Records), Vicarie Arcoleo (pop singer, on Treasure Coast Records) and Scarlett Britoni (pop singer on Octagon Records).

◐ **STANDER ENTERTAINMENT**, 6309 Ben Ave., N. Hollywood CA 91606. Phone/fax: (818)769-6365. E-mail: stander@earthlink.net. **Contact:** Jacqueline Stander, manager. Management firm, music publisher (DocRon Publishing), record company (Soaring Records) and consulting firm. Estab. 1970. Represents local individual artists, groups, film composers and songwriters; currently handles 6 acts. Receives 15% commission. Charges $50/hour consulting fee. Reviews material for acts.
How to Contact: *Call first and obtain permission to submit.* Prefers cassette or VHS videocassette with 3-5 songs and lyric sheet. If seeking management, press kit should include photo, bio, press publicity, CD or cassette. Include SASE. Responds in 3 weeks.
Music: Mostly **jazz**, **pop** and **R&B** (no rap); also **world music** and **Broadway**. Works primarily with national recording artists, film composers and singer/songwriters. Current acts include Bill Cunliffe (jazz pianist/producer), Freddie Ravel (contemporary Latin jazz keyboardist) and Lauren Wood (vocalist/songwriter).
Tips: "Always looking for long term professionals who have worked to establish themselves in their market, yet want to go to the next level. For those who have something to offer and are just starting out, I am available for consulting by phone or in person. Please call for submission request."

◐ **STARKRAVIN' MANAGEMENT**, 20501 Ventura Blvd., 217, Woodland Hills CA 91364. (818)587-6801. Fax: (818)587-6802. E-mail: bcmclane@aol.com. **Contact:** B.C. McLane, Esq. Management and law firm. Estab. 1994. Represents individual artists, groups and songwriters. Receives 20% commission (management); $175/hour as attorney.
How to Contact: Submit demo tape by mail. Unsolicited submissions are OK. Does not return material. Responds in 1 month.
Music: Mostly **rock**, **pop** and **R&B**. Works primarily with bands.

◖ **STEVENS & COMPANY MANAGEMENT**, P.O. Box 6368, Corpus Christi TX 78411. (361)888-7311. Fax: (361)888-7360. E-mail: steveco@flash.net. Website: www.fidelHernandez.co. **Contact:** Matt Stevens, owner. Management firm. Estab. 1995. Represents individual artists from anywhere. Currently handles 3 acts. Receives 20% commission. Reviews material for acts.
How to Contact: Submit demo tape by mail. Unsolicited submissions are OK. Prefers cassette or CD with lyric sheet. Include SASE. Responds in 3 weeks.
Music: Mostly **Latin**, **Mexican regional** and **country**. Works primarily with singers and individual artists. Current acts include Fidel Hernandez (country/MCA).
Tips: "Send material every time you have something new, always leave phone number on tapes."

◐ **STORMIN' NORMAN PRODUCTIONS**, 2 Front, Red Bank NJ 07701. (732)741-8733. (732)741-5353. E-mail: normanseldin@aol.com. Website: www.storminnormanproductions.com. **Contact:** Norman Seldin, Owner. Management firm, booking agency, music publisher (Noisy Joy Music/BMI) and record company (Ivory Records). Estab. 1967. Represents individual artists, groups and songwriters from anywhere; currently handles 6 acts. Receives 15-20% commission. Reviews material for acts.
How to Contact: Submit demo tape by mail. Unsolicited submissions are OK. Prefers cassette with 2-4 songs and lyric sheet. If seeking management, press kit should include demo cassette with cover and original songs, photo, song list, appearance credits, home base area, phone and address. Include SASE. Responds in 5 weeks.
Music: Mostly **country, rock** and **reggae**; also **soft rock, dynamic blues** and **folk**. Current acts include Stormin' Norman Band (R&B/nostalgia/adult contemporary), Steel Breeze (Caribbean/Latin/blues) and Bobby Vac & Everyone (adult contemporary).

✿ ✔ ◐ **STRICTLY FORBIDDEN ARTISTS**, 320 Avenue Rd., Suite 144, Toronto, Ontario M4V 2H3 Canada. (416)926-0818. Fax: (416)926-0811. E-mail: creative_agency@yahoo.com. Web-

site: http://user.netomia.com/sta/index1.html. **Contact:** Brad Black, vice president of A&R. Management firm, booking agency and record company. Estab. 1986. Represents individual artists and groups from anywhere; currently handles 8 acts. Receives 20-30% commission. Reviews material for acts.
How to Contact: Submit demo CD by mail. Unsolicited submissions are OK. Prefers CD and lyric sheet. If seeking management, press kit should include biography, press clippings, 8 × 10, photo and demo tape/CD. "Once you've sent material, don't call us, we'll call you." Does not return material. Responds in 6 weeks.
Music: Mostly **alternative rock, art rock** and **grindcore**; also **electronic, hip-hop** and **experimental**. Works primarily with performing bands, studio acts and performance artists. Current acts include Sickos (experimental/art-rock), Lazer (coldwave/electronica) and Andy Warhead (punk rock/noise).
Tips: "As long as you have faith in your music, we'll have faith in promoting you and your career."

✔ ◐ SURFACE MANAGEMENT INC., 200 Shearwater Court W., Suite #23, Jersey City NJ 10008. Phone/fax: (201)369-9784. E-mail: carolann@surfacemgmt.com. Website: www.surfacemgmt .com. **Contact:** Patti Beninati, president. Management firm. Estab. 1990. Represents local individual solo artists and groups; currently handles 3 acts. Receives 20% commission. Reviews material for acts.
How to Contact: Submit demo tape by mail or website. Unsolicited submissions are OK. Prefers CD/CDR with 5 songs and lyric sheet. If seeking management, press kit should include cover letter, bio, photo, demo, lyric sheets and press clippings. Does not return material. Responds in 1 month.
Music: Mostly **alternative pop** and **heavy rock**. Current acts include Nick Douglas, Robby and Impression.

⬛ ○ T.J. BOOKER LTD., P.O. Box 969, Rossland, British Columbia V0G 1Y0 Canada. (250)362-7795. E-mail: winterland@netidea.com. **Contact:** Tom Jones, owner. Management firm, booking agency and music publisher. Estab. 1976. Represents individual artists, groups and songwriters from anywhere; currently handles 6 acts. Receives 15% commission. Reviews material for acts.
How to Contact: Submit demo tape by mail. Unsolicited submissions are OK. Prefers CD, cassette or videocassette with 3 songs. If seeking management, include demo tape or CD, picture, cover letter and bio in press kit. Does not return material. Responds in 1 month.
Music: Mostly **MOR**, **crossover**, **rock**, **pop** and **country**. Works primarily with vocalists, show bands, dance bands and bar bands. Current acts include Kirk Orr (folk/country), Mike Hamilton (rock/blues) and Larry Hayton (rock/blues).

✔ ◐ T.L.C. BOOKING AGENCY, 37311 N. Valley Rd., Chattaroy WA 99003. (509)292-2201. Fax: (509)292-2205. E-mail: tlcagent@ix.netcom.com. Website: www.tlcagency.com. **Contact:** Tom or Carrie Lapsansky, agent/owners. Booking agency. Estab. 1970. Represents individual artists and groups from anywhere; currently handles 17 acts. Receives 10-15% commission. Reviews material for acts.
How to Contact: *Call first and obtain permission to submit.* Prefers cassette with 3-4 songs. Does not return material. Responds in 3 weeks.
Music: Mostly **rock**, **country** and **variety**; also **comedians** and **magicians**. Works primarily with bands, singles and duos. Current acts include Nobody Famous (variety), Menagerie (variety-duo) and Soul Patrol (variety/top 40).

⊠ ○ TAKE OUT MANAGEMENT, 5605 Woodman Ave. #206, Van Nuys CA 91401. (818)901-1122. Fax: (818)901-6513. E-mail: howie@howiewood.com. Website: www.howiewood.com. **Contact:** Craig Parker, artist relations. Management firm. Estab. 1985. Represents individual artists, groups and songwriters from anywhere; currently handles 4 acts. Receives 15-20% commission. Reviews material for acts.
How to Contact: Submit demo tape by mail. Unsolicited submissions are OK. Prefers cassette or CD with any number of songs and lyric sheet. If seeking management, press kit should include tape or CD, picture, bio and cover letter. Does not return material. Responds in 1 week.
Music: Mostly **pop**, **A/C** and **rock**; also **r&b** and **dance**. Works primarily with singer/songwriters, arrangers and bands. Current acts include Dan Hill (A/C) and Rodney Sheldon (r&b).

TAS MUSIC CO./DAVE TASSE ENTERTAINMENT, N2467 Knollwood Dr., Lake Geneva WI 53147-9731. E-mail: baybreeze@idcnet.com. Website: www.baybreezerecords.com. **Contact:** David Tasse. Booking agency, record company and music publisher. Represents artists, groups and songwriters; currently handles 21 acts. Receives 10-20% commission. Reviews material for acts.
How to Contact: Submit demo tape by mail. Unsolicited submissions are OK. Prefers cassette with 2-4 songs and lyric sheet. Include performance videocassette if available. If seeking management, press kit should include tape, bio and photo. Does not return material. Responds in 3 weeks.
Music: Mostly **pop** and **jazz**; also **dance**, **MOR**, **rock**, **soul** and **top 40**. Works primarily with show and dance bands. Current acts include Max Kelly (philosophic rock) and L.J. Young (rap).

TEXAS SOUNDS ENTERTAINMENT, P.O. Box 1644, Dickinson TX 77535. (281)337-2473. Fax: (281)534-1127. E-mail: mikes@texas-sounds.com. Website: www.texas-sounds.com. **Contact:** Mike Sandberg or George M. DeJesus, co-owners. Management firm, booking agency. Estab. 1980. Represents individual artists, groups and songwriters from anywhere. Currently handles 60 acts. Receives 10% commission.
How to Contact: *Write first and obtain permission to submit.* Prefers cassette with 3-4 songs and lyric and/or lead sheet. If seeking management, press kit should include bio, photo, accomplishments, demo tape. Does not return material.
Music: Mostly **country**, **R&B** and **Latin pop**. Works primarily with bands, orchestras, singer/songwriters. Current acts include Johnny Lee (country singer), Chris Chitsey (country singer/songwriter), Patrick Murphy (country singer/songwriter), Hamilton Loomis (R&B singer/musician) and Jerry Hart (country).

TIGER'S EYE ENTERTAINMENT MANAGEMENT & CONSULTING, 1876 Memorial Drive, Green Bay WI 54303. (920)494-1588. **Contact:** Thomas C. Berndt, manager/CEO. Management firm and record producer. Estab. 1992. Represents individual artists, groups and songwriters from anywhere; currently handles 3 acts. Receives 20% commission. Reviews material for acts.
How to Contact: Submit demo tape by mail. Unsolicited submissions are OK. Prefers cassette or VHS videocassette with 3-4 songs and lyric sheet. If seeking management, press kit should include tape, lyric sheet, photo, relevant press and bio. "Artist should follow up with a call after 2 weeks." Does not return material. Responds in 2 weeks.
Music: Mostly **alternative**, **hard rock** and **R&B**; also **pop**, **rap** and **gothic groove**. Works primarily with vocalists, singer/songwriters and fresh alternative grunge. Current acts include Fahenheit 420 (alternative/hard rock), Arlo Leach (folksinger) and Lethal Injection (rap).

A TOTAL ACTING EXPERIENCE, 5353 Topanga Canyon Blvd., Suite 220, Woodland Hills CA 91364-1738. **Contact:** Paul Fidele, agency director. Talent agency. Estab. 1984. Represents vocalists, lyricists, composers and groups; currently handles 30 acts. Receives 10% commission. Reviews material for acts. Agency License: TA-0698.
How to Contact: Submit demo tape by mail. Unsolicited submissions are OK. Prefers cassette or VHS videocassette with 3-5 songs and lyric or lead sheets. Please include a revealing "self talk" at the end of your tape. "Singers or groups who write their own material must submit a VHS videocassette with photo and résumé." If seeking management, press kit should include VHS videotape, five 8×10 photos, cover letter, professional résumé, bio, demo tape/CD, lyric sheets, press clippings and business card. Does not return material. Responds in 3 months only if interested. "Please include your e-mail address."
Music: Mostly **top 40/pop**, **jazz**, **blues**, **country**, **R&B**, **dance** and **MOR**; also "theme songs for new films, TV shows and special projects."
Tips: "No calls please. We will respond via your SASE. Your business skills must be strong. Please use a *new/fresh* tape and keep vocals up front. We welcome young, sincere talent who can give total

---

TO HELP YOU UNDERSTAND and use the information in these listings, see "How to Use *Songwriter's Market* to Get Your Songs Heard," on page 5.

commitment, and most important, *loyalty*, for a long-term relationship. We are seeking female vocalists (a la Streisand or Whitney Houston) who can write their own material, for a major label recording contract. Your song's story line must be as refreshing as the words you skillfully employ in preparing to build your well-balanced, orchestrated, climactic last note! Try to eliminate old, worn-out, dull, trite rhymes. A new way to write/compose or sing an old song/tune will qualify your originality and professional standing. We welcome young fresh talent who appreciate old fashioned agency nurturing, and strong guidance, in return, your honesty, commitment and growth."

N ○ TRANSATLANTIC MANAGEMENT, P.O. Box 2831, Tucson AZ 85702. (520)881-5880. Fax: (520)881-8001. E-mail: engcathy@euphoria.org. Website: www.rivergraphics.com/transmgt. Owner: English Cathy. A&R: Gina Inman. Management firm. Estab. 1979. Represents individual artists, groups and songwriters from anywhere; currently handles 4 acts. Receives 20% commission. Reviews material for acts.
How to Contact: Submit demo tape by mail. Unsolicited submissions are OK. If seeking management, press kit should include tape/CD/bio/photo. Does not return material. Responds in 6 months.
Music: Mostly **all types** from **New Age to country to hard rock**. Current acts include Kathi McDonald (rock blues singer), Mary Ann Price (jazz singer), Mary Godfrey (singer/songwriter) and Afan (Celtic music).

N ◐ TRIANGLE TALENT, INC., 10424 Watterson, Louisville KY 40299. (502)267-5466. Fax: (502)267-8244. Website: www.triangletalent.com. **Contact:** David H. Snowden, president. Booking agency. Represents artists and groups; currently handles 85 acts. Receives 10-20% commission. Reviews material for acts.
How to Contact: Submit demo tape by mail. Unsolicited submissions are OK. Prefers CD, cassette or VHS videocassette with 2-4 songs and lyric sheet. If seeking management, press kit should include photo, cassette of at least 3 songs, and video if possible. Does not return material. Responds in 1 month.
Music: Mostly **rock/top 40** and **country**. Current acts include Lee Bradley (contemporary country), Karen Kraft (country) and Four Kinsmen (Australian group).

◐ TWENTIETH CENTURY PROMOTIONS, 155 Park Ave., Cranston RI 02905. (401)467-1832. Fax: (401)467-1833. **Contact:** Gil Morse, president. Management firm, booking agency and record producer (20th Century). Estab. 1972. Represents individual artists and groups from anywhere; currently handles 9 acts. Receives 15% commission. Reviews material for acts.
How to Contact: *Call first and obtain permission to submit or to arrange personal interview.* Prefers CD or cassette. If seeking management, press kit should include photo and bio. Does not return material. Responds in 3 weeks.
Music: Mostly **country** and **blues**. Works primarily with individuals and groups. Current acts include Robbin Lynn, Charlie Brown's Costars and Bobby Buris Pickett (Monster Mash).
Tips: "Don't give up."

N ◐ UMBRELLA ARTISTS MANAGEMENT, INC., 2612 Erie Ave., P.O. Box 8369, Cincinnati OH 45208. (513)871-1500. Fax: (513)871-1510. E-mail: shertzman@cinci.rr.com. Website: www.247virtualmanagement.com. **Contact:** Stan Hertzman, president. Management consultation firm. Represents artists and groups for specific circumstances.
How to Contact: *E-mail or phone with specific need.*
Music: Mostly **progressive**, **rock** and **top 40/pop**. Works with contemporary/progressive pop/rock artists and writers on a per project basis.

◐ UMPIRE ENTERTAINMENT ENTERPRIZES, 1507 Scenic Dr., Longview TX 75604. (903)759-0300. Fax: (903)234-2944. **Contact:** Jerry Haymes, owner/president. Management firm, music publisher (Golden Guitar, Umpire Music) and record company (Enterprize Records). Estab. 1974. Represents individual artists, groups, songwriters and rodeo performers from anywhere; currently handles 6 acts. Receives 15% commission. Reviews material for acts.

How to Contact: *Contact first and obtain permission to submit.* Prefers cassette with lyric and lead sheets. If seeking management, press kit should include cover letter, bio, picture, lyric sheets, video and any recordings. Does not return material. "Submissions become part of files for two years, then disposed of." Responds in 1 month.

Music: Mostly **country, pop** and **gospel**. Artists include Johnny Patterson (instrumentalist), Larry McGuire (instrumentalist) and Crim Family (gospel).

◖ UNIVERSAL MUSIC MARKETING, P.O. Box 2297, Universal City TX 78148. (210)599-0022. E-mail: bswrl8@txdirect.net. Website: www.bswrecords.com. **Contact:** Frank Willson, president. Management firm, record company (BSW Records), booking agency, music publisher and record producer (Frank Wilson). Estab. 1987. Represents individual artists and groups from anywhere; currently handles 12 acts. Receives 15% commission. Reviews material for acts.

How to Contact: Submit demo tape by mail. Unsolicited submissions are OK. Prefers cassette or ¾″ videocassette with 3 songs and lyric sheet. If seeking management, include tape/CD, bio, photo and current activities. Include SASE. Responds in 6 weeks.

Music: Mostly **country** and **light rock**; also **blues** and **jazz**. Works primarily with vocalists, singer/songwriters and bands. Current acts include Candee Land, Darlene Austin, Larry Butler, John Wayne and Sonny Marshall.

◪ VALIANT RECORDS & MANAGEMENT, P.O. Box 180099, Dallas TX 75218. (214)327-5477. Fax: (214)327-4888. E-mail: valiant@master.net. Website: www.master.net/valiant/. President: Andy Stone. Booking agency, music publisher (Brightstone Publishing Co.), record company and record producer (Ed Loftus). Estab. 1971. Represents individual artists, groups and songwriters from anywhere; currently handles 4 acts. Receives 10-20% commission. Reviews material for acts.

How to Contact: Submit demo tape by mail. Unsolicited submissions are OK. Prefers cassette or VHS videocassette with 4 songs, lyric and/or lead sheet, if possible, and bio. "No more than four songs at a time, recorded clearly and professionally, with lyric sheets. I must be able to hear the words and melody. No arty mixes." Include SASE (no guarantees). Responds in 6 weeks, "if we like the material."

Music: Mostly **top 40** and **top 40 country**; also **children's songs** and **novelty**. Works primarily with show groups for booking/managing, songwriters for placing songs and artists for release of new product. Current acts include Vince Vance & The Valiants (pop/pop country), Edward C. Loftus (A/C singer/songwriter), Copralingus (alternative) and Mike Boyd (country/pop singer).

⊕ ✓ ◖ HANS VAN POL MANAGEMENT, Utrechtseweg 3GB, 1381 GS Weesp, Netherlands. Phone: (0)294-413-633. Fax: (0)294-480-844. E-mail: hansvanpol@yahoo.com. Managing Director: Hans Van Pol. A&R/Producer: Jochem Fluitsma. Management firm, consultant (Hans Van Pol Music Consultancy), record company (J.E.A.H.! Records) and music publisher (Blue & White Music). Estab. 1984. Represents regional (Holland/Belgium) individual artists and groups; currently handles 7 acts. Receives 20% commission. Reviews material for acts.

How to Contact: Submit demo tape by mail. Unsolicited submissions are OK. Prefers cassette or VHS videocassette with 3 songs and lyric sheets. If seeking management, press kit should include demo, possible video (VHS/PAL), bio, press clippings, photo and release information. SAE and IRC. Responds in 1 month.

Music: Mostly **MOR**, **dance**: **rap/swing beat/hip house/R&B/soul/c.a.r.** Current acts include George Bakker Selection (MOR), Fluitsma & Van Tÿn (production, commercials, MOR), Tony Scott (rap) and MC Miker "G" (rap/R&B).

◪ RICHARD VARRASSO MANAGEMENT, P.O. Box 387, Fremont CA 94537. (510)792-8910. Fax: (510)792-0891. E-mail: richard@varasso.com. Website: www.varrasso.com. President: Richard Varrasso. A&R: Saul Vigil. Management firm. Estab. 1976. Represents individual artists, groups and songwriters from anywhere; currently handles several acts. Receives 10-20% commission. Reviews material for acts.

How to Contact: Submit demo tape by mail. Unsolicited submissions are OK. Prefers cassette or CD. If seeking management, press kit should include photos, bios, cover letter, cassette, lyric sheets, press clippings, video, résumé and contact numbers. Good kits stand out. Does not return material. Responds in 2 months.

Music: Mostly **rock**, **blues** and **young country**. Works primarily with concert headliners and singers. Current acts include Gary Cambra of the Tubes, Dave Meniketti Group, Famous Hits Band featuring Rich Varasso, Alameda Allstars (Greg Allman's backup band), Richie Barron of HWY2000, Tongue N Groove, Greg Douglass (songwriter) and Blunt Force Trauma.

◑ VOKES BOOKING AGENCY, P.O. Box 12, New Kensington PA 15068-0012. (724)335-2775. President: Howard Vokes. Booking agency, music publisher (Vokes Music Publishing) and record company (Vokes Record Co.). Represents individual traditional country and bluegrass artists. Books name acts in on special occasions. For special occasions books nationally known acts from Grand Ole Opry, Jamboree U.S.A., Appalachian Jubliee, etc. Receives 10-20% commission.

How to Contact: New artists send 45 rpm record, cassette, LP or CD. Responds in 1 week.

Music: Mostly traditional **country**, **bluegrass**, **old time** and **gospel**; definitely no rock or country rock. Current acts include Howard Vokes & His Country Boys (country) and Mel Anderson.

Tips: "We work mostly with traditional country bands and bluegrass groups that play various bars, hotels, clubs, high schools, malls, fairs, lounges, or fundraising projects. We work at times with other booking agencies in bringing acts in for special occasions. Also we work directly with well-known and newer country, bluegrass and country gospel acts not only to possibly get them bookings in our area, but in other states as well. We also help 'certain artists' get bookings in the overseas marketplace."

◻ WILLIAM F. WAGNER AGENCY, 14343 Addison St. #221, Sherman Oaks CA 91423. (818)905-1033. **Contact:** Bill Wagner, owner. Management firm and record producer (Bill Wagner). Estab. 1957. Represents individual artists and groups from anywhere; currently handles 2 acts. Receives 15% commission. Reviews materials for acts.

How to Contact: Submit demo tape by mail. Unsolicited submissions are OK. Prefers cassette or CD with 5 songs and lead sheet. If seeking management, press kit should include cover letter, bio, picture, tape or CD with 5 songs. "If SASE and/or return postage are included, I will reply in 30 days. I will not reply by telephone or fax." Include SASE. Responds in 1 month.

Music: Mostly **jazz**, **contemporary pop** and **contemporary country**; also **classical**, **MOR** and **film and TV background**. Works primarily with singers, with or without band, big bands and smaller instrumental groups. Current acts include Page Cavanaugh (jazz/pop/contemporary/pianist) and Sandy Graham (jazz singer).

Tips: "Indicate in first submission what artists you are writing for, by name if possible. Don't send material blindly. Be sure all material is properly copyrighted. Be sure package shows 'all material herein copyrighted' on outside."

☑◻ WALLS & CO. MANAGEMENT/SHOWBIZ KIDZ!, 4237 Henderson Blvd., Tampa FL 33629. (813)288-2022. Fax: (813)639-1164. E-mail: showbk@excite.com. Website: www.showbizkidz.org. **Contact:** M. Susan Walls, director/personal manager. Management firm. Estab. 1988. Represents individual artists from anywhere; currently handles 4 acts. Receives 15% commission. Reviews material for acts.

How to Contact: *Call first and obtain permission to submit* or submit demo tape by mail. Prefers cassette or CD with up to 5 songs and lyric sheet. If seeking management, press kit should include appearance schedules, press releases, bio/picture, publicist's name, articles/reviews. Does not return material. Responds in 2 weeks.

Music: Mostly **country**, **jazz** and **pop**. Works primarily with bands with lead vocalists, individual artists and some songwriters. Current acts include Brandy Taylor (country), Darcy McClaren (country) and Nick Pellito (musical theatre).

Tips: "Listen, learn from experience and write every day."

☑◑ CHERYL K. WARNER PRODUCTIONS, P.O. Box 127, Hermitage TN 37076-0127. Phone/fax: (615)847-1286. E-mail: cherylkwarner@comcast.net. Website: www.cherylkwarner.com.

Contact: Cheryl K. Warner and David M. Warner, owners. Management firm, booking agency, music publisher (Cheryl K. Warner Music), record company (CKW Records) and record producer (Cheryl K. Warner). Estab. 1988. Currently handles 3 acts. Receives 20-25% commission. Reviews material for acts.

How to Contact: Submit demo tape by mail. Unsolicited submissions are OK. Prefers CD, cassette or VHS videocassette with 3 best songs, lyric or lead sheet, bio and picture. If seeking management, press kit should include CD or cassette with up-to-date bio, cover letter, lyric sheets, press clippings, video and picture. Does not return material. Responds in 6 weeks if interested.

Music: Mostly **country/traditional and contemporary**, **Christian/gospel** and **A/C/pop**. Works primarily with singer/songwriters and bands with original and versatile style. Current acts include Cheryl K. Warner (Nashville recording artist/entertainer), Cheryl K. Warner Band (support/studio alt) and Veronica (developmental/contemporary artist).

[N] ◯ WE RECORDS & MANAGEMENT, P.O. Box 684721, Austin TX 78768-4721. (512)328-5756. E-mail: werecords@aol.com. Website: www.werecords.com. **Contact:** Jason Whitmire, president. Management firm, booking agency and record company (WE Records). Estab. 1995. Represents individual artists and groups from anywhere; currently handles 3 acts. Receives 20% commission. Reviews material for acts.

How to Contact: Submit demo tape by mail. Unsolicited submissions are OK. Prefers CD. If seeking management, press kit should include cover letter, demo tape/CD, press clippings, photo and bio. "Explain, besides the music, what makes your act more appealing than others?" Does not return material. Responds in 2 months.

Music: Mostly **electronic** and **techno**. Current acts include Joey Jaime aka Derrighan, Magic Fire Sheep (techno producer), DJ Alchemy (acid trance DJ), Dj MMj (intelligent techno) and Vertigo Blue (electronica).

Tips: "Keep everyone updated on your status and keep your name in the public eye."

☑ ◎ WEMUS ENTERTAINMENT, 2006 Seaboard, Suite 400, Midland TX 79705. (915)689-3687. Fax: (915)687-0930. E-mail: wemus@aol.com. Website: www.wemus.com. **Contact:** Dennis Grubb, president. Management firm, booking agency and music publisher (Wemus Music, Inc.). Estab. 1983. Represents local and regional individual artists and groups; currently handles 6 acts. Receives 15-25% commission. Reviews material for acts.

How to Contact: Submit demo tape by mail. Unsolicited submissions are OK. Prefers cassette, CD or VHS videocassette with 3-5 songs and lyric sheet. If seeking management, press kit should include glossy head and full body shots and extensive biography. "Make sure address, phone number and possible fax number is included in the packet, or a business card." Does not return material. Responds in 1 month if interested.

Music: Mostly **country**. Current acts include The Image (variety), The Big Time (variety), The Pictures (variety), Tiffany Ammen (vocalist) and Kazzi Shae Broyles (vocalist).

Tips: "We preview and try to place good songs with national artists who are in need of good materials. We have a very tough qualification process. We refuse to forward sub-par materials to major artists or artists management."

☑ ◯ SHANE WILDER ARTISTS' MANAGEMENT, P.O. Box 335687, North Las Vegas NV 89033-0012. (702)395-5624. **Contact:** Shane Wilder, president. General Manager: Aaron Wilder. Management firm, music publisher (Shane Wilder Music/BMI) and record producer (Shane Wilder Productions). Represents artists and groups; currently handles 4 acts. Receives 10% commission. Reviews material for acts.

MARKET CONDITIONS are constantly changing! If you're still using this book and it is 2004 or later, buy the newest edition of *Songwriter's Market* at your favorite bookstore or order directly from Writer's Digest Books at (800)289-0963.

How to Contact: Submit demo tape by mail. Unsolicited submissions are OK. Prefers cassette or videocassette of performance with 4-10 songs and lyric sheet. If seeking management, send cover letter, bio, lyric sheets, cassette with 4-10 songs, photos of individuals or groups, video if possible and any press releases. "Submissions should be highly commercial." Include SASE. Responds in 2 weeks.

Music: Country. Works primarily with single artists and groups. Current acts include Isabel Marie (country), Craig Dodson (country), Darren Collier (rock), Ann Lee (country) and Lonnie Raynes (country).

☑ ◑ YVONNE WILLIAMS MANAGEMENT, 6433 Topanga Blvd. #142, Canoga Park CA 91303. (818)366-0510. Fax: (818)366-0520. E-mail: yvonne1940@aol.com. **Contact:** Yvonne Williams, president. Management firm, music publisher (Jerry Williams Music), record company (S.D.E.G.) and record producer (Jerry Williams). Estab. 1978. Represents individual artists and songwriters from anywhere; currently handles 12 acts. Receives 10-20% commission. Reviews material for acts.

How to Contact: Submit demo tape by mail. Unsolicited submissions are OK. Prefers CD/CDR only with any number of songs and lyric sheet. If seeking management, press kit should include cover letter, bio, photo, CD, press clippings, video and résumé. Include SASE, name, phone and any background in songs placed. Responds in 2 months.

Music: Mostly **rap**, **R&B**, **rock** and **country**; also **gospel** and **blues**. Works primarily with singer/songwriters and singers. Current acts include Swamp Dogg (R&B, rock, soca), Wilson Williams (blues), Clarence Carter (R&B/blues) and 20 Mill Kasino (rap).

Tips: "Make a good clean demo, with a simple pilot vocal that is understandable."

⊠ WILLIS ENTERTAINMENT, INC., 314 Stations Ave., Woodstock GA 30189. (770)592-0043. Fax: (770)517-9525. E-mail: ninjadude@mindspring.com. Website: www.willisentertainment.com. Owner/President: Mark Willis. Management firm. Estab. 1995. Represents international groups; currently handles 2 acts. Receives 20% commission. Reviews material for acts.

How to Contact: Submit demo tape by mail. Unsolicited submissions are OK. Prefers cassette or CD. If seeking management, press kit should include picture, bio, 3 song tape or CD, a list of upcoming performance dates. Does not return material. Responds in 2 months.

Music: Mostly **rock** and **alternative rock**. Works primarily with rock bands, all original, able to tour. Current acts include Stuck Mojo (metal) and Fozzy (metal).

◑ RICHARD WOOD ARTIST MANAGEMENT, 69 North Randall Ave., Staten Island NY 10301. (718)981-0641. Fax: (718)273-0797. **Contact:** Richard Wood. Management firm. Estab. 1974. Represents musical groups; currently handles 3 acts. Receives 20% commission. Reviews material for acts.

How to Contact: Submit demo tape by mail. Unsolicited submissions are OK. Prefers cassette and lead sheet. If seeking management, press kit should include demo tape, photo, cover letter and résumé. Include SASE. Responds in 1 month.

Music: Mostly **dance**, **R&B** and **top 40/pop**; also **MOR**. Works primarily with "high energy" show bands, bar bands and dance bands.

◑ WORLD WIDE MANAGEMENT, P.O. Box 536, Bronxville NY 10708. (914)337-5131. Fax: (914)337-5309. **Contact:** Jared Lloyd, A&R. Director: Steve Rosenfeld. Management firm and music publisher (Neighborhood Music/ASCAP). Estab. 1971. Represents artists, groups, songwriters and actors; currently handles 5 acts. Receives 15-20% commission. Reviews material for acts.

How to Contact: *Write first and obtain permission to submit.* Prefers CD, cassette or videocassete of performance with 3-4 songs. If seeking management, press kit should include cover letter, bio, reviews, press clippings, CD or cassette with lyrics and photo. Does not return material. Responds in 1 month.

Music: Mostly **contemporary pop**, **folk**, **folk/rock** and **New Age**; also **A/C**, **rock**, **jazz**, **bluegrass**, **blues**, **country** and **R&B**. Works primarily with self-contained bands and vocalists. Current acts include Margo Valentine Lazzara (performance artist), Rex Fowler (folk/contemporary) and Johnny Velvet Blues Band (blues).

☑ ◑ **WORLDSOUND, LLC**, (formerly Wyatt Management Worldwide, Inc.), 17651 First Ave. S., Suite 102, Seattle WA 98148-2715. (206)444-0300. Fax: (206)244-0066. E-mail: wmw@wyattworld.com. Website: www.wyattworld.com or www.worldsound.com. **Contact:** Marysia Kolodziet, A&R manager. Management firm. Estab. 1976. Represents individual artists, groups and songwriters from anywhere; currently handles 8 acts. Receives 20% commission. Reviews material for acts.
How to Contact: Submit demo tape by mail. Unsolicited submissions are OK. Prefers CD, cassette or VHS videocassette with 2-10 songs and lyric sheet. If seeking management, press kit should include band biography, photos, video, members' history, press and demo reviews. Include SASE. Responds in 1 month.
Music: Mostly **rock**, **pop** and **world**; also **heavy metal**, **hard rock** and **top 40**. Works primarily with pop/rock groups. Current acts include Carmine Appice (rock), Keali'i Reichel (world music) and Carbon 9 (tribal rock/industrial pop metal).
Tips: "Always submit new songs/material, even if you have sent material that was previously rejected; the music biz is always changing."

☑ ◑ **ZANE MANAGEMENT, INC.**, The Land Title Building, 100 S. Broad St., Suite 630, Philadelphia PA 19110. (215)640-9770. Fax: (215)640-9769. E-mail: lzr@remick-martone.com. Website: www.zanemanagement.com. **Contact:** Lloyd Z. Remick, Esq., president. Entertainment/sports consultants and managers. Represents artists, songwriters, producers and athletes; currently handles 7 acts. Receives 10-15% commission.
How to Contact: Submit demo tape by mail. Unsolicited submissions are OK. Prefers cassette, CD and lyric sheet. If seeking management, press kit should include cover letter, bio, photo, demo tape and video. Does not return material. Responds in 3 weeks.
Music: Mostly **dance**, **easy listening**, **folk**, **jazz** (fusion), **MOR**, **rock** (hard and country), **soul** and **top 40/pop**. Current acts include Bunny Sigler (disco/funk), Peter Nero and Philly Pops (conductor), Cast in Bronze (rock group), Pieces of a Dream (jazz/crossover) and Don't Look Down (rock/pop).

🔃 **D. ZIRILLI MANAGEMENT**, P.O. Box 255, Cupertino CA 95015-0255. (408)257-2535. Fax: (408)252-8938. E-mail: dz@papadoo.com. Website: www.papadoo.com. Owner: Don Zirilli. Management firm. Estab. 1965. Represents groups from anywhere; currently handles 1 act. Receives 20% commission. Reviews material for acts.
How to Contact: Submit demo tape by mail. Unsolicited submissions are OK. Prefers cassette, DAT, videocassette or CD. If seeking management, press kit should include video. Does not return material. Responds in 2 weeks.
Music: Mostly **rock**, **surf** and **MOR**. Current acts include Papa Doo Run Run (band).
Tips: "Less is more."

REMEMBER: Don't "shotgun" your demo tapes. Submit only to companies interested in the type of music you write. For more submission hints, refer to Getting Started on page 10.

Additional Managers & Booking Agents

The following companies are also managers/booking agents, but their listings are found in other sections of the book. See the General Index for page numbers, then read the listings for submission information.

Alexis
babysue
Bouquet Records
Brian Song Music Corp.
BSW Records
Capstan Record Production
Dagene Music
Dagene/Cabletown Company
De Miles Music Company, The Edward
Deadeye Records
Deep South Entertainment
Delev Music Company
Dell Music, Frank
Diamond Entertainment, Joel
Edition Rossori
Esquire International
First Time Music (Publishing) U.K.
First Time Records
Fish of Death Records and Management
Gueststar Records, Inc.
Hailing Frequency Music Productions

His Power Productions and Publishing
Kaupp Records
Kaupps & Robert Publishing Co.
L.A. Records (Canada)
Lineage Publishing Co.
Lucifer Records, Inc.
Magid Productions, Lee
Major Entertainment, Inc.
Modal Music, Inc.™
New Experience Records
Nightmare Records
Orchid Publishing
R.J. Music
Rocker Music/Happy Man Music
Safire Records
Satkowski Recordings, Steve
SDM
Silver Thunder Music Group
Sphere Group One
Stardust
Stuart Music Co., Jeb
Third Wave Productions Ltd.

Category Index

The Category Index is a good place to begin searching for a market for your songs. Below is an alphabetical list of 20 general music categories. If you write pop songs and are looking for a manager or booking agent to submit your songs to, check the Pop section in this index. There you will find a list of managers and booking agents who work with pop performers. Once you locate the entries for those publishers, read the music subheading *carefully* to determine which companies are most interested in the type of pop music you write. Some of the markets in this section do not appear in the Category Index because they have not indicated a specific preference. Most of these said they are interested in "all types" of music. Listings that were very specific, or whose description of the music they're interested in doesn't quite fit into these categories, also do not appear here.

Adult Contemporary (also easy listening, middle of the road, AAA, ballads, etc.)

All Star Talent Agency
Anderson Associates Communications Group
Brothers Management Associates
Chucker Music Inc.
Dinwoodie Management, Andrew
Five Star Entertainment
Hale Enterprises
International Entertainment Bureau
Jacobson Talent Management
Knight Agency, Bob
Kuper Personal Management
Lenthall & Associates
Levinson Entertainment Ventures International, Inc.
Lutz Entertainment Agency, Richard
M.B.H. Music Management
Management by Jaffe
Merri-Webb Productions
Prestige Artistes
Prestige Management
RadioActive Talent Inc.
Richards World Management, Inc., Diane
Risavy, Inc., A.F.
Rustron Music Productions
St. John Artists
Skorman Productions, Inc., T.
Staircase Promotion
Stormin' Norman Productions
T.J. Booker Ltd.
Take Out Management
Tas Music Co./Dave Tasse Entertainment
Total Acting Experience, A
Van Pol Management, Hans
Wagner Agency, William F.
Warner Productions, Cheryl K.
World Wide Management
Zane Management, Inc.
Zirilli Management, D.

Alternative (also modern rock, punk, college rock, new wave, hardcore, new music, industrial, ska, indie rock, garage, etc.)

American Artists Entertainment
Cotton Town Management
Countdown Entertainment
Cranium Management
DAS Communications, Ltd.
Direct Management
Doss Presents, Col. Buster
Earth Tracks Artists Agency
Hupp Enterprises, Joe
Knight Agency, Bob
Kuper Personal Management
Legacy Sound & Entertainment
M.B.H. Music Management
Management by Jaffe
Metro Talent Group, Inc.
Midnight Music Management
Monopoly Management
On the Level Music!
Outlaw Entertainment International
Performers of the World Inc. (P.O.W.)
Pillar Records
Prestige Management
RadioActive Talent Inc.
Rock Whirled Music Management
Rogue Management
Saffyre Management
Silver Bow Management
Simmons Management Group
Smeltzer Productions, Gary
Southeastern Attractions
Spoon Agency L.L.C., The
Staircase Promotion
Strictly Forbidden Artists
Surface Management Inc.
Tiger's Eye Entertainment Management & Consulting
Umbrella Artists Management, Inc.

Risavy, Inc., A.F.
Rock of Ages Productions
Rothschild Productions Inc., Charles R.
Rustron Music Productions
Sea Cruise Productions, Inc.
Serge Entertainment Group
Shute Management Pty. Ltd., Phill
Siegel Entertainment Ltd.
Silver Bow Management
Smeltzer Productions, Gary
Southeastern Attractions
SP Talent Associates
Sphere Group One
Spoon Agency L.L.C., The
Staircase Promotion
Stevens & Company Management
Stormin' Norman Productions
T.J. Booker Ltd.
T.L.C. Booking Agency
Texas Sounds Entertainment
Total Acting Experience, A
Triangle Talent, Inc.
Twentieth Century Promotions
Umpire Entertainment Enterprizes
Universal Music Marketing
Valiant Records & Management
Varrasso Management, Richard
Vokes Booking Agency
Wagner Agency, William F.
Walls & Co. Management/Showbiz Kidz!
Warner Productions, Cheryl K.
Wemus Entertainment
Wilder Artists' Management, Shane
Williams Management, Yvonne
World Wide Management

Dance (also house, hi-NRG, disco, club, rave, techno, trip-hop, trance, etc.)
Anderson Associates Communications Group
Atlantic Entertainment Group
Bassline Entertainment, Inc.
Chucker Music Inc.
Clousher Productions
Countdown Entertainment
Countrywide Producers
De Miles Company, The Edward
First Time Management
Golden City International
Kendall West Agency
Kickstart Music Ltd.
Lutz Entertainment Agency, Richard
M.B.H. Music Management
Martin Productions, Rick
Mega Music Productions
Outlaw Entertainment International
Richards World Management, Inc., Diane
Rogue Management
Skorman Productions, Inc., T.

Sound Management Direction
Southeastern Attractions
Strictly Forbidden Artists
Take Out Management
Tas Music Co./Dave Tasse Entertainment
Total Acting Experience, A
Van Pol Management, Hans
Varrasso Management, Richard
WE Records & Management
Wood Artist Management, Richard
Zane Management, Inc.

Folk (also acoustic, Celtic, etc.)
Afterschool Publishing Company
Amok Artists Agency
Concerted Efforts, Inc./Foggy Day Music
Countrywide Producers
Dinwoodie Management, Andrew
EAO Music Corporation of Canada
Five Star Entertainment
Hupp Enterprises, Joe
Immigrant Music Inc.
Knight Agency, Bob
Noteworthy Productions
Performers of the World Inc. (P.O.W.)
Rock Whirled Music Management
Rothschild Productions Inc., Charles R.
Rustron Music Productions
SP Talent Associates
Stormin' Norman Productions
World Wide Management
Zane Management, Inc.

Instrumental (also background music, musical scores, etc.)
Endangered Species Artist Management
Fiedler Management, B.C.
Jae Enterprises, Jana
Pillar Records
Wagner Agency, William F.

Jazz (also fusion, bebop, swing, etc.)
Afterschool Publishing Company
Air Tight Management
Bacchus Group Productions, Ltd.
Buxton Walker P/L
Chucker Music Inc.
Concept 2000 Inc.
Countrywide Producers
Crossfire Productions
Endangered Species Artist Management
Fox Management Inc., Mitchell
Harrell & Associates, M.
International Entertainment Bureau
Jae Enterprises, Jana
Kendall West Agency
Knight Agency, Bob
Live-Wire Management

McDonnell Group, The
Media Management
Metro Talent Group, Inc.
Music Marketing & Promotions
Noteworthy Enterprises
On the Level Music!
OTA Productions
Performers of the World Inc. (P.O.W.)
Richards World Management, Inc., Diane
Riohcat Music
Rothschild Productions Inc., Charles R.
Stander Entertainment
Tas Music Co./Dave Tasse Entertainment
Total Acting Experience, A
Universal Music Marketing
Wagner Agency, William F.
Walls & Co. Management/Showbiz Kidz!
World Wide Management
Zane Management, Inc.

Latin (also Spanish, salsa, Cuban, conga, Brazilian, cumbja, rancheras, Mexican, merengue, Tejano, Tex Mex, etc.)
Bacchus Group Productions, Ltd.
Bassline Entertainment, Inc.
Butler Music, Bill
Corvalan-Condliffe Management
Ellis International Talent Agency, The
Endangered Species Artist Management
Hansen Enterprises, Ltd.
Management Plus
Mega Music Productions
OTA Productions
Stevens & Company Management
Texas Sounds Entertainment

Metal (also thrash, grindcore, heavy metal, etc.)
Artist Representation and Management
Endangered Species Artist Management
Legacy Sound & Entertainment
Outlaw Entertainment International
Simmons Management Group
Strictly Forbidden Artists
WorldSound, LLC

New Age (also ambient)
Live-Wire Management
Richards World Management, Inc., Diane
Rustron Music Productions
Serge Entertainment Group
Sphere Group One
World Wide Management

Novelty (also comedy, humor, etc.)
Circuit Rider Talent & Management Co.
Hall Entertainment & Events, Bill

Sea Cruise Productions, Inc.
Valiant Records & Management

Pop (also top 40, top 100, popular, chart hits, etc.)
Afterschool Publishing Company
Alert Music, Inc.
All Star Talent Agency
Allen Entertainment Development, Michael
American Artists Entertainment
Anderson Associates Communications Group
Ardenne Int'l Inc.
Artist Representation and Management
Atch Records and Productions
Austex Music
Bacchus Group Productions, Ltd.
Bassline Entertainment, Inc.
Big J Productions
Bouquet-Orchid Enterprises
Brothers Management Associates
Buxton Walker P/L
Chucker Music Inc.
Circuit Rider Talent & Management Co.
Clockwork Entertainment Management Agency
Concept 2000 Inc.
Conscience Music
Corvalan-Condliffe Management
Cotton Town Management
Countdown Entertainment
Countrywide Producers
Cranium Management
Creative Star Management
Criss-Cross Industries
D&M Entertainment Agency
D&R Entertainment
DAS Communications, Ltd.
De Miles Company, The Edward
Dinwoodie Management, Andrew
Divine Industries
DMR Agency
Earth Tracks Artists Agency
Endangered Species Artist Management
Evans Productions, Scott
Fenchel Entertainment Agency, Fred T.
Fiedler Management, B.C.
First Time Management
Godtland Management, Inc., Eric
Golden City International
Golden Guru Entertainment
Gurley & Co.
Hale Enterprises
Huge Production, Inc., A
Hupp Enterprises, Joe
International Production Management
Jae Enterprises, Jana
James Management, Roger
Kagan International, Sheldon
Kickstart Music Ltd.

Rustron Music Productions
Sea Cruise Productions, Inc.
Shute Management Pty. Ltd., Phill
Silver Bow Management
Simmons Management Group
Smeltzer Productions, Gary
Sound Management Direction
Sphere Group One
Spoon Agency L.L.C., The
Stander Entertainment
Starkravin' Management
Take Out Management
Tas Music Co./Dave Tasse Entertainment
Texas Sounds Entertainment
Tiger's Eye Entertainment Management & Consult-
ing
Total Acting Experience, A
Van Pol Management, Hans
Williams Management, Yvonne
Wood Artist Management, Richard
World Wide Management
Zane Management, Inc.

Rap (also hip-hop, bass, etc.)
Afterschool Publishing Company
American Artists Entertainment
Atch Records and Productions
Bassline Entertainment, Inc.
Countdown Entertainment
Creative Star Management
First Time Management
Godtland Management, Inc., Eric
Golden City International
Hardison International Entertainment Corporation
Hes Free Productions & Publishing Company
Jacobson Talent Management
Kuper Personal Management
Precision Management
Renaissance Entertainment Group
Richards World Management, Inc., Diane
Strictly Forbidden Artists
Tiger's Eye Entertainment Management & Consult-
ing
Van Pol Management, Hans
Williams Management, Yvonne

**Religious (also gospel, sacred, Christian,
church, hymns, praise, inspirational, worship,
etc.)**
All Star Management
All Star Talent Agency
Allen Entertainment Development, Michael
Atch Records and Productions
Bouquet-Orchid Enterprises
Circuit Rider Talent & Management Co.
Concept 2000 Inc.
Cotton Town Management
Country Star Attractions

Countrywide Producers
Creative Star Management
D&R Entertainment
Direct Management
Doss Presents, Col. Buster
Exclesisa Booking Agency
Fenchel Entertainment Agency, Fred T.
First Time Management
5 Star Music Group/Mike Waddell & Associates
Golden City International
Harrell & Associates, M.
Hes Free Productions & Publishing Company
Lari-Jon Promotions
Lenthall & Associates
Mayo & Company, Phil
Merri-Webb Productions
Precision Management
Rock of Ages Productions
Silver Bow Management
Staircase Promotion
Umpire Entertainment Enterprizes
Vokes Booking Agency
Warner Productions, Cheryl K.
Williams Management, Yvonne

Rock (also rockabilly, AOR, rock 'n' roll, etc.)
Air Tight Management
Alert Music, Inc.
All Star Talent Agency
Allen Entertainment Development, Michael
American Artists Entertainment
American Bands Management
Anderson Associates Communications Group
Ardenne Int'l Inc.
Artist Representation and Management
Austex Music
Backstreet Booking
Barnard Management Services (BMS)
Barrett Rock 'n' Roll Enterprises, Paul
Big J Productions
Blowin' Smoke Productions/Records
Blue Wave Productions
Bouquet-Orchid Enterprises
Brothers Management Associates
Buxton Walker P/L
Chucker Music Inc.
Clockwork Entertainment Management Agency
Clousher Productions
Concerted Efforts, Inc./Foggy Day Music
Conscience Music
Corvalan-Condliffe Management
Cotton Town Management
Countdown Entertainment
Countrywide Producers
Crossfire Productions
D&M Entertainment Agency
DAS Communications, Ltd.
DCA Productions

De Miles Company, The Edward
Dinwoodie Management, Andrew
Divine Industries
DMR Agency
Doss Presents, Col. Buster
EAO Music Corporation of Canada
Earth Tracks Artists Agency
Endangered Species Artist Management
5 Star Music Group/Mike Waddell & Associates
Fox Management Inc., Mitchell
Godtland Management, Inc., Eric
Golden Guru Entertainment
Hale Enterprises
Hansen Enterprises, Ltd.
Harrell & Associates, M.
Hes Free Productions & Publishing Company
Huge Production, Inc., A
Hupp Enterprises, Joe
International Entertainment Bureau
Jacobson Talent Management
Kendall West Agency
Kickstart Music Ltd.
Kitchen Sync
Knight Agency, Bob
Lari-Jon Promotions
Legacy Sound & Entertainment
Levinson Entertainment Ventures International, Inc.
M.B.H. Music Management
Management by Jaffe
Martin Productions, Rick
Mayo & Company, Phil
McDonnell Group, The
Media Management
Mega Music Productions
Merri-Webb Productions
Metro Talent Group, Inc.
Midcoast, Inc.
Muse Artists Inc.
Nik Entertainment Co.
On the Level Music!
Outlaw Entertainment International
Performers of the World Inc. (P.O.W.)
Pillar Records
Prestige Artistes
Prestige Management
Pro Talent Consultants
RadioActive Talent Inc.
Rainbow Collection Ltd.
Rainbow Talent Agency
Right-On Management
Risavy, Inc., A.F.
Rock of Ages Productions
Rock Whirled Music Management
Rogue Management
Rothschild Productions Inc., Charles R.

Rustron Music Productions
Saffyre Management
St. John Artists
Sea Cruise Productions, Inc.
Serge Entertainment Group
Shute Management Pty. Ltd., Phill
Siegel Entertainment Ltd.
Silver Bow Management
Simmons Management Group
Sound Management Direction
Southeastern Attractions
SP Talent Associates
Sphere Group One
Spoon Agency L.L.C., The
Staircase Promotion
Starkravin' Management
Stormin' Norman Productions
Strictly Forbidden Artists
Surface Management Inc.
T.J. Booker Ltd.
T.L.C. Booking Agency
Take Out Management
Tas Music Co./Dave Tasse Entertainment
Tiger's Eye Entertainment Management & Consulting
Triangle Talent, Inc.
Umbrella Artists Management, Inc.
Universal Music Marketing
Varrasso Management, Richard
WE Records & Management
Williams Management, Yvonne
Willis Entertainment, Inc.
World Wide Management
WorldSound, LLC
Zane Management, Inc.
Zirilli Management, D.

World Music (also reggae, ethnic, calypso, international, world beat, etc.)

Amok Artists Agency
Bacchus Group Productions, Ltd.
Buxton Walker P/L
Concerted Efforts, Inc./Foggy Day Music
Ellis International Talent Agency, The
Endangered Species Artist Management
Fox Management Inc., Mitchell
Immigrant Music Inc.
Management Plus
Midnight Music Management
Music Marketing & Promotions
Noteworthy Productions
Performers of the World Inc. (P.O.W.)
Stander Entertainment
Stormin' Norman Productions
WorldSound, LLC

Advertising, Audiovisual & Commercial Music Firms

It's happened a million times—you hear a jingle on the radio or television and can't get it out of your head. That's the work of a successful jingle writer, writing songs to catch your attention and make you aware of the product being advertised. But the field of commercial music consists of more than just memorable jingles. It also includes background music that many companies use in videos for corporate and educational presentations, as well as films and TV shows.

SUBMITTING MATERIAL

More than any other market listed in this book, the commercial music market expects composers to have made an investment in the recording of their material before submitting. A sparse, piano/vocal demo won't work here; when dealing with commercial music firms, especially audiovisual firms and music libraries, high quality production is important. Your demo may be kept on file at one of these companies until a need for it arises, and it may be used or sold as you sent it. Therefore, your demo tape or reel must be as fully produced as possible.

The presentation package that goes along with your demo must be just as professional. A list of your credits should be a part of your submission, to give the company an idea of your experience in this field. If you have no experience, look to local television and radio stations to get your start. Don't expect to be paid for many of your first jobs in the commercial music field; it's more important to get the credits and exposure that can lead to higher-paying jobs.

Commercial music and jingle writing can be a lucrative field for the composer/songwriter with a gift for writing catchy melodies and the ability to write in many different music styles. It's a very competitive field, so it pays to have a professional presentation package that makes your work stand out.

Three different segments of the commercial music world are listed here: advertising agencies, audiovisual firms and commercial music houses/music libraries. Each looks for a different type of music, so read these descriptions carefully to see where the music you write fits in.

ADVERTISING AGENCIES

Ad agencies work on assignment as their clients' needs arise. Through consultation and input from the creative staff, ad agencies seek jingles and music to stimulate the consumer to identify with a product or service.

When contacting ad agencies, keep in mind they are searching for music that can capture and then hold an audience's attention. Most jingles are short, with a strong, memorable hook. When an ad agency listens to a demo, it is not necessarily looking for a finished product so much as for an indication of creativity and diversity. Many composers put together a reel of excerpts of work from previous projects, or short pieces of music that show they can write in a variety of styles.

AUDIOVISUAL FIRMS

Audiovisual firms create a variety of products, from film and video shows for sales meetings, corporate gatherings and educational markets, to motion pictures and TV shows. With the increase of home video use, how-to videos are a big market for audiovisual firms, as are spoken word educational videos. All of these products need music to accompany them. For your quick reference, companies working to place music in movies and TV shows (excluding commercials) have a ▣ preceding their listing (also see the Film & TV Index on page 483 for a complete list of these companies).

Like ad agencies, audiovisual firms look for versatile, well-rounded songwriters. When submitting demos to these firms, you need to demonstrate your versatility in writing specialized background music and themes. Listings for companies will tell what facet(s) of the audiovisual field they are involved in and what types of clients they serve. Your demo tape should also be as professional and fully produced as possible; audiovisual firms often seek demo tapes that can be put on file for future use when the need arises.

COMMERCIAL MUSIC HOUSES & MUSIC LIBRARIES

Commercial music houses are companies contracted (either by an ad agency or the advertiser) to compose custom jingles. Since they are neither an ad agency nor an audiovisual firm, their main concern is music. They use a lot of it, too—some composed by inhouse songwriters and some contributed by outside, freelance writers.

Music libraries are different in that their music is not custom composed for a specific client. Their job is to provide a collection of instrumental music in many different styles that, for an annual fee or on a per-use basis, the customer can use however he chooses.

In the following listings, commercial music houses and music libraries, which are usually the most open to works by new composers, are identified as such by **bold** typeface.

The commercial music market is similar to most other businesses in one aspect: experience is important. Until you develop a list of credits, pay for your work may not be high. Don't pass up opportunities if a job is non- or low-paying. These assignments will add to your list of credits, make you contacts in the field, and improve your marketability.

Money and rights

Many of the companies listed in this section pay by the job, but there may be some situations where the company asks you to sign a contract that will specify royalty payments. If this happens, research the contract thoroughly, and know exactly what is expected of you and how much you'll be paid.

Depending on the particular job and the company, you may be asked to sell one-time rights or all rights. One-time rights involve using your material for one presentation only. All rights means the buyer can use your work any way he chooses, as many times as he likes. Be sure you know exactly what you're giving up, and how the company may use your music in the future.

In the commercial world, many of the big advertising agencies have their own publishing companies where writers assign their compositions. In these situations, writers sign contracts whereby they do receive performance and mechanical royalties when applicable.

For More Information

For additional names and addresses of ad agencies that may use jingles and/or commercial music, refer to the *Standard Directory of Advertising Agencies* (National Register Publishing). For a list of audiovisual firms, check out the latest edition of *AV Marketplace* (R.R. Bowker). Both these books may be found at your local library. To contact companies in your area, see the Geographic Index at the back of this book.

THE AD AGENCY, P.O. Box 470572, San Francisco CA 94147. **Contact:** Michael Carden, creative director. Advertising agency and **jingle/commercial music production house**. Clients include business, industry and retail. Estab. 1971. Uses the services of music houses, independent songwriter/composers and lyricists for scoring of commercials, background music for video production, and jingles for commercials. Commissions 20 composers and 15 lyricists/year. Pays by the job or by the hour. Buys all or one-time rights.
How to Contact: Submit demo tape of previous work. Prefers cassette with 5-8 songs and lyric sheet. Include SASE. Responds in 3 weeks.
Music: Uses variety of musical styles for commercials, promotion, TV, video presentations.
Tips: "Our clients and our needs change frequently."

ADVERTEL, INC., P.O. Box 18053, Pittsburgh PA 15236-0053. (412)886-1400. Fax: (412)886-1411. E-mail: pberan@advertel.com. Website: www.advertel.com. **Contact:** Paul Beran, president/CEO. Telephonic/Internet production company. Clients include small and multi-national companies. Estab. 1983. Uses the services of music houses and independent songwriters/composers for scoring of instrumentals (all varieties) and telephonic production. Commissions 3-4 composers/year. Pay varies. Buys all rights and phone exclusive rights.
How to Contact: Submit demo tape of previous work. Prefers CD or cassette. "Most compositions are 2 minutes strung together in 6, 12, 18 minute length productions." Does not return material; prefers to keep on file. Responds "right away if submission fills an immediate need."
Music: Uses all varieties, including unusual; mostly subdued music beds. Radio-type production used exclusively in telephone and Internet applications.
Tips: "Go for volume. We have continuous need for all varieties of music in two minute lengths."

N ✍ ALLEGRO MUSIC, 3990 Sunsetridge, Suite 203, Moorpark CA 93021-3756. E-mail: dannymuse@aol.com. Website: www.danielobrien.com. Owner: Daniel O'Brien. Scoring service, **jingle/commercial music production house**. Clients include film-makers, advertisers, network promotions and aerobics. Estab. 1991. Uses the services of independent songwriters/composers and lyricists for scoring of films, TV and broadcast commercials, jingles for ad agencies and promotions, and commercials for radio and TV. Commissions 3 composers and 1 lyricist/year. Pays 50% royalty. Buys one-time rights.
How to Contact: Query with résumé of credits or submit demo tape of previous work. Do not call first. Prefers CD, cassette and lyric sheet. Include SASE. Responds in 1 month (if interested).
Music: Varied: Contemporary to orchestral.

✓ ✍ ANGEL FILMS COMPANY, 967 Hwy. 40, New Franklin MO 65274-9778. Phone/fax: (573)698-3900. E-mail: angelfilm@aol.com. Website: www.phoenix.org. **Contact:** Linda G. Grotzinger, vice president/marketing. Motion picture and record production company (Angel One Records). Estab. 1980. Uses the services of music houses, independent songwriters/composers and lyricists for scoring of feature films, animation, TV programs and commercials, background music for TV and radio commercials and jingles for commercials. Commissions 12-20 composers and 12-20 lyricists/year. Payment depends upon budget; each project has a different pay scale. Buys all rights.
How to Contact: Submit demo tape of previous work or query with résumé of credits. Prefers cassette or VHS videocassette with 3 pieces and lyric and lead sheet. "Do not send originals." Include SASE, but prefers to keep material on file. Responds in 6 weeks.
Music: Uses basically MOR, but will use anything (except country and religious) for record production, film, television and cartoon scores. Uses jazz—modern, classical for films.
Tips: "Send new material, not material that has old copyrights on it. Don't copy others, just do the best you can. We freelance all our work for our film and television production company, and are always looking for that one break-through artist for Angel One Records."

LISTINGS OF COMPANIES within this section which are either commercial music production houses or music libraries will have that information printed in **boldface** type.

N BLATTNER/BRUNNER INC., 11 Stanwix St., 5th Floor, Pittsburgh PA 15222-1312. (412)995-9500. Broadcast Production Coordinator: Karen Smith. Clients include retail/consumer, service, high-tech/industrial/medical. Estab. 1975. Uses the services of music houses and independent songwriters/composers for background music for TV and radio spots and jingles for TV and radio spots. Commissions 2-3 composers/year. Pays by the job. Buys all rights or one-time rights, depending on the job.
How to Contact: Submit demo tape of previous work demonstrating background music or jingle skills. Prefers CD with 3-5 songs. Does not return material. Responds in 2 months.
Music: Uses up-beat, "unique-sounding music that stands out" for commercials and industrial videos.
Tips: "Send relevant work in conjunction to the advertising business—i.e., jingles."

✔ BRg MUSIC WORKS, P.O. Box 202, Bryn Mawr PA 19010. (610)971-9490. Fax: (610)971-9630. E-mail: lnapier@brgmusicworks.com. Website: www.brgmusicworks.com. Creative Director: Doug Reed. **Contact:** Lee Napier. **Jingle producers/music library producers**. Uses independent composers and music houses for background music for radio, TV and commercials and jingles for radio and TV. Commissions 20 songwriters/year. Pays per job. Buys all rights.
How to Contact: Submit demo tape of previous work. Prefers cassette. "We are looking for quality jingle tracks already produced, as well as instrumental pieces between 2 and 3 minutes in length for use in AV music library." Include SASE. Responds in 2 weeks.
Music: All types.
Tips: "Send your best and put your strongest work at the front of your demo tape."

BRIDGE ENTERPRISES, P.O. Box 789, Marshall TX 75671-0789. (903)935-5524. Fax: (903)935-6789. **Contact:** H.A. (Tony) Bridge, Jr., sales/marketing. Hotel, restaurant and bar operator. Clients include hospitality industry. Estab. 1970. Uses the services of music houses, independent songwriters/composers and lyricists for jingles and commercials for radio and TV. Pays per job. Buys all rights.
How to Contact: Submit demo tape of previous work. Prefers cassette with lyric sheet. "No phone calls, please." Include SASE. Responds in 3 weeks.
Music: Uses various styles of music for commercials and jingles.
Tips: "Develop a good track record with radio/TV, ad agencies and hospitality industry."

BUTWIN & ASSOCIATES, INC., 8700 Westmoreland Lane, Minneapolis MN 55426. Phone/fax: (952)545-3886. **Contact:** Ron Butwin, president. Advertising agency. Clients include restaurants, banks, manufacturers, retail. Estab. 1977. Uses the services of music houses, independent songwriters/composers and lyricists for background music for videos and corporate presentations, jingles for radio and TV commercials and shows and commercials for radio and TV. Commissions 5-6 composers and 5-6 lyricists/year. Pays per job. Buys all rights "generally."
How to Contact: Submit demo tape of previous work. Prefers CD, cassette or VHS videocassette with 8-12 songs and lyric sheet. Does not return material. Prefers to keep submitted material on file. "We only respond if we're interested and either want more information or have a project in place."
Music: Uses up-tempo, pop, jazz, classical and New Age for slide presentations, jingles and commercials.
Tips: "Send us good, clean work that is truly representative of your skills. We are interested in knowing your experience and skill level. Give us some background on you and your business."

✔ CALDWELL VANRIPER/MARC, 1314 N. Meridian, Indianapolis IN 46202. (317)638-9155. Website: www.cvrmarc.com. **Contact:** Bryan Hadlock, vice president/executive creative director. Advertising agency and public relations firm. Clients include industrial, financial and consumer/trade firms. Uses the services of music houses for scoring of radio, TV and A/V projects, jingles and commercials for radio and TV.
How to Contact: Submit demo tape of previously aired work on audio cassette. Does not return material. "Sender can follow up on submission. Periodic inquiry or demo update is fine."
Tips: "We do not work directly with composers, we work with music production companies. Composers should contact the production companies directly."

☑ ⬛ **CANTRAX RECORDERS**, Dept. CM, 2119 Fidler Ave., Long Beach CA 90815. (562)498-4593. Fax: (562)498-4852. E-mail: cantrax@earthlink.net. **Contact:** Richard Cannata, owner. Recording studio. Clients include anyone needing recording services (i.e., industrial, radio, commercial). Estab. 1980. Uses the services of independent songwriters/composers and lyricists for scoring of independent features and films and background music for radio, industrials and promotions, commercials for radio and TV and jingles for radio. Commissions 10 composers/year. Pays fees set by the artist. "We take 15%."
How to Contact: Query with résumé of credits or submit demo CD of previous work. Prefers CD with lyric sheets. Does not return material. Responds in 2 weeks.
Music: Uses jazz, New Age, rock, easy listening and classical for slide shows, jingles and soundtracks.
Tips: "You must have a serious, professional attitude."

⬛ **CEDAR CREST STUDIO**, P.O. Box 28, Mountain Home AR 72653. (870)488-5777. Fax: (253)681-8194. E-mail: cedarcrest@oznet.com. Website: www.oznet.com/cedarcrest. **Contact:** Bob Ketchum, owner. Audiovisual firm and **jingle/commercial music production house**. Clients include corporate, industrial, sales, music publishing, training, educational, legal, medical, music and Internet. Estab. 1973. Sometimes uses the services of independent songwriters/composers for background music for video productions, jingles for TV spots and commercials for radio and TV. Pays by the job or by royalties. Buys all rights or one-time rights.
How to Contact: Query with résumé of credits or submit demo tape of previous work. Prefers CD, cassette, DAT, 7.5 or 15 IPS reel-to-reel or videocassette. Does not return material. "We keep it on file for future reference." Responds in 2 months.
Music: Uses up-tempo pop (not too "rocky"), unobtrusive—no solos for commercials and background music for video presentations.
Tips: "Hang, hang, hang. Be open to suggestions. Improvise, adapt, overcome."

☑ ⬛ **CINEVUE/STEVE POSTAL PRODUCTIONS**, P.O. Box 429, Bostwick FL 32007. (386)325-9356. E-mail: stepostal@aol.com. Website: www.postalproductions.com. **Contact:** Steve Postal, director/producer. Motion picture production company. Estab. 1955. Serves all types of film distributors. Uses the services of music houses, independent songwriters, composers and lyricists for scoring and background music for films and nature documentaries. Commissions 10 composers and 5 lyricists/year. Pays by the job. Buys all rights.
How to Contact: Query with résumé of credits or submit demo tape of previous work ("good tape only!"). Submit manuscript showing music scoring skills. Prefers cassette with 10 pieces and lyric or lead sheet. Only returns material if accompanied by SASE with sufficient postage for return of all materials. "Send good audio-cassette, then call me in a week." Responds in 2 weeks.
Music: Uses all styles of music for features (educational films and slide presentations). "Need horror film music on traditional instruments—no electronic music."
Tips: "Be flexible, fast—do first job free to ingratiate yourself and demonstrate your style. Follow up with two phone calls."

⬛ **COAKLEY HEAGERTY**, 1155 N. First St., San Jose CA 95112. (408)275-9400. **Contact:** Bob Meyerson, creative director. Advertising agency. Clients include consumer, business to business and high-tech firms. Estab. 1966. Uses the services of music houses for jingles for commercials for radio and TV. Commissions 15-20 songwriters/year. Pays by the job. Buys all rights.
How to Contact: Submit demo tape of previously aired work. Prefers cassette with 8-10 pieces. Does not return material; prefers to keep on file. Responds in 6 months.
Music: All kinds of music for jingles and music beds.

TO HELP YOU UNDERSTAND and use the information in these listings, see "How to Use *Songwriter's Market* to Get Your Songs Heard," on page 5.

Tips: "Send only commercials of past clients. Please don't be pushy and call over and over again. I'll call when I have something I like. Please include costs for creative and final production in a cover letter, address issues of talent availability if you are not located in a major ad market."

N COMMUNICATIONS ELECTRONICS INC., P.O. Box 1045-SWM, Ann Arbor MI 48106. (734)996-8888. Fax: (734)663-8888. Website: www.usascan.com. **Contact:** Ken Ascher, ad director. Advertising agency. Clients include electronic and hi-tech firms. Estab. 1969. Uses the services of music houses for jingles for the Web, commercials for radio and TV and background music for music on hold. Commissions 20-50 composers and 5 lyricists/year. Pays $500-3,000/job or $15-75/hour. Buys all rights.
How to Contact: Submit demo tape of previous work. Prefers CD or cassette. Prefers to keep submitted material on file. Responds in 3 weeks.
Music: Uses jazz, New Age, synthesized, MOR for music-on-hold, Internet music beds and commercials.

COMMUNICATIONS FOR LEARNING, 395 Massachusetts Ave., Arlington MA 02474. (781)641-2350. E-mail: comlearn@thecia.net. **Contact:** Jonathan L. Barkan, executive producer/ director. Video, multimedia, exhibit and graphic design firm. Clients include multi-nationals, industry, government, institutions, local, national and international nonprofits. Uses services of music houses and independent songwriters/composers as theme and background music for videos and multimedia. Commissions 1-2 composers/year. Pays $2,000-5,000/job and one-time fees. Rights purchased varies.
How to Contact: Submit demo tape of previous work. Prefers CD. Does not return material; prefers to keep on file. "For each job we consider our entire collection." Responds in 3 months.
Music: Uses all styles of music for all sorts of assignments.
Tips: "Please don't call. Just send good material and when we're interested, we'll be in touch. Make certain name and phone number are on all submitted work itself, not only cover letter."

N CREATIVE ASSOCIATES, Dept. SM, 44 Park Ave., Madison NJ 07940. (973)377-4440. **Contact:** Susan Graham, production coordinator. Audiovisual/multimedia firm and web content provider. Clients include commercial, industrial firms. Estab. 1975. Uses the services of music houses and independent songwriters/composers for scoring of video programs, background music for press tours and jingles for new products. Pays $300-5,000/job. Buys all or one-time rights.
How to Contact: Submit demo tape of previous work demonstrating composition skills or query with résumé of credits. Prefers cassette, CD-ROM or ½″ VHS videocassette. Prefers to keep material on file.
Music: Uses all styles for many different assignments.

☑ ☒ D.S.M. PRODUCERS INC., 161 W. 54th St., Suite 803, New York NY 10019. (212)245-0006. President, CEO: Suzan Bader. CFO, CPA: Kenneth R. Wiseman. **Contact:** David Fernandez, Director A&R. Vice President, National Sales Director: Doris Kaufman. Scoring service, **jingle/ commercial music production house** and original stock library called "All American Composers Library (administered world wide except USA by Warner/Chappell Music, Inc.)" Clients include networks, corporate, advertising firms, film and video, book publishers (music only). Estab. 1979. Uses the services of independent songwriters/composers for scoring of TV and feature films, background music for feature films and TV, jingles for major products and commercials for radio and TV. Pays 50% royalty. Buys all rights.
How to Contact: Write first and enclose SASE for return permission. Prefers cassette or VHS videocassette with 2 songs and lyric or lead sheet. "Use a large enough return envelope to put in a standard business reply letter." Responds in 3 months.
Music: Uses all styles including alternative, dance, New Age, country and rock for adventure films and sports programs.
Tips: "Carefully label your submissions. Include a short bio/résumé of your works. Lyric sheets are very helpful to A&R. Only send your best tapes and tunes. Invest in your profession and get a local professional to help you produce your works. A master quality tape is the standard today. This is

your competition so if you really want to be a songwriter, act like the ones who are successful—get a good tape of your tune. This makes it easier to sell overall. Never use 'samples' or any other copyrighted material in your works without a license."

dbF A MEDIA COMPANY, P.O. Box 2458, Waldorf MD 20604. (301)843-7110. E-mail: production@dbfmedia.com. Website: www.dbfmedia.com. **Contact:** Randy Runyon, general manager. Advertising agency, audiovisual and media firm and audio and video production company. Clients include business and industry. Estab. 1981. Uses the services of music houses, independent songwriters/composers and lyricists for background music for industrial, training, educational and promo videos, jingles and commercials for radio and TV. Commissions 5-12 composers and 5-12 lyricists/year. Pays by the job. Buys all rights.

How to Contact: Submit demo tape of previous work. Prefers cassette or CD or VHS videocassette with 5-8 songs and lead sheet. Include SASE, but prefers to keep material on file. Responds in 6 months.

Music: Uses up-tempo contemporary for industrial videos, slide presentations and commercials.

Tips: "We're looking for commercial music, primarily A/C."

DISK PRODUCTIONS, 1100 Perkins Rd., Baton Rouge LA 70802. Fax: (225)343-0210. E-mail: joey_decker@hotmail.com. **Contact:** Joey Decker, director. **Jingle/production house.** Clients include advertising agencies, slide production houses and film companies. Estab. 1982. Uses the services of music houses, independent songwriters/composers and lyricists for scoring and background music for TV spots, films and jingles for radio and TV. Commissions 7 songwriters/composers and 7 lyricists/year. Pays by the job. Buys all rights.

How to Contact: Submit demo tape of previous work. Prefers CD, cassette or DAT (or ½″ videocassette). Does not return material. Responds in 2 weeks.

Music: Needs all types of music for jingles, music beds or background music for TV and radio, etc.

Tips: "Advertising techniques change with time. Don't be locked in a certain style of writing. Give me music that I can't get from pay needle-drop."

ENSEMBLE PRODUCTIONS, P.O. Box 2332, Auburn AL 36831. (334)703-5963. E-mail: ensembleproductions@usa.net. **Contact:** Barry J. McConatha, owner/producer/director. Interactive multimedia and video production/post production. Clients include corporate, governmental and educational. Estab. 1984. Uses services of music houses and independent songwriters/composers for background music for corporate public relations, educational and training videos. Commissions 0-5 composers/year. Pays $25-250/job depending upon project. Buys one-time rights or all rights.

How to Contact: Send e-mail or submit demo tape of previous work demonstrating composition skills. "Needs are sporadic, write first if submission to be returned." Prefers cassette, CD or VHS videocassette with 3-5 songs. "Most needs are up-beat industrial sound but occasional mood setting music also. Inquire for details." Does not return material; prefers to keep on file. Responds in 3 months if interested. "Usually does not reply unless interested."

Music: Uses up-beat, industrial, New Age, and mood for training, PR, education and multi-media.

Tips: "Make sure your printed material is as precise as your music."

ENTERTAINMENT PRODUCTIONS, INC., 2118 Wilshire Blvd. PMB 744, Santa Monica CA 90403. (310)456-3143. Fax: (310)456-8950. **Contact:** Anne Bell, Music Director. Motion picture and television production company. Clients include motion picture and TV distributors. Estab. 1972. Uses the services of music houses and songwriters for scores, production numbers, background and theme music for films and TV and jingles for promotion of films. Commissions/year vary. Pays by the job or by royalty. Buys motion picture, video and allied rights.

How to Contact: Query with résumé of credits. Demo should show flexibility of composition skills. "Demo records/tapes sent at own risk—returned if SASE included." Responds by letter in 1 month, "but only if SASE is included."

Tips: "Have résumé on file. Develop self-contained capability."

N ESTILO COMMUNICATIONS, 1000 E. Cesar Chavez St., Austin TX 78702-4208. (512)499-0580. Fax: (512)499-0420. E-mail: estilo@estiloms.com. Website: www.estiloms.com. **Contact:** Marion Sanchez-Lozano, president. Advertising agency. Clients include Hispanic and general. Estab. 1989. Uses the services of independent songwriter/composers for jingles for radio and commercials for radio and TV. Commissions 1 composer and 2 lyricists/year. Pays by the job. Buys all rights.
How to Contact: Query with résumé of credits. Submit demo tape of previous work. Prefers cassette. Include SASE. Responds in 3 weeks.
Tips: "Keep calling and sending new materials."

FILM CLASSIC EXCHANGE, 143 Hickory Hill Circle, Osterville MA 02655-1322. Phone/fax: (508)428-7198. E-mail: moviecast@mediaone.net. Vice President: Jeffrey Aikman. Motion picture production company. Clients include motion picture industry/TV networks and affiliates. Estab. 1916. Uses the services of music houses, independent songwriters/composers and lyricists for scoring and background music for motion pictures, TV and video projects. Commissions 10-20 composers and 10-20 lyricists/year. Pays by the job. Buys all rights.
How to Contact: Submit demo tape of previous work. Prefers cassette or VHS videocassette. Include SASE, but prefers to keep material on file. Responds in 2 months.
Music: Uses pop and up-tempo for theatrical films/TV movies.
Tips: "Be persistent."

FINE ART PRODUCTIONS/RICHIE SURACI PICTURES, MULTIMEDIA, INTERACTIVE, 67 Maple St., Newburgh NY 12550-4034. Phone/fax: (845)561-5866. E-mail: rs7fap@idsi.net. Website: www.idsi.net/OPPS5.html **Contact:** Richard Suraci, owner. Advertising agency, audiovisual firm, scoring service, **jingle/commercial music production house**, motion picture production company (Richie Suraci Pictures) and **music sound effect library**. Clients include corporate, industrial, motion picture and broadcast firms. Estab. 1987. Uses services of independent songwriters/composers for scoring, background music and jingles for various projects and commercials for radio and TV. Commissions 1-2 songwriters or composers and 1-2 lyricists/year. Pays by the job, royalty or by the hours. Buys all rights.
How to Contact: Submit demo tape of previous work or tape demonstrating composition skills, query with résumé of credits or write or call first to arrange personal interview. Prefers cassette (or ½″, ¾″, or 1″ videocassette) with as many songs as possible and lyric or lead sheets. Include SASE, but prefers to keep material on file. Responds in 1 year.
Music: Uses all types of music for all types of assignments.

FITZMUSIC, 208 W. 30th St., Suite 1006, New York NY 10001. (212)695-1992. **Contact:** Gary Fitzgerald, composer/producer. **Commercial music production house**. "We service the advertising, film and television community." Estab. 1987. Uses the services of independent composers for scoring of TV, radio and industrials, background music for film and television, and jingles and commercials for radio and TV. Commissions 4-5 composers/year. *"New York talent only."* Pays per project. Buys all rights.
How to Contact: Call first to obtain permission to submit demo tape of previous work. Will not open unsolicited submissions. Prefers CD. Include SASE, but prefers to keep on file. "A follow-up call must follow submission."
Music: Uses all styles of music.
Tips: "Complete knowledge of how the advertising business works is essential. Currently looking for music for stock library."

MARKET CONDITIONS are constantly changing! If you're still using this book and it is 2004 or later, buy the newest edition of *Songwriter's Market* at your favorite bookstore or order directly from Writer's Digest Books at (800)289-0963.

N ▣ **GOLD & ASSOCIATES, INC.**, 6000 Sawgrass Village Circle #C, Ponte Vedra Beach FL 32082. Fax: (904)285-1579. E-mail: gold@strikegold.com. Website: www.strikegold.com. **Contact:** Keith Gold, Creative Director. Marketing, design and advertising firm. Clients include Time-Warner, Disney, Mercury Records, Time-Life Music and the NFL. Estab. 1988. Uses the services primarily of music houses, but also independent songwriters/composers. Agency develops its own lyrics for scoring background music for films, presentations, websites, radio and TV commercials, special events and CDs. Commissions 5-10 music projects/year. "We pay 2-3 firms $500-1,500 for demos. For the final production, we pay between $5,000 and $50,000. We normally buy all rights. However, sometimes one time rights, for a year or specific markets."

• Gold & Associates, Inc. has won over 850 regional, national and international awards, including honors from the Clio Awards, New York Advertising Awards, London International Advertising Awards, Global Awards and The Telly Awards.

How to Contact: Submit demo of previous work. Prefers CD. Will keep submitted material on file. "Sorry, but we contact writers and music houses only when we are ready to have music developed."

Music: Uses every style.

Tips: "Keep sending demos—at least one a year. Most of the time, we select and pay three companies to take our lyrics, and produce a rough demo. We select companies or individuals who have the 'sound' we are looking for. We then choose one for final production."

N **GROUP X, INC.**, P.O. Box 65, Reynoldsburg OH 43068-0065. (614)755-9565. Fax: (614)866-2636. E-mail: signsbyfasteddie@aol.com. **Contact:** Eddie Powell, president. Advertising agency. Clients include retail accounts. Estab. 1990. Uses the services of independent songwriters/composers for background music, jingles and commercials for radio and TV. Pays by the job. Buys all rights.

How to Contact: Submit demo tape of previous work. Prefers cassette, ips reel-to-reel or VHS videocassette with lyric or lead sheet. Include SASE. Responds in 3 months.

Music: Uses country and contemporary for jingles and educational projects.

Tips: "Be patient—work available on an 'as needed' basis only!"

N **HEYWOOD FORMATICS & SYNDICATION**, 1103 Colonial Blvd., Canton OH 44714. (330)456-2592. Owner: Max Heywood. Advertising agency and consultant. Clients include radio, TV, restaurants/lounges. Uses the services of music houses for commercials for radio and TV. Payment varies per project. Buys all rights.

How to Contact: Submit demo tape of previous work. Prefers cassette or 7½ or 15 ips reel-to-reel or VHS/Beta videocassette. Does not return material.

Music: Uses pop, easy listening and CHR for educational films, slide presentations and commercials.

N **THE HITCHINS COMPANY**, 22756 Hartland St., Canoga Park CA 91307-2604. (818)715-0510. Fax: (775)806-2687. E-mail: w.hitchins@socal.rr.com. President: W.E. Hitchins. Advertising agency. Estab. 1985. Uses the services independent songwriters/composers for jingles and commercials for radio and TV. Commissions 1-2 composers and 1-2 lyricists/year. Will negotiate pay. Buys all rights.

How to Contact: Query with résumé of credits. Prefers cassette, CD or VHS videocassette. "Check first to see if we have a job." Does not return material; prefers to keep on file.

Music: Uses variety of musical styles for commercials.

✔ HODGES ASSOCIATES, INC., P.O. Box 53805, 912 Hay St., Fayetteville NC 28305. (910)483-8489. Fax: (910)483-7197. E-mail: wanda@hodgesassoc.com. Website: www.hodgesassoc. com. **Contact:** Anna Smith, President, or Wanda Bullard, Production Manager. Advertising agency. Clients include industrial, retail and consumer. ("We handle a full array of clientele.") Estab. 1974. Uses the services of music houses and independent songwriters/composers for background music for industrial films and slide presentations, and commercials for radio and TV. Commissions 1-2 composers/year. Pays by the job. Buys all rights.

How to Contact: Submit demo tape of previous work. Prefers cassette or CD. Does not return material; prefers to keep on file. Responds in 3 months.

Music: Uses all styles for industrial videos, slide presentations and TV commercials.

HOME, INC., 731 Harrison Ave., Boston MA 02118. (617)266-1386. Fax: (617)266-8514. E-mail: alanmichel@homeinc.org. Director: Alan Michel. Audiovisual firm and video production company. Clients include cable television, nonprofit organizations, pilot programs, entertainment companies and industrial. Uses the services of music houses and independent songwriters/composers for scoring of music videos, background music and commercials for TV. Commissions 2-5 songwriters/year. Pays up to $200-600/job. Buys all rights and one-time rights.
How to Contact: Submit demo tape of previous work. Prefers cassette with 6 pieces. Does not return material; prefers to keep on file. Responds as projects require.
Music: Mostly synthesizer. Uses all styles of music for educational videos.
Tips: "Have a variety of products available and be willing to match your skills to the project and the budget."

K&R'S RECORDING STUDIOS, 28533 Greenfield, Southfield MI 48076. (248)557-8276. E-mail: recordav@knr.net. Website: www.knr.net. **Contact:** Ken Glaza. Scoring service and **jingle/commercial music production house**. Clients include commercial and industrial firms. Services include sound for pictures (music, dialogue). Uses the services of independent songwriters/composers and lyricists for scoring of film and video, commercials and industrials and jingles and commercials for radio and TV. Commissions 1 composer/month. Pays by the job. Buys all rights.
How to Contact: Submit demo tape of previous work. Prefers CD or VHS videocassette with 5-7 short pieces. We rack your tape for client to judge. Does not return material.
Tips: "Keep samples short. Show me what you can do in five minutes. Go to knr.net 'free samples' and listen to the sensitivity expressed in emotional music."

KEN-DEL PRODUCTIONS INC., First State Production Center, 1500 First State Blvd., Wilmington DE 19804-3596. (302)999-1164. Estab. 1950. **Contact:** Edwin Kennedy. A&R Director: Shirl Lotz. General Manager: Edwin Kennedy. Clients include publishers, industrial firms and advertising agencies, how-to's and radio/TV. Uses services of songwriters for radio/TV commercials, jingles and multimedia. Pays by the job. Buys all rights.
How to Contact: "Submit all inquiries and demos in any format to general manager." Does not return material. Will keep on file for 3 years. Generally responds in 1 month.

N̄ KJD ADVERTISING & TELEPRODUCTIONS, INC., 30 Whyte Dr., Voorhees NJ 08043. (856)751-3500. Fax: (856)751-7729. E-mail: mactoday@earthlink.net. **Contact:** Larry Scott, president/executive producer. Audio-video production and media buyers. Clients are varied. Estab. 1989. Uses the services of music houses, independent songwriters/composers or lyricists for background music for commercials, industrials, TV programming themes and jingles; also commercials for radio and TV. Commissions 1-2 composers and 1-2 lyricists/year. Pay varies. Buys all rights.
How to Contact: Query with résumé of credits or submit demo tape of previous work. Prefers cassette, DAT, ips reel-to-reel or ½″ or ¾″ Beta SP videocassette. Include SASE; but prefers to keep material on file. Responds in 6 weeks.

☑ LAPRIORE VIDEOGRAPHY, 70 James St., Worcester MA 01603. (508)755-9010. Website: www.lapriorevideo.com. **Contact:** Peter Lapriore, owner. Video production company. Clients include corporations, retail stores, educational and sports. Estab. 1985. Uses the services of music houses, independent songwriters/composers for background music for marketing, training, educational videos and TV commercials and for scoring video. "We also own several music libraries." Commissions 2 composers/year. Pays $150-1,000/job. Buys all or one-time rights.
How to Contact: Submit demo tape of previous work. Prefers cassette, CD, or VHS videocassette with 5 songs and lyric sheet. Does not return material; prefers to keep on file. Responds in 3 weeks.
Music: Uses slow, medium, up-tempo, jazz and classical for marketing, educational films and commercials.
Tips: "Be very creative and willing to work on all size budgets."

MALLOF, ABRUZINO & NASH MARKETING, 765 Kimberly Dr., Carol Stream IL 60188. (630)929-5200. Fax: (630)752-9288. E-mail: manm@kwom.com. Website: www.manmarketing.com.

Contact: Ed Mallof, president. Advertising agency. Works primarily with auto dealer jingles. Estab. 1980. Uses music houses for jingles for retail clients and auto dealers, and commercials for radio and TV. Commissions 5-6 songwriters/year. Pays $600-2,000/job. Buys all rights.

How to Contact: Submit demo tape of previous work. Prefers cassette with 4-12 songs. Include SASE. Does not return material. Responds if interested.

Tips: "Send us produced jingles we could re-lyric for our customers' needs."

N MEDIA CONSULTANTS, INC., P.O. Box 130, Sikeston MO 63801. (573)472-1116. E-mail: rwrather@sbcglobal.net. **Contact:** Richard Wrather, owner. Advertising agency. Clients are varied. Estab. 1979. Uses the services of music houses, independent songwriters/composers and lyricists for jingles and commercials for radio and TV. Commissions 10-15 composers and 10-15 lyricists/year. Pays varying amount/job. Buys all rights.

How to Contact: Submit a demo tape or CD of previous work demonstrating composition skills. Prefers cassette, CDs or ½″ or ¾″ videocassette. Does not return material; prefers to keep on file. "Send samples and prices."

Music: Uses all styles of music for varied assignments.

N ☑ PATRICK MOORE COMPOSITIONS, 236 Vancouver St., Oshawa, Ontario L1U 5X4 Canada. (905)576-9039. **Contact:** Patrick Moore, owner/president. Scoring service and **jingle/commercial music production house**. Clients include producers of documentaries/films (educational). Estab. 1988. Uses the services of orchestrators for scoring of orchestral scores. Commissions 1 composer/year. Pays by royalty. Buys synchronization rights.

How to Contact: Write first to arrange personal interview. Prefers cassette. Does not return material. Prefers to keep submitted material on file. Responds in 1 month.

Music: "I specialize in combining ethnic music with current music for educational films/documentaries."

Tips: "My needs are very specific and must meet the requirements of the producer and music editor on each project. It is not unusual for me to work with film producers and music writers from all over the world. I do a great deal of work by mailing video tapes and cassette tapes of rough drafts to producers and other professionals involved in a film production."

☑ NOVUS VISUAL COMMUNICATIONS INC., 1122 Yonkers Ave., Suite 2C, Yonkers NY 10704. (212)532-3683. E-mail: novuscom@aol.com. **Contact:** Robert Antonik, president/creative director. Advertising agency. Clients include corporations, interactive products. Estab. 1986. Uses the services of music houses, independent songwriters/composers and lyricists for scoring and background music for documentaries, commercials, multimedia applications, website, film shorts, and commercials for radio and TV. Commissions 2 composers and 4 lyricists/year. Pay varies per job. Buys one-time rights.

How to Contact: *Write first to arrange personal interview.* Query with résumé. Submit demo of previous work. Prefers cassette or VHS videocassette with 2-3 songs. "Submissions should be short and to the point." Prefers to keep submitted material on file, but will return material if SASE is enclosed. Responds in 6 weeks.

Music: Uses all styles for a variety of different assignments.

Tips: "Always present your best and don't add quantity to your reel, cassette, DAT or other submission. Novus is a full service marketing and communications agency. We work with various public relations, artists managements and legal advisors. We create multimedia events to album packaging and promotion."

N OMNI COMMUNICATIONS, Dept. SM, P.O. Box 302, Carmel IN 46032-0302. (317)846-6664. E-mail: winston@omniproductions.com. Website: www.omniproductions.com. President: W.

REMEMBER: Don't "shotgun" your demo tapes. Submit only to companies interested in the type of music you write. For more submission hints, refer to Getting Started on page 10.

H. Long. Creative Director: S.M. Long. Production Manager: Jim Mullet. Television production and audiovisual firm. Estab. 1978. Serves industrial, commercial and educational clients. Uses the services of music houses and songwriters for scoring of films and television productions, CD-ROMs and Internet streams; background music for voice overs; lyricists for original music and themes. Pays by the job. Buys all rights.

How to Contact: Submit demo tape of previous work. Prefers reel-to-reel, cassette or videocassette. Does not return material. Responds in 2 weeks.

Music: Varies with each and every project; from classical, contemporary to commercial industrial.

Tips: "Submit good demo tape with examples of your range to command the attention of our producers."

ON-Q PRODUCTIONS, INC., 618 Gutierrez St., Santa Barbara CA 93103. (805)963-1331. President: Vincent Quaranta. Audiovisual firm. Clients include corporate accounts/sales conventions. Uses the services of music houses, independent songwriters/composers and lyricists for scoring, background music and jingles for AV shows. Commissions 1-5 composers and 1-5 lyricists/year. Buys all or one-time rights.

How to Contact: Query with résumé of credits. Prefers cassette or 15 ips reel-to-reel or VHS videocassette. Prefers to keep material on file.

Music: Uses up-tempo music for slide, video and interactive presentations.

PRICE WEBER MARKETING COMMUNICATIONS, INC., Dept. SM, P.O. Box 99337, Louisville KY 40223. (502)499-9220. Fax: (502)491-5593. E-mail: cfrank@priceweber.com. Website: www.priceweber.com. **Contact:** Charles Frank, associate creative director. Advertising agency and audiovisual firm. Estab. 1968. Clients include Fortune 500, consumer durables, light/heavy industrials and package goods. Uses services of music houses and independent songwriters/composers for scoring of long format videos and corporate shows, jingles for radio and commercials for radio and TV. Commissions 6-8 composers/year. Pays by the job ($5,000-20,000). Buys all or one-time rights.

How to Contact: Submit demo tape of previous work demonstrating composition skills. Prefers CD with 10 or fewer pieces. "Enclose data sheet on budgets per selection on demo tape." Include SASE. Responds in 2 weeks.

Music: Uses easy listening, up-tempo, pop, jazz, rock and classical for corporate image industrials and commercials.

Tips: "We want fresh music. Budgets run from $5,000 to $20,000. Your music must enhance our message."

QUALLY & COMPANY INC., 2238 Central St. #3, Evanston IL 60201-5724. (847)864-6316. **Contact:** Robert Qually, creative director. Advertising agency. Uses the services of music houses, independent songwriters/composers and lyricists for scoring, background music and jingles for radio and TV commercials. Commissions 2-4 composers and 2-4 lyricists/year. Pays by the job. Buys various rights depending on deal.

How to Contact: Submit demo tape of previous work or query with résumé of credits. Prefers cassette or ¾" Beta videocassette. Include SASE, but prefers to keep material on file. Responds in 2 weeks.

Music: Uses all kinds of music for commercials.

N RBM ADVERTISING, (formerly Mitchell & Associates), 3704 Perry Ave., Kensington MD 20895. (301)949-6616. **Contact:** Ronald Mitchell, president. Advertising agency. Serves food, high-tech, transportation, financial, real estate, professional services, automotive and retail clients. Uses

LISTINGS OF COMPANIES within this section which are either commercial music production houses or music libraries will have that information printed in **boldface** type.

independent songwriters, lyricists and music houses for background music for commercials, jingles and post-TV scores for commercials. Commissions 3-5 songwriters and 3-5 lyricists/year. Pays by the job. Buys all rights.

How to Contact: Submit demo tape of previously aired work. Prefers cassette or 7½ ips reel-to-reel. Does not return material; prefers to keep on file.

Music: "Depends upon client, audience, etc."

☑ **RODEO VIDEO, INC.**, 412 S. Main St., Snowflake AZ 85937-0412. (928)536-7111. Fax: (928)536-7120. E-mail: kflake@rodeovideo.com. Website: www.rodeovideo.com. **Contact:** Keith Flake, vice president. Video and TV production company. Clients include rodeo contestants and fans. Estab. 1982. Uses the services of music houses, independent songwriters/composers and lyricists for background music for rodeo blooper videos and rodeo documentaries. Commissions 2 composers and 2 lyricists/year. Pay varies. Buys all rights or one-time rights.

How to Contact: Submit demo tape of previous work. Prefers cassette or DAT with any number of songs. Mainly interested in country/western with rodeo theme. Does not return material. Responds only if interested.

Music: Uses country/western for video backgrounds.

Tips: "Looking for uptempo songs with rodeo theme—country/western or rock."

N: SORIN PRODUCTIONS INC., 919 Highway 33, Suite 46, Freehold NJ 07728. (732)462-1785. Fax: (732)462-8411. E-mail: mail@sorinvideo.com. Website: www.sorinproductions.com. **Contact:** David Sorin, president. Audiovisual firm. Clients include corporations. Estab. 1982. Uses the services of music houses and independent songwriters/composers for background music for industrials, corporate sales, training and image, and commercials for radio and TV. Commissions 2-3 composers/year. Pays negotiable amount/job. Buys all rights.

How to Contact: Query with résumé of credits or send e-mail. Does not return material.

Music: Uses contemporary, upbeat, corporate for video, educational and local spots.

☒ **TRF PRODUCTION MUSIC LIBRARIES**, Dept. SM, 747 Chestnut Ridge Rd., Chestnut Ridge NY 10977. (845)356-0800. Fax: (845)356-0895. E-mail: info@trfmusic.com. Website: www.trfmusic.com. **Contact:** Anne Marie Russo. **Music/sound effect libraries.** Estab. 1931. Uses the services of independent composers for all categories of production music for television, film and other media. Pays 50% royalty.

How to Contact: Submit demo tape of new compositions. Prefers audio cassette or CD with 3-7 pieces. Does not return material. Responds in 3 months.

Music: Primarily interested in acoustic instrumental music for TV, film and AV/multimedia.

☑ ☒ **UTOPIAN EMPIRE CREATIVEWORKS**, 6055 Robert Dr., Traverse City MI 49684. (231)943-5050. E-mail: songwriter@utopianempire.com. Website: www.UtopianEmpire.com. **Contact:** M'Lynn Hartwell, president. Web design, multimedia firm and motion picture/video production company. Serves commercial, industrial and nonprofit clients. We provide the following services: advertising, marketing, design/packaging, distribution and booking. Uses services of music houses, independent songwriters/composers for jingles and scoring of and background music for multi-image/multimedia, film and video. Negotiates pay. Buys all or one-time rights.

How to Contact: Submit demo tape or CD of previous work, demonstrating composition skills or query with résumé of credits. Prefers CD or good quality cassette. Does not return material; prefers to keep on file. Responds only if interested.

Music: Uses mostly industrial/commercial themes.

N: VIDEO I-D, INC., Dept. SM, 105 Muller Rd., Washington IL 61571. (309)444-4323. E-mail: videoid@videoid.com. Website: www.VideoID.com. **Contact:** Gwen Wagner, manager, marketing services. Post production/teleproductions. Clients include industrial and business. Estab. 1977. Uses the services of music houses and independent songwriters/composers for background music for video productions. Pays per job. Buys one-time rights.

How to Contact: Submit demo tape of previous work. Prefers cassette or VHS videocassette with 5 songs and lyric sheet. Does not return material. Responds in 1 month.

VIP VIDEO, Film House, 143 Hickory Hill Circle, Osterville MA 02655. Phone/fax: (508)428-7198. E-mail: moviecast@mediaone.net. Website: www.jeffilms.com. **Contact:** Jeffrey H. Aikman, president. Audiovisual firm. Clients include business, industry and TV stations. Estab. 1983. Uses the services of music houses, independent songwriters/composers and lyricists for scoring andbackground music for motion pictures and home video. Commissions 15-20 composers and 15-20 lyricists/year. Pays by the job, amounts vary depending on the length and complexity of each project. Buys all rights.
How to Contact: Submit demo tape of previous work. Prefers cassette with 1-2 songs. Include SASE, but prefers to keep material on file unless specifically stated. Responds in 2 months.
Music: Uses easy listening, pop and up-tempo for feature films, TV series, TV pilots and background for videotapes. Currently working on scoring series of 26 feature length silent films. If project is successful, this series will be added to at the rate of 13 per year.

VIS/AID MARKETING/ASSOCIATES, P.O. Box 4502, Inglewood CA 90309-4502. (310)399-0696. **Contact:** Lee Clapp, manager. Advertising agency. Clients include "companies in 23 SIC codes (workable)." Estab. 1965. Uses the services of music houses, independent songwriters/composers and lyricists for background music for films, and commercials, TV jingles for radio/TV and scoring new material. Commissions 1-2 composers and 1-2 lyricists/year. Pay is negotiable. Buys all or one-time rights.
How to Contact: Query with résumé of credits. Call first to arrange personal interview or submit demo tape of previous work. Prefers cassette with 1-2 songs and lyric and lead sheet. "Do not send original material that if misplaced/lost cannot be duplicated." Does not return material. Responds in 2 weeks.
Music: Uses up-tempo, pop, jazz and classical for educational films, slide presentations and commercials.

WEISS/STAFFORD PRODUCTIONS, P.O. Box 101107, San Antonio TX 78201. Phone/fax: (210)733-7170 or (800)846-5201. E-mail: faweiss@idworld.net. President: Fred Weiss. Creative Director: Bill Stafford. Television production company. Clients include advertising and TV stations. Estab. 1996. Uses the services of independent songwriters/composers and lyricists for TV programs and music videos. Commissions 100 composers and 100 lyricists/year. Pays statutory royalty. Buys all rights.
How to Contact: Submit demo of the work to be considered. Prefers cassette with 3-4 songs and lyric sheet. "Prefer commercial cuts for young adult male and female artists and bands." Does not return material. Responds in 1 month.
Music: Uses Latin, tejano, international pop and R&B (also Christmas) for talent-search weekly TV show (22 shows/year). Also pop song "hits" for publishing.

EVANS WYATT ADVERTISING, 346 Mediterranean Dr., Suite 220, Corpus Christi TX 78418. (361)939-7200. Fax: (361)939-7999. E-mail: evanswyatt@hotmail.com. Contact: D. Spaller. Advertising agency. Clients are general/all types. Estab. 1975. Uses the services of independent songwriters/composers for background music for commercial/video, jingles for advertising, commercials, radio and TV and interactive video. Commissions 10-12 composers/year. Pays by the job. Buys all rights.
How to Contact: Submit demo, query with resume of credits or write first to arrange personal interview. Prefers CD or cassette. Does not return material. Responds in 2 months.
Music: Uses all types for commercials and videos.

THE FILM & TV INDEX found at the back of this book lists companies placing music in film and TV (excluding TV commercials).

Play Producers & Publishers

Finding a theater company willing to invest in a new production can be frustrating for an unknown playwright. But whether you write the plays, compose the music or pen the lyrics, it is important to remember not only where to start but how to start. Theater in the U.S. is a hierarchy, with Broadway, Off Broadway and Off Off Broadway being pretty much off limits to all but the Stephen Sondheims of the world.

Aspiring theater writers would do best to train their sights on nonprofit regional and community theaters to get started. The encouraging news is there is a great number of local theater companies throughout the U.S. with experimental artistic directors who are looking for new works to produce, and many are included in this section. This section covers two segments of the industry: theater companies and dinner theaters are listed under Play Producers (beginning on page 345), and publishers of musical theater works are listed under the Play Publishers heading (beginning on page 364). All these markets are actively seeking new works of all types for their stages or publications.

BREAKING IN

Starting locally will allow you to research each company carefully and learn about their past performances, the type of musicals they present, and the kinds of material they're looking for. When you find theaters you think may be interested in your work, attend as many performances as possible, so you know exactly what type of material each theater presents. Or volunteer to work at a theater, whether it be moving sets or selling tickets. This will give you valuable insight into the day-to-day workings of a theater and the creation of a new show. On a national level, you will find prestigious organizations offering workshops and apprenticeships covering every subject from arts administration to directing to costuming. But it could be more helpful to look into professional internships at theaters and attend theater workshops in your area. The more knowledgeable you are about the workings of a particular company or theater, the easier it will be to tailor your work to fit its style and the more responsive they will be to you and your work. (See the Workshops & Conferences section on page 438 for more information.) As a composer for the stage, you need to know as much as possible about a theater and how it works, its history and the different roles played by the people involved in it. Flexibility is the key to successful productions, and knowing how a theater works will only help you in cooperating and collaborating with the director, producer, technical people and actors.

If you're a playwright looking to have his play published in book form or in theater publications, see the listings under the Play Publishers section (page 364). To find play producers and publishers in your area, consult the Geographic Index at the back of this book.

Play Producers

☑ **ALLIANCE THEATRE COMPANY**, 1280 Peachtree St., Atlanta GA 30309. (404)733-4650. Fax: (404)733-4625. Website: www.alliancetheatre.org. **Contact:** Freddie Ashley, literary associate. Artistic Director: Susan V. Booth. Play producer. Estab. 1969. Produces 9-10 plays and 1 new musical/year. Audience is diverse, regional and young. Two performing spaces: 800-seat proscenium and a 200-seat flexible black box. Pays negotiable amount per performance.
How to Contact: Query with synopsis, character breakdown and set description. Include SASE. Responds in 6 months.

Musical Theater: They are primarily interested in new musicals, but also will consider works for children's theatre. Musicals for young audiences must be no longer than 1 hour in length and have a cast of 8 or fewer.

Productions: *Hot Mikado*, by David Bell/Rob Bowman/Marjorie B. Kellogg (Gilbert & Sullivan's *The Mikado* updated); *Elaborate Lives: The Legend of Aida*, by Elton John and Tim Rice (musical theatre update of legend); and *Soul Possessed*, by Debbie Allen/James Ingram/Arturo Sandoval (musical dance drama set in bayous of Louisiana).

N **AMAS MUSICAL THEATRE, INC.**, 450 W. 42nd St., Suite 2J, New York NY 10036. (212)563-2565. Fax: (212)268-5501. E-mail: amas@westegg.com. Website: www.westegg.com/am as. Producing Director: Donna Trinkoff. Play producer. Estab. 1968. Produces 2 musicals/year and musical development series (Amas Six O'clock Musical Theatre Lab) produces 5-6 concert versions of new musicals. "We seek to reach a wide and diverse audience by presenting musicals that speak to different cultures." Performance space is on Off-off Broadway theater with 76-99 seats. Payment is standard agreement.

How to Contact: Submit complete manuscript, score and tape of songs. Include SASE. Responds in 6 months.

Musical Theater: Seeks "innovative, well-written, good music. We seek musicals that lend themselves to multiracial casting."

Productions: *Little Ham: A Harlem Jazzical*, by Dan Owens/Richard Engquist/Judd Woldin (the Harlem community in the '30s); *Starmites*, by Stuart Ross/Barry Keating (a sci-fi, pop-rock adventure); and *4 Guys Named José*, by Dolores Prida, conceived by David Coffman (a Latino review).

Tips: "Submit works that speak to and about racial and cultural themes using a fresh, new, fun style."

AMERICAN LIVING HISTORY THEATER, P.O. Box 752, Greybull WY 82426. (307)765-9449. Fax: (307)765-9448. E-mail: ludwigunlimited@hotmail.com. **Contact:** Dorene Ludwig, president/artistic director. Play producer. Estab. 1975. Produces 1-2 new plays/year. Performs all over U.S.—conventions, schools, museums, universities, libraries, etc. Pays by royalty.

How to Contact: Query first. Include SASE. Responds in 1 year.

Musical Theater: "We use only primary source, historically accurate material: in music—*Songs of the Civil War* or *Songs of the Labor Movement*, etc.—presented as a program/production. We would like to keep a file of music historians who might be consulted on selection of material and accuracy."

Tips: "Do not send fictionalized historical material. We use primary source material only."

AMERICAN MUSICAL THEATRE OF SAN JOSE, 1717 Technology Dr., San Jose CA 95110-1305. (408)453-1545. Fax: (408)453-7123. E-mail: mjacobs@amtsj.org. Website: www.amtsj.org. **Contact:** Marc Jacobs, associate artistic director. Play producer. Estab. 1935. Produces 4 mainstage musicals/year. "Our season subscribers are generally upper-middle class families. Our main season is in the 2,500-seat San Jose Center for the Performing Arts. Pays variable royalty.

How to Contact: Submit complete manuscript and tape of songs. Include SASE. Responds in 3-4 months.

Musical Theater: "We are not looking for children's musicals, Christmas shows or puppet shows. We are looking for high quality (professional caliber) musicals to develop for our 2,500-seat main stage theatre, a national tour or possible Broadway production. Submissions from composers and writers with some previous track record only, please. The first thing we look for is quality and originality in the music and lyrics. Next we look for librettos that offer exciting staging possibilities. If writing original music to a pre-existing play please be sure all rights have been cleared."

Productions: Barry Manilow's *Copacabana*; *The Three Musketeers* and Disney's *Beauty and the Beast*.

MARKETS THAT WERE listed in the 2002 edition of *Songwriters Market* but do not appear this year are listed in the General Index with a notation explaining why they were omitted.

Tips: "We are a company with a $6 million per season operating budget and one of the largest subscription audiences in the country. We are looking for shows we can develop for possible main stage or Broadway productions. Therefore it is advisable that any composers or writers have professional production history before submitting to us."

N AMERICAN STAGE FESTIVAL, 14 Court St., Nashua NH 03060. (603)889-2330. Website: www.americanstage.com. **Contact:** Allison Szklarz, managing director. Play producer. Estab. 1971. Produces 6 mainstage plays, 5 children's and 2-3 musicals/year. Plays are produced in 285 seat thrust stage for a general audience. Pays 5-12% royalty.
How to Contact: Query with synopsis, character breakdown and set description. Include SASE. Responds in 3 months.
Musical Theater: "We seek stories about interesting people in compelling situations. Besides our adult audience we have an active children's theater. We will not do a large chorus musical if cast size is over 18. We use original music in plays on a regular basis, as incidental music, pre-show and between acts, or as moments in and of themselves."
Productions: *1776*, by Edwards/Stone (history); *Little Shop of Horrors*, by Alan Mencken/Howard Ashman (comedy); and *Ten Types* (musical revue of pre-WWI songs).
Tips: "We need musicals with a strong, intelligent book. Send tape of music along with initial query. Our decisions regarding musicals are based heavily upon the quality of the score."

N ARDEN THEATRE COMPANY, 40 N. Second St., Philadelphia PA 19106. (215)922-8900. E-mail: info@ardentheatre.org. Website: www.ardentheatre.org. **Contact:** Terrence J. Nolen, producing artistic director. Play producer. Estab. 1988. Produces 3-4 plays and 1-2 musicals/year. Adult audience—diverse. Mainstage: 350+ seats, flexible. Studio: 175+ seats, flexible.
How to Contact: Query with synopsis, character breakdown and set description. Include SASE. Responds in 1 year.
Musical Theater: Full length plays and musicals. The Arden Theatre Company is dedicated to bringing to life the greatest stories by the greatest storytellers of all time. We draw from any source that is inherently dramatic and theatrical—fiction, nonfiction, poetry, music and drama. Especially interested in literary adaptations. Also interested in musicals for children. Will consider original music for use in developing or pre-existing play. Composers should send samples of music on cassette.
Productions: *Baby Case*, by Michael Ozborn (Lindbergh baby kidnapping/trial of Bruno Richard Hauptman); *James Joyce's The Dead*, by Richard Nelson (adaptation of Joyce's short story); and *Baker's Wife*, by Stephen Schwartz (French fable on love and marriage).

ARKANSAS REPERTORY THEATRE, 601 Main, P.O. Box 110, Little Rock AR 72203. (501)378-0445. Fax: (501)378-0012. Website: www.therep.org. **Contact:** Brad Mooy. Play producer. Estab. 1976. Produces 8 plays and 4 musicals (1 new musical)/year. "We perform in a 354-seat house and also have a 99-seat blackbox." Pays 5-10% royalty or $75-150 per performance.
How to Contact: Query with synopsis, character breakdown and set description. Include SASE. Responds in 6 months.
Musical Theater: "Small casts are preferred, comedy or drama and prefer shows to run 1:45 to 2 hours maximum. Simple is better; small is better, but we do produce complex shows. We aren't interested in children's pieces, puppet shows or mime. We always like to receive a tape of the music with the book."
Productions: *Radio Gals*, by Mike Craver/Mark Hardwick; and *Always . . . Patsy Cline*, by Ted Swindley (bio-musical).
Tips: "Include a *good* cassette of your music, *sung well*, with the script."

N ASOLO THEATRE COMPANY, Dept. SM, 5555 N. Tamiami Trail, Sarasota FL 34243. (941)351-9010. E-mail: bruce_rodgers@asolo.org. Website: www.asolo.org. Associate Artistic Director: Bruce E. Rodgers. Play producer. Produces 7-8 plays (1 musical)/year. Plays are performed at the Asolo Mainstage (500-seat proscenium house). Pays negotiated royalty.
How to Contact: Query with synopsis, character breakdown, set description and one page of dialogue. Include SASE. Responds in 6 months.

Musical Theater: "We want small to mid-size non-chorus musicals only. They should be full-length, any subject. There are no restrictions on production demands; however, musicals with excessive scenic requirements or very large casts may be difficult to consider."

Productions: *Oh What A Lovely War*, by Joan Littlewood (WWI); and *Jane Eyre*, by Ted Davis/David Clark.

☑ **BAILIWICK REPERTORY**, Bailiwick Arts Center, 1229 W. Belmont, Chicago IL 60657. (773)883-1090. Fax: (773)883-2017. E-mail: bailiwickr@aol.com. Website: www.bailiwick.org. Director: David Zak. Producer: Rusty Hernandez. Play producer. Estab. 1982. Produces 5 mainstage, 5 one-act plays and 1-2 new musicals/year. "We do Chicago productions of new works on adaptations that are politically or thematically intriguing and relevant. We also do an annual director's festival which produces 50-75 new short works each year." Pays 5-8% royalty.

How to Contact: "Review our manuscript submission guidelines on the professional page of our website." Responds in 6 months.

Musical Theater: "We want innovative, dangerous, exciting material."

Productions: *The Christmas Schooner*, by John Reeger and Julie Shannon (holiday musical); *Bonnie and Clyde*, by Pomerantz/Eickmann/Herron/Ritchie (Roaring 20s).

Tips: "Be creative. Be patient. Be persistent. Make me believe in your dream."

☑ **BARTER THEATRE**, P.O. Box 867, Abingdon VA 24212. (276)628-2281. Fax: (276)619-3335. E-mail: barter@naxs.com. Website: www.bartertheatre.com. **Contact:** Richard Rose, artistic director. Play producer. Estab. 1933. Produces 15 plays and 5-6 musicals (1 new musical)/year. Audience "varies; middle American, middle age, tourist and local mix." 500-seat proscenium stage, 140-seat thrust stage. Pays 5% royalty.

How to Contact: Query with synopsis, character breakdown and set description. Include SASE. Responds in 1 year.

Musical Theater: "We investigate all types. We are not looking for any particular standard. Prefer sellable titles with unique use of music. Prefer small cast musicals, although have done large scale projects with marketable titles or subject matter. We use original music in almost all of our plays." Does not wish to see "political or very urban material, or material with very strong language."

Productions: *Something's Afoot*, by James McDonald, David Vos and Robert Girlach; *Oklahoma*, by Rodgers & Hammerstein; and *South Pacific*, Rodgers & Hammerstein.

Tips: "Be patient. Be talented. Don't be obnoxious. Be original and make sure subject matter fits our audience."

🄽 **BIRMINGHAM CHILDREN'S THEATRE**, P.O. Box 1362, Birmingham AL 35201-1362. (205)458-8181. Fax: (205)458-8895. E-mail: bertb@bct123.org. Website: www.bct123.org. **Contact:** Bert Brosowsky, executive director. Play producer. Estab. 1947. Produces 9 plays and 1-4 new musicals/year; "typically, original adaptations of classic children's stories for pre-school through grade 1, K-6, and junior and senior high school." "Wee Folks" Series: preschool through grade 1; Children's Series: K-6; Young Adult Series: junior and senior high. Performs in 1,072-seat flexible thrust mainstage theater, 250 seat black box theater and a 200 seat studio theater (touring venues vary). Pay is negotiable.

How to Contact: Query with synopsis, character breakdown and set description. Include SASE. Responds in 3 months.

Musical Theater: " 'Wee Folks' productions should be 40-45 minutes; Children's Series 55-60 minutes; Young Adult Series 85-95 minutes. 'Wee Folks' shows should be interactive; all others presentational. Most productions tour, so sets must be lightweight, simple and portable. 'Wee Folks' shows prefer cast of four. Touring Children's Series shows prefer cast of six. All others prefer cast of 12 or less. BCT traditionally ultilizes a great deal of music for underscoring, transitions, etc. We welcome submissions from prospective sound designers."

Productions: *To Kill a Mocking Bird*, dramatized by Christopher Sengel, book by Harper Lee; *Sleeping Beauty*, by Joe Zellner/Ed Rosendahl, music by Jay Tumminello; *Three Billy Goats Gruff*, by Jean Pierce, music by Jim Aycock; and *The Swiss Family Robinson*, adapted by Randy Marsh.

☑ **THE BLOWING ROCK STAGE COMPANY**, P.O. Box 2170, Blowing Rock NC 28605. (828)295-9168. Fax: (828)295-9104. E-mail: theatre@blowingrock.com. Website: www.blowingrock stage.com. **Contact:** Kenneth Kay, producing director. Play producer. Estab. 1986. Produces 4 shows/ year. "Blowing Rock Stage Company provides a professional summer theatre experience for the residents and the high volume of summer tourists." Performances take place in a 240-seat proscenium summer theater in the Blue Ridge Mountains. Pays flat fee/performance or 5-7% royalty.

How to Contact: Query with synopsis, character breakdown and set description. Include SASE. Responds in up to 6 months.

Musical Theater: "Casts of ten or less are preferred, with ideal show running time of two hours, intermission included. Limit set changes to three or less; or unit concept. Some comic relief, please. Not producing stark adult themes."

Productions: *Daylight Spirits*, by Charles Thomas (Appalachian music and storyline); *A Grand Night for Singing*, by Rodgers and Hammerstein (review); and *Sophie*, by Karin Baker and Tony Parise (the Sophie Tucker story).

Tips: "We're looking for inspiration. We enjoy supporting projects which are soulful and uplifting. We want light-hearted musicals with some comic relief."

BRISTOL RIVERSIDE THEATRE, Dept. SM, P.O. Box 1250, Bristol PA 19007. (215)785-6664. Fax: (215)785-2762. Website: www.brtstage.org. Artistic Director: Susan D. Atkinson. Business Manager: Jo Lalli. Play producer. Estab. 1986. Produces 5 plays and 2 musicals/year (1 new musical every 2 years) and summer concert series. "302-seat proscenium Equity theater with audience of all ages from small towns and metropolitan area." Pays 6-8% royalty.

How to Contact: Submit complete manuscript, score and tape of songs. Include SASE. Responds in 18 months.

Musical Theater: "No strictly children's musicals. All other types with small to medium casts and within reasonable artistic tastes. Prefer one-set; limited funds restrict. Do not wish to see anything catering to prurient interests."

Productions: *Sally Blane, World's Greatest Girl Detective*, by David Levy/Leslie Eberhard (spoof of teen detective genre); *Moby Dick*, by Mark St. Germain, music by Doug Katsarous; and *Texas Flyer*, by Larry Gatlin.

Tips: "You should be willing to work with small staff, open to artistic suggestion, and aware of the limitations of newly developing theaters."

Ⓝ BROADWAY ON SUNSET, 10800 Hesby St., North Hollywood CA 91601. (818)508-9270. E-mail: broadwayonsunset@cs.com. Website: www.broadwayonsunset.org. Executive Director: Kevin Kaufman. Artistic Director: Libbe S. HaLevey. Play producer. Estab. 1991. Broadway on Sunset is devoted exclusively to developing original material through various classes, workshops and staging opportunities. Produces the annual West Coast Musical Theatre Conference."

How to Contact: Query first. Include SASE. Responds in 3 months.

Musical Theater: "Seeking original, unproduced musicals, only, for mainstream audience. This is not the place for experimental, controversial material, although challenging themes and concepts are encouraged."

Productions: *American Twistory*, by Kevin Kaufman/John Everest (satirical revue); and *Mates: The Pirate Musical*, by Don Hale/Jimmy Horowitz.

CENTENARY COLLEGE, Theatre Dept., Shreveport LA 71134-1188. (318)869-5075. Fax: (318)869-5760. E-mail: rbuseick@centenary.edu. **Contact:** Robert R. Buseick, chairman. Play producer. Produces 6 plays (1-2 new musicals)/year. Plays are presented in a 350-seat playhouse to college and community audiences. Pay is negotiable.

How to Contact: Query with synopsis, character breakdown and set description. Does not return material. Responds as soon as possible.

FOR BOOKS ON THE CRAFT AND BUSINESS of songwriting, check out the website for Writer's Digest Books at www.writersdigest.com.

Productions: *Blood Brothers*; *Grand Hotel*; and *Funny Girl*.
Tips: "Keep trying. It's not easy."

CIRCA '21 DINNER PLAYHOUSE, Dept. SM, P.O. Box 3784, Rock Island IL 61204-3784.
(309)786-2667. **Contact:** Dennis Hitchcock, producer. Play producer. Estab. 1977. Produces 1-2
plays and 4-5 musicals (1 new musical)/year. Plays produced for a general audience. Three children's
works/year, concurrent with major productions. Payment is negotiable.
How to Contact: Query with synopsis, character breakdown and set description or submit complete
manuscript, score and tape of songs. Include SASE. Responds in 3 months.
Musical Theater: "We produce both full length and one act children's musicals. Folk or fairy tale
themes. Works that do not condescend to a young audience yet are appropriate for entire family.
We're also seeking full-length, small cast musicals suitable for a broad audience." Would also consider original music for use in a play being developed.
Productions: *A Closer Walk with Patsy Cline, Swingtime Canteen.*
Tips: "Small, upbeat, tourable musicals (like *Pump Boys*) and bright musically-sharp children's
productions (like those produced by Prince Street Players) work best. Keep an open mind. Stretch to
encompass a musical variety—different keys, rhythms, musical ideas and textures."

N CREEDE REPERTORY THEATRE, P.O. Box 269, Creede CO 81130. (719)658-2541. Fax:
(719)658-2343. E-mail: crt@creederep.com. **Contact:** Maurice Lamee, producing/artistic director.
Play producer. Estab. 1966. Produces 6 plays and 1 musical/year. Performs in 243-seat proscenium
theatre; audience is ½ local support and ½ tourist base from Texas, Oklahoma, New Mexico and
Colorado. Pays 7% royalty.
How to Contact: Query first. Include SASE. Responds in 1 year.
Musical Theater: "We prefer historical Western material with cast no larger than 11. Staging must
be flexible as space is limited."
Productions: *Baby Doe Tabor*, by Kenton Kersting (Colorado history); *A Frog in His Throat*, by
Feydeau, adapted by Eric Conger (French farce); and *Tommyknockers*, by Eric Engdahl, Mark Hous-
ton and Chris Thompson (mining).
Tips: "Songwriter must have the ability to accept criticism and must be flexible."

THE DIRECTORS COMPANY, 311 W. 43rd St., Suite 307, New York NY 10036. (212)246-
5877. Fax: (212)246-5882. Website: www.thedirectorscompany.org. **Contact:** Michael Parva, artistic/
producing director. Play producer. Estab. 1980. Produces 1-2 new musicals/year. Performance space
is a 99-seat theatre located in the heart of Manhattan's Theatre District. "It is beautifully equipped
with dressing rooms, box office and reception area in the lobby." Pays negotiable rate.
How to Contact: Query first. Include SASE. Responds in 1 year.
Musical Theater: "The Harold Prince Musical Theatre Program develops new musicals by incorporating the director in the early stages of collaboration. The program seeks cutting edge material that
works to break boundaries in music theatre. We produce workshops or developmental productions.
The emphasis is on the material, not on production values, therefore, we do not limit cast sizes.
However, there are limits on props and production values." No children's musicals or reviews.
Productions: Three by various authors.

N GEOF ENGLISH, PRODUCER, SADDLEBACK CIVIC LIGHT OPERA, Saddleback
College, 28000 Marguerite Pkwy., Mission Viejo CA 92692. (949)582-4763. E-mail: genglish@saddl
eback.cc.ca.us. Producer: Geofrey English. Play producer for musical theater. Produces 4 musicals/
year. Community audience of mostly senior citizens. Pays by royalty and performance.
How to Contact: Submit complete manuscript, score and tape of songs. Does not return material.
Responds in 3 months.
Musical Theater: "Looking for mainly family musicals. No limitations, open to options. It is
important that music must be sent along with scripts. Best not to call. Just send materials."
Productions: *Hello Dolly*; *Once Upon a Mattress*; and *Musical Revues* (Rodgers/Hart/various).
Tips: "Submit materials in a timely manner—usually at least one year in advance."

ENSEMBLE THEATRE, 1127 Vine St., Cincinnati OH 45210. (513)421-3555. Fax: (513)562-4104. Website: www.cincyetc.com. **Contact:** D. Lynn Meyers, producing artistic director. Play producer. Estab. 1986. Produces 14 plays and at least 1 musical (1 new musical)/year. Audience is multi-generational and multi-cultural. 191 seats, ¾ stage. Pays 5-8% royalty (negotiable).
How to Contact: Query with synopsis, character breakdown and set description. Include SASE. Responds in 6 months.
Musical Theater: "All types of musicals are acceptable. Cast not over ten; minimum set, please."
Productions: *The Adventures of Pinocchio*, a world premiere by David Kisor and Joseph McDonough; *Hedwig & The Angry Inch*, by John Cameron Mitchell; and *Violet*, by Brian Crawley.
Tips: Looking for "creative, inventive, contemporary subjects or classic tales. Send materials as complete as possible."

N FOOLS COMPANY, INC., 423 W. 46th, New York NY 10036. (212)307-6000. E-mail: foolsco @nyc.rr.com. **Contact:** Jill Russell, Executive Director. Collaborative new and experimental works producer. Estab. 1970. Produces 3 plays and 2 musicals (2 new musicals)/year. "Audience is comprised of hip, younger New Yorkers. Plays are performed at our own mid-Manhattan theater." Pay is negotiable.
How to Contact: Query first. Include SASE. Responds in 1 month.
Musical Theater: "We seek new and unusual, contemporary and experimental material. We would like small, easy-to-tour productions. Nothing classical, folkloric or previously produced." Would also consider working with composers in collaboration or original music for use in plays being developed.
Productions: *Rug Burn*; *Cathleen's Corsage*(alternative performance); and *Love Stiff*.
Tips: "Come work in NYC!"

☑ THE GASLIGHT THEATRE, 7010 E. Broadway, Tucson AZ 85710. (520)886-9428. Fax: (520)722-6232. **Contact:** Bonnie Rexroat, general manager. Play producer. Estab. 1977. Produces 5 musical melodramas (2-3 new musicals)/year. "We cater to family audiences. Our musical melodramas are always fun and never sad. Ages from toddlers to senior citizens come to our shows." Performance space is 20′w×15′d (not including the apron). Pays for outright purchase.
How to Contact: Query with synopsis, character breakdown, set description. Submit complete ms and score. Include SASE. Responds in 2 months.
Musical Theater: Prefers musical melodramas of 1 hour and 30 minutes; with an olio of 18-20 minutes. "Our shows always have a hero and villain." Cast size is usually 3 women and 5-6 men. Does not wish to see anything violent or sad. "Family entertainment only." Looking for slapstick comedy. "We always use fun sets, i.e., rolling rocks, underwater adventure, camels that move, horses, etc. Our musical melodrama is followed by a themed olio (song and dance show with jokes). Include lots of music to accompany the show."
Productions: *Zerro Rides Again*; *Robin Hood*; and *Gnatman* (Crime fighter who is a gnat. Take off of Batman), all by Peter Van Slyke.
Tips: "Think fun and comedy! Our productions always have a villian and a hero. In the conflict the hero always wins. Always fun and family entertainment. Lots of music."

THE WILL GEER THEATRICUM BOTANICUM, P.O. Box 1222, Topanga CA 90290. (310)455-2322. Fax: (310)455-3724. E-mail: theatricum@mindspring.com. Website: www.theatricum.com. **Contact:** Ellen Geer, artistic director. Literary Director: Isreal Baran. Play producer. Produces 4 plays, 1 new musical/year. Plays are performed in "large outdoor amphitheater with 60′x 25′ wooden stage. Rustic setting." Pays negotiable royalty.
How to Contact: Query with synopsis, tape of songs and character breakdown. Include SASE. Responds as soon as can be read.
Musical Theater: Seeking social or biographical works, children's works and full length musicals with cast of up to 10 equity actors (the rest non-equity). Requires "low budget set and costumes. We emphasize paying performers." Would also consider original music for use in a play being developed. Does not wish to see "anything promoting avarice, greed, violence or apathy."
Productions: *Three Penny Opera*, by Brecht; *Robber Bridegroom*, by VHRY/Waldman (country folktale); and *Pie in the Sky*, by Alsop (nuclear/3 Mile Island).

N LA JOLLA PLAYHOUSE, P.O. Box 12039, La Jolla CA 92039. (858)550-1070. Fax: (858)550-1075. E-mail: ljp@ucsd.edu. Website: www.lajollaplayhouse.com. **Contact:** Carrie Ryan, literary manager. Play producer. Estab. 1947. Produces 5 plays and 1 musical (1-2 new musicals)/year. Audience is University of California students to senior citizens. Performance space is a large proscenium theatre with 480 seats.

How to Contact: Query with synopsis, character breakdown. Include SASE. Responds in 9 months.

Musical Theater: "We prefer contemporary music but not necessarily a story set in contemporary times. Retellings of classic stories can enlighten us about the times we live in. For budgetary reasons, we'd prefer a smaller cast size."

Productions: *Jane Eyre*, book and additional lyrics by John Cairo, music and lyrics by Paul Gordon (adaptation of Charlotte Brontë's novel); *Thoroughly Modern Millie*, book by Richard Morris and Dick Scanlan, new music by Jeanine Tesori, new lyrics by Dick Scanlan (based on the 1967 movie); and *Dracula, The Musical*, book and lyrics by Don Black and Christopher Hampton, music by Frank Wildhorn (adaptation of Bram Stoker's novel).

☑ LOS ANGELES DESIGNERS' THEATRE, P.O. Box 1883, Studio City CA 91614-0883. (323)650-9600. T.D.D.: (323)654-2700. Fax: (323)654-3210. E-mail: ladesigners@juno.com. **Contact:** Richard Niederberg, artistic director. Play producer. Estab. 1970. Produces 20-25 plays and 8-10 new musicals/year. Audience is predominantly Hollywood production executives in film, TV, records and multimedia. Plays are produced at several locations, primarily Studio City, California. Pay is negotiable.

How to Contact: Query first. Does not return material. Responds in 4 months. *Send proposals only.*

Musical Theater: "We seek out controversial material. Street language OK, nudity is fine, religious themes, social themes, political themes are encouraged. Our audience is very 'jaded' as it consists of TV, motion picture and music publishing executives who have 'seen it all'." Does not wish to see bland, "safe" material. "We like first productions. In the cover letter state in great detail the proposed involvement of the songwriter, other than as a writer (i.e., director, actor, singer, publicist, designer, etc.). Also, state if there are any liens on the material or if anything has been promised."

Productions: *St. Tim*, by Fred Grab (historical '60s musical); *Slipper and the Rose* (gang musical); and *1593—The Devils Due* (historical musical).

Tips: "Make it very 'commercial' and inexpensive to produce. Allow for non-traditional casting. Be prepared with ideas as to how to transform your work to film or videotaped entertainment."

N DON AND PAT MACPHERSON PRODUCTIONS, 461 Parkway, Gatlinburg TN 37738. (865)436-4039. **Contact:** Don MacPherson and Pat MacPherson, co-owners/producers. Play producer. Estab. 1977. Produces 2 musicals/year. Plays are performed at Sweet Fanny Adams Theatre, Gatlinburg, Tennessee to tourist audience. Pays $25/per performance.

How to Contact: Query with synopsis, character breakdown and set description. Include SASE. Responds in 1 month.

Musical Theater: "Produce musicals that are funny, fast—in fact, silly; musical farces. Theater is 1890 style so shows should fit that period. Have done many westerns. Cast size limited to 7 or 8 with 2 musicians on taped music. Stage very small. Use old-time backdrops forsets. Shows should be no longer than 90 minutes." Does not wish to see "shows that would not fit 1890s style—unless it had a country theme."

Productions: *Phantom of the Opry*, by Don & Pat MacPherson/J. Lovensheimer (spoof of *Phantom of the Opera*); *Life & Times of Billy Kincaid*, by MacPherson/Lovensheimer (western); and *Not Quite Frankenstein*, by Don and Pat MacPherson.

Tips: "See a production at Sweet Fanny Adams."

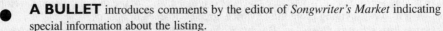

● **A BULLET** introduces comments by the editor of *Songwriter's Market* indicating special information about the listing.

N MAGIC THEATRE, Ft. Mason Center, Bldg. D, San Francisco CA 94123. (415)441-8001. Fax: (415)771-5505. E-mail: LauraO@magictheatre.org. Website: www.magictheatre.org. **Contact:** Laura Owen, literary manager. Play producer. Estab. 1968. Produces 5-6 plays/year. Audience is educated/intelligent, willing to take risks. Two performance spaces: 155-seat modified thrust and 155-seat proscenium. Pays negotiable royalty.

How to Contact: Query with synopsis, character breakdown and set description. "We prefer a smaller cast size, and nothing larger than 7 or 8." Include SASE. Responds in 2 months.

Musical Theater: Plays are innovative in form and structure. Chamber musicals are best. Cast size of 6-8. "We have only recently decided to start producing musicals. We are interested in stories with a strong book as well as music." Considers original music for use in a play being developed or for use in a pre-existing play.

Productions: *Hillary and Soon Yi Shop for Ties*, by Michelle Carter; *Schrödinger's Girlfriend*, by Matthew Wells; and *First Love*, by Charles Mee, Jr.

MANHATTAN THEATRE CLUB, 311 W. 43rd St., New York NY 10036. (212)399-3000. Fax: (212)399-4329. Website: www.mtc-nyc.org. **Contact:** Clifford Lee Johnson III, director of musical theater program. Associate Artistic Director: Michael Bush. Artistic Director: Lynne Meadow. Play producer. Estab. 1971. Produces 8 plays and sometimes 1 musical/year. Plays are performed at the Manhattan Theatre Club before varied audiences. Pays negotiated fee.

How to Contact: Query first. Include SASE. Responds in 4 months.

Musical Theater: "Original work."

Productions: *A Class Act*, by Ed Kleban/Lonny Price/Linda Kline; *The Wild Party*, by Andrew Lippa; and *Newyorkers*, by Stephen Weiner/Glenn Slater.

Tips: "Make sure your script is tightly and securely bound."

N MILL MOUNTAIN THEATRE, 1 Market Square, 2nd Floor, Roanoke VA 24011-1437. (540)342-5749. Fax: (540)342-5745. E-mail: outreach@millmountain.org. Website: www.millmountain.org. **Contact:** Literary Coordinator. Play producer. Estab. 1964. Produces 11-14 plays and generally 3 established musicals (1-2 new musicals)/year. General theater audience on mainstage; a more open minded audience in Theatre B; also children's musicals. 400-seat proscenium mainstage; 125-seat alternate space. Pays variable royalty.

How to Contact: General submission policy: query with synopsis, 10-page dialogue sample and demo tape/CD. SASE. Responds in 6 months. See website or send SASE for New Play Competition guidelines.

Musical Theater: We seek children's musicals for our main stage (especially scripts adapted from recognizable children's works). Also, plays and musicals for young audiences for our educational outreach tours to schools and community centers. We also accept contemporary musicals which explore new forms and themes. Smaller cast musicals with a minimum of technical requirements are encouraged. Musicals are also accepted in our New Play Competition.

Productions: *My Way*, by David Grapes/Todd Olson (Sinatra revue); *I Love You, You're Perfect, Now Change*, by James Hammerstein/Bernie Kukoff/Jonathan Ballard (revue of songs and scenes about dating and marriage); and *Rapunzel*, by David Crane/Marta Kauffman/Michael Skloff (one-hour family musical based on fairy tale).

MIXED BLOOD THEATRE CO., 1501 S. Fourth St., Minneapolis MN 55454. (612)338-7892. E-mail: czar@mixedblood.com. **Contact:** David Kunz, script czar. Play producer. Estab. 1976. Produces 4-5 plays/year and perhaps 1 new musical every 2 years. "We have a 200-seat theater in a converted firehouse. The audience spans the socio-economic spectrum." Pays royalty or per performance.

How to Contact: Query first (1-page cover letter, 1-page synopsis). Include SASE. Responds on queries in 2 months.

Musical Theater: "We want full-length, non-children's works with a message. Always query first. Never send unsolicited script or tape."

Productions: *Black Belts II*, musical revue (black female vocalists and their music); *Birth of the Boom* (do-wop/hip hop extravaganza); and *Vices* (musical sketch revue).

Tips: "Always query first. The direct approach is best. Be concise. Make it interesting. Surprise us. Contemporary comedies, politically-edged material and sports-oriented shows are usually of interest."

☑ **NEW REPERTORY THEATRE**, P.O. Box 610418, Newton Highlands MA 02461-0418. (617)332-7058. Fax: (617)527-5217. E-mail: info@newrep.org. Website: www.NewRep.org. **Contact:** Rick Lombardo, producing artistic director. Play producer. Estab. 1984. Produces 5 plays and 1 musical/year. Audience is Metro-Boston based. Performance space is an intimate, 170-seat thrust stage with minimal space for musicians. Pays negotiable royalty.
How to Contact: Query with synopsis, character breakdown and set description. Include SASE. Responds in 9 months.
Musical Theater: Seeks small cast (under 7), unusual stories, small orchestra. Full-length with adult themes. Does not wish to see standard musical comedies.
Productions: *Valley Song*, by Athol Fugard (South Africa); *Gifts of the Magi*, by Mark St. Germain and Randy Courrrts (musical of O'Henry); and *Moby Dick*, music by Doug Katsaros, libretto by Mark St. Germain.
Tips: "Be very clever in theatricality and style. Be unconventional."

NEW YORK STATE THEATRE INSTITUTE, 37 First St., Troy NY 12180. (518)274-3200. E-mail: nysti@capital.net. Website: www.nysti.org. **Contact:** Patricia Di Benedetto Snyder, producing artistic director. Play producer. Produces 5 plays (1 new musical)/year. Plays performed for student audiences grades K-12, family audiences and adult audiences. Theater seats 900 with full stage. Pay negotiable.
How to Contact: Query with synopsis, character breakdown, set description and tape of songs. Include SASE. *Do not send manuscript unless invited.* Responds in 6 weeks for synopsis, 4 months for manuscript.
Musical Theater: Looking for "intelligent and well-written book with substance, a score that enhances and supplements the book and is musically well-crafted and theatrical." Length: up to 2 hours. Could be play with music, musical comedy, musical drama. Excellence and substance in material is essential. Cast could be up to 20; orchestra size up to 8.
Productions: *A Tale of Cinderella*, by W.A. Frankonis/Will Severin/George David Weiss (adaptation of fairy tale); *The Silver Skates*, by Lanie Robertson/Byron Janis/George David Weiss (adaptation of book); *The Snow Queen*, by Adrian Mitchell/Richard Peaslee (adaptation of fairy tale); and *Magna Carta*, by Ed Lange/Will Severin/George David Weiss (new musical drama).
Tips: "There is a great need for musicals that are well-written with intelligence and substance which are suitable for family audiences."

☑ **NEW YORK THEATRE WORKSHOP**, 79 E. Fourth St., New York NY 10003. (212)780-9037. Fax: (212)460-8996. E-mail: info@nytw.org. Website: www.nytw.org. **Contact:** James C. Nicola, artistic director. Play producer. Produces 4-6 mainstage plays and approximately 50 readings/year. "Plays are performed in our theater on East Fourth St. Audiences include: subscription/single ticket buyers from New York area, theater professionals, and special interest groups." Pays by negotiable royalty.
How to Contact: Query with synopsis, character breakdown and set description. Include SASE. Responds in 5 months.
Musical Theater: "As with our nonmusicals, we seek musicals of intelligence and social consciousness that challenge our perceptions of the world and the events which shape our lives. We favor plays that possess a strong voice, distinctive and innovative use of language and visual imagery. Integration of text and music is particularly of interest. Musicals which require full orchestrations would generally be too big for us. We prefer 'musical theater pieces' rather than straightforward 'musicals' per-se. We often use original music for straight plays that we produce. This music may be employed as pre-show, post-show or interlude music. If the existing piece lends itself, music may also be incorporated within the play itself. Large casts (12 or more) are generally prohibitive and require soliciting of additional funds. Design elements for our productions are of the highest quality possible with our limited funds."

Productions: *The Waves*, adapted from Virginia Woolf's novel, music and lyrics by David Bucknam and text and direction by Lisa Peterson; *My Children! My Africa*, by Athol Fugard; and *Rent*, by Jonathan Larson.
Tips: "Submit ten pages of the script and a one page synopsis which captures the heart of your piece; inject your piece with a strong voice and intent and try to surprise and excite us."

N NORTH SHORE MUSIC THEATRE, 62 Dunham Rd., Beverly MA 01915. (978)232-7203. Fax: (978)921-0793. E-mail: pr@nsmt.org. Website: www.nsmt.org. **Contact:** John La Roch, associate producer. Play producer. Estab. 1955. Produces 1 play and 6 musicals (2 new musicals)/year. General audiences. Performance space is an 1800-seat arena theatre, 120-seat workshop. Pays royalty (all done via individual commission agreements).
How to Contact: Submit synopsis and CD of songs. Include SASE. Responds within 4 months.
Musical Theater: Prefers full-length adult pieces not necessarily arena-theatre oriented. Cast sizes from 1-30; orchestra's from 1-16.
Productions: *Just So*, by Anthony Drewe & George Stiles (musical based on Rudyard Kipling's fables); *Letters from 'Nam*, by Paris Barclay (Vietnam War experience as told through letters from GI's); and *Friendship of the Sea*, by Michael Wartofsky & Kathleen Cahill (New England maritime adventure musical).
Tips: "Keep at it!"

N NORTHERN LIGHTS PLAYHOUSE, P.O. Box 256, Dept. SMV, Hazelhurst WI 54531-0256. (715)356-7173, ext. 958. Fax: (715)356-1851. E-mail: nlplays@newnorth.net. **Contact:** Michael D. Cupp, producer. Play producer. Estab. 1976. Produces 5 plays and 8 musicals/year. Audience consists of conservative, wealthy, retired senior citizens. Performance space includes a proscenium and three-quarter. Pays per performance or per royalty.
How to Contact: Query with synopsis, character breakdown and set description. Include SASE. Responds in 6 months.
Musical Theater: Prefers family oriented musical comedies, 2 hours in length; children's theatre 1 hour in length. "We would love to receive a Christmas musical and/or revue." Cast limit is 12-16. "I am also in search of small musicals with 4-6 people for our smaller space." Does not wish to see anything racy or profane.
Productions: *Grease!*; *Forever Plaid*; *Jesus Christ Superstar*; *Gigi*; *Sound of Music*; *Goodbye Girl*; and *Nunsense Jamboree*.
Tips: "Consider the audience. Think commercial. Title is extremely important."

✓ ODYSSEY THEATRE ENSEMBLE, Dept. SM, 2055 S. Sepulveda Blvd., Los Angeles CA 90025. (310)477-2055. Fax: (310)444-0455. Website: www.odysseytheatre.org. **Contact:** Sally Essex-Lopresti, director of literary programs. Play producer. Estab. 1969. Produces 9 plays and 1 musical (1-2 new musicals)/year. "Our audience is predominantly over 35, upper middle-class and interested in eclectic brand of theater which is challenging and experimental." Pays negotiable royalty.
How to Contact: Query with synopsis, character breakdown, 8-10 pages of libretto, cassette of music and set description. Query should include résumé(s) of artist(s) and tape of music. Include SASE. "Unsolicited material is not read or screened at all." Responds to query in 2 weeks; ms in 6 months.
Musical Theater: "We want nontraditional forms and provocative, unusual, challenging subject matter. We are not looking for Broadway-style musicals. Comedies should be highly stylized or highly farcical. Works should be full-length only and not requiring a complete orchestra (small band preferred). Political material and satire are great for us. We're seeking interesting musical concepts and approaches. The more traditional Broadway-style musicals will generally not be done by the

REFER TO THE GEOGRAPHIC INDEX (at the back of this book) to find listings of companies by state, as well as foreign listings.

Odyssey. If we have a work in development that needs music, original music will often be used. In such a case, the writer and composer would work together during the development phase. In the case of a pre-existing play, the concept would originate with the director who would select the composer."

☑ **THE OPEN EYE THEATER**, P.O. Box 959, Margaretville NY 12455. Phone/fax: (845)586-1660. E-mail: openeye@catskill.net. Website: www.theopeneye.org. **Contact:** Amie Brockway, producing artistic director. Play producer. Estab. 1972. Produces approximately 3 full length or 3 new plays for multi-generational audiences. Pays on a fee basis.

How to Contact: Query first. "A manuscript will be accepted and read only if it is a play for all ages and is: 1) Submitted by a recognized literary agent; 2) Requested or recommended by a staff or company member; or 3) Recommended by a professional colleague with whose work we are familiar. Playwrights may submit a one-page letter of inquiry including a very brief plot synopsis. Please enclose a self-addressed (but not stamped) envelope. We will reply only if we want you to submit the script (within several months)."

Musical Theater: "The Open Eye Theater is a not-for-profit professional company working in a community context. Through the development, production and performance of plays for all ages, artists and audiences are challenged and given the opportunity to grow in the arts. In residence, on tour, and in the classroom, The Open Eye Theater strives to stimulate, educate, entertain, inspire and serve as a creative resource."

Productions: *The Weaver and the Sea*, by Julie Steiny (ancient teaching tale); *A Midsummer Night's Dream*, by Shakespeare, music by Robert Cucinotta; and *The Nightingale*, by William E. Black/Annie Brockway, music by Elliot Sokolov (freedom and nature vs. technology).

PLAYHOUSE ON THE SQUARE, 51 S. Cooper, Memphis TN 38104. (901)725-0776. Fax: (901)272-7530. **Contact:** Jackie Nichols, executive producer. Play producer. Produces 12 plays and 4 musicals/year. Plays are produced in a 260-seat proscenium resident theater. Pays $500 for outright purchase.

How to Contact: Submit complete manuscript, score and tape of songs. Unsolicited submissions OK. Include SASE. Responds in 6 months.

Musical Theater: Seeking "any subject matter—adult and children's material. Small cast preferred. Stage is 26′ deep by 43′ wide with no fly system."

Productions: *Children of Eden*; and *Tommy*, by The Who.

☑ **PLAYWRIGHTS' ARENA**, 514 S. Spring St., Los Angeles CA 90013. (213)485-1631. E-mail: jrivera923@juno.com. Website: www.playwrightsarena.org. **Contact:** Jon Lawrence Rivera, artistic director. Play producer. Estab. 1992. Produces 4 plays and 1 musical (1 new musical)/year. Audience is in their early 20s to 50s. Performance space is 26′ deep × 30′ wide proscenium stage with fly system. Pays 6% royalty.

How to Contact: Submit complete manuscript, score and tape of songs. Include SASE. Responds in 6 months.

Musical Theater: Seeking new musicals like *Rent*. Does not want old fashioned musicals.

Productions: *Bitter Homes and Gardens*, by Luis Alfaro; *Last of the Suns*, by Alice Tuan; and *Crawlspace*, by Robert Harders.

☑ **PLAYWRIGHTS HORIZONS**, 630 Ninth Ave., #708, New York NY 10036. (212)564-1235. Fax: (212)594-0296. Website: www.playwrightshorizons.org. **Contact:** Andrea Watson Canning, assistant literary manager. Artistic Director: Tim Sanford. Musical Theatre Associate Producer: Ira Weitzman. Play producer. Estab. 1971. Produces about 4 plays and 1 new musical/year. "Adventurous New York City theater-going audience." Pays general Off-Broadway contract.

How to Contact: Submit complete manuscript and tape or CD of songs. Attn: Musical Theater Program. Include SASE. Responds in 6 months.

Musical Theater: American writers. "No revivals, one-acts or children's shows; otherwise we're flexible. We have a particular interest in scores with a distinctively contemporary and American flavor. We generally develop work from scratch; we're open to proposals for shows and scripts in early stages of development."

Productions: *The Bubbly Black Girl Sheds Her Chameleon Skin*, by Kirsten Childs; *Floyd Collins*, by Adam Guettel/Tina Landau; and *The Spitfire Grill*, by James Valcq/Fred Alley.

☑ **PRIMARY STAGES**, 131 W. 45th St., 2nd Floor, New York NY 10036. (212)840-9705. Fax: (212)840-9725. **Contact:** Tyler Marchant, associate artistic director. Play producer. Estab. 1984. Produces 4-5 plays/year. "New York theater-going audience representing a broad cross-section, in terms of age, ethnicity, and economic backgrounds. 99-seat, Off-Broadway theater."
How to Contact: Query first with synopsis, character breakdown, set description and tape. "No unsolicited scripts accepted. Submissions by agents only." Include SASE. Responds in up to 8 months.
Musical Theater: "We are looking for work of heightened theatricality, that challenges realism—musical plays that go beyond film and televisions standard fare. We are looking for small cast shows under 6 characters total, with limited sets. We are interested in original works, that have not been produced in New York."
Productions: *I Sent a Letter to My Love*, by Melissa Manchester/Jeffrey Sweet; and *Nightmare Alley*, by Jonathan Brielle.

THE REPERTORY THEATRE OF ST. LOUIS, P.O. Box 191730, St. Louis MO 63119. (314)968-7340. **Contact:** Susan Gregg, associate artistic director. Play producer. Estab. 1966. Produces 9 plays and 1 or 2 musicals/year. "Conservative regional theater audience. We produce all our work at the Loretto Hilton Theatre." Pays by royalty.
How to Contact: Query with synopsis, character breakdown and set description. Does not return material. Responds in 2 years.
Musical Theater: "We want plays with a small cast and simple setting. No children's shows or foul language. After a letter of inquiry we would prefer script and demo tape."
Productions: *Almost September* and *Esmeralda*, by David Schechter and Steve Lutvak; *Jack*, by Barbara Field and Hiram Titus; and *Young Rube*, by John Pielmeier and Nattie Selman.

SECOND STAGE THEATRE, P.O. Box 1807, Ansonia Station, New York NY 10023. (212)787-8302. Fax: (212)877-9886. **Contact:** Christopher Burney, associate artistic director. Play producer. Estab. 1979. Produces 4 plays and 1 musical (1 new musical)/year. Plays are performed in a small, 108-seat Off Broadway House. Pays per performance.
 • Also offers the Constance Klinsky Award for Excellence in the Composition of Musical Theatre. Awarded annually to three composers and/or lyricists. Write for submission guidelines.
How to Contact: Query with synopsis, character breakdown, set description, tape of 5 songs (no more). No unsolicited manuscripts. Include SASE. Responds in 6 months.
Musical Theater: "We are looking for innovative, unconventional musicals that deal with sociopolitical themes."
Productions: *In a Pig's Valise*, by Eric Overmyer/Kid Creole (spoof on '40s film noir); *A . . . My Name Is Still Alice*, by various (song/sketch revue); and *Saturday Night*, by Stephen Sondheim.
Tips: "Submit through agent; have strong references; always submit the best of your material in small quantities: 5 outstanding songs are better than 10 mediocre ones."

Ⓝ **SHAKESPEARE SANTA CRUZ**, Theater Arts Center, U.C.S.C., Santa Cruz CA 95064. (831)459-2121. Fax: (831)459-3316. E-mail: iago@cats.ucsc.edu. Website: www.shakespearesantacr uz.org. **Contact:** Paul Whitworth, artistic director. Play producer. Estab. 1982. Produces 4 plays/year. Performance spaces are an outdoor redwood grove; and an indoor 540-seat thrust. Pay is negotiable.
How to Contact: Query first. Include SASE. Responds in 2 months.
Musical Theater: "Shakespeare Santa Cruz produces musicals in its Winter Holiday Season (Oct-Dec). We are also interested in composers' original music for pre-existing plays—including songs, for example, for Shakespeare's plays."
Productions: *Cinderella*, by Kate Hawley (book and lyrics) and Gregg Coffin (composer); and *Gretel and Hansel*, by Kate Hawley (book and lyrics) and composer Craig Bohmler (both are British pantomime treatment of fairy tale).
Tips: "Always contact us before sending material."

☑ **STAGE ONE**, 501 W. Main St., Louisville KY 40202. (502)589-5946. Fax: (502)588-5910. E-mail: stageone@stageone.org. Website: www.stageone.org. **Contact:** Moses Goldberg, producing director. Play producer. Estab. 1946. Produces 7-8 plays and 0-2 new musicals/year. "Audience is mainly young people ages 5-18, teachers and families." Pays 5-7% royalty, flat fee or $25-75 per performance.

How to Contact: Submit complete manuscript and tape of songs (cassette preferred). Include SASE. Responds in 4 months.

Musical Theater: "We seek stageworthy and respectful dramatizations of the classic tales of childhood, both ancient and modern. Ideally, the plays are relevant to young people and their families, as well as related to school curriculum. Cast is rarely more than 12."

Productions: *The Great Gilly Hopkins*, by David Paterson/Steve Liebman (foster home); *Pinocchio*, by Moses Goldberg/Scott Kasbaum (classic tale); and *Jack & the Beanstalk*, by Goldberg/Corrett (fairytale).

Tips: "Stage One accepts unsolicited manuscripts that meet our artistic objectives. Please do not send plot summaries or reviews. Include author's résumé, if desired. In the case of musicals, a cassette tape is preferred. Cast size is not a factor, although, in practice, Stage One rarely employs casts of over 12. Scripts will be returned in approximately 3-4 months, if SASE is included. No materials can be returned without the inclusion of a SASE. Due to the volume of plays received, it is not possible to provide written evaluations."

STAGES REPERTORY THEATRE, 3201 Allen Parkway, Houston TX 77019. (713)527-0220. Fax: (713)527-8669. Website: www.stagestheatre.com. **Contact:** Rob Bundy, artistic director. Play producer. Estab. 1979. Produces 6 plays and 1 musical/year. Performance space includes 170-seat thrust and 230-arena theatre. Pays negotiable royalty.

How to Contact: Query with synopsis, character breakdown and set description. Include SASE. Responds in 7 months.

Musical Theatre: Prefers edgy, theatrical, non-realistic stories, with a maximum cast size of 10, and single unit set with multiple locations.

Productions: *Nixon's Nixon*, by Russell Lees; *Funny Girl*, by Jules Styne; and *The Pitchfork Disney*, by Philip Ridley.

🄽 **STRAWBERRY PRODUCTIONS, INC.**, 432 Front St., Chicopee MA 01013. (413)592-4184. Fax: (413)594-7758. E-mail: info@strawberryproductions.com. Website: www.strawberryproductions.com. **Contact:** Jack Desroches, president/producer. Play producer. Estab. 1976. Produces 3-6 plays and 3-6 musicals/year. Audience is children and families. Strawberry Productions is a touring company.

How to Contact: Query first via e-mail.

Musical Theater: Seeking children's theater of 70-80 minutes in length, children's puppet theater of 30 minutes in length and educational shows. Normal touring limits vary from production to production.

Productions: *Thomas & Friends*™ "All Aboard! Tour"; *Garfield*'s "Happy Birthday to Me" 25th Anniversary Show; *Scholastic's* "Bright Idea" (light); *Scholastic's* "Recycles" (recycling); and *Alvin & The Chipmunks* "Rockin through the Decades" (music), all by John Michael Burke.

Tips: "Creativity and the ability to entertain young and old alike is very important."

🄽 **SWINE PALACE PRODUCTIONS**, The Reilly Theatre, Tower Dr.—LSU, Baton Rouge LA 70803. (225)578-3533. Fax: (225)578-9279. E-mail: info@swinepalace.org. Website: www.swinepalace.com. **Contact:** Kristin Sosnowsky, managing director. Play producer. Estab. 1991. Produces 3 productions/year. "Swine's audience is made up of the community of Louisiana which ranges from the upper-lower classes. Many college and high school students. Not for the blue-haired group. The

---

TO HELP YOU UNDERSTAND and use the information in these listings, see "How to Use *Songwriter's Market* to Get Your Songs Heard," on page 5.

brand new Reilly theatre is a traverse stage with an earth floor converted from an old livestock judging/viewing pavillion (hence "Swine" Palace). Audience sits across from each other a la stadium seating. 488 seats and one of the largest performing stages in North America. Truly unique, bold and original." Pay negotiated with the artistic staff.

How to Contact: Submit complete manuscript, score and tape of songs. Include SASE. Responds in 6 months if interested.

Musical Theater: "Swine Palace's commitment is to new work reflects the Deep South experience. Work must contain substance. No light musical comedies based on trite gimmicks. The Reilly theatre is an epic space and lends itself to large cast productions (i.e., operas are perfectly acceptable). Large casts are acceptable." Does not want works that are in no way related to the Deep South experience. Interested in musicals "that are new and rock. 5-7 piece instrumentation is best. Innovative, original and possibly dangerous material."

Productions: *A Midsummer Night's Dream*, by Shakespeare; *Gumbo Ya-Ya*, by Swine Palace Company (adaptation with music of book from 1940s Federal writer's project); *Four Joans and a Fire-Eater*, by Elizabeth Dewberry (reexamination of folk-lore, 3 women and 1 drag queen in New Orleans discover that they were all Joan of Arc in a former life—new play premiered at Swine); and *Jesus Christ Superstar*, by Andrew Lloyd Weber (fall 2000).

Tips: "Love the art in yourself not yourself in the art. Don't be afraid of work. Take the work seriously but not yourself. Live music is almost always an essential part in all of Swine Palace's work whether it be Shakespeare or Beckett. Songs and original scoring are always included in our season and audiences expect excellence in our musical support. Intelligent music based on support of the text that has been worked in through the production process is a must. Composers do not 'phone in' our scores but work alongside the design team during the production process."

TADA!, 120 W. 28th St., New York NY 10001. (212)627-1732. Fax: (212)243-6736. E-mail: tada@ta datheater.com. Website: www.tadatheater.com. **Contact:** Janine Nina Trevens, artistic director. Play producer. Estab. 1984. Produces 4 staged readings and 2-4 new musicals/year. "TADA! is a company producing works performed by children ages 6-17 for family audiences in New York City. Performances run approximately 30-45 performances. Pays varying royalty.

• Also see the listing for Free Staged Reading Series Playwriting Competition in the Contests and Awards section.

How to Contact: Submit complete manuscript with synopsis, character breakdown, score and tape of songs. Include SASE. Responds in 1 year.

Musical Theater: "We do not produce plays as full productions. At this point, we do staged readings of plays. We produce original commissioned musicals written specifically for the company."

Productions: *The History Mystery*, by Janine Nina Trevens (kids time traveling through history)' *New York New Year*, by Gary Bagley (a young midwestern girl discovers New York and herself); and *Golly Gee Whiz*, by Erick Rockwell (based on the "Mickey & Judy film classics).

Tips: "Musical playwrights should concentrate on themes and plots meaningful to children and their families as well as consider our young actors' abilities and talents as well. Vocal ranges of children 7-17 should be strongly considered when writing the score."

✔ **THEATRE THREE, INC.**, 2800 Routh St., Suite 168, Dallas TX 75201. (214)871-2933. Fax: (214)871-3139. E-mail: theatre3@airmail.net. Website: www.theatre3dallas.com. **Contact:** Terry Dobson, musical director. Artistic Director: Jac Alder. Play producer. Estab. 1961. Produces 10-12 plays and 3-4 musicals (1 or 2 new musicals)/year. "Subscription audience of 4,500 enjoys adventurous, sophisticated musicals." Performance space is an "arena stage (modified). Seats 250 per performance. Quite an intimate space." Pays varying royalty.

How to Contact: *Submit through agent only.* Include SASE. Responds in 2 months.

Musical Theater: "Off the wall topics. We have, in the past, produced *Little Shop of Horrors*, *Angry Housewives*, *Sweeney Todd*, *Groucho*, *A Life in Revue*, *The Middle of Nowhere* (a Randy Newman revue) and *A . . . My Name Is Alice*. We prefer small cast shows, but have done shows with a cast as large as 15. Orchestrations can be problematic. We usually do keyboards and percussion or some variation. Some shows can be a design problem; we cannot do 'spectacle.' Our audiences generally like good, intelligent musical properties. Very contemporary language is about the only thing that sometimes causes 'angst' among our subscribers. We appreciate honesty and forthrightness . . . and good material done in an original and creative manner."

Productions: *I Love You, You're Perfect, Now Change!*, by Jimmy Roberts/Joe Dipietro; *Blood Brothers*, by Willy Russell; and *Side Show*, by Russell & Krieger.

THEATRE WEST VIRGINIA, P.O. Box 1205, Beckley WV 25802. (800)666-9142. E-mail: twv@ cwv.net. Website: wvweb.com/www/TWV. **Contact:** Marina Dolinger, artistic director. Play producer. Estab. 1955. Produces 5 plays and 2 musicals/year. "Audience varies from mainstream summer stock to educational tours (ages K-high school)." Pays 3-6% royalty, negotiable.

How to Contact: Query with synopsis, character breakdown and set description; should include cassette tape. Include SASE. Responds in 3 months.

Musical Theater: "Theatre West Virginia is a year-round performing arts organization that presents a variety of productions including community performances and statewide educational programs on primary, elementary and secondary levels. This is in addition to our summer, outdoor dramas of *Hatfields & McCoys* and *Honey in the Rock*, now in their 42nd year." Anything suitable for school tours. No more than 6 in cast. Play should be able to be accompanied by piano/synthesizer.

Productions: *The Apple Tree*, by Sheldon Harnick and Jerry Bock (used for educational tour grades 7th-12th); *The Tinderbox*, by Mark LaPierre (musical adaptation, used for educational tour grades K-6th); and *The Sound of Music*, by Rodgers & Hammerstein.

N THEATREVIRGINIA, 2800 Grove Ave., Richmond VA 23221-2466. (804)353-6100. Fax: (804)353-8799. E-mail: tva@erols.com. Website: www.theatreva.com. **Contact:** Benny Sato Ambush, artistic director. Play producer. Estab. 1955. Produces 5-9 plays and 2-5 musicals/year. "Plays are performed in a 500-seat LORT-C house for the Richmond-area community." Payment negotiable.

How to Contact: Query first. "If material seems to be of interest to us, we will reply with a solicitation for a complete manuscript and cassette. Include SASE. Responds in 3 months for synopsis.

Musical Theater: "We do not deal in one-acts or in children's material. We would like to see full length, adult musicals. There are no official limitations. We would be unlikely to use original music as incidental/underscoring for existing plays, but there is potential for adapting existing plays into musicals."

Productions: *Bubbling Brown Sugar*, by Loften Mitchell and Rosetta Le Noice (golden years of Harlem Renaissance); *Fair and Tender Ladies*, by Eric Schmeidl, Tommy Goldsmith, Tom House and Karen Pell (folk musical from the heart of Virginia's mountain country); and *I Love You, You're Perfect, Now Change*, by Joe DiPietro and Jimmy Roberts (looking for the perfect someone).

Tips: "Read plays. Study structure. Study character. Learn how to concisely articulate the nature of your work. A beginning musical playwright wishing to work for our company should begin by writing a wonderful, theatrically viable piece of musical theater. Then he should send us the material requested in our listing, and wait patiently."

☑ THEATREWORKS/USA, 151 W. 26th St., 7th Floor, New York NY 10001. (212)647-1100. Fax: (212)924-5377. Website: www.theatreworksusa.org. Literary Manager: Michael Alltop. Play producer. Produces 10-13 plays, most are musicals (3-4 are new musicals)/year. Audience consists of children and families. Pays 6% royalty and aggregate of $1,500 commission-advance against future royalties.

How to Contact: Query with synopsis, character breakdown and sample scene and song. Include SASE. Responds in 6 months.

Musical Theater: "One hour long, 5-6 adult actors, highly portable, good musical theater structure; adaptations of children's literature, historical or biographical musicals, issues, fairy tales—all must have something to say. We demand a certain level of literary sophistication. No kiddy shows, no camp, no fractured fables, no shows written for school or camp groups to perform. Approach your material, not as a writer writing for kids, but as a writer addressing any universal audience. You have one hour to entertain, say something, make them care—don't preach, condescend. Don't forget an antagonist. Don't waste the audience's time. We always use original music—but most of the time a project team comes complete with a composer in tow."

Productions: *Island of the Blue Dolphins*, book/lyrics by Beth Blatt, music by Jennifer Giering (literary adaptation); *The Mystery of King Tut*, book/lyrics by Mindi Dickstein, music by Dan Messé (original historical); *Gold Rush!*, book by David Armstrong, music by Dick Gallagher, lyrics by Mark Waldrop (original historical); and *Sarah, Plain and Tall*, book by Julia Jordan, music by Larry O'Keefe, and lyrics by Nell Benjamin.

Tips: "Write a good show! Make sure the topic is something we can market! Come see our work to find out our style."

THUNDER BAY THEATRE, 400 N. Second Ave., Alpena MI 49707. (517)354-2267. E-mail: tbt@deepnet.com. Website: www.oweb.com/upnorth/tbt. Artistic Director: Suzanne Konicek. Play producer. Estab. 1967. Produces 12 plays and 6 musicals (1 new musical)/year. Performance space is thrust/proscenium stage. Pays variable royalty or per performance.

How to Contact: Submit complete manuscript, score and tape of songs. Include SASE. Responds in 3 months.

Musical Theater: Small cast. Not equipped for large sets. Considers original background music for use in a play being developed or for use in a pre-existing play.

Productions: *Wonderful Life*, by Holmes/Knoner/Willison (Christmas); *Smoke On the Mountain* (gospel); and *Forever Plaid*, by Stuart Ross.

VIRGINIA STAGE COMPANY, P.O. Box 3770, Norfolk VA 23514. (757)627-6988. Fax: (757)628-5958. E-mail: chensley@vastage.com. Website: www.vastage.com. **Contact:** Charlie Hensley, artistic director. Play producer. Estab. 1978. Produces 7-10 plays and 1-2 musicals (0-1 new musical)/year. "We have a diverse audience. As home to a large, well-traveled population from NATO and the U.S. Navy, we serve many sophisticated theatregoers as well as those for whom theatre is not yet a habit. Located in Southeastern Virginia, we also play to a number of people from Southern backgrounds." Performance space is a 670-seat, Beaux-Arts proscenium theatre built in 1913—a national historic landmark. This hemp house features a proscenium opening 36′ wide and 28′ high with a stage depth of 28′. Pay is negotiable.

How to Contact: Query with synopsis, character breakdown and set description. Include SASE. Responds in 6 months.

Musical Theater: "We have produced the world premieres of *The Secret Garden* and *Snapshots* (with music by Stephen Schwartz). Our tastes are eclectic and have covered a number of styles. We have recently expanded our programming for young audiences." At this time, shows with less than 20 in the cast have a better chance of production. They have commissioned original music and adaptations for plays including *Hamlet*, *Twelfth Night*, *Terra Nova* and *A Christmas Carol*.

Productions: *Appalachian Strings*, by Randal Myler/Dan Wheetman (social history of the Appalachian region); *Snapshots*, by David Stern/Michael Scheman, music by Stephen Schwartz (a middle-aged couple trying to save their marriage); *Twelfth Night*, by Shakespeare (set in 18th century Ireland with live musicians playing Celtic music); and *Blues in the Night*, by Sheldon Epps.

Tips: "Be patient. We review material as quickly as possible. It also takes time to establish the relationships and resources needed to lead us into full, top-quality productions."

☑ WALNUT STREET THEATRE, 825 Walnut St., Philadelphia PA 19107. (215)574-3550, ext. 515. Fax: (215)574-3598. E-mail: wstpc@wstonline.org. Website: www.wstonline.org. **Contact:** Literary Office. Play producer. Estab. 1809. Produces 7 plays and 3 musicals/year. Plays produced on a mainstage with seating for 1,078; and in studio theaters with seating for 90. Pays by royalty or outright purchase.

How to Contact: *Does not accept unsolicited scripts from individuals.*

MARKET CONDITIONS are constantly changing! If you're still using this book and it is 2004 or later, buy the newest edition of *Songwriter's Market* at your favorite bookstore or order directly from Writer's Digest Books at (800)289-0963.

Musical Theater: "We seek musicals with lyrical non-operatic scores and a solid book. We are looking for a small musical for springtime and one for a family audience at Christmas time. We remain open on structure and subject matter and would expect a tape with the script. Cast size: around 20 equity members (10 for smaller musical); preferably one set with variations." Would consider original music for incidental music and/or underscore. This would be at each director's discretion.
Productions: *Camila*, book, music and lyrics by Lori McKelvey (captivating new musical of forbidden love, revolution, and the tango); *My Fair Lady*, by Lerner & Loewe (a musical classic); *Damn Yankees*, book by George Abbott and Douglas Wallop, words and music by Richard Adler and Jerry Ross (a musical comedy about America's favorite pastime).

N WATERLOO COMMUNITY PLAYHOUSE, P.O. Box 433, Waterloo IA 50704. (319)235-0367. Fax: (319)235-7489. E-mail: wcpbhct@cedarnet.org. Website: www.cedarnet.org. **Contact:** Charles Stilwill, managing artistic director. Play producer. Estab. 1917. Produces 12 plays (1-2 musicals)/year. "Our audience prefers solid, wholesome entertainment, nothing risqué or with strong language. We perform in Hope Martin Theatre, a 366-seat house." Pays $15-150/performance.
How to Contact: Submit complete manuscript, score and cassette tape of songs. Include SASE. Responds in 10 months.
Musical Theater: "Casts may vary from as few as 6 people to 54. We are producing children's theater as well. We're *especially* interested in new adaptations of classic children stories."
Productions: *Jesus Christ Superstar*; *Fiddler on the Roof*; and *The Sound of Music*.
Tips: "The only 'new' musicals we are likely to produce are adaptations of name shows that would fit in our holiday slot or for our children's theater."

WEST COAST ENSEMBLE, P.O. Box 38728, Los Angeles CA 90038. (323)876-9337. **Contact:** Les Hanson, artistic director. Play producer. Estab. 1982. Produces 4-8 plays and 1 new musical/year. "Our audience is a wide variety of Southern Californians. Plays will be produced in our theater in Hollywood." Pays $35-50 per performance.
• See the listing for West Coast Ensemble—Musical Stairs in the Contests & Awards section.
How to Contact: Submit complete manuscript, score and tape of songs. Include SASE. Responds in 8 months.
Musical Theater: "There are no limitations on subject matter or style. Cast size should be no more than 12 and sets should be simple. If music is required we would commission a composer; music would be used as a bridge between scenes or to underscore certain scenes in the play."
Productions: *Cabaret* and *Merrily We Roll Along*.
Tips: "Submit work in good form and be patient. We look for musicals with a strong book and an engaging score with a variety of styles."

WEST END ARTISTS, 18034 Ventura Blvd. #291, Encino CA 91316. (818)623-0040. Fax: (818)623-0202. E-mail: egaynes@pacbell.net. **Contact:** Pamela Hall, associate artistic director. Artistic Director: Edmund Gaynes. Play producer. Estab. 1983. Produces 5 plays and 3 new musicals/year. Audience "covers a broad spectrum, from general public to heavy theater/film/TV industry crowds." Pays 6% royalty.
How to Contact: Submit complete manuscript, score and tape of songs. Include SASE. Responds in 3 months.
Musical Theater: "Prefer small-cast musicals and revues. Full length preferred. Interested in children's shows also." Cast size: "Maximum 12; exceptional material with larger casts will be considered."
Productions: *The Taffetas*, by Rick Lewis ('50s nostalgia, received 3 Ovation Award nominations); *Songs the Girls Sang*, by Alan Palmer (songs written for women now sung by men, received 1 Ovation Award nomination); *Crazy Words, Crazy Tunes* (played 2 years to Los Angeles and nationwide).
Tips: "If you feel every word or note you have written is sacred and chiseled in stone and are unwilling to work collaboratively with a professional director, don't bother to submit."

☑ WESTBETH THEATRE CENTER, 151 Bank St., New York NY 10014. (212)691-2272. Fax: (212)924-7185. E-mail: wbethjill@aol.com. Website: www.westbeththeatre.com. **Contact:** Jill

Beckman, executive assistant. Producing Director: Arnold Engleman. Play producer. Estab. 1977. Produces 1-2 musicals/year. Audience consists of artists, New York professionals and downtown theater goers. "We have five performance spaces, including a music hall and cafe theater." Pay varies. Uses usual New York showcase contract.

How to Contact: Query with résumé, one page project proposal—or one page synopsis with cast and production requirements for scripted plays and any relevant audio/visual material. Include SASE. Does not return material from outside the US. Responds in 3 months. "Artists must reside in NYC or surrounding areas and be desirous of extensive development and intense collaboration."

Musical Theater: "The New Works Program has expanded its focus to include performance proposals from a range of various disciplines including dancers, playwrights, musicians, and other performance artists. Proposals should be sharp, urban, and contemporary—period pieces or plays set in rural/regional locales will not be considered.

Productions: *20th Century Man*, by Ray Davies (bio of rock group The Kinks); *Almost Famous*, by Bruce Vilanch; and *Exactly Like You*, by Cy Coleman/E. Hutchner (musical comedy).

Tips: "Be open to the collaborative effort. We are a professional theater company, competing in the competitive world of Broadway and off-Broadway, so the work we present must reach for the highest standard of excellence."

[N] THE WILMA THEATER, 265 S. Broad St., Philadelphia PA 19107. (215)893-9456. Fax: (215)893-0895. E-mail: info@wilmatheater.org. Website: www.wilmatheater.org. **Contact:** Nakissa Etemad, literary manager. Play producer. Produces 4 shows/year. Performance space is a 300-seat, state of the art proscenium theater, with full fly system and large backstage area. Pays royalty negotiated between managing director and agent.

How to Contact: Submit through agent only. Include SASE. Responds in 6 months.

Musical Theater: "We seek to produce the most adventurous work possible. Because this is a director-driven theater, the full-length projects must pose creative challenges that engage the imaginations of our two artistic directors. The eclectic tastes of the artistic directors make it almost impossible to identify specific styles or topics. We look for work that is original, bold, challenging and stimulating."

Productions: *Bed and Sofa*, by Polly Pen/Laurence Klavan; *Tin Pan Alley Rag*, by Mark Saltzman; and *Threepenny Opera*, by Brecht/Weill.

Tips: "Please be familiar with the Wilma's production history before submitting your material."

WINGS THEATRE CO., 154 Christopher St., New York NY 10014. (212)627-2960. Fax: (212)462-0024. E-mail: jcorrick@wingstheatre.com. Website: www.wingstheatre.com. **Contact:** Tricia Gilbert, literary manager. Artistic Director: Jeffrey Corrick. Play producer. Estab. 1987. Produces 3-5 plays and 3-5 musicals/year. Performance space is a 74-seat O.O.B. proscenium; repertoire includes a New Musicals Series, a gay-play series—we produce musicals in both series. Pays $100 for limited rights to produce against 6% of gross box office receipts.

How to Contact: Submit complete manuscript, score and tape of songs (score is not essential). Include SASE. Responds in 1 year.

Musical Theater: "Eclectic. Entertaining. Enlightening. This is an O.O.B. theater. Funds are limited." Does not wish to see "movies posing as plays. Television theater."

Productions: *Scott & Zelda*, by Dave Bates (The Fitzgeralds); *Cowboys*, by Clint Jefferies (gay western spoof); and *The Three Musketeers*, by Clint Jefferies (musical adaptation).

Tips: "Book needs to have a well-developed plot line and interesting, fully-realized characters. We place emphasis on well-written scripts, as opposed to shows which rely exclusively on the quality of the music to carry the show. Also be patient—we often hold onto plays for a full year before making a final decision."

[N] WOMEN'S PROJECT AND PRODUCTIONS, 55 West End Ave., New York NY 10023. (212)765-1706. Fax: (212)765-2024. E-mail: wpp@earthlink.net. Website: www.womensproject.org. **Contact:** Karen Keagle, literary manager. Artistic Director: Julia Miles. Estab. 1978. Produces 3 plays/year. Pays by outright purchase.

How to Contact: Query with synopsis, character breakdown and set description. Include SASE. Responds in 2 months for query and 8 months for full submission. "Adult audience. Plays by women only."

Musical Theater: "We usually prefer a small to medium cast of 3-6. We produce few musicals and produce *only* women playwrights."

Productions: *Ladies*, by Eve Ensler (homelessness); *O Pioneers!*, by Darrah Cloud (adapted from Willa Cather's novel); and *Frida: The Story of Frida Kahlo*, by Hilary Blecher/Migdalia Cruz (biography of Frida Kahlo).

Tips: "Resist sending early drafts of work."

Play Publishers

AMERICAN EASTERN THEATRICAL COMPANY, (formerly Eastern Musicals), % Eastern Musicals, 136 Langley St., Fall River MA 02720. (508)676-3312. President: Raymond Carreiro. Play publisher. Estab. 1996. Publishes 3 musicals/year. Pays standard royalty.

How to Contact: Submit complete ms, score and tape of songs or VHS videocassette. Does not return material. Responds in 3 weeks.

Musical Theater: Seeks rock musicals, classical musicals, contemporary and non-musical theater. "New productions performances will be at the Cultural Center."

Publications: *Our Real World*, by Jay Brillient/Maria Esteves; *Dearest Lizzie*, by Raymond Carreiro/ Norihiko Hidino (additional lyrics by MaryAnn Thomas); *A Fifties Christmas Carol*, by Raymond Carreiro/Paul Ponte (music arrangements by Louis Terreira); *Return to Broadway* (a collaboration); and *Sideshow—the Musical*, book and lyrics by Bill Russell, music by Henry Krieger.

Tips: "Looking for new material of all subject matters. No old, dated material."

N ARAN PRESS, 1036 S. Fifth St., Louisville KY 40203. (502)568-6622. Fax: (502)561-1124. E-mail: aranpres@aye.net. Website: http://members.aye.net/~aranpres. **Contact:** Tom Eagan, editor/ publisher. Play publisher. Estab. 1983. Publishes 5-10 plays and 1-2 musicals/year. Professional, college/university, community, summer stock and dinner theater audience. Pays 50% production royalty or 10% book royalty.

How to Contact: Submit manuscript, score and tape of songs. Include SASE. Responds in 2 weeks.

Musical Theater: "The musical should include a small cast, simple set for professional, community, college, university, summer stock and dinner theater production."

Publications: *Whiskey & Wheaties*, by Bruce Feld; *Who Says Life is Fair*, by Mike Willis; and *Burning Bridges*, by Stephen Avery.

BAKER'S PLAYS, P.O. Box 699222, Quincy MA 02269-9222. (617)745-0805. Fax: (617)745-9891. E-mail: info@bakersplays.com. Website: www.bakersplays.com. **Contact:** John Welch, managing director and chief editor. Play publisher. Estab. 1845. Publishes 15-22 plays and 0-3 new musicals/ year. Plays are used by children's theaters, junior and senior high schools, colleges and community theaters. Pays negotiated book and production royalty.

● See the listing for Baker's Plays High School Playwriting Contest in the Contests & Awards section.

How to Contact: Submit complete manuscript, score and cassette tape of songs. Include SASE. Responds in 4 months.

Musical Theater: "Seeking musicals for teen production and children's theater production. We prefer large cast, contemporary musicals which are easy to stage and produce. Plot your shows strongly, keep your scenery and staging simple, your musical numbers and choreography easily explained and blocked out. Music must be camera-ready." Would consider original music for use in a play being developed or in a pre-existing play.

MARKETS THAT WERE listed in the 2002 edition of *Songwriters Market* but do not appear this year are listed in the General Index with a notation explaining why they were omitted.

Productions: *Oedipus/A New Magical Comedy*, by Bob Johnson.

Tips: "As we publish musicals that can be produced by high school theater departments with high school talent, the writer should know if their play can be done on the high school stage. I recommend that the writer go to performances of original high school musicals whenever possible."

CONTEMPORARY DRAMA SERVICE, 885 Elkton Dr., Colorado Springs CO 80907. (719)594-4422. E-mail: merpcds@aol.com. Website: www.contemporarydrama.com. **Contact:** Arthur Zapel, executive editor. Play publisher. Estab. 1979. Publishes 40-50 plays and 4-6 new musicals/year. "We publish for young children and teens in mainstream Christian churches and for teens and college level in the secular market. Our musicals are performed in churches, schools and colleges." Pays 10-50% book and performance royalty.

How to Contact: *Query first* then submit complete manuscript, score and tape of songs. Include SASE. Responds in 1 month.

Musical Theater: "For churches we publish musical programs for children and teens to perform at Easter, Christmas or some special occasion. Our school musicals are for teens to perform as class plays or special entertainments. Cast size may vary from 15-25 depending on use. We prefer more parts for girls than boys. Music must be written in the vocal range of teens. Staging should be relatively simple but may vary as needed. We are not interested in elementary school material. Elementary level is OK for church music but not public school elementary. Music must have full piano accompaniment and be professionally scored for camera-ready publication."

Publications: *Lucky, Lucky Hudson and the 12th Street Gang*, by Tim Kelly, book, and Bill Francoeur, music and lyrics (spoof of old time gangster movies); *Is There A Doctor in the House?*, by Tim Kelly, book, and Bill Francoeur, music and lyrics (adapted from Moliere comedy); and *Jitterbug Juliet*, by Mark Dissette, book, and Bill Francoeur, music and lyrics (spoof of *Romeo and Juliet*).

Tips: "Familiarize yourself with our market. Send $1 postage for catalog. Try to determine what would fit in, yet still be unique."

THE DRAMATIC PUBLISHING COMPANY, 311 Washington St., Woodstock IL 60098. (815)338-7170. E-mail: plays@dramaticpublishing.com. Website: dramaticpublishing.com. **Contact:** Linda Habjan, acquisitions editor. Play publisher. Publishes 35 plays and 3-5 musicals/year. Estab. 1885. Plays used by professional and community theaters, schools and colleges. Pays negotiable royalty.

How to Contact: Submit complete manuscript, score and tape of songs. Include SASE. Responds in 3 months.

Musical Theater: Seeking "children's musicals not over 1¼ hours, and adult musicals with 2 act format. No adaptations for which the rights to use the original work have not been cleared. If directed toward high school market, large casts with many female roles are preferred. For professional, stock and community theater small casts are better. Cost of producing a play is always a factor to consider in regard to costumes, scenery and special effects." Would also consider original music for use in a pre-existing play, "if we or the composer hold the rights to the non-musical work."

Publications: *The Little Prince*, by Rick Cummins/John Scoullar; *Hans Brinker*, by Gayle Hudson/Bobbe Bramson; and *Bubbe Meises, Bubbe Stories*, by Ellen Gould/Holly Gewandter (all are full-length family musicals).

Tips: "A complete score, ready to go is highly recommended. Tuneful songs which stand on their own are a must. Good subject matter which has wide appeal is always best but not required."

ELDRIDGE PUBLISHING CO., INC., P.O. Box 1595, Venice FL 34284. (800)HI-STAGE. E-mail: info@histage.com. Website: www.histage.com. **Contact:** Susan Shore, musical editor. Play publisher. Estab. 1906. Publishes 60 plays and 2-3 musicals/year. Seeking "large cast musicals which appeal to students. We like variety and originality in the music, easy staging and costuming. Also looking for children's theater musicals which have smaller casts and are easy to tour. We serve the school and church market, 6th grade through 12th; also Christmas and Easter musicals for churches." Would also consider original music for use in a play being developed; "music that could make an ordinary play extraordinary." Pays 50% royalty and 10% copy sales in school market.

How to Contact: Submit manuscript, score or lead sheets and tape of songs. Include SASE. Responds in 1 month.

Publications: *The Bard is Back*, by Stephen Murray ("a high school's production of Romeo & Juliet is a disaster!"); *Boogie-Woogie Bugle Girls*, book by Craig Sodaro, music and lyrics by Stephen Murray (WWII themed musical); and *Hellenback High*, book by Bill Leavengood, music and lyrics by Lee Ahlin ("a high school boy has some devilish choices to make").

Tips: "We're always looking for talented composers but not through individual songs. We're only interested in complete school or church musicals. Lead sheets, cassette tape and script are best way to submit. Let us see your work!"

THE FREELANCE PRESS, P.O. Box 548, Dover MA 02030. (508)785-8250. Managing Editor: Narcissa Campion. Play publisher. Estab. 1979. Publishes up to 3 new musicals/year. "Pieces are primarily to be acted by elementary/middle school to high school students (9th and 10th grades); large casts (approximately 30); plays are produced by schools and children's theaters." Pays 10% of purchase price of script or score, 50% of collected royalty.

How to Contact: Query first. Include SASE. Responds in 6 months.

Musical Theater: "We publish previously produced musicals and plays to be acted by children in the primary grades through high school. Plays are for large casts (approximately 30 actors and speaking parts) and run between 45 minutes to 1 hour and 15 minutes. Subject matter should be contemporary issues (sibling rivalry, friendship, etc.) or adaptations of classic literature for children (*Syrano de Bergerac*, *Rip Van Winkle*, *Pied Piper*, *Treasure Island*, etc.). We do not accept any plays written for adults to perform for children."

Publications: *Tortoise vs. Hare*, by Stephen Murray (modern version of classic); *Tumbleweed*, by Sebastian Stuart (sleepy time western town turned upside down); and *Mything Links*, by Sam Abel (interweaving of Greek myths with a great pop score).

Tips: "We enjoy receiving material that does not condescend to children. They are capable of understanding many current issues, playing complex characters, handling unconventional material, and singing difficult music."

☑ **SAMUEL FRENCH, INC.**, 45 W. 25th St., New York NY 10010. (212)206-8990. Fax: (212)206-1429. Hollywood office: 7623 Sunset Blvd., Hollywood CA 90046. (323)876-0570. Fax: (323)876-6822. Website: www.samuelfrench.com. President: Charles R. Van Nostrand. Play publisher. Estab. 1830. Publishes 40-50 plays and 2-4 new musicals/year. Amateur and professional theaters.

How to Contact: Query first. Include SASE. Responds in 10 weeks.

Musical Theater: "We publish primarily successful musicals from the NYC, London and regional stage."

Publications: *Eating Raoul*, by Paul Bartel; *Hello Muddah Hello Faddah*, by Bernstein/Krause; *Love and Shrimp*, by Judith Viorst; and *The Spitfire Grill*, *The Big Bang*, and *Smoke on the Mountain*.

HEUER PUBLISHING CO., P.O. Box 248, Cedar Rapids IA 52406. (319)364-6311. E-mail: editor @hitplays.com. Website: www.hitplays.com. Publisher: C. Emmett McMullen. Play publisher. Estab. 1928. Publishes plays and musicals for the amateur market including middle schools, junior and senior high schools and church groups. Pays by outright purchase or percentage royalty.

How to Contact: Query with synopsis, character breakdown and set description or submit complete manuscript and score. Include SASE. Responds in 2 months.

Musical Theater: "We prefer one, two or three act comedies or mystery-comedies with a large number of characters."

Publications: *Brave Buckaroo*, by Renee J. Clark (musical melodrama) and *Pirate Island*, by Martin Follose (musical comedy).

Tips: "We sell almost exclusively to junior and smaller senior high schools. Thus flexible casting is extremely important. We need plays with large, predominantly female casts and if you are writing a musical, we need more choral numbers and solos for girls than boys."

PIONEER DRAMA SERVICE, P.O. Box 4267, Englewood CO 80155. (303)779-4035. Fax: (303)779-4315. E-mail: playwrights@pioneerdrama.com. Website: www.pioneerdrama.com. **Con-**

tact: Beth Somers, assistant editor. Play publisher. Estab. 1963. "Plays are performed by junior high and high school drama departments, church youth groups, college and university theaters, semi-professional and professional children's theaters, parks and recreation departments." Playwrights paid 50% royalty (10% sales).

How to Contact: Query first with character breakdown, synopsis and set description. Include SASE. Responds in 6 months.

Musical Theater: "We seek full length children's musicals, high school musicals and one act children's musicals to be performed by children, secondary school students, and/or adults. As always, we want musicals easy to perform, simple sets, many female roles and very few solos. Must be appropriate for educational market. We are not interested in profanity, themes with exclusively adult interest, sex, drinking, smoking, etc. Several of our full-length plays are being converted to musicals. We edit them, then contract with someone to write the music and lyrics."

Publications: *The Stories of Scheherazade*, book by Susan Pargmon, music and lyrics by Bill Francoeur (musical *Arabian Nights*); *Hubba Hubba: The 1940s Hollywood Movie Musical*, by Gene Casey and Jan Casey (tribute to the 1940s Hollywood movie musical); and *Cinderella's Glass Slipper*, book by Vera Morris, music and lyrics by Bill Francoeur (musical fairy tale).

Tips: "Research and learn about our company. Our website and catalog provide an incredible amount of information."

PLAYERS PRESS, INC., P.O. Box 1132, Studio City CA 91614. (818)789-4980. Associate Editor: Karen Flathers. Vice President: Robert W. Gordon. Play publisher, music book publisher, educational publisher. Estab. 1965. Publishes 20-70 plays and 1-3 new musicals/year. Plays are used primarily by general audience and children. Pays variable royalty and variable amount/performance.

How to Contact: Query first. Include SASE. Responds in 1 year (3 weeks on queries).

Musical Theater: "We will consider all submitted works. Presently musicals for adults and high schools are in demand. When cast size can be flexible (describe how it can be done in your work) it sells better."

Publications: *Rapunzel n' The Witch*, by William-Alan Landes (children's musical); *Song of Love*, by William Alan Landes (musical); and *Curse of the Mummy's Tomb*, by Julian Harries/Pat Witymark (musical).

Tips: "For plays and musicals, have your work produced at least twice. Be present for rehearsals and work with competent people. Then submit material asked for in good clear copy with good audio tapes."

Classical Performing Arts

Finding an audience is critical to the composer of orchestral music. Fortunately, baby boomers are swelling the ranks of classical music audiences and bringing with them a taste for fresh, innovative music. So the climate is fair for composers seeking their first performance.

Finding a performance venue is particularly important because once a composer has his work performed for an audience and establishes himself as a talented newcomer, it can lead to more performances and commissions for new works.

BEFORE YOU SUBMIT

Be aware that most classical music organizations are nonprofit groups, and don't have a large budget for acquiring new works. It takes a lot of time and money to put together an orchestral performance of a new composition, therefore these groups are quite selective when choosing new works to perform. Don't be disappointed if the payment offered by these groups is small or even non-existent. What you gain is the chance to have your music performed for an appreciative audience. Also realize that many classical groups are understaffed, so it may take longer than expected to hear back on your submission. It pays to be patient, and employ diplomacy, tact and timing in your follow-up.

In this section you will find listings for classical performing arts organizations throughout the U.S. But if you have no prior performances to your credit, it's a good idea to begin with a small chamber orchestra, for example. Smaller symphony and chamber orchestras are usually more inclined to experiment with new works. A local university or conservatory of music, where you may already have contacts, is a great place to start.

All of the groups listed in this section are interested in hearing new works from contemporary classical composers. Pay close attention to the music needs of each group, and when you find one you feel might be interested in your music, follow submission guidelines carefully. To locate classical performing arts groups in your area, consult the Geographic Index at the back of this book.

N ADRIAN SYMPHONY ORCHESTRA, 110 S. Madison St., Adrian MI 49221. (517)264-3121. Fax: (517)264-3833. E-mail: aso@lni.net. Website: www.aso.org. **Contact:** John Dodson, music director. Symphony orchestra and chamber music ensemble. Estab. 1981. Members are professionals. Performs 25 concerts/year including new works. 1,200 seat hall—"Rural city with remarkably active cultural life." Pays $200-1,000 for performance.
How to Contact: Query first. Does not return material. Responds in 6 months.
Music: Chamber ensemble to full orchestra. "Limited rehearsal time dictates difficulty of pieces selected." Does not wish to see "rock music or country—not at this time."
Performances: Michael Pratt's *Dancing on the Wall* (orchestral—some aleatoric); Sir Peter Maxwell Davies' *Orkney Wedding* (orchestral); and Gwyneth Walker's *Fanfare, Interlude, Finale* (orchestral).

N THE AMERICAN BOYCHOIR, 19 Lambert Dr., Princeton NJ 08540. (609)924-5858. Fax: (609)924-5812. E-mail: jkaltenbach@americanboychoir.org. Website: www.americanboychoir.org. General Manager: Janet B. Kaitenbach. Coordinator-Tour Manager: Rosemary Hobgood. Professional boychoir. Estab. 1937. Members are musically talented boys in grades 5-8. Performs 200 concerts/year, including 10-25 new works. Commissions 1 new work approximately every 3 years. Actively seeks high quality arrangements. Performs national and international tours, orchestral engagements, church services, workshops, school programs, local concerts, and at corporate and social functions.

How to Contact: Submit complete score. Include SASE. Responds in 1 year.
Music: Choral works in unison, SA, SSA, SSAA or SATB division; unaccompanied and with piano or organ; occasional chamber orchestra or brass ensemble accompaniment. Works are usually sung by 28 to 60 boys. Composers must know boychoir sonority.
Performances: *Four Seasons*, by Michael Torke (orchestral-choral); *Garden of Light*, by Aaron Kernis (orchestral-choral); *Reasons for Loving the Harmonica*, by Libby Larsen (piano); and *Songs Eternity*, by Steven Paulus (piano).

AMERICAN OPERA MUSICAL THEATRE CO., 400 W. 43rd St. #19D, New York NY 10036. (212)594-1839. Fax: (212)695-4350. E-mail: corto@mindspring.com. **Contact:** Diana Corto, artistic director. Chamber music ensemble, chamber opera and musical theatre producing/presenting organization. Estab. 1995. Members are professionals with varying degrees of experience. Performs 2 operas and many concerts/year. Audience is sophisticated and knowledgeable about music and theatre. "We rent different performance spaces." Pays negotiable royalty.
How to Contact: Submit tape "of excerpts, not more than 15 minutes." Does not return material. Responds in up to 1 month.
Music: "Must be vocal (for opera or for music theatre) with chamber groups. Cast should not exceed 10. Orchestration should not exceed 30, smaller chamber groups preferred. No rock 'n' roll, brassy pop or theatre material."
Performances: Puccini's *La Boheme*; Verdi's *Rigoletto*; *The Jewel Box*; *Iolanta*; and *La Molinara*.

☑ **AMHERST SAXOPHONE QUARTET**, P.O. Box 29, Buffalo NY 14231-0029. (716)839-9716. Fax: (716)839-9717. E-mail: rosenthl@acsu.buffalo.edu. Website: www.amherstsaxophonequartet.buffalo.edu. **Contact:** Steve Rosenthal, director. Chamber music ensemble. Estab. 1978. Performs 80 concerts/year including 10-20 new works. Commissions 1-2 composers or new works/year. "We are a touring ensemble." Payment varies.
How to Contact: Query first. Include SASE. Responds in 1 month.
Music: "Music for soprano, alto, tenor and baritone (low A) saxophone. We are interested in great music of many styles. Level of difficulty is commensurate with full-time touring ensembles."
Performances: Lukas Foss's *Saxophone Quartet* (new music); David Stock's *Sax Appeal* (new music); and Chan Ka Nin's *Saxophone Quartet* (new music).
Tips: "Professionally copied parts help! Write what you truly want to write."

☑ **ANDERSON SYMPHONY ORCHESTRA**, P.O. Box 741, Anderson IN 46015. (765)644-2111. Fax: (765)644-7703. E-mail: aso@iquest.net or sowers@anderson.edu. Website: www.andersonsymphony.org. **Contact:** Dr. Richard Sowers, conductor. Executive Director: George W. Vinson. Symphony orchestra. Estab. 1967. Members are professionals. Performs 7 concerts/year. Performs for typical mid-western audience in a 1,500-seat restored Paramount Theatre. Pay negotiable.
How to Contact: Query first. Include SASE. Responds in several months.
Music: "Shorter lengths better; concerti OK; difficulty level: mod high; limited by typically 3 full service rehearsals."

🗣 ☑ **ARCADY**, P.O. Box 955, Simcoe, Ontario N3Y 5B3 Canada. (519)428-3185. E-mail: info@arcadyca. Website: www.arcady.ca. **Contact:** Ronald Beckett, director. Semi-professional chorus and orchestra. Members are professionals, university music majors and recent graduates from throughout Ontario. "Arcady forms the bridge between the student and the professional performing career." Performs 12 concerts/year including 1-2 new works. Commissions 1 composer or new work/year. Pay negotiable.
How to Contact: Submit complete score and tape of piece(s). Does not return material. Responds in 3 months.

REFER TO THE GEOGRAPHIC INDEX (at the back of this book) to find listings of companies by state, as well as foreign listings.

Music: "Compositions appropriate for ensemble accustomed to performance of chamber works, accompanied or unaccompanied, with independence of parts. Specialize in repetoire of 17th, 18th and 20th centuries. Number of singers does not exceed 30. Orchestra is limited to strings, supported by a professional quartet. No popular, commercial or show music."

Performances: Ronald Beckett's *I Am . . .* (opera); Ronald Beckett's *John* (opera); and David Lenson's *Prologue to Dido and Aeneas* (masque).

Tips: "Arcady is a touring ensemble experienced with both concert and stage performance."

N ATLANTA POPS ORCHESTRA, P.O. Box 723172, Atlanta GA 31139-0172. (770)435-1222. E-mail: atlantapops@mindspring.com. **Contact:** Albert Coleman, musical director/conductor. Pops orchestra. Estab. 1945. Members are professionals. Performs 5-10 concerts/year. Concerts are performed for audiences of 5,000-10,000, "all ages, all types." Composers are not paid; concerts are free to the public.

How to Contact: Call to request permission to submit. Then send cassette, and score or music, if requested. Include SASE. Responds "as soon as possible."

Performances: Vincent Montana, Jr.'s *Magic Bird of Fire*; Louis Alter's *Manhattan Serenade*; and Nelson Riddle's *It's Alright With Me*.

Tips: "My concerts are pops concerts—no deep classics."

N THE ATLANTA YOUNG SINGERS OF CALLANWOLDE, 980 Briarcliff Rd. N.E., Atlanta GA 30306. (404)873-3365. Fax: (404)873-0756. E-mail: aysc@bellsouth.org. Website: www.nysc.org. **Contact:** Paige F. Mathis, music director. Community children's chorus. Estab. 1975. Members are amateurs. Performs 25 concerts/year including a few new works. Audience consists of community churches, retirement homes, schools. Performs most often at churches. Pay is negotiable.

How to Contact: Submit complete score and tape of piece(s). Include SASE. Responds in accordance with request.

Music: "Subjects and styles appealing to grammar and junior high boys and girls. Contemporary concerns of the world of interest. Unusual sacred, folk, classic style. Internationally and ethnically bonding. Medium difficulty preferred, with keyboard accompaniment."

Tips: "Our mission is to promote service and growth through singing."

N AUGSBURG CHOIR, Augsburg College, 731 21st Ave. S., Minneapolis MN 55454. E-mail: hendricp@augsburg.edu. Website: www/augsburg.edu. Director of Choral Activities: Peter A. Hendrickson. Vocal ensemble (SATB choir). Members are amateurs. Performs 25 concerts/year, including 1-6 new works. Commissions 0-2 composers or new works/year. Audience is all ages, "sophisticated and unsophisticated." Concerts are performed in churches, concert halls and schools. Pays for outright purchase.

How to Contact: Query first. Include SASE. Responds in 1 month.

Music: Seeking "sacred choral pieces, no more than 5-7 minutes long, to be sung a cappella or with obbligato instrument. Can contain vocal solos. We have 50-60 members in our choir."

Performances: Carol Barnett's *Spiritual Journey*; Steven Heitzeg's *Litanies for the Living* (choral/orchestral); and Morton Lanriclsen's *O Magnum Mysteries* (a cappella choral).

☑ BILLINGS SYMPHONY, 201 N. Broadway., Suite 350, Billings MT 59101-1936. (406)252-3610. Fax: (406)252-3353. E-mail: symphony@billingssymphony.org. Website: www.billingssymphony.org. **Contact:** Dr. Uri Barnea, music director. Symphony orchestra, orchestra and chorale. Estab. 1950. Members are professionals and amateurs. Performs 12-15 concerts/year, including 6-7 new works. Traditional audience. Performs at Alberta Bair Theater (capacity 1,416). Pays by outright purchase (or rental).

How to Contact: Query first. Include SASE. Responds in 2 weeks.

Music: Any style. Traditional notation preferred.

Performances: Vivian Fung's *Blaze* (full orchestra); David Evan Thomas' *By Singing Light* (chamber orchestra); and Peter Schickele's *The New Century Suite* (concerto for saxophone quartet and orchestra).

Tips: "Write what you feel (be honest) and sharpen your compositional and craftsmanship skills."

BIRMINGHAM-BLOOMFIELD SYMPHONY ORCHESTRA, 1592 Buckingham, Birmingham MI 48009. (248)645-2276. Fax: (248)645-2276, *00. **Contact:** Felix Resnick, music director and conductor. Executive Director: Carla Lamphere. Symphony orchestra. Estab. 1975. Members are professionals. Performs 6 concerts including 1 new work/year. Commissions 1 composer or new work/year "with grants." Performs for middle-to-upper class audience at Temple Beth El's Sanctuary. Pays per performance "depending upon grant received."
How to Contact: Query first. Does not return material. Responds in 6 months.
Music: "We are a symphony orchestra but also play pops. Usually 3 works on program (2 hrs.) Orchestra size 65-75. If pianist is involved, they must rent piano."
Performances: Brian Belanger's *Tuskegee Airmen Suite* (symphonic full orchestra); and Larry Nazer & Friend's *Music from "Warm" CD* (jazz with full orchestra).

THE BOSTON PHILHARMONIC, 295 Huntington Ave., #210, Boston MA 02115. (617)236-0999. Fax: (617)236-8613. E-mail: office@bostonphil.org. Website: www.bostonphil.org. Music Director: Benjamin Zander. Symphony orchestra. Estab. 1979. Members are professionals, amateurs and students. Performs 9 concerts/year. Audience is ages 30-70, "though we are beginning to draw younger audience. Not very ethnically diverse." Performs at New England Conservatory's Jordan Hall, Boston's Symphony Hall and Sanders Theatre in Cambridge. Both Jordan Hall and Sanders Theatre are small (approximately 1,100 seats) and very intimate.
How to Contact: Query first. Include SASE. Responds in 2 months.
Music: Full orchestra only—moderately high level of difficulty.
Performances: Dutilleuxs' *Tout un monde lointain* for cello and orchestra (symphonic); Bernstein's *Fancy Free* (symphonic/jazzy); and Copland's *El Salon Mexico* (symphonic).

BRAVO! L.A., 16823 Liggett St., North Hills CA 91343. (818)892-8737. Fax: (818)892-1227. E-mail: info@bravo-la.com. Website: www.bravo-la.com. **Contact:** Dr. Janice Foy, director. An umbrella organization of recording/touring musicians, formed in 1994. Includes the following musical ensembles: Trio of the Americas (piano, clarinet, cello); the New American Quartet (string quartet); The Ascending Wave (harp, soprano, cello or harp/cello duo); Cellissimo! L.A. (cello ensemble); Musical Combustion (harp, flute, cello); and the Sierra Chamber Players (piano with strings or mixed ensemble). Performs 4 concerts/year, including 1 new work. "We take care of PR. There is also grant money the composer can apply for."
How to Contact: Submit complete score and tape of piece(s). Include SASE. Responds in a few months.
Music: "Classical, Romantic, Baroque, Popular (including new arrangements done by Shelly Cohen, from the 'Tonight Show Band'), ethnic (including gypsy) and contemporary works (commissioned as well). The New American Quartet has a recording project which features music of Mozart's *Eine Kleine Nachtmusik*, Borodin's *Nocturne*, a Puccini Opera Suite (S. Cohen), Strauss' *Blue Danube Waltz*, *Trepak* of Tschaikovsky, *'El Choclo'* (Argentinian tango), *Csardas!* and arrangements of Cole Porter, Broadway show tunes and popular classics."
Performances: Joe Giarrusso's *Rhapsody for Cello and Piano* (concert piece-modern romantic); Joe Giarrusso's *Cello Sonata* (concert piece); and Dan Bogley's *Foybles* (contemporary solo cello).
Tips: "Please be open to criticism/suggestions about your music and try to appeal to mixed audiences. We also look for innovative techniques, mixed styles or entertaining approaches, such as classical jazz or Bach and pop, or ethnic mixes."

CALGARY BOYS CHOIR, 1227 Browness Rd. NW, Calgary, Alberta T2N 3J6 Canada. (403)217-7790. Fax: (403)217-7796. E-mail: info@calgaryboyschoir.ab.ca. Website: www.telusplanet.net/public/cbchoir/Home.html. **Contact:** Jacquie Shand, administrator. Boys choir. Estab. 1973. Members are amateurs age 5 and up. Performs 50-70 concerts/year including 1-2 new works. Pay negotiable.
How to Contact: Query first. Submit complete score and tape of piece(s). Include SASE. Responds in 6 weeks. Does not return material.
Music: "Style fitting for boys choir. Lengths depending on project. Orchestration preferable a cappella/for piano/sometimes orchestra."

Performances: G. Wirth's *Sadhaka* and *Our Normoste*; and Shri Mataji Nirmala Devi's *Binati Suniye*.

CANADIAN OPERA COMPANY, 227 Front St. E., Toronto, Ontario M5A 1E8 Canada. (416)363-6671. E-mail: sandrag@coc.ca. Website: www.coc.ca. **Contact:** Sandra J. Gavinchuk, associate artistic administrator. Opera company. Estab. 1950. Members are professionals. 50-55 performances, including a minimum of 1 new work/year. Pays by contract.
How to Contact: Submit complete score and tapes of vocal and/or operatic works. "Vocal works please." Include SASE. Responds in 5 weeks.
Music: Vocal works, operatic in nature. "Do not submit works which are not for voice. Ask for requirements for the Composers-In-Residence program."
Performances: Louie's *Scarlett Princess* (opera in 2 acts); Burry's *Brothers Grimm* (50-minute opera for children); and Bartok's *Bluebeard and Erwartung* (operas in one act).
Tips: "We have a Composers-In-Residence program which is open to Canadian composers or landed immigrants."

CANTATA ACADEMY, 2441 Pinecrest Dr., Ferndale MI 48220. (248)358-9868. **Contact:** Phillip O'Jibway, business manager. Music Director: Dr. Michael Mitchell. music director. Vocal ensemble. Estab. 1961. Members are professionals. Performs 10-12 concerts/year including 1-3 new works. "We perform in churches and small auditoriums throughout the Metro Detroit area for audiences of about 500 people." Pays variable rate for outright purchase.
How to Contact: Submit complete score. Include SASE. Responds in 3 months.
Music: Four-part a cappella and keyboard accompanied works, two and three-part works for men's or women's voices. Some small instrumental ensemble accompaniments acceptable. Work must be suitable for forty voice choir. No works requiring orchestra or large ensemble accompaniment. No pop.
Performances: Charles S. Brown's *Five Spirituals* (concert spiritual); Kirke Mechem's *John Brown Cantata*; and Libby Larsen's *Ringeltanze* (Christmas choral with handbells & keyboard).
Tips: "Be patient. Would prefer to look at several different samples of work at one time."

CARMEL SYMPHONY ORCHESTRA, P.O. Box 761, Carmel IN 46082-0761. (317)844-9717. Fax: (317)844-9916. Website: www.carmelsymphony.org. **Contact:** Alan Davis, executive director. Symphony orchestra. Estab. 1976. Members are professionals and amateurs. Performs 15 concerts/year, including 1-2 new works. Audience is "40% senior citizens, 85% white." Performs in a 1,500-seat high school performing arts center. Pay is negotiable.
How to Contact: Query first. Include SASE. Responds in 3 months.
Music: "Full orchestra works, 10-20 minutes in length. Can be geared toward 'children's' or 'Masterworks' programs. 65-70 piece orchestra, medium difficulty."
Performances: Jim Beckel's *Glass Bead Game* (full orchestra); Percy Grainger's *Molly on the Shore* (full orchestra); and Frank Glover's *Impressions of New England* (full orchestra and jazz quartet).

CARSON CITY SYMPHONY, P.O. Box 2001, Carson City NV 89702-2001 or 191 Heidi Circle, Carson City NV 89701-6532. (775)883-4154. Fax: (775)883-4371. E-mail: dcbugli@aol.com. Website: members.aol.com/CCSymphony. **Contact:** David C. Bugli, music director/conductor. Amateur community orchestra. Estab. 1984. Members are amateurs. Performs 5 concerts, including 2 new works/year. Audience is largely Carson City/Reno area residents, many of them retirees. "Most concerts are performed in the Carson City Community Center Auditorium, which seats 800." Pay varies for outright purchase.

MARKETS THAT WERE listed in the 2002 edition of *Songwriters Market* but do not appear this year are listed in the General Index with a notation explaining why they were omitted.

How to Contact: Submit complete score and tape of works. Does not return material. Responds in 2 months.

Music: "We want classical, pop orchestrations, orchestrations of early music for modern orchestras, concertos for violin or piano, holiday music for chorus and orchestra (children's choirs and handbell ensemble available), music by women, music for brass choir. Most performers are amateurs, but there are a few professionals who perform with us. Available winds and percussion: 2 flutes and flute/ piccolo, 2 oboes (E.H. double), 2 clarinets, 1 bass clarinet, 2 bassoons, 3 or 4 horns, 3 trumpets, 3 trombones, 1 tuba, timpani, and some percussion. Harp and piano. Strings: 8-8-5-6-3. Avoid music that lacks melodic appeal. Composers should contact us first. Each concert has a different emphasis. Note: Associated choral group, Carson Chamber Singers, performs several times a year with the orchestra and independently."

Performances: Thomas Svoboda's *Overture of the Season* (minimalist overture); Gwyneth Walker's *A Concerto of Hymns and Spirituals for Trumpet and Orchestra*; and Jim Cockey's *A Land of Sage and Sun*.

Tips: "It is better to write several short movements well than to write long, unimaginative pieces, especially when starting out. Be willing to revise after submitting the work, even if it was premiered elsewhere."

N: CHAMBER ORCHESTRA OF SOUTH BAY/CARSON-DOMINIQUEZ HILLS SYM-PHONY, 21 La Vista Verde, Rancho Palos Verdes CA 90275. (310)243-3947. E-mail: FSteiner@csud h.edu. **Contact:** Dr. Frances Steiner, music director. Symphony orchestra. Estab. 1972. Members are professionals (chamber orchestra); professionals and amatuers (symphony). Performs 10-11 concerts/ year including 3-4 new works. Commissions 0-1 new works/year. Chamber orchestra audience is conservative in musical taste; symphony has an ethnically diverse and new student audience. Perform-ance spaces seat 450-480. Pays ASCAP/BMI royalty or rental fee to publisher.

How to Contact: Query first. Include SASE. Responds in 3 months.

Music: Prefers 10-15 minute works for chamber orchestra, string orchestra and symphony orchestra (winds in pairs). Works should have "audience appeal" and not be too difficult to learn; there is special interest in works by women composers of diverse ethnicity.

Performances: Michael Abels's *Global Warming* (ethinic, melodic ideas); Augusta Reid Thomas's *Flute Concerto #1* (contemporary); and Kevin O'Neal's *Japanese Sketches* (jazz and orchestra).

CHARLOTTE PHILHARMONIC ORCHESTRA, P.O. Box 470987, Charlotte NC 28247-0987. (704)846-2788. Fax: (704)847-6043. E-mail: charphilor@aol.com. Website: www.charlottephil harmonic.org. **Contact:** Albert Moehring, music director. Symphony orchestra. Estab. 1991. Members are professionals. Performs 12 concerts/year including 2-4 new works. Audience consists of music lovers, educated and uneducated. "We regularly perform Broadway/movie soundtracks, also standard classical repertoire." Performance spaces are up to 2,500 seats. Pay is negotiable.

● The Charlotte Philharmonic Orchestra was voted Charlotte's Best Entertainment in 1998.

How to Contact: Submit complete score and tape of piece(s). Does not return material. Responds in 6 weeks.

Music: Seeks full orchestrations, lush strings always popular. Maximum 8-10 minutes. Would review classical styles, but also interested in Boston Pops type selections. Require lyrical music with interest-ing melodies and good rhythms. "We are not interested in atonal, dissonant styled music. We will neither perform it, nor bother to review it. Our audiences do not like it." Players are professional. Limited rehearsals. String passages playable in limited time. Full orchestra sound—excellent brass players. 75 piece orchestra. Always interested in fine Broadway styled arrangements. Look for strong, smooth transpositions/modulations.

Performances: Davis Brown's arrangement of *Happy Holiday* (Christmas arrangement).

Tips: "With a new composer, we recommend pieces under 10 minutes, lyrical basis with definite melodies. Full use of 75 piece orchestra. Lush strings without exceedingly difficult passages for limited rehearsals. Variety of materials welcomed. Enjoy standard classics, bib band, ballroom dance-type music, ballet style. Also enjoy operatic arrangements. Use our own Philharmonic Chorus as well as regular vocalists. Good choral arrangements with full orchestra always of interest. Appreciate a tape when possible. If a composer submits during a really busy period of performances, please be patient. If there is no response in 4-6 weeks, they may contact us again."

CHATTANOOGA GIRLS CHOIR, P.O. Box 6036, 612 Maclellan Building, Chattanooga TN 37401. (423)266-9422. E-mail: girlschoir@mindspring.com. Website: www.girlschoir.home.mindspring.com. **Contact:** John E. Wigal, artistic director. Vocal ensemble. Estab. 1986. Members are amateurs. Performs 2 concerts/year including at least 1 new work. Audience consists of cultural and civic organizations and national and international tours. Performance space includes concert halls and churches. Pays for outright purchase or per performance.
How to Contact: Query first. Include SASE. Responds in 6 weeks.
Music: Seeks renaissance, baroque, classical, romantic, twentieth century, folk and musical theatre for young voices of up to 8 minutes. Performers include 5 treble choices: 4th grade (2 pts.); 5th grade (2 pts.) (SA); grades 6-9 (3 pts.) (SSA); grades 10-12 (3-4 pts.) (SSAA); and a combined choir: grades 6-12 (3-4 pts.) (SSAA). Medium level of difficulty. "Avoid extremely high Tessitura Sop I and extremely low Tessitura Alto II."
Performances: Jan Swafford's *Iphigenia Book: Meagher* (choral drama); Penny Tullock's *How Can I Keep from Singing* (Shaker hymn).

Ⓝ CIMARRON CIRCUIT OPERA COMPANY, P.O. Box 1085, Norman OK 73070. Phone/fax: (405)364-8962. E-mail: ccoc@telepath.com. **Contact:** Kevin Smith or Jennifer Baker, music directors. Opera company. Estab. 1975. Members are semi professional. Performs 75 concerts/year including 1-2 new works. Commissions 1 or less new work/year. "CCOC performs for children across the state of Oklahoma and for a dedicated audience in central Oklahoma. As a touring company, we adapt to the performance space provided, ranging from a classroom to a full raised stage." Pay is negotiable.
How to Contact: Query first. Does not return material. Responds in 6 months.
Music: "We are seeking operas or operettas in English only. We would like to begin including new, American works in our repertoire. Children's operas should be no longer than 45 minutes and require no more than a synthesizer for accompaniment. Adult operas should be appropriate for families, and may require either full orchestration or synthesizer. CCOC is a professional company whose members have varying degrees of experience, so any difficulty level is appropriate. There should be a small to moderate number of principals. Children's work should have no more than four principals. Our slogan is 'Opera is a family thing to do.' If we cannot market a work to families, we do not want to see it."
Performances: Menotti's *Amahl & the Night Visitors*; and Barab's *La Pizza Con Funghi*.
Tips: "45-minute fairy tale-type children's operas with possibly a 'moral' work well for our market. Looking for works appealing to K-8 grade students. No more than four principles."

☑ CITY SYMPHONY OF CHICAGO, (formerly Wheaton Symphony Orchestra), 344 Spring Ave., Glen Ellyn IL 60137. (630)790-1430. Fax: (630)790-9703. **Contact:** Donald C. Mattison, manager. Symphony orchestra. Estab. 1959. Members are professionals and amateurs. Performs 6 concerts/year including a varying number of new works. Pays $100/per performance.
How to Contact: Query first. Include SASE. Responds in 1 month.
Music: "This is a *good* amateur orchestra that wants pieces in a traditional idiom. Large scale works for orchestra only. No avant garde, 12-tone or atonal material. Pieces should be 20 minutes or less and must be prepared in 3 rehearsals. Instrumentation is woodwinds in 3s, full brass 4-3-3-1, 4-5 percussion and strings—minimum instrumentation only. We will read your piece several times and then record it on a cassette. Plays all months except July and August. All union players. Selections for full orchestra only. No pay for reading your piece, but we will record it at our expense."
Performances: Don Draganski's *Overtures and Fanfares* (full orchestra 3-2-2-2/brass 4331/2 percussion/timpani/strings-traditional); John Uth's *Dance Suite* (3-2-3-2/4331/percussion/timpani/strings); and Edward McKenna's *Bagatelles* (3-3-3-3/4331/timpani/percussion/strings-traditional).

☑ COMMONWEALTH OPERA INC., 140 Pine St., Florence MA 01062. (413)586-5026. Fax: (413)587-0380. E-mail: commopr1@aol.com. Website: www.commonwealthopera.org. **Contact:**

Richard R. Rescia, artistic director. Opera company. Estab. 1977. Members are professionals and amateurs. Performs 4 concerts/year. "We perform at the Calvin Theatre Northampton in an 1,200-seat opera house. Depending on opera, audience could be family oriented or adult." Pays royalty.

How to Contact: Query first. Does not return material. Response will take months.

Music: "We are open to all styles of opera. We have the limitations of a regional opera company with local chorus. Principals come from a wide area. We look only at opera scores."

Performances: Arnold Black's *The Phantom Tollbooth* (children's opera); *Diefledermaus*, and *The Magic Flute*.

Tips: "We're looking for opera that is accessible to the general public and performable by a standard opera orchestra."

CONNECTICUT CHORAL ARTISTS/CONCORA, 52 Main St., New Britain CT 06051. (860)224-7500. Website: www.concora.org. **Contact:** Richard Coffey, artistic director. Professional concert choir, also an 18-voice ensemble dedicated to contemporary a cappella works. Estab. 1974. Members are professionals. Performs 15 concerts/year, including 3-5 new works. "Mixed audience in terms of age and background; performs in various halls and churches in the region." Payment "depends upon underwriting we can obtain for the project."

How to Contact: Query first. "No unsolicited submissions accepted." Include SASE. Responds in 1 year.

Music: Seeking "works for mixed chorus of 36 singers; unaccompanied or with keyboard and/or small instrumental ensemble; text sacred or secular/any language; prefers suites or cyclical works, total time not exceeding 15 minutes. Performance spaces and budgets prohibit large instrumental ensembles. Works suited for 750-seat halls are preferable. Substantial organ or piano parts acceptable. Scores should be very legible in every way."

Performances: Wm. Schuman's *Carols of Death* (choral SATB); Charles Ives' *Psalm 90* (choral SATB); and Frank Martin's *Mass for Double Chorus* (regional premiere).

Tips: "Use conventional notation and be sure manuscript is legible in every way. Recognize and respect the vocal range of each vocal part. Work should have an identifiable *rhythmic* structure."

N DESERT CHORALE, P.O. Box 2813, Santa Fe NM 87504-2813. (505)988-2282. Fax: (505)988-7522. E-mail: sfdchorale@aol.com. Website: www.desertchorale.org. Music Director: Dennis Shrock. Executive Director: Jillian Sandrock. Business Manager: Jay Reep. Box Office Manager: Natalia Chavez. Vocal ensemble. Members are professionals. Performs 35 concerts/year including 2 new works. Commissions 1 new composer or new work/year. "Highly sophisticated audiences who are eager for interesting musical experiences. We pay $5,000 to $2,000 for premieres, often as part of consortium."

How to Contact: Query first. Submit complete score and tape *after* query. Does not return material. Responds in 2 years.

Music: "Challenging chamber choir works 6 to 20 minutes in length. Accompanied works are sometimes limited by space—normally no more than 5 or 6 players. "We sing both a cappella and with chamber orchestra; size of choir varies accordingly (20-32). No short church anthem-type pieces."

Performances: Edwin London's *Jove's Nectar* (choral with 5 instruments); Lanham Deal's *Mini-turas de Sor Juana* (unaccompanied); and Steven Sametz's *Desert Voices* (choral with 4 instruments).

Tips: "Call me or see me and I'll be happy to tell you what I need and I will also put you in touch with other conductors in the growing professional choir movement."

N DÚO CLÁSICO, 4 Essex St., Clifton NJ 07014. (973)661-1973. E-mail: wittend@mail.montcla ir.edu. Website: www.montclair.edu/pages/music/Faculty/witten.html. **Contact:** David Witten. Cham-

insider report

Composer builds eclectic musical career

At eight years old, Todd Barton got his first taste of music composition. A third grade instructor offered to teach some students the basics, with their first assignment being a trip to the movies. "He wanted us to memorize a theme from whatever movie we saw and write it down," Barton says. "And we raised our hands and said 'pardon us, but we can barely read music. What do you mean, write it down?' And he said just make little squiggles and dots, like a little artwork of what you think the music's like."

Barton completed the assignment, and his teacher correctly interpreted the squiggles and dots as the theme from *The Vikings*. "Back in the '50s there were only two or three shows in town," Barton explains. But with this little assignment, "he showed us how to create music." Barton's been creating music ever since,

Todd Barton

and for the last 33 years has served as composer in residence for the Oregon Shakespeare Festival, where he "oversees all things musical." Barton hires composers and sound designers, assembles design teams for festival productions, and composes his own work. "It's what I love—it's so eclectic," he says. "I get to have my hands and fingers, and mind and body and soul, in a lot of different areas all at the same time."

Barton also teaches composition and MetaSynth—loosely defined as a computer program which translates images into sound—at Southern Oregon University, while pursuing personal, more experimental projects on the side. He's most recently gained celebrity for his work based on the Human Genome Project, for which he used a MIDI sequencer to create music from genome DNA data for the first chromosome. Did Barton imagine in third grade he would one day have a forum for such experimental work?

"At the age of eight, you're in the sandbox," he says. "But then, at the age of 52, I'm still in the sandbox. Genome music just happened to be the sand I was playing with that day."

Here Barton talks about his eclectic body of work, his diverse career, and the professional outlook for composers starting out:

You were trained formally in music, but self-taught in composition. How did you accomplish this?
My actual formal training in composition came by studying with people I knew who were composers I respected and admired. I basically just asked them, "Will you critique my work?" And a couple of them said, "Yeah, sure." So I was writing music and sending it out and talking on the phone or corresponding by letter and learned that way, basically. I told them to be ruthless and they were. At times that was hard, but I don't think there's any other way. You have to put the time in and you have to be willing to look at yourself, and therefore your expression. They asked me questions about what I was trying to convey. They weren't trying

to impose their style on me. They were helping me learn to think like a composer.

So would you say it is or is not necessary to have a formal education to succeed in the business?
What a formal education does at its best is it stretches you to develop techniques and craft that you might not normally encounter. That's why things like orchestration, counterpoint or advanced theory may take you into realms you might not even like, but by doing the work you're expanding your personal arsenal of expression—it's much deeper and richer.

If you're a self-taught instrumentalist, for instance, you do what you do really, really well. And sometimes that's enough. That's okay. Other times, if you practice those scales and arpeggios and every day you're trying to find a new way of turning something inside out, you have a larger range of expression at your fingertips. I mean, John Coltrane was not necessarily conservatory-taught, but he took books even conservatory students wouldn't look at and memorized them—the one big one is called the *Thesaurus of Scales and Melodic Patterns*. It has every permutation available of twelve notes, and Coltrane apparently could play this inside out. So it depends on the student, the self-motivation.

If you really, really want to be a composer, you're going to do that. Academics can help, and just being tenacious and voracious in your appetite for learning can also help. And of course the tried and true way of any artist—the answer to the question, how do I become a painter, a writer, a composer?—you wake up every morning and you write music, and you try to write the music you want to hear. You do that every day. And probably many days it's not going to come out the way you want. But if you just keep doing it, and make that a lifelong commitment, then definitely down the road things are going to start to happen. Things are going to come together.

With your teaching and composer-in-residence post occupying most of your time, how do you work in your experimental side projects?
It's in between the cracks. With the festival, during January and February, I'll be working 12- to 15-hour days. Then throw in a couple of hours at the university a week. So with my personal projects, it's in the wee hours of the evening or the wee hours of the morning that something like the genome project comes. And those projects are serendipitous. I'm always exploring, everyday, even if it's 15 minutes, I try to explore something new and different. When I downloaded the human genome DNA data for chromosome one, something happened. In an hour and a half I had written a four-minute piece compiled from that data. I work fast but that was even faster.

You've said your stylistic influences range from Coltrane to Stravinsky, from Brubeck to Bartok. With such a breadth of musical tastes and interests, can you name one pivotal influence on your development that had a deep and lasting impact?
Toru Takemitsu totally blew my mind. I was in high school when I first heard his work, including a piece called "Water Music," an electronic piece based on a sample of a single drop of water that was then morphed and mutated and transformed. On that album was also a piece called "Requiem" and a piece called "Ai," which is the Japanese word for "love," a *musique concrete* piece involving layering recorded sound. "Requiem" was the most beautiful, luscious—at times, tense—piece I'd ever heard. I'd never heard anyone use harmonies like that, and I remember playing that record everyday until the grooves wore out.

Did that discovery open the door for you to more experimental work?

On that album I heard someone who was incredibly deeply classically trained, but with amazing range. I didn't understand it for awhile, but was totally fascinated by it. With that particular album, it was eclectic in many senses but it came from a single mind. I guess that unconsciously it became a model for me. It made me want to explore as much as I could pack into a single lifetime.

How has your discovery of MetaSynth influenced your work?

For me, MetaSynth is the perfect fit. It's what unknowingly I've been looking for since the age of eight. All of a sudden what a teacher taught me in third grade about how graphics can become music is real. Now I can make graphics and press a button and it renders it in the music. So I'm in heaven. What it's taught me is that the gesture, the shape, is the most important thing. The gesture and shape are indeed linked to our breath. And so what I ask about any piece of music is, "Does it breathe? Does it change my breath patterns as a listener?" What I've learned from all this is my bigger-than-life definition of music. My definition is music is sculpting energy. It's a broad definition and could be applied to just about any performing art.

Would you say now is a good time for composers to be working, both in terms of creative and employment opportunities?

I think it's a great time to be working as far as creative opportunities go because you can collaborate with just about anyone you could imagine. It doesn't have to be the stars. I'm collaborating here all the time with totally hot shot people in poetry, art, sculpture, whatever, and with the Internet I can collaborate anywhere. I can send my music and people can add to it, or they can send me their stuff and I can add to it. So yes, it's the best possible time from my point of view for creative endeavors.

As for job opportunities, once again you just have to be relentless. The opportunities are only going to open up once you know exactly what you want to do, once you know who you are musically and what you want to offer to the world community of music. Because then you'll be open to those moments where all of a sudden the opportunity will arise. It's a mystery how you get gigs. You've gotta have a demo and you've gotta have a resume, but ultimately they probably won't get you the gig. What'll get you the gig is somebody hearing your music and going "Wow, could you do this?" And then you start networking and connecting, and you just keep going. And if you know what you want, and know what you're expressing, then you become a magnet in a way.

What's the single best piece of advice you could offer aspiring composers today?

Keep doing your work, and breathe.
—*Anne Bowling*

---

ber music ensemble. Estab. 1986. Members are professionals. Performs 16 concerts/year including 4 new works. Commissions 1 composer or new work/year. Performs in small recital halls. Pays 10% royalty.

How to Contact: Query first. Include SASE. Responds in 6 weeks.

Music: "We welcome scores for flute solo, piano solo or duo. Particular interest in Latin American composers."

Performances: Diego Luzuriaga's *La Múchica* (modern, with extended techniques); Robert Starer's *Yizkor & Anima Aeterna* (rhythmic); and Piazzolla's *Etudes Tanguistiques* (solo flute).

Tips: "Extended techniques, or with tape, are fine!"

N. FONTANA CONCERT SOCIETY, 359 S. Kalamazoo Mall, Suite 200, Kalamazoo MI 49007. (616)382-7774. Fax: (616)382-0812. E-mail: fontana@iserv.net. **Contact:** Ms. Anne Berquisa, executive and artistic director. Chamber music ensemble presenter. Estab. 1980. Members are professionals. Fontana Chamber Arts presents over 45 events, including the 6-week Summer Festival of Music and Art, which runs from mid-July to the end of August. Regional and guest artists perform classical, contemporary, jazz and nontraditional music. Commissions and performs new works each year. Fontana Chamber Arts presents 7 classical and 2 jazz concerts during the Fall/Winter season. Audience consists of well-educated individuals who accept challenging new works, but like the traditional as well. Summer—180 seat hall; Fall/winter—various venues, from 400 to 1,500 seats.

How to Contact: Submit complete score, résumé and tapes of piece(s). Include SASE. Responds in approximately 1 month.

Music: Chamber music—any combination of strings, winds, piano. No "pop" music, new age type. Special interest in composers attending premiere and speaking to the audience.

Performances: George Perle's *Duos for String Quartet & Horn* (commission); Dan Welches's *Dante Dances* (U.S. premiere); and C. Curtis-Smith's *Les Adieux* for horn and string quartet (collaboration with International Horn Society).

Tips: "Provide a résumé and clearly marked tape of a piece played by live performers."

N. FORT WORTH CHILDREN'S OPERA, 3505 W. Lancaster, Fort Worth TX 76107. (817)731-0833, ext. 19. Fax: (817)731-0835. Website: www.fwopera.org. **Contact:** Alan Buratto, director of education. Opera company. Estab. 1946. Members are professionals and amateurs. Performs "upwards of 100 in-school performances/year." Audience consists of elementary and middle school-age children; performs in school auditoriums, cafetoriums and gymnasiums. Pays $45/performance.

How to Contact: Submit complete score and tape of piece(s). Include SASE. Responds in 6 months.

Music: "Familiar fairy tales or stories adapted to music of opera composers. 35-45 minutes in length. Piano or keyboard accompaniment. Prefer operatic styles with some dialogue. Must include moral, safety or school issues. Can be multi-racial and speak to all ages from pre-K through middle school-age children. Prefer pieces with easy to learn, memorable melodies. Performed by young, trained professionals for children. No greater than five performers plus accompanist/narrator."

Performances: *Little Red's Most Unusual Day* (adapted story by John Davies, music of Rossini/Offenbach, children's opera); *Wolfgang and the Three Little Pigs* (adapted story by John Davies, music of Mozart, children's opera); and *Jack and the Beanstalk* (adapted story by John Davies, music of Gilbert and Sullivan, children's opera).

Tips: "Use characters easily identifiable to children in situations which relate to their world, school and society. Adapted stories to opera music by great composers is preferred."

GREATER GRAND FORKS SYMPHONY ORCHESTRA, P.O. Box 7084, Grand Forks ND 58202-7084. (701)777-3359. Fax: (701)777-3320. E-mail: ggfso@und.nodak.edu. **Contact:** Timm Rolek, music director. Symphony orchestra. Estab. 1908. Members are professionals and/or amateurs. Performs 6 concerts/year. "New works are presented in 2-4 of our programs." Audience is "a mix of ages and musical experience. In 1997-98 we moved into a renovated, 450-seat theater." Pay is negotiable, depending on licensing agreements.

How to Contact: Submit complete score or complete score and tape of pieces. Include SASE. Responds in 6 months.

Music: "Style is open, instrumentation the limiting factor. Music can be scored for an ensemble up to but not exceeding: 3,2,3,2/4,3,3,1/3 perc./strings. Rehearsal time limited to 3 hours for new works."

REFER TO THE GEOGRAPHIC INDEX (at the back of this book) to find listings of companies by state, as well as foreign listings.

Performances: Michael Harwood's *Amusement Park Suite* (orchestra); Randall Davidson's *Mexico Bolivar Tango* (chamber orchestra); and John Corigliano's *Voyage* (flute and orchestra); Linda Tutas Haugen's *Fable of Old Turtle* (saxophone concerto).

N HASTINGS SYMPHONY ORCHESTRA, Fuhr Hall, Ninth & Ash, Hastings NE 68901. (402)461-7361. E-mail: jjohnson@hastings.edu. **Contact:** Dr. James Johnson, conductor/music director. Symphony orchestra. Estab. 1926. Members are professionals and amateurs. Performs 7-8 concerts/year including 1 new work. Commissions 0-1 new works/year. "Audience consists of conservative residents of mid-Nebraska who haven't heard most classics." Concert Hall: Masonic Temple Auditorium (950). Pays per performance.
How to Contact: Submit complete score and tapes of piece(s). Include SASE. Responds in 6 months.
Music: "We are looking for all types of music within the range of an accomplished community orchestra. Write first and follow with a phone call."
Performances: Richard Wilson's *Silhouette*; and James Oliverio's *Pilgrimage* (symphonic).
Tips: "Think about the size, ability and budgetary limits. Confer with our music director about audience taste. Think of music with special ties to locality."

HEARTLAND MEN'S CHORUS, P.O. Box 32374, Kansas City MO 64171-5374. (816)931-3338. Fax: (816)531-1367. E-mail: hmc@hmckc.org. Website: www.hmckc.org. **Contact:** Joseph Nadeau, music director. Men's chorus. Estab. 1985. Members are professionals and amateurs. Performs 3 concerts/year; 9-10 are new works. Commissions 1 composer or new works/year. Performs for a diverse audience at the Folly Theater (1,200 seats). Pay is negotiable.
How to Contact: Query first. Include SASE. Responds in 2 months.
Music: "Interested in works for male chorus (ttbb). Must be suitable for performance by a gay male chorus. We will consider any orchestration, or a cappella."
Performances: Thomas Pasatieris's *Mornings Innocent* (song cycle); Craig Carnahan's *Nutcracker: Men in Tights* (musical); and Robert Moran's *Night Passage* (opera).
Tips: "Find a text that relates to the contemporary gay experience, something that will touch peoples' lives."

✔ HELENA SYMPHONY, P.O. Box 1073, Helena MT 59624. (406)442-1860. E-mail: hss@ixi.net. Website: www.helenasymphony.org. **Contact:** Erik Funk, music director and conductor. Symphony orchestra. Estab. 1955. Members are professionals and amateurs. Performs 7-10 concerts/year including new works. Performance space is an 1,800 seat concert hall. Payment varies.
How to Contact: Query first. Include SASE. Responds in 3 months.
Music: "Imaginative, collaborative, not too atonal. We want to appeal to an audience of all ages. We don't have a huge string complement. Medium to difficult okay—at frontiers of professional ability we cannot do."
Performances: Eric Funk's *A Christmas Overture* (orchestra); Donald O. Johnston's *A Christmas Processional* (orchestra/chorale); and Elizabeth Sellers' *Prairie* (orchestra/short ballet piece).
Tips: "Try to balance tension and repose in your works. New instrument combinations are appealing."

N HENDERSONVILLE SYMPHONY ORCHESTRA, P.O. Box 1811, Hendersonville NC 28793. (828)697-5884. Fax: (828)697-5765. E-mail: hso@brinet.com. Website: www.hendersonvillesymphony.org. **Contact:** Sandie Salvaggio-Walker, general manager. Symphony orchestra. Estab. 1971. Members are professionals and amateurs. Performs 6 concerts/year. "We would welcome a new work per year." Audience is a cross-section of retirees, professionals and some children. Performance space is a 857-seat high school audiorium.
How to Contact: Query first. Include SASE. Responds in 1 month.
Music: "We use a broad spectrum of music (classical concerts and pops)."
Performances: Nelson's *Jubilee* (personal expression in a traditional method); Britten's "The Courtly Dances" from Glorina (time-tested); and Chip Davis' arrangement for Mannheim Steamroller's *Deck the Halls* (modern adaptation of traditional melody).

Tips: "Submit your work even though we are a community orchestra. We like to be challenged. We have the most heavily patronized fine arts group in the county. Our emphasis is on education."

N. HERMANN SONS GERMAN BAND, P.O. Box 162, Medina TX 78055. (830)589-2268. E-mail: fest@hctc.net. Website: www.festmusik.com. **Contact:** Herbert Bilhartz, music director. Community band with German instrumentation. Estab. 1990. Members are both professionals and amateurs. Performs 12 concerts/year including 6 new works. Commissions no new composers or new works/year. Performs for "mostly older people who like German polkas, waltzes and marches. We normally play only published arrangements from Germany."

How to Contact: Query first; then submit full set of parts and score, condensed or full. Include SASE. Responds in 6 weeks.

Music: "We like European-style polkas or waltzes (Viennese or Missouri tempo), either original or arrangements of public domain tunes. Arrangements of traditional American folk tunes in this genre would be especially welcome. Also, polkas or waltzes featuring one or two solo instruments (from instrumentation below) would be great. OK for solo parts to be technically demanding. Although we have no funds to commission works, we will provide you with a cassette recording of our performance. Also, we would assist composers in submitting works to band music publishers in Germany for possible publication. Polkas and waltzes generally follow this format: Intro; 1st strain repeated; 2nd strain repeated; DS to 1 strain; Trio: Intro; 32 bar strain; 'break-up' strain; Trio DS. Much like military march form. Instrumentation: Fl/Picc, 3 Clars in Bb, 2 Fluegelhorns in Bb; 3 Tpts in Bb, 2 or 4 Hns in F or Eb, 2 Baritones (melody/countermelody parts; 1 in Bb TC, 1 in BC), 2 Baritones in Bb TC (rhythm parts), 3 Trombones, 2 Tubas (in octaves, mostly), Drum set, Timpani optional. We don't use saxes, but a German publisher would want 4-5 sax parts. Parts should be medium to medium difficult. All brass parts should be considered one player to the part; woodwinds, two to the part. No concert type pieces; no modern popular or rock styles. However, a 'theme and variations' form with contrasting jazz, rock, country, modern variations would be clever, and our fans might go for such a piece (as might a German publisher)."

Performances: Darryl Lyman's *American Folk Music Waltz* medley and *American Folk Music Polka* medley; and David Lorrien's *Cotton-Eyed Joe* arrangement.

Tips: "German town bands love to play American tunes. There are many thousands of these bands over there and competition among band music publishers in Germany is keen. Few Americans are aware of this potential market, so few American arrangers get published over there. Simple harmony is best for this style, but good counterpoint helps a lot. Make use of the dark quality of the Fluegelhorns and the bright, fanfare quality of the trumpets. Give the two baritones (one in TC and one in BC) plenty of exposed melodic material. Keep them in harmony with each other (3rds and 6ths), unlike American band arrangements, which have only one Baritone line. If you want to write a piece in this style, give me a call, and I will send you some sample scores to give you a better idea."

HERSHEY SYMPHONY ORCHESTRA, P.O. Box 93, Hershey PA 17033. (800)533-3088. E-mail: drdackow@aol.com. **Contact:** Dr. Sandra Dackow, music director. Symphony orchestra. Estab. 1969. Members are professionals and amateurs. Performs 8 concerts/year, including 1-3 new works. Commissions "possibly 1-2" composers or new works/year. Audience is family and friends of community theater. Performance space is a 1,900 seat grand old movie theater. Pays commission fee.

How to Contact: Submit complete score and tape of piece(s). Include SASE. Responds in 3 months.

Music: "Symphonic works of various lengths and types which can be performed by a non-professional orchestra. We are flexible but like to involve all our players."

Performances: Paul W. Whear's *Celtic Christmas Carol* (orchestra/bell choir) and Linda Robbins Coleman's *In Good King Charlie's Golden Days* (overture).

Tips: "Please lay out rehearsal numbers/letter and rests according to phrases and other logical musical divisions rather than in groups of ten measures, etc., which is very unmusical and wastes time and causes a surprising number of problems. Also, please do not send a score written in concert pitch; use the usual transpositions so that the conductor sees what the players see; rehearsal is much more effective this way. Cross cue all important solos; this helps in rehearsal where instruments may be missing."

☑ **HUDSON VALLEY PHILHARMONIC**, 35 Market St., 1st Floor, Poughkeepise NY 12601. (845)473-5288. Fax: (845)473-4259. E-mail: slamarca@bardavon.org. Website: www.bardavon.org. **Contact:** Stephen LaMarca, production manager. Symphony orchestra. Estab. 1969. Members are professionals. Performs 20 concerts/year including 1-5 new works. Commissions 1 composer or new work every other year. "Classical subscription concerts: older patrons primarily; Pops concerts: all ages; New Wave concerts: baby boomers. New Wave concerts are crossover projects with a rock 'n' roll artist performing with an orchestra. HVP performs in three main theatres which are concert auditoriums with stages and professional lighting and sound." Pay is negotiable.
How to Contact: Query first. Include SASE. Responds in 8 months.
Music: "HVP is open to serious classical music, pop music and rock 'n' roll crossover projects. Desired length of work between 10-20 minutes. Orchestrations can be varied by should always include strings. There is no limit to difficulty since our musicians are professional. The ideal number of musicians to write for would include up to a Brahms-size orchestra 2222, 4231, T, 2P, piano, harp, strings."
Performances: Joan Tower's *Island Rhythms (serious classical work); Bill Vanaver's P'nai El* (symphony work with dance); and Joseph Bertolozzi's *Serenade* (light classical, pop work).
Tips: "Don't get locked into doing very traditional orchestrations or styles. Our music director is interested in fresh, creative formats. He is an orchestrator as well and can offer good advice on what works well. Songwriters who are into crossover projects should definitely submit works. Over the past four years, HVP has done concerts featuring the works of Natalie Merchant, John Cale, Sterling Morrison, Richie Havens and R. Carlos Nakaì (Native American flute player), all reorchestrated by our music director for small orchestra with the artist."

KENTUCKY OPERA, 101 S. Eighth St. at Main, Louisville KY 40202. (502)584-4500. Fax: (502)584-7484. Website: www.kyopera.org. **Contact:** Kim Cherie Lloyd, director of music. Opera. Estab. 1952. Members are professionals. Performs 3 main stage/year. Performs at Whitney Hall, The Kentucky Center for the Arts, seating is 2,400; Bomhard Theatre, The Kentucky Center for the Arts, 620; Macauley Theatre, 1,400. Pays by royalty, outright purchase or per performance.
How to Contact: *Write or call first before submitting. No unsolicited submissions.* Submit complete score. Include SASE. Responds in 6 months.
Music: Seeks opera—1 to 3 acts with orchestrations. No limitations.
Performances: *Turandot*; *Susannah!*; and *Rigaletto*.

☒ ☑ **KITCHENER-WATERLOO CHAMBER ORCHESTRA**, Box 34015, Highland Hills P.O., Kitchener, Ontario N2N 3G2 Canada. (519)744-3828. E-mail: kwchamberorchest@aol.com. **Contact:** Graham Coles, music director. Chamber Orchestra. Estab. 1985. Members are professionals and amateurs. Performs 5-6 concerts/year including 1-2 new works. "We perform mainly baroque and classical repertoire, so any contemporary works must not be too dissonant, long or far fetched." Pays per performance.
How to Contact: "It's best to query first so we can outline what not to send. Include: complete cv—list of works, performances, sample reviews." Include SAE and IRC. Responds in 2 months.
Music: "Musical style must be accessible to our audience and players (3 rehearsals). Length should be under 20 minutes. Maximum orchestration 2/2/2/2 2/2/0/0 Timp/or 1 Percussion String 5/5/3/4/2. We have limited rehearsal time, so keep technique close to that of Bach-Beethoven. We also play chamber ensemble works—octets, etc. We do not want choral or solo works."
Performances: James Grant's *Lament* (string orchestra) and Reynaldo Hahn's *La Fete Chez Therese* (ballet suite).
Tips: "If you want a first-rate performance, keep the technical difficulties minimal."

MARKETS THAT WERE listed in the 2002 edition of *Songwriters Market* but do not appear this year are listed in the General Index with a notation explaining why they were omitted.

N KNOX-GALESBURG SYMPHONY, Box 31, Knox College, Galesburg IL 61401. (309)343-0112, ext. 208. E-mail: bpolay@knox.edu. Website: www.knox.edu/knoxweb/kgs/home.html. **Contact:** Bruce Polay, music director. Symphony orchestra. Estab. 1951. Members are professionals and amateurs. Performs 7 concerts/year including 2-5 new works. Commissions 1 composer or new work/year on occasion. High diverse audience; excellent, recently renovated historical theater. Pay is negotiable.
How to Contact: Submit complete score and tapes of piece(s). "Pops material also welcome." Include SASE. Responds in 8 months.
Music: Moderate difficulty 3222/4331/T piano, harpsichord, celesta and full strings. No country.
Performances: Winstin's *5th Symphony* (orchestral); Pann's "Bullfight" from "Two Portraits of Barcelona" (orchestral); and Polay's Concerto-Fantasie (piano and orchestra).
Tips: "Looking for moderately difficult, 8-10 minute pieces for standard orchestra."

LAKESIDE SUMMER SYMPHONY, 236 Walnut Ave., Lakeside OH 43440. (419)798-4461. Fax: (419)798-5033. Website: www.lakesideohio.com. **Contact:** G. Keith Addy. Conductor: Robert L. Cronquist. Symphony orchestra. Members are professionals. Performs 8 concerts/year. Performs "Chautauqua-type programs with an audience of all ages (2-102). Hoover Auditorium is a 3,000-seat auditorium."
How to Contact: Query first. Include SASE. Material should be submitted by October 15. Responds in 6 weeks.
Music: Seeking "classical compositions for symphony composed of 50-55 musicians. The work needs to have substance and be a challenge to our symphony members. No modern jazz, popular music or hard rock."

✔ LAMARCA AMERICAN VARIETY SINGERS, 2655 W. 230th Place, Torrance CA 90505. (310)325-8708. E-mail: lamarcamusic@lycos.com. Website: www.lamarcamusic.tripod.com. **Contact:** Priscilla Kandel, director. Youth to high school vocal ensembles. Estab. 1979. Members are professionals and amateurs. Performs 10 concerts/year including 3 new works. Performs at major hotels, conventions, community theaters, fund raising events, cable TV, community fairs and Disneyland. Pays showcase only.
How to Contact: Query first. Include SASE. Responds in 2 weeks.
Music: "Seeks 3-10 or 15 minute medleys; a variety of musical styles from Broadway—pop styles to humorous specialty songs. Top 40 dance music, light rock and patriotic themes. No rap or anything not suitable for family audiences."
Performances: *Disney Movie Music* (uplifting); *Children's Music* (educational/positive); and *Beatles Medley* (love songs).

LEHIGH VALLEY CHAMBER ORCHESTRA, P.O. Box 20641, Lehigh Valley PA 18002-0641. (610)266-8555. Music Director: Donald Spieth. Chamber orchestra. Estab. 1979. Performs 25 concerts/year including 2-3 new works. Members are professionals. Commissions 1-2 composers or new works/year. Typical orchestral audience, also youth concerts. Pays commission for first 2 performances, first right for recording.
How to Contact: Submit complete score and tape of piece(s). Include SASE. Responds in 4 months.
Music: "Classical orchestral; works for youth and pops concerts. Duration 10-15 minutes. Chamber orchestra 2222-2210 percussion, strings (66442). No limit on difficulty."
Performances: February 15-16, 2002, Kyle Smith commissioned for new work.
Tips: "Send a sample tape and score of a work(s) written for the requested medium."

LEXINGTON PHILHARMONIC SOCIETY, 161 N. Mill St., Arts Place, Lexington KY 40507. (859)233-4226. Fax: (859)233-7896. Website: www.lexingtonphilharmonic.org. **Contact:** George Zack, music director. Symphony orchestra. Estab. 1961. Members are professionals. Series includes "8 serious, classical subscription concerts (hall seats 1,500); 3 concerts called Pops the Series; 10 outdoor pops concerts (from 1,500 to 5,000 tickets sold); 5-10 run-out concerts (½ serious/½ pops); and 10 children's concerts." Pays via ASCAP and BMI, rental purchase and private arrangements.
How to Contact: Submit complete score and tape of piece(s). Include SASE.

Music: Seeking "good current pops material and good serious classical works. No specific restrictions, but overly large orchestra requirements, unusual instruments and extra rentals help limit our interest."

Performances: "Visit our website for complete concert season listing."

Tips: "When working on large-format arrangement, use cross-cues so orchestra can be cut back if required. Submit good quality copy, scores and parts. Tape is helpful."

LIMA SYMPHONY ORCHESTRA, 67 Town Square, P.O. Box 1651, Lima OH 45802. (419)222-5701. Fax: (419)222-6587. **Contact:** Crafton Beck, music conductor. Symphony orchestra. Estab. 1953. Members are professionals. Performs 17-18 concerts including at least 1 new work/year. Commissions at least 1 composer or new work/year. Middle to older audience; also Young People's Series. Mixture for stage and summer productions. Performs in Veterans' Memorial Civic & Convention Center, a beautiful hall seating 1,670; various temporary shells for summer outdoors events; churches; museums and libraries. Pays $2,500 for outright purchase (Anniversary commission) or grants $1,500-5,000.

How to Contact: Submit complete score if not performed; otherwise submit complete score and tape of piece(s). Include SASE. Responds in 3 months.

Music: "Good balance of incisive rhythm, lyricism, dynamic contrast and pacing. Chamber orchestra to full (85-member) symphony orchestra." Does not wish to see "excessive odd meter changes."

Performances: Frank Proto's *American Overture* (some original music and fantasy); Werner Tharichen's *Concerto for Timpani and Orchestra*; and James Oliverio's *Pilgrimage—Concerto for Brass* (interesting, dynamic writing for brass and the orchestra).

Tips: "Know your instruments, be willing to experiment with unconventional textures, be available for in depth analysis with conductor, be at more than one rehearsal. Be sure that individual parts are correctly matching the score and done in good, neat calligraphy."

LITHOPOLIS AREA FINE ARTS ASSOCIATION, 3825 Cedar Hill Rd., Canal Winchester OH 43110-8929. (614)837-8925. **Contact:** Virginia E. Heffner, series director. Performing Arts Series. Estab. 1973. Members are professionals and amateurs. Performs 6-7 concerts/year including 2-3 new works. "Our audience consists of couples and families 30-80 in age. Their tastes run from classical, folk, ethnic, big band, pop and jazz. Our hall is acoustically excellent and seats 400. It was designed as a lecture-recital hall in 1925." Composers "may apply for Ohio Arts Council Grant under the New Works category." Pays straight fee to ASCAP.

How to Contact: Query first. Include SASE. Responds in 3 weeks.

Music: "We prefer that a composer is also the performer and works in conjunction with another artist, so they could be one of the performers on our series. Piece should be musically pleasant and not too dissonant. It should be scored for small vocal or instrumental ensemble. Dance ensembles have difficulty with 15' high 15' deep and 27' wide stage. We do not want avant-garde or obscene dance routines. No ballet (space problem). We're interested in something historical—national or Ohio emphasis would be nice. Small ensembles or solo format is fine."

Performances: Patsy Ford Simms' *Holiday Gloria* (Christmas SSA vocal); Andrew Carter's *A Maiden Most Gentle* (Christmas SSA vocal); and Luigi Zaninelli's *Alleluia, Silent Night* (Christmas SSA vocal).

Tips: "Call in September of 2001 for queries about our 2001-2002 season. We do a varied program. We don't commission artists. Contemporary music is used by some of our artist or groups. By contacting these artists, you could offer your work for inclusion in their program."

N. LYRIC OPERA OF CHICAGO, 20 N. Wacker Dr., Chicago IL 60606. (312)827-3569. Fax: (312)419-8345. E-mail: jgriffin@lyricopera.org. Website: www.lyricopera.org. **Contact:** Julie Griffin-Meadors, music administrator. Opera company. Estab. 1953. Members are professionals. Performs 80 operas/year including 1 new work in some years. Commissions 1 new work every 4 or 5 years. "Performances are held in a 3,563 seat house for a sophisticated opera audience, predominantly 30+ years old." Payment varies.

How to Contact: Query first. Does not return material. Responds in 6 months.

Music: "Full-length opera suitable for a large house with full orchestra. No musical comedy or Broadway musical style. We rarely perform one-act operas. We are only interested in works by composers and librettists with extensive theatrical experience. We have few openings for new works, so candidates must be of the highest quality. Do not send score or other materials without a prior contact."

Performances: William Bolcom's *View from the Bridge*; John Corigliano's *Ghosts of Versailles*; and Leonard Bernstein's *Candide*.

Tips: "Have extensive credentials and an international reputation."

MASTER CHORALE OF WASHINGTON, 1200 29th St. NW, Suite LL2, Washington DC 20007. (202)471-4050. Fax: (202)471-4051. E-mail: singing@masterchorale.org. Website: www.mast erchorale.org. **Contact:** Donald McCullough, music director. Vocal ensemble. Estab. 1967. Members are professionals and amateurs. Performs 8 concerts/year including 1-3 new works. Commissions one new composer or work every 2 years. "Audience covers a wide range of ages and economic levels drawn from the greater Washington DC metropolitan area. Kennedy Center Concert Hall seats 2,400." Pays by outright purchase.

How to Contact: Submit complete score and tape of piece(s). Include SASE. Responds in 9 months.

Music: Seeks new works for: 1) large chorus with or without symphony orchestras; 2) chamber choir and small ensemble.

Performances: Stephen Paulus' *Mass*; Joonas Kokkonen's *Requiem* (symphonic choral with orchestra); Morten Lauridsen's *Lux Aeterna*; Donald McCullough's *Let My People Go!: A Spiritual Journey*; and Daniel E. Gawthop's *In Quiet Resting Places*.

N! MESQUITE SYMPHONIC BAND, (formerly Mesquite Community Band), 1527 North Galloway, Mesquite TX 75149-2327. (972)216-8125. Fax: (972)288-4760. **Contact:** Dale Y. Coates, conductor. Community band. Estab. 1986. Members are both professionals and amateurs. Performs 9 (4 formal, 5 outdoor) concerts/year. Commissions 1 composer or new work/year. Audience is young-to-mature adult. Performance space is concert hall (Mesquite Arts Center). Pays variable rate for outright purchase.

How to Contact: Submit complete score and tape of piece(s). Include SASE. Responds in 1 month.

Music: Seeks full orchestration for band, approximately 4-5 minutes. "At this time we have approximately thirty-five members with the top level being level four." Does not want modern style.

Performances: James Curnow's *Olympic Fanfare & Theme*.

Tips: "Know the capability of the performing group."

MILWAUKEE YOUTH SYMPHONY ORCHESTRA, 929 N. Water St., Milwaukee WI 53202. (414)272-8540. Fax: (414)272-8549. E-mail: general@myso.org. **Contact:** Frances Richman, executive director. Multiple youth orchestras and other instrumental ensembles. Estab. 1956. Members are students. Performs 12-15 concerts/year including 1-2 new works. "Our groups perform in Uihlein Hall at the Marcus Center for the Performing Arts in Milwaukee plus area sites. The audiences usually consist of parents, music teachers and other interested community members, with periodic reviews in the *Milwaukee Journal Sentinel*." Payment varies.

How to Contact: Query first. Include SASE. Does not return material. Responds in 1 month.

Performances: James Woodward's *Tuba Concerto*.

Tips: "Be sure you realize you are working with *students* (albeit many of the best in southeastern Wisconsin) and not professional musicians. The music needs to be on a technical level students can handle. Our students are 8-18 years of age, in 2 full symphony orchestras, a wind ensemble and 2 string orchestras, plus two flute choirs, advanced chamber orchestra and 15-20 small chamber ensembles."

☑ THE MIRECOURT TRIO, 50 Orchard St., Jamaica Plain MA 02130. (617)524-2495. E-mail: tkingcello@aol.com. **Contact:** Terry King. Chamber music ensemble; violin, cello, piano. Estab. 1973. Members are professionals. Performs 2-4 concerts/year including 1 new work. Commissions

1 composer or new work/year. Concerts are performed for university, concert series, schools, societies and "general chamber music audiences of 100-1,500." Pays for outright purchase, percentage royalty or per performance.

How to Contact: Query first. Include SASE. Responds in 6 months.

Music: Seeks "music of short to moderate duration (5-20 minutes) that entertains, yet is not derivative or clichéd. Orchestration should be basically piano, violin, cello, occasionally adding voice or instrument. We do not wish to see academic or experimental works."

Performances: Otto Leuning's *Solo Sonata* (solo cello); Lukas Foss's *Three American Pieces* (cello, piano premiere); and Coolidge's *Dialectic No. 1 for piano trio.*

Tips: "Submit works that engage the audience or relate to them, that reward the players as well."

 MOHAWK TRAIL CONCERTS, P.O. Box 75, Shelburne Falls MA 01370. (413)625-9511. 1-888-MTC-MUSE. E-mail: info@mohawktrailconcerts.org. Website: www.mohawktrailconcerts.org. Director: Polesny Bartoli. Artistic Director: Ruth Black. Chamber music presenter. Estab. 1969. Members are professionals. Performs 22 concerts/year including 3-5 new works. Conducts school performances. "Audience ranges from farmers to professors, children to elders. Concerts are performed in Federated Church, Charlemont, MA." Pays by variable rate.

How to Contact: Query first. (Attention: Arnold Black, Artistic Director). Include SASE. Responds in months.

Music: "We want chamber music, generally not longer than 30 minutes. We are open to a variety of styles and orchestrations for a maximum of 8 performers. We don't want pop, rock or theater music."

Performances: Michael Cohen's *Fantasia for Flute, Piano and Strings* (chamber); William Bolcom's *Nes Songs* (piano/voice duo); and Arnold Black's *Laments & Dances* (string quartet and guitar duo).

Tips: "We are looking for artistic excellence, a committment to quality performances of new music, and music that is accessible to a fairly conservative (musically) audience."

  MONTREAL CHAMBER ORCHESTRA, 1155 René Lévesque Blvd. W, Suite 2500, Montreal, Quebec H3B 2K4 Canada. (514)871-1224. Fax: (514)871-8967. E-mail: mcoocm@aol.com. Website: www.mco-ocm.qc.ca. Conductor and Music Director: Wanda Kaluzny. Chamber orchestra. Estab. 1974. Members are professionals. Performs 6 concerts including 1-3 new works/year. Commissions various new works/year (Canadian composers only). Audience is mixed ages, mixed income levels. Orchestra performs in Pollack Hall, seating 600. Pays "through the composer's performing arts organization."

How to Contact: Submit complete score. Does not return material. Responds "only if performing the work."

Music: Works with string orchestra (6 / 4 / 2 / 2 / 1), 8-12 min. duration. Strings (6 / 4 / 2 / 2 / 1).

Performances: Anne Lauber's *Piano Concerto No. 2* (piano concerto); Heather Schmidt's *Serenade* (string orchestra, 1 movement); and Michael Matthews' *Between the Wings of the Earth* (chamber orchestra).

 MOORES OPERA CENTER, Moores School of Music, University of Houston, Houston TX 77204-4201. (713)743-3162. E-mail: bross@www.music.uh.edu. Director of Opera: Buck Ross. Opera/music theater program. Members are professionals, amateurs and students. Performs 12-14 con-

FOR EXPLANATIONS OF THESE SYMBOLS,
SEE THE INSIDE FRONT AND BACK COVERS OF THIS BOOK.

certs/year including 1 new work. Performs in a proscenium theater which seats 800. Pit seats approximately up to 75 players. Audience covers wide spectrum, from first time opera-goers to very sophisticated. Pays per performance.

How to Contact: Submit complete score and tapes of piece(s). Include SASE. Responds in 6 months.

Music: "We seek music that is feasible for high graduate level student singers. Chamber orchestras are very useful. No more than two and a half hours. No children's operas."

Performances: John Corigliano's *The Ghosts of Versailles*; Carlisle Floyd's *Bilby's Doll*; Robert Nelson's *A Room With a View*; Conrad Susa's *The Dangerous Liaisons*; and Dominick Argento's *Casanova's Homecoming*.

MOZART FESTIVAL ORCHESTRA, INC., 33 Greenwich Ave., New York NY 10014. (212)675-9127. **Contact:** Dr. Baird Hastings, conductor. Symphony orchestra. Estab. 1960. Members are professionals. Audience members are Greenwich Village residents of all ages, largely professionals. Performances are held at the First Presbyterian Church, Fifth Ave. and 12th St., ("wonderful acoustics"). Payment varies.

How to Contact: Query first. Include SASE. Responds in 2 weeks.

Music: "We are an established chamber orchestra interested in *unusual* music of all periods, but not experimental. Orchestra size usually under 20 performers."

Performances: Gary Sunden's *Sganarelle* (prelude); and Virgil Thomson's *Portrait* (strings).

NATIONAL ASSOCIATION OF COMPOSERS/USA (NACUSA), P.O. Box 49256, Los Angeles CA 90049. (310)541-8213. E-mail: bia@flash.net. Website: www.thebook.com/nacusa. **Contact:** Marshall Bialosky, president. Chamber music ensemble and composers' service organization. Estab. 1932. Members are professionals. Performs 10-15 concerts/year in L.A.; 10-11 nationally with other chapters—all new works. Usually perform at universities in Los Angeles and at a mid-town church in New York. Paid by ASCAP or BMI (NACUSA does not pay composers).

How to Contact: To submit, you must be a member of NACUSA. Submit complete score and tape of pieces. Include SASE. Responds in 3 months.

Music: Chamber music for five or fewer players; usually in the 5-20 minute range. "Level of difficulty is not a problem; number of performers is solely for financial reasons. We deal in serious, contemporary concert hall music. No 'popular' music."

Performances: Robert Linn's *Piano Variations*; Aurelio dela Vega's *Transparent Songs* (voice, piano); and Michelle Green's *At Ends* (solo violin).

Tips: "Send in modest-sized pieces—not symphonies and concertos."

N NEW JERSEY SYMPHONY ORCHESTRA/GREATER NEWARK YOUTH ORCHESTRA, 2 Central Ave., Newark NJ 07102. (973)624-3713. Fax: (973)624-2115. E-mail: information@njsymphony.org. Website: www.njsymphony.org. Symphony orchestra and youth orchestra. Estab. 1922. Members are professionals and students for youth orchestra. Performs 2-10 new works/year. Commissions 1-3 composers or new works/year.

How to Contact: Query first or submit complete score and tape of piece(s). Include SASE. Responds in 2 months.

Music: Classical with jazz, pop influence, or the fusion of the above. Compositions for young people's concerts.

N THE NEW YORK CONCERT SINGERS, 75 East End Ave., Suite 9L, New York NY 10028. (212)879-4412. Music Director/Conductor: Judith Clurman. Chorus. Estab. 1988. Performs 3-4 concerts/year including new works. Frequently commissions new composers. "Audience is mixture of young and old classical music 'lovers.' Chorus performs primarily at Carnegie Hall and Lincoln Center, NYC." ASCAP, BMI fees paid. Records for New World and Delos Records.

How to Contact: Submit complete score with tape of piece(s). Include SASE. Responds in 2 months.

Music: Seeks music "for professional ensemble, with or without solo parts, a cappella, small instrumental ensemble or full orchestra. Looking for pieces ranging from 7-20 minutes."

Performances: Ellen Taaffe Zurlich's *Magnificat*; Stephen Paulus' *Meditation of Li Po* and William Bokom's *The Mask* (all traditional oratorio).

Tips: "When choosing a piece for a program I study both the text and music. Both are equally important."

■ NORFOLK CHAMBER MUSIC FESTIVAL/YALE SUMMER SCHOOL OF MUSIC,

Box 208246, New Haven CT 06520-8246. (203)432-1966. E-mail: norfolk@yale.edu. Website: www. yale.edu/norfolk. **Contact:** Elaine C. Carroll, festival manager. Summer music festival. Estab. 1941. Members are international faculty/artists plus young professionals. Performs 20 concerts, 15 recitals/ year, including 6 new works. Commissions 1 composer or new work/year. Audience is "highly motivated with interests in traditional chamber and serious music." Pays a commission fee. Also offers a Composition Search and Residency biennially. The Norfolk Chamber Music Festival-Yale Summer School of Music seeks new chamber music works from American composers. The goal of this search is to identify promising young composers and to provide a visible and high quality venue for the premiere of their work. A maximum of two winning compositions are selected. Winners are invited to the Norfolk Chamber Music Festival for a week-long residency.

● The Norfolk Chamber Music Festival/Yale Summer School of Music has won an ASCAP/ Chamber Music America award for adventurous programming.

How to Contact: Query first. Include SASE. Responds in 6 months.

Music: "Chamber music of combinations, particularly for strings, woodwinds, brass and piano."

Performances: Yehudi Wyner's *Epilogue 1996* (commission); Jennifer Higdon's *Autumn Quintet* (Norfolk prize); Martin Bresnick's *The Bucketrider and Be Just!*; and Joan Tower's *Tres Lent*.

▩ OPERA MEMPHIS,

Box 171413, Memphis TN 38187. (901)257-3100. Fax: (901)257-3109. E-mail: michael@operamemphis.org. Website: www.operamemphis.org. **Contact:** Michael Ching, artistic director. Opera company. Estab. 1955. Members are professionals. Performs 8-12 concerts/ year including 1 new work. Commissions 1 composer or new work/year. Audience consists of older, wealthier patrons, along with many students and young professionals. Pay is negotiable.

How to Contact: Query first. Include SASE. Responds in 1 year.

Music: Accessible practical pieces for educational or main stage programs. Educational pieces should not exceed 90 minutes or 4-6 performers. We encourage songwriters to contact us with proposals or work samples for theatrical works. We are very interested in crossover work.

Performances: Mike Reid's *Different Fields* (one act opera); David Olney's *Light in August* (folk opera); and Sid Selvidge's *Riversongs* (one act blues opera).

Tips: "Spend many hours thinking about the synopsis (plot outline)."

☑ OPERA ON THE GO,

1212 Huntcliff Trace, Aiken SC 29803. (803)643-7633. E-mail: Jodirose 11@aol.com. Website: http://operaonthego.org. **Contact:** Jodi Rose, artistic director. American opera chamber ensemble. Estab. 1985. Members are professionals. Performs about 100 operas/year includ- ing 1-2 new works. Commissions variable number of new works/year. "We perform primarily in schools and community theaters. We perform only American contemporary opera. It must be lyrical in sound and quality as we perform for children as well as adults. We prefer pieces written for children based on fairy tales needing 2-4 singers." Pays royalties of $20-30 per performance."We also help composers acquire a 'Meet the Composer' grant."

How to Contact: Query first, then submit complete score and tapes of piece(s). Include SASE. Responds in 2 months.

Music: Need works in all age groups including adults. For older ages the pieces can be up to 60 minutes. Rarely use orchestra. "Keep the music about 45 minutes long since we do a prelude (spoken) and postlude involving the children's active participation and performance. If it is totally atonal it will never work in the schools we perform in."

Performances: Arne Christiansen's *Tumbleweeds* (performed by children); Noel Katz's *Pirate Cap- tains* (opera for 6 grade-adult); and Seymour Barab's *Little Red Riding Hood* (children's opera).

Tips: "Be flexible. Through working with children we know what works best with different ages. If this means editing music to guarantee its performance, don't get offended or stubborn. All operas must have audience participatory sections."

OPERAWORKS, 170 W. 73rd St., New York NY 10023. (212)873-9531. E-mail: david@opera works.org. Website: www.operaworks.org. **Contact:** David Leighton, music director. Opera producers. Estab. 1983. Members are professionals. Performs 50 times including 5 new works/year. Commissions new composers or new works each year. Diverse audience—classical music enthusiasts and avant-garde art scene. Spaces: 100-400 seat theaters, traditional and experimental. Pay is negotiable.
How to Contact: Submit complete score and tape of piece(s). Include SASE. Responds in 3 months.
Music: The Virtual Orchestra-realistic orchestral sound produced by state-of-the-art electronic technology.
Performances: Martin Halpern's *The Satin Cloak*; Thea Musgrave's *Occurrence at Owl Creek Bridge*; and Antonio Bibalo's *The Glass Menagerie*.

ORCHESTRA SEATTLE/SEATTLE CHAMBER SINGERS, 1305 Fourth Ave. #402, Seattle WA 98101. (206)682-5208. E-mail: osscs@osscs.org. Website: www.osscs.org. **Contact:** Andrew Danilchik, librarian. Symphony orchestra, chamber music ensemble and community chorus. Estab. 1969. Members are amateurs and professionals. Performs 8 concerts/year including 2-3 new works. Commissions 1-2 composers or new works/year. "Our audience is made up of both experienced and novice classical music patrons. The median age is 45 with an equal number of males and females in the upper income range. Most concerts now held in Benaroya Hall."
How to Contact: Query first. Include SASE. Responds in 1 year.
Performances: Robert Kechley's *Psalm 100*; Huntley Beyer's *The Mass of Life and Death*; and Carol Sams's *Marches of Glynn* (choral work); and William Wilde Zeitler's *Beyond the Frontier of the Known* (glass armonica concerto).

PALMETTO MASTERSINGERS, P.O. Box 7441, Columbia SC 29202. (803)765-0777. Fax: (928)441-6083. E-mail: info@palmettomastersingers.org. Website: www.palmettomastersingers.org. **Contact:** Walter Cuttino, music director. 80 voice male chorus. Estab. 1981 by the late Dr. Arpad Darasz. Members are professionals and amateurs. Performs 8-10 concerts/year. Commissions 1 composer of new works every other year (on average). Audience is generally older adults, "but it's a wide mix." Performance space for the season series is the Koger Center (approximately 2,000 seats) in Columbia, SC. More intimate venues also available. Fee is negotiable for outright purchase.
How to Contact: Query first. Include SASE. Or e-mail to info@palmettomastersingers.org.
Music: Seeking music of 10-15 minutes in length, "not too far out tonally. Orchestration is negotiable, but chamber size (10-15 players) is normal. We rehearse once a week and probably will not have more than 8-10 rehearsals. These rehearsals (2 hours each) are spent learning a 1½-hour program. Only 1-2 rehearsals (max) are with the orchestra. Piano accompaniments need not be simplified, as our accompanist is exceptional."
Performances: Randal Alan Bass' *Te Deum* (12-minute, brass and percussion); and Dick Goodwin's *Mark Twain Remarks* (40 minute, full symphony).
Tips: "Contact us as early as possible, given that programs are planned by July. Although this is an amateur chorus, we have performed concert tours of Europe, performed at Carnegie Hall, The National Cathedral and the White House in Washington, DC. We are skilled amateurs."

PICCOLO OPERA COMPANY INC., 24 Del Rio Blvd., Boca Raton FL 33432-4734. (800)282-3161. Fax: (561)394-0520. E-mail: leejon51@msn.com. **Contact:** Lee Merrill, executive assistant. Traveling opera company. Estab. 1962. Members are professionals. Performs 1-50 concerts/year including 1-2 new works. Commissions 0-1 composer or new work/year. Operas are performed for a mixed audience of children and adults. Pays by performance or outright purchase.
How to Contact: Query first. Include SASE.

   A BULLET introduces comments by the editor of *Songwriter's Market* indicating special information about the listing.

Music: "Musical theater pieces, lasting about one hour, for adults to perform for adults and/or youngsters. Performers are mature singers with experience. The cast should have few performers (up to 10), no chorus or ballet, accompanied by piano or local orchestra. Skeletal scenery. All in English."
Performances: Menotti's *The Telephone*; Mozart's *Cosi Fan Tutte*; and Puccini's *La Boheme* (repertoire of more than 22 productions).

☑ **PRINCETON SYMPHONY ORCHESTRA**, P.O. Box 250, Princeton NJ 08542. (609)497-0020. Fax: (609)497-0904. E-mail: info@princetonsymphony.org. Website: www.princetonsymphony.org. **Contact:** Mark Laycock, music director. Symphony orchestra. Estab. 1980. Members are professionals. Performs 6-10 concerts/year including some new works. Commissions 1 composer or new work/year. Performs in a "beautiful, intimate 800-seat hall with amazing sound." Pays by arrangement.
How to Contact: Submit through agent only. Include SASE. Responds in 6 months.
Music: "Orchestra usually numbers 40-60 individuals."

Ⓝ **PRISM SAXOPHONE QUARTET**, 257 Harvey St., Philadelphia PA 19144. (215)438-5282. President, New Sounds Music Inc. Prism Quartet: Matthew Levy. Chamber music ensemble. Estab. 1984. Members are professionals. Performs 80 concerts/year including 10-15 new works. Commissions 4 composers or new works/year. "Ours are primarily traditional chamber music audiences." Pays royalty per performance from BMI or ASCAP or commission range from $100 to $15,000.
How to Contact: Submit complete score (with parts) and tape of piece(s). Does not return material. Responds in 3 months.
Music: "Orchestration—sax quartet, SATB. Lengths—5-25 minutes. Styles—contemporary, classical, jazz, crossover, ethnic, gospel, avant-garde. No limitations on level of difficulty. No more than 4 performers (SATB sax quartet). No transcriptions. The Prism Quartet places special emphasis on crossover works which integrate a variety of musical styles."
Performances: David Liebman's *The Gray Convoy* (jazz); Bradford Ellis's *Tooka-Ood Zasch* (ethnic-world music); and William Albright's *Fantasy Etudes* (contemporary classical).

Ⓝ **QUEENS OPERA**, P.O. Box 1311, Jackson NJ 08527. (732)833-8214. General Director: Joe Messina. Opera company. Estab. 1961. Members are professionals. Performs 8 concerts and operas/year including 1 new work.
How to Contact: Include SASE. Responds in 1 month.
Music: "Operatic scores and songs, small orchestra."
Performances: Strauss' *Die Fledermaus*; Puccini's *La Boheme*; Lehar's *Merry Widow*; and Three Divas concerts.

☑ **RIDGEWOOD SYMPHONY ORCHESTRA**, P.O. Box 176, Ridgewood NJ 07451. (201)612-0118. Fax: (201)445-2762. E-mail: info@ridgewoodssymphony.org. Website: www.ridgewoodsymphony.org. **Contact:** Edmund A. Moderacki, artistic director. Symphony orchestra. Estab. 1939. Members are professionals and amateurs. Performs 4-6 concerts/year and 2-3 children's concerts including 1-2 new works. Commissions possibly 1 new work/year. Audience is "sophisticated." Performance space is 744-seat school auditorium. Pays commission fee.
How to Contact: Submit complete score and tape of piece(s). Include SASE. Responds in 3 months ("it depends on how busy we are").
Music: "Symphonic works of various lengths and types which can be performed by a nonprofessional orchestra. We are flexible but would like to involve all of our players; very restrictive instrumentations do not suit our needs."
Performances: Shostakovich's *Festive Overture*; Gerschwin's *Piano Concerto in F*; Gerschwin's *American in Paris* (rhapsody); Dvorak's *Symphony No. 7 in D Minor*; Mussorgsky's *Pictures at an Exhibition*; and Elgar's *Enigma Variations*.
Tips: "Please lay out rehearsal numbers/letters and rests according to phrases and other logical musical divisions rather than in groups of ten measures, etc., which is very unmusical, wastes time and causes a surprising number of problems. Also, please *do not* send a score written in concert pitch;

use the usual transpositions so that the conductor sees what the players see. Rehearsal is much more effective this way. Cross cue all important solos; this helps in rehearsal where instruments may be missing."

☑ **SACRAMENTO MASTER SINGERS**, P.O. Box 215501, Sacramento CA 95821. (916)338-0300. Fax: (916)334-1808. E-mail: smscbarb@aol.com. Website: www.mastersingers.org. **Contact:** Ralph Hughes, conductor/artistic director. Vocal ensemble. Estab. 1984. Members are professionals and amateurs. Performs 9 concerts/year including 5-6 new works. Commissions 2 new works/year. Audience is made up of mainly college age and older patrons. Performs mostly in churches with 500-900 seating capacity. Pays $200 for outright purchase.
How to Contact: Submit complete score and tape of piece(s). Include SASE. Responds in 5 weeks.
Music: "A cappella works; works with small orchestras or few instruments; works based on classical styles with a 'modern' twist; multi-cultural music; shorter works probably preferable, but this is not a requirement. We usually have 38-45 singers capable of a high level of difficulty, but find that often simple works are very pleasing."
Performances: Joe Jennings' *An Old Black Woman, Homeless and Indistinct* (SATB, oboe, strings, dramatic).
Tips: "Keep in mind we are a chamber ensemble, not a 100-voice choir."

☑ **ST. LOUIS CHAMBER CHORUS**, P.O. Box 11558, Clayton MO 63105. (636)458-4343. E-mail: maltworm@inlink.com. Website: www.chamberchorus.org. **Contact:** Philip Barnes, artistic director. Vocal ensemble, chamber music ensemble. Estab. 1956. Members are professionals and amateurs. Performs 6 concerts/year including 5-10 new works. Commissions 1-2 new works/year. Audience is "diverse and interested in unaccompanied choral work and outstanding architectural/acoustic venues." Performances take place at various auditoria noted for their excellent acoustics—churches, synagogues, schools and university halls. Pays by arrangement.
How to Contact: Query first. Does not return material. "Panel of 'readers' submit report to Artistic Director. Responds in 3 months. 'General Advice' leaflet available on request."
Music: "*Only a cappella* writing; no contemporary 'popular' works; historical editions welcomed. No improvisatory works. Our programs are tailored for specific acoustics—composers should indicate their preference."
Performances: Sir Richard Rodney Bennett's *A Contemplation Upon Flowers* (a cappella madrigal); Stuart McIntosh's *Can Thou Lov'st Me, Lady?* (a cappella glee for men's voices); and Sasha Johnson Manning's *Dies Irae* (a cappella motet).
Tips: "We only consider a cappella works which can be produced in five rehearsals. Therefore pieces of great complexity or duration are discouraged."

☑ **THE SAINT THOMAS CHOIR OF MEN AND BOYS**, One W. 53rd St., New York NY 10019. (212)664-9360. E-mail: concerts@saintthomaschurch.org. Website: www.saintthomaschurch.org. **Contact:** Dr. Gerre Hancock, organist/director of music, master of choiristers, or Michael Monaco, concert series director. Church choir. Estab. 1919. Performs 4 concerts/year including 1 new work. Commissions 1 composer or new work every other year. Performs for a cosmopolitan New York audience in a Gothic Church. Pays by outright purchase or per performance.
How to Contact: Query first. Include SASE. Responds in 2 weeks.
Music: "Music for chorus appropriate to religious observances and Anglican liturgies: unaccompanied, organ accompaniment with or without chamber orchestra. The choir consists of 16-20 boy choristers/sopranos (unchanged voices), 4 adult male altos, 4 tenors, 4 basses. All adults are professional singers."
Performances: Gunther Schuller's *Magnificat and Nonc Dimittis (chorus and organ); Randall Thompson's Place of the Blest* (chorus and orchestra); and William Walton's *The Twelve* (chorus and orchestra).

🆕 **SAULT STE. MARIE SYMPHONY ORCHESTRA**, 3508 Bermuda Ave., Sault Ste. Marie MI 49783. (906)635-2265. **Contact:** Dr. John Wilkinson, music director. Symphony orchestra. Estab. 1972. Members are professionals and amateurs. Performs 8 full orchestra concerts/year including 1-2 new works. "Our audience is conservative. Our performance hall seats 964."

How to Contact: Query first. Include SASE.

Music: "We have traditional orchestra size 2222/4231/2, plus strings. String 10-12-5-5-3. We want pieces of length (5-15 minutes) in approachable styles. We have 55-60 performers. Pieces should be of moderate difficulty. Engage the listener; make it playable."

Performances: Ridout-Quesnel's *Colas et Colinette* (light overture); S. Glick's *Elegy* (elegy); L. Kuzmenko's *Prayer*; and J. Weinzweig's *The Red Ear of Corn* (ballet suite).

SINGING BOYS OF PENNSYLVANIA, P.O. Box 206, Wind Gap PA 18091. (610)759-6002. **Contact:** K. Bernard Schade, Ed. D., director. Vocal ensemble. Estab. 1970. Members are professional children. Performs 100 concerts/year including 3-5 new works. "We attract general audiences: family, senior citizens, churches, concert associations, university concert series and schools." Pays $300-3,000 for outright purchase.

How to Contact: Query first. Does not return material. Responds in 3 weeks.

Music: "We want music for commercials, voices in the SSA or SSAA ranges, sacred works or arrangements of American folk music with accompaniment. Our range of voices are from G below middle C to A (13th above middle C). Reading ability of choir is good but works which require a lot of work with little possibility of more than one performance are of little value. We sing very few popular songs except for special events. We perform music by composers who are well-known and works by living composers who are writing in traditional choral forms. Works which have a full orchestral score are of interest. The orchestration should be fairly light, so as not to cover the voices. Works for Christmas have more value than some other, since we perform with orchestras on an annual basis."

Performances: Don Locklair's *The Columbus Madrigals* (opera).

Tips: "It must be appropriate music and words for children. We do not deal in pop music. Folk music, classics and sacred are acceptable."

N: SOLI DEO GLORIA CANTORUM, 3402 Woolworth Ave., Omaha NE 68105. (402)341-4111. E-mail: cantorum@berkey.com. Website: www.berkey.com. **Contact:** Almeda Berkey, music director. Professional choir. Estab. 1988. Members are professionals. Performs 5-7 concerts/year; several are new works. Commissions 1-2 new works/year. Performance space: "cathedral, symphony hall, smaller intimate recital halls as well." Payment is "dependent upon composition and composer."

How to Contact: Submit complete score and tape of piece(s). Include SASE. Responds in 2 months.

Music: "Chamber music mixed with topical programming (e.g., all Celtic or all Hispanic programs, etc.). Generally a cappella compositions from very short to extended range (6-18 minutes) or multi-movements. Concerts are of a formal length (approx. 75 minutes) with 5 rehearsals. Difficulty must be balanced within program in order to adequately prepare in a limited rehearsal time. 28 singers. Not seeking orchestral pieces, due to limited budget."

Performances: Jackson Berkey's *Native Am Ambience* (eclectic/classical); John Rutter's *Hymn to the Creator of Light* (classical); and Arvo Part's *Te Deum* (multi-choir/chant-based classical).

N: SOUTHERN ARIZONA SYMPHONY ORCHESTRA, P.O. Box 43131, Tucson AZ 85733-3131. (520)323-7166. Fax: (480)585-4485. E-mail: saso@zerogee.com. Website: www.zerogee.com/saso. **Contact:** Warren Cohen, musical director. Symphony orchestra. Estab. 1979. Members are amateurs. Performs 9 concerts/year at least 2 new works every year. Commissions 1 composer or new work/year. Audience is a cross-section of Tucson as well as retirees. Perfoms in the 400-seat Berger Performing Arts Center and the 700-seat Saddlebrooke Arts Center. Pay varies. "We arrange each case differently, usually pay per performance."

How to Contact: Submit complete score and tape of piece(s). Include SASE. Responds in 4 months "or longer."

MARKET CONDITIONS are constantly changing! If you're still using this book and it is 2004 or later, buy the newest edition of *Songwriter's Market* at your favorite bookstore or order directly from Writer's Digest Books at (800)289-0963.

Music: Seeking works for a full symphony or chamber orchestra. Open to all styles of music, and will consider works of any length under 30 minutes. "Concertos are harder to program, as are works with chorus, but we will consider them. We have an amateur orchestra, but we have played a good deal of fairly difficult music. We could not, however, do Bruckner or Mahler symphonies. Most contemporary music has been fairly conservative in style, but we are open to things that are different, as long as it's not extremely difficult. Please keep orchestration fairly standard; no bass oboes or theremins."

Performances: 1999-2000 season included world premiere of James Barnes' *Autumn Soliloquy.* Other performances include Richard Arnell's *Symphony No. 6*, and Malcolm Arnold's *Clarinet Concerto No. 2.*

Tips: "Send a nice clean score. Don't get discouraged as we only have limited performance options. We appreciate knowing if you have orchestral parts available. We are especially excited by the possibility of discovering talented, unknown composers who have not had the opportunities available to those who are well-connected."

☑ **SPACE COAST POPS, INC.**, P.O. Box 3344, Cocoa FL 32924 or 2150 Lake Dr., Cocoa FL 32926. (321)632-7445. Fax: (321)632-1611. E-mail: popsorch@aol.com. **Contact:** Robert Coleman, music director and conductor. Pops orchestra and chamber music ensemble. Estab. 1986. Members are professionals. Performs 7 concerts/year, including 1-2 new works. Concerts are performed for "average audience—they like familiar works and pops. Concert halls up to 2,000 seats."

How to Contact: Query first. Include SASE. Responds in 6 months.

Music: Seeks "pops and serious music for full symphony orchestra, but not an overly large orchestra with unusual instrumentation. We use about 60 musicians because of hall limitations. Works should be medium difficulty—not too easy and not too difficult—and not more than ten minutes long." Does not wish to see avant-garde music.

Performances: Dussich's *First March* (march).

Tips: "If we would commission a work it would be to feature the space theme in our area."

⬛ **STAR-SCAPE**, P.O. Box 793, Station F, Toronto, Ontario M4Y 2N7 Canada. (905)951-3155 or (800)437-1454. Fax: (905)951-9712. E-mail: info@sun-scape.com. Website: www.sun-scape.com or www.kennethgmills.com. **Contact:** Ellen Mann, assistant to the conductor. A cappella choir (10-12 voices). Estab. 1976. Members are professionals. Performs 15 concerts/year including over 170 original works. Audience is appreciative of extraordinary technical ability of the ensemble and recognize that "this music, this art opens up the soul." Performances take place in concert halls and churches.

● See the listing for Sun-Scape Enterprises Limited in the Record Companies section.

How to Contact: Query first. Include SASE.

Performances: Kenneth G. Mills/Christopher Dedrick's *The Fire Mass* and arrangement of *The Battle Hymn of the Republic*; *He's Got The Whole World In His Hands* (spiritual); and Rachmaninoff's *Vespers.*

☑ **SUSQUEHANNA SYMPHONY ORCHESTRA**, P.O. Box 485, Forest Hill MD 21050. (410)838-6465. E-mail: sheldon.bair@ssorchestra.org or sbzbair@erols.com. Website: www.ssorchestra.org. **Contact:** Sheldon Bair, music director. Symphony orchestra. Estab. 1978. Members are amateurs. Performs 6 concerts/year including 1-2 new works. Composers paid depending on the circumstances. "We perform in 1 hall, 600 seats with fine acoustics. Our audience encompasses all ages."

How to Contact: Query first. Include SASE. Responds in 3 or more months.

Music: "We desire works for large orchestra, any length, in a 'conservative 20th and 21st century' style. Seek fine music for large orchestra. We are a community orchestra, so the music must be within our grasp. Violin I to 7th position by step only; Violin II—stay within 5th position; English horn and harp are OK. Full orchestra pieces preferred."

Performances: Malcolm Arnold's *Symphony No. 1* (US premiere); Daniel Dorff's *Goldilocks and the Three Bears*; and Tracey Rush's *Spirit of Freedom* (all orchestral works).

Ⓝ **SYMPHONY OF THE AMERICAS**, 199 N. Ocean Blvd., Suite 200, Pompano Beach FL 33062. (954)545-0088. Fax: (954)545-9088. E-mail: sympamer@aol.com. Website: www.symphamer

.com. **Contact:** Dr. James Brooks-Bruzzese, conductor/artistic director. Symphony orchestra and chamber music ensemble (strings). Estab. 1988. Members are professionals. Performs 8 concerts/year including 1 new work. Commissions 1 composer or new work/year. Audience is very conservative. Performance space is the 600-seat Broward Center for the Arts. Pays royalty.

How to Contact: Query first or submit complete score and tape of piece(s). Include SASE. Responds in 3 weeks.

Music: Seeking contemporary neo-romantic and classical for a small classical size orchestra. "At times we add trombones, extra percussion and harp but we prefer not to do this. It is too costly. No 12-tone music. Must be pleasing to the ear."

Performances: Villa-bobos's *Mono Precoce* (piano concerto); Robert Beaser's *Song of the Bells* (flute concerto); and David Heckendorn's *Environment Symphony* (symphony in three movements).

Tips: "Make it cost effective, pleasing to the ear and dramatic."

TORONTO MENDELSSOHN CHOIR, 60 Simcoe St., Toronto, Ontario M5J 2H5 Canada. (416)598-0422. Fax: (416)598-2992. Website: www.tmchoir.org. **Contact:** Eileen Keown, executive director. Vocal ensemble. Members are professionals and amateurs. Performs 25 concerts/year including 1-3 new works. "Most performances take place in Roy Thomson Hall. The audience is reasonably sophisticated, musically knowledgeable but with moderately conservative tastes." Pays by commission and ASCAP/SOCAN.

How to Contact: Query first or submit complete score and tapes of pieces. Include SASE. Responds in 6 months.

Music: All works must suit a large choir (180 voices) and standard orchestral forces or with some other not-too-exotic accompaniment. Length should be restricted to no longer than ½ of a nocturnal concert. The choir sings at a very professional level and can sight-read almost anything. "Works should fit naturally with the repertoire of a large choir which performs the standard choral orchestral repertoire."

Performances: Holman's *Jezebel*; Orff's *Catulli Carmina*; and Lambert's *Rio Grande*.

TOURING CONCERT OPERA CO. INC., 228 E. 80th, New York NY 10021. (212)988-2542. Fax: (518)851-6778. E-mail: tcoc@mhonline.net. **Contact:** Anne DeFigols, director. Opera company. Estab. 1971. Members are professionals. Performs 30 concerts/year including 1 new work. Payment varies.

How to Contact: Submit complete score and tape of piece(s). Does not return material. Response time varies.

Music: "Operas or similar with small casts."

Tips: "We are a touring company which travels all over the world. Therefore, operas with casts that are not large and simple but effective sets are the most practical."

VANCOUVER CHAMBER CHOIR, 1254 W. Seventh Ave., Vancouver, British Columbia V6H 1B6 Canada. E-mail: info@vancouverchamberchoir.com. Website: www.vancouverchamberchoir.com. **Contact:** Jon Washburn, artistic director. Vocal ensemble. Members are professionals. Performs 40 concerts/year including 5-8 new works. Commissions 2-4 composers or new works/year. Pays SOCAN royalty or negotiated fee for commissions.

How to Contact: Submit complete score and tape of piece(s). Does not return material. Responds in 6 months if possible.

Music: Seeks "choral works of all types for small chorus, with or without accompaniment and/or soloists. Concert music only. Choir made up of 20 singers. Large or unusual instrumental accompaniments are less likely to be appropriate. No pop music."

Performances: The VCC has commissioned and premiered over 150 new works by Canadian and international composers, including Alice Parker's *That Sturdy Vine* (cantata for chorus, soloists and orchestra); R. Murray Schafer's *Magic Songs* (SATB a cappella); and Jon Washburn's *A Stephen Foster Medley* (SSAATTBB/piano).

Tips: "We are looking for choral music that is performable yet innovative, and which has the potential to become 'standard repertoire.' Although we perform much new music, only a small portion of the many scores which are submitted can be utilized."

N ♻ VANCOUVER YOUTH SYMPHONY ORCHESTRA SOCIETY, 3214 W. 10th Ave., Vancouver, British Columbia V6K 2L2 Canada. (604)737-0714. Fax: (604)737-0739. E-mail: vyso@t elus.net. Website: www.vyso-web.com. Music Directors: Arthur Polson (senior orchestra conductor), Jim Zhang (intermediate orchestra conductor), and Margerita Kress (introductory string orchestra and junior string orchestra conductor). Youth orchestra. "There are four divisions with students ranging from 8-21 years old." Estab. 1930. Members are amateurs. Performs 6-8 concerts/year. Performs in various venues from churches to major concert halls.

How to Contact: Query first. Does not return material.

Music: "The Senior Orchestra performs the standard symphony repertoire. Programs usually consist of an overture, a major symphony and perhaps a concerto or shorter work. The Christmas concert and tour programs are sometimes lighter works. Extensive repertoire for all divisions. Please contact the VYSO for specific information."

Performances: Glen Morley's *Salish Lullaby*; Victor Davies' *The Big Top*; and Michael Conway Baker's *Challenge for the Future*.

N VIRGINIA OPERA, P.O. Box 2580, Norfolk VA 23501. (757)627-9545. Fax:(757)622-0058. E-mail: information@vaopera.com. Website: www.vaopera.org. Director of Education: Jeff Corrirean. Artistic Director: Peter Mark. Opera company. Estab. 1974. Members are professionals. Performs more than 560 concerts/year. Commissions vary on number of composers or new works/year. Concerts are performed for school children throughout Virginia, grades K-5, 6-8 and 9-12 at the Harrison Opera House in Norfolk, and at public/private schools in Virginia. Pays on commission.

How to Contact: Query first. Include SASE. Response time varies.

Music: "Audience accessible style approximately 45 minutes in length. Limit cast list to three vocal artists of any combination. Accompanied by piano and/or keyboard. Works are performed before school children of all ages. Pieces must be age appropriate both aurally and dramatically. Musical styles are encouraged to be diverse, contemporary as well as traditional. Works are produced and presented with sets, costumes, etc." Limitations: "Three vocal performers (any combination). One keyboardist. Medium to difficult acceptable, but prefer easy to medium. Seeking only pieces which are suitable for presentation as part of an opera education program for Virginia Opera's education and outreach department. Subject matter must meet strict guidelines relative to Learning Objectives, etc. Musical idiom must be representative of current trends in opera, musical theater. Extreme dissonance, row systems not applicable to this environment."

Performances: Seymour Barab's *Cinderella*; John David Earnest's *The Legend of Sleepy Hollow*; and Seymour Barab's *The Pied Piper of Hamelin*.

Tips: "Theatricality is very important. New works should stimulate interest in musical theater as a legitimate art form for school children with no prior exposure to live theatrical entertainment. Composer should be willing to create a product which will find success within the educational system."

MARKETS THAT WERE listed in the 2002 edition of *Songwriters Market* but do not appear this year are listed in the General Index with a notation explaining why they were omitted.

Contests & Awards

Participating in contests is a great way to gain exposure for your music. Prizes vary from contest to contest, from cash to musical merchandise to studio time, and even publishing and recording deals. For musical theater and classical composers, the prize may be a performance of your work. Even if you don't win, valuable contacts can be made through contests. Many times, contests are judged by music publishers and other industry professionals, so your music may find its way into the hands of key industry people who can help further your career.

HOW TO SELECT A CONTEST

It's important to remember when entering any contest to do proper research before signing anything or sending any money. We have confidence in the contests listed in *Songwriter's Market*, but it pays to read the fine print. First, be sure you understand the contest rules and stipulations once you receive the entry forms and guidelines. Then you need to weigh what you will gain against what they're asking you to give up. If a publishing or recording contract is the only prize a contest is offering, you may want to think twice before entering. Basically, the company sponsoring the contest is asking you to pay a fee for them to listen to your song under the guise of a contest, something a legitimate publisher or record company would not do. For those contests offering studio time, musical equipment or cash prizes, you need to decide if the entry fee you're paying is worth the chance to win such prizes.

Be wary of exorbitant entry fees, and if you have any doubts whatsoever as to the legitimacy of a contest, it's best to stay away. Songwriters need to approach a contest, award or grant in the same manner as they would a record or publishing company. Make your submission as professional as possible; follow directions and submit material exactly as stated on the entry form.

Contests in this section encompass all types of music and levels of competition. Read each listing carefully and contact them if the contest interests you. Many contests now have websites that offer additional information and even entry forms you can print. Be sure to read the rules carefully and be sure you understand exactly what a contest is offering before entering.

☑ AFRICAN AMERICAN COMPOSER'S PROGRAM, (formerly Unisys African American Composer's Residency and National Symposium), 3663 Woodward Ave., Suite 100, Detroit MI 48201-2403. (313)576-5162. Fax: (313)576-5101. E-mail: dnewman@dsa.org. Website: www.detroit symphony.com. **Contact:** Daisy Newman, director of education. Estab. 1989. For composers. Annual award.
Purpose: "Program was designed to identify and perform significant orchestral works by contemporary African American Composers."
Requirements: Send for application. Samples of work upon request. Pieces should be scored for traditional orchestra.
Awards: Applications are judged by Adjudication Committee (conductor and resident conductor).

☑ ALEA III INTERNATIONAL COMPOSITION PRIZE, 855 Commonwealth Ave., Boston MA 02215. (617)353-3340. E-mail: kalogeras@earthlink.com. For composers. Annual award.
Purpose: To promote and encourage young composers in the composition of new music.
Requirements: Composers 40 years of age and younger may apply; 1 score per composer. Works may be for solo voice or instrument or for chamber ensemble up to 15 members lasting between 6

and 15 minutes. All works must be unpublished. Deadline: March 15. Send for application. Submitted work required with application. "Real name should not appear on score; a nom de plume should be signed instead. Sealed envelope with entry form should be attached to each score."

Awards: ALEA III International Composition Prize: $2,500. Awarded once annually. Between 8-10 finalists are chosen and their works are performed in a competition concert by the ALEA III contemporary music ensemble. One grand prize winner is selected by a panel of judges.

Tips: "Emphasis placed on works written in 20th century compositional idioms."

AMERICAN SONGWRITER LYRIC CONTEST, 1009 17th Ave. S., Nashville TN 37212-2201. (615)321-6096 or (800)739-8712. Fax: (615)321-6097. E-mail: contest@americansongwriter.com. Website: www.americansongwriter.com. Contact: Lou Heffernan, managing editor. Estab. 1984. For songwriters and composers. Award for each bimonthly issue of *American Songwriter* magazine, plus grand prize at year-end.

Purpose: To promote the art of songwriting.

Requirements: Lyrics must be typed and a check for $10 (per entry) must be enclosed. Deadlines: January 25, March 22, May 17, July 19, September 20, November 15. Call for required official form or get it from our website. Lyrics only, no cassettes.

Awards: A Martin guitar to each contest winner. Awards airfare to Nashville and a demo session for yearly winner; certificates to all winners; and top 5 winning lyrics reprinted in each magazine. Lyrics judged by 6-7 industry people—songwriters, publishers, journalists.

Tips: "You do not have to be a subscriber to enter or win. Pick your best lyric (limit three), don't just send them at random."

BAKER'S PLAYS HIGH SCHOOL PLAYWRITING CONTEST, Baker's Plays, P.O. Box 699222, Quincy MA 02269-9222. (617)745-0805. Fax: (617)745-9891. E-mail: info@bakersplay.c om. Website: www.bakersplays.com. **Contact:** John Welch, managing director & chief editor. Estab. 1990. For high school students. Annual award.

Requirements: Plays should be about the "high school experience," but may also be about any subject and of any length, so long as the play can be reasonably produced on the high school stage. Plays must be accompanied by the signature of a sponsoring high school drama or English teacher, and it is recommended that the play receive a production or a public reading prior to the submission. Multiple submissions and co-authored scripts are welcome. Teachers may not submit a student's work. The manuscript must be firmly bound, typed and come with a SASE. Include enough postage to cover the return of the manuscript. Scripts that do not come with an SASE will not be returned. Do not send originals; copies only. Deadline: January 31, 2002. Send for guidelines.

Awards: 1st Place: $500 and the play will be published by Baker's Plays; 2nd Place: $250 and an Honorable Mention; 3rd Place: $100 and an Honorable Mention.

☑ **BILLBOARD SONG CONTEST**, P.O. Box 470306, Tulsa OK 74147-0306. (918)627-0351. Fax: (918)624-2104. E-mail: bbsc@jimhalsey.com. Website: www.billboard.com/songcontest. **Contact:** David Kindred, Director. Estab. 1988. For songwriters, composers and performing artists. Annual international contest.

Purpose: "To reward deserving songwriters and performers for their talent."

Requirements: Entry fee: $30.

Awards: To be announced. For entry forms and additional information send SASE to the above address or visit website.

Tips: "Participants should understand popular music structure."

REFER TO THE GEOGRAPHIC INDEX (at the back of this book) to find listings of companies by state, as well as foreign listings.

THE BLANK THEATRE COMPANY YOUNG PLAYWRIGHTS FESTIVAL, 1301 Lucile Ave., Los Angeles CA 90026. (323)662-7734. Fax: (323)661-3903. E-mail: info@theblank.com. Website: www.youngplaywrights.com. **Contact:** Christopher Steele, producer. Estab. 1993. For both musical and non-musical playwrights. Annual award.

Purpose: "To give young playwrights an opportunity to learn more about playwriting and to give them a chance to have their work mentored, developed, and presented by professional artists."

Requirements: Playwrights must be 19 years old or younger on March 15, 2003. Send legible, original plays of any length and on any subject (co-written plays are acceptable provided all co-writers meet eligibility requirements). Submissions must be postmarked by March 15, 2003 and must include a cover sheet with the playwright's name, date of birth, school (if any), home address, home phone number, e-mail address and production history. Pages must be numbered and submitted unbound (unstapled). For musicals, a tape or CD of a selection from the score should be submitted with the script. Manuscripts will not be returned. Please do not send originals. Semi-finalists and winners will be contacted in May.

Awards: Winning playwrights receive a workshop presentation of their work.

BUSH ARTIST FELLOWS PROGRAM, E-900 First National Bank Bldg., 332 Minnesota St., St. Paul MN 55101. (651)227-5222. E-mail: kpolley@bushfound.org. Website: www.bushfoundation. org. **Contact:** Kathi Polley, program assistant. Estab. 1976. For songwriters, composers and musical playwrights. Applications in music composition are accepted in even-numbered years.

Purpose: "To provide artists with significant financial support that enables them to further their work and their contribution to their communities."

Requirements: Applicant must be a Minnesota, North Dakota, South Dakota or western Wisconsin resident for 12 of preceeding 36 months, 25 years or older, not a student. Deadline: late October. Send for application. Samples of work on cassette required with application. "Music composition applications will not be taken again until the fall of 2002. Applications will be taken in the fall of 2002 in the following areas: music composition, scriptworks (screenwriting and playwriting), literature (creative non-fiction, fiction, poetry) and film/video.

Awards: Fellowships: $44,000 stipend for a period of 12-18 months. "Five years after completion of preceeding fellowship, one may apply again." Applications are judged by peer review panels.

COLUMBIA ENTERTAINMENT COMPANY'S JACKIE WHITE MEMORIAL PLAYWRITING CONTEST, 309 Parkade Blvd., Columbia MO 65202. (573)874-5628. **Contact:** Betsy Phillips, director, CEC contest. For musical playwrights. Annual award.

Purpose: "We are looking for top-notch scripts for theater school use to challenge and expand the talents of our students, ages 10-15. We want good plays with large casts (20-30 characters) suitable for use with our theater school students."

Requirements: "Must be large cast plays, original story lines and cannot have been previously published. Because theater school enrollment is typically composed of more girls than boys, scripts should have at least 50% of characters female. Please write or call for complete rules." Send SASE for application; then send scripts to address above. Full-length play, neatly typed. No name on title page, but name, address and name of play on a 3×5 index card and full musical score as well as tape of musical numbers. $10 entry fee. Include SASE for entry form.

Awards: $250 1st Prize. Production likely but play may not be produced at discretion of CEC. If produced, travel expenses will be available to author. Award given after any revisions required are completed. "The judging committee is taken from members of Columbia Entertainment Company's Executive and Advisory boards, and from theater school parents. Readings by at least eight members, with at least three readings of all entries, and winning entries being read by entire committee. We are looking for plays that will work with our theater school students."

Tips: "Remember the play we are looking for will be performed by 10-15 year old students with normal talents—difficult vocal ranges, a lot of expert dancing and so forth will eliminate the play. We especially like plays that deal with current day problems and concerns. However, if the play is good enough, any suitable subject matter is fine. It should be fun for the audience to watch."

COMPOSERS COMMISSIONING PROGRAM, ACF, 332 Minnesota St., #E-145, St. Paul MN 55101. (651)228-1407. Fax: (651)291-7978. E-mail: pblackburn@composersforum.org. Website: www.composersforum.org. **Contact:** Philip Blackburn, program director. Estab. 1979. For songwriters, musical playwrights, composers and performers. Annual award.

Purpose: "CCP provides grants to support the commissioning of new works by emerging composers."

Requirements: Not for students. Deadline: end of July. Application available on website. Samples of work are required with application. Send score/tape.

Awards: 18-22 commissioning grants of $1,500-8,000; each grant good for 5 years. Applications are judged by peer review panel (anonymous).

Tips: "Composers pair up with performers: one party must be based in Minnesota or New York City."

COMPOSERS GUILD ANNUAL COMPOSITION CONTEST, P.O. Box 586, Farmington UT 84025-0586. (801)451-2275. **Contact:** Ruth B. Gatrell, president. Estab. 1963. For songwriters, musical playwrights and composers. Annual award.

Purpose: "To stimulate musical composition and help composers through judge's comments on each composition submitted. Composers can broaden their creative skills by entering different categories. Categories: Arrangements (original in public domain or with composer's permission); music for children; choral; instrumental; jazz/New Age; keyboard; orchestra/band; popular (all types); vocal solo; young composer (18 or under on August 31)."

Requirements: Score and/or cassette. Entry fee: $20 for work 7 minutes or more in length (may include multimovements on compositions), $15 for work less than 7 minutes. Dues are $25/year. Member entry fees: $10 for work 7 minutes or more, $5 less than 7 minutes. Deadline: August 31. Send or call for application.

Awards: Award of Excellence $500; 1st Prize in each category except Award of Excellence category $100; 2nd Prize in each category $50; 3rd Prize in each category $25; Honorable Mention certificate. Judge has a doctorate in music, plus compositions published and performed (usually has vast teaching experience). Same judge never used in successive years.

Tips: "Submit good clear copies of score. Have cassette cued up. Only one composition per cassette (each entry requires separate cassette). No composer names to appear on score or cassette. Enter as many categories and compositions as you wish. Separate entry fee for each. One check can cover all entries and dues."

CRS NATIONAL COMPOSERS COMPETITION, 724 Winchester Rd., Broomall PA 19008. (610)544-5920. Fax: (215)544-5921. E-mail: crsnews@erols.com. Website: www.erols.com/crsnews. **Contact:** Caroline Hunt, administrative assistant. Senior Representative: Jack Shusterman. Estab. 1981. For songwriters, composers and performing artists. College faculty. Annual award.

Requirements: For composers, songwriters, performing artists and ensembles. The work submitted must be non-published (prior to acceptance) and not commercially recorded on any label. The work submitted must not exceed nine performers. Each composer may submit one work for each application submitted. (Taped performances are additionally encouraged.) Composition must not exceed twenty-five minutes in length. CRS reserves the right not to accept a First Prize Winner. Write with SASE for application or visit website. Add $3.50 for postage and handling. Deadline: October 28. Send a detailed résumé with application form. Samples of work required with application. Send score and parts on cassette or DAT. Application fee: $50.

Awards: 1st Prize: Commercial recording grant. Applications are judged by panel of judges determined each year.

☑ CUNNINGHAM COMMISSION FOR YOUTH THEATRE, (formerly Cunningham Prize for Playwriting), The Theatre School, DePaul University, 2135 N. Kenmore Ave., Chicago IL 60614. (773)325-7938. Fax: (773)325-7920. E-mail: lgoetsch@depaul.edu. Website: theatreschool.depaul.edu. **Contact:** Lara Goetsch, director of marketing/public relations. Estab. 1990. For musical playwrights. Annual award.

Purpose: "The purpose of the Commission is to encourage the writing of dramatic works for young audiences that affirm the centrality of religion, broadly defined, and the human quest for meaning, truth, and community. The Theatre School intends to produce the plays created through this commission in its award-winning Chicago Playworks for Families and Young Audiences series at the historic Merle Ruskin Theatre. Each year Chicago Playworks productions are seen by 35,000 students and families from throughout the Chicago area."

Requirements: "Candidates for the commission must be writers whose residence is in the Chicago area, defined as within 100 miles of the Loop. Playwrights who have won the award within the last five years are not eligible. Deadline: annually by October 1. Candidates should submit a résumé, a 20 page sample of their work, and a brief statement about their interest in the commission. The submission should not include a proposal for a project the playwright would complete it awarded the commission. The writing sample may be from a play of any genre for any audience."

Awards: $5,000. "Winners will be notified by February 1. The Selection Committee is chaired by the Dean of the Theatre School and is composed of members of the Cunningham Commission advisory committee and faculty of The Theatre School."

N KENNETH DAVENPORT NATIONAL COMPETITION FOR ORCHESTRAL WORKS, School of Fine & Performing Arts, SUNY New Paltz, 75 S. Manheim Blvd., Suite 9, New Paltz NY 12561-2443. (845)257-3860. Fax: (845)257-3860. E-mail: fpa@newpaltz.edu. Website: www.newpaltz.edu. Dean: Patricia C. Phillips. Estab. 1988. For composers. Annual award.

Requirements: Deadline: March 31. Send for application. Works requiring chorus or solo voice are not eligible.

Awards: Panel of judges reviews all scores submitted. $4,000 award and performance of winning composition by the Hudson Valley Philharmonic.

Tips: "Apply for prize by sending your score for orchestral works."

DELTA OMICRON INTERNATIONAL COMPOSITION COMPETITION, 12297 W. Tennessee Place, Lakewood CO 80228. (303)989-2871. Composition Competition Chairman: Judith L. Eidson. For composers. Triennial award.

Purpose: "To encourage composers worldwide to continually add to our wonderful heritage of musical creativity instrumentally and/or vocally."

Requirements: People from college age on (or someone younger who is enrolled in college). Work must be unpublished and unperformed in public. The composition should be for Solo Flute or Flute Quartet with a time length from a minimum of seven minutes to a maximum of fifteen minutes. Manuscripts should be legibly written in ink or processed, signed with *nom de plume*, and free from any marks that would identify the composer to the judges. Entry fee: $25. Deadline: all entries postmarked no later than March 20, 2002. Send for application. Samples of work are required with application.

Awards: 1st Place: $600 and world premiere at Delta Omicron Triennal Conference. Judged by 2-3 judges (performers and/or composers).

☑ EUROPEAN INTERNATIONAL COMPETITION FOR COMPOSERS/IBLA FOUNDATION, 226 E. 2nd St., Suite 5D, New York NY 10009. (212)387-0111. Fax: (212)214-0701. E-mail: iblanyc@aol.com. Website: www.ibla.org. **Contact:** Mr. Gregory Nuber, assistant director. Chairman: Dr. S. Moltisanti. Estab. 1995. For songwriters and composers. Annual award.

Purpose: "To promote the winners' career through exposure, publicity, recordings with Athena Records and nationwide distribution with the Empire Group."

Requirements: Deadline: March 15. Send for application. Samples of work are required with application.

MARKET CONDITIONS are constantly changing! If you're still using this book and it is 2004 or later, buy the newest edition of *Songwriter's Market* at your favorite bookstore or order directly from Writer's Digest Books at (800)289-0963.

Awards: $10,000 to sponsor the promotion of the winners.

FREE STAGED READING SERIES PLAYWRITING COMPETITION, 120 W. 28th St., New York NY 10001. (212)627-1732. Fax: (212)243-6736. E-mail: tada@tadatheater.com. Website: www.t adatheater.com. **Contact:** Janine Nina Trevens, assistant to the artistic director. Estab. 1984. For musical playwrights or anyone wanting to write a play.
Purpose: "The series was initiated to encourage playwrights, composers, and lyricists to write for family audiences and to involve children and their parents in the excitement of the play development process."
Requirements: "Script must be original, unproduced and unpublished. Any age may apply. One act musical or non-musical cast must be primarily youth ages 7-18; children do not play adults—adult actors can be hired. Script must be typed, include character breakdown, set and costume description. Playwrights should adhere to the topic given—teen topics—and take into consideration that they need to not only write for young audiences but young performers as well. Meaningful family topics are also appropriate for this particular staged reading contest with an emphasis on the children's relationship with parents rather than a spotlight on the parents." Deadline: July 15. Send for guidelines.
Tips: "Issues having to do with children and what they are going through in life and good teen issues are especially relevant."

FULBRIGHT SCHOLAR PROGRAM, COUNCIL FOR INTERNATIONAL EXCHANGE OF SCHOLARS, 3007 Tilden St. NW, Suite 5L, Washington DC 20008-3009. (202)686-7877. Fax: (202)362-3442. E-mail: scholars@cies.iie.org. Website: www.cies.org. Estab. 1946. For composers and academics. Annual award.
Purpose: "Awards for university lecturing and advanced research abroad are offered annually in virtually all academic disciplines including musical composition."
Requirements: "U.S. citizenship at time of application; M.F.A., Ph.D. or equivalent professional qualifications; for lecturing awards, university teaching experience (some awards are for professionals non-academic)." Applications become available in March each year, for grants to be taken up 1½ years later. Application deadlines: August 1, all world areas. Write or call for application. Samples of work are required with application.
Awards: "Benefits vary by country, but generally include round-trip travel for the grantee and for most full academic-year awards, one dependent; stipend in U.S. dollars and/or local currency; in many countries, tuition allowance for school age children; and book and baggage allowance. Grant duration ranges from 2 months-1 academic year."

HARVEY GAUL COMPOSITION CONTEST, The Pittsburgh New Music Ensemble, Inc., P.O. Box 99476, Pittsburgh PA 15233. Phone/fax: (412)682-2955. E-mail: pnme@pnme.org. Website: www.pnme.org. **Contact:** Kevin Noe, artistic director. For composers. Biennial.
Purpose: Objective is to encourage composition of new music. Winning piece to be premiered by the PNME.
Requirements: "Must be citizen of the US. New works scored for 6 to 16 instruments drawn from the following: flute, oboe, 2 clarinets, bassoon, horn, trumpet, trombone, tuba, 2 violins, cello, bass, 2 percussion, piano, harp, electronic tape." Deadline: April 15. Send SASE for application. Samples of work are required with application. "Real name must not appear on score—must be signed with a 'nom de plume'." Entry fee: $50.
Awards: Harvey Gaul Composition Contest: $3,000.

☑ **GREAT AMERICAN SONG CONTEST**, PMB 135, 6327-C SW Capitol Hill Hwy., Portland OR 97201-1937. E-mail: info@GreatAmericaSong.com. Website: www.GreatAmericaSong.com. **Contact:** Carla Starrett, event coordinator. Estab. 1998. For songwriters, composers and lyricists. Annual award.
Purpose: To help songwriters get their songs heard by music-industry professionals; to generate educational and networking opportunities for participating songwriters; to help songwriters open doors in the music business.

Requirements: Entry fee: $15. "Annual deadline. Check our website for details or send SASE along with your mailed request for information."

Awards: Winners receive a mix of cash awards and prizes. The focus of the contest is on networking and educational opportunities. (All participants receive detailed evaluations of their songs by industry professionals.) Songs are judged by knowledgeable music-industry professionals, including prominent hit songwriters, producers and publishers.

Tips: "The quality of the demo recording is not important. Focus should be on the song—not on fancy production or complex arrangements. Judges will be looking for excellent songwriting, not great performances."

☑ **HENRICO THEATRE COMPANY ONE-ACT PLAYWRITING COMPETITION**, P.O. Box 27032, Richmond VA 23273. (804)501-5115. (804)501-5115 or (804)501-5138. Fax: (804)501-5284. E-mail: per22@co.henrico.va.us. **Contact:** Amy A. Perdue, cultural arts coordinator. Cultural Arts Assistant: Cindy Warren. For musical playwrights, songwriters, composers and performing artists. Annual award.

Purpose: Original one-act musicals for a community theater organization.

Requirements: "Only one-act plays or musicals will be considered. The manuscript should be a one-act original (not an adaptation), unpublished, and unproduced, free of royalty and copyright restrictions. Scripts with smaller casts and simpler sets may be given preference. Controversial themes and excessive language should be avoided. Standard play script form should be used. All plays will be judged anonymously; therefore, there should be two title pages; the first must contain the play's title and the author's complete address and telephone number. The second title page must contain only the play's title. The playwright must submit two excellent quality copies. Receipt of all scripts will be acknowledged by mail. Scripts will be returned if SASE is included. No scripts will be returned until after the winner is announced. The HTC does not assume responsibility for loss, damage or return of scripts. All reasonable care will be taken." Deadline: July 1st. Send for application first.

Awards: 1st Prize $300; 2nd Prize $200; 3rd Prize $200.

☑ **INDIANA OPERA THEATRE/MACALLISTER AWARDS FOR OPERA SINGERS**, 7515 E. 30th St., Indianapolis IN 46219. (317)202-0634. Fax: (317)202-0637. E-mail: opera@iquest.n et. Website: www.macallisterawards.com. Artister/General Director: E. Bookwalter. Estab. 1980. For college and professional opera singers.

Requirements: For professional and amateurs. Entry fee: $25 professional, free for college students. Send for application or visit website. Auditions are held throughout the year; check the website.

Awards: "The Final Awards Program dates are August 23-25."

⌶N⌶ **KATE NEAL KINLEY MEMORIAL FELLOWSHIP**, University of Illinois, College of Fine and Applied Arts, 608 E. Lorado Taft Dr. #115, Champaign IL 61820. (217)333-1661. **Contact:** Dr. Kathleen F. Conlin, chair. Estab. 1931. For students of architecture, art or music. Annual award.

Purpose: The advancement of study in the fine arts.

Requirements: "The Fellowship will be awarded upon the basis of unusual promise in the fine arts. Open to college graduates whose principal or major studies have been in the fields of architecture, art or music." Write or call for fall deadline. Send for application or call. Samples of work are required with application.

Awards: "Two or three major Fellowships which yield the sum of $7,500 each which is to be used by the recipients toward defraying the expenses of advanced study of the fine arts in America or abroad." Good for 1 year. Grant is nonrenewable.

☑ **L.A. DESIGNERS' THEATRE MUSIC AWARDS**, P.O. Box 1883, Studio City CA 91614-0883. (323)650-9600. (323)654-3210 (T.D.D.). Fax: (323)654-3210. E-mail: ladesigners@juno.com. Artistic Director: Richard Niederberg. For songwriters, composers, performing artists, musical playwrights and rights holders of music.

Purpose: To produce new musicals, operettas, opera-boufes and plays with music, as well as new dance pieces with new music scores.

Requirements: Submit nonreturnable cassette, tape, CD or any other medium by first or 4th class mail. "*We prefer proposals* to scripts." Acceptance: continuous. Submit nonreturnable materials with cover letter. No application form or fee is necessary.

Awards: Music is commissioned for a particular project. Amounts are negotiable. Applications judged by our artistic staff.

Tips: "Make the material 'classic, yet commercial' and easy to record/re-record/edit. Make sure rights are totally free of all 'strings,' 'understandings,' 'promises,' etc. ASCAP/BMI/SESAC registration is OK, as long as 'grand' or 'performing rights' are available."

☑ **THE JOHN LENNON SONGWRITING CONTEST**, 459 Columbus Ave., Box 120, New York NY 10024. Fax: (212)579-4320. E-mail: info@jlsc.com. Website: www.jlsc.com. **Contact:** Marc Hassan, associate director. Estab. 1996. For songwriters. Annual award.

Purpose: "The purpose of the John Lennon Songwriting Contest is to promote the art of songwriting by assisting in the discovery of new talent as well as providing more established songwriters with an opportunity to advance their careers."

Requirements: Each entry must consist of the following: completed and signed application; audio cassette containing one song only, 5 minutes or less in length; lyric sheet typed or printed legibly (English translation is required when applicable); $30 entry fee. Deadline: August 28, 2002. Applications can be found in various music-oriented magazines. Prospective entrants can send for an application or contact the contest via e-mail at info@jlsc.com.

Awards: Entries are accepted in the following 12 categories: rock, country, jazz, pop, world, gospel/inspirational, R&B, hip-hop, Latin, electronic, folk and a special category of children's music. 2002 prize packages: 12 Grand Prize winners (one in each category) receive $2,000 in cash, $5,000 in Yamaha project studio equipment, and a $5,000 advance from EMI Music Publishing. One Grand Prize winner receives an additional $20,000 for the "Song of the Year" courtesy of Maxell. Finalists receive $1,000. 72 additional winners receive $100 from Guitar Center. Winners are chosen by an Executive Committee comprised of noted songwriters, producers and recording artists. Songs will be judged based upon melody, composition and lyrics (when applicable). The quality of performance and production will not be considered during the adjudication process.

☑ **MID-ATLANTIC SONG CONTEST**, Songwriters' Association of Washington, PMB 106-137, 4200 Wisconsin Ave., NW, Washington DC 20016. (800)218-5996 or (301)654-8434. E-mail: masc@saw.org. Website: www.saw.org. For songwriters and composers. Estab. 1982. Annual award.

Purpose: This is one of the longest-running contests in the nation; SAW has organized eighteen contests since 1982. The competition is designed to afford rising songwriters in a wide variety of genres the opportunity to receive awards and exposure in an environment of peer competition.

Requirements: Amateur status is important. Applicants should request a brochure/application using the contact information above. Rules and procedures are clearly explained in that brochure. Cassette or CD and 3 copies of the lyrics are to be submitted with an application form and fee for each entry. Reduced entry fees are offered to members of Songwriters' Association of Washington; membership can be arranged for simultaneously with entering. Applications are mailed out in late spring; the submission deadline is usually sometime in August; awards are typically announced late in the fall.

Awards: The two best songs in each of ten categories win prize packages donated by the contest's corporate sponsors: Writer's Digest Books, BMI, Oasis CD and Cassette Duplication, Omega Recording Studios, and TAXI. Winning songwriters are invited to perform in Washington, DC at the Awards Ceremony Gala, and the twenty winning songs are included on a compilation CD. The best song in each category is eligible for two grand cash prizes. Certificates are awarded to other entries meriting honorable mention.

MARKETS THAT WERE listed in the 2002 edition of *Songwriters Market* but do not appear this year are listed in the General Index with a notation explaining why they were omitted.

Tips: "Enter the song in the most appropriate category. Make the sound recording the best it can be (even though judges are asked to focus on melody and lyric and not on production.) Avoid clichés, extended introductions, and long instrumental solos."

NACUSA YOUNG COMPOSERS' COMPETITION, Box 49256 Barrington Station, Los Angeles CA 90049. (310)541-8213. Fax: (310)544-1413. E-mail: biaaflash.net. Website: www.theboo k.com/nacusa. **Contact:** Marshall Bialosky, president, NACUSA. Estab. 1978. For composers. Annual award.

Purpose: To encourage the composition of new American concert hall music.

Requirements: Entry fee: $20 (membership fee). Deadline: October 30. Send for application. Samples are not required.

Awards: 1st Prize: $200; 2nd Prize: $50; and possible Los Angeles performances. Applications are judged by a committee of experienced NACUSA composer members.

☑ SAMMY NESTICO AWARD/USAF BAND AIRMEN OF NOTE, 201 McChord St., Bolling AFB, Washington DC 20332-0202. (202)767-1756. Fax: (202)767-0686. E-mail: tyler.kuebler@b olling.af.mil. **Contact:** Alan Baylock, master sergeant. Estab. 1995. For composers. Annual award.

Purpose: To carry on the tradition of excellence of Sammy Nestico's writing through jazz composition. The winner will have their composition performed by the USAF Airmen of Note, have it professionally recorded and receive a $1,000 follow up commission for a second work.

Requirements: Unpublished work for jazz ensemble instrumentation (5,4,4,4) style, form and length are unrestricted. Deadline: October 1, 2002. Send for application. Samples of work are required with full score and set of parts (or cassette recording).

Awards: Performance by the USAF Band Airmen of Note; expense paid travel to Washington, DC for the performance; professionally produced recording of the winning composition; and $1,000 follow up commission for second work. Applications are judged by panel of musicians.

NEW FOLK CONCERTS FOR EMERGING SONGWRITERS, P.O. Box 29, Kerrville TX 78029. (800)435-8429 or (830)257-3600. Fax: (830)257-8680. E-mail: rod@kerrville-music.com. Website: www.kerrville-music.com. **Contact:** Rod Kennedy, producer. For songwriters. Annual award.

Purpose: "To provide an opportunity for unknown songwriters to be heard and rewarded for excellence."

Requirements: Songwriter enters 2 original previously unrecorded songs on same side of cassette tape with entry fee; no more than one tape may be entered; 6-8 minutes total for 2 songs. No written application necessary; no lyric sheets or press material needed. Deadline: April 6 or first 600 entries received prior to that date. Call to request rules. Entry fee: $16.

Awards: New Folk Award Winner. 32 semi-finalists invited to sing the 2 songs entered during The Kerrville Folk Festival. 6 writers are chosen as award winners. Each of the 6 receives a cash award of $450 or more and performs at a winner's concert during the Kerrville Folk Festival, May 27-28, 2001. Initial round of entries judged by the Festival Producer. 32 finalists judged by panel of 3 performer/songwriters.

Tips: "Make certain cassette is rewound and ready to play. Do not allow instrumental accompaniment to drown out lyric content. Don't enter without complete copy of the rules. Former winners and finalists include Lyle Lovett, Nanci Griffith, Hal Ketchum, John Gorka, David Wilcox, Lucinda Williams and Robert Earl Keen, David Wilcox, Tish Hinojosa, Carrie Newcomer, Jimmy Lafave, etc."

N NSAI ANNUAL SONG CONTEST, 1701 West End Ave, 3rd Floor, Nashville TN 37203. (615)256-3354. Fax: (615)256-0034. E-mail: deanie@nashvillesongwriters.com. Website: www.nash villesongwriters.com. **Contact:** Deanie Williams, director. Annual award for songwriters.

Purpose: "A chance for aspiring songwriters to be heard by music industry decision makers. Winners are flown to Nashville for a recording session and an appointment with Music Row executives."

Requirements: In order to be eligible contestants must not be receiving income from any work submitted—original material only. Submissions must include both lyrics and melody. Deadline is different each year; check website or send for application. Samples are required with application in the format of cassette or CD.
Awards: Varies from year to year; check website.

PLAYHOUSE ON THE SQUARE NEW PLAY COMPETITION, 51 S. Cooper, Memphis TN 38104. (901)725-0776. **Contact:** Jackie Nichols, executive director. For musical playwrights. Annual award. Estab. 1983.
Requirements: Send script, tape and SASE. "Playwrights from the South will be given preference." Open to full-length, unproduced plays. Musicals must be fully arranged for piano when received. Deadline: April 1.
Awards: Grants may be renewed. Applications judged by 3 readers.

☑ **PORTLAND SONGWRITERS ASSOCIATION ANNUAL SONGWRITING COMPETITION**, P.O. Box 16985, Portland OR 97292-0985. (503)727-8546. Fax: (503)241-9104. E-mail: info@pdxsongwriters.org. Website: www.pdxsongwriters.org. **Contact:** JC Tubbs, President. Vice President: Bill Wood. Estab. 1991. For songwriters and composers. Annual award.
Purpose: To provide opportunities for songwriters to improve their skills in the art and craft of songwriting, to connect our performing songwriters with the public through PSA sponsored venues and to create a presence and an avenue of approach for members' songs to be heard by industry professionals.
Requirements: For information, send SASE. All amateur songwriters may enter. Entries taken between March 1 and August 31. Entry fee: $15 members; $20 nonmembers.
Awards: Multiple awards totaling $1,000 in prizes. All songs will be reviewed by at least three qualified judges, including industry pros. Finalists may have their songs reviewed by celebrity judges.

PULITZER PRIZE IN MUSIC, 709 Journalism, Columbia University, New York NY 10027. (212)854-3841. Fax: (212)854-3342. E-mail: pulitzer@pulitzer.org. Website: www.pulitzer.org. **Contact:** Elizabeth Mahaffey, music secretary. For composers and musical playwrights. Annual award.
Requirements: "For distinguished musical composition of significant dimension by an American that has had its American premiere between March 2 and March 1 of the one-year period in which it is submitted for consideration." Deadline: March 1. Samples of work are required with application, biography and photograph of composer, date and place of performance, score or manuscript and recording of the work, entry form and $50 entry fee.
Awards: "One award: $7,500. Applications are judged first by a nominating jury, then by the Pulitzer Prize Board."

ROCKY MOUNTAIN FOLKS FESTIVAL SONGWRITER SHOWCASE, P.O. Box 769, Lyons CO 80540. (800)624-2422 or (303)823-0848. Fax: (303)823-0849. E-mail: kahlie@bluegrass.com. Website: www.bluegrass.com. **Contact:** Steve Szymanski, director. Estab. 1993. For songwriters, composers and performers. Annual award.
Purpose: Award based on having the best song and performance.
Requirements: Deadline: June 29. Finalists notified by July 13. Send for rules or find rules available on website. Samples of work are required with application. Send CD or cassette with $10 entry fee.
Awards: 1st Place is a custom Hayes Guitar and Festival Main Stage Set; 2nd: $400; 3rd: $300; 4th: $200; 5th: $100. Applications judged by panel of judges.

RICHARD RODGERS AWARDS, American Academy of Arts and Letters, 633 W. 155th St., New York NY 10032. (212)368-5900. **Contact:** Lydia Kaim, coordinator. Estab. 1978. Deadline: November 1, 2002. "The Richard Rodgers Awards subsidize full productions, studio productions, and staged readings by nonprofit theaters in New York City of works by composers and writers who are not already established in the field of musical theater. The awards are only for musicals—songs by themselves are not eligible. The authors must be citizens or permanent residents of the United States." Guidelines for this award may be obtained by sending a SASE to above address.

ROME PRIZE COMPETITION FELLOWSHIP, American Academy in Rome, 7 E. 60th St., New York NY 10022-1001. (212)751-7200. Fax: (212)751-7220. E-mail: info@aarome.org. Website: www.aarome.org. **Contact:** Programs Department. For composers. Annual award.

Purpose: "Rome Prize Competition winners pursue independent projects."

Requirements: "Applicants for 11-month fellowships must hold a bachelor's degree in music, musical composition or its equivalent." Deadline: November 1. Entry fee: $25. Application guidelines are available to download through the Academy's website.

Awards: "Up to two awards are made annually. Fellowship stipend is up to $20,000 and includes room and board, and a study or studio at Academy facilities in Rome. In all cases, excellence is the primary criterion for selection, based on the quality of the materials submitted. Winners are announced in mid-April."

LOIS AND RICHARD ROSENTHAL NEW PLAY PRIZE, % Cincinnati Playhouse in the Park, P.O. Box 6537, Cincinnati OH 45206-0537. (513)345-2242. Website: www.cincyplay.com **Contact:** Literary Associate. For playwrights and musical playwrights. Annual award.

Purpose: The Lois and Richard Rosenthal New Play Prize was established in 1987 to encourage the development of new plays that are original, theatrical, strong in character and dialogue, and make a significant contribution to the literature of American theatre. Residents of Cincinnati, the Rosenthals are committed to supporting arts organizations and social agencies that are innovative and foster social change.

Requirements: "Plays must be full-length in any style: comedy, drama, musical, etc. Translations, adaptations, individual one-acts and any play previously submitted for the Rosenthal Prize are not eligible. Collaborations are welcome, in which case the prize benefits are shared. Plays must be unpublished prior to submission and may not have received a full-scale, professional production. Plays that have had a workshop, reading or non-professional production are still eligible. Playwrights with past production experience are especially encouraged to submit new work. Submit a two-page maximum abstract of the play including title, character breakdown, story synopsis and playwright information (bio or résumé). Also include up to five pages of sample dialogue. If submitting a musical, please include a tape or CD of selections from the score. All abstracts and dialogue samples will be read. From these, selected manuscripts will be solicited. Do not send a manuscript with or instead of the abstract. Unsolicited manuscripts will not be read. Submitted materials, including tapes and CDs, will be returned only if a SASE with adequate postage is provided. The Rosenthal Prize is open for submission from July 1st to December 31st. Only one submission per playwright each year."

Awards: The Rosenthal Prize play receives a full production at Cincinnati Playhouse in the Park as part of the theater's annual season and is given regional and national promotion. The playwright receives a $10,000 award plus travel and residency expenses for the Cincinnati rehearsal period.

TELLURIDE TROUBADOUR CONTEST, P.O. Box 769, Lyons CO 80540. (303)823-0848 or (800)624-2422. Fax: (303)823-0849. E-mail: kahlie@bluegrass.com. Website: www.bluegrass.com. **Contact:** Steve Szymanski, director. Estab. 1991. For songwriters, composers and performers. Annual award.

Purpose: Award based on having best song and performance.

Requirements: Deadline: must be postmarked by April 26; notified May 10, if selected. Send for rules or find rules available on website. Send cassette or CD and $10 entry fee.

Awards: 1st: custom Shanti Guitar and main stage set; 2nd: $400 and Crate acoustic amp; 3rd: $300 and Martin backpacker guitar; 4th: $200 and Martin backpacker guitar; 5th: $100. Applications judged by panel of judges.

FOR BOOKS ON THE CRAFT AND BUSINESS of songwriting, check out the website for Writer's Digest Books at www.writersdigest.com.

U.S.A. SONGWRITING COMPETITION, 4331 N. Federal Hwy., Suite 403A, Ft. Lauderdale FL 33308. (954)776-1577. Fax: (954)776-1132. E-mail: info@songwriting.net. Website: www.songw riting.net. **Contact:** Contest Manager. Estab. 1994. For songwriters, composers, performing artists and lyricists. Annual award.

Purpose: "To honor good songwriters/composers all over the world, especially the unknown ones."

Requirements: Open to professional and beginner songwriters. No limit on entries. Each entry must include an entry fee, a cassette tape of song(s) and lyric sheet(s). Judged by music industry representatives. Past judges have included record label representatives and publishers from Arista Records, EMI and Warner/Chappell. Deadline: To be announced. Entry fee: To be announced. Send SASE with request or e-mail for entry forms at any time. Samples of work are not required.

Awards: Prizes include cash and merchandise in 15 different categories: pop, rock, country, Latin, R&B, gospel, folk, jazz, "lyrics only" category, instrumental and many others.

Tips: "Judging is based on lyrics, originality, melody and overall composition. CD quality production is great but not a consideration in judging."

U.S.-JAPAN CREATIVE ARTISTS EXCHANGE FELLOWSHIP PROGRAM, Japan-U.S. Friendship Commission, 1120 Vermont Ave., NW, Suite 925, Washington DC 20005-3523. (202)418-9800. Fax: (202)418-9802. E-mail: artist@jusfc.gov. Website: www.jusfc.gov. **Contact:** Roberta Stewart, secretary. Estab. 1980. For all creative artists. Annual award.

Purpose: "For artists to go as seekers, as cultural visionaries, and as living liaisons to the traditional and contemporary life of Japan."

Requirements: "Artists' works must exemplify the best in U.S. arts." Deadline: June. Send for application and guidelines. Applications available via Internet. Samples of work are required with application. Requires 2 pieces on cassette or CD, cued to the 3-5 minute section to be reviewed.

Awards: Five artists are awarded a six-month residency anywhere in Japan. Awards monthly stipend for living expenses, housing and professional support services; up to $6,000 for pre-departure costs, including such items as language training and economy class roundtrip airfare. Residency is good for 1 year. Applications are judged by a panel of previous recipients of the awards, as well as other arts professionals with expertise in Japanese culture.

Tips: "Applicants should anticipate a highly rigorous review of their artistry and should have compelling reasons for wanting to work in Japan."

U.S.-MEXICO FUND FOR CULTURE, Londres 16-PB, 3er. Piso, Col. Juarez Mexico City Mexico 06600. (525)592-5386. Fax: (525)566-8071. E-mail: usmexcult@fidemexusa.org.mx. Website: www.fidemexusa.org.mx. **Contact:** Beatriz E. Nava, program officer. Estab. 1991. For composers, choreographers, musical playwrights and performers. Annual award.

Purpose: "The U.S.-Mexico Fund for Culture, an independent body created through a joint initiative of the Bancomer Cultural Foundation, The Rockefeller Foundation and Mexico's National Fund for Culture and the Arts, provides financial support for the development of cultural binational projects in music, theater, dance, visual arts, cultural studies, literary and cultural publications, media arts and libraries."

Requirements: Deadline: April 16, 2001 (postmarked). Send for application with SASE ($8\frac{1}{2} \times 11$ envelope) or contact us at our website. Samples of work are required with application in duplicate.

Awards: Range from $2,000-25,000. Award is good for 1 year. Judged by binational panel of experts in each of the disciplines, one from Mexico and one from the USA.

Tips: "Proposals must be binational in character and have a close and active collaboration with artists from Mexico. The creation of new works is highly recommendable."

"UNISONG" INTERNATIONAL SONG CONTEST, 5198 Arlington Ave., PMB 513, Riverside CA 92504. (213)673-4067. E-mail: entry@unisong.com. Website: www.unisong.com. Co-Founders: Alan Roy Scott and David Stark. London office: P.O. Box 13383, London, NW3 5ZR United Kingdom. (44)(0208)387-9293. Estab. 1997. For songwriters, composers and lyricists. Annual songwriting contest.

Purpose: "Unisong was created by songwriters for songwriters. Helping songwriters around the world by making donations from every entry fee to songwriter organizations and Amnesty International."

Requirements: Send for an entry form or request one by phone or e-mail. Download entry form from website or enter online. Send cassette or CD only. No DATs. Entries also accepted via MP3.
Awards: Over $50,000 in cash and prizes. Grand Prize winner to write with professional writers and artists through Music Bridges Around The World. Songs judged on song quality only, not demo.
Tips: "Please make sure your song is professionally presented. Make sure lyrics are typed or printed clearly. Print your personal information clearly. Enter your song in the most appropriate categories."

WEST COAST ENSEMBLE–MUSICAL STAIRS, P.O. Box 38728, Los Angeles CA 90038. (323)876-9337. **Contact:** Les Hanson, artistic director. For composers and musical playwrights. Annual award.
Purpose: To provide an arena and encouragement for the development of new musicals for the theater.
Requirements: No entry fee. Submit book and a cassette or CD of the score to the above address.
Awards: The West Coast Ensemble Musical Stairs Competition Award includes a production of the selected musical and $500 prize. Panel of judges reads script and listen to cassette or CD. Final selection is made by Artistic Director.
Tips: "Submit libretto in standard playscript format along with professional sounding cassette or CD of songs."

☑ **Y.E.S. FESTIVAL OF NEW PLAYS**, Northern Kentucky University Dept. of Theatre, FA-205, Highland Heights KY 41099-1007. (859)572-6303. Fax: (859)572-6057. E-mail: forman@nku.edu. **Contact:** Sandra Forman, project director. Estab. 1983. For musical playwrights. Biennial award (odd numbered years).
Purpose: "The festival seeks to encourage new playwrights and develop new plays and musicals. Three plays or musicals are given full productions."
Requirements: "No entry fee. Submit a script with a completed entry form. Musicals should be submitted with a piano/conductor's score and a vocal parts score. Scripts may be submitted May 1 through Oct. 31, for the New Play Festival occuring April. Send for application. Samples of work are required with application."
Awards: Three awards of $500. "The winners are brought to NKU at our expense to view late rehearsals and opening night." Applications are judged by a panel of readers.
Tips: "Plays/musicals which have heavy demands for mature actors are not as likely to be selected as an equally good script with roles for 18-25 year olds."

YOUNG COMPOSERS AWARDS, % NGCSA and the Hartt School, University of Hartford, 200 Bloomfield Ave., West Hartford CT 06117. (860)768-4451. E-mail: yaffe@mail.hartford.edu or info@natguild.org. Website: www.nationalguild.org. **Contact:** Michael Yaffe, director. For composers. Open to students age 13-18. Annual award.
Purpose: "To encourage young students to write music, so that the art of composition—with no restrictions as to the category of music in which the works are written—will once again occupy the place in the center of music education where it belongs. It takes tons of ore to extract one ounce of gold: by focusing on the inventiveness of many students, the Awards may lead to the discovery of genuine creative talents—that is the eventual goal." Young Composers Awards was established by the late Dr. Herbert Zipperin in 1985 with the initial support of the Rockefeller Foundation. Since 1985, awards in the amount of $42,500 have been granted to 67 young composers.
Requirements: "Applicants must be enrolled in a public or private secondary school, in a recognized musical institution, or be engaged in the private study of music with an established teacher. No compositions will be considered without certification by the applicant's teacher. Student composers must not be enrolled in an undergraduate program when they apply. This competition is open to residents of the United States and Canada. Each applicant may submit only one work. Deadline: all submissions must be postmarked on or before early April 2002. Check website for exact date. Send for application. Samples of work are required with application. Four photocopies of the work must be submitted. All manuscripts must be in legible form and may be submitted on usual score paper or reduced under a generally accepted process. The composer's name must not appear on the composition submitted. The composition must be marked with a pseudonym on the manuscript. Copies must be

submitted with a check in the amount of $5 made payable to the Hartt School. One copy of score will be returned if entrant sends SASE with application. Entrants must be certain postage purchased has no expiration date. Composers retain full and all legal rights to their submitted composition. Students who have previously won this award are not eligible to reapply."

Awards: Herbert Zipper Prizes: 2 separate categories—age group 13-15 (Junior) and 16-18 (Senior). 2 prizes are awarded in each of the Senior and Junior categories—Senior: 1st Place: $1,000; 2nd Place: $500. Junior: 1st Place: $500; 2nd Place: $250. "Announcement of the Awards are made no later than mid-June each year. In the event that no entry is found to be worthy of the $1,000 Prize, the jury may award one or both of the other prizes or none at all. NGCSA appoints an independent jury to review all entries submitted. The jury consists of not less than three qualified judges. Prizes shall be awarded at the discretion of the jury. The decision of the judges is final."

Tips: "Paramount would be neatness and legibility of the manuscript submitted. The application must be complete in all respects."

Resources

Organizations

One of the first places a beginning songwriter should look for guidance and support is a songwriting organization. Offering encouragement, instruction, contacts and feedback, these groups of professional and amateur songwriters can help an aspiring songwriter hone the skills needed to compete in the ever-changing music industry.

The type of organization you choose to join depends on what you want to get out of it. Local groups can offer a friendly, supportive environment where you can work on your songs and have them critiqued in a constructive way by other songwriters. They're also great places to meet collaborators. Larger, national organizations can give you access to music business professionals and other songwriters across the country.

Most of the organizations listed in this book are non-profit groups with membership open to specific groups of people—songwriters, musicians, classical composers, etc. They can be local groups with a membership of less than 100 people, or large national organizations with thousands of members from all over the country. In addition to regular meetings, most organizations occasionally sponsor events such as seminars and workshops to which music industry personnel are invited to talk about the business, and perhaps listen to and critique demo tapes.

Check the following listings, bulletin boards at local music stores and your local newspapers for area organizations. If you are unable to locate an organization within an easy distance of your home, you may want to consider joining one of the national groups. These groups, based in New York, Los Angeles and Nashville, keep their members involved and informed through newsletters, regional workshops and large yearly conferences. They can help a writer who feels isolated in his hometown get his music heard by professionals in the major music centers.

In the following listings, organizations describe their purpose and activities, as well as how much it costs to join. Before joining any organization, consider what they have to offer and how becoming a member will benefit you. To locate organizations close to home, see the Geographic Index at the back of this book.

N ACADEMY OF COUNTRY MUSIC, 4100 W. Alameda Ave., Burbank CA 91505. (818)842-8400. Fax: (818)842-8535. E-mail: acmoffice@value.net. Website: www.acmcountry.com. **Contact:** Fran Boyd, executive director. Estab. 1964. Serves producers, artists, songwriters, talent buyers and others involved with the country music industry. Eligibility for professional members is limited to those individuals who derive some portion of their income directly from country music. Each member is classified by one of the following categories: artist/entertainer, club operator/employee, musician/trend leader, DJ, manager/booking agent, composer, music publisher, promotion, publications, radio, TV/motion picture, record company or affiliated (general). The purpose of ACM is to promote and enhance the image of country music. The Academy is involved year-round in activities important to the country music community. Some of these activities include charity fund-raisers, participation in country music seminars, talent contests, artist showcases, assistance to producers in placing country music on television and in motion pictures and backing legislation that benefits the interests of the country music community. The ACM is governed by directors and run by officers elected annually. Applications are accepted throughout the year. Membership is $60/year.

ALABAMA SONGWRITER'S GUILD, P.O. Box 272, Garden City AL 35070. (256)352-4873. E-mail: lithics@hiwaay.net. **Contact:** Dennis N. Kahler. Estab. 1992. "The Alabama Songwriter's Guild is comprised of songwriters and their supporters, with no restrictions. We have members who are just beginning to write, and others who have number one hits under their belts on the *Billboard* charts. We welcome all genres of songwriting, and count several non-writers as members of our network efforts. The main purpose of the ASG is to help link Alabama and outside songwriters to information on seminars, showcases, publishing and song-plugging opportunities, local associations, workshops, and other events from one end of the state to the other. We help spread word of the induction ceremonies and other events at the Alabama Music Hall of Fame, report on the annual Frank Brown International Songwriter's Festival in Gulf Shores/Orange Beach every November, and help link writers together with like-minded individuals for co-writes. Any purpose that serves the songwriter is of interest to us." Queries welcomed anytime.

Tips: "Networking is crucial! Wherever you live, develop your network. If you need songwriting contacts in Alabama, contact us."

ALL SONGWRITERS NETWORK (ASN), (formerly American Songwriters Network), Dept A95, Box 23912, Ft. Lauderdale FL 33307. (954)537-3463. E-mail: asn@tiac.net. Website: www.tiac. net/users/asn. **Contact:** Network Manager. Estab. 1995. Serves "professional level songwriters/composers with monthly music industry leads tipsheet. The tipsheet includes the most current listing of producers, A&R managers, record labels, entertainment attorneys, agents and publishing companies looking for specific material for their projects/albums. Any songwriter from any part of the country or world can be a member of this organization. The purpose of this organization is to foster a better professional community by helping members to place their songs." Membership fee: $140/year.

Tips: "Please send SASE or e-mail for application form."

 AMERICAN COMPOSERS FORUM, 332 Minnesota St. #E145, St. Paul MN 55101. (651)228-1407. Fax: (651)291-7978. E-mail: mail@composersforum.org. Website: www.composersf orum.org. **Contact:** Wendy Collins, member services manager. Estab. 1973. "The American Composers Forum links communities with composers and performers, encouraging the making, playing and enjoyment of new music. Building two-way relationships between artists and the public, the Forum develops programs that educate today's and tomorrow's audiences, energize composers' and performers' careers, stimulate entrepreneurship and collaboration, promote musical creativity, and serve as models of effective support for the arts. Programs include residencies, fellowships, commissions, producing and performance opportunities, a recording assistance program and a widely-distributed recording label. The Forum's members, more than 1,200 strong, live in 49 states and 16 countries; membership is open to all." Dues: $50, students/seniors: $35.

 AMERICAN SOCIETY OF COMPOSERS, AUTHORS AND PUBLISHERS (ASCAP), One Lincoln Plaza, New York NY 10023. (212)621-6000 (administration); (212)621-6240 (membership). E-mail: info@ascap.com. Website: www.ascap.com. President and Chairman of the Board: Marilyn Bergman. CEO: John LoFrumento. Executive Vice President/Membership: Todd Brabec. **Contact:** Member Services at (800)95-ASCAP. **Regional offices: West Coast:** 7920 Sunset Blvd., 3rd Floor, Los Angeles CA 90046, (323)883-1000; **Nashville:** 2 Music Square W., Nashville TN 37203, (615)742-5000; **Chicago:** 1608 N. Milwaukee Ave., Suite 1007, Chicago IL 60647, (773)394-4286; **Atlanta:** PMB 400-541 10th St. NW, Atlanta GA 30318, (404)351-1252; **Florida:** 420 Lincoln Rd., Suite 385, Miami Beach FL 33139, (305)673-3446; **United Kingdom:** 8 Cork St., London WIX 1PB England, 011-44-202-439-0909; **Puerto Rico:** 510 Royal Bank Center, 255 Ponce De Leon Ave., Hato Rey, Puerto Rico 00917, (787)281-0782. ASCAP is a membership association of over 130,000 composers, lyricists, songwriters, and music publishers, whose function is to protect the rights of its members by licensing and collecting royalties for the nondramatic public performance

**FOR EXPLANATIONS OF THESE SYMBOLS,
SEE THE INSIDE FRONT AND BACK COVERS OF THIS BOOK.**

of their copyrighted works. ASCAP licensees include radio, television, cable, live concert promoters, bars, restaurants, symphony orchestras, new media, and other users of music. ASCAP is the leading performing rights society in the world, with 2001 revenues of more than $647 million. All revenues, less operating expenses, are distributed to members (about 85 cents of each dollar, $511 million, in 2001). ASCAP was the first US performing rights organization to distribute royalties from the Internet. Founded in 1914, ASCAP is the only society created and owned by writers and publishers. The ASCAP Board of Directors consists of 12 writers and 12 publishers, elected by the membership. ASCAP's Member Card provides exclusive benefits geared towards working music professionals. Among the benefits are health, musical instrument and equipment, tour and studio liability, term life and long term care insurance, discounts on musical instruments, equipment and supplies, access to a credit union, and much more. ASCAP hosts a wide array of showcases and workshops throughout the year, and offers grants, special awards, and networking opportunities in a variety of genres. Visit their website listed above for more information.

ARIZONA SONGWRITERS ASSOCIATION, P.O. Box 678, Phoenix AZ 85001-0678. (602)973-1988. Website: www.punkfolker.com. **Contact:** Gavan Wieser, membership director. Estab. 1977. Members are all ages with wide variety of interests; beginners and those who make money from their songs. Most members are residents of Arizona. Purpose is to educate about the craft and business of songwriting and to facilitate networking with business professionals and other local songwriters. Offers instruction, newsletter, lectures, workshops and performance opportunities. Applications accepted year-round. Membership fee: $25/year.

ASSOCIATED MALE CHORUSES OF AMERICA, 773 Cedar Glen Rd., RR1, Dunsford, Ontario K0M 1L0 Canada. E-mail: internationaloffice@ameachorus.org. Website: www.amcofa. org. **Contact:** William J. Bates, executive secretary. Estab. 1924. Serves musicians and male choruses of US and Canada. "Our members are people from all walks of life. Many of our directors and accompanists are professional musicians. Age ranges from high school students to members in their '70s and '80s. Potential members must be supportive of Male Chorus Singing. They do not have to belong to a chorus to join. We have both Associate and Affiliate memberships. Our purpose is to further the power of music, not only to entertain and instruct, but to uplift the spirit, arouse the finest instincts, and develop the soul of man. With so little male chorus music being written, we as a 1,500 member organization provide a vehicle for songwriters, so that the music can be performed." Offers competitions, instruction, lectures, library, newsletter, performance opportunities, social outings and workshops. Also sponsors annual Male Chorus Songwriters Competition Contest. Applications accepted year-round. Membership fees are Chorus Members: $7 (per singer); Affiliate (Individual or Organization) Members: $10; Student Members: $2; Life Members: $125 (one time fee). "Information and application forms can be found on our website."

ASSOCIATION DES PROFESSIONEL.LE.S DE LA CHANSON ET DE LA MUSIQUE, 255 ch. Montréal, Suite 200, Ontario K1L 6C4 Canada. (613)745-5642. Fax: (613)745-1733. E-mail: apcm@sympatico.ca. Website: www.apcm.ca. **Contact:** Laurent de Crombruggne, director. Estab. 1989. Members are French Canadian singers and musicians. Members must be French singing and may have a CD/cassette to be distributed. Purpose is to gather French speaking artists (outside of Quebec, mainly in Ontario) to distribute their material, other workshops, instructions, lectures, etc. Offers instruction, newsletter, lectures, workshops, and distribution. Applications accepted year-round. Membership fee: $50 (Canadian).

ATLANTIC CANADIAN COMPOSERS ASSOCIATION, 22 Portledge Ave., Moncton, New Brunswick E1C 5C6 Canada. (506)388-4224. E-mail: lhoffman@is.dal.ca. **Contact:** Richard Gibson, member at large. Estab. 1980. "Our membership consists of people who write 'serious' (as opposed to commercial, pop, jazz, industrial) music. An applicant must be resident in one of the four Atlantic Canadian provinces and must be able to demonstrate a fluency with a variety of genres of notated music. An applicant must be prepared to submit five completed scores." Offers performance opportunities. Applications accepted year-round. Membership fee is 35 Canadian dollars.

AUSTIN SONGWRITERS GROUP, P.O. Box 2578, Austin TX 78768. (512)442-TUNE. E-mail: asginfo@aol.com. Website: www.austinsongwriter.org. **Contact:** Polk Shelton, president. Vice President of Membership: John Hudson. Estab. 1986. Serves all ages and all levels, from just beginning to advanced. Perspective members should have an interest in the field of songwriting, whether it be for profit or hobby. The main purpose of this organization is "to educate members in the craft and business of songwriting; to provide resources for growth and advancement in the area of songwriting; and to provide opportunities for performance and contact with the music industry." The primary benefit of membership to a songwriter is "exposure to music industry professionals, which increases contacts and furthers the songwriter's education in both craft and business aspects." Offers competitions, instruction, lectures, library, newsletter, performance opportunities, evaluation services, workshops and "contact with music industry professionals through special guest speakers at meetings, plus our yearly 'Austin Songwriters Conference,' which includes instruction, song evaluations, and song pitching direct to those pros currently seeking material for their artists, publishing companies, etc." Applications accepted year-round. Membership fee: $40/year.
Tips: "Our newsletter is top-quality—packed with helpful information on all aspects of songwriting—craft, business, recording and producing tips, and industry networking opportunities."

☑ **THE BLACK COUNTRY MUSIC SHOWCASE**, (formerly The Black Country Music Association), 629 Shady Lane, Nashville TN 37206. (615)227-5570. Co-Founder/Chair: Frankie Staton. Estab. 1997. Members are all ages and all people who perform or support country music. "Purpose is to have a platform for African Americans who love and perform country music in an industry that does not realize how much African-Americans want to participate in this genre. Forming the Black Country Music Showcase, the traveling group of the BCMA. Appearing at festivals, fairs and other functions." Offers instruction, newsletter, workshops, performance opportunities and evaluation services. Applications accepted year-round.
Tips: "With respect to the Black country artist and songwriter, the BCMA acts as an historical/educational entity. We have a quarterly newsletter. Send all promotional material (picture, bio, tape) to Frankie Staton."

🇳 **THE BLACK ROCK COALITION**, P.O. Box 1054, Cooper Station, New York NY 10276. (212)713-5097. E-mail: info@blackrockcoalition.org. Website: www.blackrockcoalition.org. **Contact:** Darrell McNeill, membership manager. President: Bruce Mack. Estab. 1985. Serves musicians, songwriters—male and female ages 18-40 (average). Also engineers, entertainment attorneys and producers. Looking for members who are "mature and serious about music as an artist or activist willing to help fellow musicians. The BRC independently produces, promotes and distributes Black alternative music acts as a collective and supportive voice for such musicians within the music and record business. The main purpose of this organization is to produce, promote and distribute the full spectrum of black music along with educating the public on what black music is. The BRC is now soliciting recorded music by bands and individuals for Black Rock Coalition Records. Please send copyrighted and original material only." Offers instruction, newsletter, lectures, free seminars and workshops, monthly membership meeting, quarterly magazine, performing opportunities, evaluation services, business advice, full roster of all members. Applications accepted year-round. Bands must submit a tape, bio with picture and a self-addressed, stamped envelope before sending their membership fee. Membership fee: $25 per individual/$100 per band.

☑ **THE BOSTON SONGWRITERS WORKSHOP**. (617)499-6932. Website: www.bostonsongwriters.org. Estab. 1988. "The Boston Songwriters Workshop is made up of a very diverse group of people, ranging in age from late teens to people in their sixties, and even older. The interest areas are also diverse, running the gamut from folk, pop and rock to musical theater, jazz, R&B, dance, rap and classical. Skill levels within the group range from relative newcomers to established veterans that have had cuts and/or songs published. By virtue of group consensus, there are no eligibility requirements other than a serious desire to pursue one's songwriting ventures, and availability and interest in volunteering for the various activities required to run the organization. The purpose of the BSW is to establish a community of songwriters and composers within the greater Boston area, so that its members may better help each other to make further gains in their respective musical careers."

Offers performance opportunities, instruction, newsletter, workshops and bi-weekly critique sessions. Applications accepted year-round. Membership: $35/year; newsletter subscription only: $10/year; guest (nonmember) fees: free, limited to two meetings.

BROADCAST MUSIC, INC. (BMI), 320 W. 57th St., New York NY 10019. (212)586-2000; 8730 Sunset Blvd., Los Angeles CA 90069, (310)659-9109. Website: www.bmi.com. **Nashville:** 10 Music Square East, Nashville TN 37203, (615)401-2000. **Miami:** 5201 Blue Lagoon Dr., Suite 310, Miami FL 33126, (305)266-3636; **United Kingdom:** 84 Harley House, Marylebone Rd., London NW1 5HN, United Kingdom, 011-44-207-486-2036. President and CEO: Frances W. Preston. Senior Vice President, Performing Rights: Del R. Bryant. Vice Presidents, California: Barbara Cane and Doreen Ringer Ross. Vice President, New York: Charlie Feldman. Vice President, Nashville: Paul Corbin. Vice President, London: Phil Graham. Assistant Vice President, Miami: Diane J. Almodovar. BMI is a performing rights organization representing approximately 300,000 songwriters, composers and music publishers in all genres of music, including pop, rock, country, R&B, rap, jazz, Latin, gospel and contemporary classical. "Applicants must have written a musical composition, alone or in collaboration with other writers, which is commercially published, recorded or otherwise likely to be performed." Purpose: BMI acts on behalf of its songwriters, composers and music publishers by insuring payment for performance of their works through the collection of licensing fees from radio stations, broadcast and cable TV stations, hotels, nightclubs, aerobics centers and other users of music. This income is distributed to the writers and publishers in the form of royalty payments, based on how the music is used. BMI also undertakes intensive lobbying efforts in Washington D.C. on behalf of its affiliates, seeking to protect their performing rights through the enactment of new legislation and enforcement of current copyright law. In addition, BMI helps aspiring songwriters develop their skills through various workshops, seminars and competitions it sponsors throughout the country. Applications accepted year-round. There is no membership fee for songwriters; a one-time fee of $150 is required to affiliate an individually-owned publishing company; $250 for partnerships, corporations and limited-liability companies. "Visit our website for specific contacts, e-mail addresses and additional membership information."

N BROADWAY ON SUNSET, 10800 Hesby, Suite 9, North Hollywood CA 91601. (818)508-9270. Fax: (818)508-1806. E-mail: broadwayonsunset@cs.com. Website: www.broadwayonsunset.o rg. Executive Director: Kevin Kaufman. Literary Director: Libbe S. Halevy. Estab. 1991. Sponsored by the National Academy of Songwriters. Members are musical theater writers (composers, lyricists, librettists) at all skill levels. All styles of music and musicals accepted. Participants should have access to the Los Angeles area to attend our programs. "We provide writers of new musicals with a structured development program that gives them a full understanding of the principles and standards of Broadway-level craft, and provide them with opportunities to test their material in front of an audience." We produce the annual West Coast Musical Theatre Conference. Offers lectures, symposia, interviews with Broadway writers and other crafts, production opportunities, evaluation and consultation services, workshops and instruction. Co-produces full productions of developed original musicals in various local theaters. Applications accepted year-round. No membership fee per se; writers pay nominal fees to participate in classes and workshops. Certain scholarships are available.

CALIFORNIA LAWYERS FOR THE ARTS, 1641 18th St., Santa Monica CA 90404. (310)998-5590. Fax: (310)998-5594. E-mail: usercla@aol.com. Website: www.calawyersforthearts.o rg. **Contact:** Audrey Greenberg, Program Director. L.A. Director: Jane Hall. Systems Coordinator: Josie Porter. Estab. 1974. "For artists of all disciplines, skill levels, and ages, supporting individuals and organizations, and arts organizations. Artists of all disciplines are welcome, whether professionals or amateurs. We also welcome groups and individuals who support the arts. We work most closely with the California arts community. Our mission is to establish a bridge between the legal and arts

---

REFER TO THE GEOGRAPHIC INDEX (at the back of this book) to find listings of companies by state, as well as foreign listings.

communities so that artists and art groups may handle their creative activities with greater business and legal competence; the legal profession will be more aware of issues affecting the arts community; and the law will become more responsive to the arts community." Offers newsletter, lectures, library, workshops, mediation service, attorney referral service, housing referrals, publications and advocacy. Membership fee: $20 for senior citizens and full-time students; $25 for working artists; $40 for general individual; $55 for panel attorney; $100 to $1,000 for patrons. Organizations: $45 for small organizations (budget under $50,000); $80 for large organizations (budget of $50,000 or more); $100 to $1,000 for corporate sponsors.

CANADA COUNCIL FOR THE ARTS/CONSEIL DES ARTS DU CANADA, 350 Albert St., P.O. Box 1047, Ottawa, Ontario K1P 5V8 Canada. (613)566-4414, ext. 5060. Website: www.canadacouncil.ca. **Contact:** Michelle Legaut, Danielle Sarault, or Lise Rochon, information offices. Estab. 1957. An independent agency that fosters and promotes the arts in Canada by providing grants and services to professional artists including songwriters and musicians. "Individual artists must be Canadian citizens or permanent residents of Canada, and must have completed basic training and/or have the recognition as professionals within their fields. The Canada Council offers grants to professional musicians to pursue their own personal and creative development. There are specific deadline dates for the various programs of assistance." Call or write for more details.

CANADIAN ACADEMY OF RECORDING ARTS & SCIENCES (CARAS), 124 Merton St., Suite 305, Toronto, Ontario M4S 2Z2 Canada. (416)485-3135 or (800)440-JUNO. Fax: (416)485-4978. E-mail: caras@juno-awards.ca. Website: www.juno-awards.ca. President: Daisy C. Falle. Awards and Events Coordinator: Leisa Peacock. Communications Co-ordinator: Tammy Watson. Membership is open to all employees (including support staff) in broadcasting and record companies, as well as producers, personal managers, recording artists, recording engineers, arrangers, composers, music publishers, album designers, promoters, talent and booking agents, record retailers, rack jobbers, distributors, recording studios and other music industry related professions (on approval). Applicants must be affliliated with the Canadian recording industry. Offers newsletter, nomination and voting privileges for Juno Awards and discount tickets to Juno awards show. Also discount on trade magazines. "CARAS strives to foster the development of the Canadian music and recording industries and to contribute toward higher artistic standards." Applications accepted year-round. Membership fee is $50/year (Canadian) + GST = $53.50. Applications accepted from individuals only, not from companies or organizations.

CANADIAN COUNTRY MUSIC ASSOCIATION (CCMA), 5 Director Court, Unit 102, Woodbridge, Ontario L4L 4S5 Canada. (905)850-1144. Fax: (905)850-1330. E-mail: country@ccma.org. Website: www.ccma.org. **Contact:** Colleen MacIntyre, Membership Services Coordinator. Executive Director: Sheila Hamilton. Estab. 1976. Members are songwriters, musicians, producers, radio station personnel, managers, booking agents and others. Offers newsletter, workshops, performance opportunities and annual awards. "Through our newsletters and conventions we offer a means of meeting and associating with artists and others in the industry. During our workshops or seminars (Country Music Week), we include a songwriters' seminar. The CCMA is a federally chartered, nonprofit organization, dedicated to the promotion and development of Canadian country music throughout Canada and the world and to providing a unity of purpose for the Canadian country music industry." Send for application.

CANADIAN MUSICAL REPRODUCTION RIGHTS AGENCY LTD., 56 Wellesley St. W, #320, Toronto, Ontario M5S 2S3 Canada. (416)926-1966. Fax: (416)926-7521. E-mail: inquiries@cmrra.ca. Website: www.cmrra.ca. **Contact:** Kevin Shaver, publisher relations. Estab. 1975. Members are music copyright owners, music publishers, sub-publishers and administrators. Representation by CMRRA is open to any person, firm or corporation anywhere in the world, which owns and/or administers one or more copyrighted musical works. CMRRA is a music licensing agency—Canada's largest—which represents music copyright owners, publishers and administrators for the purpose of mechanical and synchronization licensing in Canada. Offers mechanical and synchronization licensing. Applications accepted year-round.

CENTER FOR THE PROMOTION OF CONTEMPORARY COMPOSERS, P.O. Box 631043, Nacogdoches TX 75963. E-mail: cpcc@under.org. Website: www.under.org/cpcc. Director: Dr. Stephen Lias. Estab. 1996. "Our members range from student composers to composers with international reputations." Purpose is to promote the works and activities of contemporary composers by creating custom composer web pages, posting composer opportunities (competitions, calls for scores, grants, faculty openings, etc.), maintaining a catalogue of members' works and a calendar of upcoming performances of new music. Offers competitions, newsletter, performance opportunities and custom web pages and listings in online catalog. Applications accepted year-round. Membership fee: $12 regular; $10/month resident ($120/year).

CENTRAL CAROLINA SONGWRITERS ASSOCIATION (CCSA), 1144 Amber Acres Lane, Knightdale NC 27545. (919)266-5791. Fax: (919)460-6284. E-mail: davisshantel@hotmail.com. Website: www.NCneighbors.com/147/. **Contact:** Shantel R. Davis, Founder. Vice President: Dawn Williams. Estab. 1996. "CCSA welcomes all songwriters and musicians, regardless of age. Our members vary in musical interests, and we cover all types of music. From the beginning songwriter to the experienced professional, all songwriters and musicians can find benefit in joining CCSA. We meet monthly in Raleigh, NC. We are open to all songwriters who could possibly make it to our meetings, or those who are too far away could use our Critique-By-Mail service. All members must be active participants in CCSA for the benefit of the group, as well as for their own benefit, dedicated songwriters/musicians. The main purpose of the CCSA is to provide each songwriter and musician a resourceful organization where members can grow musically by learning and sharing with one another. We want to reach every songwriter we can and attend to his/her musical needs. CCSA has formed KIDSN2MUSIC, a division for songwriters under 18. The webpage can be viewed at www.NCneighbors.com/2154. We are also forming CCSA-Charlotte for those songwriters in the western part of the state. Call the Knightdale number or e-mail us for more information." Offers instruction, newsletter, library, workshops, evaluation services, open-mic nights and musicians/collaborators network. Applications accepted quarterly. Dues are $20 per year.

☑ **CENTRAL OREGON SONGWRITERS ASSOCIATION**, 68978 Graham Court, Sisters OR 97759. (541)923-3505. Fax: (541)549-1811. E-mail: cosa@teleport.com. Website: http://COSA4 U.tripod.com. **Contact:** Al Byer, Secretary/Treasurer. Organizer: Earl Richards. President: Matt Engle. Estab. 1993. "Our members range in age from their 20s into their 80s. Membership includes aspiring beginners, accomplished singer/songwriter performing artists and all in between. Anyone with an interest in songwriting (any style) is invited to and welcome at COSA. COSA is a nonprofit organization to promote, educate and motivate members in the skills of writing, marketing and improving their craft." Offers competitions, instruction, newsletter, lectures, library, workshops, performance opportunities, songwriters round, awards, evaluation services and collaboration. Applications accepted year-round. Membership fee is $25.
Tips: "COSA enjoys a close association with other like associations, thereby increasing and expanding the benefits of association."

N **CHICAGO DANCE AND MUSIC ALLIANCE**, (formerly Chicago Music Alliance), 410 S. Michigan Ave., Suite 819, Chicago IL 60605. (312)987-9296. Fax: (312)987-1127. E-mail: cmanet@voyager.net. Website: www.chicagoperformances.org. Executive Director: Matthew Brockmeier. Estab. 1984. "Chicago Dance and Music Alliance is comprised of not-for-profit organizations and individuals involved in dance and music of all styles at all levels of skill. Administrators, composers, choreographers, performers, students, performers, educators and others are members as well as groups from the smallest ensemble to full symphony orchestras and major dance companies. Ensembles should reside and perform in the Chicago area, as should individuals. Individuals across the country are CDMA members, but they have a connection with Chicago in some way (want to stay in touch, are interested in moving to Chicago, their work is performed in Chicago, etc). Our mission is to provide direct services to members engaged in all genres of dance and music in the Chicago area, act as an advocate on their behalf, and disseminate information about their activities to the general public. As a service organization we are committed to meeting the needs of our members. We act as a center for the exchange of ideas and resources, maintain ties with the educational community, and develop programs to serve our members with their direct input. Our activities include workshops, events listings, music performance and merchandise discounts, and résumé/career counseling." Offers newsletter, lectures, workshops, research and information finding services, information on auditions and competitions. Website offers a searchable performance guide and directories by performing skills and teaching activities. Also offers financial services, including credit union membership. Applications accepted year-round. All memberships expire December 31. Individual dues are $40 per year. Fees for ensembles vary by budget size.

THE COLLEGE MUSIC SOCIETY, 202 W. Spruce St., Missoula MT 59802-4202. (406)721-9616. Fax: (406)721-9419. E-mail: cms@music.org. Website: www.music.org. Estab. 1959. Serves college, university and conservatory professors, as well as independent musicians. "The College Music Society is a consortium of college, conservatory, university and independent musicians and scholars interested in all disciplines of music. Its mission is to promote music teaching and learning, musical creativity and expression, research and dialogue, and diversity and interdisciplinary interaction." Offers journal, newsletter, lectures, workshops, performance opportunities, job listing service, databases of organizations and institutions, music faculty and mailing lists. Applications accepted year-round. Membership fee: $55 (regular dues).

☑ **COLORADO MUSIC ASSOCIATION**, 8 E. First Ave., Denver CO 80203. (720)570-2280. E-mail: dolly@coloradomusic.org. Website: http://coloradomusic.org. **Contact:** David Barber, president. Estab. 1999. Members are musicians of all ages and skill levels, songwriters, recording studios, music business merchants, teachers, performers, attorneys, agents, managers, publicists, promoters, venue owners and operators, and others connected to local music communities. Purpose is to support the local music community and encourage the development of skills, creativity and production. Offers instruction, lectures, workshops, performance and showcase opportunities, evaluation services, music directory, and free UPC (barcode) numbers for CD and other music products. Applications accepted year-round. Membership fee: $35/individual; $60/band; $115/business.
Tips: "We meet monthly in Denver and present speakers on topics of interest to the group. Our Internet site is being expanded to provide extensive educational features relative to the music biz."

COMPOSERS GUILD, 40 N. 100 West, P.O. Box 586, Farmington UT 84025-0586. (801)451-2275. **Contact:** Ruth Gatrell, president. Estab. 1963. Serves all ages, including children. Musical skill varies from beginners to professionals. An interest in composing is the only requirement. The purpose of this organization is to "help composers in every way possible through classes, workshops and symposiums, concerts, composition contests and association with others of similar interests." Offers competitions, instruction, lectures, newsletter, performance opportunities, evaluation services and workshops. Applications accepted year-round. Membership fee is $25/year. Associate memberships for child, spouse, parent, grandchild or grandparent of member: $15. "Holds four concerts/year. See our listing in the Contests & Awards section for details."

CONNECTICUT SONGWRITERS ASSOCIATION, 51 Hillcrest Ave., Watertown CT 06795. (860)945-1272. E-mail: paul4csa@aol.com. Website: www.ctsongs.com. **Contact:** Paul Chapin, president. Vice President: Ric Speck. "We are an educational, nonprofit organization dedicated to improving the art and craft of original music. Founded in 1979 by Don Donegan, CSA has grown to over 250 active members and has become one of the best known songwriters' associations in the country. Membership in the CSA admits you to 12-18 seminars/workshops/song critique sessions per year at 3-5 locations in Connecticut. Out of state members may mail in songs for free critique at our meetings. Noted professionals deal with all aspects of the craft and business of music including lyric writing, music theory, music technology, arrangement and production, legal and business aspects, performance techniques, song analysis and recording techniques. CSA offers 2-3 song screening sessions per year

---

MARKETS THAT WERE listed in the 2002 edition of *Songwriters Market* but do not appear this year are listed in the General Index with a notation explaining why they were omitted.

for members (songs which are voted on by the panel). Songs that 'pass' are then eligible for inclusion on the CSA sampler anthology CD series. Eight 16-20 song tapes have been released so far and are for sale at local retail outlets and are given to speakers and prospective buyers. CSA has produced three holiday CDs of member songs. CSA also offers showcases and concerts which are open to the public and designed to give artists a venue for performing their original material for an attentive, listening audience. CSA benefits help local soup kitchens, group homes, hospice, world hunger, libraries, nature centers, community centers and more. CSA shows encompass ballads to bluegrass and Bach to rock. Our monthly newsletter, *Connecticut Songsmith*, offers free classified advertising for members, and has been edited and published by Bill Pere since 1980. In addition, CSA offers members free web pages on their website. Annual dues: $40; senior citizen and full time students $30; organizations $80. Memberships are tax-deductible as business expenses or as charitable contributions to the extent allowed by law."

COUNTRY LEGENDS ASSOCIATION, 5 N. Third Ave. W, Suite 300, Duluth MN 55807-7171. (218)628-3003. E-mail: cla@clabranson.org. Website: www.clabranson.org. **Contact:** Frank Dell, president. Estab. 1997. Members are professional/nonprofessional industry people, fans of classic country music. Members must be active in the country music industry (classic country music)—artists, songwriters, promoters, record companies, merchandisers, musicians, country radio station disc jockeys and fans of classic country music. Purpose is to promote classic country music, educate, establish the country classic legends Hall of Fame in Branson, Missouri, help new talent, hold annual conventions and award shows. Offers competitions, instruction, newsletter, lectures, workshops, performance opportunities and evaluation services. Applications accepted year-round. Membership fee: $100/industry; $50/artist, musician, songwriters; $25/fans; $20 senior citizens.

COUNTRY MUSIC ASSOCIATION OF TEXAS, P.O. Box 549, Troy TX 76579. (254)938-2454. Fax: (254)938-2049. **Contact:** Bud Fisher, founder/director. Estab. 1989. Open to songwriters, singers, pickers, fans and other professionals of all ages from all over the world. Members are interested in country music, especially traditional, classics. Purpose is to promote traditional and independent country music. Offers newsletter, workshops, performance opportunities and evaluation services. Applications accepted year-round. Membership fee: $23.95/year.
Tips: "Membership has grown to over 4,000 fans, musicians and songwriters, making it one of the largest state organizations in America. We hold numerous functions throughout the year and we have helped many local recording artists chart their releases nationwide and in Europe. Texas country music is hot!"

☑ COUNTRY MUSIC SHOWCASE INTERNATIONAL, INC., P.O. Box 368, Carlisle IA 50047. (515)989-3748. Fax: (515)989-0235. E-mail: haroldl@cmshowcase.org. Website: www.cmshowcase.org or www.cmshowcase.org/doorway.htm. **Contact:** Harold L. Luick, CEO. "We are an online nonprofit website for public use, supported by donations, free will offerings, and operated, maintained entirely by volunteers. We can put you on the Internet with or without you having a computer, so you can advertise, sell, market, promote yourself or your product to Internet buyers and consumers. Ideal for songwriters, musicians, entertainers, bands and music publishers. A great way to do business with the Internet is through our Internet Provider Service. Other services offered are: song critique service, private individual music business consulting service, booking agency service, an Online Music Product Store to market your CD, tapes or product, directory and listings of bands, entertainers, available for hire through our agency, country music festivals, events, stageshows, contests and music activities in the Iowa/Midwest area. We are the #1 traditional, old-time, classic country and Cajun music website destination for search engines in the USA. A non-profit organization for those that believe in keeping country music and Cajun music art forms alive and well. For free brochure/information send a #10 SASE to the above address, e-mail, phone or Fax or visit our website. "New addition to our website for 2002 is the Iowa/Midwest 'Virtual' Country Music Heritage Museum, Library and Hall of Fame at www.cmshowcase.org/doorway.htm."

DALLAS SONGWRITERS ASSOCIATION, Sammons Center for the Arts, 3036 Harry Hines, Box 20, Dallas TX 75219. (214)750-0916. Fax: (214)692-1392. E-mail: info@dallassongwrite rs.org. Website: www.dallassongwriters.org. **Contact:** Kay Seamayer, Membership Director. President: James Cornelius. Founding President Emeritis: Barbara McMillen. Estab. 1986. Serves songwriters and lyricists of Dallas/Ft. Worth metroplex. Members are adults ages 18-65, Dallas/Ft. Worth area songwriters/lyricists who are or aspire to be professionals. Purpose is to provide songwriters an opportunity to meet other songwriters, share information, find co-writers and support each other through group discussions at monthly meetings; to provide songwriters an opportunity to have their songs heard and critiqued by peers and professionals by playing cassettes and providing an open mike at monthly meetings and by offering contests judged by publishers; to provide songwriters opportunities to meet other music business professionals by inviting guest speakers to monthly meetings and the Dallas Songwriters Seminar; and to provide songwriters opportunities to learn more about the craft of songwriting and the business of music by presenting mini-workshops at each monthly meeting. "We offer a chance for the songwriter to learn from peers and industry professionals and an opportunity to belong to a supportive group environment to encourage the individual to continue his/her songwriting endeavors." Offers competitions, field trips, instruction, lectures, newsletter, performance opportunities, social outings, workshops and seminars. "Our members are eligible for discounts at several local music stores and seminars." Applications accepted year-round. Membership fee: $45. "When inquiring by phone, please leave complete mailing address and phone number where you can be reached day and night."

N THE DRAMATISTS GUILD OF AMERICA, INC., (formerly The Dramatists Guild, Inc.), 1501 Broadway, Suite 701, New York NY 10036. (212)398-9366. Fax: (212)944-0420. E-mail: membership@dramaguild.com. Website: www.dramaguild.com. **Contact:** Tom Epstein, executive director. "For over three-quarters of a century, The Dramatists Guild has been the professional association of playwrights, composers and lyricists, with more than 6,000 members across the country. All theater writers, whether produced or not, are eligible for Associate membership ($75/year); those who are engaged in a drama-related field but are not a playwright are eligible for Subscribing membership ($50/year); students enrolled in writing degree programs at colleges or universities are eligible for Student membership ($35/year); writers who have been produced on Broadway, Off-Broadway or on the main stage of a resident theater are eligible for Active membership ($125/year). The Guild offers its members the following activities and services: use of the Guild's contracts (including the Approved Production Contract for Broadway, the Off-Broadway contract, the LORT contract, the collaboration agreements for both musicals and drama, the 99 Seat Theatre Plan contract, the Small Theatre contract, commissioning agreements, and the Underlying Rights Agreements contract; advice on all theatrical contracts including Broadway, Off-Broadway, regional, showcase, Equity-waiver, dinner theater and collaboration contracts); a nationwide toll-free number for all members with business or contract questions or problems; advice and information on a wide spectrum of issues affecting writers; free and/or discounted ticket service; symposia led by experienced professionals in major cities nationwide; access to a health insurance program and a group term life insurance plan; and a spacious meeting room which can accommodate up to 50 people for readings and auditions on a rental basis. The Guild's publications are: *The Dramatist*, a bimonthly journal containing articles on all aspects of the theater (which includes *The Dramatists Guild Newsletter*, with announcements of all Guild activities and current information of interest to dramatists); and an annual resource directory with up-to-date information on agents, grants, producers, playwriting contests, conferences and workshops.

☑ THE FIELD, 161 Sixth Ave., New York NY 10013. (212)691-6969. Fax: (212)255-2053. E-mail: info@thefield.org. Website: www.thefield.org. **Contact:** Diane Vivona, director art-based programs. Estab. 1986. "The Field gives independent performing artists the tools to develop and sustain their creative and professional lives, while allowing the public to have immediate, direct access to a remarkable range of contemporary artwork. The organization was started by eight emerging artists who shared common roots in contemporary dance and theater. Meeting regularly, these artists created a structure to help each other improve their artwork, and counter the isolation that often comes with the territory of an artistic career. The Field offers a comprehensive program structure similar to an urban artists' residency or graduate program. Participants select from a broad array of services focused in three basic areas: Art, Career and Exploration. These include: workshops and performance opportunities; management training and career development; fundraising consultations, fiscal sponsorship, and informational publications; and residencies. The Field's goal is to help artists develop their best artwork by deepening the artistic process and finding effective ways to bring that art into the market-place. Most Field programs cost under $85, and tickets to our performance events average $8. In addition, since 1992, The Field has coordinated a network of satellite sites in Atlanta, Chicago, Dallas, Houston, Miami, Philadelphia, San Francisco, Seattle, Toronto, Washington D.C. and most recently, Japan. The Field is the only organization in New York that provides comprehensive programming for independent performing artists on a completely non-exclusive basis. Programs are open to artists from all disciplines, aesthetic viewpoints, and levels of development." Offers newsletter, workshops and performance opportunities. Applications accepted year-round. Membership fee: $85/year.

THE FOLK ALLIANCE (North American Folk Music and Dance Alliance), 962 Wayne Ave., Suite 902, Silver Springs MD 20910-4480. (301)588-8185. Fax: (301)588-8186. E-mail: fa@fol k.org. Website: www.folk.org. **Contact:** Tony Ziselberger, director of member services. Executive Director: Phyllis Barney. Estab. 1989. Members are organizations and individuals involved in tradi-tional and contemporary folk music and dance in the US and Canada (in any genre—blues, bluegrass, Celtic, Latino, old-time, singer/songwriter, etc.). The Folk Alliance hosts its annual conference (which includes performance showcases) in late February at different locations in the US and Canada. The conferences include workshops, panel discussions, the largest all folk exhibit hall and showcases. The Folk Alliance also serves members with their newsletter and through education, advocacy and field development. Memberships accepted year-round. Membership fee: $60 ($80 Canadian)/year for individual (voting); $140-495 ($190-690 Canadian)/year for organizational. Upcoming conference sites: 2001: Vancouver BC, Canada. 2002: Jacksonville, FL. "We *do not* offer songwriting contests. We are *not* a publisher—no demo tapes, please."

☑ **FORT WORTH SONGWRITERS ASSOCIATION**, P.O. Box 162443, Fort Worth TX 76161. (817)654-5400. E-mail: info@fwsa.com. Website: www.fwsa.com. President: Rose Jeffus. Executive Vice President: Tim Blazer; Vice President Publications: John Terry; Vice President Web Operations/Webmaster: Dennis Coble. Estab. 1992. Members are ages 18-75, beginners up to and including published writers. Interests cover gospel, country, western swing, rock, pop, bluegrass and blues. Purpose is to allow songwriters to become more proficient at songwriting; to provide an opportunity for their efforts to be performed before a live audience; to provide songwriters an opportu-nity to meet co-writers. "We provide our members free critiques of their efforts. We provide a monthly newsletter outlining current happenings in the business of songwriting. We offer competitions and mini workshops with guest speakers from the music industry. We promote a weekly open 'mic' for singers of original material. Our main contest is for Best Song of the Year which is selected by publishers and producers from Nashville. We also offer showcases and web pages for members." Applications accepted year-round. Membership fee: $25.

GEORGIA MUSIC INDUSTRY ASSOCIATION, INC., P.O. Box 550314, Atlanta GA 30355. (404)266-2666. Website: www.gmia.org. **Contact:** Cindy Lou Harrington, president. Vice President: Chip Martin. Secretary/Treasurer: Janet Eller. Estab. 1978. "The Georgia Music Industry Association (GMIA), formerly the Atlanta Songwriter's Association, was formed in 1979 by a group of songwrit-ers to provide an outlet to create and collaborate with fellow songwriters, and to provide an avenue for networking within the music community. The group's main purpose has always been to promote and encourage the craft of songwriting and to offer opportunities to those writers and performers who have set goals for themselves in the music business. GMIA does this by tying together talented performance artists and songwriters with music industry professionals, media representatives, and financial institutions. GMIA has formed alliances with an advisory board that is national in scope

FOR BOOKS ON THE CRAFT AND BUSINESS of songwriting, check out the website for Writer's Digest Books at www.writersdigest.com.

and that offers expertise to GMIA members at educational panels, seminars, and showcases." Events include songwriting showcase competitions in the Spring and Fall, "Georgia's Best" Performance Showcase in January, Monthly Song Critiques, and a quarterly newsletter.

GOSPEL MUSIC ASSOCIATION, 1205 Division St., Nashville TN 37203. (615)242-0303. E-mail: joy@gospelmusic.org. Website: www.gospelmusic.org. **Contact:** Joy T. Fletcher, director of member development. Estab. 1964. Serves songwriters, musicians and anyone directly involved in or who supports gospel music. Professional members include advertising agencies, musicians, agents/managers, composers, retailers, music publishers, print and broadcast media, and other members of the recording industry. Associate members include supporters of gospel music and those whose involvement in the industry does not provide them with income. The primary purpose of the GMA is to promote the industry of gospel music, and provide professional development series for industry members. Offers library, newsletter, performance opportunities and workshops. Applications accepted year-round. Membership fee: $85/year (professional) and $60/year (associate).

⊕ THE GUILD OF INTERNATIONAL SONGWRITERS & COMPOSERS, Sovereign House, 12 Trewartha Rd., Praa Sands, Penzance, Cornwall TR20 9ST England. Phone: (01736)762826. Fax: (01736)763328. E-mail: songmag@aol.com. Website: www.songwriters-guild.c om. **Contact:** C.A. Jones, secretary. Serves songwriters, musicians, record companies, music publishers, etc. "Our members are amateur and professional songwriters and composers, musicians, publishers, studio owners and producers. Membership is open to all persons throughout the world of any age and ability, from amateur to professional. The Guild gives advice and services relating to the music industry. A free magazine is available upon request with an SAE or 3 IRCs. We provide contact information for artists, record companies, music publishers, industry organizations; free copyright service; *Songwriting & Composing Magazine*; and many additional free services." Applications accepted year-round. Annual dues: £40 in the U.K.; £50 in E.E.C. countries; £50 overseas (subscriptions in pounds sterling only).

Ⓝ HAWAI'I SONGWRITERS ASSOCIATION, P.O. Box 88129, Honolulu HI 96830. (808)988-6878. Fax: (808)988-6236. E-mail: stanrubens@aol.com Website: members.aol.com/hsas ong/hsa.html. **Contact:** Stan Rubens, secretary. Estab. 1972. "We have two classes of membership: Professional (must have had at least one song commercially published and for sale to general public) and Regular (any one who wants to join and share in our activities). Both classes can vote equally, but only Professional members can hold office. Must be 18 years old to join. Our members include musicians, entertainers and record producers. Membership is world-wide and open to all varieties of music, not just ethnic Hawaiian. President, Stan Rubens, has published 4 albums." Offers competitions, instruction, newsletter, lectures, workshops, performance opportunities and evaluation services. Applications accepted year-round. Membership fee: $24.

Ⓝ INTERNATIONAL BLUEGRASS MUSIC ASSOCIATION (IBMA), 1620 Frederica St., Owensboro KY 42301. (270)684-9025. Fax: (270)686-7863. E-mail: ibma@ibma.org. Website: www. ibma.org. Member Services: Jill Snider. Estab. 1985. Serves songwriters, musicians and professionals in bluegrass music. "IBMA is a trade association composed of people and organizations involved professionally and semi-professionally in the bluegrass music industry, including performers, agents, songwriters, music publishers, promoters, print and broadcast media, local associations, recording manufacturers and distributors. Voting members must be currently or formerly involved in the bluegrass industry as full or part-time professionals. A songwriter attempting to become professionally involved in our field would be eligible. Our mission statement reads: "IBMA: Working together for high standards of professionalism, a greater appreciation for our music, and the success of the worldwide bluegrass music community." IBMA publishes a bimonthly *International Bluegrass*, holds an annual trade show/convention with a songwriters showcase in the fall, represents our field outside the bluegrass music community, and compiles and disseminates databases of bluegrass related resources and organizations. Market research on the bluegrass consumer is available and we offer Bluegrass in the Schools information and matching grants. The primary value in this organization for a songwriter is having current information about the bluegrass music field and contacts with other songwriters, publishers, musicians and record companies." Offers workshops, liability insurance, rental car discounts, consultation and databases of record companies, radio stations, press, organizations and gigs. Applications accepted year-round. Membership fee: for a non-voting patron $25/year; for an individual voting professional $50/year; for an organizational voting professional $125/year.

INTERNATIONAL SONGWRITERS ASSOCIATION LTD., 37b New Cavendish St., London WI England. (0171)486-5353. E-mail: jliddane@songwriter.iol.ie. Website: www.songwriter. co.uk. **Contact:** Anna M. Sinden, membership department. Serves songwriters and music publishers. "The ISA headquarters is in Limerick City, Ireland, and from there it provides its members with assessment services, copyright services, legal and other advisory services and an investigations service, plus a magazine for one yearly fee. Our members are songwriters in more than 50 countries worldwide, of all ages. There are no qualifications, but applicants under 18 are not accepted. We provide information and assistance to professional or semi-professional songwriters. Our publication, *Songwriter*, which was founded in 1967, features detailed exclusive interviews with songwriters and music publishers, as well as directory information of value to writers." Offers competitions, instruction, library, newsletter and a weekly e-mail newsletter *Songwriter Newswire*. Applications accepted year-round. Membership fee for European writers is £19.95; for non-European writers, US $30.

INTERNATIONAL SONGWRITERS GUILD, 5108 Louvre Ave., Orlando FL 31028. (407)851-5328. **Contact:** Russ Robinson, president. Estab. 1977.
 • Russ Robinson, President of the Guild, played piano for Judy Garland and Frank Sinatra, among others, and was a member of "The Modernairs" (five-part harmony vocals). He is a writer of national commercials, and is well-known in the music and film industry.
Members are lyricists, composers, performers, arrangers, publishers, songwriters of all ages, backgrounds and skill levels. Open to anyone interested in songwriting and in improving their songwriting skills. The main purpose of the organization is to guide and educate those people wanting to write commercial music successfully. We use monthly critiquing sessions of approximately 10 songs, where the top 5 winners are announced in the next monthly newsletter, "Guild Tidings." Offers competitions, lectures, performance opportunities, instruction, evaluation services, newsletters, workshops and industry contacts. Applications accepted year-round. Membership fee: $35 annually.

JUST PLAIN FOLKS MUSIC ORGANIZATION (www.jpfolks.com), 1315 N. Butler, Indianapolis IN 46219. (317)513-6557. E-mail: JPFolksPro@jpfolks.com. Website: www.jpfolks.com. **Contact:** Brian Austin Whitney (brian@jpfolks.com), founder or Linda Berger (linda@jpfolks.com), projects director. Estab. 1998. "Just Plain Folks is among the world's largest Music Organizations. Our members cover nearly every musical style and professional field, from songwriters, artists, publishers, producers, record labels, entertainment attorneys, publicists and PR experts, performing rights organization staffers, live and recording engineers, educators, music students, musical instrument manufacturers, TV, Radio and Print Media and almost every major Internet Music entity. Representing all 50 US States and over 60 countries worldwide, we have members of all ages, musical styles and levels of success, including winners and nominees of every major music industry award, as well as those just starting out. A complete demographics listing of our group is available on our website. Whether you are a #1 hit songwriter or artist, or the newest kid on the block, you are welcome to join. We're all in this together!" The purpose of this organization is "to share wisdom, ideas and experiences with others who have been there, and to help educate those who have yet to make the journey. Just Plain Folks provides its members with a friendly networking and support community that uses the power of the Internet and combines it with good old-fashioned human interaction. We help promote our members ready for success and educate those still learning." Offers special programs to members, including:
 • *Just Plain Notes Newsletter:* Members receive our frequent e-mail newsletters full of expert info on how to succeed in the music business, profiles of members successes and advice, opportunities to develop your career and first-person networking contacts to help you along the way. (Note: We send this out 2-3 times/month via e-mail only.)
 • *Just Plain Mentors:* We have some of the friendliest expert educators, writers, artists and industry folks in the business who volunteer their time as part of our Mentor Staff. Included

are John and JoAnn Braheny, Jason Blume, Harriet Schock, Pat and Pete Luboff, Derek Sivers, Jodi Krangle, Holly Figueroa, Steve Seskin, Alan O'Day, Walter Egan, Sara Light, Danny Arena, Barbara Cloyd, Michael Laskow, Janet Fisher, Anne Leighton, Mark Keefner, Valerie DeLaCruz, Karen Angela Moore, Ben McLane, Jack Perricone, Pat Pattison, Mark Baxter, Josh Whitmore, Harold Payne, Joey Arreguin, John Beland, Susan Gibson, Art Twain and many others.

● *JPFolks.com Website:* Our home page serves as your pathway to the resources and members of the group worldwide. With message boards, lyric feedback forums, featured members music, member profiles, member contact listings, member links pages, chapter homepages, demographics information, our Internet radio station and all the back issues of our newsletter, "Just Plain Notes."

● *Just Plain Folks/Radio Free Virgin Channel:* We have partnered with our friends at Radio Free Virgin on a channel playing our members music 24/7. This network is among the largest in the world and our channel gives exposure to our members' music to millions of RFV's listeners via the Internet. All music is selected by the staff of Just Plain Folks directly from music submitted from our membership.

● *Roadtrips:* We regularly tour the US and Canada, hosting showcases, workshops and friendly member gatherings in each city we visit. We provide opportunities for all our members, at all levels and welcome everyone to our events. Most events are free of charge.

● *Music Awards:* Just Plain Folks has one of the largest and most diverse Member Music Awards programs in the world. The most recent awards involved over 7,500 albums and 100,000 songs in over 35 genres. Music Award nominees and winners receive featured performance slots at showcases around the world throughout the year. Awards are given out at the end of a special ceremony and awards show. Current submission instructions can be found on the website.

Membership requests are accepted year-round. "To become a member, simply send an e-mail to join@jpfolks.com with the words 'I Want To Join Just Plain Folks.' In the e-mail, include your name, address, website (if applicable) and phone number for our files." There are currently no membership fees.

Tips: "Our motto is 'We're All In This Together!'"

N KNOXVILLE SONGWRITERS ASSOCIATION, P.O. Box 603, Knoxville TN 37901. (865)588-0934. E-mail: greatsongs@yahoo.com. **Contact:** Dana Correll, Newsletter Editor. President: Richard McKee. Estab. 1982. Serves songwriters of all ages. "Some have been members since 1982, others are beginners. Members must be interested in learning the craft of songwriting. Not only a learning organization but a support group of songwriters who wants to learn what to do with their song after it has been written. We open doors for aspiring writers. The primary benefit of membership is to supply information to the writer on how to write a song. Many members have received major cuts." Offers showcases, instruction, lectures, library, newsletter, performance opportunities, evaluation services and workshops. Applications accepted year-round. Membership fee: $30/year.

☑ THE LAS VEGAS SONGWRITERS ASSOCIATION, P.O. Box 42683, Las Vegas NV 89116-0683. (702)223-7255. Website: www.lasvegassongwriters.com. **Contact:** Betty Kay Miller, president. Secretary: Barbara Jean Smith. Estab. 1980. "We are an educational, nonprofit organization dedicated to improving the art and craft of the songwriter. We want members who are serious about their craft. We want our members to respect their craft and to treat it as a business. Members must be at least 18 years of age. We offer quarterly newsletters, monthly information meetings, workshops three times a month and quarterly seminars with professionals in the music business. We provide support and encouragement to both new and more experienced songwriters. We critique each song

---

⬛ ⊕ SENDING TO A COUNTRY other than your own? Be sure to send International Reply Coupons (IRCs) instead of stamps for replies or return of your materials.

or lyric that's presented during workshops, we make suggestions on changes—if needed. We help turn amateur writers into professionals. Several of our songwriters have had their songs recorded on both independent and major labels." Dues: $30/year.

☑ **LOS ANGELES MUSIC NETWORK**, P.O. Box 8934, Universal City CA 91618-8934. (818)769-6095. E-mail: info@lamn.com. Website: www.lamn.com. **Contact:** Che Wang, membership director. Estab. 1988. "Ours is an association of music industry professionals, i.e., people who work at music companies, in publishing, management, entertainment law, etc. Members are ambitious and interested in advancing their careers. LAMN is an association created to promote career advancement, communication and continuing education among music industry professionals and top executives. LAMN sponsors industry events and educational panels held bi-monthly at venues in the Los Angeles area." Offers instruction, newsletter, lectures, seminars, music industry job listings, career counseling, résumé publishing, mentor network, résumé resource guide and many professional networking opportunities. See our website for current job listings and a calendar of upcoming events. Applications accepted year-round. Annual membership fee is $95 (subject to change without notice).

LOUISIANA SONGWRITERS ASSOCIATION, P.O. Box 80425, Baton Rouge LA 70898-0425. (504)443-5390. E-mail: zimshah@aol.com. Website: www.lasongwriters.org. **Contact:** Connie Zimmerman, membership coordinator. Serves songwriters. "LSA was organized to educate songwriters in all areas of their trade, and promote the art of songwriting in Louisiana. LSA is honored to have a growing number of songwriters from other states join LSA and fellowship with us. LSA membership is open to people interested in songwriting, regardless of age, musical ability, musical preference, ethnic background, etc. "This year marks our 20th anniversary and also a new direction for our organization. Our group is now driven by special projects (short term), which are coordinated and implemented by our membership. This arms our members with the knowledge and experience necessary to succeed within the industry." LSA offers competitions, lectures, library, newsletter, directory, marketing, performance opportunities, workshops, discounts on various music-related books and magazines, discounts on studio time, and we are developing a service manual that will contain information on music related topics, such as copyrighting, licensing, etc." Also offers regular showcases in Baton Rouge and New Orleans. General membership dues: $25/year, 45/2 years.

▟ **MANITOBA AUDIO RECORDING INDUSTRY ASSOCIATION (MARIA)**, 407-100 Arthur St., Winnipeg, Manitoba R3B 1H3 Canada. (204)942-8650. Fax: (204)942-1555. E-mail: info@manaudio.mb.ca. Website: www.manaudio.mb.ca. **Contact:** Hal Brolund, member services/office coordinator. Estab. 1987. Organization consists of "songwriters, producers, agents, musicians, managers, retailers, publicists, radio, talent buyers, media, record labels, etc. (no age limit, no skill level minimum). Must have interest in the future of Manitoba's sound recording industry." The main purpose of MARIA is to foster growth in all areas of the Manitoba music industry primarily through education, promotion and lobbying. Offers newsletter, lectures, directory of Manitoba's music industry, workshops and performance opportunities; also presents demo critiquing sessions and comprehensive member discount program featuring a host of participating Manitoba businesses. MARIA is also involved with the Prairie Music Weekend festival, conference and awards show. Applications accepted year-round. Membership fee: $50 (Canadian funds).

MEET THE COMPOSER, 2112 Broadway, Suite 505, New York NY 10023. (212)787-3601. Fax: (212)787-3745. E-mail: mtrevino@meetthecomposer.org. Website: www.meetthecomposer.org. Estab. 1974. "Meet The Composer serves composers working in all styles of music, at every career stage, through a variety of grant programs and information resources. A nonprofit organization, Meet The Composer raises money from foundations, corporations, individual patrons and government sources and designs programs that support all genres of music—from folk, ethnic, jazz, electronic, symphonic, and chamber to choral, music theater, opera and dance. Meet The Composer awards grants for composer fees to non-profit organizations that perform, present, or commission original works. This is not a membership organization; all composers are eligible for support. Meet The Composer was founded in 1974 to increase artistic and financial opportunities for composers by fostering the creation, performance, dissemination, and appreciation of their music." Offers grant programs and information services. Deadlines vary for each grant program.

MEMPHIS SONGWRITERS' ASSOCIATION, 4500 Summer Ave., Suite #127, Memphis TN 38122. (901)577-0906. E-mail: admin@memphissongwriters.com. Website: www.memphissong writers.com. **Contact:** Dennis Burroughs, president. Estab. 1973. "MSA is a nonprofit songwriters organization serving songwriters nationally. Our mission is to dedicate our services to promote, advance, and help songwriters in the composition of music, lyrics and songs; to work for better conditions in our profession; and to secure and protect the rights of MSA songwriters. We also supply copyright forms. We offer critique sessions for writers at our monthly meetings. We also have monthly open mic songwriters night to encourage creativity, networking and co-writing. We host an annual songwriter's seminar and an annual songwriter's showcase, as well as a bi-monthly guest speaker series, which provide education, competition and entertainment for the songwriter. In addition, our members receive a bimonthly newsletter to keep them informed of MSA activities, demo services and opportunities in the songwriting field." Annual fee: $50.

MISSOURI SONGWRITERS ASSOCIATION, INC., 693 Green Forest Dr., Fenton MO 63026. Phone/fax: (636)343-4765. **Contact:** John G. Nolan, Jr., president. Serves songwriters and musicians. No eligibility requirements. "The MSA (a non-profit organization founded in 1979) is a tremendously valuable resource for songwriting and music business information outside of the major music capitals. Only with the emphasis on education can the understanding of craft and the utilization of skill be fully realized and in turn become the foundation for the ultimate success of MSA members. Songwriters gain support from their fellow members when they join the MSA, and the organization provides 'strength in numbers' when approaching music industry professionals. As a means toward its goals the organization offers: (1) an extremely informative newsletter; (2) Songwriting Contest; prizes include CD and/or cassette release of winners, publishing contract, free musical merchandise and equipment, free recording studio time, plaque or certificate; (3) St. Louis Original Music Celebration featuring live performances, recognition, showcase, radio simulcast, videotape for later broadcast and awards presentation; (4) seminars on such diverse topics as creativity, copyright law, brainstorming, publishing, recording the demo, craft and technique, songwriting business, collaborating, etc.; (5) workshops including song evaluation, establishing a relationship with publishers, hit song evaluations, the writer versus the writer/artist, the marriage of collaborators, the business side of songwriting, lyric craft, etc.; (6) services such as collaborators referral, publisher contracts, consultation, recording discounts, musicians referral, library, etc. The Missouri Songwriters Association belongs to its members and what a member puts into the organization is returned dynamically in terms of information, education, recognition, support, camaraderie, contacts, tips, confidence, career development, friendships and professional growth." Due to various circumstances, some functions or services occasionally may not be active or available. Applications accepted year-round. Tax deductible dues: $30/year.

MUSICIANS CONTACT, P.O. Box 788, Woodland Hills CA 91365. (818)888-7879. Fax: (818)227-5919. E-mail: muscontact@aol.com. Website: www.musicianscontact.com. **Contact:** Sterling, president. Estab. 1969. "The primary source of paying jobs for musicians and vocalists nationwide. Job opportunities arrive by phone and e-mail and are posted daily on the Internet and a 24 hour hotline. Also offers exposure to the music industry for solo artists and complete acts seeking representation."

NASHVILLE SONGWRITERS ASSOCIATION INTERNATIONAL (NSAI), 1701 W. End Ave., 3rd Floor, Nashville TN 37203. (615)256-3354 or (800)321-6008. Fax: (615)256-0034. E-mail: nsai@nashvillesongwriters.com. Website: www.nashvillesongwriters.com. Executive Director: Barton Herbison. Purpose: a not-for-profit service organization for both aspiring and professional songwriters in all fields of music. Membership: Spans the United States and several foreign countries. Songwriters may apply in one of four annual categories: Active ($100—for songwriters who have at least one song contractually signed to a publisher affiliated with ASCAP, BMI or SESAC); Associate ($100—for songwriters who are not yet published or for anyone wishing to support songwriters); Student ($80—for full-time college students or for students of an accredited senior high school); Professional ($100—for songwriters who derive their primary source of income from songwriting or who are generally recognized as such by the professional songwriting community); Foreign ($75— for Active, Associate, and Student members residing outside the US). Membership benefits: music industry information and advice, song evaluations by mail, quarterly newsletter, access to industry professionals through weekly Nashville workshop and several annual events, regional workshops, use of office facilities, discounts on books and discounts on NSAI's three annual events. There are also "branch" workshops of NSAI. Workshops must meet certain standards and are accountable to NSAI. Interested coordinators may apply to NSAI.

 NASHVILLE SONGWRITERS ASSOCIATION INTERNATIONAL-DETROIT, P.O. Box 26044, Fraser MI 48026. (586)493-7643. Fax: (810)498-8636. E-mail: senecal@earthlink.net. **Contact:** Terri Senecal, coordinator. Estab. 1967. Serves songwriters, musicians, artists and beginners. "Members are from Detroit with interests in country, pop, rock and R&B. The main purpose of this organization is to educate songwriters, artists and musicians in the craft of songwriting." NSAI offers song critique services, instruction, and monthly workshops on the first Tuesday of each month. Applications accepted year-round. Membership fee: $100/year.

NATIONAL ACADEMY OF POPULAR MUSIC (NAPM), 330 W. 58th St., Suite 411, New York NY 10019-1827. (212)957-9230. Fax: (212)957-9227. E-mail: 73751.1142@compuserve.com. Website: www.songwritershalloffame.org. **Contact:** Bob Leone, projects director. Managing Director: April Anderson. Estab. 1969. "The majority of our members are songwriters, but also on NAPM's rolls are music publishers, producers, record company executives, music attorneys, and lovers of popular music of all ages. Professional members are affiliated with ASCAP, BMI and/or SESAC; or are employed by music industry firms. Associate membership, however, merely requires a completed application and $25 dues. NAPM was formed to determine a variety of ways to celebrate the songwriter (e.g., induction into the Songwriters' Hall of Fame). We also provide educational and networking opportunities to our members through our workshop and showcase programs." Offers newsletter, workshops, performance opportunities, monthly networking meetings with industry pros and scholarships for excellence in songwriting. Applications accepted year-round. Membership fee: $25.
Tips: "Our priority at this time is to locate a site for the re-establishment of the Songwriters' Hall of Fame Museum in New York City."

NATIONAL ACADEMY OF SONGWRITERS (NAS). E-mail: nassong@aol.com. Website: www.nassong.org.
   • The National Academy of Songwriters and Songwriters Guild of America have merged. National Academy of Songwriter's no longer exists as an organization. Also see the Songwriters Guild of America listing in this section.

 THE NATIONAL ASSOCIATION OF COMPOSERS/USA (NACUSA), P.O. Box 49256, Barrington Station, Los Angeles CA 90049. (310)541-8213. Fax: (310)544-1413. E-mail: bia@flash.net. **Contact:** Marshall Bialosky, president. Estab. 1932. Serves songwriters, musicians and classical composers. "We are of most value to the concert hall composer. Members are serious music composers of all ages and from all parts of the country, who have a real interest in composing, performing, and listening to modern concert hall music. The main purpose of our organization is to perform, publish, broadcast and write news about composers of serious concert hall music—mostly chamber and solo pieces. Composers may achieve national notice of their work through our newsletter and concerts, and the fairly rare feeling of supporting a non-commercial music enterprise dedicated to raising the musical and social position of the serious composer." Offers competitions, lectures,

FOR EXPLANATIONS OF THESE SYMBOLS,
SEE THE INSIDE FRONT AND BACK COVERS OF THIS BOOK.

performance opportunities, library and newsletter. Applications accepted year-round. Membership fee: $20; $40 for Los Angeles, San Francisco, Philadelphia, Tidewater VA, Baton Rouge and New York chapter members.

Tips: "99% of the money earned in music is earned, or so it seems, by popular songwriters who might feel they owe the art of music something, and this is one way they might help support that art. It's a chance to foster fraternal solidarity with their less prosperous, but wonderfully interesting classical colleagues at a time when the very existence of serious art seems to be questioned by the general populace."

N. NATIONAL MUSIC DAY FOUNDATION, 132 W. Main St., Aspen CO 81611. (970)920-2101. Fax: (970)925-5847. Website: www.nationalmusicday.org. **Contact:** Sharon Hope, director. Estab. 2001. "The purpose of the National Music Day Foundation is to create and coordinate a national day of recognition and appreciation of music." Offers performance opportunities.

☑ NATIONAL SOCIETY OF MEN AND WOMEN OF THE MUSIC BUSINESS (WOMB), P.O. Box 5170, Beverly Hills CA 90209-5170. (323)464-4300. Fax: (323)467-8468. E-mail: luckyjaq@aol.com. Website: www.YuleJam.org. **Contact:** Director. Estab. 1996. "WOMB is a non-profit organization of top music industry professionals keeping music education and dreams alive for kids who attend inner-city high schools and community organizations around the U.S. Music industry professionals are encouraged to participate and make a difference in a child's life!" Programs include "WOMB's School Music Network": top music industry professionals volunteer 2-3 hours to visit inner-city high schools; "WOMB's Music for Music": organizes music instrument and material donation drives for schools through corporate sponsorships and events; Yule Jam, a charity concert and music instrument drive with proceeds going to local school music departments. Offers corporate sponsorships, events, performance opportunities and an e-mail newsletter. Future programs include afterschool music programs, college scholarships and special events. Volunteers, music instrument, material donations and corporate sponsorships accepted year-round.

☑ NORTH FLORIDA CHRISTIAN MUSIC WRITERS ASSOCIATION, P.O. Box 61113, Jacksonville FL 32236. (904)786-2372. E-mail: justsongs@aol.com or sueannray@hotmail.com. Website: www.christiansongwriter.com. **Contact:** Jackie Hand, president. Estab. 1974. "Members are people from all walks of life who promote Christian music—not just composers or performers, but anyone who wants to share today's message in song with the world. No age limit. Anyone interested in promoting Christian music is invited to join. If you are talented in several areas you might be asked to conduct a training session or workshop. Your expertise is wanted and needed by our group. The group's purpose is to serve God by using our God-given talents and abilities and to assist our fellow songwriters, getting their music in the best possible form to be ready for whatever door God chooses to open for them concerning their music. Members' works are included in song-books published by our organization—also biographies." Offers competitions, performance opportunities, field trips, instruction, newsletter, workshops and critiques. This year we offer a new website featuring song clips by members as well as a short bio. Also featured is a special "Memorial Members" list honoring deceased members by keeping their music alive. The one time fee of $100 to place loved ones on the list includes a song clip on our website and entry privileges in our songwriting contest. Applications accepted year-round. Membership fee: $15/year ($20 for outside US), $20 for husband/wife team ($25 for outside US). Make checks payable to Jackie Hand.

Tips: "If you are serious about your craft, you need fellowship with others who feel the same. A Christian songwriting organization is where you belong if you write Christian songs. We are now in a position to offer Sound Trax of your original music. Contact Winston Miller at #14 Blanding Blvd., Orange Park FL 32073 for prices. Phone him at (904)276-5022 or fax (904)276-2840."

NORTHERN CALIFORNIA SONGWRITERS ASSOCIATION, 1724 Laurel St., Suite 120, San Carlos CA 94070. (650)654-3966. Fax: (650)654-2156, or (800)FORSONG (California and Nashville only). E-mail: info@ncsasong.org. Website: www.ncsasong.org. **Contact:** Ian Crombie, executive director. Serves songwriters and musicians. Estab. 1979. "Our 1,200 members are lyricists and composers from ages 16-80, from beginners to professional songwriters. No eligibility requirements. Our purpose is to provide the education and opportunities that will support our writers in creating and marketing outstanding songs. NCSA provides support and direction through local networking and input from Los Angeles and Nashville music industry leaders, as well as valuable marketing opportunities. Most songwriters need some form of collaboration, and by being a member they are exposed to other writers, ideas, critiquing, etc." Offers annual Northern California Songwriting Conference, "the largest event in northern California. This 2-day event held in September features 16 seminars, 50 screening sessions (over 1,200 songs listened to by industry profesionals) and a sunset concert with hit songwriters performing their songs." Also offers monthly visits from major publishers, songwriting classes, competitions, seminars conducted by hit songwriters ("we sell audio tapes of our seminars—list of tapes available on request"), mail-in song-screening service for members who cannot attend due to time or location, a monthly newsletter, monthly performance opportunities and workshops. Applications accepted year-round. Dues: $40/year, student; $75/year, regular membership; $150/year, pro-membership; $250/year, contributing membership.

Tips: "NCSA's functions draw local talent and nationally recognized names together. This is of a tremendous value to writers outside a major music center. We are developing a strong songwriting community in Northern California. We serve the San Jose, Monterey Bay, East Bay, San Francisco and Sacramento areas and we have the support of some outstanding writers and publishers from both Los Angeles and Nashville. They provide us with invaluable direction and inspiration."

☑ **OKLAHOMA SONGWRITERS & COMPOSERS ASSOCIATION**, 105 S. Glenn English, Cordell OK 73632. E-mail: arfnannie@hotmail.com. Website: www.oksongwriters.com. **Contact:** Ann Wilson, membership. Estab. 1983. Serves songwriters, musicians, professional writers and amateur writers. "A nonprofit, all-volunteer organization sponsored by Rose State College providing educational and networking opportunities for songwriters, lyricists, composers and performing musicians. All styles of music. We sponsor major workshops, open-mic nights, demo critiques and the *OSCA News*. Throughout the year we sponsor contests and original music showcases." Applications accepted year-round. Membership fee: $25 for new members, $15 for renewal, $15 for out of state newsletter only.

☑ **OPERA AMERICA**, 1156 15th St., NW, Suite 810, Washington DC 20005-1704. (202)293-4466. Fax: (202)393-0735. E-mail: frontdesk@operaamerica.org. Website: www.operaamerica.org. Membership Services Manager: Ronni Levine. Membership Assistant: Warren Lee. Estab. 1970. Members are composers, librettists, musicians and opera/music theater producers. "OPERA America maintains an extensive library of reference books and domestic and foreign music periodicals, and the most comprehensive operatic archive in the United States. OPERA America draws on these unique resources to supply information to its members." Offers conferences. Publishes online database of opera/music theater companies in the US and Canada, online directory of opera and musical performances world-wide and US, and a online directory of new works created and being developed by current-day composers and librettists, to encourage the performance of new works. Applications accepted year-round. Publishes 40-page news bulletin 10 times/year. Membership fee is on a sliding scale.

OUTMUSIC, P.O. Box 376, Old Chelsea Station, New York NY 10113-0376. (212)330-9197. E-mail: info@outmusic.com. Website: www.outmusic.com. **Contact:** Jon Gilber Leavitt, membership director. Estab. 1990. "OUTMUSIC is comprised of gay men, lesbians, bisexuals and transgenders. They represent all different musical styles from rock to classical. Many are writers of original material. We are open to all levels of accomplishment—professional, amateur, and interested industry people. The only requirement for membership is an interest in the growth and visibility of music and lyrics created by the LGBT community. We supply our members with support and networking opportunities. In addition, we help to encourage artists to bring their work 'OUT' into the world." Offers newsletter, lectures, workshops, performance opportunities, networking, industry leads and monthly open mics. Sponsors Outmusic Awards. Applications accepted year-round. For membership information go to www.outmusic.com.

Tips: "OUTMUSIC has spawned *The Gay Music Guide*, The Gay and Lesbian American Music Awards (GLAMA), several compilation albums and many independent recording projects."

OZARK NOTEWORTHY SONGWRITERS ASSOCIATION, INC., 2303 S. Luster, Springfield MO 65804. (417)883-3385. **Contact:** Betty Hickory, president. Vice President: Mary Hickory. Estab. 1992. Purpose is to help songwriters find co-writers, keep writers updated about what is selling in the music world and explain the copyright law. Offers newsletter and workshops. Applications accepted year-round. Membership fee: $30/year. "Members will be notified of meeting dates as to when and where."

PACIFIC MUSIC INDUSTRY ASSOCIATION. (604)873-1914. E-mail: info@pmia.org. Website: www.pmia.org. Estab. 1990. Serves "mostly young adults and up from semi-pro to professional. Writers, composers, performers, publishers, engineers, producers, broadcasters, studios, retailers, manufacturers, managers, publicists, entertainment lawyers and accountants, etc. Must work in some area of music industry." The main purpose of this organization is "to promote B.C. music and music industry; stimulate activity in B.C. industry; promote communication and address key issues." Offers competitions, newsletters, ongoing professional development and directory for the BC music industry. Applications accepted year-round. Membership fee: $50 Canadian (plus 7% GST).

PACIFIC NORTHWEST SONGWRITERS ASSOCIATION, P.O. Box 98564, Seattle WA 98198. (206)824-1568. E-mail: pnsapals@hotmail.com. "PNSA is a nonprofit organization, serving the songwriters of the Puget Sound area since 1977. Members have had songs recorded by national artists on singles, albums, videos and network television specials. Several have released their own albums and the group has done an album together. For only $45 per year, PNSA offers monthly workshops, a quarterly newsletter and direct contact with national artists, publishers, producers and record companies. New members are welcome and good times are guaranteed. And remember, the world always needs another great song!"

PITTSBURGH SONGWRITERS ASSOCIATION, 523 Scenery Dr., Elizabeth PA 15037. E-mail: psa@trfn.clpgh.org. Website: trfn.clpgh.org/psa. **Contact:** Van Stragand, president. Estab. 1983. "We are a non-profit organization dedicated to helping its members develop and market their songs. Writers of any age and experience level welcome. Current members are from 20s to 50s. All musical styles and interests are welcome. Our organization wants to serve as a source of quality material for publishers and other industry professionals. We assist members in developing their songs and their professional approach. We provide meetings, showcases, collaboration opportunities, instruction, industry guests, library and social outings. Annual dues: $25. We have no initiation fee. Prospective members are invited to attend two free meetings. Interested parties please call Van Stragand at (412)751-9584."

POP RECORD RESEARCH, 10 Glen Ave., Norwalk CT 06850. Director: Gary Theroux. Estab. 1962. Serves songwriters, musicians, writers, researchers and media. "We maintain archives of materials relating to music, TV and film, with special emphasis on recorded music (the hits and hitmakers 1877-present): bios, photos, reviews, interviews, discographies, chart data, clippings, films, videos, etc." Offers library and clearinghouse for accurate promotion/publicity to biographers, writers, reviewers, the media. Offers programming, annotation and photo source for reissues or retrospective album collections on any artist (singers, songwriters, musicians, etc.), also music consultation services for film or television projects. "There is no charge to include publicity, promotional or biographical materials in our archives. Artists, writers, composers, performers, producers, labels and publicists are always invited to add or keep us on their publicity/promotion mailing list with career data, updates, new releases and reissues of recorded performances, etc. Fees are assessed only for reference use by

MARKET CONDITIONS are constantly changing! If you're still using this book and it is 2004 or later, buy the newest edition of *Songwriter's Market* at your favorite bookstore or order directly from Writer's Digest Books at (800)289-0963.

researchers, writers, biographers, reviewers, etc. Songwriters and composers (or their publicists) should keep or put us on their publicity mailing lists to ensure that the information we supply others on their careers, accomplishments, etc. is accurate and up-to-date."

☑ **PORTLAND SONGWRITERS ASSOCIATION**, P.O. Box 16985, Portland OR 97292-0985. (503)727-9072. E-mail: info@pdxsongwriters.org. Website: www.pdxsongwriters.org. Estab. 1991. **Contact:** JC Tubbs, President. "The PSA is a nonprofit organization providing education and opportunities that will assist writers in creating and marketing their songs. The PSA offers an annual National Songwriting Contest, monthly workshops, songwriter showcases, special performance venues, quarterly newsletter, mail-in critique service, discounted seminars by music industry pros." Annual dues: $35. Newsletter only: $15 (no eligibility requirements).
Tips: "Although most of our members are from the Pacific Northwest, we offer services that can assist songwriters anywhere. Our goal is to provide information and contacts to help songwriters grow artistically and gain access to publishing, recording and related music markets. For more information, please call, write or e-mail."

RHODE ISLAND SONGWRITERS' ASSOCIATION (RISA), 159, Elmgrove Ave., Providence RI 02906. (401)461-6153. E-mail: rhodysong@aol.com. Website: http://members.aol.com/rhodysong. Co-Chairs: Deb DoVale and David Fontaine. Regional Secretary: Michael Khouri. Estab. 1993. "Membership consists of novice and professional songwriters. RISA provides opportunities to the aspiring writer or performer as well as the established regional artists who have recordings, are published and perform regularly. The only eligibility requirement is an interest in the group and the group's goals. Non-writers are welcome as well." The main purpose is to "encourage, foster and conduct the art and craft of original musical and/or lyrical composition through education, information, collaboration and performance." Offers instruction, newsletter, lectures, workshops, performance opportunities and evaluation services. Applications accepted year-round. Membership fee: $25/year. "The group holds twice monthly critique sessions; twice monthly performer showcases (one performer featured) at a local coffeehouse; songwriter showcases (usually 6-8 performers); weekly open mikes; and a yearly songwriter festival called 'Hear In Rhode Island,' featuring approximately 50 Rhode Island acts, over two days."

☑ **SAN FRANCISCO FOLK MUSIC CLUB**, 885 Clayton, San Francisco CA 94117. (415)661-2217. E-mail: sffolk@aol.com. Website: www.sffmc.org. **Contact:** SF FMC. Serves songwriters, musicians and anyone who enjoys folk music. "Our members range from ages 2 to 80. The only requirement is that members enjoy, appreciate and be interested in sharing folk music. As a focal point for the San Francisco Bay Area folk music community, the SFFMC provides opportunities for people to get together to share folk music, and the newsletter *The Folknik* disseminates information. We publish two songs by our members an issue (six times a year) in our newsletter, our meetings provide an opportunity to share new songs, and at our camp-outs there are almost always songwriter workshops." Offers library, newsletter, informal performance opportunities, annual free folk festival, social outings and workshops. Applications accepted year-round. Membership fee: $7/year.

SESAC INC., 421 W. 54th St., New York NY 10019. (212)586-3450; 55 Music Square East, Nashville TN 37203. (615)320-0055. Website: sesac.com. Chief Operating Officer: Bill Velez. Coordinator-Writer/Publisher Relations: Mandy Reilly. SESAC is a selective organization taking pride in having a repertory based on quality rather than quantity. Serves writers and publishers in all types of music who have their works performed by radio, television, nightclubs, cable TV, etc. Purpose of organization is to collect and distribute performance royalties to all active affiliates. As a SESAC affiliate, the individual may obtain equipment insurance at competitive rates. Tapes are reviewed upon invitation by the Writer/Public Relations dept.

THE SINGER SONGWRITER INFORMATION LINE, 9 Music Square S. #145, Nashville TN 37203. Information Hotline: (800)345-2694. Office: (615)792-2222. Fax: (615)792-1509. E-mail: cjstarlit@aol.com. **Contact:** C.J. Reilly, owner. Estab. 1988. Purpose is to give advice over a free 1-800 number to anyone who writes music. All callers will receive a free publisher's list. Offers instruction, newsletter, performance opportunities and evaluation services.

Tips: "We are a Nashville-based company. When people call, we try to answer questions regarding music publishing and record production."

N: SOCIETY OF COMPOSERS & LYRICISTS, 400 S. Beverly Dr., Suite 214, Beverly Hills CA 90212. (310)281-2812. Fax: (310)284-4861. E-mail: administrator@filmscore.org. Website: www .filmscore.org. The professional nonprofit trade organization for members actively engaged in writing music/lyrics for films or TV, or are students of film composition or songwriting. Primary mission is to advance the interests of the film and TV music community. Offers instruction, lectures, and annual conference. Applications accepted year-round. Membership fee: $135 Full Membership (composers, lyricists, songwriters—film/TV music credits must be submitted); $85 Associate/Student Membership; $135 Sponsor Membership (music editors, music supervisors, music attorneys, etc.).

SOCIETY OF COMPOSERS, AUTHORS AND MUSIC PUBLISHERS OF CANADA/ SOCIÉTÉ CANADIENNE DES AUTEURS, COMPOSITEURS ET ÉDITEURS DE MUSI- QUE (SOCAN), Head Office: 41 Valleybrook Dr., Toronto, Ontario M3B 2S6 Canada. (800)55- SOCAN. Fax: (416)445-7108. E-mail: socan.ca. Website: www.socan.ca. CEO: André LeBel. Vice President, Quebec & Atlantic Division and National Licensing: France Lafleur. Vice President, West Coast Division and National Member Services: Kent Sturgeon. The Society licenses public perform- ance of music and distributes performance royalties to composers, lyricists, authors and music publish- ers. ASCAP, BMI and SESAC license the public performance of SOCAN's repertoire in the US.

SODRAC INC., 759 Victoria Square, Suite 420, Montreal, Quebec H2Y 2J7 Canada. (514)845- 3268. Fax: (514)845-3401. E-mail: sodrac@sodrac.com. Website: www.sodrac.com. **Contact:** Chan- tel Beandoin, membership department (author, composer and publisher) or Diane Lamarre, member- ship department (visual artist and rights owner). Estab. 1985. "Sodrac was founded in 1985 on the initiative of songwriters and composers in order to manage the reproduction rights of authors, compos- ers and publishers of music works. In September 1997, a new department was created specifically to manage the rights of visual artists. SODRAC represents the musical repertoire of about 83 countries and more than 5,000 Canadian members." Serves those with an interest in songwriting and music publishing no matter what their age or skill level is. "Members must have written or published at least one musical work that has been reproduced on an audio (CD, cassette, LP) or audio-visual support (TV, video). The new member will benefit of a society working to secure his reproduction rights (mechanicals) and broadcast mechanicals." Applications accepted year-round. "There is no membership fee or annual dues. SODRAC retains a commission currently set at 10% for amounts collected in Canada and 5% for amounts collected abroad. SODRAC is the only Reproduction Rights Society in Canada where both songwriters and music publishers are represented, directly and equally."

THE SONGWRITERS ADVOCATE (TSA), 18 Dortmund Circle, Rochester NY 14624. (716)266-0679. E-mail: jerrycme@aol.com. **Contact:** Jerry Englerth, director. "TSA is a nonprofit educational organization that is striving to fulfill the needs of the songwriter. We offer opportunities for songwriters which include song evaluation workshops to help songwriters receive an objective critique of their craft. TSA evaluates tapes and lyric sheets via the mail. We do not measure success on a monetary scale, ever. It is the craft of songwriting that is the primary objective. If a songwriter can arm himself with knowledge about the craft and the business, it will increase his confidence and effectiveness in all his dealings. However, we feel that the songwriter should be willing to pay for professional help that will ultimately improve his craft and attitude." One-time membership dues: $15. Must be member to receive discounts or services provided.

SONGWRITERS & LYRICISTS CLUB, % Robert Makinson, P.O. Box 605, Brooklyn NY 11217- 0605. **Contact:** Robert Makinson, founder/director. Estab. 1984. Serves songwriters and lyricists. Gives information regarding songwriting: creation of songs, reality of market and collaboration. Only requirement is the ability to write lyrics or melodies. Beginners are welcome. The primary benefits of membership for the songwriter are opportunities to collaborate and assistance with creative aspects and marketing of songs through publications and advice. Offers newsletter and assistance with lead sheets and demos. *Songwriters & Lyricists Club Newsletter* will be mailed semi-annually to members.

Other publications, such as *Climbing the Songwriting Ladder* and *Roster of Songs by Members* are mailed to new members upon joining. Applications accepted year-round. Dues: $35/year; remit to Robert Makinson. Write with SASE for more information.

Tips: "Plan and achieve realistic goals. We specialize in country, gospel and novelty songs and lyrics."

SONGWRITERS AND POETS CRITIQUE, P.O. Box 21065, Columbus OH 43221. (614)777-0326. E-mail: spcmusic@yahoo.com. Website: www.songwriterscritique. **Contact:** Brian Preston. Estab. 1985. Serves songwriters, musicians, poets, lyricists and performers. Meets second and fourth Friday of every month to discuss club events and critique one another's work. Offers seminars and workshops with professionals in the music industry. Has established Nashville contacts. "We critique mail-in submissions from long-distance members. Our goal is to provide support and opportunity to anyone interested in creating songs or poetry." Applications are accepted year-round. Annual dues: $30.

N **SONGWRITERS ASSOCIATION OF NOVA SCOTIA**, P.O. Box 272, Dartmouth, Nova Scotia B2Y 3Y3 Canada. Phone/fax: (902)465-3174. E-mail: bkershaw@supercity.ns.ca. Website: sans.nf.ca. President: Becky Kershaw. Vice President: Al Gallagher. Estab. 1989. Members are professionals, apprentices and hobbyists, age 18-98. "Must be a songwriter living in Atlantic Canada; however, we do accept membership from songwriters who reside in the province part time." Purpose is to create and promote a support base for Nova Scotia songwriters through workshops, song circles, concerts and networking opportunities. Offers newsletter, membership directory, workshops, performance opportunities and evaluation services. Applications accepted year-round. Membership fee: $20.

SONGWRITERS ASSOCIATION OF WASHINGTON, PMB 106-137, 4200 Wisconsin Ave. NW, Box 100-137, Washington DC 20016. (301)654-8434. E-mail: membership@SAW.org. Website: www.SAW.org. Estab. 1979. "SAW is a nonprofit organization operated by a volunteer board of directors. It is committed to providing its members opportunities to learn more about the art of songwriting, to learn more about the music business, to perform in public, and to connect with fellow songwriters. SAW sponsors various events to achieve this goals: workshops, open mics, song swaps, and showcases. In addition, SAW organizes the Mid-Atlantic Song Contest open to entrants nationwide each year; since 1982 there have been eighteen competitions. (Contest information 800-218-5996). As well as maintaining a website, SAW publishes *SAW Notes*, a bimonthly newsletter for members containing information on upcoming local events, members news, contest information, and articles of interest. Joint introductory membership with the Washington Area Music Association is available at a savings. Use the contact information above for membership inquiries."

THE SONGWRITERS GUILD OF AMERICA(SGA), 1560 Broadway, Suite #1306, New York NY 10036. (212)768-7902. Fax: (212)768-9048. E-mail: songnews@aol.com. Website: www.songwriters.org. New Jersey: 1500 Harbor Blvd, Weehawken NJ 07087-6732. (201)867-7603. West Coast: 6430 Sunset Blvd., Suite 705, Hollywood CA 90028, (323)462-1108. Fax: (323)462-5430; Nashville: 1222 16th Ave. S., Nashville TN 37203, (615)329-1782.

• Also see the listings for The Songwriters Guild Foundation and The Songwriters Guild of America in the Workshops & Conferences section.

President: Rick Carnes. Executive Director: Lewis M. Bachman. National Projects Director: George Wurzbach. West Coast Regional Director: Aaron Meza. Southern Regional Director: Rundi Ream. Estab. 1931. "The Songwriters Guild of America (SGA) is a voluntary songwriter association run by and for songwriters. It is devoted exclusively to providing songwriters with the services and activities they need to succeed in the business of music. The preamble to the SGA constitution charges the board to take such lawful actions as will advance, promote and benefit the profession. Services

REFER TO THE GEOGRAPHIC INDEX (at the back of this book) to find listings of companies by state, as well as foreign listings.

of SGA cover every aspect of songwriting including the creative, administrative and financial." A full member must be a published songwriter. An associate member is any unpublished songwriter with a desire to learn more about the business and craft of songwriting. The third class of membership comprises estates of deceased writers. Membership dues: $85-450/regular; $70/associate; $70-400/ estate. Regular and estate members pay annual dues on a graduated scale, determined by the amount of royalties collected by SGA in the previous year on behalf of that member. The Guild contract is considered to be the best available in the industry, having the greatest number of built-in protections for the songwriter. The Guild's Royalty Collection Plan makes certain that prompt and accurate payments are made to writers. The ongoing Audit Program makes periodic checks of publishers' books. For the self-publisher, the Catalogue Administration Program (CAP) relieves a writer of the paperwork of publishing for a fee lower than the prevailing industry rates. The Copyright Renewal Service informs members a year in advance of a song's renewal date. Other services include workshops in New York and Los Angeles, free Ask-A-Pro sessions with industry pros, critique sessions, collaborator service and newsletters. In addition, the Guild reviews your songwriter contract on request (Guild or otherwise); fights to strengthen songwriters' rights and to increase writers' royalties by supporting legislation which directly affects copyright; offers a group medical and life insurance plan; issues news bulletins with essential information for songwriters; provides a songwriter collaboration service for younger writers; financially evaluates catalogues of copyrights in connection with possible sale and estate planning; operates an estates administration service; and maintains a nonprofit educational foundation (The Songwriters Guild Foundation)."

SONGWRITERS OF OKLAHOMA, P.O. Box 4121, Edmond OK 73083-4121. (405)348-6534. **Contact:** Harvey Derrick, president. Offers information on the music industry: reviews publishing/ artist contracts, where and how to get demo tapes produced, presentation of material to publishers or record companies, royalties and copyrights. Also offers information on the craft of songwriting: cowriters, local songwriting organizations, a written critique of lyrics, songs and compositions on tapes as long as a SASE is provided for return of critique. A phone service is available to answer any questions writers, composers or artists may have. "Calls accepted between 10 and 11 pm CST Tuesday through Thursday only." All of these services are provided at no cost; there is no membership fee. A SASE must be included with all submissions/inquiries.

☑ **SONGWRITERS OF WISCONSIN INTERNATIONAL**, P.O. Box 1027, Neenah WI 54957-1027. (920)722-0122. E-mail: sowtoner@aol.com. **Contact:** Tony Ansems, president. Workshops Coordinator: Mike Heath. Estab. 1983. Serves songwriters. "Membership is open to songwriters writing all styles of music. Residency in Wisconsin is recommended but not required. Members are encouraged to bring tapes and lyric sheets of their songs to the meetings, but it is not required. We are striving to improve the craft of songwriting in Wisconsin. Living in Wisconsin, a songwriter would be close to any of the workshops and showcases offered each month at different towns. The primary value of membership for a songwriter is in sharing ideas with other songwriters, being critiqued and helping other songwriters." Offers competitions (contest entry deadline: May 15), field trips, instruction, lectures, newsletter, performance opportunities, social outings, workshops and critique sessions. Applications accepted year-round. Membership dues: $25/year.
Tips: "Critique meetings every last Thursday of each month, January through October, 7 p.m.-10 p.m. at The Hampton Inn, 350 N. Fox River Dr., Appleton, WI."

SONGWRITERS RESOURCE NETWORK, PMB 135, 6327-C SW Capitol Hill, Portland OR 97201-1937. E-mail: info@SongwritersResourceNetwork.com. Website: www.SongwritersResource Network.com. **Contact:** Steve Cahill, president. Estab. 1998. "For songwriters and lyricists of every kind, from beginners to advanced." No eligibility requirements. "Purpose is to provide free information to help songwriters develop their craft, market their songs, and learn about songwriting opportunities." Sponsors the annual Great American Song Contest, offers marketing tips and website access to music industry contacts. "We provide leads to publishers, producers and other music industry professionals." Visit website or send SASE for more information.

SOUTHEAST TEXAS BLUEGRASS MUSIC ASSOCIATION, 130 Willow Run, Lumberton TX 77657-9210. (409)755-0622. E-mail: PickNBow@aol.com. **Contact:** Edy Mathews, editor. Estab.

1976. Members are musicians and listeners of all ages. Purpose is to promote bluegrass, gospel and old time music. Offers newsletter and monthly shows which are free. Applications accepted year-round. Membership fee: $12/year.

☑ **SOUTHERN SONGWRITERS GUILD, INC.**, P.O. Box 52656, Shreveport LA 71136-2656. (318)424-7000. E-mail: songguild@aol.com. Website: www.southernsongwritersguild.org. **Contact:** Cathy Williams, president. Estab. 1984. "The purpose of the Southern Songwriters Guild is to promote the art and craft of songwriting through all available educational and charitable means and to endeavor to uphold its objectives in harmony with society. SSG hosts an annual Awards Banquet that features winners of our 'Song of the Year' contest that provides cash prizes; and to induct new members into 'SSG Songwriters Hall of Fame', who may have local or regional roots in either heritage or career development. SSG has monthly Board and General Membership meetings aimed toward education. Fundraiser benefits are occasionally conducted for specific needs. A small educational scholarship program is infrequently available for those who meet certain criteria for need and purpose. SSG offers an opportunity to network or collaborate with other songwriters and songwriter organizations and encourages dual or multi-memberships with other organizations whose purposes are consistent with those of SSG. A newsletter is distributed to the membership and to non-member related entities. Performance opportunities, open mic sessions, songwriting workshops, clinics, annual family picnic, Christmas party and song critiques are additional functions. Please send SASE for membership application or other information." Applications accepted year-round. Membership fee: $30/year, $25 for each additional family member, $100 for organization or institution.

SOUTHWEST VIRGINIA SONGWRITERS ASSOCIATION, P.O. Box 698, Salem VA 24153. Phone/fax: (540)586-5000. E-mail: kirasongs@aol.com. **Contact:** Greg Trafidlo. Estab. 1981. 80 members of all ages and skill all levels, mainly country, folk, gospel, contemporary and rock but other musical interests too. "The purpose of SVSA is to increase, broaden and expand the knowledge of each member and to support, better and further the progress and success of each member in songwriting and related fields of endeavor." Offers performance opportunities, evaluation services, instruction, newsletter, workshops, monthly meetings and monthly newsletter. Application accepted year-round. Membership fee: $18/year.

SPARS (Society of Professional Audio Recording Services), 364 Clove Dr., Memphis TN 38117-4009. 1-800-771-7727 or (901)821-9111. Fax: (901)682-9177. E-mail: spars@spars.com. Website: www.spars.com. **Contact:** Larry Lipman, executive director. Estab. 1979. Members are recording studios, manufacturers of audio recording equipment, individual project studio owners, mastering engineers, regular audio engineers, providers of services to the audio recording industry. Call for application/brochure describing membership. Non-profit professional organization focused on the business issues of multimedia facility ownership; management and operations; and educational networking and communion. Offers newsletter, publications, workshops, evaluation services and SPARS test. Applications accepted year-round. Call or write for information.

THE TENNESSEE SONGWRITERS INTERNATIONAL, P.O. Box 2664, Hendersonville TN 37077-2664. TSA Hotline: (615)969-5967. (615)824-4555. Fax: (615)822-2048. E-mail: asktsai@aol.com Website: www.clubnashville.com/tsai.htm. Executive Director: Jim Sylvis. Serves songwriters. "Our membership is open to all ages and consists of both novice and experienced professional songwriters. The only requirement for membership is a serious interest in the craft and business of songwriting. Our main purpose and function is to educate and assist the songwriter, both in the art/craft of songwriting and in the business of songwriting. In addition to education, we also provide an opportunity for camaraderie, support and encouragement, as well a chance to meet co-writers. We also critique each others' material and offer suggestions for improvement, if needed. We offer the following to our members: Informative monthly newsletters; 'Pro-Rap'—once a month a key person from the music industry addresses our membership on their field of specialty. They may be writers, publishers, producers and sometimes even the recording artists themselves; 'Pitch-A-Pro'—we schedule a publisher, producer or artist who is currently looking for material to come to our meeting and listen to songs pitched by our members; 'Legends Night'—several times a year, a 'legend' in the music business will be our guest speaker. Annual Awards Dinner—honoring the most accomplished of our TSAI membership during the past year; Tips—letting our members know who is recording and how to get their songs to the right people. Workshops are held at Belmont University, Wedgewood Ave., Nashville TN in the Massey Business Center Building, Room 20013 on Wednesday evenings from 7-9 p.m. Other activities—a TSAI summer picnic, parties throughout the year, and opportunities to participate in music industry-related charitable events." Applications accepted year-round. Membership runs for one year from the date you join. Membership fee is $50/year.

N. TEXAS ACCOUNTANTS & LAWYERS FOR THE ARTS, 1540 Sul Ross, Houston TX 77006-4730. (713)526-4876 or (800)526-TALA. Fax: (713)526-1299. E-mail: info@talarts.org. Website: www.talarts.org. **Contact:** Jane S. Lowery, executive director. Estab. 1979. TALA's members include accountants, attorneys, museums, theatre groups, dance groups, actors, artists, musicians and filmmakers. Our members are of all age groups and represent all facets of their respective fields. TALA is a nonprofit organization that provides pro bono legal and accounting services to income-eligible artists from all disciplines and to nonprofit arts organizations. TALA also provides mediation services for resolving disputes as a low cost-nonadversarial alternative to litigation. Offers newsletter, lectures, library and workshops. Applications accepted year-round. Membership fee for artists: $25. **Tips:** TALA's speakers program presents low-cost seminars on topics such as The Music Business, Copyright and Trademark, and The Business of Writing. These seminars are held annually at a location in Houston. TALA's speaker's program also provides speakers for seminars by other organizations.

TEXAS MUSIC OFFICE, P.O. Box 13246, Austin TX 78711. (512)463-6666. (512)463-4114. E-mail: music@governor.state.tx.us. Website: www.governor.state.tx.us/music. **Contact:** Casey Monahan, director. Estab. 1990. "The main purpose of the Texas Music Office is to promote the Texas music industry and Texas music, and to assist music professionals around the world with information about the Texas market. The Texas Music Office serves as a clearinghouse for Texas music industry information using their seven databases: Texas Music Industry (5,800 Texas music businesses in 94 music business categories); Texas Music Events (700 Texas music events); Texas Talent Register (900 Texas recording artists); Texas Radio Stations (733 Texas stations); U.S. Record Labels; Classical Texas (detailed information for all classical music organizations in Texas); and International (450 foreign businesses interested in Texas music). Provides referrals to Texas music businesses, talent and events in order to attract new business to Texas and/or to encourage Texas businesses and individuals to keep music business in-state. Serves as a liaison between music businesses and other government offices and agencies. Publicizes significant developments within the Texas music industry." Publishes the *Texas Music Industry Directory* (see the Publications of Interest section for more information).

N. TORONTO MUSICIANS' ASSOCIATION, 15 Gervais Dr., Suite 500, Toronto, Ontario M3C 1Y3 Canada. (416)421-1020. Fax: (416)421-7011. Executive Director: Bill Skolnick. Executive Assistant: Nancy Neal. Estab. 1887. Serves musicians—*All* musical styles, background, areas of the industry. "Must be a Canadian citizen, show proof of immigration status, or have a valid work permit for an extended period of time." The purpose of this organization is "to unite musicians into one organization, in order that they may, individually and collectively, secure, maintain and profit from improved economic, working and artistic conditions." Offers newsletter. Applications accepted year-round. Joining fee is $225.

VOLUNTEER LAWYERS FOR THE ARTS, 1 E. 53rd St., 6th Floor, New York NY 10022. (212)319-ARTS (2787), ext. 1 (Monday-Friday 9:30-12 and 1-4 EST). Fax: (212)752-6575. E-mail: vlany@vlany.org or vlany@vlany.org. Website: www.vlany.org. **Contact:** Elena M. Paul, esq., executive director. Estab. 1969. Serves songwriters, musicians and all performing, visual, literary and fine

---

FOR BOOKS ON THE CRAFT AND BUSINESS of songwriting, check out the website for Writer's Digest Books at www.writersdigest.com.

arts artists and groups. Offers legal assistance and representation to eligible individual artists and arts organizations who cannot afford private counsel and a mediation service. VLA sells publications on arts-related issues and offers educational conferences, lectures, seminars and workshops. In addition, there are affiliates nationwide who assist local arts organizations and artists. Call for information.
Tips: "VLA now offers a monthly copyright seminar, 'Copyright Basics,' for songwriters and musicians as well as artists in other creative fields."

WASHINGTON AREA MUSIC ASSOCIATION, 1101 17th St. NW, Suite 1100, Washington DC 20036. (202)338-1134. Fax: (703)393-1028. E-mail: dcmusic@wamadc.com. Website: www.wamadc.com. **Contact:** Mike Schreibman, president. Estab. 1985. Serves songwriters, musicians and performers, managers, club owners and entertainment lawyers; "all those with an interest in the Washington music scene." The organization is designed to promote the Washington music scene and increase its visibility. Its primary value to members is its seminars and networking opportunities. Offers lectures, newsletter, performance opportunities and workshops. WAMA sponsors the annual Washington Music Awards (The Wammies) and The Crosstown Jam or annual showcase of more than 300 artists at 60 venues in the DC area. Applications accepted year-round. Annual dues: $30.

WOMEN IN MUSIC, P.O. Box 441, Radio City Station, New York NY 10101. (212)459-4580. Website: www.womeninmusic.org. **Contact:** Gina Andriolo, president. Estab. 1985. Members are professionals in the business and creative areas: record company executives, managers, songwriters, musicians, vocalists, attorneys, recording engineers, agents, publicists, studio owners, music publishers and more. Purpose is to support, encourage and educate as well as provide networking opportunities. Offers newsletter, lectures, workshops, performance opportunities and business discounts. Presents annual "Touchstone Award" luncheon helping to raise money to support other organizations and individuals through WIM donations and scholarships. Applications accepted year-round. Membership fee: Professional $75; Associate $45; Student $25.

Workshops & Conferences

For a songwriter just starting out, conferences and workshops can provide valuable learning opportunities. At conferences, songwriters can have their songs evaluated, hear suggestions for further improvement and receive feedback from music business experts. They are also excellent places to make valuable industry contacts. Workshops can help a songwriter improve his craft and learn more about the business of songwriting. They may involve classes on songwriting and the business, as well as lectures and seminars by industry professionals.

Get the Most From a Conference

Before You Go:
- **Save money**. Sign up early for a conference and take advantage of the early registration fee. Don't put off making hotel reservations either—the conference will usually have a block of rooms reserved at a discounted price.
- **Become familiar with all the pre-conference literature**. Study the maps of the area, especially the locations of the rooms in which your meetings/events are scheduled.
- **Make a list of three to five objectives you'd like to obtain**, e.g., what you want to learn more about, what you want to improve on, how many new contacts you want to make.

At the Conference:
- **Budget your time**. Label a map so you know where, when and how to get to each session. Note what you want to do most. Then, schedule time for demo critiques if they are offered.
- **Don't be afraid to explore new areas**. You are there to learn. Pick one or two sessions you wouldn't typically attend. Keep your mind open to new ideas and advice.
- **Allow time for mingling**. Some of the best information is given after the sessions. Find out "frank truths" and inside scoops. Asking people what they've learned at the conference will trigger a conversation that may branch into areas you want to know more about, but won't hear from the speakers.
- **Attend panels**. Panels consist of a group of industry professionals who have the capability to further your career. If you're new to the business you can learn so much straight from the horse's mouth. Even if you're a veteran, you can brush up on your knowledge or even learn something new. Whatever your experience, the panelist's presence is an open invitation to approach him with a question during the panel or with a handshake afterwards.
- **Collect everything**: especially informational materials and business cards. Make notes about the personalities of the people you meet to later remind you who to contact and who to avoid.

After the Conference:
- **Evaluate**. Write down the answers to these questions: Would I attend again? What were the pluses and minuses, e.g., speakers, location, food, topics, cost, lodging? What do I want to remember for next year? What should I try to do next time? Who would I like to meet?
- **Write a thank-you letter** to someone who has been particularly helpful. They'll remember you when you later solicit a submission.

Each year, hundreds of workshops and conferences take place all over the country. Songwriters can choose from small regional workshops held in someone's living room to large national conferences such as South by Southwest in Austin, Texas, which hosts more than 6,000 industry people, songwriters and performers. Many songwriting organizations—national and local—host workshops that offer instruction on just about every songwriting topic imaginable, from lyric writing and marketing strategy to contract negotiation. Conferences provide songwriters the chance to meet one on one with publishing and record company professionals and give performers the chance to showcase their work for a live audience (usually consisting of industry people) during the conference. There are conferences and workshops that address almost every type of music, offering programs for songwriters, performers, musical playwrights and much more.

This section includes national and local workshops and conferences with a brief description of what they offer, when they are held and how much they cost to attend. Write or call any that interest you for further information. To find out what workshops or conferences take place in specific parts of the country, see the Geographic Index at the end of this book.

APPEL FARM ARTS AND MUSIC FESTIVAL, P.O. Box 888, Elmer NJ 08318. (856)358-2472. Fax: (856)358-6513. E-mail: appelarts@aol.com. Website: www.appelfarm.org. **Contact:** Sean Timmons, artistic director. Estab. Festival: 1989; Series: 1970. "Our annual open air festival is the highlight of our year-round Performing Arts Series which was established to bring high quality arts programs to the people of South Jersey. Festival includes acoustic and folk music, blues, etc." Past performers have included Indigo Girls, John Prine, Ani DiFranco, Randy Newman, Nanci Griffith, Shawn Colvin, Arlo Guthrie and Madeleine Peyroux. In addition, our Country Music concerts have featured Toby Keith, Joe Diffie, Ricky Van Shelton, Doug Stone and others. Programs for songwriters and musicians include performance opportunities as part of Festival and Performing Arts Series. Programs for musical playwrights also include performance opportunities as part of Performing Arts Series. Festival is a one-day event held in June, and Performing Arts Series is held year-round. Both are held at the Appel Farm Arts and Music Center, a 176-acre farm in Southern New Jersey. Up to 20 songwriters/musicians participate in each event. Participants are songwriters, individual vocalists, bands, ensembles, vocal groups, composers, individual instrumentalists and dance/mime/movement. Participants are selected by demo tape submissions. Applicants should send a press packet, demonstration tape and biographical information. Application materials accepted year round. Faculty opportunities are available as part of residential Summer Arts Program for children, July/August.

☑ **ARCADY MUSIC FESTIVAL**, P.O. Box 780, Bar Harbor ME 04609. Phone/fax: (207)288-2141. E-mail: arcady@arcady.org. Website: www.arcady.org. **Contact:** Patricia Ciraulo, executive director. Artistic Director: Masanobu Ikemiya. Estab. 1980. Promotes classical chamber music, chamber orchestra concerts, master classes and a youth competition in Maine. Offers programs for performers. Workshops take place year-round in several towns in Eastern Maine. 30-50 professional, individual instrumentalists participate each year. Performers selected by invitation. "Sometimes we premiere new music by songwriters but usually at request of visiting musician."

☑ **ASCAP MUSICAL THEATRE WORKSHOP**, 1 Lincoln Plaza, New York NY 10023. (212)621-6234. Fax: (212)621-6558. E-mail: mkerker@ascap.com. Website: www.ascap.com. **Contact:** Michael A. Kerker, director of musical theatre. Estab. 1981. Workshop is for musical theatre composers and lyricists only. Its purpose is to nurture and develop new musicals for the theatre. Offers programs for songwriters. Offers programs annually, usually April through May. Event took place in New York City. Six musical works are selected. Others are invited to audit the workshop. Participants are amateur and professional songwriters, composers and musical playwrights. Participants are selected by demo tape submission. Send for application. Deadline: mid-March.

☑ **ASCAP WEST COAST/LESTER SILL SONGWRITER'S WORKSHOP**, 7920 Sunset Blvd., 3rd Floor, Los Angeles CA 90046. (323)883-1000. Fax: (323)883-1049. E-mail: jsimms@ascap.com. Website: www.ascap.com. **Contact:** Jackey Simms, director of repertory/creative affairs. Estab. 1963. Offers programs for songwriters. Offers programs annually. Event takes place mid-January through mid-February. 14 songwriters/musicians participate in each event. Participants are amateur and professional songwriters. Participants are selected by demo tape submission or by invitation. "Send in two songs with lyrics, bio and brief explanation why you'd like to participate." Deadline: November 30.

 ASPEN MUSIC FESTIVAL AND SCHOOL, 2 Music School Rd., Aspen CO 81611. (970)925-3254. Fax: (970)925-5708. E-mail: school@aspenmusic.org. Website: www.aspenmusicfest ival.com. Estab. 1949. Promotes classical music by offering programs for composers, including an advanced master class in composition which meets weekly during the nine-week season. Offers several other music programs as well. School and Festival run June 12 to August 18 in Aspen CO. Participants are amateur and professional composers, individual instrumentalists and ensembles. Send for application. Deadline: February 22. Charges $2,750 for full 9 weeks, $1,725 for one of two 4½ week sessions. Fee: $80 until February 1, $100 after February. Scholarship assistance is available.

 BMI-LEHMAN ENGEL MUSICAL THEATRE WORKSHOP, 320 W. 57th St., New York NY 10019. (212)830-2508. Fax: (212)262-2824. E-mail: jbanks@bmi.com. Website: www.bmi.com. **Contact:** Jean Banks, senior director of musical theatre. Estab. 1961. "BMI is a music licensing company which collects royalties for affiliated writers. We have departments to help writers in jazz, concert, Latin, pop and musical theater writing." Offers programs "to musical theater composers, lyricists and librettists. The BMI-Lehman Engel Musical Theatre Workshops were formed in an effort to refresh and stimulate professional writers, as well as to encourage and develop new creative talent for the musical theater." Each workshop meets 1 afternoon a week for 2 hours at BMI, New York. Participants are professional songwriters, composers and playwrights. "BMI-Lehman Engel Musical Theatre Workshop Showcase presents the best of the workshop to producers, agents, record and publishing company execs, press and directors for possible option and production." Call for application. Tape and lyrics of 3 compositions required with application. "BMI also sponsors a jazz composers workshop. For more information call Burt Korall at (212)586-2000."

BROADWAY TOMORROW PREVIEWS, % Science of Light, Inc., 191 Claremont Ave., Suite 53, New York NY 10027. E-mail: solight@worldnet.att.net. Website: home.att.net/~solight. **Contact:** Elyse Curtis, artistic director. Estab. 1983. Purpose is the enrichment of American theater by nurturing new musicals. Offers series in which composers living in New York city area present scores of their new musicals in concert. 2-3 composers/librettists/lyricists of same musical and 1 musical director/ pianist participate. Participants are professional singers, composers and opera/musical theater writers. Submission is by audio cassette of music, synopsis, cast breakdown, résumé, reviews, if any, acknowledgement postcard and SASE. Participants selected by screening of submissions. Programs are presented in fall and spring with possibility of full production of works presented in concert. Membership fee: $50.

  CANADIAN MUSIC WEEK, 5355 Vail Court, Mississauga, Ontario L5M 6G9 Canada. (905)858-4747. Fax: (905)858-4848. Website: www.cmw.net. **Contact:** Neill Dixon, president. Estab. 1985. Offers annual programs for songwriters, composers and performers. Event takes place mid-March in Toronto. 100,000 public, 300 bands and 1,200 delegates participate in each event. Participants are amateur and professional songwriters, vocalists, composers, bands and instrumentalists.

**FOR EXPLANATIONS OF THESE SYMBOLS,
SEE THE INSIDE FRONT AND BACK COVERS OF THIS BOOK.**

Participants are selected by submitting demonstration tape. Send for application and more information. Concerts take place in 25 clubs and 5 concert halls, and 3 days of seminars and exhibits are provided. Fee: $375 (Canadian).

N CUTTING EDGE MUSIC BUSINESS CONFERENCE, 1524 N. Claiborne Ave., New Orleans LA 70119. (504)945-1800. Fax: (504)945-1873. E-mail: cut_edge@bellsouth.net. Website: www.jass.com/cuttingedge. Executive Producer: Eric L. Cager. Showcase Producer: Nathaniel Franklin. Estab. 1993. "The conference is a five-day international conference which covers the business and educational aspects of the music industry. As part of the conference, the New Works showcase features over 200 bands and artists from around the country and Canada in showcases of original music. All music genres are represented." Offers programs for songwriters and performers. "Bands and artists should submit material for consideration of entry into the New Works showcase." Event takes place late August in New Orleans. 1,000 songwriters/musicians participate in each event. Participants are songwriters, vocalists and bands. Send for application. Deadline: June 1. Fee: $175 general registration; $25 showcase registration. "The Music Business Institute offers a month-long series of free educational workshops for those involved in the music industry. The workshops take place each October. Further information is available via our website."

PETER DAVIDSON'S WRITER'S SEMINAR, P.O. Box 497, Arnolds Park IA 51331. **Contact:** Peter Davidson, seminar presenter. Estab. 1985. "Peter Davidson's Writer's Seminar is for persons interested in writing all sorts of materials, including songs. Emphasis is placed on developing salable ideas, locating potential markets for your work, copyrighting, etc. The seminar is not specifically for writers of songs, but is very valuable to them, nevertheless." Offers programs year-round. One-day seminar, 9:00 a.m.-4:00 p.m. Event takes place on various college campuses. In even-numbered years offers seminars in Minnesota, Iowa, Nebraska, South Dakota, Kansas, Colorado and Wyoming. In odd-numbered years offers seminars in Minnesota, Iowa, Nebraska, South Dakota, Missouri, Illinois, Arkansas and Tennessee. Anyone can participate. Send SASE for schedule. Deadline: day of the seminar. Fee: $40-59. "All seminars are held on college campuses in college facilities—various colleges sponsor and promote the seminars."

N EMERGING ARTISTS & TALENT IN MUSIC (EAT'M) CONFERENCE AND FESTIVAL, 2341A Renaissance Dr., Las Vegas NV 89119. (631)547-0800. Fax: (631)293-3996. E-mail: dbard@pulver.com. Website: www.EAT-M.com. **Contact:** David Bard, director of operations. Founder: Lisa Tenner. Co-director: Sue Shifrin-Cassidy. Estab. 1998. Annual music conference which addresses both recording and touring. Offers programs for songwriters, performers, managers and attorneys. Offers 3 days of educational panels, mentor sessions, continuing legal education, also the 3rd Annual David Cassidy Celebrity Golf Tournament benefitting Special Olympics. The event will be held May 28-31, 2002 at the MGM Grand Hotel and Casino. Participants are amateur and professional songwriters, vocalists, composers and instrumentalists. Participants are selected by showcase submissions. "Register for conference now." Artists will appear on 10 stages on the Las Vegas Strip.

☑ FOLK ALLIANCE ANNUAL CONFERENCE, 962 Wayne Ave., Suite 902, Silver Spring MD 20910. (301)588-8185. Fax: (301)588-8186. E-mail: fa@folk.org. Website: www.folk.org. Estab. 1989. Conference/workshop topics change each year. Conference takes place mid-February and lasts 4 days at a different location each year. 1,500 attendees include artists, agents, arts administrators, print/broadcast media, folklorists, folk societies, merchandisers, presenters, festivals, recording companies, fans, etc. Artists wishing to showcase should contact the office for a showcase application form. Closing date for application is June 1. Application fee is $35 for members, $75 for nonmembers. $200 on acceptance. Additional costs vary from year to year. Housing is separate for the event, scheduled for Feb. 21-24, 2002 in Jacksonville, FL; Feb. 6-9, 2003 in Nashville, TN; Feb. 26-29, 2004 in San Diego, CA; Feb. 24-27, 2005 in Montreal, Quebec Canada.

☑ GENESIUS GUILD, P.O. Box 2213, New York NY 10108-2213. (212)946-5625. E-mail: info@genesiusguild.org. Website: www.genesiusguild.org. **Contact:** Stephen Bishop Seely, artistic director. Estab. 1994. Purpose is to create and develop new musical theatre, opera, dance and other musical performance art. Offers programs for songwriters, composers and musical playwrights. Offers programs year round including stage reading series, workshops, productions, roundtable sessions and cabaret program. Event takes place at various venues in New York City. Participants are professional songwriters, vocalists, composers, bands, musical playwrights and instrumentalists. Participants are selected by demo tape submission. Send tape, synopsis and letter. Series takes place at various venues and theatre spaces with 100-200 seats.

I WRITE THE SONGS, PMB 208, 2250 Justin Rd., Suite 108, Highland Village TX 75077-7164. (972)317-2760. Fax: (972)317-4737. E-mail: info@cqkmusic.com. Website: www.cqkmusic.com. **Contact:** Sarah Marshall, administrative director. Estab. 1996. "I Write the Songs is an on-the-air songwriting seminar. It is a syndicated radio talk show available both on the radio and on the Internet. A detailed description of the program and its hosts, Mary Dawson and Sharon Braxton, can be found on the website. The website address will also link you to the Internet broadcasts and list the radio stations that carry the program. I Write the Songs has been created to inspire and instruct aspiring songwriters of all genres of music in the craft and business of songwriting." Offers programs, including weekly programs on radio and the Internet, for songwriters, composers and performers. "Occasionally we hold competitions. All aspiring songwriters earning less than $5,000 annually from song royalties are eligible." I Write the Songs features "Critique Shows" every 4-6 weeks. Songwriters can submit demos on cassette or CD with typed lyric sheet. Does not return material. Featured songs are selected at random. Writers whose songs are selected for a show will receive a taped copy of the program on which their song is critiqued. Mary Dawson conducts songwriting seminars across the country and internationally. For a list of upcoming seminars, check the website.

KERRVILLE FOLK FESTIVAL, Kerrville Festivals, Inc., P.O. Box 291466, Kerrville TX 78029. (830)257-3600. E-mail: staff@kerrville-music.com. Website: www.kerrville-music.com. **Contact:** Rod Kennedy, producer. Estab. 1972. Hosts 3-day songwriters' school, a 4-day music business school and New Folk concert competition sponsored by *Performing Songwriter* magazine. Festival produced in late spring and late summer. Spring festival lasts 18 days and is held outdoors at Quiet Valley Ranch. 110 or more songwriters participate. Performers are professional songwriters and bands. Participants selected by submitting demo, by invitation only. Send cassette, or CD, promotional material and list of upcoming appearances. "Songwriter and music schools include lunch, experienced professional instructors, camping on ranch and concerts. Rustic facilities. Food available at reasonable cost. Audition materials accepted at above address. These three-day and four-day seminars include noon meals, handouts and camping on the ranch. Usually held during Kerrville Folk Festival, first and second week in June. Write for contest rules, schools and seminars information, and festival schedules. Also establishing a Phoenix Fund to provide assistance to ill or injured singer/songwriters who find themselves in distress. Listen to 'Music from Kerrville' 7 pm, Monday through Friday on www.kerrville-music.com."

LAMB'S RETREAT FOR SONGWRITERS presented by SPRINGFED ARTS, a nonprofit organization, P.O. Box 304, Royal Oak MI 48068-0304. (248)589-1594. Fax: (248)589-3913. E-mail: johndlamb@ameritech.net. Website: www.springfed.org. **Contact:** John D. Lamb, director. Estab. 1995. Offers programs for songwriters on annual basis; November 7-10, 2002 at The Birchwood Inn, Harbor Springs, MI. 60 songwriters/musicians participate in each event. Participants are amateur and professional songwriters. Anyone can participate. Send for application or e-mail. Deadline: day before event begins. Fee: $200-400, includes all meals. Facilities are single/double occupancy lodging with private baths; 2 conference rooms and hospitality lodge. Offers song assignments, songwriting workshops, song swaps, open mic and one-on-one mentoring. Faculty are noted songwriters, such as Michael Smith. Partial scholarships may be available by writing: Blissfest Music Organization, % Jim Gillespie, P.O. Box 441, Harbor Springs, MI 49740. Deadline: day before event.

☑ MANCHESTER MUSIC FESTIVAL, P.O. Box 1165, Manchester Center VT 05255. (802)362-1956. Fax: (802)362-0711. E-mail: mmf@vermontel.net. Website: www.mmfvt.org. **Contact:** Robyn Pruett, managing director. Estab. 1974. Offers classical music education and performances. Summer program for young professional musicians offered in tandem with a professional concert series in the mountains of Manchester, VT. Up to 23 young professionals, age 18 and up, are selected by audition for the Young Artists Program, which provides instruction, performance and teaching opportunities, with full scholarship for all participants. Printable application available on website. Application fee: $40. Commissioning opportunities for new music, and performance opportunities for professional chamber ensembles and soloists for both summer and fall/winter concert series. "Celebrating 28 years of fine music."

☑ **MUSIC BUSINESS SOLUTIONS/CAREER BUILDING WORKSHOPS**, P.O. Box 266, Boston MA 02123-0266. (888)655-8335. E-mail: peter@mbsolutions.com. Website: www.mbsolutions.com. **Contact:** Peter Spellman, director. Estab. 1991. Workshop titles include "How to Succeed in Music Without Overpaying Your Dues," "How to Release an Independent Record" and "Promoting and Marketing Music Toward the Year 2000." Offers programs for music entrepreneurs, songwriters, musical playwrights, composers and performers. Offers programs year-round, annually and bi-annually. Event takes place at various colleges, recording studios, hotels, conferences. 10-100 songwriters/musicians participate in each event. Participants are both amateur and professional songwriters, vocalists, music business professionals, composers, bands, musical playwrights and instrumentalists. Anyone can participate. Call or write (regular or e-mail) for application. Fee: varies. "Music Business Solutions offers a number of other services and programs for both songwriters and musicians including: private music career counseling, business plan development and internet marketing; publication of *Music Biz Insight: Power Reading for Busy Music Professionals*, a bimonthly e-zine chock full of music management and marketing tips and resources. Free subscription with e-mail address."

NASHVILLE MUSIC FESTIVAL, P.O. Box 291827, Nashville TN 37229-1827. (615)252-8202. Fax: (615)321-0384. E-mail: c4promo@aol.com. Website: www.radiocountry.org (festivals). **Contact:** Ambassador Charlie Ray, director. Estab. 2000. Offers 100 booth spaces for makers of instruments, craftspeople, independent record companies, and unsigned artists; seminars by successful music industry professionals; contests; and stages on which to perform. "Nashville record companies big and small are looking for new talent. A lot of them will have talent scouts at the festival. If they see you on stage and like what they see, you could be signed to a recording contract. There will also be a songwriter's stage in 2002." Event takes place May 25-27, 2002. "Complete directions to festival location will be mailed with your tickets and posted on our webpage." Fee: $50, adult 3-day ticket.

NATIONAL ACADEMY OF POPULAR MUSIC SONGWRITING WORKSHOP PROGRAM, 330 W. 58th St. Suite 411, New York NY 10019. (212)957-9230. Fax: (212)957-9227. E-mail: 73751.1142@compuserve.com. Website: www.songwritershalloffame.org. **Contact:** Bob Leone, projects director. Managing Director: April Anderson. Estab. 1969. "For all forms of pop music, from rock to R&B to dance." Offers programs for member lyricists and composers including songwriting workshops (beginning to master levels) and songwriters showcases. "The Abe Olman Scholarship for excellence in songwriting is awarded ($1,200) to a student who has been in our program for at least 4 quarters." Offers programs 3 times/year: fall, winter and spring. Event takes place mid-September to December, mid-January to April, mid-April to July (10 2-3 hour weekly sessions) at New York Spaces, 131 W. 72nd St., New York. Also offer monthly networking meetings with industry pros and biweekly open mics. 50 students involved in 4 different classes. Participants are amateur and professional lyricists and composers. Some participants are selected by submitting demonstration tape (pro-song class), and by invitation (master class). Send for application. Deadline: first week of classes. Annual dues: $25. Sponsors songwriter showcases in March, June, September and December.

☑ **NEMO MUSIC SHOWCASE & CONFERENCE**, Zero Governors Ave. #6, Boston MA 02155. (781)306-0441. Fax: (781)306-0442. E-mail: cavery@nemoboston.com. Website: www.nemoboston.com. **Contact:** Candace Avery, founder/director. Estab. 1996. Music showcase and conference,

REFER TO THE GEOGRAPHIC INDEX (at the back of this book) to find listings of companies by state, as well as foreign listings.

featuring the Boston Music Awards and 3 days/nights of a conference with trade show and more than 200 nightly showcases in Boston. Offers showcases for songwriters. Offers programs annually. Event takes place in April. 1,500 songwriters/musicians participate at conference; 3,000 at awards show; 20,000 at showcases. Participants are professional songwriters, vocalists, composers, bands and instrumentalists. Participants are selected by invitation. Send for application or visit website. Fee: $30.

☑ **THE NEW HARMONY PROJECT**, 613 N. East St., Indianapolis IN 46202. (317)464-1103. Fax: (317)635-4201. Website: www.newharmonyproject.org. **Contact:** Anna D. Shapiro, artistic director. Estab. 1986. Selected scripts receive various levels of development with rehearsals and readings, both public and private. "Our mission is to nurture writers and their life-affirming scripts. This includes plays, screenplays, musicals and TV scripts." Offers programs for musical playwrights. Event takes place in May/June in southwest Indiana. Participants are amateur and professional writers and media professionals. Send for application.

🍁 ☑ **NEW MUSIC WEST**, 1062 Homer St., #300, Vancouver, British Columbia V6B 2W9 Canada. (604)684-9338. Fax: (604)684-9337. E-mail: info@newmusicwest.com. Website: www.new musicwest.com/. Producer: Frank Weipert. Co-Producer: Umeeda Switlow. Estab. 1990. A four day music festival and conference held May each year in Vancouver, B.C. The conference offers songwriter intensive workshops; demo critique sessions with A&R and publishers; information on the business of publishing; master producer workshops: "We invite established hit record producers to conduct three-hour intensive hands-on workshops with 30 young producers/musicians in studio environments. The festival offers songwriters in the round and 250 original music showcases. Largest music industry event in the North Pacific Rim. Entry fee: $20.

☑ **NORFOLK CHAMBER MUSIC FESTIVAL**, September-May address: 165 Elm St., Suite 101, Box 208246, New Haven CT 06520. (203)432-1966. Fax: (203)432-2136. June-August address: Ellen Battell, Stoeckel Estate, Box 545, Norfolk CT 06058. (860)542-3000. Fax: (860)542-3004. E-mail: norfolk@yale.edu. Website: www.yale.edu/norfolk. **Contact:** Deanne E. Chin, operations manager. Estab. 1941. Festival season of chamber music. Offers programs for composers and performers. Offers programs summer only. Approximately 45 fellows participate. Participants are up-and-coming composers and instrumentalists. Participants are selected by following a screening round. Auditions are held in New Haven, CT. Send for application. Deadline: January 16. Fee: $50. Held at the Ellen Battell Stoeckel Estate, the Festival offers a magnificent Music Shed with seating for 1,000, practice facilities, music library, dining hall, laundry and art gallery. Nearby are hiking, bicycling and swimming.

🍁 ☑ **NORTH BY NORTHEAST MUSIC FESTIVAL AND CONFERENCE (NXNE)**, 189 Church St., Lower Level, Toronto, Ontario M5B 1Y7 Canada. (416)863-6963. Fax: (416)863-0828. E-mail: tbird@nxnc.com. Website: www.nxne.com. **Contact:** Travis Bird, festival coordinator. Estab. 1995. "Our festival takes place mid-June at over 25 venues and 2 outdoor stages in downtown Toronto, drawing over 2,000 conference delegates, 400 bands and 50,000 music fans. Musical genres include everything from folk to funk, roots to rock, polka to punk and all points in between, bringing exceptional new talent, media front-runners, music business heavies and music fans from all over the world to Toronto." Participants include emerging and established songwriters, vocalists, composers, bands and instrumentalists. Festival performers are selected by submitting a CD or tape and accompanying press kit. Application forms are available by website or by calling the office. Submission period each year is from November 1 to the third weekend in January. Submissions fee: $20. Conference registration fee: $115-195 (US), $145-250 (Canadian). "Our conference is held at the deluxe Holiday Inn King and the program includes mentor sessions—15-minute one-on-one opportunities for songwriters and composers to ask questions of industry experts. North By Northeast 2002 will be held June 6-8, 2002 and North By Northeast 2003 will be held June 12-14, 2003."

NORTHERN CALIFORNIA SONGWRITERS ASSOCIATION CONFERENCE, 1724 Laurel St., Suite 120, San Carlos CA 94070. (650)654-3966 or (800)FOR-SONG. Fax: (650)654-2156. E-mail: info@ncsasong.org. Website: www.ncsasong.org. **Contact:** Ian Crombie, executive director.

Estab. 1980. "Conference offers opportunity and education. 16 seminars, 50 song screening sessions (1,500 songs reviewed), performance showcases, one on one sessions and concerts." Offers programs for lyricists, songwriters, composers and performers. "During the year we have competitive open mics. Winners go into the playoffs. Winners of the playoffs perform at the sunset concert at the conference." Event takes place second weekend in September at Foothill College, Los Altos Hills, CA. Over 500 songwriters/musicians participate in this event. Participants are songwriters, composers, musical playwrights, vocalists, bands, instrumentalists and those interested in a career in the music business. Send for application. Deadline: September 1. Fee: $90-175. "See our listing in the Organizations section."

NSAI SONG CAMPS, 1701 West End Ave., Nashville TN 37023. 1-800-321-6008 or (615)256-3354. Fax: (615)256-0034. E-mail: claudiayoung@nashvillesongwriters.com. Website: www.nashvill esongwriters.com. **Contact:** Claudia Young, director of song camps and cruises. Estab. 1992. Offers programs strictly for songwriters. Event held 5 times/year at Montgomery Bell State Park about 45 minutes west of Nashville, except for one, which is a cruise ("Song Camp at Sea"). Participants stay, eat meals and hold classes at Montgomery Bell Inn. "We provide most meals and lodging is available. We also bus the campers into town for an evening of music presented by the faculty." Camps are 3 days long, except the cruise, which is 5 days long, with 30-85 participants, depending on the camp. "There are different levels of camps, some having preferred prerequisites. Each camp varies. Please call, e-mail or refer to website. It really isn't about the genre of music, but the quality of the song itself. Song Camp strives to strengthen the writer's vision and skills, therefore producing the better song. Song Camp is known as 'boot camp' for songwriters. It is guaranteed to catapult you forward in your writing! Participants are all aspiring songwriters led by a pro faculty. We do accept lyricists only and composers only with the hopes of expanding their scope." Participants are selected through submission of 2 songs with lyric sheet. Song Camp is open to NSAI members, although anyone can apply and upon acceptance join the organization. There is no formal application form. See website for membership and event information.

NSAI SONGWRITERS SYMPOSIUM, 1701 West End Ave., Nashville TN 37203. (615)256-3354. Fax: (615)256-0034. E-mail: membership@NashvilleSongwriters.com. Website: www.nashvill esongwriters.com. Membership Director: David Mark Thomas. Covers "all types of music. Participants take part in publisher evaluations, as well as large group sessions with different guest speakers." Offers annual programs for songwriters. Event takes place in April in downtown Nashville. 300 amateur songwriters/musicians participate in each event. Send for application. Deadline: March 1. Fee: $225, member; $300, non-member; after March 1: $275 for members; $350 for nonmembers.

ORFORD FESTIVAL, Orford Arts Centre, 3165 Chemim DuParc, Orford, Quebec J1X 7A2 Canada. (819)843-3981. E-mail: arts.orford@sympatico.ca. Website: www.arts-orford.org. **Contact:** Isabelle Langlois, communications coordinator. Artistic Director: Agnes Grossman. Estab. 1951. "Each year, the Orford Arts Centre produces up to 35 concerts in the context of its Music Festival. It receives artists from all over the world in classical and chamber music." Offers master classes for music students, young professional classical musicians and chamber music ensembles. New offerings include master classes for all instruments and voice, opera and jazz workshops. Master classes last 2 months and take place at Orford Arts Centre from the end of June to the middle of August. 350 students participate each year. Participants are selected by demo tape submissions. Send for application. Closing date for application is mid to late March. Check our website for specific dates and deadlines. Scholarships for qualified students. Registration fees $50 (Canadian). Tuition fees $250 (Canadian)/week. Accommodations $250 (Canadian)/week.

MARKETS THAT WERE listed in the 2002 edition of *Songwriters Market* but do not appear this year are listed in the General Index with a notation explaining why they were omitted.

THE SHIZNIT MUSIC CONFERENCE, P.O. Box 1881, Baton Rouge LA 70821. (225)231-2739. Fax: (225)926-5055. E-mail: staffers@bellsouth.net. Website: www.theshiznit.com. Public Relations: Lee Williams. Vice President: Sedrick Hills. Purpose is to provide performance and networking opportunities for a wide variety of music and music related businesses, from urban to country, from blues to zydeco. Showcases, networking, trade shows and seminars offer information about the music industry. Offers programs annually for songwriters and performers. Event takes place June 22-24, 2001 at over 40 venues in Baton Rouge and New Orleans. 400 songwriters/musicians participate in each event. Participants are amateur and professional songwriters, vocalists and bands. Participants are selected by demo tape audition. Fee: $185. Send for application.

☑ **THE SONGWRITERS GUILD FOUNDATION**, 6430 Sunset Blvd., Suite 705, Hollywood CA 90028. (323)462-1108. Fax: (323)462-5430. E-mail: lasga@aol.com. Website: www.songwriterso rg.com. West Coast Regional Director: B. Aaron Meza. Assistant West Coast Regional Director: Eric Morimisato. Nashville office: 1222 16th Ave., S, Nashville TN 37212. (615)329-1782. Fax: (615)329-2623. Southern Regional Director: Rundi Ream. Assistant Southern Regional Director: Kimberly Maiers. E-mail: sganash@aol.com. New York office: 1560 Broadway, Suite 1306, New York NY 10036. (212)768-7902. Fax: (212)768-9048. National Projects Director: George Wurzbach. E-mail: songnews@aol.com. Website: www.songwritersorg.com. Offers a series of workshops with discounts to members. "There is a charge for each songwriting class. Charges vary depending on the class. SGA members receive discounts! Also, the Re-write workshop and Ask-A-Pro/Song Critique are free!"

• Also see the Songwriters Guild of America listing in the Organizations section.

Ask-A-Pro/Song Critique (Hollywood and Nashville offices): SGA members are given the opportunity to present their songs and receive constructive feedback from industry professionals. A great chance to meet industry people, make contacts, ask questions and get your song heard! Free to SGA members. Reservations required. Call for schedule. Free.

Phil Swan Song Styles/Songwriting Workshops (Hollywood and Nashville offices): This 8-week workshop taught by Phil Swann, Dreamworks SKG staff writer, is perfect for those writers who want to become better songwriters in the country, pop, and rock genres as well as more savvy about the changing marketplaces. Fee.

Special Seminars and Workshops: Other special seminars have been presented by such industry professionals as Dale Kawashima, John Braheny and Dr. George Gamez. Fee.

Building a Songwriting Career: A 3-day workshop for songwriters, musicians and recording artists, etc. to help them discover how they can establish a career in the exciting world of songwriting. Features SGA professional songwriters and music business executives in panel discussions about intellectual property, creativity, the craft and business of songwriting and more. Fee.

Re-Write Workshop (Hollywood office): (Hollywood office)Conducted by Michael Allen. Songwriters will have the chance to have their songs critiqued by their peers with an occasional guest critique. Free.

Harriet Schock Songwriting Workshop (Hollywood office): A 10-week course consisting of nine lessons which help create a solid foundation for writing songs effortlessly. Fee.

Jai Josefs Writing Music For Hit Songs (Hollywood office): This 10-week course will show songwriters how to integrate the latest chord progressions, melodies, and grooves from all styles of music into their writing.

Song Critique: New York's oldest ongoing song critique. Guild songwriters are invited to either perform their song live or present a cassette demo for feedback. A Guild moderator is on hand to direct comments. Nonmembers may attend and offer comments. Free.

Street Smarts (New York office): Street Smarts is a 3-hour orientation session for new SGA members. It introduces the basics in areas such as: contracts, copyrights, royalties, song marketing and more. The session is free to members and is scheduled whenever there is a minimum of 8 participants.

Pro-Shop: For each of 6 sessions an active publisher, producer or A&R person is invited to personally screen material from professional Guild writers. Participation is limited to 10 writers, and audit of 1 session. Audition of material is required. Coordinator is producer/musician/award winning singer, Ann Johns Ruckert. Fee; $75 (SGA members only).

SGA Week: Held in spring/summer of each year, this is a week of scheduled events and seminars of interest to songwriters at each of SGA's regional offices. Events include workshops, seminars and showcases. For schedule and details contact the SGA office beginning several weeks prior to SGA Week.

SONGWRITERS PLAYGROUND®, 75-A Lake Rd., #366, Congers NY 10920. (845)267-0001. E-mail: heavyhitters@earthlink.net. **Contact:** Barbara Jordan, director. Estab. 1990. "To help songwriters, performers and composers develop creative and business skills through the critically acclaimed programs *Songwriters Playground*®, *The 'Reel' Deal on Getting Songs Placed in Film and Television*, and the *Mind Your Own Business* Seminars. We offer programs year-round. Workshops last anywhere from 2-15 hours. Workshops are held at various venues throughout the United States. Prices vary according to the length of the workshop." Participants are amateur and professionals. Anyone can participate. Send or call for application.

SOUTH BY SOUTHWEST MUSIC AND MEDIA CONFERENCE, P.O. Box 4999, Austin TX 78765. (512)467-7979. Fax: (512)451-0754. E-mail: sxsw@sxsw.com. Website: sxsw.com/sxsw. Estab. 1987. "We have over 1,000 bands perform in over 50 venues over 5 nights featuring every genre of alternative-based music." Offers programs for songwriters and performers. Annual event takes place in March, at the Austin Convention Center, Austin, TX. Participants are songwriters, vocalists, bands, instrumentalists and representatives of almost all areas of the music business. Participants are selected by demo tape audition. Submissions accepted September through mid-November. Fee: $10 early fee; $20 late fee. Application is required. Forms are available by request or on the SXSW website. "We have a mentor program during the conference where participants can have a one-on-one with professionals in the music business. Also of interest to musicians are the SXSW film and interactive/multimedia festivals held the week before the music conference, and the North By Northwest music conference held annually in Autumn in Portland, OR. For more information, see the website."

☑ **THE SWANNANOA GATHERING—CONTEMPORARY FOLK WEEK**, Warren Wilson College, P.O. Box 9000, Asheville NC 28815-9000. (828)298-3434 or (828)771-3761. Fax: (828)299-3326. E-mail: gathering@warren-wilson.edu. Website: www.swangathering.com. Director: Jim Magill. Coordinator: Eric Garrison. "For anyone who ever wanted to make music for an audience, we offer a comprehensive week in artist development, divided into four major subject areas: Songwriting, Performance, Sound & Recording and Vocal Coaching, along with daily panel discussions of other business matters such as promotion, agents and managers, logistics of touring, etc. 2002 staff includes Steve Seskin, Kim and Reggie Harris, Ray Chesna, John Smith, Tena Moyer, Penny Nichols, Mae Robertson, Sloan Wainwright, Eric Garrison, Christine Kane, Tom Paxton, Crow Johnson, Billy Jonas and Doc & Jean Russell. For a brochure or other info contact Jim Magill, Director, The Swannanoa Gathering, at the phone number/address above. Tuition: $340. Takes place last week in July. Housing (including all meals): $260. Annual program of The Swannanoa Gathering Folk Arts Workshops."

UNDERCURRENTS, P.O. Box 94040, Cleveland OH 44101-6040. (216)397-9921. Fax: (216)932-1143. E-mail: music@undercurrents.com. Website: www.undercurrents.com. **Contact:** John Latimer, president. Estab. 1989. A yearly music industry expo with online exposure featuring seminars, trade show, media center and showcases of rock, alternative, metal, folk, jazz and blues music. Offers programs for songwriters, composers, music industry professionals and performers. Dates for Under-

---

MARKET CONDITIONS are constantly changing! If you're still using this book and it is 2004 or later, buy the newest edition of *Songwriter's Market* at your favorite bookstore or order directly from Writer's Digest Books at (800)289-0963.

currents 2001 were May 18-19. Deadline for showcase consideration is February 1. Participants are selected by demo tape, biography and 8×10 photo audition. Send for application. Fee: $25 for 3-day event.

N: WESTERN WIND WORKSHOP IN ENSEMBLE SINGING, 263 W. 86 St., New York NY 10024. (212)873-2848 or (800)788-2187. Fax: (212)873-2849. E-mail: workshops@westernwind.org. Website: www.westernwind.org. **Contact:** William Zuhof, executive producer. Estab. 1981. Participants learn the art of ensemble singing—no conductor, one on-a-part. Workshop focuses on blend, diction, phrasing and production. Offers programs for performers. Limited talent-based scholarship available. Offers programs annually. Takes place June, July and August in the music department at Smith College, Northampton MA. 70-80 songwriters/musicians participate in each event. Participants are amateur and professional vocalists. Anyone can participate. Send for application or register at their website. Workshop takes place in the Smith College music department. Arrangers' works are frequently studied and performed. Also offers additional workshops President's Day weekend in Brattleboro VT and Columbus Day weekend in Woodstock VT.

Retreats & Colonies

This section provides information on retreats and artists' colonies. These are places for creatives, including songwriters, to find solitude and spend concentrated time focusing on their work. While a residency at a colony may offer participation in seminars, critiques or performances, the atmosphere of a colony or retreat is much more relaxed than that of a conference or workshop. Also, a songwriter's stay at a colony is typically anywhere from one to twelve weeks (sometimes longer), while time spent at a conference may only run from one to fourteen days.

Like conferences and workshops, however, artists' colonies and retreats span a wide range. Yaddo, perhaps the most well-known colony, limits its residencies to artists "working at a professional level in their field, as determined by a judging panel of professionals in the field." The Brevard Music Center offers residencies only to those involved in classical music. Despite different focuses, all artists' colonies and retreats have one thing in common: They are places where you may work undisturbed, usually in nature-oriented, secluded settings.

SELECTING A COLONY OR RETREAT

When selecting a colony or retreat, the primary consideration for many songwriters is cost, and you'll discover that arrangements vary greatly. Some colonies provide residencies as well as stipends for personal expenses. Some suggest donations of a certain amount. Still others offer residencies for substantial sums but have financial assistance available.

When investigating the various options, consider meal and housing arrangements and your family obligations. Some colonies provide meals for residents, while others require residents to pay for meals. Some colonies house artists in one main building; others provide separate cottages. A few have provisions for spouses and families. Others prohibit families altogether.

Overall, residencies at colonies and retreats are competitive. Since only a handful of spots are available at each place, you often must apply months in advance for the time period you desire. A number of locations are open year-round, and you may find planning to go during the "off-season" lessens your competition. Other colonies, however, are only available during certain months. In any case, be prepared to include a sample of your best work with your application. Also, know what project you'll work on while in residence and have alternative projects in mind in case the first one doesn't work out once you're there.

Each listing in this section details fee requirements, meal and housing arrangements, and space and time availability, as well as the retreat's surroundings, facilities and special activities. Of course, before making a final decision, send a SASE to the colonies or retreats that interest you to receive their most up-to-date details. Costs, application requirements and deadlines are particularly subject to change.

For More Information

For other listings of songwriter-friendly colonies, see *Musician's Resource* (available from Watson-Guptill Publications, 1695 Oak St., Lakewood NJ 08701, 1-800-451-1741), which not only provides information about conferences, workshops and academic programs but also residencies and retreats. Also check the Publications of Interest section in this book for newsletters and other periodicals providing this information.

■ **BREVARD MUSIC CENTER**, P.O. Box 312, Brevard NC 28712-0312. (828)884-2975. Fax: (828)884-2036. E-mail: bmcadmission@brevardmusic.org. Website: www.brevardmusic.org. **Contact:** Lynn Johnson, admissions coordinator. Estab. 1936. Offers 6-week residencies from the last week in June through the first week of August. Open to professional and student composers, pianists, vocalists and instrumentalists of classical music. A 2-week advanced conducting workshop (orchestral and opera) with David Effron and Gunther Schuller is offered, as well as a collaborative pianist program. 2002 composers in residence are Karel Husa and Dan Locklair. Accommodates 400 at one time. Personal living quarters include cabins. Offers rehearsal, teaching and practice cabins.
Costs: $3,600 for tuition, room and board. Scholarships are available.
Requirements: Call for application forms and guidelines. $50 application fee. Participants are selected by audition or demonstration tape and then by invitation. There are 60 different audition sites throughout the US.

BYRDCLIFFE ARTS COLONY, 34 Tinker St., Woodstock NY 12498. (845)679-2079. Fax: (845)679-4529. E-mail: wguild@ulster.net. Website: www.woodstockguild.org. **Contact:** Carla T. Smith, executive director. Estab. 1991. Offers 1-month residencies June-September. Open to composers, writers and visual artists. Accommodates 10 at one time. Personal living quarters include single rooms, shared baths and kitchen facilities. Offers separate private studio space. Composers must provide their own keyboard with headphone. Activities include open studio, readings, followed by pot luck dinner once a month. The Woodstock Guild, parent organization, offers music and dance performances, gallery exhibits and book signings.
Costs: $600/month. Residents are responsible for own meals and transportation.
Requirements: Send SASE for application forms and guidelines. Accepts inquiries via fax or e-mail. $5 application fee. Submit a score of at least 10 minutes with 2 references, résumé and application.

DORLAND MOUNTAIN ARTS COLONY, P.O. Box 6, Temecula CA 92593. (909)302-3837. Fax: (909)696-2855. E-mail: dorland@ez2.net. Website: www.ez2.net/dorland. **Contact:** Director. Estab. 1979. Offers 1- or 2-month residencies, year-round, on availability. Open to composers, playwrights, writers, visual artists, sculptors, etc. Personal living quarters include 6 individual rustic cottages with private baths and private kitchen facilities. Propane gas is provided for cooking, refrigeration and hot water. Lighting is by kerosene lamps and heat is by wood stoves. There is no electricity. Two Composer studios are equipped with pianos, including 1 concert grand Steinway, and 1 baby grand Chickering.
Costs: $50 non-refundable scheduling fee. Cabin donation: $300 per month.
Requirements: Send SASE for application forms and guidelines. Accepts inquiries via fax or e-mail. Deadline: March 1 and September 1.

DORSET COLONY HOUSE, P.O. Box 510, Dorset VT 05251-0510. (802)867-2223. Fax: (802)867-0144. E-mail: theatre@sover.net. Website: www.theatredirectories.com. **Contact:** John Nassivera, executive director. Estab. 1980. Offers up to 1-month residencies September-November and April-May. Open to writers, composers, directors, designers and collaborators of the theatre. Accommodates 8 at one time. Personal living quarters include single rooms with desks with shared bath and shared kitchen facilities.
Costs: $120/week. Meals not included. Transportation is residents' responsibility.
Requirements: Send SASE for application forms and guidelines. Accepts inquiries via fax or e-mail. Submit letter with requested dates, description of project and résumé of productions.

🌐 ■ **THE TYRONE GUTHRIE CENTRE**, Annaghmakerrig, Newbliss, County Monaghan, Ireland. Phone: (353)(47)54003. Fax: (353)(47)54380. E-mail: thetgc@indigo.ie. Website: www.tyro neguthrie.ie. **Contact:** Sheila Pratschke, director. Estab. 1981. Offers year-round residencies. Artists

REFER TO THE GEOGRAPHIC INDEX (at the back of this book) to find listings of companies by state, as well as foreign listings.

may stay for anything from 1 week to 3 months in the Big House, or for up to 6 months at a time in one of the 5 self-catering houses in the old farmyard. Open to artists of all disciplines. Accommodates 15 at one time. Personal living quarters include bedroom with bathroom en suite. Offers a variety of workspaces. There is a music room for composers and musicians, a large rehearsal and performance space for theatre groups and music ensembles. Activities include informal readings and performances. At certain times of the year it is possible, by special arrangement, to accommodate groups of artists, symposiums, master classes, workshops and other collaborations.

Costs: Artists who are not Irish must pay £760 per week, all found, for a residency in the Big House and £380 per week for one of the self-catering farmyard houses. To qualify for a residency, it is necessary to show evidence of a significant level of achievement in the relevant field.

Requirements: Send SAE and IRC for application forms and guidelines. Accepts inquiries via fax or e-mail. Fill in application form with cv to be reviewed by the board members at regular meetings.

☑ **THE HAMBIDGE CENTER**, P.O. Box 339, Rabun Gap GA 30568-0339. (706)746-5718. Fax: (706)746-9933. E-mail: center@hambidge.org. Website: www.hambidge.org. **Contact:** Peggy McBride, residency director. Estab. 1934 (Center); 1988 (residency). Offers 2-week to 2-month residencies year round. Open to all artists. Accommodates 8 at one time. Personal living quarters include a private cottage with kitchen, bath, living/studio space and bedroom. Offers composer/musical studio equipped with piano. Activities include communal dinners April through November and nightly or periodic sharing of works-in-progress.

Costs: $125/week.

Requirements: Send SASE for application forms and guidelines, or available on website. Accepts inquiries via fax and e-mail. Application fee: $20. Deadlines: November 1 for May to October; May 1 for November to April.

ISLE ROYALE NATIONAL PARK ARTIST-IN-RESIDENCE PROGRAM, 800 E. Lakeshore Dr., Houghton MI 49931-1869. (906)482-0984. Fax: (906)482-8753. E-mail: isro_parkinfo@nps.gov. Website: www.nps.gov/ISRO/. **Contact:** Greg Blust, coordinator. Estab. 1991. Offers 2-3 week residencies from mid-June to mid-September. Open to all art forms. Accommodates 1 artist with 1 companion at one time. Personal living quarters include cabin with solar powered generators for enough electricity for computer use; shared outhouse. A canoe is provided for transportation. Offers a guest house at the site that can be used as a workroom. The artist is asked to contribute a piece of work representative of their stay at Isle Royale, to be used by the park in an appropriate manner. During their residency, artists will be asked to share their experience (1 presentation per week of residency, about 1 hour/week) with the public by demonstration, talk, or other means.

Requirements: Send for application forms and guidelines. Accepts inquiries via fax or e-mail. A panel of professionals from various disciplines, and park representatives will choose the finalists. The selection is based on artistic integrity, ability to reside in a wilderness environment, a willingness to donate a finished piece of work inspired on the island, and the artist's ability to relate and interpret the park through their work.

KALANI OCEANSIDE RETREAT, RR 2 Box 4500, Pahoa-Beach Road HI 96778-9724. (808)965-7828. Fax: (808)965-0527. E-mail: kalani@kalani.com. Website: www.kalani.com. **Contact:** Richard Koob, director. Estab. 1980. Offers 2-week to 2-month residencies. Open to all artists who can verify professional accomplishments. Accommodates 80 at one time. Personal living quarters include private cottage or lodge room with private or shared bath. Full (3 meals/day) dining service, also shared kitchens available. Offers shared studio/library spaces. Activities include opportunity to share works in progress, ongoing yoga, hula and other classes; beach, thermal springs, Volcanos National Park nearby; olympic pool/spa on 113-acre facility.

Cost: $55-105/night lodging with 50% stipend. Meals separate at $29/day. Transportation by rental car from $25/day, Kalani service $50/trip, or taxi $70/trip. 50% discount ("stipend") on lodging only.

Requirements: Send SASE for application forms and guidelines. Accepts inquiries via fax or e-mail. $10 application fee.

☑ **THE MACDOWELL COLONY**, 100 High St., Peterborough NH 03458. (603)924-3886. Fax: (603)924-9142. Website: www.macdowellcolony.org. Admissions Coordinator: Courtney Bethel. Es-

tab. 1907. Offers year-round residencies of up to 2 months (average length is 6 weeks). Open to writers, composers, film/video makers, visual artists, architects and interdisciplinary artists. Personal living quarters include single rooms. Offers private studios on 450-acre grounds.
Cost: None (contributions accepted).
Requirements: Send SASE or visit website for application forms and guidelines. Composers should send 2 clearly reproduced scores, one of which was completed in the last 5 years, along with audiocassette (1 piece per cassette) or both works on 1 CD. Application deadline: January 15, April 15 and September 15.

NORTHWOOD UNIVERSITY ALDEN B. DOW CREATIVITY CENTER, 4000 Whitring Dr., Midland MI 48640-2398. (989)837-4478. Fax: (989)837-4468. E-mail: creativity@nort hwood.edu. Website: www.northwood.edu/abd. **Contact:** Director. Estab. 1979. Offers 10-week summer residencies (mid-June through mid-August). Fellowship Residency is open to individuals in all fields (the arts, humanities or sciences) who have innovative, creative projects to pursue. Accommodates 4 at one time. Each Fellow is given a furnished apartment on campus, complete with 2 bedrooms, kitchen, bath and large living room. Fellows' apartments serve as their work space as well as their living quarters unless special needs are requested.
Cost: $10 application fee. Room and board is provided plus a $750 stipend to be used toward project costs or personal needs. "We look for projects which are innovative, creative, unique. We ask the applicant to set accomplishable goals for the 10-week residency."
Requirements: Send for application information and guidelines. Accepts inquiries via fax or e-mail. Applicants submit 2-page typed description of their project; cover page with name, address, phone numbers plus summary (30 words or less) of project; support materials such as tapes, CDs; personal résumé; facilities or equipment needed; and $10 application fee. Application deadline: December 31 (postmarked).

SITKA CENTER FOR ART & ECOLOGY, P.O. Box 65, Otis OR 97368-0065. (541)994-5485. Fax: (541)994-8024. E-mail: info@sitkacenter.org. Website: www.sithacenter.org. **Contact:** Randall Koch, executive director. Estab. 1971. Offers 4-month residencies in October through January or February through May; shorter residencies are available upon arrangement. Open to artists or naturalists who have earned a BA, BS, BFA and/or MA, MS, MFA, PhD degree, or equivalent professional experience. Personal living quarters include 3 living quarters, each self-contained with a sleeping area, kitchen and bathroom. Offers 4 studios. Workshops or presentations are encouraged; an exhibition/presentation to share residents' works is held in January and May.
Cost: The resident is encouraged to hold an open studio or community outreach program at Sitka one day per month during the residency, exceptions by arrangements with the director. The resident is asked to provide some form of community service on behalf of Sitka.
Requirements: Send SASE for application forms and guidelines. Accepts inquiries via fax. Send completed application with résumé, 2 letters of recommendation, work samples and SASE.

VILLA MONTALVO ARTIST RESIDENCY PROGRAM, P.O. Box 158, Saratoga CA 95071-0158. (408)961-5822. Fax: (408)961-5850. E-mail: kfunk@villamontalvo.org. Website: www.villamo ntalvo.org. **Contact:** Dakin Hart, artist residency director. Estab. 1942. "Offers 1- to 3-month residencies year-round. Open to writers (prose, poetry, playwrights, screen writers, etc.), visual artists, musicians and composers, architects, filmmakers. Residents are provided with fully equipped apartments/cottages, with kitchens and baths. Four to five apartments/cottages have pianos. The composer's apartment has a grand piano. Activities include weekly gatherings of the residents.
Cost: Residencies are free, but artists must provide food, materials and transportation. There are 7 fellowships ($400) awarded to highest ranking artists based on panelist's review of work samples.

FOR BOOKS ON THE CRAFT AND BUSINESS of songwriting, check out the website for Writer's Digest Books at www.writersdigest.com.

Requirements: Send self addressed label and 55¢ postage. Accepts inquiries via fax or e-mail. $20 application fee plus work samples as defined by discipline. Application deadline: March 1 and September 1.

VIRGINIA CENTER FOR THE CREATIVE ARTS, Box VCCA, Sweet Briar VA 24595. (804)946-7236. Fax: (804)946-7239. E-mail: vcca@vcca.com. Website: www.vcca.com. **Contact:** Sheila Gulley Pleasants, director of artists' services. Estab. 1971. Offers residencies year-round, typical residency lasts 1 month. Open to originating artists: composers, writers and visual artists. Accommodates 22 at one time. Personal living quarters include 20 single rooms, 2 double rooms, bathrooms shared with one other person. All meals are served. Kitchens for fellows' use available at studios and residence. Activities include trips in the VCCA van twice a week into town. Fellows share their work regularly. Three studios have pianos.
Cost: No transportation costs are covered. The suggested daily fee is $30 which includes meals.
Requirements: Send SASE for application forms and guidelines or call the above number. Applications are reviewed by a panel of judges. Application fee: $20. Deadline: May 15 for October-January residency; September 15 for February-May residency; January 15 for June-September residency.

☑ **YADDO ARTISTS' COMMUNITY**, P.O. Box 395, Union Ave., Saratoga Springs NY 12866-0395. (518)584-0746. Fax: (518)584-1312. E-mail: yaddo@yaddo.org. Website: www.yaddo.org. **Contact:** Candace Wait, program coordinator. Estab. 1900. Offers residencies of 2 weeks to 2 months, year-round except for a brief 2-3 week period in September. Open to those working at a professional level in their field, as determined by a judging panel of professionals in the field. Accommodates 12-15 in winter, up to 35 in spring and summer at one time. Personal living quarters include private rooms and studios, some with private baths and some with shared baths. All meals are provided; breakfast and dinner are communal; lunches packed in lunch pails. Offers composers' studios equipped with pianos. Several small libraries are available on the grounds; guests have access to a college and municipal library nearby.
Cost: No fees are charged for any services. Limited help with travel expenses available.
Requirements: Send SASE with 57¢ postage for application forms and guidelines. Accepts inquiries via fax or e-mail. $20 non-refundable filing fee, work samples required (2 musical scores and audio cassette of one of the scores) and 2 letters of support sent directly to Yaddo by the sponsors. Deadline: January 15 and August 1.

State & Provincial Grants

Arts councils in the United States and Canada provide assistance to artists (including poets) in the form of fellowships or grants. These grants can be substantial and confer prestige upon recipients; however, **only state or province residents are eligible**. Because deadlines and available support vary annually, query first (with a SASE).

UNITED STATES ARTS AGENCIES

Alabama State Council on the Arts, *201 Monroe St., Montgomery AL 36130-1800. (334)242-4076. E-mail: staff@arts.state.al.us. Website: www.arts.state.al.us.*

Alaska State Council on the Arts, *411 W. Fourth Ave., Suite 1-E, Anchorage AK 99501-2343. (907)269-6610 or (888)278-7424. E-mail: akso_info@eed.state.ak.us. Website: www.aksca.org.*

Arizona Commission on the Arts, *417 W. Roosevelt, Phoenix AZ 85003-1326. (602)255-5882. E-mail: general@arizonaarts.org. Website: www.arizonaarts.org.*

Arkansas Arts Council, *1500 Tower Bldg., 323 Center St., Little Rock AR 72201. (501)324-9766. E-mail: info@arkansasarts.com. Website: www.arkansasarts.com.*

California Arts Council, *1300 I St., Suite 930, Sacramento CA 95814. (916)322-6555 or (800)201-6201. E-mail: cac@cwo.com. Website: www.cac.ca.gov/.*

Colorado Council on the Arts, *750 Pennsylvania St., Denver CO 80203-3699. (303)894-2617. E-mail: coloarts@state.co.us. Website: www.coloarts.state.co.us.*

Connecticut Commission on the Arts, *755 Main St., 1 Financial Plaza, Hartford CT 06103. (860)566-4770. E-mail: artsinfo@ctarts.org. Website: www.ctarts.org.*

Delaware Division of the Arts, *Carvel State Office Building, 820 N. French St., Wilmington DE 19801. (302)577-8278. E-mail: delarts@state.de.us. Website: www.artsdel.org.*

District of Columbia Commission on the Arts & Humanities, *410 Eighth St. NW, 5th Floor, Washington DC 20004. (202)724-5613. E-mail: dcarts@dc.gov. Website: http://dcarts.dc.gov.*

Florida Arts Council, *Division of Cultural Affairs, Florida Dept. of State, 1001 DeSoto Park Dr., Tallahassee FL 32301. (850)487-2980. Website: www.dos.state.fl.us/dca.*

Georgia Council for the Arts, *260 14th St. NW, Suite 401, Atlanta GA 30318-5793. (404)685-2787. E-mail: goarts@gaarts.org. Website: www.gaarts.org.*

Hawaii State Foundation on Culture & Arts, *250 S. Hotel St., 2nd Floor, Honolulu HI 96813. (808)586-0300. E-mail: sfca@sfca.state.hi.us. Website: www.state.hi.us/sfca.*

Idaho Commission on the Arts, *P.O. Box 83720, Boise ID 83720-0008. (208)334-2119 or (800)278-3863. E-mail: mestrada@ica.state.id.us. Website: www2.state.id.us/arts.*

Illinois Arts Council, *100 W. Randolph, Suite 10-500, Chicago IL 60601. (312)814-6750. E-mail: info@arts.state.il.us. Website: www.state.il.us/agency/iac.*

Indiana Arts Commission, *402 W. Washington St., Indianapolis IN 46204-2243. (317)232-1268. E-mail: arts@state.in.us. Website: www.state.in.us/iac.*

Iowa Arts Council, *600 E. Locust, Capitol Complex, Des Moines IA 50319-0290. (515)281-6412. Website: www.culturalaffairs.org/iac.*

Kansas Arts Commission, *700 SW Jackson, Suite 1004, Topeka KS 66603. (785)296-3335. E-mail: KAC@arts.state.ks.us. Website: http://arts.state.ks.us.*

Kentucky Arts Council, *Old Capital Annex, 300 W. Broadway, Frankfort KY 40601-1980. (502)564-3757. E-mail: kyarts@mail.state.ky.us. Website: www.kyarts.org.*

Louisiana State Arts Council, *P.O. Box 44247, Baton Rouge LA 70804-4247. (225)342-8180.*
E-mail: arts@crt.state.la.us. Website: www.crt.state.la.us/arts.

Maine Arts Commission, *193 State St., 25 State House Station, Augusta ME 04333-0025. (207)287-2724.*
E-mail: jan.poulin@state.me.us. Website: www.mainearts.com.

Maryland State Arts Council, *175 West Ostend Street, Suite E, Baltimore MD 21230. (410)767-6555.*
E-mail: tcolvin@mdbusiness.state.md.us. Website: www.msac.org.

Massachusetts Cultural Council, *10 St. James Ave., 3rd Floor, Boston MA 02116-3803. (617)727-3668.*
E-mail: web@art.state.ma.us. Website: www.massculturalcouncil.org.

Michigan Council for Arts & Cultural Affairs, *Dept. of Consumer & Industry Services, 525 W. Ottawa,*
P.O. Box 30004, Lansing, MI 48909. (517)373-1820. E-mail: artsinfo@cis.state.mi.us.
Website: www.commerce.state.mi.us/arts/home.htm.

Minnesota State Arts Board, *Park Square Court, 400 Sibley St., Suite 200, St. Paul MN 55101-1928.*
(651)215-1600. E-mail: msab@state.mn.us. Website: www.arts.state.mn.us.

Mississippi Arts Commission, *239 N. Lamar St., Suite 207, Jackson MS 39201. (601)359-6030.*
E-mail: hedgepet@arts.state.ms.us. Website: www.arts.state.ms.us.

Missouri Arts Council, *111 N. Seventh St., Suite 105, St. Louis MO 63101-2188. (314)340-6845.*
E-mail: moarts@mail.state.mo.us. Website: www.missouriartscouncil.org.

Montana Arts Council, *P.O. Box 202201, Helena MT 59620-2201. (406)444-6430. E-mail: mac@state.mt.us.*
Website: www.art.state.mt.us.

National Endowment for the Arts, *1100 Pennsylvania Ave. NW, Washington DC 20506. (202)682-5400.*
E-mail: webmgr@arts.endow.gov. Website: www.arts.endow.gov.

Nebraska Arts Council, *3838 Davenport St., Omaha NE 68131-2329. (402)595-2122.*
E-mail: cmalloy@nebraskaartscouncil.org. Website: www.nebraskaartscouncil.org.

Nevada State Council on the Arts, *716 N. Curry St., Carson City NV 89701. (775)687-6680.*
E-mail: kjodonne@clan.lib.nv.us. Website: www.dmla.clan.lib.nv.us/docs/arts/

New Hampshire State Council on the Arts, *40 N. Main St., Concord NH 03301-4974. (603)271-2789.*
E-mail: mdurkee@nharts.state.nh.us. Website: www.state.nh.us/nharts.

New Jersey State Council on the Arts, *P.O. Box 306, 225 W. State St., Trenton NJ 08625. (609)292-6130.*
E-mail: njsca@arts.sos.state.nj.us. Website: www.njartscouncil.org.

New Mexico Arts Division, *228 E. Palace Ave., Santa Fe NM 87501. (505)827-6490.*
E-mail: vcastell@oca.state.nm.us. Website: www.nmarts.org.

New York State Council on the Arts, *175 Varick St., 3rd Floor, New York NY 10014. (212)627-6562.*
E-mail: msc@nysca.org. Website: www.nysca.org.

North Carolina Arts Council, *Department of Cultural Resources and Service Center,*
Raleigh NC 27699-4632. (919)733-2111. E-mail: lawson@nemail.net. Website: www.ncarts.org.

North Dakota Council on the Arts, *418 E. Broadway, Suite 70, Bismarck ND 58501-4086. (701)328-3954.*
E-mail: comserv@state.nd.us. Website: www.state.nd.us/arts.

Ohio Arts Council, *727 E. Main St., Columbus OH 43205-1796. (614)466-2613.*
E-mail: shannon.ford@oac.state.oh.us. Website: www.oac.state.oh.us.

Oklahoma Arts Council, *P.O. Box 52001-2001, Oklahoma City OK 73152-2001. (405)521-2931.*
E-mail: okarts@arts.state.ok.us. Website: www.state.ok.us/~arts.

Oregon Arts Commission, *775 Summer St. NE, Suite 200, Salem OR 97301-1284. (503)986-0088.*
E-mail: oregon.artscomm@state.or.us. Website: http://art.econ.state.or.us.

Pennsylvania Council on the Arts, *Room 216, Finance Bldg., Harrisburg PA 17120. (717)787-6883.*
E-mail: mcaszatt@state.pa.us. Website: www.artsnet.org/pca.

Institute of Puerto Rican Culture, *P.O. Box 9024184, San Juan PR 00902-4184. (787)725-5137.*
Website: http://icp.prstar.net.

Rhode Island State Council on the Arts, *83 Park St., 6th Floor, Providence RI 02903. (401)222-3880.*
E-mail: info@risca.state.ri.us. Website: www.risca.state.ri.us.

South Carolina Arts Commission, *1800 Gervais St., Columbia SC 29201. (803)734-8696.*
E-mail: burnette@arts.state.sc.us. Website: www.state.sc.us/arts.

South Dakota Arts Council, *800 Governors Dr., Pierre SD 57501-2294. (605)773-3131. E-mail: sdac@stlib.state.sd.us. Website: www.state.sd.us/deca/sdarts.*

Tennessee Arts Commission, *401 Charlotte Ave., Nashville TN 37243-0780. (615)741-1701. Website: www.arts.state.tn.us.*

Texas Commission on the Arts, *P.O. Box 13406, Austin TX 78711-3406. (512)463-5535. E-mail: front.desk@arts.state.tx.us. Website: www.arts.state.tx.us.*

Utah Arts Council, *617 E. South Temple, Salt Lake City UT 84102-1177. (801)236-7555. E-mail: swadding@arts.state.ut.us. Website: www.dced.state.ut.us/arts.*

Vermont Arts Council, *136 State St., Drawer 33, Montpelier VT 05633-6001. (802)828-3291. E-mail: info@vermontartscouncil.org. Website: www.vermontartscouncil.org.*

Virgin Islands Council on the Arts, *41-42 Norre Gada, P.O. Box 103, St. Thomas VI 00804. (340)774-5984. E-mail: vicouncil@islands.vi. Website: www.nasaa-arts.org/gateway/VI.html.*

Virginia Commission for the Arts, *Lewis House, 2nd Floor, 223 Governor St., Richmond VA 23219-2010. (804)225-3132. E-mail: arts@state.va.us. Website: www.artswire.org/~vacomm/.*

Washington State Arts Commission, *P.O. Box 42675, Olympia WA 98504-2675. (360)753-3860. E-mail: krist@arts.wa.gov. Website: www.arts.wa.gov.*

West Virginia Arts Commission, *Cultural Center, 1900 Kanawha Blvd. E., Charleston WV 25305-0300. (304)558-0220. E-mail: barbie.anderson@wvculture.org. Website: www.wvculture.org.*

Wisconsin Arts Board, *101 E. Wilson St., 1st Floor, Madison WI 53702. (608)266-0190. E-mail: artsboard@arts.state.wi.us. Website: www.arts.state.wi.us.*

Wyoming Arts Council, *2320 Capitol Ave., Cheyenne WY 82002. (307)777-7742. Website: http://wyoarts.state.wy.us.*

CANADIAN PROVINCES ARTS AGENCIES

Alberta Foundation for the Arts, *901 Standard Life Centre, 10405 Jasper Ave., Edmonton, Alberta T5J 4R7. (780)427-6315. E-mail: afa@mcd.gov.ab.ca. Website: www.cd.gov.ab.ca/affta.*

British Columbia Arts Council, *P.O. Box 9819, Stn Prov Govt, Victoria, British Columbia V8W 9W3. (250)356-1718. E-mail: bcartscouncil@gems2.gov.bc.ca. Website: www.bcartscouncil.gov.bc.ca.*

Manitoba Arts Council, *525 - 93 Lombard Ave., Winnipeg, Manitoba R3B 3B1. (204)945-2237. E-mail: info@artscouncil.mb.ca. Website: www.artscouncil.mb.ca.*

New Brunswick Department of Economic Development, Tourism & Culture, *Arts Branch, P.O. Box 6000, Fredericton, New Brunswick E3B 5H1. (506)453-3984. Website: www.gnb.ca.*

Newfoundland & Labrador Arts Council, *P.O. Box 98, St. John's, Newfoundland A1C 5H5. (709)726-2212. E-mail: nlacmail@newcomm.net. Website: www.nlac.nf.ca.*

Nova Scotia Arts Council, *(902)424-1593. Website: www.novascotiaartscouncil.ns.ca.*

The Canada Council, *350 Albert St., P.O. Box 1047, Ottawa, Ontario K1P 5V8. (613)566-4414. Website: www.canadacouncil.ca.*

Ontario Arts Council, *151 Bloor St. W., 5th Floor, Toronto, Ontario M5S 1T6. (416)961-1660. E-mail: info@arts.on.ca. Website: www.arts.on.ca/.*

Prince Edward Island Council of the Arts, *115 Richmond, Charlottetown, Prince Edward Island C1E 1H7. (902)368-6176. E-mail: artscouncil@pei.aibn.com.*

Saskatchewan Arts Board, *2135 Broad St., Regina, Saskatchewan S4P 3V7. (306)787-4056. E-mail: sab@artsboard.sk.ca. Website: www.artsboard.sk.ca.*

Yukon Arts Branch, *Box 2703, Whitehorse, Yukon Y1A 2C6. (867)667-8589. E-mail: arts@gov.yk.ca. Website: www.artsyukon.com.*

Publications of Interest

Knowledge about the music industry is essential for both creative and business success. Staying informed requires keeping up with constantly changing information. Updates on the evolving trends in the music business are available to you in the form of music magazines, music trade papers and books. There is a publication aimed at almost every type of musician, songwriter and music fan, from the most technical knowledge of amplification systems to gossip about your favorite singer. These publications can enlighten and inspire you and provide information vital in helping you become a more well-rounded, educated, and, ultimately, successful musical artist.

This section lists all types of magazines and books you may find interesting. From songwriters' newsletters and glossy music magazines to tip sheets and how-to books, there should be something listed here that you'll enjoy and benefit from.

PERIODICALS

THE ALBUM NETWORK, *120 N. Victory Blvd., Burbank CA 91502. (818)955-4000. Website: www.musicbiz. com. Weekly music industry trade magazine.*

AMERICAN SONGWRITER MAGAZINE, *1009 17th Ave. S., Nashville TN 37212-2201. (615)321-6096. E-mail: info@americansongwriter.com. Website: www.americansongwriter.com. Bimonthly publication for and about songwriters.*

BACK STAGE and BACK STAGE WEST, *P.O. Box 5026, Brentwood TN 37024. (800)437-3183. Website: www.back stage.com. Weekly East and West Coast performing artist trade papers.*

BASS PLAYER, *2800 Campus Dr., San Mateo CA 94403. (650)513-4400. E-mail: bassplayer@ musicplayer.com. Website: www.bassplayer.com. Monthly magazine for bass players with lessons, interviews, articles, and transcriptions.*

BILLBOARD, *1515 Broadway, New York NY 10036. (800)745-8922. E-mail: bbstore@billboard.com. Website: www. billboard.com. Weekly industry trade magazine.*

CANADIAN MUSICIAN, *23 Hannover Dr., Suite 7, St. Catharines, Ontario L2W 1A3 Canada. (877)746-4692. Website: www.canadianmusician.com. Bimonthly publication for amateur and professional Canadian musicians.*

CHART, *200-41 Britain St., Toronto, Ontario M5A 1R7 Canada. (416)363-3101. E-mail: chart@chartnet.com. Website: www.chartnet.com. Monthly magazine covering the Canadian and international music scenes.*

CMJ NEW MUSIC REPORT, *11 Middle Neck Rd., Suite 400, Great Neck NY 11021-2301. (800)CMJ-WKLY or (516)466-6000. E-mail: subscriptions@cmj.com. Website: www.cmjmusic.com. Weekly college radio and alternative music tip sheet.*

CONTEMPORARY SONGWRITER, *P.O. Box 25879, Colorado Springs CO 80936-5879. E-mail: contemposong@ yahoo.com. Website: www.contemposong.bigfoot.com. Monthly songwriter's magazine.*

COUNTRY LINE MAGAZINE, *P.O. Box 17245, Austin TX 78760. (512)292-1113. E-mail: editor@countrylinemaga zine.com. Website: http://countrylinemagazine.com. Monthly Texas-only country music cowboy and lifestyle magazine.*

DAILY VARIETY, *5700 Wilshire Blvd., Suite 120, Los Angeles CA 90036. (323)857-6600. Website: www.variety.com. Daily entertainment trade newspaper.*

DRAMALOGUE, *1456 N. Gordon, Hollywood CA 90028. L.A.-based entertainment newspaper with an emphasis on theatre and cabaret.*

THE DRAMATIST, *1501 Broadway, Suite 701, New York NY 10036. (212)398-9366. Fax: (212)944-0420. Website: www.dramaguild.com. The quarterly journal of the Dramatists Guild, the professional association of playwrights, composers and lyricists.*

ENTERTAINMENT LAW & FINANCE, *New York Law Publishing Co., 345 Park Ave. S., 8th Floor, New York NY 10010. (917)256-2115. E-mail: leader@ljextra.com. Monthly newsletter covering music industry contracts, lawsuit filings, court rulings and legislation.*

EXCLAIM!, *7-B Pleasant Blvd., Suite 966, Toronto, Ontario M4T 1K2 Canada. (416)535-9735. E-mail: exclaim@ex claim.ca. Website: http://exclaim.ca. Canadian music monthly covering all genres of non-mainstream music.*

FAST FORWARD, *Disc Makers, 7905 N. Rt. 130, Pennsauken NJ 08110-1402. (800)468-9353. Website: www.disc makers.com/music/ffwd. Quarterly newsletter featuring companies and products for performing and recording artists in the independent music industry.*

THE GAVIN REPORT, *140 Second St., 5th Floor, San Francisco CA 94105. (415)495-1990. Website: www.gavin.com. Weekly listing of radio charts.*

GUITAR PLAYER, *2800 Campus Dr., San Mateo CA 94403. (650)513-4300. E-mail: guitplyr@musicplayer.com. Website: www.guitarplayer.com. Monthly guitar magazine with transcriptions, columns, and interviews, including occasional articles on songwriting.*

HITS MAGAZINE, *14958 Ventura Blvd., Sherman Oaks CA 91403. (818)501-7900. Website: www.hitsmagazine.com. Weekly music industry trade publication.*

JAZZTIMES, *P.O. Box 99050, Collingswood NJ 08108. (888)279-7444. Website: http://jazztimes.com. 10 issues/year magazine covering the American jazz scene.*

THE LEADS SHEET, *Allegheny Music Works, 1611 Menoher Blvd., Johnstown PA 15905. (814)535-3373. Monthly tip sheet.*

LYRICIST REVIEW, *P.O. Box 2167, North Canton OH 44720-0167. E-mail: lyricaslit@aol.com. Website: www.lyricist review.com. Quarterly commentaries on song lyrics and previously unpublished lyrics available to performing musicians.*

MUSIC BOOKS PLUS, *P.O. Box 670, 240 Portage Rd., Lewiston NY 14092. (800)265-8481. E-mail: mail@nor.com. Website: www.musicbooksplus.com.*

MUSIC BUSINESS INTERNATIONAL MAGAZINE, *1 Penn Plaza, 11th Floor, New York NY 10119. (212)615-2925. E-mail: mbi@dotmusic.com. Bimonthly magazine for senior executives in the music industry.*

MUSIC CONNECTION MAGAZINE, *4731 Laurel Canyon Blvd., N. Hollywood CA 91607. (818)755-0101. E-mail: mc@musicconnection.com. Website: www.musicconnection.com. Biweekly music industry trade publication.*

MUSIC MORSELS, *P.O. Box 672216, Marietta GA 30006-0037. (770)850-9560. Fax: (770)850-9646. E-mail: musmor sels@aol.com. Website: www.serge.org/musicmorsels.htm. Monthly songwriting publication.*

MUSIC ROW MAGAZINE, *P.O. Box 158542, Nashville TN 37215. (615)321-3617. E-mail: news@musicrow.com. Website: www.musicrow.com. Biweekly Nashville industry publication.*

OFFBEAT MAGAZINE, *OffBeat Publications, 421 Frenchman St., Suite 200, New Orleans LA 70116-2506. (504)944-4300. E-mail: editor@offbeat.com. Website: www.offbeat.com. Monthly magazine covering Louisiana music and artists.*

PERFORMANCE MAGAZINE, *1101 University Dr., Suite 108, Fort Worth TX 76107-3000. (817)338-9444. Fax: (817)877-4273. E-mail: performmag@aol.com. Website: www.performancemagazine.com. Weekly publication on touring itineraries, artist availability, upcoming tours, and production and venue news.*

THE PERFORMING SONGWRITER, *2805 Azalea Place, Nashville TN 37204. (800)883-7664. E-mail: order@perf ormingsongwriter.com. Website: www.performingsongwriter.com. Bimonthly songwriters' magazine.*

PRODUCER REPORT, *415 S. Topanga Canyon Blvd., Suite 114, Topanga CA 90290. (310)455-0888. Fax: (310)455-0894. E-mail: web@mojavemusic.com. Website: www.mojavemusic.com. Semimonthly newsletter covering which producers are working on which acts, and upcoming, current and recently completed projects.*

PROFESSIONAL SOUND, *23 Hannover Dr., Suite 7, St. Catharine's, Ontario L2W 1A3 Canada. (800)265-8481. Fax: (905)641-1648. E-mail: mail@nor.com. Website: www.professional-sound.com. Bimonthly publication for professionals in the sound and light industry.*

PUBLIC DOMAIN REPORT, *P.O. Box 3102, Margate NJ 08402. (609)822-9401. Website: www.pubdomain.com. Monthly guide to significant titles entering the public domain.*

RADIO AND RECORDS, *10100 Santa Monica Blvd., 5th Floor, Los Angeles CA 90067-4004. (310)553-4330. Fax: (310)203-9763. E-mail: mailroom@rronline.com. Website: www.rronline.com. Weekly newspaper covering the radio and record industries.*

RADIR, *Radio Mall, 2412 Unity Ave. N., Dept. WEB, Minneapolis MN 55422. (800)759-4561. E-mail: info@bbhsoftwar e.com. Website: www.bbhsoftware.com. Quarterly radio station database on disk.*

SING OUT!, *P.O. Box 5460, Bethlehem PA 18015. (888)SING-OUT. Fax: (610)865-5129. E-mail: info@singout.org. Website: www.singout.org. Quarterly folk music magazine.*

SONGCASTING, *15445 Ventura Blvd. #260, Sherman Oaks CA 91403. (818)377-4084. Monthly tip sheet.*

SONGLINK INTERNATIONAL, *23 Belsize Crescent, London NW3 5QY England. E-mail: david@songlink.com. Website: www.songlink.com. 10 issues/year newsletter including details of recording artists looking for songs; contact details for industry sources; also news and features on the music business.*

SONGWRITER MAGAZINE, *P.O. Box 25879, Colorado Springs CO 80936. Monthly magazine especially for songwriters.*

SONGWRITER PRODUCTS, IDEAS AND NECESSITIES, *2520 CR 427 North, Suite 100, Longwood FL 32750. (407)834-8555. Fax: (407)834-9997. Website: www.songwriterproducts.com. Free semi-annual catalog of songwriting tips, tools and accessories, including tapes, CDs, duplication products and music business career packages.*

SONGWRITER'S MONTHLY, The Stories Behind Today's Songs, *332 Eastwood Ave., Feasterville PA 19053. (215)953-0952. E-mail: a1foster@aol.com. Website: www.lafay.com. Monthly songwriters' magazine.*

THE TEXAS POLKA NEWS, *P.O. Box 800183, Houston TX 77280. (281)480-8624. Fax: (713)462-7213. Website: www.angelfive.com/folk/polka/news.html. Monthly publication on Texas dancehalls, record releases, festival and dance listings, and radio station information.*

VARIETY, *5700 Wilshire Blvd., Suite 120, Los Angeles CA 90036. (323)857-6600. Fax: (323)857-0494. Website: www.variety.com. Weekly entertainment trade newspaper.*

WORDS AND MUSIC, *41 Valleybrook Dr., Don Mills, Ontario M3B 2S6 Canada. (416)445-8700. Website: www. socan.ca. Monthly songwriters' magazine.*

BOOKS & DIRECTORIES

88 SONGWRITING WRONGS & HOW TO RIGHT THEM, *by Pat & Pete Luboff, Writer's Digest Books, 1507 Dana Ave., Cincinnati OH 45207. (800)289-0963. Website: www.writersdigest.com.*

THE A&R REGISTRY, *by Ritch Esra, SRS Publishing, 7510 Sunset Blvd. #1041, Los Angeles CA 90046-3418. (800)377-7411 or (800)552-7411. E-mail: musicregistry@compuserve.com.*

ATTENTION: A&R, *by Teri Muench and Susan Pomerantz, Alfred Publishing Co. Inc., P.O. Box 10003, Van Nuys CA 91410-0003. (818)892-2452. Website: www.alfredpub.com.*

THE BILLBOARD GUIDE TO MUSIC PUBLICITY, *revised edition, by Jim Pettigrew, Jr., Billboard Books, 1695 Oak St., Lakewood NJ 08701. (800)344-7119.*

BREAKIN' INTO NASHVILLE, *by Jennifer Ember Pierce, Madison Books, University Press of America, 4720 Boston Way, Lanham MD 20706.*

CMJ DIRECTORY, *11 Middle Neck Rd., Suite 400, Great Neck NJ 11021-2301. (516)466-6000. Website: www.cmj.com.*

CONTRACTS FOR THE MUSIC INDUSTRY, *P.O. Box 952063, Lake Mary FL 32795-2063. (407)834-8555. E-mail: info@songwriterproducts.com. Website: www.songwriterproducts.com. Book and computer software of a variety of music contracts.*

THE CRAFT AND BUSINESS OF SONGWRITING, *by John Braheny, Writer's Digest Books, 1507 Dana Ave., Cincinnati OH 45207. (800)289-0963. Website: www.writersdigest.com.*

THE CRAFT OF LYRIC WRITING, *by Sheila Davis, Writer's Digest Books, 1507 Dana Ave., Cincinnati OH 45207. (800)289-0963. Website: www.writersdigest.com.*

CREATING MELODIES, *by Dick Weissman, Writer's Digest Books, 1507 Dana Ave., Cincinnati OH 45207. (800)289-0963. Website: www.writersdigest.com.*

DIRECTORY OF INDEPENDENT MUSIC DISTRIBUTORS, *by Jason Ojalvo, Disc Makers, 7905 N. Rt. 130, Pennsauken NJ 08110. (800)468-9353. E-mail: discman@discmakers.com. Website: www.discmakers.com.*

EASY TOOLS FOR COMPOSING, *by Charles Segal, Segal's Publications, 16 Grace Rd., Newton MA 02159. (617)969-6196.*

FILM/TV MUSIC GUIDE, *by Ritch Esra, SRS Publishing, 7510 Sunset Blvd. #1041, Los Angeles CA 90046-3418. (800)552-7411. E-mail: musicregistry@compuserve.com or srspubl@aol.com.*

FINDING FANS & SELLING CDs, *by Veronique Berry and Jason Ojalvo, Disk Makers, 7905 N. Rt. 130, Pennsauken NJ 08110-1402. (800)468-9353. E-mail: discman@diskmakers.com. Website: www.discmakers.com.*

GUIDE TO INDEPENDENT MUSIC PUBLICITY, *by Veronique Berry, Disc Makers, 7905 N. Rt. 130, Pennsauken NJ 08110-1402. (800)468-9353. E-mail: discman@discmakers.com.*

GUIDE TO MASTER TAPE PREPARATION, *by Dave Moyssiadis, Disk Makers, 7905 N. Rt. 130, Pennsauken NJ 08110-1402. (800)468-9353. E-mail: discman@discmakers.com.*

HOLLYWOOD CREATIVE DIRECTORY, *3000 W. Olympic Blvd. #2525, Santa Monica CA 90404. (800)815-0503. Website: www.hcdonline.com. Lists producers in film and TV.*

THE HOLLYWOOD REPORTER BLU-BOOK PRODUCTION DIRECTORY, *5055 Wilshire Blvd., Los Angeles CA 90036. (323)525-2150. Website: www.hollywoodreporter.com.*

HOT TIPS FOR THE HOME RECORDING STUDIO, *by Hank Linderman, Writer's Digest Books, 1507 Dana Ave., Cincinnati OH 45207. (800)289-0963. Website: www.writersdigest.com.*

HOW TO PROMOTE YOUR MUSIC SUCCESSFULLY ON THE INTERNET, *by David Nevue, Midnight Rain Productions, P.O. Box 21831, Eugene OR 97402. Website: www.rainmusic.com.*

HOW YOU CAN BREAK INTO THE MUSIC BUSINESS, *by Marty Garrett, Lonesome Wind Corporation, P.O. Box 2143, Broken Arrow OK 74013-2143. (800)210-4416. Website: www.telepath.com/bizbook.*

LOUISIANA MUSIC DIRECTORY, *OffBeat, Inc., 421 Frenchmen St., Suite 200, New Orleans LA 70116. (504)944-4300. Website: www.offbeat.com.*

MUSIC ATTORNEY LEGAL & BUSINESS AFFAIRS REGISTRY, *by Ritch Esra and Steve Trumbull, SRS Publishing, 7510 Sunset Blvd. #1041, Los Angeles CA 90046-3418. (800)552-7411. E-mail: musicregistry@compuserve.com or srspubl@aol.com.*

MUSIC DIRECTORY CANADA, *seventh edition, Norris-Whitney Communications Inc., 23 Hannover Dr., Suite 7, St. Catherines, Ontario L2W 1A3 Canada. (877)RING-NWC. E-mail: mail@nor.com. Website: http://nor.com.*

MUSIC LAW: HOW TO RUN YOUR BAND'S BUSINESS, *by Richard Stin, Nolo Press, 950 Parker St., Berkeley CA 94710-9867. (510)549-1976. Website: www.nolo.com.*

MUSIC, MONEY AND SUCCESS: THE INSIDER'S GUIDE TO THE MUSIC INDUSTRY, *by Jeffrey Brabec and Todd Brabec, Schirmer Books, 1633 Broadway, New York NY 10019. Website: http://w3.mlr.com/mlr/schirmer.*

THE MUSIC PUBLISHER REGISTRY, *by Ritch Esra, SRS Publishing, 7510 Sunset Blvd. #1041, Los Angeles CA 90046-3418. (800)552-7411. E-mail: musicregistry@compuserve.com or srspubl@aol.com.*

MUSIC PUBLISHING: A SONGWRITER'S GUIDE, *revised edition, by Randy Poe, Writer's Digest Books, 1507 Dana Ave., Cincinnati OH 45207. (800)289-0963. Website: www.writersdigest.com.*

THE MUSICIAN'S GUIDE TO MAKING & SELLING YOUR OWN CDs & CASSETTES, *by Jana Stanfield, Writer's Digest Books, 1507 Dana Ave., Cincinnati OH 45207. (800)289-0963. Website: www.writersdigest.com.*

MUSICIANS' PHONE BOOK, THE LOS ANGELES MUSIC INDUSTRY DIRECTORY, *Get Yourself Some Publishing, 28336 Simsalido Ave., Canyon Country CA 91351. (805)299-2405. E-mail: mpb@earthlink.net. Website: www.musiciansphonebook.com.*

NASHVILLE MUSIC BUSINESS DIRECTORY, *by Mark Dreyer, NMBD Publishing, P.O. Box 120675, Nashville TN 37212. Phone/Fax: (615)826-4141. E-mail: nashvillemusicbusinessdirectory@juno.com.*

NASHVILLE'S UNWRITTEN RULES: INSIDE THE BUSINESS OF THE COUNTRY MUSIC MACHINE, *by Dan Daley, Overlook Press, 2568 Rt. 212, Woodstock NY 12498. (914)679-6838.*

NATIONAL DIRECTORY OF INDEPENDENT RECORD DISTRIBUTORS, *P.O. Box 452063, Lake Mary FL 32795-2063. (407)834-8555. E-mail: info@songwriterproducts.com. Website: www.songwriterproducts.com.*

THE OFFICIAL COUNTRY MUSIC DIRECTORY, *P.O. Box 7000, Rancho Mirage CA 92270. (760)773-0995.*

RADIO STATIONS OF AMERICA: A NATIONAL DIRECTORY, *P.O. Box 452063, Lake Mary FL 32795-2063. (407)834-8555. E-mail: info@songwriterproducts.com. Website: www.songwriterproducts.com.*

THE REAL DEAL—HOW TO GET SIGNED TO A RECORD LABEL FROM A TO Z, *by Daylle Deanna Schwartz, Billboard Books, 1695 Oak St., Lakewood NJ 08701. (800)344-7119.*

RECORDING INDUSTRY SOURCEBOOK, *Music Books Plus, P.O. Box 670, 240 Portage Rd., Lewiston NY 14092. (800)265-8481. Website: www.musicbooksplus.com.*

THE SONGWRITERS IDEA BOOK, *by Sheila Davis, Writer's Digest Books, 1507 Dana Ave., Cincinnati OH 45207. (800)289-0963. Website: www.writersdigest.com.*

SONGWRITER'S MARKET GUIDE TO SONG & DEMO SUBMISSION FORMATS, *Writer's Digest Books, 1507 Dana Ave., Cincinnati OH 45207. (800)289-0963. Website: www.writersdigest.com.*

SONGWRITER'S PLAYGROUND—INNOVATIVE EXERCISES IN CREATIVE SONGWRITING, *by Barbara L. Jordan, Creative Music Marketing, 1085 Commonwealth Ave., Suite 323, Boston MA 02215. (617)926-8766.*

SONGWRITING AND THE CREATIVE PROCESS, *by Steve Gillette, Sing Out! Publications, P.O. Box 5253, Bethlehem PA 18015-0253. (888)SING-OUT. E-mail: singout@libertynet.org. Website: www.singout.org/sopubs. html.*

SONGWRITING: ESSENTIAL GUIDE TO LYRIC FORM AND STRUCTURE, *by Pat Pattison, Berklee Press, 1140 Boylston St., Boston MA 02215. (617)747-2146. Website: www.www.berkleepress.com.*

THE SOUL OF THE WRITER, *by Susan Tucker with Linda Lee Strother, Journey Publishing, P.O. Box 92411, Nashville TN 37209. (800)776-4231. Website: www.journeypublishing.com.*

SUCCESSFUL LYRIC WRITING, *by Sheila Davis, Writer's Digest Books, 1507 Dana Ave., Cincinnati OH 45207. (800)289-0963. Website: www.writersdigest.com.*

THIS BUSINESS OF MUSIC MARKETING AND PROMOTION, *by Tad Lathrop and Jim Pettigrew, Jr., Billboard Books, Watson-Guptill Publications, 1515 Broadway, New York NY 10036-8986. (800)344-7119.*

TIM SWEENEY'S GUIDE TO RELEASING INDEPENDENT RECORDS, *by Tim Sweeney, TSA Books, 21213-B Hawthorne Blvd. #5255, Torrance CA 90503. (310)542-1322. Website: www.tsamusic.com.*

TIM SWEENEY'S GUIDE TO SUCCEEDING AT MUSIC CONVENTIONS, *by Tim Sweeney, TSA Books, 21213-B Hawthorne Blvd. #5255, Torrance CA 90503. (310)542-1322. Website: www.tsamusic.com.*

TEXAS MUSIC INDUSTRY DIRECTORY, *Texas Music Office, Office of the Governor, P.O. Box 13246, Austin TX 78711. (512)463-6666. E-mail: music@governor.state.tx.us. Website: www.governor.state.tx.us/music.*

TUNESMITH: INSIDE THE ART OF SONGWRITING, *by Jimmy Webb, Hyperion, 114 Fifth Ave., New York NY 10011. (800)343-9204.*

VOLUNTEER LAWYERS FOR THE ARTS GUIDE TO COPYRIGHT FOR MUSICIANS AND COMPOSERS, *One E. 53rd St., 6th Floor, New York NY 10022. (212)319-2787.*

WRITING BETTER LYRICS, *by Pat Pattison, Writer's Digest Books, 1507 Dana Ave., Cincinnati OH 45207. (800)289-0963. Website: www.writersdigest.com.*

THE YELLOW PAGES OF ROCK, *The Album Network, 120 N. Victory Blvd., Burbank CA 91502. (818)955-4000.*

Websites of Interest

The Internet can provide a wealth of information for songwriters and performers, and the number of sites devoted to music grows each day. Below is a list of some websites that can offer you information, links to other music sites, contact with other songwriters and places to showcase your songs. Since the online world is changing and expanding at such a rapid pace, this is hardly a comprehensive list, and some of these addresses may be obsolete by the time this book goes to print. But it gives you a place to start on your journey through the Internet to search for opportunities to get your music heard.

ABOUT.COM MUSICIANS' EXCHANGE: *http://musicians.miningco.com*
Site featuring headlines and articles of interest to independent musicians, as well as numerous links.

AMERICAN MUSIC CENTER: *www.amc.net*
Classical/jazz archives, includes a list of composer organizations and contacts.

AMERICAN SOCIETY OF COMPOSERS, AUTHORS AND PUBLISHERS (ASCAP) *www.ascap.com*
Database of performed works in ASCAP's repertoire. Also includes songwriter, performer and publisher information, ASCAP membership information and industry news.

AMPCAST.COM: *www.ampcast.com*
Online musicians community and music hosting site.

ARCANA, Artist Research, Composer's Aid & Network Access: *www.musicnotes.com*
Reference site for classical composers and musicians, including collaboration opportunities, contests and music archives, in addition to industry news.

ASSOCIATION FOR INDEPENDENT MUSIC: *www.afim.org*
AFIM's mission is to establish channels of effective communication for independent distribution. They sponsor an annual convention of retailers, distributors, labels and artists.

THE BANDIT A&R NEWSLETTER: *www.banditnewsletter.com*
Offers newsletter to help musicians target demos and press kits to labels, publishers, managers and production companies actively looking for new talent.

BANDSTAND: *www.bandstand.com*
Music news and links.

THE BARD'S CRIER: *http://thebards.net/crier/*
A free guerilla music marketing e-zine.

THE BLUES FOUNDATION: *www.blues.org*
Information on the foundation, its membership and events.

BROADCAST MUSIC, INC. (BMI): *www.bmi.com*
Offers lists of song titles, songwriters and publishers of the BMI repertoire. Also includes BMI membership information, and general information on songwriting and licensing.

THE BUZZ FACTOR: *www.thebuzzfactor.com*
Offers press kit evaluation, press release writing, guerrilla music marketing, tips and weekly newsletter.

CDBABY: *www.cdbaby.com*
An online CD store dedicated solely to independent music.

CDSTREET.COM: *www.cdstreet.com*
Offers secure online ordering support to artist websites for a 15% commission.

CHILDREN'S MUSIC WEB: *www.childrensmusic.org*
Website dedicated to music for kids.

CHORUS AMERICA: *www.chorusamerica.org*
The website of Chorus America, a national service organization for professional and volunteer choruses, including job listings and professional development information.

COMPOSERS CONCORDANCE: *www.musicnotes.com*
The website of the ARCANA-sponsored group which promotes performance of new American music through concert series and public awareness.

CPCC: *www.under.org/cpcc*
Website for the Center for the Promotion of Contemporary Composers.

CREATIVE MUSICIANS COALITION (CMC): *www.aimcmc.com*
Website of the CMC, an international organization dedicated to the advancement of independent musicians, links to artists, and tips and techniques for musicians.

DIY TOUR GUIDE: *http://industrial.org/tour.html*
Directory of venues and promoters.

ENSEMBLE 21: *www.ensemble21.com/e21.html*
Website of the New York contemporary music performance group dedicated to promotion and performance of new orchestral compositions.

FILM MUSIC: *www.filmmusic.com*
Website relating to film and TV music composition.

FOURFRONT MEDIA AND MUSIC: *www.knab.com*
This site by music industry consultant Christopher Knab offers in-depth information on product development, promotion, publicity and performance.

GAJOOB MAGAZINE: *www.gajoob.com*
Online magazine offering information on labels looking for artists, radio stations looking for independent artists, festivals, publications, collaborations, etc.

GETSIGNED.COM: *www.getsigned.com*
Interviews with industry executives, how-to business information and more.

GOVERNMENT LIAISON SERVICES: *www.trademarkinfo.com*
An intellectual property research firm. Offers a free online trademark search.

GUITAR NINE RECORDS: *www.guitar9.com*
Offers articles by music professionals and insiders.

HARRY FOX AGENCY: *www.nmpa.org/hfa/licensing.html*
Offers a comprehensive FAQ about licensing songs for use in recording, performance and film.

INDEPENDENT ARTISTS' SERVICES: *www.idiom.com/~upend/*
Full of information including searchable databases of bands and booking/touring information and other resources.

INDEPENDENT DISTRIBUTION NETWORK: *www.idnmusic.com/*
Website of independent bands distributing their music, with advice on everything from starting a band to finding labels.

INDEPENDENT SONGWRITER WEB MAGAZINE: *www.independentsongwriter.com*
Independent music reviews, classifieds, message board and chat sessions.

INDIE CENTRE: *www.indiecentre.com*
An independent label information site created to share ideas on releasing albums, including creating a label, distribution and touring.

INDIE CORNER: *http://theglobalmuse.com/indiecorner/index.html*
Offers tips and articles on promotion and marketing, demos, dealing with A&R persons and designing a website geared toward promoting and selling your music.

INDIE-MUSIC.COM: *http://indie-music.com*
Full of how-to articles, record label directory, radio links and venue listing.

INTERNET UNDERGROUND MUSIC ARCHIVE (IUMA): *www.iuma.com*
Online musicians community and music hosting site.

JAZZ COMPOSERS COLLECTIVE: *www.jazzcollective.com*
Industry information on composers, projects, recordings, concerts and events.

JAZZ CORNER: *www.jazzcorner.com*
Website for musicians and organizations featuring links to 70 websites for jazz musicians and organizations and the Speakeasy, an interactive conference area.

JUST PLAIN FOLKS: *www.jpfolks.com*
Online songwriting organization featuring messageboards, lyric feedback forums, member profiles, featured members'

music, contact listings, chapter homepages, and an Internet radio station. (See the Just Plain Folks listing in the Organizations section).

KATHODE RAY MUSIC: *www.kathoderaymusic.com*
Specializes in marketing and promotion consultation and offers a business forum, e-newsletter and a free classified ads board.

LAW CYBERCENTER: *www.hollywoodnetwork.com/Law/music/survival2.html*
Tips on negotiating and dealing with songwriting contracts.

LI'L HANK'S GUIDE FOR SONGWRITERS IN L.A.: *www.halsguide.com*
Website for songwriters with information on clubs, publishers, books, etc. as well as links to other songwriting sites.

LIVECONCERTS.COM: *www.liveconcerts.com*
Features interactive interviews with artists, concert dates and industry news.

LOS ANGELES GOES UNDERGROUND: *http://lagu.somaweb.org*
Website dedicated to underground rock bands from Los Angeles and Hollywood.

LOS ANGELES MUSIC ACCESS (LAMA): *http://lama.com*
Database of Los Angeles bands, clubs and resources sponsored by a group that promotes independent artists.

LYRICAL LINE: *www.lyricalline.com*
Offers places to market your songs, critique service, industry news and more.

LYRICIST.COM: *www.lyricist.com*
Jeff Mallet's songwriter site offering contests, tips and job opportunities in the music industry.

MEDIA BUREAU: *www.mediabureau.com*
Live Internet radio programs where guests perform and talk about songwriting.

MI2N (THE MUSIC INDUSTRY NEWS NETWORK): *www.mi2n.com*
Offers news on happenings in the music industry and career postings.

MP3.COM: *www.mp3.com*
Currently the most well-known online musicians community and music hosting site with thousands of songs available for free download.

THE MUSE'S MUSE: *www.musesmuse.com*
Classifieds, catalog of lyric samples, songwriting articles, organizations and chat room.

MUSIC & AUDIO CONNECTION: *www.musicandaudio.com*
Guide to Canadian artists, associations and other resources from Norris-Whitney Communications, Inc.

MUSIC INDUSTRY PAGES: *www.musicindustry.com*
Listings of labels, magazines, products, music schools, retailers, etc.

MUSIC PUBLISHERS ASSOCIATION: *http://host.mpa.org*
Provides a copyright resource center, directory of member publishers and information on the organization.

MUSIC YELLOW PAGES: *www.musicyellowpages.com*
Phone book listings of music-related businesses.

MUSICIANS ASSISTANCE SITE (MAS): *www.musicianassist.com*
Features site reviews and databases of venues, contacts, promoters, manufacturers and record labels. Also includes an archive of music business articles, columns, and pre-made contracts and agreements.

THE MUSICIANS GUIDE THROUGH THE LEGAL JUNGLE: *www.legaljungleguide.com/resource.htm*
Offers articles on copyright law, music publishing and talent agents.

NATIONAL ASSOCIATION OF COMPOSERS USA (NACUSA): *www.music-usa.org/nacusa*
Website of the organization dedicated to promotion and performance of new music by Americans, featuring a young composers' competition, concert schedule, job opportunities and more.

NATIONAL MUSIC PUBLISHERS ASSOCIATION: *www.nmpa.org*
The organization's online site with information about copyright, legislation and other concerns of the music publishing world.

ONLINE ROCK: *www.onlinerock.com*
Offers e-mail, marketing and free webpage services. Also features articles, chat rooms, links, etc.

OPERA AMERICA: *www.operaam.org*
Website of Opera America, featuring information on advocacy and awareness programs, publications, conference schedules and more.

OUTERSOUND: *www.outersound.com*
Information on finding a recording studio, educating yourself in the music industry, and a list of music magazines to advertise in or get reviewed by.

PUBLIC DOMAIN MUSIC: *www.pdinfo.com*
Articles on public domain works and copyright, including public domain song lists, research resources, tips and a FAQ.

RES ROCKET SURFER: *www.resrocket.com or www.rocketnetwork.com*
Offers collaboration opportunities and industry news.

RHYTHM NET: *www.rhythmnet.com*
Information on artists, labels, entertainment establishments and more.

SESAC INC.: *www.sesac.com*
Includes SESAC performing rights organization information, songwriter profiles, organization news, licensing information and links to other sites.

SONG SHARK: *www.geocities.com/songshark*
Website of information on known song sharks.

SONGCATALOG.COM: *www.songcatalog.com*
Online song catalog database for pitching and licensing.

SONGFILE.COM: *www.songfile.com*
Online song catalog database for pitching and licensing.

SONGLINK: *www.songlink.com*
Offers opportunities to pitch songs to music publishers for specific recording projects, also industry news.

SONGNET.COM: *www.songnet.com*
Information, bulletin boards and links related to songwriting.

SONGSCAPE: *www.songscape.com*
Music database and music industry news service.

SONGSCOPE.COM: *www.songscope.com*
Online song catalog database for pitching and licensing.

SONGWRITER PRODUCTS IDEAS & NECESSITIES (SPIN): *www.songwriterproducts.com*
Offer songwriting tips, tools and accessories, including tapes, CDs, duplication products and music business career packages.

SONGWRITER'S GUILD OF AMERICA (SGA): *www.songwriters.org*
Offers industry news, members services information, newsletters, contract reviews and more.

SONGWRITER'S RESOURCE NETWORK: *www.songwritersresourcenetwork.com*
Online information and services designed especially for songwriters.

THE SONGWRITING EDUCATION RESOURCE: *www.craftofsongwriting.com*
An educational site for Nashville songwriters offering discussion boards, articles and links.

SONIC NET: *www.sonicnet.com*
Music news, chat and reviews.

STOMPINGGROUND: *www.stompinground.com*
Provides bands with Real Audio concerts, free listings, promotion and a list of record labels.

STUDIO FINDER: *www.studiofinder.com*
Locate more than 5,000 recording studios anywhere in the U.S.

TAXI: *www.taxi.com*
Independent A&R vehicle that shops tapes to A&R professionals.

ULTIMATE BAND LIST: *www.ubl.com*
Lists record labels and their artists, posts calendar of events, festivals and club dates for artists nationwide; also includes chart information and artist news.

UNITED STATES COPYRIGHT OFFICE: *http://lcweb.loc.gov/copyright*
The homepage for the U.S. copyright office, offering information on registering songs.

YAHOO!: *www.yahoo.com/Entertainment/Music/*
Use this search engine to retrieve over 20,000 music listings.

ONLINE SHOWCASES
These sites offer places for you to post your music for a fee as a way of marketing your songs to music executives.

INTERNET UNDERGROUND MUSIC ARCHIVE (IUMA): *www.iuma.com.*

KALEIDOSPACE: *http://kspace.com*

MUSIC SPOTLIGHT WEB: *www.musicspotlight.com*

Contributors to the Insider Reports

TRAVIS ADKINS was an intern for Writer's Digest Books and is now a copy editor for an advertising company. During his tour of duty he worked on many of the market books, including *Songwriter's Market* and *Writer's Market*. He also contributed articles to *WritersMarket.com*.

ANNE BOWLING is editor of *Novel & Short Story Writer's Market* and a Cincinnati-based freelance writer.

DAN KIMPEL is the author of the best-selling book *Networking in the Music Business* (Writer's Digest Books). Since 1998, he has taught a course based on his book at Sir Paul McCartney's Liverpool Institute for Performing Arts (LIPA) in the U.K. He contributes to a variety of print mediums, and passengers on United Airlines hear Kimpel's interviews with songwriters and recording artists on the United Entertainment Network. He lives in Los Angeles, California.

CANDI LACE is the assistant editor of *Children's Writer's & Illustrator's Market*. Her writings have been published in *Clamor*, *Art Papers*, *Alternative Cinema* and *DJ Mixed* magazine, among other venues. Lace was listed in the *Millennium Edition of Who's Who of American Women*.

AMY RATTO is a freelance writer based in Missoula, Montana.

RACHEL VATER is editor for *Guide to Literary Agents* and *Guide to Talent & Modeling*, and is a Cincinnati-based novelist and scriptwriter.

Glossary

A cappella. Choral singing without accompaniment.

AAA form. A song form in which every verse has the same melody; often used for songs that tell a story.

AABA, ABAB. A commonly used song pattern consisting of two verses, a bridge and a verse, or a repeated pattern of verse and bridge, where the verses are musically the same.

A&R Director. Record company executive in charge of the Artists and Repertoire Department who is responsible for finding and developing new artists and matching songs with artists.

A/C. Adult contemporary music.

Advance. Money paid to the songwriter or recording artist, which is then recouped before regular royalty payment begins. Sometimes called "up front" money, advances are deducted from royalties.

AFIM. Association for Independent Music (formerly NAIRD). Organization for independent record companies, distributors, retailers, manufacturers, etc.

AFM. American Federation of Musicians. A union for musicians and arrangers.

AFTRA. American Federation of Television and Radio Artists. A union for performers.

AIMP. Association of Independent Music Publishers.

Airplay. The radio broadcast of a recording.

AOR. Album-Oriented Rock. A radio format that primarily plays selections from rock albums as opposed to hit singles.

Arrangement. An adaptation of a composition for a recording or performance, with consideration for the melody, harmony, instrumentation, tempo, style, etc.

ASCAP. American Society of Composers, Authors and Publishers. A performing rights society. (See the Organizations section.)

Assignment. Transfer of rights of a song from writer to publisher.

Audio Visual Index (AVI). A database containing title and production information for cue sheets which are available from a performing rights organization. Currently, BMI, ASCAP, SOCAN, PRS, APRA and SACEM contribute their cue sheet listings to the AVI.

Audiovisual. Refers to presentations that use audio backup for visual material.

Background music. Music used that creates mood and supports the spoken dialogue of a radio program or visual action of an audiovisual work. Not feature or theme music.

b&w. Black and white.

Bed. Prerecorded music used as background material in commercials. In rap music, often refers to the sampled and looped drums and music over which the rapper performs.

Black box. Theater without fixed stage or seating arrangements, capable of a variety of formations. Usually a small space, often attached to a major theater complex, used for workshops or experimental works calling for small casts and limited sets.

BMI. Broadcast Music, Inc. A performing rights society. (See the Organizations section.)

Booking agent. Person who schedules performances for entertainers.

Bootlegging. Unauthorized recording and selling of a song.

Business manager. Person who handles the financial aspects of artistic careers.

Buzz. Attention an act generates through the media and word of mouth.

b/w. Backed with. Usually refers to the B-side of a single.

C&W. Country and western.

Catalog. The collected songs of one writer, or all songs handled by one publisher.

CD. Compact Disc (see below).

CD-R. A recordable CD.

CD-ROM. Compact Disc-Read Only Memory. A computer information storage medium capable of holding enormous amounts of data. Information on a CD-ROM cannot be deleted. A computer user must have a CD-ROM drive to access a CD-ROM.

Chamber music. Any music suitable for performance in a small audience area or chamber.

Chamber orchestra. A miniature orchestra usually containing one instrument per part.

Chart. The written arrangement of a song.

Charts. The trade magazines' lists of the best-selling records.

CHR. Comtemporary Hit Radio. Top 40 pop music.

Collaboration. Two or more artists, writers, etc., working together on a single project; for instance, a playwright and a songwriter creating a musical together.

Compact disc. A small disc (about 4.7 inches in diameter) holding digitally encoded music that is read by a laser beam in a CD player.

Composers. The men and women who create musical compositions for motion pictures and other audio visual works, or the creators of classical music composition.

Co-publish. Two or more parties own publishing rights to the same song.

Copyright. The exclusive legal right giving the creator of a work the power to control the publishing, reproduction and selling of the work. Although a song is technically copyrighted at the time it is written, the best legal protection of that copyright comes through registering the copyright with the Library of Congress.

Copyright infringement. Unauthorized use of a copyrighted song or portions thereof.

Cover recording. A new version of a previously recorded song.

Crossover. A song that becomes popular in two or more musical categories (e.g., country and pop).

Cut. Any finished recording; a selection from a LP. Also to record.

DAT. Digital Audio Tape. A professional and consumer audio cassette format for recording and playing back digitally-encoded material. DAT cassettes are approximately one-third smaller than conventional audio cassettes.

DCC. Digital Compact Cassette. A consumer audio cassette format for recording and playing back digitally-encoded tape. DCC tapes are the same size as analog cassettes.

Demo. A recording of a song submitted as a demonstration of a writer's or artist's skills.

Derivative work. A work derived from another work, such as a translation, musical arrangement, sound recording, or motion picture version.

Distributor. Wholesale marketing agent responsible for getting records from manufacturers to retailers.

Donut. A jingle with singing at the beginning and end and instrumental background in the middle. Ad copy is recorded over the middle section.

E-mail. Electronic mail. Computer address where a company or individual can be reached via modem.

Engineer. A specially-trained individual who operates recording studio equipment.

Enhanced CD. General term for an audio CD that also contains multimedia computer information. It is playable in both standard CD players and CD-ROM drives.

EP. Extended play record or cassette containing more selections than a standard single, but fewer than a standard album.

Exploit. To seek legitimate uses of a song for income.

Final mix. The art of combining all the various sounds that take place during the recording session into a two-track stereo or mono tape. Reflects the total product and all of the energies and talents the artist, producer and engineer have put into the project.

Fly space. The area above a stage from which set pieces are lowered and raised during a performance.

Folio. A softcover collection of printed music prepared for sale.

Following. A fan base committed to going to gigs and buying albums.

Foreign rights societies. Performing rights societies other than domestic which have reciprocal agreements with ASCAP and BMI for the collection of royalties accrued by foreign radio and television airplay and other public performance of the writer members of the above groups.

Harry Fox Agency. Organization that collects mechanical royalties.

Grammy. Music industry awards presented by the National Academy of Recording Arts and Sciences.

Hip-hop. A dance oriented musical style derived from a combination of disco, rap and R&B.

Hit. A song or record that achieves top 40 status.

Hook. A memorable "catch" phrase or melody line that is repeated in a song.

House. Dance music created by remixing samples from other songs.

Hypertext. Words or groups of words in an electronic document that are linked to other text, such as a definition or a related document. Hypertext can also be linked to illustrations.

Indie. An independent record label, music publisher or producer.

Infringement. A violation of the exclusive rights granted by the copyright law to a copyright owner.

Internet. A worldwide network of computers that offers access to a wide variety of electronic resources.

ips. Inches per second; a speed designation for tape recording.

IRC. International reply coupon, necessary for the return of materials sent out of the country. Available at most post offices.

Jingle. Usually a short verse set to music designed as a commercial message.

Lead sheet. Written version (melody, chord symbols and lyric) of a song.

Leader. Plastic (non-recordable) tape at the beginning and between songs for ease in selection.

Libretto. The text of an opera or any long choral work. The booklet containing such text.

Listing. Block of information in this book about a specific company.

LP. Designation for long-playing record played at 33⅓ rpm.

Lyric sheet. A typed or written copy of a song's lyrics.

Market. A potential song or music buyer; also a demographic division of the record-buying public.

Master. Edited and mixed tape used in the production of records; the best or original copy of a recording from which copies are made.

MD. MiniDisc. A 2.5 inch disk for recording and playing back digitally-encoded music.

Mechanical right. The right to profit from the physical reproduction of a song.

Mechanical royalty. Money earned from record, tape and CD sales.

MIDI. Musical instrument digital interface. Universal standard interface that allows musical instruments to communicate with each other and computers.

Mini Disc. (See **MD** above.)

Mix. To blend a multi-track recording into the desired balance of sound, usually to a 2-track stereo master.

Modem. MOdulator/DEModulator. A computer device used to send data from one computer to another via telephone line.

MOR. Middle of the road. Easy-listening popular music.

MP3. File format of a relatively small size that stores audio files on a computer. Music saved in a MP3 format can be played only with a MP3 player (which can be downloaded onto a computer).

Ms. Manuscript.

Multimedia. Computers and software capable of integrating text, sound, photographic-quality images, animation and video.

Music bed. (See **Bed** above.)

Music jobber. A wholesale distributor of printed music.

Music library. A business that purchases canned music, which can then be bought by producers of radio and TV commercials, films, videos and audiovisual productions to use however they wish.

Music publisher. A company that evaluates songs for commercial potential, finds artists to record them, finds other uses (such as TV or film) for the songs, collects income generated by the songs and protects copyrights from infringement.

Music Row. An area of Nashville, TN, encompassing Sixteenth, Seventeeth and Eighteenth avenues where most of the major publishing houses, recording studios, mastering labs, songwriters, singers, promoters, etc. practice their trade.

NARAS. National Academy of Recording Arts and Sciences.

The National Academy of Songwriters (NAS). The largest U.S. songwriters' association. (See the Organizations section.)

Needle-drop. Refers to a type of music library. A needledrop music library is a licensed library that allows producers to borrow music on a rate schedule. The price depends on how the music will be used.

Network. A group of computers electronically linked to share information and resources.

NMPA. National Music Publishers Association.

One-off. A deal between songwriter and publisher which includes only one song or project at a time. No future involvement is implicated. Many times a single song contract accompanies a one-off deal.

One-stop. A wholesale distributor of who sells small quantities of records to "mom and pop" record stores, retailers and jukebox operators.

Operetta. Light, humorous, satiric plot or poem, set to cheerful light music with occasional spoken dialogue.

Overdub. To record an additional part (vocal or instrumental) onto a basic multi-track recording.

Parody. A satirical imitation of a literary or musical work. Permission from the owner of the copyright is generally required before commercial exploitation of a parody.

Payola. Dishonest payment to broadcasters in exchange for airplay.

Performing rights. A specific right granted by U.S. copyright law protecting a composition from being publicly performed without the owner's permission.

Performing rights organization. An organization that collects income from the public performance of songs written by its members and then proportionally distributes this income to the individual copyright holder based on the number of performances of each song.

Personal manager. A person who represents artists to develop and enhance their careers. Personal managers may negotiate contracts, hire and dismiss other agencies and personnel relating to the artist's career, review material, help with artist promotions and perform many services.

Piracy. The unauthorized reproduction and selling of printed or recorded music.

Pitch. To attempt to solicit interest for a song by audition.

Playlist. List of songs a radio station will play.

Points. A negotiable percentage paid to producers and artists for records sold.

Producer. Person who supervises every aspect of a recording project.

Production company. Company specializing in producing jingle packages for advertising agencies. May also refer to companies specializing in audiovisual programs.

Professional manager. Member of a music publisher's staff who screens submitted material and tries to get the company's catalog of songs recorded.

Proscenium. Permanent architectural arch in a theater that separates the stage from the audience.

Public domain. Any composition with an expired, lapsed or invalid copyright, and therefore belonging to everyone.

Purchase license. Fee paid for music used from a stock music library.

Query. A letter of inquiry to an industry professional soliciting his interest.

R&B. Rhythm and blues.

Rack Jobber. Distributors who lease floor space from department stores and put in racks of albums.

Rate. The percentage of royalty as specified by contract.

Release. Any record issued by a record company.

Residuals. In advertising or television, payments to singers and musicians for use of a performance.

RIAA. Recording Industry Association of America.

Royalty. Percentage of money earned from the sale of records or use of a song.

RPM. Revolutions per minute. Refers to phonograph turntable speed.

SAE. Self-addressed envelope (with no postage attached).

SASE. Self-addressed stamped envelope.

SATB. The abbreviation for parts in choral music, meaning Soprano, Alto, Tenor and Bass.

Score. A complete arrangement of all the notes and parts of a composition (vocal or instrumental) written out on staves. A full score, or orchestral score, depicts every orchestral part on a separate staff and is used by a conductor.

Self-contained. A band or recording act that writes all their own material.

SESAC. A performing rights organization, originally the Society of European Stage Authors and Composers. (See the Organizations section.)

SFX. Sound effects.

Shop. To pitch songs to a number of companies or publishers.

Single. 45 rpm record with only one song per side. A 12″ single refers to a long version of one song on a 12″ disc, usually used for dance music.

Ska. Fast tempo dance music influenced primarily by reggae and punk, usually featuring horns, saxophone and bass.

SOCAN. Society of Composers, Authors and Music Publishers of Canada. A Canadian performing rights organization. (See the Organizations section.)

Solicited. Songs or materials that have been requested.

Song plugger. A songwriter representative whose main responsibility is promoting uncut songs to music publishers, record companies, artists and producers.

Song shark. Person who deals with songwriters deceptively for his own profit.

SoundScan. A company that collates the register tapes of reporting stores to track the actual number of albums sold at the retail level.

Soundtrack. The audio, including music and narration, of a film, videotape or audiovisual program.

Space stage. Open stage that features lighting and, perhaps, projected scenery.

Split publishing. To divide publishing rights between two or more publishers.

Staff songwriter. A songwriter who has an exclusive agreement with a publisher.

Statutory royalty rate. The maximum payment for mechanical rights guaranteed by law that a record company may pay the songwriter and his publisher for each record or tape sold.

Subpublishing. Certain rights granted by a U.S. publisher to a foreign publisher in exchange for promoting the U.S. catalog in his territory.

Synchronization. Technique of timing a musical soundtrack to action on film or video.

Take. Either an attempt to record a vocal or instrument part, or an acceptable recording of a performance.

Tejano. A musical form begun in the late 1970s by regional bands in south Texas, its style reflects a blended Mexican-American culture. Incorporates elements of rock, country, R&B and jazz, and often features accordion and 12-string guitar.

Thrust stage. Stage with audience on three sides and a stagehouse or wall on the fourth side.

Top 40. The first 40 songs on the pop music charts at any given time. Also refers to a style of music which emulates that heard on the current top 40.

Track. Divisions of a recording tape (e.g., 24-track tape) that can be individually recorded in the studio, then mixed into a finished master.

Trades. Publications covering the music industry.

DISCOVER
A WORLD OF
WRITING
SUCCESS

Are you ready to be praised, published, and paid for your writing? It's time to invest in your future with *Writer's Digest*! Beginners and experienced writers alike have been enjoying *Writer's Digest*, the world's leading magazine for writers, for more than 80 years — and it keeps getting better! Each issue is brimming with:

- Inspiration from writers who have been in your shoes
- Detailed info on the latest contests, conferences, markets, and opportunities in every genre
- Tools of the trade, including reviews of the latest writing software and hardware
- Writing prompts and exercises to overcome writer's block and rekindle your creative spark
- Expert tips, techniques, and advice to help you get published
- And so much more!

That's a lot to look forward to every month. Let *Writer's Digest* put you on the road to writing success!

Get 2 FREE ISSUES of Writer's Digest!

NO RISK!
Send No Money Now!

☐ **Yes!** Please rush me my 2 FREE issues of *Writer's Digest* — the world's leading magazine for writers. If I like what I read, I'll get a full year's subscription (12 issues, including the 2 free issues) for only $19.96. That's 67% off the newsstand rate! If I'm not completely happy, I'll write "cancel" on your invoice, return it and owe nothing. The 2 FREE issues are mine to keep, no matter what!

Name_____

Address_____

City_____

State_____ZIP_____

Annual newsstand rate is $59.88. Orders outside the U.S. will be billed an additional $10 (includes GST/HST in Canada.) Please allow 4-6 weeks for first-issue delivery.

www.writersdigest.com

T6SM4

Get 2 FREE TRIAL ISSUES of Writer's® Digest

Packed with creative inspiration, advice, and tips to guide you on the road to success, *Writer's Digest* will offer you everything you need to take your writing to the next level! You'll discover how to:

- Create dynamic characters and page-turning plots
- Submit query letters that publishers won't be able to refuse
- Find the right agent or editor for you
- Make it out of the slush-pile and into the hands of the right publisher
- Write award-winning contest entries
- And more!

See for yourself by ordering your 2 FREE trial issues today!

RUSH! 2 Free Issues!

12″ Single. A 12-inch record containing one or more remixes of a song, originally intended for dance club play.

Unsolicited. Songs or materials that were not requested and are not expected.

VHS. ½″ videocassette format.

Vocal score. An arrangement of vocal music detailing all vocal parts, and condensing all accompanying instrumental music into one piano part.

Website. An address on the World Wide Web that can be accessed by computer modem. It may contain text, graphics and sound.

Wing space. The offstage area surrounding the playing stage in a theater, unseen by the audience, where sets and props are hidden, actors wait for cues, and stagehands prepare to chance sets.

World music. A general music category which includes most musical forms originating outside the U.S. and Europe, including reggae and calypso. World music finds its roots primarily in the Caribbean, Latin America, Africa and the south Pacific.

World Wide Web (WWW). An Internet resource that utilizes hypertext to access information. It also supports formatted text, illustrations and sounds, depending on the user's computer capabilities.

Indexes

Openness to Submissions Index

Use this index to find companies open to your level of experience. Be sure to read the Openness to Submissions sidebar on page 8 for more information. It is recommended to use this index in conjunction with the Category Indexes found at the end of the following sections: Music Publishers, Record Companies, Record Producers, Managers & Booking Agents. Once you have compiled a list of companies open to your experience and music, read the information in these listings, paying close attention to **How to Contact**

☐ OPEN TO BEGINNERS

Music Publishers
Abalone Publishing
Alco Music
Alexander Sr. Music
Alexis
Alias John Henry Tunes
All Rock Music
Allegheny Music Works
ARAS Music
Audio Music Publishers
Avalon Music
Barkin' Foe the Master's Bone
Barren Wood Publishing
Bay Ridge Publishing Co.
Black Market Entertainment Recordings
Bradley Music, Allan
BSW Records
Buckeye Music Group
Buried Treasure Music
Burnsongs
California Country Music
Corelli's Music Box
Cotton Town Music Company
Country Showcase America
Crowe Entertainment
Cupit Music
Dagene Music
Dapmor Publishing
Delev Music Company
Doss Music, Buster
Dream Seekers Publishing
Duane Music, Inc.
Earitating Music Publishing
East Coast Music Publishing
Edition Rossori
Egyptianman Productions
Emandell Tunes
Emstone, Inc. Music Publishing
Faverett Group

Fifth Avenue Media, Ltd.
Fresh Entertainment
Frick Enterprises, Bob Scott
Furrow Music
Gary Music, Alan
Glad Music Co.
Golden Music, August
Goodland Music Group Inc., The
Hammel Associates, Inc., R.L.
His Power Productions and Publishing
Hitsburgh Music Co.
Holy Spirit Music
Interplanetary Music
Iron Skillet Music
Ja/Nein Musikverlag GmbH
Jerjoy Music
JPMC Music Inc.
Kansa Records Corporation
Kaupps & Robert Publishing Co.
Kaysarah Music
Leigh Music, Trixie
Les Music Group
M & T Waldoch Publishing, Inc.
Mayfair Music
McConkey Artists Agency Music Publishing
McCoy Music, Jim
Mellow House Music
Mighty Blue Music Machine, The
Moon June Music
Nervous Publishing
New Clarion Music Group
Ontrax Companies
Oyster Bay Music Publishing
Pecos Valley Music
PEN Music Group, Inc.
Peters Music, Justin
QUARK, Inc.
R.T.L. Music
Ridge Music Corp.
Rustron Music Publishers
Sabteca Music Co.

◑ PREFERS EXPERIENCED, BUT OPEN TO BEGINNERS

Music Publishers

AlliSongs Inc.
Alpha Music Inc.
Amen, Inc.
Americatone International
Bagatelle Music Publishing Co.
Bal & Bal Music Publishing Co.
Bernard Enterprises, Inc., Hal
Big Fish Music Publishing Group
Blue Dog Publishing and Records
BME Publishing
Branson Country Music Publishing
Camex Music
Cherri/Holly Music
Christmas & Holiday Music
Christopher Publishing, Sonny
Cimirron Music
Coffee and Cream Publishing Company
Cornelius Companies, The
Country Star Music
De Miles Music Company, The Edward
Del Camino Music Publishing
Demi Monde Records & Publishing Ltd.
Drive Music, Inc.
EMF Productions
Ever-Open-Eye Music
First Time Music (Publishing) U.K.
Fricon Music Company
Frozen Inca Music
G Major Music
G-String Publishing
Happy Melody
High-Minded Moma Publishing & Productions
Hitsource Publishing
Inside Records/OK Songs
Jae Music, Jana
Jaelius Enterprises
Jasper Stone Music (ASCAP)/JSM Songs (BMI)
Jolson Black & White Music, Al
Juke Music
KeyShavon Music Publishing
Lari-Jon Publishing
Lexington Alabama Music Publishing
Lilly Music Publishing
Lineage Publishing Co.
Luick & Associates Music Publisher, Harold
Major Entertainment
Makers Mark Gold
Marvin Publishing, John Weller
Master Source
Mento Music Group
Musikuser Publishing
New Rap Jam Publishing, A

Northwest Alabama Music Publishing
Orchid Publishing
Piano Press
Pollybyrd Publications Limited
Presser Co., Theodore
Pritchett Publications
R.J. Music
Rhythms Productions
Rock N Metal Music Publishing Co.
Rocker Music/Happy Man Music
Rockford Music Co.
Rosebowl Music
Shawnee Press, Inc.
Shu'Baby Montez Music
Silver Thunder Music Group
Sinus Musik Produktion, Ulli Weigel
Spradlin/Gleich Publishing
Starbound Publishing Co.
Stellar Music Industries
Stuart Music Co., Jeb
Sunsongs Music/Dark Son Music
T.C. Productions/Etude Publishing Co.
Tower Music Group
Transamerika Musikverlag KG
Transition Music Corporation
Unknown Source Music
Vaam Music Group
Vokes Music Publishing
Weaver of Words Music
Westwood Music Group
Whiting Music
Wilcom Publishing
Zettitalia Music International
Zitel Publishing Co.
Zomba Music Publishing

Record Companies

Afterschool Records, Inc.
All Star Record Promotions
Americatone Records International USA
AMP Records & Music
Asylum Records Nashville
Awal.com
Bagatelle Record Company
Belmont Records
BMX Entertainment
Bolivia Records
Bouquet Records
Broken Note Records
C.P.R.
Candyspiteful Productions
Capricorn Records
Capstan Record Production
Case Entertainment Group/C.E.G. Records, Inc.
Cherry Street Records
Chiaroscuro Records

New Experience Records
Pacific North Studios Ltd.
Parker, Patty
Pierce, Jim
Shu'Baby Montez Music
Silver Thunder Music Group
Sphere Group One
Stuart Audio Services
Valtec Productions
Westwires Digital USA
Wilbur Productions
Willson, Frank
WLM Music/Recording
World Records
Wytas Productions, Steve

Managers & Booking Agents
Air Tight Management
Alert Music, Inc.
All Star Management
All Star Talent Agency
Allen Entertainment Development, Michael
American Artists Entertainment
Amok Artists Agency
Anderson Associates Communications Group
Ardenne Int'l Inc.
Artist Representation and Management
Atlantic Entertainment Group
Austex Music
Backstreet Booking
Barrett Rock 'n' Roll Enterprises, Paul
Big J Productions
Blank & Blank
Blowin' Smoke Productions/Records
Bouquet-Orchid Enterprises
Brothers Management Associates
Chucker Music Inc.
Circuit Rider Talent & Management Co.
Class Act Productions/Management
Clockwork Entertainment Management Agency
Clousher Productions
Cody Entertainment Group
Concept 2000 Inc.
Concerted Efforts, Inc./Foggy Day Music
Corvalan-Condliffe Management
Countrywide Producers
Cranium Management
Criss-Cross Industries
Crossfire Productions
D&M Entertainment Agency
DCA Productions
Dinwoodie Management, Andrew
Direct Management
Divine Industries
Doss Presents, Col. Buster
EAO Music Corporation of Canada

Evergreen Entertainment Services Ltd.
Feldman & Associates, S.L.
Fenchel Entertainment Agency, Fred T.
Fiedler Management, B.C.
First Time Management
Five Star Entertainment
Fox Management Inc., Mitchell
Godtland Management, Inc., Eric
Golden Guru Entertainment
Greif-Garris Management
Gurley & Co.
Hale Enterprises
Hall Entertainment & Events, Bill
Hansen Enterprises, Ltd.
Hawkeye Attractions
Immigrant Music Inc.
International Production Management
J & V Management
Jacobson Talent Management
Jae Enterprises, Jana
James Management, Roger
Kagan International, Sheldon
Kendall West Agency
Kitchen Sync
Knight Agency, Bob
Lari-Jon Promotions
Lawrence, Ltd., Ray
Legacy Sound & Entertainment
Lenthall & Associates
Levinson Entertainment Ventures International, Inc.
Live-Wire Management
Lutz Entertainment Agency, Richard
Management Plus
Management Trust Ltd., The
Mayo & Company, Phil
Mazur Entertainment
McDonnell Group, The
Media Management
Mega Music Productions
Metro Talent Group, Inc.
Mirkin Management
Montgomery Management, Gary F.
Muse Artists Inc.
Nik Entertainment Co.
OTA Productions
Pillar Records
Prestige Management
Rainbow Collection Ltd.
Rainbow Talent Agency
Right-On Management
Riohcat Music
Risavy, Inc., A.F.
Rogue Management
Rothschild Productions Inc., Charles R.

Saffyre Management
Sa'Mall Management
Scott Entertainment, Craig
SDM, Inc.
Shute Management Pty. Ltd., Phill
Siddons & Associates
Skorman Productions, Inc., T.
Sound Management Direction
Southeastern Attractions
SP Talent Associates
Sphere Group One
Staircase Promotion
Stander Entertainment
Starkravin' Management
Stormin' Norman Productions
Strictly Forbidden Artists
Surface Management Inc.
T.L.C. Booking Agency
Tas Music Co./Dave Tasse Entertainment
Texas Sounds Entertainment
Tiger's Eye Entertainment Management & Consulting
Triangle Talent, Inc.
Twentieth Century Promotions
Umpire Entertainment Enterprizes
Varrasso Management, Richard
Vokes Booking Agency
Warner Productions, Cheryl K.
Wemus Entertainment
Williams Management, Yvonne
World Wide Management
WorldSound, LLC
Zane Management, Inc.

☑ ONLY OPEN TO PREVIOUSLY PUBLISHED SONGWRITERS/WELL-ESTABLISHED ACTS

Music Publishers
Baitstring Music
Brian Song Music Corp.
Dell Music, Frank
Disney Music Publishing
Flying Red Horse Publishing
Goodnight Kiss Music
Markea Music/Gina Pie Music
Montina Music
Pegasus Music
Segal's Publications
Sellwood Publishing
Sun Star Songs
Winston & Hoffman House Music Publishers

Record Companies
American Recordings
Arkadia Entertainment Corp.

Astralwerks
Broken Records International
Cambria Records & Publishing
Cantilena Records
Griffin Music
Heads Up Int., Ltd.
Kingston Records
Lucifer Records, Inc.
Malaco Records
Monticana Records
Robbins Entertainment LLC
Trac Record Co.

Record Producers
Cacophony Productions
Kingston Records and Talent
Marenco, Cookie
Monticana Productions
Segal's Productions
Texas Fantasy Music Group
Trac Record Co.

Managers & Booking Agents
Buxton Walker P/L
DAS Communications, Ltd.
De Miles Company, The Edward
Levy Management, Rick
Management by Jaffe
Noteworthy Productions
Performers of the World Inc. (P.O.W.)
Prestige Artistes
Serge Entertainment Group
Siegel Entertainment Ltd.
Van Pol Management, Hans

☑ DOES NOT ACCEPT UNSOLICITED MATERIAL/ ONLY ACCEPTS MATERIAL REFERRED BY AN INDUSTRY SOURCE

Music Publishers
A Ta Z Music
Balmur Entertainment
Bixio Music Group & Associates/IDM Music
Bourne Co. Music Publishers
Brentwood-Benson Music Publishing
Bug Music, Inc.
Cheavoria Music Co. (BMI)
Chrysalis Music
CTV Music (Great Britain)
DreamWorks SKG Music Publishing
EMI Christian Music Publishing
EMI Music Publishing
Famous Music Publishing Companies
Green One Music

Film & TV Index

This index lists companies who place music in motion pictures and TV shows (excluding commercials). To learn more about their film/TV experience, read the information under **Film & TV** in their listings. It is recommended to use this index in conjunction with the Openness to Submissions Index beginning on page 483.

Music Publishers

Alexander Sr. Music
Alpha Music Inc.
Big Fish Music Publishing Group
Bixio Music Group & Associates/IDM Music
Brentwood-Benson Music Publishing
BSW Records
Christmas & Holiday Music
CTV Music (Great Britain)
De Miles Music Company, The Edward
Famous Music Publishing Companies
Fresh Entertainment
Golden Music, August
Goodnight Kiss Music
Heupferd Musikverlag GmbH
Holy Spirit Music
Jaelius Enterprises
Lilly Music Publishing
Manuiti L.A.
Markea Music/Gina Pie Music
Master Source
McConkey Artists Agency Music Publishing
McJames Music Inc.
MIDI Track Publishing/ALLRS Music Publishing Co.
Naked Jain Records
Old Slowpoke Music
Pas Mal Publishing Sarl
PEN Music Group, Inc.
Presser Co., Theodore
QUARK, Inc.
Rainbow Music Corp.
Saddlestone Publishing
Shu'Baby Montez Music
Silver Blue Music/Oceans Blue Music
Still Working Music Group
Succes
Tower Music Group
Transamerika Musikverlag KG
Transition Music Corporation
Winston & Hoffman House Music Publishers
Zettitalia Music International

Record Companies

Sahara Records and Filmworks Entertainment

Record Producers

Craig, Douglas
Texas Fantasy Music Group

Managers & Booking Agents

American Artists Entertainment
Hansen Enterprises, Ltd.
Total Acting Experience, A

Advertising, Audiovisual & Commercial Music Firms

Allegro Music
Angel Films Company
Cantrax Recorders
Cinevue/Steve Postal Productions
D.S.M. Producers Inc.
Disk Productions
Entertainment Productions, Inc.
Film Classic Exchange
Gold & Associates, Inc.
TRF Production Music Libraries
Utopian Empire Creativeworks
Vis/Aid Marketing/Associates

Geographic Index

This Geographic Index will help you locate companies by state, as well as those in countries outside of the U.S. It is recommended to use this index in conjunction with the Openness to Submissions Index on page 475. Once you find the names of companies in this index you are interested in, check the listings within each section for addresses, phone numbers, contact names and submission details.

Drive Music, Inc.
Duane Music, Inc.
Emandell Tunes
EMI Music Publishing
Famous Music Publishing Companies
Goodnight Kiss Music
His Power Productions and Publishing
Hitsource Publishing
Jones Music, Quincy
Kaupps & Robert Publishing Co.
Lake Transfer Productions & Music
Manuiti L.A.
Master Source
Maverick Music
MCA Music Publishing
McConkey Artists Agency Music Publishing
McJames Music Inc.
Mellow House Music
Music Bridge, The
Music Room Publishing Group, The
Musikuser Publishing
Naked Jain Records
PEN Music Group, Inc.
Piano Press
Platinum Gold Music
Pollybyrd Publications Limited
PolyGram Music Publishing
Ren Zone Music
Rhythms Productions
Rondor Music International/Almo/Irving
    Music, A Universal Music Group Company
Sabteca Music Co.
Sellwood Publishing
Silver Blue Music/Oceans Blue Music
Sony Music Publishing
Transition Music Corporation
Vaam Music Group
Warner/Chappell Music, Inc.
Wemar Music Corp.
Wilcom Publishing
Winston & Hoffman House Music Publishers
Zettitalia Music International
Zomba Music Publishing

Record Companies

ABL Records
American Recordings
Arista Records
Atlantic Records
Awal.com
Big Beat Records
Blue Gem Records
Cambria Records & Publishing
Cantilena Records
Capitol Records
Chattahoochee Records

Cleopatra Records
Columbia Records
Crank! A Record Company
Curb Records
Dagene/Cabletown Company
Deadeye Records
Del-Fi Records, Inc.
Discmedia
DreamWorks Records
Drive Entertainment
Drool Records
Edmonds Record Group
Elektra Records
EMF Records & Affiliates
Entourage Music Group
Epic Records
Flood Recording Corp.
Gallery II Records/Jumpin' Jack Records
Geffen/DGC Records
Gonzo! Records Inc.
Grass Roots Record & Tape/LMI Records
Hollywood Records
Horizon Records, Inc.
Interscope/Geffen/A&M Records
Island/Def Jam Music Group
Jive Records
Kaupp Records
London Sire Records
Loud Records
Maverick Records
MCA Records
Metal Blade Records
Moody Prodx, Doug
Motown Records
Oglio Records
Only New Age Music, Inc.
Outstanding Records
Pentacle Records
Polydor Records
PPL Entertainment Group
Priority Records
Rampant Records
RCA Records
Reprise Records
Road Records
Roll On Records®
Sabteca Record Co.
Siltown Records
Solana Records
Sureshot Records
Thump Records, Inc.
Trac Record Co.
Triple X Records
Universal Records
Valtec Productions

Workshops & Conferences
ASCAP West Coast/Lester Sill Songwriter's
     Workshop
Northern California Songwriters Association
     Conference
Songwriters Guild Foundation, The

Retreats & Colonies
Dorland Mountain Arts Colony
Villa Montalvo Artist Residency Program

Contests & Awards
Blank Theatre Company Young Playwrights
     Festival, The
L.A. Designers' Theatre Music Awards
NACUSA Young Composers' Competition
"Unisong" International Song Contest
West Coast Ensemble—Musical Stairs

COLORADO

Record Companies
Case Entertainment Group/C.E.G. Records, Inc.
Silver Wave Records

Play Producers & Publishers
Contemporary Drama Service
Creede Repertory Theatre
Pioneer Drama Service

Organizations
Colorado Music Association
National Music Day Foundation

Workshops & Conferences
Aspen Music Festival and School

Contests & Awards
Delta Omicron International Composition
     Competition
Rocky Mountain Folks Festival Songwriter
     Showcase
Telluride Troubadour Contest

CONNECTICUT

Music Publishers
Ridge Music Corp.

Record Companies
BMX Entertainment
Generic Records, Inc.

Record Producers
Wytas Productions, Steve

Managers & Booking Agents
Air Tight Management
Martin Productions, Rick
Rustron Music Productions

Classical Performing Arts
Connecticut Choral Artists/Concora
Norfolk Chamber Music Festival/Yale Summer
     School of Music

Organizations
Connecticut Songwriters Association
Pop Record Research

Workshops & Conferences
Norfolk Chamber Music Festival

Contests & Awards
Young Composers Awards

DELAWARE

*Advertising, Audiovisual &
Commercial Music Firms*
Ken-Del Productions Inc.

DISTRICT OF COLUMBIA

Record Companies
Rags to Records, Inc.
Smithsonian Folkways Recordings

Classical Performing Arts
Master Chorale of Washington

Organizations
Opera America
Songwriters Association of Washington
Washington Area Music Association

Contests & Awards
Fulbright Scholar Program, Council for
     International Exchange of Scholars
Mid-Atlantic Song Contest
Nestico Award, Sammy/USAF Band Airmen of
     Note
U.S.-Japan Creative Artists Exchange Fellowship
     Program

FLORIDA

Music Publishers
Alco Music
ARAS Music
Emstone, Inc. Music Publishing
Mighty Blue Music Machine, The
Pritchett Publications
Rocker Music/Happy Man Music
Rustron Music Publishers
Stuart Music Co., Jeb

Record Companies
Alco Recordings
CPA Records
Discos Fuentes/Miami Records & Edimusica
     USA

Get Your 2004 Edition Delivered Right to Your Door—and Save!

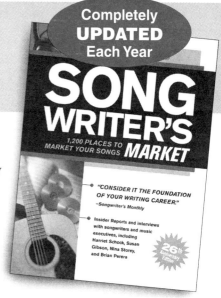

Completely UPDATED Each Year

SONG WRITER'S MARKET

1,200 PLACES TO MARKET YOUR SONGS

"CONSIDER IT THE FOUNDATION OF YOUR WRITING CAREER." —*Songwriter's Monthly*

Insider Reports and interviews with songwriters and music executives, including Harriet Schock, Susan Gibson, Nina Storey, and Brian Perera

26th Annual Edition

Finding the right markets for your songs is crucial to your success! With constant changes in the music industry, staying informed as to who, where, and why is a challenge. That's why every year the songwriters turn to the new edition of *Songwriter's Market* for the most up-to-date information on the people and places that will get their songs heard. This indispensable guide includes more than 2,000 listings of music publishers, record producers, managers, booking agents, and more. You'll also find insider tips from industry professionals which will further increase your opportunities.

2004 Songwriter's Market will be published and ready for shipment in August 2003.

Through this special offer, you can reserve your 2004 *Songwriter's Market* at the 2003 price—just $24.99. Order today and save!

Turn over for more books to help write and market your songs!

Yes! I want the most current edition of *Songwriter's Market*. Please send me the 2004 edition at the 2003 price—$24.99. (#10850-K)

| # 10850-K | $ 24.99 |

(NOTE: *2004 Songwriter's Market* will be shipped in August 2003.)

I also want these books listed on back:

Book		Price
#	-K	$
#	-K	$
#	-K	$
#	-K	$
Subtotal		$
Postage & Handling		$

In the U.S., please add $3.95 s&h for the first book, $1.95 for each additional book. In OH, NY, CO and MI add applicable sales tax. In Canada, add US$5.00 for the first book, US$3.00 for each additional book, and 7% GST. Payment in U.S. funds must accompany order.

| **Total** | $ |

Credit card orders call
TOLL FREE 1-800-448-0915
or visit
www.writersdigest.com/catalog

☐ Payment enclosed $ _____ (or)

Charge my: ☐ VISA ☐ MC ☐ AmEx Exp._____

Account # _____

Signature _____

Name _____

Address _____

City_____

State/Prov._____ ZIP/PC_____

☐ Check here if you do not want your name added to our mailing list.

30-Day Money Back Guarantee on every book you buy!

ZAH02B4

Mail to: Writer's Digest Books • PO Box 9274 • Central Islip, NY 11722-9274

More Great Books to Help You Market Your Songs!

You Can Write Song Lyrics
by Terry Cox
An experienced and successful lyric writer guides you step by step through the process of lyric writing. Learn about basic song components, collaborative song-writing, and creative ways to come up with song ideas. Cox also walks you through the stages of writing lyrics for a song—from choosing a title, to the chorus, verses, and bridge. You'll even find valuable information on the next steps of getting your song performed and recorded.
#10685-K/$14.99/144 p/pb

The Craft and Business of Songwriting
2nd Edition
by John Braheny
Want to be a professional songwriter? Then get Braheny's must-have insider info on being competitive in this crowded market. You'll learn how to overcome writer's block, focus ideas, handle business concerns, and much more. Plus, up-to-date Web references, video info, and software advice.
#10767-K/$22.99/322 p/pb

The Musician's Guide to Making & Selling Your Own CDs & Cassettes
by Jana Stanfield
Learn how to produce the kind of recordings that will launch your music career. It doesn't take a major label to be successful in the music industry. Stanfield shows you how she made it to the top, and how you can, too.
#10522-K/$18.99/160 p/pb

The Songwriter's Market Guide to Song & Demo Submission Formats
by the editors of Songwriter's Market
Get your foot in the door with knock-out query letters, slick demo presentation, and the best advice for dealing with every player in the industry!
#10401-K/$19.99/160 p/hc

Writing Better Lyrics
by Pat Pattison
Make every song sizzle using this unique, in-depth approach to lyric writing. You'll examine extraordinary songs to determine what makes them so effective. Plus, work through more than 30 language exercises to find snappy rhymes and create meaningful metaphors and similes.
#10742-K/$15.99/192 p/pb

Cellar Records
Griffin Music
Modal Music, Inc.™
Nation Records Inc.
Pravda Records
Sahara Records and Filmworks Entertainment
UAR Records
Waterdog Music

Record Producers
Coachouse Music
De Miles, Edward
Neu Electro Productions

Managers & Booking Agents
Bacchus Group Productions, Ltd.
Conscience Music
Risavy, Inc., A.F.

Advertising, Audiovisual &
Commercial Music Firms
Mallof, Abruzino & Nash Marketing
Qually & Company Inc.
Video I-D, Inc.

Plays Producers & Publishers
Bailiwick Repertory
Circa '21 Dinner Playhouse
Dramatic Publishing Company, The

Classical Performing Arts
City Symphony of Chicago
Knox-Galesburg Symphony
Lyric Opera of Chicago

Organizations
American Society of Composers, Authors and
    Publishers (ASCAP)
Chicago Dance and Music Alliance

Contests & Awards
Cunningham Commission for Youth Theatre
Kinley Memorial Fellowship, Kate Neal

INDIANA
Music Publishers
Hammel Associates, Inc., R.L.
Interplanetary Music
Ontrax Companies

Record Companies
Dale Productions, Alan
P.M. Records

Managers & Booking Agents
De Miles Company, The Edward
Hale Enterprises
Harrell & Associates, M.
Hawkeye Attractions
International Entertainment Bureau

Advertising, Audiovisual &
Commercial Music Firms
Caldwell Vanriper/Marc
Omni Communications

Classical Performing Arts
Anderson Symphony Orchestra
Carmel Symphony Orchestra

Organizations
Just Plain Folks

Workshops & Conferences
New Harmony Project, The

Contests & Awards
Indiana Opera Theatre/MacAllister Awards for
    Opera Singers

IOWA
Music Publishers
JoDa Music
Luick & Associates Music Publisher, Harold
Rock N Metal Music Publishing Co.

Record Producers
Heart Consort Music
Luick & Country Music Showcase Intl.
    Associates, Harold

Managers & Booking Agents
Fenchel Entertainment Agency, Fred T.

Play Producers & Publishers
Heuer Publishing Co.
Waterloo Community Playhouse

Organizations
Country Music Showcase International, Inc.

Workshops & Conferences
Davidson's Writer's Seminar, Peter

KANSAS
Music Publishers
Dave Music, Jof
Kansa Records Corporation

KENTUCKY
Music Publishers
Holy Spirit Music
Just a Note

Record Producers
Glocc Cocced Records

Managers & Booking Agents
Triangle Talent, Inc.

**Advertising, Audiovisual &
Commercial Music Firms**
Price Weber Marketing Communications, Inc.

Play Producers & Publishers
Aran Press
Stage One

Classical Performing Arts
Kentucky Opera
Lexington Philharmonic Society

Organizations
International Bluegrass Music Association
    (IBMA)

Contests & Awards
Y.E.S. Festival of New Plays

LOUISIANA
Music Publishers
Dapmor Publishing
EMF Productions
Melody Hills Ranch Publishing Co.

Record Companies
EMF Productions

Managers & Booking Agents
Big J Productions
Sea Cruise Productions, Inc.

**Advertising, Audiovisual &
Commercial Music Firms**
Disk Productions

Play Producers & Publishers
Centenary College, Theatre Department
Swine Palace Productions

Organizations
Louisiana Songwriters Association
Southern Songwriters Guild, Inc.

Workshops & Conferences
Cutting Edge Music Business Conference
Shiznit Music Conference, The

MAINE
Record Producers
Stuart Audio Services

Workshops & Conferences
Arcady Music Festival

MARYLAND
Music Publishers
Country Showcase America
Leigh Music, Trixie

Record Companies
Banana Records

Managers & Booking Agents
Noteworthy Productions

**Advertising, Audiovisual &
Commercial Music Firms**
dbF A Media Company
RBM Advertising

Classical Performing Arts
Susquehanna Symphony Orchestra

Organizations
Folk Alliance

Workshops & Conferences
Folk Alliance Annual Conference

MASSACHUSETTS
Music Publishers
East Coast Music Publishing
Scott Music Group, Tim
Segal's Publications

Record Companies
Anisette Records
Belmont Records
Fish of Death Records and Management
Night Owl Records
Stargard Entertainment

Record Producers
Mona Lisa Records/Bristol Recording Studios
Segal's Productions

Managers & Booking Agents
Clockwork Entertainment Management Agency
Concerted Efforts, Inc./Foggy Day Music
Huge Production, Inc., A

**Advertising, Audiovisual &
Commercial Music Firms**
Communications for Learning
Film Classic Exchange
Home, Inc.
Lapriore Videography
VIP Video

Play Producers & Publishers
American Eastern Theatrical Company
Baker's Plays
Freelance Press, The
New Repertory Theatre
North Shore Music Theatre
Strawberry Productions, Inc.

Classical Performing Arts
Boston Philharmonic, The
Commonwealth Opera, Inc.

Mirecourt Trio, The
Mohawk Trail Concerts

Organizations
Boston Songwriters Workshop, The

Workshops & Conferences
Music Business Solutions/Career Building
    Workshops
NEMO Music Showcase & Conference

Contests & Awards
ALEA III International Composition Prize
Baker's Plays High School Playwriting Contest

MICHIGAN
Music Publishers
Abalone Publishing

Record Companies
Afterschool Records, Inc.
Gueststar Records, Inc.
L.A. Records (Michigan)
RAVE Records, Inc.
Small Stone Records
Wall Street Music

Record Producers
Theoretical Reality
World Records

Managers & Booking Agents
Afterschool Publishing Company
Gueststar Entertainment Agency
J & V Management
Monopoly Management
Right-On Management

**Advertising, Audiovisual &
Commercial Music Firms**
Communications Electronics Inc.
K&R's Recording Studios
Utopian Empire Creativeworks

Play Producers & Publishers
Thunder Bay Theatre

Classical Performing Arts
Adrian Symphony Orchestra
Birmingham-Bloomfield Symphony Orchestra
Cantata Academy
Fontana Concert Society
Sault Ste. Marie Symphony Orchestra

Organizations
Nashville Songwriters Association International-
    Detroit

Workshops & Conferences
Lamb's Retreat for Songwriters

Retreats & Colonies
Isle Royale National Park Artist-in-Residence
    Program

Northwood University Alden B. Dow Creativity
    Center

Contests & Awards
African American Composer's Program

MINNESOTA
Music Publishers
Dell Music, Frank
Portage Music

Record Companies
Nightmare Records

Managers & Booking Agents
Artist Representation and Management

**Advertising, Audiovisual &
Commercial Music Firms**
Butwin & Associates, Inc.

Play Producers & Publishers
Mixed Blood Theatre Co.

Classical Performing Arts
Augsburg Choir

Organizations
American Composers Forum
Country Legends Association

Contests & Awards
Bush Artist Fellows Program
Composers Commissioning Program

MISSISSIPPI
Music Publishers
Bay Ridge Publishing Co.

Record Companies
Malaco Records
Missile Records

Managers & Booking Agents
Exclesisa Booking Agency

MISSOURI
Music Publishers
Blue Dog Publishing and Records
Green One Music
Lineage Publishing Co.
Southern Most Publishing Company

Record Companies
Capstan Record Production
Green Bear Records

Record Producers
Angel Films Company
Haworth Productions

Scott Entertainment, Craig
Sphere Group One
Stormin' Norman Productions
Surface Management Inc.

Advertising, Audiovisual & Commercial Music Firms
Creative Associates
KJD Advertising & Teleproductions, Inc.
Sorin Productions Inc.

Classical Performing Arts
American Boychoir, The
Dúo Clásico
New Jersey Symphony Orchestra/Greater Newark Youth Orchestra
Princeton Symphony Orchestra
Queens Opera
Ridgewood Symphony Orchestra

Organizations
Songwriters Guild of America, The

Workshops & Conferences
Appel Farm Arts and Music Festival

NEW MEXICO

Music Publishers
Pecos Valley Music

Record Companies
SunCountry Records

Classical Performing Arts
Desert Chorale

NEW YORK

Music Publishers
Alpha Music Inc.
Bixio Music Group & Associates/IDM Music
BMG Music Publishing
Bourne Co. Music Publishers
Bug Music, Inc.
Camex Music
EMI Music Publishing
Famous Music Publishing Companies
Fifth Avenue Media, Ltd.
Jasper Stone Music (ASCAP)/JSM Songs (BMI)
Major Entertainment
MCA Music Publishing
MIDI Track Publishing/ALLRS Music Publishing Co.
PolyGram Music Publishing
QUARK, Inc.
Rainbow Music Corp.
Rockford Music Co.
Sony Music Publishing

Sunsongs Music/Dark Son Music
Warner/Chappell Music, Inc.
Zomba Music Publishing

Record Companies
Amigos Music & Marketing
Angel/EMI Records
Arista Records
Arkadia Entertainment Corp.
Astralwerks
Atlantic Records
Blue Wave
C.P.R.
Candyspiteful Productions
Capitol Records
Chiaroscuro Records
Columbia Records
Com-Four Distribution
Creative Improvised Music Projects (CIMP) Records
Dental Records
DreamWorks Records
Elektra Records
Epic Records
Evil Teen Records
Factory Beat Records, Inc.
Geffen/DGC Records
Gold City Records, Inc.
Hollywood Records
Hot Wings Entertainment
Interscope/Geffen/A&M Records
Island/Def Jam Music Group
Jive Records
Lamar Music Marketing
Loud Records
Major Entertainment, Inc.
Marvel Records, Andy
MCA Records
Mighty Records
Motown Records
NPO Records, Inc.
Omega Record Group, Inc.
Pacific Time Entertainment
Paint Chip Records
Polydor Records
Priority Records
Quark Records
Radical Records
Razor & Tie Entertainment
RCA Records
Reprise Records
Robbins Entertainment LLC
Select Records
Tommy Boy Records
TVT Records
Universal Records

GEOGRAPHIC INDEX

Managers & Booking Agents
D&R Entertainment
Hupp Enterprises, Joe
Jae Enterprises, Jana

Classical Performing Arts
Cimarron Circuit Opera Company

Organizations
Oklahoma Songwriters & Composers
    Association
Songwriters of Oklahoma

Contests & Awards
Billboard Song Contest

OREGON
Music Publishers
Earitating Music Publishing
High-Minded Moma Publishing & Productions
Moon June Music

Record Companies
Flying Heart Records

Record Producers
Celt Musical Services, Jan

Organizations
Central Oregon Songwriters Association
Portland Songwriters Association
Songwriters Resource Network

Retreats & Colonies
Sitka Center for Art & Ecology

Contests & Awards
Great American Song Contest
Portland Songwriters Association Annual
    Songwriting Competition

PENNSYLVANIA
Music Publishers
Allegheny Music Works
Coffee and Cream Publishing Company
Country Star Music
Delev Music Company
Makers Mark Gold
Presser Co., Theodore
Shawnee Press, Inc.
Shu'Baby Montez Music
Vokes Music Publishing

Record Companies
Allegheny Music Works
Country Star International
Golden Triangle Records
Q Records
Ruffnation Records

Sound Gems
Vokes Music Record Co.

Record Producers
Baird Enterprises, Ron
Big Sky Audio Productions
Coffee and Cream Productions
Country Star Productions
Integrated Entertainment
Makers Mark Music Productions
Philly Breakdown Recording Co.
Shu'Baby Montez Music
Westwires Digital USA

Managers & Booking Agents
Blank & Blank
Clousher Productions
Country Star Attractions
Countrywide Producers
Golden Guru Entertainment
Hall Entertainment & Events, Bill
McDonnell Group, The
Pillar Records
Rock Whirled Music Management
Vokes Booking Agency
Zane Management, Inc.

*Advertising, Audiovisual &
Commercial Music Firms*
Advertel, Inc.
Blattner/Brunner
BRg Music Works

Play Producers & Publishers
Arden Theatre Company
Bristol Riverside Theatre
Walnut Street Theatre
Wilma Theater, The

Classical Performing Arts
Hershey Symphony Orchestra
Lehigh Valley Chamber Orchestra
Prism Saxophone Quartet
Singing Boys of Pennsylvania

Organizations
Pittsburgh Songwriters Association

Contests & Awards
CRS National Composers Competition
Gaul Composition Contest, Harvey

RHODE ISLAND
Record Companies
North Star Music

Managers & Booking Agents
D&M Entertainment Agency
Twentieth Century Promotions

Organizations
Rhode Island Songwriters' Association

SOUTH CAROLINA

Music Publishers
Brian Song Music Corp.

Record Companies
Street Records

Classical Performing Arts
Opera on the Go
Palmetto Mastersingers

TENNESSEE

Music Publishers
Alias John Henry Tunes
AlliSongs Inc.
Avalon Music
Balmur Entertainment
Beaverwood Audio-Video
BMG Music Publishing
Brentwood-Benson Music Publishing
Bug Music, Inc.
Buried Treasure Music
Burnsongs
Cornelius Companies, The
Crowe Entertainment
Cupit Music
Doss Music, Buster
EMI Christian Music Publishing
Famous Music Publishing Companies
Faverett Group
Frick Enterprises, Bob Scott
Fricon Music Company
Golden Music, August
Goodland Music Group Inc., The
Hitsburgh Music Co.
Iron Skillet Music
Jolson Black & White Music, Al
Juke Music
Lita Music
Markea Music/Gina Pie Music
MCA Music Publishing
McJames Music Inc.
Monk Family Music Group
New Clarion Music Group
NSAI Song Camps
Peters Music, Justin
Platinum Planet Music, Inc.
Schafer Music Group
SDM
Silver Thunder Music Group
Simply Grand Music, Inc.
Sizemore Music

Sony Music Publishing
Stevens Music, Ray
Still Working Music Group
Sun Star Songs
Talbot Music Group
Tourmaline Music, Inc.
Tower Music Group
Ultimate Peak Music
Universal Music Publishing
Whiting Music

Record Companies
Arista Records
Asylum Records Nashville
Atlantic Records
Avalon Recording Group
Avita Records
Brentwood Records/Diadem Records
Capitol Records
Columbia Records
Curb Records
DreamWorks Records
Epic Records
Imaginary Records
Inside Sounds
Island/Def Jam Music Group
Jive Records
MCA Records
PBM Talent & Publishing
Plateau Music
RCA Records
Stardust
Warner Bros. Records
Word Records & Music

Record Producers
Aberdeen Productions
Avalon Productions
Birthplace Productions
Cold Creek Records (CCR)
Cupit Productions, Jerry
DeLory and Music Makers, Al
Doss Presents, Col. Buster
Pierce, Jim
Schafer Music
Silver Thunder Music Group
Swift River Productions

Managers & Booking Agents
All Star Talent Agency
Allen Entertainment Development, Michael
Circuit Rider Talent & Management Co.
Doss Presents, Col. Buster
5 Star Music Group/Mike Waddell & Associates
Fox Management Inc., Mitchell
Gurley & Co.

Hardison International Entertainment
  Corporation
Midcoast, Inc.
Monterey Artists, Inc.
Riohcat Music
Warner Productions, Cheryl K.

Play Producers & Publishers
MacPherson Productions, Don and Pat
Playhouse on the Square

Classical Performing Arts
Chattanooga Girls Choir
Opera Memphis

Organizations
American Society of Composers, Authors and
  Publishers (ASCAP)
Black Country Music Showcase, The
Broadcast Music, Inc. (BMI)
Gospel Music Association
Knoxville Songwriters Association
Memphis Songwriters' Association
Nashville Songwriters Association International
SESAC Inc.
Singer Songwriter Information Line, The
Songwriters Guild of America, The
Tennessee Songwriters International, The

Workshops & Conferences
Nashville Music Festival
NSAI Songwriters Symposium

Contests & Awards
American Songwriter Lyric Contest
NSAI Annual Song Contest
Playhouse on the Square New Play Competition

TEXAS
Music Publishers
Amen, Inc.
Bagatelle Music Publishing Co.
BSW Records
Christopher Publishing, Sonny
Flying Red Horse Publishing
Glad Music Co.
Hes Free Productions & Publishing Company
Jaelius Enterprises
Les Music Group
Silicon Music Publishing Co.
Starbound Publishing Co.
Valiant Records & Management
Zitel Publishing Co.

Record Companies
Albatross Records
Arista Records
Bagatelle Record Company

Broken Note Records
BSW Records
CKB Records/Helaphat Entertainment
Cosmotone Records
Enterprize Records-Tapes
Front Row Records
Groove Makers' Recordings
Hacienda Records & Recording Studio
Heart Music, Inc.
Idol Records
Inner Soul Records, Inc.
Joey Records
Sonar Records & Production
Southland Records, Inc.
Texas Rose Records
Topcat Records
World Beatnik Records

Record Producers
ACR Productions
Dixon III, Philip D., Attorney at Law
Hes Free Productions & Publishing
Mittelstedt, A.V.
RN'D Productions
Texas Fantasy Music Group
TMC Productions
Trinity Studio, The
Willson, Frank

Managers & Booking Agents
American Bands Management
Atch Records and Productions
Austex Music
Butler Music, Bill
Crossfire Productions
Direct Management
Hes Free Productions & Publishing Company
Kendall West Agency
Kuper Personal Management
Legacy Sound & Entertainment
Management Plus
Mirkin Management
Smeltzer Productions, Gary
SP Talent Associates
Spoon Agency L.L.C., The
Stevens & Company Management
Texas Sounds Entertainment
Umpire Entertainment Enterprizes
Universal Music Marketing
Valiant Records & Management
WE Records & Management
Wemus Entertainment

**Advertising, Audiovisual &
Commercial Music Firms**
Bridge Enterprises
Estilo Communications

Weiss/Stafford Productions
Wyatt Advertising, Evans

Play Producers & Publishers
Stages Repertory Theatre
Theatre Three, Inc.

Classical Performing Arts
Fort Worth Children's Opera
Hermann Sons German Band
Mesquite Symphonic Band
Moores Opera Center

Organizations
Austin Songwriters Group
Center for the Promotion of Contemporary
    Composers
Country Music Association of Texas
Dallas Songwriters Association
Fort Worth Songwriters Association
Southeast Texas Bluegrass Music Association
Texas Accountants & Lawyers for the Arts
Texas Music Office

Workshops & Conferences
I Write the Songs
Kerrville Folk Festival
South by Southwest Music and Media
    Conference

Contests & Awards
New Folk Concerts for Emerging Songwriters

UTAH
Organizations
Composers Guild

Contests & Awards
Composers Guild Annual Composition Contest

VERMONT
Music Publishers
A Ta Z Music
JPMC Music Inc.

Record Companies
Big Heavy World

Managers & Booking Agents
Evergreen Entertainment Services Ltd.
Mayo & Company, Phil

Workshops & Conferences
Manchester Music Festival

Retreats & Colonies
Dorset Colony House

VIRGINIA
Music Publishers
Cimirron Music
Weaver of Words Music

Record Companies
Cimirron/Rainbird Records
Leatherland Productions
Warehouse Creek Recording Corp.

Managers & Booking Agents
Cody Entertainment Group
Precision Management

Play Producers & Publishers
Barter Theatre
Mill Mountain Theatre
Theatrevirginia
Virginia Stage Company

Classical Performing Arts
Virginia Opera

Organizations
Southwest Virginia Songwriters Association

Contests & Awards
Henrico Theatre Company One-Act Playwriting
    Competition

WASHINGTON
Music Publishers
Corelli's Music Box
Your Best Songs Publishing

Record Companies
Seafair/Bolo Records

Managers & Booking Agents
T.L.C. Booking Agency
WorldSound, LLC

Classical Performing Arts
Orchestra Seattle/Seattle Chamber Singers

Organizations
Pacific Northwest Songwriters Association

WEST VIRGINIA
Music Publishers
McCoy Music, Jim

Record Companies
Winchester Records

Record Producers
Blues Alley Records

Play Producers & Publishers
Theatre West Virginia

WISCONSIN
Music Publishers
KeyShavon Music Publishing
M & T Waldoch Publishing, Inc.

Record Companies
Safire Records

Managers & Booking Agents
Ellis International Talent Agency, The
St. John Artists
Tas Music Co./Dave Tasse Entertainment
Tiger's Eye Entertainment Management &
    Consulting

Play Producers & Publishers
Northern Lights Playhouse

Classical Performing Arts
Milwaukee Youth Symphony Orchestra

Organizations
Songwriters of Wisconsin International

WYOMING
Play Producers & Publishers
American Living History Theater

AUSTRALIA
Managers & Booking Agents
Buxton Walker P/L
Cranium Management
Dinwoodie Management, Andrew
Music Marketing & Promotions
Shute Management Pty. Ltd., Phill

AUSTRIA
Music Publishers
Edition Rossori

BELGIUM
Music Publishers
Happy Melody
Inside Records/OK Songs
Succes

Record Producers
Jump Productions

CANADA
Music Publishers
G-String Publishing
Hickory Lane Publishing and
    Recording
Lilly Music Publishing
Mayfair Music
Montina Music
Saddlestone Publishing
Third Wave Productions Limited

Record Companies
Hi-Bias Records Inc.
L.A. Records (Canada)
Mayfair Music
Monticana Records
P. & N. Records
sonic unyon records canada
Sun-Scape Enterprises Limited
Synergy Records
Third Wave Productions Ltd.

Record Producers
"A" Major Sound Corporation
DaVinci's Notebook Records
Jay Bird Productions
Kane Producer/Engineer, Karen
Monticana Productions
Pacific North Studios Ltd.
Panio Brothers Label
Silver Bow Productions
Soul Candy Productions

Managers & Booking Agents
Alert Music, Inc.
Amok Artists Agency
Ardenne Int'l Inc.
Divine Industries
EAO Music Corporation of Canada
Feldman & Associates, S.L.
Fiedler Management, B.C.
Immigrant Music Inc.
Kagan International, Sheldon
Lenthall & Associates
M.B.H. Music Management
Management Trust Ltd., The
Outlaw Entertainment International
Siegel Entertainment Ltd.
Silver Bow Management
Strictly Forbidden Artists
T.J. Booker Ltd.

**Advertising, Audiovisual &
Commercial Music Firms**
Moore Compositions, Patrick

Classical Performing Arts
Arcady
Calgary Boys Choir
Canadian Opera Company
Kitchener-Waterloo Chamber Orchestra
Montreal Chamber Orchestra
Star-Scape
Toronto Mendelssohn Choir
Vancouver Chamber Choir
Vancouver Youth Symphony Orchestra Society

Organizations
Associated Male Choruses of America
Association des Professionel.le.s de la chanson
    et de la musique

WALES

General Index

Use this index to locate specific markets and resources. Also, we list companies that appeared in the 2002 edition of *Songwriter's Market*, but do not appear this year. Instead of page numbers beside these markets you will find two-letter codes in parenthesis that explain why these markets no longer appear. The codes are: (**ED**)—Editorial Decision, (**NS**)—Not Accepting Submissions, (**NR**)—No (or late) Response to Listing Request, (**OB**)—Out of Business, (**RR**)—Removed by Listing's Request, (**UC**)—Unable to Contact.

C

GENERAL INDEX

GENERAL INDEX

GENERAL INDEX

Companies that appeared in the 2002 edition of *Songwriter's Market,* **but do not appear this year, are
listed in this General Index with the following codes explaining why these markets were omitted: (ED)—
Editorial Decision, (NS)—Not Accepting Submissions, (NR)—No (or late) Response to Listing Request,
(OB)—Out of Business, (RR)—Removed by Listing's Request, (UC)—Unable to Contact.**